12 DESIGNING EFFECTIVE INPUT

12.1 This Form May Be Hazardous to Your Health 442
12.2 Squeezin' Isn't Pleasin' 445
12.3 What's That Thing Supposed to Be? 448
12.4 It's Only Skin Deep 459

13 DESIGNING DATABASES

13.1 Hitch Your Cleaning Cart to a Star 481
13.2 Storing Minerals for Health, Data for Mining 516
13.3 Losing Prospects 518

14 HUMAN-COMPUTER INTERACTION

14.1 School Spirit Comes in Many Sizes 544
14.2 I'd Rather Do It Myself 549
14.3 Don't Slow Me Down 551
14.4 That's Not a Lightbulb 552
14.5 Waiting to Be Fed 559
14.6 When You Run A Marathon It Helps to Know Where You're Going 564
14.7 Hey, Look Me Over (Reprise) 570

15 DESIGNING ACCURATE DATA ENTRY PROCEDURES

15.1 It's a Wilderness in Here 599
15.2 Catching a Summer Code 602
15.3 To Enter or Not to Enter: That is the Question 610
15.4 Do You Validate Parking? 616

16 QUALITY ASSURANCE THROUGH SOFTWARE ENGINEERING

16.1 The Quality of MIS Is Not Strained 634
16.2 Write Is Right 653
16.3 Cramming for Your Systems Test 656

17 SUCCESSFULLY IMPLEMENTING THE INFORMATION SYSTEM

17.1 You Can Lead a Fish to Water...But You Can't Make It Drink 685
17.2 The Sweet Smell of Success 696
17.3 Mopping Up with the New System 697

18 OBJECT-ORIENTED SYSTEMS ANALYSIS AND DESIGN USING UML

18.1 Making the Magic Reel 713
18.2 Recycling the Programming Environment 723
18.3 Developing a Fine System That Was Long Overdue: Using Object-Oriented Analysis for the Ruminski Public Library System 744
18.4 C-Shore++ 747

To the memory of Julia A. Kendall and memory of Edward J. Kendall, whose lifelong example of working together will inspire us forever.

Library of Congress Cataloging-in-Publication Data

Kendall, Kenneth E.
Systems analysis and design / Kenneth E. Kendall, Julie E. Kendall. -- 7th ed.
p. cm.
ISBN 0-13-615405-0
1. System design. 2. System analysis. 3. Systems programming (Computer science)
I. Kendall, Julie E. II. Title.

QA76.9.S88K45 2007
003--dc22 2007002228

AVP/Executive Editor: Bob Horan
VP/Editorial Director: Jeff Shelstad
Manager, Product Development: Pamela Hersperger
Project Manager: Ana Jankowski
Editorial Assistant: Kelly Loftus
Associate Director, Production Editorial: Judy Leale
Managing Editor: Cynthia Zonneveld
Production Editor: Melissa Feimer
Permissions Coordinator: Charles Morris
Associate Director, Manufacturing: Vinnie Scelta
Manufacturing Buyer: Arnold Vila
Design/Composition Manager: Christy Mahon
Composition Liaison: Suzanne Duda
Designer: Suzanne Duda
Cover Design: Suzanne Duda
Cover Illustration: Richard Kalina, "Carthage" collage, acrylic, flashe on linen; © 2006
Composition: ICC Macmillan Inc.
Full-Service Project Management: ICC Macmillan Inc.
Printer/Binder: Quebecor
Typeface: 10.5/13 Berling

Pearson Education LTD.
Pearson Education Singapore, Pte. Ltd
Pearson Education, Canada, Ltd
Pearson Education–Japan
Pearson Education Australia PTY, Limited
Pearson Education North Asia Ltd
Pearson Educación de Mexico, S.A. de C.V.
Pearson Education Malaysia, Pte. Ltd.

PEARSON
Prentice Hall

10 9 8 7 6 5 4 3 2 1
ISBN-13: 978-0-13-224085-7
ISBN-10: 0-13-224085-8

SYSTEMS ANALYSIS AND DESIGN

SEVENTH EDITION

KENNETH E. KENDALL
Rutgers University
School of Business–Camden
Camden, New Jersey

JULIE E. KENDALL
Rutgers University
School of Business–Camden
Camden, New Jersey

PEARSON
Prentice Hall
Upper Saddle River, New Jersey 07458

COMPANY TRADEMARKS

BRIEF CONTENTS

PART I SYSTEMS ANALYSIS FUNDAMENTALS

1 ASSUMING THE ROLE OF THE SYSTEMS ANALYST 1
2 UNDERSTANDING ORGANIZATIONAL STYLE AND ITS IMPACT ON INFORMATION SYSTEMS 27
3 PROJECT MANAGEMENT 57

PART II INFORMATION REQUIREMENTS ANALYSIS

4 INFORMATION GATHERING: INTERACTIVE METHODS 109
5 INFORMATION GATHERING: UNOBTRUSIVE METHODS 143
6 AGILE MODELING AND PROTOTYPING 171

PART III THE ANALYSIS PROCESS

7 USING DATA FLOW DIAGRAMS 217
8 ANALYZING SYSTEMS USING DATA DICTIONARIES 267
9 DESCRIBING PROCESS SPECIFICATIONS AND STRUCTURED DECISIONS 305
10 PREPARING THE SYSTEMS PROPOSAL 339

PART IV THE ESSENTIALS OF DESIGN

11 DESIGNING EFFECTIVE OUTPUT 379
12 DESIGNING EFFECTIVE INPUT 433
13 DESIGNING DATABASES 479
14 HUMAN–COMPUTER INTERACTION 533
15 DESIGNING ACCURATE DATA ENTRY PROCEDURES 591

PART V SOFTWARE ENGINEERING AND IMPLEMENTATION

16 QUALITY ASSURANCE THROUGH SOFTWARE ENGINEERING 631
17 SUCCESSFULLY IMPLEMENTING THE INFORMATION SYSTEM 671
18 OBJECT-ORIENTED SYSTEMS ANALYSIS AND DESIGN USING UML 709

GLOSSARY 753
ACRONYMS 763
INDEX 764

CONTENTS

PART I SYSTEMS ANALYSIS FUNDAMENTALS

1 ASSUMING THE ROLE OF THE SYSTEMS ANALYST 1

Types of Systems 2
Transaction Processing Systems 2 / Office Automation Systems and Knowledge Work Systems 3 / Management Information Systems 3 / Decision Support Systems 3 / Expert Systems and Artificial Intelligence 3 / Group Decision Support Systems and Computer-Supported Collaborative Work Systems 4 / Executive Support Systems 4

Integrating Technologies for Systems 4
Ecommerce Applications and Web Systems 5 / Enterprise Resource Planning Systems 5 / Systems for Wireless and Handheld Devices 6 / Open Source Software 6

Need for Systems Analysis and Design 7

Roles of the Systems Analyst 7
Systems Analyst as Consultant 8

Consulting Opportunity 1.1 Healthy Hiring: Ecommerce Help Wanted 8
Systems Analyst as Supporting Expert 9 / Systems Analyst as Agent of Change 9 / Qualities of the Systems Analyst 9

The Systems Development Life Cycle 10
Incorporating Human–Computer Interaction Considerations 10 / Identifying Problems, Opportunities, and Objectives 11 / Determining Human Information Requirements 12 / Analyzing System Needs 13 / Designing the Recommended System 13 / Developing and Documenting Software 13 / Testing and Maintaining the System 14 / Implementing and Evaluating the System 14 / The Impact of Maintenance 14

Using CASE Tools 16
Reasons for Using CASE Tools 16

Upper and Lower CASE 17
Upper CASE Tools 17 / Lower CASE Tools 18

Object-Oriented Systems Analysis and Design 19

The Agile Approach and Other Alernative Methodologies 20

SUMMARY 21
HYPERCASE® EXPERIENCE 1 22
KEYWORDS AND PHRASES 23
REVIEW QUESTIONS 23
SELECTED BIBLIOGRAPHY 24
CPU CASE EPISODE 1: THE CASE OPENS 26

2 UNDERSTANDING ORGANIZATIONAL STYLE AND ITS IMPACT ON INFORMATION SYSTEMS 27

Organizations as Systems 27
Interrelatedness and Interdependence of Systems 28 / Virtual Organizations and Virtual Teams 29 / Taking a Systems Perspective 30

Consulting Opportunity 2.1 The E in Vitamin E Stands for Ecommerce 30
Enterprise Resource Planning: Viewing the Organization as a System 32

Depicting Systems Graphically 32
Systems and the Context-Level Data Flow Diagram 32 / Systems and the Entity-Relationship Model 34

Use Case Modeling 39
Use Case Symbols 39 / Use Case Relationships 40 / Developing Use Case Diagrams 42 / Developing Use Case Scenarios 42 / Why Use Case Diagrams are Helpful 45

Levels of Management 46

Consulting Opportunity 2.2 Where There's Carbon, There's a Copy 47

Consulting Opportunity 2.3 Pyramid Power 48
Implications for Information Systems Development 48

Organizational Culture 49
SUMMARY 49
HYPERCASE® EXPERIENCE 2 50
KEYWORDS AND PHRASES 51
REVIEW QUESTIONS 52
PROBLEMS 52
GROUP PROJECTS 54
SELECTED BIBLIOGRAPHY 54
CPU CASE EPISODE 2: PICTURING THE RELATIONSHIPS 55

3 PROJECT MANAGEMENT 57

Project Initiation 57
Problems in the Organization 58

Consulting Opportunity 3.1 The Sweetest Sound I've Ever Sipped 59
Defining the Problem 59 / Selection of Projects 62

Determining Feasibility 63
Defining Objectives 64 / Determining Resources 66 / Judging Feasibility 68

Activity Planning and Control 68
Estimating Time Required 68

Consulting Opportunity 3.2 Food for Thought 69
Using Gantt Charts for Project Scheduling 70 / Using PERT Diagrams 71

Computer-Based Project Scheduling 74
Timeboxing 75 / Managing the Project 76 / Addressing System Complexity 76

Function Point Analysis 76
Estimating Staffing Requirements for the Project 79 / Managing Risk 80

Managing Analysis and Design Activities 81
Assembling a Team 81 / Communication Strategies for Managing Teams 82

Consulting Opportunity 3.3 Goal Tending 83
Setting Project Productivity Goals 83 / Motivating Project Team Members 84 / Managing Projects Using COTS Software 84 / Managing Ecommerce Projects 85 / Creating the Project Charter 85 / Avoiding Project Failures 86

Agile Development 86
Resource Trade-Offs Using an Agile Approach 87 / Core Practices and Roles of the Agile Approach 89 / Developmental Process for an Agile Project 94
SUMMARY 96
HYPERCASE® EXPERIENCE 3 97
KEYWORDS AND PHRASES 99
REVIEW QUESTIONS 99
PROBLEMS 100
GROUP PROJECTS 103
SELECTED BIBLIOGRAPHY 104
CPU CASE EPISODE 3: GETTING TO KNOW U 105

PART II INFORMATION REQUIREMENTS ANALYSIS

4 INFORMATION GATHERING: INTERACTIVE METHODS 109

Interviewing 109
Five Steps in Interview Preparation 110 / Question Types 112 / Arranging Questions in a Logical Sequence 114

Consulting Opportunity 4.1 Strengthening Your Question Types 115
Writing the Interview Report 116

Consulting Opportunity 4.2 Skimming the Surface 117

Joint Application Design 118
Conditions That Support the Use of JAD 118 / Who Is Involved 118
HYPERCASE® EXPERIENCE 4.1 119
Where to Hold JAD Meetings 120 / Accomplishing a Structured Analysis of Project Activities 120

Consulting Opportunity 4.3 A Systems Analyst, I Presume? 121
Potential Benefits of Using JAD in Place of Traditional Interviewing 121 / Potential Drawbacks of Using JAD 121

Using Questionnaires 122
Planning for the Use of Questionnaires 122 / Writing Questions 123 / Using Scales in Questionnaires 126 / Designing the Questionnaires 128

Consulting Opportunity 4.4 The Unbearable Questionnaire 129
Administering Questionnaires 130

Consulting Opportunity 4.5 Order in the Courts 130
SUMMARY 131
HYPERCASE® EXPERIENCE 4.2 132
KEYWORDS AND PHRASES 133
REVIEW QUESTIONS 133
PROBLEMS 134
GROUP PROJECTS 137
SELECTED BIBLIOGRAPHY 138
CPU CASE EPISODE 4: I'LL LISTEN NOW, ASK QUESTIONS LATER 139

5 INFORMATION GATHERING: UNOBTRUSIVE METHODS 143

Sampling 143
The Need for Sampling 144 / Sampling Design 144 / The Sample Size Decision 146

Consulting Opportunity 5.1 Trapping a Sample 148

Investigation 148
Analyzing Quantitative Documents 149

Consulting Opportunity 5.2 A Rose by Any Other Name . . . or Quality, Not Quantities 151
Analyzing Qualitative Documents 153
HYPERCASE® EXPERIENCE 5.1 155

Observing a Decision Maker's Behavior 155
Observing a Typical Manager's Decision-Making Activities 155

Observing the Physical Environment 157
Structured Observation of the Environment (STROBE) 157 / Applying STROBE 160

Consulting Opportunity 5.3 Don't Bank on Their Self-Image or Not Everything Is Reflected in a Mirror 160
SUMMARY 162
HYPERCASE® EXPERIENCE 5.2 163
KEYWORDS AND PHRASES 164
REVIEW QUESTIONS 164
PROBLEMS 165
GROUP PROJECTS 167
SELECTED BIBLIOGRAPHY 168
CPU CASE EPISODE 5: SEEING IS BELIEVING 169

6 AGILE MODELING AND PROTOTYPING 171

Prototyping 172
Kinds of Prototypes 172 / Prototyping as an Alternative to the Systems Development Life Cycle 174

Developing a Prototype 175
Guidelines for Developing a Prototype 175 / Disadvantages of Prototyping 177

Consulting Opportunity 6.1 Is Prototyping King? 177
Advantages of Prototyping 178
Prototyping Using COTS Software 178

Consulting Opportunity 6.2 Clearing the Way for Customer Links 178

Consulting Opportunity 6.3 To Hatch a Fish 179

Users' Role in Prototyping 179
Interaction with the Prototype 180

Consulting Opportunity 6.4 This Prototype Is All Wet 180

Rapid Application Development 181
Phases of RAD 182 / Comparing RAD to the SDLC 183

Agile Modeling 185
Values and Principles of Agile Modeling 186 / Activities, Resources, and Practices of Agile Modeling 189 / The Agile Development Process and Tools 190 / Lessons Learned from Agile Modeling 195

Comparing Agile Modeling and Structured Methods 197
Reducing the Interface Time and Errors 198 / Reducing the Process Learning Time and Dual Processing Losses 199 / Reducing the Time and Effort to Structure Tasks and Format Outputs 199 / Reducing the Nonproductive Expansion of Work 199 / Reducing the Data and Knowledge Search and Storage Time and Costs 199 / Reducing Communication and Coordination Time and Costs 200 / Reducing Losses from Human Information Overload 200 / Risks Inherent in Organizational Innovation 201

SUMMARY 203

HYPERCASE® EXPERIENCE 6 205

KEYWORDS AND PHRASES 206

REVIEW QUESTIONS 206

PROBLEMS 207

GROUP PROJECTS 209

SELECTED BIBLIOGRAPHY 209

CPU CASE EPISODE 6: REACTION TIME 211

PART III THE ANALYSIS PROCESS

7 USING DATA FLOW DIAGRAMS 217

The Data Flow Approach to Human Requirements Determination 217
Advantages of the Data Flow Approach 218 / Conventions Used in Data Flow Diagrams 218

Developing Data Flow Diagrams 220
Creating the Context Diagram 220 / Drawing Diagram 0 (The Next Level) 221 / Creating Child Diagrams (More Detailed Levels) 221 / Checking the Diagrams for Errors 223

Logical and Physical Data Flow Diagrams 225
Developing Logical Data Flow Diagrams 227 / Developing Physical Data Flow Diagrams 228 / Partitioning Data Flow Diagrams 232 / A Data Flow Diagram Example 234 / Creating the Context Diagram 235 / Drawing Diagram 0 235 / Creating a Child Diagram 237

Creating a Physical Data Flow Diagram 238
Partitioning the Data Flow Diagram 240

A Second Data Flow Diagram Example 241

Partitioning Web Sites 246

Consulting Opportunity 7.1 There's No Business Like Flow Business 249

Communicating Using Data Flow Diagrams 250

SUMMARY 250

HYPERCASE® EXPERIENCE 7 251

KEYWORDS AND PHRASES 252

REVIEW QUESTIONS 252

PROBLEMS 252

GROUP PROJECTS 255

SELECTED BIBLIOGRAPHY 255

CPU CASE EPISODE 7: JUST FLOWING ALONG 256

8 ANALYZING SYSTEMS USING DATA DICTIONARIES 267

The Data Dictionary 267
Need for Understanding the Data Dictionary 268

The Data Repository 268
Defining the Data Flows 269 / Describing Data Structures 271 / Logical and Physical Data Structures 273 / Data Elements 274 / Data Stores 277

Creating the Data Dictionary 279
Analyzing Input and Output 280

Consulting Opportunity 8.1 Want to Make It Big in the Theatre? Improve Your Diction(ary)! 281
Developing Data Stores 281

Using the Data Dictionary 282
Using Data Dictionaries to Create XML 284 / XML Document Type Definitions 287 / XML Schemas 289

SUMMARY 289

HYPERCASE® EXPERIENCE 8 290

KEYWORDS AND PHRASES 291

REVIEW QUESTIONS 291

PROBLEMS 291

GROUP PROJECTS 294

SELECTED BIBLIOGRAPHY 294

CPU CASE EPISODE 8: DEFINING WHAT YOU MEAN 296

9 DESCRIBING PROCESS SPECIFICATIONS AND STRUCTURED DECISIONS 305

Overview of Process Specifications 305
Process Specification Format 306

Structured English 308
Writing Structured English 309

Consulting Opportunity 9.1 Kit Chen Kaboodle, Inc. 310

Consulting Opportunity 9.2 Kneading Structure 311
Data Dictionary and Process Specifications 312

Decision Tables 313
Developing Decision Tables 315

Consulting Opportunity 9.3 Saving a Cent on Citron Car Rental 316
Checking for Completeness and Accuracy 318 / More Advanced Decision Tables 319

Decision Trees 319

Consulting Opportunity 9.4 A Tree for Free 320
Drawing Decision Trees 320

Choosing a Structured Decision Analysis Technique 321

Physical and Logical Process Specifications 323
Using Process Specifications: Horizontal Balancing 324

SUMMARY 327

HYPERCASE® EXPERIENCE 9 328

KEYWORDS AND PHRASES 329

REVIEW QUESTIONS 329

PROBLEMS 330

GROUP PROJECTS 332

SELECTED BIBLIOGRAPHY 332

CPU CASE EPISODE 9: TABLING A DECISION 333

10 PREPARING THE SYSTEMS PROPOSAL 339

Ascertaining Hardware and Software Needs 339
Inventorying Computer Hardware 340 / Estimating Workloads 341 / Evaluating Computer Hardware 341 / Acquisition of Computer Equipment 342 / Software Evaluation 345 / Decision Support Tools 348

Consulting Opportunity 10.1 Veni, Vidi, Vendi, or, I Came, I Saw, I Sold 349
Expert Systems, Neural Nets, and Other Decision Tools 350
HYPERCASE® EXPERIENCE 10.1 351

Identifying and Forecasting Costs and Benefits 351
Forecasting Costs and Benefits 352

Consulting Opportunity 10.2 We're Off to See the Wizards 354
Identifying Benefits and Costs 354

Comparing Costs and Benefits 355
Break-Even Analysis 355
HYPERCASE® EXPERIENCE 10.2 357
Cash-Flow Analysis 357 / Present Value Analysis 358 / Guidelines for Analysis 359 / Examining Alternative Systems 359

The Systems Proposal 360
Organizing the Systems Proposal 360 / Using Figures for Effective Communication 361

Presenting the Systems Proposal 366
Understanding the Audience 366

Consulting Opportunity 10.3 Should This Chart Be Barred? 367
Organizing the Systems Proposal Presentation 368 / Principles of Delivery 368
SUMMARY 368
HYPERCASE® EXPERIENCE 10.3 369
KEYWORDS AND PHRASES 370
REVIEW QUESTIONS 370
PROBLEMS 371
GROUP PROJECTS 375
SELECTED BIBLIOGRAPHY 375
CPU CASE EPISODE 10: PROPOSING TO GO FORTH 376

PART IV THE ESSENTIALS OF DESIGN

11 DESIGNING EFFECTIVE OUTPUT 379

Output Design Objectives 379
Designing Output to Serve the Intended Purpose 380 / Designing Output to Fit the User 380 / Delivering the Appropriate Quantity of Output 380 / Making Sure the Output Is Where It Is Needed 380 / Providing the Output on Time 380 / Choosing the Right Output Method 381

Relating Output Content to Output Method 381
Output Technologies 381

Consulting Opportunity 11.1 Your Cage or Mine? 386
Factors to Consider When Choosing Output Technology 389

Consulting Opportunity 11.2 A Right Way, a Wrong Way, and a Subway 393

Realizing How Output Bias Affects Users 394
Recognizing Bias in the Way Output Is Used 394 / Avoiding Bias in the Design of Output 396 / Designing Printed Output 396 / Guidelines for Printed Report Design 396

Designing Output for Displays 398
Guidelines for Display Design 398 / Using Graphical Output in Screen Design 400 / Dashboards 400

Consulting Opportunity 11.3 Is Your Work a Grind? 402
Widgets and Gadgets—Changing the Desktop Metaphor 402

Designing a Web Site 403
General Guidelines for Designing Web Sites 403 / Creating Blogs (Web Logs) 412

Consulting Opportunity 11.4 A Field Day 412

Output Production and XML 413
Ajax 415
SUMMARY 416
HYPERCASE® EXPERIENCE 11 417
KEYWORDS AND PHRASES 418
REVIEW QUESTIONS 418
PROBLEMS 419
GROUP PROJECTS 423
SELECTED BIBLIOGRAPHY 424
CPU CASE EPISODE 11: REPORTING ON OUTPUTS 425

12 DESIGNING EFFECTIVE INPUT 433

Good Form Design 433
Making Forms Easy to Fill In 434 / Meeting the Intended Purpose 437 / Ensuring Accurate Completion 437 / Keeping Forms Attractive 437 / Computer-Assisted Form Design 438 / Controlling Business Forms 440

Good Display and Web Forms Design 441
Keeping the Display Simple 441

Consulting Opportunity 12.1 This Form May be Hazardous to Your Health 442
Keeping the Display Consistent 443 / Facilitating Movement 443 / Designing an Attractive and Pleasing Display 443

Consulting Opportunity 12.2 Squeezin' Isn't Pleasin' 445
Using Icons in Display Design 446 / Graphical User Interface Design 446

Consulting Opportunity 12.3 What's That Thing Supposed to Be? 448
Form Controls and Values 449 / Hidden Fields 450 / Event-Response Charts 451 / Dynamic Web Pages 453 / Ajax (Asynchronous Javascript and XML) 455 / Tab Control Dialog Boxes 457 / Using Color in Display Design 458

Consulting Opportunity 12.4 It's Only Skin Deep 459

Intranet and Internet Page Design 460
SUMMARY 462
HYPERCASE® EXPERIENCE 12 463
KEYWORDS AND PHRASES 464
REVIEW QUESTIONS 464
PROBLEMS 465
GROUP PROJECTS 470
SELECTED BIBLIOGRAPHY 470
CPU CASE EPISODE 12: FORMING SCREENS AND SCREENING FORMS 471

13 DESIGNING DATABASES 479

Databases 480

Data Concepts 480

Consulting Opportunity 13.1 Hitch Your Cleaning Cart to a Star 481
Reality, Data, and Metadata 481 / File Organization 488 / Relational Databases 490

Normalization 492
The Three Steps of Normalization 492 / A Normalization Example 493 / Using the Entity-Relationship Diagram to Determine Record Keys 502 / One-to-Many Relationship 502 / Many-to-Many Relationship 502

Guidelines for Master File/Database Relation Design 503
Integrity Constraints 504 / Anomalies 505

Making Use of the Database 506
Steps in Retrieving and Presenting Data 506

Denormalization 511

Data Warehouses 512
Online Analytic Processing 514

Consulting Opportunity 13.2 Storing Minerals for Health, Data for Mining 516
Data Mining 516

Consulting Opportunity 13.3 Losing Prospects 518

SUMMARY 519

HYPERCASE® EXPERIENCE 13 520

KEYWORDS AND PHRASES 521

REVIEW QUESTIONS 521

PROBLEMS 522

GROUP PROJECT 524

SELECTED BIBLIOGRAPHY 524

CPU CASE EPISODE 13: BACK TO DATA BASICS 525

14 HUMAN–COMPUTER INTERACTION 533

Understanding Human–Computer Interaction 533
How Fit Affects Performance and Well-Being 534 / The Technology Acceptance Model and Attitude 536 / Usability 536 / Designing for the Cognitive Styles of Individual Users 537 / Physical Considerations in HCI Design 542 / Considering Human Limitations, Disabilities, and Design 543

Consulting Opportunity 14.1 School Spirit Comes in Many Sizes 544

Implementing Good HCI Practices 545

Types of User Interface 545
Natural-Language Interfaces 546 / Question-and-Answer Interfaces 546 / Menus 547 / Form-Fill Interfaces (Input/Output Forms) 549

Consulting Opportunity 14.2 I'd Rather Do It Myself 549
Command-Language Interfaces 550

Consulting Opportunity 14.3 Don't Slow Me Down 551
Graphical User Interfaces 551

Consulting Opportunity 14.4 That's Not a Lightbulb 552
Other User Interfaces 552

Guidelines for Dialog Design 554
Meaningful Communication 554 / Minimal User Action 555 / Standard Operation and Consistency 557

Feedback for Users 558
Consulting Opportunity 14.5 Waiting to Be Fed 559
Types of Feedback 559 / Including Feedback in Design 562
Special Design Considerations for Ecommerce 563
Soliciting Feedback from Ecommerce Web Site Customers 563
Consulting Opportunity 14.6 When You Run a Marathon, It Helps to Know Where You're Going 564
Easy Navigation for Ecommerce Web Sites 565
Mashups 566
Designing Queries 567
Query Types 567
Consulting Opportunity 14.7 Hey, Look Me Over (Reprise) 570
Query Methods 570
SUMMARY 573
HYPERCASE® EXPERIENCE 14 574
KEYWORDS AND PHRASES 576
REVIEW QUESTIONS 576
PROBLEMS 577
GROUP PROJECTS 578
SELECTED BIBLIOGRAPHY 579
CPU CASE EPISODE 14: UP TO THE USERS 581

15 DESIGNING ACCURATE DATA ENTRY PROCEDURES 591

Effective Coding 591
Keeping Track of Something 592 / Classifying Information 593 / Concealing Information 595 / Revealing Information 596 / Unicode 597 / Requesting Appropriate Action 598 / General Guidelines for Coding 598
Consulting Opportunity 15.1 It's a Wilderness in Here 599
Effective and Efficient Data Capture 601
Deciding What to Capture 601
Consulting Opportunity 15.2 Catching a Summer Code 602
Letting the Computer Do the Rest 602 / Avoiding Bottlenecks and Extra Steps 604 / Starting with a Good Form 604 / Choosing a Data Entry Method 605
Ensuring Data Quality Through Input Validation 608
Validating Input Transactions 609
Consulting Opportunity 15.3 To Enter or Not to Enter: That Is the Question 610
Validating Input Data 610 / The Process of Validation 614
Consulting Opportunity 15.4 Do You Validate Parking? 616
Accuracy Advantages in Ecommerce Environments 616
Customers Keying Their Own Data 617 / Storing Data for Later Use 617 / Using Data Through the Order Fulfillment Process 617 / Providing Feedback to Customers 617
SUMMARY 618
HYPERCASE® EXPERIENCE 15 619
KEYWORDS AND PHRASES 619
REVIEW QUESTIONS 620
PROBLEMS 621
GROUP PROJECTS 623
SELECTED BIBLIOGRAPHY 624
CPU CASE EPISODE 15: ENTERING NATURALLY 625

PART V SOFTWARE ENGINEERING AND IMPLEMENTATION

16 QUALITY ASSURANCE THROUGH SOFTWARE ENGINEERING 631

The Total Quality Management Approach 631
Six Sigma 632 / Responsibility for Total Quality Management 632

Consulting Opportunity 16.1 The Quality of MIS Is Not Strained 634
Structured Walkthrough 634 / Systems Design and Development 635 / Modular Development 637 / Modularity in the Windows Environment 638

Using Structure Charts to Design Systems 638
Drawing a Structure Chart 642 / Types of Modules 644 / Module Subordination 646

Software Engineering and Documentation 648
Pseudocode 649 / Procedure Manuals 650 / The Folklore Method 651

Consulting Opportunity 16.2 Write Is Right 653
Choosing a Design and Documentation Technique 653

Testing, Maintenance, and Auditing 653
The Testing Process 654

Consulting Opportunity 16.3 Cramming for Your Systems Test 656
Maintenance Practices 657 / Auditing 657

SUMMARY 658

HYPERCASE® EXPERIENCE 16 659

KEYWORDS AND PHRASES 660

REVIEW QUESTIONS 660

PROBLEMS 661

GROUP PROJECTS 662

SELECTED BIBLIOGRAPHY 662

CPU CASE EPISODE 16: CHARTING THE STRUCTURE 663

17 SUCCESSFULLY IMPLEMENTING THE INFORMATION SYSTEM 671

Implementing Distributed Systems 672
Client/Server Technology 672 / Types of Distributed Systems Networks 674 / Network Modeling 677 / Groupware 681

Training Users 683
Training Strategies 683 / Guidelines for Training 684

Consulting Opportunity 17.1 You Can Lead a Fish to Water . . . But You Can't Make It Drink 685

Conversion 686
Conversion Strategies 686

Security Concerns for Traditional and Web-Based Systems 688
Physical Security 688 / Logical Security 689 / Behavioral Security 689 / Special Security Considerations for Ecommerce 690 / Privacy Considerations for Ecommerce 691 / Disaster Recovery Planning 691

Other Conversion Considerations 693
Organizational Metaphors and Their Relationship to Successful Systems 693

Evaluation 694
Evaluation Techniques 694 / The Information System Utility Approach 695

Consulting Opportunity 17.2 The Sweet Smell of Success 696
Evaluating the System 696

Consulting Opportunity 17.3 Mopping Up with the New System 697

Evaluating Corporate Web Sites 697
SUMMARY 700
HYPERCASE® EXPERIENCE 17 701
KEYWORDS AND PHRASES 702
REVIEW QUESTIONS 702
PROBLEMS 703
GROUP PROJECTS 705
SELECTED BIBLIOGRAPHY 705
CPU CASE EPISODE 17: SEMPER REDUNDATE 707

18 OBJECT-ORIENTED SYSTEMS ANALYSIS AND DESIGN USING UML 709

Object-Oriented Concepts 710
Objects 710 / Classes 710 / Inheritance 711

CRC Cards and Object Think 712

Consulting Opportunity 18.1 Making the Magic Reel 713
Interacting During a CRC Session 713

The Unified Modeling Language (UML) Concepts and Diagrams 715

Use Case Modeling 717

Activity Diagrams 720
Creating Activity Diagrams 722

Consulting Opportunity 18.2 Recycling the Programming Environment 723

Sequence and Communication Diagrams 724
Sequence Diagrams 724 / Communication Diagrams 726

Class Diagrams 727
Method Overloading 728 / Types of Classes 729 / Defining Messages and Methods 730 / A Class Example for the Web 730 / Relationships 733 / Generalization/Specialization (Gen/Spec) Diagrams 736

Statechart Diagrams 740
State Transition Example 741

Packages and Other UML Artifacts 742

Consulting Opportunity 18.3 Developing a Fine System That Was Long Overdue: Using Object-Oriented Analysis for the Ruminski Public Library System 744

Putting UML to Work 744

The Importance of Using UML for Modeling 746

Consulting Opportunity 18.4 C-Shore++ 747
SUMMARY 748
KEYWORDS AND PHRASES 748
REVIEW QUESTIONS 749
PROBLEMS 749
SELECTED BIBLIOGRAPHY 751

GLOSSARY 753

ACRONYMS 763

INDEX 764

PREFACE

NEW TO THIS EDITION

The seventh edition of Kendall & Kendall *Systems Analysis and Design* includes many new and updated features. In particular:

- New chapter of HCI (human–computer interaction)
- Early introduction of use cases
- Expanded coverage of project management
- New approaches to creating a project charter
- New methods for creating a problem definition
- Expanded coverage of human-centered approach including usability and human values
- New techniques to estimate the size of a systems project
- New, in-depth coverage of the agile approach and agile modeling
- New discussion of designing for emerging information technologies
- Expanded coverage of ecommerce analysis and design
- New coverage of mashups, dashboards, widgets, gadgets, and application programming interfaces.
- Expanded coverage of object-oriented analysis and design
- New end-of-chapter Review Questions, Problems, and Group Exercises
- Updated HyperCase 2.7, a graphical simulation for the Web that allows students to apply their new skills

DESIGN FEATURES

Figures take on a stylized look in order to help students more easily grasp the subject matter.

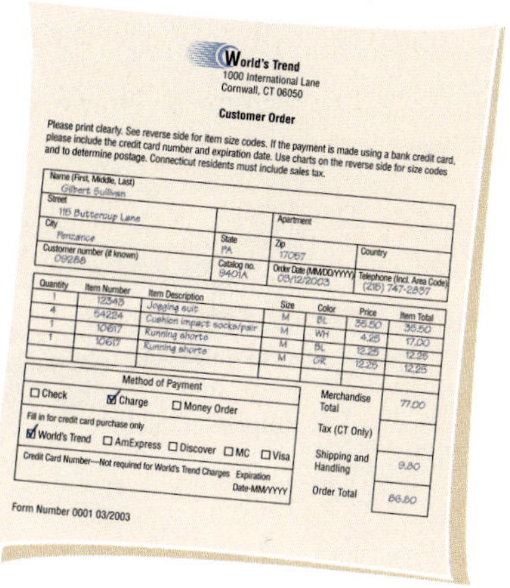
World's Trend
1000 International Lane
Cornwall, CT 06050

Customer Order

Please print clearly. See reverse side for item size codes. If the payment is made using a bank credit card, please include the credit card number and expiration date. Use charts on the reverse side for size codes and to determine postage. Connecticut residents must include sales tax.

Name (First, Middle, Last): Gilbert Sullivan
Street: 115 Buttercup Lane
Apartment:
City: Penzance
State: PA
Zip: 17057
Country:
Customer number (if known): 09288
Catalog no.: 9401A
Order Date (MM/DD/YYYY): 03/12/2003
Telephone (Incl. Area Code): (215) 747-2837

Quantity	Item Number	Item Description	Size	Color	Price	Item Total
1	12343	Jogging suit	M	BL	35.50	35.50
4	54224	Cushion impact socks/pair	M	WH	4.25	17.00
1	10617	Running shorts	M	BL	12.25	12.25
1	10617	Running shorts	M	GR	12.25	12.25

Method of Payment
☐ Check ☑ Charge ☐ Money Order
Fill in for credit card purchase only
☑ World's Trend ☐ AmExpress ☐ Discover ☐ MC ☐ Visa
Credit Card Number—Not required for World's Trend Charges Expiration Date-MM/YYYY

Merchandise Total: 77.00
Tax (CT Only):
Shipping and Handling: 9.80
Order Total: 86.80

Form Number 0001 03/2003

Paper forms are used throughout to show input and output design as well as the design of questionnaires. Blue ink is always used to show writing or data input, thereby making it easier to identify what was filled in by users. Although most organizations have computerization of manual processes as their eventual goal, much data capture is still done using paper forms. Improved form design enables analysts to ensure accurate and complete input and output. Better forms can also help streamline new internal workflows that result from newly automated business-to-consumer (B2C) applications for ecommerce on the Web.

Computer displays demonstrate important software features that are useful to the analyst. This example shows how a Web site can be evaluated for broken links by using a package such as Microsoft Visio. Actual screen shots show important aspects of design. Analysts are continuously seeking to improve the appearance of the screens and Web pages they design. Colorful examples help to illustrate why some screen designs are particularly effective.

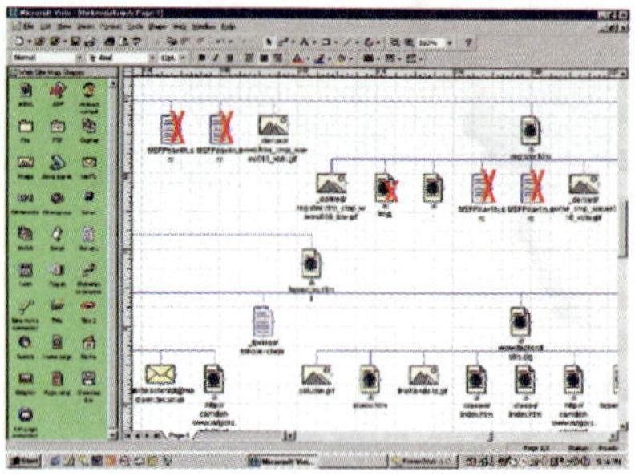

Conceptual diagrams are used to introduce the many tools that systems analysts have at their disposal. This example shows the differences between logical data flow diagrams and physical data flow diagrams. Conceptual diagrams are color coded so that students can distinguish easily among them, and their functions are clearly indicated. Many other important tools are illustrated, including entity-relationship diagrams, structure charts, and structured English.

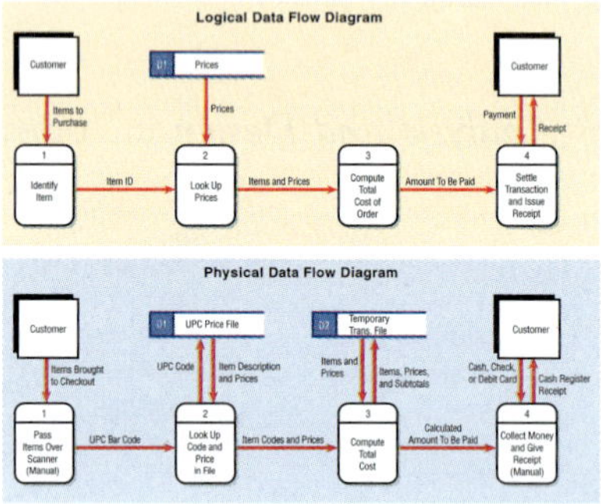

Tables are used when an important list needs special attention, or when information needs to be organized or classified. In addition, tables are used to supplement the understanding of the reader in a way that is different from how material is organized in the narrative portion of the text. Most analysts find tables a useful way to organize numbers and text into a meaningful "snapshot."

This example of a table from Chapter 3 shows how analysts can refine their activity plans for analysis by breaking them down into smaller tasks and then estimating how much time it will take to complete them. The underlying philosophy of our book is that systems analysis and design is a process that integrates the use of many tools with the unique talents of the systems analyst to systematically

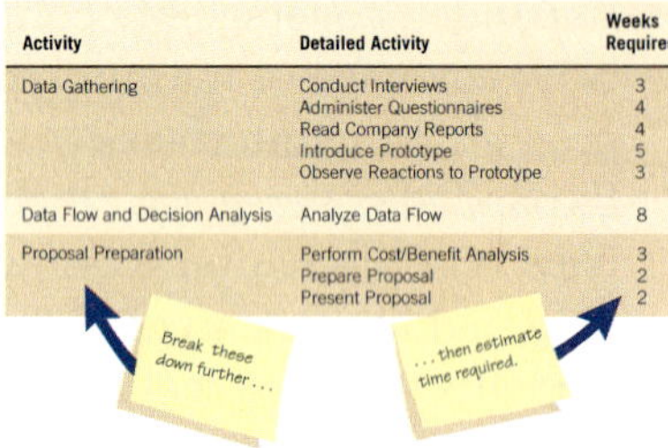

Activity	Detailed Activity	Weeks Required
Data Gathering	Conduct Interviews Administer Questionnaires Read Company Reports Introduce Prototype Observe Reactions to Prototype	3 4 4 5 3
Data Flow and Decision Analysis	Analyze Data Flow	8
Proposal Preparation	Perform Cost/Benefit Analysis Prepare Proposal Present Proposal	3 2 2

improve business through the implementation or modification of computerized information systems. Systems analysts can grow in their work by taking on new IT challenges and keeping current in their profession through the application of new techniques and tools.

A BRIEF TOUR OF THE SEVENTH EDITION

Systems analysis and design is typically taught in one or two semesters. Our book may be used in either situation. The text is appropriate for undergraduate (junior or senior) curricula at a four-year university, graduate school, or community college. The level and length of the course can be varied and supplemented by using real-world projects, HyperCase, or other materials available on the instructor's resource section of our companion Web site.

The text is divided into five major parts: Systems Analysis Fundamentals (Part I), Information Requirements Analysis (Part II), The Analysis Process (Part III), The Essentials of Design (Part IV), and Software Engineering and Implementation (Part V).

Part I (Chapters 1–3) stresses the basics that students need to know about what an analyst does; how a variety of emerging information systems, including handheld computers, wireless technologies, and ERP systems, fit into organizations; how to determine whether a systems project is worthy of commitment; new coverage of ecommerce project management; and how to manage a systems project using special software tools. There is expanded material on virtual teams and virtual organizations. Techniques for drawing entity-relationship diagrams and context-level data flow diagrams when first entering the organization are introduced. Chapter 2 includes expanded coverage of use cases. Chapter 3 introduces new material to explain how an alternative approach called agile modeling, or the agile approach, balances objectives to manage the analysis and design process. New techniques to estimate project size, to create a project charter, and to create a problem definition are all covered. The three roles of the systems analyst as consultant, supporting expert, and agent of change are also introduced, and there are updated ideas on ethical issues and professional guidelines for serving as a systems consultant.

Part II (Chapters 4–6) emphasizes the use of systematic and structured methodologies for performing information requirements analysis. Attention to analysis helps analysts ensure that they are addressing the correct problem before designing the system.

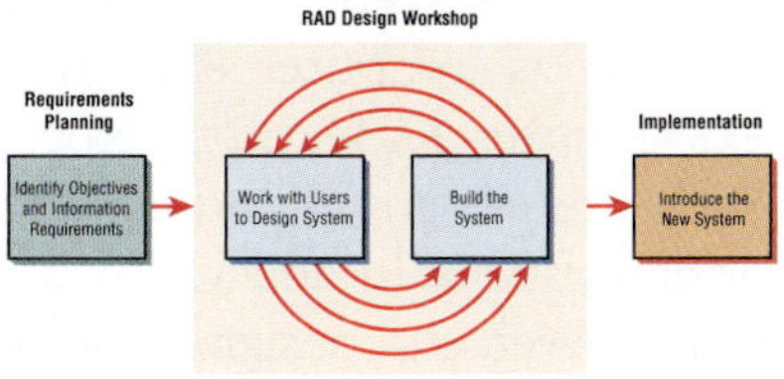

Chapter 4 introduces a group of interactive methods, including interviewing, joint application design (JAD), and constructing questionnaires. Chapter 5 introduces a group of unobtrusive methods for ascertaining information requirements of users. These methods include sampling, investigating hard and archival data, and observation of decision-makers' behavior and their physical environment. Chapter 6 is especially innovative in its treatment of prototyping as another data gathering technique that enables the analyst to solve the right problem by getting users involved from the start. This chapter also includes material on rapid application development (RAD). New material in this chapter enables students to understand the agile approach to systems development. The core practices that differentiate the agile approach from other methodologies are explained. In addition, the values critical to agile modeling are introduced.

Part III (Chapters 7–10) details the analysis process. It builds on the previous two parts to move students into analysis of data flows as well as structured and semistructured decisions. It provides step-by-step details on how to use structured techniques to draw data flow diagrams (DFDs). Chapter 7 provides coverage of how to create child diagrams; how to develop both logical and physical data flow diagrams; and how to partition data flow diagrams. The object-oriented approach of use cases and data flow diagrams is included. The object-oriented approach in Chapter 8 features material on the data repository and vertical balancing of data flow diagrams. Chapter 8 also includes extensive coverage of extensible markup language (XML) and demonstrates how to use data dictionaries to create XML. Chapter 9 includes material on developing process specifications. A discussion of both logical and physical process specifications shows how to use process specifications for horizontal balancing.

Part III also covers how to diagram structured decisions with the use of structured English, decision tables, and decision trees. In addition, push technologies are introduced.

Chapter 10 teaches several methods for forecasting costs and benefits, which are necessary to the discussion of acquiring software and hardware. Chapter 10 helps students evaluate software by assessing trade-offs among creating custom software, purchasing commercial-off-the-shelf (COTS) software, or outsourcing to an application service provider (ASP). Additionally, this chapter shows students how to assist decision makers in choosing decision support software, recommendation systems, and using neural nets. Chapter 10 also guides students in professionally writing and presenting an effective systems proposal, incorporating figures and graphs to communicate with users.

Part IV (Chapters 11–15) covers the essentials of design. It begins with designing output, because many practitioners believe systems to be output driven. The design of Web-based forms is covered in detail. Particular attention is paid to relating output method to content, the effect of output on users, and designing good forms and screens. Chapter 11 compares advantages and disadvantages of output, including Web displays, audio, CD-ROM, DVD, and electronic output such as email, faxes, and bulletin boards. Designing a Web site for ecommerce purposes is emphasized, and output production and XML is covered. Chapter 12 includes innovative material on designing Web-based input forms, as well as other electronic form design. Also included is computer-assisted form design.

Chapter 12 features expanded coverage of Web site design, including guidelines on when designers should add video, audio, and animation to Web site designs. The uses of Web push and pull technologies for output design are covered. There is detailed consideration of how to create effective graphics for corporate Web sites and designing effective onscreen navigation for Web site users.

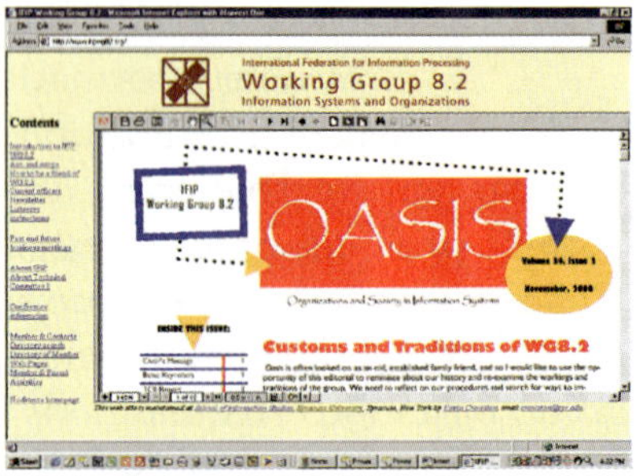

Coverage of intranet and extranet page design is also included. Consideration of database integrity constraints has been included, and how the user interacts with the computer and how to design an appropriate interface are also covered. The importance of user feedback is also found in Part IV. How to design accurate data entry procedures that take full advantage of computer and human capabilities to assure entry of quality data is emphasized here.

Chapter 13 demonstrates how to use the entity-relationship diagram to determine record keys, as well as providing guidelines for file/database relation design.

Students are shown the relevance of database design for the overall usefulness of the system, and how users actually use databases.

Chapter 14 is a new chapter on human–computer interaction (HCI). It introduces HCI, discussing its importance in designing systems that suit individuals and assisting them in achieving personal and organizational goals through their use of information technology. The concepts of usability, fit, perceived usefulness, and perceived ease of use are introduced, as is the Technology Acceptance Model (TAM), so that systems students can knowledgeably incorporate HCI practices into their designs. Chapter 14 also features material on designing easy onscreen navigation for Web site visitors. Innovative approaches to searching on the Web are also presented. Material on GUI design is also highlighted, and innovative approaches to designing dialogs are provided. Chapter 14 articulates specialized design considerations for ecommerce Web sites. Mashups, new applications created by combining two or more Web-based application programming interfaces, are also introduced. Chapter 14 also includes extensive coverage on how to formulate queries, all within the framework of HCI. Chapter 15 includes material on managing the supply chain through the effective design of business-to-business (B2B) ecommerce systems.

Part V (Chapters 16–18) introduces students to structured software engineering and documentation techniques as ways to implement a quality system. Chapter 16 provides material on taking the Six Sigma approach to quality for software and systems design. Chapter 16 also includes a section on the important concepts of code generation and design reengineering. We also cover developments in structured techniques, teaching students which techniques are appropriate for particular situations.

The material on structure charts includes details on how to use data flow diagrams to draw structure charts. In addition, material on system security and firewalls is included. Testing, auditing, and maintenance of systems are discussed in the context of total quality management. Chapter 17 presents innovative tools for modeling networks, which can be done with popular tools such as Microsoft Visio. A discussion of groupware is also included. Part V also introduces the student to designing client/server systems, distributed systems, and multiple wireless systems, including WLANs, Wi-Fi networks, and Bluetooth networks.

Material on security and privacy in relation to designing ecommerce applications is included. Expanded coverage on security, specifically firewalls, gateways, public key infrastructure (PKI), secure electronic translation (SET), secure socket layering (SSL), virus protection software, URL filtering products, email filtering products, and virtual private networks (VPN), is included. Additionally, current topics of interest to designers of ecommerce applications, including the development of audience profiling and the development and posting of corporate privacy policies, are covered.

Important coverage of how the analyst can promote and then monitor a corporate Web site is included in this section, which features Web activity monitoring, Web site promotion, Web traffic analysis, and audience profiling to ensure the effectiveness of new ecommerce systems. Techniques for evaluating the completed information systems project are covered systematically as well.

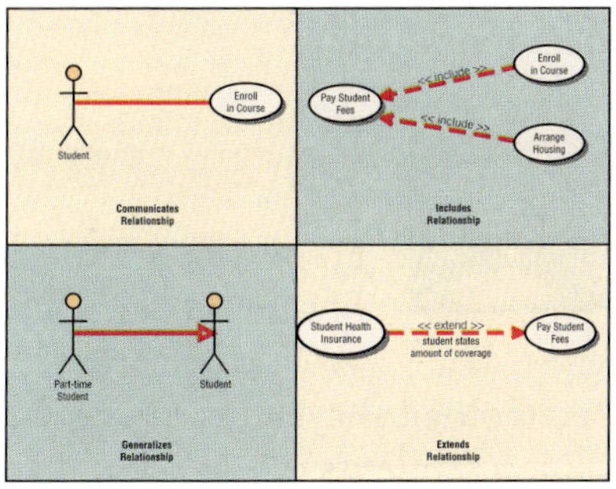

Part V concludes with Chapter 18 on object-oriented systems analysis and design, which includes an in-depth section on using unified modeling language (UML). There is detailed coverage of the use case model, creating the class model diagram with UML, creating gen/spec diagrams, use case scenarios, and activity diagrams. Through several examples and Consulting Opportunities, this chapter demonstrates how to use an object-oriented approach. Consulting Opportunities, diagrams, and problems enable students to learn and use UML to model systems from an object-oriented perspective.

The seventh edition contains an updated **Glossary** of terms and a separate list of updated **Acronyms** used in the book and in the systems analysis and design field.

PEDAGOGICAL FEATURES

Chapters in the Seventh Edition contain:

- **Learning Objectives** at the beginning of each chapter
- **Summaries** that tie together the salient points of each chapter while providing an excellent source of review for exams
- **Keywords and Phrases**
- **Review Questions**
- **Problems**
- **Group Projects** that help students work together in a systems team to solve important problems that are best solved through group interaction
- **Consulting Opportunities**—now more than 65 minicases throughout the book
- **HyperCase Experiences**
- **CPU Episodes**—parts of an ongoing case threaded throughout the book

CONSULTING OPPORTUNITIES

The seventh edition presents more than 65 Consulting Opportunities, and many of them address relevant and emerging topics that have arisen in the field, including designing systems from an HCI perspective, ecommerce applications for the Web, COTS software, and using UML to model information systems from an object-oriented perspective. Consulting Opportunities can be used for stimulating in-class discussions, or assigned as homework or take-home exam questions. Because not all systems are extended two- or three-year projects, our book contains many Consulting Opportunities that can be solved quickly in 20 to 30 minutes of group discussion or individual writing. These minicases, written in a humorous manner to enliven the material, require students to synthesize what they have learned up to that point in the course, ask students to mature in their professional and ethical judgment, and expect students to articulate the reasoning that led to their systems decisions.

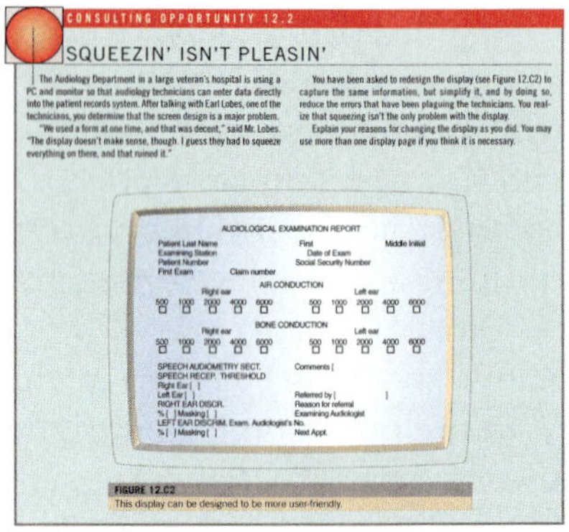

HYPERCASE EXPERIENCES

HyperCase Experiences that pose challenging student exercises are present in each chapter. HyperCase version 2.7 is now available on the Web. HyperCase has organizational problems featuring state-of-the-art technological systems. HyperCase represents an original virtual organization that allows students who access it to become immediately immersed in organizational

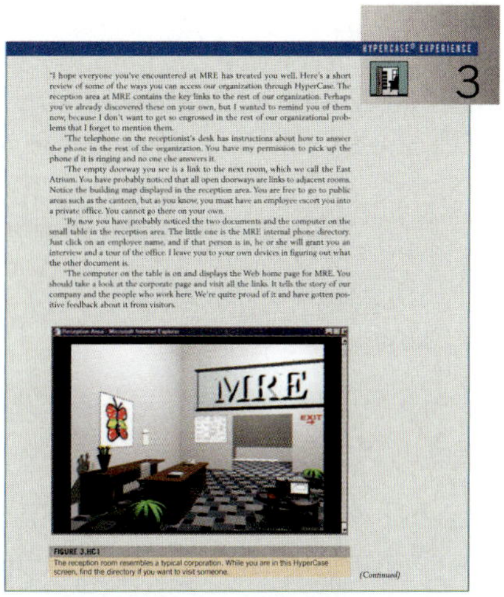

HYPERCASE® EXPERIENCE 3

"I hope everyone you've encountered at MRE has treated you well. Here's a short review of some of the ways you can access our organization through HyperCase. The reception area at MRE contains the key links to the rest of our organization. Perhaps you've already discovered these on your own, but I wanted to remind you of them now, because I don't want to get so engrossed in the rest of our organizational problems that I forget to mention them.

"The telephone on the receptionist's desk has instructions about how to answer the phone in the rest of the organization. You have my permission to pick up the phone if it is ringing and no one else answers it.

"The empty doorway you see is a link to the next room, which we call the East Atrium. You have probably noticed that all open doorways are links to adjacent rooms. Notice the building map displayed in the reception area. You are free to go to public areas such as the canteen, but as you know, you must have an employee escort you into a private office. You cannot go there on your own.

"By now you have probably noticed the two documents and the computer on the small table in the reception area. The little one is the MRE internal phone directory. Just click on an employee name, and if that person is in, he or she will grant you an interview and a tour of the office. I leave you to your own devices in figuring out what the other document is.

"The computer on the table is on and displays the Web home page for MRE. You should take a look at the corporate page and visit all the links. It tells the story of our company and the people who work here. We're quite proud of it and have gotten positive feedback about it from visitors.

FIGURE 3.HC1
The reception room resembles a typical corporation. While you are in this HyperCase screen, find the directory if you want to visit someone.

(Continued)

life. Students will interview people, observe office environments, analyze their prototypes, and review the documentation of their existing systems. HyperCase 2.7 is Web-based, interactive software that presents an organization called Maple Ridge Engineering (MRE) in a colorful, three-dimensional graphics environment. HyperCase permits professors to begin approaching the systems analysis and design class with exciting multimedia material. Carefully watching their use of time and managing multiple methods, students use the hypertext characteristics of HyperCase on the Web to create their own individual paths through the organization.

Maple Ridge Engineering is drawn from the actual consulting experiences of the authors of the original version (Raymond Barnes, Richard Baskerville, Julie E. Kendall, and Kenneth E. Kendall). Allen Schmidt joined the project for Version 2.0. Peter Schmidt was the HTML programmer, and Jason Reed created the images for the Web version.

In each chapter, there are special HyperCase Experiences that include assignments (and even some clues) to help students solve the difficult organizational problems they encounter at MRE. HyperCase has been fully tested in classrooms, and was an award winner in the Decision Sciences Institute Innovative Instruction competition.

CPU CASE EPISODES

In keeping with our belief that a variety of approaches is important, we have once again integrated the Central Pacific University (CPU) case into every chapter of the seventh edition. The CPU case makes use of the popular CASE tool Visible Analyst by Visible Systems, Inc., as well as Microsoft Access for the example screen shots and the student exercises.

The CPU case takes students through all phases of the systems development life cycle, demonstrating the capabilities of Visible Analyst, a student edition of which can be bundled with our book. This CASE tool gives students an opportunity to solve problems on their own, using Visible Analyst and data that users of the book can download from the Web containing Visible Analyst exercises specifically keyed to each chapter of the book. Additionally, partially completed exercises in Microsoft Access files are available for student use on the Web. The CPU case has been fully tested in classrooms around the world with a variety of students over numerous terms. The case is detailed, rigorous, and rich enough to stand alone as a systems analysis and design project spanning one or two terms. Alternatively, the CPU case can be used as a way to teach the use of CASE tools in conjunction with the assignment of a one- or two-term, real-world project outside the classroom.

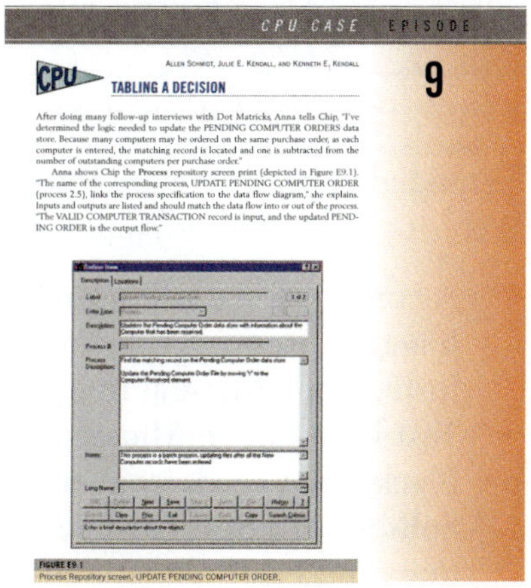

CPU CASE EPISODE 9

ALLEN SCHMIDT, JULIE E. KENDALL, AND KENNETH E. KENDALL

TABLING A DECISION

After doing many follow-up interviews with Dot Matricks, Anna tells Chip, "I've determined the logic needed to update the PENDING COMPUTER ORDERS data store. Because many computers may be ordered on the same purchase order, as each computer is entered, the matching record is located and one is subtracted from the number of outstanding computers per purchase order."

Anna shows Chip the **Process** repository screen print (depicted in Figure E9.1). "The name of the corresponding process, UPDATE PENDING COMPUTER ORDER (process 2.5), links the process specification to the data flow diagram," she explains. Inputs and outputs are listed and should match the data flow into or out of the process. "The VALID COMPUTER TRANSACTION record is input, and the updated PENDING ORDER is the output flow."

FIGURE E9.1
Process Repository screen, UPDATE PENDING COMPUTER ORDER.

SOFTWARE

Kendall & Kendall's *Systems Analysis and Design*, Seventh Edition, can be bundled with the following software for student use:

- Visible Analyst 7.6 Educational Edition.
- Microsoft Project 2003.
- Microsoft Visio 2003.
- Oracle10g.

EXPANDED WEB SUPPORT

Kendall & Kendall's *Systems Analysis and Design*, Seventh Edition, features Web-based support to solid but lively pedagogical techniques in the information systems field.

- The Web site, located at **www.prenhall.com/kendall,** contains a wealth of critical learning and support tools, which keep class discussions exciting.
- **HyperCase 2.7,** an award-winning, virtually interactive organization game. Students are encouraged to interview people in the organization, analyze problems, modify data flow diagrams and data dictionaries, react to prototypes, and design new input and output. HyperCase now has a distinctive 3-D look.
- **Student Exercises based on the ongoing CPU case,** with partially solved problems and examples stored in Visible Analyst files and Microsoft Access files, so students can develop a Web-based computer management system.

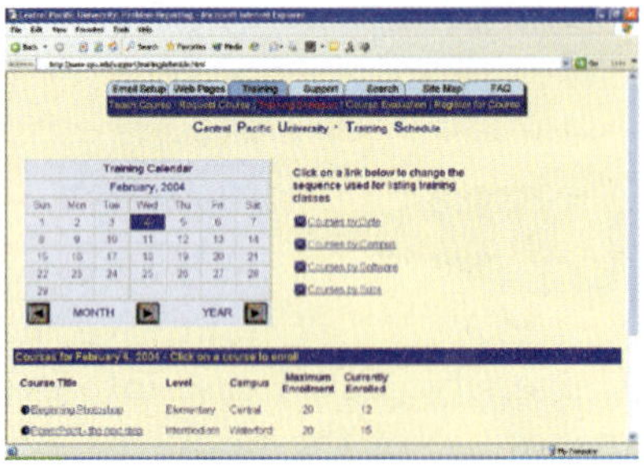

- **Interactive Study Guide,** featuring true or false and multiple-choice questions for each chapter. Students receive automatic grading and feedback on completing each quiz.
- **Instructor's Manual** (within a secure faculty section) with answers to problems, solutions to cases, and suggestions for approaching the subject matter.
- **A complete set of PowerPoint presentation slides** for use in lectures, which includes *all* of the technical figures from the seventh edition.
- **Solutions to Student Exercises** based on the ongoing CPU case, with solutions and examples stored in Visible Analyst files and Microsoft Access files.

EXPANDED INSTRUCTOR SUPPLEMENTAL WEB SUPPORT

Extended support for instructors using this edition can be found at the official Web site located at www.prenhall.com/kendall. Resources include:

- A complete set of **PowerPoint presentation slides** for use in lectures
- **Image Library,** a collection of all text art organized by chapter
- **Instructor's Manual** in Microsoft Word
- **Test Item File** in Microsoft Word and TestGen with WebCT- and Blackboard-ready conversions.
- **Solutions to Student Exercises** based on the ongoing CPU case, with solutions and examples stored in Visible Analyst files and Microsoft Access files.

ACKNOWLEDGMENTS

When we began working on the seventh edition of *Systems Analysis and Design*, we observed an increasing awareness of the need for using a human-centered and often agile approach to systems design. We also noticed a rising interest in using IT and new systems to foster social inclusion; bridge the digital divide; improve productivity and the quality of individual lives, as well as the quality of established and developing societies. Many people all over the world are becoming systems designers, and even more people around the globe are required to become sophisticated consumers of information, conveyed by Web-based systems and emerging information technologies. Users respond to and participate with the information systems that surround them. Good systems analysts and designers use both art and science to reply to the feedback they receive in order to develop systems that are in tune with their users, their environments, and even society.

Our cover artist, Richard Kalina, comments about his artwork saying, "*Carthage* attempts to link logic with beauty by establishing certain structural parameters, such as multiple overlaid grid systems and a menu of color choices, and then allowing artistic intuition to intercede. While *Carthage* has an overall feeling of crispness and geometric clarity, any severity is undercut by the painting's freely drawn edges and a sense that the whole composition has somehow been tugged and pulled into place. Similarly, the symmetrical ordering of the white lines and the linen squares is balanced by the dynamic (yet modular) asymmetrical configuration of the colored bars. Color is a vital part of the painting. Though delimited in certain ways, it is absolutely direct in terms of visceral appeal. Using hundreds of pieces of transparently painted and collaged paper, color is created that is rich and glowing, speaking to the heart as well as to the mind."

We think you will come to recognize that the creation of the painting is similar to what happens in the creation of new information systems to support people in their organizational tasks. You learn and apply numerous structured techniques, methods, tools, and approaches. But when the time comes to interpret what is happening in the organization and to develop meaningful information systems from the application of rules to your analysis, your training combines with creativity to produce a system that is in some ways a surprise: it is structured, yet intuitive; multi-layered and complex, in keeping with the character of the organization and uniquely reflective of you as a systems analyst and a human being.

Our students deserve credit for this new edition by helping us to continuously improve the book through the sharing of their reactions and suggestions. They told us that they rapidly put to use the new material on HCI and agile modeling. We appreciate their eagerness to teach us new things. We want to thank our co-author, Allen Schmidt, for all of the wit, insight, and creativity he brings to our collaborations. He is a superb human being. Our enthusiastic thanks also go to Peter Schmidt and Jason Reed for their improvements to the early HyperCase. We also want to thank the other two original authors of HyperCase, Richard Baskerville and Raymond Barnes, who contributed so much.

We would like to thank our editor, Bob Horan, who encouraged us to make this an engaging and vital edition. Ana Jankowski also helped us succeed in making this a robust revision. Their experience, insight, and capabilities have kept this project moving toward our common goals.

Melissa Feimer, our production editor at Prentice Hall, also deserves praise for graciously helping us with the difficult task of publishing a new edition. Because of her efforts, along with those of many others, this edition went very smoothly. There were many people we did not meet face-to-face, but rather worked with in virtual teams at Prentice Hall, including Mohinder Singh, our project manager; Fred Dahl of Inkwell, and many others elsewhere who helped us by designing the book, drawing the art, composing the pages, and securing permissions. We appreciate their efforts and want to thank them all.

We are also grateful for the encouragement and support of our Dean, Mitchell P. Koza and our Provost, Roger J. Dennis. The entire Rutgers community, from the administrative staff to the board, has been very enthusiastic about this edition as well as the many translations of *Systems Analysis and Design* into Spanish, Chinese, and Indonesian.

All of the reviewers for the seventh edition deserve our thanks as well. Their thoughtful comments and suggestions helped to strengthen the book. They are:

Michel Avital, Case Western Reserve University
Joseph Blankenship, Youngstown State University
James W. Gabberty, Pace University
Lori Kelley, Madison Area Technical College
Paul Mangiameli, University of Rhode Island
Lin Qui, SUNY Oswego
Keng Siau, University of Nebraska–Lincoln
Merrill Warkentin, Mississippi State University

Many of our colleagues and friends have encouraged us through the process of writing this book. We thank them for their comments on our work. They include: Ayman Abu Hamdieh; Charles P. Bonini: Jim and Jan Buffington; the Ciupeks; Charles J. Coleman; Derek Travis Collard; Roger T. Danforth; Gordon Davis; Dorothy Dologite; Jim Evans; Bruce Fanning; Paul Gray; Varun Grover; Nancy V. Gulick; Andy and Pam Hamingson; Chung Kwong Han; Art and Joan Kraft; Lee and Judie Krajewski; Muhammadou and Jainaba Kah; Stefan Lano; Carol Latta; Ken and Jane Laudon; Richard Levao; Bob Mankoff; Robert Mockler; Bill and Phyllis Perkins; Joel and Bobbie Porter; Ron Rice; Caryn Schmidt; Marc and Jill Schniederjans; Gabriel Jeffrey Shanks; Detmar W. Straub, Jr.; James T. C. Teng; the Vargos; Merrill Warkentin; Jeff and Bonnie Weil; Shaker and Patricia Zahra; Ping Zhang, and all of our friends and colleagues in the Association for Information Systems, the Decision Sciences Institute, IFIP Working Group 8.2, and all those involved in the KPMG PhD Project for minority doctoral students in information systems.

Our heartfelt thanks go to the memory of Julia A. Kendall and to the memory of Edward J. Kendall. Their belief that love, goals, and hard work are an unbeatable combination continues to infuse our every endeavor.

ASSUMING THE ROLE OF THE SYSTEMS ANALYST

1

Learning Objectives

Once you have mastered the material in this chapter you will be able to:

1. **Recall the basic types of computer-based systems that a systems analyst needs to address.**
2. **Understand how users working in context with new technologies change the dynamics of a system.**
3. **Realize what the many roles of a systems analyst are.**
4. **Know the steps of the SDLC as they relate to HCI and how to apply them to a real system.**
5. **Understand what CASE tools are and how they help a systems analyst.**
6. **Explore other methodologies such as object-oriented systems design and prototyping.**

Organizations have long recognized the importance of managing key resources such as people and raw materials. Information has now moved to its rightful place as a key resource. Decision makers now understand that information is not just a byproduct of conducting business; rather, it fuels business and can be the critical factor in determining the success or failure of a business.

To maximize the usefulness of information, a business must manage it correctly, just as it manages other resources. Managers need to understand that costs are associated with the production, distribution, security, storage, and retrieval of all information. Although information is all around us, it is not free, and its strategic use for positioning a business competitively should not be taken for granted.

The ready availability of networked computers, along with access to the Internet and the World Wide Web, has created an information explosion throughout society in general and business in particular. Managing computer-generated information differs in significant ways from handling manually produced data. Usually there is a greater quantity of computer information to administer. Costs of organizing and maintaining it can increase at alarming rates, and users often treat it less skeptically than information obtained in different ways. This chapter examines the fundamentals of different kinds of information systems, the varied roles of systems analysts, and the phases in the systems development life cycle as they relate to Human–Computer Interaction (HCI) factors; it also introduces Computer-Aided Software Engineering (CASE) tools.

TYPES OF SYSTEMS

Information systems are developed for different purposes, depending on the needs of human users and the business. Transaction processing systems (TPS) function at the operational level of the organization; office automation systems (OAS) and knowledge work systems (KWS) support work at the knowledge level. Higher-level systems include management information systems (MIS) and decision support systems (DSS). Expert systems apply the expertise of decision makers to solve specific, structured problems. On the strategic level of management we find executive support systems (ESS). Group decision support systems (GDSS) and the more generally described computer-supported collaborative work systems (CSCWS) aid group-level decision making of a semistructured or unstructured variety.

The variety of information systems that analysts may develop are shown in Figure 1.1. Notice that the figure presents these systems from the bottom up, indicating that the operational, or lowest, level of the organization is supported by TPS, and the strategic, or highest, level of semistructured and unstructured decisions is supported by ESS, GDSS, and CSCWS at the top. This text uses the terms *management information systems, information systems* (IS), *computerized information systems,* and *computerized business information systems* interchangeably to denote computerized information systems that support the broadest range of user interactions with technologies and business activities through the information they produce in organizational contexts.

TRANSACTION PROCESSING SYSTEMS

Transaction processing systems (TPS) are computerized information systems that were developed to process large amounts of data for routine business transactions such as payroll and inventory. A TPS eliminates the tedium of necessary operational transactions and reduces the time once required to perform them manually, although people must still input data to computerized systems.

Transaction processing systems are boundary-spanning systems that permit the organization to interact with external environments. Because managers look to the data generated by the TPS for up-to-the-minute information about what is

FIGURE 1.1
A systems analyst may be involved with any or all of these systems.

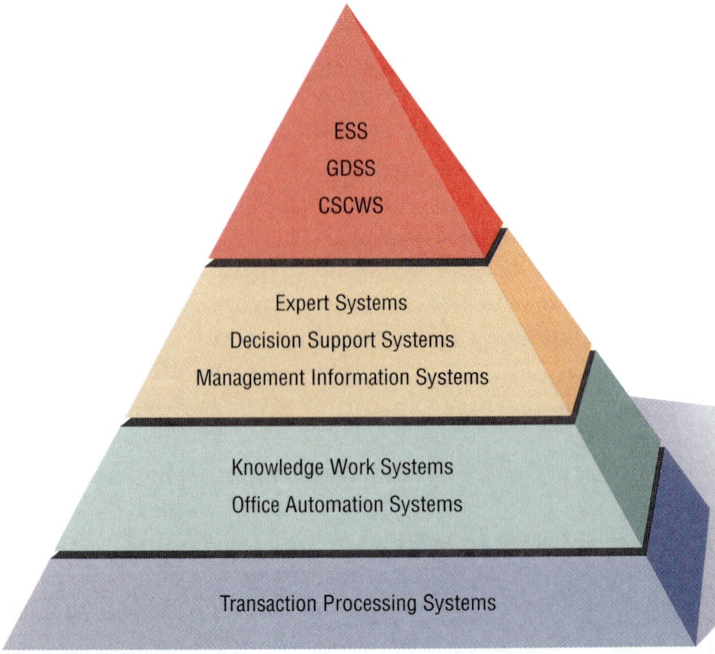

happening in their companies, it is essential to the day-to-day operations of business that these systems function smoothly and without interruption.

OFFICE AUTOMATION SYSTEMS AND KNOWLEDGE WORK SYSTEMS

At the knowledge level of the organization are two classes of systems. Office automation systems (OAS) support data workers, who do not usually create new knowledge but rather analyze information so as to transform data or manipulate it in some way before sharing it with, or formally disseminating it throughout, the organization and, sometimes, beyond. Familiar aspects of OAS include word processing, spreadsheets, desktop publishing, electronic scheduling, and communication through voice mail, email (electronic mail), and video conferencing.

Knowledge work systems (KWS) support professional workers such as scientists, engineers, and doctors by aiding them in their efforts to create new knowledge (often in teams) and by allowing them to contribute it to their organization or to society at large.

MANAGEMENT INFORMATION SYSTEMS

Management information systems (MIS) do not replace transaction processing systems; rather, all MIS include transaction processing. MIS are computerized information systems that work because of the purposeful interaction between people and computers. By requiring people, software (computer programs), and hardware (computers, printers, etc.) to function in concert, management information systems support users in accomplishing a broader spectrum of organizational tasks than transaction processing systems, including decision analysis and decision making.

To access information, users of the management information system share a common database. The database stores both data and models that help the user interact with, interpret, and apply that data. Management information systems output information that is used in decision making. A management information system can also help unite some of the computerized information functions of a business, although it does not exist as a singular structure anywhere in the business.

DECISION SUPPORT SYSTEMS

A higher-level class of computerized information systems are decision support systems (DSS). DSS are similar to the traditional management information system because they both depend on a database as a source of data. A decision support system departs from the traditional management information system because it emphasizes the support of decision making in all its phases, although the actual decision is still the exclusive province of the decision maker. Decision support systems are more closely tailored to the person or group using them than is a traditional management information system. Sometimes they are discussed as systems that focus on business intelligence.

EXPERT SYSTEMS AND ARTIFICIAL INTELLIGENCE

Artificial intelligence (AI) can be considered the overarching field for expert systems. The general thrust of AI has been to develop machines that behave intelligently. Two avenues of AI research are understanding natural language and analyzing the ability to reason through a problem to its logical conclusion. Expert systems use the approaches of AI reasoning to solve the problems put to them by business (and other) users.

Expert systems are a very special class of information system that have been made practicable for use by business as a result of widespread availability of hardware and software such as personal computers (PCs) and expert system shells. An expert system (also called a knowledge-based system) effectively captures and uses the knowledge of a human expert or experts for solving a particular problem experienced in an organization. Notice that unlike DSS, which leave the ultimate judgment to the decision maker, an expert system selects the best solution to a problem or a specific class of problems.

The basic components of an expert system are the knowledge base, an inference engine connecting the user with the system by processing queries via languages such as SQL (structured query language), and the user interface. People called knowledge engineers capture the expertise of experts, build a computer system that includes this expert knowledge, and then implement it. It is entirely possible that building and implementing expert systems will be the future work of many systems analysts.

GROUP DECISION SUPPORT SYSTEMS AND COMPUTER-SUPPORTED COLLABORATIVE WORK SYSTEMS

Organizations are becoming increasingly reliant on groups or teams to make decisions together. When groups make semistructured or unstructured decisions, a group decision support system may afford a solution. Group decision support systems (GDSS), which are used in special rooms equipped in a number of different configurations, permit group members to interact with electronic support—often in the form of specialized software—and a special group facilitator. Group decision support systems are intended to bring a group together to solve a problem with the help of various supports such as polling, questionnaires, brainstorming, and scenario creation. GDSS software can be designed to minimize typical negative group behaviors such as lack of participation due to fear of reprisal for expressing an unpopular or contested viewpoint, domination by vocal group members, and "group think" decision making. Sometimes GDSS are discussed under the more general term *computer-supported collaborative work systems* (CSCWS), which might include software support called groupware for team collaboration via networked computers. Group decision support systems can also be used in a virtual setting.

EXECUTIVE SUPPORT SYSTEMS

When executives turn to the computer, they are often looking for ways to help them make decisions on the strategic level. Executive support systems (ESS) help executives organize their interactions with the external environment by providing graphics and communications technologies in accessible places such as boardrooms or personal corporate offices. Although ESS rely on the information generated by TPS and MIS, executive support systems help their users address unstructured decision problems, which are not application specific, by creating an environment that helps them think about strategic problems in an informed way. ESS extend and support the capabilities of executives, permitting them to make sense of their environments.

INTEGRATING TECHNOLOGIES FOR SYSTEMS

As users adopt new technologies, some of the systems analyst's work will be devoted to integrating traditional systems with new ones to ensure a useful context, as shown in Figure 1.2. This section describes some of the new information technologies

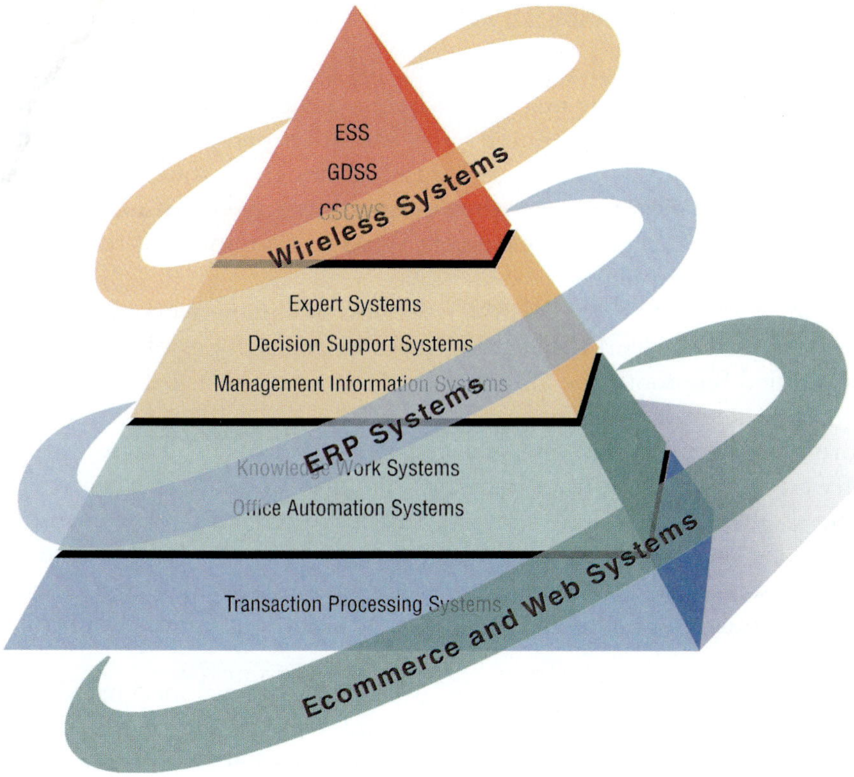

FIGURE 1.2

Systems analysts need to be aware that integrating technologies affect all types of users and systems.

systems analysts will be using as people work to integrate their ecommerce applications into their traditional businesses or as they begin entirely new ebusinesses.

ECOMMERCE APPLICATIONS AND WEB SYSTEMS

Many of the systems discussed here can be imbued with greater functionality if they are migrated to the World Wide Web or if they are originally conceived and implemented as Web-based technologies. There are many benefits to mounting or improving an application on the Web:

1. Increasing user awareness of the availability of a service, product, industry, person, or group.
2. The possibility of 24-hour access for users.
3. Improving the usefulness and usability of the interface design.
4. Creating a system that can extend globally rather than remain local, thus reaching people in remote locations without worry of the time zone in which they are located.

ENTERPRISE RESOURCE PLANNING SYSTEMS

Many organizations envision potential benefits from the integration of many information systems existing on different management levels and within different functions. Enterprise resource planning (ERP) systems are designed to perform this integration. Instituting ERP requires enormous commitment and organizational change. Often systems analysts serve as consultants to ERP endeavors that use proprietary software. Popular ERP software includes that from SAP and Oracle. Some of these packages are targeted toward moving enterprises onto the Web. Typically, analysts as well as some users require vendor training, support, and maintenance to be able to properly design, install, maintain, update, and use a particular ERP package.

SYSTEMS FOR WIRELESS AND HANDHELD DEVICES

Analysts are being called to design a plethora of new systems and applications for adventurous users, including many for wireless devices and handheld computers such as the popular Palm computer series and other personal digital assistants (PDAs). In addition, analysts may find themselves designing standard or wireless communications networks for users that integrate voice, video, and email into organizational intranets or industry extranets. Wireless ecommerce is referred to as mcommerce (mobile commerce).

Wireless local area networks (WLANs), wireless fidelity networks, called Wi-Fi, and personal wireless networks that bring together many types of devices under the standard called Bluetooth, are all systems that you may be asked to design. (For more on wireless networks see Chapter 17.)

In more advanced settings, analysts may be called on to design intelligent agents, software that can assist users with tasks in which the software learns preferences of the users over time and then acts on those preferences. For example, in the use of pull technology, an intelligent agent would search the Web for stories of interest to the user, having observed the user's behavior patterns with information over time, and would conduct searches on the Web without continual prompting from the user.

One example of this type of software is that being developed by Microsoft based on Bayesian statistics (using statistics to infer probabilities) and decision-making theory in combination with monitoring a user's behavior concerning the handling of incoming information (such as a message from home, a phone call from a client, a call on a cell phone, or updated analysis of one's stock portfolio). The result is notification manager software that also places a dollar value on each piece of incoming information from a variety of sources and how it should best be displayed. For instance, based on decision theory, probability, statistics, and the user's own previous behavior, a phone call from home could be valued at $1.00 and could pop up on their computer screen, whereas a cold sales call could be valued at 20¢ (i.e., lower value) and could appear as a text message.

OPEN SOURCE SOFTWARE

An alternative to traditional software development in which proprietary code is hidden from the users is called open source software (OSS). With OSS, the code, or computer instructions, can be studied, shared, and modified by many users and programmers. Rules of this community include the idea that any program modifications must be shared with all the people on the project.

Development of open source software has also been characterized as a philosophy rather than simply as the process of creating new software. Often those involved in OSS communities view it as a way to help societies change. Widely known open source projects include Apache for developing a Web server, the browser called Mozilla Firefox, and Linux, which is a Unixlike open source operating system.

However, it would be an oversimplification to think of OSS as a monolithic movement, and it does little to reveal what type of users or user-analysts are developing open source software projects and on what basis. To help us understand the open source movement, researchers have recently categorized open source communities into four community types along six different dimensions. They describe them as ad hoc, standardized, organized, and commercial. The four communities differ from each other on six key dimensions: general structure, environment, goals, methods, user community, and licensing. Some researchers argue that OSS is at a crossroads and that the commercial and community open source software groups need to understand where they converge and where the potential for conflict exists.

Open source development is useful for many applications running on diverse technologies, including handheld devices and communication equipment. Its use may encourage progress in creating standards for devices to communicate more easily. Widespread use of open source software may alleviate some of the severe shortages of programmers, and some large problems may be solved through intense and extensive collaboration.

NEED FOR SYSTEMS ANALYSIS AND DESIGN

Systems analysis and design, as performed by systems analysts, seeks to understand what humans need to analyze data input or data flow systematically, process or transform data, store data, and output information in the context of a particular business. Furthermore, systems analysis and design is used to analyze, design, and implement improvements in the support of users and the functioning of businesses that can be accomplished through the use of computerized information systems.

Installing a system without proper planning leads to great user dissatisfaction and frequently causes the system to fall into disuse. Systems analysis and design lends structure to the analysis and design of information systems, a costly endeavor that might otherwise have been done in a haphazard way. It can be thought of as a series of processes systematically undertaken to improve a business through the use of computerized information systems. Systems analysis and design involves working with current and eventual users of information systems to support them in working with technologies in an organizational setting.

User involvement throughout the systems project is critical to the successful development of computerized information systems. Systems analysts, whose roles in the organization are discussed next, are the other essential component in developing useful information systems.

Users are moving to the forefront as software development teams become more international in their composition. This means that there is more emphasis on working with software users; on performing analysis of their business, problems, and objectives; and on communicating the analysis and design of the planned system to all involved.

New technologies also are driving the need for systems analysis. Ajax (Asynchronous JavaScript and XML) is not a new programming language, but a technique that uses existing languages to make Web pages function more like a traditional desktop application program. Building and redesigning Web pages that utilize Ajax technologies will be a task facing analysts. New programming languages, such as Ruby on Rails, which is a combination programming language and code generator for creating Web applications, will require more analysis.

ROLES OF THE SYSTEMS ANALYST

The systems analyst systematically assesses how users interact with technology and businesses function by examining the inputting and processing of data and the outputting of information with the intent of improving organizational processes. Many improvements involve better support of users' work tasks and business functions through the use of computerized information systems. This definition emphasizes a systematic, methodical approach to analyzing—and potentially improving—what is occurring in the specific context experienced by users and created by a business.

CONSULTING OPPORTUNITY 1.1

HEALTHY HIRING: ECOMMERCE HELP WANTED

"You'll be happy to know that we made a strong case to management that we should hire a new systems analyst to specialize in ecommerce development," says Al Falfa, a systems analyst for the multioutlet international chain of Marathon Vitamin Shops. He is meeting with his large team of systems analysts to decide on the qualifications that their new team member should possess. Al continues, saying, "In fact, they were so excited by the possibility of our team helping to move Marathon into an ecommerce strategy that they've said we should start our search now and not wait until the fall."

Ginger Rute, another analyst, agrees, saying, "As long as the economy is healthy, the demand for Web site developers is far outstripping the supply. We should move quickly. I think our new person should be knowledgeable in CASE tools, Visual Basic, and JavaScript, just to name a few."

Al looks surprised at Ginger's long list of languages, but then replies, "Well, that's certainly one way we could go. But I would also like to see a person with some business savvy. Most of the people coming out of school will have solid programming skills, but they should know about accounting, inventory, and distribution of goods and services, too."

The newest member of the systems analysis group, Vita Minn, finally breaks into the discussion. She says, "One of the reasons I chose to come to work with all of you was that I thought we all got along quite well together. Because I had some other opportunities, I looked very carefully at what the atmosphere was here. From what I've seen, we're a friendly group. Let's be sure to hire someone who has a good personality and who fits in well with us."

Al concurs, continuing, "Vita's right. The new person should be able to communicate well with us, and with business clients, too. We are always communicating in some way, through formal presentations, drawing diagrams, or interviewing users. If they understand decision making, it will make their job easier, too. Also, Marathon is interested in integrating ecommerce into the entire business. We need someone who at least grasps the strategic importance of the Web. Page design is such a small part of it."

Ginger interjects again with a healthy dose of practicality, saying, "Leave that to management. I still say the new person should be a good programmer." Then she ponders aloud, "I wonder how important UML will be?"

After listening patiently to everyone's wish list, one of the senior analysts, Cal Siem, speaks up, joking, "We'd better see if Superman is available!"

As the group shares a laugh, Al sees an opportunity to try for some consensus, saying, "We've had a chance to hear a number of different qualifications. Let's each take a moment and make a list of the qualifications we personally think are essential for the new ecommerce development person to possess. We'll share them and continue discussing until we can describe the person in enough detail to turn a description over to the human resources group for processing."

What qualifications should the systems analysis team be looking for when hiring their new ecommerce development team member? Is it more important to know specific languages or to have an aptitude for picking up languages and software packages quickly? How important is it that the person being hired have some basic business understanding? Should all team members possess identical competencies and skills? What personality or character traits are desirable in a systems analyst who will be working in ecommerce development?

Our definition of a systems analyst is necessarily broad. The analyst must be able to work with people of all descriptions and be experienced in working with computers. The analyst plays many roles, sometimes balancing several at the same time. The three primary roles of the systems analyst are consultant, supporting expert, and agent of change.

SYSTEMS ANALYST AS CONSULTANT

The systems analyst frequently acts as a systems consultant to humans and their businesses and, thus, may be hired specifically to address information systems issues within a business. Such hiring can be an advantage because outside consultants can bring with them a fresh perspective that other people in an organization do not possess. It also means that outside analysts are at a disadvantage because the true organizational culture can never be known to an outsider. As an outside consultant, you will rely heavily on the systematic methods discussed throughout this text to analyze and design appropriate information systems for users working in a particular business. In addition, you will rely on information systems users to help you understand the organizational culture from others' viewpoints.

SYSTEMS ANALYST AS SUPPORTING EXPERT

Another role that you may be required to play is that of supporting expert within a business for which you are regularly employed in some systems capacity. In this role the analyst draws on professional expertise concerning computer hardware and software and their uses in the business. This work is often not a full-blown systems project, but rather it entails a small modification or decision affecting a single department.

As the support expert, you are not managing the project; you are merely serving as a resource for those who are. If you are a systems analyst employed by a manufacturing or service organization, many of your daily activities may be encompassed by this role.

SYSTEMS ANALYST AS AGENT OF CHANGE

The most comprehensive and responsible role that the systems analyst takes on is that of an agent of change, whether internal or external to the business. As an analyst, you are an agent of change whenever you perform any of the activities in the systems development life cycle (discussed in the next section) and are present and interacting with users and the business for an extended period (from two weeks to more than a year). An agent of change can be defined as a person who serves as a catalyst for change, develops a plan for change, and works with others in facilitating that change.

Your presence in the business changes it. As a systems analyst, you must recognize this fact and use it as a starting point for your analysis. Hence, you must interact with users and management (if they are not one and the same) from the very beginning of your project. Without their help you cannot understand what they need to support their work in the organization, and real change cannot take place.

If change (that is, improvements to the business that can be realized through information systems) seems warranted after analysis, the next step is to develop a plan for change along with the people who must enact the change. Once a consensus is reached on the change that is to be made, you must constantly interact with those who are changing.

As a systems analyst acting as an agent of change, you advocate a particular avenue of change involving the use of information systems. You also teach users the process of change, because changes in the information system do not occur independently but cause changes in the rest of the organization as well.

QUALITIES OF THE SYSTEMS ANALYST

From the foregoing descriptions of the roles the systems analyst plays, it is easy to see that the successful systems analyst must possess a wide range of qualities. Many different kinds of people are systems analysts, so any description is destined to fall short in some way. There are some qualities, however, that most systems analysts seem to display.

Above all, the analyst is a problem solver. He or she is a person who views the analysis of problems as a challenge and who enjoys devising workable solutions. When necessary, the analyst must be able to systematically tackle the situation at hand through skillful application of tools, techniques, and experience. The analyst must also be a communicator capable of relating meaningfully to other people over extended periods of time. Systems analysts need to be able to understand humans' needs in interacting with technology, and they need enough computer experience to program, to understand the capabilities of computers, to glean information requirements from users, and to communicate what is needed to programmers.

They also need to possess strong personal and professional ethics to help them shape their client relationships.

The systems analyst must be a self-disciplined, self-motivated individual who is able to manage and coordinate other people, as well as innumerable project resources. Systems analysis is a demanding career, but, in compensation, an ever-changing and always challenging one.

THE SYSTEMS DEVELOPMENT LIFE CYCLE

Throughout this chapter we have referred to the systematic approach analysts take to the analysis and design of information systems. Much of this is embodied in what is called the systems development life cycle (SDLC). The SDLC is a phased approach to analysis and design that holds that systems are best developed through the use of a specific cycle of analyst and user activities.

Analysts disagree on exactly how many phases there are in the systems development life cycle, but they generally laud its organized approach. Here we have divided the cycle into seven phases, as shown in Figure 1.3. Although each phase is presented discretely, it is never accomplished as a separate step. Instead, several activities can occur simultaneously, and activities may be repeated. It is more useful to think of the SDLC as accomplished in phases (with activities in full swing overlapping with others and then tapering off) and not in separate steps.

INCORPORATING HUMAN–COMPUTER INTERACTION CONSIDERATIONS

In recent years, the study of human–computer interaction (HCI) has become increasingly important for systems analysts. Although the definition is still evolving, researchers characterize HCI as the "aspect of a computer that enables communications and interactions between humans and the computer. It is the layer of the computer that is between humans and the computer" (Zhang, Carey, Te'eni, & Tremaine, 2005, p. 518). Analysts using an HCI approach are emphasizing people rather than the work to be done or the IT that is involved. Their approach to a problem is multifaceted, looking at the "human ergonomic, cognitive, affective, and behavioral factors involved in user tasks, problem solving processes and interaction context" (Zhang, Carey, Te'eni, & Tremaine, 2005, p. 518). Human computer interaction moves away from focusing first on organizational and system needs and instead concentrates on human needs. Analysts adopting HCI principles examine a variety of user needs in the context of humans interacting with information

FIGURE 1.3
The seven phases of the systems development life cycle.

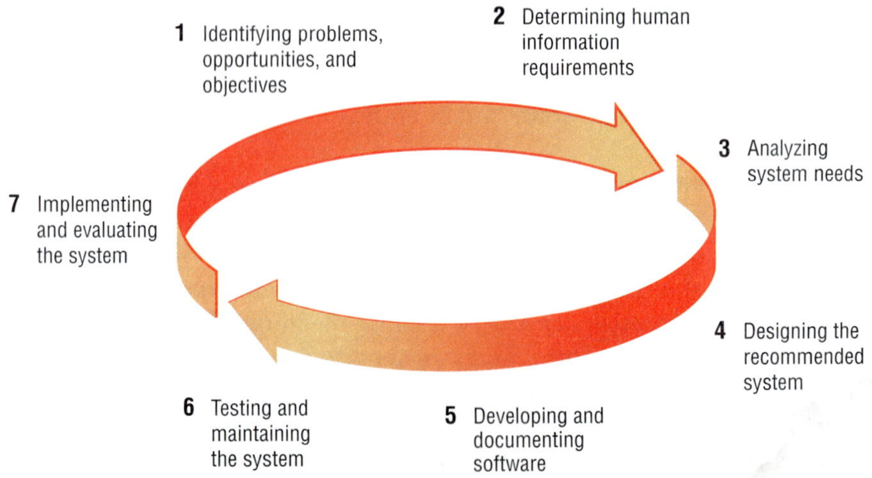

technology to complete tasks and solve problems. These include taking into account physical or ergonomic factors; usability factors that are often labeled cognitive matters; the pleasing, aesthetic and enjoyable aspects of using the system; and behavioral aspects that center around the usefulness of the system.

Another way to think about HCI is to think of it as a human-centered approach that puts people ahead of organizational structure or culture when creating new systems. When analysts employ HCI as a lens to filter the world, their work will possess a different quality than those who do not possess this perspective.

Your career can benefit from a strong grounding in HCI. The demand for analysts who are capable of incorporating HCI into the systems development process keeps increasing, as companies increasingly realize that the quality of systems and the quality of work life can both be improved by taking a human-centered approach at the outset of a project.

The application of human–computer interaction principles tries to uncover and address the frustrations that users voice over their use of information technology. These concerns include a suspicion that systems analysts misunderstand the work being done, the tasks involved, and how they can best be supported; a feeling of helplessness or lack of control when working with the system; intentional breaches of privacy; trouble navigating through system screens and menus; and a general mismatch between the system designed and the way users themselves think of their work processes.

Misjudgments and errors in design that cause users to neglect new systems or that make systems fall into disuse soon after their implementation can be eradicated or minimized when systems analysts adopt an HCI approach.

Researchers in HCI see advantages to the inclusion of HCI in every phase of the systems development life cycle. This is a worthwhile approach, and we will try to mirror this by bringing human concerns explicitly into each phase of the SDLC. As a person who is learning systems analysis, you can also bring a fresh eye to the SDLC to identify opportunities for designers to address HCI concerns and ways for users to become more central to each phase of the systems development life cycle. Chapter 14 is devoted to examining the role of the systems analyst in designing human-centered systems and interfaces from an HCI perspective.

IDENTIFYING PROBLEMS, OPPORTUNITIES, AND OBJECTIVES

In this first phase of the systems development life cycle, the analyst is concerned with identifying problems, opportunities, and objectives. This stage is critical to the success of the rest of the project, because no one wants to waste subsequent time addressing the wrong problem.

The first phase requires that the analyst look honestly at what is occurring in a business. Then, together with other organizational members, the analyst pinpoints problems. Often these problems will be brought up by others, and they are the reason the analyst was initially called in. Opportunities are situations that the analyst believes can be improved through the use of computerized information systems. Seizing opportunities may allow the business to gain a competitive edge or set an industry standard.

Identifying objectives is also an important component of the first phase. First, the analyst must discover what the business is trying to do. Then the analyst will be able to see if some aspect of information systems applications can help the business reach its objectives by addressing specific problems or opportunities.

The people involved in the first phase are the users, analysts, and systems managers coordinating the project. Activities in this phase consist of interviewing user management, summarizing the knowledge obtained, estimating the scope of the project, and documenting the results. The output of this phase is a feasibility report containing a problem definition and summarizing the objectives. Management must then make a decision on whether to proceed with the proposed project. If the user group does not have sufficient funds in its budget or wishes to tackle unrelated problems, or if the problems do not require a computer system, a different solution may be recommended, and the systems project does not proceed any further.

DETERMINING HUMAN INFORMATION REQUIREMENTS

The next phase the analyst enters is that of determining the human needs of the users involved, using a variety of tools to understand how users interact in the work context with their current information systems. The analyst will use interactive methods such as interviewing, sampling and investigating hard data, and questionnaires, along with unobtrusive methods, such as observing decision makers' behavior and their office environments, and all-encompassing methods, such as prototyping.

The analyst will use these methods to pose and answer many questions concerning human-computer interaction, including questions such as, "What are the users' physical strengths and limitations?" In other words, "What needs to be done to make the system audible, legible, and safe?" "How can the new system be designed to be easy to use, learn, and remember?" "How can the system be made pleasing or even fun to use?" "How can the system support a user's individual work tasks and make them more productive in new ways?"

In the information requirements phase of the SDLC, the analyst is striving to understand what information users need to perform their jobs. At this point the analyst is examining how to make the system useful to the people involved. How can the system better support individual tasks that need doing? What new tasks are enabled by the new system that users were unable to do without it? How can the new system be created to extend a user's capabilities beyond what the old system provided? How can the analyst create a system that is rewarding for workers to use?

The people involved in this phase are the analysts and users, typically operations managers and operations workers. The systems analyst needs to know the details of current system functions: the who (the people who are involved), what (the business activity), where (the environment in which the work takes place), when (the timing), and how (how the current procedures are performed) of the business under study. The analyst must then ask why the business uses the current system. There may be good reasons for doing business using the current methods, and these should be considered when designing any new system.

Rapid application development (RAD) is an object-oriented approach (OOA) to systems development that includes a method of development (including generating information requirements) as well as software tools. In this text it is paired with prototyping in Chapter 6, because the philosophical approach it takes is similar to prototyping, even though the method for creating a design quickly and getting rapid feedback from users differs somewhat. (There is more about object-oriented approaches in Chapter 18.)

If the reason for current operations is that "it's always been done that way," however, the analyst may wish to improve on the procedures. At the completion of this phase, the analyst should understand how users accomplish their work when interacting with a computer and begin to know how to make the new system more useful and usable. The analyst should also know how the business functions and have complete information on the people, goals, data, and procedures involved.

ANALYZING SYSTEM NEEDS

The next phase that the systems analyst undertakes involves analyzing system needs. Again, special tools and techniques help the analyst make requirement determinations. One such tool is the use of data flow diagrams to chart the input, processes, and output of the business's functions in a structured graphical form. From the data flow diagrams, a data dictionary is developed that lists all the data items used in the system, as well as their specifications.

During this phase the systems analyst also analyzes the structured decisions made. Structured decisions are those for which the conditions, condition alternatives, actions, and action rules can be determined. There are three major methods for analysis of structured decisions: structured English, decision tables, and decision trees.

At this point in the systems development life cycle, the systems analyst prepares a systems proposal that summarizes what has been found out about the users, usability, and usefulness of current systems; provides cost/benefit analyses of alternatives; and makes recommendations on what (if anything) should be done. If one of the recommendations is acceptable to management, the analyst proceeds along that course. Each systems problem is unique, and there is never just one correct solution. The manner in which a recommendation or solution is formulated depends on the individual qualities and professional training of each analyst and the analyst's interaction with users in the context of their work environment.

DESIGNING THE RECOMMENDED SYSTEM

In the design phase of the systems development life cycle, the systems analyst uses the information collected earlier to accomplish the logical design of the information system. The analyst designs procedures for users to help them accurately enter data so that data going into the information system are correct. In addition, the analyst provides for users to complete effective input to the information system by using techniques of good form and screen design.

Part of the logical design of the information system is devising the human–computer interface. The interface connects the user with the system and is thus extremely important. The user interface is designed with the help of users to make sure that the system is audible, legible, and safe, as well as attractive and enjoyable to use. Examples of physical user interfaces include a keyboard (to type in questions and answers), onscreen menus (to elicit user commands), and a variety of graphical user interfaces (GUIs) that use a mouse or touch screen.

The design phase also includes designing files or databases that will store much of the data needed by decision makers in the organization. Users benefit from a well organized database that is logical to them and corresponds to the way they view their work. In this phase the analyst also works with users to design output (either onscreen or printed) that meets their information needs.

Finally, the analyst must design controls and backup procedures to protect the system and the data, and to produce program specification packets for programmers. Each packet should contain input and output layouts, file specifications, and processing details; it may also include decision trees or tables, data flow diagrams, a system flowchart, and the names and functions of any prewritten code routines.

DEVELOPING AND DOCUMENTING SOFTWARE

In the fifth phase of the systems development life cycle, the analyst works with programmers to develop any original software that is needed. Some of the structured techniques for designing and documenting software include structure charts and pseudocode. The systems analyst uses one or more of these devices to communicate to the programmer what needs to be programmed.

During this phase the analyst also works with users to develop effective documentation for software, including procedure manuals, online help, and Web sites featuring Frequently Asked Questions (FAQ), on Read Me files shipped with new software. Because users are involved from the beginning, phase documentation should address the questions they have raised and solved jointly with the analyst. Documentation tells users how to use software and what to do if software problems occur.

Programmers have a key role in this phase because they design, code, and remove syntactical errors from computer programs. To ensure quality, a programmer may conduct either a design or a code walkthrough, explaining complex portions of the program to a team of other programmers.

TESTING AND MAINTAINING THE SYSTEM

Before the information system can be used, it must be tested. It is much less costly to catch problems before the system is signed over to users. Some of the testing is completed by programmers alone, some of it by systems analysts in conjunction with programmers. A series of tests to pinpoint problems is run first with sample data and eventually with actual data from the current system.

Maintenance of the system and its documentation begins in this phase and is carried out routinely throughout the life of the information system. Much of the programmer's routine work consists of maintenance, and businesses spend a great deal of money on maintenance. Some maintenance, such as program updates, can be done automatically via a vendor site on the Web. Many of the systematic procedures the analyst employs throughout the systems development life cycle can help ensure that maintenance is kept to a minimum.

IMPLEMENTING AND EVALUATING THE SYSTEM

In this last phase of systems development, the analyst helps implement the information system. This phase involves training users to handle the system. Some training is done by vendors, but oversight of training is the responsibility of the systems analyst. In addition, the analyst needs to plan for a smooth conversion from the old system to the new one. This process includes converting files from old formats to new ones, or building a database, installing equipment, and bringing the new system into production.

Evaluation is included as part of this final phase of the systems development life cycle mostly for the sake of discussion. Actually, evaluation takes place during every phase. A key criterion that must be satisfied is whether the intended users are indeed using the system.

It should be noted that systems work is often cyclical. When an analyst finishes one phase of systems development and proceeds to the next, the discovery of a problem may force the analyst to return to the previous phase and modify the work done there.

THE IMPACT OF MAINTENANCE

After the system is installed, it must be maintained, meaning that the computer programs must be modified and kept up to date. Figure 1.4 illustrates the average amount of time spent on maintenance at a typical MIS installation. Estimates of the time spent by departments on maintenance have ranged from 48 to 60 percent

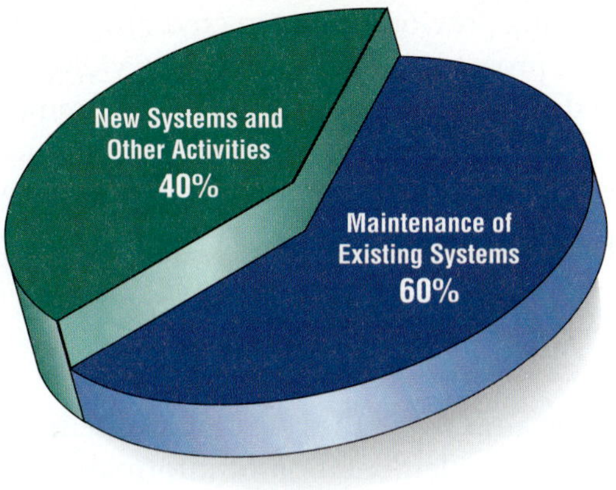

FIGURE 1.4

Some researchers estimate that the amount of time spent on system maintenance may be as much as 60 percent of the total time spent on systems projects.

of the total time spent developing systems. Very little time remains for new systems development. As the number of programs written increases, so does the amount of maintenance they require.

Maintenance is performed for two reasons. The first of these is to correct software errors. No matter how thoroughly the system is tested, bugs or errors creep into computer programs. Bugs in commercial PC software are often documented as "known anomalies," and are corrected when new versions of the software are released or in an interim release. In customized software, bugs must be corrected as they are detected.

The other reason for performing system maintenance is to enhance the software's capabilities in response to changing organizational needs, generally involving one of the following three situations:

1. Users often request additional features after they become familiar with the computer system and its capabilities.
2. The business changes over time.
3. Hardware and software are changing at an accelerated pace.

Figure 1.5 illustrates the amount of resources—usually time and money—spent on systems development and maintenance. The area under the curve represents the total dollar amount spent. You can see that over time the total cost of maintenance is likely to exceed that of systems development. At a certain point it becomes more feasible to perform a new systems study, because the cost of continued maintenance is clearly greater than that of creating an entirely new information system.

In summary, maintenance is an ongoing process over the life cycle of an information system. After the information system is installed, maintenance usually

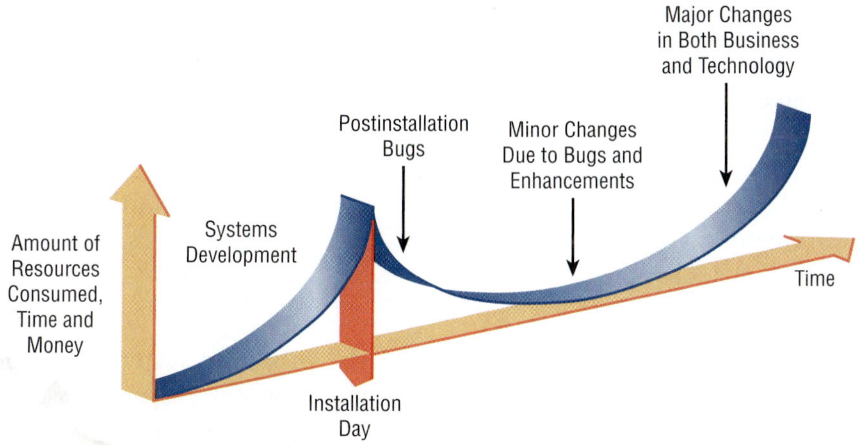

FIGURE 1.5

Resource consumption over the system life.

takes the form of correcting previously undetected program errors. Once these are corrected, the system approaches a steady state, providing dependable service to its users. Maintenance during this period may consist of removing a few previously undetected bugs and updating the system with a few minor enhancements. As time goes on and the business and technology change, however, the maintenance effort increases dramatically.

USING CASE TOOLS

Throughout this book we emphasize the need for a systematic, thorough approach to the analysis, design, and implementation of information systems. We recognize that to be productive, systems analysts must be organized, accurate, and complete in what they set out to do. Since the early 1990s, analysts have begun to benefit from productivity tools, called Computer-Aided Software Engineering (CASE) tools, that have been created explicitly to improve their routine work through the use of automated support. In a recent study it was found that larger IS departments, those with more than 10 employees, were more likely than smaller IS departments to adopt CASE tools. Organizational systems, procedures, and management practices may constrain the spread of CASE tools. Analysts rely on CASE tools to increase productivity, communicate more effectively with users, and integrate the work that they do on the system from the beginning to the end of the life cycle.

REASONS FOR USING CASE TOOLS

Increasing Analyst Productivity Visible Analyst (VA) is a CASE tool that enables systems analysts to do graphical planning, analysis, and design in order to build complex client/server applications and databases. It allows data, processes, and objects to be modeled in multiple notations. Visible Analyst generates model information in many different forms, including COBOL, C, Visual Basic, SQL, and XML. (An educational version of Visible Analyst is available with this text, and there are partially completed VA exercises on the Web for the HyperCase Experiences and the continuing CPU Case.)

Visible Analyst allows its users to draw and modify diagrams easily. The analyst can thus become more productive simply by reducing the considerable time typically spent in manually drawing and redrawing data flow diagrams until they are acceptable.

A tools package such as Visible Analyst also enhances group productivity by allowing analysts to share work easily with other team members, who can simply access the file on their PCs and review or modify what has been done. Such sharing reduces the time necessary to reproduce data flow diagrams and distribute them among team members. Thus, rather than mandating a strict distribution and feedback response schedule, such a tools package further allows members of the systems analysis team to work with the diagrams whenever they have the time.

CASE tools also facilitate interaction among team members by making diagramming a dynamic, iterative process, rather than one in which changes are cumbersome and therefore tend to become a drain on productivity. In this instance the CASE tool for drawing and recording data flow diagrams affords a record of the team's changing thinking regarding data flows.

Improving Analyst–User Communication For the proposed system to come into being and actually be used, excellent communication among analysts and users throughout the systems development life cycle is essential. The success of the eventual system implementation rests on the capability of analysts and users to communicate in a meaningful way at every phase. So far, it has been the experience of analysts currently using CASE tools that their use fosters greater, more meaningful communication among users and analysts.

Analysts and users alike report that CASE tools afford them a means of communication about the system during its conceptualization. Through the use of automated support featuring onscreen output, clients can readily see how data flows and other system concepts are depicted, and they can then request corrections or changes that would have taken too much time with older tools.

Whether a particular diagram will be adjudged useful by users or analysts at the end of the project is questionable. What is important is that such automated support for many life cycle design activities serves as a means to an end by acting as a catalyst for analyst–user interaction. The same arguments used to support CASE tools' role in increasing productivity are equally valid in this arena; that is, the tasks of drawing, reproducing, and distributing take much less time, so work in progress can be shared more easily with users.

Integrating Life Cycle Activities The third reason for using CASE tools is to integrate activities and provide continuity from one phase to the next throughout the systems development life cycle.

CASE tools are especially useful when a particular phase of the life cycle requires several iterations of feedback and modification. Recall that user involvement can be important in each of the phases. Integration of activities through the underlying use of technologies makes it easier for users to understand how all the life cycle phases are interrelated and interdependent.

Accurately Assessing Maintenance Changes The fourth and possibly one of the most important reasons for using CASE tools is that they enable users to analyze and assess the impact of maintenance changes. For example, the size of an element such as a customer number may need to be made larger. The CASE tool can cross-reference every screen, report, and file in which the element is used, leading to a comprehensive maintenance plan.

UPPER AND LOWER CASE

CASE tools are classified as lower CASE, upper CASE, and integrated CASE, which combines both upper and lower CASE in one toolset. Although experts disagree about what precisely constitutes an upper CASE tool versus a lower CASE tool, it might be helpful to conceptualize upper CASE tools on the basis of whom they support. Upper CASE tools primarily help analysts and designers. Lower CASE tools are used more often by programmers and workers who must implement the systems designed via upper CASE tools.

UPPER CASE TOOLS

An upper CASE tool allows the analyst to create and modify the system design. All the information about the project is stored in an encyclopedia called the CASE repository, a large collection of records, elements, diagrams, screens, reports, and other information (see Figure 1.6). Analysis reports may be produced using the repository information to show where the design is incomplete or contains errors.

Upper CASE tools can also help support the modeling of an organization's functional requirements, assist analysts and users in drawing the boundaries for a

FIGURE 1.6
The repository concept.

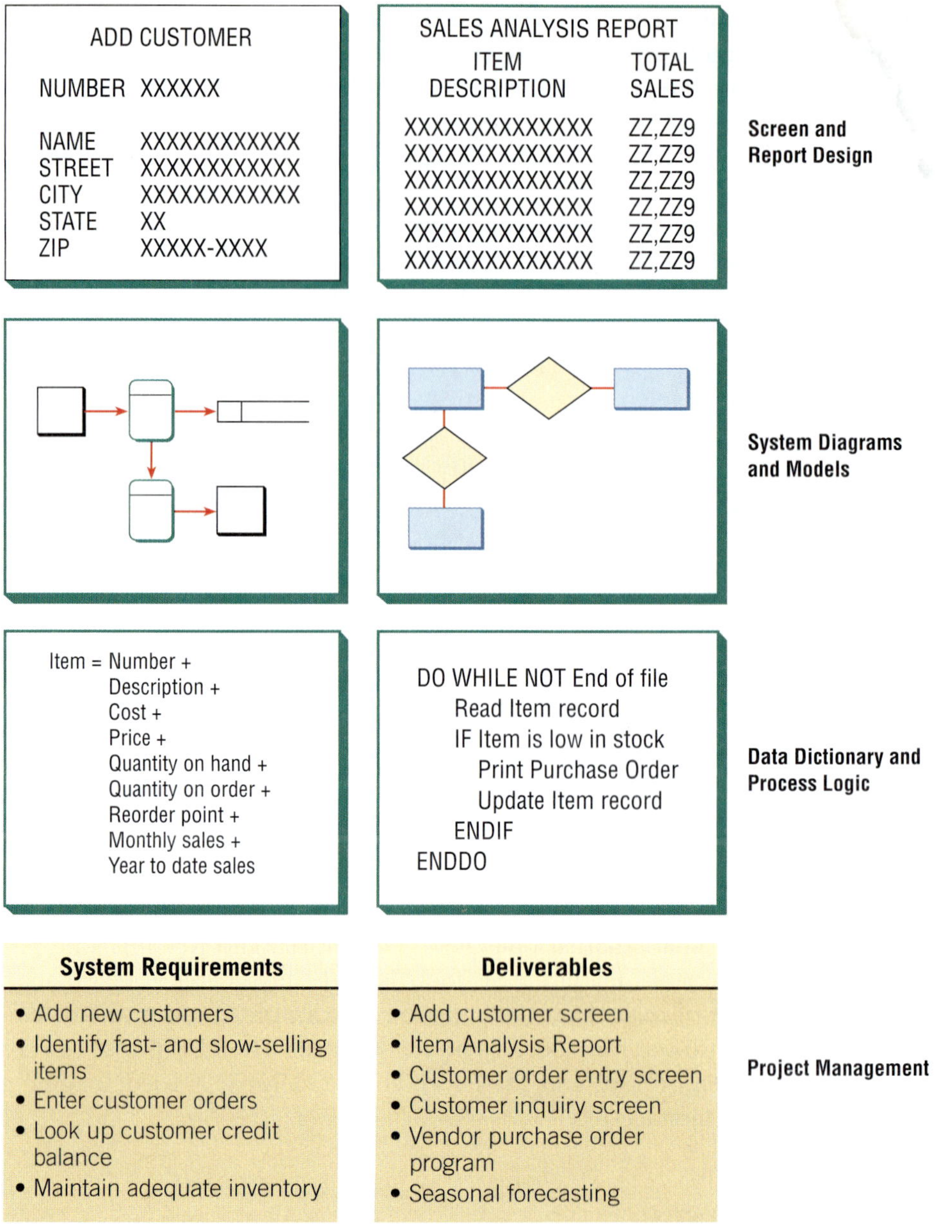

given project, and help them visualize how the project meshes with other parts of the organization. In addition, some upper CASE tools can support prototyping of screen and report designs.

LOWER CASE TOOLS

Lower CASE tools are used to generate computer source code, eliminating the need for programming the system. Code generation has several advantages:

1. The system can be produced more quickly than by writing computer programs. Becoming familiar with the methodology used by the code generator, however, often takes a great deal of time, so program generation may initially be slower. In addition, the design must be thoroughly entered into the toolset, which may require a lengthy period of time.
2. The amount of time spent on maintenance decreases with code generation. There is no need to modify, test, and debug computer programs. Instead, the

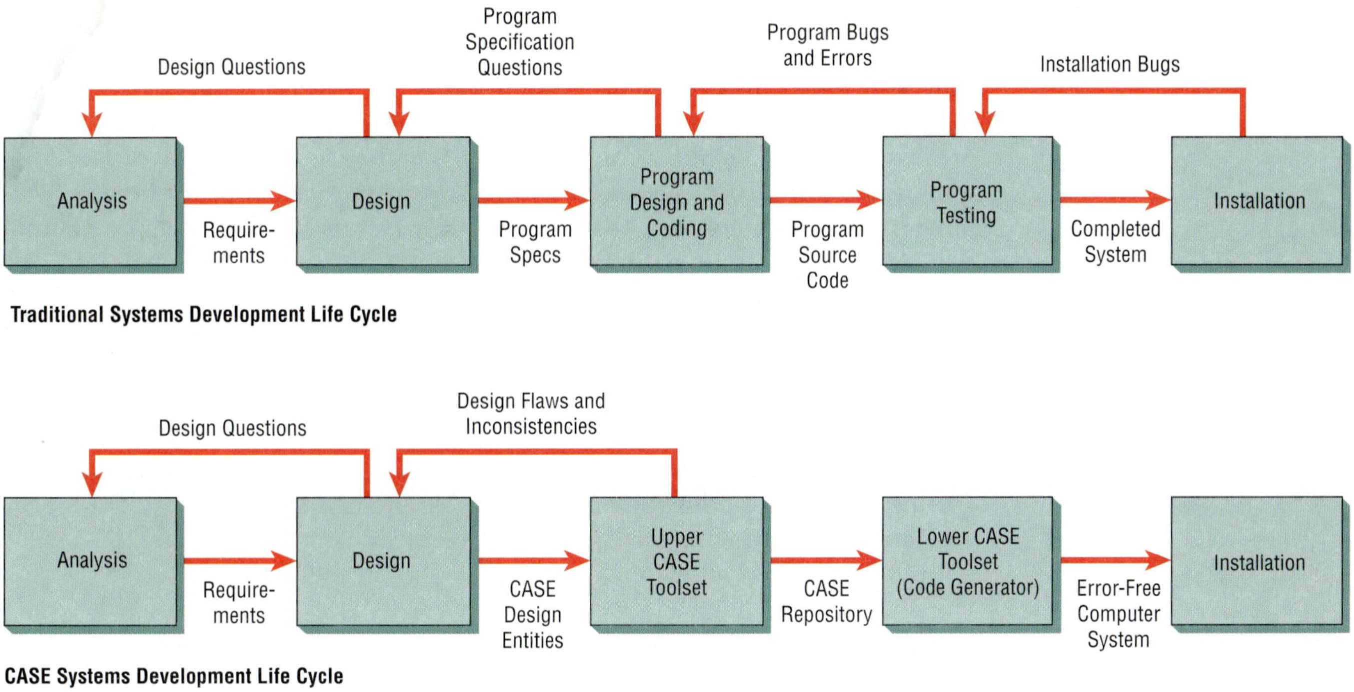

FIGURE 1.7

Traditional versus CASE systems development life cycles.

CASE design is modified, and the code is regenerated. Decreased time spent on maintenance results in more time to develop new systems and helps to relieve a backlog of projects under consideration for development.

3. Code can be generated in more than one computer language, so it is easier to migrate systems from one platform, such as a mainframe, to another, perhaps a PC. For example, VA Corporate Edition, can generate full ANSI, COBOL, or C-language 3 GL source code.
4. Code generation provides a cost-effective way of tailoring systems purchased from third-party vendors to the needs of the organization. Often, modifying purchased software requires such great effort that the cost of doing so exceeds that of the software. With code generation software, purchasing CASE design and a CASE repository for the application enables the analyst to modify the design and generate the revised computer system.
5. Generated code is free of computer program errors. The only potential errors are design errors, which can be minimized by running CASE analysis reports to ensure that the system design is complete and correct.

Figure 1.7 illustrates the traditional systems development life cycle and the CASE life cycle. Notice that the program coding, testing, and debugging portions of the cycle are eliminated from the CASE life cycle.

OBJECT-ORIENTED SYSTEMS ANALYSIS AND DESIGN

Object-oriented (O-O) analysis and design is an approach that is intended to facilitate the development of systems that must change rapidly in response to dynamic business environments. Chapter 18 helps you understand what object-oriented systems analysis and design is, how it differs from the structured approach of the SDLC, and when it may be appropriate to use an object-oriented approach.

Object-oriented techniques are thought to work well in situations in which complicated information systems are undergoing continuous maintenance, adaptation, and redesign. Object-oriented approaches use the industry standard for modeling object-oriented systems, called the unified modeling language (UML), to break down a system into a use case model.

Object-oriented programming differs from traditional procedural programming by examining objects that are part of a system. Each object is a computer representation of some actual thing or event. Objects may be customers, items, orders, and so on. Objects are represented by and grouped into classes that are optimal for reuse and maintainability. A class defines the set of shared attributes and behaviors found in each object in the class.

Object-oriented methodologies often focus on small, quick iterations of development, sometimes called the spiral model. Analysis is performed on a small part of the system, usually starting with a high-priority item or perhaps one that has the greatest risk. This is followed by design and implementation. The cycle is repeated with analysis of the next part, design, and some implementation, and it is repeated until the project is completed.

THE AGILE APPROACH AND OTHER ALTERNATIVE METHODOLOGIES

Although this text focuses on the most widely used approach in practice, at times the analyst will recognize that the organization could benefit from an alternative approach. Perhaps a systems project using a structured approach has recently failed, or perhaps the organizational subcultures, composed of several different user groups, seem more in step with an alternative method. We cannot do justice to these methods in a small space; each deserves and has inspired its own books and research. By mentioning these approaches here, however, we hope to help you become aware that under certain circumstances, your organization may want to consider an alternative or supplement to structured analysis and design and to the systems development life cycle.

The agile approach is a software development approach based on values, principles, and core practices. The four values are communication, simplicity, feedback, and courage. We recommend that systems analysts adopt these values in all projects they undertake, not just when adopting the agile approach.

In order to finish a project, adjustments often need to be made in project management. In Chapter 3 we will see that agile methods can ensure successful completion of a project by adjusting the important resources of time, cost, quality, and scope. When these four control variables are properly included in the planning, there is a state of balance between the resources and the activities needed to complete the project.

Taking development practices to the extreme is most noticeable when one pursues practices that are unique to agile development. In Chapter 6 we discuss four core agile practices: short releases, the 40-hour work week, hosting an onsite customer, and using pair programming. At first glance these practices appear extreme, but as you will see, we can learn some important lessons from incorporating many of the values and practices of the agile approach into systems analysis and design projects.

Among the most popular alternative methods are prototyping (distinct from the prototyping we discuss in Chapter 6), ETHICS, the project champion approach, Soft Systems Methodology, and Multiview. Prototyping, established in other disciplines and applied to IS, was offered as a response to the long development times associated with the systems development life cycle approach and to the uncertainty often surrounding user requirements. ETHICS was introduced as a sociotechnical methodology combining social and technical solutions. The project champion approach, a concept borrowed from marketing, adopts the strategy of involving one key person from each area affected by the system to ensure the system's success. Soft Systems Methodology was envisioned as a way to model a world that is often chaotic by using "rich pictures," ideographs that capture characteristic organizational narratives. Multiview was proposed as a way to organize and use elements of several competing methodologies.

SUMMARY

Information can be viewed as an organizational resource just as humans are. As such, it must be managed carefully, just as other resources are. The availability of affordable computer power to organizations has meant an explosion of information, and consequently, more attention must be paid to coping with the information generated.

Systems analysts recommend, design, and maintain many types of systems for users, including transaction processing systems (TPS), office automation systems (OAS), knowledge work systems (KWS), and management information systems (MIS). They also create decision-oriented systems for specific users. These include decision support systems (DSS), expert systems (ES), group decision support systems (GDSS), computer-supported collaborative work systems (CSCWS), and executive support systems (ESS). Many applications are either originating on, or moving to, the Web to support ecommerce.

Systems analysis and design is a systematic approach to identifying problems, opportunities, and objectives; to analyzing human and computer-generated information flows in organizations; and to designing computerized information systems to solve a problem. Systems analysts are required to take on many roles in the course of their work. Some of these roles are (1) an outside consultant to business, (2) a supporting expert within a business, and (3) an agent of change in both internal and external situations.

Analysts possess a wide range of skills. First and foremost, the analyst is a problem solver, someone who enjoys the challenge of analyzing a problem and devising a workable solution. Systems analysts require communication skills that allow them to relate meaningfully to many different kinds of people on a daily basis, as well as computer skills. Understanding and relating well to users is critical to their success.

Analysts proceed systematically. The framework for their systematic approach is provided in what is called the systems development life cycle (SDLC). This life cycle can be divided into seven sequential phases, although in reality the phases are interrelated and are often accomplished simultaneously. The seven phases are identifying problems, opportunities, and objectives; determining human information requirements; analyzing system needs; designing the recommended system; developing and documenting software; testing and maintaining the system; and implementing and evaluating the system.

Automated, PC-based software packages for systems analysis and design are called Computer-Aided Software Engineering (CASE) tools. The four reasons for adopting CASE tools are increasing analyst productivity, improving communication among analysts and users, integrating life cycle activities, and analyzing and assessing the impact of maintenance changes.

A different approach to systems development is object-oriented analysis (OOA) and object-oriented design (OOD). These techniques are based on

HYPERCASE® EXPERIENCE 1

"Welcome to Maple Ridge Engineering, what we call MRE. We hope you'll enjoy serving as a systems consultant for us. Although I've worked here five years in different capacities, I've just been reassigned to serve as an administrative aide to Snowden Evans, the head of the new Training and Management Systems Department. We're certainly a diverse group. As you make your way through the company, be sure to use all your skills, both technical and people oriented, to understand who we are and to identify the problems and conflicts that you think should be solved regarding our information systems.

"To bring you up to date, let me say that Maple Ridge Engineering is a medium-sized medical engineering company. Last year, our revenues exceeded $287 million. We employ about 335 people. There are about 150 administrative employees as well as management and clerical staff like myself; approximately 75 professional employees, including engineers, physicians, and systems analysts; and about 110 trade employees, such as drafters and technicians.

"There are four offices. You will visit us through HyperCase in our home office in Maple Ridge, Tennessee. We have three other branches in the southern United States as well: Atlanta, Georgia; Charlotte, North Carolina; and New Orleans, Louisiana. We'd love to have you visit when you're in the area.

"For now, you should explore HyperCase using either Netscape Navigator or Microsoft Internet Explorer.

"To learn more about Maple Ridge Engineering as a company or to find out how to interview our employees, who will use the systems you design, and how to observe their offices in our company, you may want to start by going to the Web site found at www.prenhall.com/kendall. Then click on the link labeled **HyperCase.** At the HyperCase display screen, click on **Start** and you will be in the reception room for Maple Ridge Engineering. From this point, you can start consulting right away."

This Web site contains useful information about the project as well as files that can be downloaded to your computer. One file is a set of Visible Analyst data files that match HyperCase. They contain a partially constructed series of data flow diagrams, entity-relationship diagrams, and repository information. The HyperCase Web site also contains additional exercises that may be assigned. HyperCase is designed to be explored, and you should not overlook any object or clue on a Web page.

object-oriented programming concepts that have become codified in the UML, a standardized modeling language in which objects that are created include not only code about data but also instructions about the operations to be performed on the data.

When the organizational situation demands it, the analyst may depart from the SDLC to try an alternative methodology. The agile approach, also called agile methods, has a specific philosophy, practices, and values to address rapidly changing user requirements. Prototyping, ETHICS, the project champion approach, Soft Systems Methodology, and Multiview are all development approaches that offer a different perspective.

KEYWORDS AND PHRASES

agent of change
agile approach
agile methods
Ajax
artificial intelligence (AI)
Computer-Assisted Software Engineering (CASE)
CASE tools
computer-supported collaborative work systems (CSCWS)
decision support systems (DSS)
ecommerce applications
enterprise resource planning (ERP) systems
ETHICS
executive support systems (ESS)
expert systems
group decision support systems (GDSS)
human–computer interaction (HCI)
knowledge work systems (KWS)
management information systems (MIS)
mcommerce (mobile commerce)
migrate systems
Multiview
object-oriented analysis (OOA)
object-oriented design (OOD)
object-oriented (O-O) systems analysis and design
office automation systems (OAS)
open source software (OSS)
personal digital assistant (PDA)
project champion approach
prototyping
rapid application development (RAD)
Soft Systems Methodology
systems analysis and design
systems analyst
systems consultant
systems development life cycle (SDLC)
transaction processing systems (TPS)
unified modeling language (UML)

REVIEW QUESTIONS

1. Compare treating information as a resource to treating humans as a resource.
2. List the differences between OAS and KWS.
3. Define what is meant by MIS.
4. How does MIS differ from DSS?
5. Define the term *expert systems.* How do expert systems differ from decision support systems?
6. List the problems of group interaction that group decision support systems (GDSS) and computer-supported collaborative work systems (CSCWS) were designed to address.
7. Which is the more general term, CSCWS or GDSS? Explain.
8. Define the term *mcommerce.*
9. List the advantages of mounting applications on the Web.
10. What is the overarching reason for designing ERP systems?
11. Provide an example of an open source software project.
12. List the advantages of using systems analysis and design techniques in approaching computerized information systems for business.
13. List three roles that the systems analyst is called upon to play. Provide a definition for each one.
14. What personal qualities are helpful to the systems analyst? List them.
15. List and briefly define the seven phases of the systems development life cycle (SDLC).

16. What is rapid application development (RAD)?
17. List the four reasons for adopting CASE tools.
18. Define what is meant by the agile approach.
19. Define the terms *object-oriented analysis* and *object-oriented design*.
20. What is UML?

SELECTED BIBLIOGRAPHY

Avison, D. E., and A. T. Wood-Harper. *Multiview: An Exploration in Information Systems Development.* Oxford: Blackwell Scientific Publications, 1990.

Beath, C. M. "Supporting the Information Technology Champion." *MIS Quarterly,* Vol. 15, No. 3, September 1991, pp. 355–372.

Carey, J. D., Galletta, J. Kim, D. Te'eni, B. Wildemuth, and P. Zhang. "The Role of Human–Computer Interaction in Management Information Systems Curricula: A Call to Action." *Communications of the Association for Information Systems,* Vol. 13, 2004, pp. 357–379.

Checkland, P. B. "Soft Systems Methodology." *Human Systems Management*, Vol. 8, No. 4, 1989, pp. 271–289.

Coad, P., and E. Yourdon. *Object-Oriented Analysis,* 2d ed. Englewood Cliffs, NJ: Prentice Hall, 1991.

Davis, G. B., and M. H. Olson. *Management Information Systems: Conceptual Foundation, Structure, and Development,* 2d ed. New York: McGraw-Hill, 1985.

Feller, J., P. Finnegan, D. Kelly, and M. MacNamara. "Developing Open Source Software: A Community-Based Analysis of Research." In IFIP International Federation for Information Processing, Vol. 208, *Social Inclusion: Societal and Organizational Implications for Information Systems.* Edited by E. Trauth, D. Howcroft, T. Butler, B. Fitzgerald, and J. DeGross, pp. 261–278. Boston: Springer, 2006.

Garretson, C. "What Users Hate about IT Pros." *Networkworld*. Available at: http://www.networkworld.com.news/2006/071706widernet-end-users.html. Last accessed July 30, 2006.

Hirschheim, R., J. Iivari, and H. K. Klein. "A Comparison of Five Alternative Approaches to Information Systems Development." *Australian Journal of Information Systems,* Vol. 5, No. 1, September 1997.

Hirschheim, R., and H. K. Klein. "Four Paradigms of Information Systems Development." *Communications of the ACM,* Vol. 32, No. 10, October 1989, pp. 1199–1216.

Holsapple, C. W., and A. B. Whinston. *Business Expert Systems.* Homewood, IL: Irwin, 1987.

Kendall, J. E., and K. E. Kendall. "Information Delivery Systems: An Exploration of Web Push and Pull Technologies." *Communications of AIS,* Vol. 1, Article 14, April 23, 1999.

Kendall, J. E., and K. E. Kendall. "Outsourcing and Information Systems Development: How Complementary Corporate Cultures Minimize the Risks of Outsourced Systems Projects." In *Outsourcing Management Information Systems.* Edited by M. J. Schniederjans, A. M. Schniederjans, and D. G. Schniederjans, pp. 225–241. Hershey, PA: Idea Group Publishing, 2007.

Kendall, J. E. and K. E. Kendall. "Agile Methodologies and the Lone Systems Analyst: When Individual Creativity and Organizational Goals Collide in the Global IT Environment." *Journal of Individual Employment Rights,* Vol. 11, No. 4, 2004–2005, pp. 333–347.

Kendall, J. E., K. E. Kendall, and S. Kong. "Improving Quality Through the Use of Agile Methods in Systems Development: People and Values in the Quest for Quality." In

Measuring Information Systems Delivery Quality. Edited by E. W. Duggan and H. Reichgelt, pp. 201–222. Hershey, PA: Idea Group Publishing, 2006.

Laudon, K. C., and J. P. Laudon. *Management Information Systems,* 9th ed. Upper Saddle River, NJ: Prentice Hall, 2006.

Lessig, L. *Free Culture: The Nature and Future of Creativity.* New York: Penguin Press, 2005.

Mumford, E., and M. Weir. *Computer Systems in Work Design—The ETHICS Method.* London: Associated Business Press, 1979.

Sharma, S., and A. Rai. "CASE Deployment in IS Organizations." *Communications of the ACM,* Vol. 43, No. 1, January 2000, pp. 80–88.

Stohr, E. A., and S. Viswanathan. "Recommendation Systems." In *Emerging Information Technologies: Improving Decisions, Cooperation, and Infrastructure.* Edited by K. E. Kendall, pp. 21–44. Thousand Oaks, CA: Sage Publications, 1999.

Verma, S. "Software Quality and the Open Source Process." In *Measuring Information Systems Delivery Quality.* Edited by E. W. Duggan and H. Reichgelt, pp. 284–303. Hershey, PA: Idea Group Publishing, 2006.

www.visible.com/Products/index.htm. Last accessed July 30, 2006.

Yourdon, E. *Modern Structured Analysis.* Englewood Cliffs, NJ: Prentice Hall, 1989.

Zhang, P., J. Carey, D. Te'eni, and M. Tremaine, M. "Integrating Human–Computer Interaction Development into the Systems Development Life Cycle: A Methodology." *Communications of the Association for Information Systems,* Vol. 15, 2005, pp. 512–543.

EPISODE 1 CPU CASE

Allen Schmidt, Julie E. Kendall, and Kenneth E. Kendall

THE CASE OPENS

On a warm, sunny day in late October, Chip Puller parks his car and walks into his office at Central Pacific University. It felt good to be starting as a systems analyst, and he was looking forward to meeting the other staff.

In the office, Anna Liszt introduces herself. "We've been assigned to work as a team on a new project. Why don't I fill you in with the details, and then we can take a tour of the facilities."

"That sounds good to me," Chip replies. "How long have you been working here?"

"About five years," answers Anna. "I started as a programmer analyst, but the last few years have been dedicated to analysis and design. I'm hoping we'll find some ways to increase our productivity," Anna continues.

"Tell me about the new project," Chip says.

"Well," Anna replies, "like so many organizations, we have a large number of microcomputers with different software packages installed on them. In the 1980s there were few microcomputers and a scattered collection of software, but there has been a rapid increase in recent years. The current system used to maintain software and hardware has been overwhelmed."

"What about the users? Who should I know? Who do you think will be important in helping us with the new system?" Chip asks.

"You'll meet everyone, but there are key people I've recently met, and I'll tell you what I've learned so you'll remember them when you meet them.

"Dot Matricks is manager of all microcomputer systems at Central Pacific. We seem to be able to work together well. She's very competent. She'd really like to be able to improve communication among users and analysts."

"It will be a pleasure to meet her," Chip speculates.

"Then there's Mike Crowe, the micromaintenance expert. He really seems to be the nicest guy, but too busy. We need to help lighten his load. The software counterpart to Mike is Cher Ware. She's a free spirit, but don't get me wrong, she knows her job," Anna says.

"She could be fun to work with," Chip says.

"Could be," Anna agrees. "You'll meet the financial analyst, Paige Prynter, too. I haven't figured her out yet."

"Maybe I can help," Chip says.

"Last, you should—I mean, you will—meet Hy Perteks, who does a great job running the Information Center. He'd like to see us be able to integrate our life cycle activities."

"It sounds promising," Chip says. "I think I'm going to like it here."

EXERCISE

E-1. From the introductory conversation Chip and Anna shared, which elements mentioned might suggest the use of CASE tools

UNDERSTANDING ORGANIZATIONAL STYLE AND ITS IMPACT ON INFORMATION SYSTEMS

2

LEARNING OBJECTIVES

Once you have mastered the material in this chapter you will be able to:

1. **Understand that organizations and their members are systems and that analysts need to take a systems perspective.**
2. **Depict systems graphically using context-level data flow diagrams, entity-relationship models, and use cases and use case scenarios.**
3. **Recognize that different levels of management require different systems.**
4. **Comprehend that organizational culture impacts the design of information systems.**

To analyze and design appropriate information systems, systems analysts need to comprehend the organizations they work in as systems shaped through the interactions of three main forces: the levels of management, design of organizations, and organizational cultures.

Organizations are large systems composed of interrelated subsystems. The subsystems are influenced by three broad levels of management decision makers (operations, middle management, and strategic management) that cut horizontally across the organizational system. Organizational cultures and subcultures all influence the way people in subsystems interrelate. These topics and their implications for information systems development are considered in this chapter.

ORGANIZATIONS AS SYSTEMS

Organizations and their members are usefully conceptualized as systems designed to accomplish predetermined goals and objectives through people and other resources that they employ. Organizations are composed of smaller, interrelated systems (departments, units, divisions, etc.) serving specialized functions. Typical functions include accounting, marketing, production, data processing, and management. Specialized functions (smaller systems) are eventually reintegrated through various mechanisms to form an effective organizational whole.

The significance of conceptualizing organizations as complex systems is that systems principles allow insight into how organizations work. To ascertain information requirements properly and to design appropriate information systems, it is of primary importance to understand the organization as a whole. All systems are composed of subsystems (which include information systems); therefore, when studying an organization, we also examine how smaller systems are involved and how they function.

INTERRELATEDNESS AND INTERDEPENDENCE OF SYSTEMS

All systems and subsystems are interrelated and interdependent. This fact has important implications both for organizations and for those systems analysts who seek to help them better achieve their goals. When any element of a system is changed or eliminated, the rest of the system's elements and subsystems are also significantly affected.

For example, suppose that the administrators of an organization decide not to hire personal secretaries any longer and to replace their functions with networked PCs. This decision has the potential to significantly affect not only the secretaries and the administrators but also all the organizational members who built up communications networks with the now departed secretaries.

All systems process inputs from their environments. By definition, processes change or transform inputs into outputs. Whenever you examine a system, check to see what is being changed or processed. If nothing is changed, you may not be identifying a process. Typical processes in systems include verifying, updating, and printing.

Another aspect of organizations as systems is that all systems are contained by boundaries separating them from their environments. Organizational boundaries exist on a continuum ranging from extremely permeable to almost impermeable. To continue to adapt and survive, organizations must be able first to import people, raw materials, and information through their boundaries (inputs), and then to exchange their finished products, services, or information with the outside world (outputs).

Feedback is one form of system control. As systems, all organizations use planning and control to manage their resources effectively. Figure 2.1 shows how system outputs are used as feedback that compares performance with goals. This comparison in turn helps administrators formulate more specific goals as inputs. An example is a manufacturing company that produces red-white-and-blue weight-training sets as well as gun-metal gray sets. The company finds that one year after the Olympics, very few red-white-and-blue sets are purchased. Production managers use that information as feedback to make decisions about what quantities of each color to produce. Feedback in this instance is useful for planning and control.

The ideal system, however, is one that self-corrects or self-regulates in such a way that decisions on typical occurrences are not required. An example is a computerized information system for production planning that takes into account current and projected demand and formulates a proposed solution as output. An Italian knitwear manufacturer that markets its clothing in the United States has just

FIGURE 2.1
System outputs serve as feedback that compares performance with goals.

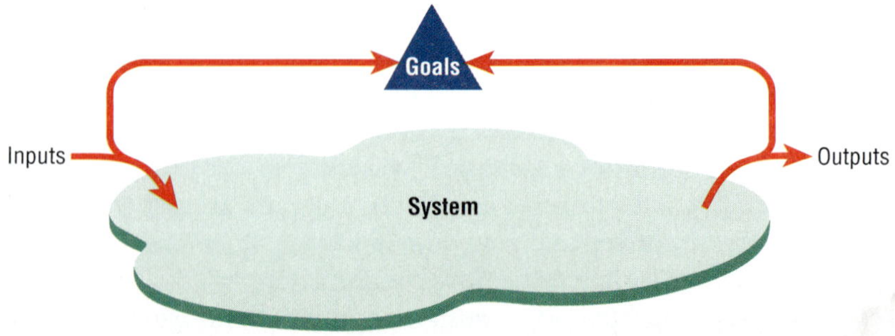

such a system. This company produces most of its sweaters in white, uses its computerized inventory information system to find out what colors are selling best, and then dyes sweaters in hot-selling colors immediately before shipping them.

Feedback is received from within the organization and from the outside environments around it. Anything external to an organization's boundaries is considered to be an environment. Numerous environments, with varying degrees of stability, constitute the milieu in which organizations exist.

Among these environments are (1) the environment of the community in which the organization is physically located, which is shaped by the size of its population and its demographic profile, including factors such as education and average income; (2) the economic environment, influenced by market factors, including competition; and (3) the political environment, controlled through state and local governments. Although changes in environmental status can be planned for, they often cannot be directly controlled by the organization.

Related and similar to the concept of external boundary permeability is the concept of internal openness or closedness of organizations. Openness and closedness also exist on a continuum, because there is no such thing as an absolutely open or completely closed organization.

Openness refers to the free flow of information within the organization. Subsystems such as creative or art departments often are characterized as open, with a free flow of ideas among participants and very few restrictions on who gets what information at what time when a creative project is in its infancy.

At the opposite end of the continuum might be a defense department unit assigned to work on top-secret defense planning affecting national security. Each person needs to receive clearance, timely information is a necessity, and access to information is only on a "need to know" basis. This sort of unit is limited by numerous rules.

Using a systems overlay to understand organizations allows us to acknowledge the idea of systems composed of subsystems; their interrelatedness and their interdependence; the existence of boundaries that allow or prevent interaction between various departments and elements of other subsystems and environments; and the existence of internal environments characterized by degrees of openness and closedness, which might differ across departments, units, or even projects.

VIRTUAL ORGANIZATIONS AND VIRTUAL TEAMS

Not all organizations or parts of organizations are visible in a physical location. Entire organizations or units of organizations can now possess virtual components that permit them to change configurations to adapt to changing project or marketplace demands. Virtual enterprises use networks of computers and communications technology to bring people with specific skills together electronically to work on projects that are not physically located in the same place. Information technology enables coordination of these remote team members. Often virtual teams spring up in already-established organizations; in some instances, however, organizations of remote workers have been able to succeed without the traditional investment in infrastructure.

There are several potential benefits to virtual organizations, such as the possibility of reducing costs of physical facilities, more rapid response to customer needs, and helping virtual employees to fulfill their familial obligations to children or aging parents. Just how important it will be to meet the social needs of virtual workers is still open to research and debate. One example of a need for tangible identification with a culture arose when students who were enrolled in an online virtual university, with no physical campus (or sports teams), kept requesting

CONSULTING OPPORTUNITY 2.1

THE E IN VITAMIN E STANDS FOR ECOMMERCE

"Our retail shops and mail-order division are quite healthy," says Bill Berry, one of the owners of Marathon Vitamin Shops, "but to be competitive, we must establish an ecommerce Web site." His father, and coowner, exclaims, "I agree, but where do we start?" The elder Berry knew, of course, that it wasn't a case of setting up a Web site and asking customers to email their orders to the retail store. He identified eight different parts to ecommerce and realized that they were all part of a larger system. In other words, all the parts had to work together to create a strong package. His list of elements essential to ecommerce included the following:

1. Attracting customers to an ecommerce Web site.
2. Informing customers about products and services offered.
3. Allowing customers to customize products online.
4. Completing transactions with customers.
5. Accepting payment from customers in a variety of forms.
6. Supporting customers after the sale via the Web site.
7. Arranging for the delivery of goods and services.
8. Personalizing the look and feel of the Web site for different customers.

Bill Berry read the list and contemplated it for a while. "It is obvious that ecommerce is more complex than I thought," he says. You can help the owners of Marathon Vitamin Shops in the following ways:

1. Make a list of the elements that are interrelated or interdependent. Then write a paragraph stating why it is critical to monitor these elements closely.
2. Decide on the boundaries of the system. That is, write a paragraph expressing an opinion on which elements are critical for Marathon Vitamin Shops and which elements can be explored at a later date.
3. Suggest which elements should be handled in-house and which should be outsourced to another company that may be better able to handle the job. Justify your suggestions in two paragraphs, one for the in-house jobs and one for the outsourced tasks.

items such as sweatshirts, coffee mugs, and pennants with the virtual university's logo imprinted on them. These items are meaningful cultural artifacts that traditional brick-and-mortar schools have long provided.

Many systems analysis and design teams are now able to work virtually, and in fact, many of them marked the path for other types of employees to follow in accomplishing work virtually. Some applications permit analysts who are providing technical assistance over the Web to "see" the software and hardware configuration of the user requesting help, in this way creating an ad hoc virtual team composed of the analyst and user.

TAKING A SYSTEMS PERSPECTIVE

Taking a systems perspective allows systems analysts to start broadly clarifying and understanding the various businesses with which they will come into contact. It is important that members of subsystems realize that their work is interrelated. Notice in Figure 2.2 that the outputs from the production subsystems serve as inputs for marketing and that the outputs of marketing serve as new inputs for production. Neither subsystem can properly accomplish its goals without the other.

Problems occur when each manager possesses a different picture of the importance of his or her own functional subsystem. In Figure 2.3 you can see that the marketing manager's personal perspective shows the business as driven by marketing, with all other functional areas interrelated but not of central importance. By the same token, the perspective of a production manager positions production at the center of the business, with all other functional areas driven by it.

The relative importance of functional areas as revealed in the personal perspectives of managers takes on added significance when managers rise to the top

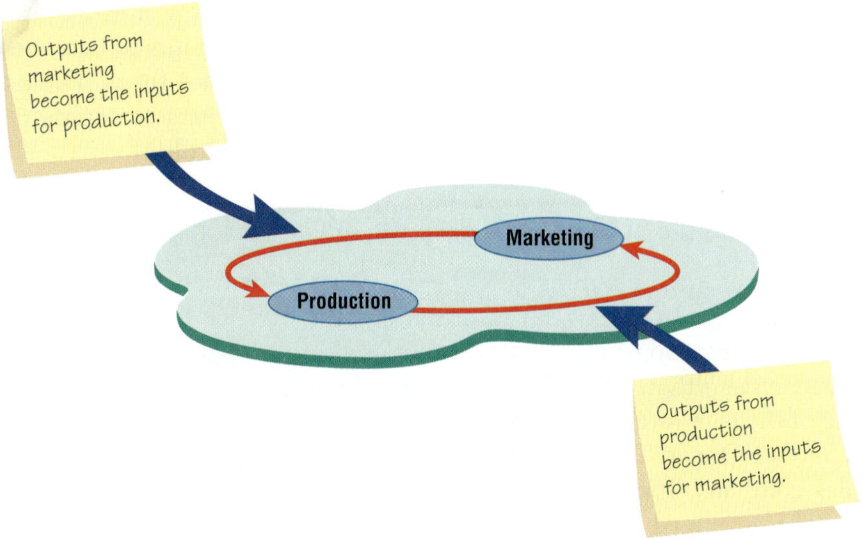

FIGURE 2.2
Outputs from one department serve as inputs for another such that subsystems are interrelated.

through the ranks, becoming strategic managers. They can create problems if they overemphasize their prior functional information requirements in relation to the broader needs of the strategic manager.

For example, if a production manager is promoted but continues to stress production scheduling and performance of line workers, the broader aspects of forecasting and policy making may suffer. This tendency is a danger in all sorts of

How a Marketing Manager May View the Organization

How a Production Manager May See the Organization

FIGURE 2.3
A depiction of the personal perspective of functional managers shows that they feature their own functional area as central to the organization.

businesses: where engineers work their way up to become administrators of aerospace firms, college professors move from their departments to become deans, or programmers advance to become executives of software firms. Their tunnel vision often creates problems for the systems analyst trying to separate actual information requirements from desires for a particular kind of information.

ENTERPRISE RESOURCE PLANNING: VIEWING THE ORGANIZATION AS A SYSTEM

An enterprise resource planning (ERP) system is a term used to describe an integrated organizational (enterprise) information system. ERP is software that helps the flow of information between the functional areas in the organization. It is a customized system that, rather than being developed in-house, is usually purchased from one of the software development companies well-known for its ERP packages, such as SAP or Oracle. The product is then customized to fit the requirements of a particular company. Typically, the vendor requires an organizational commitment in terms of specialized user or analyst training. Many ERP packages are designed to run on the Web. ERP, although growing in popularity, is also being viewed with some skepticism.

ERP evolved from materials requirements planning (MRP), the information systems designed to improve manufacturing in general and assembly in particular. ERP systems now include manufacturing components and thus help with capacity planning, material production scheduling, and forecasting. Beyond manufacturing (and its service counterpart), ERP includes sales and operations planning, distribution, procurement, and managing the supply chain. It therefore significantly affects all the areas in the organization, including accounting, finance, management, marketing, and information systems.

Implementing an ERP solution may be frustrating because it is difficult to analyze a system currently in use and then fit the ERP model to that system. Furthermore, companies tend to design their business processes before ERP is implemented. Unfortunately, this process is often rushed and the proposed business model does not always match the ERP functionality. The result is further customizations, extended implementation time frames, higher costs, and often the loss of user confidence. Analysts need to be aware of the magnitude of the problem they are tackling when trying to implement ERP packages.

DEPICTING SYSTEMS GRAPHICALLY

A system or subsystem as it exists within the corporate organization may be graphically depicted in several ways. The various graphical models show the boundaries of the system and the information used in the system.

SYSTEMS AND THE CONTEXT-LEVEL DATA FLOW DIAGRAM

The first model is the context-level data flow diagram (also called an environmental model). Data flow diagrams focus on the data flowing into and out of the system and the processing of the data. These basic components of every computer program can be described in detail and used to analyze the system for accuracy and completeness.

As shown in Figure 2.4, the context-level data flow diagram employs only three symbols: (1) a rectangle with rounded corners, (2) a square with two shaded edges, and (3) an arrow. Processes transform incoming data into outgoing information, and the content level has only one process, representing the entire system. The external entity represents any entity that supplies or receives information

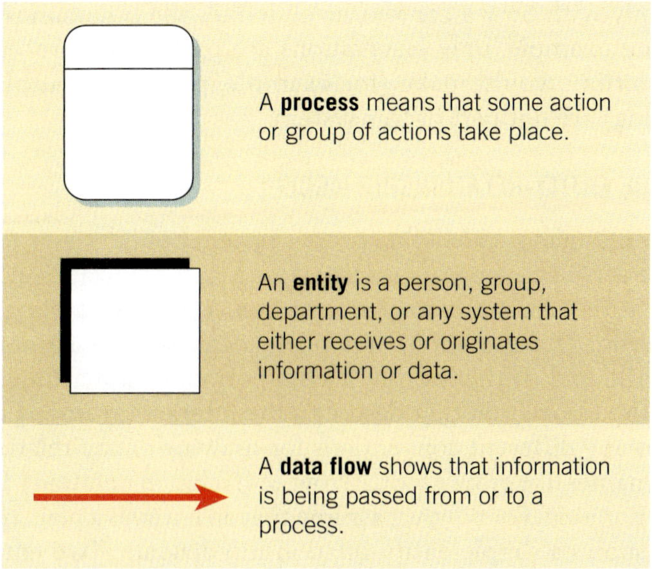

FIGURE 2.4
The basic symbols of a data flow diagram.

from the system but is not a part of the system. This entity may be a person, a group of people, a corporate position or department, or other systems. The lines that connect the external entities to the process are called data flows, and they represent data.

An example of a context-level data flow diagram is found in Figure 2.5. In this example, the most basic elements of an airline reservation system are represented. The passenger (an entity) initiates a travel request (data flow). The context-level diagram doesn't show enough detail to indicate exactly what happens (it isn't supposed to), but we can see that the passenger's preferences and the available flights are sent to the travel agent, who sends ticketing information back to the process. We can also see that the passenger reservation is sent to the airline.

In Chapter 7 we see that a data flow contains much information. For example, the passenger reservation contains the passenger's name, airline, flight number(s), date(s) of travel, price, seating preference, and so on. For now, however, we are

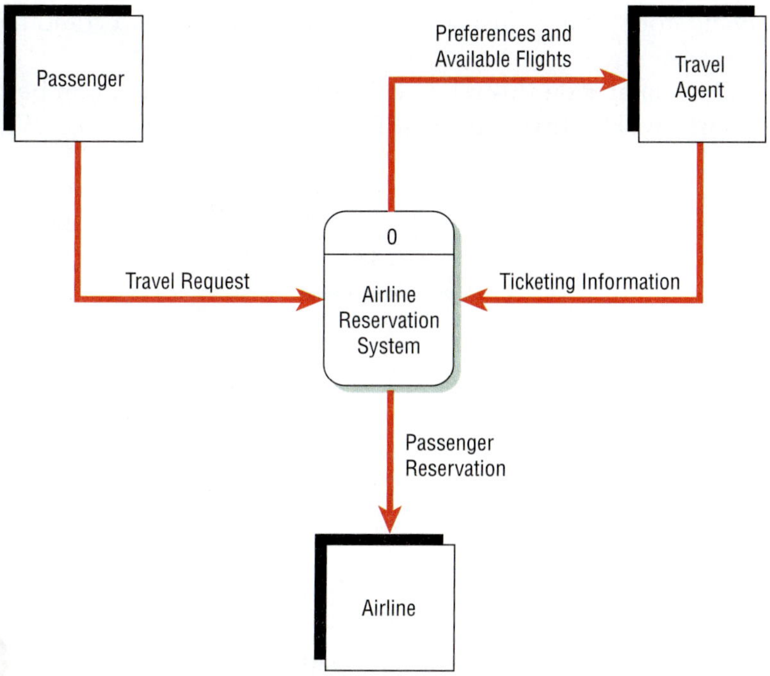

FIGURE 2.5
A context-level data flow diagram for an airline reservation system.

concerned mainly with how a context level defines the boundaries of the system. In the preceding example, only reservations are part of the process. Other decisions that the airline would make (for example, purchasing airplanes, changing schedules, pricing) are not part of this system.

SYSTEMS AND THE ENTITY-RELATIONSHIP MODEL

One way a systems analyst can define proper system boundaries is to use an entity-relationship model. The elements that make up an organizational system can be referred to as entities. An entity may be a person, a place, or a thing, such as a passenger on an airline, a destination, or a plane. Alternatively, an entity may be an event, such as the end of the month, a sales period, or a machine breakdown. A relationship is the association that describes the interaction among the entities.

There are many different conventions for drawing entity-relationship, or E-R, diagrams (with names like crow's foot, Arrow, or Bachman notation). In this book, we use crow's foot notation. For now, we assume that an entity is a plain rectangular box.

Figure 2.6 shows a simple entity-relationship diagram. Two entities are linked together by a line. In this example, the end of the line is marked with two short parallel marks (||), signifying that this relationship is one-to-one. Thus, exactly one employee is assigned to one phone extension. No one shares the same phone extension in this office.

The red arrows are not part of the entity-relationship diagram. They are present to demonstrate how to read the entity-relationship diagram. The phrase on the right side of the line is read from top to bottom as follows: "One EMPLOYEE is assigned to one PHONE EXTENSION." On the left side, as you read from bottom to top, the arrow says, "One PHONE EXTENSION is listed for one EMPLOYEE."

Similarly, Figure 2.7 shows another relationship. The crow's foot notation (>+) is obvious on this diagram, and this particular example is a many-to-one example. As you read from left to right, the arrow signifies, "Many EMPLOYEES are members of a DEPARTMENT." As you read from right to left, it implies, "One DEPARTMENT contains many EMPLOYEES."

Notice that when a many-to-one relationship is present, the grammar changes from "is" to "are" even though the singular "is" is written on the line. The crow's foot and the single mark do not literally mean that this end of the relationship must be a mandatory "many." Instead, they imply that this end could be anything from one to many.

Figure 2.8 elaborates on this scheme. Here we have listed a number of typical entity relationships. The first, "An EMPLOYEE is assigned to an OFFICE," is a

FIGURE 2.6
An entity-relationship diagram showing a one-to-one relationship.

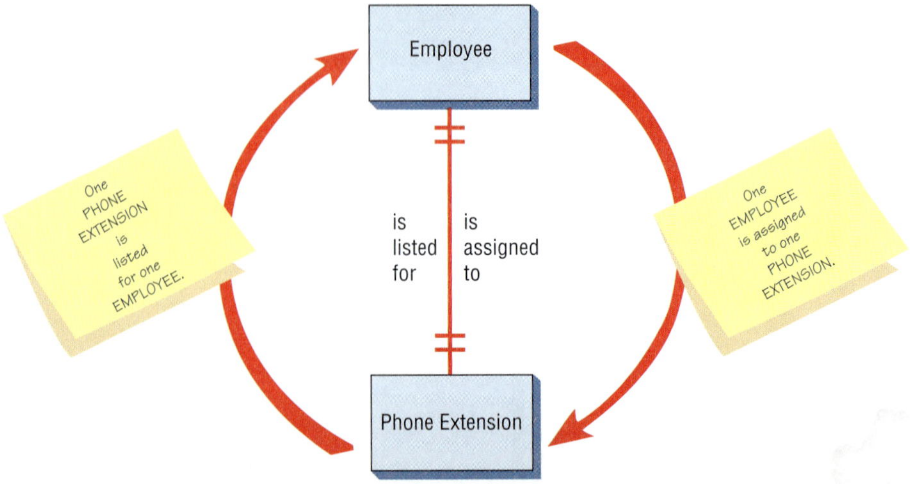

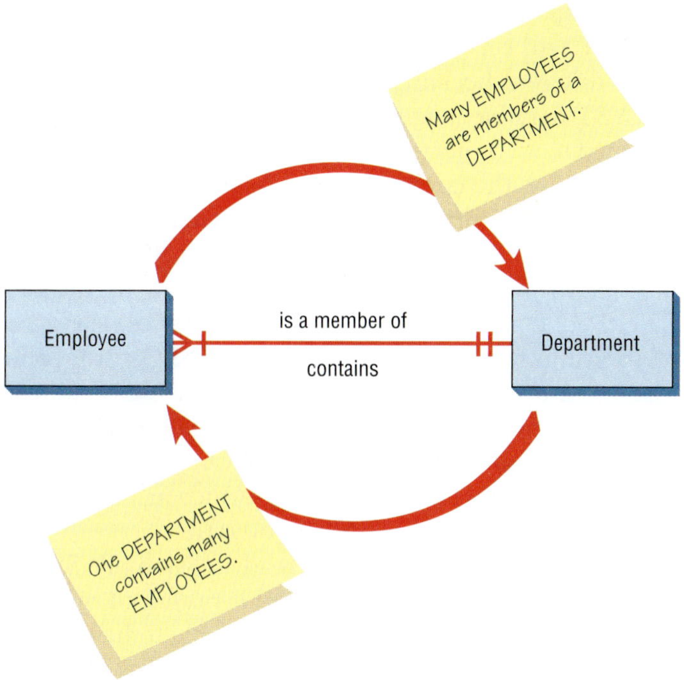

FIGURE 2.7
An entity-relationship diagram showing a many-to-one relationship.

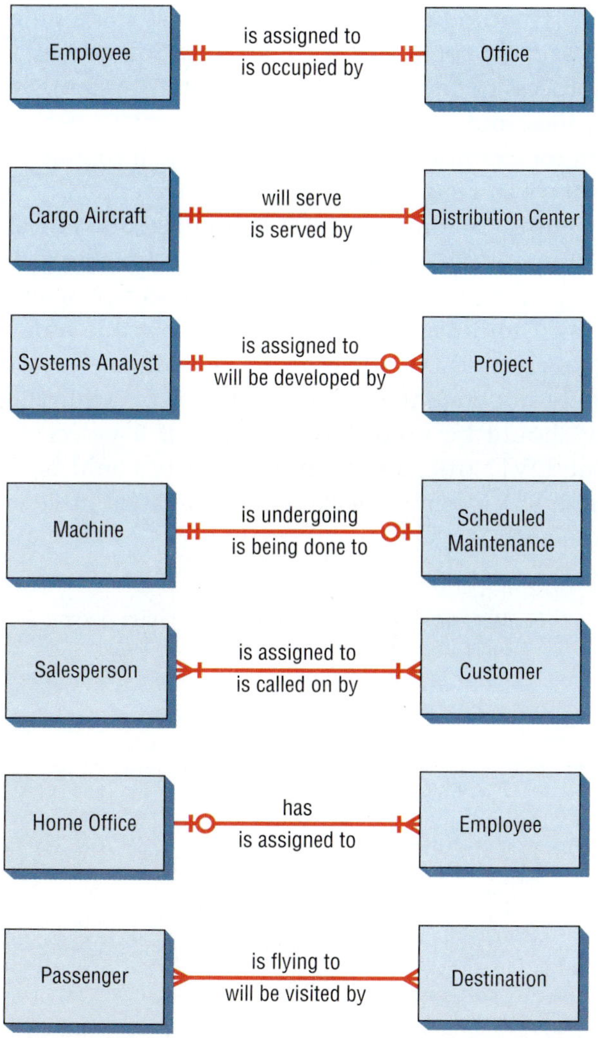

FIGURE 2.8
Examples of different types of relationships in E-R diagrams.

one-to-one relationship. The second one is a one-to-many relationship: "One CARGO AIRCRAFT will serve one or more DISTRIBUTION CENTERs." The third one is slightly different because it has a circle at one end. It can be read as "A SYSTEMS ANALYST may be assigned to MANY PROJECTS," meaning that the analyst can be assigned to no projects [that is what the circle (O), for zero, is for], one, or many projects. Likewise, the circle (O) indicates that none is possible in the next relationship. Recall that the short mark means one. Therefore, we can read it as follows: "A MACHINE may or may not be undergoing SCHEDULED MAINTENANCE." Notice that the line is written as "is undergoing," but the end marks on the line indicate that either no maintenance (O) or maintenance (I) is actually going on.

The next relationship states, "One or many SALESPEOPLE (plural of SALESPERSON) are assigned to one or more CUSTOMERs." It is the classic many-to-many relationship. The next relationship can be read as follows: "The HOME OFFICE can have one or many EMPLOYEEs," or "One or more EMPLOYEEs may or may not be assigned to the HOME OFFICE." Once again, the I and O together imply a Boolean situation, in other words, one or zero.

The final relationship shown here can be read as, "Many PASSENGERs are flying to many DESTINATIONs." This symbol [—<] is preferred by some to indicate a mandatory "many" condition. (Would it ever be possible to have only one passenger or only one destination?) Even so, some CASE tools such as Visible Analyst do not offer this possibility, because the optional one-or-many condition as shown in the SALESPERSON-CUSTOMER relationship will do.

Up to now we have modeled all our relationships using just one simple rectangle and a line. This method works well when we are examining the relationships of real things such as real people, places, and things. Sometimes, though, we create new items in the process of developing an information system. Some examples are invoices, receipts, files, and databases. When we want to describe how a person relates to a receipt, for example, it becomes convenient to indicate the receipt in a different way, as shown in Figure 2.9 as an associative entity.

An associative entity can only exist if it is connected to at least two other entities. For that reason, some call it a gerund, a junction, an intersection, or a concatenated entity. This wording makes sense because a receipt wouldn't be necessary unless there were a customer and a salesperson making the transaction.

Another type of entity is the attributive. When an analyst wants to show data that are completely dependent on the existence of a fundamental entity, an attributive entity should be used. For example, if a video store had multiple copies of the same DVD title, an attributive entity could be used to designate which copy of the DVD is being checked out. The attributive entity is useful for

FIGURE 2.9
Three different types of entities used in E-R diagrams.

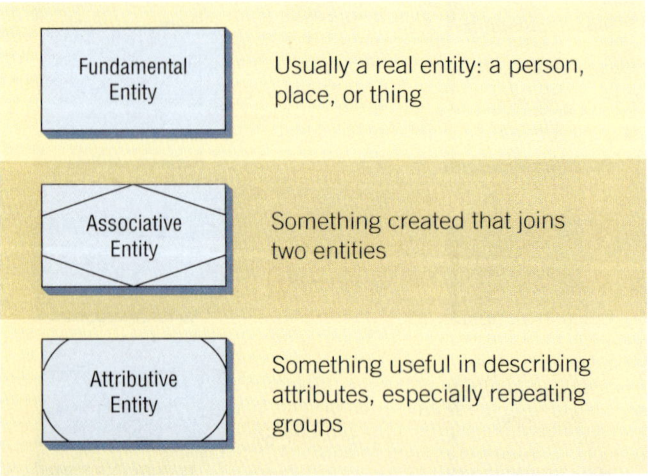

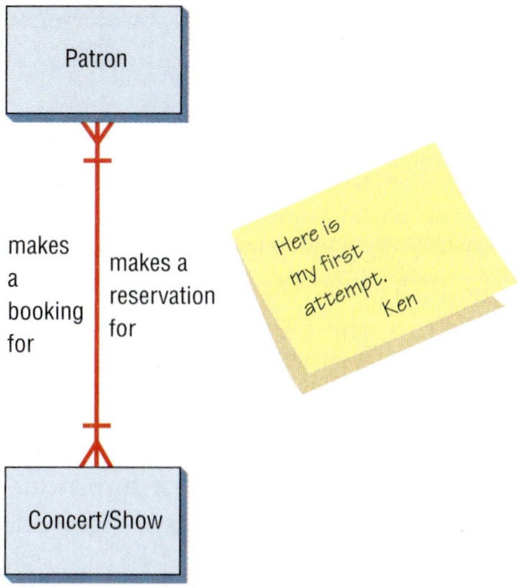

FIGURE 2.10
The first attempt at drawing an E-R diagram.

showing repeating groups of data. For example, suppose we are going to model the relationships that exist when a patron gets tickets to a concert or show. The entities seem obvious at first: "a PATRON and a CONCERT/SHOW," as shown in Figure 2.10. What sort of relationship exists? At first glance the PATRON gets a reservation for a CONCERT/SHOW, and the CONCERT/SHOW can be said to have made a booking for a PATRON.

The process isn't that simple, of course, and the E-R diagram need not be that simple either. The PATRON actually makes a RESERVATION, as shown in Figure 2.11. The RESERVATION is for a CONCERT/SHOW. The CONCERT/SHOW holds the RESERVATION, and the RESERVATION is in the name of

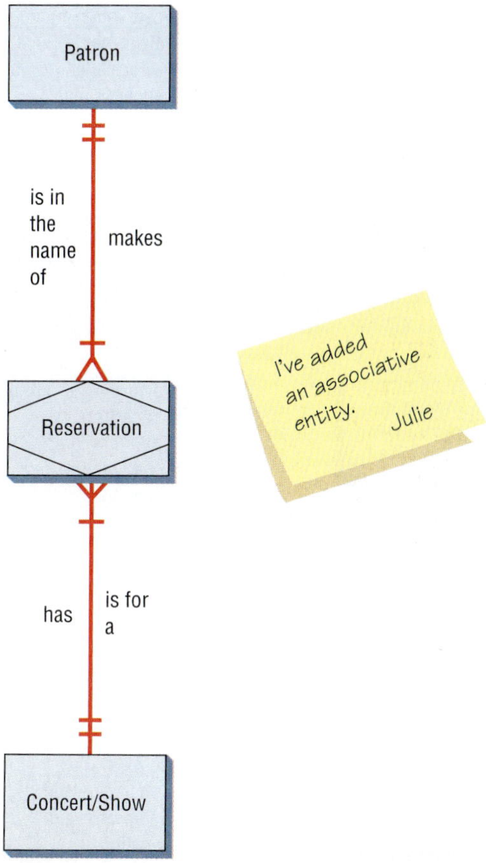

FIGURE 2.11
Improving the E-R diagram by adding an associative entry called RESERVATION.

the PATRON. We added an associative entity here because a RESERVATION was created due to the information system required to relate the PATRON and the CONCERT/SHOW.

Again this process is quite simple, but because concerts and shows have many performances, the entity-relationship diagram is drawn once more in Figure 2.12. Here we add an attributive entity to handle the many performances of the CONCERT/SHOW. In this case the RESERVATION is made for a particular PERFORMANCE, and the PERFORMANCE is one of many that belong to a specific CONCERT/SHOW. In turn the CONCERT/SHOW has many performances, and one PERFORMANCE has a RESERVATION that is in the name of a particular PATRON.

To the right of this E-R diagram is a set of data attributes that make up each of the entities. Some entities may have attributes in common. The attributes that are underlined can be searched for. The attributes are referred to as keys and are discussed in Chapter 13.

FIGURE 2.12
A more complete E-R diagram showing data attributes of the entities.

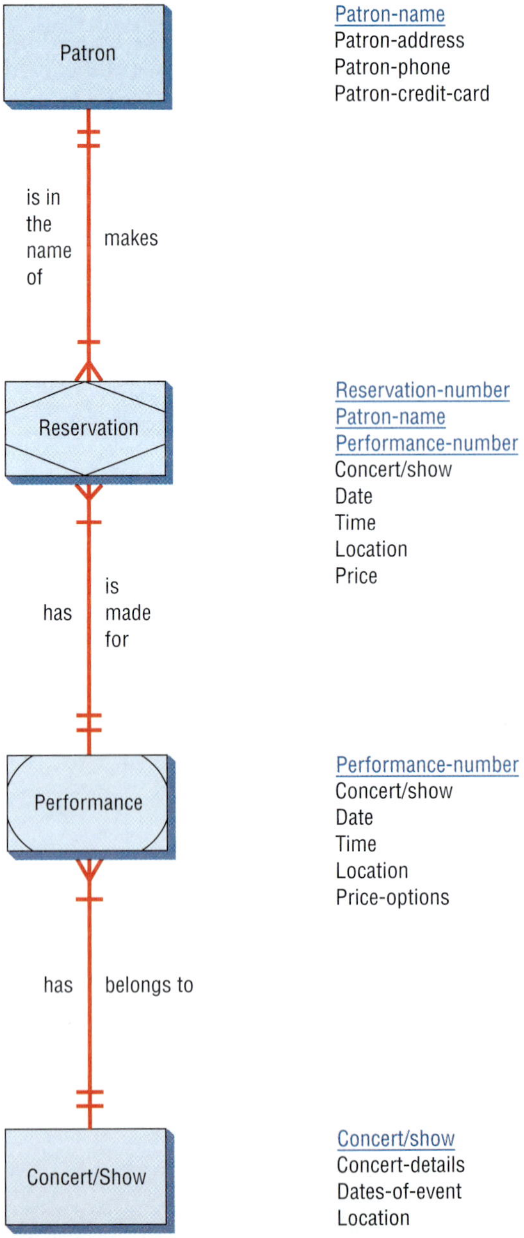

Entity-relationship diagrams are often used by systems designers to help model the file or database. It is even more important, however, that the systems analyst understand early both the entities and relationships in the organizational system. In sketching out some basic E-R diagrams, the analyst needs to:

1. List the entities in the organization to gain a better understanding of the organization.
2. Choose key entities to narrow the scope of the problem to a manageable and meaningful dimension.
3. Identify what the primary entity should be.
4. Confirm the results of steps 1 through 3 through other data-gathering methods (investigation, interviewing, administering questionnaires, observation, and prototyping), as discussed in Chapters 4 through 6.

It is critical that the systems analyst begin to draw E-R diagrams upon entering the organization rather than waiting until the database needs to be designed, because E-R diagrams help the analyst understand what business the organization is actually in, determine the size of the problem, and discern whether the right problem is being addressed. The E-R diagrams need to be confirmed or revised as the data-gathering process takes place.

USE CASE MODELING

Originally introduced as a diagram for use in the object-oriented UML, use cases are now being used regardless of the approach to systems development. It can be used as part of the SDLC or in agile modeling. The word *use* is pronounced as a noun (yoos) rather than a verb (yooz). A use case model describes *what* a system does without describing *how* the system does it; that is, it is a logical model of the system. (Logical or conceptual models will be further discussed in Chapter 7.) The use case model reflects the view of the system from the perspective of a user outside of the system (i.e., the system requirements).

An analyst develops use cases in a cooperative effort with the business experts who help define the requirements of the system. The use case model provides an effective means of communication between the business team and the development team. A use case model partitions the way the system works into behaviors, services, and responses (the use cases) that are significant to the users of the system.

From the perspective of an actor (or user), a use case should produce something that is of value. Therefore, the analyst must determine what is important to the user, and remember to include it in the use case diagram. For example, is entering a password something of value to the user? It may be included if the user has a concern about security or if it is critical to the success of the project.

USE CASE SYMBOLS

A use case diagram contains the actor and use case symbols, along with connecting lines. Actors are similar to external entities; they exist outside of the system. The term *actor* refers to a particular role of a user of the system. For example, an actor may be an employee, but also may be a customer at the company store. Even though it is the same person in the real world, it is represented as two different symbols on a use case diagram, because the person interacts with the system in different roles. The actor exists outside of the system and interacts with the system in a specific way. An actor can be a human, another system, or a device such as a keyboard or Web connection. Actors can initiate an instance of a use case. An actor may interact with one or more use cases, and a use case may involve one or more actors.

Actors may be divided into two groups. Primary actors supply data or receive information from the system. Some users directly interact with the system (system actors), but primary actors may also be businesspeople who do not directly interact with the system but have a stake in it. Primary actors are important because they are the people who use the system and can provide details on what the use case should do. They can also provide a list of goals and priorities. Supporting actors (also called secondary actors) help to keep the system running or provide other services. These are the people who run the help desk, the analysts, programmers, and so on.

Sometimes it is useful to create an actor profile that lists the actors, their background, and their skills in a simple table format. This may be useful to understand how the actor interacts with the system. An example is an Order Processing Specialist. The profile would be, "A regular user of the software, familiar with minor features, order exceptions, and order customization."

A use case provides developers with a view of what the users want. It is free of technical or implementation details. We can think of a use case as a sequence of transactions in a system. The use case model is based on the interactions and relationships of individual use cases.

A use case always describes three things: an actor that initiates an event; the event that triggers a use case; and the use case that performs the actions triggered by the event. In a use case, an actor using the system initiates an event that begins a related series of interactions in the system. Use cases are used to document a single transaction or event. An event is an input to the system that happens at a specific time and place and causes the system to do something.

It is better to create fewer use cases rather than more. Often queries and reports are not included; 20 use cases (and no more than 40 or 50) are sufficient for a large system. Use cases may also be nested, if needed. You can include a use case on several diagrams, but the actual use case is defined only once in the repository. A use case is named with a verb and a noun.

USE CASE RELATIONSHIPS

Active relationships are referred to as behavioral relationships and are used primarily in use case diagrams. There are four basic types of behavioral relationships: communicates, includes, extends, and generalizes. Notice that all these terms are action verbs. Figure 2.13 shows the arrows and lines used to diagram each of the four types of behavioral relationships. The four relationships are described below.

FIGURE 2.13

Some components of use case diagrams showing actors, use cases, and relationships for a student enrollment example.

Relationship	Symbol	Meaning
Communicates	————————	An actor is connected to a use case using a line with no arrowheads.
Includes	<< include >> <- - - - - - - - - - - -	A use case contains a behavior that is common to more than one other use case. The arrow points to the common use case.
Extends	<< extend >> - - - - - - - - - - - - ->	A different use case handles exceptions from the basic use case. The arrow points from the extended to the basic use case.
Generalizes	————————▷	One UML "thing" is more general than another "thing." The arrow points to the general "thing."

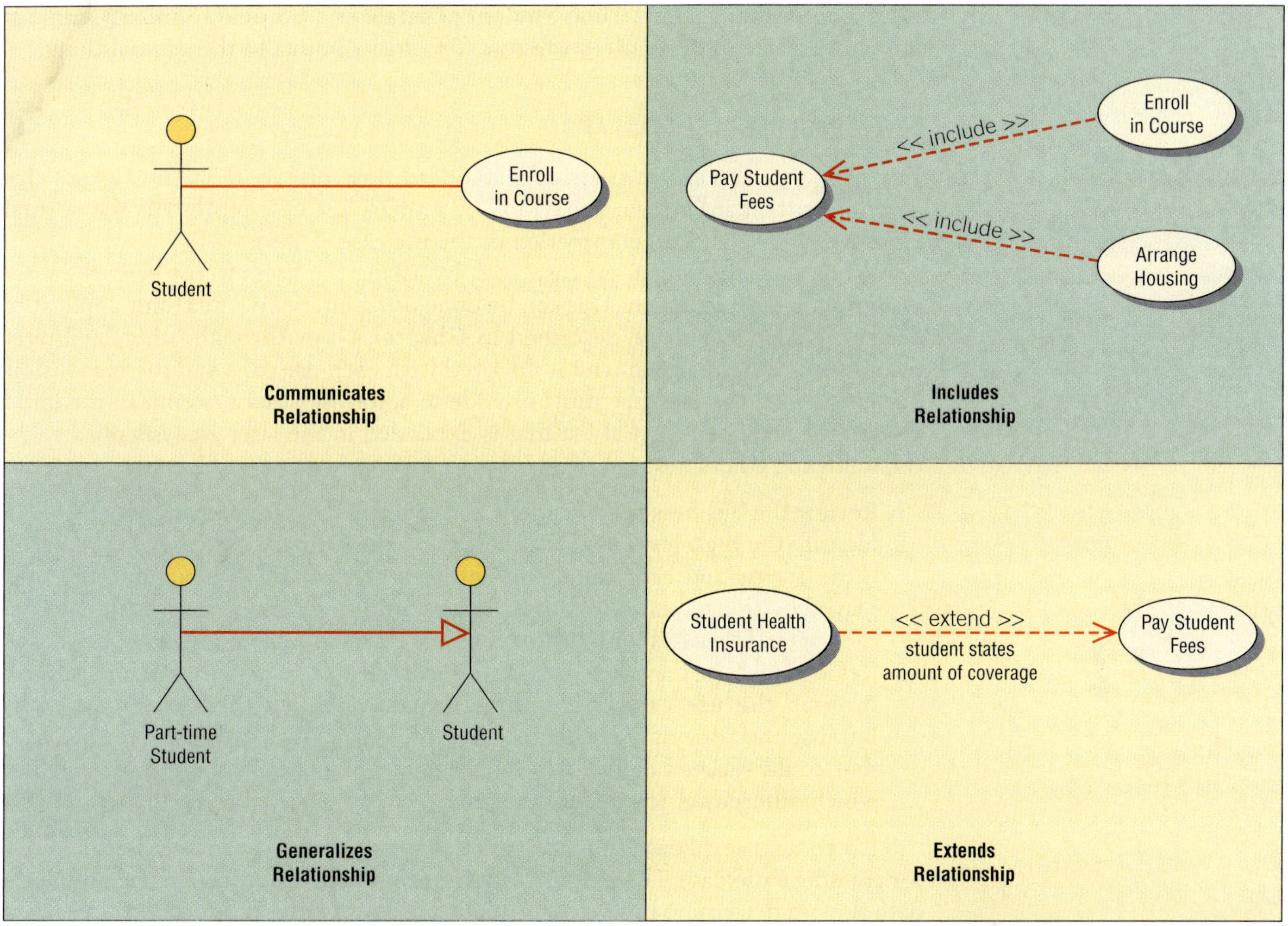

FIGURE 2.14

Examples of use cases and behavioral relationships for student enrollment.

Communicates The behavioral relationship communicates is used to connect an actor to a use case. Remember that the task of the use case is to give some sort of result that is beneficial to the actor in the system. Therefore, it is important to document these relationships between actors and use cases. In our first example, a **Student** communicates with **Enroll in Course.** Examples of some components of a student enrollment example are shown in the use case diagrams in Figure 2.14.

Includes The includes relationship (also called uses relationship) describes the situation in which a use case contains behavior that is common to more than one use case. In other words, the common use case is included in the other use cases. A dotted arrow that points to the common use case indicates the includes relationship. An example would be a use case **Pay Student Fees** that is included in **Enroll in Course** and **Arrange Housing,** because in both cases students must pay their fees. This may be used by several use cases. The arrow points toward the common use case.

Extends The extends relationship describes the situation in which one use case possesses the behavior that allows the new use case to handle a variation or exception from the basic use case. For example, the extended use case **Student Health Insurance** extends the basic use case **Pay Student Fees.** The arrow goes from the extended to the basic use case.

Generalizes The generalizes relationship implies that one thing is more typical than the other thing. This relationship may exist between two actors or two use cases. For example, a **Part-Time Student** generalizes a **Student.** Similarly, some of the university employees are professors. The arrow points to the general thing.

DEVELOPING USE CASE DIAGRAMS

The primary use case consists of a standard flow of events in the system that describes a standard system behavior. The primary use case represents the normal, expected, and successful completion of the use case.

When diagramming a use case, start by asking the users to list everything the system should do for them. This can be done using interviews, in a joint application design session (as will be described in Chapter 4), or through other facilitated team sessions. Write down who is involved with each use case, and the responsibilities or services the use case must provide to actors or other systems. In the initial phases, this may be a partial list that is expanded in the later analysis phases. Use the following guidelines:

1. Review the business specifications and identify the actors involved.
2. Identify the high-level events and develop the primary use cases that describe those events and how the actors initiate them. Carefully examine the roles played by the actors to identify all the possible primary use cases initiated by each actor. Use cases with little or no user interaction do not have to be shown.
3. Review each primary use case to determine the possible variations of flow through the use case. From this analysis, establish the alternative paths. Because the flow of events is usually different in each case, look for activities that could succeed or fail. Also look for any branches in the use case logic in which different outcomes are possible.

If a context-level data flow diagram has been created, it can be a starting point for creating a use case. The external entities are potential actors. Then examine the data flow to determine if it would initiate a use case or be produced by a use case.

Figure 2.15 is an example of a use case diagram representing a system used to plan a conference. The actors are the **Conference Chair,** responsible for planning and managing the conference, the conference **Participant, Speakers,** a **Keynote Speaker, Hotel Reservations,** and a **Caterer.** Actors represent the *role* the user plays, and the **Caterer** may be either a hotel employee or an external catering service.

Both the **Conference Chair** and the **Caterer** are involved in planning meals and banquets. The **Conference Chair** is also responsible for arranging speakers. The **Participant** registers for the conference. Notice that the **Reserve Room** use case is involved in an *includes* relationship with the **Arrange Speaker** and **Register for Conference** use cases, since both speakers and participants will need lodging. The **Arrange Language Translation** use case extends the **Register for Conference** use case because not all participants will require language translation services. The **Speaker** actor is a generalization of **Keynote Speaker.**

DEVELOPING USE CASE SCENARIOS

Each use case has a description. We will refer to the description as a use case scenario. As mentioned, the primary use case represents the standard flow of events in the system, and alternative paths describe variations to the behavior. Use case scenarios may describe what happens if an item purchased is out of stock, or if a credit card company rejects a customer's requested purchase.

There is no standardized use case scenario format, so each organization is faced with specifying what standards should be included. Often the use cases are documented using a use case document template predetermined by the organization,

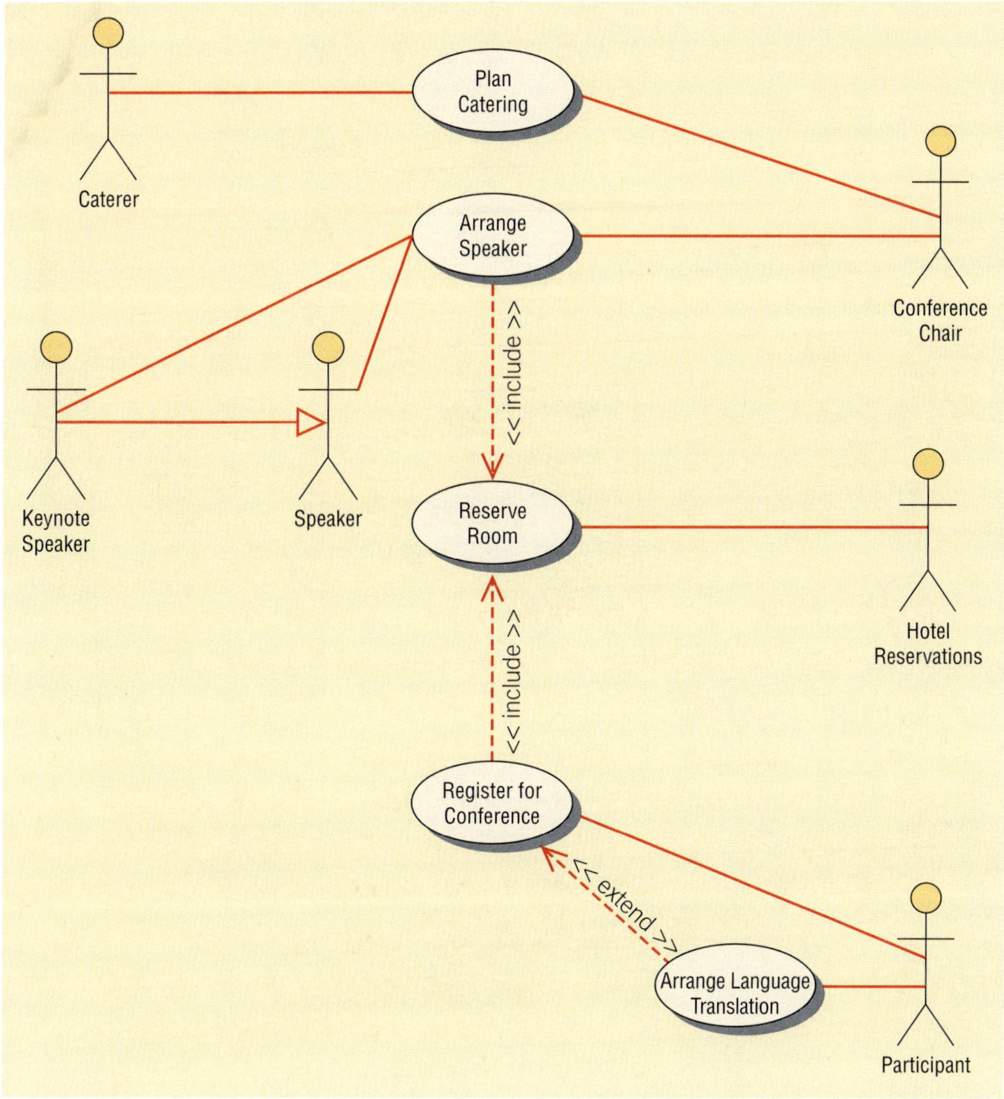

FIGURE 2.15
A use case diagram representing a system used to plan a conference.

which makes the use cases easier to read and provides standardized information for each use case in the model.

A use case scenario example is shown in Figure 2.16. Some of the areas included are optional, and may not be used by all organizations. The three main areas are:

1. Use case identifiers and initiators.
2. Steps performed.
3. Conditions, assumptions, and questions.

The first area, use case identifiers and initiators, orients the reader and contains the use case name and a unique ID; the application area or system that this use case belongs to; the actors involved in the use case; a brief description of what the use case accomplishes; and the initiating (triggering) event, that is, what caused the use case to start, and the type of trigger, either external or temporal. External events are those started by an actor, either a person or another system requesting information, such as an airline reservation system requesting flight information from an airline system. Temporal events are those that are triggered or started by time. Events occur at a specific time, such as sending an email about special offers once a week on a Sunday evening, sending bills on a specific day, or generating

Use case name:	Register for Conference	**UniqueID:**	Conf RG 003
Area:	Conference Planning		
Actor(s):	Participant		
Description:	Allow conference participant to register online for the conference using a secure Web site.		
Triggering Event:	Participant uses Conference Registration Web site, enters userID and password, and clicks the logon button.		
Trigger type:	☒ External ☐ Temporal		

Steps Performed (Main Path)	**Information for Steps**
1. Participant logs in using the secure Web server.	userID, Password
2. Participant record is read and password is verified.	Participant Record, userID, Password
3. Participant and session information is displayed on the Registration Web page.	Participant Record, Session Record
4. Participant enters information on the Registration Web form and clicks **Submit** button.	Registration Web Form
5. Registration information is validated on the Web server.	Registration Web Form
6. Registration Confirmation page is displayed to confirm registration information.	Confirmation Web Page
7. Credit card is charged for registration fees.	Secure Credit Card Web Page
8. Add Registration Journal record is written.	Confirmation Web Page
9. Registration record is updated on the Registration Master.	Confirmation Web Page, Registration Record
10. Session record is updated for each selected session on the Session Master.	Confirmation Web Page, Session Record
11. Participant record is updated for the participant on the Participant Master.	Confirmation Web Page, Participant Record
12. Successful Registration Confirmation Web page is sent to the participant.	Registration Record Confirmation Number

Preconditions:	Participant has already registered and has created a user account.
Postconditions:	Participant has successfully registered for the conference.
Assumptions:	Participant has a browser and a valid userID and password.
Requirements Met:	Allow conference participants to be able to register for the conference using a secure Web site.
Outstanding Issues:	How should a rejected credit card be handled?
Priority:	High
Risk:	Medium

FIGURE 2.16

A use case scenario is divided into three sections: identification and initiation; steps performed; and conditions, assumptions, and questions.

government statistics on a specified date every quarter. In addition to actors, a use case may list stakeholders and their interest in the use case. Stakeholders are individuals or organizations that are not actors but have some vested interest in the behavior of the use case.

The second area of the use case includes the steps performed, and the information required for each of the steps. These statements represent the standard flow of events and the steps taken for the successful completion of the use case. It is desirable to write up a use case for the main path, and then to write up one for each of the alternative paths separately, rather than using IF . . . THEN . . . statements. The steps may come from a detailed interview with users or may be derived from agile modeling stories (as described in Chapter 6). These steps should be reviewed with the users for clarification. The analyst should examine each of the steps and determine the information required for each step. If the analyst cannot determine the information, he or she should schedule a follow-up interview with the user. Some use case descriptions include the exceptions as additional sections following the standard flow of events.

The third area of the use case includes:

- Preconditions, or the condition of the system before the use case may be performed, which may be another use case.
- Postconditions, or the state of the system after the use case has finished, including output people have received, transmissions to other systems, and data that have been created or updated.
- Assumptions made that would affect the method of the use case and that could stipulate required technology, such as the minimum technology requirements in a browser or even a specific or higher version of a browser.
- Any outstanding issues or questions that must be answered before implementation of the use case.
- An optional statement of priority of the use case, which may come from the problem definition.
- An optional statement of risk involved in creating the use case.

The "requirements met" area links the use case to user requirements or objectives from a problem definition. Once you develop the use case scenarios, be sure to review your results with the business experts to verify and refine the use cases if needed.

In this particular use case scenario, called **Register for Conference,** is the only actor involved is the **Participant.** The overall area is **Conference Planning,** and the use case is triggered by the participant logging on to the **Registration Web page.** The **Steps Performed** area lists the sequence of events that must occur for a successful conference registration. Notice that the information needed to perform each of the steps is listed on the right. This may include Web pages and forms, as well as database tables and records.

The **Preconditions** area in the footer section of the use case scenario lists what must occur before the participant can register for a conference. In this example, the participant must have already signed up as a member of the society and have a valid userID and password. The **Postconditions** area lists what has been accomplished by the use case. The **Assumptions** area lists any basic premises the analyst assumes are fulfilled by the actor beforehand. The **Requirements Met** area shows why this use case is important and necessary for the business area to be successful. **Priority** is an indication of which use cases should be developed first and which may be delayed. **Risk** is a rough assessment of whether there may be problems or difficulties developing the use case. In this case, the risk is medium because the registration use case requires a secure server and is accepting credit card information.

WHY USE CASE DIAGRAMS ARE HELPFUL

No matter what method you use to develop your system (traditional SDLC methods, agile methods, or object-oriented methods), you will find that use cases are very valuable. The use case diagrams identify all of the actors in the

FIGURE 2.17

The main reasons for writing use cases are their effectiveness in communicating with users and their capturing of user stories.

- Use cases effectively communicate systems requirements because the diagrams are kept simple.
- Use cases allow people to tell stories.
- Use case stories make sense to nontechnical people.
- Use cases do not depend on a special language.
- Use cases can describe most functional requirements (such as interactions between actors and applications).
- Use cases can describe nonfunctional requirements (such as performance and maintainability) through the use of stereotypes.
- Use cases help analysts define boundaries.
- Use cases can be traceable, allowing analysts to identify links between use cases and other design and documentation tools.

problem domain and a systems analyst can concentrate on what humans want and need to use the system, extend their capabilities, and enjoy their interaction with technology.

The actions that need to be completed are also clearly shown on the use case diagram. This not only makes it easy for the analyst to identify processes, but it also aids in communication with other analysts on the team and business executives.

The use case scenario is also worthwhile. Since a lot of the information the users impart to the analyst already takes the form of stories, it is easy to capture the stories on a use case scenario form. The use case scenario always documents the triggering event so that an analyst can always trace the steps that led to other use cases. Since the steps performed are noted, it is possible to employ use case scenarios to write logical processes.

Use case diagrams are becoming popular because of their simplicity and lack of technical detail. They are used to show the scope of a system, along with the major features of the system and the actors who work with those major features. The main reasons for writing use cases are shown in Figure 2.17.

LEVELS OF MANAGEMENT

Management in organizations exists on three broad, horizontal levels: operational control, managerial planning and control (middle management), and strategic management, as shown in Figure 2.18. Each level carries its own responsibilities, and all work toward achieving organizational goals and objectives in their own ways.

FIGURE 2.18

Management in organizations exists on three horizontal levels: operational control, managerial planning and control, and strategic management.

CONSULTING OPPORTUNITY 2.2

WHERE THERE'S CARBON, THERE'S A COPY

"I don't know what we do with the pink ones yet," Richard Russell admitted. "They're part of a quadruplicate form that rips apart. All I know is that we keep them for the filing clerk, and he files them when he has time."

Richard is a newly hired junior account executive for Carbon, Carbon & Rippy, a brokerage house. You are walking through the steps he takes in making a stock purchase "official" because his boss has asked you to streamline the process whereby stock purchase information is stored in the computer and retrieved.

After you leave, Richard continues thinking about the pink forms. He tells his clerk, Harry Schultz, "In my two months here, I haven't seen anyone use those. They take up my time and yours, not to mention all the filing space. Let's pitch them."

Richard and Harry proceed to open all the old files kept by Richard's predecessor and throw out the filed pink forms, along with those accumulated but not yet filed. It takes hours, but they make a lot of room. "Definitely worth the time," Richard reassures Harry.

Three weeks later, an assistant to Richard's boss, Carol Vaness, appears. Richard is happy to see a familiar face, greeting her with, "Hi, Carol. What's new?"

"Same old thing," Carol sighs. "Well, I guess it isn't old to you, because you're the newcomer. But I need all those pesky pink forms."

Almost in shock, Richard exchanges looks with Harry, then mumbles, "You're kidding, of course."

Carol looks more serious than Richard ever thought possible, replying, "No joke. I summarize all the pink forms from all the brokers, and then my totals are compared with computerized stock purchase information. It's part of our routine, three-month audit for transaction accuracy. My work depends on yours. Didn't Ms. McCue explain that to you when you started?"

What systems concept did Richard and Harry ignore when tossing out the pink forms? What are the possible ramifications for systems analysts if general systems concepts are ignored?

Operational control forms the bottom tier of three-tiered management. Operations managers make decisions using predetermined rules that have predictable outcomes when implemented correctly.

They make decisions that affect implementation in work scheduling, inventory control, shipping, receiving, and control of processes such as production. Operations managers oversee the operating details of the organization.

Middle management forms the second, or intermediate, tier of the three-tiered management system. Middle managers make short-term planning and control decisions about how resources may best be allocated to meet organizational objectives.

Their decisions range all the way from forecasting future resource requirements to solving employee problems that threaten productivity. The decision-making domain of middle managers can usefully be characterized as partly operational and partly strategic, with constant fluctuations.

Strategic management is the third level of three-tiered management control. Strategic managers look outward from the organization to the future, making decisions that will guide middle and operations managers in the months and years ahead.

Strategic managers work in a highly uncertain decision-making environment. Through statements of goals and the determination of strategies and policies to achieve them, strategic managers actually define the organization as a whole. Theirs is the broad picture, wherein the company decides to develop new product lines, divest itself of unprofitable ventures, acquire other compatible companies, or even allow itself to be sold.

There are sharp contrasts among the decision makers on many dimensions. For instance, strategic managers have multiple decision objectives, whereas operations managers have single ones. It is often difficult for high-level managers to identify problems, but it is easy for operations managers to do so. Strategic managers are faced with semistructured problems, whereas lower-level managers deal mostly with structured problems.

CONSULTING OPPORTUNITY 2.3

PYRAMID POWER

"We really look up to you," says Paul LeGon. As a systems analyst, you have been invited to help Pyramid, Inc., a small, independent book-publishing firm that specializes in paperback books outside of the publishing mainstream.

Paul continues, "We deal with what some folks think are fringe topics. You know, pyramid power, end-of-the-world prophecies, and healthier living by thinking of the color pink. Sometimes when people see our books, they just shake their heads and say, 'Tut—uncommon topic.' But we're not slaves to any particular philosophy, and we've been very successful. So much so that because I'm 24, people call me the 'boy king.'" Paul pauses to decipher your reaction.

Paul continues, "I'm at the top as president, and functional areas such as editorial, accounting, production, and marketing are under me."

Paul's assistant, Ceil Toom, who has been listening quietly up to now, barges in with her comments: "The last systems experts that did a project for us recommended the creation of liaison committees of employees between accounting, production, and marketing, so that we could share newly computerized inventory and sales figures across the organization. They claimed that committees such as that would cut down on needless duplication of output, and each functional area would be better integrated with all the rest."

Paul picks up the story, saying, "It was fair—oh, for a while—and the employees shared information, but the reason you're here is that the employees said they didn't have time for committee meetings and were uncomfortable sharing information with people from other departments who were further up the ladder than they were here at Pyramid."

According to Paul and Ceil, what were the effects of installing a management information system at Pyramid, Inc., that required people to share information in ways that were not consistent with their structure? Propose some general ways to resolve this problem so that Pyramid employees can still get the sales and inventory figures they need.

The alternative solutions to a problem facing the strategic managers are often difficult to articulate, but the alternatives that operations managers work with are usually easy to enumerate. Strategic managers most often make one-time decisions, whereas the decisions made by operations managers tend to be repetitive.

IMPLICATIONS FOR INFORMATION SYSTEMS DEVELOPMENT

Each of the three management levels holds differing implications for developing information systems. Some of the information requirements for managers are clear-cut, whereas others are fuzzy and overlap.

Operations managers need internal information that is of a repetitive, low-level nature. They are highly dependent on information that captures current performance, and they are large users of online, real-time information resources. The need of operations managers for past performance information and periodic information is only moderate. They have little use for external information that allows future projections.

On the next management level, middle managers are in need of both short- and longer-term information. Due to the troubleshooting nature of their jobs, middle managers experience extremely high needs for information in real time. To control properly, they also need current information on performance as measured against set standards. Middle managers are highly dependent on internal information. In contrast to operations managers, they have a high need for historical information, along with information that allows prediction of future events and simulation of numerous possible scenarios.

Strategic managers differ somewhat from both middle and operations managers in their information requirements. They are highly dependent on information from external sources that supply news of market trends and the strategies of competing corporations. Because the task of strategic managing demands projections into the uncertain future, strategic managers have a high need for information of a predictive nature and information that allows creation of many different what-if scenarios. Strategic managers also exhibit strong needs for periodically reported information as they seek to adapt to fast-moving changes.

ORGANIZATIONAL CULTURE

Organizational culture is an established area of research that has grown remarkably in the last generation. Just as it is appropriate to think of organizations as including many technologies, it is similarly appropriate to see them as hosts to multiple, often competing subcultures.

There is still little agreement on what precisely constitutes an organizational subculture. It is agreed, however, that competing subcultures may be in conflict, attempting to gain adherents to their vision of what the organization should be. Research is in progress to determine the effects of virtual organizations and virtual teams on the creation of subcultures when members do not share a physical workspace but share tasks.

Rather than thinking about culture as a whole, it is more useful to think about the researchable determinants of subcultures, such as shared verbal and nonverbal symbolism. Verbal symbolism includes shared language used to construct, convey, and preserve subcultural myths, metaphors, visions, and humor. Nonverbal symbolism includes shared artifacts, rites, and ceremonies; clothing of decision makers and workers; the use, placement, and decoration of offices; and rituals for celebrating members' birthdays, promotions, and retirements.

Subcultures coexist within "official" organizational cultures. The officially sanctioned culture may prescribe a dress code, suitable ways to address superiors and coworkers, and proper ways to deal with the outside public. Subcultures may be powerful determinants of information requirements, availability, and use.

Organizational members may belong to one or more subcultures in the organization. Subcultures may exert a powerful influence on member behavior, including sanctions for or against the use of information systems.

Understanding and recognizing predominant organizational subcultures may help the systems analyst overcome the resistance to change that arises when a new information system is installed. For example, the analyst might devise user training to address specific concerns of organizational subcultures. Identifying subcultures may also help in the design of decision support systems that are tailored for interaction with specific user groups.

SUMMARY

There are three broad organizational fundamentals to consider when analyzing and designing information systems: the concept of organizations as systems, the various levels of management, and the overall organizational culture.

Organizations are complex systems composed of interrelated and interdependent subsystems. In addition, systems and subsystems are characterized by their internal environments on a continuum from open to closed. An open system allows free passage of resources (people, information, materials) through its boundaries; closed systems do not permit free flow of input or output. Organizations and teams can also be organized virtually with remote members connected electronically who are not in the same physical workspace. Enterprise resource planning systems are integrated organizational (enterprise) information systems

2

"You seem to have already made a good start at MRE. Even though I can tell you a lot about the company, remember that there are a number of ways to orient yourself within it. You will want to interview users, observe their decision-making settings, and look at archival reports, charts, and diagrams. To do so, you can click on the telephone directory to get an appointment with an interviewee, click on the building map to view the layout of the building, or click on organizational charts that show you the functional areas and formal hierarchical relationships at MRE.

"Many of the rules of corporate life apply in the MRE HyperCase. For instance, there are many public areas in which you are free to walk. If you want to tour a private corporate office, however, you must first book an appointment with one of our employees. Some secure areas are strictly off limits to you, just because you are an outsider and could pose a security risk.

"I don't think you'll find us excessively secretive, however, because you may assume that any employee who grants you an interview will also grant you access to the archival material in his or her files as well as to current work. You'll be able to go about your consulting freely in most cases. If you get too curious or invade our privacy in some way, we'll let you know. We're not afraid to tell you what the limits are.

"Unfortunately, some people in the company never seem to make themselves available to consultants. If you need to know more about these hard-to-get interviewees, I suggest you be persistent. There are lots of ways to find out about the people and the systems of MRE, but much of the time creativity is what pays off. You will notice that the systems consultants who follow their hunches, sharpen their technical skills, and never stop thinking about piecing together the puzzles here at MRE are the ones who are the best.

FIGURE 2.HC1

"Remember to use multiple methods—interviewing, observation, and investigation—to understand what we at MRE are trying to tell you. Sometimes actions, documents, and offices actually speak louder than words!"

HYPERCASE QUESTIONS

1. What major organizational change recently took place at MRE? What department(s) was involved, and why was the change made?
2. What does the Management Systems Unit at MRE do? Who are its clients?
3. What are the goals and strategies of the Engineering and Systems Division at MRE? What are the goals of the Training and Management Systems Department?
4. Would you categorize MRE as a service industry, a manufacturer, or both? What kind of "products" does MRE "produce" (i.e., does it offer material goods, services, or both)? Suggest how the type of industry MRE is in affects the information systems it uses.
5. What type of organizational structure does MRE have? What are the implications of this structure for MIS?
6. Describe in a paragraph the "politics" of the Training and Management Systems Department at MRE. Who is involved, and what are some of the main issues?

developed with customized, proprietary software that help the flow of information between the functional areas in the organization. They support a systems view of the organization.

There are many ways to graphically depict the system. The analyst should choose among these tools early on to get an overview of the system. These approaches include drawing context-level data flow diagrams, capturing relationships early on with entity-relationship diagrams; drawing use case diagrams or writing use case scenarios based on user stories. Using these diagrams and techniques at the beginning of analysis can help the analyst define the boundaries of the system, and can help bring into focus which people and systems are external to the system being developed.

Entity-relationship diagrams help the systems analyst understand the entities and relationships that comprise the organizational system. E-R diagrams can depict a one-to-one relationship, a one-to-many relationship, a many-to-one relationship, and a many-to-many relationship.

The three levels of managerial control are operational, middle management, and strategic. The time horizon of decision making is different for each level.

Organizational cultures and subcultures are important determinants of how people use information and information systems. By grounding information systems in the context of the organization as a larger system, it is possible to realize that numerous factors are important and should be taken into account when ascertaining information requirements and designing and implementing information systems.

KEYWORDS AND PHRASES

actor
associative entity
attributive entity
closedness
context-level data flow diagram
crow's foot notation
enterprise resource planning (ERP)
entity (fundamental entity)

- entity-relationship (E-R) diagrams
- environment
- feedback
- interdependent
- interrelatedness
- middle management
- openness
- operations management
- organizational boundaries
- organizational culture
- strategic management
- systems
- use case
- use case diagram
- use case scenario
- virtual enterprise
- virtual organization
- virtual team

REVIEW QUESTIONS

1. What are the three groups of organizational fundamentals that carry implications for the development of information systems?
2. What is meant by saying that organizational subsystems are interrelated and interdependent?
3. Define the term *organizational boundary.*
4. What are the two main purposes for feedback in organizations?
5. Define openness in an organizational environment.
6. Define closedness in an organizational environment.
7. What is the difference between a traditional organization and a virtual one?
8. What are the potential benefits and a drawback of a virtual organization?
9. Give an example of how systems analysts could work with users as a virtual team.
10. What is ERP, and what is its purpose?
11. What problems do analysts often encounter when they try to implement an ERP package?
12. What are the two symbols on a use case diagram and what do they represent?
13. What is a use case scenario?
14. What are the three main parts of a use case scenario?
15. What does a process represent on a context-level data flow diagram?
16. What is an entity on a data flow diagram?
17. What is meant by the term *entity-relationship diagram*?
18. What symbols are used to draw E-R diagrams?
19. List the types of E-R diagrams.
20. How do an entity, an associative entity, and an attributive entity differ?
21. List the three broad, horizontal levels of management in organizations.
22. How can understanding organizational subcultures help in the design of information systems?

PROBLEMS

1. "It's hard to focus on what we want to achieve. I look at what our real competitors, the convenience stores, are doing and think we should copy that. Then a hundred customers come in, and I listen to each of them, and they say we should keep our little store the same, with friendly clerks and old-fashioned cash registers. Then, when I pick up a copy of SuperMarket News, they say that the wave of the future is super grocery stores, with no individual prices marked and UPC scanners replacing clerks. I'm pulled in so many directions

I can't really settle on a strategy for our grocery store," admits Geoff Walsham, owner and manager of Jiffy Geoff's Grocery Store.

In a paragraph, apply the concept of permeable organizational boundaries to analyze Geoff's problem in focusing on organizational objectives.

2. Write seven sentences explaining the right-to-left relationships in Figure 2.8.
3. Draw an entity-relationship diagram of a patient–doctor relationship.
   a. Which of the types of E-R diagrams is it?
   b. In a sentence or two, explain why the patient–doctor relationship is diagrammed in this way.
4. You began drawing E-R diagrams soon after your entry into the health maintenance organization for which you're designing a system. Your team member is skeptical about using E-R diagrams before the design of the database is begun. In a paragraph, persuade your team member that early use of E-R diagrams is worthwhile.
5. Neil is an decision maker for Pepe's Atlantic Sausage Company. Because there are several suppliers of ingredients and their prices fluctuate, he has come up with several different formulations for the various sausages that he makes, depending on the availability of particular ingredients from particular suppliers. He then orders ingredients accordingly twice a week. Even though he cannot predict when ingredients will become available at a particular price, his ordering of supplies can be considered routine.
   a. On what level of management is Neil working? Explain in a paragraph.
   b. What attributes of his job would have to change before you would categorize him as working on a different level of management? List them.
6. Many of the people who work at Pepe's (Problem 5) are extremely dedicated to Pepe's and have devoted their lives to the company. Others feel that company is behind the times and should use more sophisticated production systems, information systems, and supply chain management to make the company more competitive. Members of a third group feel that what they do is unappreciated. Describe the various subculture in words. Assign them a name based on their emotions.
7. Alice in the human resources department at the Cho Manufacturing plant is constantly being asked by employees how much is taken out of their paychecks for insurance, taxes, medical, manadatory retirement, and voluntary retirement. "It takes up to a few hours every day," says Alice.

   She would like a Web system that would allow employees to use a secure logon to view the information. Alice wants the system to interface with health and dental insurance companies to obtain the amount remaining in the employee's account for the year. She would also like to obtain retirement amounts saved along with investment results. Alice has a high regard for privacy and wants the system to have employees register and give permission to obtain financial amounts from the dental insurance and retirement companies. Draw a use case diagram representing the activities of the Employee Benefit system.
8. Write up a use case scenario for the use case diagram you constructed for Cho Manufacturing.
9. Create a context-level data flow diagram for the Employee Benefit system in Problem 7. Make any assumptions about the data to and from the central process. Do you find this to be better or not as good at explaining the system to Alice than the use case and use case scenarios?
10. Draw a use case and write up a use case scenario for getting two or three email accounts. Think about the steps that are needed to ensure security.

GROUP PROJECTS

1. Break up into groups of five. Assign one person to act as the Web site designer, one to write copy for a company's product, one to keep track of customer payments, one to monitor distribution, and one to satisfy customers who have questions about using the product. Then select a simple product (one that does not have too many versions). Good examples are a digital camera, a DVD player, a GPS, a box of candy, or a specialty travel hat (rainproof or sunblocker). Now spend 20 minutes trying to explain to the Web site designer what to include on the Web site. Describe in about three paragraphs what experience your group had in coordination. Elaborate on the interrelatedness of subsystems in the organization (your group).
2. In a small group, develop a use case and a use case scenario for making air, hotel, and car reservations for domestic travel.
3. Change your answer in Group Project 2 to include foreign travel. How does the use case and use case scenario change?
4. With your group, draw a context-level data flow diagram of your school's or university's registration system. Label each entity and process. Discuss why there appear to be different ways to draw the diagram. Reach consensus as a group about the best way to draw the diagram and defend your choice in a paragraph. Now, working with your group's members, follow the appropriate steps for developing an E-R diagram and create one for your school or university registration system. Make sure your group indicates whether the relationship you depict is one-to-one, one-to-many, many-to-one, or many-to-many.

SELECTED BIBLIOGRAPHY

Bleeker, S. E. "The Virtual Organization." *Futurist*, Vol. 28, No. 2, 1994, pp. 9–14.

Chen, P. "The Entity-Relationship Model—Towards a Unified View of Data." *ACM Transactions on Database Systems*, Vol. 1, March 1976, pp. 9–36.

Ching, C., C. W. Holsapple, and A. B. Whinston. "Toward IT Support for Coordination in Network Organizations." *Information Management*, Vol. 30, No. 4, 1996, pp. 179–199.

Davis, G. B., and M. H. Olson. *Management Information Systems, Conceptual Foundations, Structure, and Development*, 2d ed. New York: McGraw-Hill, 1985.

Galbraith, J. R. *Organizational Design*. Reading, MA: Addison-Wesley, 1977.

Kendall, K. E., J. R. Buffington, and J. E. Kendall. "The Relationship of Organizational Subcultures to DSS User Satisfaction." *Human Systems Management*, March 1987, pp. 31–39.

Kulak, D., and E. Guiney. *Use Cases: Requirement in Context*, 2d ed. Boston: Pearson Education, 2004.

PeopleSoft. Available at: www.peoplesoft.com/corplen/public_index.jsp. Accessed June 3, 2003.

Warkentin, M., L. Sayeed, and R. Hightower. "Virtual Teams versus Face-to-Face Teams; An Exploratory Study of a Web-Based Conference System." In *Emerging Information Technologies: Improving Decisions, Cooperation, and Infrastructure.* Edited by K. E. Kendall, pp. 241–262. Thousand Oaks, CA: Sage Publications, 1999.

Yager, S. E. "Everything's Coming Up Virtual." Available at: www.acm.org/crossroads/xrds4-1/organ.html. Accessed June 3, 2003.

ALLEN SCHMIDT, JULIE E. KENDALL, AND KENNETH E. KENDALL

PICTURING THE RELATIONSHIPS

"So the project involves more than simply performing maintenance work on the current programs," Chip says. "Are we using a formal methodology for analyzing and designing the new system?"

"Yes," replies Anna. "We are also using a CASE tool, Visible Analyst, to analyze and design the system.[1] We've recently installed the product on our PC in the office."

With a few easy mouse clicks Anna comes to a context-level data flow diagram (see Figure E2.1). "It's very useful to begin thinking of the system this way," Anna says as they look at the diagram on the screen.

Chip agrees, saying, "I can very easily see what you think is happening with the system. For instance, I see that the external entity Management supplies hardware and software inquiries and receives the corresponding responses in return. It shows the system within the larger organization."

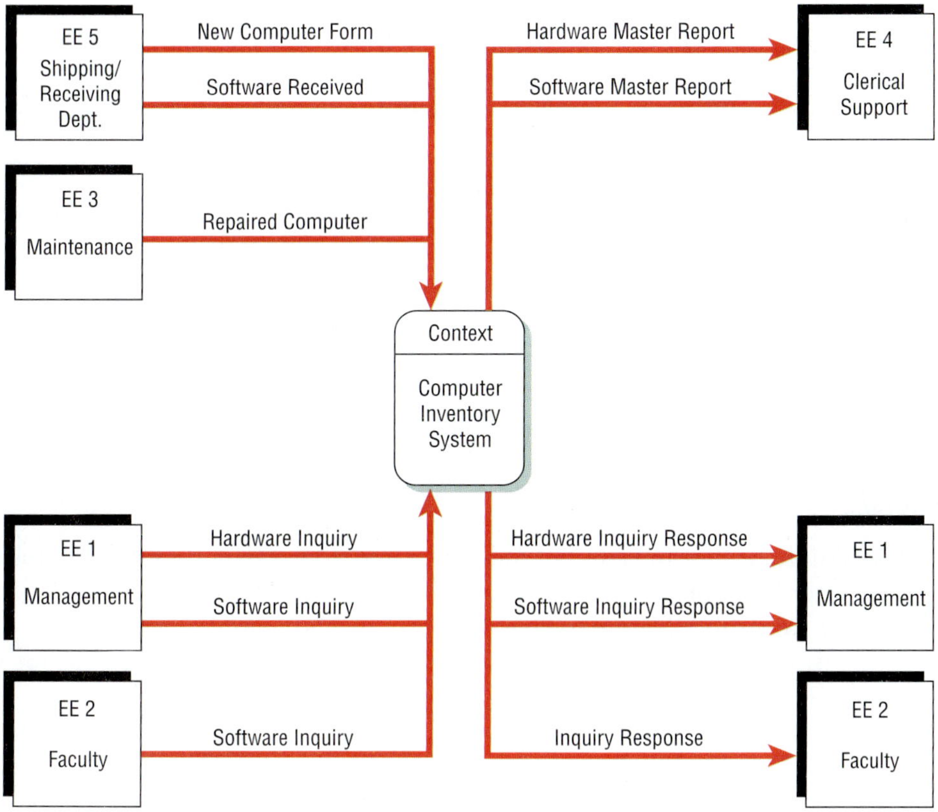

FIGURE E2.1

[1]For more details on how to begin using Visible Analyst, see Allen Schmidt, *Working with Visible Analyst*, 2d ed. (Upper Saddle River, NJ: Prentice Hall, 2004).

The Central Pacific University case can be adapted to other CASE tools. Other tools include Microsoft Visio. Alternatively, many of the exercises can be accomplished manually if CASE tools are unavailable.

2

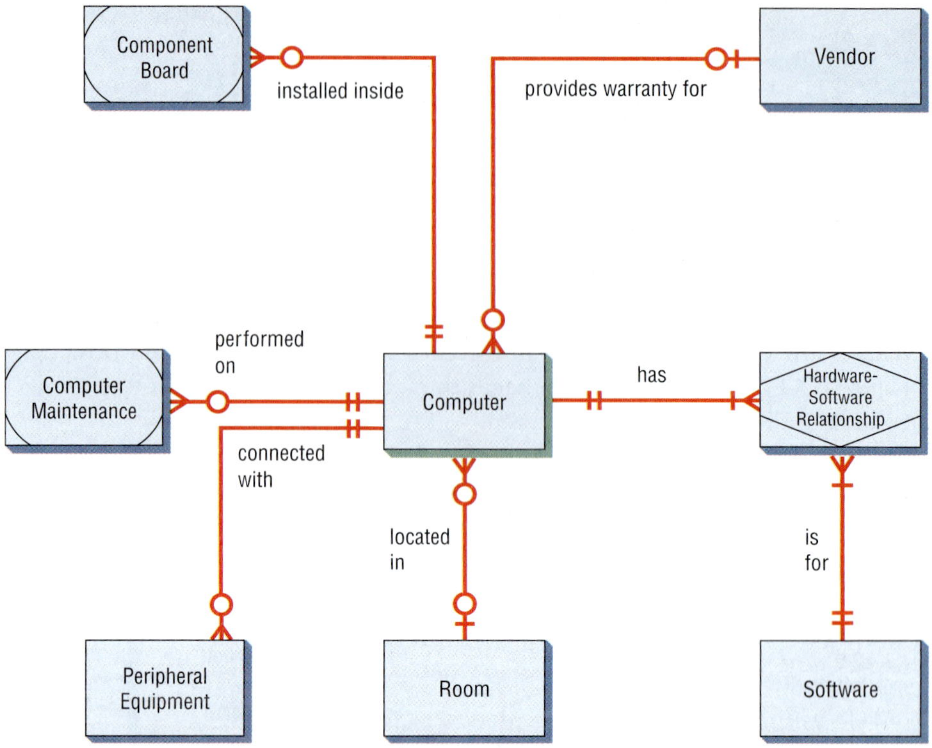

FIGURE E2.2

"I've also drawn an E-R diagram of the system," Anna says as she brings up the entity-relationship diagram on the screen (see Figure E2.2).

"Yes, the many-to-many and one-to-many relationships are very clear when you look at this," Chip says, viewing the screen. "You've got a good start here," Chip continues. "Let's get to work and see what needs to be done next."

EXERCISES

E-1. Use Visible Analyst to view and print the context-level data flow diagram for the computer inventory system, as Chip and Anna did.

E-2. Use the Repository feature to view the entry for the central process.

E-3. Use Visible Analyst to view and print the entity-relationship diagram for the computer inventory system.

E-4. Explain why the external entities on the context-level diagram are not found on the entity-relationship diagram.

E-5. Explain why the entities MANAGEMENT and FACULTY are found on both sides of the process on the context-level diagram.

The exercises preceded by a Web icon indicate value-added material is available from the Web site at www.prenhall.com/kendall. Students can download a sample Visible Analyst Project and a Microsoft Access database that can be used to complete the exercises. Visible Analyst software can be packaged with this text for an additional fee.

PROJECT MANAGEMENT

3

LEARNING OBJECTIVES

Once you have mastered the material in this chapter you will be able to:

1. **Understand how projects are initiated and selected.**
2. **Define a business problem and determine the feasibility of a proposed project.**
3. **Plan a project by identifying activities and scheduling them.**
4. **Understand how an alternative approach called agile development balances objectives to manage the analysis and design process.**
5. **Manage team members and analysis and design activities so that the project objectives are met while the project remains on schedule.**

Initiating projects, determining project feasibility, scheduling projects, and planning and then managing activities and team members for productivity are all important capabilities for the systems analyst to master. As such, they are considered project management fundamentals.

A systems project begins with problems or with opportunities for improvement in a business that often come up as the organization adapts to change. The increasing popularity of ecommerce means that some fundamental changes are occurring as businesses either originate their enterprises on, or move their internal operations as well as external relationships to, the Internet. Changes that require a systems solution occur in the legal environment as well as in the industry's environment. Analysts work with users to create a problem definition reflecting current business systems and concerns. Once a project is suggested, the systems analyst works quickly with decision makers to determine whether it is feasible. If a project is approved for a full systems study, the project activities are scheduled through the use of tools such Gantt charts and Program Evaluation and Review Techniques (PERT) diagrams so that the project can be completed on time. Part of assuring the productivity of systems analysis team members is effectively managing their scheduled activities. This chapter is devoted to a discussion of project management fundamentals.

PROJECT INITIATION

Systems projects are initiated by many different sources for many reasons. Some of the projects suggested will survive various stages of evaluation to be worked on by you (or you and your team); others will not and should not get that far.

Businesspeople suggest systems projects for two broad reasons: (1) because they experience problems that lend themselves to systems solutions, and (2) because they recognize opportunities for improvement through upgrading, altering, or installing new systems when they occur. Both situations can arise as the organization adapts to and copes with natural, evolutionary change.

PROBLEMS IN THE ORGANIZATION

Managers do not like to conceive of their organization as having problems, let alone talk about them or share them with someone from outside. Good managers, however, realize that recognizing symptoms of problems or, at a later stage, diagnosing the problems themselves and then confronting them are imperative if the business is to keep functioning at its highest potential.

Problems surface in many different ways. One way of conceptualizing what problems are and how they arise is to think of them as situations in which goals have never been met or are no longer being met. Useful feedback gives information about the gap between actual and intended performance. In this way feedback spotlights problems.

In some instances problems that require the services of systems analysts are uncovered because performance measures are not being met. Problems (or symptoms of problems) with processes that are visible in output and that could require the help of a systems analyst include excessive errors and work performed too slowly, incompletely, incorrectly, or not at all. Other symptoms of problems become evident when people do not meet baseline performance goals. Changes in employee behavior such as unusually high absenteeism, high job dissatisfaction, or high worker turnover should alert managers to potential problems. Any of these changes, alone or in combination, might be sufficient reason to request the help of a systems analyst.

Although difficulties such as those just described occur in the organization, feedback on how well the organization is meeting intended goals may come from outside, in the form of complaints or suggestions from customers, vendors, or suppliers, and lost or unexpectedly lower sales. This feedback from the external environment is extremely important and should not be ignored.

A summary of symptoms of problems and approaches useful in problem detection is provided in Figure 3.1. Notice that checking output, observing or researching employee behavior, and listening to feedback from external sources are all valuable in problem finding. When reacting to accounts of problems in the

FIGURE 3.1
Checking output, observing employee behavior, and listening to feedback are all ways to help the analyst pinpoint systems problems and opportunities.

To Identify Problems	Look for These Specific Signs:
Check output against performance criteria.	• Too many errors • Work completed slowly • Work done incorrectly • Work done incompletely • Work not done at all
Observe behavior of employees.	• High absenteeism • High job dissatisfaction • High job turnover
Listen to external feedback from: Vendors. Customers. Suppliers.	• Complaints • Suggestions for improvement • Loss of sales • Lower sales

CONSULTING OPPORTUNITY 3.1

THE SWEETEST SOUND I'VE EVER SIPPED

Felix Straw, who represents one of the many U.S. distributors of the European soft drink Sipps, gazes unhappily at a newspaper weather map, which is saturated with dark red, indicating that most of the United States is experiencing an early spring heat wave with no signs of a letup. Pointing to the paper as he speaks, he tells your systems group, "It's the best thing that could happen to us, or at least it should be. But when we had to place our orders three months ago, we had no idea that this spring monster heat wave was going to devour the country this way!" Nodding his head toward a picture of their European plant on the wall, he continues. "We need to be able to tell them when things are hot over here so we can get enough product. Otherwise, we'll miss out every time. This happened two years ago and it just about killed us.

"Each of us distributors meets with our district managers to do three-month planning. When we agree, we fax our orders into European headquarters. They make their own adjustments, bottle the drinks, and then we get our modified orders about 9 to 15 weeks later. But we need ways to tell them what's going on now. Why, we even have some new superstores that are opening up here. They should know we have extra-high demand."

Corky, his assistant, agrees, saying, "Yeah, they should at least look at our past sales around this time of year. Some springs are hot, others are just average."

Straw concurs, saying, "It would be music to my ears, it would be really sweet, if they would work with us to spot trends and changes—and then respond quickly."

Stern's, based in Blackpool, England, is a European beverage maker and the developer and producer of Sipps. Sipps is a sweet, fruit-flavored, nonalcoholic, noncarbonated drink, which is served chilled or with ice, and it is particularly popular when the weather is hot. Selling briskly in Europe and growing in popularity in the United States since its introduction five years ago, Sipps has had a difficult time adequately managing inventory and keeping up with U.S. customer demand, which is affected by seasonal temperature fluctuations. Places with year-round, warm-temperature climates and lots of tourists (such as Florida and California) have large standing orders, but other areas of the country could benefit from a less cumbersome, more responsive order-placing process. Sipps is distributed by a network of local distributors located throughout the United States and Canada.

As one of the systems analysts assigned to work with the U.S. distributors of Sipps, begin your analysis by listing some of the key symptoms and problems you have identified after studying the information flows, ordering process, and inventory management, and after interviewing Mr. Straw and his assistant. In a paragraph describe which problems might indicate the need for a systems solution.

Note: This consulting opportunity is loosely based on J. C. Perez, "Heineken's HOPS Software Keeps A-Head on Inventory," *PC Week*, Vol. 14, No. 2, January 13, 1997, pp. 31 and 34.

organization, the systems analyst plays the roles of consultant, supporting expert, and agent of change, as discussed in Chapter 1. As you might expect, roles for the systems analyst shift subtly when projects are initiated because the focus is on opportunities for improvement rather than on the need to solve problems.

DEFINING THE PROBLEM

Whether using the classical systems development life cycle or an object-oriented approach, the analyst first defines the problems and objectives of the system. These form the foundation of determining what needs to be accomplished by the system. Methods like Six Sigma (refer to Chapter 16 for details) start with a problem definition.

A problem definition usually contains some sort of problem statement, summarized in a paragraph or two. This is followed by a series of issues, or major, independent pieces of the problem. The issues are followed by a series of objectives, or goals that match the issues point by point. Issues are the current situation; objectives are the desired situation. The objectives may be very specific or worded using a general statement.

Here are some examples of business questions relating to business objectives:

- What are the purposes of the business?
- Is the business profit or nonprofit?

- Does the company plan to grow or expand?
- What is the business's attitude (culture) about technology?
- What is the business's budget for IT?
- Does the business's staff have the expertise?

Needless to say, the systems analyst needs to understand how a business works.

The last part of the problem definition contains requirements, the things that must be accomplished, along with the possible solutions and the constraints that limit the development of the system. The requirements section may include security, usability, government requirements, and so on. Constraints often include the word "not," indicating a limitation and may contain budget restrictions or time limitations.

The problem definition is produced after completing interviews, observations, and document analysis with the users. The result of gathering this information is a wealth of facts and important opinions in need of summary. The first step in producing the problem definition is to find a number of points that may be included in one issue. Major points can be identified in the interview in a number of ways:

1. Identifying an issue, topic, or theme that is repeated several times, sometimes by different people in several interviews.
2. Users may communicate the same metaphors, such as saying the business is a journey, war, game, organism, machine, and so on.
3. Users may speak at length on a topic.
4. Users may tell you outright that "This is a major problem."
5. Users may communicate importance by body language or may speak emphatically on an issue.
6. The problem may be the first thing mentioned by the user.

Once the issues have been created, the objectives must be stated. At times the analyst may have to do a follow-up interview to obtain more precise information about the objectives. After the objectives are stated, the relative importance of the issues or objectives must be determined. If there are not enough funds to develop the complete system, the most critical objectives must be completed first. The identification of the most critical objectives is best done by users (with the support of analysts), because users are domain experts in their business area and in how they work best with technologies in the organization.

One technique is to ask the users to assign a weight for each issue or objective of the first draft of the problem definition. This is a subjective judgment by the user, but, if a number of users all assign weights and they are averaged together, the result might reflect the bigger picture. After the weights have been determined, the problem definition issues and objectives are resequenced in order of decreasing importance, the most important issues listed first. There is software such as Expert Choice (www.expertchoice.com) and other decision support software that can assist with the weighting and prioritizing of objectives.

Besides looking through data and interviewing people, try to witness the problem first hand. When looking at the same situation, an employee may view a problem very differently than a systems analyst does. This also gives analysts the opportunity to confirm their findings. In this way they use multiple methods, thereby strengthening the case for taking appropriate action.

A Problem Definition Example: Catherine's Catering Catherine's Catering is a small business that caters meals, receptions, and banquets for business and social occasions such as luncheons and weddings. It was inspired by Catherine's love of cooking and her talent for preparing fine meals. At first it was a small company with a handful of employees working on small projects. Catherine met with customers to determine the number of people, the type of meals, and other information necessary to cater an event. As their reputation for creating superb food and the quality of the service began to blossom, the number of events started to increase. The building of a new convention center, along with a prospering business community in the city, increased the number of catering events.

Catherine was able to manage the business using spreadsheets and word processing but found difficulty in keeping up with endless phone calls about what types of meals were available, changes to the number of guests attending the event, and the availability of specialty dietary items, such as vegan, vegetarian, low-fat, low-carbohydrate, and so on. Catherine's decisions to hire a number of part-time employees to cook and cater the events meant that the complexity of scheduling personnel was becoming overwhelming to the new human resources manager. Catherine decided to hire an IT and business consulting company to help her address the problems her catering enterprise was facing.

After performing interviews and observing a number of key staff, the consultants found the following concerns:

1. The master chef ordered supplies (produce, meat, and so on) from suppliers for each event. The suppliers would provide discounts if greater quantities were ordered at a single time for all events occurring in a given time frame.
2. Customers often called to change the number of guests for an event, with some changes made only one or two days before the event was scheduled.
3. It was too time-consuming for Catherine and her staff to handle each request for catering, with about 60 percent of the calls resulting in a contract.
4. Conflicts in employee schedules were occurring and some events were understaffed. Complaints about the timeliness of service were becoming more frequent.
5. Catherine does not have any summary information about the number of events and types of meals. It would be helpful to have trend information that would help guide her customers in their choice of meals.
6. Events are often held at hotels or other meeting halls, which provide table settings for sit-down meals. There are problems with having sufficient wait staff and changes with the number of guests.

The problem definition is shown in Figure 3.2. Notice the weights on the right, representing an average of the weights assigned by each employee. Objectives match the issues. Each objective is used to create user requirements.

User requirements are then used to create use cases and a use case diagram. Each objective may create one or more user requirement or several objectives may create one or perhaps no use cases (use cases are not often created for simple reports).

The user requirements for Catherine's Catering are to:

1. Create a dynamic Web site to allow current and potential clients to view and obtain pricing information for a variety of different products.
2. Allow current and potential clients to submit a request with their catering choices, with the request routed to an account manager.
3. Add clients to the client database, assigning them a userID and a password for access to their projects.
4. Create a Web site for clients to view and update the number of guests for an event and restrict changing the number of guests when the event day is less than five days in the future.
5. Obtain or create software to communicate directly with event facility personnel.

Catherine's Catering

Problem Definition

Catherine's Catering is experiencing problems with handling the number of routine calls with customers, as well as coordinating with external partners such as suppliers and meeting facilities. The growth in the number of part-time staff is leading to scheduling conflicts and understaffed events.

Issues

Issue	Weight
1. Customer contact takes an inordinate amount of time for routine questions.	10
2. Managing part-time employees is time-consuming and leads to scheduling errors.	9
3. It is difficult to accommodate last-minute changes for events.	7
4. Supplies are ordered for each event. Often shipments are received several times a day.	6
5. There are often problems communicating changes to event facilities.	5
6. There is little historical information about customers and meals.	3

Objectives

1. Provide a Web system for customers to obtain pricing information and place orders.
2. Create or purchase a human resources system with a scheduling component.
3. After customers have signed an event contract, provide them with Web access to their account and a means for them to update the number of guests. Notify management of changes.
4. Provide a means to determine overall quantities of supplies for events occurring within a concurrent time frame.
5. Provide a system for communicating changes to key personnel at event facilities.
6. Store all event data and make summary information available in a variety of formats.

Requirements

1. The system must be secure.
2. Feedback must be entered by event managers at the close of each event.
3. There must be a means for event facilities to change their contact person.
4. The system must be easy to use by nontechnical people.

Constraints

1. Development costs must not exceed $50,000.
2. The initial Web site for customer orders must be ready by March 1 to accommodate requests for graduation parties and weddings.

FIGURE 3.2
Problem definition for Catherine's Catering, developed with the help of users.

6. Create or purchase a human resources system for scheduling part-time employees, allowing management to add employees and schedule them using a number of constraints.
7. Provide queries or reports with summary information.

SELECTION OF PROJECTS

Projects come from many different sources and for many reasons. Not all should be selected for further study. You must be clear in your own mind about the reasons for recommending a systems study on a project that seems to address a problem or could bring about improvement. Consider the motivation that prompts a proposal on the project. You need to be sure that the project under consideration is not being proposed simply to enhance your own political reputation or power, or that of the person or group proposing it, because there is a high probability that such a project will be ill-conceived and eventually ill-accepted.

As outlined in Chapter 2, prospective projects need to be examined from a systems perspective in such a way that you are considering the impact of the proposed change on the entire organization. Recall that the various subsystems of the organization are interrelated and interdependent, so a change to one subsystem might affect all the others. Even though the decision makers directly involved ultimately set the boundaries for the systems project, a systems project cannot be contemplated or selected in isolation from the rest of the organization.

Beyond these general considerations are five specific criteria for project selection:

1. Backing from management.
2. Appropriate timing of project commitment.
3. Possibility of improving attainment of organizational goals.
4. Practical in terms of resources for the systems analyst and organization.
5. Worthwhile project compared with other ways the organization could invest resources.

First and foremost is backing from management. Absolutely nothing can be accomplished without the endorsement of the people who eventually will foot the bill. This statement does not mean that you lack influence in directing the project or that people other than management can't be included, but management backing is essential.

Another important criterion for project selection includes timing for you and the organization. Ask yourself and the others who are involved if the business is presently capable of making a time commitment for installation of new systems or improvement to existing ones. You must also be able to commit all or a portion of your time for the duration.

A third criterion is the possibility of improving attainment of organizational goals. The project should put the organization on target, not deter it from its ultimate goals.

A fourth criterion is selecting a project that is practicable in terms of your resources and capabilities as well as those of the business. Some projects will not fall within your realm of expertise, and you must be able to recognize them.

Finally, you need to come to a basic agreement with the organization about the worthiness of the systems project relative to any other possible project being considered. Remember that when a business commits to one project, it is committing resources that thereby become unavailable for other projects. It is useful to view all possible projects as competing for the business resources of time, money, and people.

DETERMINING FEASIBILITY

Once the number of projects has been narrowed according to the criteria discussed previously, it is still necessary to determine if the selected projects are feasible. Our definition of feasibility goes much deeper than common usage of the term, because systems projects feasibility is assessed in three principal ways: operationally, technically, and economically. The feasibility study is not a full-blown systems study. Rather, the feasibility study is used to gather broad data for the members of management that in turn enables them to make a decision on whether to proceed with a systems study.

Data for the feasibility study can be gathered through interviews, which are covered in detail in Chapter 4. The kind of interview required is directly related to the problem or opportunity being suggested. The systems analyst typically interviews those requesting help and those directly concerned with the decision-making process, typically management. Although it is important to address the correct problem, the systems analyst should not spend too much time doing feasibility studies, because many projects will be requested and only a few can or should be executed. The feasibility study must be highly time compressed, encompassing several activities in a short span of time.

DEFINING OBJECTIVES

The systems analyst serves as catalyst and supporting expert primarily by being able to see where processes can be improved. Optimistically, opportunities can be conceived of as the obverse of problems; yet, in some cultures, crisis also means opportunity. What looms as a disturbing problem for a manager might be turned into an opportunity for improvement by an alert systems analyst.

Improvements to systems can be defined as changes that will result in incremental but worthwhile benefits. There are many possibilities for improvements, including:

1. Speeding up a process.
2. Streamlining a process through the elimination of unnecessary or duplicated steps.
3. Combining processes.
4. Reducing errors in input through changes of forms and display screens.
5. Reducing redundant storage.
6. Reducing redundant output.
7. Improving integration of systems and subsystems.

It is well within the systems analyst's capabilities to notice opportunities for improvements. People who come into daily contact with the system, however, may be even better sources of information about improvements that should be made. If improvements have already been suggested, your expertise is needed to help determine whether the improvement is worthwhile and how it can be implemented.

It is worthwhile for an analyst to create a feasibility impact grid (FIG) for understanding and assessing what impacts (if any) improvements to existing systems can make. Figure 3.3 maps out such a grid. The labels on the far left-hand side describe a variety of systems that exist currently or are proposed. They are categorized into three system types: ecommerce systems, management information systems (MIS), and transaction processing systems (TPS). Listed at the top are the seven process objectives. Red check marks in the grid show that a positive impact can be made when a system improvement is made. Green check marks indicate that the system has been implemented and that the improvement positively impacted the process objective.

Notice that the transaction processing systems show a positive effect on the process objectives in almost every case. Traditional management information systems may help make better decisions, but sometimes they do not help the efficient collecting, storing, or retrieving of data. Thus, there are fewer check marks in that part of the grid. When entering the world of ecommerce, the analyst needs to be aware of how each system improvement may effect process objectives. Notice that the analyst who completed this grid recognized that although some process objectives were effected, others were not.

	System Components	Process Objectives: Speeding Up a Process	Streamlining a Process	Combining Processes	Reducing Errors in Input	Reducing Redundant Data Storage	Reducing Redundant Output	Improving Integration of Systems
Ecommerce Systems	Online catalog	✓ (red)	✓ (red)				✓ (red)	✓ (red)
	Online order processing	✓ (red)	✓ (red)		✓ (red)	✓ (red)		✓ (red)
	Online technical support		✓ (red)					
	Banner advertisements							
	Web-based intelligent push agent							
MIS	Inventory management		✓ (green)					✓ (green)
	Production scheduling		✓ (green)					✓ (green)
	Monthly sales reports				✓ (green)			✓ (green)
	Regional sales analysis				✓ (red)			✓ (red)
	Logistics management					✓ (green)		✓ (green)
TPS	Payroll	✓ (green)	✓ (green)	✓ (green)	✓ (green)	✓ (green)	✓ (green)	✓ (green)
	Order processing	✓ (green)	✓ (green)	✓ (green)	✓ (green)	✓ (green)	✓ (green)	✓ (green)
	Order tracking	✓ (green)	✓ (green)	✓ (green)	✓ (green)	✓ (green)	✓ (green)	✓ (green)
	Accounts payable	✓ (green)			✓ (green)	✓ (green)	✓ (green)	✓ (green)
	Accounts receivable	✓ (green)	✓ (green)	✓ (green)	✓ (green)	✓ (green)	✓ (green)	✓ (green)

Symbol	Meaning
✓ (red)	Proposed information system component or improvement can contribute positively to the process objective when implemented in the future.
✓ (green)	Existing information system component is contributing positively to the process objective.

FIGURE 3.3

An analyst can use a feasibility impact grid to show how each system component affects process objectives.

Of equal importance is how corporate objectives are affected by improvements to information systems. These corporate objectives include:

1. Improving corporate profits.
2. Supporting the competitive strategy of the organization.
3. Improving cooperation with vendors and partners.
4. Improving internal operations support so that goods and services are produced efficiently and effectively.
5. Improving internal decision support so that decisions are more effective.
6. Improving customer service.
7. Increasing employee morale.

Once again a feasibility impact grid can be drawn to increase awareness of the impacts made on the achievement of corporate objectives. The grid shown in Figure 3.4 is similar to the process objectives grid described earlier, but it emphasizes the point that improvements to the management information system greatly affect corporate objectives. You may recall that traditional MIS did not affect many process objectives, but on the other hand, they do affect most of the corporate objectives.

It is essential that analysts systematically go through the steps in developing feasibility impact grids. By understanding process and corporate objectives, an analyst realizes why he or she is building systems and comprehends what the importance of

FIGURE 3.4

An analyst can use a feasibility impact grid to show how each system component affects corporate objectives.

	System Components	Corporate Objectives: Corporate Profits	Competitive Strategy	Cooperative Ventures	Internal Operations Support	Internal Decision Support	Customer Service	Employee Morale
Ecommerce Systems	Online catalog		✓ (red)				✓ (red)	✓ (red)
	Online order processing		✓ (red)	✓ (red)			✓ (red)	✓ (red)
	Online technical support		✓ (red)				✓ (red)	✓ (red)
	Banner advertisements	✓ (red)		✓ (red)			✓ (red)	
	Web-based intelligent push agent						✓ (red)	
MIS	Inventory management	✓ (green)	✓ (red)		✓ (green)	✓ (green)	✓ (green)	
	Production scheduling	✓ (green)	✓ (red)		✓ (green)	✓ (green)	✓ (green)	✓ (green)
	Monthly sales reports	✓ (green)	✓ (red)		✓ (green)	✓ (green)		✓ (green)
	Regional sales analysis	✓ (red)			✓ (red)	✓ (red)		✓ (red)
	Logistics management	✓ (green)	✓ (red)		✓ (green)	✓ (green)		
TPS	Payroll				✓ (green)			✓ (green)
	Order processing	✓ (green)			✓ (green)		✓ (green)	
	Order tracking	✓ (green)			✓ (green)		✓ (green)	
	Accounts payable			✓ (green)	✓ (green)		✓ (green)	
	Accounts receivable			✓ (green)	✓ (green)		✓ (green)	

Symbol	Meaning
✓ (red)	Proposed information system component or improvement can contribute positively to the corporate objective when implemented in the future.
✓ (green)	Existing information system component is contributing positively to the corporate objective.

designing efficient and effective systems might be. Analysts can communicate those impacts to the decision makers evaluating (and paying for) the project.

An analyst should be aware that there also are some unacceptable objectives for systems projects. As mentioned before, they include undertaking a project solely to prove the prowess of the systems analysis team or purely to assert the superiority of one department over another in terms of its power to command internal resources. Without a consideration of its true contribution to the achievement of the organization's goals, it is also unacceptable to automate manual procedures for the sake of automation alone or to invest in new technology because of infatuation with the "bells and whistles" it provides over and above what the present system offers.

The objectives of the project need to be cleared formally on paper as well as informally by talking to people in the business. Find out what problem they believe the systems project would solve or what situation it would improve, and what their expectations are for the proposed system.

DETERMINING RESOURCES

Resource determination for the feasibility study follows the same broad pattern discussed previously and will be revised and reevaluated if and when a formal systems study is commissioned. A project must be feasible in all three ways to merit

The Three Key Elements of Feasibility

Technical Feasibility
    Add on to present system
    Technology available to meet users' needs

Economic Feasibility
    Systems analysts' time
    Cost of systems study
    Cost of employees' time for study
    Estimated cost of hardware
    Cost of packaged software or software development

Operational Feasibility
    Whether the system will operate when installed
    Whether the system will be used

FIGURE 3.5
The three key elements of feasibility include technical, economic, and operational feasibility.

further development, as shown in Figure 3.5. Resources are discussed in relationship to three areas of feasibility: technical, economic, and operational.

Technical Feasibility A large part of determining resources has to do with assessing technical feasibility. The analyst must find out whether current technical resources can be upgraded or added to in a manner that fulfills the request under consideration. Sometimes, however, "add-ons" to existing systems are costly and not worthwhile, simply because they meet needs inefficiently. If existing systems cannot be added onto, the next question becomes whether there is technology in existence that meets the specifications.

At this point the expertise of systems analysts is beneficial, because by using their own experience and their contacts with vendors, systems analysts will be able to answer the question of technical feasibility. Usually the response to whether a particular technology is available and capable of meeting the users' requests is "yes," and then the question becomes an economic one.

Economic Feasibility Economic feasibility is the second part of resource determination. The basic resources to consider are your time and that of the systems analysis team, the cost of doing a full systems study (including the time of employees you will be working with), the cost of the business employee time, the estimated cost of hardware, and the estimated cost of software or software development.

The concerned business must be able to see the value of the investment it is pondering before committing to an entire systems study. If short-term costs are not overshadowed by long-term gains or produce no immediate reduction in operating costs, the system is not economically feasible and the project should not proceed any further.

Operational Feasibility Suppose for a moment that technical and economic resources are both judged adequate. The systems analyst must still consider the operational feasibility of the requested project. Operational feasibility is dependent on the human resources available for the project and involves projecting whether the system will operate and be used once it is installed.

If users are virtually wed to the present system, see no problems with it, and generally are not involved in requesting a new system, resistance to implementing the new system will be strong. Chances for it ever becoming operational are low.

Alternatively, if users themselves have expressed a need for a system that is operational more of the time, in a more efficient and accessible manner, chances are better that the requested system will eventually be used. Much of the art of determining operational feasibility rests with the user interfaces that are chosen, as we see in Chapter 14.

At this point, determining operational feasibility requires creative imagination on the part of the systems analyst, as well as the powers of persuasion to let users know which interfaces are possible and which will satisfy their needs. The systems analyst must also listen carefully to what users really want and what it seems they will use. Ultimately, however, assessing operational feasibility largely involves educated guesswork.

JUDGING FEASIBILITY

From the foregoing discussion, it is evident that judging the feasibility of systems projects is never a clear-cut or easy task. Furthermore, project feasibility is a decision to be made not by the systems analyst but instead by management. Decisions are based on feasibility data expertly and professionally gathered and presented by the analyst.

The systems analyst needs to be sure that all three areas of technical, economic, and operational feasibility are addressed in the preliminary study. The study of a requested systems project must be accomplished quickly so that the resources devoted to it are minimal, the information output from the study is solid, and any existing interest in the project remains high. Remember that this is a preliminary study, which precedes the system study, and it must be executed rapidly and competently.

Projects that meet the criteria discussed in the "Selection of Projects" subsection earlier in the chapter, as well as the three criteria of technical, economic, and operational feasibility, should be chosen for a detailed systems study. At this point the systems analyst must act as a supporting expert, advising management that the requested systems project meets all the selection criteria and has thus qualified as an excellent candidate for further study. Remember that a commitment from management now means only that a systems study may proceed, not that a proposed system is accepted. Generally, the process of feasibility assessment is effective in screening out projects that are inconsistent with the business's objectives, technically impossible, or economically without merit. Although it is painstaking, studying feasibility is worthwhile and saves businesses and systems analysts a good deal of time and money in the end.

ACTIVITY PLANNING AND CONTROL

Systems analysis and design involves many different types of activities that together make up a project. The systems analyst must manage the project carefully if the project is to be successful. Project management involves the general tasks of planning and control.

Planning includes all the activities required to select a systems analysis team, assign members of the team to appropriate projects, estimate the time required to complete each task, and schedule the project so that tasks are completed in a timely fashion. Control means using feedback to monitor the project, including comparing the plan for the project with its actual evolution. In addition, control means taking appropriate action to expedite or reschedule activities to finish on time while motivating team members to complete the job properly.

ESTIMATING TIME REQUIRED

The systems analyst's first decision is to determine the amount of detail that goes into defining activities. The lowest level of detail is the systems development life

CONSULTING OPPORTUNITY 3.2

FOOD FOR THOUGHT

We could really make some changes. Shake up some people. Let them know we're with it. Technologically, I mean," said Malcolm Warner, vice president for AllFine Foods, a wholesale dairy products distributor. "That old system should be overhauled. I think we should just tell the staff that it's time to change."

"Yes, but what would we actually be improving?" Kim Han, assistant to the vice president, asks. "I mean, there aren't any substantial problems with the system input or output that I can see."

Malcolm snaps, "Kim, you're purposely not seeing my point. People out there see us as a stodgy firm. A new computer system could help change that. Change the look of our invoices. Send jazzier reports to the food store owners. Get some people excited about us as leaders in wholesale food distributing and computers."

"Well, from what I've seen over the years," Kim replies evenly, "a new system is very disruptive, even when the business really needs it. People dislike change, and if the system is performing the way it should, maybe there are other things we could do to update our image that wouldn't drive everyone nuts in the process. Besides, you're talking big bucks for a new gimmick."

Malcolm says, "I don't think just tossing it around here between the two of us is going to solve anything. Check on it and get back to me. Wouldn't it be wonderful?"

A week later Kim enters Malcolm's office with several pages of interview notes in hand. "I've talked with most of the people who have extensive contact with the system. They're happy, Malcolm. And they're not just talking through their hats. They know what they're doing."

"I'm sure the managers would like to have a newer system than the guys at Quality Foods," Malcolm replies. "Did you talk to them?"

Kim says, "Yes. They're satisfied."

"And how about the people in systems? Did they say the technology to update our system is out there?" Malcolm inquires insistently.

"Yes. It can be done. That doesn't mean it should be," Kim says firmly.

As the systems analyst for AllFine Foods, how would you assess the feasibility of the systems project Malcolm is proposing? Based on what Kim has said about the managers, users, and systems people, what seems to be the operational feasibility of the proposed project? What about the economic feasibility? What about the technological feasibility? Based on what Kim and Malcolm have discussed, would you recommend that a full-blown systems study be done? Discuss your answer in a paragraph.

cycle itself, whereas the highest extreme is to include every detailed step. The optimal answer to planning and scheduling lies somewhere in between.

A structured approach is useful here. In Figure 3.6 the systems analyst beginning a project has broken the process into three major phases: analysis, design, and implementation. Then the analysis phase is further broken down into data gathering, data flow and decision analysis, and proposal preparation. Design is broken down into data entry design, input and output design, and data organization. The implementation phase is divided into implementation and evaluation.

In subsequent steps the systems analyst needs to consider each of these tasks and break them down further so that planning and scheduling can take place. Figure 3.7 shows how the analysis phase is described in more detail. For example, data gathering is broken down into five activities, from conducting interviews to

Phase	Activity
Analysis	Data gathering Data flow and decision analysis Proposal preparation
Design	Data entry design Input design Output design Data organization
Implementation	Implementation Evaluation

Break apart the major activities into smaller ones.

FIGURE 3.6

Beginning to plan a project by breaking it into three major activities.

FIGURE 3.7

Refining the planning and scheduling of analysis activities by adding detailed tasks and establishing the time required to complete the tasks.

Activity	Detailed Activity	Weeks Required
Data gathering	Conduct interviews	3
	Administer questionnaires	4
	Read company reports	4
	Introduce prototype	5
	Observe reactions to prototype	3
Data flow and decision analysis	Analyze data flow	8
Proposal preparation	Perform cost/benefit analysis	3
	Prepare proposal	2
	Present proposal	2

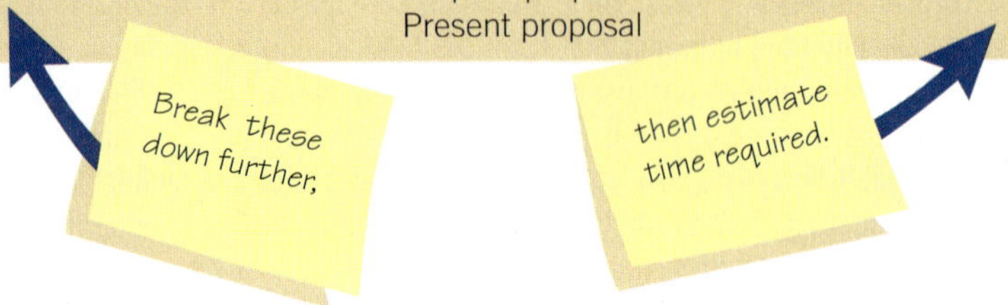

observing reactions to the prototype. This particular project requires data flow analysis but not decision analysis, so the systems analyst has written in "analyze data flow" as the single step in the middle phase. Finally, proposal preparation is broken down into three steps: perform cost/benefit analysis, prepare proposal, and present proposal.

The systems analyst, of course, has the option to break down steps further. For instance, the analyst could specify each of the persons to be interviewed. The amount of detail necessary depends on the project, but all critical steps need to appear in the plans.

Sometimes the most difficult part of project planning is the crucial step of estimating the time it takes to complete each task or activity. When quizzed about reasons for lateness on a particular project, project team members cited poor scheduling estimates that hampered the success of projects from the outset. There is no substitute for experience in estimating time requirements, and systems analysts who have had the opportunity of an apprenticeship are fortunate in this regard.

Planners have attempted to reduce the inherent uncertainty in determining time estimates by projecting most likely, pessimistic, and optimistic estimates and then using a weighted average formula to determine the expected time an activity will take. This approach offers little more in the way of confidence, however. Perhaps the best strategy for the systems analyst is to adhere to a structured approach in identifying activities and describing these activities in sufficient detail. In this manner, the systems analyst will at least be able to limit unpleasant surprises.

USING GANTT CHARTS FOR PROJECT SCHEDULING

A Gantt chart is an easy way to schedule tasks. It is a chart on which bars represent each task or activity. The length of each bar represents the relative length of the task.

Figure 3.8 is an example of a two-dimensional Gantt chart in which time is indicated on the horizontal dimension and a description of activities makes up the vertical dimension. In this example the Gantt chart shows the analysis or information gathering phase of the project. Notice on the Gantt chart that conducting interviews will take three weeks, administering the questionnaire will take four weeks, and so on. These activities overlap part of the time. In the chart the special

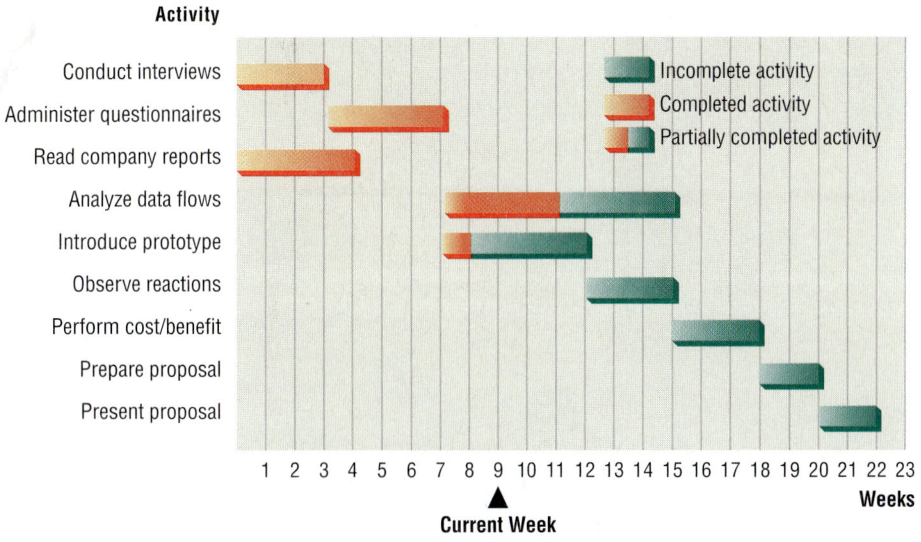

FIGURE 3.8
Using a two-dimensional Gantt chart for planning activities that can be accomplished in parallel.

symbol ▲ signifies that it is week 9. The bars with color shading represent projects or parts of projects that have been completed, telling us that the systems analyst is behind in introducing prototypes but ahead in analyzing data flows. Action must be taken on introducing prototypes soon so that other activities or even the project itself will not be delayed as a result.

The main advantage of the Gantt chart is its simplicity. The systems analyst will find not only that this technique is easy to use but also that it lends itself to worthwhile communication with end users. Another advantage of using a Gantt chart is that the bars representing activities or tasks are drawn to scale; that is, the size of the bar indicates the relative length of time it will take to complete each task.

USING PERT DIAGRAMS

PERT is an acronym for Program Evaluation and Review Techniques. A program (a synonym for a project) is represented by a network of nodes and arrows that are then evaluated to determine the critical activities, improve the schedule if necessary, and review progress once the project is undertaken. PERT was developed in the late 1950s for use in the U.S. Navy's Polaris nuclear submarine project. It reportedly saved the U.S. Navy two years' development time.

PERT is useful when activities can be done in parallel rather than in sequence. The systems analyst can benefit from PERT by applying it to systems projects on a smaller scale, especially when some team members can be working on certain activities at the same time that fellow members are working on other tasks.

Figure 3.9 compares a simple Gantt chart with a PERT diagram. The activities expressed as bars in the Gantt chart are represented by arrows in the PERT diagram. The length of the arrows has no direct relationship with the activity durations. Circles on the PERT diagram are called events and can be identified by numbers, letters, or any other arbitrary form of designation. The circular nodes are present to (1) recognize that an activity is completed and (2) indicate which activities need to be completed before a new activity may be undertaken (precedence).

In reality activity C may not be started until activity A is completed. Precedence is not indicated at all in the Gantt chart, so it is not possible to tell whether activity C is scheduled to start on day 4 on purpose or by coincidence.

A project has a beginning, a middle, and an end; the beginning is event 10 and the end is event 50. To find the length of the project, each path from beginning to end is identified, and the length of each path is calculated. In this example path

FIGURE 3.9
Gantt charts compared with PERT diagrams for scheduling activities.

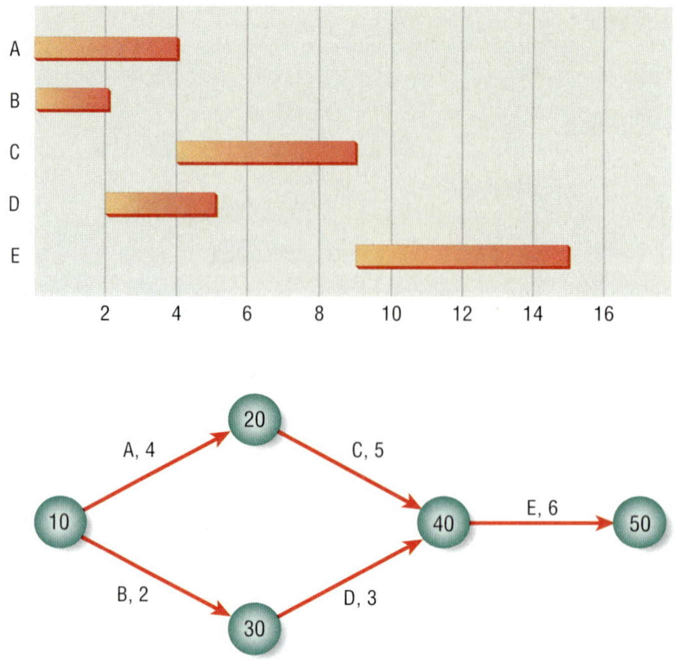

10–20–40–50 has a length of 15 days, whereas path 10–30–40–50 has a length of 11 days. Even though one person may be working on path 10–20–40–50 and another on path 10–30–40–50, the project is not a race. The project requires that both sets of activities (or paths) be completed; consequently, the project takes 15 days to complete.

The longest path is referred to as the critical path. Although the critical path is determined by calculating the longest path, it is defined as the path that will cause the whole project to fall behind if even one day's delay is encountered on it. Note that if you are delayed one day on path 10–20–40–50, the entire project will take longer, but if you are delayed one day on path 10–30–40–50, the entire project will not suffer. The leeway to fall behind somewhat on noncritical paths is called slack time.

Occasionally, PERT diagrams need pseudo-activities, referred to as dummy activities, to preserve the logic of or clarify the diagram. Figure 3.10 shows two

FIGURE 3.10
Precedence of activities is important in determining the length of the project when using a PERT diagram.

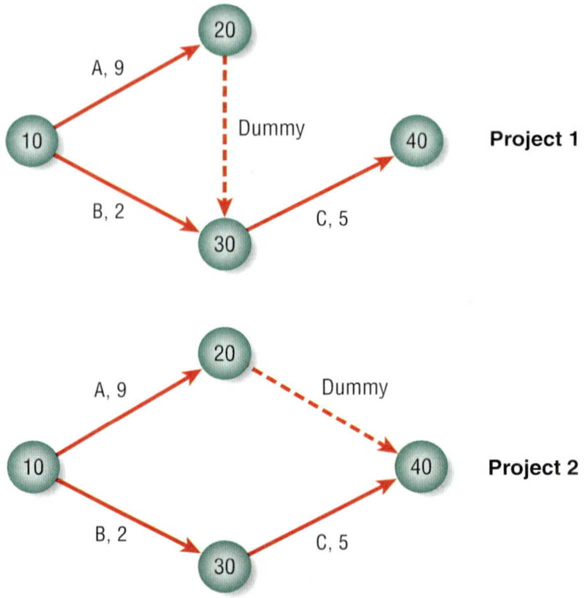

Activity		Predecessor	Duration
A	Conduct interviews	None	3
B	Administer questionnaires	A	4
C	Read company reports	None	4
D	Analyze data flow	B, C	8
E	Introduce prototype	B, C	5
F	Observe reactions to prototype	E	3
G	Perform cost/benefit analysis	D	3
H	Prepare proposal	F, G	2
I	Present proposal	H	2

FIGURE 3.11
Listing activities for use in drawing a PERT diagram.

PERT diagrams with dummies. Project 1 and project 2 are quite different, and the way the dummy is drawn makes the difference clear. In project 1 activity C can only be started if both A and B are finished, because all arrows coming into a node must be completed before leaving the node. In project 2, however, activity C requires only activity B's completion and can therefore be under way while activity A is still taking place.

Project 1 takes 14 days to complete, whereas project 2 takes only 9 days. The dummy in project 1 is necessary, of course, because it indicates a crucial precedence relationship. The dummy in project 2, on the other hand, is not required, and activity A could have been drawn from 10 to 40 and event 20 may be eliminated completely.

Therefore, there are many reasons for using a PERT diagram over a Gantt chart. The PERT diagram allows:

1. Easy identification of the order of precedence.
2. Easy identification of the critical path and thus critical activities.
3. Easy determination of slack time.

A PERT Example Suppose a systems analyst is trying to set up a realistic schedule for the data gathering and proposal phases of the systems analysis and design life cycle. The systems analyst looks over the situation and lists activities that need to be accomplished along the way. This list, which appears in Figure 3.11, also shows that some activities must precede other activities. The time estimates were determined as discussed in an earlier section of this chapter.

Drawing the PERT Diagram In constructing the PERT diagram, the analyst looks first at those activities requiring no predecessor activities, in this case A (conduct interviews) and C (read company reports). In the example in Figure 3.12, the analyst chose to number the nodes 10, 20, 30, and so on, and he or she drew two arrows out of the beginning node 10. These arrows represent activities A and C

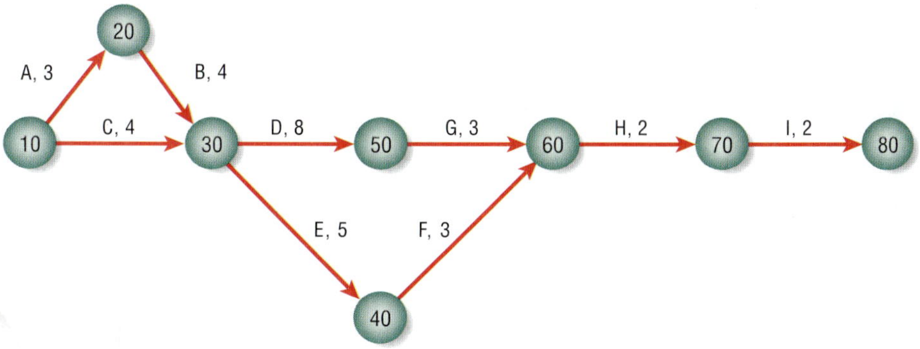

FIGURE 3.12
A completed PERT diagram for the analysis phase of a systems project.

and are labeled as such. Nodes numbered 20 and 30 are drawn at the end of these respective arrows. The next step is to look for any activity requiring only A as a predecessor; task B (administer questionnaires) is the only one, so it can be represented by an arrow drawn from node 20 to node 30.

Because activities D (analyze data flow) and E (introduce prototype) require both activities B and C to be finished before they are started, arrows labeled D and E are drawn from node 30, the event that recognizes the completion of both B and C. This process is continued until the entire PERT diagram is completed. Notice that the entire project ends at an event called node 80.

Identifying the Critical Path Once the PERT diagram is drawn, it is possible to identify the critical path by calculating the sum of the activity times on each path and choosing the longest path. In this example, there are four paths: 10–20–30–50–60–70–80, 10–20–30–40–60–70–80, 10–30–50–60–70–80, and 10–30–40–60–70–80. The longest path is 10–20–30–50–60–70–80, which takes 22 days. It is essential that the systems analyst carefully monitor the activities on the critical path so as to keep the entire project on time or even shorten the project length if warranted.

COMPUTER-BASED PROJECT SCHEDULING

Using PCs for project scheduling has now become practical and straightforward. Microsoft Project is a good example of a powerful program.

An example of project management from Microsoft Project can be found in Figure 3.13. New tasks can be entered in either the top or the bottom part of the display, whichever is easier for the user. Let's assume we want to enter the task "Conduct needs analysis" on the bottom half of the screen. First, we enter the name of the activity, then its duration, 5d (including a qualifier: d for day, w for week, etc.), and the ID for any predecessors. The ID, or identifier, is simply the

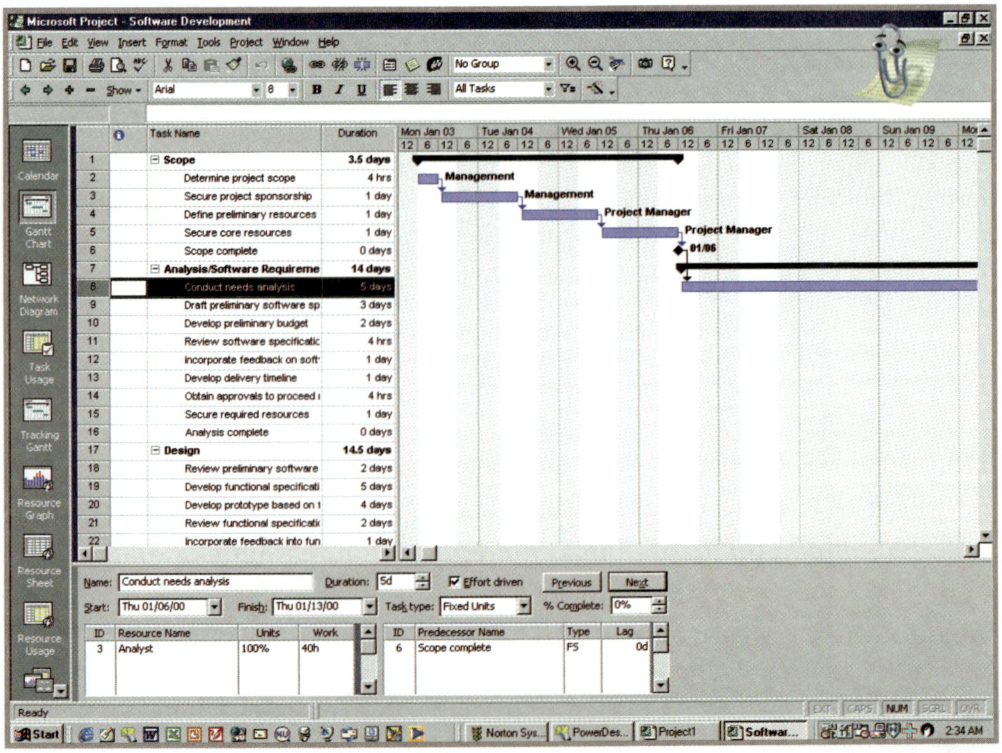

FIGURE 3.13

This screen from Microsoft Project illustrates a Gantt chart.

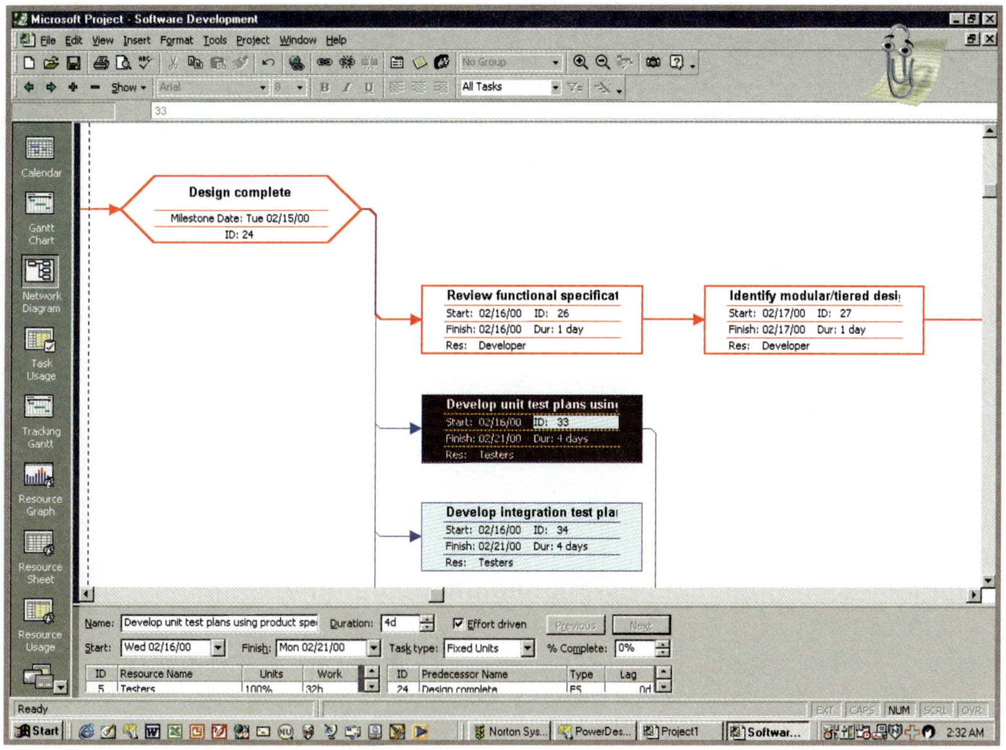

FIGURE 3.14

Microsoft Project shows activities in a PERT diagram as rectangles, not arrows.

number of the task. We don't have to enter a start date if we want the computer program to schedule it for us (as soon as possible, given the predecessors). The upper left part of the table lists the activities in the order in which we entered them. In the upper right a Gantt chart is shown.

Figure 3.14 is another display from Microsoft Project. The top half now shows a PERT diagram. Microsoft Project takes the liberty of representing the tasks or activities with rectangles rather than with arrows. Although this goes against the traditional conventions used in PERT diagrams, the software authors feel that it is easier to read tasks in rectangular boxes than to read them on arrows. A bold line, shown in red on the display, indicates the critical path. Once activities are drawn on the display, they can be repositioned using a mouse to enhance readability and communication with others. The dark box indicates that we are looking at that activity now. The dotted vertical line on the left side of the display shows the user where the page break will occur. The icons at the top of the page are familiar to anyone who uses Microsoft products.

TIMEBOXING

A recent development in project management is the concept of timeboxing. Traditionally, a project is broken down into phases, milestones, and tasks, but the timeboxing approach uses an absolute due date for the project and whatever has been accomplished by that due date is implemented. It is important to set a reasonable due date given the project size and goals. It is also important to prioritize the project goals so that the most important ones are delivered to the users by the due date. Lesser goals may be implemented later in the project. An example of timeboxing is creating a Web site that contains the most important features, with some of the minor pages containing an "Under Construction" image.

Other approaches to scheduling include integrated personal information managers, or PIMs. Some examples of a PIM include Microsoft Outlook and Palm Desktop. These PIMs are useful because they are a repository for phone and fax numbers of business associates; for daily, weekly, or monthly planners; and for to-do lists. Some PIMs are designed to be shells that enable you to launch other programs and even allow you to store similar data from word processing and spreadsheet programs in folders organized around a particular topic. Some are good at sharing data with other programs, whereas others include Gantt charts to aid in project management. Most PIMs can be synchronized with PIMs in Palm computers and other handheld devices, cell phones, and watches, allowing for excellent, wireless portability.

MANAGING THE PROJECT

The process of analysis and design can become unwieldy, especially when the system being developed is large. To keep the development activities as manageable as possible, we usually employ some of the techniques of project management to help us get organized.

One important aspect of project management is how to manage one's schedule to finish the system on time, but it is not the only thing needed. The person in charge, called the project manager, is often the lead systems analyst. The project manager needs to understand how to determine what is needed and how to initiate a project; how to develop a problem definition; how to examine feasibility of completing the systems project; how to reduce risk; how to identify and manage activities; and how to hire, manage, and motivate other team members.

ADDRESSING SYSTEM COMPLEXITY

Estimating models, such as Costar (www.softstarsystems.com) or Construx (http://www.construx.com) work as follows: First the systems analyst enters an estimate of the size of the system. This can be entered in a number of different ways, including the lines of source code of the current system. Then it may be helpful to adjust the degree of difficulty based on how familiar the analyst is with this type of project.

Also considered are other variables, like the experience or capability of the team, the type of platform or operating system, the level of usability of the finished software (for example, what languages are necessary), and other factors that can drive up costs. Once the data are entered, calculations are made, and a rough projection of the completion date is produced. As the project gets underway, more specific estimates are possible.

FUNCTION POINT ANALYSIS

You can see that experience has a lot to do with shaping the estimates. If a project manager keeps track of the time it takes each member of the team to complete specific activities, then in future projects it becomes much easier to come up with accurate estimates. As mentioned previously, one way to predict the time it will take to complete a systems project is to estimate the necessary lines of code directly. Another way to estimate size is by using function point analysis. Function point analysis is based on five main components of computers systems.

1. External inputs.
2. External outputs.
3. External queries.
4. Internal logical files.
5. External interface files.

To determine the function point count (FPC), count the preceding components, rate each of them in terms of complexity, assign numbers to them based on their complexity, arrive at a subtotal, then multiply that number by an adjustment factor based on systems characteristics that make the system more complex. The entire process is accomplished using rules of thumb, so the function point count becomes an estimator of how complex a project will be. In this book, we use estimates or rules of thumb developed by the International Function Point User Group. To understand more about function points, go to www.ifpug.org.

As you can see immediately, it is first necessary to define a boundary (as covered in Chapter 2) so that we know what is internal and what is external to the system. Once this is accomplished, the components can be placed into one of the preceding categories.

An external input can be data from another application or even data entered on an input screen. External outputs are usually derived variables, calculated within the system, that transfer to another system or are used to prepare a report. External queries are actions that retrieve data from internal files or databases but do not change them.

Internal logical files are clusters of logically identifiable data that are stored entirely within the system. Finally, external interface files are groups of logically related data maintained by applications outside the system and used for reference purposes only. (Note that in that last two instances we are referring to logical, not physical, groups and storage. Where data are physically stored does not matter.)

For example, a spell checker would have external input keyed in by a user. External output would include an error message with suggested alternative spellings. An external query is a lookup table for each word against the internal dictionary. The standard dictionary and a second, user-entered dictionary would be included as internal logical files. An example of an external interface file would be an external dictionary, such as www.wiktionary.org, that could be referenced if the user required more information to answer a question such as, "Is JAVA (all caps) or Java (upper and lower case) the correct way to express the programming language?" (The correct answer is "Java.")

Calculating function point values is a five-step process, as shown in Figure 3.15.

1. Determine the complexity (low, average, or high) of external inputs, external outputs, and external queries based on the number of files updated or referenced and the number of different data element types. (For now picture "data elements" as the last name, first name, address, city, etc.) Assume that two or three files updated or referenced and 6 to 20 data elements are "average." If the number of either files or data elements increases, the complexity increases to "high." If the number decreases, the complexity decreases to "low."

   Therefore, if an external input referenced two files and there are 10 data elements, a Step 1 table lookup would determine that this external input was rated "average." If an external output referenced two files and there are 25 data elements, a Step 1 table lookup would determine that this external input was rated "high." This table lookup would be repeated for each external input, external output, and external query.
2. Determine the complexity (low, average, or high) of internal logical files and external interface files based on the number of groups of data elements and the number of different element types. (For example, a person resides at an address that is composed of a group of data elements including last name, first name, address, city, state, and so on.) Assume two to five logical groups of data elements and 20 to 50 different data element types are average. If either the

FIGURE 3.15

Function point counts can be accomplished in five steps.

STEP 1: Look up low, average, and high values for external inputs, external outputs, and external queries.

File Types Referenced	Number of Data Elements Included		
	1–5	6–20	21+
0	Low	Low	Average
1–3	Low	Average	High
4+	Average	High	High

STEP 2: Look up low, average and high values for internal logical files and external interface files.

Group of Elements	Number of Data Elements Included		
	1–19	20–50	51+
0–1	Low	Low	Average
2–5	Low	Average	High
6+	Average	High	High

STEP 3: Calculate the number of unadjusted functions points (UFP) using predetermined weights. (The weights are the numbers in blue after the × sign.)

Type of Component	Number of Components	Low	Complexity of Average	Components High	Total
External inputs	5 (2, 1, 2)	2 × 3	1 × 4	2 × 6	22
External outputs	12 (4, 6, 2)	4 × 4	6 × 5	2 × 7	60
External queries	20 (5, 10, 5)	5 × 3	10 × 4	5 × 6	85
Internal logical files	13 (3, 5, 5)	3 × 7	5 × 10	5 × 15	146
External interface files	2 (1, 0, 1)	1 × 5	0 × 7	1 × 10	15
Total unadjusted function points					**328**

STEP 4: Determine the value adjustment factor (VAF) by rating each system characteristic and calculating a subtotal, then dividing it by 100.

System Characteristic (Rate 0 for no effect; 5 for strong effect)	Rating
Data communications	2
Distributed data processing	2
Performance	0
Heavily used configuration	0
Transaction rate	0
Online data entry	0
End user efficiency	0
Online update	0
Complex processing	0
Reusability	2
Installation ease	3
Operational ease	3
Multiple sites	3
Facilitate change	1
VAF = Total divided by 100 =	**16/100 = 0.16**

STEP 5: Calculate the number of adjusted function points using the following formula:

$$FPC = UFP \times (0.65 + VAF) = 328 + (0.65 + 0.16) = 328 \times 0.81 = 266$$

groups of data elements or the data elements increase, the complexity increases to "high." If either decrease, the complexity decreases to "low."

Therefore, if an external logical file contains only one group of data elements and there are 25 different types of data elements, a Step 2 table lookup would determine that this external logical file was rated "low." This table lookup would be repeated for each internal logical file and external interface file.

3. Calculate the number of unadjusted function points (UFP) by assigning predetermined weights (numbers) to low, medium, and high complexity for each of the five components and calculate the result. For example, the weights for external inputs were assigned values of low = 3, average = 4, and high = 6. Then multiple the number of external inputs (2 of low complexity, 1 of average, and 2 of high) times these weights. Subtotal them. Once you have done this for all of the components, sum the subtotals to calculate the number of unadjusted function points.
4. Determine the value adjustment factor (VAF) based on 14 general characteristics of the system. To complete this table, you may need to ask questions: "How are distributed data functions handled?" "Does the application have extensive logic processing?" "To what extent are start-up, backup, and recovery procedures automatic?" These questions allow you to assign a rating of 0 (no effect on the complexity) to 3 (great effect on the complexity). Once you do this for all of the standard 14 characteristics, calculate the total and divide by 100 to get the value adjustment factor (VAF).
5. Calculate the function point count (FPC) by multiplying the number of unadjusted function points (UAF in Step 3) by the total of 0.65, plus the value adjustment factor (VAF in Step 4).

Note that 0.65 (or 65 percent) has been predetermined and represents the multiplier when there is no effect on complexity. The VAF is a number that can range between 0.00 and 0.70 (if all 14 systems characteristics are rated as 5, having a strong effect on complexity). Therefore the number you multiply by the UAF is always a number between 0.65 (if system characteristics have no effect on complexity) and 1.35 (if system characteristics have a strong effect on complexity). If all of the system characteristics have an average effect on complexity, the VAF would be 1.02.

The function point count can be used to estimate lines of code and differs for various languages. Software Product Research (www.spr.com/products/programming.shtm) claims that, if a developer is using a second-generation language, the default is to multiply the number of function points by 107, a third-generation language by 80, and a fourth generation language by 20. In our example we determined that the function point count was 266, so using COBOL our system might require approximately 28,000 lines of code, Java or C++ may require 21,000 lines, and PowerBuilder or HTML might require only 5,000 lines.

This approach has merit, but only if the project manager has prior experience developing systems. Otherwise, it is very difficult to estimate how many external inputs, outputs, and the like are created in developing the system. After the system development is underway, it becomes a bit easier to estimate the number of these components and consequently this approach has more value.

ESTIMATING STAFFING REQUIREMENTS FOR THE PROJECT

One of the key lessons from the last section is to make sure you are alert to how much your choice of software can influence the amount of effort that goes into system development. If COBOL is chosen, the team will be responsible for writing 28,000 lines of code, but if PowerBuilder is chosen, the project could be done in about 5,000 lines. The choice of language may have an enormous effect on the time it takes to complete the project and the number of analysts and programmers needed to complete the work.

A rule of thumb commonly used to estimate a project in person-months is:

$$\text{Number of person months} = 1.4 \times \frac{\text{Number of lines of code}}{1{,}000}$$

Therefore, our system would take $(1.4 \times 28{,}000/1{,}000) = 39.2$ or about 39 months to develop the system in COBOL, 29 months to finish it in C++ or Java, and only seven months to complete the project in PowerBuilder.

But, once again, project managers who are experienced in thinking in terms of person-months realize that it does not work to say, "If it takes seven months to finish a project, let's hire seven people and complete it in one month!" Picture the following. If you wanted to replace a roof, one person can do the work, but two can do it faster. Three may be faster yet. But teams of people need to communicate. Otherwise, they get in each other's way. Maybe one of them even falls off the roof. This principle applies to systems projects as well. When two systems developers are involved, there is one set of two-way communication. If three are involved there are three sets. If four developers are on the project, there are 12 sets of two-way communication, and so on.

One rule of thumb that used for calculating months scheduled is:

$$\text{Scheduled months} = 3 \times \text{Person months}^{1/3}$$

For our example of a project using COBOL:

$$\begin{aligned}\text{Scheduled months} &= 3 \times 39^{1/3} \\ &= 3 \times 3.39 \\ &= 10.17 = \text{or about 10 months}\end{aligned}$$

Using C++ or Java:

$$\begin{aligned}\text{Scheduled months} &= 3 \times 29^{1/3} \\ &= 3 \times 3.07 = 9.21 = \text{approximately 9 months}\end{aligned}$$

Using PowerBuilder:

$$\begin{aligned}\text{Scheduled months} &= 3 \times 7^{1/3} \\ &= 3 \times 1.91 \\ &= 5.73 = \text{approximately 6 months}\end{aligned}$$

(Note that the function in Microsoft Excel for the cube root or raising to the 1/3 power is [CellName] ^ [1/3].)

So the project manager would need to allow from 6 to 10 months, depending on the language selected to perform the analysis, design, and implementation phases of the project. The project manager would need to add additional time for planning at the beginning and for training and maintenance at the end.

MANAGING RISK

Although much effort is put into function point analysis to arrive at reasonable estimates, many projects actually fail. Studies have shown that about 30 percent of

Potential Problem That May Risk Completion of the Entire Project	Problem Probability	Delay if Problem Occurs	Budgeted Delay
Team is delayed because they are finishing another project.	0.50	60 days	30 days
Executives are not present during requirements phase.	0.25	20 days	5 days
Time budgeted to compensate delays to the project			**35 days**

FIGURE 3.16
Calculating the extra time required to ensure that a project is completed on time.

all projects succeed (that is, they were delivered with all the necessary features, on time, and within budget), but as many as 20 percent fail (were never completed or used). The remaining 50 percent of the projects are either late, over budget, or offer fewer features than originally promised.

The system we looked at earlier in this chapter had a function point count of only 266. In that range, projects terminate prior to completion at a rate of about 10 percent. Large systems projects (those with 10,000 lines of code) are less likely to be completed, with a rate of failure of about 50 percent. Project managers must realize they need to break complex projects down into smaller projects to increase their probability of success.

Projects often fail because things happen unexpectedly, but a good project manager can identify potential problems. For example, if some members of the team are currently wrapping up another project, a project manger can assume some probability that the teams members may take longer than expected and not be able to give full time to the new project. Suppose the probability of this is 50 percent and, if it happens, it would delay the project 30 days (6 work weeks).

Another possibility is that key managers would not be available to interview during the needs requirement phase because of other work on their agenda. Suppose this had a probability of 25 percent and, if it occurs, it would cause a delay of 20 days.

By carefully thinking about scenarios that could cause potential problems and calculating the expected value of all delays, the project manager is able to add additional time as a buffer to protect against the entire project failing. Figure 3.16 shows how to list all the potential problems and calculate the extra time that should be budgeted if the project manager wants to ensure the project is completed on time.

MANAGING ANALYSIS AND DESIGN ACTIVITIES

Along with managing time and resources, systems analysts must also manage people. Management is accomplished primarily by communicating accurately to team members who have been selected for their competency and compatibility. Goals for project productivity must be set, and members of systems analysis teams must be motivated to achieve them.

ASSEMBLING A TEAM

Assembling a team is desirable. If a project manager has the opportunity to create a dream team of skilled people to develop a system, whom should they choose? In general, project managers need to look for others who share their values of teamwork guided by the desire to deliver a high-quality system on time and on budget. Other desirable team member characteristics include a good work ethic, honesty, competency; a readiness to take on leadership based on expertise; motivation, enthusiasm for the project, and trust of teammates.

The project manager needs to know about business principles, but it doesn't hurt to have at least one other person on the team who understands how a business operates. Perhaps this person should be a specialist in the same area as the system being developed. When developing an ecommerce site, teams can enlist the help of someone in marketing; those developing an inventory system can ask a person versed in production and operations to provide expertise.

A team ideally should have two systems analysts on it. They can help each other, check each other's work, and shift their workloads accordingly. There is certainly a need to have people with programming skills on board. Coding is important, but people who know how to conduct walk-throughs, reviews, testing, and documenting systems are important as well. Some people are good at seeing the big picture, while others perform well when tasks are broken down into smaller ones for them. Every team should have both types of individuals.

Beyond the basics, a project manager should look for people with both experience and enthusiasm. Experience is especially important when trying to estimate the time required to complete a project. Experience in programming can mean code is developed five times faster than if it is developed by an inexperienced team. A usability expert is also a useful addition to the team.

The team must be motivated. One way to keep the team positively oriented throughout the entire process is to select good people at the outset. Look for enthusiasm, imagination, and an ability to communicate with different kinds of people. These basic attributes hold the potential for success. It also helps to hire superior writers and articulate speakers who can present proposals and work directly with customers.

Trust is an important part of a team. All members of the project need to act responsibly and agree to do their best and complete their part of the project. People may have different work styles, but they all need to agree to work together toward a common goal.

COMMUNICATION STRATEGIES FOR MANAGING TEAMS

Teams have their own personalities, a result of combining each individual team member with every other in a way that creates a totally new network of interactions. A way to organize your thinking about teams is to visualize them as always seeking a balance between accomplishing the work at hand and maintaining the relationships among team members.

In fact, teams will often have two leaders, not just one. Usually one person will emerge who leads members to accomplish tasks, and another person will emerge who is concerned with the social relationships among group members. Both are necessary for the team. These individuals have been labeled by other researchers as, respectively, task leader and socioemotional leader. Every team is subject to tensions that are an outgrowth of seeking a balance between accomplishing tasks and maintaining relationships among team members.

For the team to continue its effectiveness, tensions must be continually resolved. Minimizing or ignoring tensions will lead to ineffectiveness and eventual disintegration of the team. Much of the tension release necessary can be gained through skillful use of feedback by all team members. All members, however, need to agree that the way they interact (i.e., process) is important enough to merit some time. Productivity goals for processes are discussed in a later section.

Securing agreement on appropriate member interaction involves creating explicit and implicit team norms (collective expectations, values, and ways of

CONSULTING OPPORTUNITY 3.3

GOAL TENDING

"Here's what I think we can accomplish in the next five weeks," says Hy, the leader of your systems analysis team, as he confidently pulls out a schedule listing each team member's name alongside a list of short-term goals. Just a week ago your systems analysis team went through an intense meeting on expediting their project schedule for the Kitchener, Ontario, Redwings, a hockey organization whose management is pressuring you to produce a prototype.

The three other members of the team look at the chart in surprise. Finally, one of the members, Rip, speaks: "I'm in shock. We each have so much to do as it is, and now this."

Hy replies defensively, "We've got to aim high, Rip. They're in the off-season. It's the only time to get them. If we set our goals too low, we won't finish the system prototype, let alone the system itself, before another hockey season passes. The idea is to give the Kitchener Redwings the fighting edge through the use of their new system."

Fiona, another team member, enters the discussion, saying, "Goodness knows their players can't give them that!" She pauses for the customary groan from the assembled group, then continues. "But seriously, these goals are killers. You could have at least asked us what we thought, Hy. We may even know better than you what's possible."

"This is a pressing problem, not a tea party, Fiona," Hy replies. "Polite polling of team members was out of the question. Something had to be done quickly. So I went ahead with these. I say we submit our schedule to management based on this. We can push back deadlines later if we have to. But this way they'll know we're committed to accomplishing a lot during the off-season."

As a fourth team member listening to the foregoing exchange, formulate three suggestions that would help Hy improve his approach to goal formation and presentation. How well motivated do you think the team will be if they share Fiona's view of Hy's goals? What are the possible ramifications of supplying management with overly optimistic goals? Write one paragraph devoted to short-term effects and another one discussing the long-term effects of setting unrealistically high goals.

behaving) that guide members in their relationships. A team's norms belong to it and will not necessarily transfer from one team to another. These norms change over time and are better thought of as a team process of interaction rather than a product.

Norms can be functional or dysfunctional. Just because a particular behavior is a norm for a team does not mean it is helping the team to achieve its goals. For example, an expectation that junior team members should do all project scheduling may be a team norm. By adhering to this norm, the team is putting extreme pressure on new members and not taking full advantage of the experience of the team. It is a norm that, if continued, could make team members waste precious resources.

Team members need to make norms explicit and periodically assess whether norms are functional or dysfunctional in helping the team achieve its goals. The overriding expectation for your team must be that change is the norm. Ask yourself whether team norms are helping or hindering the team's progress.

SETTING PROJECT PRODUCTIVITY GOALS

When you have worked with your team members on various kinds of projects, you or your team leader will acquire acumen for projecting what the team can achieve in a specific amount of time. Using the hints discussed in the earlier section in this chapter on methods for estimating time required and coupling them with experience will enable the team to set worthwhile productivity goals.

Systems analysts are accustomed to thinking about productivity goals for employees who show tangible outputs, such as the number of blue jeans sewn per hour, the number of entries keyed in per minute, or the number of items scanned per second. As manufacturing productivity rises, however, it is becoming clear that managerial productivity must keep pace. It is with this aim in mind that productivity goals for the systems analysis team are set.

Goals need to be formulated and agreed to by the team, and they should be based on team members' expertise, former performance, and the nature of the specific project. Goals will vary somewhat for each project undertaken, because sometimes an entire system will be installed, whereas other projects might involve limited modifications to a portion of an existing system.

MOTIVATING PROJECT TEAM MEMBERS

Although motivation is an extremely complex topic, it is a good one to consider, even if briefly, at this point. To oversimplify, recall that people join organizations to provide for some of their basic needs such as food, clothing, and shelter. All humans, however, also have higher-level needs, which include affiliation, control, independence, and creativity. People are motivated to fulfill unmet needs on several levels.

Team members can be motivated, at least partially, through participation in goal setting, as described in the previous section. The very act of setting a challenging but achievable goal and then periodically measuring performance against the goal seems to work in motivating people. Goals act almost as magnets in attracting people to achievement.

Part of the reason goal setting motivates people is that team members know prior to any performance review exactly what is expected of them. The success of goal setting for motivating can also be ascribed to it, affording each team member some autonomy in achieving the goals. Although a goal is predetermined, the means to achieve it may not be. In this instance team members are free to use their own expertise and experience to meet their goals.

Setting goals can also motivate team members by clarifying for them and others what must be done to get results. Team members are also motivated by goals because goals define the level of achievement that is expected of them. This use of goals simplifies the working atmosphere, but it also electrifies it with the possibility that what is expected can indeed be done.

MANAGING PROJECTS USING COTS SOFTWARE

Sometimes commercial off-the-shelf (COTS) software is used to finish the project faster or to decrease the risk involved. Managing such projects still requires careful planning.

Some people define COTS software very broadly. That is, they consider a wide range of packages such as Microsoft Word and Microsoft Access to be COTS software packages. COTS software for the PC would therefore include off-the-shelf virus protection, graphical software, and income tax packages. Others define it as industry-specific software. The result is the same—rather than writing your own code, you can simply adopt these packages.

COTS software packages allow some customization. Macros and templates can be used to customize them to a particular business. COTS software packages, however, often pose compatibility problems and do not work well together. Before Windows XP, in fact, the installation of some packages disabled others (the authors have suffered through this problem themselves many times). But even now, two packages offered by WordPerfect Corporation (CorelDraw Graphics Suite and Corel Designer) have keystrokes and commands that are not shared, but rather independent of one another. Because one of the arguable advantages of COTS software packages includes the ability to train people easily, this lack of common keystrokes and commands is a contradiction. Other COTS software packages for decision support will be discussed in Chapter 10.

MANAGING ECOMMERCE PROJECTS

Many of the approaches and techniques discussed earlier are transferable to ecommerce project management. You should be cautioned, however, that although there are many similarities, there are also many differences. One difference is that the data used by ecommerce systems are scattered all over the organization. Therefore, you are not just managing data in a self-contained department or even one solitary unit. Hence, many organizational politics can come into play, because units often feel protective of the data they generate and do not understand the need to share them across the organization.

Another stark difference is that ecommerce project teams typically need more staff with a variety of skills, including developers, consultants, database experts, and system integrators, from across the organization. Neatly defined, stable project groups that exist within a cohesive IS group or systems development team will be the exception rather than the rule. In addition, because so much help may be required initially, ecommerce project managers need to build partnerships externally and internally well ahead of the implementation, perhaps sharing talent across projects to defray costs of ecommerce implementations and to muster the required numbers of people with the necessary expertise. The potential for organizational politics to drive a wedge between team members is very real.

One way to prevent politics from sabotaging a project is for the ecommerce project manager to emphasize the integration of the ecommerce with the organization's internal systems and in so doing emphasize the organizational aspect embedded in the ecommerce project. As one ecommerce project manager told us, "Designing the front end [what the consumer sees] is the easy part of all this. The real challenge comes from integrating ecommerce strategically into all the organization's systems."

A fourth difference between traditional project management and ecommerce project management is that because the system will be linking with the outside world via the Internet, security is of the utmost importance. Developing and implementing a security plan before the new system is in place is a project in and of itself and must be managed as such.

CREATING THE PROJECT CHARTER

Part of the planning process is to agree on what will be done and at what time. Analysts who are external consultants, as well as those who are organization members, need to specify what they will eventually deliver and when they will deliver it. This chapter has elaborated on ways to estimate the delivery date for the completed system and also how to identify organizational goals and assess the feasibility of the proposed system.

The project charter is a written narrative that clarifies the following questions:

1. What does the user expect of the project (what are the objectives)? What will the system do to meet the needs (achieve the objectives)?
2. What is the scope (or what are the boundaries) of the project? (What does the user consider to be beyond the project's reach?)
3. What analysis methods will the analyst use to interact with users in gathering data, developing, and testing the system?
4. Who are the key participants? How much time are users willing and able to commit to participating?
5. What are the project deliverables? (What new or updated software, hardware, procedures, and documentation do the users expect to have available for interaction when the project is done?)

6. Who will evaluate the system and how will they evaluate it? What are the steps in the assessment process? How will the results be communicated and to whom?
7. What is the estimated project timeline? How often will analysts report project milestones?
8. Who will train the users?
9. Who will maintain the system?

The project charter describes in a written document the expected results of the systems project (deliverables) and the time frame for delivery. It essentially becomes a contract between the chief analyst (or project manager) and their analysis team with the organizational users requesting the new system.

AVOIDING PROJECT FAILURES

The early discussions you have with management and others requesting a project, along with the feasibility studies you do, are usually the best defenses possible against taking on projects that have a high probability of failure. Your training and experience will improve your ability to judge the worthiness of projects and the motivations that prompt others to request projects. If you are part of an in-house systems analysis team, you must keep current with the political climate of the organization as well as with financial and competitive situations.

You can also learn from the wisdom gained by people involved in earlier project failures. When asked to reflect on why projects had failed, professional programmers cited the setting of impossible or unrealistic dates for completion by management, belief in the myth that simply adding more people to a project would expedite it (even though the original target date on the project was unrealistic), and management behaving unreasonably by forbidding the team to seek professional expertise from outside of the group to help solve specific problems.

Remember that you are not alone in the decision to begin a project. Although apprised of your team's recommendations, management will have the final say about whether a proposed project is worthy of further study (that is, further investment of resources). The decision process of your team must be open and stand up to scrutiny from those outside of it. The team members should consider that their reputation and standing in the organization are inseparable from the projects they accept.

AGILE DEVELOPMENT

The agile approach (also called agile methods or agile development) is an innovative philosophy and methodology comprised of systems development practices, techniques, values, and principles (including XP, extreme programming) intended for use in developing systems in a dynamic way.

Often posed as an alternative way to develop systems, the agile approach seeks to address common complaints arising over the traditional SDLC approach (for being too time-consuming, focusing on data rather than on humans, and being too costly) by being rapid, iterative, flexible, and participative in responding to changing human information requirements, business conditions, and environments.

We explore agile methods in greater detail in Chapter 6, but it is very relevant in this chapter, because the agile approach also implies agile project management.

This section is devoted to agile practices that ensure that the project is completed on schedule. The four variables that a systems developer can control are time, cost, quality, and scope. When these four control variables are properly included in the planning, there exists a state of balance between the resources and the activities needed to complete the project, as noted in Figure 3.17.

Use These Four Control Variables	To Balance These Four Activities
• Time	• Coding
• Cost	• Testing
• Quality	• Listening
• Scope	• Designing

FIGURE 3.17
The analyst can control the time, cost, quality, and scope of the project to balance the activities.

The activities of the agile approach are coding, testing, listening, and designing. Coding is, of course, essential in any software project. Testing for functionality, performance, and conformance is mandatory. Listening to the customer and other programmers and analysts is essential. Designing a system that is functional, aesthetic, and maintainable is critically important.

The major difference between agile project management and other more traditional types of project management is that as you listen to what users want, you can figure out how much of each resource is required. In order to balance the project outcomes, the analyst using an agile approach can adjust any of these four resource variables.

The agile philosophy assumes, for example, that if the analyst determines the scope, quality, and amount of time needed to complete the project, the analyst can adjust cost. If the project is running behind schedule, simply increase spending by hiring more people. Alternatively, if the analyst predetermined the amount of time, quality, and cost that is required, the analyst could adjust the scope accordingly. In this case, if the project is running late, the analyst may want to consult with the customer to forego some feature, for example. The following subsection elaborates on adjusting each of the resource control variables.

RESOURCE TRADE-OFFS USING AN AGILE APPROACH

Completing all of the activities in the project on time within all of the constraints is admirable, but, as you probably have realized by now, in order to accomplish this, project management is crucial. Managing a project doesn't mean simply getting all the tasks and resources together. It also means that the analyst is faced with a number of trade-offs. Sometimes cost may be predetermined, at other junctures time may be the most important factor. These resource control variables (time, cost, quality, and scope) are discussed below.

Time You need to allow enough time to complete your project. Time, however, is split into many separate pieces. You need time to listen to the customers, time to design, time to code, and time to test.

One of our friends is an owner of a Chinese restaurant. Recently, he found himself short-staffed as one of the members of his reliable crew returned to Hong Kong to get married. The owner placed himself in the kitchen so the food was served on time, but stopped greeting his customers out front in the usual way. He sacrificed the listening activity to achieve another, but in this case he found out it was hurting his business. Customers wanted the attention.

It is the same in systems development. You can create quality software, but fail to listen. You can design a perfect system, but not allow enough time to test it. Time is difficult to manage. If you find yourself running short of time, what do you do?

The agile approach challenges the notion that more time will give you the results you want. Perhaps the customer would prefer that you finish on time rather than extending the deadline to add another feature. Customers, we often find, are happy if some of the functionality is up and running on time. Our experience shows that often a customer is 80-percent satisfied with the first 20 percent of the functionality. This means that when you complete the final 80 percent of the project, the customer may be only slightly happier than they were after you completed the first 20 percent. The message here is be careful not to extend your deadline. The agile approach insists on finishing on time.

Cost Cost is the second variable we can consider adjusting. Suppose that the activities of coding, designing, testing, and listening are weighing the project down, and the resources we put into time, scope, and quality are not sufficient, even with a normal amount devoted to cost, to balance the project. Essentially we might be required to contribute more resources that require money to balance the project.

The easiest way to increase spending (and hence costs) is to hire more people. This may appear to be the perfect solution. If we hire more programmers, we'll finish faster. Right? Not necessarily. Picture hiring two people to repair a roof and increase that number to four. Soon the people are bumping into one another. Furthermore, they need to ask each other what still needs to be done. And if there's a lightning storm, no one will be working. Going from two to four doesn't mean it will take half of the time. Consider the required increase in communication and other intangible costs when you are considering hiring more people. Remember that when a person joins a team, they do not know the project or the team. They will slow the original members down, because the original members must devote time to getting new members up to speed.

Overtime doesn't help much either. It increases the cost, but the productivity doesn't always follow. Tired programmers are less effective than alert programmers. Tired programmers take a long time to complete a task, and they also make mistakes that are even more time consuming to fix.

Is there anything else we can spend our money on? Perhaps. As you read later chapters you will read about a variety of tools that support analysts and programmers. These tools are often a wise investment. Analysts, for example, use graphical packages such as Microsoft Visio to communicate ideas about the project to others, and CASE tools such as Visible Analyst also help speed up projects.

Even new hardware could be a worthwhile expenditure. Laptops and cell phones improve productivity away from the office. Larger visual displays, Bluetooth-enabled keyboards and mice, and more powerful graphics cards can also increase productivity.

Quality The third resource control variable is quality. If ideal systems are perfect, why is so much effort placed in maintaining systems? Are we already practicing agile development by sacrificing quality in software development? In Chapter 16 we will see the importance of quality and methods (such as TQM and Six Sigma) that help ensure software quality is high.

The agile philosophy, however, does allow the analyst to adjust this resource, and perhaps put less effort into maintaining quality than otherwise would be expected. Quality can be adjusted both internally and externally. Internal quality involves testing software for factors such as functionality (Does a program do what it is supposed to do?) and conformance (Does the software meet certain conformance standards and is it maintainable?). It usually doesn't pay to tinker with internal quality.

That leaves us with external quality, or how the customer perceives the system. The customer is interested in performance. Some of the questions a customer may ask are: Does the program act reliably (or do software bugs still exist)? Is the output effective? Does the output reach me on time? Does the software run effortlessly? Is the user interface easy to understand and use?

The extreme philosophy of agile development allows some of the external quality issues to be sacrificed. In order for the system to be released on time, the customer may have to contend with some software bugs. If we want to meet our deadline, the user interface may not be perfect. We can make it better in a follow-up version.

Commercial off-the-shelf software manufacturers do sacrifice quality, and it is debatable whether this is the correct approach. So don't be surprised when your PC software applications (not to mention your operating system and Web browser) are updated often, if developers are using extreme programming as one of their agile practices.

Scope Finally, there is scope. In the agile approach, scope is determined by listening to customers and getting them to write down their stories. Then the stories are examined to see how much can be done in a given time to satisfy the customer. Stories should be brief and easy to grasp. Stories will be described in more detail in Chapter 6, but here is a brief example showing four short stories from an online air travel system. Each story is shown in bold type:

Display alternative flights.

Prepare a list of the five cheapest flights.

Offer cheaper alternatives.

Suggest to the customer that they travel on other days, make weekend stays, take special promotions, or use alternate airports.

Purchase a ticket.

Allow the customer to purchase a ticket directly using a credit card (check validity).

Allow the customer to choose his or her seat.

Direct the customer to a visual display of the airplane and ask the customer to select a seat.

Ideally, the analyst would be able to determine how much time and money was needed to complete each of these stories and be able to set the level of quality for them as well. It is obvious that this system must not sacrifice quality, or credit card purchases may be invalid or customers may show up at the airport without reservations.

Once again agile practices allow extreme measures, so in order to maintain quality, manage cost, and complete the project on time, the agile analyst may want to adjust the scope of the project. This can be accomplished by agreeing with the customer that one or more of the stories can be delayed until the next version of the software. For example, maybe the functionality of allowing customers to choose their own seats can be put off for another time.

In summary, the agile analyst can control any of the four resource variables of time, cost, quality, and scope. Agility calls for extreme measures and places a great deal of importance on completing a project on time. In doing so, sacrifices must be made and the agile analyst will find out that the trade-offs available involve difficult decisions.

CORE PRACTICES AND ROLES OF THE AGILE APPROACH

Now that we have discussed how we can manage systems projects using agile concepts, let's turn our attention to how to develop and plan agile systems. In this section, we will introduce you to core agile practices that differentiate agile

FIGURE 3.18

Four core practices distinguish agile modeling from other systems development approaches.

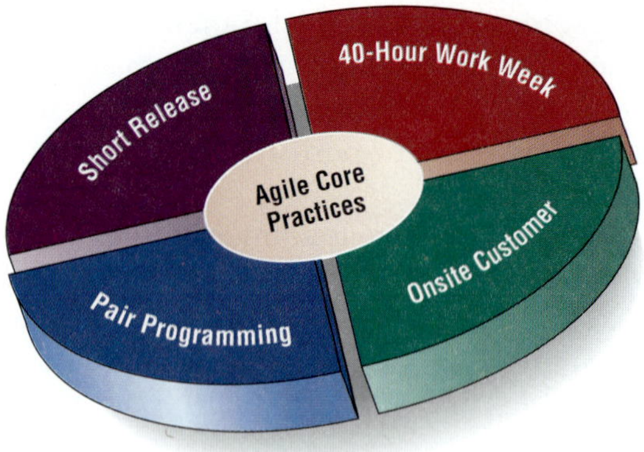

development from the SDLC approach and other types of development methodologies. Then we will elaborate on some of the roles that participants in agile development play. Next we will describe how agile projects are planned using a concept called the planning game. Finally, we will address some risks and fears of systems development and how the agile approach addresses these risks.

Four Core Agile Practices Balancing resources to complete a project on time is one way to manage a project. The best way to manage, however, is to develop practices that yield outstanding results. The agile movement has developed a set of core practices that have changed the way systems are developed. Following are four extreme practices. As you can see, they are radical compared to what we have discussed so far in project management. Figure 3.18 illustrates the four core practices.

1. Short release. In order for agile development to be successful, products must be released quickly. That means that even if the programmers couldn't get all of the features into a piece of software, the version must be released on schedule. Yes, this is extreme, but customers are pleased because they have a product to use. Any improvements can be made later. This practice is widely used in PC software development and is even more common for cell phones and other mobile devices. In the U.S., even tax software is released early in the tax season before all of the IRS tax laws (and forms) are finalized. The tax software developers know that the customer wants the product as soon as possible.
2. 40-hour work week. The Silicon Valley model for software development encouraged programmers to live at the office, working around the clock. Not so with the agile movement. Agile development teams purposely endorse a cultural core practice in which the team works intensely together during a typical 40-hour work week. This practice attempts to motivate team members to work intensely at the job, and then to take time off so that when they return to work they are relaxed, less stressed, able to see problems, and less prone to make costly errors and omissions because of ineffectual performance or burnout.
3. Onsite customer. Most systems developers claim that the customer is vital to system success, but wind up meeting only once or twice with the customer to determine system requirements. The core practice of the onsite customer goes to the extreme by insisting that an expert in the business should work onsite during the entire development process. This person is active in the process, writing user stories (explained in Chapters 2 and 6), communicating to team members, and helping to set priorities. This works well with adoption of an HCI approach, which is user-centered as well.
4. Pair programming. We are very familiar with the concept of systems analyst teams; why not have teams of programmers? No, one programmer doesn't look

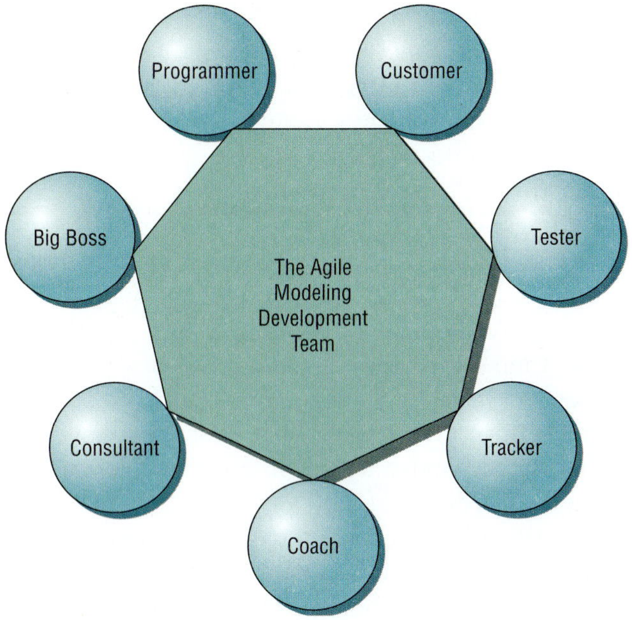

FIGURE 3.19
Roles in the agile approach include members from inside of the development team as well as at least one onsite customer.

over the other's shoulder to see whether any errors are made. Rather, pair programming means that two programmers who choose to work together both do the programming, run the tests, and talk to one another about ways to efficiently and effectively get the job done. Working with another programmer helps you clarify your thinking. Pair programming saves time, cuts down on careless thinking, sparks creativity, and is a fun way to program.

Roles for People There are many roles people must play in agile development projects, and some people will even be called on to play multiple roles during the effort. The seven roles include those of programmer, customer, tester, tracker, coach, consultant, and something referred to (only half in jest) as the "big boss." The seven roles are shown in Figure 3.19.

The programmer is often discussed as the heart of the agile development effort. However, agile programmers are quite different in emphasis than other programmers, because they are asked to be excellent communicators. Communication skills are put into play as soon as a development effort begins, because the agile approach encourages working in programming pairs, in which each person codes, although often there is a junior and senior person on a given task. As an analyst/programmer, you also need to have outstanding technical skills to program well, to be able to refactor, and to be able to unit test the code you have written. In addition you need a willingness to approach the hardest problems with simplicity, learn from others, share in coding and design, and have courage to face any fears of inadequacy or failure you may have in approaching new problems.

The next role we discuss is that of customer. The best way to describe it is that the customer must take on new qualities, some of them very much like a developer, while still retaining the essence of what is needed in the system. The most ideally suited customer for the agile team is someone who will be a user of the system and who possesses business knowledge of it. With that in mind, the customer must learn to write user stories, learn to write functional tests for the applications that the programmers create, and make sound decisions about the essential features of the system and even adjustments in project schedules and delivery dates. Customers also need to show that they have courage in the face of difficult scheduling or functional decisions.

A third role is that of tester on an agile development team. Programmers are called on to do both unit and functional testing of any new coding that has been done. Someone who is a programmer also needs to communicate with the customer about functional tests, run tests regularly, maintain the testing tools, and communicate clearly the results of tests.

Another role on the agile development team is that of tracker. This person tracks the overall progress of the group by estimating the time of its tasks and its overall progress toward its goals. The tracker does estimates, but also provides feedback about the team's estimates. Were they too low or too high? By what percentage were they incorrect? As a tracker you will be able to tell the team this valuable information, so that their estimates improve in accuracy. Trackers also serve as the team memory, keeping track of all of the functional test scores. Defects that are reported are also tracked, and the name of the programmer who took responsibility for handling that defect is also noted. In addition, you track what test cases were added to address each defect.

We next consider the role of coach, who often is an invisible hand guiding the overall process. Because one of the hallmarks of agile development is that each person accepts responsibility for their actions, a coach may seem unnecessary. However, coaches are critical. For instance, they display a calm demeanor when everyone else on the team is panicking. They shape situations indirectly (most of the time), and only occasionally do they need to assertively pull control away from an errant developer, get them back on track, and then turn over the reins to them again. A good coach keeps reminding the team members about the way they agreed to act when everything first started. A coach might remind a programmer, "You agreed to share ownership of the code," or "You vowed to take the simplest approach first." Coaches try to bring out the best qualities in all of the other team members, while remaining in the background most of the time.

The next role we examine is that of consultant. The role of a consulting technical expert is a very odd one. If you are serving as a consultant to the team, they will ask you to solve the problem with them, badgering you all the while to challenge any assumptions that you are glossing over. What agile development teams want out of consultants is to learn how to solve their own problems. As they learn from you they grow confident again, and when you have left them they may or may not use the solution you presented, but be forewarned, this is typical.

The last role we consider for the agile development team is that of big boss. The team expects the big boss to demonstrate confidence in them, exhibit courage to adhere to the basic values and principles they have agreed to, and have the potential to point out a mistake if your team drifts off course. The team will want to keep communicating to you (even small changes from the design, or deviations from other goals). Your task as big boss is to figure out how to keep communication flowing without making it a tidal wave. Above all, you do not want to be an obstacle to anything reasonable the team is trying to do. This is a role that demands complete conviction to the agile approach, and a strong sense that if everyone on the team adheres to their basic values and principles, they will probably come up with something worthwhile.

The Planning Game The entire planning process has been characterized using the idea of a *planning game* (Beck, 2000, p. 86). The planning game spells out rules that can help formulate the agile development team's relationship with their business customers. Although the rules form an idea of how you want each party to act during development, they are not meant as a replacement for a relationship. They are a basis for building and maintaining a relationship.

So, we use the metaphor of a game. To that end we talk in terms of the goal of the game, the strategy to pursue, the pieces to move, and the players involved. The goal of the game is to maximize the value of the system produced by the agile team. In order to figure the value, you have to deduct costs of development, and the time, expense, and uncertainty taken on so that the development project could go forward.

The strategy pursued by the agile development team is always one of limiting uncertainty (downplaying risk). To do that they design the simplest solution possible, put the system into production as soon as possible, get feedback from the business customer about what's working, and adapt their design from there.

Story cards become the pieces in the planning game that briefly describe the task, provide notes, and provide an area for task tracking.

There are two main players in the planning game: the development team and the business customer. Deciding which business group in particular will be the business customer is not always easy, because the agile process is an unusually demanding role for the customer to play. Customers decide what the development team should tackle first. Their decisions will set priorities and check functionalities throughout the process.

How Project Risks Are Handled with the Agile Approach Up until now our discussion about extreme programming has focused on planning and how to adjust our resources as needed. It is important, however, to note that systems projects can and do have serious problems. Those that are developed using agile methods are not immune to such troubles. In order to illustrate what can go wrong in a project, a systems analyst may want to draw a fishbone diagram (also called a cause-and-effect diagram or an Ishikawa diagram). When you examine Figure 3.20, you will see that it is called a fishbone diagram because it resembles the skeleton of a fish.

The value of fishbone diagrams is to systematically list all of the possible problems that can occur. In the case of the agile approach, it is useful to organize the

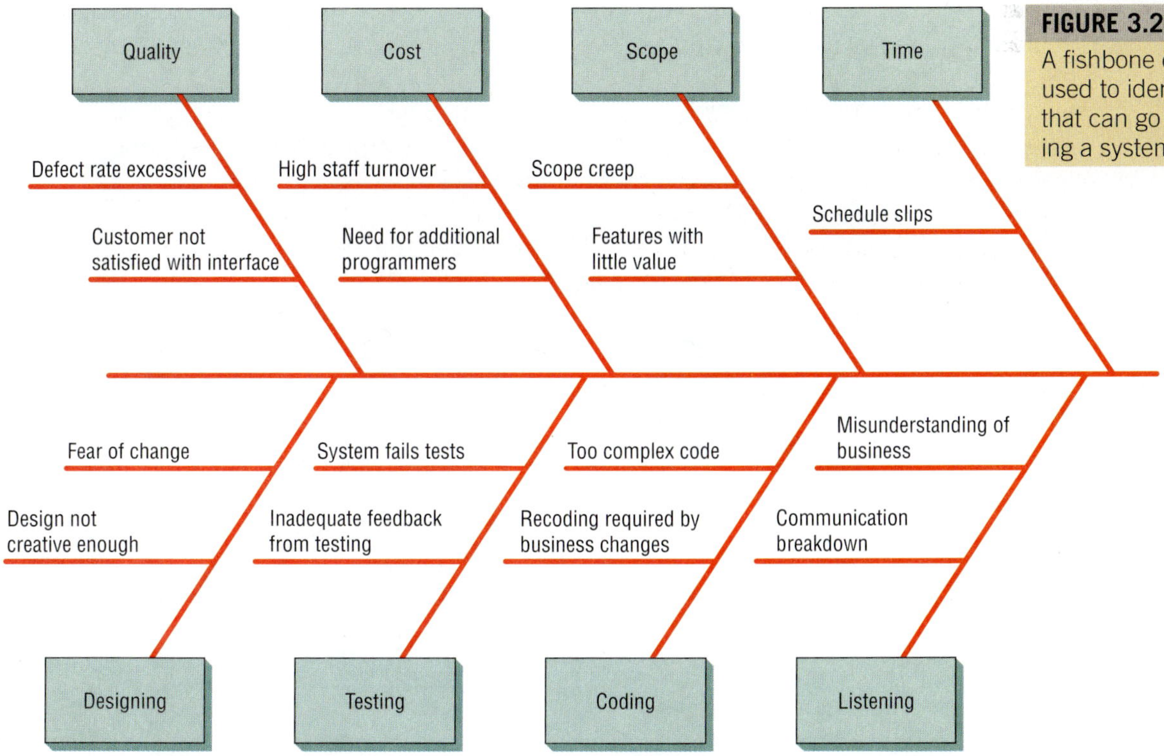

FIGURE 3.20
A fishbone diagram may be used to identify all the things that can go wrong in developing a system.

fishbone diagram by listing all of the resource control variables on the top and all of the activities on the bottom. Some problems such as schedule slips might be obvious, but others such as scope creep (the desire to add features after the analyst hears new stories) or developing features with little value are not as obvious.

Many of these problems can be avoided using the agile philosophy. Agile development has very short release cycles, so customers have ample opportunity to influence the design and help increase quality. Schedule slips are kept to a minimum. Pair programming helps maintain quality, reduce turnover, minimize scope creep, and keep defects to a minimum.

Listening and responding to customers' written and spoken stories minimizes situations in which a business is misunderstood. Having an onsite customer minimizes the chance that a project will be cancelled or the business will change dramatically without the agile team knowing it. In many ways extreme programming reduces potential problems. All in all, it is valuable to identify places where things may go wrong, but it is certainly not productive to fear them.

Many other developmental approaches would blame the analysts for problems due to lack of communication, a tendency toward complexity, or fear. However, the agile approach handles these situations by insisting that analysts and customers share values that enable them to stay away from these problems. There is more detail on these shared values in Chapter 6.

DEVELOPMENTAL PROCESS FOR AN AGILE PROJECT

There are activities and behaviors that shape the way development team members and customers act during the development of an agile project. Two words that characterize a project done with an agile approach are interactive and incremental. By examining Figure 3.21, you can see that there are five distinct stages: exploration,

FIGURE 3.21

The five stages of the agile modeling development process show that frequent iterations are essential to successful system development.

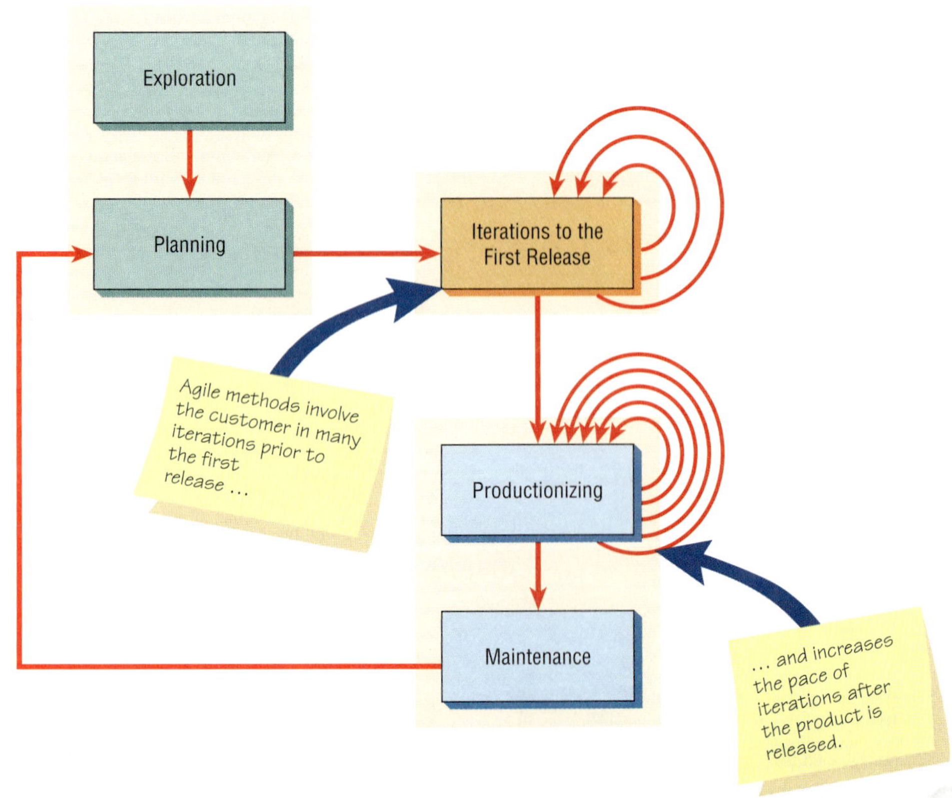

planning, iterations to the first release, productionizing, and maintenance. Notice that the three red arrows that loop back into the "Iterations" box symbolize incremental changes created through repeated testing and feedback that eventually lead to a stable but evolving system. Also note that there are multiple looping arrows that feed back into the productionizing phase. These symbolize that the pace of iterations is increased after a product is released. The red arrow is shown leaving the maintenance stage and returning to the planning stage, so that there is a continuous feedback loop involving customers and the development team as they agree to alter the evolving system.

During exploration, you will explore your environment, asserting your conviction that the problem can and should be approached with extreme programming, assemble the team, and assess team member skills. This stage will take anywhere from a few weeks (if you already know your team members and technology) to a few months (if everything is new). You also will be actively examining potential technologies needed to build the new system. During this stage you should practice estimating the time needed for a variety of tasks. In exploration, customers also are experimenting with writing user stories. The point is to get the customer to refine a story enough so that you can competently estimate the amount of time it will take to build the solution into the system you are planning. This stage is all about adopting a playful and curious attitude toward the work environment, its problems, technologies, and people.

The next stage of the agile development process is called planning. In contrast to the first stage, planning may only take a few days to accomplish. In this stage you and your customers agree on a date anywhere from two months to half a year from the current date to deliver solutions to their most pressing business problems (you will be addressing the smallest, most valuable set of stories). If your exploration activities were sufficient, this stage should be very short.

The third stage in the agile development process is composed of iterations to the first release. Typically these are iterations (cycles of testing, feedback, and change) of about three weeks in duration. You will be pushing yourself to sketch out the entire architecture of the system, even though it is just in outline or skeletal form. One goal is to run customer-written functional tests at the end of each iteration. During the iterations stage you should also question whether the schedule needs to be altered or whether you are tackling too many stories. Make small rituals out of each successful iteration, involving customers as well as developers. Always celebrate your progress, even if it is small, because this is part of the culture of motivating everyone to work extremely hard on the project.

When all iterations are complete, the system is ready to go to the next stage, known as productionizing. Several activities occur during this phase. In this phase the feedback cycle speeds up so that rather than receiving feedback for an iteration every three weeks, software revisions are being turned around in one week. You may institute daily briefings so everyone knows what everyone else is doing. The product is released in this phase, but may be improved by adding other features. Getting a system into production is an exciting event. Make time to celebrate with your teammates and mark the occasion. One of the watchwords of the agile approach, with which we heartily agree, is that it is supposed to be fun to develop systems!

The last stage we consider is maintenance. Once the system has been released, it needs to be kept running smoothly. New features may be added, riskier customer suggestions may be considered, and team members may be rotated on or off the team. The attitude you take at this point in the developmental process is more conservative than at any other time. You are now in a "keeper of the flame" mode rather than the playful one you experienced during exploration.

The philosophy behind the agile development approach is more than just planning and managing a systems project in extreme ways. It is about values and principles.

SUMMARY

The five major project management fundamentals that the systems analyst must handle are (1) project initiation, defining the problem (2) determining project feasibility, (3) activity planning and control, (4) project scheduling, and (5) managing systems analysis team members. Projects may be requested by many different people in the business or by systems analysts themselves. When faced with questions of how businesses can meet their goals and solve systems problems, the analyst creates a problem definition. A problem definition is a formal statement of the problem, including (1) the issues of the present situation, (2) the objectives for each issue, (3) the requirements that must be included in all proposed systems, and (4) the constraints that limit system development.

Selecting a project is a difficult decision, because more projects will be requested than can actually be done. Five important criteria for project selection are (1) that the requested project be backed by management, (2) that it be timed appropriately for a commitment of resources, (3) that it move the business toward attainment of its goals, (4) that it be practical, and (5) that it be important enough to be considered over other possible projects.

If a requested project meets these criteria, a feasibility study of its operational, technical, and economic merits can be done. Through the feasibility study, systems analysts gather data that enable management to decide whether to proceed with a full systems study. Project planning includes the estimation of time required for each of the analyst's activities, scheduling them, and expediting them if necessary to ensure that a project is completed on time. One technique available to the systems analyst for scheduling tasks is the Gantt chart, which displays activities as bars on a graph.

Another technique, called PERT (for Program Evaluation and Review Techniques), displays activities as arrows on a network. PERT helps the analyst determine the critical path and slack time, which is the information required for effective project control. The timeboxing approach uses an absolute due date for the project, and whatever has been accomplished by that due date is implemented. Function point analysis helps the analyst quantitatively estimate the overall length of the software development efforts.

Computer-based project scheduling using PCs is now practical. In addition, personal information managers can be used by analysts to do planning, create repositories for phone and fax numbers, or even launch other programs. Most PIMs can be synchronized with PIMs in Palm computers and other handheld devices, allowing for excellent portability.

Once a project has been judged feasible, the systems analyst must manage the team members and their activities, time, and resources. Such management is accomplished by communicating with team members. Teams are constantly seeking a balance between working on tasks and maintaining relationships in the team. Tensions arising from attempting to achieve this balance must be addressed. Often two leaders of a team will emerge, a task leader and a socioemotional leader. Members must periodically assess team norms to ensure that the norms are functional rather than dysfunctional for the attainment of team goals.

"I hope everyone you've encountered at MRE has treated you well. Here's a short review of some of the ways you can access our organization through HyperCase. The reception area at MRE contains the key links to the rest of our organization. Perhaps you've already discovered these on your own, but I wanted to remind you of them now, because I don't want to get so engrossed in the rest of our organizational problems that I forget to mention them.

"The telephone on the receptionist's desk has instructions about how to answer the phone in the rest of the organization. You have my permission to pick up the phone if it is ringing and no one else answers it.

"The empty doorway you see is a link to the next room, which we call the East Atrium. You have probably noticed that all open doorways are links to adjacent rooms. Notice the building map displayed in the reception area. You are free to go to public areas such as the canteen, but as you know, you must have an employee escort you into a private office. You cannot go there on your own.

"By now you have probably noticed the two documents and the computer on the small table in the reception area. The little one is the MRE internal phone directory. Just click on an employee name, and if that person is in, he or she will grant you an interview and a tour of the office. I leave you to your own devices in figuring out what the other document is.

"The computer on the table is on and displays the Web home page for MRE. You should take a look at the corporate page and visit all the links. It tells the story of our company and the people who work here. We're quite proud of it and have gotten positive feedback about it from visitors.

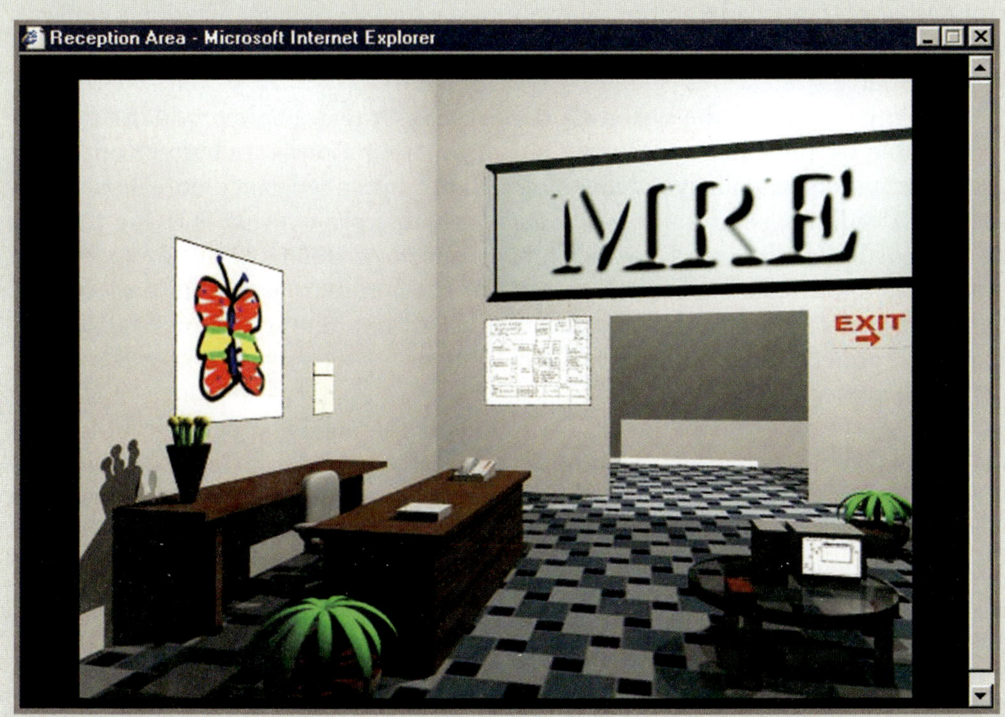

FIGURE 3.HC1

The reception room resembles a typical corporation. While you are in this HyperCase screen, find the directory if you want to visit someone.

(Continued)

"If you have had a chance to interview a few people and see how our company works, I'm sure you are becoming aware of some of the politics involved. We are also worried, though, about more technical issues, such as what constitutes feasibility for a training project and what does not."

HYPERCASE QUESTIONS

1. What criteria does the Training Unit use to judge the feasibility of a new project? List them.
2. List any changes or modifications to these criteria that you would recommend.
3. Snowden Evans has asked you to help prepare a proposal for a new project tracking system for the Training Unit. Briefly discuss the technical, economic, and operational feasibility of each alternative for a proposed project tracking system for the Training Unit.
4. Which option would you recommend? Use evidence from HyperCase to support your decision.

Managing ecommerce projects is similar to managing traditional IS projects in a number of ways, but there are four ways in which it departs significantly from these practices. The first is that the data you will be coordinating are scattered all over the organization (which has political ramifications); another is that specialized team members are drawn from across the organization (so organizational politics may also loom); a third is that the ecommerce project manager should be emphasizing strategic integration of ecommerce into all the organization's systems; and the fourth is that security concerns must be managed first when establishing an ecommerce site.

It is important that the systems analysis team set reasonable productivity goals for tangible outputs and process activities. Creating a project charter containing user expectations and analyst deliverables is recommended, since unrealistic management deadlines, adding unneeded personnel to a project that is trying to meet an unrealistic deadline, and not permitting developer teams to seek expert help outside their immediate group, were cited by programmers as reasons projects had failed. Project failures can usually be avoided by examining the motivations for requested projects, as well as your team's motives for recommending or avoiding a particular project.

One alternative to the SDLC is the agile approach. The agile development methodology adopts extreme techniques that can be used to manage projects and keep them on schedule. In the agile approach, the resources that an analyst has available must be balanced against the activities performed.

Agile development is different from other project development processes; it utilizes the practices of short releases, a 40-hour work week, an onsite customer, and pair programming. The seven different roles important in the agile development process are programmer, customer, tester, tracker, coach, consultant, and big boss.

In the agile approach, planning is accomplished by a technique called the planning game, which provides rules for the agile development team to follow when structuring their relationships with a customer. Five broad stages in the agile development process are exploration, planning, iterations to the first release, productionizing, and maintenance.

KEYWORDS AND PHRASES

- 40-hour work week
- agile approach
- computer-based project scheduling
- critical path
- ecommerce project management
- economic feasibility
- exploration phase
- extreme programming (XP)
- feasibility impact grid (FIG)
- function point analysis
- Gantt chart
- iterations to the first release phase
- maintenance phase
- onsite customer
- operational feasibility
- pair programming
- personal information managers (PIMs)
- PERT diagram
- planning phase
- problem definition
- productionizing phase
- productivity goals
- project charter
- short release
- socioemotional leader
- task leader
- team motivation
- team norms
- team process
- technical feasibility
- the planning game
- timeboxing

REVIEW QUESTIONS

1. What are the five major project fundamentals?
2. List three ways to find out about problems or opportunities that might call for a systems solution.
3. List the five criteria for systems project selection.
4. Examine the feasibility impact grid shown in Figure 3.3. List the corporate objectives that seem to be affected positively by ecommerce systems.
5. Define technical feasibility.
6. Define economic feasibility.
7. Define operational feasibility.
8. When is a two-dimensional Gantt chart more appropriate than a one-dimensional Gantt chart?
9. When is a PERT diagram useful for systems projects?
10. List three advantages of a PERT diagram over a Gantt chart for scheduling systems projects.
11. Define the term *critical path*.
12. Define the technique of timeboxing.
13. What is function point analysis?
14. Explain how different programming languages affect the time it takes to develop a system.
15. How does a project manager assess the risk of things going wrong and take that into consideration of the time needed to complete the project?
16. List the functions of computer-based project scheduling that are available in common software packages.
17. List the functions of some commonly used personal information manager (PIM) software.
18. List the two types of team leaders.
19. What is meant by a dysfunctional team norm?
20. What is meant by team process?
21. What are three reasons that goal setting seems to motivate systems analysis team members?
22. What are four ways in which ecommerce project management differs from traditional project management?

23. What are three reasons programmers cite for project failure?
24. What elements are contained in a project charter?
25. Name the four resource control variables used in the agile approach.
26. Name the four activities referred to in agile modeling.
27. Describe how control variables are used to balance activities so that agile projects are successful.
28. What are the four core practices of the agile modeling approach that distinguish it from other approaches to development?
29. What are seven roles that must be played during the agile development process?
30. What is the meaning of the phrase "the planning game"?
31. What are the stages in agile development?

PROBLEMS

1. Williwonk's Chocolates of St. Louis makes an assortment of chocolate candy and candy novelties. The company has six in-city stores, five stores in major metropolitan airports, and a small mail order branch. Williwonk's has a small, computerized information system that tracks inventory in its plant, helps schedule production, and so on, but this system is not tied directly into any of its retail outlets. The mail order system is handled manually.

   Recently, several Williwonk's stores experienced a rash of complaints from mail order customers that the candy was spoiled upon arrival, that it did not come when promised, or that it never arrived; the company also received several letters complaining that candy in various airports tasted stale. Williwonk's has been selling a new, low-carb, dietetic form of chocolate made with sugar-free, artificial sweetener. Sales have been brisk, but there have been problems shipping the wrong type of chocolate to an address with a diabetic person. There were a number of complaints and Williwonk's sent a number of free boxes of chocolate to ease the situation.

   Management would like to sell products using the Web but only has a few Web pages with information about the company and an order form that could be printed. Web ordering does not exist. One of the senior executives would like to sell customized chocolates with the name of a person on each piece. Although the production area has assured management that this could be easily done, there is no method to order customized chocolates.

   Another senior executive has mentioned that Williwonk's has partnered with several European chocolate manufacturers and will be importing chocolate from a variety of countries. At present, this must be done over the phone, with email, or by mail. The executive wants an internal Web site that will enable employees to order directly from the partner companies. All this has led a number of managers to request trend analysis. Too much inventory results in stale chocolate, while at other times there is a shortage of a certain kind of chocolate.

   Seasonal and holiday variation trends would help Williwonk's maintain an adequate inventory. The inventory control manager has insisted that all changes must be implemented before the next holiday season. "The time for this to be complete is an absolute due date," remarked Candy, a senior manager. "Make sure that everything works perfectly before the site goes public," she continues. "I don't want any customers receiving the wrong customers!" In addition, the order processing manager has mentioned that the system must be secure.

   You had been working for two weeks with Williwonk's on some minor modifications for its inventory information system when you overheard two

Description	Task	Must Follow	Time (Weeks)
Draw data flow	A	None	5
Draw decision tree	B	A	4
Revise tree	C	B	10
Write up project	D	C, I	4
Organize data dictionary	E	A	7
Do output prototype	F	None	2
Revise output design	G	F	9
Write use cases	H	None	10
Design database	I	H, E, and G	8

FIGURE 3.EX1
Data to help in the organization of a design project for creating an information system that tracks shipments of frozen foods to warehouses.

managers discussing these occurrences. List the possible opportunities or problems among them that might lend themselves to systems projects.

2. Where is most of the feedback on problems with Williwonk's products coming from in Problem 1? How reliable are the sources? Explain in a paragraph.
3. After getting to know them better, you have approached Williwonk's management people with your ideas on possible systems improvements that could address some of the problems or opportunities given in Problem 1.
   a. In two paragraphs, provide your suggestions for systems projects. Make any realistic assumptions necessary.
   b. Are there any problems or opportunities discussed in Problem 1 that are not suitable? Explain your response.
4. Create a problem definition for the Williwonk's, as described in Problem 1. Estimate the weights of importance. Include at least one requirement and one constraint.
5. Create a list of user requirements for the problem definition created in Problem 4.
6. Brian F. O'Byrne ("F," he says, stands for "frozen.") owns a frozen food company and wants to develop an information system for tracking shipments to warehouses.
   a. Using the data from the table in Figure 3.EX1, draw a Gantt chart to help Brian organize his design project.
   b. When is it appropriate to use a Gantt chart? What are the disadvantages? Explain in a paragraph.
7. In addition to a Gantt chart, you've drawn Brian a PERT diagram so that you can communicate the necessity to keep an eye on the critical path. Consult Figure 3.EX2, which was derived from the data from Problem 4. List all paths, and calculate and identify the critical path.
8. Cherry Jones owns a homeopathic medicine company called Faithhealers. She sells vitamins and other relatively nonperishable products for those who want choices regarding alternative medicine. Cherry is developing a new system that

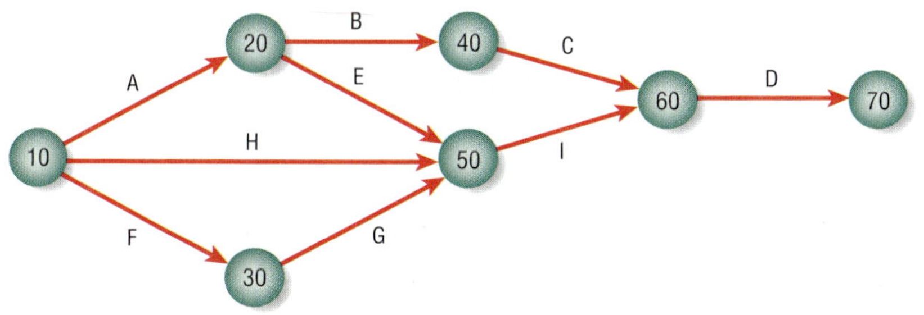

FIGURE 3.EX2
The PERT diagram from Brian's Frozen Foods.

FIGURE 3.EX3

Tasks to be performed during systems development of an order fulfillment system.

Description	Task	Must Follow	Time (Weeks)
Interview executives	A	None	6
Interview staff in order fulfillment	B	None	3
Design input prototype	C	B	2
Design output prototype	D	A, C	3
Write use cases	E	A, C	4
Record staff reactions to prototypes	F	D	2
Develop system	G	E, F	5
Write up training manual	H	B, G	3
Train staff working in order fulfillment	I	H	2

would require her staff to be retrained. Given the information in Figure 3.EX3, make a PERT diagram for her and identify the critical path. If Cherry could find a way to save time on the "write use cases" phase, would it help? Why or why not?

9. Angus McIndoe wants to modernize his popular restaurant by adapting it more closely to his the preferences of his repeat customers. Keeping track of his customers' likes and dislikes. Information such as where they like to sit, what they like to eat, when they normally arrive at the restaurant are all items of interest to him, since he believes that in this way he can better serve his customers. Angus has asked you to develop a system for him that will help make his customers happy while increasing his business.

   You have heard what Angus had to say about his customers. There are certainly more preferences that he can keep track of.

   Develop a problem definition for Angus, similar to one developed for Catherine's Catering in this chapter.

10. Michael Cerveris owns a business that distributes commercial barber and hairdresser equipment to a large group of independently owned shops across the country. He needs a system but is concerned about how long it will take to develop a working one.

    Use the following information, along with the example earlier in the book, to calculate the time it would take a team of analysts to develop an operational system.

    a. There are three external inputs. Input A references two files and four data elements. Input B references two files and eight data elements. Input C references four files and ten data elements. Using the table in step 1, look up the values for inputs A, B, and C. Are they low, average, or high?
    b. There are two external interface files. The first one contains three groups of elements consisting of 50 different data elements. The second contains six groups of elements consisting of 20 different data elements. Using the table in step 2, look up the values for the first and second external interface files. Are they low, average, or high?
    c. Using the information in parts a and b, plus the additional information in the table in Figure 3.EX4, calculate the total unadjusted function points using the table in step 3.

FIGURE 3.EX4

Some data to use in function point analysis for the commercial hairdresser equipment problem.

Component	Total Number	Low	Average	High
External inputs	See part a.			
External outputs	10	2	7	1
External queries	18	3	13	2
Internal logical files	15	3	8	4
External interface files	See part b.			

d. Assume the first three systems characteristics had no effect on the complexity of the system, but the remaining 11 had a strong effect (rating = 5) on the complexity. Calculate the value adjustment factor (VAF) using step 4.
e. Calculate the function point count using the formula in step 5.

11. Michael still needs to know how long it will take to complete the system. Taking the result you obtained in the previous problem, tell Michael how many months it would normally take to finish a system using:
    a. COBOL.
    b. C++ or Java.
    c. PowerBuilder.
12. Michael is razor sharp. You have just given him your estimate, but he asks you further questions about risk. He admits three possible problems that might delay the problem. Each delay would set the project back 40 days (eight work weeks). You feel that the risk is moderately low; perhaps 20 percent on the first two and only 10 percent on the third. How much time (in days) should be added to the project timetable for these possible delays?
13. Recently, two analysts just out of college have joined your systems analyst group at the newly formed company, Mega Phone. When talking to you about the group, they mention that some things strike them as odd. One is that group members seem to look up to two group leaders, Bill and Penny, not just one.

    Their observation is that Bill seems pretty relaxed, whereas Penny is always planning and scheduling activities. They have also observed that everyone "just seems to know what to do" when they get into a meeting, even though no instructions are given. Finally, they have remarked on the openness of the group in addressing problems as they arise, instead of letting things get out of hand.
    a. By way of explanation to the new team members, label the types of leaders Bill and Penny appear to be, respectively.
    b. Explain the statement that "everyone just seems to know what to do." What is guiding their behavior?
    c. What concept best describes the openness of the group that the new team members commented on?
14. Prepare a list of activities for a systems development team for an online travel agent that is setting up a Web site for customers. Now suppose you are running out of time. Describe some of your options. Describe what you will trade off to get the Web site released in time.
15. Given the situation for Williwonk's chocolates (Problem 1), which of the four agile modeling resource variables may be adjusted?

GROUP PROJECTS

1. With your group members, explore project management software such as Microsoft Project. What features are available? Work with your group to list them. Have your group evaluate the usefulness of the software for managing a systems analysis and design team project. In a paragraph, state whether the software you are evaluating facilitates team member communication and management of team activities, time, and resources. State which particular features support these aspects of any project. Note whether the software falls short of these criteria in any regard.
2. Within your group, assign some of the roles that people take on in agile development. Make sure that one person is an onsite customer and at least two people are programmers. Assign other roles, such as coach, as you see fit. Simulate

the systems development situation discussed in Problem 7, or have the person acting as the onsite customer choose an ecommerce business with which they are familiar. Assume that the customer wants to add some functionality to their Web site. Role-play a scenario showing what each person would do if this was being approached through agile methods. Write a paragraph that discusses the constraints that each person faces in enacting his or her role.

SELECTED BIBLIOGRAPHY

Adam, E. E., Jr., and R. J. Ebert. *Production and Operations Management*, 3d ed. Englewood Cliffs, NJ: Prentice Hall, 1986.

Bales, R. F. *Personality and Interpersonal Behavior.* New York: Holt, Rinehart and Winston, 1970.

Beck, K. *Extreme Programming Explained: Embrace Change.* Boston: Addison-Wesley Publishing Co., 2000.

Beck, K., and M. Fowler. *Planning Extreme Programming.* Boston: Addison-Wesley Publishing Co., 2001.

Construx Software Builders. Available at: www.construx.com. Accessed August 10, 2006.

Costar Web site. Available at: www.softstarsystems.com. Accessed August 8, 2006.

Glass, R. "Evolving a New Theory of Project Success." *Communications of the ACM*, Vol. 42, No. 11, 1999, pp. 17–19.

Linberg, K. R. "Software Perceptions about Software Project Failure: A Case Study." *Journal of Systems and Software*, Vol. 49, Nos. 2 and 3, 1999, pp. 177–92.

Longstreet Consulting. www.ifpug.org. Accessed August 14, 2006.

McBreen, P. *Questioning Extreme Programming*, Boston: Addison-Wesley Co., 2003.

Schein, E. H. *Process Consultation: Its Role in Organization Development.* Reading, MA: Addison-Wesley, 1969.

Shtub, A., J. F. Bard, and S. Globerson. *Project Management: Processes, Methodologies, and Economics*, 3d ed. Upper Saddle River, NJ: Pearson, 2005.

Software Product Research. Available at: www.spr.com/products/programming.shtm. Accessed August 11, 2006.

Walsh, B. "Your Network's Not Ready for E-Commerce." *Network Computing.* Available at: www.networkcomputing.com/922/922colwalsh.html. Last updated October 19, 1999.

Weinberg, G. M. *Rethinking Systems Analysis and Design.* Boston: Little, Brown, 1982.

Allen Schmidt, Julie E. Kendall, and Kenneth E. Kendall

GETTING TO KNOW U

Chip enters Anna's office one day, saying, "I think the project will be a good one, even though it's taking some long hours to get started."

Anna looks up from her screen and smiles. "I like what you've done in getting us organized," she says. "I hadn't realized Visible Analyst could help us this much with project management. I've decided to do a PERT diagram for the data gathering portion of the project. It should help us plan our time and work as a team on parallel activities."

"Can I take a look at the PERT diagram?" asks Chip.

Anna shows him a screen with a PERT diagram on it (see Figure E3.1) and remarks, "This will help immensely. It is much easier than planning haphazardly."

"I notice that you have Gather Reports, Gather Records and Data Capture Forms, and Gather Qualitative Documents as parallel tasks," notes Chip, gazing at the screen.

"Yes," replies Anna. "I thought that we would split up the time that it takes to gather the information. We can also divide up the task of analyzing what we have learned."

"I notice that you have a rather large number of days allocated for interviewing the users," notes Chip.

"Yes," replies Anna. "This activity also includes creating questions, sequencing them, and other tasks, such as taking notes of the office environment and analyzing them. I've also assumed a standard of six productive hours per day."

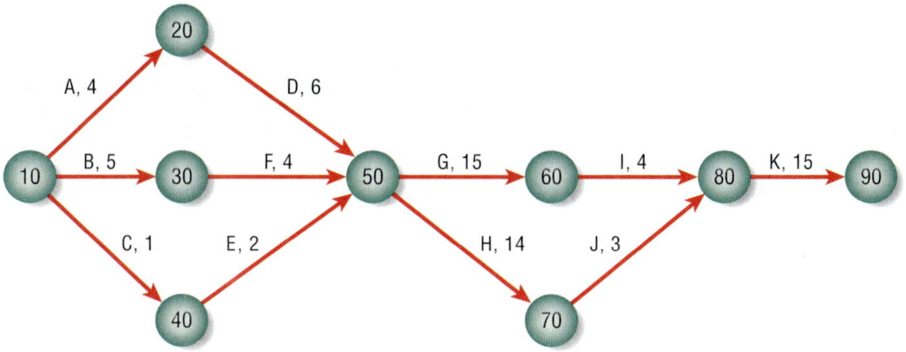

A Gather reports
B Gather records and data capture forms
C Gather qualitative documents
D Analyze reports
E Understand corporate culture
F Analyze records and forms
G Interview users
H Administer questionnaires
I Summarize interviews
J Summarize survey results
K Prototype system

FIGURE E3.1
A PERT diagram for Central Pacific University that is used for gathering information.

EPISODE 3 CPU CASE

Anna glances at her watch. "But now it's getting late. I think we've made a lot of progress in setting up our project. Let's call it a day, or should I say evening? Remember, I got us tickets for the football game."

Chip replies, "I haven't forgotten. Let me get my coat, and we'll walk over to the stadium together."

Walking across campus later, Chip says, "I'm excited. It's my first game here at CPU. What's the team mascot, anyway?"

"Chipmunks, of course," says Anna.

"And the team colors?" Chip asks, as they enter the stadium.

"Blue and white," Anna replies.

"Oh, that's why everyone's yelling, 'Go Big Blue!'" Chip says, listening to the roar of the crowd.

"Precisely," says Anna.

EXERCISES

E-1. Use Visible Analyst to view the Gathering Information PERT diagram.

E-2. List all paths and calculate and determine the critical path for the Gathering Information PERT diagram.

E-3. Use Visible Analyst to create the PERT diagram shown in Figure E3.2. It represents the activities involved in interviewing the users and observing their offices.

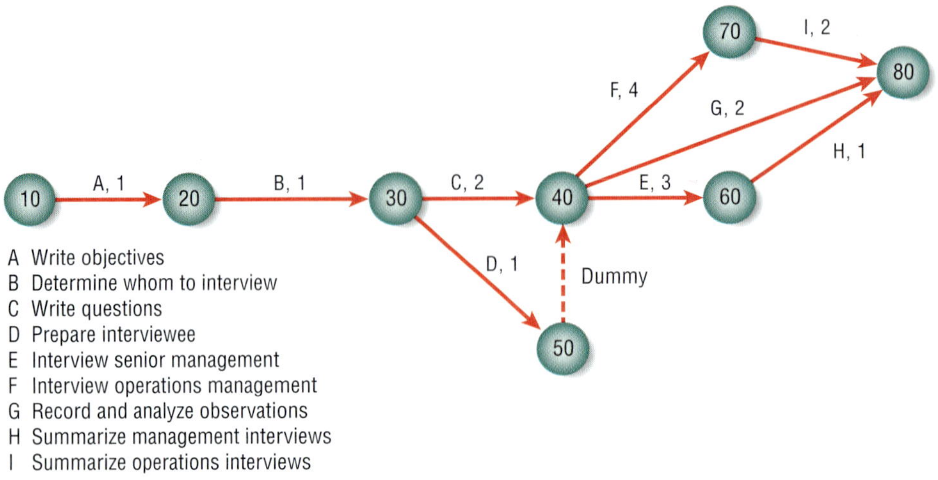

FIGURE E3.2
A PERT diagram for Central Pacific University that is used for interviewing users phase.

The exercises preceded by a Web icon indicate value-added material is available from the Web site at www.prenhall.com/kendall. Students can download a sample Visible Analyst Project and a Microsoft Access database that can be used to complete the exercises. Visible Analyst software can be packaged with this text for an additional fee.

E-4. List all paths and calculate and determine the critical path for the Interviewing Users PERT diagram.

E-5. Use Visible Analyst to create a PERT diagram for creating system prototypes. The activity information is shown in Figure E3.3.

Activity		Predecessor	Duration
A	Determine overall prototype screens and reports	None	2
B	Determine report and screen contents	A	4
C	Create report prototypes	B	3
D	Create screen prototypes	B	4
E	Obtain report prototype feedback	C	1
F	Obtain screen prototype feedback	D	2
G	Modify report prototypes	E	2
H	Modify screen prototypes	F	4
I	Obtain final approval	G, H	2

FIGURE E3.3
A list of activities and estimated duration times for the CPU project.

INFORMATION GATHERING: INTERACTIVE METHODS

4

LEARNING OBJECTIVES

Once you have mastered the material in this chapter you will be able to:

1. **Recognize the value of interactive methods for information gathering.**
2. **Construct interview questions to elicit human information requirements.**
3. **Structure interviews in a way that is meaningful to users.**
4. **Understand the concept of JAD and when to use it.**
5. **Write effective questions to survey users about their work.**
6. **Design and administer effective questionnaires.**

There are three key interactive methods that you can use to elicit human information requirements from organizational members. These three methods are interviewing, joint application design (JAD), and surveying people through questionnaires. Although different in their implementation, these methods have a great deal in common, too. The basis of their shared properties is talking with and listening to people in the organization to understand their interactions with technology through a series of carefully composed questions.

Each of the three interactive methods for information gathering possesses its own established process for you to follow in interacting with users. If followed, these systematic approaches will help ensure proper design and implementation of interviews, JAD workshops, and questionnaires, as well as support insightful analysis of the resulting data. Unobtrusive methods (sampling, investigation, and observing a decision maker's behavior and physical environment) that do not require the same degree of interactivity between analysts and users will be covered in an upcoming chapter. By using interactive methods with unobtrusive methods you will achieve a more complete portrait of the organization's information requirements.

INTERVIEWING

Before you interview someone else, you must in effect interview yourself. You need to know your biases and how they will affect your perceptions. Your education, intellect, upbringing, emotions, and ethical framework all serve as powerful filters for what you will be hearing in your interviews.

You need to think through the interview thoroughly before you go. Visualize why you are going, what you will ask, and what will make it a successful interview in your eyes. You must anticipate how to make the interview fulfilling for the individual you interview, as well.

An information gathering interview is a directed conversation with a specific purpose that uses a question-and-answer format. In the interview you want to get the opinions of the interviewee and his or her feelings about the current state of the system, organizational and personal goals, and informal procedures for interacting with information technologies.

Above all, seek the opinions of the person you are interviewing. Opinions may be more important and more revealing than facts. For example, imagine asking the owner of a traditional store who has recently added an online store how many customer refunds she typically gives for Web transactions each week. She replies, "About 20 to 25 a week." When you monitor the transactions and discover that the average is only 10.5 per week, you might conclude that the owner is overstating the facts and the problem.

Imagine instead that you ask the owner what her major concerns are and that she replies, "In my opinion, customer returns of goods purchased over the Web are way too high." By seeking opinions rather than facts, you discover a key problem that the owner wants addressed.

In addition to opinions, you should try to capture the feelings of the interviewee. Remember that the interviewee knows the organization better than you do. You can understand the organization's culture more fully by listening to the feelings of the respondent.

Goals are important information that can be gleaned from interviewing. Facts that you obtain from hard data may explain past performance, but goals project the organization's future. Try to find out as many of the organization's goals as possible from interviewing. You may not be able to determine goals through any other data gathering methods.

The interview is also a valuable time to explore key HCI (human–computer interaction) concerns, including the ergonomic aspects, the system usability, how pleasing and enjoyable the system is, and how useful it is in supporting individual tasks.

In the interview you are setting up a relationship with someone who is probably a stranger to you. You need to build trust and understanding quickly, but at the same time you must maintain control of the interview. You also need to sell the system by providing needed information to your interviewee. Do so by planning for the interview before you go so that conducting it is second nature to you. Fortunately, effective interviewing can be learned. As you practice, you will see yourself improving. Later in the chapter we discuss joint application design (JAD) (pronounced as one word, jăd, rhymes with add), which can serve as an alternative to one-on-one interviewing in certain situations.

FIVE STEPS IN INTERVIEW PREPARATION

The five major steps in interview preparation are shown in Figure 4.1. These steps include a range of activities from gathering basic background material to deciding who to interview.

Read Background Material Read and understand as much background information about the interviewees and their organization as possible. This material can often be obtained on the corporate Web site, from a current annual report, a corporate newsletter, or any publications sent out to explain the organization to the

Steps in Planning the Interview

1. Read background material.
2. Establish interviewing objectives.
3. Decide whom to interview.
4. Prepare the interviewee.
5. Decide on question types and structure.

FIGURE 4.1
Steps the systems analyst follows in planning the interview.

public. Check the Internet for any corporate information such as that in Standard and Poor's.

As you read through this material, be particularly sensitive to the language the organizational members use in describing themselves and their organization. What you are trying to do is build up a common vocabulary that will eventually enable you to phrase interview questions in a way that is understandable to your interviewee. Another benefit of researching your organization is to maximize the time you spend in interviews; without such preparation you may waste time asking general background questions.

Establish Interviewing Objectives Use the background information you gathered as well as your own experience to establish interview objectives. There should be four to six key areas concerning HCI, information processing, and decision-making behavior about which you will want to ask questions. These areas include HCI concerns (the usefulness and usability of the system; how it fits physical aspects; how it suits a user's cognitive capabilities, whether it is engaging or aesthetically pleasing; and whether using the system is rewarded with desired consequences), information sources, information formats, decision-making frequency, qualities of information, and decision-making style.

Decide Whom to Interview When deciding whom to interview, include key people at all levels who will be affected by the system in some manner. Strive for balance so that as many users' needs are addressed as possible. Your organizational contact will also have some ideas about whom should be interviewed.

Prepare the Interviewee Prepare the person to be interviewed by calling ahead or sending an email message and allowing the interviewee time to think about the interview. If you are doing an in-depth interview, it is permissible to email your questions ahead of time to allow your interviewee time to think over their responses. Because there are many objectives to fulfill in the interview (including building trust and observing the workplace), however, interviews should typically be conducted in person and not via email. Interviews should be kept to 45 minutes or an hour at the most. No matter how much your interviewees seem to want to extend the interview beyond this limit, remember that when they spend time with you, they are not doing their work. If interviews go over an hour, it is likely that the interviewees will resent the intrusion, whether or not they articulate their resentment.

Decide on Question Types and Structure Write questions to cover the key areas of HCI and decision making that you discovered when you ascertained interview objectives. Proper questioning techniques are the heart of interviewing. Questions have some basic forms you need to know. The two basic question types are open-ended and closed. Each question type can accomplish something a little different from the other, and each has benefits and drawbacks. You need to think about the effect each question type will have.

FIGURE 4.2

Open-ended interview questions allow the respondent open options for responding. The examples were selected from different interviews and are not shown in any particular order.

Open-Ended Interview Questions

- What's your opinion of the current state of business-to-business ecommerce in your firm?
- What are the critical objectives of your department?
- Once the data are submitted via the Web site, how are they processed?
- Describe the monitoring process that is available online.
- What are some of the common data entry errors made in this department?
- What are the biggest frustrations you've experienced during the transition to ecommerce?

It is possible to structure your interview in three different patterns: a pyramid structure, a funnel structure, or a diamond structure. Each is appropriate under different conditions and serves a different function, and each one is discussed later in this chapter.

QUESTION TYPES

Open-Ended Questions Open-ended questions include those such as "What do you think about putting all the managers on an intranet?" "Please explain how you make a scheduling decision." "In what ways does the system extend your capability to do tasks that would not be possible otherwise?" Consider the term *open-ended.* "Open" actually describes the interviewee's options for responding. They are open. The response can be two words or two paragraphs. Some examples of open-ended questions are found in Figure 4.2.

The benefits of using open-ended questions are numerous and include the following:

1. Putting the interviewee at ease.
2. Allowing the interviewer to pick up on the interviewee's vocabulary, which reflects their education, values, attitudes, and beliefs.
3. Providing richness of detail.
4. Revealing avenues of further questioning that may have gone untapped.
5. Making it more interesting for the interviewee.
6. Allowing more spontaneity.
7. Making phrasing easier for the interviewer.
8. Using them in a pinch if the interviewer is caught unprepared.

As you can see, there are several advantages to using open-ended questions. There are, however, also many drawbacks:

1. Asking questions that may result in too much irrelevant detail.
2. Possibly losing control of the interview.
3. Allowing responses that may take too much time for the amount of useful information gained.
4. Potentially seeming that the interviewer is unprepared.
5. Possibly giving the impression that the interviewer is on a "fishing expedition" with no real objective for the interview.

You must carefully consider the implications of using open-ended questions for interviewing.

Closed Questions The alternative to open-ended questions is found in the other basic question type: closed questions. Such questions are of the basic form "Is it

Closed Interview Questions

- How many times a week is the project repository updated?
- On average, how many calls does the call center receive monthly?
- Which of the following sources of information is most valuable to you?
  - Completed customer complaint forms
  - Email complaints from consumers who visit the Web site
  - Face-to-face interaction with customers
  - Returned merchandise
- List your top two priorities for improving the technology infrastructure.
- Who receives this input?

FIGURE 4.3
Closed interview questions limits the respondents options. The examples were selected from different interviews and are not shown in any particular order.

easy to use the current system?" and, "How many subordinates do you have?" The possible responses are closed to the interviewee, because he or she can only reply with a finite number such as "None," "One," or "Fifteen." Some examples of closed questions can be found in Figure 4.3.

A closed question limits the response available to the interviewee. You may be familiar with closed questions through multiple-choice exams in college. You are given a question and five responses, but you are not allowed to write down your own response and still be counted as having correctly answered the question.

A special kind of closed question is the bipolar question. This type of question limits the interviewee even further by only allowing a choice on either pole, such as yes or no, true or false, agree or disagree. Examples of bipolar questions can be found in Figure 4.4.

The benefits of using closed questions of either type include the following:

1. Saving time.
2. Easily comparing interviews.
3. Getting to the point.
4. Keeping control over the interview.
5. Covering lots of ground quickly.
6. Getting to relevant data.

The drawbacks of using closed questions are substantial, however. They include the following:

1. Being boring for the interviewee.
2. Failing to obtain rich detail (because the interviewer supplies the frame of reference for the interviewee).
3. Missing main ideas for the preceding reason.
4. Failing to build rapport between interviewer and interviewee.

Thus, as the interviewer, you must think carefully about the question types you will use.

Bipolar Interview Questions

- Do you use the Web to provide information to vendors?
- Do you agree or disagree that ecommerce on the Web lacks security?
- Do you want to receive a printout of your account status every month?
- Does your Web site maintain a FAQ page for employees with payroll questions?
- Is this form complete?

FIGURE 4.4
Bipolar interview questions are a special kind of closed question. The examples were selected from different interviews and are not shown in any particular order.

FIGURE 4.5
Attributes of open-ended and closed questions.

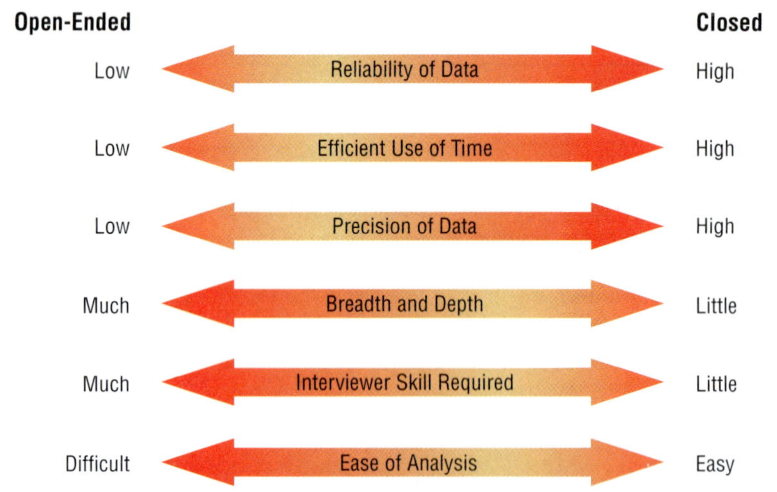

Both open-ended and closed questions have advantages and drawbacks, as shown in Figure 4.5. Notice that choosing one question type over the other actually involves a trade-off; although an open-ended question affords breadth and depth of reply, responses to open-ended questions are difficult to analyze.

Probes A third type of question is the probe or follow-up. The strongest probe is the simplest: the question, "Why?" Other probes are "Can you give me an example of a time you did not find the system trustworthy?" and "Will you elaborate on that for me?" Some examples of probing questions can be found in Figure 4.6. The purpose of the probe is to go beyond the initial answer to get more meaning, to clarify, and to draw out and expand on the interviewee's point. Probes may be either open-ended or closed questions.

It is essential to probe. Most beginning interviewers are reticent about probing and consequently accept superficial answers. They are usually grateful that employees have granted interviews and feel somewhat obligated to accept unqualified statements politely.

ARRANGING QUESTIONS IN A LOGICAL SEQUENCE

Just as there are two generally recognized ways of reasoning—inductive and deductive—there are two similar ways of organizing your interviews. A third way combines both inductive and deductive patterns.

Using a Pyramid Structure Inductive organization of interview questions can be visualized as having a pyramid shape. Using this form, the interviewer begins with

FIGURE 4.6
Probes allow the systems analyst to follow up on questions to get more detailed responses. The examples were selected from different interviews and are not shown in any particular order.

Probes

- Why?
- Give an example of how ecommerce has been integrated into your business processes.
- Please give an illustration of the security problems you are experiencing with your online bill payment system.
- You mentioned both an intranet and an extranet solution. Please give an example of how you think each differs.
- What makes you feel that way?
- Tell me step by step what happens after a customer clicks the "Submit" button on the Web registration form.

CONSULTING OPPORTUNITY 4.1

STRENGTHENING YOUR QUESTION TYPES

Strongbodies, a large, local chain of sports clubs, has experienced phenomenal growth in the past five years. Management would like to refine its decision-making process for purchasing new bodybuilding equipment. Currently, managers listen to customers, attend trade shows, look at advertisements, and put in requests for new equipment purchases based on their subjective perceptions. These are then approved or denied by Harry Mussels.

Harry is the first person you will interview. He is a 37-year-old division manager who runs five area clubs. He travels all over the city to their widespread locations. He keeps an office at the East location, although he is there less than a quarter of the time.

In addition, when Harry is present at a club, he is busy answering business-related phone calls, solving on-the-spot problems presented by managers, and interacting with club members. His time is short, and to compensate for that he has become an extremely well-organized, efficient divisional manager. He cannot grant you a lot of interview time. However, his input is important, and he feels he would be the main beneficiary of the proposed system.

What type of interview question might be most suitable for your interview with Harry? Why is this type most appropriate? How will your choice of question type affect the amount of time you spend in preparation for interviewing Harry? Write 5 to 10 questions of this type. What other techniques might you use to supplement information unavailable through that type of question? Write a paragraph to explain.

very detailed, often closed, questions. The interviewer then expands the topics by allowing open-ended questions and more generalized responses, as shown in Figure 4.7.

A pyramid structure should be used if you believe your interviewee needs to warm up to the topic. Using a pyramid structure for question sequencing is also useful when you want an ending determination about the topic. Such is the case in the final question, "In general, how do you feel about security of data versus the importance of Internet access?"

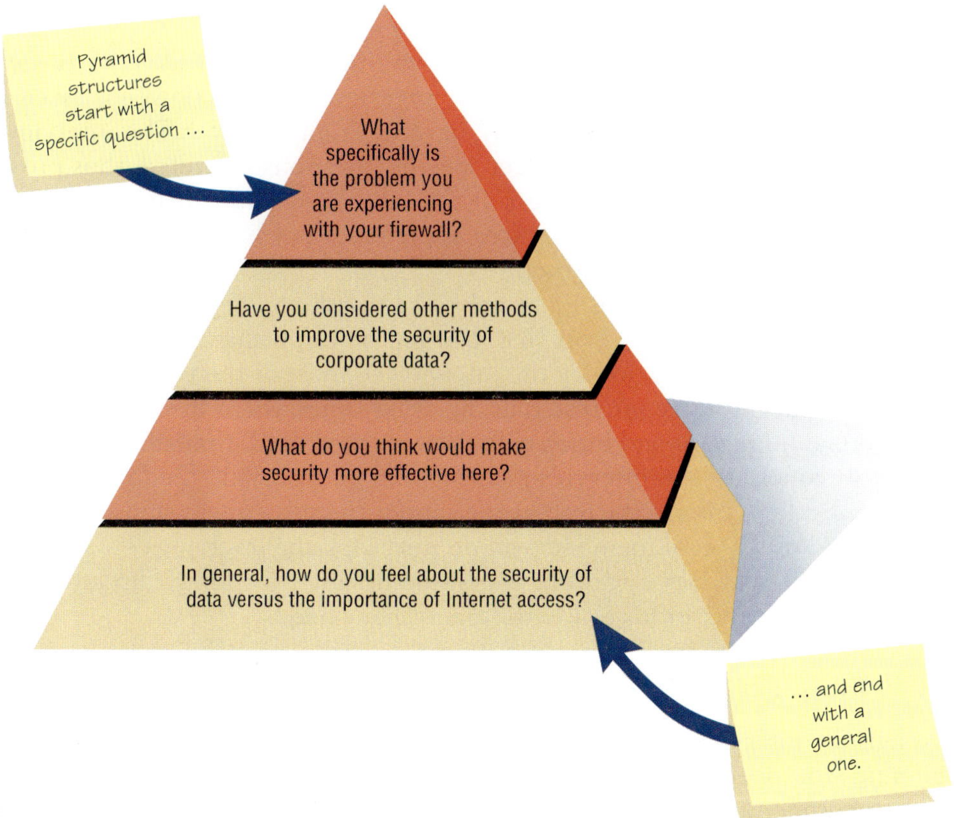

FIGURE 4.7
Pyramid structure for interviewing goes from specific to general questions.

FIGURE 4.8

Funnel structure for interviewing begins with broad questions, then funnels to specific questions.

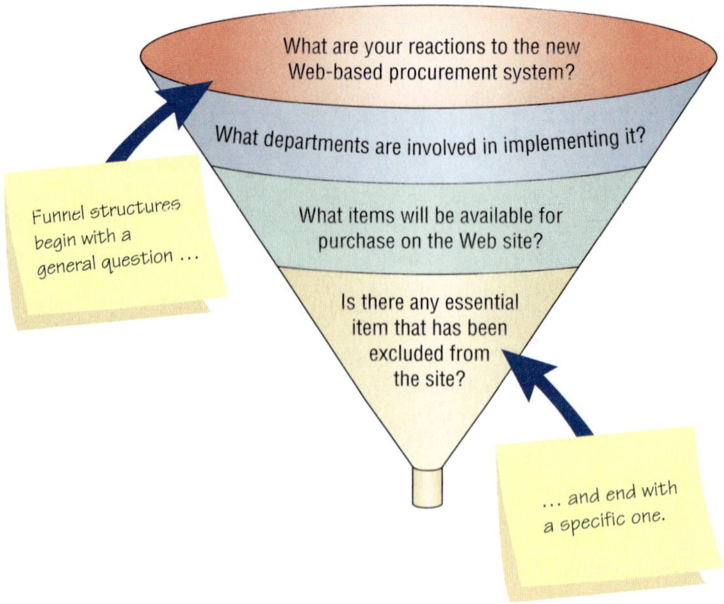

Using a Funnel Structure In the second kind of structure, the interviewer takes a deductive approach by beginning with generalized, open-ended questions and then narrowing the possible responses by using closed questions. This interview structure can be thought of as funnel shaped, as that depicted in Figure 4.8. Using the funnel structure method provides an easy, nonthreatening way to begin an interview. A funnel-shaped question sequence is also useful when the interviewee feels emotional about the topic and needs freedom to express those emotions.

Using a Diamond-Shaped Structure Often a combination of the two structures, resulting in a diamond-shaped interview structure, is best. This structure entails beginning in a very specific way, then examining general issues, and finally coming to a very specific conclusion, as shown in Figure 4.9.

The interviewer begins with easy, closed questions that provide a warm-up to the interview process. In the middle of the interview, the interviewee is asked for opinions on broad topics that obviously have no "right" answer. The interviewer then narrows the questions again to get specific questions answered, thus providing closure for both the interviewee and the interviewer. The diamond structure combines the strengths of the other two approaches but has the disadvantage of taking longer than either other structure.

The end of the interview is a natural place to ask one key question: "Is there anything we haven't touched on that you feel is important for me to know?" Considered a formula question by the interviewee most of the time, the response will often be "No." You are interested in the other times, when this question opens the proverbial floodgates and much new data are presented, though.

As you conclude the interview, summarize and provide feedback on your overall impressions. Inform the interviewee about the subsequent steps to take and what you and other team members will do next. Ask the interviewee with whom you should talk next. Set up future appointment times for follow-up interviews, thank the interviewee for his or her time, and shake hands.

WRITING THE INTERVIEW REPORT

Although the interview itself is complete, your work on the interview data is just beginning. You need to capture the essence of the interview through a written report. It is imperative that you write the interview report as soon as possible after

CONSULTING OPPORTUNITY 4.2

SKIMMING THE SURFACE

You are about to leave SureCheck Dairy after a preliminary tour when another member of your systems analysis team calls you at the dairy to say he cannot make his interview appointment with the plant manager because of illness. The plant manager is extremely busy, and you want to keep his enthusiasm for the project going by doing things as scheduled. You also realize that without the initial interview data, the rest of your data gathering will be slowed. Although you have no interview questions prepared, you make the decision to go ahead and interview the plant manager on the spot.

You have learned that SureCheck is interested in processing its own data on quantities and kinds of dairy products sold so that its people can use that information to better control production of the company's large product line (it includes whole, skim, 2 percent, and 1 percent milk, half-and-half, cottage cheese, yogurt, and frozen novelties). Sales managers are currently sending their sales figures to corporate headquarters, 600 miles away, and processing turnaround seems slow. You will base your ad-libbed questions on what you have just found out on the tour.

In the few minutes before your interview begins, decide on a structure for it: funnel, pyramid, or diamond. In a paragraph, justify why you would proceed with the interview structure you have chosen based on the unusual context of this interview. Write a series of questions and organize them in the structure you have chosen.

the interview. This step is another way you can ensure quality of interview data. The longer you wait to write up your interview, the more suspect the quality of your data becomes.

After this initial summary, go into more detail, noting main points of the interview and your own opinions. Review the interview report with the respondent at a

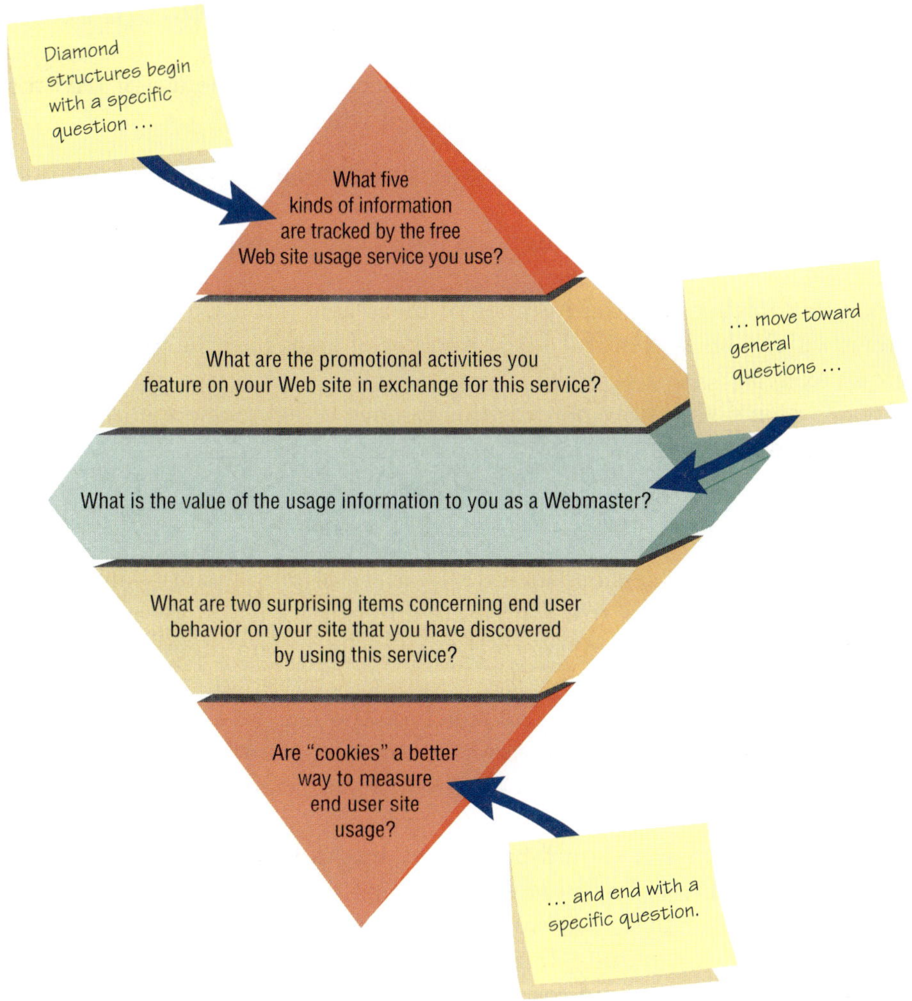

FIGURE 4.9
Diamond-shaped structure for interviewing combines the pyramid and funnel structures.

follow-up meeting. This step helps clarify the meaning the interviewee had in mind and lets the interviewee know that you are interested enough to take the time to understand their point of view and perceptions.

JOINT APPLICATION DESIGN

No matter how adept you become as an interviewer, you will inevitably experience situations in which one-on-one interviews do not seem to be as useful as you would like. Personal interviews are time consuming and subject to error, and their data are prone to misinterpretation. An alternative approach to interviewing users one by one, called joint application design (JAD), was developed by IBM. The motivation for using JAD is to cut the time (and hence the cost) required by personal interviews, to improve the quality of the results of information requirements assessment, and to create more user identification with new information systems as a result of the participative processes.

Although JAD can be substituted for personal interviews at any appropriate juncture during the systems development life cycle, it has usually been employed as a technique that allows you, as a systems analyst, to accomplish requirements analysis and to design the user interface jointly with users in a group setting. The many intricacies of this approach can only be learned in a paid seminar demonstrating proprietary methods. We can, however, convey enough information about JAD here to make you aware of some of its benefits and drawbacks in comparison with one-on-one interviews.

CONDITIONS THAT SUPPORT THE USE OF JAD

The following list of conditions will help you decide when the use of JAD may be fruitful. Consider using joint application design when:

1. User groups are restless and want something new, not a standard solution to a typical problem.
2. The organizational culture supports joint problem-solving behaviors among multiple levels of employees.
3. Analysts forecast that the number of ideas generated via one-on-one interviews will not be as plentiful as the number of ideas possible from an extended group exercise.
4. Organizational workflow permits the absence of key personnel during a two-to-four-day block of time.

WHO IS INVOLVED

Joint application design sessions include a variety of participants—analysts, users, executives, and so on—who will contribute differing backgrounds and skills to the sessions. Your primary concern here is that all project team members are committed to the JAD approach and become involved. Choose an executive sponsor, a senior person who will introduce and conclude the JAD session. Preferably, select an executive from the user group who has some sort of authority over the IS people working on the project. This person will be an important, visible symbol of organizational commitment to the systems project.

At least one IS analyst should be present, but the analyst usually takes a passive role, unlike traditional interviewing in which the analyst controls the interaction. As the project analyst, you should be present during JAD to listen to what users say and what they require. In addition, you will want to give an expert opinion about any disproportionate costs of solutions proposed during the JAD session

HYPERCASE® EXPERIENCE 4.1

"Well, I did warn you that things weren't always smooth here at MRE. By now you've met many of our key employees and are starting to understand the 'lay of the land.' Who would have thought that some innocent decisions about hardware, like whether to buy a COMTEX or Shiroma, would cause such hostility? Well, live and learn, I always say. At least now you'll know what you're up against when you have to start recommending hardware!

"It's funny that not all questions are created equal. I myself favor asking open-ended questions, but when I have to answer them, it is not always easy. Have you been taking the opportunity to view people's offices when you've been in there to do your interviews? You can learn a lot more by using a structured observation method such as STROBE."

HYPERCASE QUESTIONS

1. Using the interview questions posed in HyperCase, give five examples of open-ended questions and five examples of closed questions. Explain why your examples are correctly classified as either open-ended or closed question types.
2. List three probing questions that are part of the HyperCase interviews. In particular, what did you learn by following up on the questions you asked Snowden Evans?

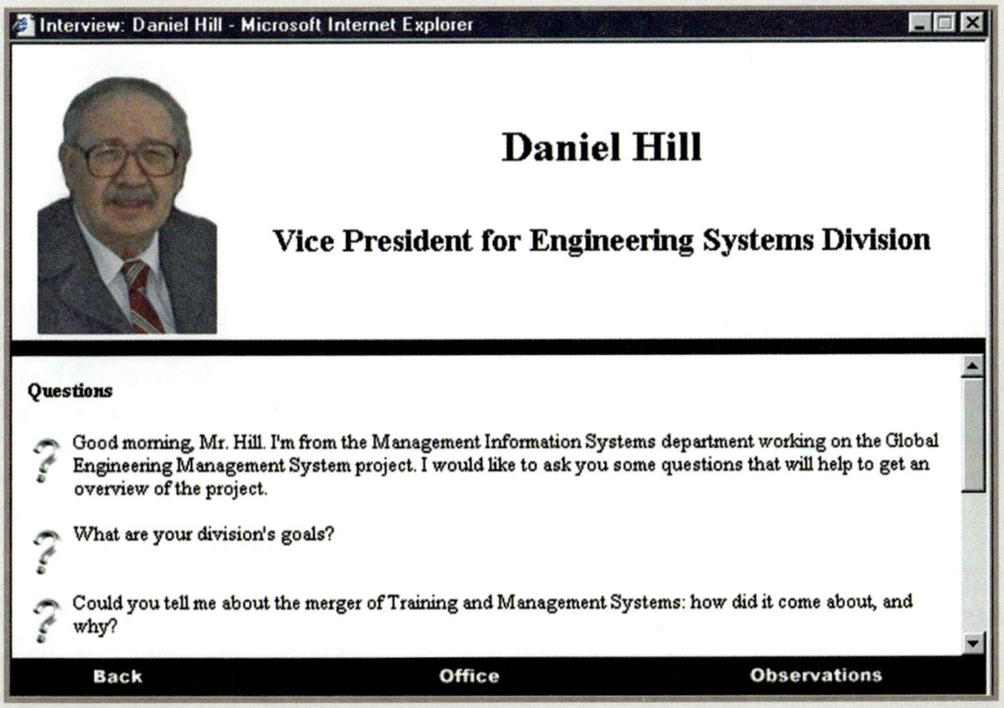

FIGURE 4.HC1

Pointing to a question in HyperCase will reveal an answer.

itself. Without this kind of immediate feedback, unrealistic solutions with excessive costs may creep into the proposal and prove costly to discourage later on.

From eight to a dozen users can be chosen from any rank to participate in JAD sessions. Try to select users who can articulate what information they need to perform their jobs as well as what they desire in a new or improved computer system.

The session leader should not be an expert in systems analysis and design but rather someone who has excellent communication skills to facilitate appropriate interactions. Note that you do not want to use a session leader who reports to another person in the group. To avoid this possibility, an organization may want to retain an outside management consultant to serve as session leader. The point is to get a person who can bring the group's attention to bear on important systems issues, satisfactorily negotiate and resolve conflicts, and help group members reach a consensus.

Your JAD session should also include one or two observers who are analysts or technical experts from other functional areas to offer technical explanations and advice to the group during the sessions. In addition, one scribe from the IS department should attend the JAD sessions to formally write down everything that is done.

WHERE TO HOLD JAD MEETINGS

If at all possible, we recommend holding the two-to-four-day sessions offsite, away from the organization, in comfortable surroundings. Some groups use executive centers or even group decision support facilities that are available at major universities. The idea is to minimize the daily distractions and responsibilities of the participants' regular work. The room itself should comfortably hold the number of people invited. Minimal presentation support equipment includes two overhead projectors, a whiteboard, a flip chart, and easy access to a copier. Group decision support rooms will also provide networked PCs, a projection system, and software written to facilitate group interaction while minimizing unproductive group behaviors.

Schedule your JAD session when all participants can commit to attending. Do not hold the sessions unless everyone who has been invited can actually attend. This rule is critical to the success of the sessions. Ensure that all participants receive an agenda before the meeting, and consider holding an orientation meeting for a half-day one week or so before the workshop so that those involved know what is expected of them. Such a premeeting allows you to move rapidly and act confidently once the actual meeting is convened.

ACCOMPLISHING A STRUCTURED ANALYSIS OF PROJECT ACTIVITIES

IBM recommends that the JAD sessions examine these points in the proposed systems project: planning, receiving, receipt processing/tracking, monitoring and assigning, processing, recording, sending, and evaluating. For each topic, the questions who, what, how, where, and why should also be asked and answered. Clearly, ad hoc interactive systems such as decision support systems and other types of systems dependent on decision-maker style (including prototype systems) are not as easily analyzed with the structured approach of JAD.

As the analyst involved with the JAD sessions, you should receive the notes of the scribe and prepare a specifications document based on what happened at the meeting. Systematically present the management objectives as well as the scope and boundaries of the project. Specifics of the system, including details on screen and report layouts, should also be included.

CONSULTING OPPORTUNITY 4.3

A SYSTEMS ANALYST, I PRESUME?

"Know what I think of the work the last systems analyst team did? The printouts created are a jungle. To figure out the cost of raw materials to us, I have to cut my way through the overgrowth of data, hacking my path with a pen. I cross out everything that's irrelevant. Sometimes I physically rip out the excess vegetation until I reach the numbers I need," says Henry Stanley, accounting supervisor for Zenith Glass Company. As you interview him, he points unhappily to an untidy stack of mutilated printouts sprouting beside his desk.

Identify the overriding metaphor Henry is using to describe the printouts he is receiving and the accessibility of information in them. In a paragraph, describe how this step helps you understand Henry's attitude toward any work proposed by your systems analysis team. In a paragraph, adopt Henry's metaphor and extend it in a more positive sense during your interview with him.

POTENTIAL BENEFITS OF USING JAD IN PLACE OF TRADITIONAL INTERVIEWING

There are four major potential benefits that you, the users, and your systems analysis team should consider when you weigh the possibilities of using joint application design. The first potential benefit is time savings over traditional one-on-one interviews. Some organizations have estimated that JAD sessions have provided a 15-percent time savings over the traditional approach.

Hand-in-hand with time savings is the rapid development possible via JAD. Because user interviews are not accomplished serially over a period of weeks or months, the development can proceed much more quickly.

A third benefit to weigh is the possibility of improved ownership of the information system. As analysts, we are always striving to involve users in meaningful ways and to encourage users to take early ownership of the systems we are designing. Due to its interactive nature and high visibility, JAD helps users become involved early in systems projects and treats their feedback seriously. Working through a JAD session eventually helps reflect user ideas in the final design.

A final benefit of participating in JAD sessions is the creative development of designs. The interactive character of JAD has a great deal in common with brainstorming techniques that generate new ideas and new combinations of ideas because of the dynamic and stimulating environment. Designs can evolve through facilitated interactions, rather than in relative isolation.

POTENTIAL DRAWBACKS OF USING JAD

There are three drawbacks or pitfalls that you should also weigh when making a decision on whether to do traditional one-on-one interviews or to use joint application design. The first drawback is that JAD requires the commitment of a large block of time from all participants. Because JAD requires a two-to-four-day commitment, it is not possible to do any other activities concurrently or to time-shift any activities, as is typically done in one-on-one interviewing.

A second pitfall occurs if preparation for the JAD sessions is inadequate in any regard or if the follow-up report and documentation of specifications is incomplete. In these instances resulting designs could be less than satisfactory. Many variables need to come together correctly for JAD to be successful. Conversely, many things can go wrong. The success of designs resulting from JAD sessions is less predictable than that achieved through standard interviews.

Finally, the necessary organizational skills and organizational culture may not be sufficiently developed to enable the concerted effort required to be productive in a JAD setting. In the end you will have to judge whether the organization is truly committed to, and prepared for, this approach.

USING QUESTIONNAIRES

The use of questionnaires is an information gathering technique that allows systems analysts to study attitudes, beliefs, behavior, and characteristics of several key people in the organization who may be affected by the current and proposed systems. Attitudes are what people in the organization say they want (in a new system, for instance); beliefs are what people think is actually true; behavior is what organizational members do; and characteristics are properties of people or things.

Responses gained through questionnaires (also called surveys) using closed questions can be quantified. If you are surveying people via email or the Web, you can use software to turn electronic responses directly into data tables for analysis using a spreadsheet application or statistical software packages. Responses to questionnaires using open-ended questions are analyzed and interpreted in other ways. Answers to questions on attitudes and beliefs are sensitive to the wording chosen by the systems analyst.

Through the use of questionnaires, the analyst may be seeking to quantify what was found in interviews. In addition, questionnaires may be used to determine how widespread or limited a sentiment expressed in an interview really is. Conversely, questionnaires can be used to survey a large sample of system users to sense problems or raise important issues before interviews are scheduled.

Throughout this chapter, we compare and contrast questionnaires with interviews. There are many similarities between the two techniques, and perhaps the ideal would be to use them in conjunction with each other, either following up unclear questionnaire responses with an interview or designing the questionnaire based on what is discovered in the interview. Each technique, however, has its own specific functions, and it is not always necessary or desirable to use both.

PLANNING FOR THE USE OF QUESTIONNAIRES

At first glance questionnaires may seem to be a quick way to gather massive amounts of data about how users assess the current system, about what problems they are experiencing with their work, and about what people expect from a new or modified system. Although it is true that you can gather a lot of information through questionnaires without spending time in face-to-face interviews, developing a useful questionnaire takes extensive planning time in its own right. When you decide to survey users via email or the Web, you face additional planning considerations concerning confidentiality, authentication of identity, and problems of multiple responses.

You must first decide what you are attempting to gain through using a survey. For instance, if you want to know what percentage of users prefers a FAQ page as a means of learning about new software packages, a questionnaire might be the right technique. If you want an in-depth analysis of a manager's decision-making process, an interview is a better choice.

Here are some guidelines to help you decide whether use of questionnaires is appropriate. Consider using questionnaires if:

1. The people you need to question are widely dispersed (different branches of the same corporation).
2. A large number of people are involved in the systems project, and it is meaningful to know what proportion of a given group (for example, management) approves or disapproves of a particular feature of the proposed system.

3. You are doing an exploratory study and want to gauge overall opinion before the systems project is given any specific direction.
4. You wish to be certain that any problems with the current system are identified and addressed in follow-up interviews.

Once you have determined that you have good cause to use a questionnaire and have pinpointed the objectives to be fulfilled through its use, you can begin formulating questions.

WRITING QUESTIONS

The biggest difference between the questions used for most interviews and those used on questionnaires is that interviewing permits interaction between the questions and their meanings. In an interview the analyst has an opportunity to refine a question, define a muddy term, change the course of questioning, respond to a puzzled look, and generally control the context.

Few of these opportunities are possible on a questionnaire. Thus, for the analyst, questions must be transparently clear, the flow of the questionnaire cogent, the respondent's questions anticipated, and the administration of the questionnaire planned in detail. (A respondent is the person who responds to or answers the questionnaire.)

The basic question types used on the questionnaire are open-ended and closed, as discussed for interviewing. Due to the constraints placed on questionnaires, some additional discussion of question types is warranted.

Open-Ended Questions Recall that open-ended questions (or statements) are those that leave all possible response options open to the respondent. For example, open-ended questions on a questionnaire might read, "Describe any problems you are currently experiencing with output reports" or "In your opinion, how helpful are the user manuals for the current system's accounting application?"

When you write open-ended questions for a questionnaire, anticipate what kind of response you will get. For instance, if you ask a question such as, "How do you feel about the system?" the responses are apt to be too broad for accurate interpretation or comparison. Therefore, even when you write an open-ended question, it must be narrow enough to guide respondents to answer in a specific way. (Examples of open-ended questions can be found in Figure 4.10.)

Open-ended questions are particularly well suited to situations in which you want to get at organizational members' opinions about some aspect of the system, whether product or process. In such cases you will want to use open-ended questions when it is impossible to list effectively all the possible responses to the question.

Closed Questions Recall that closed questions (or statements) are those that limit or close the response options available to the respondent. For example, in Figure 4.11 the statement in question 23 ("Below are the six software packages currently available. Please check the software package(s) you personally use most frequently") is closed. Notice that respondents are not asked why the package is preferred, nor are they asked to select more than one, even if that is a more representative response.

Closed questions should be used when the systems analyst is able to list effectively all the possible responses to the question and when all the listed responses are mutually exclusive, so that choosing one precludes choosing any of the others.

Use closed questions when you want to survey a large sample of people. The reason becomes obvious when you start imagining how the data you are collecting

FIGURE 4.10

Open-ended questions used for questionnaires.

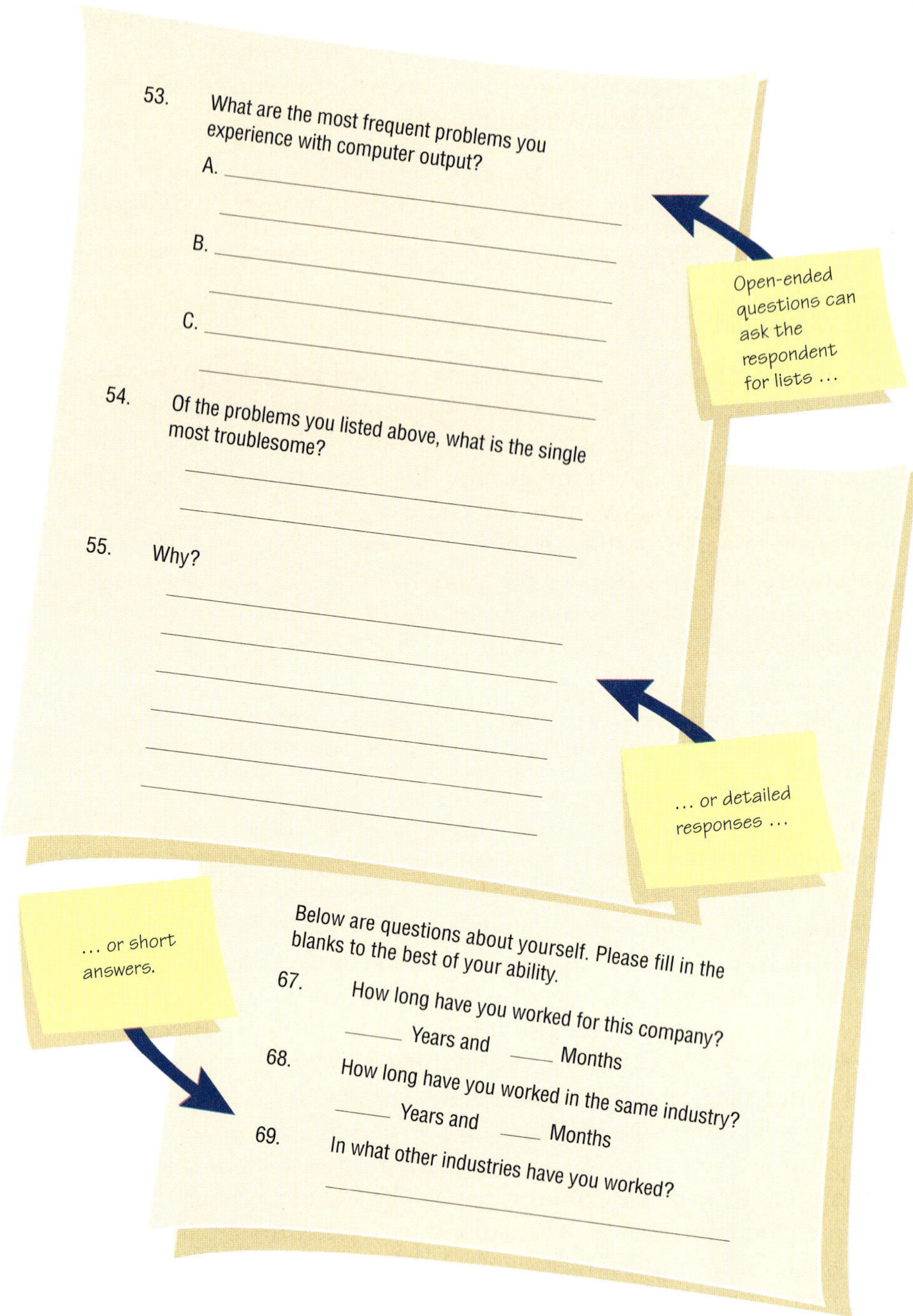

will look. If you use only open-ended questions for hundreds of people, correct analysis and interpretation of their responses becomes impossible without the aid of a computerized content analysis program.

There are trade-offs involved in choosing either open-ended or closed questions for use on questionnaires. Figure 4.12 summarizes these trade-offs. Notice that responses to open-ended questions can help analysts gain rich, exploratory insights as well as breadth and depth on a topic. Although open-ended questions can be written easily, responses to them are difficult and time consuming to analyze.

When we refer to the writing of closed questions with either ordered or unordered answers, we often refer to the process as scaling. The use of scales in surveys is discussed in detail in a later section.

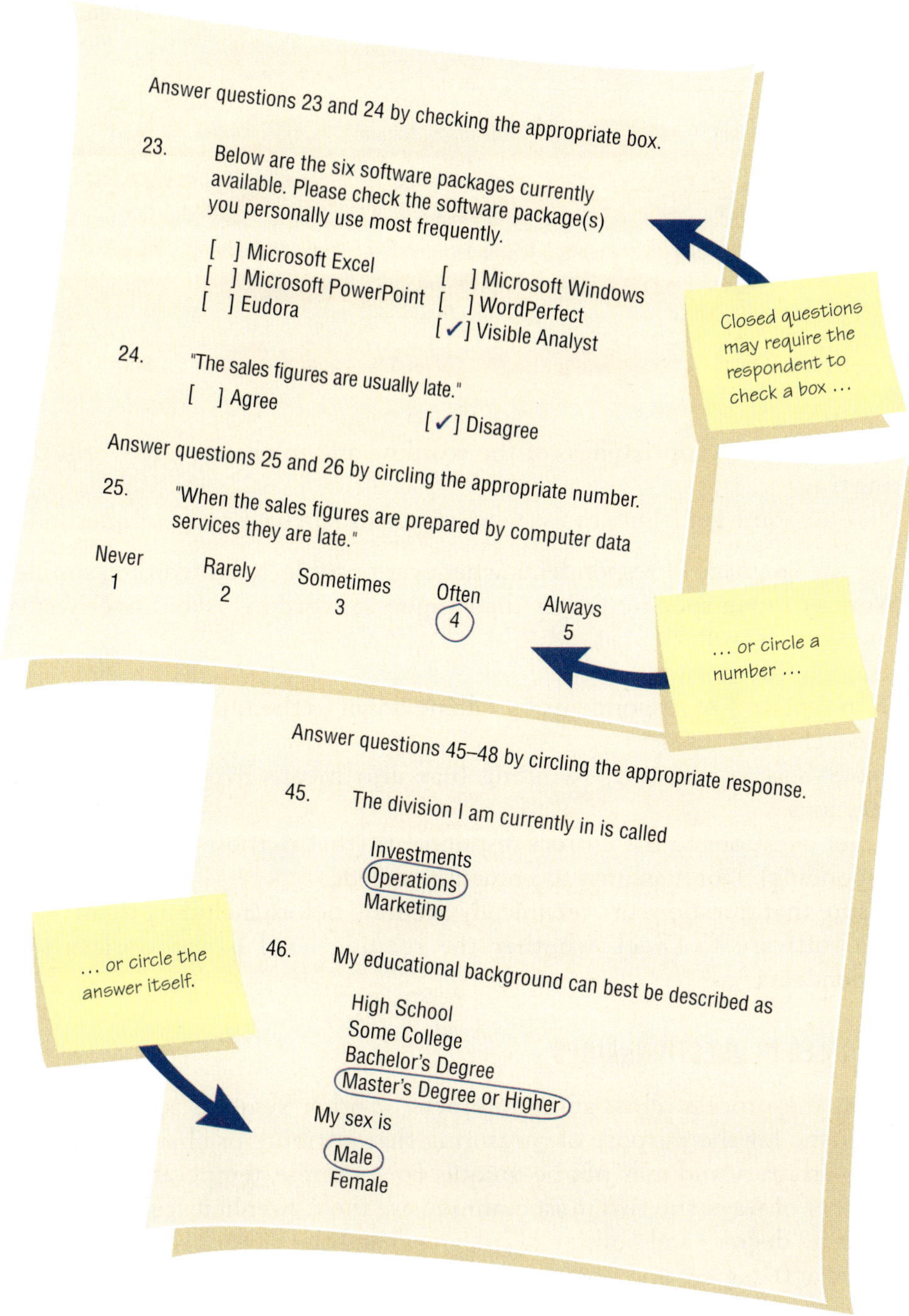

FIGURE 4.11

Closed questions on questionnaires helps ensure responses.

Choice of Words Just as with interviews, the language of questionnaires is an extremely important aspect of their effectiveness. Even if the systems analyst has a standard set of questions concerning systems development, it is wise to write them to reflect the business's own terminology.

Respondents appreciate the efforts of someone who bothers to write a questionnaire reflecting their own language usage. For instance, if the business uses the term *supervisors* instead of *managers*, or *units* rather than *departments*, incorporating the preferred terms in the questionnaire helps respondents relate to the meaning of the questions. Responses will be easier to interpret accurately, and respondents will be more enthusiastic overall.

To check whether language used on the questionnaire is that of the respondents, try some sample questions on a pilot (test) group. Ask them to pay particular

FIGURE 4.12

Trade-offs between the use of open-ended and closed questions on questionnaires.

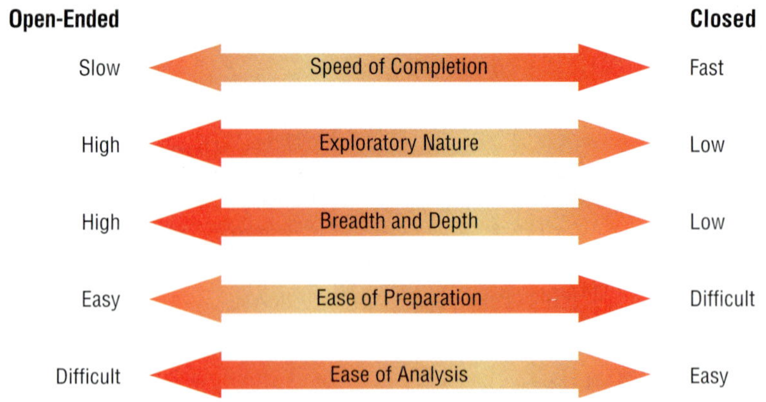

attention to the appropriateness of the wording and to change any words that do not ring true.

Here are some guidelines to use when choosing language for your questionnaire:

1. Use the language of respondents whenever possible. Keep wording simple.
2. Work at being specific rather than vague in wording. Avoid overly specific questions as well.
3. Keep questions short.
4. Do not patronize respondents by talking down to them through low-level language choices.
5. Avoid bias in wording. Avoiding bias also means avoiding objectionable questions.
6. Target questions to the correct respondents (that is, those who are capable of responding). Don't assume too much knowledge.
7. Ensure that questions are technically accurate before including them.
8. Use software to check whether the reading level is appropriate for the respondents.

USING SCALES IN QUESTIONNAIRES

Scaling is the process of assigning numbers or other symbols to an attribute or characteristic for the purpose of measuring that attribute or characteristic. Scales are often arbitrary and may not be unique. For example, temperature is measured in a number of ways; the two most common are the Fahrenheit scale (where water freezes at 32 degrees and boils at 212 degrees) and the Celsius scale (where freezing occurs at 0 degrees and boiling at 100 degrees).

Measurement There are two different forms of measurement scales commonly used by systems analysts:

1. nominal scales and
2. interval scales.

Nominal scales are used to classify things. A question such as:

What type of software do you use the most?

1 = A Word Processor
2 = A Spreadsheet
3 = A Database
4 = An Email Program

uses a nominal scale. Obviously, nominal scales are the weakest of the forms of measurement. Generally, all the analyst can do with them is obtain totals for each classification.

Interval scales possess the characteristic that the intervals between each of the numbers are equal. Due to this characteristic, mathematical operations can be performed on the questionnaire data, resulting in a more complete analysis. Examples of interval scales are the Fahrenheit and Celsius scales, which measure temperature.

The foregoing example of the Information Center is definitely not that of an interval scale, but by anchoring the scale on either end, the analyst may want to assume the respondent perceives the intervals to be equal:

How useful is the support given by the Technical Support Group?

Not Useful At All				Extremely Useful
1	2	3	4	5

If the systems analyst makes this assumption, more quantitative analysis is possible.

Validity and Reliability There are two measures of performance in constructing scales: validity and reliability. The systems analyst should be aware of these concerns.

Validity is the degree to which the question measures what the analyst intends to measure. For example, if the purpose of the questionnaire is to determine whether the organization is ready for a major change in computer operations, do the questions measure that?

Reliability measures consistency. If the questionnaire was administered once and then again under the same conditions and if the same results were obtained both times, the instrument is said to have external consistency. If the questionnaire contains subparts and these parts have equivalent results, the instrument is said to have internal consistency. Both external and internal consistency are important.

Constructing Scales The actual construction of scales is a serious task. Careless construction of scales can result in one of the following problems:

1. Leniency.
2. Central tendency.
3. Halo effect.

Leniency is a problem caused by respondents who are easy raters. A systems analyst can avoid the problem of leniency by moving the "average" category to the left (or right) of center.

Central tendency is a problem that occurs when respondents rate everything as average. The analyst can improve the scale (1) by making the differences smaller at the two ends, (2) by adjusting the strength of the descriptors, or (3) by creating a scale with more points.

The halo effect is a problem that arises when the impression formed in one question carries into the next question. For example, if you are rating an employee about whom you have a very favorable impression, you may give a high rating in every category or trait, regardless of whether or not it is a strong point of the employee's. The solution is to place one trait and several employees on each page, rather than one employee and several traits on a page.

DESIGNING THE QUESTIONNAIRES

Many of the same principles that are relevant to the design of forms for data input (as covered in Chapter 12) are important here as well. Although the intent of the questionnaire is to gather information on attitudes, beliefs, behavior, and characteristics whose impact may substantially alter users' work, respondents are not always motivated to respond. Remember that organizational members as a whole tend to receive too many surveys, many of which are often ill-conceived and trivial.

A well-designed, relevant questionnaire can help overcome some of this resistance to respond. Here are some rules for designing a good questionnaire:

1. Allow ample white space.
2. Allow ample space to write or type in responses.
3. Make it easy for respondents to clearly mark their answers.
4. Be consistent in style.

When you design questionnaires for the Web, apply the same rules you use when designing paper questionnaires. Most software packages allow you to insert one of the commonly used data entry formats shown in Figure 4.13. Following the four guidelines should help you gain a better response rate to the questionnaire.

Order of Questions There is no best way to order questions on the questionnaire. Once again, as you order questions, you must think about your objectives in using the questionnaire and then determine the function of each question in helping you to achieve your objectives. It is also important to see the questionnaire through the respondent's eyes. Some guidelines for ordering questions are:

1. Place questions that are important to respondents first.
2. Cluster items of similar content together.
3. Introduce less controversial questions first.

You want respondents to feel as unthreatened by and interested in the questions being asked as possible, without getting overwrought about a particular issue.

FIGURE 4.13

When designing a Web survey, keep in mind that there are different ways to capture responses.

Name	Appearance	Purpose
One-line text box		Used to obtain a small amount of text and limit the answer to a few words
Scrolling text box		Used to obtain one or more paragraphs of text
Check box		Used to obtain a yes-no answer (e.g., Do you wish to be included on the mailing list?)
Radio button		Used to obtain a yes-no or true-false answer
Drop-down menu		Used to obtain more consistent results (Respondent is able to choose the appropriate answer from a predetermined list [e.g., a list of state abbreviations])
Push button		Most often used for an action (e.g., a respondent pushes a button marked "Submit" or "Clear")

CONSULTING OPPORTUNITY 4.4

THE UNBEARABLE QUESTIONNAIRE

"I'm going to go into a depression or at least a slump if someone doesn't figure this out soon," say Penny Stox, office manager for Carbon, Carbon, & Rippy, a large brokerage firm. Penny is sitting across a conference table from you and two of her most productive account executives, By Lowe and Sal Hy. You are all mulling over the responses to a questionnaire that has been distributed among the firm's account executives, which is shown in Figure 4.C1.

"We need a crystal ball to understand these," By and Sal call out together.

"Maybe it reflects some sort of optimistic cycle, or something," Penny says as she reads more of the responses. "Who designed this gem, anyway?"

"Rich Kleintz," By and Sal call out in unison.

"Well, as you can see, it's not telling us anything," Penny exclaims.

Penny and her staff are dissatisfied with the responses they have received on the unbearable questionnaire, and they feel that the responses are unrealistic reflections of the amount of information account executives want. In a paragraph, state why these problems are occurring. On a separate sheet, change the scaling of the questions to avoid these problems.

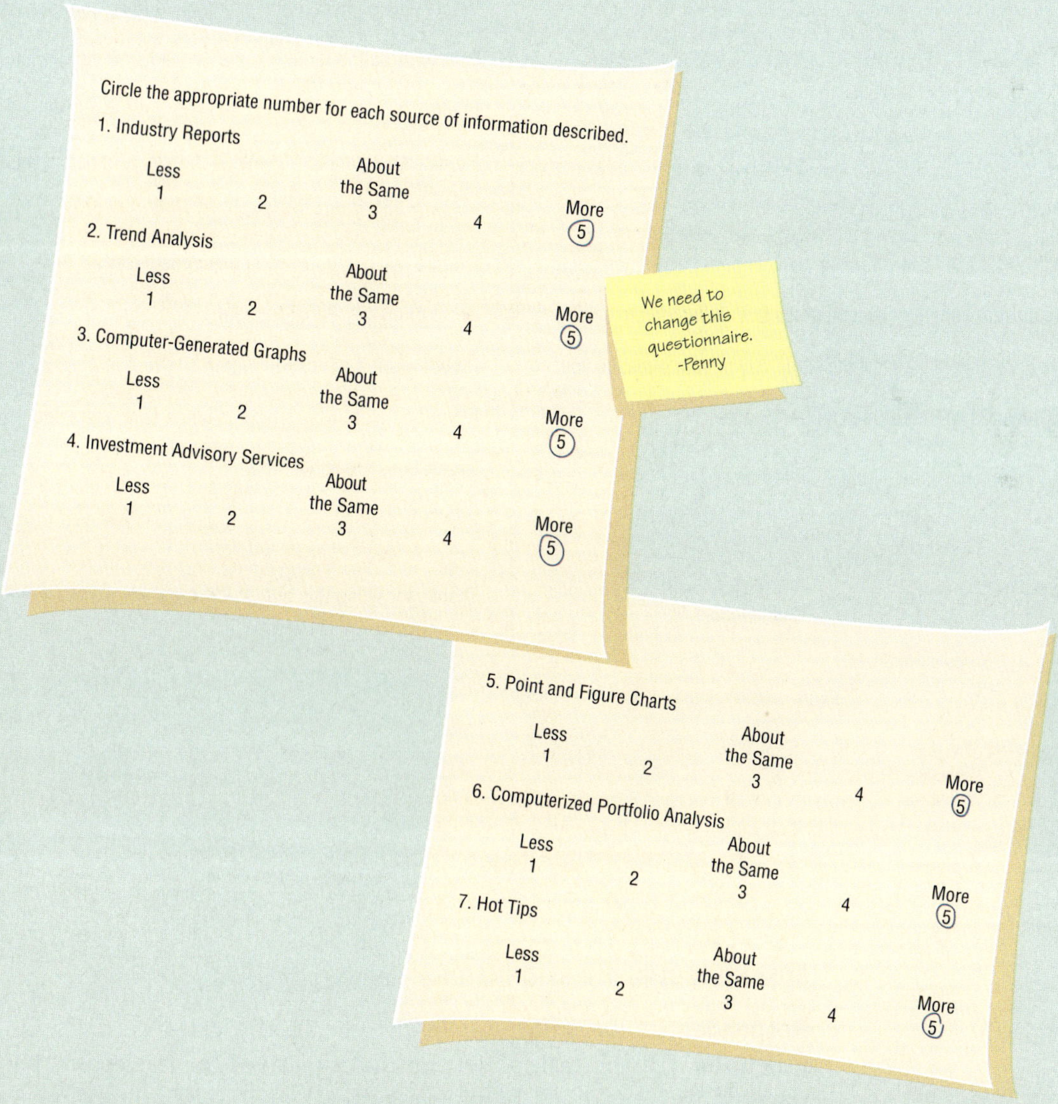
Circle the appropriate number for each source of information described.

1. Industry Reports
Less 1 — 2 — About the Same 3 — 4 — More (5)

2. Trend Analysis
Less 1 — 2 — About the Same 3 — 4 — More (5)

3. Computer-Generated Graphs
Less 1 — 2 — About the Same 3 — 4 — More (5)

4. Investment Advisory Services
Less 1 — 2 — About the Same 3 — 4 — More (5)

5. Point and Figure Charts
Less 1 — 2 — About the Same 3 — 4 — More (5)

6. Computerized Portfolio Analysis
Less 1 — 2 — About the Same 3 — 4 — More (5)

7. Hot Tips
Less 1 — 2 — About the Same 3 — 4 — More (5)

FIGURE 4.C1
Questionnaire developed for the brokerage firm of Carbon, Carbon, & Rippy by Rich Kleintz.

CONSULTING OPPORTUNITY 4.5

ORDER IN THE COURTS

"I love my work," Tennys says, beginning the interview with a volley. "It's a lot like a game. I keep my eye on the ball and never look back," he continues. Tennyson "Tennys" Courts is a manager for Global Health Spas, Inc., which has popular health and recreation spas worldwide.

"Now that I've finished my M.B.A., I feel like I'm on top of the world with Global," Tennys says. "I think I can really help this outfit shape up with its computers and health spas."

Tennys is attempting to help your systems group, which is developing a system to be used by all 80 outlets (where currently each group handles its paperwork in its own way). "Can I bounce this off you?" he asks Terri Towell, a member of your team of systems analysts. "It's a questionnaire I designed for distribution to all spa managers."

Ever the good sport, Terri tells Tennys that she'd love to take a look at the form. But back in the office, Terri puts the ball in your court. Systematically critique Tennys's technique as depicted in Figure 4.C2, and explain to him point by point what it needs to be a matchless questionnaire with a winning form. Building on your critique, tell Tennys what he should do to rewrite the form as an email survey instead.

QUESTIONNAIRE FOR ALL MANAGERS OF HEALTH SPAS

URGENTFILL OUT IMMEDIATELY AND RETURN PERSONALLY TO YOUR DIVISION MANAGER. YOUR NEXT PAYCHECK WILL BE WITHHELD UNTIL IT IS CONFIRMED THAT YOU HAVE TURNED THIS IN.

In 10 words or fewer, what complaints have you lodged about the current computer system in the last six months to a year?

Are there others who feel the same way in your outlet as you do? Who? List their names and positions.

1.   2.

3.   4.

5.

7.

What is the biggest problem you have when communicating your information requirements to headquarters? Describe it briefly.

How much computer downtime did you experience last year?

1 - 2 - 3 - 4 - 5 - 6 - 7 - 8 - 9 - 10 -

Is there any computer equipment you never use?

Description   Serial Number

Do you want it removed? Agree   Neutral   Disagree

In your opinion, what's next as far as computers and Global Health Spas are concerned?

Thanks for filling this out. • • • • • • • • • • • • • • • •

Terri
Please help me improve this form.
Tennys

FIGURE 4.C2
Questionnaire developed for managers of Global Health spas by Tennys Court.

ADMINISTERING QUESTIONNAIRES

Respondents Deciding who will receive the questionnaire is handled in conjunction with the task of setting up objectives for its results. Sampling, which is covered in Chapter 5, helps the systems analyst to determine what sort of representation is necessary and hence what kind of respondents should receive the questionnaire.

Recipients are often chosen as representative because of their rank, length of service with the company, job duties, or special interest in the current or proposed system. Be sure to include enough respondents to allow for a reasonable sample in the event that some questionnaires are not returned or some response sheets are incorrectly completed and thus must be discarded.

Methods of Administering the Questionnaire The systems analyst has several options for administering the questionnaire, and the choice of administration method is often determined by the existing business situation. Options for administering the questionnaire include the following:

1. Convening all concerned respondents together at one time.
2. Personally handing out blank questionnaires and taking back completed ones.
3. Allowing respondents to self-administer the questionnaire at work and drop it in a centrally located box.
4. Mailing questionnaires to employees at branch sites and supplying a deadline, instructions, and return postage.
5. Administering the questionnaire electronically either via email or on the Web.

Each of these five methods has advantages and disadvantages. Most commonly, respondents are allowed to self-administer the questionnaire. Response rates with this method are a little lower than with the other methods, because people may forget about the form, lose it, or purposely ignore it. Self-administration, however, allows people to feel that their anonymity is ensured and may result in less guarded answers from some respondents. Both email and Web surveys fall into the category of self-administered questionnaires.

Administering the questionnaire electronically, either via email or posted on the Web, is one way to quickly reach current system users. Costs of duplication are minimized. In addition, responses can be made at the convenience of the respondent and then can be automatically collected and stored electronically. Some software permits respondents to begin answering a survey, save their answers, and return to it for completion if they are interrupted. Reminders to respondents can be easily and inexpensively sent via email, as can notifications to the analyst about when the respondent has opened the email. Some software now turns email data into data tables for use in spreadsheet or statistical analysis software.

Research shows that respondents are willing to respond to questions about highly sensitive matters via the Internet. Thus, questions that may be difficult to pose in person regarding systems problems may be acceptable to ask on a Web survey.

SUMMARY

This chapter covers three of the key interactive methods for information gathering that the systems analyst can use, including interviewing, JAD, and construction of questionnaires. During the process of interviewing, which is one method systems analysts use for collecting data on human and system information requirements, analysts listen for HCI concerns relating to ergonomics, aesthetics, usability, and usefulness, as well as goals, feelings, opinions, and informal procedures in interviews with organizational decision makers. Interviews are preplanned question-and-answer dialogues between two people. The analyst uses the interview to develop their relationship with a client, to observe the workplace, and to collect data regarding human information requirements. Although email can be used to prepare the interviewee by posing questions prior to meeting, interviews should typically be conducted in person and not electronically.

HYPERCASE® EXPERIENCE

4.2

"You've probably noticed by now that not everyone enjoys filling out questionnaires at MRE. We seem to get more questionnaires than most organizations. I think it's because many of the employees, especially those from the old Training Unit, value the contributions of questionnaire data in our work with clients. When you examine the questionnaire that Snowden distributed, you'll probably want not only to look at the results but also to critique it from a methods standpoint. I always feel strongly that we can improve our internal performance so that eventually we can better serve our clients. The next time we construct a questionnaire, we want to be able to improve three things: the reliability of the data, the validity of the data, and the response rate we get."

HYPERCASE QUESTIONS

1. What evidence of questionnaires have you found at MRE? Be specific about what you have found and where.
2. Critique the questionnaire that Snowden circulated. What can be done to it to improve its reliability, validity, and response rate? Provide three practical suggestions.
3. Write a short questionnaire to follow up on some aspects of the merger between Management Systems and the Training Unit at MRE that are still puzzling you. Be sure to observe all the guidelines for good questionnaire design.
4. Redesign the questionnaire you wrote in question 3 so that it can be used as a Web survey.

There are five steps to be taken in preplanning the interview:

1. Read background material.
2. Establish interviewing objectives.
3. Decide whom to interview.
4. Prepare the interviewee.
5. Decide on question types and structure.

Questions are of two basic types: open-ended or closed. Open-ended questions leave open all response options for the interviewee. Closed questions limit the possible options for response. Probes or follow-up questions can be either open-ended or closed, but they ask the respondent for a more detailed reply.

Interviews can be structured in three basic ways: pyramid, funnel, or diamond. Pyramid structures begin with detailed, closed questions and broaden to more generalized questions. Funnel structures begin with open-ended, general questions and then funnel down to more specific, closed questions. Diamond-shaped structures combine the strengths of the other two structures, but they take longer to conduct. There are trade-offs involved when deciding how structured to make interview questions and question sequences.

To cut both the time and cost of personal interviews, analysts may want to consider joint application design as an alternative. Using JAD, analysts can both analyze human information requirements and design a user interface with users in a group setting. Careful assessment of the particular organizational culture will help the analyst judge whether JAD is a suitable alternative.

By using questionnaires, systems analysts can gather data on HCI concerns attitudes, beliefs, behavior, and characteristics from key people in the organization.

Questionnaires are useful if people in the organization are widely dispersed, many people are involved with the systems project, exploratory work is necessary before recommending alternatives, or there is a need for problem sensing before interviews are conducted.

Once objectives for the questionnaire are articulated, the analyst can begin writing either open-ended or closed questions. Choice of wording is extremely important and should reflect the language of the organizational members. Ideally, the questions should be simple, specific, short, free of bias, not patronizing, technically accurate, addressed to those who are knowledgeable, and written at an appropriate reading level.

Scaling is the process of assigning numbers or other symbols to an attribute or characteristic. The systems analyst may want to use scales either to measure the attitudes or characteristics of respondents or to have respondents act as judges for the subject of the questionnaire.

Systems analysts most commonly use either a nominal or interval scale and need to be concerned with validity and reliability. Validity means that the questionnaire measures what the systems analyst intended to measure. Reliability means that the results are consistent. Analysts should be careful to avoid problems such as leniency, central tendency, and the halo effect when constructing scales.

Consistent control of the questionnaire format and style can result in a better response rate. Web surveys can be designed to encourage consistent responses by including radio buttons, drop-down menus, and scrolling text boxes to pose both open-ended and closed questions. In addition, the meaningful ordering and clustering of questions is important for helping respondents understand the questionnaire. Surveys can be administered in a variety of ways, including (but not limited to) electronically via email or the Web, or with the analyst present in a group of users.

KEYWORDS AND PHRASES

- bipolar closed questions
- central tendency
- check box
- closed questions
- diamond-shaped structure
- drop-down menu
- funnel structure
- halo effect
- human–computer interaction (HCI)
- informal procedures
- interval scale
- interviewee feelings
- interviewee goals
- interviewee opinions
- joint application design (JAD)
- leniency
- nominal scale
- open-ended questions
- probes
- pyramid structure
- questionnaire
- radio button
- reliability
- scrolling text box
- survey respondents
- validity

REVIEW QUESTIONS

1. What kinds of information should be sought in interviews?
2. List the five steps in interview preparation.
3. Define what is meant by open-ended interview questions. Give eight benefits and five drawbacks of using them.
4. When are open-ended questions appropriate for use in interviewing?
5. Define what is meant by closed interview questions. Give six benefits and four drawbacks of using them.
6. When are closed questions appropriate for use in interviewing?

7. What is a probing question? What is the purpose of using a probing question in interviews?
8. Define what is meant by pyramid structure. When is it useful to employ it in interviews?
9. Define what is meant by funnel structure. When is it useful to employ it in interviews?
10. Define what is meant by diamond-shaped structure. When is it useful to employ it in interviews?
11. Define joint application design (JAD).
12. List the situations that warrant use of JAD in place of personal organizational interviews.
13. List the potential benefits of using joint application design.
14. List the three potential drawbacks of using JAD as an alternative to personal interviews.
15. What kinds of information is the systems analyst seeking through the use of questionnaires or surveys?
16. List four situations that make the use of questionnaires appropriate.
17. What are the two basic question types used on questionnaires?
18. List two reasons why a systems analyst would use a closed question on a questionnaire.
19. List two reasons why a systems analyst would use an open-ended question on a questionnaire.
20. What are the seven guidelines for choosing language for the questionnaire?
21. Define what is meant by scaling.
22. What are two kinds of information or scales that are most commonly used by systems analysts?
23. What are nominal scales used for?
24. Give an example of an interval scale.
25. When should the analyst use interval scales?
26. Define reliability as it refers to the construction of scales.
27. Define validity as it refers to the construction of scales.
28. List three problems that can occur because of careless construction of scales.
29. What are four actions that can be taken to ensure that the questionnaire format is conducive to a good response rate?
30. Which questions should be placed first on the questionnaire?
31. Why should questions on similar topics be clustered together?
32. What is an appropriate placement of controversial questions?
33. List five methods for administering the questionnaire.
34. What considerations are necessary when questionnaires are Web-based?

PROBLEMS

1. As part of your systems analysis project to update the automated accounting functions for Xanadu Corporation, a maker of digital cameras, you will interview Leo Blum, the chief accountant. Write four to six interview objectives covering his use of information sources, information formats, decision-making frequency, desired qualities of information, and decision-making style.
   a. In a paragraph, write down how you will approach Leo to set up an interview.
   b. State which structure you will choose for this interview. Why?
   c. Leo has four subordinates who also use the system. Would you interview them also? Why or why not?
   d. Would you also try to interview customers (visitors to the Web site)? Are there better ways to get the opinions of customers? Why or why not?

e. Write three open-ended questions that you will email to Leo prior to your interview. Write a sentence explaining why it is preferable to conduct an interview in person rather than via email.

2. Here are five questions written by one of your systems analysis team members. Her interviewee is the local manager of LOWCO, an outlet of a national discount chain, who has asked you to work on a management information system to provide inventory information. Review these questions for your team member.
   1. When was the last time you thought seriously about your decision-making process?
   2. Who are the trouble makers in your store, I mean the ones who will show the most resistance to changes in the system that I have proposed?
   3. Are there any decisions you need more information about to make them?
   4. You don't have any major problems with the current inventory control system, do you?
   5. Tell me a little about the output you'd like to see.

   a. Rewrite each question to be more effective in eliciting information.
   b. Order your questions in either a pyramid, funnel, or diamond-shaped structure, and label the questions with the name of the structure you used.
   c. What guidelines can you give your team member for improving her interviewing questions for the future? Make a list of them.
3. Ever since you entered the door, your interviewee, Max Hugo, has been shuffling papers, looking at his watch, and drumming on his desk with his fingers. Based on what you know about interviews, you guess that Max is nervous because of the other work he needs to do. In a paragraph, describe how you would deal with this situation so that the interview can be accomplished with Max's full attention. (Max cannot reschedule the interview for a different day.)
4. Write a series of six *closed* questions that cover the subject of decision-making style for the manager described in Problem 2.
5. Write a series of six *open-ended* questions that cover the subject of decision-making style for the manager described in Problem 2.
6. Examine the interview structure presented in the sequencing of the following questions:
   1. How long have you been in this position?
   2. What are your key responsibilities?
   3. What reports do you receive?
   4. How do you view the goals of your department?
   5. How would you describe your decision-making process?
   6. How can that process best be supported?
   7. How frequently do you make those decisions?
   8. Who is consulted when you make a decision?
   9. What is the one decision you make that is essential to departmental functioning?

   a. What structure is being used? How can you tell?
   b. Restructure the interview by changing the sequence of the questions (you may omit some if necessary). Label the reordered questions with the name of the structure you have used.
7. The following is the first interview report filed by one of your systems analysis team members: "In my opinion, the interview went very well. The subject allowed me to talk with him for an hour and a half. He told me the whole history of the business, which was very interesting. The subject also mentioned that things have not changed all that much since he has been with the firm, which is about 16 years. We are meeting again soon to finish the interview, because we did not have time to go into the questions I prepared."

a. In two paragraphs, critique the interview report. What critical information is missing?
b. What information is extraneous to the interview report?
c. If what is reported actually occurred, what three suggestions do you have to help your teammate conduct a better interview next time?

8. Cab Wheeler is a newly hired systems analyst with your group. Cab has always felt that questionnaires are a waste. Now that you will be doing a systems project for MegaTrucks, Inc., a national trucking firm with branches and employees in 130 cities, you want to use a questionnaire to elicit some opinions about the current and proposed systems.
   a. Based on what you know about Cab and MegaTrucks, give three persuasive reasons why he should use a survey for this study.
   b. Given your careful arguments, Cab has agreed to use a questionnaire but strongly urges that all questions be open-ended so as not to constrain the respondents. In a paragraph, persuade Cab that closed questions are useful as well. Be sure to point out trade-offs involved with each question type.
9. "Every time we get consultants in here, they pass out some goofy questionnaire that has no meaning to us at all. Why don't they bother to personalize it, at least a little?" asks Ray Dient, head of emergency systems. You are discussing the possibility of beginning a systems project with Pohattan Power Company (PPC) of Far Meltway, New Jersey.
   a. What steps will you follow to customize a standardized questionnaire?
   b. What are the advantages of adapting a questionnaire to a particular organization? What are the disadvantages?
10. A sample question from the draft of the Pohattan Power Company questionnaire reads:
    I have been with the company:

    20–upwards years
    10–15 years upwards
    5–10 years upwards
    less than a year
    Check one that most applies.
    a. What kind of a scale is the question's author using?
    b. What errors have been made in the construction of the question, and what might be the possible responses?
    c. Rewrite the question to achieve clearer results.
    d. Where should the question you've written appear on the questionnaire?
11. Also included on the PPC questionnaire is this question:
    When residential customers call, I always direct them to our Web site to get an answer.

Sometimes	***Never***	***Always***	***Usually***
1	2	3	4

   a. What type of scale is this one intended to be?
   b. Rewrite the question and possible responses to achieve better results.
12. Figure 4.EX1 is a questionnaire designed by an employee of Green Toe Textiles, which specializes in manufacturing men's socks. Di Wooly wrote the questionnaire because, as the office manager at headquarters in Juniper, Tennessee, she is concerned with the proposed purchase and implementation of a new computer system.
    a. Provide a one-sentence critique for each question given.
    b. In a paragraph, critique the layout and style in terms of white space used, room for responses, ease of responding, and so on.

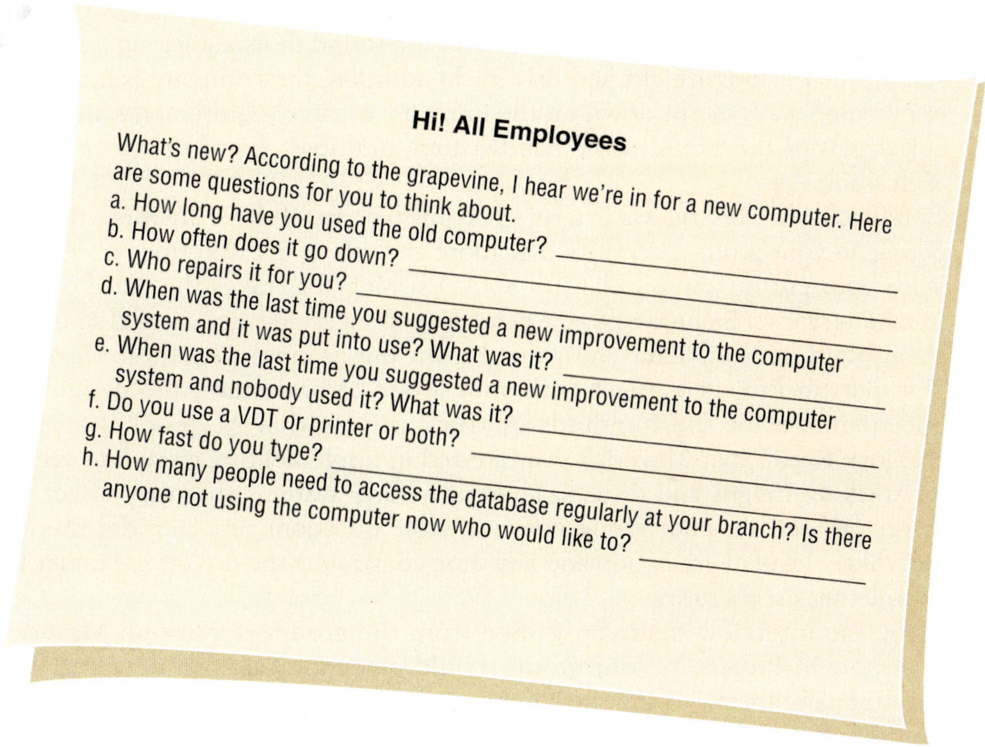
Hi! All Employees

What's new? According to the grapevine, I hear we're in for a new computer. Here are some questions for you to think about.

a. How long have you used the old computer? ______
b. How often does it go down? ______
c. Who repairs it for you? ______
d. When was the last time you suggested a new improvement to the computer system and it was put into use? What was it? ______
e. When was the last time you suggested a new improvement to the computer system and nobody used it? What was it? ______
f. Do you use a VDT or printer or both? ______
g. How fast do you type? ______
h. How many people need to access the database regularly at your branch? Is there anyone not using the computer now who would like to? ______

FIGURE 4.EX1
Questionnaire developed by Di Wooly.

13. Based on what you surmise Ms. Wooly is trying to get through the questionnaire, rewrite and reorder the questions (use both open-ended and closed questions) so that they follow good practice and result in useful information for the systems analysts. Indicate next to each question that you write whether it is open-ended or closed, and write a sentence indicating why you have written the question this way.
14. Redesign the questionnaire you created for Ms. Wooly in Problem 13 for use on email. Write a paragraph saying what changes were necessary to accommodate users on email.
15. Redesign the questionnaire you created for Ms. Wooly in Problem 13 as a Web survey. Write a paragraph saying what changes were necessary to accommodate users on the Web.

GROUP PROJECTS

1. With your group members, role play a series of interviews with various system users at Maverick Transport. Each member of your group should choose one of the following roles: company president, information technology director, dispatcher, customer service agent, or truck driver. Those group members playing roles of Maverick Transport employees should attempt to briefly describe their job responsibilities, goals, and informational needs.

   Remaining group members should play the roles of systems analysts and devise interview questions for each employee. If there are enough people in your group, each analyst may be assigned to interview a different employee. Those playing the roles of systems analysts should work together to develop common questions that they will ask, as well as questions tailored to each individual employee. Be sure to include open-ended, closed, and probing questions in your interviews.

   Maverick Transport is attempting to change from outdated and unreliable technology to more state-of-the-art, dependable technology. The company is seeking to move from dumb terminals attached to a mainframe because it wants to use PCs in some way, and is also interested in investigating a satellite system for tracking freight and drivers. In addition, the company is interested in pursuing ways to cut down on the immense storage requirements and difficult access of the troublesome handwritten, multipart forms that accompany each shipment.

2. Conduct all five interviews in a role-playing exercise. If there are more than 10 people in your group, permit two or more analysts to ask questions.
3. With your group, write a plan for a JAD session that takes the place of personal interviews. Include relevant participants, suggested setting, and so on.
4. Using the interview data you gained from the group exercise on Maverick Transport in Project 1, meet with your group to brainstorm the design of a questionnaire for the hundreds of truck drivers that Maverick Transport employs. Recall that Maverick is interested in implementing a satellite system for tracking freight and drivers. There are other systems that may affect the drivers as well. As your group constructs the questionnaire, consider the drivers' likely level of education and any time constraints the drivers are under for completing such a form.
5. Using the interview data you gained from the group exercise on Maverick Transport in Project 1, your group should meet to design an email or Web questionnaire for surveying the company's 20 programmers (15 of whom have been hired in the past year) about their skills, ideas for new or enhanced systems, and so on. As your group constructs the programmer survey, consider what you have learned about users in the other interviews as well as what vision the director of information technology holds for the company.

SELECTED BIBLIOGRAPHY

Ackroyd, S., and J. A. Hughes. *Data Collecting in Context*, 2d ed. New York: Longman, 1992.

Babbie, E. R. *Survey Research Methods.* Belmont, CA: Wadsworth, 1973.

Cash, C. J., and W. B. Stewart, Jr. *Interviewing Principles and Practices*, 4th ed. Dubuque, IA: Wm. C. Brown, 1986.

Cooper, D. R., and P. S. Schindler. *Business Research Methods*, 6th ed. New York: Irwin/McGraw-Hill, 1998.

Deetz, S. *Transforming Communication, Transforming Business: Building Responsive and Responsible Workplaces.* Cresskill, NJ: Hampton Press, 1995.

Dillman, D. A. *Mail and Telephone Surveys.* New York: Wiley, 1978.

Di Salvo, V. *Business and Professional Communication.* Columbus, OH: Merrill, 1977.

Emerick, D., K. Round, and S. Joyce. *Exploring Web Marketing and Project Management.* Upper Saddle River, NJ: Prentice Hall PTR, 2000.

Gane, C. *Rapid System Development.* New York: Rapid System Development, 1987.

Georgia Tech's Graphic, Visualization, and Usability Center. "GVU WWW Survey through 1998." Available at: www.cc.gatech.edu/gvu/. Accessed May 23, 2003.

Hessler, R. M. *Social Research Methods.* New York: West, 1992.

Joint Application Design. GUIDE Publication GPP-147. Chicago: GUIDE International, 1986.

Peterson, R. A. *Constructing Effective Questionnaires.* Thousand Oaks, CA: Sage Publications, 1999.

Strauss, J., and R. Frost. *E-Marketing*, 2d ed. Upper Saddle River, NJ: Prentice Hall, 2001.

Sudman, S., and N. M. Bradburn. *Asking Questions: A Practical Guide to Questionnaire Design.* San Francisco: Jossey-Bass, 1988.

Emory, C. W. *Business Research Methods*, 3d ed. Homewood, IL: Irwin, 1985.

Allen Schmidt, Julie E. Kendall, and Kenneth E. Kendall

4

I'LL LISTEN NOW, ASK QUESTIONS LATER

"I've scheduled preliminary interviews with five key people. Because you've been so busy with Visible Analyst, I decided to do the first round of interviews myself," Anna tells Chip as they begin their morning meeting.

"That's fine with me," Chip says. "Just let me know when I can fill in. Who will you be talking to first? Dot?"

"No secret there, I guess," replies Anna. "She's critical to the success of the system. Her word is it when it comes to whether a project will fly or not."

"Who else?" asks Chip.

"I'll see who Dot refers me to, but I set up appointments with Mike Crowe, the maintenance expert; Cher Ware, the software specialist; and Paige Prynter, CPU's financial analyst."

"Don't forget Hy Perteks," says Chip.

"Right. The Information Center will be important to our project," says Anna. "Let me call and see when he's available."

After a brief phone conversation with Hy, Anna turns once again to Chip.

"He'll meet with me later today," Anna confirms.

After completing her interviews, Anna sits at her desk, reviewing the interview summaries and the memos that were gathered during the summer. Several stacks of papers are neatly filed in expansion folders.

"We have so much information," she remarks to Chip, "yet I sense that we are only working with the tip of the iceberg. I don't have a solid feeling for the difficulties of faculty members and research staff. Are there additional problems we haven't heard about?"

Chip looks up from his work of trying to extract key points for defining the problems. "I wonder if we should do more interviews, or perhaps gather more documents," he says.

But how many interviews should we conduct and who should we interview?" Anna replies. "Suppose we interview several staff members and base the new system on the results. We could interview the wrong people and design a system to satisfy only their needs, missing key problems that the majority of faculty and staff need to have solved."

"I see what you mean," Chip answers. "Perhaps we should design a questionnaire and survey the faculty and research staff."

"Great idea!" Anna says. "How should we decide which questions to include on the survey?"

"Let's speak with some key people and base the survey on the results. A good starting point would be Hy Perteks, because he is always talking with the faculty and staff. I'll give him a call and arrange a meeting," Chip says.

Chip arranged the meeting for the following morning. It would be held in a conference room adjacent to the Information Center.

"Thanks for meeting with us on such short notice," Chip opens. "We're thinking about surveying the faculty and research staff to obtain additional information that will help us define the system concerns."

4

"I think it's a tremendous idea," Hy replies. "I would also like to find out what type of software should be available in the Information Center and the type of training we should provide. Information about the major package types used should be obtained," Hy continues. "Word processing software is essential. We should find out which package each user likes and, equally important, which version of the package. I know that many are using Microsoft Word and others are using WordPerfect. Database software also varies although many are using Access. Same for spreadsheets with Excel being the most popular.

"Another consideration would be what type of specialized software is used by groups of faculty members," muses Hy. "Many of the people in the math department are using Exp, a math word processor. Others are using various software packages for a number of courses. For instance, the information science people are using Visible Analyst, but a few are using Visio. I've also heard that we're getting some biology and astronomy software. And the art department uses Macs almost exclusively. Many of the faculty are getting heavily into software for constructing Web sites, such as Dreamweaver and FrontPage."

"Other than software packages and versions, what types of information should we capture?" asks Chip.

"I would like to know what level of expertise each person has," responds Hy. "No doubt, some are beginners, whereas others have a good knowledge but have not mastered all the features of a particular package. Some are experts. They know the software inside and out. I'm interested in the beginners and intermediate users, because we should be providing different training for them. Knowing who's an expert helps, too."

"Is there anything else you feel we should find out about in the survey?" asks Chip.

"The only other thing that I worry about are problems that result in a faculty or staff member not using the software," Hy replies.

"What do you mean?" asks Chip.

"Well, suppose a person has the software but it is installed incorrectly or displays a message, such as 'Not enough memory to run,' or 'This wizard isn't installed,'" replies Hy. "I've had some inquiries about this matter recently. One person said that they couldn't use Access except for simple tasks because he always got a message saying that the wizards weren't installed. It turned out that the system was not configured correctly to run over a network. It was a simple matter to fix the problem, but it had been going on for a long time! There's a faculty member in math, Rhoda Booke, who has consistently shown interest in hardware and software issues. I've helped her a number of times, and she's always friendly and grateful. You should interview her for sure."

"Thanks once again for all your help," says Chip. "We'll get back to you later with the results of the survey."

Anna arranges a meeting with Rhoda and explains the nature of the project and why she was selected as a faculty representative. The meeting was held in a small conference room in the math department.

"We'd like to have the faculty perspective on problems encountered with PCs and the associated software," says Anna. "Our goal is to provide the faculty with the best possible resources with the least number of problems."

"I'm really glad to be a part of the project," exclaims Rhoda. "I've been using classroom software for about five years, and what a learning experience it has been! Thank goodness that Hy is available as a resource. I've taken hours of his time, and it's been well worth the effort. I feel much more productive, and the students are using software that helps them grasp the material more thoroughly."

"That's good, but are there some difficulties that you've been experiencing?" asks Chip.

"Well, becoming familiar with the software is a major hurdle. I spent a good portion of last summer, when I wasn't working on my book, learning how to use some of the classroom software for both algebra and calculus. The stuff's great, but I got stuck several times and had to call for help. It's necessary to understand the software to prepare lesson plans and explain to the students how to use it."

"How about problems with installing the software or hardware?" Anna asks.

"Oh, yes!" exclaims Rhoda. "I tried to install the software, and it went smoothly until the part where the screen asked questions about a number of import file formats for graphics, such as PSD and PNG. I didn't even know what those letters meant," laughs Rhoda.

"Then there were setup problems," Rhoda continues. "I needed to figure out what to install on the network and what to include on the local hard drive. Some of the computers in the student lab gave us 'Not enough memory' error messages, and we learned that they had been installed with minimum memory. The physics faculty had the same problem."

"Are there any other concerns you feel that we should include on our survey to the faculty and research staff?" Chip asks.

"It would be useful to know who is using the same software in different departments and what software is supplied by which vendor. Perhaps if we purchase many packages from one vendor, we could get a larger discount for software. The department software budget is already overwhelmed," Rhoda says.

"Thanks for all your help," Anna says. "If you think of any additional questions we should include on the survey, please do not hesitate to call us."

Back in their office, the analysts start compiling a list of the issues to be contained on the survey.

"We certainly need to ask about the software in use and about training needs," remarks Anna. "We should also address the problems that are occurring."

"Agreed," replies Chip. "I feel that we should include questions on software packages, vendors, versions, level of expertise, and training concerns. What I'm not so sure about is how to obtain information on problems the faculty and staff are encountering. How should we approach these issues?"

"Well," replies Anna, "we should focus on matters with which they are familiar. We might ask questions about the type of problems that are occurring, but certainly not technical ones. And the survey should not ask any questions that we could easily look up answers to, such as 'Who is the vendor for the software?'"

"I see," replies Chip. "Let's divide the questions into categories. Some would be closed questions and some would be open-ended. Then there's the matter of which structure to use."

EXERCISES

The first three exercises require that you visit the Web site to obtain the text of the interviews with CPU staff members. Please visit the Web site at www.prenhall.com/kendall and look for the "CPU Interviews."

EPISODE 4 *CPU CASE*

E-1. Analyze the five interviews. In a paragraph, discuss what type of structure each interview had.

E-2. List each interview, 1 through 5, and then write a paragraph for each, discussing ways that Anna might improve on her interviews for next time.

E-3. Analyze the questions used in the five interviews. In a paragraph, discuss the question types used and whether they were appropriate for getting needed information.

E-4. From the list of concerns presented earlier in this chapter, select the issues that would best be phrased as closed questions.

E-5. From the list of concerns, select the issues that would best be phrased as open-ended questions.

E-6. On the basis of Exercises E-4 and E-5, design a questionnaire to be sent to the faculty and research staff.

E-7. Pilot your questionnaire by having other students in class fill it out. On the basis of their feedback and your capability to analyze the data you receive, revise your questionnaire.

INFORMATION GATHERING: UNOBTRUSIVE METHODS

5

Learning Objectives

Once you have mastered the material in this chapter you will be able to:

1. **Recognize the value of unobtrusive methods for information gathering.**
2. **Understand the concept of sampling for human information requirements analysis.**
3. **Construct useful samples of people, documents, and events for determining human information requirements.**
4. **Create an analyst's playscript to observe decision-maker activities.**
5. **Apply the STROBE technique to observe and interpret the decision maker's environment and their interaction with technologies.**

Just by being present in an organization, the systems analyst changes it. However, unobtrusive methods such as sampling, investigation, and observing a decision maker's behavior and interaction with physical environment are less disruptive than other ways of eliciting human information requirements. Unobtrusive methods are considered to be insufficient information gathering methods when used alone. Rather, they should be used in conjunction with one or many of the interactive methods studied in the previous chapter. This is called a multiple methods approach. Using both interactive and unobtrusive methods in approaching the organization is a wise practice that will result in a more complete picture of human information requirements.

SAMPLING

Sampling is the process of systematically selecting representative elements of a population. When these selected elements are examined closely, it is assumed that the analysis will reveal useful information about the population as a whole.

The systems analyst has to make a decision on two key issues. First, there are many reports, forms, output documents, memos, and Web sites that have been generated by people in the organization. Which of these should the systems analyst pay attention to, and which should the systems analyst ignore?

Second, a great many employees can be affected by the proposed information system. Which people should the systems analyst interview, seek information from via questionnaires, or observe in the process of carrying out their decision-making roles?

THE NEED FOR SAMPLING

There are many reasons a systems analyst would want to select either a representative sample of data to examine or representative people to interview, question, or observe. They include:

1. Containing costs.
2. Speeding up the data gathering.
3. Improving effectiveness.
4. Reducing bias.

Examining every scrap of paper, talking with everyone, and reading every Web page from the organization would be far too costly for the systems analyst. Copying reports, asking employees for valuable time, and duplicating unnecessary surveys would result in much needless expense.

Sampling helps accelerate the process by gathering selected data rather than all data for the entire population. In addition, the systems analyst is spared the burden of analyzing data from the entire population.

Effectiveness in data gathering is an important consideration as well. Sampling can help improve effectiveness if information that is more accurate can be obtained. Such sampling is accomplished, for example, by talking to fewer employees but asking them questions that are more detailed. In addition, if fewer people are interviewed, the systems analyst can afford the time to follow up on missing or incomplete data, thus improving the effectiveness of data gathering.

Finally, data gathering bias can be reduced by sampling. When the systems analyst interviews an executive of the corporation, for example, the executive is involved with the project, because this person has already given a certain amount of time to the project and would like it to succeed. When the systems analyst asks an opinion about a permanent feature of the installed information system, the executive interviewed may provide a biased evaluation, because there is little possibility of changing it.

SAMPLING DESIGN

A systems analyst must follow four steps to design a good sample:

1. Determine the data to be collected or described.
2. Determine the population to be sampled.
3. Choose the type of sample.
4. Decide on the sample size.

These steps are described in detail in the following subsections.

Determining the Data to Be Collected or Described The systems analyst needs a realistic plan about what will be done with the data once they are collected. If irrelevant data are gathered, then time and money are wasted in the collection, storage, and analysis of useless data.

The duties and responsibilities of the systems analyst at this point are to identify the variables, attributes, and associated data items that need to be gathered in the sample. The objectives of the study must be considered as well as the type of data gathering method (investigation, interviews, questionnaires, observation) to be used. The kinds of information sought when using each of these methods are discussed in more detail in this and subsequent chapters.

	Not Based on Probability	Based on Probability
Sample elements are selected directly without restrictions	Convenience	Simple random
Sample elements are selected according to specific criteria	Purposive	Complex random (systematic, stratified, and cluster)

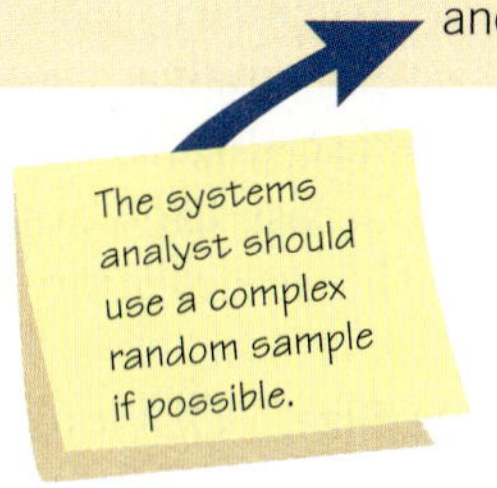

FIGURE 5.1
Four main types of samples the analyst has available.

Determining the Population to Be Sampled Next, the systems analyst must determine what the population is. In the case of hard data, the systems analyst needs to decide, for example, if the last two months are sufficient, or if an entire year's worth of reports are needed for analysis.

Similarly, when deciding whom to interview, the systems analyst has to determine whether the population should include only one level in the organization or all the levels, or maybe the analyst should even go outside of the system to include the reactions of customers, vendors, suppliers, or competitors. These decisions are explored further in the chapters on interviewing, questionnaires, and observation.

Choosing the Type of Sample The systems analyst can use one of four main types of samples, as pictured in Figure 5.1. They are convenience, purposive, simple, and complex. Convenience samples are unrestricted, nonprobability samples. A sample could be called a convenience sample if, for example, the systems analyst posts a notice on the company's intranet asking for everyone interested in working with the new sales performance reports to come to a meeting at 1 P.M. on Tuesday the 12th. Obviously, this sample is the easiest to arrange, but it is also the most unreliable. A purposive sample is based on judgment. A systems analyst can choose a group of individuals who appear knowledgeable and who are interested in the new information system. Here the systems analyst bases the sample on criteria (knowledge about and interest in the new system), but it is still a nonprobability sample. Thus, purposive sampling is only moderately reliable. If you choose to perform a simple random sample, you need to obtain a numbered list of the population to ensure that each document or person in the population has an equal chance of being selected. This step often is not practical, especially when sampling involves documents and reports. The complex random samples that are most appropriate for the systems analyst are (1) systematic sampling, (2) stratified sampling, and (3) cluster sampling.

In the simplest method of probability sampling, systematic sampling, the systems analyst would, for example, choose to interview every *k*th person on a list of company employees. This method has certain disadvantages, however. You would not want to use it to select every *k*th day for a sample because of the potential periodicity problem. Furthermore, a systems analyst would not use this approach if the list were ordered (for example, a list of banks from the smallest to the largest), because bias would be introduced.

Stratified samples are perhaps the most important to the systems analyst. Stratification is the process of identifying subpopulations, or strata, and then selecting objects or people for sampling in these subpopulations. Stratification is often essential if the systems analyst is to gather data efficiently. For example, if you want to seek opinions from a wide range of employees on different levels of the organization, systematic sampling would select a disproportionate number of employees from the operational control level. A stratified sample would compensate for this. Stratification is also called for when the systems analyst wants to use different methods to collect data from different subgroups. For example, you may want to use a survey to gather data from middle managers, but you might prefer to use personal interviews to gather similar data from executives.

Sometimes the systems analyst must select a group of people or documents to study. This process is referred to as cluster sampling. Suppose an organization had 20 helpdesks scattered across the country. You may want to select one or two of these helpdesks under the assumption that they are typical of the remaining ones.

Deciding on the Sample Size Obviously, if everyone in the population viewed the world the same way or if each of the documents in a population contained exactly the same information as every other document, a sample size of one would be sufficient. Because that is not the case, it is necessary to set a sample size greater than one but less than the size of the population itself.

It is important to remember that the absolute number is more important in sampling than the percentage of the population. We can obtain satisfactory results sampling 20 people in 200 or 20 people in 2,000,000.

THE SAMPLE SIZE DECISION

The sample size often depends on the cost involved or the time required by the systems analyst, or even the time available by people in the organization. This subsection gives the systems analyst some guidelines for determining the required sample size under ideal conditions, for example, to determine what percentage of input forms contain errors, or alternatively what proportion of people to interview.

The systems analyst needs to follow seven steps, some of which are subjective judgments, to determine the required sample size:

1. Determine the attribute (in this case, the type of errors to look for).
2. Locate the database or reports in which the attribute can be found.
3. Examine the attribute. Estimate p, the proportion of the population having the attribute.
4. Make the subjective decision regarding the acceptable interval estimate, i.
5. Choose the confidence level and look up the confidence coefficient (z value) in a table.
6. Calculate σ_p, the standard error of the proportion as follows:

$$\sigma_p = \frac{i}{z}$$

7. Determine the necessary sample size, n, using the following formula:

$$n = \frac{p(1-p)}{\sigma_p^2} + 1$$

The first step, of course, is to determine which attribute you will be sampling. Once this is done, you can find out where this data is stored, perhaps in a database, on a form, or in a report.

It is important to estimate p, the proportion of the population having the attribute, so that you set the appropriate sample size. Many textbooks on systems analysis suggest using a heuristic of 0.25 for $p(1 - p)$. This value almost always results in a sample size larger than necessary because 0.25 is the maximum value

First decide on the confidence level . . .

Confidence Level	Confidence Coefficient (z value)
99%	2.58
98	2.33
97	2.17
96	2.05
95	1.96
90	1.65
80	1.28
50	0.67

. . . then look up the z value.

FIGURE 5.2

A table of area under a normal curve can be used to look up a value once the systems analyst decides on the confidence level.

of $p(1-p)$, which occurs only when $p = 0.50$. When $p = 0.10$, as is more often the case, $p(1-p)$ becomes 0.09, resulting in a much smaller sample size.

Steps 4 and 5 are subjective decisions. The acceptable interval estimate of ± 0.10 means that you are willing to accept an error of no more than 0.10 in either direction from the actual proportion, p. The confidence level is the desired degree of certainty, say, for example, 95 percent. Once the confidence level is chosen, the confidence coefficient (also called a z value) can be looked up in a table like the one found in Figure 5.2.

Steps 6 and 7 complete the process by taking the parameters found or set in steps 3 through 5 and entering them into two equations to eventually solve for the required sample size.

Example

The foregoing steps can best be illustrated by an example. Suppose the A. Sembly Company, a large manufacturer of shelving products, asks you to determine what percentage of orders contain mistakes. You agree to do this job and perform the following steps. You:

1. Determine that you will be looking for orders that contain mistakes in names, addresses, quantities, or model numbers.
2. Locate copies of order forms from the past six months.
3. Examine some of the order forms and conclude that only about 5 percent (0.05) contain errors.
4. Make a subjective decision that the acceptable interval estimate will be ± 0.02.
5. Choose a confidence level of 95 percent. Look up the confidence coefficient (z value) in Figure 5.2. The z value equals 1.96.
6. Calculate σ_p as follows:

$$\sigma_p = \frac{i}{z} = \frac{0.02}{1.96} = 0.0102$$

7. Determine the necessary sample size, n, as follows:

$$n = \frac{p(1-p)}{\sigma_p^2} + 1 = \frac{0.05(0.95)}{(0.0102)(0.0102)} + 1 = 458$$

The conclusion, then, is to set the sample size at 458. Obviously, a greater confidence level or a smaller acceptable interval estimate would require a larger sample

CONSULTING OPPORTUNITY 5.1

TRAPPING A SAMPLE

"Real or fake? Fake or real? Who would have thought it, even five years ago?" howls Sam Pelt, a furrier who owns stores in New York, Washington, D.C., Beverly Hills, and Copenhagen. Sylva Foxx, a systems analyst with her own consulting firm, is talking with Sam for the first time. Currently, P & P, Ltd. (which stands for Pelt and Pelt's son) is using a PC that supports package software for a select customer mailing list, accounts payable and accounts receivable, and payroll.

Sam is interested in making some strategic decisions that will ultimately affect the purchasing of goods for his four fur stores. He feels that although the computer might help, other approaches should also be considered.

Sam continues, "I think we should talk to all of the customers when they come in the door. Get their opinions. You know, some of them are getting very upset about wearing fur from endangered species. They're very environmentally minded. They prefer fake to real, if they can save a baby animal. Some even like fakes better, calling them 'fun furs.' And I can charge almost the same for a good look-alike.

"It's a very fuzzy proposition, though. If I get too far away from my suppliers of pelts, I may not get what I want when I need it. They see the fake fur people as worms, worse then moths! If I deal with them, the real fur men might not talk to me. They can be animals. On the other hand, I feel strange showing fakes in my stores. All these years, we've prided ourselves on having only the genuine article."

Sam continues, in a nearly seamless monologue, "I want to talk to each and every employee, too."

Sylva glances at him furtively and begins to interrupt. "But that will take months, and purchasing may come apart at the seams unless they know soon what—"

Pelt interrupts, "I don't care how long it takes, if we get the right answers. But they have to be right. Not knowing how to solve this dilemma about fake furs is making me feel like a leopard without its spots."

Sylva talks to Sam Pelt a bit longer and then ends the interview by saying, "I'll talk it all over with the other analysts at the office and let you know what we come up with. I think we can outfox the other furriers if we use the computer to help us sample opinions, rather than trapping unsuspecting customers into giving an opinion. But I'll let you know what they say. This much is for sure: If we can sample and not talk to everybody before making a decision, every coat you sell will have a silver lining."

As one of the systems analysts who is part of Sylva Foxx's firm, suggest some ways that Sam Pelt can use the PC he has to adequately sample the opinions of his customers, store managers, buyers, and any others you feel will be instrumental in making the strategic decision regarding the stocking of fake furs in what has always been a real fur store. Suggest a type of sample for each group and justify it. The constraints you are subject to include the need to act quickly so as to remain competitive, the need to retain a low profile so that competing furriers are unaware of your fact gathering, and the need to keep costs of data gathering to a reasonable level.

size. If we keep the acceptable interval estimate the same but increase the confidence level to 99 percent (with a z value of 2.58), the necessary sample size becomes 1,827, a figure much larger than the 458 we originally decided to sample.

Determining Sample Size When Interviewing There are no magic formulas to help the systems analyst set the sample size for interviewing. The overriding variable that determines how many people the systems analyst should interview in depth is the time an interview takes. A true in-depth interview and follow-up interview is very time consuming for both the interviewer and the participant.

A good rule of thumb is to interview at least three people on every level of the organization and at least one from each of the organization's functional areas (as described in Chapter 2) who will work directly with a new or updated system. Remember also that one does not have to interview more people just because it is a larger organization. If the stratified sample is done properly, a small number of people will adequately represent the entire organization.

INVESTIGATION

Investigation is the act of discovery and analysis of data. While investigating evidence in an organization, the analyst acts like Sherlock Holmes, the fabled detective from 221B Baker Street.

As the systems analyst works to understand users, their organization, and its information requirements, it will become important to examine different types of hard data that offer information unavailable through any other method of data gathering. Hard data reveal where the organization has been and where its members believe it is going. To piece together an accurate picture, the analyst needs to examine both quantitative and qualitative hard data.

ANALYZING QUANTITATIVE DOCUMENTS

Many quantitative documents are available for interpretation in any business, and they include reports used for decision making, performance reports, records, and a variety of forms. All these documents have a specific purpose and audience for which they are targeted.

Reports Used for Decision Making A systems analyst needs to obtain some of the documents that are used in running the business. These documents are often paper reports regarding the status of inventory, sales, or production. Many of these reports are not complex, but they serve mainly as feedback for quick action. For example, a sales report may summarize the amount sold and the type of sales. In addition, sales reports might include graphical output comparing revenue and income over a set number of periods. Such reports enable the decision maker to spot trends easily.

Production reports include recent costs, current inventory, recent labor, and plant information. Beyond these key reports, many summary reports are used by decision makers to provide background information, spot exceptions to normal occurrences, and afford strategic overviews of organizational plans.

Performance Reports Most performance reports take on the general form of actual versus intended performance. One important function of performance reports is to assess the size of the gap between actual and intended performance. It is also important to be able to determine if that gap is widening or narrowing as an overall trend in whatever performance is being measured. Figure 5.3 shows a clear

Week	Number of Batches Produced	Number of Batches Rejected	Percentage Rejected	Amount Away from 5% Goal
2/2	245	19	7.8	2.8
2/9	229	19	8.3	3.3
2/16	219	14	6.3	1.3
2/23	252	13	5.2	0.2
3/2	245	13	5.3	0.3
3/9	260	13	5.0	* * *
3/16	275	14	5.1	0.1
3/23	260	13	5.0	* * *
3/30	260	13	5.0	* * *
4/6	244	12	4.9	* * *
4/13	242	11	4.5	* * *
4/20	249	11	4.4	* * *
4/27	249	11	4.4	* * *

* * * indicates met or exceeded the < 5% goal

Performance reports show goals . . .

. . . and trends.

FIGURE 5.3

A performance report showing improvement.

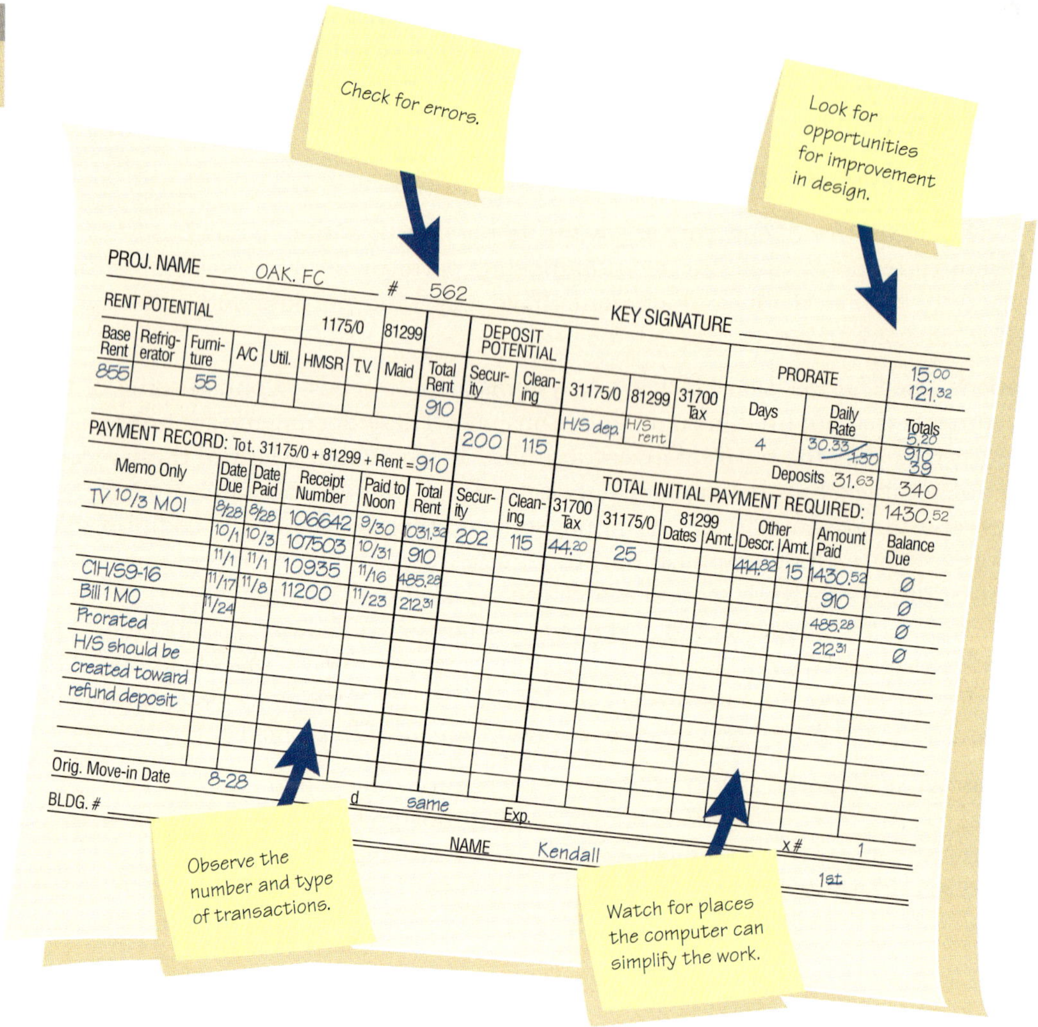

FIGURE 5.4

A manually completed payment record.

improvement in sales performance over two to three months. The analyst will want to note if performance measurement is available and adequate for key organizational areas.

Records Records provide periodic updates of what is occurring in the business. If the record is updated in a timely fashion by a careful recorder, it can provide much useful information to the analyst. Figure 5.4 is a manually completed payment record for apartment rental. There are several ways that the analyst can inspect a record, many of which are indicative of their usability:

1. Checking for errors in amounts and totals.
2. Looking for opportunities for improving the recording form design.
3. Observing the number and type of transactions.
4. Watching for instances in which the computer can simplify the work (i.e., calculations and other data manipulation).

Data Capture Forms Before you set out to change the information flows in the organization, you need to be able to understand the system that is currently in place. You or one of your team members may want to collect and catalog a blank copy of each form (official or unofficial) that is in use. (Sometimes businesses have a person already charged with forms management, who would be your first source for forms in use.)

CONSULTING OPPORTUNITY 5.2

A ROSE BY ANY OTHER NAME . . . OR QUALITY, NOT QUANTITIES

"I think we have everything we need. I've sampled financial statements, sales figures for each branch, wastage for each shop—we have it all. With all these numbers, we should be able to figure out how to keep Fields in the green, or at least at the forefront of the flower business. We can even show Seymour Fields himself how his new computer system can make it all happen," says Rod Golden, a junior systems analyst working for a medium-sized consulting group.

The firm, under the supervision of its head systems analyst, Clay Potts, has been working on a systems project for the entire chain of 15 successful florist shops and indoor floral markets called Fields. Each of three Midwestern cities has five Fields outlets.

"Although it's just a budding enterprise now, eventually we want to grow with offshoots to half a dozen states," says Seymour Fields, the owner. "I want to reap the benefits of all the happiness we've sown so far. I think we can do it by playing my hunches about what is the best time to purchase flowers at each European market we buy from, and then we should prune back our purchases.

"Over the past three years, I've written lots of memos to our managers about this plan. They've written some good ones back, too. I think we're ready to stake out some territory on this soon," continues Seymour, painting a rosy picture of Fields's future.

"I agree," says Rod. "When I come back from my analysis of these figures," he says, indicating a large stack of material he has unearthed from Fields field offices, "we'll be able to deliver."

Three weeks later, Rod returns to Clay with wilting confidence. "I don't know what to make of all this. I can't seem to get at what's causing the company's growth, or how it's managed. They've been expanding, but I've been through all the figures, and nothing really seems to make sense yet."

Clay listens empathetically, then says, "You've given me a germ of an idea. What we need is some cross-pollination, a breath of fresh air. We need to dig a little deeper. Did you examine anything but their bottom line?"

Rod looks startled and replies, "No, I—uh—what do you mean?"

How can Clay Potts tactfully explain to Rod Golden that examination of qualitative as well as quantitative documents could be important to delivering an accurate assessment of Fields's potential to be a more fruitful enterprise? In a paragraph, recommend some specific documents that should be read. List the specific steps Rod should follow in evaluating qualitative documents obtained from Fields. Write a paragraph to explain how qualitative documents help in presenting an overall account of Fields's success.

Blank forms, along with their instructions for completion and distribution, can be compared with filled-in forms to see if any data items are consistently left blank on the forms; whether the people who are supposed to receive the forms actually do get them; and if they follow standard procedures for using, storing, and discarding them. Remember to print out any Web-based forms that require users to print them. Alternatively, electronic versions that can be submitted via the Web or email can be identified and stored in a database for later inspection.

To proceed when creating a catalog of forms to help you understand the information flow currently in use in the business:

1. Collect examples of all the forms in use, whether officially sanctioned by the business or not (official versus bootleg forms).
2. Note the type of form (whether printed in-house, handwritten, computer-generated in-house, online forms, Web fill-in forms, printed externally and purchased, etc.).
3. Document the intended distribution pattern.
4. Compare the intended distribution pattern with who actually receives the form.

Although this procedure is time consuming, it is useful. Another approach is to sample data capture forms that have already been completed. Remember to check databases that store consumer data when sampling input from ecommerce transactions. The analyst must keep in mind many particular questions, as

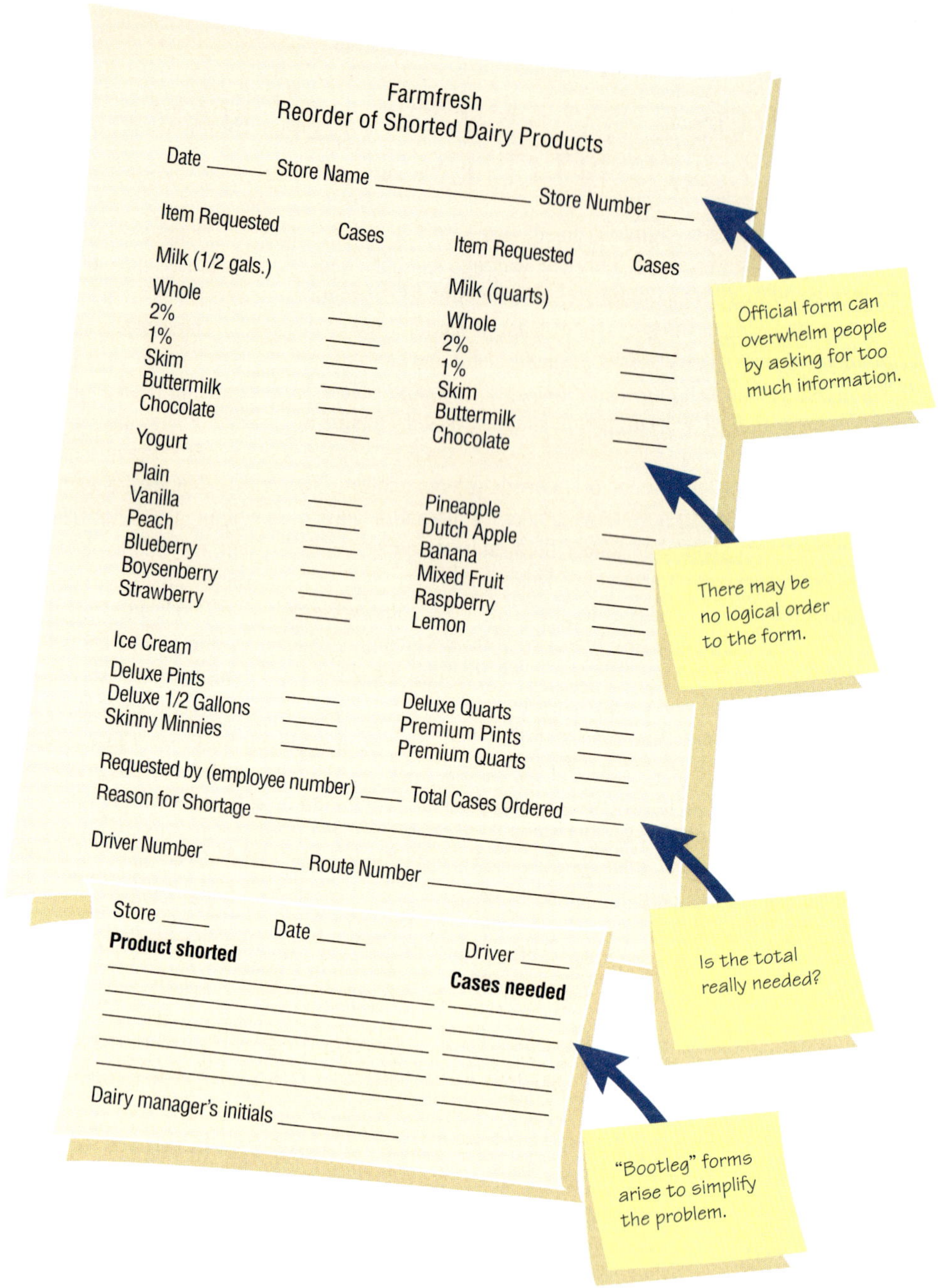

FIGURE 5.5

Questions to ask about official and bootleg forms that are already filled out.

illustrated in Figure 5.5. They include the following aspects of HCI relating to usability, aesthetics, and usefulness:

1. Is the form filled out in its entirety? If not, what items have been omitted, and are they consistently omitted? Why?
2. Are there forms that are never used? Why? (Check the design and appropriateness of each form for its purported function.)
3. Are all copies of forms circulated to the proper people or filed appropriately? If not, why not? Can people who must access online forms do so?
4. If there is a paper form that is offered as an alternative to a Web-based form, compare the completion rates for both.
5. Are "unofficial" forms being used on a regular basis? (Their use might indicate a problem in standard procedures or may indicate political battles in the organization.)

ANALYZING QUALITATIVE DOCUMENTS

Qualitative documents include email messages, memos, signs on bulletin boards and in work areas, Web pages, procedure manuals, and policy handbooks. Many of these documents are rich in details revealing the expectations for behavior of others that their writers hold and the ways in which users expect to interact with information technologies.

Although many systems analysts are apprehensive about analyzing qualitative documents, they need not be. Several guidelines can help analysts take a systematic approach to this sort of analysis. Many of these relate to the affective, emotional, and motivational aspects of human–computer interaction, as well as interpersonal relationships in the organization.

1. Examine documents for key or guiding metaphors.
2. Look for insiders versus outsiders or an "us against them" mentality.
3. List terms that characterize good or evil and appear repeatedly in documents.
4. Look for the use of meaningful messages and graphics posted on common areas or on Web pages.
5. Recognize a sense of humor, if present.

Examining documents for key or guiding metaphors is done because language shapes behavior; thus, the metaphors we employ are critical. For example, an organization that discusses employees as "part of a great machine" or "cogs in a wheel" might be taking a mechanistic view of the organization. Notice that the guiding metaphor in the memo in Figure 5.6 is, "We're one big happy family." The analyst can use this information to predict the kinds of metaphors that will be persuasive in the organization. Obviously, if one department is battling another, it may be impossible to gain any cooperation on a systems project until the politics are resolved in a satisfactory manner. Assessing the use of humor provides a quick and accurate barometer of many HCI, interpersonal, and organizational variables, including which subculture a person belongs to and what kind of morale exists.

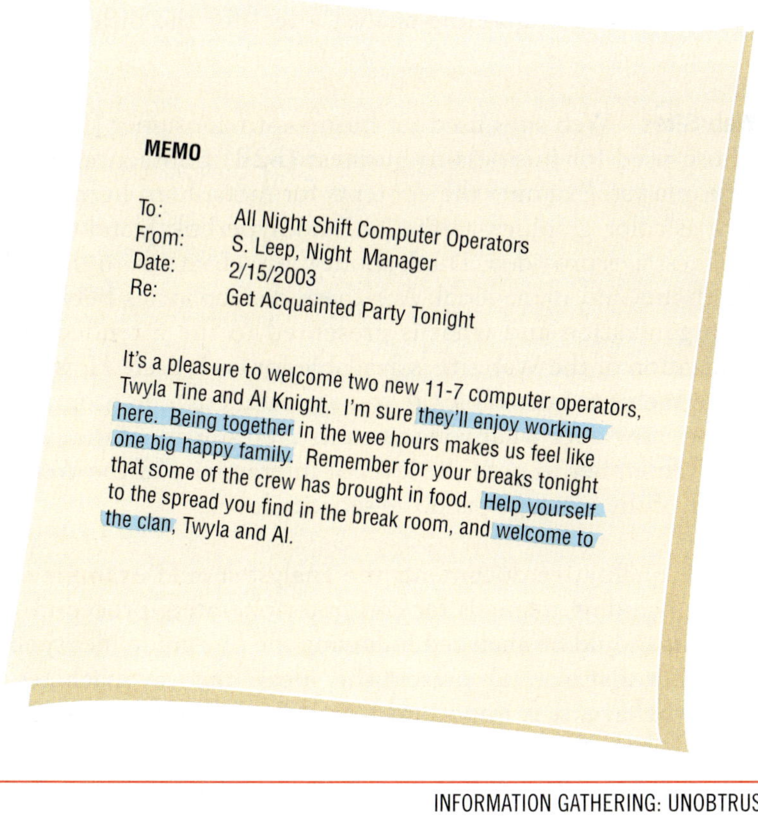
MEMO

To: All Night Shift Computer Operators
From: S. Leep, Night Manager
Date: 2/15/2003
Re: Get Acquainted Party Tonight

It's a pleasure to welcome two new 11-7 computer operators, Twyla Tine and Al Knight. I'm sure they'll enjoy working here. Being together in the wee hours makes us feel like one big happy family. Remember for your breaks tonight that some of the crew has brought in food. Help yourself to the spread you find in the break room, and welcome to the clan, Twyla and Al.

FIGURE 5.6
Analysis of memos provides insight into the metaphors that guide the organization's thinking.

FIGURE 5.7

Posted signs reveal the official organizational culture.

Memos Along with the five preceding guidelines, the analyst should also consider who sends memos and who receives them. Typically, most information flows downward and horizontally rather than upward in organizations, and extensive email systems mean messages are sent to many workgroups and individuals. Memos reveal a lively, continuing dialogue in the organization. Analysis of memo content will provide you with a clear idea of the values, attitudes, and beliefs of organizational members.

Signs or Posters on Bulletin Boards or in Work Areas Although signs may seem incidental to what is happening in the organization, they serve as subtle reinforcers of values to those who read them, as depicted in Figure 5.7. Signs such as "Quality Is Forever" or "Safety First" give the analyst a feel for the official organizational culture.

Corporate Web Sites Web sites used for business-to-consumer (B2C) ecommerce as well as those used for business-to-business (B2B) transactions should also be viewed by the analyst. Examine the contents for metaphors, humor, use of design features (such as color, graphics, animation, and hyperlinks), and the meaning and clarity of any messages provided. Think about the Web site from three dimensions: technical, aesthetic, and managerial. Are there discrepancies between the stated goals of the organization and what is presented to the intended viewer? How much customization of the Web site is available for each user? How much personalization of the Web site is possible? If you are not designing ecommerce sites for the organization, how does what you see on its Web site affect the systems you are investigating? Remember to note the level of interactivity of the Web site or sites, the accessibility of the messages, and the security level.

Manuals Other qualitative documents the analyst should examine are organizational manuals, including manuals for computer operating procedures and online manuals. Manuals should be analyzed following the five guidelines spelled out previously. Remember that manuals present the "ideal," the way machines and people are expected to behave. It is important to recall that printed manuals are rarely kept current and are sometimes relegated to a shelf, unused.

HYPERCASE® EXPERIENCE

5.1

"We're glad you find MRE an interesting place to consult. According to the grapevine, you've been busy exploring the home office. I know, there's so much going on. We find it hard to keep track of everything ourselves. One thing we've made sure of over the years is that we try to use the methods that we believe in. Have you seen any of our reports? How about the data that were collected on one of Snowden's questionnaires? He seems to favor questionnaires over any other method. Some people resent them, but I think you can learn a lot from the results. Some people have been good about cooperating on these projects. Have you met Kathy Blandford yet?"

HYPERCASE QUESTIONS

1. Use clues from the case to evaluate the Training Unit's computer experience and its staff's feeling about a computerized project tracking system. What do you think the consensus is in the Training Unit toward a computerized tracking system?
2. What reports and statements are generated by the Training Unit during project development? List each with a brief description.
3. According to the interview results, what are the problems with the present project tracking system in the Training Unit?
4. Describe the "project management conflict" at MRE. Who is involved? Why is there a conflict?
5. How does the Management Systems Unit keep track of project progress? Briefly describe the method or system.

Policy Handbooks The last type of qualitative document we consider is the policy handbook. Although these documents typically cover broad areas of employee and corporate behavior, you can be primarily concerned with those that address policies about computer services, use, access, security, and charges. Examining policies allows the systems analyst to gain an awareness of the values, attitudes, and beliefs guiding the corporation.

OBSERVING A DECISION MAKER'S BEHAVIOR

Observing decision makers, their physical environment, and their interaction with their physical, ergonomic environment is an important unobtrusive method for the systems analyst. Through observing activities of decision makers, the analyst seeks to gain insight about what is actually done, not just what is documented or explained. In addition, through observation of the decision maker, the analyst attempts to see firsthand the relationships that exist between decision makers and other organizational members. Observation of decision makers' interactions with technologies can also reveal important clues regarding HCI concerns, such as how well the system fits with the user.

OBSERVING A TYPICAL MANAGER'S DECISION-MAKING ACTIVITIES

Managers' workdays have been described as a series of interruptions punctuated by short bursts of work. In other words, pinning down what a manager "does" is a slippery proposition even under the best of circumstances. For the systems analyst to grasp adequately how managers characterize their work, interactive interviews and questionnaires are used. Observation, however, allows the analyst to see firsthand how managers gather, process, share, and use information and technology to get work done.

Although it is possible to describe and document how managers make decisions using boxes and arrows, we are primarily describing humans and their activities. Therefore, we suggest that systems analysts use a more humanistic approach to describe what managers do. This method is called the analyst's playscript. With this technique the "actor" is the decision maker who is observed "acting" or making decisions. In setting up a playscript, the actor is listed in the left-hand column and all their actions are listed in the right-hand column, as shown in Figure 5.8. All activities are recorded with action verbs, so that a decision maker would be described as "talking," "sampling," "corresponding," and "deciding."

FIGURE 5.8

A sample page from the analyst's playscript describing decision making.

Playscript Analysis Company: Solid Steel Shelving Analyst: L. Bracket Scenario: Quality Assurance Date: 9/3/2003

Decision Maker (Actor)	Information-Related Activity (Script)
Quality Assurance Manager	Asks shop floor supervisor for the day's production report
Shop Floor Supervisor	Prints out daily computerized production report
	Discusses recurring problems in production runs with quality assurance (QA) manager
Quality Assurance Manager	Reads production report
	Compares current report with other reports from the same week
	Inputs data from daily production run into QA model on computer
	Observes onscreen results of QA model
	Calls steel suppliers to discuss deviations from quality standards
Shop Floor Supervisor	Attends meeting on new quality specifications with quality assurance manager and vice president of production
Quality Assurance Manager	Drafts letter to inform suppliers on new quality specifications agreed on in meeting
	Sends draft to vice president via email
Vice President of Production	Reads drafted letter
	Returns corrections and comments via email
Quality Assurance Manager	Reads corrected letter on email
	Rewrites letter to reflect changes

Playscript is an organized and systematic approach that demands the analyst be able to understand and articulate the action taken by each observed decision maker. This approach eventually assists the systems analyst in determining what information is required for major or frequent decisions made by the observed people. For instance, from the quality assurance manager example in the playscript, it becomes clear that even though this decision maker is on the middle management level, he or she still requires a fair amount of external information to perform the required activities of this specific job.

OBSERVING THE PHYSICAL ENVIRONMENT

Observing the activities of decision makers is just one way to assess their information requirements. Observing the physical environment in which decision makers work also reveals much about their human information requirements. Most often, such observing means systematically examining the offices of decision makers, because offices constitute their primary workplace. Decision makers influence and are in turn influenced by their physical environments and by their interactions with the technology that takes place there. Many HCI concerns can be identified through structured observation and confirmed with other techniques, such as interviews or questionnaires.

STRUCTURED OBSERVATION OF THE ENVIRONMENT (STROBE)

Film critics sometimes use a structured form of criticism called mise-en-scène analysis to systematically assess what is in a single shot of the film. They look at editing, camera angle, set decor, and the actors and their costumes to find out how they are shaping the meaning of the film as intended by the director. Sometimes the film's mise-en-scène will contradict what is said in the dialogue. For information requirements analysis, the systems analyst can take on a role similar to that of the film critic. It often is possible to observe the particulars of the surroundings that will confirm or negate the organizational narrative (also called "stories" or "dialogue") that is found through interviews or questionnaires.

The method for *STR*uctured *OB*servation of the *E*nvironment is referred to as STROBE. Successful application of STROBE requires that an analyst explicitly observe seven concrete elements commonly found in offices. The seven observable elements and some key questions that may arise are listed in Figure 5.9. These elements can reveal much about the way a decision maker gathers, processes, stores, and shares information, as well as about the decision maker's credibility in the workplace.

Office Location One of the first elements a systems analyst should observe is the location of a particular decision maker's office with respect to other offices. Accessible offices tend to increase interaction frequency and informal messages, whereas inaccessible offices tend to decrease the interaction frequency and increase task-oriented messages. Offices distributed along the perimeter of the building usually result in a report or memo being held up in one of the offices, whereas office clusters encourage information sharing. It is also likely that the people whose offices are separated from others may tend to view the organization differently and so drift further apart from other organization members in their objectives.

Desk Placement Placement of a desk in the office can provide clues to the exercise of power by the decision maker. Executives who enclose a visitor in a tight space with the visitor's back to the wall while allowing themselves a lot of room

FIGURE 5.9
Seven concrete observable elements of STROBE and example of questions an analyst may want to ask.

Observable Element	Questions an Analyst Might Investigate
Office location	Who has the corner office? Are the key decision makers dispersed over separate floors?
Desk placement	Does the placement of the desk encourage communication? Does the placement demonstrate power?
Stationary equipment	Does the decision maker prefer to gather and store information personally? Is the storage area large or small?
Props	Is there evidence that the decision maker uses the PC? Are there any handheld computers or tablet computers in the office?
External information sources	Does the decision maker get much information from external sources such as trade journals or the Web?
Office lighting and color	Is the lighting set up to do detailed work or more appropriate for casual communication? Are the colors warm and inviting?
Clothing worn by decision makers	Does the decision maker show authority by wearing conservative suits? Are employees required to wear uniforms?

put themselves into the strongest possible power position. An executive who positions his or her desk facing the wall with a chair at the side for a visitor is probably encouraging participation and equal exchanges. The systems analyst should notice the arrangement of the office furniture and in particular the placement of the desk. Figure 5.10 shows an example of desk placement as well as many of the other elements of STROBE, such as props, stationary office equipment, lighting, color, and external sources of information.

Stationary Office Equipment File cabinets, bookshelves, and other large equipment for storing items are all included in the category of stationary office equipment. If

FIGURE 5.10
Observe a decision maker's office for clues concerning his or her personal storage, processing, and sharing of information.

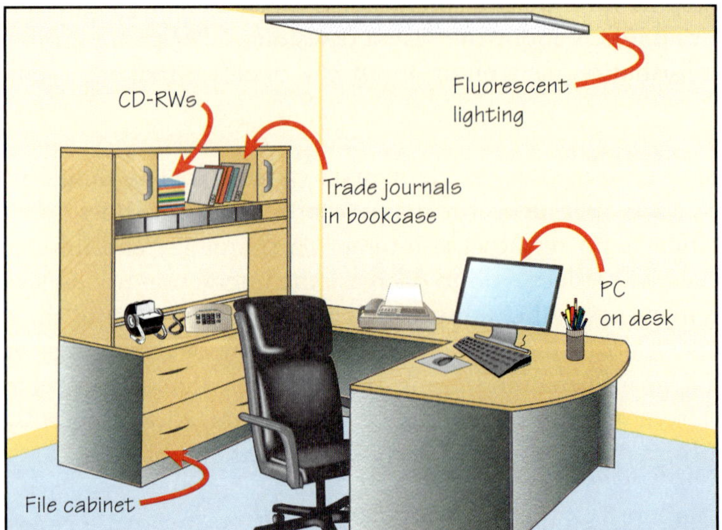

there is no such equipment, it is likely the decision maker stores very few items of information personally. If there is an abundance of such equipment, it is presumed the decision maker stores and values much information.

Props The term *props* (an abbreviation of the theatre/film term *properties*) refers to all the small equipment used to process information, including PDAs, calculators, PCs, pens, pencils, and rulers. The presence of handhelds, calculators, and PCs suggests that a decision maker who possesses such equipment is more likely to use it personally than one who must leave the room to use it.

External Information Sources A systems analyst needs to know what type of information is used by the decision maker. Observation of the type of publications stored in the office can reveal whether the decision maker is looking for external information (found in trade journals, newspaper clippings about other companies in the industry, and so on) or relies more on internal information (company reports, intraoffice correspondence, policy handbooks). The analyst should also observe whether the decision maker prefers to get external information from the Web.

Office Lighting and Color Lighting and color play an important role in how a decision maker gathers information. An office lighted with warm, incandescent lighting indicates a tendency toward more personal communication. An executive in a warmly lit office will gather more information informally, whereas another organizational member working in a brightly lit, brightly colored office may gather information through more formal memos and official reports.

Clothing Worn by Decision Makers Much has been written about the clothing worn by executives and others in authority. The systems analyst can gain an understanding of the credibility exhibited by managers in the organization by observing the clothing they wear on the job. The two-piece suit for a man or the skirted suit for a woman represents the maximum authority, according to some researchers who have studied perceptions of executive appearance. Casual dressing by leaders tends to open the door for more participative decision making, but such attire often results in some loss of credibility in the organization if the predominant culture values traditional, conservative clothing.

Through the use of STROBE, the systems analyst can gain a better understanding of how managers gather, process, store, and use information. A summary of the characteristics exhibited by decision makers and the corresponding observable elements is shown in Figure 5.11.

Characteristics of Decision Makers	Corresponding Elements in the Physical Environment
Gathers information informally	Warm, incandescent lighting and colors
Seeks extraorganizational information	Trade journals present in office
Processes data personally	PCs, handhelds present in office
Stores information personally	Equipment/files present in office
Exercises power in decision making	Desk placed for power
Exhibits credibility in decision making	Wears authoritative clothing
Shares information with others	Office easily accessible

FIGURE 5.11
A summary of decision-maker characteristics that correspond to observable elements in the physical environment.

CONSULTING OPPORTUNITY 5.3

DON'T BANK ON THEIR SELF-IMAGE
OR
NOT EVERYTHING IS REFLECTED IN A MIRROR

"I don't want any power here," demurs Dr. Drew Charles, medical director of the regional blood center where your systems group has just begun a project. "I'm up to my neck in work just keeping the regional physicians informed so they follow good bloodbanking practices," he says, as he shields his eyes from the bright sunlight streaming into his office. He clicks off the monitor connected to his PC and turns his attention to you and the interview.

Dr. Charles is dressed in a conservative, dark wool suit and is wearing a red-striped silk necktie. He continues, "In fact, I don't make decisions. I'm here purely in a positive support role." He pulls out the organizational chart shown in Figure 5.C1 to illustrate his point. "It is as clear as a fracture. The chief administrator is the expert on all administrative matters. I am the medical consultant only."

Dr. Charles's office is stacked high not only with medical journals such as *Transfusion* but also with *BYTE* magazine and *Business Week*. Each is opened to a different page, as if the doctor were in the process of devouring each new morsel of information. The overflow journals, however, are not stored meticulously on metal bookshelves as expected. In sharp contrast to the gleaming new equipment you saw being used in the donor rooms, the journals are piled a foot high on an old blood-donating bed that has been long retired from its intended use.

Next, you decide to interview the chief administrator, Craig Bunker, to whom Dr. Charles has alluded. Fifteen minutes after the scheduled start of your appointment, Bunker's secretary, Dawn Upshaw, finally allows you to enter his office. Bunker, who has just finished a phone call, is dressed in a light-blue sport coat, checkered slacks, light-blue shirt, and a necktie. "How are you doing? I've just been checking around to see how everything's perking along," Bunker says by way of introduction. He is outgoing and very friendly.

As you glance around the room, you notice that there are no filing cabinets, nor is there a PC such as the one Dr. Charles was using. There are lots of photos of Craig Bunker's family, but the only item resembling a book or magazine is the center's newsletter, *Bloodline*. As the interview begins in earnest, Bunker cheerfully launches into stories about the Pennsylvania Blood Center, where he held the position of assistant administrator six years ago.

Finally, you descend the stairs to the damp basement level of the Heath Lambert Mansion. The bloodmobiles have just returned, and processed blood has been shipped to area hospitals. You decide to talk with Sang Kim, a bloodmobile driver; Jenny McLaughlin, the distribution manager; and Roberta Martin, a lab technician who works the night shift.

Roberta begins, "I don't know what we'd do without the doctor." In the same vein, though, Sang feeds the conversation by remarking, "Yeah, he helped us by thinking up a better driving schedule last week."

Jenny adds, "Dr. Charles is invaluable in setting the inventory levels for each hospital, and if it wasn't for him, we wouldn't have word processing yet, let alone our new computer."

As one of the systems analysis team members assigned to the blood center project, develop an anecdotal checklist using STROBE to help you systematically interpret the observations you made about the offices of Dr. Charles and Craig Bunker. Consider any disparities between a decision maker's clothing, what a decision maker states, and what is said by others; between office location and what is stated; and between office equipment and policies stated. In addition, in a paragraph, suggest possible follow-up interviews and observations to help settle any unresolved questions.

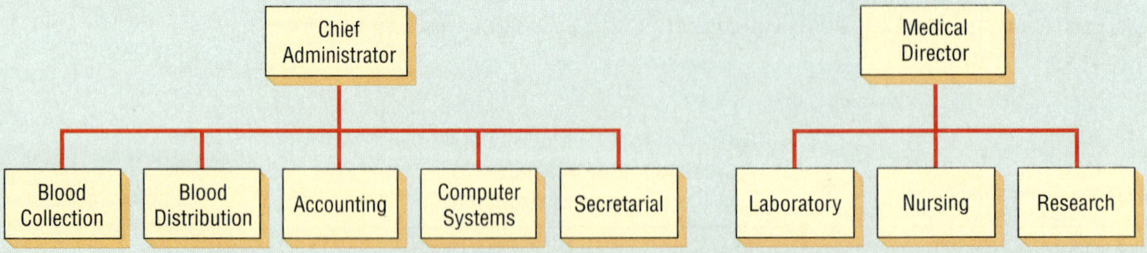

FIGURE 5.C1
Organizational chart of the regional blood center.

APPLYING STROBE

One way to implement STROBE is through the use of an anecdotal checklist with meaningful shorthand symbols. This approach to STROBE was useful in ascertaining the information requirements for four key decision makers in a franchise clothing store.

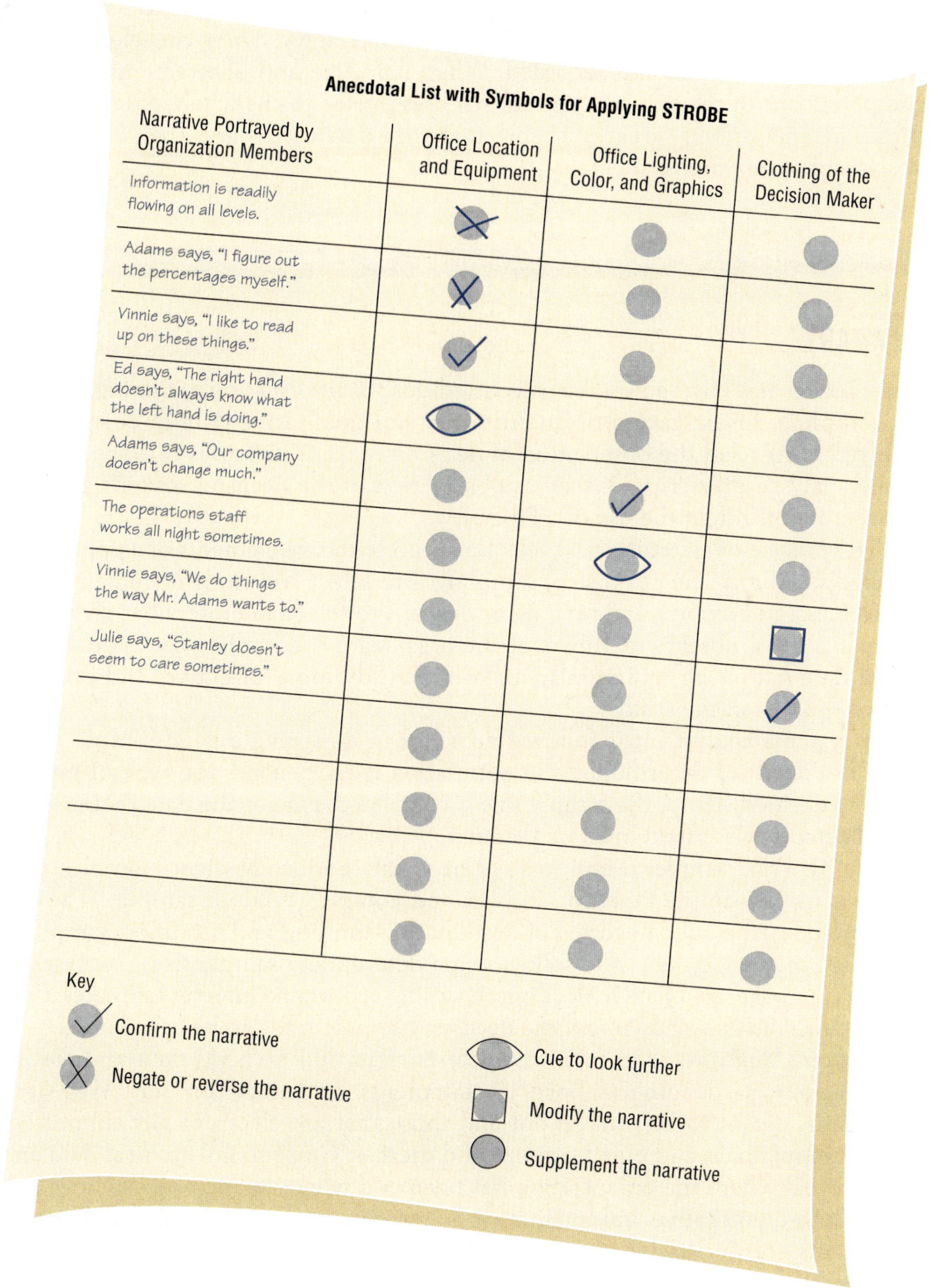

FIGURE 5.12

An anecdotal list with symbols for use in applying STROBE.

As can be seen in Figure 5.12, five shorthand symbols were used by the systems analysts to evaluate how observation of the elements of STROBE compared with the organizational narrative generated through interviews. The five symbols are as follows:

1. A check mark means the narrative is confirmed.
2. An "X" means the narrative is reversed.
3. An oval or eye-shaped symbol serves as a cue for the systems analyst to look further.
4. A square means observation of the elements of STROBE modifies the narrative.
5. A circle means the narrative is supplemented by what is observed.

When STROBE is implemented in this manner, the first step is to write down key organizational themes growing out of interviews. Then the elements of STROBE are observed and recorded. When narrative and observations are then compared, one of the five appropriate symbols is used to characterize the relationship. The analyst thus creates a table that first documents and then aids in the analysis of observations.

SUMMARY

This chapter has covered unobtrusive methods for information gathering, including sampling; investigation of quantitative and qualitative data in current and archived forms; and the observation of decision maker's activities through the use of the analyst's playscript, as well as observation of the decision maker's physical environment through the use of STROBE.

The process of systematically selecting representative elements of a population is called sampling. The purpose of sampling is to select and study documents such as invoices, sales reports, and memos, or perhaps to select and interview, give questionnaires to, or observe members of the organization. Sampling can reduce cost, speed data gathering, potentially make the study more effective, and possibly reduce the bias in the study.

A systems analyst must follow four steps in designing a good sample. First, there is a need for determining the population itself. Second, the type of sample must be decided. Third, the sample size is calculated. Finally, the data that need to be collected or described must be planned.

The types of samples useful to a systems analyst are convenience samples, purposive samples, simple random samples, and complex random samples. The last type includes the subcategories of systematic sampling and stratified sampling. There are several guidelines to follow when determining sample size. The systems analyst can make a subjective decision regarding acceptable interval estimates, then a confidence level is chosen and the necessary sample size can be calculated.

Systems analysts need to investigate current and archival data and forms, including reports, documents, financial statements, content of corporate Web sites, Web forms meant to be printed out and those that are electronically submitted, procedure manuals, and email content and memos. Current and archival data and forms reveal where the organization has been and where its members believe it is going. Both quantitative and qualitative documents need to be analyzed. Because documents are persuasive messages, it must be recognized that changing them might well change the organization.

Analysts use observation as an information gathering technique. Through observation they gain insight into what is actually done as users interact with information technology. One way to describe how decision makers behave is to use an analyst's playscript that documents each of the major player's activities.

In addition to observing a decision maker's behavior, the systems analyst should observe the decision maker's surroundings for important clues as to how well the system fits the user. One method is Structured Observation of the Environment, or STROBE. A systems analyst uses STROBE in the same way that a film critic uses a method called mise-en-scène analysis to analyze a shot in a film.

Several concrete elements in the decision maker's environment can be observed and interpreted. These elements include (1) office location, (2) placement of the decision maker's desk, (3) stationary office equipment, (4) props such

"We're proud of our building here in Tennessee. In fact, we used the architectural firm of I. M. Paid to carry the same theme, blending into the local landscape while still reaching out to our clients throughout all the branches. We get lots of people coming through just to admire the building once they catch on to where it is exactly. In fact, by Tennessee standards, we get so many sightseers that it might as well be the pyramids! Well, you can see for yourself as you go through. The East Atrium is my favorite place: plenty of light, lots of louvered blinds to filter it. Yet it has always fascinated me that the building and its furnishings might tell a story quite different from the one its occupants tell.

"Sometimes employees complain that the offices all look the same. The public rooms are spectacular, though. Even the lunchroom is inviting. Most people can't say that about their cafeterias at work. You'll notice that we all personalize our offices, anyway. So even if the offices were of the 'cookie cutter' kind, their occupants' personalities seem to take over as soon as they have been here a while. What have you seen? Was there anything that surprised you so far?"

HYPERCASE QUESTIONS

1. Use STROBE to compare and contrast Snowden Evans's and Ketcham's offices. What sort of conclusion about each person's use of information technology can you draw from your observations? How compatible do Evans and Ketcham seem in terms of the systems they use? What other clues to their storage, use, and sharing of information can you discover based on your observations of their offices?

FIGURE 5.HC1
There are hidden clues in HyperCase. Use STROBE to discover them.

(Continued)

2. Carefully examine Kathy Blandford's office. Use STROBE to confirm, reverse, or negate what you have learned during your interview with her. List anything you found out about Ms. Blandford from observing her office that you did not know from the interview.
3. Carefully examine the contents of the MRE reception area using STROBE. What inferences can you make about the organization? List them. What interview questions would you like to ask, based on your observations of the reception area? Make a list of people you would like to interview and the questions you would ask each of them.
4. Describe in a paragraph the process you would go through in applying STROBE to observing an MRE office setting. List all elements in the MRE offices that seem important to understanding the users' decision-making behavior.

as handheld devices and PCs, (5) external information sources such as trade journals and use of the Web, (6) office lighting and color, and (7) clothing worn by the decision maker. STROBE can be used to gain a better understanding of how decision makers actually gather, process, store, and share information in order to get their work done.

KEYWORDS AND PHRASES

- analyst's playscript
- business-to-business (B2B) ecommerce
- business-to-consumer (B2C) ecommerce
- clothing worn by decision makers
- cluster sampling
- complex random sample
- confidence level
- convenience sample
- corporate Web sites
- desk placement
- external information sources
- office lighting and color
- office location
- props (handheld devices and PCs)
- purposive sample
- sample population
- sampling
- simple random sample
- stationary office equipment
- stratified sampling
- STROBE
- systematic observation
- systematic sampling

REVIEW QUESTIONS

1. Define what is meant by sampling.
2. List four reasons why the systems analyst would want to sample data or select representative people to interview.
3. What are the four steps to follow to design a good sample?
4. List the three approaches to complex random sampling.
5. Define what is meant by stratification of samples.
6. What effect on sample size does using a greater confidence level have when sampling attribute data?
7. What is the overriding variable that determines how many people the systems analyst should interview in depth?

8. What information about the decision maker does the analyst seek to gain from observation?
9. List five steps to help the analyst observe the decision maker's typical activities.
10. In the technique known as the analyst's playscript, who is the actor?
11. In the analyst's playscript, what information about mangers is recorded in the right-hand column?
12. Noting that the idea of STROBE originally came from the world of film, what does the systems analyst's role resemble?
13. List the seven concrete elements of the decision maker's physical environment that can be observed by the systems analyst using STROBE.

PROBLEMS

1. Cheyl Stake is concerned that too many forms are being filled out incorrectly. She feels that about 8 percent of all the forms have an error.
   a. How large a sample size should Ms. Stake use to be 99 percent certain she will be within 0.02?
   b. How large a sample size should Ms. Stake use to be 90 percent certain she will be within 0.02?
   c. Explain the difference between parts a and b in words.
   d. Suppose Ms. Stake will accept a confidence level of 95 percent that she will be within 0.02. What will the sample size of forms be now?
2. "I see that you have quite a few papers there. What all do you have in there?" asks Betty Kant, head of the MIS task force that is the liaison group between your systems group and Sawder's Furniture Company. You are shuffling a large bundle of papers as you prepare to leave the building.

   "Well, I've got some financial statements, production reports from the last six months, and some performance reports that Sharon gave me that cover goals and work performance over the last six months," you reply as some of the papers fall to the floor. "Why do you ask?"

   Betty takes the papers from you and puts them on the nearest desk. She answers, "Because you don't need all this junk. You're here to do one thing, and that's talk to us, the users. Bet you can't read one thing in there that'll make a difference."
   a. The only way to convince Betty of the importance of each document is to tell her what you are looking for in each one. Use a paragraph to explain what each kind of document contributes to the systems analyst's understanding of the business.
   b. While you are speaking with Betty, you realize you actually need other quantitative documents as well. List any you are missing.
3. You've sampled the email messages that have been sent to several middle managers of Sawder's Furniture Company, which ships build-your-own particle-board furniture across the country. Here is one that repeats a message found in several other memos:

   To: Sid, Ernie, Carl
   From: Imogene
   Re: computer/printer supplies
   Date: November 10, 2006

   It has come to my attention that I have been waging a war against requests for computer and printer supplies (writable CDs, toner, paper, etc.) that are all out of proportion to what has been negotiated for in the current budget. Because we're all good soldiers here, I hope you will take whatever our supply sergeant says is standard issue. Please, no "midnight requisitioning" to make up for shortages. Thanks for being GI in this regard; it makes the battle easier for us all.

a. What metaphor(s) is (are) being used? List the predominant metaphor and other phrases that play on that theme.
b. If you found repeated evidence of this idea in other email messages, what interpretation would you have? Use a paragraph to explain.
c. In a paragraph, describe how the people in your systems analysis group can use the information from the email messages to shape their systems project for Sawder's.
d. In interviews with Sid, Ernie, and Carl, there has been no mention of problems with obtaining enough computer and printer supplies. In a paragraph, discuss why such problems may not come up in interviews and discuss the value of examining email messages and other memos in addition to interviewing.

4. "Here's the main policy manual we've put together over the years for system users," says Al Bookbinder, as he blows the dust off the manual and hands it to you. Al is a document keeper for the systems department of Prechter and Gumbel, a large manufacturer of health and beauty aids. "Everything any user of any part of the system needs to know is in what I call the Blue Book. I mean it's chockablock with policies. It's so big, I'm the only one with a complete copy. It costs too much to reproduce it." You thank Al and take the manual with you. When you read through it, you are astonished at what it contains. Most pages begin with a message such as: "This page supersedes page 23.1 in manual Vol. II. Discard previous inserts; do not use."
   a. List your observations about the frequency of use of the Blue Book.
   b. How user friendly are the updates in the manual? Write a sentence explaining your answer.
   c. Write a paragraph commenting on the wisdom of having all-important policies for all systems users in one book.
   d. Suggest a solution that incorporates the use of online policy manuals for some users.
5. "I think I'll be able to remember most everything he does," says Ceci Awll. Ceci is about to interview Biff Welldon, vice president of strategic planning of OK Corral, a steak restaurant chain with 130 locations. "I mean, I've got a good memory. I think it's much more important to listen to what he says than to observe what he does anyway." As one of your systems analysis team members, Ceci has been talking with you about the desirability of writing down her observations of Biff's office and activities during the interview.
   a. In a paragraph, persuade Ceci that listening is not enough in interviews and that observing and recording those observations are also important.
   b. Ceci seems to have accepted your idea that observation is important but still doesn't know what to observe. Make a list of items and behaviors to observe, and in a sentence beside each behavior, indicate what information Ceci should hope to gain through observation of it.
6. "We're a progressive company, always looking to be ahead of the power curve. We'll give anything a whirl if it'll put us ahead of the competition, and that includes every one of us," says I. B. Daring, an executive with Michigan Manufacturing (2M). You are interviewing him as a preliminary step in a systems project, one in which his subordinates have expressed interest. As you listen to I. B., you look around his office to see that most of the information he has stored on shelves can be classified as internal procedures manuals. In addition, you notice a PC on a back table of I. B.'s office. The monitor's screen is covered with dust, and the manuals stacked beside the PC are still encased in

their original shrink-wrap. Even though you know that 2M uses an intranet, no cables are visible going to or from I. B.'s PC. On the wall behind I. B.'s massive mahogany desk you see five framed oil portraits of 2M's founders, all clustered around a gold plaque bearing the corporate slogan, which states, "Make sure you're right, then go ahead."

a. What is the organizational narrative or storyline as portrayed by I. B. Daring? Rephrase it in your own words.
b. List the elements of STROBE that you have observed during your interview with I. B.
c. Next to each element of STROBE that you have observed, write a sentence on how you would interpret it.
d. Construct a table with the organizational story line down the left-hand side of the page and the elements of STROBE across the top. Using the symbols from the "anecdotal list" application of STROBE, indicate the relationship between the organizational story line as portrayed by I. B. and each element you have observed (that is, indicate whether each element of STROBE confirms, reverses, causes you to look further, modifies, or supplements the narrative).
e. Based on your observations of STROBE and your interview, state in a paragraph what problems you are able to anticipate in getting a new system approved by I. B. and others. In a sentence or two, discuss how your diagnosis might have been different if you had only talked to I. B. over the phone or had read his written comments on a systems proposal.

GROUP PROJECTS

1. Assume your group will serve as a systems analysis and design team for a project designed to computerize or enhance the computerization of all business aspects of a 15-year-old, national U.S. trucking firm called Maverick Transport. Maverick is a less-than-a-truckload (LTL) carrier. The people in management work from the philosophy of just in time (JIT), in which they have created a partnership that includes the shipper, the receiver, and the carrier (Maverick Transport) for the purpose of transporting and delivering the materials required just in time for their use on the production line. Maverick maintains 626 tractors for hauling freight, and has 45,000 square feet of warehouse space and 21,000 square feet of office space.
   a. Along with your group members, develop a list of sources of archival data that should be checked when analyzing the information requirements of Maverick.
   b. When this list is complete, devise a sampling scheme that would permit your group to get a clear picture of the company without having to read each document generated in its 15-year history.
2. Arrange to visit a local organization that is expanding or otherwise enhancing its information systems. To allow your group to practice the various observation methods described in this chapter, assign either of these two methods to each team member: (1) developing the analyst's playscript, or (2) using STROBE. Many of these strategies can be employed during one-on-one interviews, whereas some require formal organizational meetings. Try to accomplish several objectives during your visit to the organization by scheduling it at an appropriate time, one that permits all team members to try their assigned method of observation. Using multiple methods such as interviewing and observation (often simultaneously) is the only cost-effective way to get a true, timely picture of the organization's information requirements.

3. The members of your group should meet and discuss their findings after completing Project 2. Were there any surprises? Did the information garnered through observation confirm, reverse, or negate what was learned in interviews? Were any of the findings from the observational methods in direct conflict with each other? Work with your group to develop a list of ways to address any puzzling information (for example, by doing follow-up interviews).

SELECTED BIBLIOGRAPHY

Babbie, R. R. *Survey Research Methods.* Belmont, CA: Wadsworth, 1973.

Edwards, A., and R. Talbot. *The Hard-Pressed Researcher.* New York: Longman, 1994.

Emory, C. W. *Business Research Methods,* 3d ed. Homewood, IL: Irwin, 1985.

Kendall, J. E., "Examining the Relationship Between Computer Cartoons and Factors in Information Systems Use, Success, and Failure: Visual Evidence of Met and Unmet Expectations," *The DATA BASE for Advances in Information Systems,* Vol. 28, No. 2, Spring 1997, pp. 113–126.

Kendall, J. E., and K. E. Kendall. "Metaphors and Methodologies: Living Beyond the Systems Machine." *MIS Quarterly,* Vol. 17, No. 2, June 1993, pp. 149–171.

Kendall J. E., and K. E. Kendall. "Metaphors and Their Meaning for Information Systems Development." *European Journal of Information Systems,* 1994, pp. 37–47.

Kendall, K. E., and J. E. Kendall. "Observing Organizational Environments: A Systematic Approach for Information Analysts." *MIS Quarterly,* Vol. 5, No. 1, 1981, pp. 43–55.

Kendall, K. E., and J. E. Kendall. "STROBE: A Structured Approach to the Observation of the Decision-Making Environment." *Information and Management,* Vol. 7, No. 1, 1984, pp. 1–11.

Kendall, K. E., and J. E. Kendall. "Structured Observation of the Decision-Making Environment: A Validity and Reliability Assessment." *Decision Sciences,* Vol. 15, No. 1, 1984, pp. 107–118.

Markus, M. L., and A. S. Lee. "Special Issue on Intensive Research in Information Systems: Using Qualitative, Interpretive, and Case Methods to Study Information Technology—Second Installment." *MIS Quarterly,* Vol. 24, No. 1, March 2000, p. 1.

Sano, D. *Designing Large-Scale Web Sites: A Visual Methodology.* New York: Wiley Computer Publishing, 1996.

Schultze, U. "A Confessional Account of an Ethnography about Knowledge Work." *MIS Quarterly,* Vol. 24, No. 1, March 2000, pp. 3–41.

Shultis, R. L. "'Playscript'—A New Tool Accountants Need." *NAA Bulletin,* Vol. 45, No. 12, August 1964, pp. 3–10.

Webb, E. J., D. T. Campbell, R. D. Schwartz, and L. Sechrest. *Unobtrusive Measures: Nonreactive Research in the Social Sciences.* Chicago: Rand McNally College Publishing, 1966.

ALLEN SCHMIDT, JULIE E. KENDALL, AND KENNETH E. KENDALL

5

SEEING IS BELIEVING

"Chip, I know the interviews took a long time, but they were worth it," Anna says defensively as Chip enters her office with a worried look on his face.

"I'm sure of that," Chip says. "You really made a good impression on them. People have stopped me in the hall and said they're glad we're working on the new system. I'm not worried about the interviews themselves. But I was concerned that we didn't have time to discuss observations before you did them."

"Rest assured, I was all eyes," Anna laughs. "I used a technique called STROBE, or Structured Observation of the Environment, to see our decision maker's habitats systematically. You'll be interested in these notes I wrote up for each person I interviewed," says Anna, as she hands Chip her written, organized observations from each interview.

EXERCISES

These exercises require that you visit the Web site to obtain observations of the decision makers' offices. Please visit the Web site at www.prenhall.com/kendall and look for "CPU Observations of Decision Makers' Offices."

E-1. Based on Anna's written observation of Dot's office and clothing, use STROBE to analyze Dot as a decision maker. In two paragraphs, compare and contrast what you learned in Dot's interview and what you learned via STROBE.

E-2. After examining Anna's written observations about Mike Crowe's office, use STROBE to analyze Mike as a decision maker. What differences (if any) did you see between Mike in his interview and Mike in Anna's observations? Use two paragraphs to answer.

E-3. Use STROBE to analyze Anna's written observations about Cher Ware and Paige Prynter. Use two paragraphs to compare and contrast the decision-making style of each person as it is revealed by their offices and clothing.

E-4. Use STROBE to analyze Anna's written observations about Hy Perteks. Now compare your analysis with Hy's interview. Use two paragraphs to discuss whether STROBE confirms, negates, reverses, or serves as a cue to look further in Hy's narrative. (Include any further questions you would ask Hy to clarify your interpretation.)

6

AGILE MODELING AND PROTOTYPING

Learning Objectives

Once you have mastered the material in this chapter you will be able to:

1. **Understand the roots of agile modeling in prototyping and the four main types of prototyping.**
2. **Be able to use prototyping for human information requirements gathering.**
3. **Understand the concept of RAD for use in human information requirements gathering and interface design.**
4. **Understand agile modeling and the core practices that differentiate it from other development methodologies.**
5. **Learn the importance of values critical to agile modeling.**
6. **Understand how to improve efficiency for users who are knowledge workers using either structured methods or agile modeling.**

This chapter explores agile modeling, which is a collection of innovative, user-centered approaches to systems development. You will learn the values and principles, activities, resources, practices, processes, and tools associated with agile methodologies. Agile approaches (as well as much of the human–computer interaction material you will learn in Chapter 14), have their roots in prototyping. So this chapter begins with prototyping to provide a proper context for understanding, and then takes up the agile approach in the last half of the chapter.

Prototyping of information systems is a worthwhile technique for quickly gathering specific information about users' information requirements. Generally speaking, effective prototyping should come early in the systems development life cycle, during the requirements determination phase. Prototyping, however, is a complex technique that requires knowledge of the entire systems development life cycle before it is successfully accomplished.

Prototyping is included at this point in the text to underscore its importance as an information gathering technique. When using prototyping in this way, the systems analyst is seeking initial reactions from users and management to the prototype, user suggestions about changing or cleaning up the prototyped system, possible innovations for it, and revision plans detailing which parts of the system need to be done first or which branches of an organization to prototype next.

One special instance of prototyping that uses an object-oriented approach is called rapid application development, or RAD. Prototyping and RAD can also be used as an alternative method to SDLC.

PROTOTYPING

As the systems analyst presenting a prototype of the information system, you are keenly interested in the reactions of users and management to the prototype. You want to know in detail how they react to working with the prototype and how good the fit is between their needs and the prototyped features of the system. Reactions are gathered through observation, interviews, and feedback sheets (possibly questionnaires) designed to elicit each person's opinion about the prototype as he or she interacts with it.

Information gathered in the prototyping phase allows the analyst to set priorities and redirect plans inexpensively, with a minimum of disruption. Because of this feature, prototyping and planning go hand-in-hand.

KINDS OF PROTOTYPES

The word *prototype* is used in many different ways. Rather than attempting to synthesize all these uses into one definition or trying to mandate one correct approach to the somewhat controversial topic of prototyping, we illustrate how each of several conceptions of prototyping may be usefully applied in a particular situation, as shown in Figure 6.1.

FIGURE 6.1
Four kinds of prototypes (clockwise, starting from the upper left).

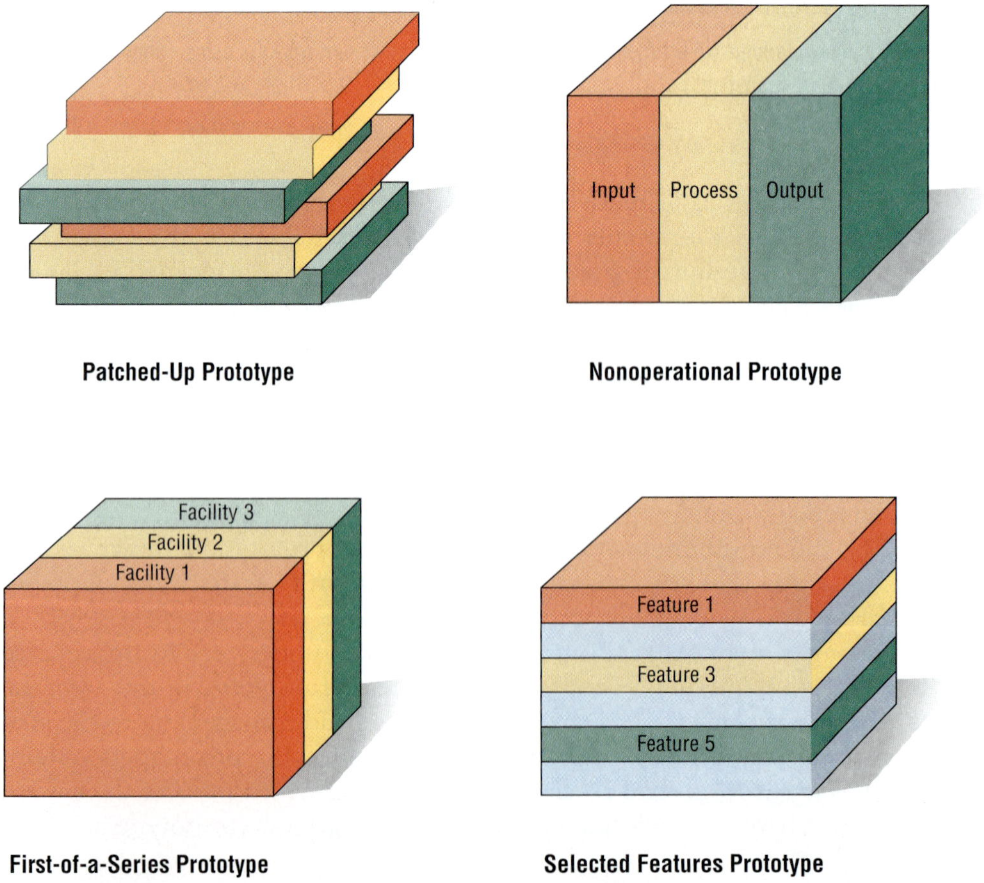

Patched-Up Prototype The first kind of prototyping has to do with constructing a system that works but is patched up or patched together. In engineering this approach is referred to as breadboarding: creating a patched-together, working model of an (otherwise microscopic) integrated circuit.

An example in information systems is a working model that has all the necessary features but is inefficient. In this instance of prototyping, users can interact with the system, getting accustomed to the interface and types of output available. The retrieval and storage of information may be inefficient, however, because programs were written rapidly with the objective of being workable rather than efficient.

Nonoperational Prototype The second conception of a prototype is that of a nonworking scale model that is set up to test certain aspects of the design. An example of this approach is a full-scale model of an automobile that is used in wind tunnel tests. The size and shape of the auto are precise, but the car is not operational. In this case only features of the automobile essential to wind tunnel testing are included.

A nonworking scale model of an information system might be produced when the coding required by the applications is too extensive to prototype but when a useful idea of the system can be gained through the prototyping of the input and output only. In this instance, processing, because of undue cost and time, would not be prototyped. Users could still make decisions on the utility of the system, based on their use of prototyped input and output.

First-of-a-Series Prototype A third conception of prototyping involves creating a first full-scale model of a system, often called a pilot. An example is prototyping the first airplane of a series. The prototype is completely operational and is a realization of what the designer hopes will be a series of airplanes with identical features.

This type of prototyping is useful when many installations of the same information system are planned. The full-scale working model allows users to experience realistic interaction with the new system, but it minimizes the cost of overcoming any problems that it presents. Creation of a working model is one of the types of prototyping done with RAD, covered later in this chapter.

For example, when a retail grocery chain intends to use EDI (electronic data interchange) to check in suppliers' shipments in a number of outlets, a full-scale model might be installed in one store so users could work through any problems before the system is implemented in all the others. Another example is found in banking installations for electronic funds transfer. A full-scale prototype is installed in one or two locations first, and if successful, duplicates are installed at all locations based on customer usage patterns and other key factors.

Selected Features Prototype A fourth conception of prototyping concerns building an operational model that includes some, but not all, of the features that the final system will have. An analogy would be a new retail shopping mall that opens before the construction of all shops is complete.

When prototyping information systems in this way, some, but not all, essential features are included. For example, users may view a system menu on a screen that lists six features: add a record, update a record, delete a record, search a record for a key word, list a record, or scan a record. In the prototyped system, however, only three of the six may be available for use, so that the user may add a record (feature 1), delete a record (feature 3), and list a record (feature 5). User feedback can help analysts understand what is working and what isn't. It can also help with suggestions on what features to add next.

When this kind of prototyping is done, the system is accomplished in modules so that if the features that are prototyped are evaluated by users as successful, they can be incorporated into the larger, final system without undertaking immense work in interfacing. Prototypes done in this manner are part of the actual system. They are *not* just a mock-up as in nonoperational prototyping considered previously.

PROTOTYPING AS AN ALTERNATIVE TO THE SYSTEMS DEVELOPMENT LIFE CYCLE

Some analysts argue that prototyping should be considered as an alternative to the systems development life cycle (SDLC). Recall that the SDLC, introduced in Chapter 1, is a logical, systematic approach to follow in the development of information systems.

Complaints about going through the SDLC process center around two interrelated concerns. The first concern is the extended time required to go through the development life cycle. As the investment of analyst time increases, the cost of the delivered system rises proportionately.

The second concern about using the SDLC is that user requirements change over time. During the long interval between the time that user requirements are analyzed and the time that the finished system is delivered, user requirements are evolving. Thus, because of the extended development cycle, the resulting system may be criticized for inadequately addressing current user information requirements.

A corollary of the problem of keeping up with user information requirements is the suggestion that users cannot really know what they do or do not want until they see something tangible. In the traditional SDLC, it often is too late to change an unwanted system once it is delivered.

To overcome these problems, some analysts propose that prototyping be used as an alternative to the systems development life cycle. When prototyping is used in this way, the analyst effectively shortens the time between ascertainment of human information requirements and delivery of a workable system. In addition, using prototyping instead of the traditional SDLC might overcome some of the problems of accurately identifying user information requirements.

Drawbacks to supplanting the SDLC with prototyping include prematurely shaping a system before the problem or opportunity being addressed is thoroughly understood. Also, using prototyping as an alternative may result in producing a system that is accepted by specific groups of users but that is inadequate for overall system needs.

The approach we advocate here is to use prototyping as a part of the traditional SDLC. In this view prototyping is considered as an additional, specialized method for ascertaining users' information requirements as they interact with prototypes and provide feedback for the analyst.

DEVELOPING A PROTOTYPE

In this section guidelines for developing a prototype are advanced. The term *prototyping* is taken in the sense of the last definition that was discussed, that is, a selected-features prototype that will include some but not all features; one that, if successful as judged by users and analysts in consultation, will eventually be part of the larger, final system that is delivered.

Prototyping is a superb way to elicit feedback about the proposed system and about how readily it is fulfilling the information needs of its users, as depicted in Figure 6.2. The first step of prototyping is to estimate the costs involved in building a module of the system. If costs of programmers' and analysts' time as well as equipment costs are within the budget, building of the prototype can proceed. Prototyping is an excellent way to facilitate the integration of the information system into the larger system and culture of the organization.

GUIDELINES FOR DEVELOPING A PROTOTYPE

Once the decision to prototype has been made, four main guidelines must be observed when integrating prototyping into the requirements determination phase of the SDLC:

1. Work in manageable modules.
2. Build the prototype rapidly.
3. Modify the prototype in successive iterations.
4. Stress the user interface.

As you can see, the guidelines suggest ways of proceeding with the prototype that are necessarily interrelated. Each guideline is explained in the following subsections.

Working in Manageable Modules When prototyping some of the features of a system into a workable model, it is imperative that the analyst work in manageable modules. One distinct advantage of prototyping is that it is not necessary or desirable to build an entire working system for prototype purposes.

A manageable module is one that allows users to interact with its key features but can be built separately from other system modules. Module features that are deemed less important are purposely left out of the initial prototype. As you will see later in this chapter, this is very similar to the agile approach that emphasizes small releases.

Building the Prototype Rapidly Speed is essential to the successful prototyping of an information system. Recall that one complaint voiced against following the

FIGURE 6.2
Analysts should modify their original screen designs based on user reactions to the prototype.

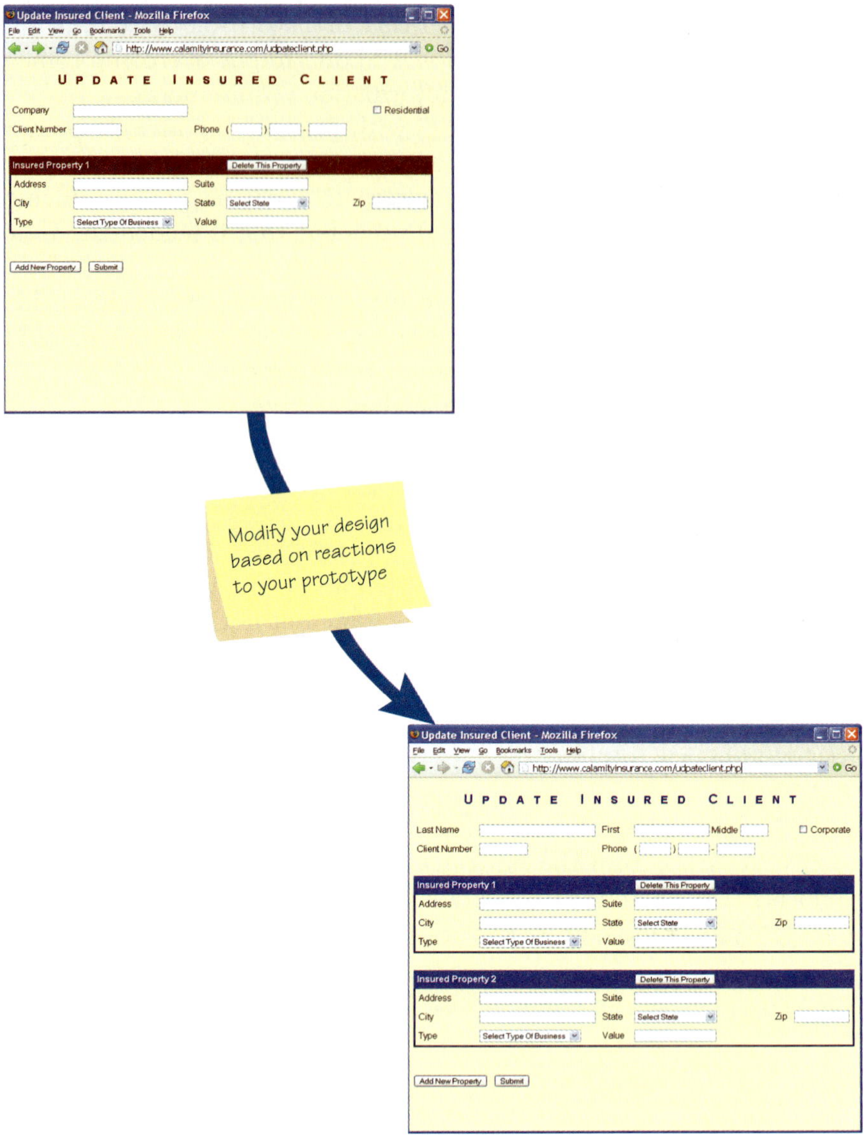

traditional SDLC is that the interval between requirements determination and delivery of a complete system is far too long to address evolving user needs effectively.

Analysts can use prototyping to shorten this gap by using traditional information gathering techniques to pinpoint salient information requirements, and then quickly make decisions that bring forth a working model. In effect the user sees and uses the system very early in the SDLC instead of waiting for a finished system to gain hands-on experience.

Putting together an operational prototype both rapidly and early in the SDLC allows the analyst to gain valuable insight into how the remainder of the project should go. By showing users very early in the process how parts of the system actually perform, rapid prototyping guards against overcommitting resources to a project that may eventually become unworkable. Later, when RAD is discussed, you again see the importance of rapid systems building. In addition, agile modeling also builds on the practice of quick turnaround times.

Modifying the Prototype A third guideline for developing the prototype is that its construction must support modifications. Making the prototype modifiable means

CONSULTING OPPORTUNITY 6.1

IS PROTOTYPING KING?

"As you know, we're an enthusiastic group. We're not a dynasty yet, but we're working on it," Paul Le Gon tells you. Paul (introduced in Consulting Opportunity 2.3), at 24 years of age, is the "boy king" of Pyramid, Inc., a small but successful independent book-publishing firm that specializes in paperback books outside of the publishing mainstream. As a systems analyst, you have been hired by Pyramid, Inc., to help develop a computerized warehouse inventory and distribution information system.

"We're hiring lots of workers," Paul continues, as if to convince you of the vastness of Pyramid's undertaking. "And we feel Pyramid is positioned perfectly as far as our markets in the north, south, east, and west are concerned.

"My assistant, Ceil Toom, and I have been slaving away, thinking about the new system. And we've concluded that what we really need is a prototype. As a matter of fact, we've tunneled through a lot of material. Our fascination with the whole idea has really pyramided."

As you formulate a response to Paul, you think back over the few weeks you've worked with Pyramid, Inc. You think that the business problems its information system must resolve are very straightforward. You also know that the people in the company are on a limited budget and cannot afford to spend like kings. Actually, the entire project is quite small.

Ceil, building on what Paul has said, tells you, "We don't mean to be too wrapped up with it, but we feel prototyping represents the new world. And that's where we all want to be. We know we need a prototype. Have we convinced you?"

Based on Paul's and Ceil's enthusiasm for prototyping and what you know about Pyramid's needs, would you support construction of a prototype? Why or why not? Formulate your decision and response in a letter to Paul Le Gon and Ceil Toom. Present a justification for your decision based on overall criteria that should be met to justify prototyping.

creating it in modules that are not highly interdependent. If this guideline is observed, less resistance is encountered when modifications in the prototype are necessary.

The prototype is generally modified several times, going through several iterations. Changes in the prototype should move the system closer to what users say is important. Each modification necessitates another evaluation by users.

The prototype is not a finished system. Entering the prototyping phase with the idea that the prototype will require modification is a helpful attitude that demonstrates to users how necessary their feedback is if the system is to improve.

Stressing the User Interface The user's interface with the prototype (and eventually the system) is very important. Because what you are really trying to achieve with the prototype is to get users to further articulate their information requirements, they must be able to interact easily with the system's prototype. They should be able to see how the prototype will enable them to accomplish their tasks. For many users the interface is the system. It should not be a stumbling block.

Although many aspects of the system will remain undeveloped in the prototype, the user interface must be well developed enough to enable users to pick up the system quickly and not be put off. Online, interactive systems using GUI interfaces are ideally suited to prototypes. Chapter 14 describes in detail the considerations that are important in designing human–computer interaction.

DISADVANTAGES OF PROTOTYPING

As with any information gathering technique, there are several disadvantages to prototyping. The first is that it can be quite difficult to manage prototyping as a project in the larger systems effort. The second disadvantage is that users and analysts may adopt a prototype as a completed system when it is in fact inadequate and was never intended to serve as a finished system. Analysts need to work to ensure that communication with users is clear regarding the timetable for interacting with and improving the prototype.

CONSULTING OPPORTUNITY 6.2

CLEARING THE WAY FOR CUSTOMER LINKS

World's Trend (see Chapter 7 for a detailed corporate description) is building a Web site on which to sell clearance merchandise usually sold through the Web and through its catalog operation. As a newly hired Web consultant, Lincoln Cerf finds himself in a very cold, wintry city, fighting his way through several inches of snow to meet with one of the systems team members, Mary Maye, at World's Trend headquarters.

Mary welcomes Lincoln, saying, "At least the weather doesn't seem to affect our Web sales! They're brisk no matter what." Lincoln groans appreciatively at her weak attempt at humor, smiles, and says, "I gathered from your email last week that you are trying to determine the type of information that needs to be displayed on our clearance Web site."

Mary replies, "Yes, I'm trying to get it organized in the best possible way. Our customers are all so busy. I know photos of all our merchandise can take a long time to appear on the page if a customer is accessing the Web via a slower modem from home." Mary continues by saying, "Linc, I'm not even that concerned about how to design our clearance site at this time. I am worried, though, about how much information we need to include on a page. For example, when items are on clearance, not all colors and sizes are available. Which do you think is better, to include some basic information and let the customer click a button to ask for more information, or to be as complete as possible on one page? If I use the linking method, then I could fit more items on the screen . . . but it might be too orderly. Customers like the look and feel of a sale in which merchandise is kind of jumbled together."

Linc continues her line of thought, saying, "Yeah, I wonder how customers want the information organized. Have you actually watched them use the Web? I mean, do they look for shoes when they buy a suit? If so, should shoes appear on the suit page or be linked in some way?"

Mary comments, "Those are my questions, too. Then I wonder if we should just try this approach for men's clothes first, before we implement it for women's clothing. What if men's and women's approaches to shopping on the Web are different?"

As a third member of the World's Trend Web site development group, respond in a brief written report to Lincoln and Mary about whether you should use a prototype to elicit recommendations from potential customers about the proposed Web site. What type of prototype is appropriate? Consider each form of prototype and explain why each type would apply (or would not apply) to this problem. Devote a paragraph to each explanation.

The analyst needs to weigh these disadvantages against the known advantages when deciding whether to prototype, when to prototype, and how much of the system to prototype.

ADVANTAGES OF PROTOTYPING

Prototyping is not necessary or appropriate in every systems project, as we have seen. The advantages, however, should also be given consideration when deciding whether to prototype. The three major advantages of prototyping are the potential for changing the system early in its development, the opportunity to stop development on a system that is not working, and the possibility of developing a system that more closely addresses users' needs and expectations.

Successful prototyping depends on early and frequent user feedback, which analysts can use to modify the system and make it more responsive to actual needs. As with any systems effort, early changes are less expensive than changes made late in the project's development. In the later part of the chapter, you will see how the agile approach to development uses an extreme form of prototyping that requires an onsite customer to provide feedback during all iterations.

PROTOTYPING USING COTS SOFTWARE

Sometimes the quickest way to prototype is through the modular installation of COTS software. Although the concept of COTS software can be easily grasped by looking at familiar and relatively inexpensive packages such as the Microsoft Office products, some COTS software is elaborate and expensive, but highly useful. One example of rapid implementation of COTS software can be found in Catholic

CONSULTING OPPORTUNITY 6.3

TO HATCH A FISH

"Just be a little patient. I think we need to add a few more features before we turn it over to them. Otherwise, this whole prototype will sink, not swim," says Sam Monroe, a member of your systems analysis team. All four members of the team are sitting together in a hurriedly called meeting, and they are discussing the prototype that they are developing for an information system to help managers monitor and control water temperature, number of fish released, and other factors at a large, commercial fish hatchery.

"They've got plenty to do already. Why, the system began with four features and we're already up to nine. I feel like we're swimming upstream on this one. They don't need all that. They don't even want it," argues Belle Uga, a second member of the systems analysis team. "I don't mean to carp, but just give them the basics. We've got enough to tackle as it is."

"I think Monroe is more on target," volunteers Wally Ide, a third member of the team, baiting Belle a little. "We have to show them our very best, even if it means being a few weeks later in hatching our prototype than we promised."

"Okay," Belle says warily, "but I want the two of you to tell the managers at the hatchery why we aren't delivering the prototype. I don't want to. And I'm not sure they'll let you off the hook that easily."

Monroe replies, "Well, I guess we could, but we probably shouldn't make a big deal out of being later than we wanted. I don't want to rock the boat."

Wally chimes in, "Yeah. Why point out our mistakes to everyone? Besides, when they see the prototype, they'll forget any complaints they had. They'll love it."

Belle finds a memo in her notebook from their last meeting with the hatchery managers and reads it aloud. "Agenda for meeting of September 22. 'Prototyping—the importance of rapid development, putting together the user analyst team, getting quick feedback for modification . . . .'" Belle's voice trails off, omitting the last few agenda items. In the wake of her comments, Monroe and Wally look unhappily at each other.

Monroe speaks first. "I guess we did try to get everyone primed for receiving a prototype quickly and to be involved from day one." Noting your silence up until now, Monroe continues, "But still waters run deep. What do you think we should do next?" he asks you.

As the fourth member of the systems analysis team, what actions do you think should be taken? In a one- or two-paragraph email message to your teammates, answer the following questions: Should more features be added to the hatchery system prototype before giving it to the hatchery managers to experiment with? How important is the rapid development of the prototype? What are the trade-offs involved in adding more features to the prototype versus getting a more basic prototype to the client when it was promised? Complete your message with a recommendation.

University's use of the ERP COTS software package called PeopleSoft, which is handling many of its Web-based functions.

Catholic University, along with a higher education consulting group and PeopleSoft, successfully undertook rapid implementation of a recruiting and admissions module of their COTS software. They launched the implementation in April 1999, and by that October they had successfully implemented recruiting and admissions for undergraduates. By November of the same year, they implemented the same functions for graduate students. Other modules of the PeopleSoft COTS software that are implemented at Catholic University include a complete online course catalog, online registration, and the capability for students to check grades, transcripts, bills, and financial aid payments online from anywhere.

USERS' ROLE IN PROTOTYPING

The users' role in prototyping can be summed up in two words: honest involvement. Without user involvement there is little reason to prototype. The precise behaviors necessary for interacting with a prototype can vary, but it is clear that the user is pivotal to the prototyping process. Realizing the importance of the user to the success of the process, the members of the systems analysis team must encourage and welcome input and guard against their own natural resistance to changing the prototype. For more in-depth material on how to design human-centered systems, see the HCI material in Chapter 14.

CONSULTING OPPORTUNITY 6.4

THIS PROTOTYPE IS ALL WET

"It can be changed. It's not a finished product, remember," affirms Sandy Beach, a systems analyst for RainFall, a large manufacturer of fiberglass bathtub and shower enclosures for bathrooms. Beach is anxiously reassuring Will Lather, a production scheduler for RainFall, who is poring over the first hard-copy output produced for him by the prototype of the new information system.

"Well, it's okay," Lather says quietly. "I wouldn't want to bother you with anything. Let's see, . . . yes, *here* they are," he says as he finally locates the monthly report summarizing raw materials purchased, raw materials used, and raw materials in inventory.

Lather continues paging through the unwieldy computer printout. "This will be fine." Pausing at a report, he remarks, "I'll just have Miss Fawcett copy this part for the people in Accounting." Turning a few more pages, he says, "And the guy in Quality Assurance should really see this column of figures, although the rest of it isn't of much interest to him. I'll circle it and make a copy of it for him. Maybe I should phone part of this in to the warehouse, too."

As Sandy prepares to leave, Lather bundles up the pages of the reports, commenting, "The new system will be a big help. I'll make sure everybody knows about it. Anything will be better than the 'old monster' anyway. I'm glad we've got something new."

Sandy leaves Will Lather's office feeling a little lost at sea. Thinking it over, he starts wondering why Accounting, QA, and the warehouse aren't getting what Will thinks they should. Sandy phones a few people, and he confirms that what Lather has told him is true. They need the reports and they're not getting them.

Later in the week Sandy approaches Lather about rerouting the output as well as changing some of the features of the system. These modifications would allow Lather to get onscreen answers regarding what-if scenarios about changes in the prices suppliers are charging or changes in the quality rating of the raw materials available from suppliers (or both), as well as allow him to see what would happen if a shipment was late.

Lather is visibly upset with Sandy's suggestions for altering the prototype and its output. "Oh, don't do it on my account. It's okay really. I don't mind taking the responsibility for routing information to people. I'm always showering them with stuff anyway. Really, this is working pretty well. I would hate to have you take it away from us at this point. Let's just leave it in place."

Sandy is pleased that Lather seems so satisfied with the prototyped output, but he is concerned about Lather's unwillingness to change the prototype, because he has been encouraging users to think of it as an evolving product, not a finished one.

Write a brief report to Sandy listing changes to the prototype prompted by Lather's reactions. In a paragraph, discuss ways that Sandy can calm Lather's fears about having the prototype "taken away." Discuss in a paragraph some actions that can be taken *before* a prototype is tried out to prepare users for its evolutionary nature.

INTERACTION WITH THE PROTOTYPE

There are three main ways a user can be of help in prototyping:

1. Experimenting with the prototype.
2. Giving open reactions to the prototype.
3. Suggesting additions to or deletions from the prototype.

Users should be free to experiment with the prototype. In contrast to a mere list of systems features, the prototype allows users the reality of hands-on interaction. Mounting a prototype on an interactive Web site is one way to facilitate this interaction.

Another aspect of the users' role in prototyping requires that they give open reactions to the prototype. Unfortunately, these reactions are not something that occur on demand. Rather, making users secure enough to give an open reaction is part of the relationship between analysts and users that your team works to build.

Analysts need to be present at least part of the time when experimentation is occurring. They can then observe users' interactions with the system, and they are bound to see interactions they never planned. A filled-in form for observing user experimentation with the prototype is shown in Figure 6.3. Some of the variables you should observe include user reactions to the prototype, user suggestions for changing or expanding the prototype, user innovations for using the system in completely new ways, and any revision plans for the prototype that aid in setting priorities.

Prototype Evaluation Form

Observer Name: Chip Puller — Date: 1/06/2003

System or Project Name: Microcomputer System — Company or Location: Central Pacific University

Program Name or Number: Prev. Maint. — Version: 1

	User 1	User 2	User 3	User 4
User Name	Mike C.	Dot M.		
Period Observed	1/06/2003 A.M.	1/06/2003 A.M.		
User Reactions	Generally favorable, got excited about project	Excellent!		
User Suggestions	Add the date when maintenance was performed.	Place a form number on top for reference. Place word WEEKLY in title.		
Innovations				
Revision Plans	Modify on 1/08/2003. Review with Dot and Mike.			

FIGURE 6.3

An important step in prototyping is to properly record user reactions, user suggestions, innovations, and revision plans.

A third aspect of the users' role in prototyping is their willingness to suggest additions to or deletions from the features being tried. The analyst's role is to elicit such suggestions by assuring users that the feedback they provide is taken seriously, by observing users as they interact with the system, and by conducting short, specific interviews with users concerning their experiences with the prototype. Although users will be asked to articulate suggestions and innovations for the prototype, in the end it is the analyst's responsibility to weigh this feedback and translate it into workable changes where necessary. To facilitate the prototyping process, the analyst must clearly communicate the purposes of prototyping to users, along with the idea that prototyping is valuable only when users are meaningfully involved.

RAPID APPLICATION DEVELOPMENT

Rapid application development (RAD) is an object-oriented approach to systems development that includes a method of development as well as software tools. It makes sense to discuss RAD and prototyping in the same chapter, because they are conceptually very close. Both have as their goal the shortening of time typically needed in a traditional SDLC between the design and implementation of the information system. Ultimately, both RAD and prototyping are trying to meet rapidly changing business requirements more closely. Once you have learned the concepts of prototyping, it is much easier to grasp the essentials of RAD, which can be thought of as a specific implementation of prototyping.

Some developers are looking at RAD as a helpful approach in new ecommerce, Web-based environments in which so-called first-mover status of a business might be important. In other words, to deliver an application to the Web before their competitors, businesses may want their development team to experiment with RAD.

FIGURE 6.4

The RAD design workshop is the heart of the interactive development process.

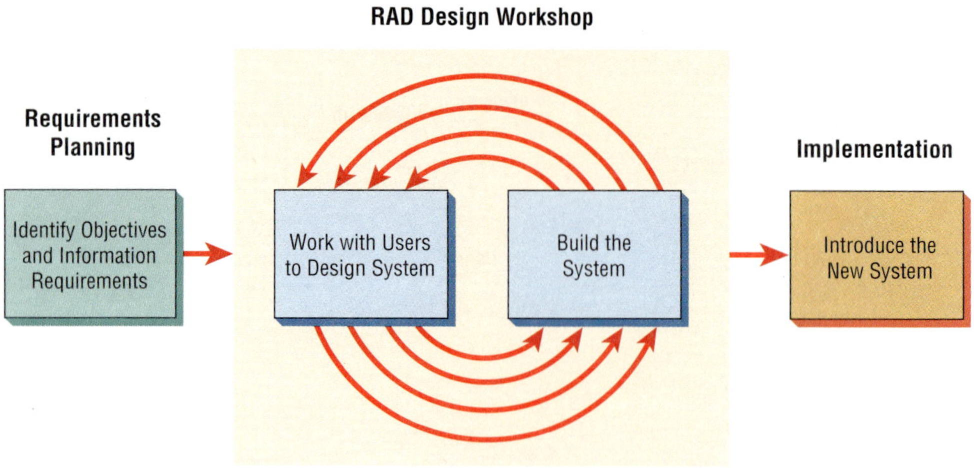

PHASES OF RAD

There are three broad phases to RAD that engage both users and analysts in assessment, design, and implementation. Figure 6.4 depicts these three phases. Notice that RAD involves users in each part of the development effort, with intense participation in the business part of the design.

Requirements Planning Phase In the requirements planning phase, users and analysts meet to identify objectives of the application or system and to identify information requirements arising from those objectives. This phase requires intense involvement from both groups; it is not just signing off on a proposal or document. In addition, it may involve users from different levels of the organization (as covered in Chapter 2). In the requirements planning phase, when information requirements are still being addressed, you may be working with the CIO (if it is a large organization) as well as with strategic planners, especially if you are working with an ecommerce application that is meant to further the strategic aims of the organization. The orientation in this phase is toward solving business problems. Although information technology and systems may even drive some of the solutions proposed, the focus will always remain on reaching business goals.

RAD Design Workshop The RAD design workshop phase is a design-and-refine phase that can best be characterized as a workshop. When you imagine a workshop, you know that participation is intense, not passive, and that it is typically hands on. Usually participants are seated at round tables or in a U-shaped configuration of chairs with attached desks where each person can see the other and where there is space to work on a notebook computer. If you are fortunate enough to have a group decision support systems (GDSS) room available at the company or through a local university, use it to conduct at least part of your RAD design workshop.

During the RAD design workshop, users respond to actual working prototypes and analysts refine designed modules (using some of the software tools mentioned later) based on user responses. The workshop format is very exciting and stimulating, and if experienced users and analysts are present, there is no question that this creative endeavor can propel development forward at an accelerated rate.

Implementation Phase In the previous figure, you can see that analysts are working with users intensely during the workshop to design the business or nontechnical aspects of the system. As soon as these aspects are agreed on and the systems are built and refined, the new systems or part of systems are tested and then introduced

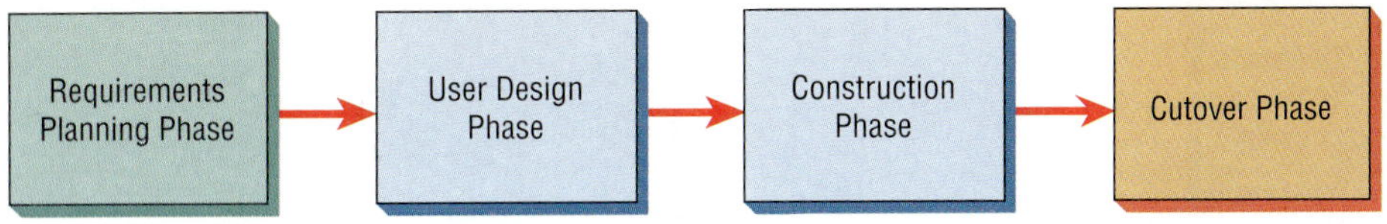

FIGURE 6.5
Martin's phases of RAD.

to the organization. Because RAD can be used to create new ecommerce applications for which there is no old system, there is often no need to (and no real way to) run the old and new systems in parallel before implementation.

By this time, the RAD design workshop will have generated excitement, user ownership, and acceptance of the new application. Typically, change brought about in this manner is far less wrenching than when a system is delivered with little or no user participation.

Martin's Pioneering Approaches to RAD In Figure 6.5 you can see our conceptualization of James Martin's original RAD phases. In the first phase Martin discusses requirements planning. Here high-level users decide on what functions the application should feature.

In the second phase, here called the user design phase, Martin characterizes users as being engaged in discussing the nontechnical design aspects of the system, with the assistance of analysts. The RAD design workshop phase incorporates both the user phase and the construction phase into one, because the highly interactive and visual nature of the design-and-refine process is occurring in an interactive, participative way.

In the construction phase many different activities are going on. Any designs that were created in the previous phase are further enhanced with RAD tools. As soon as the new functions become available, they are shown to users for interaction, comments, and review. With RAD tools, analysts are able to make continuous changes in the design of applications.

In Martin's fourth and final phase, the cutover phase, the newly developed application will replace the old one. While it is being run in parallel with the old application, the new one is tested, users are trained, and organizational procedures are changed before the cutover occurs.

Software Tools for RAD As you would expect, RAD software tools are often newer, often object-oriented tools. They include such familiar programs as Microsoft Access, Microsoft Visual Basic, Visual C++, and Microsoft .NET. (For more on taking a thoroughly object-oriented approach, see Chapter 18.)

One way the tools differ from one another is in their capabilities to support client/server applications (for example, MS Access does not, Visual Basic does) as well as their ease of use and the amount of programming skill that is required. Most RAD applications have stayed on the small, PC-based side, although their true power may be for client/server applications that need to run across multiple platforms.

Although there are almost as many different phases of RAD identified as there are analysts, the four phases proposed by Martin—requirements planning, user design, construction, and cutover—are useful. Let's examine each in a little more detail, comparing and contrasting them to the features of classic prototyping and the traditional SDLC.

COMPARING RAD TO THE SDLC

In Figure 6.6 you can compare the phases of the SDLC with those detailed for RAD at the beginning of this section. Notice that the ultimate purpose of RAD is to shorten the SDLC and in this way respond more rapidly to dynamic information

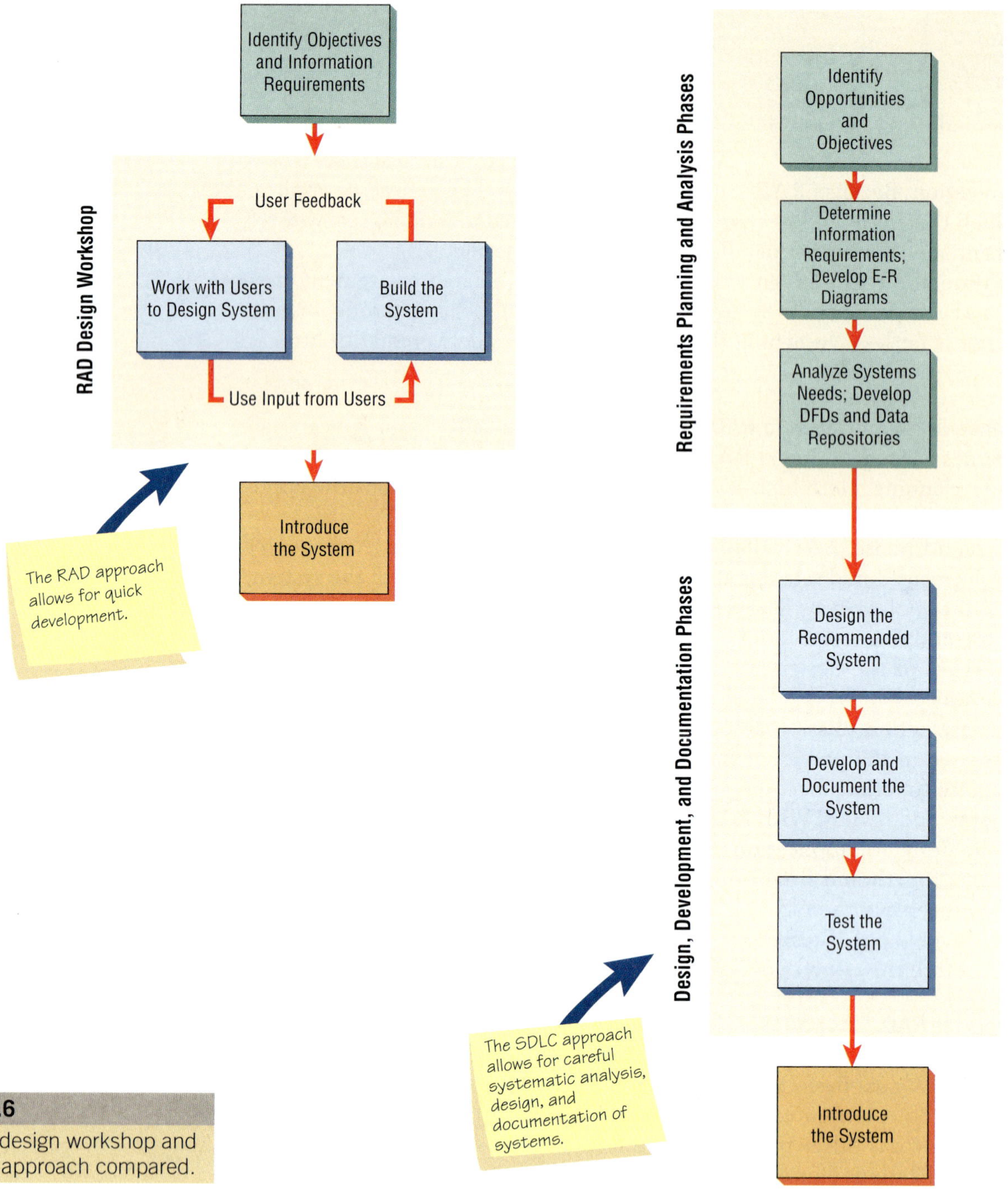

FIGURE 6.6
The RAD design workshop and the SDLC approach compared.

requirements of organizations. The SDLC takes a more methodical, systematic approach that ensures completeness and accuracy and has as its intention the creation of systems that are well integrated into standard business procedures and culture.

The RAD design workshop phase is a departure from the standard SDLC design phases, because RAD software tools are used to generate screens and to exhibit the overall flow of the running of the application. Thus, when users approve this design, they are signing off on a visual model representation, not just a conceptual design represented on paper, as is traditionally the case.

The implementation phase of RAD is in many ways less stressful than others, because the users have helped to design the business aspects of the system and are well aware of what changes will take place. There are few surprises, and the change is something that is welcomed. Often when using the SDLC, there is a lengthy time during development and design when analysts are separated from users. During this period, requirements can change and users can be caught off guard if the final product is different than anticipated over many months.

When to Use RAD As an analyst, you want to learn as many approaches and tools as possible to facilitate getting your work done in the most appropriate way. Certain applications and systems work will call forth certain methodologies. Consider using RAD when:

1. Your team includes programmers and analysts who are experienced with it; and
2. There are pressing business reasons for speeding up a portion of an application development; or
3. When you are working with a novel ecommerce application and your development team believes that the business can sufficiently benefit over their competitors from being an innovator if this application is among the first to appear on the Web; or
4. When users are sophisticated and highly engaged with the organizational goals of the company.

Disadvantages of RAD The difficulties with RAD, as with other types of prototyping, arise because systems analysts try to hurry the project too much. Suppose two carpenters are hired to build two storage sheds for two neighbors. The first carpenter follows the SDLC philosophy, whereas the second follows the RAD philosophy.

The first carpenter is systematic, inventorying every tool, lawn mower, and piece of patio furniture to determine the correct size for the shed, designing a blueprint of the shed, and writing specifications for every piece of lumber and hardware. The carpenter builds the shed with little waste and has precise documentation about how the shed was built if anyone wants to build another just like it, repair it, or paint it using the same color.

The second carpenter jumps right into the project by estimating the size of the shed, getting a truckload of lumber and hardware, building a frame and discussing it with the owner of the property as modifications are made when certain materials are not available, and making a trip to return the lumber not used. The shed gets built faster, but if a blueprint is not drawn, the documentation never exists.

AGILE MODELING

Agile methods are a collection of innovative, user-centered approaches to systems development. You will learn the values and principles, activities, resources, practices, processes, and tools associated with agile methodologies in the upcoming section. Agile practices are becoming accepted, increasing in popularity, and reportedly working. Agile methods can be credited with many successful systems development projects and in numerous cases even credited with rescuing companies from a failing system that was designed using a structured methodology.

Project management is important (as we saw in Chapter 3), so the agile approach tries to define an overall system plan quickly, develop and release software quickly, and then continuously revise the software to add additional features. Ordinary programmers, analysts, and designers who work independently and then integrate their work achieve solid results; agile programmers who work in pairs can be outstanding. But agile the approach is not based just on results. It is based on values, principles, and practices. We will now examine how the values and principles of agile modeling, including extreme programming (XP), shape the development of agile systems.

FIGURE 6.7
Values are crucial to the agile approach.

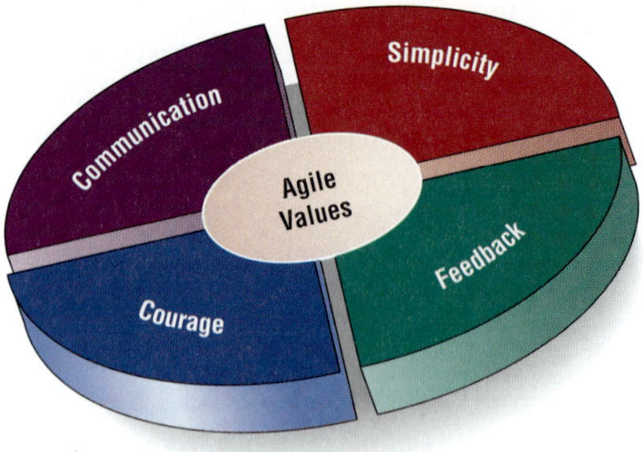

VALUES AND PRINCIPLES OF AGILE MODELING

Essential to agile programming are stated values and principles that create the context for collaboration among programmers and customers. In order to be agile analysts, you must adhere to the following values and principles as developed by Beck (2000) in his work on agile modeling that he called "extreme programming."

Four Values of Agile Modeling There are four values that create an environment in which both developers and businesses can be adequately served. Because there is often tension between what developers do in the short term and what is commercially desirable in the long term, it is important that you knowingly espouse values that will form a basis for acting together on a software project. The four values are communication, simplicity, feedback, and courage, as shown in Figure 6.7.

Let's begin with communication. Every human endeavor is fraught with possibilities for miscommunication. Systems projects that require constant updating and technical design are especially prone to such errors. Add to this tight project deadlines, specialized jargon, and the stereotype that programmers would prefer to talk to machines rather than people, and you have the potential for some serious communication problems. Projects can be delayed; the wrong problem can be solved; programmers are punished for even bringing up problems to managers; people leave or join the project in midstream without proper updates; and so the litany goes.

Typical agile practices such as pair programming (two programmers collaborating, described later in the chapter), estimating tasks, and unit testing rely heavily on good communication. Problems are fixed rapidly, holes are closed, and weak thinking is quickly strengthened through interaction with others on the team. An agile coach, as described in Chapter 3, is present to observe whether anyone has stopped communicating, and to reunite them.

A second value of the agile approach is that of simplicity. When we are working on a software development project, our first inclination is to become overwhelmed with the complexity and bigness of the task. However, you cannot run until you know how to walk, nor walk until you know how to stand. Simplicity for software development means that we will begin with the simplest possible thing we can do.

Simplicity takes practice, and is something that the agile coach may have to help with. The agile value of simplicity asks us to do the simplest thing today, with the understanding that it might have to be changed a little tomorrow. This requires a clear focus on the goals of the project and really is a basic value.

Feedback is the third basic value that is important to taking an extreme programming approach. When you think of feedback in this context, it is good to consider that feedback is wrapped up with the concept of time. Good, concrete feedback that is useful to the programmer, analyst, and customer can occur within seconds, minutes, days, weeks, or months, depending on what is needed, who is communicating, and what will be done with the feedback. A fellow programmer may hand you a test case that breaks the code you wrote only hours before, but that feedback is almost priceless in terms of being able to change what is not working before it is accepted and further embedded in the system.

Feedback occurs when customers create functional tests for all of the stories that programmers have subsequently implemented. (See more on user stories later in this chapter.) Critical feedback about the schedule comes from customers who compare the goal of the plan to the progress that has been made. Feedback helps programmers to make adjustments and lets the business start experiencing very early on what the new system will be like once it is fully functional.

Courage is the fourth value enunciated in agile programming. The value of courage has to do with a level of trust and comfort that must exist in the development team. It means not being afraid to throw out an afternoon or a day of programming and begin again if all is not right. It means being able to stay in touch with one's instincts (and test results) concerning what is working and what is not.

Courage also means responding to concrete feedback, acting on a teammate's hunch when they believe that they have a simpler, better way to accomplish your goal. Courage is a high-risk, high-reward value that encourages experimentation that can take the team to its goal more rapidly, in an innovative way. Courage means that you and your teammates trust each other and your customers enough to act in ways that will continuously improve what is being done on the project, even if they require throwing out code, rethinking solutions, or further simplifying approaches. Courage also implies that you, as a systems analyst, eagerly apply the practices of the agile approach.

Analysts can best reflect all of the four values through an attitude of humility. Historically, computer software was developed by experts who often thought they knew how to run a business better than the local customers who were the true domain experts. Computer experts were often referred to as "gurus." Some of the gurus displayed large egos and insisted on their infallibility, even when customers did not believe it. Many gurus lacked the virtue of humility.

However, maintaining a humble attitude during systems development is critical. You must continually embrace the idea that if the user is expressing a difficulty, then that difficulty must be addressed. It cannot be ignored. Agile modelers are systems analysts who make suggestions, voice opinions, but never insist that they are right 100 percent of the time. Agile modelers possess the self-confidence to allow their customers to question, critique, and sometimes complain about the system under development. Analysts learn from their customers, who have been in business a long time.

The Basic Principles of Agile Modeling In a perfect world, customers and your software development team would see eye to eye and communication would not be necessary. We would all be in agreement at all times. We know that the ideal world doesn't exist. But how can we bring our software development projects closer to the ideal? Part of why this will not happen is that so far we are trying to operate on a vague system of shared values. They're a good beginning, but they are really not operationalized to the point at which we can measure our success in any meaningful way. So we work to derive the basic principles that can help us check whether what we are doing in our software project is actually measuring up to the values that we share.

Although there are about a dozen principles that we can usefully derive from our values, the basic principles that we describe are providing rapid feedback,

FIGURE 6.8

Five agile principles guide the systems analyst through a successful project.

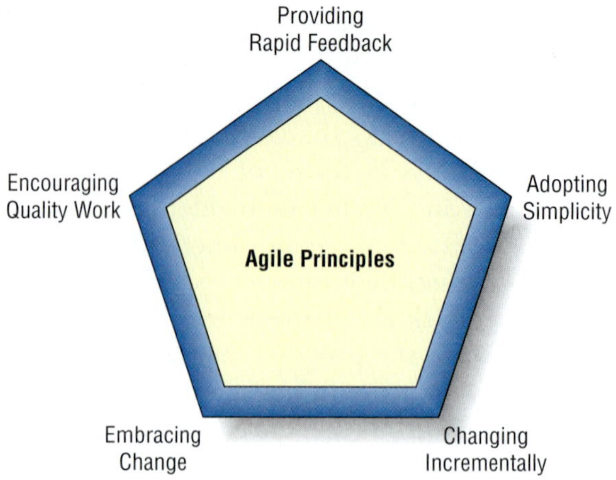

assuming simplicity, changing incrementally, embracing change, and encouraging quality work. These principles are illustrated in Figure 6.8.

The organizing principle to remember regarding rapid feedback is that in order for humans or the system to make a connection between a stimulus and reaction, the feedback must occur at a reasonable interval. If a printer runs out of paper, it must display an "out of paper" message instantly as feedback to the user, so that the situation can be remedied and the printing can continue. Rapid feedback for the development team means that the closer to the time of an action (coding a feature derived from a user story) to the time of the testing, the more meaningful the feedback (test results) will be. The earlier in the life of a system it is brought into production (rather than just being in development), the more value the feedback has to the business for gauging whether the system is meeting its goals.

The next basic principle is that the development team must assume simplicity. The premise is that over 90 percent of problems can be solved with utter simplicity. Notice that this flies in the face of most traditional training, which asks developers to plan for the future, figure out all of the interfaces, and so on, before beginning. Extreme programming (XP), an agile method that takes principles and practices to the extreme, says that "Simplicity rules the day." Complexity can be added later. This is a very difficult principle for many developers to master.

Accepting incremental change is the third basic principle that we examine. This means that you are constantly making the smallest change possible that still results in a difference in the development effort. No sweeping changes. This goes for the code, the team, and the business requirements. They will all change incrementally, even after the product is released. This fits well with the agile idea of evolution.

A fourth basic principle that we can derive from the agile values is that of embracing change. We want to keep all of our options open, but we want to be able to simultaneously solve whatever presents the biggest obstacle. Though there are always trade-offs involved, we will know for sure that change is welcomed. That dynamism keeps the project moving forward and animates the spirit of the project team. Change is good.

The last principle is the notion of performing quality work. The principle stems from the idea that all participants want to do quality work. Otherwise, why would they even be involved in an agile effort? The point is to make work enjoyable, work well with the team, and keep the project alive and well.

There are a handful of other principles that will help developers know how to proceed when a certain situation comes up. Briefly, they include the mandate to teach learning; encouragement to make a small initial investment so that good, but not extravagant, work is done; play to win, don't play to avoid losing; and use concrete experiments to test the work that is being done.

Other important concepts that support the agile approach are the idea of using open and honest communication without fear; working with people's natural tendencies (to want to succeed, interact with others, have autonomy in their work, be part of a winning team, be trusted, have their software work); claiming responsibility for a task rather than ordering others to do something; locally adapting the approach you are learning for agile development and seeking to use honest measurement that doesn't pretend a preciseness that doesn't exist. Agile modeling adds other principles such as "model with a purpose," "software is your primary goal," and "travel light," a way of saying a little documentation is good enough.

ACTIVITIES, RESOURCES, AND PRACTICES OF AGILE MODELING

Agile modeling involves a number of activities that need to be completed sometime during the agile development process. This section discusses these activities, the resources, and the practices that are unique to extreme programming.

Four Basic Activities of Agile Development There are four basic activities of development that agile methods use. They are coding, testing, listening, and designing. The agile analyst needs to identify the amount of effort that will go into each activity and balance that with the resources needed to complete the project.

Coding is designated as the one activity that it is not possible to do without. One author states that the most valuable thing that we receive from code is "learning." The process is basically this: have a thought, code it, test it, and see whether the thought was a logical one. Code can also be used to communicate ideas that would otherwise remain fuzzy or unshaped. When I see your code, I may get a new thought. Source code is the basis for a living system. It is essential for development.

Testing is the second basic activity of development. The agile approach views automated tests as critical. Extreme programming advocates writing tests to check the coding, functionality, performance, and conformance. Agile modeling relies on automated tests, and large libraries of tests exist for most programming languages. These tests need to be updated as necessary during the progress of the project.

There are both long-term and short-term reasons for testing. Testing in the short term provides you with extreme confidence in what you are building. If tests run perfectly you can continue on with renewed confidence. In the long term, testing keeps a system alive and allows you to make changes longer than would be possible if no tests were written or run.

The third basic activity of development is listening. In Chapter 4, we learned about the importance of listening during interviews. In the agile approach, listening is done in the extreme. Developers use active listening to hear their programming partner. In agile modeling there is less reliance on formal, written communication, and so listening becomes a paramount skill.

The developer also uses active listening with the customer. Developers assume that they know nothing about the business they are helping, and so they must listen carefully to businesspeople to get the answers to their questions. The developer needs to come to an understanding of what effective listening is. If you don't listen, you will not know what you should code or what you should test.

The fourth basic activity in development is designing, which is a way of creating a structure to organize all of the logic in the system. Designing is evolutionary, and so systems that are designed using the agile approach are conceptualized as evolving, always being designed.

Good design is often simple. Design should allow flexibility as well. Designing well permits you to make extensions to the system by making changes only in one place. Effective design locates logic near the data on which it will be operating. Above all, design should be useful to all those who will need it as the development effort proceeds, including customers as well as programmers.

Four Resource Control Variables of Agile Modeling In order to accomplish the activities described above, agile analysts need resources. Four resources can be adjusted to complete the project by its due date: time, cost, quality, and scope. When these four control variables are properly included in the planning, there is a state of balance between the resources and the activities needed to complete the project. A complete discussion of these resources and how they can be adjusted can be found in Chapter 3.

Four Core Agile Practices Four core practices markedly distinguish the agile approach from other approaches: short releases; the 40-hour work week; hosting an onsite customer; and using pair programming.

1. Short releases means that the development team compresses the time between releases of their product. Rather than releasing a full-blown version in a year, using the short release practice they will shorten the release time by tackling the most important features first, releasing that system or product, and then improving it later.
2. Forty-hour work week means that agile development teams purposely endorse a cultural core practice in which the team works intensely together during a typical 40-hour work week. As a corollary to this practice, the culture reinforces the idea that working overtime for more than a week in a row is very bad for the health of the project and the developers. This core practice attempts to motivate team members to work intensely at the job, and then to take time off so that when they return they are relaxed and less stressed. This helps team members spot problems more readily, and prevents costly errors and omissions due to ineffectual performance or burnout.
3. Onsite customer means that a user who is an expert in the business aspect of the systems development work is onsite during the development process. This person is integral to the process, writes user stories, communicates to team members, helps prioritize and balance the long-term business needs, and makes decisions about which feature should be tackled first.
4. Pair programming is an important core practice. It means that you work with another programmer of your own choosing. You both do coding, you both run tests. Often the senior person will take the coding lead initially, but as the junior person becomes involved, whoever has the clear vision of the goal will typically do the coding for the moment. When you ask another person to work with you, the protocol of pair programming says they are obligated to consent. Working with another programmer helps you clarify your thinking. Pairs change frequently, especially during the exploration stage of the development process. Pair programming saves time, cuts down on sloppy thinking, sparks creativity, and is a fun way to program.

How core agile practices interrelate with and support agile development activities, resources, and values is shown in Figure 6.9.

THE AGILE DEVELOPMENT PROCESS AND TOOLS

Now that you have learned about the activities, resources, and core practices of agile modeling, we can put that knowledge about agile modeling to work. This

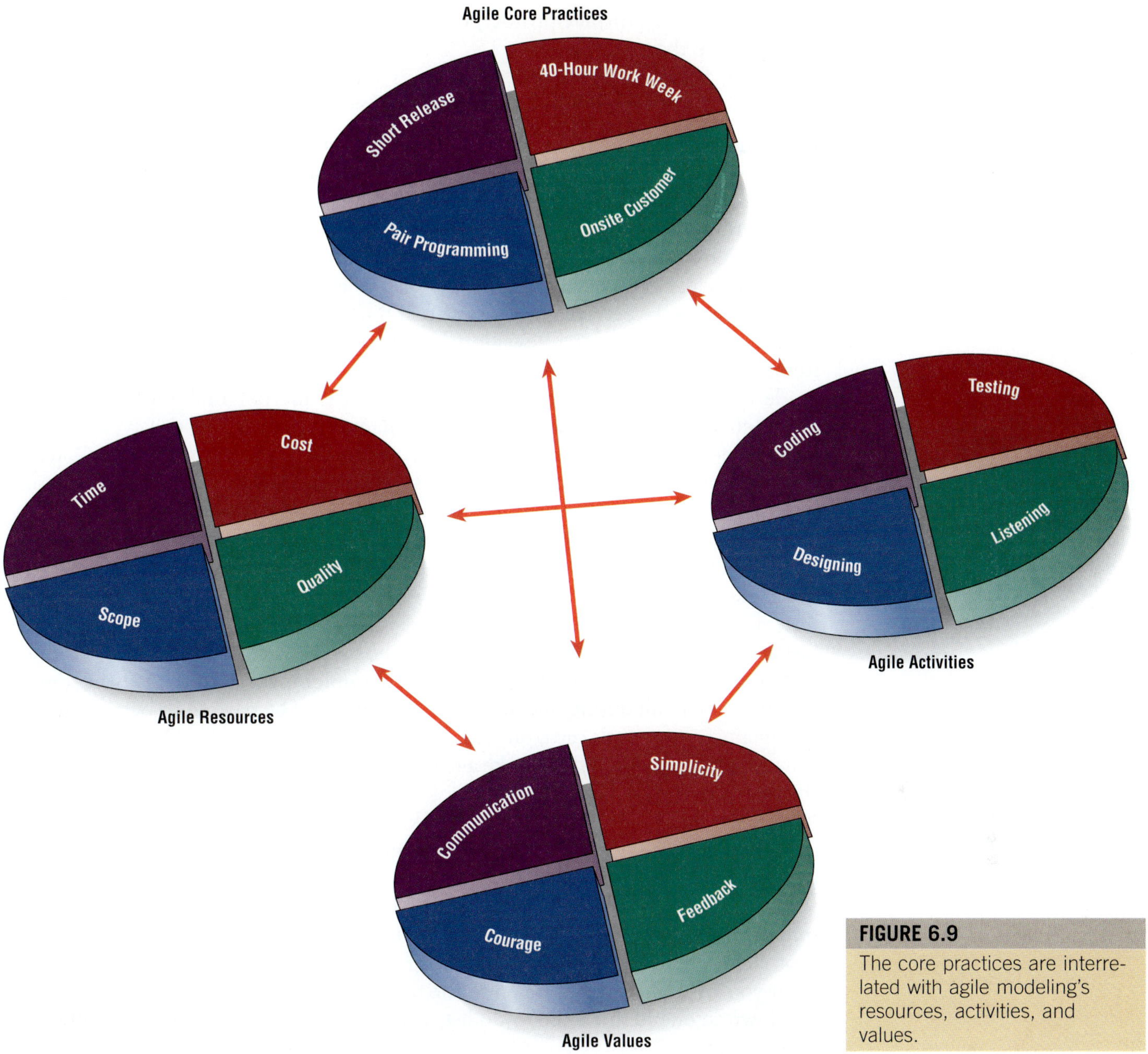

FIGURE 6.9
The core practices are interrelated with agile modeling's resources, activities, and values.

section describes the agile programming development process, explains the details involved in writing user stories, and examines some of the tools currently available for developing systems with an agile approach.

The Agile Development Process Modeling is a keyword in agile methods. Agile modeling seizes on the opportunity to create models. These can be logical models such as drawings of systems, or mock-ups such as the prototypes described earlier in this chapter. A typical agile modeling process would go something like this:

1. Listen for user stories from the customer.
2. Draw a logical workflow model to gain an appreciation for the business decisions represented in the user story.
3. Create new user stories based on the logical model.

4. Develop some display prototypes. In doing so, show the customer what sort of interface they will have.
5. Using feedback from the prototypes and the logical workflow diagrams, develop the system until you create a physical data model.

Agile is the other keyword in agile modeling. Agile implies maneuverability. Today's systems, especially those that are Web-based, pose twin demands: getting software released as soon as possible and continually improving the software to add new features. The systems analyst needs to have the ability and methods to create dynamic, context-sensitive, scalable, and evolutionary applications. Agile modeling as such is a change-embracing method, not dissimilar to extreme programming.

In Chapter 1 you learned about the SDLC and its many phases. Extreme programming also possesses a development process, but it is much more interactive, iterative, and integrative than the SDLC. However, the agile approach does not guide the developer through phases. Rather it is incremental and the activities are often done concurrently. Notice that many of the steps of the cycle for agile development are done every day. This is clearly in contrast to the SDLC, which proceeds at a much slower pace, and for which some activities (requirements analysis, testing, and so on) would be completed in distinct phases.

The five phases of the agile development process are exploration, planning, iterations to the first release, productionizing, and maintenance (for a detailed description of the stages, see Chapter 3). The following section describes specifically how a typical agile work session unfolds during the development process. For instance, the typical process would be to take on a task that is directly related to a system feature that a customer desires, test it, implement it into the existing design, and integrate it, all during one development episode. The day might begin by scrutinizing a user story task card, on which a specific task is written. During a brief, so-called stand-up meeting, you make a few inquiries about work done the previous day that could help in this task. You then ask another programmer to help on the task.

Other onsite experts who might know answers to specific questions are quickly consulted. Then the existing group of test cases is consulted. There are probably some that will apply and some that must be written.

A next step would be to write down the next task on the to-do list. Then you might write a test case for whatever you are trying to find out. You finish and run it. It probably will fail. Together you and your partner look at other test cases and debug what you wrote. You continue on to the next test case and the next. Eventually, you are down to one item on the to-do list, which would be restructuring the other test cases. You do so.

You load the updated release and the changes. You then run all the test cases, debug any that are not running, and fix the code. When you rerun it and it works, you're done. The code can then be released.

You may still be wondering just how to begin an agile development task. One wise author getting directly to the heart of the matter and being only slightly facetious, wrote, "Pick your worst problem, solve it the XP way. When it is no longer your worst problem, repeat" (Wells, as quoted in Beck, 2000, p. 123). In this way, you are showing great courage. You are daring to focus on solving your most pressing problem first, and you are applying the agile development strategies to work through that problem by testing, coding, listening, designing, and integrating. You are completing all the tasks of agile development in each daily programming assignment, and you are recognizing that the process of improving the system and addressing the hard problems simply and directly are keys to success.

Writing User Stories Even though the title of this section is "Writing User Stories," the emphasis in the creation of user stories is on spoken interaction between developers and users, not the written communication. In user stories, the developer is seeking first and foremost to identify valuable business user requirements. Users will typically engage in conversations every day with the developers about the meaning of the user stories they have written. These frequent conversations are purposeful interactions that have as their goal the prevention of misunderstandings or misinterpretations of user requirements. Therefore, user stories serve as reminders to the developers that they must hold conversations devoted to those requirements.

The following is an example of a series of stories written for an ecommerce application for an online merchant of books, CDs, and other media products. The stories give a fairly complete picture of what is needed at each of the stages in the purchase process, but the stories are very short and easy to comprehend. The point here is to get all of the needs and concerns of the online store out in the open. Although there is not enough of a story to begin programming, an agile developer might begin to see the overall picture clearly enough to begin estimating what it takes to complete the project. The stories are as follows:

Welcome the customer.

If the customer has been at this site before using this same computer, welcome the customer back to the online store.

Show specials on home page.

Show any recent books or other products that have recently been introduced. If the customer is identified, tailor the recommendations to that specific customer.

Search for desired product.

Include an effective search engine that will locate the specific product and similar products.

Show matching titles and availability.

Display the results of the search on a new Web page.

Allow customer to ask for greater detail.

Offer the customer more product details, such as sample pages in a book, more photos of a product, or to play a partial track from a CD.

Display reviews of the product.

Share the comments that other customers have about the product.

Place a product into a shopping cart.

Make it easy for the customer to click on a button that places the product into a shopping cart of intended purchases.

Keep purchase history on file.

Keep details about the customer and their purchases in a cookie on the customer's computer. Also keep credit card information for faster checkout.

Suggest other books that are similar.

Include photos of other books that have similar themes or were written by the same authors.

Proceed to checkout.

Confirm the identity of the customer.

Review the purchases.

Allow the customer to review the purchases.

Continue shopping.

Offer the customer a chance to make further purchases at the same time.

Apply shortcut methods for faster checkout.

If the identity of the customer is known and the delivery address matches, speed up the transaction by accepting the credit card on file and the remainder of the customer's preferences, such as shipping method.

Add names and shipping addresses.

If the purchase is a gift, allow the customer to enter the name and address of the recipient.

Offer options for shipping.

Allow the customer to choose a shipping method based on cost.

Complete the transaction.

Finish the transaction. Ask for credit card confirmation if the shipping address is different from the customer's address on file.

As you can easily see, there is no shortage of stories. The agile analyst needs to choose a few stories, complete the programming, and release a product. Once this is done, more stories are selected and a new version is released until all of the stories are included in the system (or the analyst and customer agree that a particular story lacks merit, or is not pressing, and so need not be included).

An example of a user story as it might appear to an agile developer is shown in Figure 6.10. On cards (or electronically), an analyst might first identify the need or opportunity, and then follow it with a brief story description. The analyst might take the opportunity to begin thinking broadly about the activities that need to be completed as well as the resources it will take to finish the project. In this example from the online merchant, the analyst indicates that the designing activity will take above-average effort, and the time and quality resources are required to rise above average. Notice that the analyst is not trying to be more precise than currently possible on this estimate, but it is still a useful exercise.

FIGURE 6.10
User stories can be recorded on cards. The user story should be brief enough for an analyst to determine what systems features are needed.

Development Tools for Agile Modeling There are several tools that are favored by agile developers. The original creators of the XP approach were working in

Need or Opportunity:	Apply shortcut methods for faster checkout.					
Story:	If the identity of the customer is known and the delivery address matches, speed up the transaction by accepting the credit card on file and the rest of the customer's preferences such as shipping method.					
		Well Below	**Below Average**	**Average**	**Above Average**	**Well Above**
Activities:	**Coding**			✓		
	Testing			✓		
	Listening			✓		
	Designing				✓	
Resources:	**Time**				✓	
	Cost		✓			
	Quality				✓	
	Scope			✓		

SmallTalk, and eventually ported their unit testing framework (SUnit) to Java, which is now called JUnit. There are many resources on the Web that allow you to download xUnit testing frameworks for whatever software development language you are using.

The creators of XP and other agile approaches were careful not to saddle their principles with any particular development tool. This means that the agile approach can be as flexible as needed over time, and can also evolve with new tools that become available. Tools come and go, but the principles should remain intact regardless of that fluctuation.

Many of the tools used in agile development are inexpensive or entirely free. There is an excellent Web site, SourceForge.net, at which most of the software development tools can be found. As you will see from examining the site, extreme programming is used across many languages and software platforms, but the two clear leaders in terms of widespread use and popularity are Java and Microsoft .NET.

There are many different types of tools available that support the activities you would need to accomplish when doing agile development. These include tools that facilitate collaboration such as Wiki Wiki, Whiteboard, Project Web, NetMeeting, and IBM's Rational ProjectConsole. There are also tools such as IBM's Rational ClearCase, Visual Intercept, Compuware Track Record, and BlipIt that support defect management.

Automated unit testers, acceptance testers, and GUI testers include JUnit, ComUnit, VBUnit, Nunit, httpUnit, and Rational Visual Test Tools. DevPartner Code Review helps with quality assurance. In addition there are tools that help with measuring system and component performance such as Jmeter, JUnitPerf, PerfMon, TrueTime, RealTime, and Microsoft Visual Studio Analyzer. There are also tools that assist with source code configuration management, including CVS, Visual Source Safe, and PVCS. Finally, there is a class of tools that you are probably already familiar with, the development environments of IBM VisualAge, Microsoft Visual Studio .NET, and JBuilder.

LESSONS LEARNED FROM AGILE MODELING

Several agile development projects have been chronicled in books, articles, and on Web sites. Many of them were successes, some have been failures, but we can learn a great deal from studying them, as well as the agile values, principles, and core practices. Following are the six major lessons we draw from our examination of agile modeling. Figure 6.11 depicts the six lessons.

The first lesson is that short releases allow systems to evolve. Product updates are made often, and changes are incorporated quickly. In this way the system is permitted to grow and expand in ways that the customer finds useful. Through the use of short releases, the development team compresses the time between releases of their product, improving the product later as the dynamic situation demands.

The second lesson is that pair programming enhances overall quality. Although pair programming is controversial, it clearly fosters other positive activities necessary in systems development such as good communication, identifying with the customer, focusing on the most valuable aspects of the project first, testing all code as it is developed, and integrating the new code after it successfully passes its tests.

The third lesson is that onsite customers are mutually beneficial to the business and the agile development team. Customers serve as a ready reference and reality check, and the focus of the system design will always be maintained via their presence: customers become more like developers and developers empathize more fully with customers.

FIGURE 6.11

There are six vital lessons that can be drawn from the agile approach to systems.

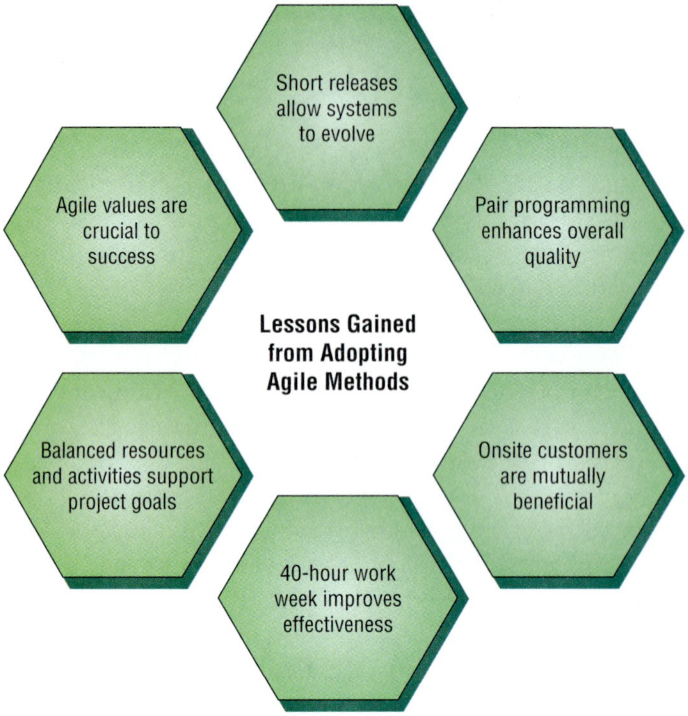

The fourth lesson we take from the agile approach is that the 40-hour work week improves effectiveness. Even the hardest-hitting developers are susceptible to errors and burnout if they work too hard for too long a period. When the development team is together, however, every moment counts. Working at a sustainable pace is much more desirable for the life of the project, the life of the system, and the life of the developer! We all know the parable of the hare and the tortoise.

The fifth lesson we draw from taking the agile approach is that balanced resources and activities support project goals. Managing a project doesn't mean simply getting all resources and tasks together. It also means that the analyst is faced with a number of trade-offs. Sometimes cost may be predetermined, at other junctures time may be the most important factor. The resource control variables of time, cost, quality, and scope need to be properly balanced with the activities of coding, designing, testing, and listening.

The last lesson we take from agile modeling approaches is that agile values are crucial to success. It is essential to the overall success of the project that analysts wholeheartedly embrace the values of communication, simplicity, feedback, and courage in all of the work that they do. This type of personal and team commitment enables the analyst to succeed where others, who possess similar technical competencies but who lack values, will fail. True dedication to these values is fundamental to successful development.

Another agile approach is named Scrum. The word *scrum* is taken from a starting position in rugby in which the rugby teams form a huddle and fight for possession of the ball. Scrum is really about teamwork, similar to what is needed in playing a game of rugby.

Just as rugby teams will come to a game with an overall strategy, development teams begin the project with a high-level plan that can be changed on the fly as the "game" progresses. Systems development team members realize that the success of the project is most important, and their individual success is secondary. The project leader has some, but not much, influence on the detail. Rather, the tactical game is left up to the team members, just as if they were on the field. The systems team works within a strict time frame (30 days for development), just as a rugby team would play in a strict time constraint of a game.

We can describe the components of the Scrum methodology as:

1. Product backlog, in which a list is derived from product specifications.
2. Sprint backlog, a dynamically changing list of tasks to be completed in the next sprint.
3. Sprint, a 30-day period in which the development team transforms the backlog into software that can be demonstrated.
4. Daily scrum, a brief meeting in which communication is the number-one rule. Team members need to explain what they did since the last meeting, whether they encountered any obstacles, and what they plan to do before the next daily scrum.
5. Demo, working software that can be demonstrated to the customer.

Scrum is indeed a high-intensity methodology. It is just one of the approaches that adopts the philosophy of agile modeling.

COMPARING AGILE MODELING AND STRUCTURED METHODS

As you have seen, agile methods are developed quickly; they reportedly work; users are customers who are directly involved. While it is true that projects developed by agile methods often require tweaking to work properly, agile developers admit that tweaking is part of the process. The agile approach implies many short releases with features added along the way.

This section examines how agile practices differ from structured methodologies in improving the efficiency of systems development. We then go on to examine what happens when organizations, analysts, and programmers are asked to adopt the agile approach after becoming accustomed to structured methodologies. Our goal is to raise awareness of the risks encountered by organizations and individuals when adopting innovations, specifically in adopting agile methodologies for systems development.

Researchers (Davis & Naumann, 1999) developed a list of seven strategies that can improve the efficiency of knowledge work: reducing interface time and errors; reducing process learning time and dual processing losses; reducing time and effort to structure tasks and format outputs; reducing nonproductive expansion of work; reducing data and knowledge search and storage time and costs; reducing communication and coordination time and costs; and reducing losses from human information overload. They believe this is important, since based on their study of a group of programmers, they claim that the best programmers are five to ten times more productive than the worst ones. They further point out this ratio is only two to one for workers in clerical or physical tasks. Their suggestion is that software can help improve many situations.

We use the standard, traditional systems development approach of structured methods to compare and contrast how structured approaches versus agile methods would implement the seven strategies proposed to improve the efficiency of knowledge workers.

While adopting more software may indeed improve performance, it is reasonable to suggest that changing an approach or methodology may also improve performance. Consequently, we will examine each aspect of knowledge work productivity through lenses from both structured and agile methodologies. Figure 6.12 lists the original seven strategies for productivity improvement and then explains what methods are used to improve the efficiency of systems development for both structured and agile methodologies.

Strategies for Improving Efficiency in Knowledge Work	Implementation Using Structured Methodologies	Implementation Using Agile Methodologies
Reduce interface time and errors	Adopting organizational standards for coding, naming, etc.; using forms	Adopting pair programming
Reduce process learning time and dual processing losses	Managing when updates are released so the user does not have to learn and use software at the same time	Ad hoc prototyping and rapid development
Reduce time and effort to structure tasks and format outputs	Using CASE tools and diagrams; using code written by other programmers	Encouraging short releases
Reduce nonproductive expansion of work	Project management; establishing deadlines	Limiting scope in each release
Reduce data and knowledge search and storage time and costs	Using structured data gathering techniques, such as interviews, observation, sampling	Allowing for an onsite customer
Reduce communication and coordination time and costs	Separating projects into smaller tasks; establishing barriers	Timeboxing
Reduce losses from human information overload	Applying filtering techniques to shield analysts and programmers	Sticking to a 40-hour work week

FIGURE 6.12
How Davis and Naumann's (1999) strategies for improving efficiency can be implemented using two different development approaches.

In the upcoming sections we will compare and contrast structured approaches with the agile approach. An overarching observation about the agile methodology is that it is a human-oriented approach that permits people to create nuanced solutions that are impossible to create through formal specifications of process.

REDUCING THE INTERFACE TIME AND ERRORS

Systems analysts and programmers need to analyze, design, and develop systems using knowledge work tools that range from Microsoft Office to sophisticated and costly CASE tools. They also need to document as they develop systems. It is important that analysts and programmers are capable of understanding the interface they use. They need to know how to classify, code, store, and write about the data they gather. Systems developers also need to quickly access a program, enter the required information, and retrieve it when it is needed again.

Structured approaches encourage adopting standards for everything. Rules set forth include items such as, "Everyone must use Microsoft Word rather than Word Perfect." They may be more detailed instructions to ensure clean data such as, "Always use M for Male and F for Female," thereby ensuring that analysts do not unthinkingly choose codes of their own, such as 0 for Male and 1 for Female. These rules then become part of the data repository. Forms are also useful, requiring all personnel to document their procedures so that another programmer might be able to take over if necessary.

In an agile approach, forms and procedures work well too, but another element is added. The additional practice of pair programming assures that one programmer will check the work of another, thereby reducing the number of errors. Pair programming means that ownership of the design or software itself is shared as in a partnership. Both partners (typically one a programmer, often a senior one) will say they chose a programming partner who desired to have a quality product that is error-free. Since two people work on the same design and code, interface time is not an issue; it is an integral part of the process. The authors have noted that programmers are quite emotional when the topic of pair programming is broached.

REDUCING THE PROCESS LEARNING TIME AND DUAL PROCESSING LOSSES

Analysts and programmers learn specific techniques and software languages required for the completion of a current project. Inefficiencies often result when some analysts and programmers already know the products used while others still need to learn them. Typically, we ask that developers learn these products at the same time they are using them to build the system. This on-the-job training slows down the entire systems development project considerably.

A traditional, structured project requires more learning. If CASE tools were used, an analyst may need to learn the proprietary CASE tools used in the organization. The same applies to the use of a specific computer language. Documentation is also a concern.

Using an agile philosophy, the ability to launch projects without using CASE tools and detailed documentation allows the analysts and programmers to spend most of their time on system development rather than on learning specific tools.

REDUCING THE TIME AND EFFORT TO STRUCTURE TASKS AND FORMAT OUTPUTS

Whenever a project is started, a developer needs to determine the boundaries. In other words, the developers need to know what the deliverable will be and how they will go about organizing the project so they can complete all the necessary tasks.

A traditional approach would include using CASE tools; drawing diagrams (such as E-R diagrams and data flow diagrams); using project management software (such as Microsoft Project); writing detailed job descriptions; using and reusing forms and templates; and reusing code written by other programmers.

Systems development using an agile approach addresses the need to structure tasks by scheduling short releases. The agile philosophy suggests that system developers create a series of deadlines for many releases of the system. The first releases would possess fewer features, but, with each new release, additional features would be added.

REDUCING THE NONPRODUCTIVE EXPANSION OF WORK

Parkinson's law states that "work expands so as to fill the time available for its completion." If there are no specified deadlines, it is possible that knowledge work will continue to expand.

With traditional structured methodologies, deadlines at first seem far into the future. Analysts may use project management techniques to try to schedule the activities, but there is a built-in bias to extend earlier tasks longer than they need to be and then try to shorten tasks later on in the development. Analysts and programmers are less concerned about distant deadlines than approaching ones.

Once again, the agile approach stresses short releases. Releases can be delivered at the time promised, minus some of the features originally promised. Making all deadlines imminent pushes a realistic expectation for (at least partial) completion to the fore.

REDUCING THE DATA AND KNOWLEDGE SEARCH AND STORAGE TIME AND COSTS

System developers need to gather information about the organization, goals, priorities, and details about current information systems before they can proceed to develop a new system. Data-gathering methods include interviewing, administering questionnaires, observation, and investigation by examining reports and memos.

Structured methodologies encourage structured data-gathering methods. Structured techniques would normally be used to structure interviews and design the interview process. Questionnaires would be developed in a structured way, and structured observational techniques such as STROBE would encourage the analyst to specifically observe key elements and form conclusions based on the observations of the physical environment. A sampling plan would be determined quantitatively, in order for the systems analyst to select reports and memos to examine.

Knowledge searches are less structured in an agile modeling environment. The practice of having an onsite customer greatly enhances access to information. The onsite customer is present to answer questions about the organization itself, its goals, the priorities of organizational members and customers, and whatever knowledge is necessary about existing information systems. As the project continues, the picture of customer requirements becomes clearer. This approach seems relatively painless because, when the system developers want to know something, they can just ask. The downside, however, is that the onsite representative may make up information if it is unknown or unavailable or evade telling the truth for some ulterior purpose.

REDUCING COMMUNICATION AND COORDINATION TIME AND COSTS

Communication between analysts and users, as well as among analysts themselves, is at the heart of developing systems. Poor communication is certainly the root of multiple development problems. We know that communication increases when more people join the project. When two people work on a project, there is one opportunity for a one-to-one conversation; when three people are involved, there are three possibilities; when four are involved, there are six possibilities, and so on. Inexperienced team members need time to get up to speed, and they can slow down a project even though they are meant to help expedite it.

Traditional structured development encourages the separation of big tasks into smaller tasks. This allows more tightly knit groups and decreases the time spent communicating. Another approach involves setting up barriers. For example, customers may not be given access to programmers. This is a common practice in many industries. However, increased efficiency often means decreased effectiveness, and it has been noted that dividing up groups and setting up barriers often introduce errors.

Agile methods, on the other hand, limit time instead of tasks. Timeboxing is used in agile methodologies to encourage completion of activities in shorter periods. Timeboxing is simply setting a time limit of one or two weeks to complete a feature or module. The agile method scrum puts a premium on time, while the developers communicate effectively as a team. Since communication is one of the four values of the agile philosophy, communication costs tend to increase rather than decrease.

REDUCING LOSSES FROM HUMAN INFORMATION OVERLOAD

We have long known that people do not react well in information overload situations. When telephones were an emerging technology, switchboard operators manually connected calls between two parties. It was demonstrated that this system would work until an information overload occurred, at which point the entire system broke down. When too many calls came in, the overwhelmed switchboard operator would simply stop working and give up completely on connecting callers. An analogous overload situation can occur anytime to anyone, including systems analysts and programmers.

A traditional approach would be to try to filter information to shield analysts and programmers from customer complaints. This approach allows developers to continue working on the problem without the interference and subjectivity that would normally occur.

Using an agile philosophy, analysts and programmers are expected to stick to a 40-hour work week. This might be viewed by some as a questionable practice. How will all the work ever get done? The agile philosophy states, however, that quality work is usually done during a routine schedule, and it is only when overtime is added that problems of poor quality design and programming enter the scene. By sticking to a 40-hour week schedule, agile methodology claims you will eventually come out ahead.

RISKS INHERENT IN ORGANIZATIONAL INNOVATION

In consultation with users, analysts must consider the risks that organizations face when adopting new methodologies. Clearly this is part of a larger question of when is the appropriate time to upgrade human skills, adopt new organizational processes, and institute internal change.

In the larger sense, these are questions of a strategic dimension for organizational leadership. Specifically, we consider the case of the systems analysis team adopting agile methods in light of the risks to the organization and the eventual successful outcome for the systems development team and their clients. Figure 6.13 shows many of the variables that need to be considered when assessing the risk of adopting organizational innovation.

The Culture of the Organization and the Culture of the Systems Development Team

A key consideration is the overall culture of the organization and how the culture of the development team fits within it. A conservative organizational culture with many stable features that does not seek to innovate may be an inappropriate or even inhospitable context for the adoption of agile methodologies by the systems development group.

Analysts and other developers must use caution in introducing new techniques into this type of setting, since their success is far from assured, and long-standing

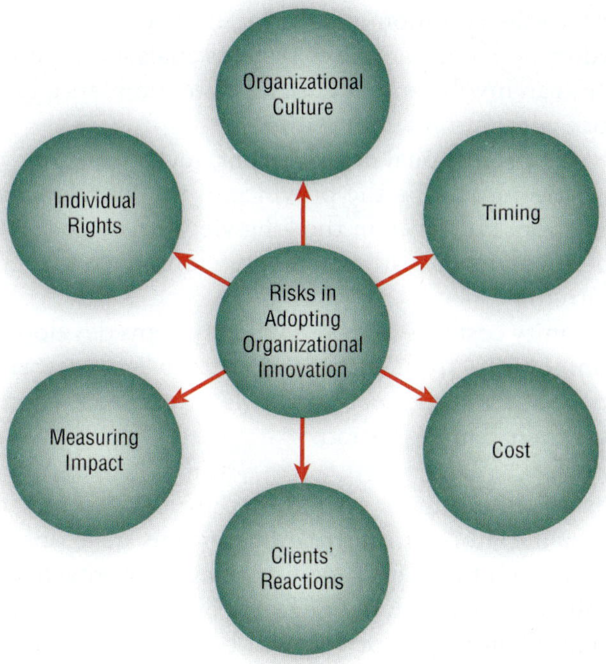

FIGURE 6.13
Adopting new information systems involves balancing several risks.

development team members or other organizational members may be threatened by new ways of working that depart from customary, dependable approaches with proven results.

Conversely, an organization that is dependent on innovation to retain its cutting edge in its industry might be the organization most welcoming toward agile innovations in systems development methods. In this instance, the culture of the organization is already permeated with the understanding of the critical nature of many of the core principles of agile development methodologies. From the strategic level downward, the company's members have internalized the need for rapid feedback, dynamic responses to changing environments in real time, dependence on the customer for guidance and participation in problem solving, and so on.

Located between these extremes are organizations that do not rely on innovation as a key strategic strength (in other words, they are not dependent on research and development of new products or services to remain afloat) but that might still wish to adopt innovative practices in small units or groups. Indeed, such small, innovative centers or kernels might eventually drive the growth or competitive advantage of this type of organization.

In those situations, systems development groups that adopt agile methods might find some initial resistance but might succeed if the groups are kept independent of the dominant, conservative culture. The systems group would then be permitted to experiment or innovate among their group and within their client relationship.

Specifically, agile methods might be considered a proving ground or incubator for more widespread adoption of innovative methods. Alternatively, it might be classified or interpreted as the province of a creative group, as is often the case for marketing, art, and other innovative departments in a larger corporation.

Timing Organizations must ask and answer the question of when is the best time to innovate with the adoption of new systems development methodologies, when all other projects and factors (internally and externally) are taken into account.

Organizations must consider the entire panoply of projects in which they are investing, looking ahead at project deadlines, scheduling the upgrading of physical plants, and absorbing key industry and economic forecasts.

Cost Another risk to the adoption of agile methodologies for organizations is the cost involved in education and training of systems analysts and programmers in the new approach. This can involve either costly offsite seminars and courses or hiring consultants to work with current staff onsite.

In many instances, professional development, such as learning new methodologies or languages, is deemed to be the province of the individual and not the concern of the organization. However, in the long view, it is recognized that the organization should be involved in fostering the development of its employees. Either way costs are incurred.

Further, opportunity costs are involved when systems developers are necessarily diverted (albeit temporarily) from ongoing projects to learn new skills. Education in itself can be costly, but an additional burden is recognized when analysts cannot earn income during their training period.

Clients' Reactions When clients (whether they are internal or external) are involved as users or initiators of information systems development efforts, reactions to the use of new methods entailed by the agile approach are also a key consideration. Some clients react with joy once the benefits of timeliness and involvement are described. Others do not want to be used as human guinea pigs for systems "experiments" with uncertain outcomes.

The behaviors expected of clients change when developers adopt agile methods. Therefore, the adoption of agile methodologies is not a one-sided decision that is solely the province of the developers. The client-analyst relationship must be resilient enough to absorb and adapt to changes in expected behaviors. For example, the onsite presence of a client during development is a major commitment that should be thoroughly understood and agreed upon by those adopting agile methods.

Measuring Impact Another consideration for organizations adopting agile methodologies is how to certify and measure that the new methods are going to facilitate successful systems development. The strengths and weaknesses of traditional structured methods used to develop information systems are well-known.

While there is ample anecdotal evidence that agile methodologies are superior for development under some conditions, their history is short-lived and not yet empirically supported. Therefore, the adoption of agile methodologies carries with it the risk that systems created with them will not be successful or will not adequately interface with legacy systems. Measuring the impact of the use of agile methodologies has begun, but organizations need to be vigilant in proposing impact measurements in tandem with the adoption of new methods.

The Individual Rights of Programmers/Analysts Successful systems developers (analysts and programmers) exercise creativity in their approach to their work, and they deserve the right to work in the most fruitful configuration possible. It is possible that the working requirements of new agile methods (for example, pair programming) encroach upon some basic rights of creative people to work alone or in groups as the design work dictates. Analysts should not be enslaved by the dictates of agile or any other methods, but rather should be free to pursue development in the way they deem the most productive.

There is no "one best way" to design a system, a module, interface, form, or Web page. Decisions made about systems design, about user interfaces, about who should access information which information, about information sharing, and about the distribution of knowledge are all potentially value-laden and subject to expert judgment. In the instance of systems developers, creativity, subjectivity, and the right to achieve design objectives through numerous individual paths need to be balanced against the organizational adoption of innovative approaches such as agile methodologies.

As you can see, adopting organizational innovations poses many risks to the organization as well as to individuals. We have examined the specific implications of adopting systems development through the use of agile methods. We examined risks to the organization as a whole as well as to those posed to the individual systems analyst who is caught up in the organization's desire to innovate.

SUMMARY

Prototyping is an information gathering technique useful for supplementing the traditional systems development life cycle; however, both agile methods and human–computer interaction share roots in prototyping. When systems analysts use prototyping, they are seeking user reactions, suggestions, innovations, and revision plans to make improvements to the prototype, and thereby modify system plans with a minimum of expense and disruption. Systems that support semistructured decision making (as decision support systems do) are prime candidates for prototyping.

The term *prototyping* carries several different meanings, four of which are commonly used. The first definition of prototyping is that of constructing a prototype as a patched-up system. A second definition of prototyping is a nonoperational prototype that is used to test certain aspects of the design. A third conception of prototyping is creating the first-of-a-series prototype that is fully operational. This kind of prototype is useful when many installations of the same information system (under similar conditions) are planned. The fourth kind of prototyping is a selected-features prototype that has some, but not all, of the essential system features. It uses self-contained modules as building blocks so that if prototyped features are successful, they can be kept and incorporated into the larger, finished system.

The four major guidelines for developing a prototype are to (1) work in manageable modules, (2) build the prototype rapidly, (3) modify the prototype, and (4) stress the user interface.

One disadvantage of prototypes is that managing the prototyping process is difficult because of the rapidity of the process and its many iterations. A second disadvantage is that an incomplete prototype may be pressed into service as if it were a complete system.

Although prototyping is not always necessary or desirable, it should be noted that there are three main, interrelated advantages to using it: (1) the potential for changing the system early in its development, (2) the opportunity to stop development on a system that is not working, and (3) the possibility of developing a system that more closely addresses users' needs and expectations.

Users have a distinct role to play in the prototyping process. Their main concern must be to interact with the prototype through experimentation. Systems analysts must work systematically to elicit and evaluate users' reactions to the prototype.

One particular use of prototyping is rapid application development, or RAD. It is an object-oriented approach with three phases: requirements planning, the RAD design workshop, and implementation.

Agile modeling is a software development approach that defines an overall plan quickly, develops and releases software quickly, and then continuously revises software to add additional features. Agile programmers work in pairs to develop quality systems.

The five values of the agile approach that are shared by the commercial customer as well as the development team are communication, simplicity, feedback, courage and humility. The five basic principles of agile development are providing rapid feedback; assuming simplicity when approaching a new programming task; changing code, design, and even the development team only incrementally; embracing change as the normal state of work; and doing quality work. Agile activities include coding, testing, listening, and designing. Resources available include time, cost, quality, and scope.

The four core practices of the agile approach are (1) short releases, (2) 40-hour work week, (3) onsite customer, and (4) pair programming. These core practices distinguish extreme programming from other systems development processes. Five broad stages in the agile developmental process are exploration, planning, iterations to the first release, productionizing, and maintenance.

The agile development process includes choosing a task that is directly related to a customer-desired feature based on user stories; choosing a programming partner; selecting and writing appropriate test cases; writing the code; running the test cases; debugging it until all test cases run; implementing it with the existing design; and integrating it into what currently exists.

"Thank goodness it's the time of year when everything is new. I love spring; it's the most exhilarating time here at MRE. The trees are so green, with leaves in so many different shades. So many new projects to do, too; so many new clients to meet. It's really exciting. It reminds me of prototyping. Or what I know about prototyping, anyway. It's something new and fresh, a quick way to find out what's happening.

"In fact, I believe that we have a few prototypes already going on here. The best thing about them is that they can change. I don't know anyone who's really been satisfied with a first pass at a prototype. But it is fun to be involved with something that is happening fast, and something that will change."

HYPERCASE QUESTIONS

1. Locate the prototype currently proposed for use in one of MRE's departments. Suggest a few modifications that would make this prototype even more responsive to the unit's needs.
2. Using a word processor, construct a nonoperational prototype for a Training Unit Project Reporting System. If you have a hypertext program available, attempt to create partial functionality by making the menus functional. *Hint:* See sample screens in Chapters 11 and 12 to help you in your design.

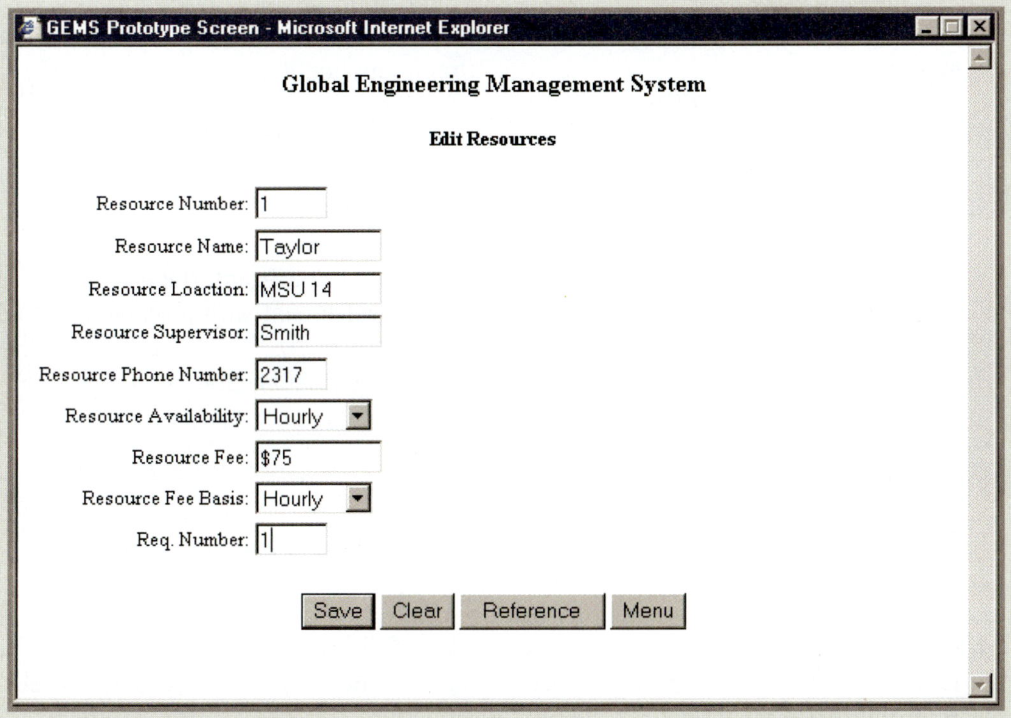

FIGURE 6.HC1
One of the many prototype screens found in HyperCase.

There are six lessons to be learned from the agile approach. The first lesson is that short releases allow systems to evolve. The second lesson is that pair programming enhances overall quality. The third lesson is that onsite customers are mutually beneficial to the business and the agile development team. The fourth lesson is that the 40-hour work week improves effectiveness. The fifth lesson is that balanced resources and activities support project goals. The last lesson we take from extreme programming is that agile development values are crucial to success.

Agile modeling embraces a set of core principles. One way to implement agile modeling is through the Scrum methodology.

We classified and discussed several inherent dangers to organizations adopting innovative approaches, including an incompatible organizational culture, poor timing of the project in comparison to other projects being undertaken, cost of training systems analysts and customers in new approaches (as well as opportunity costs when analysts are taken away from projects to undergo training seminars), unfavorable client reactions to new behavioral expectations, difficulties in measuring the impact of new methodologies, and the possible compromise of the individual creative rights of programmers and analysts.

KEYWORDS AND PHRASES

40-hour work week
agile modeling
agile principles
agile values
assume simplicity
embracing change
exploration phase
extreme programming (XP)
first-of-a-series prototype
implementation
incremental change
iterations to the first release phase
maintenance phase
modifying the prototype
nonoperational prototype
onsite customer
pair programming
patched-up prototype
planning phase
productionizing phase
prototype
RAD design workshop
rapid application development (RAD)
rapid feedback
requirements planning phase
Scrum methodology
selected-features prototype
short release
stressing the user interface
user involvement with prototyping
user stories
working in manageable modules

REVIEW QUESTIONS

1. What four kinds of information is the analyst seeking through prototyping?
2. What is meant by the term *patched-up prototype*?
3. Define a prototype that is a nonworking scale model.
4. Give an example of a prototype that is a first full-scale model.
5. Define what is meant by a prototype that is a model with some, but not all, essential features.
6. List the advantages and disadvantages of using prototyping to *replace* the traditional systems development life cycle.
7. Describe how prototyping can be used to augment the traditional systems development life cycle.
8. What are the criteria for deciding whether a system should be prototyped?
9. List four guidelines the analyst should observe in developing a prototype.
10. What are the two main problems identified with prototyping?

11. List the three main advantages in using prototyping.
12. How can a prototype mounted on an interactive Web site facilitate the prototyping process? Answer in a paragraph.
13. What are three ways that a user can be of help in the prototyping process?
14. Define what is meant by RAD.
15. What are the three phases of RAD?
16. Define extreme programming.
17. What are the four values that must be shared by the development team and business customers when taking an agile approach?
18. What are the five basic principles of the agile approach?
19. What are the four core practices of the agile approach?
20. Outline the typical steps in an agile development episode.
21. What is a user story? Is it primarily written or spoken? State your choice, then defend your answer with an example.
22. List software tools that can aid the developer in doing a variety of tests of code.
23. What are six lessons taken from experience with agile development efforts?
24. What is Scrum?

PROBLEMS

1. As part of a larger systems project, Clone Bank of Clone, Colorado, wants your help in setting up a new monthly reporting form for its checking and savings account customers. The president and vice presidents are very attuned to what customers in the community are saying. They think that their customers want a checking account summary that looks like the one offered by the other three banks in town. They are unwilling, however, to commit to that form without a formal summary of customer feedback that supports their decision. Feedback will not be used to change the prototype form in any way. They want you to send a prototype of one form to one group and to send the old form to another group.
   a. In a paragraph discuss why it probably is not worthwhile to prototype the new form under these circumstances.
   b. In a second paragraph discuss a situation under which it would be advisable to prototype a new form.
2. C. N. Itall has been a systems analyst for Tun-L-Vision Corporation for many years. When you came on board as part of the systems analysis team and suggested prototyping as part of the SDLC for a current project, C. N. said, "Sure, but you can't pay any attention to what users say. They have no idea what they want. I'll prototype, but I'm not 'observing' any users."
   a. As tactfully as possible, so as not to upset C. N. Itall, make a list of the reasons that support the importance of observing user reactions, suggestions, and innovations in the prototyping process.
   b. In a paragraph, describe what might happen if part of a system is prototyped and no user feedback about it is incorporated into the successive system.
3. "Every time I think I've captured user information requirements, they've already changed. It's like trying to hit a moving target. Half the time, I don't think they even know what they want themselves," exclaims Flo Chart, a systems analyst for 2 Good 2 Be True, a company that surveys product use for the marketing divisions of several manufacturing companies.
   a. In a paragraph, explain to Flo Chart how prototyping can help her to better define users' information requirements.

b. In a paragraph, comment on Flo's observation: "Half the time, I don't think they even know what they want themselves." Be sure to explain how prototyping can actually help users better understand and articulate their own information requirements.

c. Suggest how an interactive Web site featuring a prototype might address Flo's concerns about capturing user information requirements. Use a paragraph.

4. Harold, a district manager for the multioutlet chain of Sprocket's Gifts, thinks that building a prototype can mean only one thing: a nonworking scale model. He also believes that this way is too cumbersome to prototype information systems and thus is reluctant to do so.
   a. Briefly (in two or three paragraphs) compare and contrast the other three kinds of prototyping that are possible so that Harold has an understanding of what prototyping can mean.
   b. Harold has an option of implementing one system, trying it, and then having it installed in five other Sprocket locations if it is successful. Name a type of prototyping that would fit well with this approach, and in a paragraph defend your choice.
5. "I've got the idea of the century!" proclaims Bea Kwicke, a new systems analyst with your systems group. "Let's skip all this SDLC garbage and just prototype everything. Our projects will go a lot more quickly, we'll save time and money, and all the users will feel as if we're paying attention to them instead of going away for months on end and not talking to them."
   a. List the reasons you (as a member of the same team as Bea) would give her to dissuade her from trying to scrap the SDLC and prototype every project.
   b. Bea is pretty disappointed with what you have said. To encourage her, use a paragraph to explain the situations you think would lend themselves to prototyping.
6. The following remark was overheard at a meeting between managers and a systems analysis team at the Fence-Me-In fencing company: "You told us the prototype would be finished three weeks ago. We're still waiting for it!"
   a. In a paragraph, comment on the importance of rapid delivery of a portion of a prototyped information system.
   b. List three elements of the prototyping process that must be controlled to ensure prompt delivery of the prototype.
   c. What are some elements of the prototyping process that are difficult to manage? List them.
7. Examine the collection of user stories from the online merchant shown earlier in the chapter. The online media store would now like to have you add some features to its Web site. Following the format shown in Figure 6.11 write a user story for the features listed below:
   a. Include pop-up ads.
   b. Offer to share the details of the customer's purchases with their friends.
   c. Extend offer to purchase other items.
8. Go to the Palm gear Web site at www.palmgear.com. Explore the Web site and write up a dozen brief user stories for improving the Web site.
9. Go to the techtv Web site at www.techtv.com and write up a dozen brief user stories for improving the Web site.
10. Using the stories you wrote for Problem 7, walk through the five stages of the agile development process and describe what happens at each one of the stages.

GROUP PROJECTS

1. Divide your group into two smaller subgroups. Have group 1 follow the processes specified in this chapter for creating prototypes. Using a CASE tool or a word processor, group 1 should devise two nonworking prototype screens using the information collected in the interviews with Maverick Transport employees accomplished in the group exercise in Chapter 4. Make any assumptions necessary to create two screens for truck dispatchers. Group 2 (playing the roles of dispatchers) should react to the prototype screens and provide feedback about desired additions and deletions.
2. The members of group 1 should revise the prototype screens based on the user comments they received. Those in group 2 should respond with comments about how well their initial concerns were addressed with the refined prototypes.
3. As a united group, write a paragraph discussing your experiences with prototyping for ascertaining information requirements.

SELECTED BIBLIOGRAPHY

Alavi, M. "An Assessment of the Prototyping Approach to Information Systems Development." *Communications of the ACM*, Vol. 27, No. 6, June 1984, pp. 556–563.

Avison, D., and D. N. Wilson. "Controls for Effective Prototyping." *Journal of Management Systems*, Vol. 3, No. 1, 1991.

Baird, S. *SAMS Teach Yourself Extreme Programming in 24 Hours.* Indianapolis, IN: SAMS Publishing, 2003.

Beck, K. *Extreme Programming Explained: Embrace Change.* Boston: Addison-Wesley Publishing Co., 2000.

Beck, K., and M. Fowler. *Planning Extreme Programming.* Boston: Addison-Wesley Publishing Co., 2001.

Billings, C., M. Billings, and J. Tower. *Rapid Application Development with Oracle Designer/2000.* Reading, MA: Addison-Wesley, 1996.

Cockburn, A. *Agile Software Development.* Boston: Addison-Wesley Publishing Co., 2002.

Davis, G. B., and M. H. Olson. *Management Information Systems: Conceptual Foundations, Structure, and Development*, 2d ed. New York: McGraw-Hill, 1985.

Davis, G. B., and J. D. Naumann. "Knowledge Work Productivity." In *Emerging Information Technologies: Improving Decisions, Cooperation, and Infrastructure.* Edited by K. E. Kendall, pp. 343–357. Thousand Oaks, CA: Sage, 1999.

Dearnley, P., and P. Mayhew. "In Favour of System Prototypes and Their Integration into the Systems Development Cycle." *Computer Journal*, Vol. 26, February 1983, pp. 36–42.

Fitzgerald, B., and Hartnett G. (2005). "A Study of the Use of Agile Methods Within Intel," Matthiassen, L., Pries-Heje, J. and DeGross, J. (Eds.) Business Agility & IT Diffusion, Proc Conference, Atlanta, May 2005, Springer, New York, pp. 187–202.

Ghione, J. "A Web Developer's Guide to Rapid Application Development Tools and Techniques." *Netscape World*, June 1997.

Gremillion, L. L., and P. Pyburn. "Breaking the Systems Development Bottleneck." *Harvard Business Review*, March–April 1983, pp. 130–137.

Harrison, T. S. "Techniques and Issues in Rapid Prototyping." *Journal of Systems Management*. Vol. 36, No. 6, June 1985, pp. 8–13.

Kendall, J. E., and K. E. Kendall. "Agile Methodologies and the Lone Systems Analyst: When Individual Creativity and Organizational Goals Collide in the Global IT Environment." *Journal of Individual Employment Rights*, Vol. 11, No. 4, 2004–2005, pp. 333–347.

Kendall, J. E., K. E. Kendall, and S. Kong. "Improving Quality Through the Use of Agile Methods in Systems Development: People and Values in the Quest for Quality." In *Measuring Information Systems Delivery Quality.* Edited by E. W. Duggan and H. Reichgelt, pp. 201–222. Hershey, PA: Idea Group Publishing, 2006.

Liang, D. *Rapid Java Application Development Using JBuilder 3*. Upper Saddle River, NJ: Prentice Hall, 2000.

McBreen, P. *Questioning Extreme Programming.* Boston: Addison-Wesley Publishing Co., 2003.

McMahon, D. *Rapid Application Development with Visual Basic 6 (Enterprise Computing)*. New York: McGraw-Hill Professional Publishing, 1999.

McMahon, D. *Rapid Application Development with Visual* C++. New York: McGraw-Hill Professional Publishing, 1999.

Naumann, J. D., and A. M. Jenkins. "Prototyping: The New Paradigm for Systems Development." *MIS Quarterly,* september 1982, pp. 29–44.

ALLEN SCHMIDT, JULIE E. KENDALL, AND KENNETH E. KENDALL

REACTION TIME

"We need to get a feel for some of the output needed by the users," Anna comments. "It will help to firm up some of our ideas on the information they require."

"Agreed," replies Chip. "It will also help us determine the necessary input. From that we can design corresponding data entry screens. Let's create prototype reports and screens and get some user feedback. Why don't we use Microsoft Access to quickly create screens and reports? I'm quite familiar with the software."

Anna starts by developing the PREVENTIVE MAINTENANCE REPORT prototype. Based on interview results, she sets to work creating the report she feels Mike Crowe will need.

"This report should be used to predict when machines should have preventive maintenance," Anna thinks. "It seems to me that Mike would need to know *which* machine needs work performed as well as *when* the work should be scheduled. Now let's see, what information would identify the machine clearly? The inventory number, brand name, and model would identify the machine. I imagine the room and campus should be included to quickly locate the machine. A calculated maintenance date would tell Mike when the work should be completed. What sequence should the report be in? Probably the most useful would be by location."

The PREVENTIVE MAINTENANCE REPORT prototype showing the completed report is shown in Figure E6.1. Notice that Xxxxxxx's and generic dates are used to indicate where data should be printed. Realistic campus and room locations as well as inventory numbers are included. They are necessary for Microsoft Access to accomplish group printing.

The report prototype is soon finished. After printing the final copy, Anna takes the report to both Mike Crowe and Dot Matricks. Mike Crowe is enthusiastic about the project and wants to know when the report will be in production. Dot is similarly impressed.

Several changes come up. Mike wants an area to write in the completion date of the preventive maintenance so the report can be used to reenter the dates into the computer. Dot wants the report number assigned by data control to appear at the top of the form for reference purposes. She also suggests that the report title be changed to WEEKLY PREVENTIVE MAINTENANCE REPORT. The next steps are to modify the prototype report to reflect the recommended changes and then have both Mike and Dot review the result.

The report is easily modified and printed. Dot is pleased with the final result. "This is really a fine method for designing the system," she comments. "It's so nice to feel that we are a part of the development process and that our opinions count. I'm starting to feel quite confident that the final system will be just what we've always wanted."

Mike has similar praise, observing, "This will make our work so much smoother. It eliminates the guesswork about which machines need to be maintained. And sequencing them by room is a fine idea. We won't have to spend so much time returning to rooms to work on machines."

Chip makes a note about each of these modifications on a Prototype Evaluation Form. This form gets Chip organized and documents the prototyping process. (See Figure 6.3 for an example of this screen.)

6

Preventive Maintenance Report

Week of 1/11/2004

1/11/04

Page 1 of 1

Campus Location	Room Location	Inventory Number	Brand Name	Model	Last Preventive Maintenance Date	Done
Central Administration	11111	84004782	Xxxxxxxxxxxxxxxx	Xxxxxxxxxxxxxxxxxxxx	11/4/03	___
Central Administration	11111	90875039	Xxxxxxxxxxxxxx	Xxxxxxxxxxxxxxxx	10/24/03	___
Central Administration	11111	93955411	Xxxxxxxxxxxxxxxx	Xxxxxxxxxxxxxxxxxxxx	11/4/03	___
Central Administration	11111	99381373	Xxxxxxxxxxxxxxxx	Xxxxxxxxxxxxxxxxxxxx	10/24/03	___
Central Administration	22222	10220129	Xxxxxxxxxxxxxx	Xxxxxxxxxxxxxxxxxx	10/24/03	___
Central Administration	99999	22838234	Xxxxxxxxxxxxxx	Xxxxxxxxxxxxxxxx	10/24/03	___
Central Administration	99999	24720952	Xxxxxxxxxxxxxx	Xxxxxxxxxxxxxxxxxx	10/24/03	___
Central Administration	99999	33453403	Xxxxxxxxxxxxxxxx	Xxxxxxxxxxxxxxxx	11/4/03	___
Central Administration	99999	34044449	Xxxxxxxxxxxx	Xxxxxxxxxxxxxxxxxx	11/4/03	___
Central Administration	99999	40030303	Xxxxxxxxxxxxxxxx	Xxxxxxxxxxxxxxxxxxxx	11/4/03	___
Central Administration	99999	47403948	Xxxxxxxxxxxxxxxx	Xxxxxxxxxxxxxxxx	10/24/03	___
Central Administration	99999	56620548	Xxxxxxxxxxxxxxxx	Xxxxxxxxxxxxxxxx	11/4/03	___
Central Computer Science	22222	34589349	Xxxxxxxxxxxx	Xxxxxxxxxxxxxxxxxx	10/24/03	___
Central Computer Science	22222	38376910	Xxxxxxxxxxxx	Xxxxxxxxxxxxxxxxxx	10/24/03	___
Central Computer Science	22222	94842282	Xxxxxxxxxxxxxxxx	Xxxxxxxxxxxxxxxxxxxx	10/24/03	___
Central Computer Science	99999	339393	Xxxxxxxxxxxxxx	Xxxxxxxxxxxxxxxx	11/4/03	___
Central Zoology	22222	11398423	Xxxxxxxxxxxxxxxx	Xxxxxxxxxxxxxxxxxxxx	10/24/03	___
Central Zoology	22222	28387465	Xxxxxxxxxxxxxxxx	Xxxxxxxxxxxxxxxxxxxx	11/4/03	___
Central Zoology	99999	70722533	Xxxxxxxxxxxxxx	Xxxxxxxxxxxxxxxx	10/24/03	___
Central Zoology	99999	99481102	Xxxxxxxxxxxxxxxx	Xxxxxxxxxxxxxxxxxxxx	10/24/03	___

FIGURE E6.1

Prototype for PREVENTIVE MAINTENANCE REPORT. This report needs to be revised.

Chip and Anna next turn their attention to creating screen prototypes. "Because I like the hardware aspect of the system, why don't I start working on the ADD NEW COMPUTER screen design?" asks Chip.

"Sounds good to me," Anna replies. "I'll focus on the software aspects."

Chip analyzes the results of detailed interviews with Dot and Mike. He compiles a list of elements that each user would need when adding a computer. Other elements, such as location and maintenance information, would update the COMPUTER MASTER later, after the machine was installed.

The ADD NEW COMPUTER prototype screen created with the Access form feature is shown in Figure E6.2. Placed on the top of the screen are the current date and time as well as a centered screen title. Field captions are placed on the screen, with the characters left aligned. Check boxes are included for several fields, as well as drop-down lists for the type of monitor, printer, and network connections. A small Board

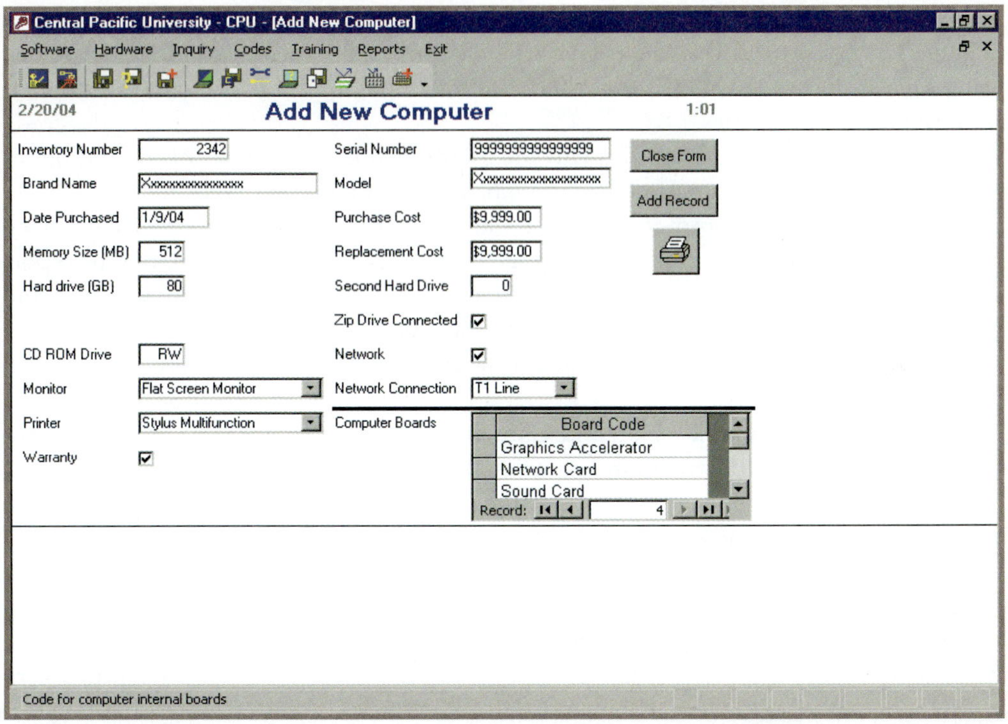

FIGURE E6.2

Prototype for the ADD NEW COMPUTER screen. Microsoft Access was used as the prototyping tool. Improvements can be made at this stage.

Code table is included to add several internal boards for one computer. "Add Record" and "Print" buttons are included.

"Having the database tables defined sure helps to make quick prototypes," Chip comments. "It didn't take very long to complete the screen. Would you like to watch me test the prototype?"

"Sure," replies Anna. "This is my favorite part of prototyping."

Chip executes the screen design as Anna, Mike, and Dot watch. The drop-down lists and check boxes make it easy to enter accurate data.

"I really like this," Dot says. "May I try adding some data?"

"Be my guest," replies Chip. "Try to add both invalid and valid data. And notice the help messages that appear at the bottom of the screen to indicate what should be entered."

Anna returns to her desk and creates the ADD SOFTWARE RECORD screen design.

When Anna completes the screen design, she asks Cher to test the prototype. Cher keys information in, checks the drop-down list values, and views help messages.

"I really like the design of this screen and how it looks," remarks Cher. "It lacks some of the fields that would normally be included when a software package is entered, though, like the computer brand and model that the software runs on, the memory required, monitor, and the printer or plotter required. I would also like buttons to save the record and exit the screen."

"Those are all doable. I'll make the changes and get back to you," replies Anna, making some notes to herself.

6

A short time later, Cher again tests the ADD SOFTWARE RECORD screen. It includes all the features that she requires. The completed screen design may be viewed using Microsoft Access. Notice that there is a line separating the software information from the hardware entries.

"Chip, I was speaking with Dot and she mentioned that there has been funding for putting some of the information on the Web, as part of a unified Web site for technology support at CPU," comments Anna, looking up from her computer. "I have been busy creating a prototype for the Web page menus and the first screen, one to report technology problems. Because solving problems is Mike's area, I have invited him and Dot to review the prototype. Care to join the session?"

"Sure," replies Chip. "I am interested in working on the design of some of the Web pages."

A short time later Mike, Dot, and Chip are gathered around Anna as she demonstrates the Web page, illustrated in Figure E6.3.

"I really like the menu style," comments Dot. "The main feature tabs on the top are easy to use, and I like the way they change color when one is clicked."

"Yes, and having submenus underneath the main one for the features of each tab makes it easy to find what you are looking for," adds Mike. "I do have some suggestions for the Web page for reporting problems, though. It would be more useful if the Problem Category selection area were moved to the top of the page. Each problem type is assigned to a different technician, one who is more or less an expert in that area. We need an additional check box to identify if it is Macintosh- or IBM-compatible

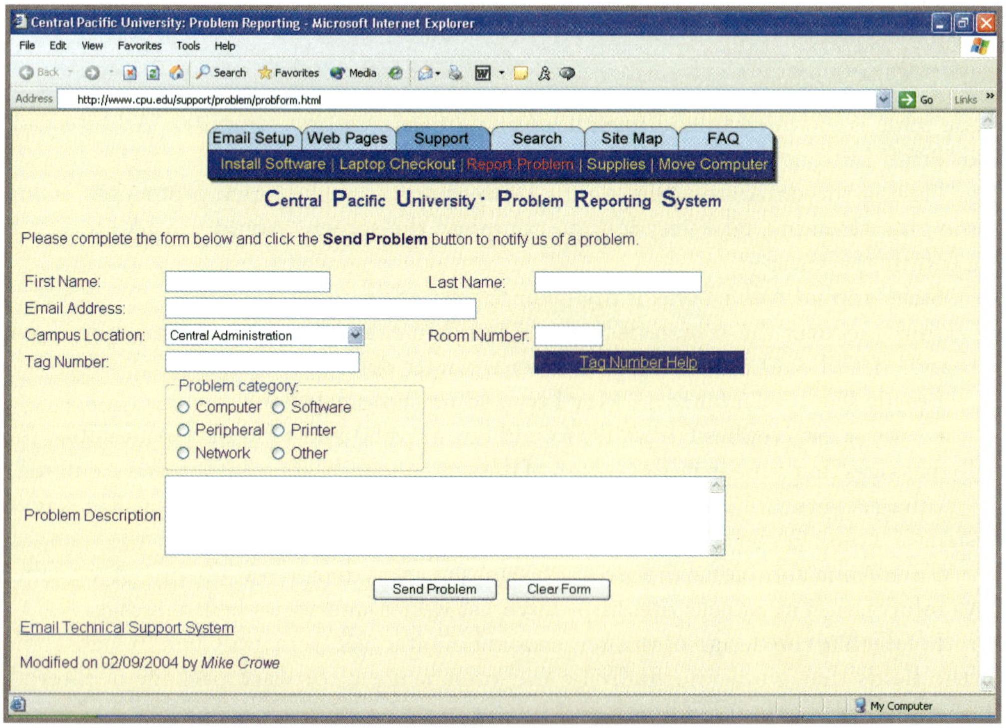

FIGURE E6.3
Prototype for the PROBLEM REPORTING SYSTEM Web page. This Web page needs some improvement.

equipment or software we are working with. The Tag Number help is a great idea. Many people do not realize that each piece of equipment has a small metal identifying tag on it with a unique inventory number. Hmmm. . . . That large blue area seems to stand out too much. After all, it is just help. I think that it would be better to replace it with a small graphic image."

"I think that these changes will be easy to do," remarks Anna.

"Great," replies Mike. "It would also be useful to include the tech support hot line phone number on the Web page. If it's a real emergency, it might speed up our resolution to the problem. We should add an entry field for their phone number as well. Of course, we could always look it up, but the person reporting the problem may be in a computer lab or another location away from their office."

"Good idea!" exclaims Dot. "This is going to be extremely helpful to the faculty and staff. I think that we should prototype all the Web pages for the site. I realize that Web pages are supposed to change from time to time, but let's get these as good as possible from the start!"

Anna glances at Chip and grins. "I guess you'll be working on Web page design sooner than you think!"

Anna and Chip continued to work on prototypes by designing, obtaining user feedback, and modifying the design to accommodate user changes. Now that the work is complete, they have a solid sense of the requirements of the system.

EXERCISES

Critique the report and screen prototypes for the exercises below (E-1 through E-10). Record the changes on a copy of the Prototype Evaluation Form. Use Microsoft Access to view the prototypes, then modify the report and screen prototypes with the suggested changes. Print the final prototypes.

Use the following guidelines to help in your analysis:

1. *Alignment of fields on reports.* Are the fields aligned correctly? Are report column headers aligned correctly over the columns? If the report has captions to the left of data fields, are they aligned correctly (usually on the left)? Are the data aligned correctly *within* each entry field?
2. *Report content.* Does the report contain all the necessary data? Are appropriate and useful totals and subtotals present? Are there extra totals or data that should not be on the report? Are codes or the meaning of the codes printed on the report (codes should be avoided because they may not clearly present the user with information)?
3. *Check the visual appearance of the report.* Does it look pleasing? Are repeating fields group printed (that is, the data should print only once, at the beginning of the group)? Are there enough blank lines between groups to easily identify them?
4. *Screen data and caption alignment.* Are the captions correctly aligned on the screens? Are the data fields correctly aligned? Are the data *within* a field correctly aligned?
5. *Screen visual appearance.* Does the screen have a pleasing appearance? Is there enough vertical spacing between fields? Is there enough horizontal spacing between columns? Are the fields logically grouped together? Are features, such as buttons and check boxes, grouped together?
6. *Does the screen contain all the necessary functional elements?* Look for missing buttons that would help the user work smoothly with the screen; also look for missing data,

extra unnecessary data, or fields that should be replaced with a check box or drop-down list.

E-1. The HARDWARE INVENTORY LISTING. It shows all personal computers, sorted by campus and room.

E-2. The SOFTWARE INVESTMENT REPORT is used to calculate the total amount invested in software.

E-3. The INSTALLED COMPUTER REPORT shows the information for installed machines.

E-4. The prototype for the COMPUTER PROBLEM REPORT lists all machines sorted by the total cost of repairs and includes the number of repairs (some machines do not have a high cost, because they are still under warranty). This prototype is used to calculate the total cost of repairs for the entire university, as well as to identify the problem machines.

E-5. The NEW SOFTWARE INSTALLED REPORT shows the number of machines with each software package that are installed in each room of each campus.

E-6. The SOFTWARE CROSS-REFERENCE REPORT lists all locations for each version of each software package.

E-7. The DELETE COMPUTER RECORD screen is used to select computers to remove from the system. The entry area is the Hardware Inventory Number field. The other fields are for display only, to identify the machine. The users would like the ability to print each record before they delete it. They also want to scroll to the next and previous records. *Hint:* Examine the fields shown in the HARDWARE INVENTORY LISTING report.

E-8. An UPDATE MAINTENANCE INFORMATION screen enables Mike Crowe to change maintenance information about personal computers. Sometimes these are routine changes, such as the LAST PREVENTIVE MAINTENANCE DATE or the NUMBER OF REPAIRS, but other changes may occur only sporadically, such as the expiration of a warranty. The HARDWARE INVENTORY NUMBER is entered, and the matching COMPUTER RECORD is found. The BRAND and MODEL are displayed for feedback. The operator may then change the WARRANTY, MAINTENANCE INTERVAL, NUMBER OF REPAIRS, LAST PREVENTIVE MAINTENANCE DATE, and TOTAL COST OF REPAIRS fields. Mike would like to print the screen information, as well as undo any changes, easily.

E-9. The SOFTWARE LOCATION INQUIRY displays information about rooms and machines containing selected software. The TITLE, VERSION NUMBER, and OPERATING SYSTEM are entered. The output portion of the screen should show the CAMPUS LOCATION, ROOM LOCATION, HARDWARE INVENTORY NUMBER, BRAND NAME, and MODEL. Buttons allow the user to move to the next record, the previous record, and to close and exit the screen.

E-10. The HARDWARE CHARACTERISTIC INQUIRY is used to locate machines with certain hardware characteristics. The operator enters a BRAND NAME and CD-ROM DRIVE type. The MONITOR and PRINTER CODE fields have drop-down lists to select the appropriate codes. The display portion of the inquiry screen consists of CAMPUS, ROOM, and INVENTORY NUMBER.

The exercises preceded by a Web-icon indicate value-added material is available from the Web site at www.prenhall.com/kendall. Students can download a sample Visible Analyst Project and a Microsoft Access database that can be used to complete the exercises. Visible Analyst software can be packaged with this text for an additional fee.

USING DATA FLOW DIAGRAMS

7

LEARNING OBJECTIVES

Once you have mastered the material in this chapter you will be able to:

1. **Comprehend the importance of using logical and physical data flow diagrams (DFDs) to graphically depict data movement for humans and systems in an organization.**
2. **Create, use, and explode logical DFDs to capture and analyze the current system through parent and child levels.**
3. **Develop and explode logical DFDs that illustrate the proposed system.**
4. **Produce physical DFDs based on logical DFDs you have developed.**
5. **Understand and apply the concept of partitioning of physical DFDs.**

The systems analyst needs to make use of the conceptual freedom afforded by data flow diagrams, which graphically characterize data processes and flows in a business system. In their original state, data flow diagrams depict the broadest possible overview of system inputs, processes, and outputs, which correspond to those of the general systems model discussed in Chapter 2. A series of layered data flow diagrams may be used to represent and analyze detailed procedures in the larger system.

THE DATA FLOW APPROACH TO HUMAN REQUIREMENTS DETERMINATION

When systems analysts attempt to understand the information requirements of users, they must be able to conceptualize how data move through the organization, the processes or transformation that the data undergo, and what the outputs are. Although interviews and the investigation of hard data provide a verbal narrative of the system, a visual depiction can crystallize this information for users and analysts in a useful way.

Through a structured analysis technique called data flow diagrams (DFDs), the systems analyst can put together a graphical representation of data processes throughout the organization. By using combinations of only four symbols, the systems analyst can create a pictorial depiction of processes that will eventually provide solid system documentation.

ADVANTAGES OF THE DATA FLOW APPROACH

The data flow approach has four chief advantages over narrative explanations of the way data move through the system:

1. Freedom from committing to the technical implementation of the system too early.
2. Further understanding of the interrelatedness of systems and subsystems.
3. Communicating current system knowledge to users through data flow diagrams.
4. Analysis of a proposed system to determine if the necessary data and processes have been defined.

Perhaps the biggest advantage lies in the conceptual freedom found in the use of the four symbols (covered in the upcoming subsection on DFD conventions). (You will recognize three of the symbols from Chapter 2.) None of the symbols specifies the physical aspects of implementation. DFDs emphasize the processing of data or the transforming of data as they move through a variety of processes. In logical DFDs, there is no distinction between manual or automated processes. Neither are the processes graphically depicted in chronological order. Rather, processes are eventually grouped together if further analysis dictates that it makes sense to do so. Manual processes are put together, and automated processes can also be paired with each other. This concept, called *partioning*, is taken up in a later section.

CONVENTIONS USED IN DATA FLOW DIAGRAMS

Four basic symbols are used to chart data movement on data flow diagrams: a double square, an arrow, a rectangle with rounded corners, and an open-ended rectangle (closed on the left side and open ended on the right), as shown in Figure 7.1.

FIGURE 7.1
The four basic symbols used in data flow diagrams, their meanings, and examples.

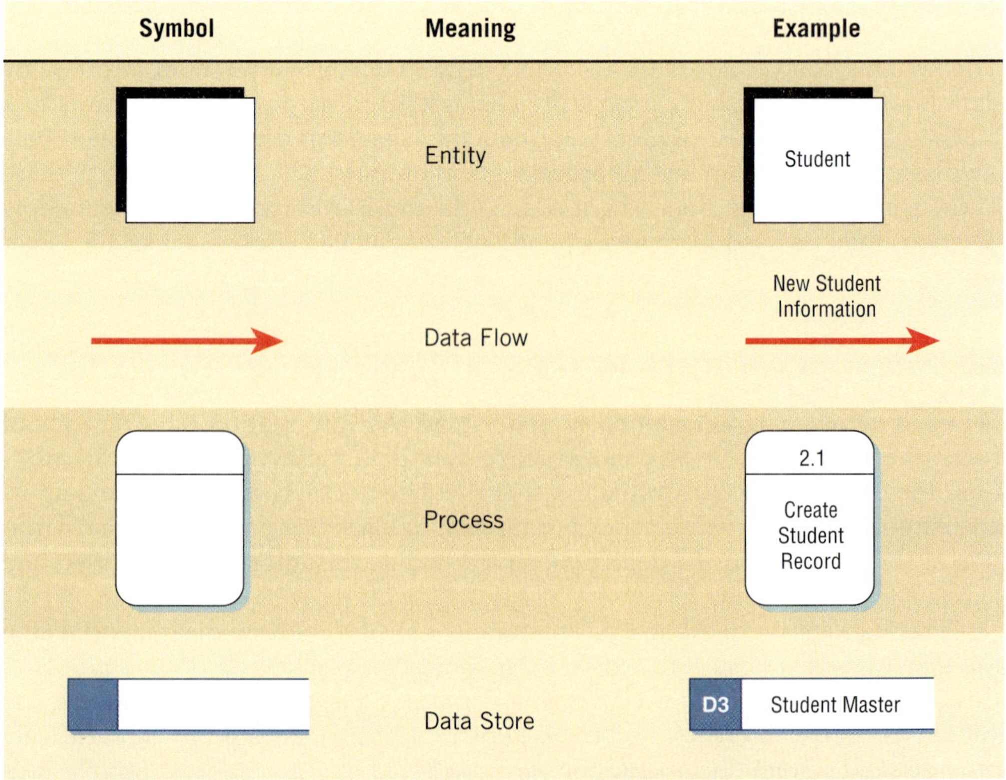

An entire system and numerous subsystems can be depicted graphically with these four symbols in combination.

The double square is used to depict an external entity (another department, a business, a person, or a machine) that can send data to or receive data from the system. The external entity, or just entity, is also called a source or destination of data, and it is considered to be external to the system being described. Each entity is labeled with an appropriate name. Although it interacts with the system, it is considered as outside the boundaries of the system. Entities should be named with a noun. The same entity may be used more than once on a given data flow diagram to avoid crossing data flow lines.

The arrow shows movement of data from one point to another, with the head of the arrow pointing toward the data's destination. Data flows occurring simultaneously can be depicted doing just that through the use of parallel arrows. Because an arrow represents data about a person, place, or thing, it too should be described with a noun.

A rectangle with rounded corners is used to show the occurrence of a transforming process. Processes always denote a change in or transformation of data; hence, the data flow leaving a process is *always* labeled differently than the one entering it. Processes represent work being performed in the system and should be named using one of the following formats. A clear name makes it easier to understand what the process is accomplishing.

1. Assign the name of the whole system when naming a high-level process. An example is INVENTORY CONTROL SYSTEM.
2. To name a major subsystem, use a name such as INVENTORY REPORTING SUBSYSTEM or INTERNET CUSTOMER FULFILLMENT SYSTEM.
3. Use a verb-adjective-noun format for detailed processes. The verb describes the type of activity, such as COMPUTE, VERIFY, PREPARE, PRINT, or ADD. The noun indicates what the major outcome of the process is, such as REPORT or RECORD. The adjective illustrates which specific output, such as BACKORDERED or INVENTORY, is produced. Examples of complete process names are COMPUTE SALES TAX, VERIFY CUSTOMER ACCOUNT STATUS, PREPARE SHIPPING INVOICE, PRINT BACKORDERED REPORT, SEND CUSTOMER EMAIL CONFIRMATION, VERIFY CREDIT CARD BALANCE, and ADD INVENTORY RECORD.

A process must also be given a unique identifying number indicating its level in the diagram. This organization is discussed later in this chapter. Several data flows may go into and out of each process. Examine processes with only a single flow in and out for missing data flows.

The last basic symbol used in data flow diagrams is an open-ended rectangle, which represents a data store. The rectangle is drawn with two parallel lines that are closed by a short line on the left side and are open ended on the right. These symbols are drawn only wide enough to allow identifying lettering between the parallel lines. In logical data flow diagrams, the type of physical storage is not specified. At this point the data store symbol is simply showing a depository for data that allows examination, addition, and retrieval of data.

The data store may represent a manual store, such as a filing cabinet, or a computerized file or database. Because data stores represent a person, place, or thing, they are named with a noun. Temporary data stores, such as scratch paper or a temporary computer file, are not included on the data flow diagram. Give each data store a unique reference number, such as D1, D2, D3, and so on, to identify its level as described in the following section.

DEVELOPING DATA FLOW DIAGRAMS

Data flow diagrams can and should be drawn systematically. Figure 7.2 summarizes the steps involved in successfully completing data flow diagrams. First, the systems analyst needs to conceptualize data flows from a top-down perspective.

To begin a data flow diagram, collapse the organization's system narrative (or story) into a list with the four categories of external entity, data flow, process, and data store. This list in turn helps determine the boundaries of the system you will be describing. Once a basic list of data elements has been compiled, begin drawing a context diagram.

CREATING THE CONTEXT DIAGRAM

With a top-down approach to diagramming data movement, the diagrams move from general to specific. Although the first diagram helps the systems analyst grasp basic data movement, its general nature limits its usefulness. The initial context diagram should be an overview, one including basic inputs, the general system, and outputs. This diagram will be the most general one, really a bird's-eye view of data movement in the system and the broadest possible conceptualization of the system.

The context diagram is the highest level in a data flow diagram and contains only one process, representing the entire system. The process is given the number zero. All external entities are shown on the context diagram, as well as major data flow to and from them. The diagram does not contain any data stores and is fairly

FIGURE 7.2
Steps in developing data flow diagrams.

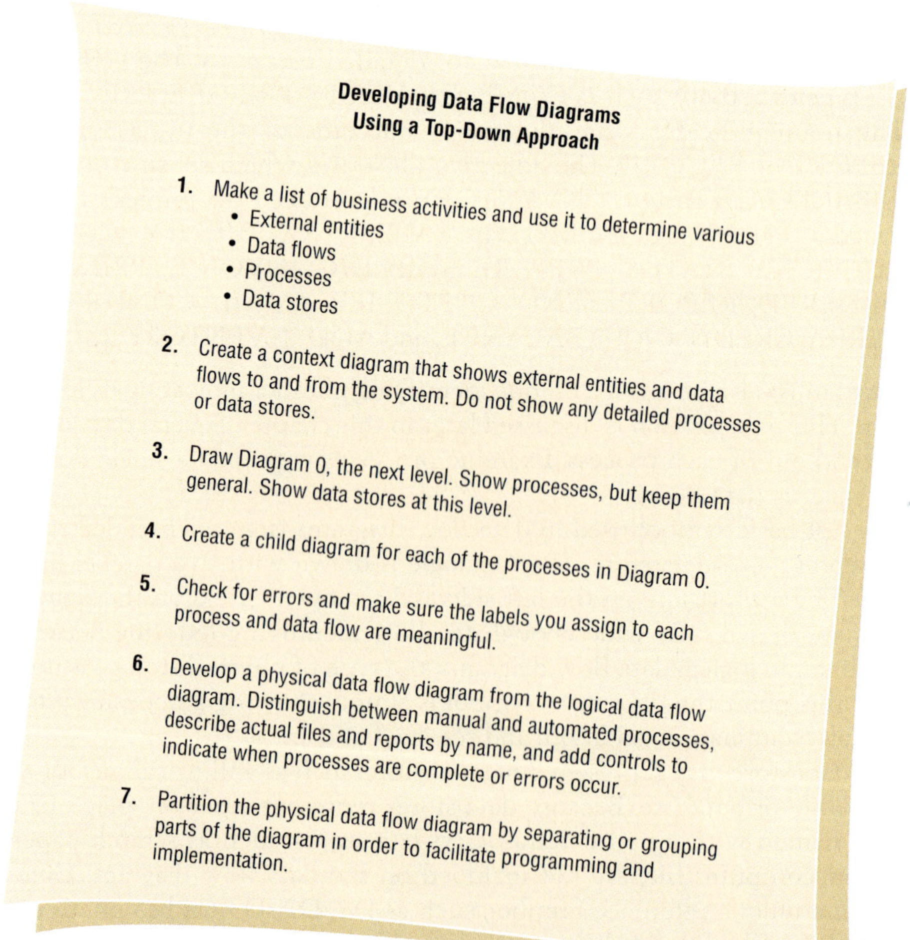
Developing Data Flow Diagrams
Using a Top-Down Approach

1. Make a list of business activities and use it to determine various
   - External entities
   - Data flows
   - Processes
   - Data stores
2. Create a context diagram that shows external entities and data flows to and from the system. Do not show any detailed processes or data stores.
3. Draw Diagram 0, the next level. Show processes, but keep them general. Show data stores at this level.
4. Create a child diagram for each of the processes in Diagram 0.
5. Check for errors and make sure the labels you assign to each process and data flow are meaningful.
6. Develop a physical data flow diagram from the logical data flow diagram. Distinguish between manual and automated processes, describe actual files and reports by name, and add controls to indicate when processes are complete or errors occur.
7. Partition the physical data flow diagram by separating or grouping parts of the diagram in order to facilitate programming and implementation.

simple to create, once the external entities and the data flow to and from them are known to analysts.

DRAWING DIAGRAM 0 (THE NEXT LEVEL)

More detail than the context diagram permits is achievable by "exploding the diagrams." Inputs and outputs specified in the first diagram remain constant in all subsequent diagrams. The rest of the original diagram, however, is exploded into close-ups involving three to nine processes and showing data stores and new lower-level data flows. The effect is that of taking a magnifying glass to view the original data flow diagram. Each exploded diagram should use only a single sheet of paper. By exploding DFDs into subprocesses, the systems analyst begins to fill in the details about data movement. The handling of exceptions is ignored for the first two or three levels of data flow diagramming.

Diagram 0 is the explosion of the context diagram and may include up to nine processes. Including more processes at this level will result in a cluttered diagram that is difficult to understand. Each process is numbered with an integer, generally starting from the upper left-hand corner of the diagram and working toward the lower right-hand corner. The major data stores of the system (representing master files) and all external entities are included on Diagram 0. Figure 7.3 schematically illustrates both the context diagram and Diagram 0.

Because a data flow diagram is two-dimensional (rather than linear), you may start at any point and work forward or backward through the diagram. If you are unsure of what you would include at any point, take a different external entity, process, or data store, and then start drawing the flow from it. You may:

1. Start with the data flow from an entity on the input side. Ask questions such as: "What happens to the data entering the system?" "Is it stored?" "Is it input for several processes?"
2. Work backwards from an output data flow. Examine the output fields on a document or screen. (This approach is easier if prototypes have been created.) For each field on the output, ask: "Where does it come from?" or "Is it calculated or stored on a file?" For example, when the output is a PAYCHECK, the EMPLOYEE NAME and ADDRESS would be located on an EMPLOYEE file, the HOURS WORKED would be on a TIME RECORD, and the GROSS PAY and DEDUCTIONS would be calculated. Each file and record would be connected to the process that produces the paycheck.
3. Examine the data flow to or from a data store. Ask: "What processes put data into the store?" or "What processes use the data?" Note that a data store used in the system you are working on may be produced by a different system. Thus, from your vantage point, there may not be any data flow into the data store.
4. Analyze a well-defined process. Look at what input data the process needs and what output it produces. Then connect the input and output to the appropriate data stores and entities.
5. Take note of any fuzzy areas where you are unsure of what should be included or what input or output is required. Awareness of problem areas will help you formulate a list of questions for follow-up interviews with key users.

CREATING CHILD DIAGRAMS (MORE DETAILED LEVELS)

Each process on Diagram 0 may in turn be exploded to create a more detailed child diagram. The process on Diagram 0 that is exploded is called the *parent process*, and the diagram that results is called the *child diagram*. The primary rule for creating child diagrams, vertical balancing, dictates that a child diagram cannot

FIGURE 7.3

Context diagrams (above) can be "exploded" into Diagram 0 (below). Note the greater detail in Diagram 0.

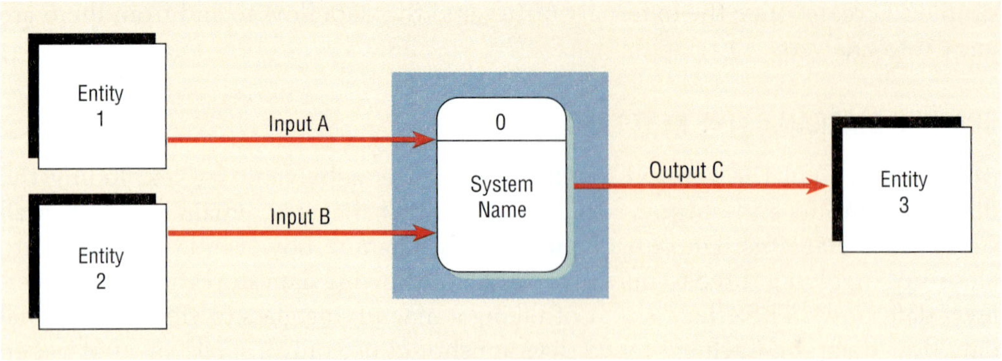

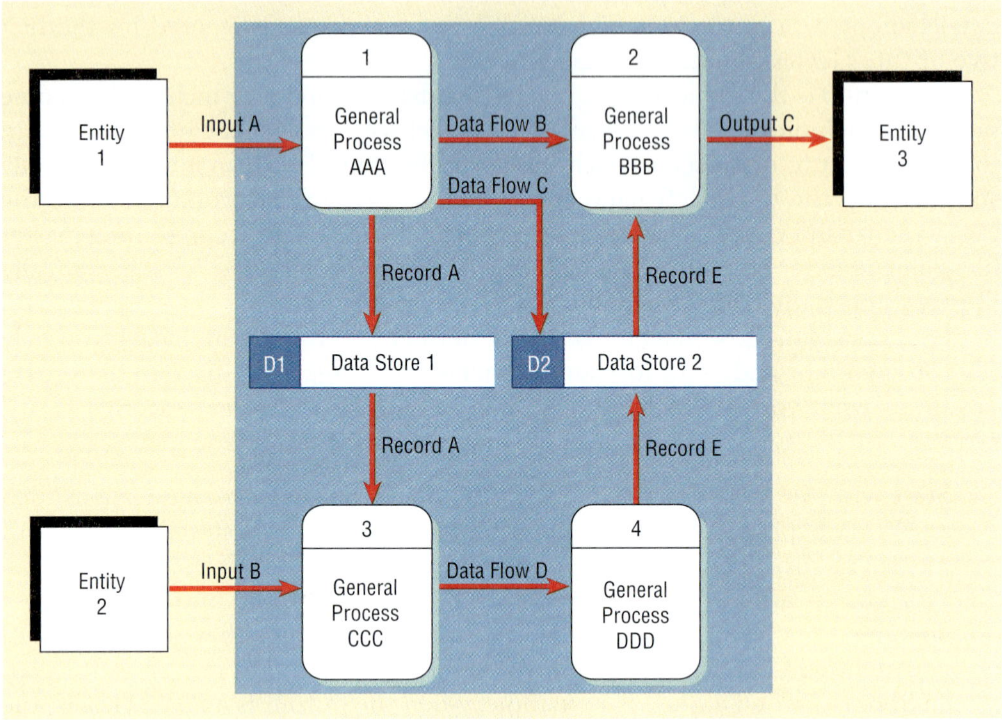

produce output or receive input that the parent process does not also produce or receive. All data flow into or out of the parent process must be shown flowing into or out of the child diagram.

The child diagram is given the same number as its parent process in Diagram 0. For example, process 3 would explode to Diagram 3. The processes on the child diagram are numbered using the parent process number, a decimal point, and a unique number for each child process. On Diagram 3, the processes would be numbered 3.1, 3.2, 3.3, and so on. This convention allows the analyst to trace a series of processes through many levels of explosion. If Diagram 0 depicts processes 1, 2, and 3, the child diagrams 1, 2, and 3 are all on the same level.

Entities are usually not shown on the child diagrams below Diagram 0. Data flow that matches the parent flow is called an *interface data flow* and is shown as an arrow from or into a blank area of the child diagram. If the parent process has data flow connecting to a data store, the child diagram may include the data store as well. In addition, this lower-level diagram may contain data stores not shown on the parent process. For example, a file containing a table of information, such as a tax table, or a file linking two processes on the child diagram may be included. Minor data flow, such as an error line, may be included on a child diagram but not on the parent.

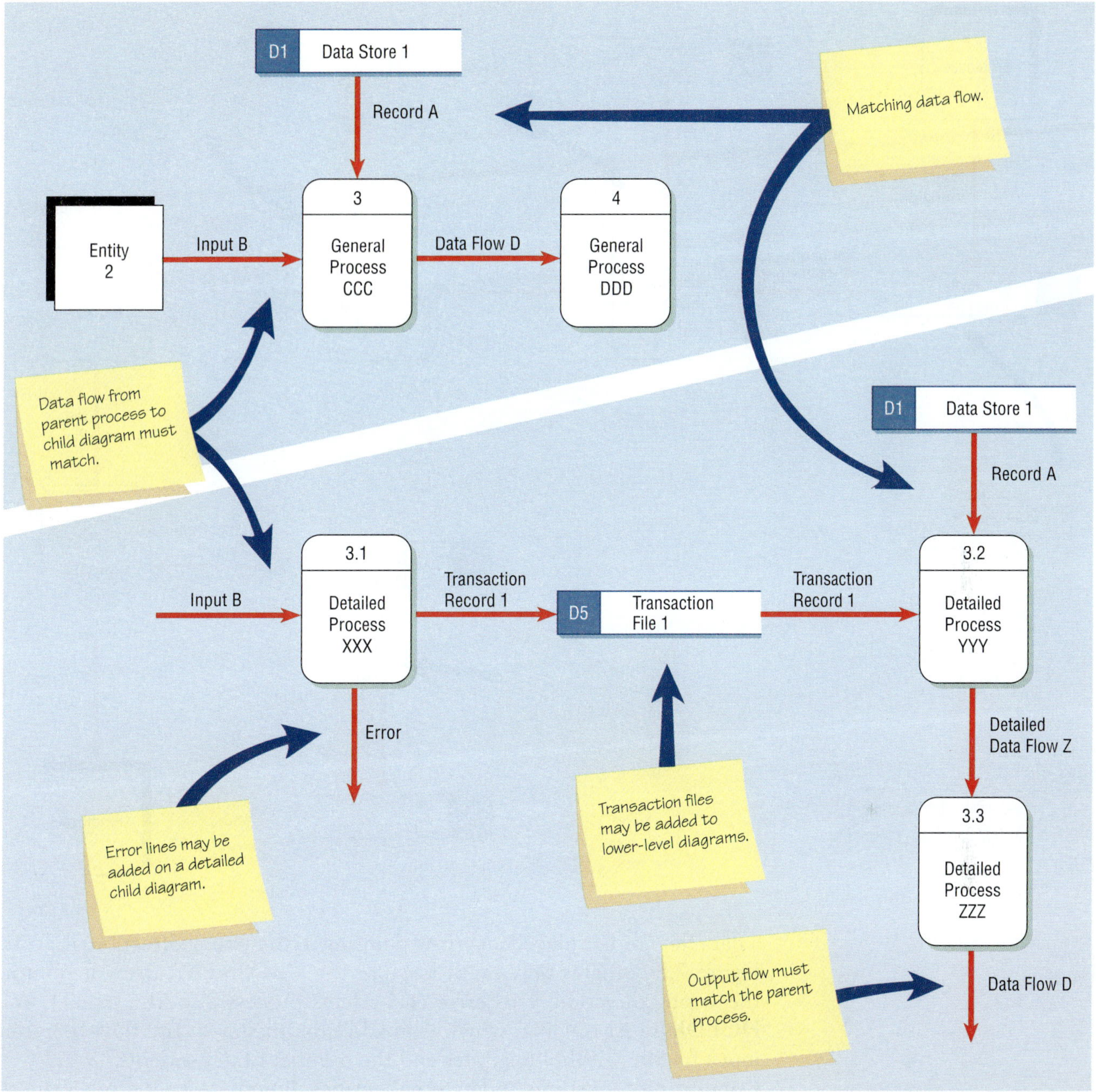

FIGURE 7.4
Differences between the parent diagram (above) and the child diagram (below).

Processes may or may not be exploded, depending on their level of complexity. When a process is not exploded, it is said to be functionally primitive and is called a *primitive process*. Logic is written to describe these processes and is discussed in detail in Chapter 9. Figure 7.4 illustrates detailed levels in a child data flow diagram.

CHECKING THE DIAGRAMS FOR ERRORS

Several common errors made when drawing data flow diagrams are as follows:

1. Forgetting to include a data flow or pointing an arrow in the wrong direction. An example is a drawn process showing all its data flow as either input or output. Each process transforms data and must receive input and produce output. This type of error usually occurs when the analyst has forgotten to include

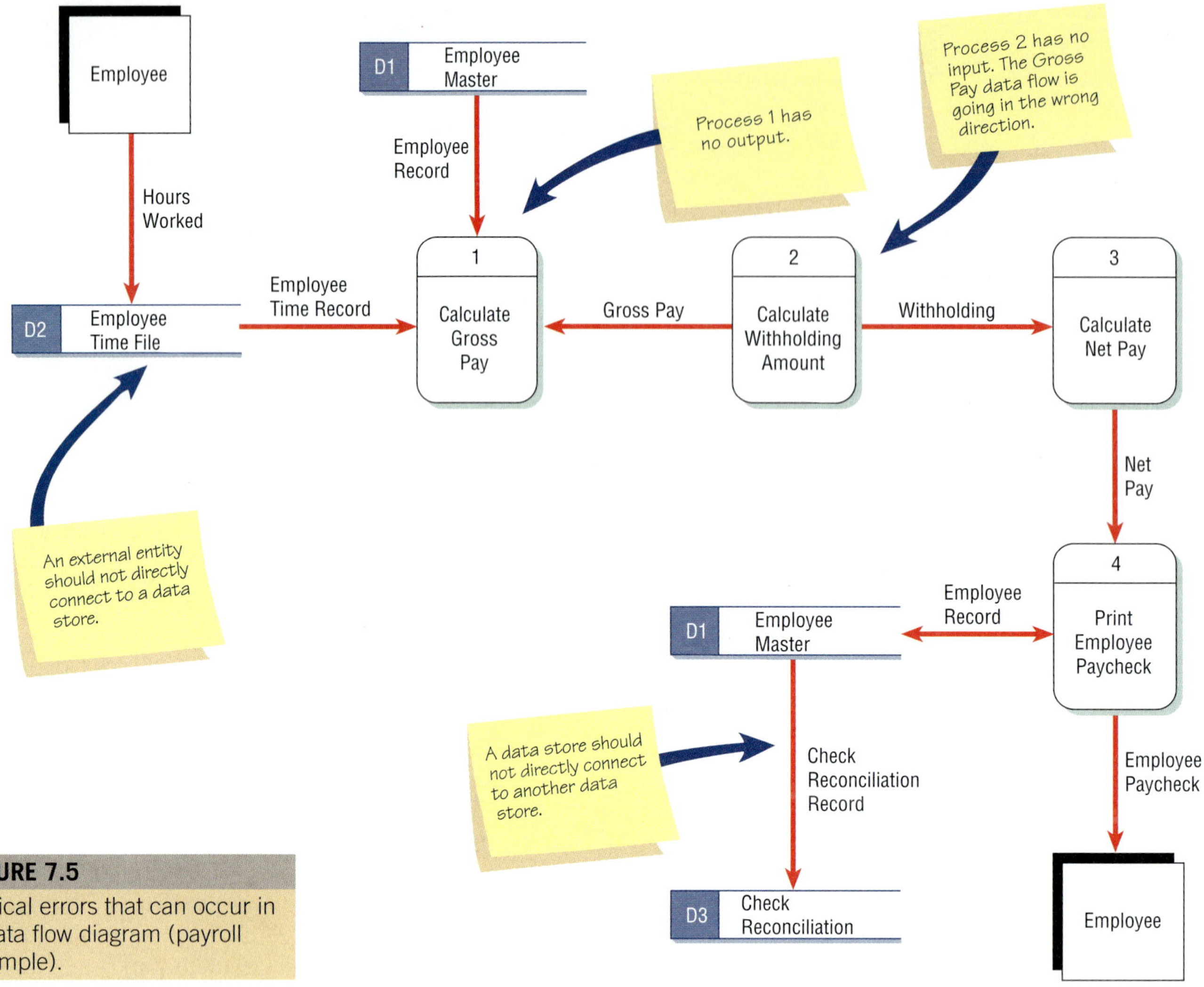

FIGURE 7.5
Typical errors that can occur in a data flow diagram (payroll example).

a data flow or has placed an arrow pointing in the wrong direction. Process 1 in Figure 7.5 contains only input because the GROSS PAY arrow is pointing in the wrong direction. This error also affects process 2, CALCULATE WITHHOLDING AMOUNT, which is in addition missing a data flow representing input for the withholding rates and the number of dependents.

2. Connecting data stores and external entities directly to each other. Data stores and entities may not be connected to each other; data stores and external entities must connect only with a process. A file does not interface with another file without the help of a program or a person moving the data, so EMPLOYEE MASTER cannot directly produce the CHECK RECONCILIATION file. External entities do not directly work with files. For example, you would not want a customer rummaging around in the customer master file. Thus, the EMPLOYEE does not create the EMPLOYEE TIME FILE. Two external entities directly connected indicate that they wish to communicate with each other. This connection is not included on the data flow diagram unless the system is facilitating the communication. Producing a report is an instance of this sort of communication. A process must still be interposed between the entities to produce the report, however.
3. Incorrectly labeling processes or data flow. Inspect the data flow diagram to ensure that each object or data flow is properly labeled. A process should

indicate the system name or use the verb-adjective-noun format. Each data flow should be described with a noun.

4. Including more than nine processes on a data flow diagram. Having too many processes creates a cluttered diagram that is confusing to read and hinders rather than enhances communication. If more than nine processes are involved in a system, group some of the processes that work together into a subsystem and place them in a child diagram.
5. Omitting data flow. Examine your diagram for linear flow, that is, data flow in which each process has only one input and one output. Except in the case of very detailed child data flow diagrams, linear data flow is somewhat rare. Its presence usually indicates that the diagram has missing data flow. For instance, the process CALCULATE WITHHOLDING AMOUNT needs the number of dependents that an employee has and the WITHHOLDING RATES as input. In addition, NET PAY cannot be calculated solely from the WITHHOLDING, and the EMPLOYEE PAYCHECK cannot be created from the NET PAY alone; it also needs to include an EMPLOYEE NAME, as well as the current and year-to-date payroll and WITHHOLDING AMOUNT figures.
6. Creating unbalanced decomposition (or explosion) in child diagrams. Each child diagram should have the same input and output data flow as the parent process. An exception to this rule is minor output, such as error lines, which are included only on the child diagram. The data flow diagram in Figure 7.6 is correctly drawn. Note that although the data flow is not linear, you can clearly follow a path directly from the source entity to the destination entity.

LOGICAL AND PHYSICAL DATA FLOW DIAGRAMS

Data flow diagrams are categorized as either logical or physical. A logical data flow diagram focuses on the business and how the business operates. It is not concerned with how the system will be constructed. Instead, it describes the business events that take place and the data required and produced by each event. Conversely, a physical data flow diagram shows how the system will be implemented, including the hardware, software, files, and people involved in the system. The chart shown in Figure 7.7 contrasts the features of logical and physical models. Notice that the logical model reflects the business, whereas the physical model depicts the system.

Ideally, systems are developed by analyzing the current system (the current logical DFD) and then adding features that the new system should include (the proposed logical DFD). Finally, the best methods for implementing the new system should be developed (the physical DFD). This progression is shown in Figure 7.8.

Developing a logical data flow diagram for the current system affords a clear understanding of how the current system operates, and thus a good starting point for developing the logical model of the current system. This time-consuming step is often omitted so as to go straight to the proposed logical DFD. An example of one type of logical model is the navigation charts created for Web sites when using Microsoft FrontPage.

One argument in favor of taking the time to construct the logical data flow diagram of the current system is that it can be used to create the logical data flow diagram of the new system. Processes that will be unnecessary in the new system may be dropped, and new features, activities, output, input, and stored data may be added. This approach provides a means of ensuring that the essential features of the old system are retained in the new system. In addition, using the logical model for the current system as a basis for the proposed system provides for a gradual transition to

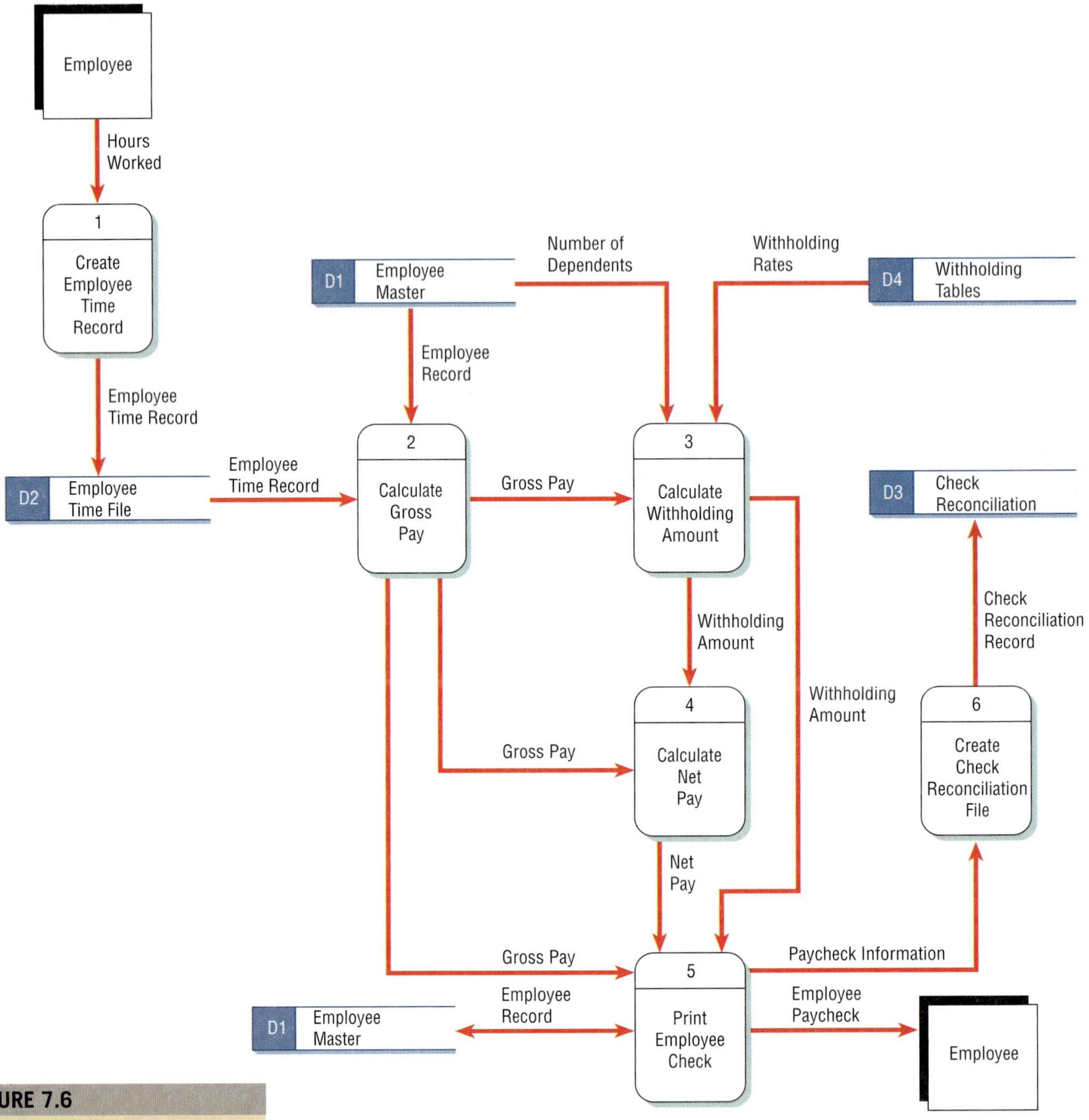

FIGURE 7.6
The correct data flow diagram for the payroll example.

the design of the new system. After the logical model for the new system has been developed, it may be used to create a physical data flow diagram for the new system.

Figure 7.9 shows a logical data flow diagram and a physical data flow diagram for a grocery store cashier. The CUSTOMER brings the ITEMS to the register; PRICES for all ITEMS are LOOKED UP and then totaled; next, PAYMENT is given to the cashier; finally, the CUSTOMER is given a RECEIPT. The logical data flow diagram illustrates the processes involved without going into detail about the physical implementation of activities. The physical data flow diagram shows that a bar code—the universal product code (UPC) BAR CODE found on most grocery store items—is used. In addition, the physical data flow diagram mentions manual processes such as scanning, explains that a temporary file is used to keep a subtotal of items, and indicates that the PAYMENT could be made by CASH, CHECK, or DEBIT CARD. Finally, it refers to the receipt by its name, CASH REGISTER RECEIPT.

Design Feature	Logical	Physical
What the model depicts	How the business operates.	How the system will be implemented (or how the current system operates).
What the processes represent	Business activities.	Programs, program modules, and manual procedures.
What the data stores represent	Collections of data regardless of how the data are stored.	Physical files and databases, manual files.
Type of data stores	Show data stores representing permanent data collections.	Master files, transition files. Any processes that operate at two different times must be connected by a data store.
System controls	Show business controls.	Show controls for validating input data, for obtaining a record (record found status), for ensuring successful completion of a process, and for system security (example: journal records).

FIGURE 7.7
Features common of logical and physical data flow diagrams.

DEVELOPING LOGICAL DATA FLOW DIAGRAMS

To develop such a diagram, first construct a logical data flow diagram for the current system. There are a number of advantages to using a logical model, including:

1. Better communication with users.
2. More stable systems.
3. Better understanding of the business by analysts.
4. Flexibility and maintenance.
5. Elimination of redundancies and easier creation of the physical model.

A logical model is easier to use when communicating with users of the system because it is centered on business activities. Users will thus be familiar with the essential activities and many of the human information requirements of each activity.

Systems formed using a logical data flow diagram are often more stable because they are based on business events and not on a particular technology or

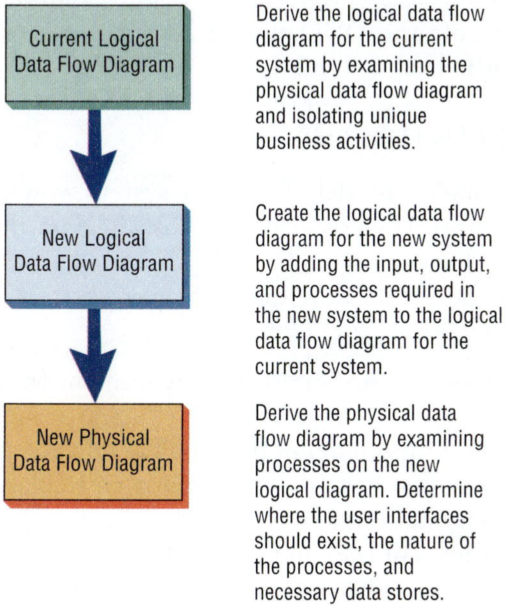

FIGURE 7.8
The progression of models from logical to physical.

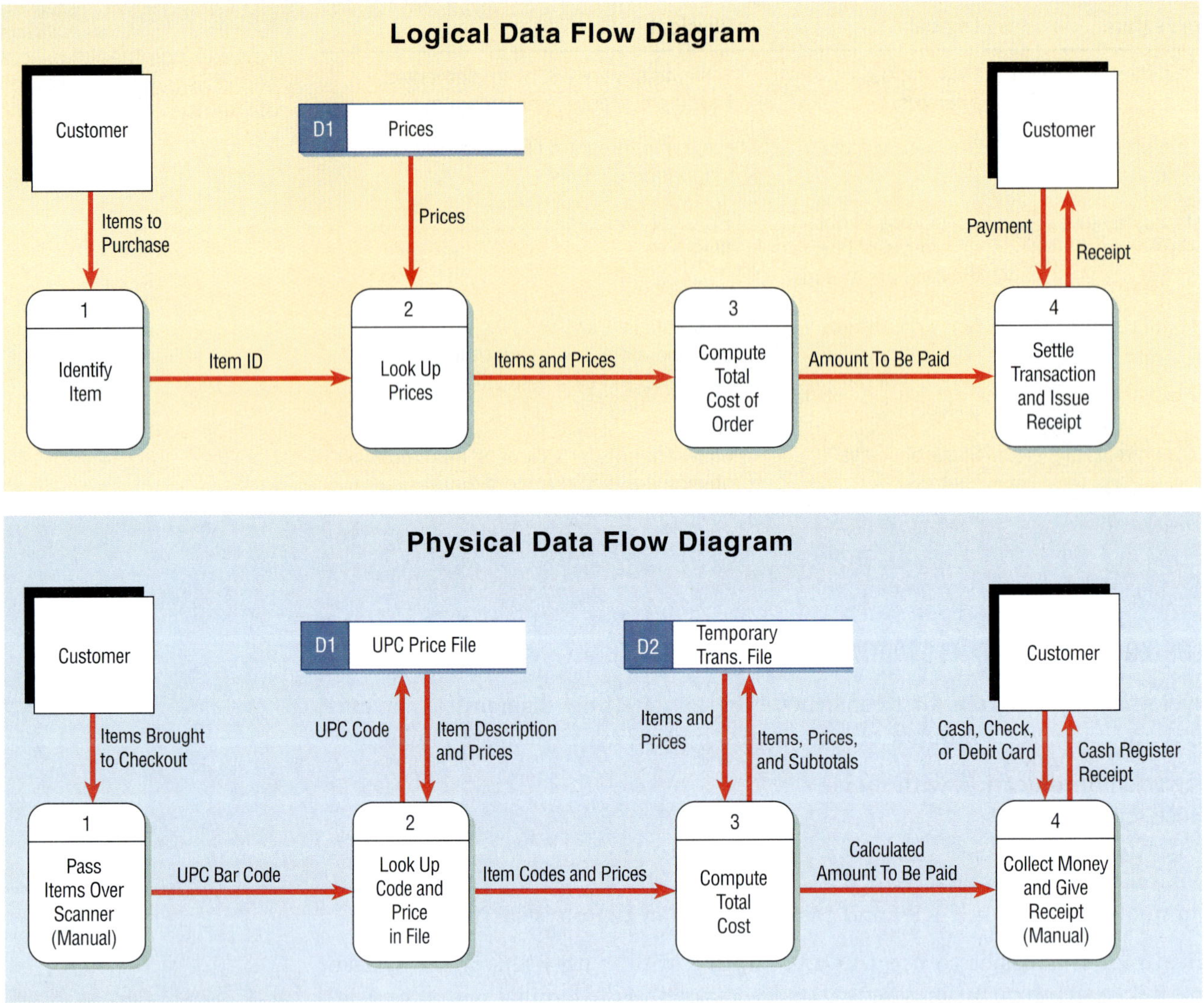

FIGURE 7.9
The physical data flow diagram (below) shows certain details not found on the logical data flow diagram (above).

method of implementation. Logical data flow diagrams represent features of a system that would exist no matter what the physical means of doing business are. For example, activities such as applying for a video store membership card, checking out a DVD, and returning the DVD, would all occur whether the store had an automated, manual, or hybrid system.

DEVELOPING PHYSICAL DATA FLOW DIAGRAMS

After you develop the logical model of the new system, you may use it to create a physical data flow diagram. The physical data flow diagram shows how the system will be constructed, and usually contains most, if not all, of the elements found in Figure 7.10. Just as logical data flow diagrams have certain advantages, physical data flow diagrams have others, including:

1. Clarifying which processes are performed by humans (manual) and which are automated.
2. Describing processes in more detail than logical DFDs.
3. Sequencing processes that have to be done in a particular order.
4. Identifying temporary data stores.
5. Specifying actual names of files and printouts.
6. Adding controls to ensure the processes are done properly.

Contents of Physical Data Flow Diagrams

- Manual processes
- Processes for adding, deleting, changing, and updating records
- Data entry and verifying processes
- Validation processes for ensuring accurate data input
- Sequencing processes to rearrange the order of records
- Processes to produce every unique system output
- Intermediate data stores
- Actual file names used to store data
- Controls to signify completion of tasks or error conditions

FIGURE 7.10
Physical data flow diagrams contain many items not found in logical data flow diagrams.

Physical data flow diagrams are often more complex than logical data flow diagrams simply because of the many data stores present in a system. The acronym CRUD is often used for Create, Read, Update, and Delete, the activities that must be present in a system for each master file. A CRUD matrix is a tool to represent where each of these processes occurs in a system. Figure 7.11 is a CRUD matrix for an Internet storefront. Notice that some of the processes include more than one activity. Data entry processes such as keying and verifying are also part of physical data flow diagrams.

Physical data flow diagrams also have intermediate data stores, often a transaction file or a temporary database table. Intermediate data stores often consist of transaction files used to store data between processes. Because most processes that require access to a given set of data are unlikely to execute at the same instant in time, transaction files must hold the data from one process to the next. An easily understood example of this concept is found in the everyday experiences of grocery shopping, meal preparation, and eating. The activities are:

1. Selecting items from shelves.
2. Checking out and paying the bill.
3. Transporting the groceries home.
4. Preparing a meal.
5. Eating the meal.

Activity	Customer	Item	Order	Order Detail
Customer Logon	R			
Item Inquiry		R		
Item Selection		R	C	C
Order Checkout	U	U	U	R
Add Account	C			
Add Item		C		
Close Customer Account	D			
Remove Obsolete Item		D		
Change Customer Demographics	RU			
Change Customer Order	RU	RU	RU	CRUD
Order Inquiry	R	R	R	R

FIGURE 7.11
A CRUD matrix for an Internet storefront. This tool can be used to represent where each of four processes (Create, Read, Update, and Delete) occurs within a system.

Each of these five activities would be represented by a separate process on a physical data flow diagram, and each one occurs at a different time. For example, you would not typically transport the groceries home and eat them at the same time. Therefore, a "transaction data store" is required to link each task. When you are selecting items, the transaction data store is the shopping cart. After the next process (checking out), the cart is unnecessary. The transaction data store linking checking out and transporting the groceries home is the shopping bag (cheaper than letting you take the cart home!). Bags are an inefficient way of storing the groceries once they are home, so cupboards and a refrigerator are used as a transaction data store between the activity of transporting the goods home and preparing the meal. Finally, a plate, bowl, and cup constitute the link between preparing and eating the meal.

Timing information may also be included. For example, a physical DFD may indicate that an edit program must be run before an update program. Updates must be performed before producing a summary report, or an order must be entered on a Web site before the amount charged to a credit card may be verified with the financial institution. Note that because of such considerations, a physical data flow diagram may appear more linear than a logical model.

Create the physical data flow diagram for a system by analyzing its output and input. When creating a physical data flow diagram, input data flow from an external entity is sometimes called a trigger because it starts the activities of a process, and output data flow to an external entity is sometimes called a response because it is sent as the result of some activity. Determine which data fields or elements need to be keyed. These fields are called *base elements* and must be stored in a file.

FIGURE 7.12

An event response table for an Internet storefront.

Event	Source	Trigger	Activity	Response	Destination
Customer logs on	Customer	Customer number and password	Find customer record and verify password. Send Welcome Web page.	Welcome Web page	Customer
Customer browses items at Web storefront	Customer	Item information	Find item price and quantity available. Send Item Response Web page.	Item Response Web page	Customer
Customer places item into shopping basket at Web storefront	Customer	Item purchase (item number and quantity)	Store data on Order Detail Record. Calculate shipping cost using shipping tables. Update customer total. Update item quantity on hand.	Items Purchased Web page	Customer
Customer checks out	Customer	Clicks "Check Out" button on Web page	Display Customer Order Web page.	Verification Web page	
Obtain customer payment	Customer	Credit card information	Verify credit card amount with credit card company. Send.	Credit card data Customer feedback	Credit card company Customer
Send customer email		Temporal, hourly	Send customer an email confirming shipment.		Customer

Elements that are not keyed but are rather the result of a calculation or logical operation are called *derived elements*.

Sometimes it is not clear how many processes to place in one diagram and when to create a child diagram. One suggestion is to examine each process and count the number of data flows entering and leaving it. If the total is greater than four, the process is a good candidate for a child diagram. Physical data flow diagrams are illustrated later in this chapter.

Event Modeling and Data Flow Diagrams A practical approach to creating physical data flow diagrams is to create a simple data flow diagram fragment for each unique system event. Events cause the system to do something and act as a trigger to the system. Triggers start activities and processes, which in turn use data or produce output. An example of an event is a customer reserving a flight on the Web. As each Web form is submitted, processes are activated, such as validating and storing the data and formatting and displaying the next Web page.

Events are usually summarized in an event response table. An example of an event response table for an Internet storefront business is illustrated in Figure 7.12. A data flow diagram fragment is represented by a row in the table. Each DFD fragment is a single process on a data flow diagram. All the fragments are then combined to form Diagram 0. The trigger and response columns become the input and output data flows, and the activity becomes the process. The analyst must determine the data stores required for the process by examining the input and output data flows. Figure 7.13 illustrates a portion of the data flow diagram for the first three rows of the event response table.

FIGURE 7.13

Data flow diagrams for the first three rows of the Internet storefront event response table.

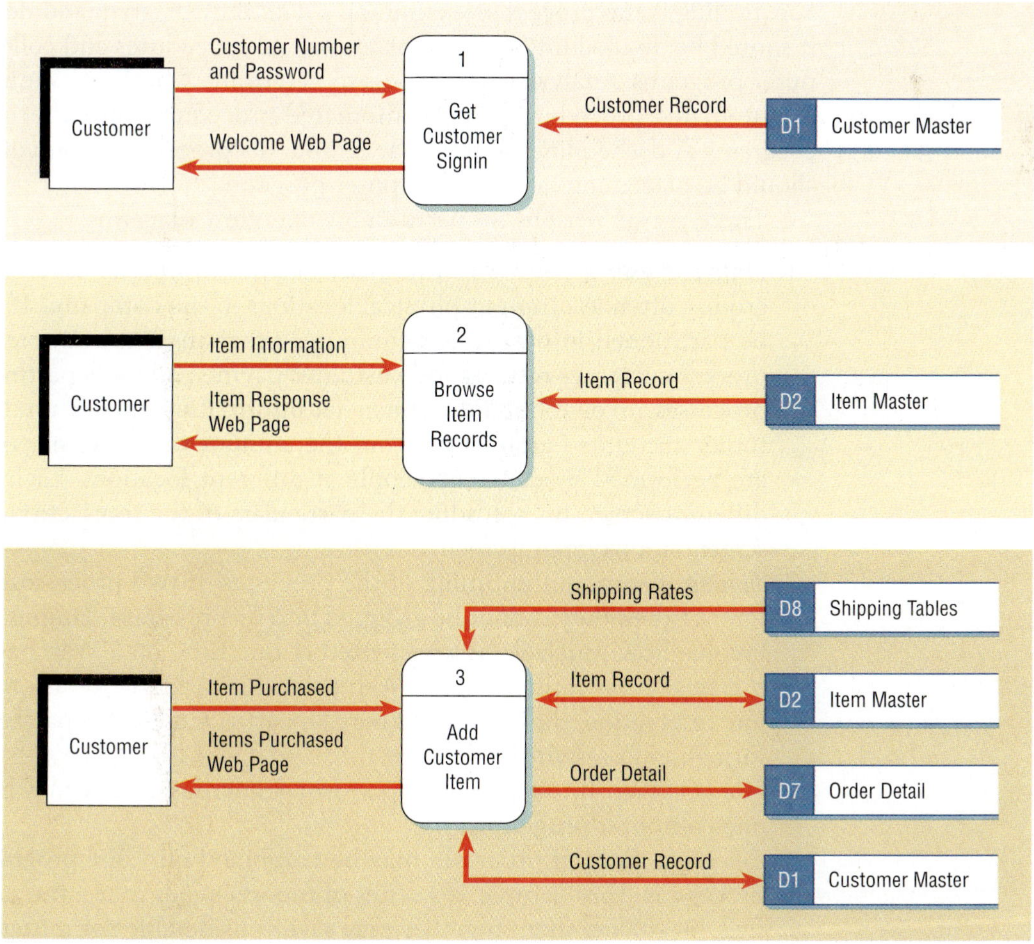

The advantage of building data flow diagrams based on events is that the users are familiar with the events that take place in their business area and know how the events drive other activities.

Use Cases and Data Flow Diagrams In Chapter 2, we introduced the concept of a *use case* .We use this notion of a use case in creating data flow diagrams. A use case summarizes an event and has a similar format to process specifications (described in Chapter 9). Each use case defines one activity and its trigger, input, and output. Figure 7.14 illustrates a use case for Process 3, Add Customer Item.

This approach allows the analyst to work with users to understand the nature of the processes and activities and then create a single data flow diagram fragment. When creating use cases, first make an initial attempt to define the use cases without going into detail. This step provides an overview of the system and leads to the creation of Diagram 0. Decide what the names should be and provide a brief description of the activity. List the activities, inputs, and outputs for each one.

Make sure you document the steps used in each use case. These should be in the form of business rules that list or explain the human and system activities completed for each use case. If at all possible, list them in the sequence that they would normally be executed. Next, determine the data used by each step. This step is easier if a data dictionary has been completed. Finally, ask the users to review and suggest modifications of the use cases. It is important that the use cases are written clearly. (See Chapter 18 for a further discussion of UML, use cases, and use case diagrams.)

PARTITIONING DATA FLOW DIAGRAMS

Partitioning is the process of examining a data flow diagram and determining how it should be divided into collections of manual procedures and collections of computer programs. Analyze each process to determine whether it should be a manual or automated procedure. Group automated procedures into a series of computer programs. A dashed line is often drawn around a process or group of processes that should be placed into a single computer program.

There are six reasons for partitioning data flow diagrams:

1. *Different user groups.* Are the processes performed by several different user groups, often at different physical locations in the company? If so, they should be partitioned into different computer programs. An example is the need to process customer returns and customer payments in a department store. Both processes involve obtaining financial information that is used to adjust customer accounts (subtracting from the amount the customer owes), but they are performed by different people at different locations. Each group needs a different screen for recording the particulars of the transaction, either a credit screen or a payment screen.
2. *Timing.* Examine the timing of the processes. If two processes execute at different times, they cannot be grouped into one program. Timing issues may also involve how much data is presented at one time on a Web page. If an ecommerce site has rather lengthy Web pages for ordering items or making an airline reservation, the Web pages may be partitioned into separate programs that format and present the data.
3. *Similar tasks.* If two processes perform similar tasks, they may be grouped into one computer program.
4. *Efficiency.* Several processes may be combined into one program for efficient processing. For example, if a series of reports needs to use the same large input files, producing them together may save considerable computer run time.

Use case name: Add Customer Item	
Description: Adds an item for a customer Internet order.	Process ID: 3
Trigger: Customer places an order item in the shopping basket.	
Trigger type: External ■ Temporal ☐	

Input Name	Source	Output Name	Destination
Item Purchased (Item Number and Quantity)	Customer	Items Purchased Confirmation Web Page	Customer

Steps Performed	Information for Steps
1. Find Item Record using the Item Number. If the item is not found, place a message on the Items Purchased Web page.	Item Number, Item Record
2. Store item data on Order Detail Record.	Order Detail Record
3. Use the Customer Number to find the Customer Record.	Customer Number, Customer Record
4. Calculate Shipping Cost using shipping tables. Using the Item Weight from the Item Record and the Zip Code from the Customer Record, look up the Shipping Cost in the Shipping Tables.	Zip Code, Item Weight, Shipping Table
5. Modify the Customer Total using the Quantity Purchased and the Item Price. Add the Shipping Cost. Update the Customer Record.	Item Record, Quantity Purchased, Shipping Cost, Customer Record
6. Modify the Item Quantity On Hand and update the Item Record.	Quantity Ordered, Item Record

FIGURE 7.14

A Use Case form for the Internet storefront describes the Add Customer Item activity and its triggers, input, and output.

5. *Consistency of data.* Processes may be combined into one program for consistency of data. For example, a credit card company may take a "snapshot" and produce a variety of reports at the same time just so figures are consistent.
6. *Security.* Processes may be partitioned into different programs for security reasons. A dashed line may be placed around Web pages that are on a secure

server to separate them from those Web pages on a server that is not secured. A Web page that is used for obtaining the user's identification and password is usually partitioned from order entry or other business pages.

A DATA FLOW DIAGRAM EXAMPLE

The corporation in our example is FilmMagic, a video rental chain founded by three people with expertise in the video rental business. A summary of the business activities obtained from interviews with the owners of FilmMagic is illustrated in Figure 7.15. The plan is to have a series of stores scattered strategically around a metropolitan area. The company has also adopted a unique policy of giving free DVD or game rentals to its high-volume customers in an attempt to gain a large market share. According to one of the company's owners, "If the airlines can have frequent flyer programs, our video stores can have a recurrent rental program." Consequently, a monthly customer bonus program will be part of the system.

FIGURE 7.15
Start with a list of business activities, which will help you identify processes, external entities, and data flows.

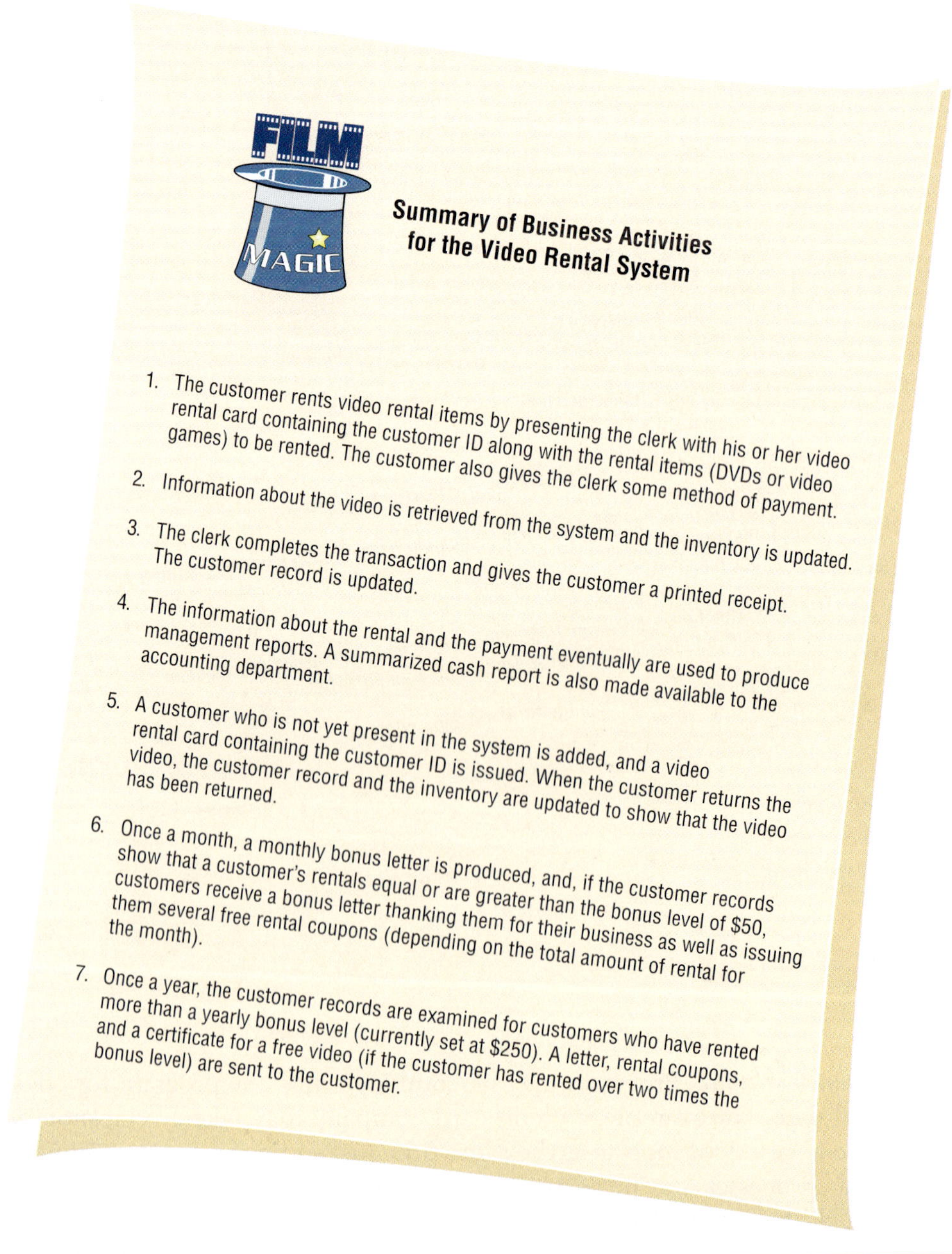

Summary of Business Activities for the Video Rental System

1. The customer rents video rental items by presenting the clerk with his or her video rental card containing the customer ID along with the rental items (DVDs or video games) to be rented. The customer also gives the clerk some method of payment.
2. Information about the video is retrieved from the system and the inventory is updated.
3. The clerk completes the transaction and gives the customer a printed receipt. The customer record is updated.
4. The information about the rental and the payment eventually are used to produce management reports. A summarized cash report is also made available to the accounting department.
5. A customer who is not yet present in the system is added, and a video rental card containing the customer ID is issued. When the customer returns the video, the customer record and the inventory are updated to show that the video has been returned.
6. Once a month, a monthly bonus letter is produced, and, if the customer records show that a customer's rentals equal or are greater than the bonus level of $50, customers receive a bonus letter thanking them for their business as well as issuing them several free rental coupons (depending on the total amount of rental for the month).
7. Once a year, the customer records are examined for customers who have rented more than a yearly bonus level (currently set at $250). A letter, rental coupons, and a certificate for a free video (if the customer has rented over two times the bonus level) are sent to the customer.

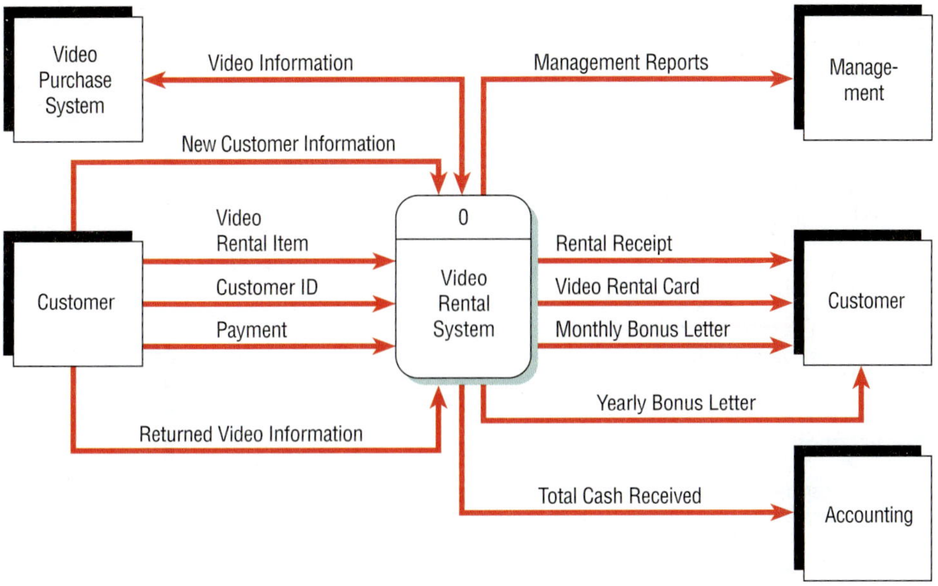

FIGURE 7.16
Context level diagram for the FilmMagic video rental stores.

CREATING THE CONTEXT DIAGRAM

The context-level data flow diagram, representing an overview of the entire system, appears in Figure 7.16. Because the system must keep track of the number of DVDs a customer has rented, the external CUSTOMER has the most data flow to and from it.

DRAWING DIAGRAM 0

Diagram 0, shown in Figure 7.17, depicts the major activities for the FilmMagic video rental system. Note that there is one process for each major activity. Each process is analyzed to determine the data required and the output produced. Process 1, RENT VIDEO ITEMS, summarizes the main function of the system, and is thus a complex process. Notice the many input and output data flows.

To draw the data flow diagram correctly, questions must be asked such as, "What information is needed to rent a DVD?" A VIDEO RENTAL ITEM (which may be either a DVD or a video game), a PAYMENT, and a CUSTOMER ID (a rental card) are required from the CUSTOMER. The VIDEO RENTAL ITEM is used to find matching information about the DVD, such as the price and description. The process creates a CASH TRANSACTION, which will eventually produce information about the TOTAL CASH RECEIVED. The CUSTOMER RECORD is obtained and updated with the total amount of the rental. A double-headed arrow indicates that the CUSTOMER RECORD is obtained from and replaced in the same file location. The RENTAL RECEIPT and DVD are given to the CUSTOMER. RENTAL INFORMATION, such as the date and the item rented, is produced for later use to PRODUCE MANAGEMENT REPORTS.

The other processes are simpler, with fewer inputs and outputs. Process 3, CHECK IN CUSTOMER VIDEO RETURN, updates the CUSTOMER data store indicating that items are no longer checked out. New customers must be added to the CUSTOMER data store before a DVD may be checked out. Process 5, ADD NEW CUSTOMER, takes NEW CUSTOMER INFORMATION and issues the customer a VIDEO RENTAL CARD. The card must be presented each time a customer wishes to check out a DVD.

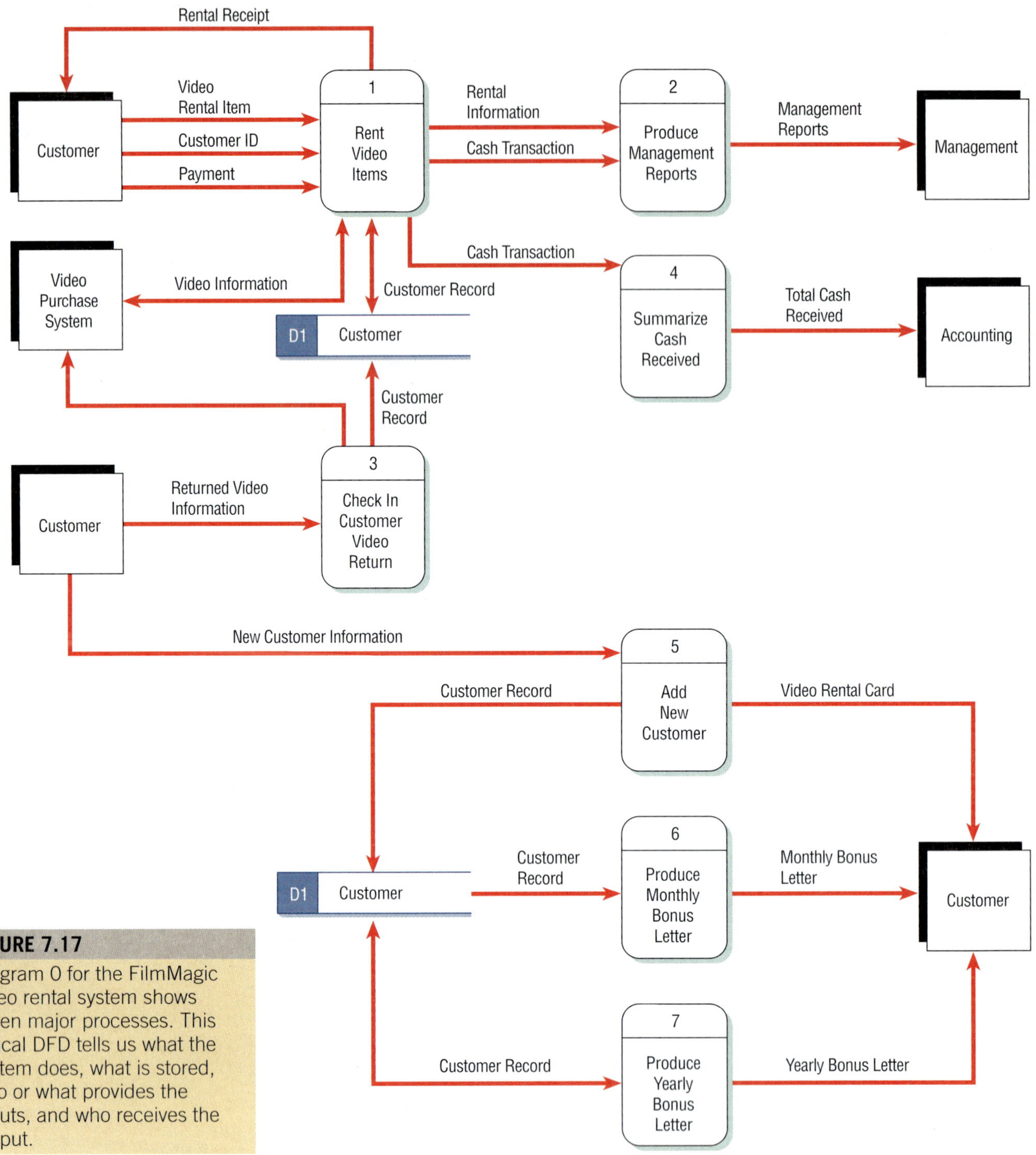

FIGURE 7.17

Diagram 0 for the FilmMagic video rental system shows seven major processes. This logical DFD tells us what the system does, what is stored, who or what provides the inputs, and who receives the output.

Processes 2 and 4 produce useful information for managing the business and making decisions, such as when to lower the price of DVDs that are in demand and when to advertise to draw more customers, thereby increasing cash flow. Processes 6 and 7 use CUSTOMER data store information to PRODUCE MONTHLY and YEARLY CUSTOMER BONUS LETTERS. Notice that the names of the data flows going out of the processes are different, indicating that something has transformed input data to produce output data. All processes start with a verb such as RENT, PRODUCE, CHECK IN, SUMMARIZE, or ADD.

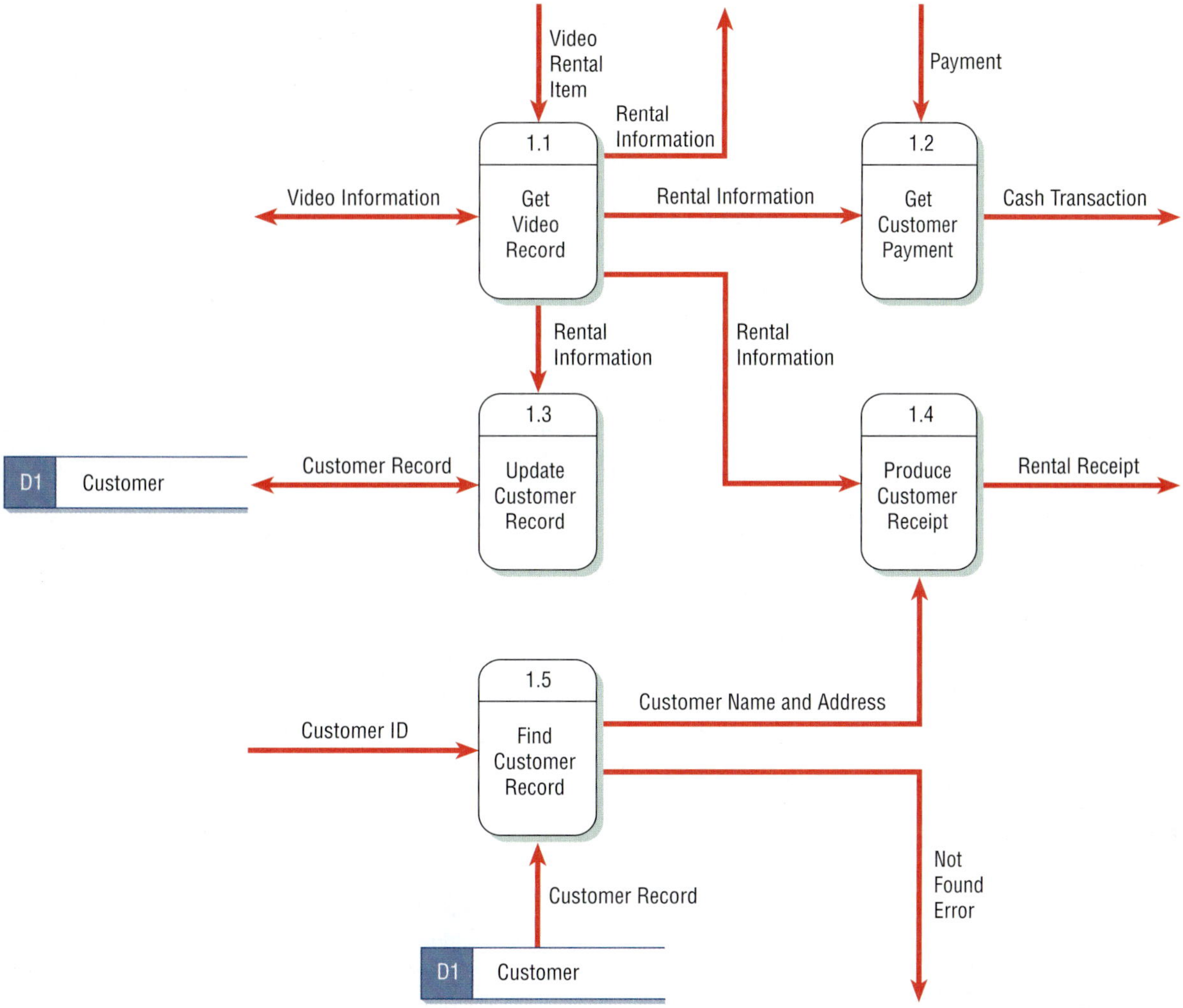

FIGURE 7.18

The child diagram for process 1 shows more detail than does Diagram 0. Process 1.1 is GET VIDEO RECORD. The logical DFD tells us what is accomplished but not how to do it.

CREATING A CHILD DIAGRAM

Figure 7.18 is the child diagram of process 1, RENT VIDEO ITEMS, in the FilmMagic example. The input data flow VIDEO INFORMATION is connected only to the process GET VIDEO RECORD. The source of this input is a blank area in the drawing. This incomplete interface flow matches the flow into process 1 on Diagram 0. The same is true for VIDEO RENTAL, PAYMENT, and CUSTOMER ID.

The CUSTOMER RECORD is also an interface data flow, but it is connected on Diagram 1 to the CUSTOMER data store because data stores in the parent diagram may also be included on the child diagram. The output data flows CASH TRANSACTION and RENTAL RECEIPT are interface flows that match the parent process output. The flow NOT FOUND ERROR is not depicted in the parent process because an error line is considered a minor output.

Child diagram processes are more detailed, illustrating the logic required to produce the output. The process GET VIDEO RECORD uses VIDEO RENTAL, which indicates which DVD the customer wishes to rent, to find the matching VIDEO INFORMATION (title, price, and so on). Process 1.5, FIND CUSTOMER RECORD, uses the CUSTOMER ID on the video rental card to locate the CUSTOMER record. The CUSTOMER NAME AND ADDRESS are printed on the RENTAL RECEIPT printed from process 1.4.

CREATING A PHYSICAL DATA FLOW DIAGRAM

FIGURE 7.19
This physical data flow diagram corresponds to logical Diagram 0. Note the subtle differences. CUSTOMER ID is now CUSTOMER ID BAR CODE, emphasizing physical implementation.

Figure 7.19 is the physical data flow diagram corresponding to the FilmMagic logical Diagram 0. Data flow names have been changed to reflect implementation. The customer now supplies a VIDEO RENTAL BAR CODE and a CUSTOMER ID BAR CODE to process 1, RENT VIDEO ITEMS. The entity VIDEO PURCHASE SYSTEM has been replaced with a VIDEO MASTER file because files are used to communicate between systems. There are now two transaction files. The RENTAL TRANSACTION file is used to store information from the time the videos are rented until they are returned. The CASH TRANSACTIONS file is necessary because videos are rented throughout the day, but the CASH RECEIVED REPORT is produced only once a week. Data are entered using the RETURNED VIDEO screen (and any late charges are calculated in process 3, CHECK IN CUSTOMER VIDEO RETURN). New customers fill out the NEW

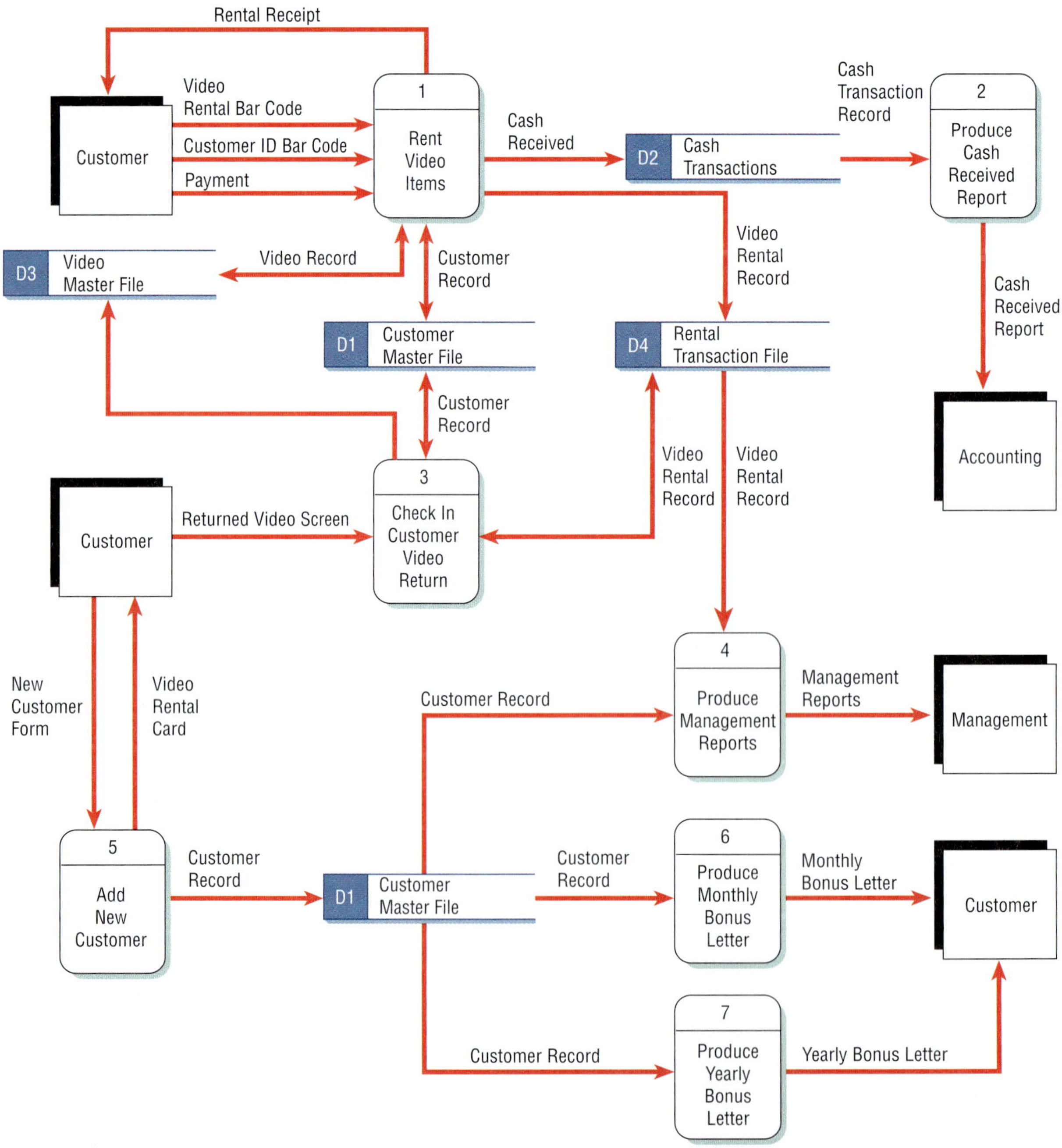

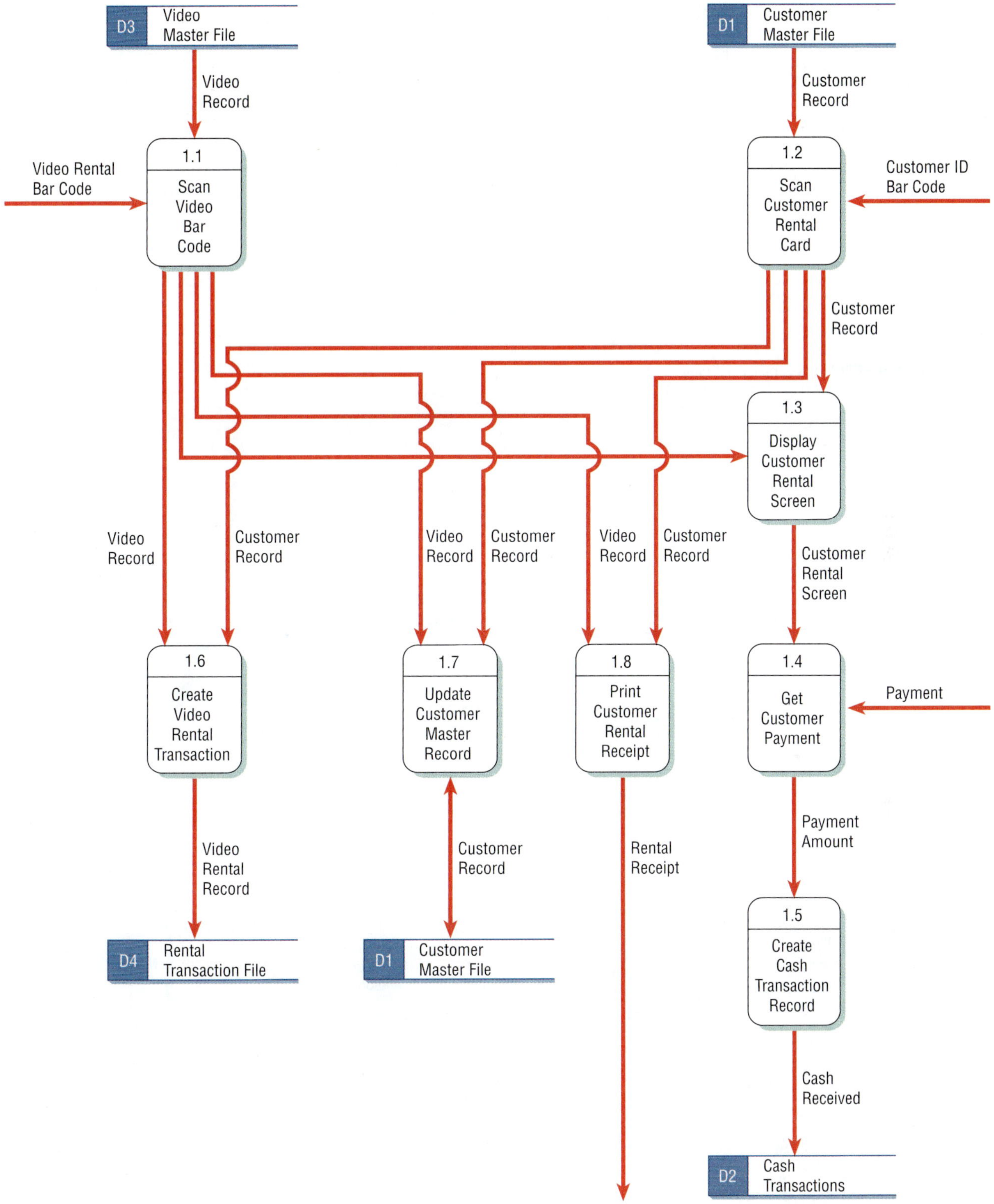

CUSTOMER FORM, whereas on the logical data flow diagram this step is simply called NEW CUSTOMER INFORMATION.

An example of a physical child data flow diagram is Diagram 1 of the FilmMagic example, which is illustrated in Figure 7.20. Notice that there are processes for scanning bar codes, displaying screens, locating records, and creating and updating files. The sequence of activities is important here, because the emphasis is on how the system will work and in what order events happen.

FIGURE 7.20

This physical child data flow diagram shows details about real world implementation. The logical diagram process 1.1 was GET VIDEO RECORD, but the physical diagram process 1.1 tells us how (SCAN VIDEO BAR CODE).

PARTITIONING THE DATA FLOW DIAGRAM

FIGURE 7.21

Partitioning the FilmMagic physical data flow diagram. Partitioning takes the physical DFD and makes programming and implementation manageable.

Figure 7.21 illustrates partitioning for the FilmMagic physical data flow diagram. Notice the use of dotted lines to indicate which processes should be in separate programs. The process RENT VIDEO ITEMS operates on a minute-by-minute basis. The process CHECK IN CUSTOMER VIDEO RETURN also operates on a minute-by-minute basis. Returns, however, are handled at a time later than the rental process, and both procedures should thus be in separate programs.

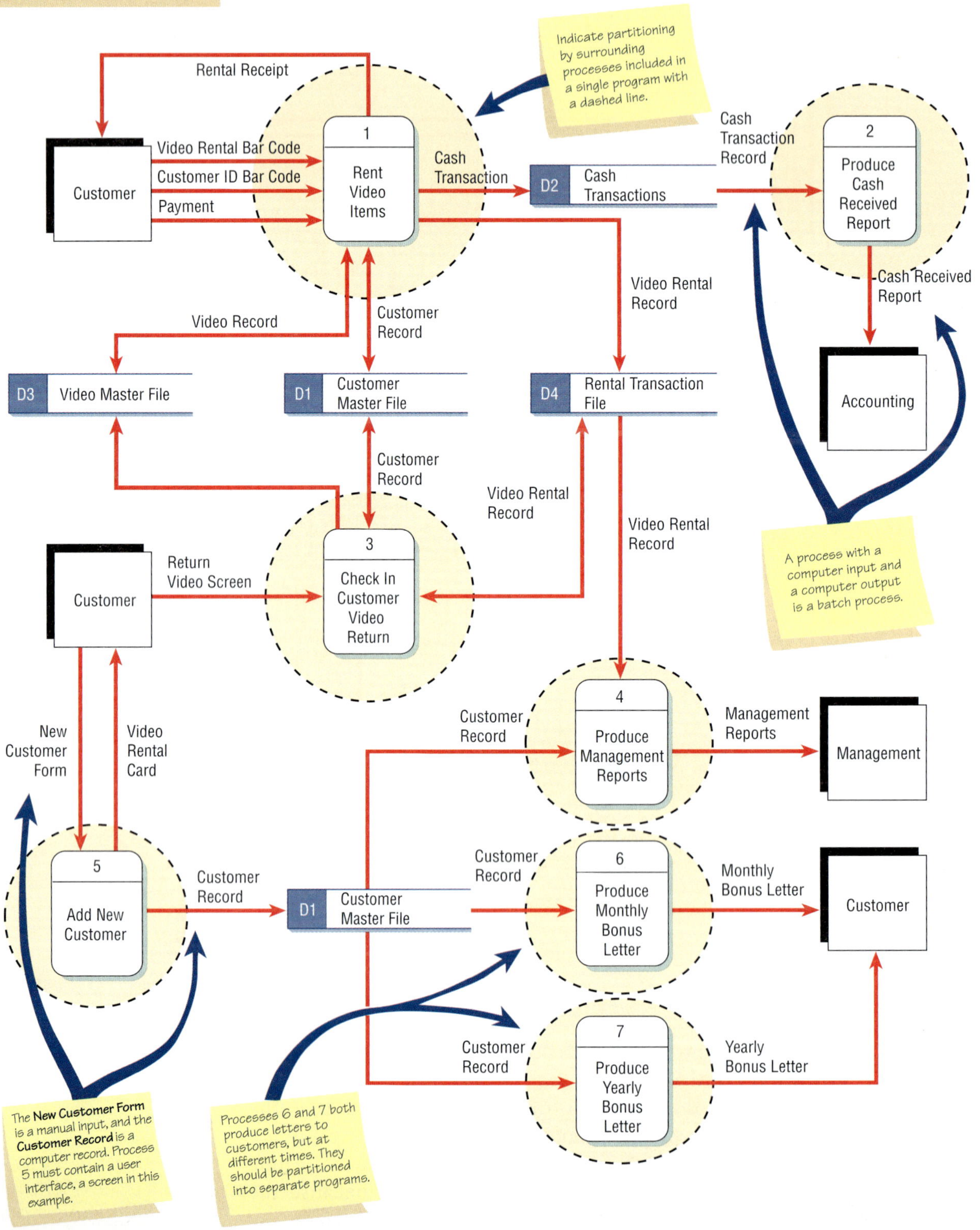

The PRODUCE CASH RECEIVED REPORT process is weekly and therefore must also be in a separate program. Because the CASH TRANSACTION RECORD that goes into this process and the CASH RECEIVED REPORT that comes out of the process are both computer information, the process should be implemented as a batch program. The same is true for process 4, PRODUCE MANAGEMENT REPORTS; for process 6, PRODUCE MONTHLY BONUS LETTER; and for process 7, PRODUCE YEARLY BONUS LETTER.

Process 5, ADD NEW CUSTOMER, could be either batch or online. Because the customer is probably waiting for the video rental card on the other side of a counter, an online process would provide the best customer service.

A SECOND DATA FLOW DIAGRAM EXAMPLE

Often, a person's first exposure to data flow diagrams seems confusing because there are so many new concepts and definitions. This next example is intended to illustrate the development of a data flow diagram by selectively looking at each of the components explored earlier in this chapter. The example, called "World's Trend Catalog Division," will also be used to illustrate concepts covered in Chapters 8 and 9.

A list of business activities for World's Trend can be found in Figure 7.22. You could develop this list using information obtained through interacting with people in interviews, through investigation, and through observation. The list can be

World's Trend
1000 International Lane
Cornwall, CT 06050

World's Trend is a mail order supplier of high-quality, fashionable clothing. Customers place orders by telephone, by mailing an order form included with each catalog, or via the Web site.

Summary of Business Activities

1. When customer orders come in, the item master and the customer master files are both updated. If an item is out of stock, the inventory control department is notified.
2. If the order is from a new customer, a new record is created in the customer master file.
3. Picking slips are produced for the customer order and sent to the warehouse.
4. A shipping statement is prepared.
5. The process of shipping a customer order involves getting the goods from the warehouse and matching up the customer shipping statement, getting the correct customer address, and shipping it all to the customer.
6. The customer statement is generated and a billing statement is sent to a customer once a month.
7. An accounts receivable report is sent to the accounting department.

FIGURE 7.22
A summary of business activities for World's Trend Catalog Division.

used to identify external entities such as CUSTOMER, ACCOUNTING, and WAREHOUSE as well as data flows such as ACCOUNTS RECEIVABLE REPORT and CUSTOMER BILLING STATEMENT. Later (when developing level 0 and child diagrams), the list can be used to define processes, data flows, and data stores.

Once this list of activities is developed, create a context-level data flow diagram as shown in Figure 7.23. This diagram shows the ORDER PROCESSING SYSTEM in the middle (no processes are described in detail in the context-level diagram) and five external entities (the two separate entities both called CUSTOMER are really one and the same). The data flows that come from and go to the external entities are shown as well (for example, CUSTOMER ORDER and ORDER PICKING LIST).

Next, go back to the activity list and make a new list of as many processes and data stores as you can find. You can add more later, but start making the list now. If you think you have enough information, draw a level 0 diagram such as the one found in Figure 7.24. Call this Diagram 0 and keep the processes general so as not to overcomplicate the diagram. Later, you can add detail. When you are finished drawing the seven processes, draw data flows between them and to the external entities (the same external entities shown in the context-level diagram). If you think there need to be data stores such as ITEM MASTER or CUSTOMER MASTER, draw those in and connect them to processes using data flows. Now take the time to number the processes and data stores. Pay particular attention to making the labels meaningful. Check for errors and correct them before moving on.

At this point try to draw a child diagram (sometimes also called a level 1 diagram) such as the one in Figure 7.25. Number your child diagrams Diagram 1, Diagram 2, and so on, in accordance with the number you assigned to each process in the level 0 diagram. When you draw Diagram 1, make a list of subprocesses first. A process such as ADD CUSTOMER ORDER can have subprocesses (in this case,

FIGURE 7.23
A context-level data flow diagram for the order processing system at World's Trend.

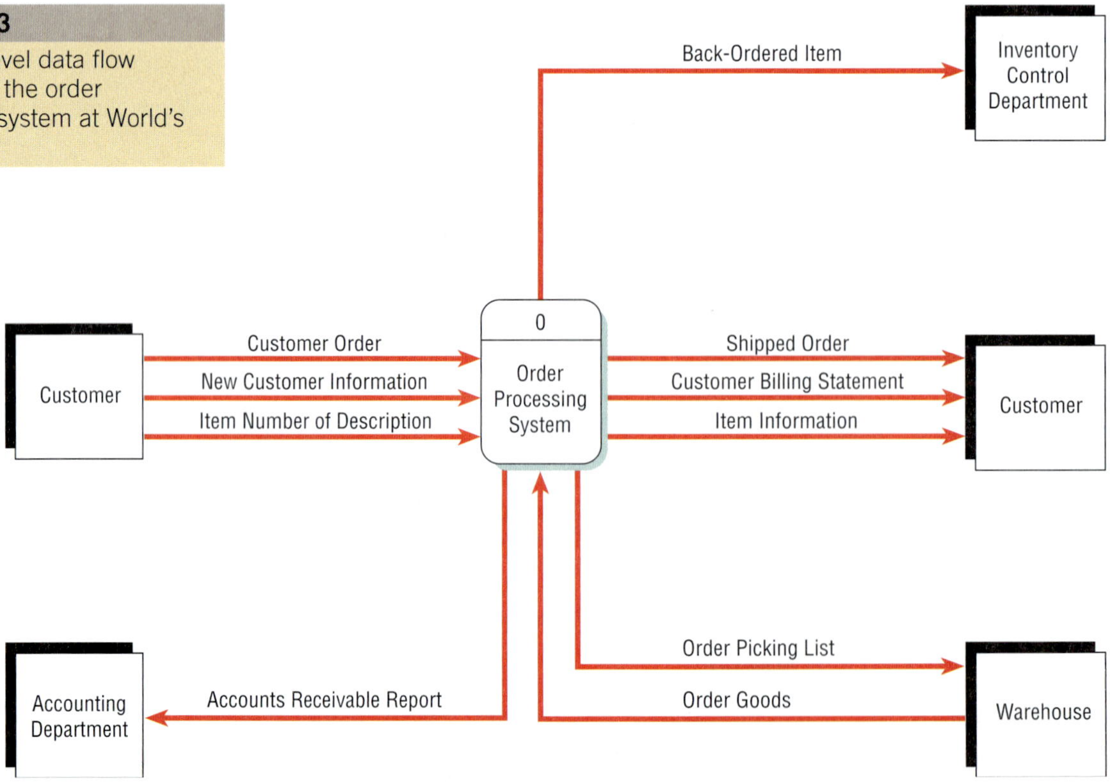

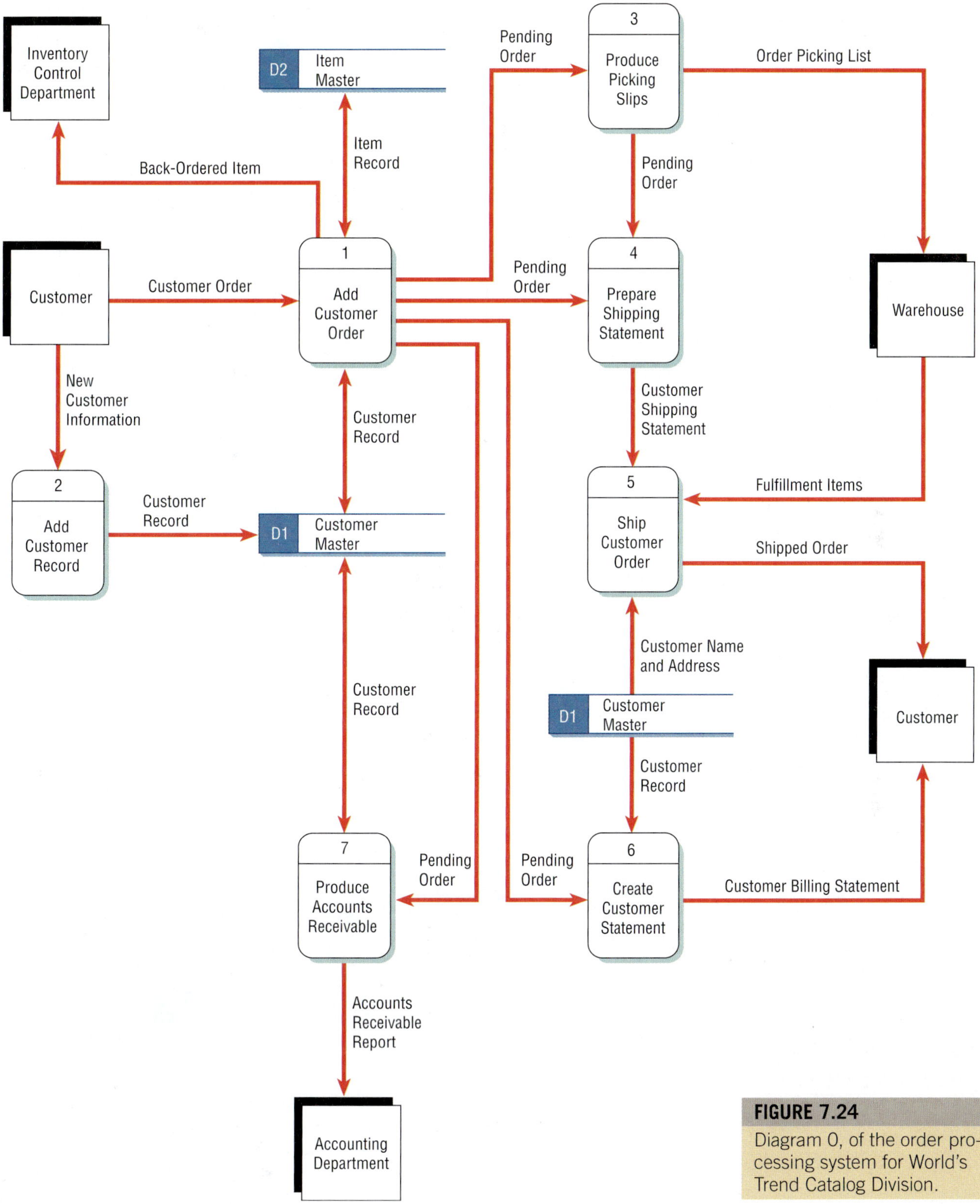

FIGURE 7.24
Diagram 0, of the order processing system for World's Trend Catalog Division.

there are seven). Connect these subprocesses to one another and also to data stores when appropriate. Subprocesses do not have to be connected to external entities, because we can always refer to the parent (or level 0) data flow diagram to identify these entities. Label the subprocesses 1.1, 1.2, 1.3, and so on. Take the time to check for errors and make sure the labels make sense.

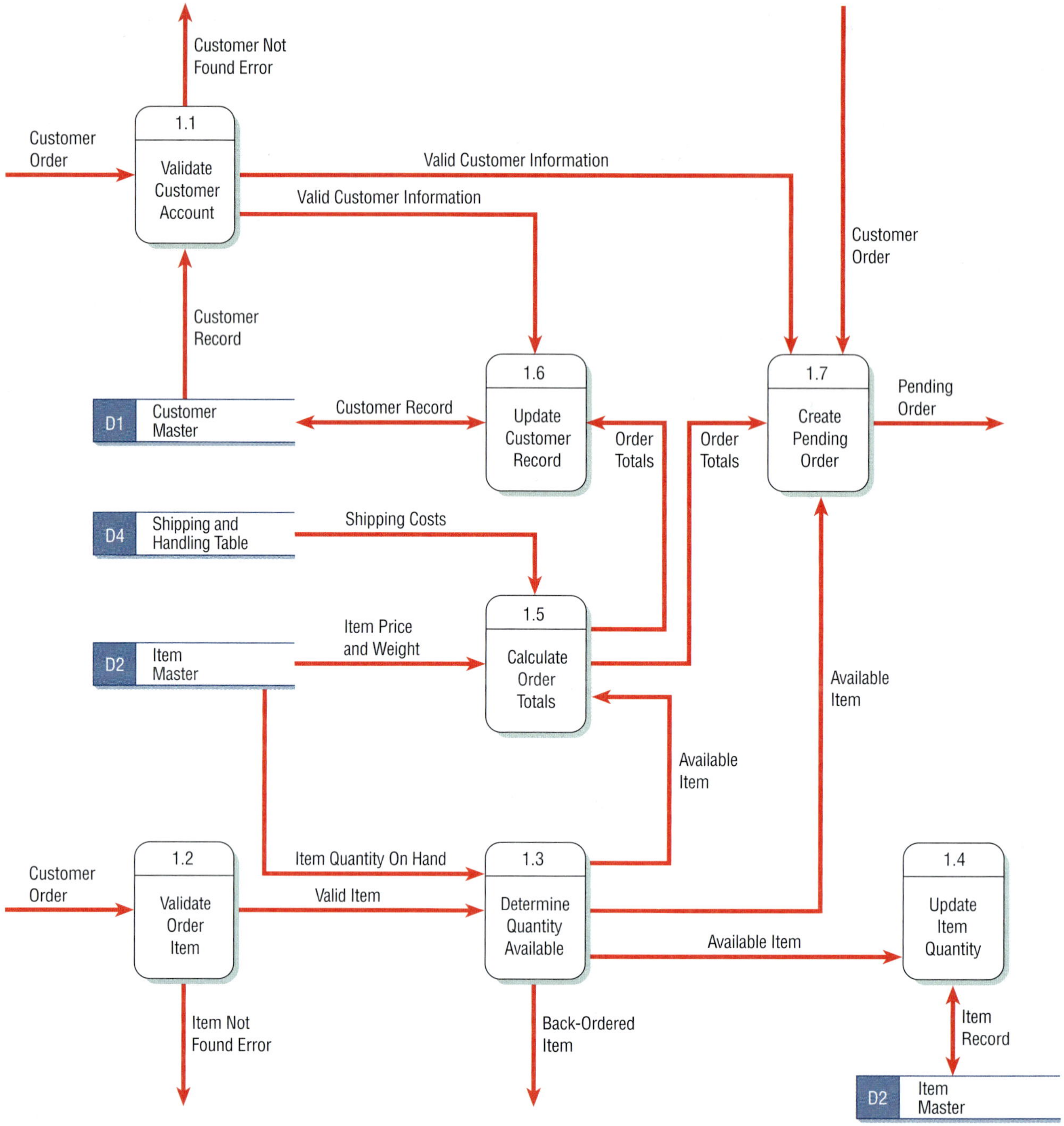

FIGURE 7.25
Diagram 1, of the order processing system for World's Trend Catalog Division.

If you want to go beyond the logical model and draw a physical model as well, look at Figure 7.26, which is an example of a physical data flow child diagram of process 3, PRODUCE PICKING SLIPS. When you label a physical model, take care to describe the process in great detail. For example, subprocess 3.3 in a logical model could simply be SORT ORDER ITEM, but in the physical model, a better label is SORT ORDER ITEM BY LOCATION WITHIN CUSTOMER. When you write a label for a data store, refer to the actual file or database, such as CUSTOMER MASTER FILE or SORTED ORDER ITEM FILE. When you describe data flows, describe the actual form, report, or screen. For example, when you print a slip for order picking, call the data flow ORDER PICKING SLIP.

Finally, take the physical data flow diagram and suggest partitioning through combining or separating the processes. As stated earlier, there are many reasons for

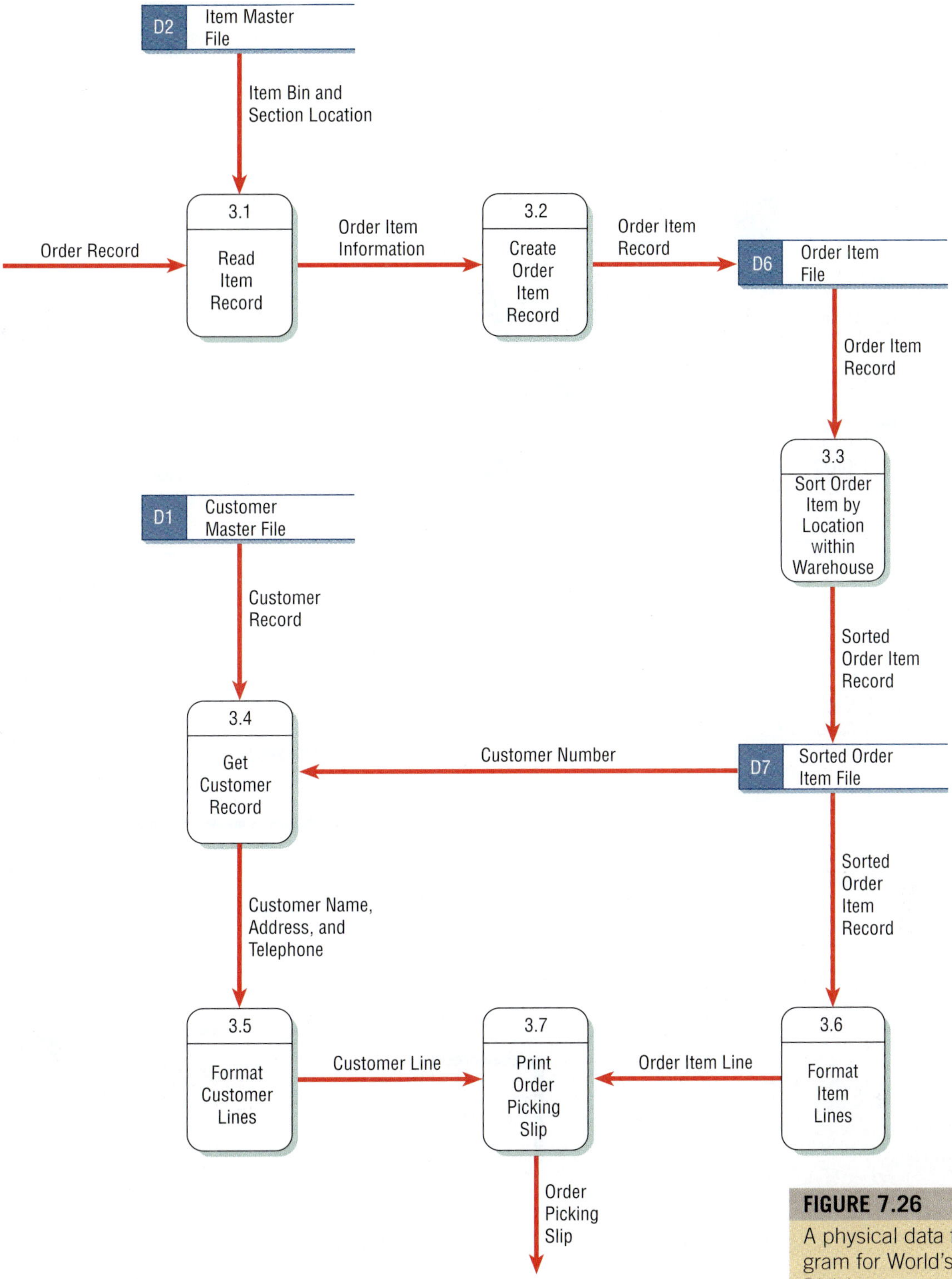

FIGURE 7.26
A physical data flow child diagram for World's Trend Catalog Division.

partitioning: identifying distinct processes for different user groups, separating processes that need to be performed at different times, grouping similar tasks, grouping processes for efficiency, combining processes for consistency, or separating them for security. Figure 7.27 shows that partitioning is useful in the case of World's Trend Catalog Division. You would first group processes 1 and 2 because it would make sense to add new customers at the same time their first order was placed. You would then put processes 3 and 4 in two separate partitions. Although both are batch processes, they must be done at different times from each other and thus cannot be grouped into a single program.

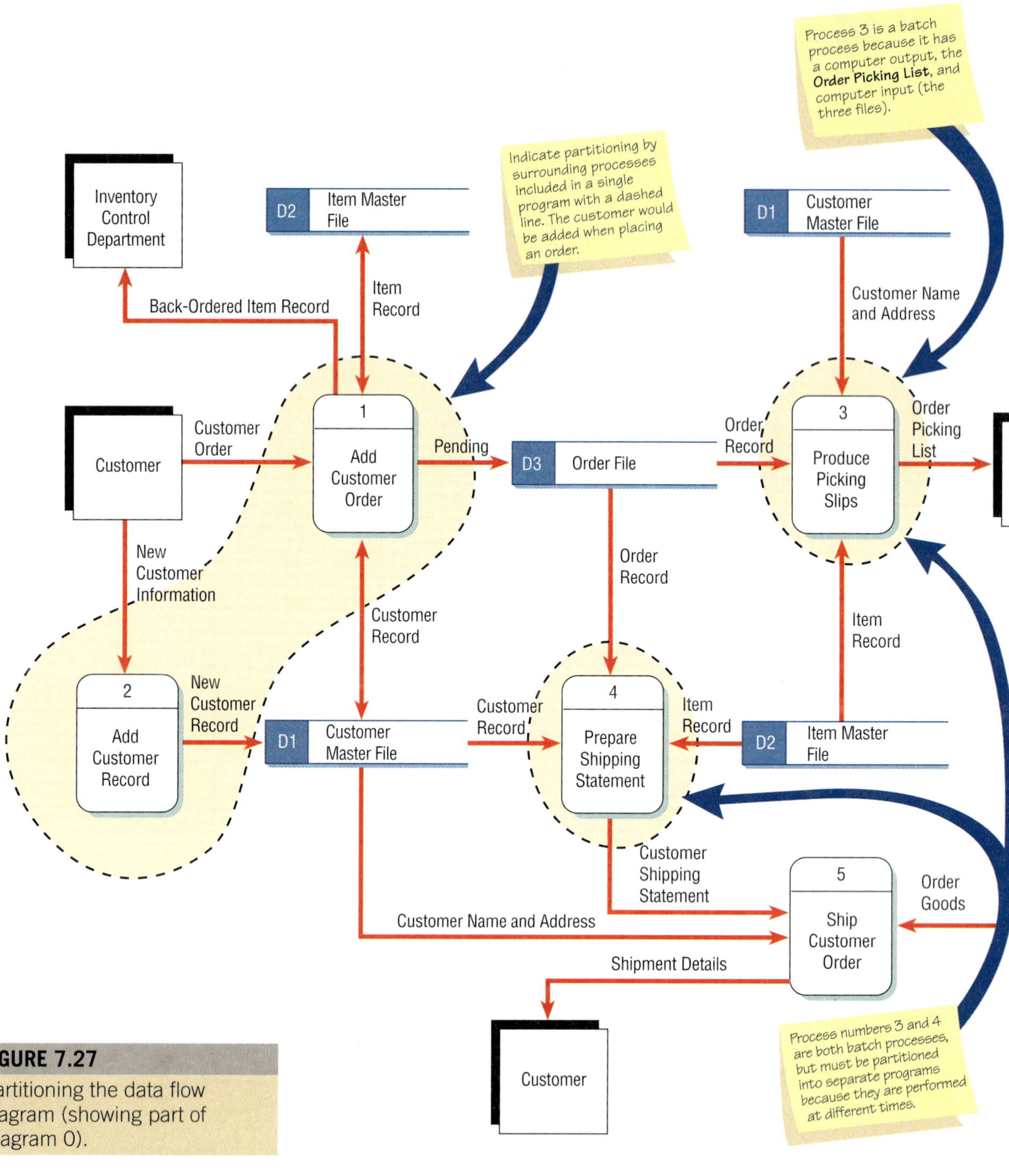

FIGURE 7.27
Partitioning the data flow diagram (showing part of Diagram 0).

The process of developing a data flow diagram is now completed from the top down, first drawing a companion physical data flow diagram to accompany the logical data flow diagram, then partitioning the data flow diagram by grouping or separating the processes. The World's Trend example is used again in Chapters 8 and 9.

PARTITIONING WEB SITES

Partitioning is a very useful principle when designing a Web site. Web site designers who use forms to collect data may find it more appropriate to divide a Web site into a series of Web pages, which will improve the way humans use the site, the speed of processing, and the ease of maintaining the site. Each time data must be obtained from a data store or an external partner, a Web site designer might consider creating a unique Web form and DFD process to validate and process the data.

The Web developer may also use Ajax, sending a request to the server and obtaining a small amount of data or an XML document returned to the same page. Ajax may be used to avoid creating too many small pages containing only a few extra or changed Web form elements. However, the analyst should create several pages when needed. One consideration is when a large amount of data needs to be obtained from the server, such as a list of all the flights that match starting and destination airports for specific travel days. When accessing different database tables on the same database, the data may be obtained containing fields from different database tables and passed to one process. However, if different databases are involved, the analyst may decide to use separate Web pages. When user input is required, the analyst may either use separate Web pages or use Ajax to facilitate a change in a drop-down list or to change a small amount of data.

A good example of partitioning can be seen in the development of a Web-based travel booking site. To simplify, we will only look at the airline booking portion of the Web site, shown in the data flow diagram in Figure 7.28. Notice that the Web designer has chosen to create several processes and unique partitions in making a flight reservation. Process 1 receives and validates the dates and airports entered by the customer (or travel agent acting for a customer). The selection data is used to obtain flight details and create a transaction data store of flight details that match the flight request.

It is advisable to partition the process of finding the flight information as a separate process, because a data store must be searched and the flight details are used to display a series of successive Web pages with matching flights. Then, once a customer chooses a flight, the information must be sent to a selected airline. It is important to have the FLIGHT DETAILS transaction file available to display each Web page of new flights, because redoing the search may take a lengthy amount of time that is unacceptable to a human user trying to complete a transaction.

The selection of available flights (process 2) uses an internal database, but this database does not have information about availability of seats, because the airlines are receiving reservations from many travel service organizations. This means that there must be a separate process and small program partitioned for determining if seats are available and for reserving specific seats.

Because there is a lot of user input, forms are designed to handle all of the user requests. Having separate forms means that the forms are less complex, and therefore users will find them more attractive and easier to fill out. This design meets both the usability and usefulness criteria important when designing Web sites for human–computer interaction. It also means that processing will take place more quickly, because once the flight is chosen, the next step involving the choice of seats should not require the customer to input or even see the flight details again at this time. Air France, for example, uses pop-up windows in which customers point to their seat selection.

Another reason for partitioning is to keep the transaction secure. Once the seat has been selected, the customer must confirm the reservation and supply credit card information. This is done using a secure connection, and the credit card company is involved in validating the amount of purchase. The secure connection means a separate process must be used. Once the credit card has been confirmed, two additional processes must be included, one to format and send an email confirmation and an eticket to the customer, and another to send notification of the flight purchase to the airline.

The entire procedure must be partitioned into a series of interacting processes, each with a corresponding Web page or interaction with an external system. Each

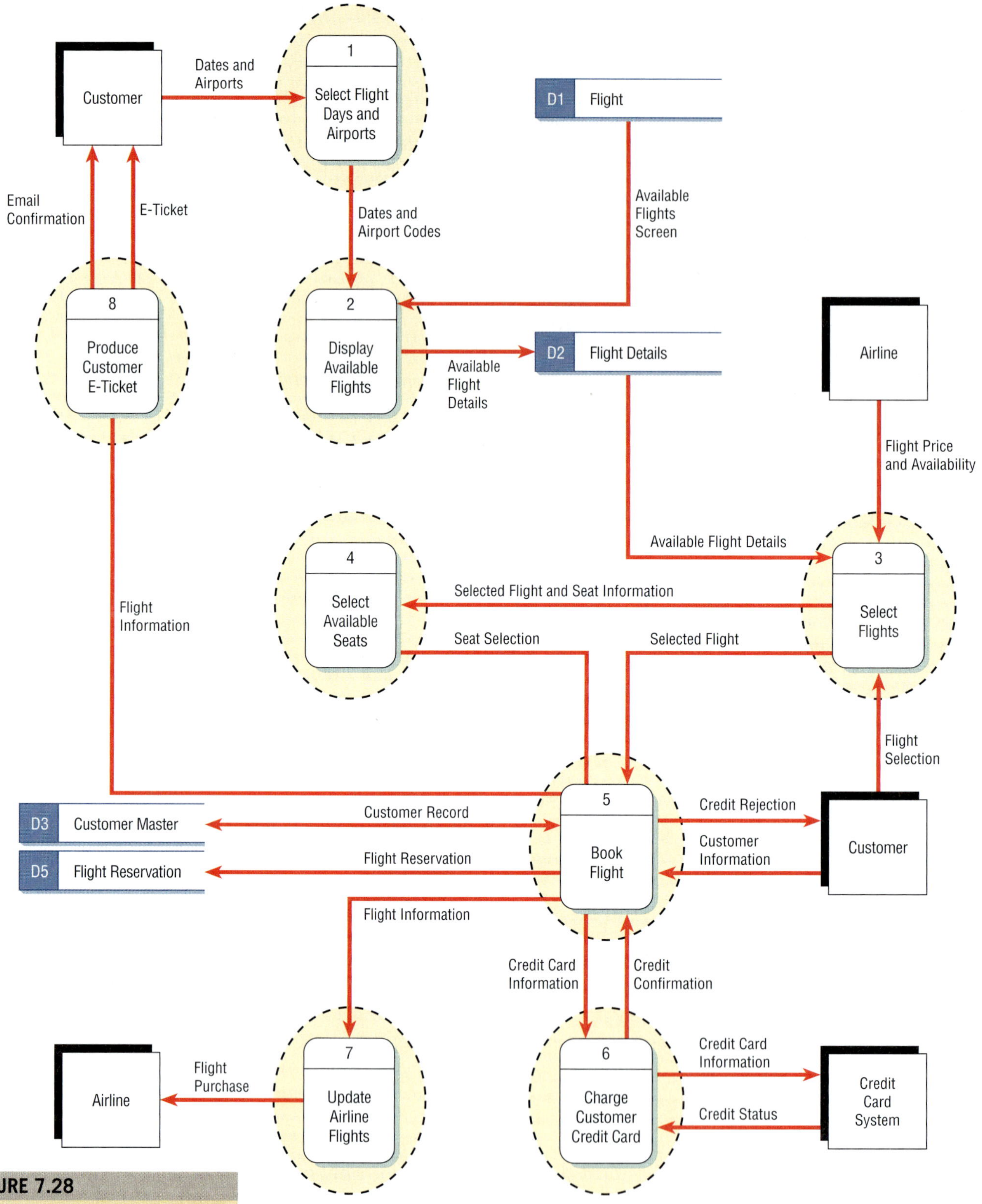

FIGURE 7.28
Partitioning is important for Web-based systems, as this physical data flow diagram of an online ticket purchasing system demonstrates.

time a new data store is used to obtain additional data, a process must be included to format or obtain the data. Each time an external company or system is involved, a process needs to be partitioned into a separate program. When processes or forms need to be revised, it is not a major task. The small size of the programs makes them easy to change. In this way, the Web site is secure, efficient, and more easily maintained.

CONSULTING OPPORTUNITY 7.1

THERE'S NO BUSINESS LIKE FLOW BUSINESS

The phone at Merman's Costume Rentals rings, and Annie Oaklea, head of costume inventory, picks it up and answers a query by saying, "Let me take a look at my inventory cards. Sorry, it looks as if there are only two male bear suits in inventory, with extra growly expressions at that. We've had a great run on bear. When do you need them? Perhaps one will be returned. No, can't do it, sorry. Would you like these two sent, regardless? The name of your establishment? Manhattan Theatre Company? London branch? Right. Delightful company! I see by our account card that you've rented from us before. And how long will you be needing the costumes?"

Figure 7.C1 is a data flow diagram that sets the stage for processing of costume rentals from Merman's. It shows rentals such as the one Annie is doing for Manhattan Theatre Company.

After conversing for another few moments about shop policy on alterations, Annie concludes her conversation by saying, "You are very lucky to get the bears on such short notice. I've got another company reserving them for the first week in July. I'll put you down for the bear suits, and they'll be taken to you directly by our courier. As always, prompt return will save enormous trouble for us all."

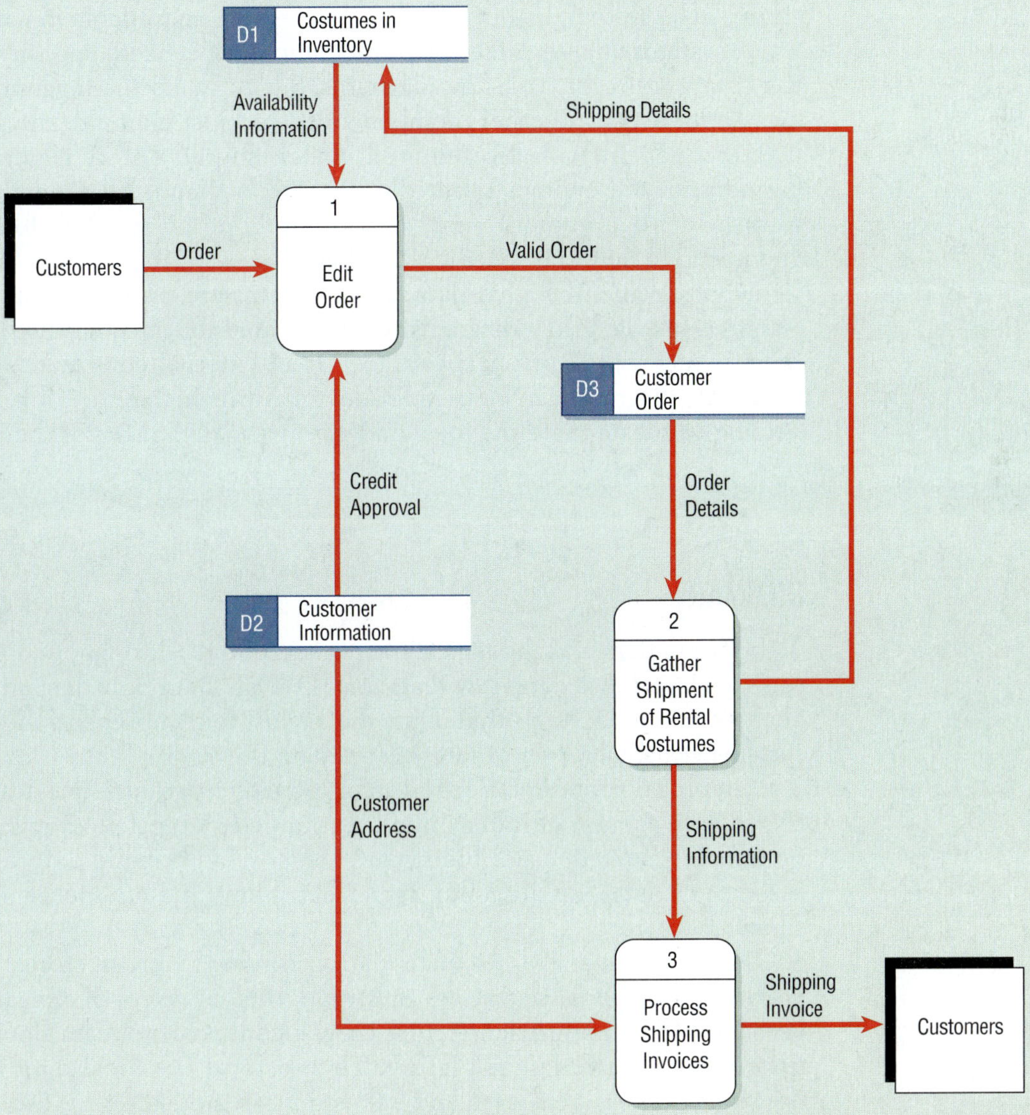

FIGURE 7.C1
A data flow diagram for Merman's Costume Rentals.

(Continued)

Merman's costume rental enterprise is located in London's world-famous West End theatre district. When a theatre or television production company lacks the resources (either time or expertise) to construct a costume in its own shop, the cry goes up to "Ring up Merman's!" and it proceeds to rent what it needs with a minimum of fuss.

The shop (more aptly visualized as a warehouse) goes on for three floors full of costume racks, holding thousands of costumes hung together by historical period, then grouped as to whether they are for men or women, and then by costume size.[1] Most theatre companies are able to locate precisely what they need through Annie's capable assistance.

Now tailor-make the *rental return* portion of the data flow diagram given earlier. Remember that timely returns are critical for keeping the spotlight on costumes rented from Merman's.

[1]Western Costume Company in Hollywood, California, is said to have more than 1 million costumes worth about $40 million.

COMMUNICATING USING DATA FLOW DIAGRAMS

Data flow diagrams are useful throughout the analysis and design process. Use original, unexploded data flow diagrams early when ascertaining information requirements. At this stage they can help provide an overview of data movement through the system, lending a visual perspective unavailable in narrative data.

A systems analyst might be quite competent at sketching through the logic of the data stream for data flow diagrams, but to make the diagrams truly communicative to users and other members of the project team, meaningful labels for all data components are also required. Labels should not be generic, because then they do not tell enough about the situation at hand. All general systems models bear the configuration of input, process, and output, so labels for a data flow diagram need to be more specific than that.

Finally, remember that data flow diagrams are used to document the system. Assume that data flow diagrams will be around longer than the people who drew them, which is, of course, always true if an external consultant is drawing them. Data flow diagrams can be used for documenting high or low levels of analysis and helping to substantiate the logic underlying the data flows of the organizations.

SUMMARY

To better understand the logical movement of data throughout a business, the systems analyst draws data flow diagrams (DFDs). Data flow diagrams are structured analysis and design tools that allow the analyst to comprehend the system and subsystems visually as a set of interrelated data flows.

Graphical representations of data movement storage and transformation are drawn with the use of four symbols: a rounded rectangle to depict data processing or transformations, a double square to show an outside data entity (source or receiver of data), an arrow to depict data flow, and an open-ended rectangle to show a data store.

The systems analyst extracts data processes, sources, stores, and flows from early organizational narratives or stories told by users or revealed by data and uses a top-down approach to first draw a context-level data flow diagram of the system within the larger picture. Then a level 0 logical data flow diagram is drawn. Processes are shown and data stores are added. Next, the analyst creates a child diagram for each of the processes in Diagram 0. Inputs and outputs remain constant, but the data stores and sources change. Exploding the original data flow diagram allows the systems analyst to focus on ever more detailed depictions of data movement in the system. The analyst then develops a physical data flow

"You take a very interesting approach to the problems we have here at MRE. I've seen you sketching diagrams of our operation almost since the day you walked in the door. I'm actually getting used to seeing you doodling away now. What did you call those? Oh, yes. Context-level diagrams. And flow charts? Oh, no. Data flow diagrams. That's it, isn't it?"

HYPERCASE QUESTIONS

1. Find the data flow diagrams already drawn in MRE. Make a list of those you found and add a column to show where in the organization you found them.
2. Draw a context-level diagram modeling the Training Unit Project Development process, one that is based on case interviews with relevant Training Unit staff. Then draw a level 0 diagram detailing the process.

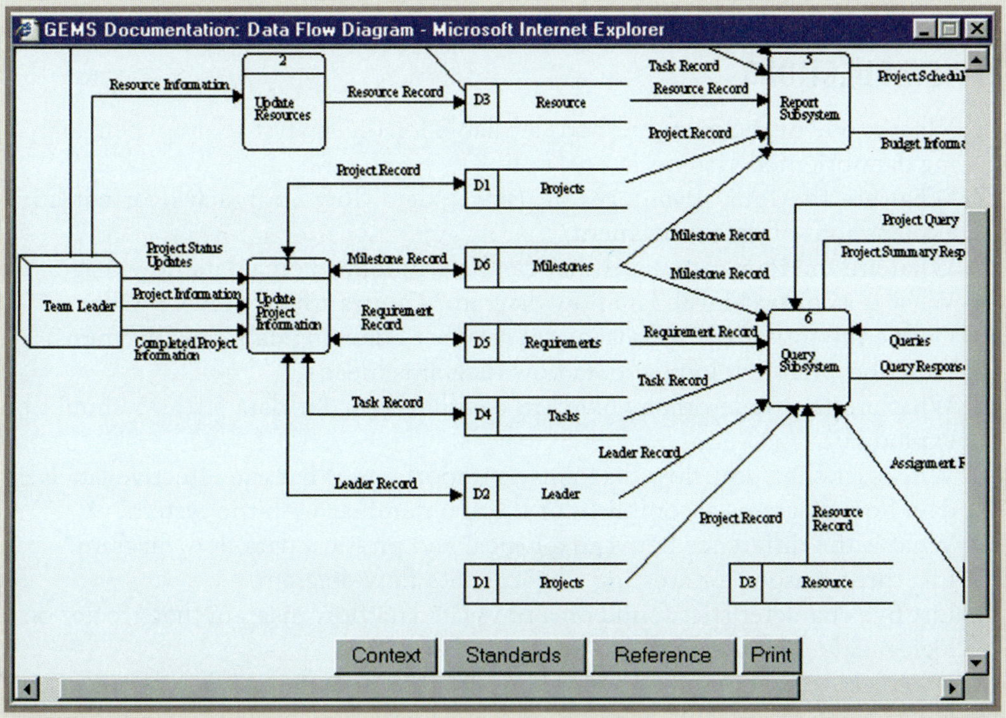

FIGURE 7.HC1
In Hypercase you can click on elements in a data flow diagram.

diagram from the logical data flow diagram, partitioning it to facilitate programming. Each process is analyzed to determine whether it should be a manual or automated procedure.

Six considerations for partitioning data flow diagrams include whether processes are performed by different user groups, processes execute at the same times, processes perform similar tasks, batch processes can be combined for efficient processing, processes may be combined into one program for consistency of data, or processes may be partitioned into different programs for security reasons.

KEYWORDS AND PHRASES

- Ajax
- base element
- child diagram
- context-level data flow diagram
- data flow diagram
- data flow diagram fragment
- data-oriented system
- data store
- derived elements
- event modeling
- event response table
- event trigger
- exploding
- external entity (source or destination)
- functionally primitive
- interface data flow
- level 0 diagram
- logical model
- online process
- parent process
- partitioning
- physical data store
- physical model
- primitive process
- top-down approach
- transaction data store
- transforming process
- unified modeling language (UML)
- use case
- vertical balancing

REVIEW QUESTIONS

1. What is one of the main methods available for the analyst to use when analyzing data-oriented systems?
2. What are the four advantages of using a data flow approach over narrative explanations of data movement?
3. What are the four data items that can be symbolized on a data flow diagram?
4. What is a context-level data flow diagram? Contrast it to a level 0 DFD.
5. Define the top-down approach as it relates to drawing data flow diagrams.
6. Describe what "exploding" data flow diagrams means.
7. What are the trade-offs involved in deciding how far data streams should be exploded?
8. Why is labeling data flow diagrams so important? What can effective labels on data flow diagrams accomplish for those unfamiliar with the system?
9. What is the difference between a logical and physical data flow diagram?
10. List three reasons for creating a logical data flow diagram.
11. List five characteristics found on a physical data flow diagram that are not on a logical data flow diagram.
12. When are transaction files required in the system design?
13. How can an event table be used to create a data flow diagram?
14. List the major sections of a use case.
15. How can a use case be used to create a data flow diagram?
16. What is partitioning, and how is it used?
17. How can an analyst determine when a user interface is required?
18. List three ways of determining partitioning in a data flow diagram.
19. List three ways to use completed data flow diagrams.

PROBLEMS

1. Up to this point you seem to have had excellent rapport with Kevin Cahoon, the owner of a musical instrument manufacturing company. When you showed him a set of data flow diagrams you drew, he wasn't able to see how the system you were proposing was described in the diagrams.
   a. In a paragraph, write down in general terms how to explain a data flow diagram to a user. Be sure to include a list of symbols and what they mean.

b. It takes some effort to educate users about data flow diagrams. Is it worthwhile to share them with users? Why or why not? Defend your response in a paragraph.
c. Compare data flow diagrams to use cases and use case scenarios. What do data flow diagrams show that use case diagrams have a difficult time trying to explain?

2. Your latest project is to combine two systems used by Producers Financial. Angie Schworer's loan application system is fairly new, but has no documentation. Scott Wittman's loan management system is older, needs much revision, and the records are coded and kept independently of the other system. The loan application system accepts applications, processes them, and recommends loans for approval. The loan management system takes loans that have been approved and follows them through their final disposition (paid, sold, or defaulted). Draw a context diagram and a level 1data flow diagram that shows what an idealized combined system would look like.
3. One common experience that students in every college and university share is enrolling in a college course.
   a. Draw a level 1 data flow diagram of data movement for enrollment in a college course. Use a single sheet and label each data item clearly.
   b. Explode one of the processes in your original data flow diagram into subprocesses, adding data flows and data stores.
   c. List the parts of the enrollment process that are "hidden" to the outside observer and about which you have had to make assumptions to complete a second-level diagram.
4. Figure 7.EX1 is a level 1 data flow diagram of data movement in a Niagara Falls tour agency called Marilyn's Tours. Read it over, checking for any inaccuracies.
   a. List and number the errors that you have found in the diagram.
   b. Redraw and label the data flow diagram of Marilyn's so that it is correct. Be sure that your new diagram employs symbols properly so as to cut down on repetitions and duplications where possible.

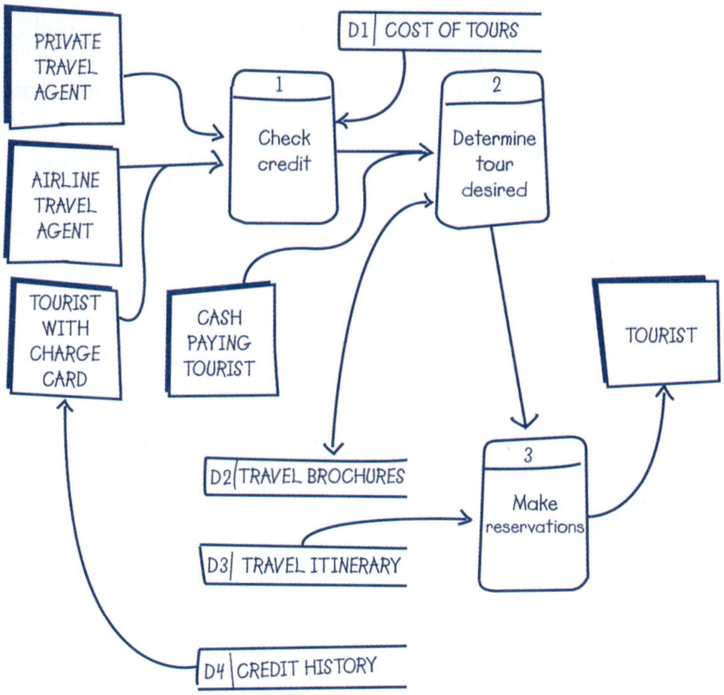

FIGURE 7.EX1
A hand-sketched data flow diagram for Marilyn's Tours.

5. Perfect Pizza wants to install a system to record orders for pizza and chicken wings. When regular customers call Perfect Pizza on the phone, they are asked their phone number. When the number is typed into a computer, the name, address, and last order date is automatically brought up on the screen. Once the order is taken, the total, including tax and delivery, is calculated. Then the order is given to the cook. A receipt is printed. Occasionally, special offers (coupons) are printed so the customer can get a discount. Drivers who make deliveries give customers a copy of the receipt and a coupon (if any). Weekly totals are kept for comparison with last year's performance. Write a summary of business activities for taking an order at Perfect Pizza.
6. Draw a context-level data flow diagram for Perfect Pizza (Problem 5).
7. Explode the context-level diagram in Problem 6 showing all the major processes. Call this Diagram 0. It should be a logical data flow diagram.
8. Draw a logical child diagram for Diagram 0 in Problem 7 for the process that adds a new customer if he or she is not currently in the database (has never ordered from Perfect Pizza before).
9. Draw a physical data flow diagram for Problem 7.
10. Draw a physical data flow diagram for Problem 8.
11. Partition the physical data flow diagram in Problem 7, grouping and separating processes as you deem appropriate. Explain why you partitioned the data flow diagram in this manner. (Remember that you do not have to partition the entire diagram, only the parts that make sense to partition.)
12. a. Draw a logical child diagram for process 6 in Figure 7.24.
    b. Draw a physical child diagram for process 6 in Figure 7.24.
13. Draw a physical data flow diagram for process 1.1 in Figure 7.25.
14. Create a context diagram for a real estate agent trying to create a system that matches buyers with potential houses.
15. Draw a logical data flow diagram showing general processes for Problem 14. Call it Diagram 0.
16. Create a context-level diagram for billing in a dental office. External entities include the patients and insurance companies.
17. Draw a logical data flow diagram showing general processes for Problem 16. Call it Diagram 0.
18. Create a use case for the list of six activities for the FilmMagic video rental system. Refer to Figure 7.17.
19. Create an event response table for the six activities of the FilmMagic video rental system.
20. Create an event response table for the activities listed for World's Trend order processing system.
21. Create a use case for the list of seven processes for the World's Trend order processing system.
22. Create a CRUD matrix for FilmMagic.
23. Create a CRUD matrix for the files of World's Trend.
24. Use the principles of partitioning to determine which of the processes in Problem 19 should be included in separate programs.
25. Create a physical data flow child diagram for the following situation: The local PC Users Group holds meetings once a month with informative speakers, door prizes, and sessions for special interest groups. A laptop computer is taken to the meetings, and is used to add the names of new members to the group. The diagram represents an online process and is the child of process 1, ADD NEW MEMBERS. The following tasks are included:
    a. Key the new member information.
    b. Validate the information. Errors are displayed on the screen.

c. When all the information is valid, a confirmation screen is displayed. The operator visually confirms that the data are correct and either accepts the transaction or cancels it.
d. Accepted transactions add new members to the MEMBERSHIP MASTER file, which is stored on the laptop hard drive.
e. Accepted transactions are written to a MEMBERSHIP JOURNAL file, which is stored on a disk.

GROUP PROJECTS

1. Meet with your group to develop a context-level data flow diagram for Maverick Transport (first introduced in Chapter 4). Use any data you have subsequently generated with your group about Maverick Transport. (*Hint:* Concentrate on one of the company's functional areas rather than try to model the entire organization.)
2. Using the context-level diagram developed in Problem 1, develop with your group a level 0 logical data flow diagram for Maverick Transport. Make any assumptions necessary to draw it. List them.
3. With your group, choose one key process and explode it into a logical child diagram. Make any assumptions necessary to draw it. List follow-up questions and suggest other methods to get more information about processes that are still unclear to you.
4. Use the work your group has done to date to create a physical data flow diagram of a portion of the new system you are proposing for Maverick Transport.

SELECTED BIBLIOGRAPHY

Ambler, S. W. am L. L. Constantine (eds). *The Unified Process Inception Phase: Best Practices for Implementing the UP.* Lawrence, KS: CMP Books, 2000.

Gane, C., and T. Sarson. *Structured Systems Analysis and Design Tools and Techniques.* Englewood Cliffs, NJ: Prentice Hall, 1979.

Kotonya, G., and I. Sommerville. *Requirements Engineering: Processes and Techniques.* New York: John Wiley & Sons, 1999.

Lucas, H. *Information Systems Concepts for Management,* 3d ed. New York: McGraw-Hill, 1986.

Martin, J. *Strategic Data-Planning Methodologies.* Englewood Cliffs, NJ: Prentice Hall, 1982.

McFadden, F. R., and J. A. Hoffer. *Data Base Management.* Menlo Park, CA: Benjamin/Cummings, 1985.

Thayer, R. H., M. Dorfman, and D. Garr. *Software Engineering: Vol. 1: The Development Process,* 2nd ed. New York: Wiley-IEEE Computer Society Press, 2002.

7

ALLEN SCHMIDT, JULIE E. KENDALL, AND KENNETH E. KENDALL

CPU

JUST FLOWING ALONG

After the results of interviews, questionnaires, and prototyping are gathered and analyzed, Anna and Chip move to the next step, modeling the system. Their strategy is to create a layered set of data flow diagrams and then describe the components.

Modeling starts with analyzing the context-level diagram of the current computer inventory system. This diagram is simple to create and is the foundation for successive levels because it describes the external entities and the major data flow.

"Shall we create a physical data flow diagram of the current system?" asks Chip.

Anna replies, "No, it's fairly simple to understand, and we wouldn't gain any significant new knowledge of how the system operates. Let's start by creating a logical model of the current system."

The logical data flow diagrams are completed in a few days. Anna and Chip hold an afternoon meeting to review the diagrams and give each other feedback. "These look good," remarks Chip. "We can clearly see the business events that comprise the current system."

Anna replies, "Yes, let's take the current logical data flow diagrams and add all the requirements and desired features of the new system. We can also eliminate any of the unnecessary features that wouldn't be implemented in the new system."

Anna takes the context-level diagram (shown in Chapter 2) and adds many of the reports, inquiries, and other information included in the new system. The finished context-level diagram is shown in Figure E7.1. Notice the many new data flows. The maintenance department will receive reports that currently are not available. One report, for example, helps to automate the installation of new computers, the INSTALLATION LISTING, and another report intended for management shows which software is located on which machines, the SOFTWARE CROSS-REFERENCE REPORT.

Chip reviews the finished diagram, commenting, "This is more art than science. It looks like all the requirements of the new system are included. But it is far more complex than I originally thought it would be."

Anna replies, "Let's expand this to Diagram 0 for the new system. This will be a logical data flow diagram because we want to focus on the business needs. Perhaps it would be best if we work in a team for this diagram."

After working for several hours that afternoon and a good portion of the next morning, they complete the diagram. It is reviewed and modified with some minor changes. The finished Diagram 0 is shown in Figure E7.2 and Figure E7.3. Because it is a logical diagram, it shows no keying or validation operations, nor does it show any temporary data stores or transaction files. Timing is not a consideration (an example is the ADD NEW COMPUTER process, in which it appears that orders are updated and reports produced simultaneously).

"This finally looks right," muses Chip. "All the major processes, data flows, and data stores are accounted for. And the overall diagram doesn't look too complicated."

"Putting all of the inquiries into one subsystem and all the reports into another helped. Remember how complex the original diagram was?" asks Anna.

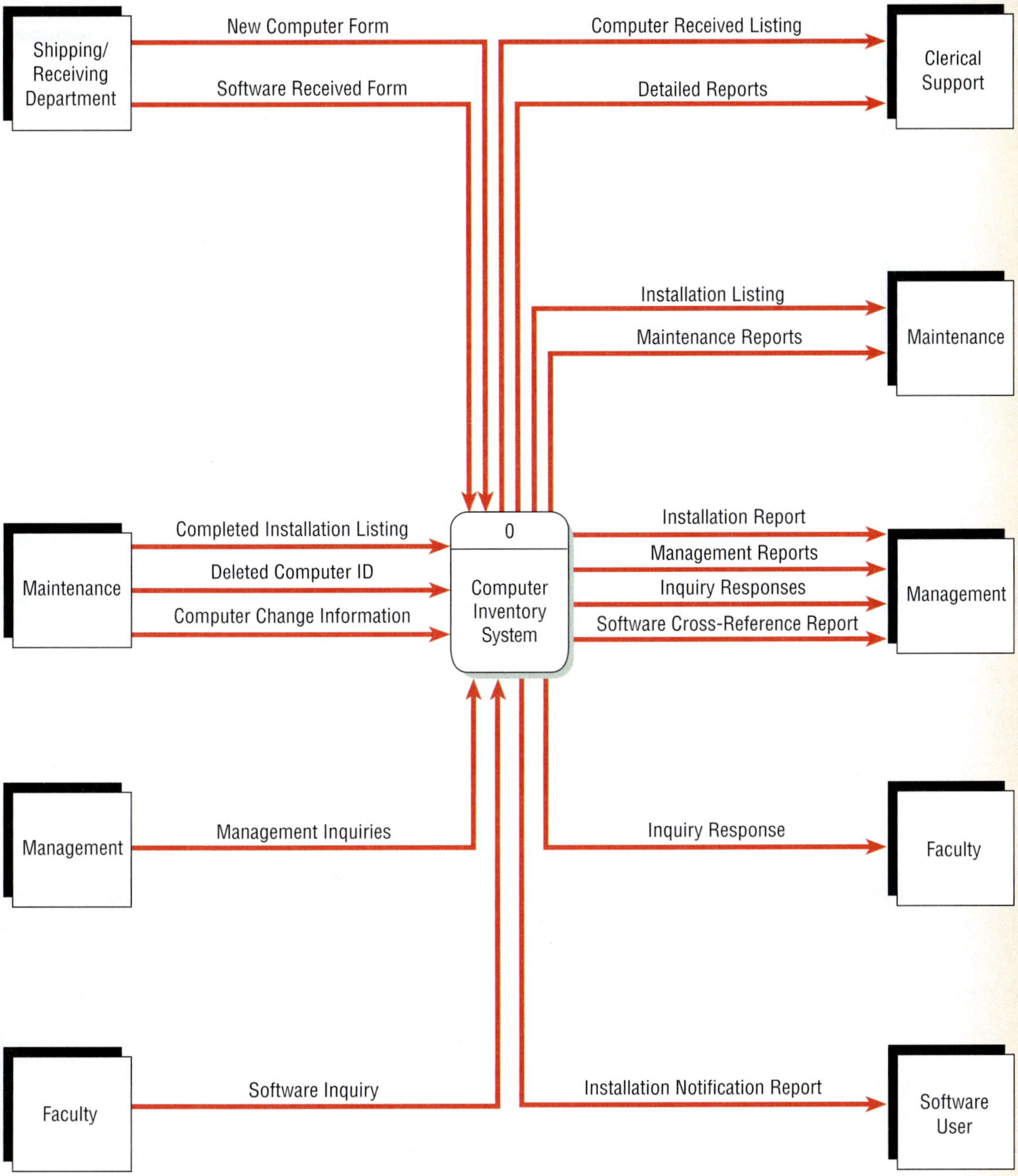

FIGURE E7.1
Context-level data flow diagram, Proposed System.

"I sure do," Chip replies. "I started to think we were tackling too much at once with this system. At least it's more manageable now. Now that this is finished, what's the next step?"

"We need to decide how to implement the data flow diagram into a series of steps, which are shown on the physical data flow diagram," Anna says. "This logical data flow

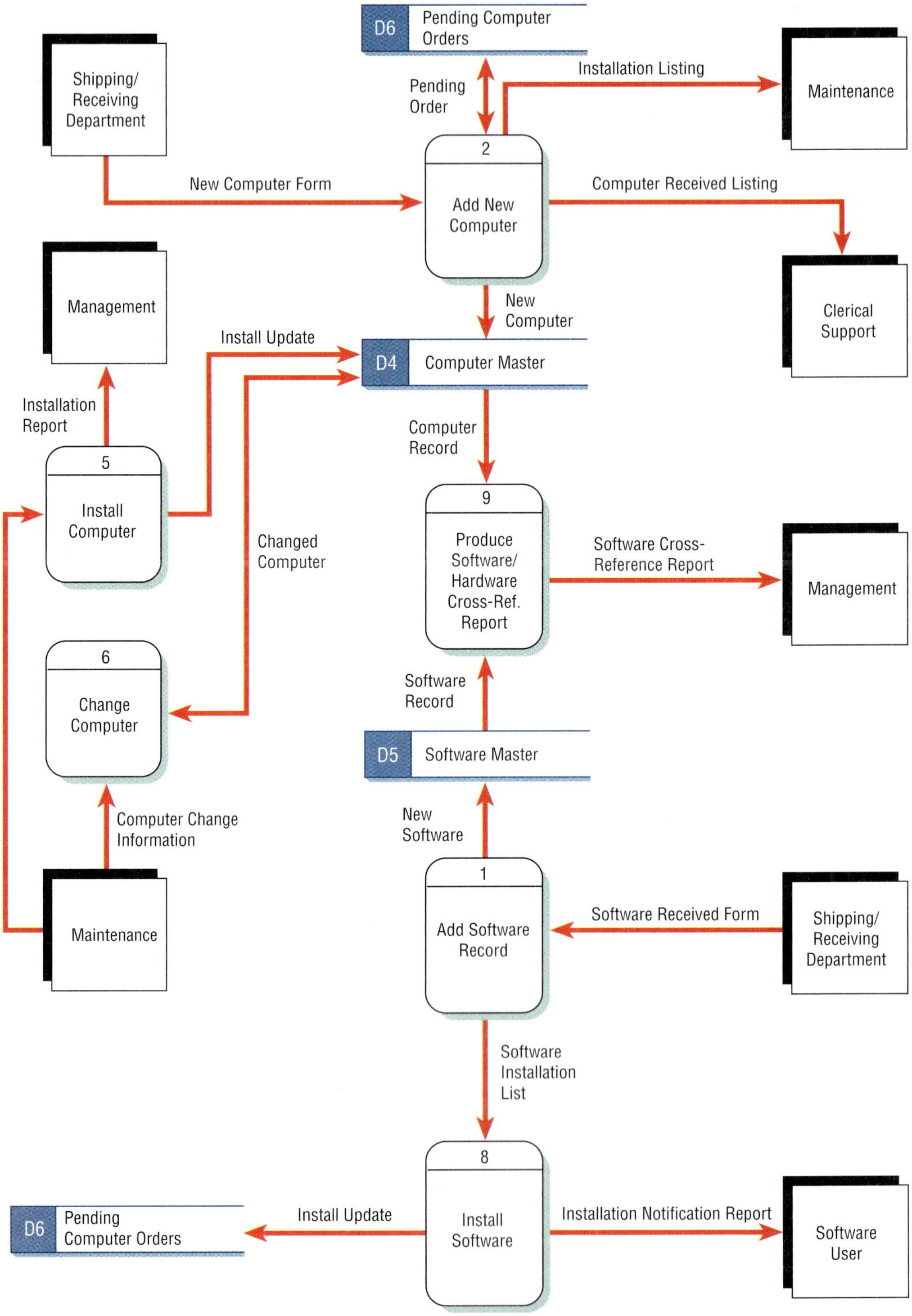

FIGURE E7.2
Diagram 0: Proposed Computer Inventory System (part 1).

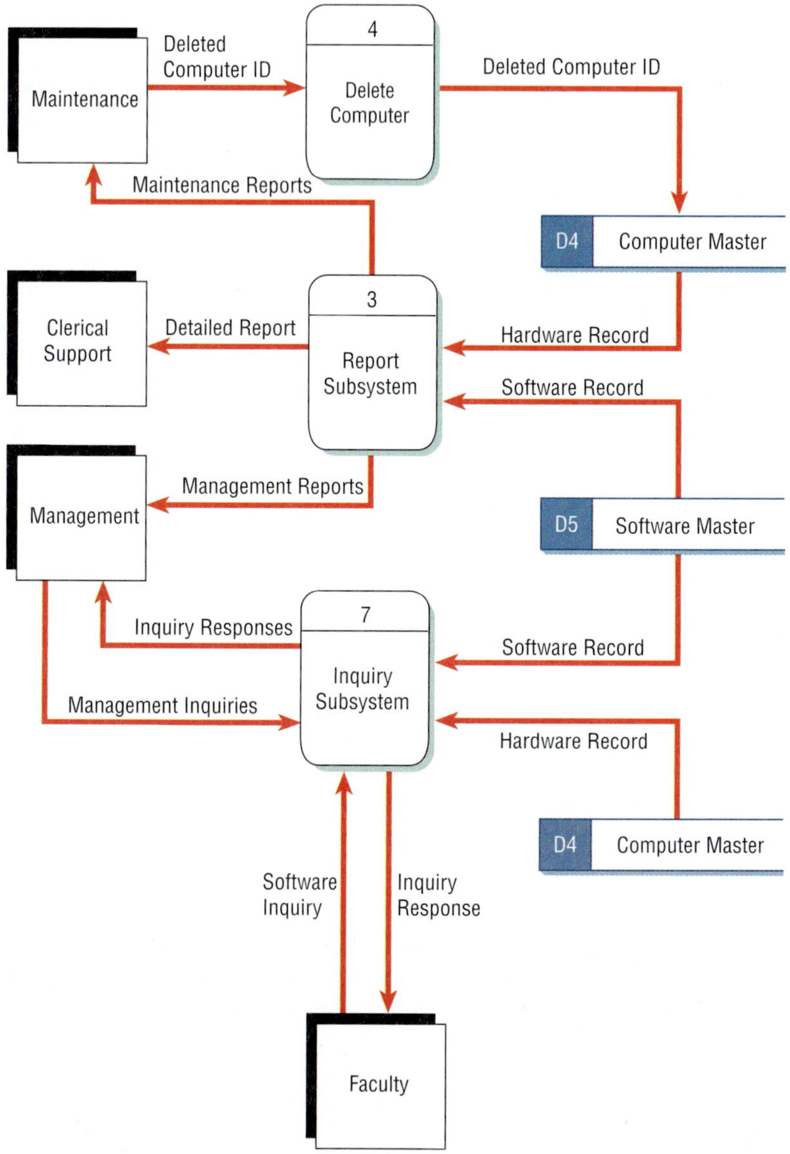

FIGURE E7.3
Diagram 0: Proposed Computer Inventory System (part 2).

diagram shows the business tasks, or *what* should be accomplished. Now we need to show *how* the system will work. Keying, validation, visually confirming the data, and transaction files need to be added."

Chip and Anna divide up the work by major tasks to be accomplished. Chip starts working on the ADD COMPUTER process.

When Chip draws the diagrams, he sees that he is drawing a level 0 diagram and then exploding it into many level 1 diagrams. Just as a parent may have many children, there may be many level 1 diagrams for a specific level 0 diagram. For this reason some analysts refer to them as parent and child diagrams.

Chip and Anna decide to abbreviate the level 0 diagram as Diagram 0. The details are shown on a child diagram, Diagram 2. The external entities do not appear on the diagram, because they are only shown on the context-level diagram and Diagram 0, the context-level diagram explosion.

"I've been working on Diagram 1, an explosion of process 1, ADD SOFTWARE RECORD. Perhaps you would like to review the finished result," remarks Anna.

"Sure," replies Chip. "I'll check it for omissions and errors."

Diagram 1 is shown in Figure E7.4. NEW SOFTWARE INFORMATION is keyed and edited. Errors are reported on the screen and corrected by the operator. After all errors have been corrected, the operator has a chance to visually confirm the data. If correct, the operator clicks a button to accept the data; otherwise the transaction may be canceled or corrected.

Confirmed data are added to the SOFTWARE MASTER file and used to create a SOFTWARE LOG RECORD. This record contains all the keyed information, as well as the date, time, and user ID of the person entering the transaction. In the ADD SOFTWARE diagram, this record is used to create the SOFTWARE INSTALLATION LIST, as well as to provide a backup of all new transactions and an audit trail of entries.

When a specified data flow diagram is analyzed, the resultant report may reveal that any of the following data flow diagram syntax errors exist in that DFD:

1. The data flow diagram must have at least one process, and must not have any free-standing objects or objects connected to themselves.
2. A process must receive at least one data flow and create at least one data flow. Processes with all inputs or all outputs should not occur.
3. A data store should be connected to at least one process.
4. External entities should not be connected to each other. Although they communicate independently, that communication is not part of the system being designed.

Visible Analyst does not show the following errors or check the standards set by Chip and Anna for the project:

1. Data flow names into and out of a process should be different (with exceptions).
2. Linear flow (several processes with only one input and output) is rarely found. Except in very low-level processes, it is a warning sign that some of the processes may be missing input or output flows.
3. External entities should not be connected directly to data stores. For example, you would not let an employee rummage through the EMPLOYEE MASTER file!
4. Process names should contain a verb describing the work being performed (with exceptions, such as INQUIRY SUBSYSTEM). Data flow names should be nouns.

Chip and Anna both use Visible Analyst to verify that the data flow diagram syntax is correct. The analysis report is shown in Figure E7.5. Notice that a descriptive error message is given for each error, with the diagram object that relates to the problem

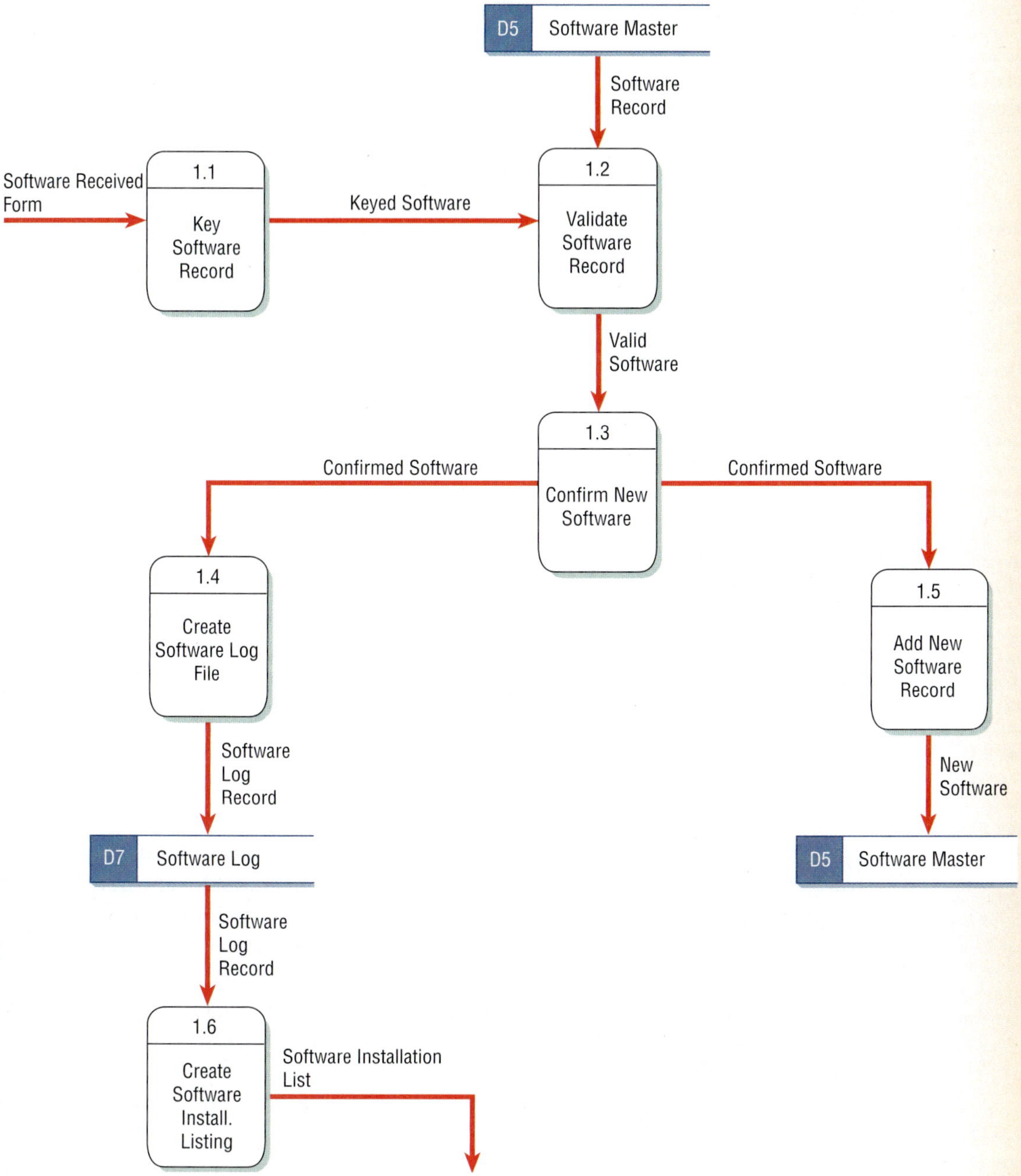

FIGURE E7.4
Diagram 1: Proposed Computer System.

indicated with quotation marks. This error report was generated because of the syntactical errors in the data flow diagram shown in Figure E7.6.

Visible Analyst will also check that the levels balance among data flow diagram processes and the child diagrams. Inputs and outputs that do not match are shown.

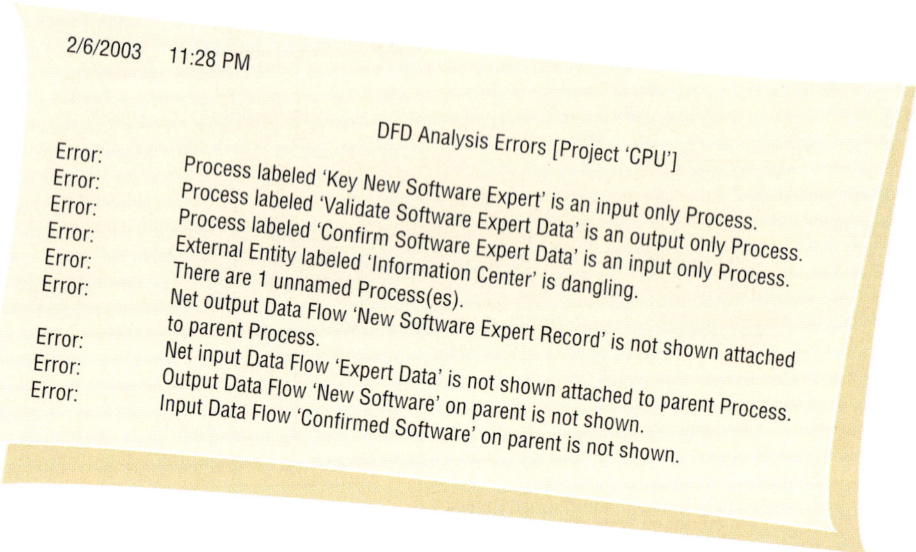

2/6/2003 11:28 PM

DFD Analysis Errors [Project 'CPU']

Error: Process labeled 'Key New Software Expert' is an input only Process.
Error: Process labeled 'Validate Software Expert Data' is an output only Process.
Error: Process labeled 'Confirm Software Expert Data' is an input only Process.
Error: External Entity labeled 'Information Center' is dangling.
Error: There are 1 unnamed Process(es).
Error: Net output Data Flow 'New Software Expert Record' is not shown attached to parent Process.
Error: Net input Data Flow 'Expert Data' is not shown attached to parent Process.
Error: Output Data Flow 'New Software' on parent is not shown.
Error: Input Data Flow 'Confirmed Software' on parent is not shown.

FIGURE E7.5
Data flow diagram error report.

EXERCISES

E-1. Use Visible Analyst to view the context-level diagram for the proposed computer system. Experiment with the **Zoom** controls on the lower toolbar to change from a global to a detailed view of the diagram. Double click on the central process to examine the repository entry for it. Click **Exit** to return to the diagram. Right click on the central process to display the object menu for the central process. Use the **Explode** option to display Diagram 0, representing the details of the central process. Maximize the window and double click on some of the data stores and data flows to examine their repository entries. Click **Exit** to return to the diagram. Zoom to 100 percent and scroll around the screen to view different regions of the diagram; then print the diagram using a landscape orientation. Click FILE, NEST, and PARENT to return to the context-level diagram. Maximize the window.

E-2. Modify Diagram 0 of the proposed computer system. Add process 10, UPDATE SOFTWARE RECORD. You will have to move the MANAGEMENT external entity lower in the diagram; place it to the left of process 7, INQUIRY SUBSYSTEM. Create a repository entry for the process and then click **Exit** to return to the diagram. Print the diagram using a landscape orientation.

Input:	1.	SOFTWARE CHANGE DATA, from CLERICAL SUPPORT
	2.	SOFTWARE DELETE ID, from MANAGEMENT
Output:	1.	SOFTWARE RECORD, an update from the SOFTWARE MASTER data store

The exercises preceded by a Web icon indicate value-added material is available from the Web site at www.prenhall.com/kendall. Students can download a sample Visible Analyst Project and a Microsoft Access database that can be used to complete the exercises. Visible Analyst software can be packaged with this text for an additional fee.

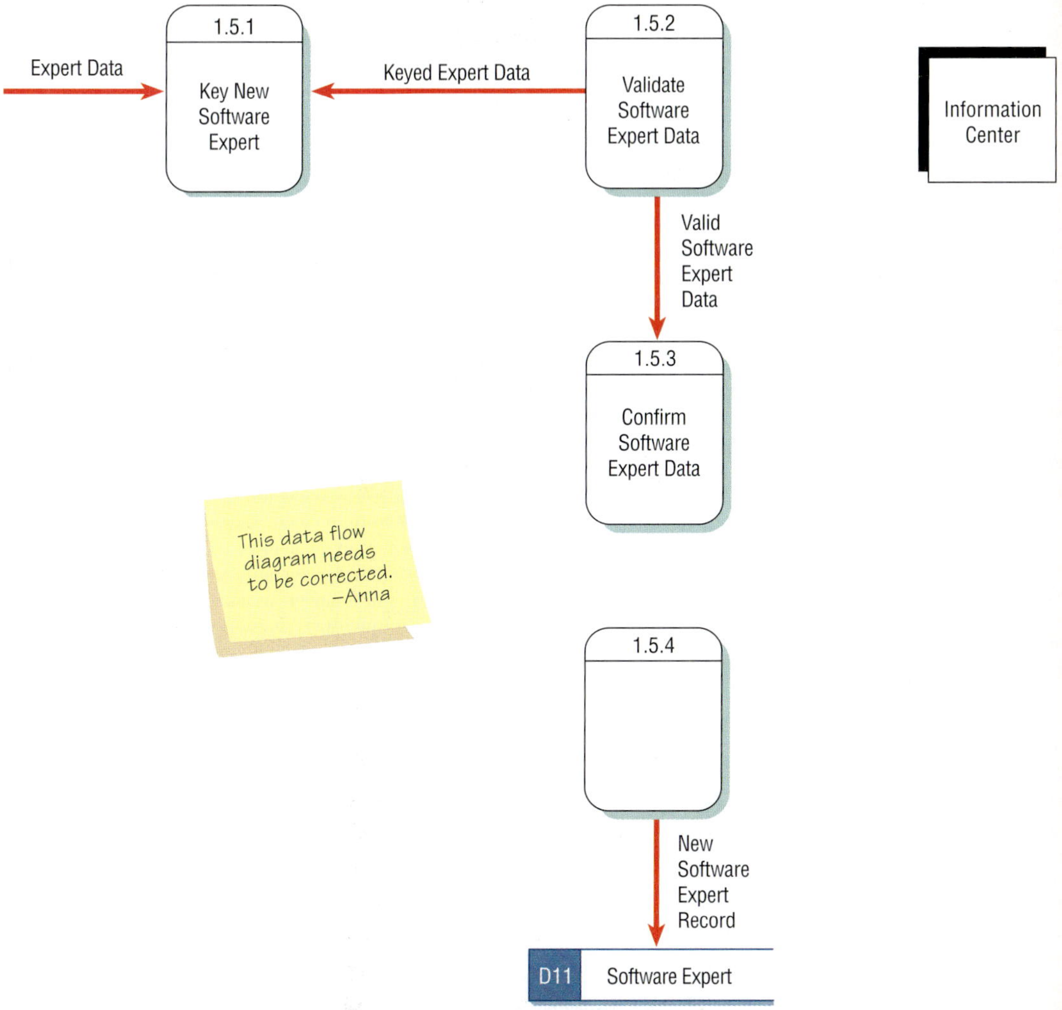

FIGURE E7.6
Data flow diagram with errors.

E-3. Explode to Diagram 10, UPDATE SOFTWARE RECORD. Maximize the window and create the diagram illustrated in Figure E7.7. Connect to the SOFTWARE MASTER using a double-headed arrow. (*Hint:* Right click on the data flow, select **Change Item,** then select **Change Type,** and **Terminator Type, Double Filled.**) Print the final diagram.

E-4. Modify Diagram 8, INSTALL SOFTWARE. Add the following processes, describing each in the repository. Zoom to 100 percent and scroll around the screen, checking your diagram for a professional appearance. Print the final result.

Process:		8.2 INSTALL COMPUTER SOFTWARE
Description:		Manual process, place software on machine
Input:	1.	COMPUTER LOCATION, from process 8.1
	2.	SOFTWARE TITLE AND VERSION, from process 8.1
Output:	1.	INSTALLED SOFTWARE FORM

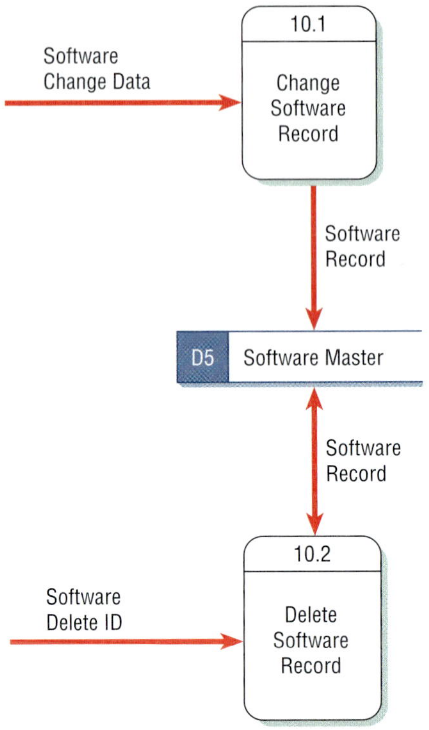

FIGURE E7.7
Data flow diagram, UPDATE SOFTWARE RECORD.

Process:		8.3 CREATE INSTALLED SOFTWARE TRANSACTION
Description:		Batch data entry process for creating installed software transactions, including validation
Input:	1.	INSTALLED SOFTWARE FORM
Output:	1.	INSTALLED SOFTWARE TRANSACTION, to INSTALLED SOFTWARE data store
Process:		8.4 UPDATE SOFTWARE MASTER
Description:		Random update of the SOFTWARE MASTER data store with update information
Input:	1.	INSTALLED SOFTWARE TRANSACTION
Output:	1.	SOFTWARE MASTER, update
Process:		8.5 PRODUCE INSTALLATION NOTIFICATION
Description:		Produce an installation notification informing users onto which machines the software has been installed
Input:	1.	INSTALLED SOFTWARE TRANSACTION
	2.	SOFTWARE MASTER, from the SOFTWARE MASTER data store
	3.	HARDWARE MASTER, from the COMPUTER MASTER data store

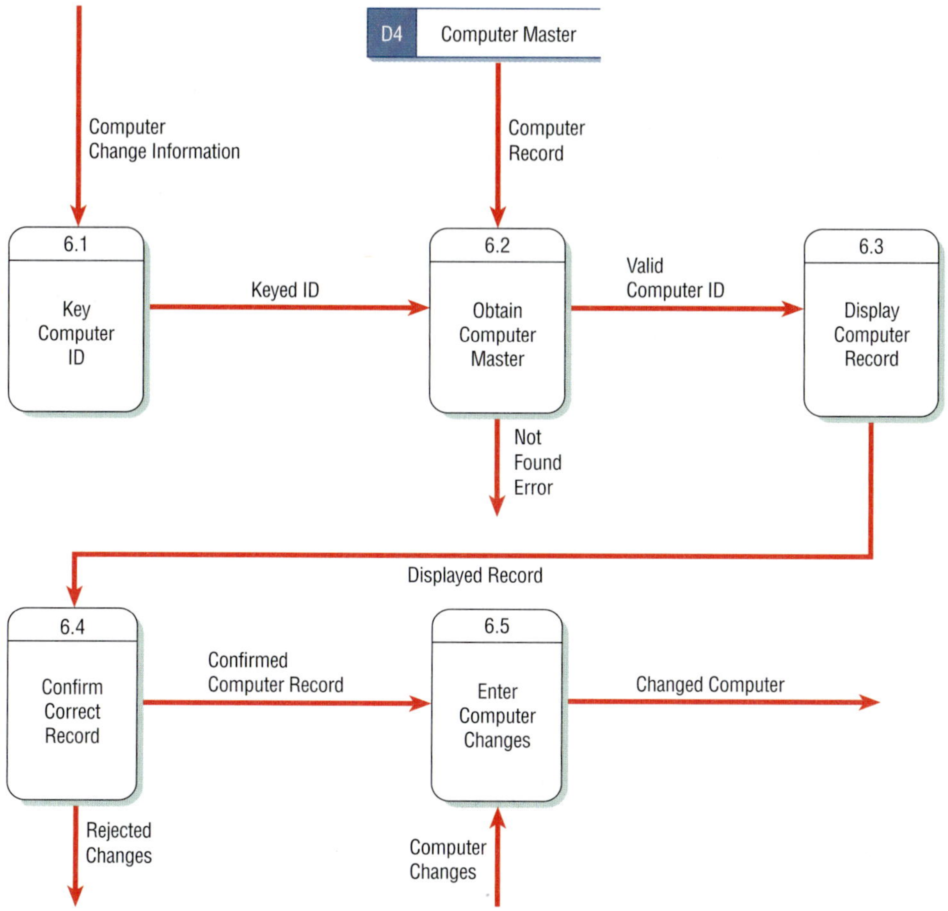

FIGURE E7.8
Data flow diagram, CHANGE COMPUTER RECORD.

Output: 1. INSTALLATION NOTIFICATION LISTING, an interface flow

E-5. Modify Diagram 6, CHANGE COMPUTER RECORD, which is shown in Figure E7.8. This is an interactive, online program to change computer information. Add the following three processes. Create repository entries for each of the processes, as well as the data flow. When completed, zoom to 100 percent and change any data flow arrows that are not straight, and move data flow labels for a professional-looking graph. Print the diagram using landscape orientation.

a. Process 6.6, VALIDATE CHANGES. This process edits each change field for validity. The input is the KEYED CHANGES. The output fields are CHANGE ERRORS (interface flow) and VALID CHANGES (to process 6.7).

b. Process 6.7, CONFIRM CHANGES. This process is a visual confirmation of the changes. The operator has a chance to reject the changes or accept them. Input is the VALID CHANGES. The output fields are REJECTED CHANGES (interface flow) and CONFIRMED CHANGES (to process 6.8).

c. Process 6.8, REWRITE COMPUTER MASTER. This process rewrites the COMPUTER MASTER record with the changes on the record. Input is the CONFIRMED CHANGES. Output flow is the COMPUTER MASTER record, to the COMPUTER MASTER data store.

E-6. Create the explosion data flow diagram for process 4, DELETE COMPUTER. The following table summarizes input, process, and output. Describe each process and data flow in the repository. When completed, zoom to 100 percent, move any data flow lines that are not aligned correctly, move the data flow labels for a professional-looking graph, and print the diagram.

Process:		4.1 KEY DELETE ID
Description:		The computer ID is keyed interactively
Input:	1.	DELETED COMPUTER ID
Output:	1.	KEYED DELETE
Process:		4.2 OBTAIN COMPUTER RECORD
Description:		COMPUTER MASTER record is read to ensure that it exists
Input:	1.	KEYED DELETE (interface)
	2.	COMPUTER RECORD, from the COMPUTER MASTER data store
Output:	1.	NOT FOUND ERROR (interface)
	2.	VALID COMPUTER RECORD
Process:		4.3 CONFIRM COMPUTER DELETION
Description:		The computer information is displayed on the screen for operator confirmation or rejection
Input:	1.	VALID COMPUTER RECORD
Output:	1.	REJECTED DELETION (interface)
	2.	CONFIRMED DELETION
Process:		4.4 DELETE COMPUTER RECORD
Description:		The computer record is *logically* (not physically) deleted from the COMPUTER MASTER data store by rewriting the record with an I for inactive in the Record Code field
Input:	1.	CONFIRMED DELETION
Output:	1.	DELETED COMPUTER, a double-headed arrow to the COMPUTER MASTER data store

E-7. Run the data flow diagram analysis feature (select **Diagram Analyze** and select **Current Diagram**). Print the report for each of the data flow diagrams described in previous problems. Examine the diagrams and note the problems detected.

ANALYZING SYSTEMS USING DATA DICTIONARIES

8

Learning Objectives

Once you have mastered the material in this chapter you will be able to:

1. **Understand how analysts use data dictionaries for analyzing data-oriented systems.**
2. **Create data dictionary entries for data processes, stores, flows, structures, and logical and physical elements of the systems being studied, based on DFDs.**
3. **Understand the concept of a repository for analysts' project information and the role of CASE tools in creating them.**
4. **Recognize the functions of data dictionaries in helping users update and maintain information systems.**

After successive levels of data flow diagrams are complete, systems analysts use them to help catalog the data processes, flows, stores, structures, and elements in a data dictionary. Of particular importance are the names used to characterize data items. When given an opportunity to name components of data-oriented systems, the systems analyst needs to work at making the name meaningful but exclusive of other existing data component names. This chapter covers the data dictionary, which is another method to aid in the analysis of data-oriented systems.

THE DATA DICTIONARY

The data dictionary is a specialized application of the kinds of dictionaries used as references in everyday life. The data dictionary is a reference work of data about data (that is, *metadata*), one that is compiled by systems analysts to guide them through analysis and design. As a document, the data dictionary collects and coordinates specific data terms, and it confirms what each term means to different people in the organization. The data flow diagrams covered in Chapter 7 are an excellent starting point for collecting data dictionary entries.

One important reason for maintaining a data dictionary is to keep clean data. This means that data must be consistent. If you store data about a man's sex as "M" in one record, "Male" in a second record, and as the number "1" in a third record, the data are not clean. Keeping a data dictionary will help in this regard.

Automated data dictionaries (part of the CASE tools mentioned earlier) are valuable for their capacity to cross-reference data items, thereby allowing necessary program changes to all programs sharing a common element. This feature supplants changing programs on a haphazard basis, or it prevents waiting until the program won't run because a change has not been implemented across all programs sharing the updated item. Clearly, automated data dictionaries become important for large systems that produce several thousand data elements requiring cataloging and cross-referencing.

NEED FOR UNDERSTANDING THE DATA DICTIONARY

Many database management systems now come equipped with an automated data dictionary. These dictionaries can be either elaborate or simple. Some computerized data dictionaries automatically catalog data items when programming is done; others simply provide a template to prompt the person filling in the dictionary to do so in a uniform manner for every entry.

Despite the existence of automated data dictionaries, understanding what data compose a data dictionary, the conventions used in data dictionaries, and how a data dictionary is developed, are issues that remain pertinent for the systems analyst during the systems effort. Understanding the process of compiling a data dictionary can aid the systems analyst in conceptualizing the system and how it works. The upcoming sections allow the systems analyst to see the rationale behind what exists in automated data dictionaries.

In addition to providing documentation and eliminating redundancy, the data dictionary may be used to:

1. Validate the data flow diagram for completeness and accuracy.
2. Provide a starting point for developing screens and reports.
3. Determine the contents of data stored in files.
4. Develop the logic for data flow diagram processes.
5. Create XML (extensible markup language).

THE DATA REPOSITORY

Although the data dictionary contains information about data and procedures, a larger collection of project information is called a repository. The repository concept is one of the many impacts of CASE tools and may contain the following:

1. Information about the data maintained by the system, including data flows, data stores, record structures, elements, entities, and messages.
2. Procedural logic and use cases.
3. Screen and report design.
4. Data relationships, such as how one data structure is linked to another.
5. Project requirements and final system deliverables.
6. Project management information, such as delivery schedules, achievements, issues that need resolving, and project users.

The data dictionary is created by examining and describing the contents of the data flows, data stores, and processes, as illustrated by Figure 8.1. Each data store and data flow should be defined and then expanded to include the details of the elements it contains. The logic of each process should be described using the data flowing into or out of the process. Omissions and other design errors should be noted and resolved.

The four data dictionary categories—data flows, data structures, data elements, and data stores—should be developed to promote understanding of the data of the system. Procedural logic is presented in Chapter 9, entities are discussed in Chapter 13, and messages and use cases are presented in Chapters 2 and 18.

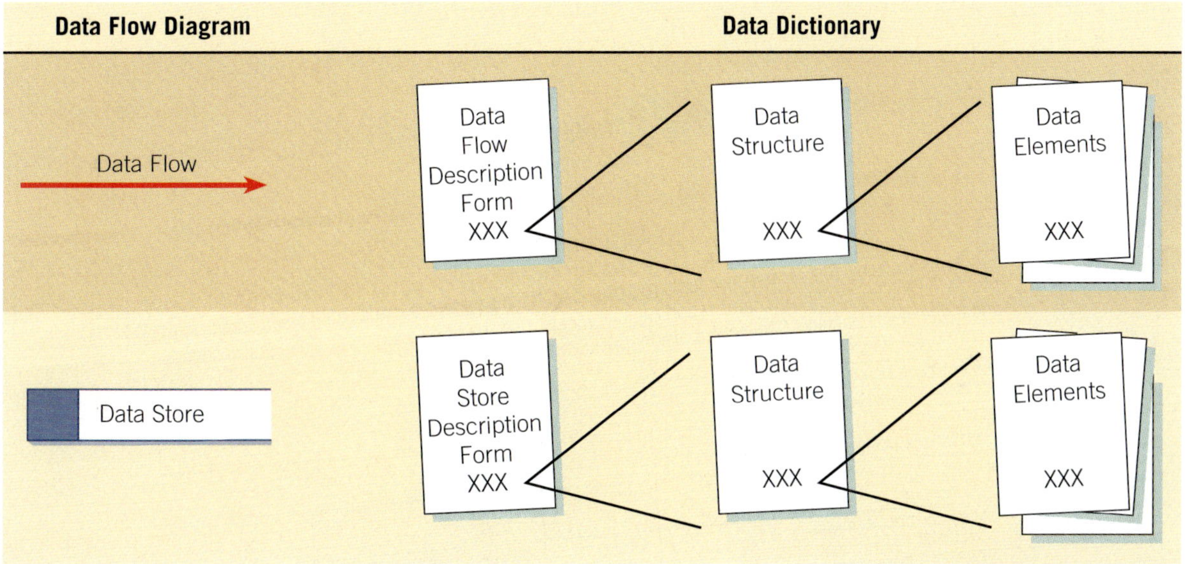

FIGURE 8.1
How data dictionaries relate to data flow diagrams.

To illustrate how data dictionary entries are created, we use an example for World's Trend Catalog Division. This company sells clothing and other items by mail order using a toll-free phone order system (or faxing the mail order form), and via the Internet using customized Web forms. Regardless of the origin of the order, the underlying data captured by the system are the same for all three methods.

The World's Trend order form shown in Figure 8.2 gives some clues about what to enter into a data dictionary. First, you need to capture and store the name, address, and telephone number of the person placing the order. Then you need to address the details of the order: the item description, size, color, price, quantity, and so on. The customer's method of payment must also be determined. Once you have done this, these data may be stored for future use. This example is used throughout this chapter to illustrate each part of the data dictionary.

DEFINING THE DATA FLOWS

Data flows are usually the first components to be defined. System inputs and outputs are determined from interviewing, observing users, and analyzing documents and other existing systems. The information captured for each data flow may be summarized using a form containing the following information:

1. ID, an optional identification number. Sometimes the ID is coded using a scheme to identify the system and the application in the system.
2. A unique descriptive name for this data flow. This name is the text that should appear on the diagram and be referenced in all descriptions using the data flow.
3. A general description of the data flow.
4. The source of the data flow. The source could be an external entity, a process, or a data flow coming from a data store.
5. The destination of the data flow (same items listed under the source).
6. An indication of whether the data flow is a record entering or leaving a file or a record containing a report, form, or screen. If the data flow contains data that are used between processes, it is designated as *internal.*
7. The name of the data structure describing the elements found in this data flow. For a simple data flow, it could be one or several elements.

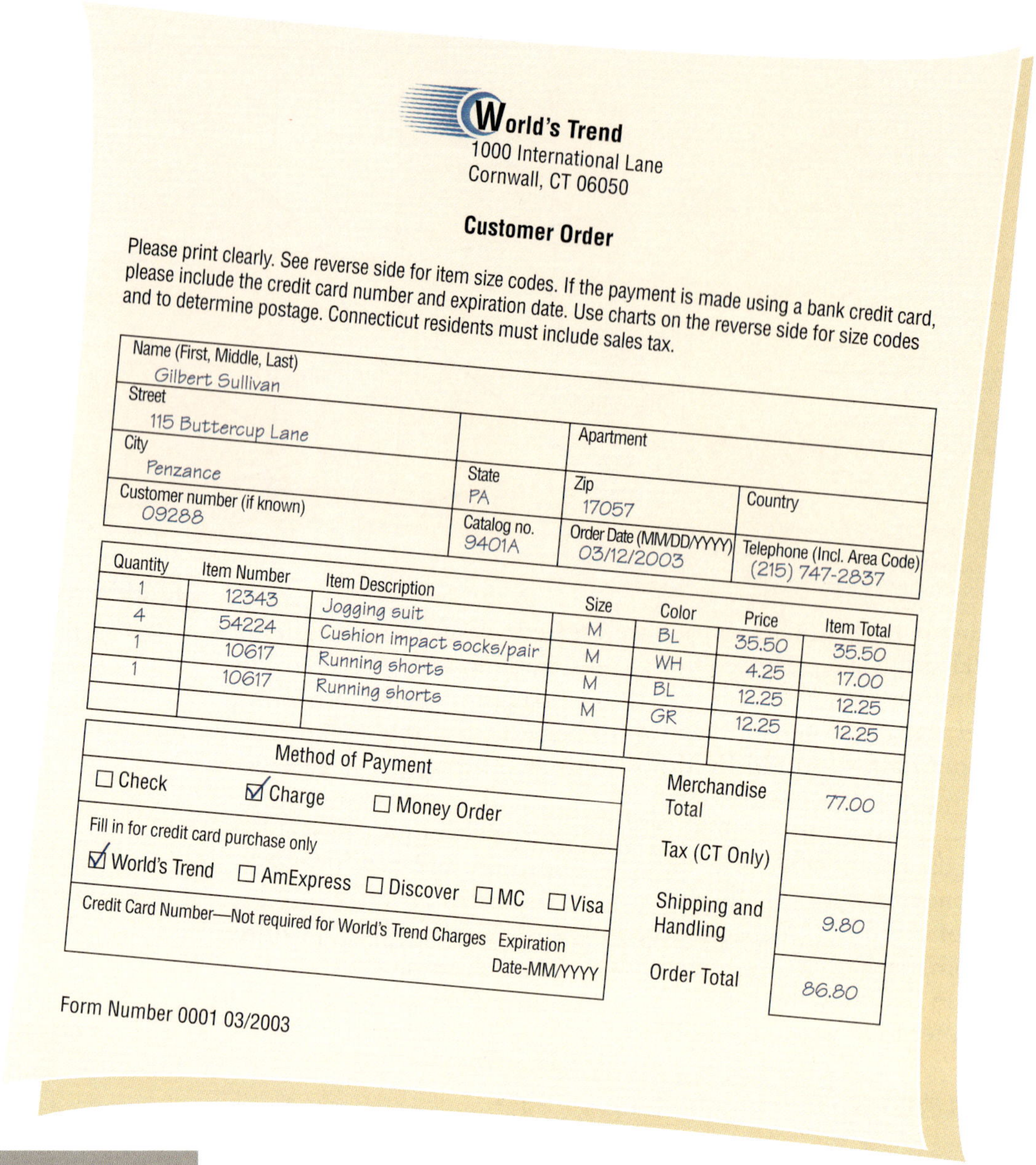

World's Trend
1000 International Lane
Cornwall, CT 06050

Customer Order

Please print clearly. See reverse side for item size codes. If the payment is made using a bank credit card, please include the credit card number and expiration date. Use charts on the reverse side for size codes and to determine postage. Connecticut residents must include sales tax.

Name (First, Middle, Last) Gilbert Sullivan			
Street 115 Buttercup Lane		Apartment	
City Penzance	State PA	Zip 17057	Country
Customer number (if known) 09288	Catalog no. 9401A	Order Date (MM/DD/YYYY) 03/12/2003	Telephone (Incl. Area Code) (215) 747-2837

Quantity	Item Number	Item Description	Size	Color	Price	Item Total
1	12343	Jogging suit	M	BL	35.50	35.50
4	54224	Cushion impact socks/pair	M	WH	4.25	17.00
1	10617	Running shorts	M	BL	12.25	12.25
1	10617	Running shorts	M	GR	12.25	12.25

Method of Payment

☐ Check ☑ Charge ☐ Money Order

Fill in for credit card purchase only

☑ World's Trend ☐ AmExpress ☐ Discover ☐ MC ☐ Visa

Credit Card Number—Not required for World's Trend Charges Expiration Date-MM/YYYY

Merchandise Total	77.00
Tax (CT Only)	
Shipping and Handling	9.80
Order Total	86.80

Form Number 0001 03/2003

FIGURE 8.2
An order form from World's Trend Catalog Division.

8. The volume per unit of time. The data could be records per day or any other unit of time.
9. An area for further comments and notations about the data flow.

Once again we can use our World's Trend Catalog Division example from Chapter 7 to illustrate a completed form. Figure 8.3 is an example of the data flow description representing the screen used to add a new CUSTOMER ORDER and to update the customer and item files. Notice that the external entity CUSTOMER is the source and that PROCESS 1 is the destination, providing linkage back to the data flow diagram. The checked box for "Screen" indicates that the flow represents an input screen. It could be any screen, such as a Web page, graphical user interface (GUI), mobile phone, or perhaps a mainframe screen. The detailed description of the data flow could appear on this form, or it could be represented as a data structure.

Data flows for all inputs and outputs should be described first, because they usually represent the human interface, followed by the intermediate data flows

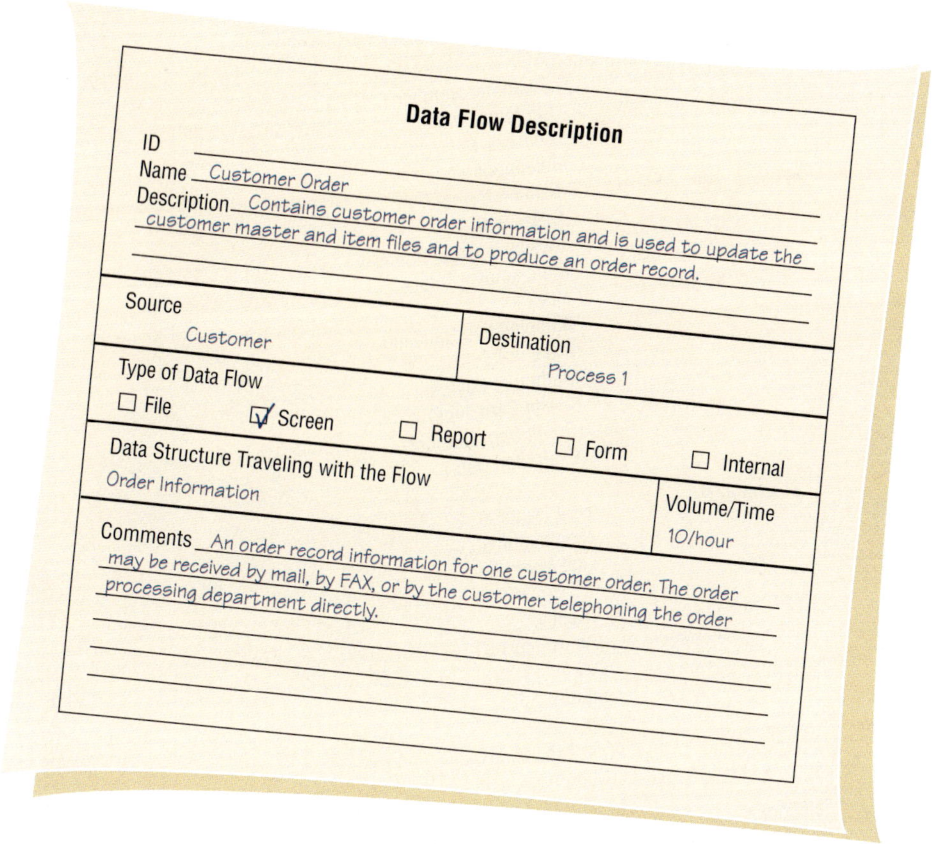

Data Flow Description

ID
Name Customer Order
Description Contains customer order information and is used to update the customer master and item files and to produce an order record.

Source: Customer
Destination: Process 1

Type of Data Flow
☐ File ☑ Screen ☐ Report ☐ Form ☐ Internal

Data Structure Traveling with the Flow: Order Information
Volume/Time: 10/hour

Comments An order record information for one customer order. The order may be received by mail, by FAX, or by the customer telephoning the order processing department directly.

FIGURE 8.3
An example of a data flow description from World's Trend Catalog Division.

and the data flows to and from data stores. The detail of each data flow is described using elements, sometimes called fields, a data structure, or a group of elements.

A simple data flow may be described using a single element, such as a customer number used by an inquiry program to find the matching customer record.

DESCRIBING DATA STRUCTURES

Data structures are usually described using algebraic notation. This method allows the analyst to produce a view of the elements that make up the data structure along with information about those elements. For instance, the analyst will denote whether there are many of the same element in the data structure (a repeating group), or whether two elements may exist mutually exclusive of each other. The algebraic notation uses the following symbols:

1. An equal sign (=) means "is composed of."
2. A plus sign (+) means "and."
3. Braces { } indicate repetitive elements, also called repeating groups or tables. There may be one repeating element or several in the group. The repeating group may have conditions, such as a fixed number of repetitions, or upper and lower limits for the number of repetitions.
4. Brackets [ ] represent an either/or situation. Either one element may be present or another, but not both. The elements listed between the brackets are mutually exclusive.
5. Parentheses ( ) represent an optional element. Optional elements may be left blank on entry screens and may contain spaces or zeros for numeric fields in file structures.

FIGURE 8.4

Data structure example for adding a customer order at World's Trend Catalog Division.

```
Customer Order =          Customer Number +
                          Customer Name +
                          Address +
                          Telephone +
                          Catalog Number +
                          Order Date +
                          {Available Order Items} +
                          Merchandise Total +
                          (Tax) +
                          Shipping and Handling +
                          Order Total +
                          Method of Payment +
                          (Credit Card Type) +
                          (Credit Card Number) +
                          (Expiration Date)
Customer Name =           First Name +
                          (Middle Initial) +
                          Last Name
Address =                 Street +
                          (Apartment) +
                          City +
                          State +
                          Zip +
                          (Zip Expansion) +
                          (Country)
Telephone =               Area Code +
                          Local Number
Available Order Items =   Quantity Ordered +
                          Item Number +
                          Item Description +
                          Size +
                          Color +
                          Price +
                          Item Total
Method of Payment =       [Check ¦ Charge ¦ Money Order]
Credit Card Type =        [World's Trend ¦ American Express ¦ MasterCard ¦ Visa]
```

Figure 8.4 is an example of the data structure for adding a customer order at World's Trend Catalog Division. Each NEW CUSTOMER screen consists of the entries found on the right side of the equal signs. Some of the entries are elements, but others, such as CUSTOMER NAME, ADDRESS, and TELEPHONE, are groups of elements or structural records. For example, CUSTOMER NAME is made up of FIRST NAME, MIDDLE INITIAL, and LAST NAME. Each structural record must be further defined until the entire set is broken down into its component elements. Notice that following the definition for the CUSTOMER ORDER screen are definitions for each structural record. Even a field as simple as the TELEPHONE NUMBER is defined as a structure so that the area code may be processed individually.

Structural records and elements that are used in many different systems are given a nonsystem-specific name, such as street, city, and zip, that does not reflect the functional area in which they are used. This method allows the analyst to define these records once and use them in many different applications. For example, a city may be a customer city, supplier city, or employee city. Notice the use of parentheses to indicate that (MIDDLE INITIAL), (APARTMENT), and (ZIP EXPANSION) are optional ORDER information (but not more than one). Indicate the OR condition by enclosing the options in square brackets and separating them with the symbol ¦.

LOGICAL AND PHYSICAL DATA STRUCTURES

When data structures are first defined, only the data elements that the user would see, such as a name, address, and balance due, are included. This stage is the logical design, showing what data the business needs for its day-to-day operations. As we learned from HCI, it is important that the logical design accurately reflect the mental model of how the user views the system. Using the logical design as a basis, the analyst then designs the physical data structures, which include additional elements necessary for implementing the system. Examples of physical design elements are the following:

1. Key fields used to locate records in a database table. An example is an item number, which is not required for a business to function but is necessary for identifying and locating computer records.
2. Codes to identify the status of master records, such as whether an employee is active (currently employed) or inactive. Such codes can be maintained on files that produce tax information.
3. Transaction codes are used to identify types of records when a file contains different record types. An example is a credit file containing records for returned items as well as records of payments.
4. Repeating group entries containing a count of how many items are in the group.
5. Limits on the number of items in a repeated group.
6. A password used by a customer accessing a secure Web site.

Figure 8.5 is an example of the data structure for a CUSTOMER BILLING STATEMENT, one showing that the ORDER LINE is both a repeating item and a

Customer Billing Statement = Current Date +
Customer Number +
Customer Name +
Address +
$^{5}_{1}${Order Line} +
(Previous Payment Amount) +
Total Amount Owed +
(Comment)

Order Line = Order Number +
Order Date +
Order Total

FIGURE 8.5
Physical elements added to a data structure.

structural record. The ORDER LINE limits are from 1 to 5, indicating that the customer may order from one to five items on this screen. Additional items would appear on subsequent orders.

The repeating group notation may have several other formats. If the group repeats a fixed number of times, that number is placed next to the opening brace, as in 12 {Monthly Sales}, where there are always 12 months in the year. If no number is indicated, the group repeats indefinitely. An example is a table containing an indefinite number of records, such as Customer Master Table = {Customer Records}.

The number of entries in repeating groups may also depend on a condition, such as an entry on the Customer Master Record for each item ordered. This condition could be stored in the data dictionary as {Items Purchased} 5, where 5 is the number of items.

DATA ELEMENTS

Each data element should be defined once in the data dictionary and may also be entered previously on an element description form, such as the one illustrated

FIGURE 8.6

An element description form example from World's Trend Catalog Division.

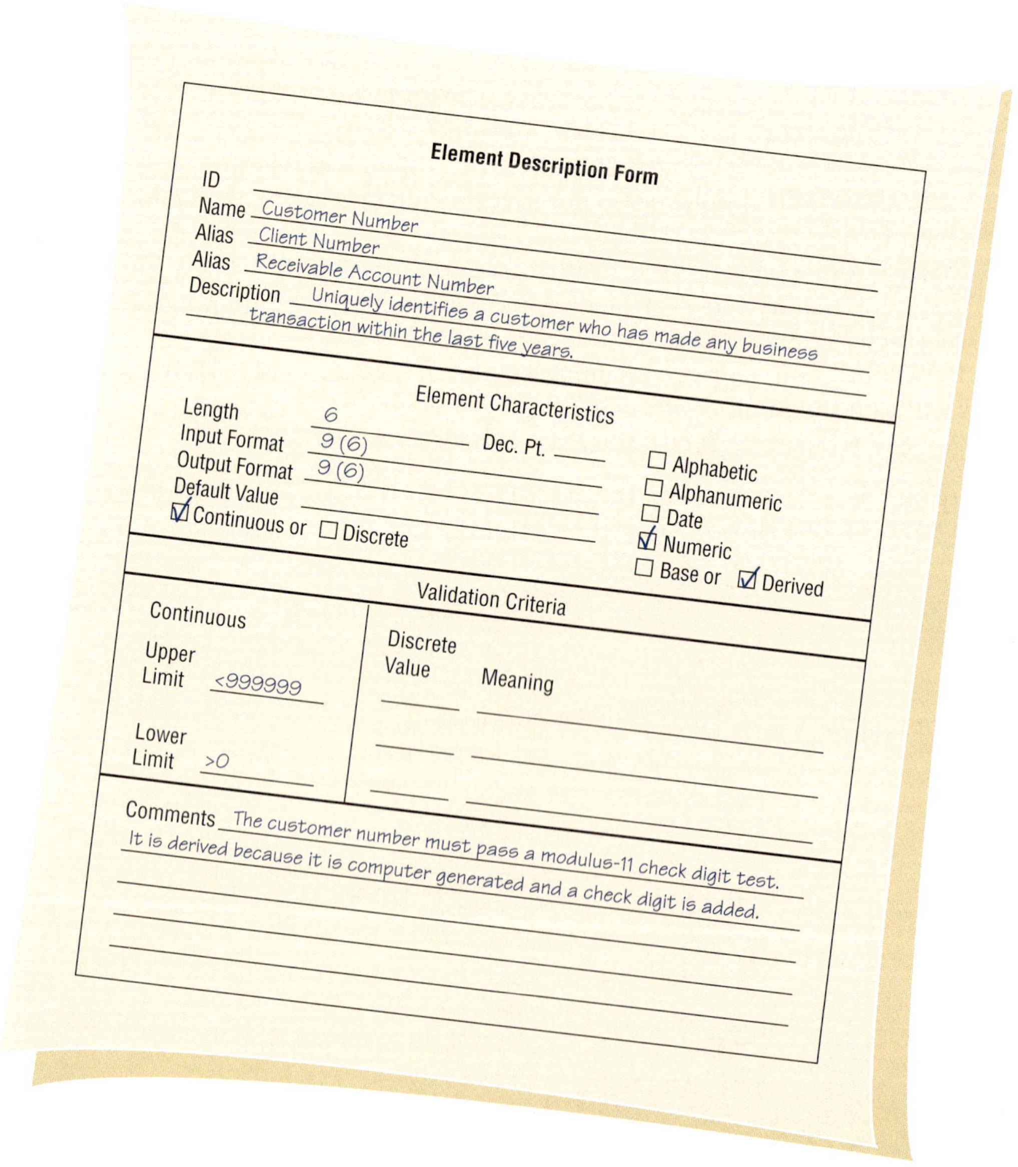

Element Description Form

ID
Name Customer Number
Alias Client Number
Alias Receivable Account Number
Description Uniquely identifies a customer who has made any business transaction within the last five years.

Element Characteristics

Length 6
Input Format 9 (6) Dec. Pt.
Output Format 9 (6)
Default Value
☑ Continuous or ☐ Discrete

☐ Alphabetic
☐ Alphanumeric
☐ Date
☑ Numeric
☐ Base or ☑ Derived

Validation Criteria

Continuous
Upper Limit <999999
Lower Limit >0

Discrete Value | Meaning

Comments The customer number must pass a modulus-11 check digit test. It is derived because it is computer generated and a check digit is added.

in Figure 8.6. Characteristics commonly included on the element description form are the following:

1. Element ID. This optional entry allows the analyst to build automated data dictionary entries.
2. The name of the element. The name should be descriptive, unique, and based on what the element is commonly called in most programs or by the major user of the element.
3. Aliases, which are synonyms or other names for the element. Aliases are names used by different users in different systems. For example, a CUSTOMER NUMBER may also be called a RECEIVABLE ACCOUNT NUMBER or a CLIENT NUMBER.
4. A short description of the element.
5. Whether the element is base or derived. A base element is one that is initially keyed into the system, such as a customer name, address, or city. Base elements must be stored in files. Derived elements are created by processes as the result of a calculation or a series of decision-making statements.
6. The length of an element. Some elements have standard lengths. In the United States, for example, lengths for state name abbreviations, zip codes, and telephone numbers are all standard. For other elements, the lengths may vary, and the analyst and user community must jointly decide the final length based on the following considerations:
   a. Numeric amount lengths should be determined by figuring the largest number the amount will probably contain and then allowing reasonable room for expansion. Lengths designated for totals should be large enough to accommodate the sum of the numbers accumulated in them.
   b. Name and address fields may be given lengths based on the following table. For example, a last name field of 11 characters will accommodate 98 percent of the last names in the United States.
   c. For other fields, it is often useful to examine or sample historical data found in the organization to determine a suitable field length.

Field	*Length*	*Percentage of Data That Will Fit (U.S.)*
Last Name	11	98
First Name	18	95
Company Name	20	95
Street	18	90
City	17	99

   If the element is too small, the data that need to be entered will be truncated. The analyst must decide how that will affect the system outputs. For example, if a customer's last name is truncated, mail would usually still be delivered; if an email address is truncated, however, it will be returned as not found.
7. The type of data—numeric, date, alphabetic, varchar, or character, which is sometimes called alphanumeric or text data. Varchar data may contain any number of characters, up to a limit set by the database software. When using varchar, specifying the length is optional. Several of these formats are shown in Figure 8.7. Character fields may contain a mixture of letters, numbers, and special characters. If the element is a date, its format—for example, MMDDYYYY—must be determined. If the element is numeric, its storage type should be determined.

   Personal computer formats, such as currency, number, or scientific, depend on how the data will be used. Number formats are further defined as integer,

FIGURE 8.7
Some examples of data formats used in PC systems.

Data Type	Meaning
Bit	A value of 1 or 0, a true/false value
Char, varchar, text	Any alphanumeric character
Datetime, smalldatetime	Alphanumeric data, several formats
Decimal, numeric	Numeric data that are accurate to the least significant digit; can contain a whole and decimal portion
Float, real	Floating-point values that contain an approximate decimal value
Int, smallint, tinyint	Only integer (whole digit) data
Currency, money, smallmoney	Monetary numbers accurate to four decimal places
Binary, varbinary, image	Binary strings (sound, pictures, video)
Cursor, timestamp, uniqueidentifier	A value that is always unique within a database
Autonumber	A number that is always incremented by one when a record is added to a database table

long integer, single precision, double precision, and so on. There are many other types of formats used with PC systems. Unicode is a standardized coding system for defining graphic symbols, such as Chinese or Japanese characters. Unicode is described in greater detail in a later chapter. There are three standard formats for mainframe computers: zoned decimal, packed decimal, and binary. The zoned decimal format is used for printing and displaying data. The packed decimal format is commonly used to save space on file layouts and for elements that require a high level of arithmetic to be performed on them. The binary format is suitable for the same purposes as the packed decimal format but is less commonly used.

8. Input and output formats should be included, using special coding symbols to indicate how the data should be presented. These symbols and their uses are illustrated in Figure 8.8. Each symbol represents one character or digit. If the same character repeats several times, the character followed by a number in parentheses indicating how many times the character repeats is substituted for the group. For example, XXXXXXXX would be represented as X(8).
9. Validation criteria for ensuring that accurate data are captured by the system. Elements are either discrete, meaning they have certain fixed values, or continuous, with a smooth range of values. Here are common editing criteria:
   a. A range of values is suitable for elements that contain continuous data. For example, in the United States a student grade point average may be from

FIGURE 8.8
Format character codes.

Formatting Character	Meaning
X	May enter or display/print any character
9	Enter or display only numbers
Z	Display leading zeros as spaces
,	Insert commas into a numeric display
.	Insert a period into a numeric display
/	Insert slashes into a numeric display
-	Insert a hyphen into a numeric display
V	Indicate a decimal position (when the decimal point is not included)

0.00 through 4.00. If there is only an upper or lower bound to the data, a limit is used instead of a range.
b. A list of values is indicated if the data are discrete. Examples are codes representing the colors of items for sale in World's Trend's catalog.
c. A table of codes is suitable if the list of values is extensive (for example, state abbreviations, telephone country codes, or U.S. telephone area codes.)
d. For key or index elements, a check digit is often included.

10. Any default value the element may have. The default value is displayed on entry screens and is used to reduce the amount of keying that the operator may have to do. Usually, several fields in each system have default values. When using GUI lists or drop-down lists, the default value is the one currently selected and highlighted. When using radio buttons, the option for the default value is selected, and when using check boxes, the default value (either "yes" or "no") determines whether or not the check box will have an initial check in it.
11. An additional comment or remarks area. This might be used to indicate the format of the date, special validation that is required, the check digit method used (explained in Chapter 15), and so on.

Data element descriptions such as CUSTOMER NUMBER may be called CLIENT NUMBER elsewhere in the system (perhaps old code written with this alias needs to be updated).

Another kind of data element is an alphabetic element. At World's Trend Catalog Division, codes are used to describe colors: for example, BL for blue, WH for white, and GR for green. When this element is implemented, a table will be needed for users to look up the meanings of these codes. (Coding is discussed further in Chapter 15.)

DATA STORES

All base elements must be stored in the system. Derived elements, such as the employee year-to-date gross pay, may also be stored in the system. Data stores are created for each different data entity being stored. That is, when data flow base elements are grouped together to form a structural record, a data store is created for each unique structural record.

Because a given data flow may only show part of the collective data that a structural record contains, you may have to examine many different data flow structures to arrive at a complete data store description.

Figure 8.9 is a typical form used to describe a data store. The information included on the form is as follows:

1. The data store ID. The ID is often a mandatory entry to prevent the analyst from storing redundant information. An example would be D1 for the CUSTOMER MASTER.
2. The data store name, which is descriptive and unique.
3. An alias for the table, such as CLIENT MASTER for the CUSTOMER MASTER.
4. A short description of the data store.
5. The file type, either computer or manual.
6. The format designates whether the file is a database table or if it has the format of a simple flat file. (File formats are detailed in Chapter 13.)
7. The maximum and average number of records on the file as well as the growth per year. This information helps the analyst to predict the amount of disk space required for the application and is necessary for hardware acquisition planning.

FIGURE 8.9

An example of a data store form for World's Trend Catalog Division.

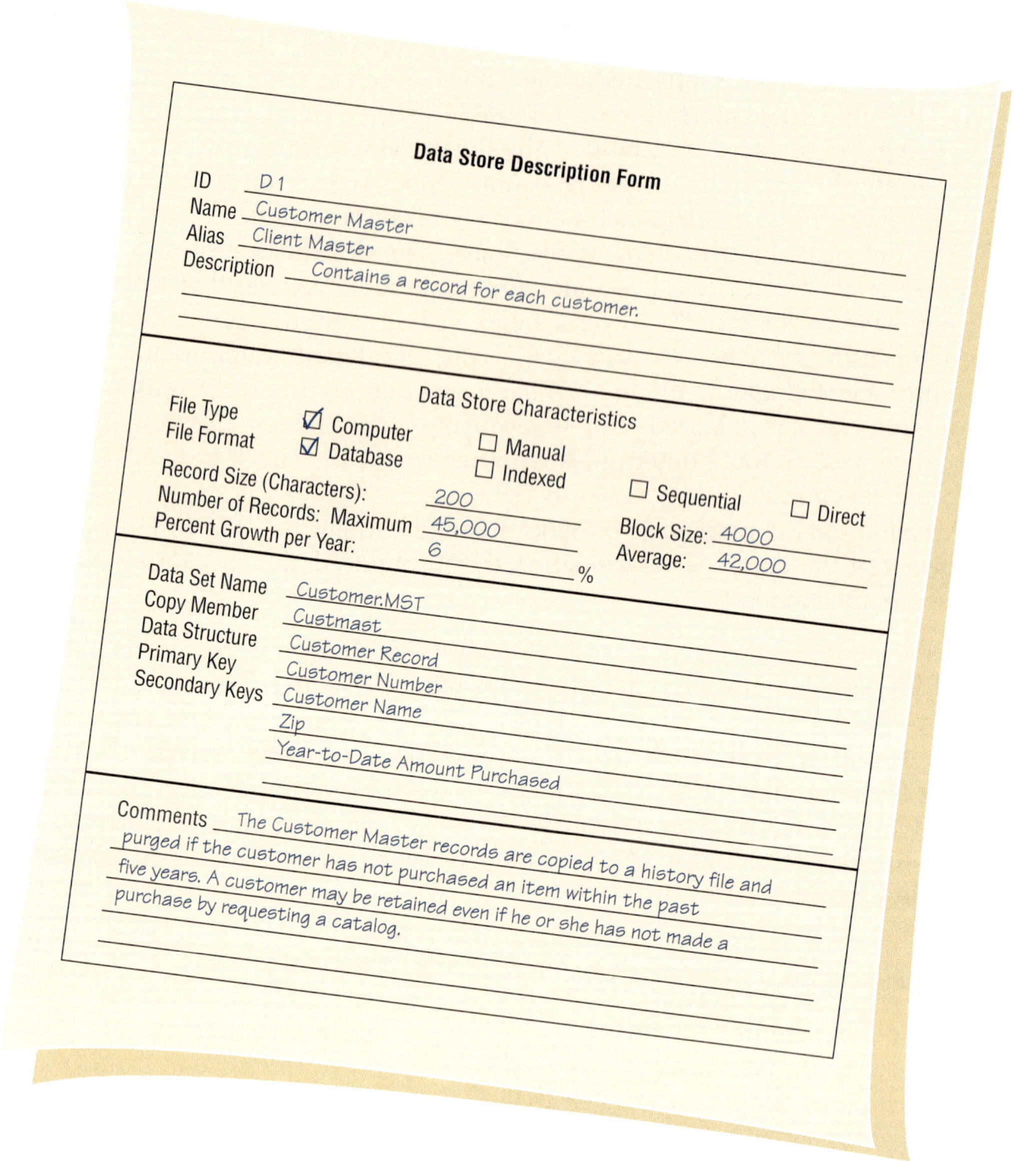

Data Store Description Form

ID D1

Name Customer Master

Alias Client Master

Description Contains a record for each customer.

Data Store Characteristics

File Type ☑ Computer ☐ Manual

File Format ☑ Database ☐ Indexed ☐ Sequential ☐ Direct

Record Size (Characters): 200 Block Size: 4000

Number of Records: Maximum 45,000 Average: 42,000

Percent Growth per Year: 6 %

Data Set Name Customer.MST

Copy Member Custmast

Data Structure Customer Record

Primary Key Customer Number

Secondary Keys Customer Name

Zip

Year-to-Date Amount Purchased

Comments The Customer Master records are copied to a history file and purged if the customer has not purchased an item within the past five years. A customer may be retained even if he or she has not made a purchase by requesting a catalog.

8. The file or data set name specifies the file name, if known. In the initial design stages, this item may be left blank. An electronic form produced using Visible Analyst is shown in Figure 8.10. This example shows that the CUSTOMER MASTER is stored on a computer in the form of a database with a maximum number of 45,000 records. (Records and the keys used to sort the database are explained in Chapter 13.)
9. The data structure should use a name found in the data dictionary, providing a link to the elements for this data store. Alternatively, the data elements could be described on the data store description form or on the CASE tool screen for the data store. Primary and secondary keys must be elements (or a combination of elements) found in the data structure. In the example, the CUSTOMER NUMBER is the primary key and should be unique. The CUSTOMER NAME, ZIP, and YEAR-TO-DATE AMOUNT PURCHASED are secondary keys used to control record sequencing on reports and to locate records directly. (Keys are discussed in Chapter 13.) Comments are used for information that does not fit into any of the above categories. They may include update or backup timing, security, or other considerations.

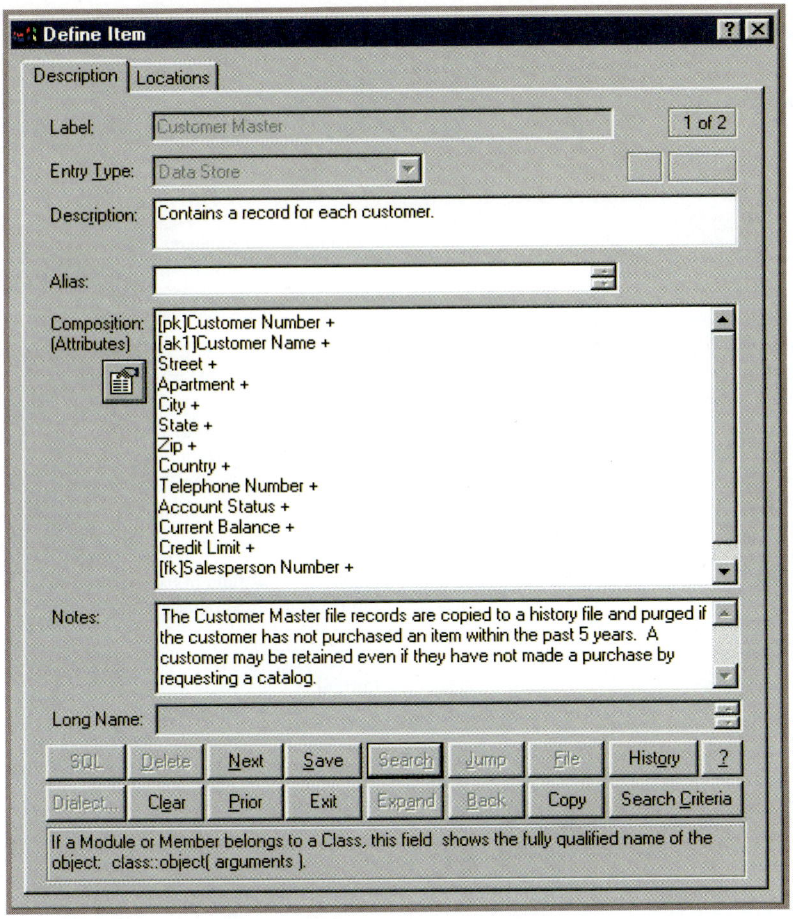

FIGURE 8.10

Visible Analyst screen showing a data store description.

CREATING THE DATA DICTIONARY

Data dictionary entries may be created after the data flow diagram has been completed, or they may be constructed as the data flow diagram is being developed. The use of algebraic notation and structural records allows the analyst to develop the data dictionary and the data flow diagrams using a top-down approach. For instance, the analyst may create a Diagram 0 data flow after the first few interviews and, at the same time, make the preliminary data dictionary entries. Typically, these entries consist of the data flow names found on the data flow diagram and their corresponding data structures.

After conducting several additional interviews with users to learn the details of the system and the ways they interact with it, the analyst will expand the data flow diagram and create the child diagrams. The data dictionary is then modified to include the new structural records and elements gleaned from further interviews, observation, and document analysis.

Each level of a data flow diagram should use data appropriate for the level. Diagram 0 should include only forms, screens, reports, and records. As child diagrams are created, the data flow into and out of the processes becomes more and more detailed, including structural records and elements.

Figure 8.11 illustrates a portion of two data flow diagram levels and corresponding data dictionary entries for producing an employee paycheck. Process 5, found on Diagram 0, is an overview of the production of an EMPLOYEE PAYCHECK. The corresponding data dictionary entry for EMPLOYEE RECORD shows the EMPLOYEE NUMBER and four structural records, the view of the data

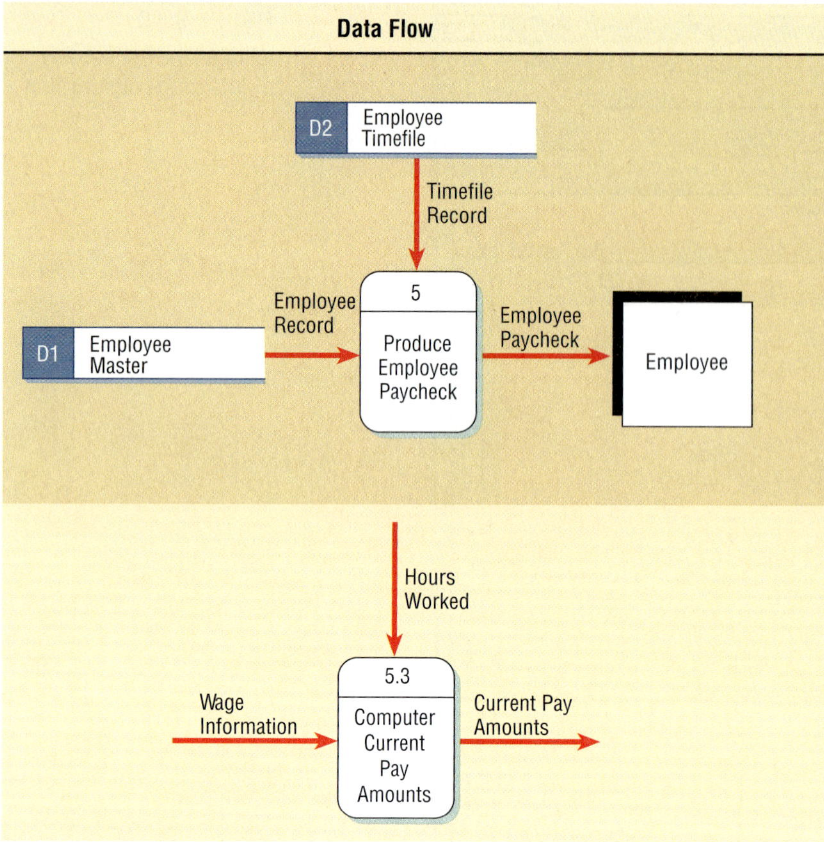

Data Structure

Employee Record	=	Employee Number + Personal Information + Wage Information + Current Pay Information + Year-to-Date Information
Timefile Record	=	Employee Number + Employee Name + Hours Worked
Employee Paycheck	=	Employee Number + Employee Name + Address + Current Pay Amounts + Year-to-Date Figures
Wage Information	=	Rate of Pay + Number of Dependents
Current Pay Amounts	=	Gross Pay + Federal Withholding + State Withholding + Social Security Withholding + Net Pay

FIGURE 8.11
Two data flow diagrams and corresponding data dictionary entries for producing an employee paycheck.

obtained early in the analysis. Similarly, TIMEFILE RECORD and the EMPLOYEE PAYCHECK are also defined as series of structures.

It is important that the data flow names on the child data flow diagram are contained as elements or structural records in the data flow on the parent process. Returning to the example, WAGE INFORMATION (input into process 5.3, COMPUTE CURRENT PAY AMOUNTS) is a structural record contained in the EMPLOYEE RECORD (input to process 5). Similarly, GROSS PAY (output from process 5.3.4, a lower-level process not shown in the figure) is contained in the structural record CURRENT PAY AMOUNTS (output from the parent process 5.3, COMPUTE CURRENT PAY AMOUNTS).

ANALYZING INPUT AND OUTPUT

An important step in creating the data dictionary is to identify and categorize system input and output data flow. Input and output analysis forms contain the following commonly included fields:

1. A descriptive name for the input or output. If the data flow is on a logical diagram, the name should identify what the data are (for example, CUSTOMER INFORMATION). If the analyst is working on the physical design or if the user has explicitly stated the nature of the input or output, however, the name should include that information regarding the format. Examples are CUSTOMER BILLING STATEMENT and CUSTOMER DETAILS INQUIRY.
2. The user contact responsible for further details clarification, design feedback, and final approval.
3. Whether the data is input or output.

CONSULTING OPPORTUNITY 8.1

WANT TO MAKE IT BIG IN THE THEATRE? IMPROVE YOUR DICTION(ARY)!

As you enter the door of Merman's, Annie Oaklea greets you warmly, saying, "I'm delighted with the work you have done on the data flow diagrams. I would like you to keep playing the role of systems analyst for Merman's and see if you can eventually get a new information system for our costume inventory sewn up. Unfortunately, some of the terms you're using don't come off very well in the language of Shakespeare. Bit of a translation problem, I suspect."

Clinging to Annie's initial praise, you are undaunted by her exit line. You determine that a data dictionary based on the rental and return data flow diagrams would make a big hit.

Begin by writing entries for a manual system in as much detail as possible. Prepare two data process entries, two data flow entries, two data store entries, one data structure entry, and four data element entries using the formats in this chapter. Portraying interrelated data items with preciseness will result in rave reviews. (Refer to Consulting Opportunity 7.1.)

4. The format of the data flow. In the logical design stage, the format may be undetermined.
5. Elements indicating the sequence of the data on a report or screen (perhaps in columns).
6. A list of elements, including their names, lengths, and whether they are base or derived, and their editing criteria.

Once the form has been completed, each element should be analyzed to determine whether the element repeats, whether it is optional, or whether it is mutually exclusive of another element. Elements that fall into a group or that regularly combine with several other elements in many structures should be placed together in a structural record.

These considerations can be seen in the completed Input and Output Analysis Form for World's Trend Catalog Division (see Figure 8.12). In this example of a CUSTOMER BILLING STATEMENT, the CUSTOMER FIRST NAME, CUSTOMER LAST NAME, and CUSTOMER MIDDLE INITIAL should be grouped together in a structural record.

DEVELOPING DATA STORES

Another activity in creating the data dictionary is developing data stores. Up to now, we have determined what data needs to flow from one process to another. This information is described in data structures. The information, however, may be stored in numerous places, and in each place the data store may be different. Whereas data flows represent data in motion, data stores represent data at rest.

For example, when an order arrives at World's Trend (see Figure 8.13), it contains mostly temporary information, that is, the information needed to fill that particular order, but some information might be stored permanently. Examples of the latter include information about customers (so catalogs can be sent to them) and information about items (because these items will appear on many other customers' orders).

Data stores contain information of a permanent or semipermanent (temporary) nature. An ITEM NUMBER, DESCRIPTION, and ITEM COST are examples of information that is relatively permanent. So is the TAX RATE. When the ITEM COST is multiplied by the TAX RATE, however, the TAX CHARGED is calculated (or derived). Derived values do not have to be stored in a data store.

FIGURE 8.12

An example of an input/output analysis form for World's Trend Catalog Division.

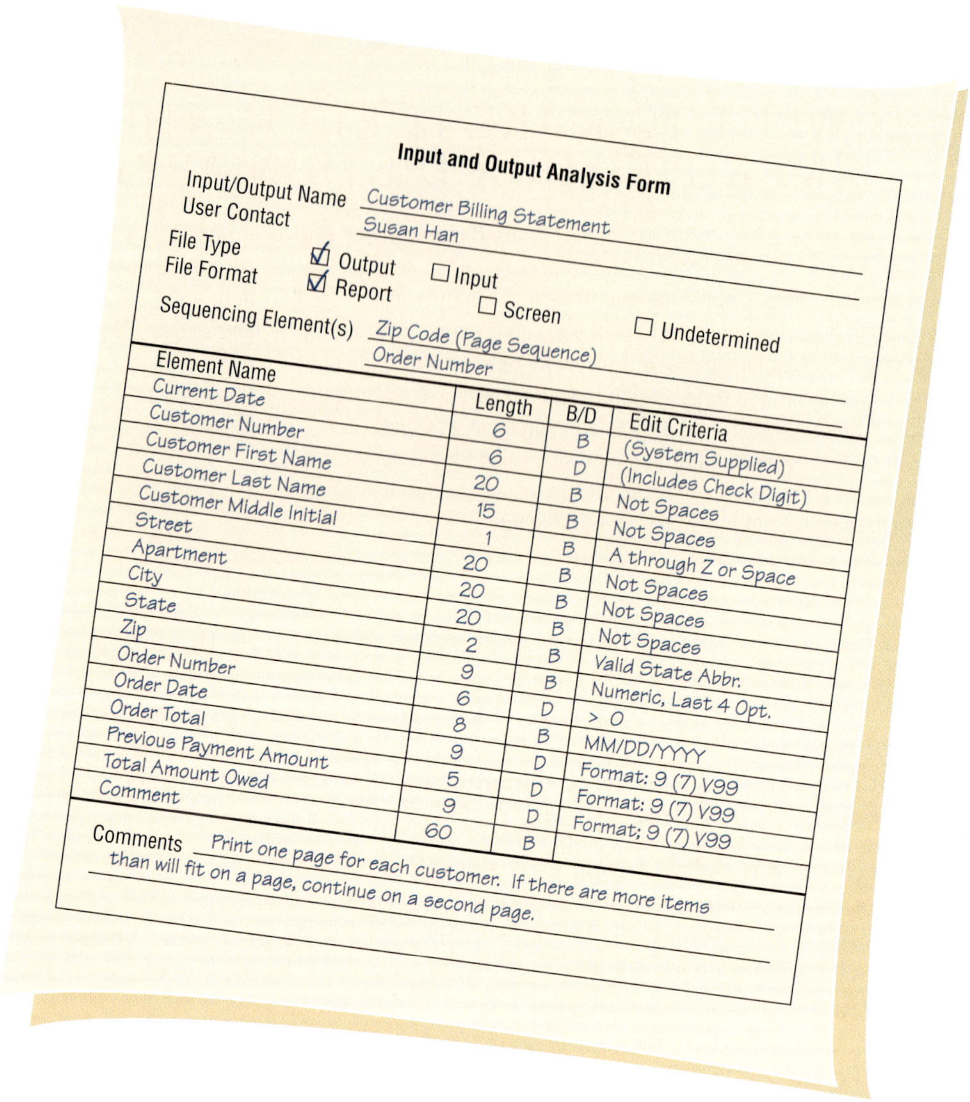

Input and Output Analysis Form

Input/Output Name: Customer Billing Statement
User Contact: Susan Han
File Type: ☑ Output ☐ Input
File Format: ☑ Report ☐ Screen ☐ Undetermined
Sequencing Element(s): Zip Code (Page Sequence)
Order Number

Element Name	Length	B/D	Edit Criteria
Current Date	6	B	(System Supplied)
Customer Number	6	D	(Includes Check Digit)
Customer First Name	20	B	Not Spaces
Customer Last Name	15	B	Not Spaces
Customer Middle Initial	1	B	A through Z or Space
Street	20	B	Not Spaces
Apartment	20	B	Not Spaces
City	20	B	Not Spaces
State	2	B	Valid State Abbr.
Zip	9	B	Numeric, Last 4 Opt.
Order Number	6	D	> 0
Order Date	8	B	MM/DD/YYYY
Order Total	9	D	Format: 9 (7) V99
Previous Payment Amount	5	D	Format: 9 (7) V99
Total Amount Owed	9	D	Format; 9 (7) V99
Comment	60	B	

Comments: Print one page for each customer. If there are more items than will fit on a page, continue on a second page.

When data stores are created for only one report or screen, we refer to them as "user views," because they represent the way that the user wants to see the information.

USING THE DATA DICTIONARY

The ideal data dictionary is automated, interactive, online, and evolutionary. As the systems analyst learns about the organization's systems, data items are added to the data dictionary. On the other hand, the data dictionary is not an end in itself and must never become so. To avoid becoming sidetracked with the building of a complete data dictionary, the systems analyst should view it as an activity that parallels systems analysis and design.

To have maximum power, the data dictionary should be tied into a number of systems programs so that when an item is updated or deleted from the data dictionary, it is automatically updated or deleted from the database. The data dictionary becomes simply a historical curiosity if it is not kept current.

The data dictionary may be used to create screens, reports, and forms. For example, examine the data structure for the World's Trend ORDER PICKING

```
Customer Master =        Customer Number +
                         Customer Name +
                         Address +
                         Telephone +
                         Corporate Credit Card Number +
                         Expiration Date
Item Master =            Item Number +
                         Price +
                         Quantity on Hand
Order Record =           Customer Number +
                         Catalog Number +
                         Order Date +
                         {Available Order Items} +
                         Merchandise Total +
                         (Tax) +
                         Shipping and Handling +
                         Order Total +
                         Method of Payment +
                         (Credit Card Type) +
                         (Credit Card Number) +
                         (Expiration Date)
Available Order Items =  Item Number +
                         Quantity Ordered +
                         Quantity Shipped +
                         Current Price
Method of Payment =      [Check | Charge | Money Order]
Credit Card Type =       [World's Trend | American Express | MasterCard | Visa]
```

FIGURE 8.13

Data stores derived from a pending order at World's Trend Catalog Division.

SLIP in Figure 8.14. Because the necessary elements and their lengths have been defined, the process of creating physical documents consists of arranging the elements in a pleasing and functional way using design guidelines and common sense. Repeating groups become columns, and structural records are grouped together on the screen, report, or form. The report layout for the World's Trend ORDER PICKING SLIP is shown in Figure 8.15. Notice that FIRST NAME and LAST NAME are grouped together in NAME, and that QUANTITY (PICKED and ORDERED), SECTION, SHELF NUMBER, ITEM NUMBER, ITEM DESCRIPTION, SIZE, and COLOR form a series of columns, because they are the repeating elements.

The data structure and elements for a data store are commonly used to generate corresponding computer language source code, which is then incorporated into computer programs. The data dictionary may be used in conjunction with a data flow diagram to analyze the system design, detecting flaws and areas that need clarification. Some considerations are:

1. All base elements on an output data flow must be present on an input data flow to the process producing the output. Base elements are keyed and should never be created by a process.

FIGURE 8.14

Data structure for an order picking slip at World's Trend Catalog Division.

Order Picking Slip =	Order Number + Order Date + Customer Number + Customer Name + Customer Address + Customer Telephone + {Order Item Selection} + Number of Items
Order Item Selection =	Item Number + Item Description + Size Description + Color Description + Warehouse Section + Shelf Number + Quantity Ordered + Quantity Picked
Customer Name =	First Name + (Middle Initial) + Last Name
Address =	Street + (Apartment) + City + State + Zip + (Zip Expansion) + (Country)
Telephone =	Area Code + Local Number

2. A derived element must be created by a process and should be output from at least one process into which it is not input.
3. The elements that are present in a data flow coming into or going out of a data store must be contained in the data store.

If begun early, a data dictionary can save many hours of time in the analysis and design phases. The data dictionary is the one common source in the organization for answering questions and settling disputes about any aspect of data definition. An up-to-date data dictionary can serve as an excellent reference for maintenance efforts on unfamiliar systems. Automated data dictionaries can serve as references for both people and programs.

USING DATA DICTIONARIES TO CREATE XML

Extensible markup language (XML) is a language that can be used to exchange data between businesses or between systems within a business. It is similar to HTML,

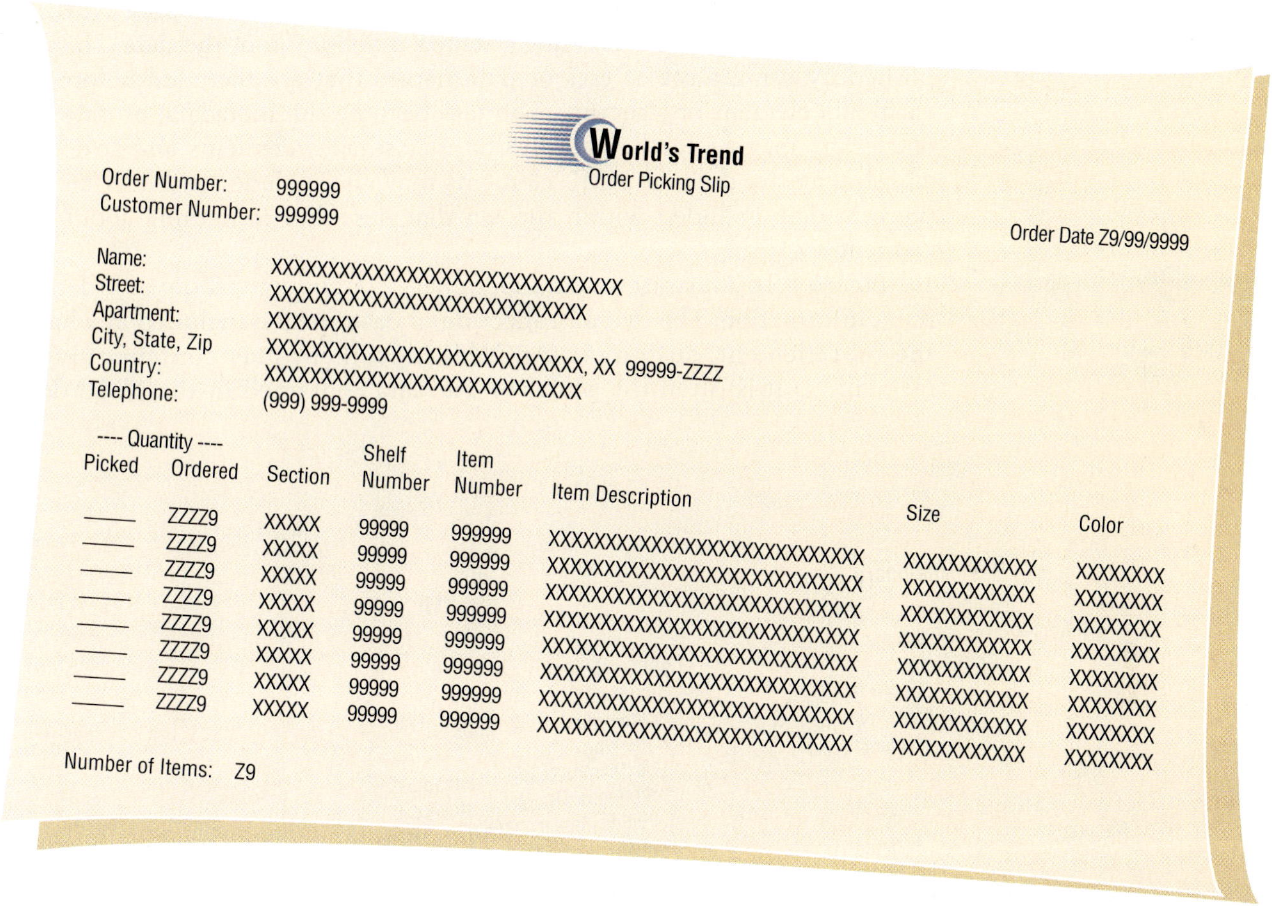

World's Trend
Order Picking Slip

Order Number: 999999
Customer Number: 999999

Order Date Z9/99/9999

Name: XXXXXXXXXXXXXXXXXXXXXXXXXXXXXX
Street: XXXXXXXXXXXXXXXXXXXXXXXXXXX
Apartment: XXXXXXXX
City, State, Zip XXXXXXXXXXXXXXXXXXXXXXXXXXX, XX 99999-ZZZZ
Country: XXXXXXXXXXXXXXXXXXXXXXXXXXX
Telephone: (999) 999-9999

---- Quantity ----							
Picked	Ordered	Section	Shelf Number	Item Number	Item Description	Size	Color
____	ZZZZ9	XXXXX	99999	999999	XXXXXXXXXXXXXXXXXXXXXXXXXXX	XXXXXXXXXXXX	XXXXXXXX
____	ZZZZ9	XXXXX	99999	999999	XXXXXXXXXXXXXXXXXXXXXXXXXXX	XXXXXXXXXXXX	XXXXXXXX
____	ZZZZ9	XXXXX	99999	999999	XXXXXXXXXXXXXXXXXXXXXXXXXXX	XXXXXXXXXXXX	XXXXXXXX
____	ZZZZ9	XXXXX	99999	999999	XXXXXXXXXXXXXXXXXXXXXXXXXXX	XXXXXXXXXXXX	XXXXXXXX
____	ZZZZ9	XXXXX	99999	999999	XXXXXXXXXXXXXXXXXXXXXXXXXXX	XXXXXXXXXXXX	XXXXXXXX
____	ZZZZ9	XXXXX	99999	999999	XXXXXXXXXXXXXXXXXXXXXXXXXXX	XXXXXXXXXXXX	XXXXXXXX
____	ZZZZ9	XXXXX	99999	999999	XXXXXXXXXXXXXXXXXXXXXXXXXXX	XXXXXXXXXXXX	XXXXXXXX
____	ZZZZ9	XXXXX	99999	999999	XXXXXXXXXXXXXXXXXXXXXXXXXXX	XXXXXXXXXXXX	XXXXXXXX

Number of Items: Z9

FIGURE 8.15
Order picking slip created from the data dictionary.

the markup language used to create Web pages, but is more powerful. HTML is concerned primarily with formatting a document; XML addresses the problem of sharing data when users have different computer systems and software or different database management systems (for example, one company using Oracle and another using IBM's DB2). If everyone used the same software or database management system, there would be little need for XML.

Once an XML document has been created, the data may be transformed into a number of different output formats and displayed in many different ways, including printed output, Web pages, output for a handheld device, and portable document format (PDF) files. Thus, the document's data content is separated from the output format. The XML content is defined once as data and then transformed as many times as necessary.

The advantage of using an XML document is that the analyst may select only the data that an internal department or external partner needs to have in order to function. This helps to ensure the confidentiality of data. For example, a shipping company may receive only the customer name, the address, the item number, and the quantity to ship, but *not* credit card information or other financial data. This efficient approach also cuts down on information overload.

XML therefore is a way to define, sort, filter, and translate data into a universal data language that can be used by anyone. XML may be created from databases, a form, or software programs, or it may be keyed directly into a document, text editor, or XML entry program.

The data dictionary is an ideal starting point for developing XML content. The key to using XML is creating a standard definition of the data. This is accomplished by using a set of tags or data names that are included before and after each data element or structure. The tags become the metadata, or data about the data. Data may be further subdivided into smaller elements and structures until all elements are defined. XML elements may also include attributes, an additional piece of data included within the tag that describes something about the XML element.

Figure 8.16 illustrates a data dictionary containing customer, order, and payment information. The overall collection of customers is included in what is called the root element, customers. An XML document may contain only one root element, so it is often the plural of the data contained in the XML document.

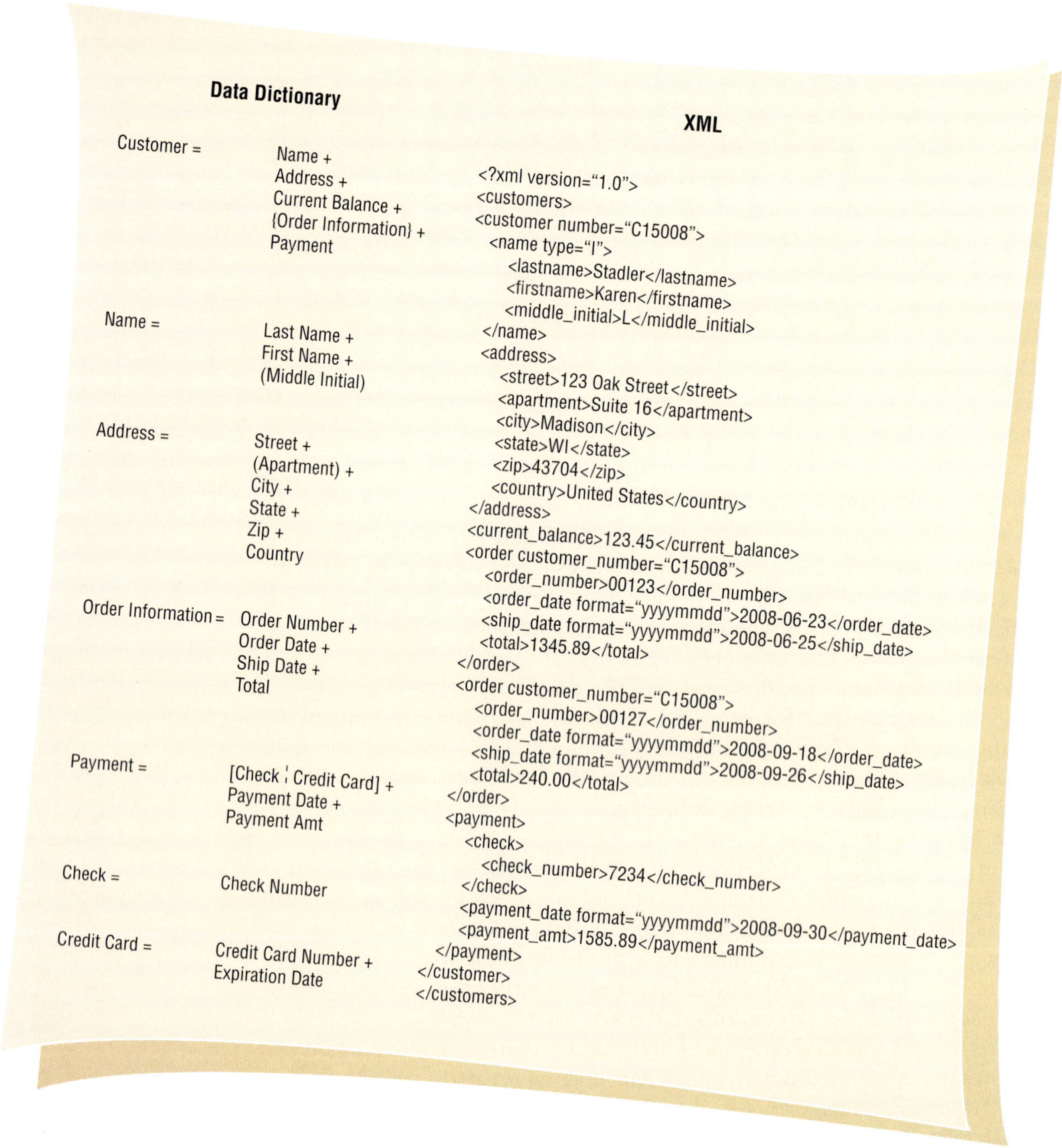

FIGURE 8.16

Using a data dictionary entry to develop XML content. The XML document mirrors the data dictionary structure.

Each customer may place many orders. The structure is defined in the two left columns, and the XML code appears on the right. CUSTOMER, as you can see, consists of a NAME, ADDRESS, CURRENT BALANCE, multiple ORDER INFORMATION entries, and a PAYMENT. Some of these structures are further subdivided.

The XML document tends to mirror the data dictionary structure. The first entry (other than an XML line identifying the document) is <customer>, which defines the entire collection of customer information. The less than (<) and greater than (>) symbols are used to identify tag names (similar to HTML). The last line of the XML document is a closing tag, </customer>, signifying the end of the customer information.

Customer is defined first and contains an attribute, the customer number. There is often a discussion about whether data should be stored as an element or an attribute. In this case, they are stored as an attribute.

The name tag, <name>, is defined next because it is the first entry in the data dictionary. NAME is a structure consisting of LAST NAME, FIRST NAME, and an optional MIDDLE INITIAL. In the XML document, this structure starts with <name> and is followed by <lastname>, <firstname>, and <middle_initial>. Because spaces are not allowed in XML tag names, an underscore is typically used to separate words. The closing </name> tag signifies the end of the group of elements. Using a structure such as name saves time and coding if the transformation displays the full name. Each of the child elements will be on one line separated by a space. Name also contains an attribute, either I for individual or C for corporation.

Indentation is used to show which structures contain elements. Note that <address> is similar to <customer>, but when we get to <order_information> there is a big difference.

There are multiple entries for <order_information>, each containing an <order_number>, <order_date>, <shipping_date>, and <total>. Because the payment is made either by check or credit card, only one of these may be present. In our example, payment is by check. The dates have an attribute called format that indicates whether the date appears as month, day, year; year, month, day; or day, month, year. If a credit card is used to make a payment, a TYPE attribute contains either an M, V, A, D, or an O indicating the type of credit card (MasterCard, Visa, and so on).

XML DOCUMENT TYPE DEFINITIONS

Often the element structure of XML content is defined using a document type definition (DTD). A DTD is used to determine whether the XML document content is valid, that is, whether it conforms to the order and type of data that must be present in the document. The DTD is easy to create and well supported by standard software. Once the DTD has been completed, it may be used to validate the XML document using standard XML tools. The DTD is easier to create if a data dictionary has been completed, since the analyst has worked with users and made decisions on the structure of the data.

Figure 8.17 illustrates the document type definition for the Customer XML document. Keywords, such as !DOCTYPE, indicating the start of the DTD, must be in capital letters. !ELEMENT describes an element, and !ATTLIST describes an attribute, listing the element name followed by the attribute name. An element that has the keyword #PCDATA, for parsed character data, is a primitive element, not further defined. An element that has a series of other elements

```
< !DOCTYPE  customers  [
  < !ELEMENT  customers                    (customer) + >
  < !ELEMENT  customer                     (name, address, current_balance, order*) >
  < !ATTLIST  customer number              ID #REQUIRED>
  < !ELEMENT  name                         (lastname, firstname, middle_initial?) >
  < !ATTLIST  name type                    (I|C) #REQUIRED>
  < !ELEMENT  lastname                     (#PCDATA) >
  < !ELEMENT  firstname                    (#PCDATA) >
  < !ELEMENT  middle_initial               (#PCDATA) >
  < !ELEMENT  address                      (street, apartment?, city, state, zip, country) >
  < !ELEMENT  street                       (#PCDATA) >
  < !ELEMENT  apartment                    (#PCDATA) >
  < !ELEMENT  city                         (#PCDATA) >
  < !ELEMENT  state                        (#PCDATA) >
  < !ELEMENT  zip                          (#PCDATA) >
  < !ELEMENT  country                      (#PCDATA) >
  < !ELEMENT  current_balance              (#PCDATA) >
  < !ELEMENT  order                        (order_number, order_date, ship_date, total) >
  < !ATTLIST  order customer_number        IDREF #REQUIRED>
  < !ELEMENT  order_number                 (#PCDATA) >
  < !ELEMENT  order_date                   (#PCDATA) >
  < !ATTLIST  order_date format            (mmddyyyy|yyyymmdd|ddmmyyyy) #REQUIRED>
  < !ELEMENT  payment                      (check|credit_card) >
  < !ELEMENT  check                        (check_number) >
  < !ELEMENT  credit_card                  (credit_card_number, expiration_date) >
  < !ATTLIST  credit_card type             (M|V|A|D|O) #REQUIRED>
  < !ELEMENT  credit_card_number           (#PCDATA) >
  < !ELEMENT  expiration_date              (#PCDATA) >
  < !ELEMENT  payment_date                 (#PCDATA) >
  < !ATTLIST  payment_date format          (mmddyyyy|yyyymmdd|ddmmyyyy) #REQUIRED>
  < !ELEMENT  payment_amt                  (#PCDATA) >
] >
```

FIGURE 8.17

A document type definition for the customer XML document.

within parenthesis means that they are child elements and must be in the order listed. The statement <!ELEMENT name (lastname, firstname, middle_initial?)> means that the name must have the last name followed by the first name followed by the middle initial. The question mark after "middle_initial" means that the element is optional and may be left out of the document for a particular customer. A plus sign means that there are one or more repeatable elements. Customers must contain at least one customer tag but could contain many customer tags. An asterisk means that there is zero or more of the elements. Each customer may have zero to many orders. A vertical bar separates two or more child elements that are mutually exclusive. Payment contains by either check or credit card.

The attribute list definition for a customer number contains a keyword ID (in uppercase letters). This means that the attribute number must appear only once in the XML document as an attribute for an element with an ID and that it is somewhat similar to a primary key. The difference is that, if the document had several different elements, each with an ID attribute, the given ID (C15008 in this example) could appear only once. An ID must start with a letter or an underscore and cannot be solely a number. The reason behind putting the customer number as an ID is to ensure that it is not repeated in a longer document. The keyword

#REQUIRED means that the attribute must be present. A keyword of #IMPLIED means that the attribute is optional. A document may also have an IDREF attribute, which links one element with another that is an ID. The ORDER tag has a customer_number attribute defined as an IDREF, and the value C15008 must be present in an ID somewhere in the document. An attribute list containing values in parentheses means that the attribute must contain one of the values. A DTD definition <!ATTLIST credit_card type (M|V|A|D|O) #REQUIRED>, means that the credit card type must be either an M, V, A, D, or O.

XML SCHEMAS

A schema is another, more precise way to define the content of an XML document. Schemas may include the exact number of times an element may occur as well as the type of data within elements, such as character or numeric values, including the length of the element, limits on the data, and the number of places to the left and right of a decimal number.

A data dictionary is an excellent starting point for developing an XML document and a document type of definition or schema. The advantage of using XML to define data is that, in the XML format, data are stored in a pure text format and not dependent on any proprietary software. The document may be easily validated and transformed into many different output formats.

Industry groups or organizations may be involved in defining an industry-specific XML structure so that all involved parties understand what the data mean. This is very important when an element name may have several meanings. An example is "state," which may mean a postal state abbreviation or the state of an order or account. Examples of industry-specific XML document type definitions and schemas may be found at www.xml.org.

SUMMARY

Using a top-down approach, the systems analyst uses data flow diagrams to begin compiling a data dictionary, which is a reference work containing data about data, or metadata, on all data processes, stores, flows, structures, and logical and physical elements in the system being studied. One way to begin is by including all data items from data flow diagrams.

A larger collection of project information is called a repository. CASE tools permit the analyst to create a repository that may include information about data flows, stores, record structures, and elements; about procedural logic screen and report design; and about data relationships. A repository can also contain information about project requirements and final system deliverables; and about project management information.

Each entry in the data dictionary contains the item name, an English description, aliases, related data elements, the range, the length, encoding, and necessary editing information. The data dictionary is useful in all phases of analysis, design, and ultimately documentation, because it is the authoritative source on how a data element is used and defined by users in the system. Many large systems feature computerized data dictionaries that cross-reference all programs in the database using a particular data element. The data dictionary can also be used to create XML that enables businesses with different systems, software, or database management systems to exchange data.

HYPERCASE® EXPERIENCE 8

"You're really doing very well. Snowden says you've given him all sorts of new ideas for running the new department. That's saying quite a lot, when you consider that he has a lot of his own ideas. By now I hope you've had a chance to speak with everyone you would like to: certainly Snowden himself, Tom Ketcham, Daniel Hill, and Mr. Hyatt.

"Mr. Hyatt is an elusive soul, isn't he? I guess I didn't meet him until well into my third year. I hope you get to find out about him much sooner. Oh, but when you do get to see him, he cuts quite a figure, doesn't he? And those crazy airplanes. I've almost been conked on the head by one in the parking lot. But how can you get angry, when it's The Boss who's flying it? He's also got a secret—or should I say private—oriental garden off his office suite. No, you'll never see it on the building plans. You have to get to know him very well before he'll show you that, but I would wager it's the only one like it in Tennessee and maybe in the whole U.S. He fell in love with the wonderful gardens he saw in Southeast Asia as a young man. It goes deeper than that, however. Mr. Hyatt knows the value of contemplation and meditation. If he has an opinion, you can be sure it has been well thought through."

HYPERCASE QUESTIONS

1. Briefly list the data elements that you have found on three different reports produced at MRE.
2. Based on your interviews with Snowden Evans and others, list the data elements that you believe you should add to the Management Unit's project reporting systems to better capture important data on project status, project deadlines, and budget estimates.
3. Create a data dictionary entry for a new data store, a new data flow, and a new data process that you are suggesting based on your response to Question 2.
4. Suggest a list of new data elements that might be helpful to Jimmie Hyatt but are clearly not being made available to him currently.

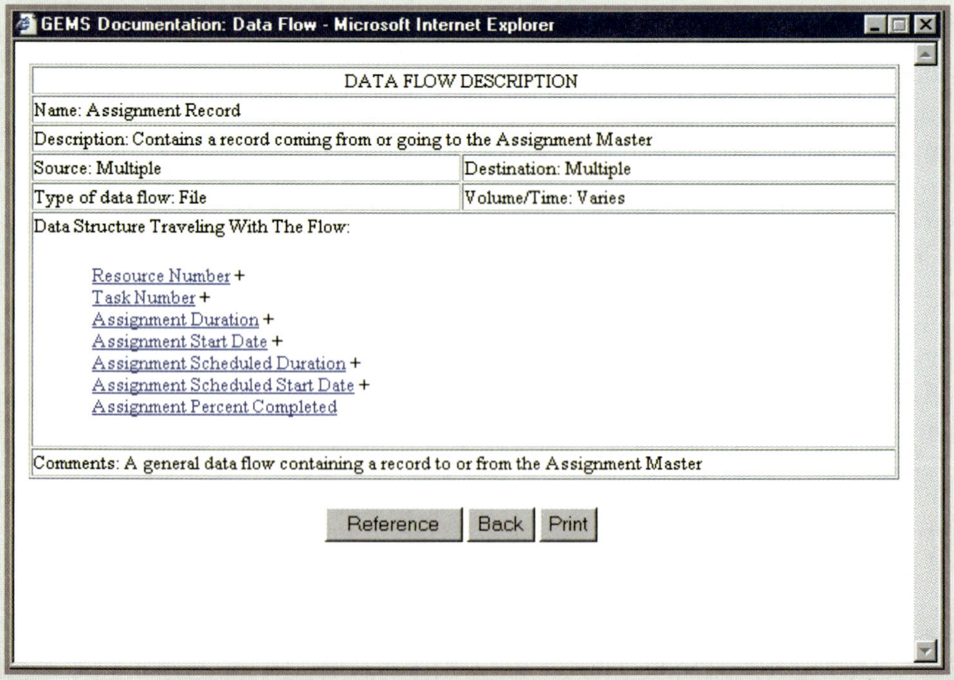

FIGURE 8.HC1

In HyperCase, you can look at the data dictionary kept at MRE.

KEYWORDS AND PHRASES

- base element
- binary format
- data dictionary
- data element
- data structure
- derived element
- document type definition (DTD)
- extensible markup language (XML)
- ID
- IDREF
- packed decimal
- physical data structure
- repeating group
- repeating item
- repository
- schema
- structural record
- system deliverables
- varchar
- zoned decimal

REVIEW QUESTIONS

1. Define the term *data dictionary*. Define *metadata*.
2. What are four reasons for compiling a complete data dictionary?
3. What information is contained in the data repository?
4. What is a structural record?
5. List the eight specific categories that each entry in the data dictionary should contain. Briefly give the definition of each category.
6. What are the basic differences among data dictionary entries prepared for data stores, data structures, and data elements?
7. Why are structural records used?
8. What is the difference between logical and physical data structures?
9. Describe the difference between base and derived elements.
10. How do the data dictionary entries relate to levels in a set of data flow diagrams?
11. List the four steps to take in compiling a data dictionary.
12. Why shouldn't compiling the data dictionary be viewed as an end in itself?
13. What are the main benefits of using a data dictionary?
14. What does extensible markup language (XML) describe?
15. What is a document type definition?
16. How does a document type definition help to ensure that an XML document contains all necessary elements?
17. When should attributes be used in an XML document?
18. What does an ID attribute ensure?
19. What does an IDREF attribute validate?

PROBLEMS

1. Based on Figure 7.EX1 in Chapter 7, Joe, one of your systems analysis team members, made the following entry for the data dictionary used by Marilyn's Tours:

   DATA ELEMENT = TOURIST* * * * PAYMENT
   ALIAS = TOURIST PAY
   CHARACTERS = 12–24
   RANGE = $5.00–$1,000
   VARIABLES = $5.00, $10.00, $15.00 up to $1,000, and anything in between in dollars and cents.

TO CALCULATE = TOTAL COST OF ALL TOURS, ANY APPLICABLE N.Y. STATE TAX, minus any RESERVATION DEPOSITS made.

   a. Is this truly a data element? Why or why not?
   b. Rewrite the data dictionary entry for TOURIST PAYMENT, reclassifying it if necessary. Use the proper form for the classification you choose.

2. Sue Kong, the systems analyst, has made significant progress in understanding the data movement at Shanghai Megabank. To share what she has done with other members of her team as well as the head of regional operations, she is composing a data dictionary.
   a. Write an entry in Sue's data dictionary for three of the data flows in regional banking. Be as complete as possible.
   b. Write an entry in Sue's data dictionary for three of the data stores in regional banking. Be as complete as possible.
3. Jorge Alvarez, the manager of the bookstore that your systems analysis team has been working with to build a computerized inventory system, thinks that one of your team members is making a nuisance of himself by asking him extremely detailed questions about data items used in the system. For example, he asks, "Jorge, how much space, in characters, does the listing of an ISBN take?"
   a. What are the problems created by going directly to the manager with questions concerning data dictionary entries? Use a paragraph to list the problems you can see with your team member's approach.
   b. In a paragraph, explain to your team member how he can better gather information for the data dictionary.
4. Michael Bush owns a store specializing in travel gear and clothes. Manufacturers have their own coding, but there are many manufacturers. Set up data elements for six different travel hats from three different suppliers.
5. Michael (from Problem 4) also assembles packages of camping kits. Each kit is a group of separate products that are sold as a package. Each package (called a PRODUCT) is built using many parts, which vary from product to product. Interviews with the head parts clerk have resulted in a list of elements for the PRODUCT PART Web page, showing which parts are used in

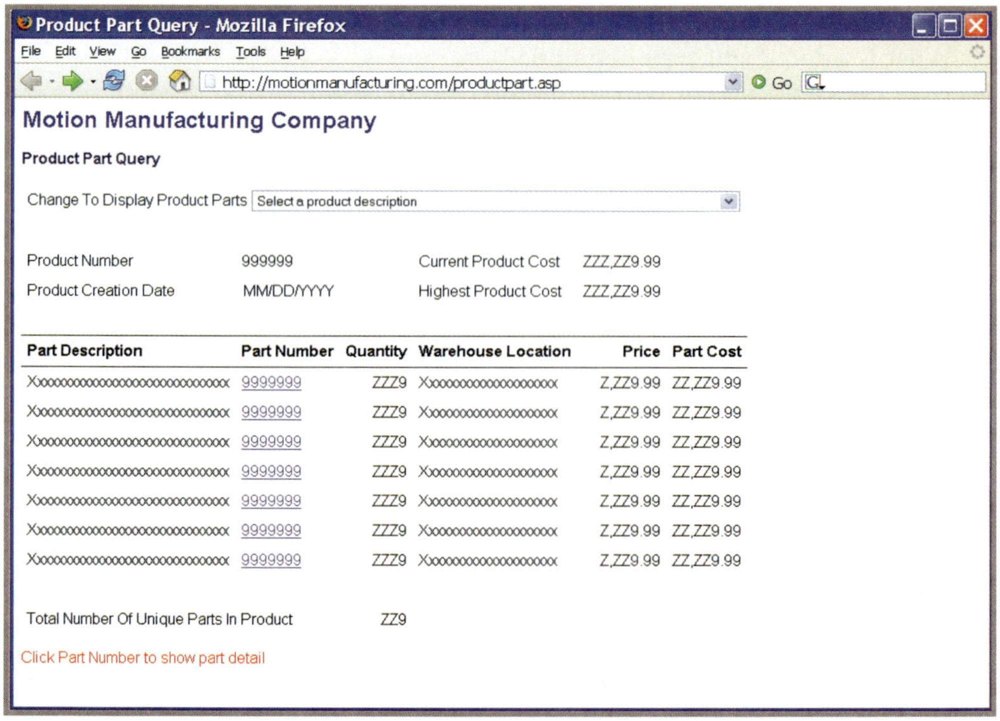

FIGURE 8.EX1
A prototype of the PRODUCT-PART Web page.

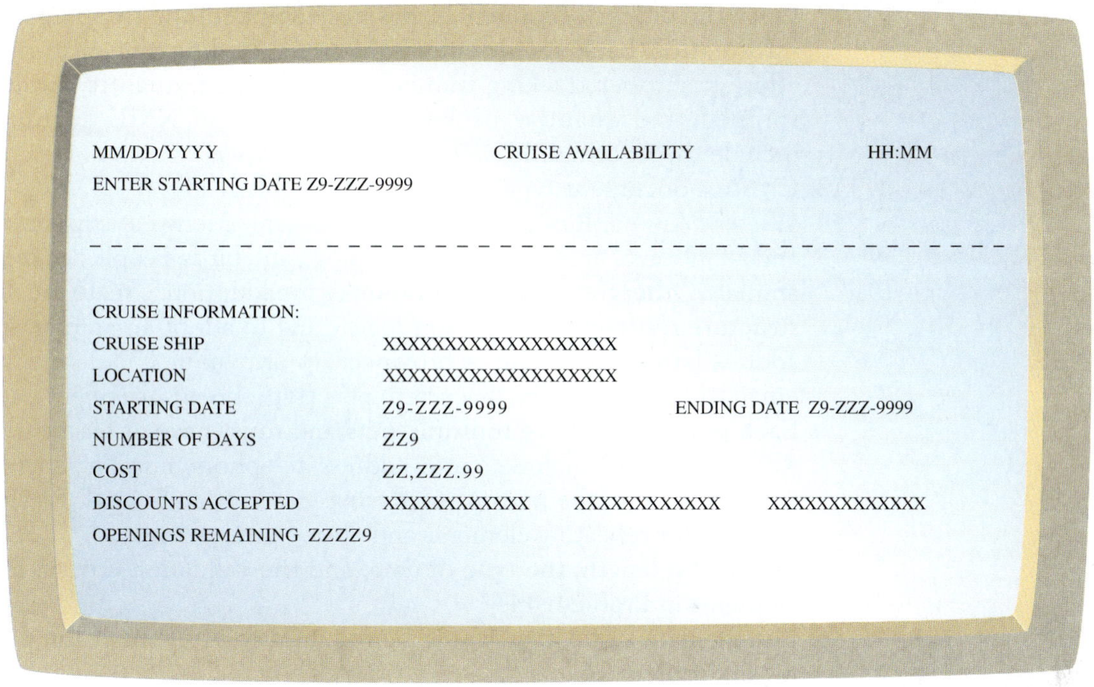

FIGURE 8.EX2
A display screen showing cruise availability.

the manufacture of each product. A prototype of the PRODUCT-PART Web page is illustrated in Figure 8.EX1. Create a data structure dictionary entry for the PRODUCT-PART.

6. Analyze the elements found on the PRODUCT-PART Web page and create the data structure for the PRODUCT MASTER and the PART MASTER data stores.
7. Which of the elements on the PRODUCT-PART Web page are derived elements?
8. The Pacific Holiday Company arranges cruise vacations of varying lengths at several locations. When customers call to check on the availability of a cruise, a CRUISE AVAILABILITY INQUIRY, illustrated in Figure 8.EX2, is used to supply them with information. Create the data dictionary structure for the CRUISE AVAILABILITY INQUIRY.
9. List the master files that would be necessary to implement the CRUISE AVAILABILITY INQUIRY.
10. The following ports of call are available for the Pacific Holiday Company:

Apia	Nuku Hiva	Auckland
Pago Pago	Papeete	Wellington
Bora Bora	Raiatea	Christ Church
Moorea	Napier	Dunedin

Create the PORT OF CALL element. Examine the data to determine the length and format of the element.

11. Raul Esparza, the ecommerce manager for Moonlight Mugs, a company that sells customized coffee mugs, would like to send information to another company that maintains the warehouse and provides shipping services. Order information is obtained from a secure Web site, including customer number, name and address, telephone number, email address, product number and quantity, as well as credit card information. There may be several different products shipped on one order. The shipping company handles items for other small businesses as well. Define an XML document that will include only the information that the shipping company needs to ship goods to the customer.

12. Once the order in Problem 11 has been shipped, the shipping company sends information back to Moonlight Mugs, including the customer name and address, shipper tracking number, data shipped, quantity ordered, quantity shipped, and quantity backordered. Define an XML document that will include the information sent to Moonlight Mugs.
13. Create a document type definition for Problem 11.
14. Western Animal Rescue is a nonprofit organization that supports the fostering and adoption of animals, such as cats, dogs, and birds. People can register to adopt animals. Others register and add animals for adoption. Create the data dictionary structure representing a person registering to adopt an animal. Include name, address (street, city, state or province, zip or mailing code), telephone number, email address, date of birth, current pets (type, breed, age of pet), and references. Each person may have multiple pets and must have at least three references. References must include name, address, telephone number, email address, and how they know the person registering to adopt an animal. Be sure to include notation for repeating elements and optional elements.
15. Define the length, the type of data, and the validation criteria for each of the elements in Problem 14.
16. List the data stores that would be required to implement the person registering in Problem 14.
17. Create an XML document with sample data for one person registering to adopt an animal.

GROUP PROJECTS

1. Meet with your group and use a CASE tool or a manual procedure to develop data dictionary entries for a process, data flow, data store, and data structure based on the data flow diagrams you completed for Maverick Transport in the Chapter 7 group exercises. As a group, agree on any assumptions necessary to make complete entries for each data element.
2. Your group should develop a list of methods to help you make complete data dictionary entries for this exercise as well as for future projects. For example, study existing reports, base them on new or existing data flow diagrams, and so on.

SELECTED BIBLIOGRAPHY

Baskerville, R., and J. Pries-Heje. "Short Cycle Time Systems Development." *Information Systems Journal*, Vol. 14, 2004, pp. 237–264.

Conboy, K., and B. Fitzgerald. "Toward a Conceptual Framework of Agile Methods: A Study of Agility in Different Disciplines." *WISER '04*, November 5, 2004, Newport Beach, CA, pp. 37–44.

Davis, G. B., and M. H. Olson. *Management Information Systems, Conceptual Foundations, Structure, and Development*, 2d ed. New York: McGraw-Hill, 1985.

Gane, C., and T. Sarson. *Structured Systems Analysis and Design Tools and Techniques*. Englewood Cliffs, NJ: Prentice Hall, 1979.

Lucas, H. *Information Systems Concepts for Management*, 3d ed. New York: McGraw-Hill, 1986.

Martin, J. *Strategic Data-Planning Methodologies*. Englewood Cliffs, NJ: Prentice Hall, 1982.

McFadden, F. R., and J. A. Hoffer. *Data Base Management*. Menlo Park, CA: Benjamin/Cummings, 1985.
Sagheb-Tehrani, M. "Expert Systems Development and Some Ideas of Design Process." *ACM SIGSOFT Software Engineering Notes*, Vol. 30, No. 2, March 2005, pp. 1–5.
Schmidt, A. *Working with Visible Analyst Workbench for Windows*. Upper Saddle River, NJ: Prentice Hall, 1996.
Semprevivo, P. C. *Systems Analysis and Design: Definition, Process, and Design*. Chicago: Science Research Associates, Inc., 1982.
Subramaniam, V., and A. Hunt. *Practices of an Agile Developer*. Raleigh, NC: Pragmatic Bookshelf, 2006.

8

ALLEN SCHMIDT, JULIE E. KENDALL, AND KENNETH E. KENDALL

CPU DEFINING WHAT YOU MEAN

"We can use the data flow diagrams we completed to create data dictionary entries for all data flow and data stores," Chip says to Anna at their next meeting. Each of these components has a composition entry in the repository. The records created for the computer system are thus linked directly to the data flow diagram components that describe data.

Anna and Chip meet to divide the work of creating records and elements. "I'll develop the data dictionary for the software portion of the system," Anna says.

"Good thing I enjoy doing the hardware," Chip kids her good-naturedly.

Records, or data structures, are created first. They may contain elements, the basic building blocks of the data structure, and they may also contain other records in them called structural records. Visible Analyst also maintains relationships among graph components, records, and elements that may be used for analysis and reporting.

Using information from interviews and the prototype screens, Anna starts to create the Software records. Because the output of a system will determine what data need to be both stored and obtained via data entry screens, the starting point is the output data flow SOFTWARE INSTALLATION LIST. This prototype identifies some of the elements that should be stored in the SOFTWARE MASTER:

SOFTWARE INVENTORY NUMBER
VERSION NUMBER
NUMBER OF CDs
CAMPUS LOCATION
TITLE
HARDWARE INVENTORY
NUMBER
ROOM LOCATION

Other output prototype reports and screens are also examined. Additional elements are obtained from the ADD SOFTWARE prototype screen. These elements are arranged into a logical sequence for the SOFTWARE MASTER file. The following standards for arranging elements within a record are used:

1. The major key element that uniquely identifies the record. An example is the SOFTWARE INVENTORY NUMBER.
2. Descriptive information, such as TITLE, VERSION NUMBER, and PUBLISHER.
3. Information that is periodically updated, such as NUMBER OF COPIES.
4. Any repeating elements, such as HARDWARE INVENTORY NUMBER, denoting the machines on which the software has been installed.

Next, the SOFTWARE MASTER record is created using the Visible Analyst repository. The description screen for creating a record is shown in Figure E8.1. (*Note:* This screen may differ from the data structure screen in your copy of Visible Analyst. To view the screen that is in the same format, click the **Options** menu and then click so there is a check in front of **Classical User Interface.**) Notice the entry area for an alias, or a different name for the record, used by a different user group. Because each user may refer to the same record by a different name, all such names should be documented, resulting in enriched communication among users.

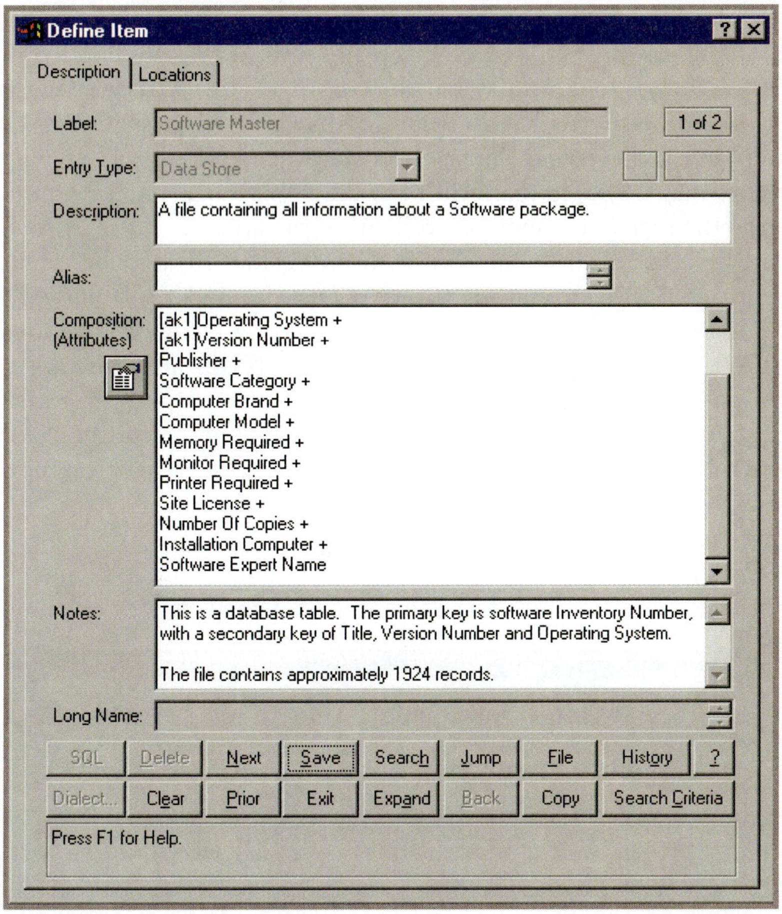

FIGURE E8.1
Record description screen, SOFTWARE MASTER.

Each element or structural record needs to be defined as part of the whole record, and it is entered in the **Composition** area. If the element or structural record is a repeating group, the name is enclosed in curly brackets ({ }) and the number of times it repeats is placed in front of the name. If the data are keys, a code is put in brackets ([ ]) in front of the name. The symbol [pk] represents a primary key. The symbol [akn] represents an alternate key, where n is 1, 2, 3 and so on and defines each different key or group of fields that, when combined, make a secondary key. When a group of fields makes up a secondary key, that key is called a concatenated key.

Examine the SOFTWARE MASTER. It contains a primary key of SOFTWARE INVENTORY NUMBER and a concatenated secondary key of TITLE, OPERATING SYSTEM, and VERSION NUMBER.

Visible Analyst allows you to easily describe each structural record or element composing the larger record. Anna places the cursor in each name in the **Composition** area and clicks the **Jump** button. Further record and element screens are displayed and detailed information is entered.

"This is great!" Anna thinks to herself. "It's so easy to enter the details, and by using this method, I won't accidentally forget to describe an element."

8

Chip is also impressed with the simplicity of creating the data dictionary. Following a process similar to Anna's, he creates a record description for the COMPUTER MASTER. It contains a table of five internal boards and two structural records, PERIPHERAL EQUIPMENT and MAINTENANCE INFORMATION. The **Composition** area for entering element or record names is a scroll region, meaning that more lines may be keyed than will fit in the display area. As entries are added to the bottom of the region, top entries scroll out of the area.

As elements are added to the record, Chip decides to describe each in detail. The element description screen for the HARDWARE INVENTORY NUMBER is shown in Figure E8.2. Observe the areas for entering element attributes. Several aliases may be included along with a definition. A **Notes** area contains any other useful information about the element. Chip and Anna employ this area to enter further edit criteria and other useful notation. The description for the HARDWARE INVENTORY NUMBER details how this number is used to keep physical track of the machines.

Clicking on the **Physical Characteristics** tab displays a second screen for the HARDWARE INVENTORY NUMBER, illustrated in Figure E8.3. It contains an area showing within which structures the element is contained, as well as an area for the

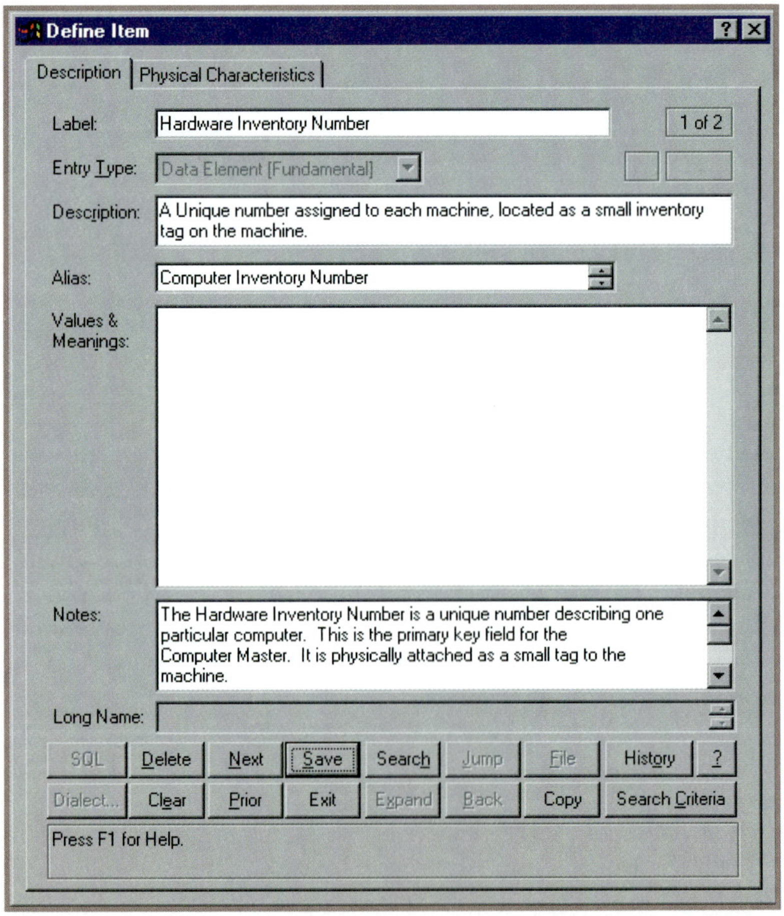

FIGURE E8.2
Element description screen, HARDWARE INVENTORY NUMBER.

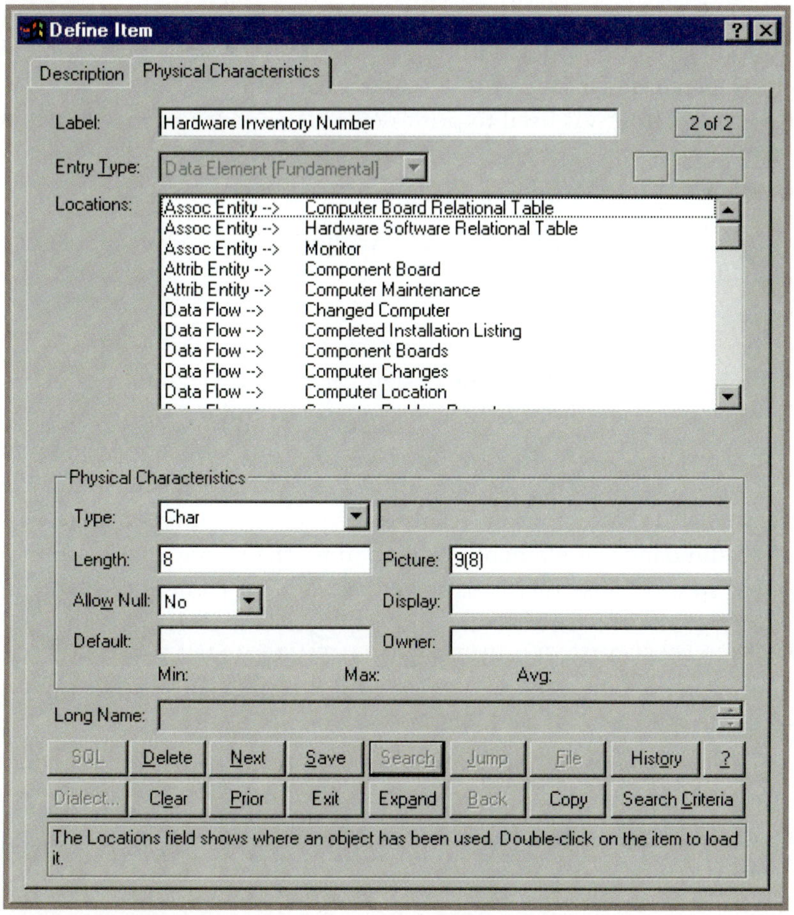

FIGURE E8.3
HARDWARE INVENTORY NUMBER, element characteristics display.

type of data, the length, and the picture used to describe how the data are formatted. Each such picture is a coded entry, similar to those used in programming languages. Examples of some of the codes are as follows:

- 9 Represents numeric data: Only numbers may be entered when prototyping.
- A Alphabetic: Only alphabetic characters may be entered.
- X Alphanumeric: Any characters may be entered.
- Z Zero suppression: Replace leading zeros with spaces.
- $ Dollar sign: Replace leading zeros with a dollar sign.

Chip is careful to include complete entries for these areas, including any default values and whether the entry may be null or not.

Anna and Chip repeat this process for all elements found on each record. This effort is time consuming but worthwhile. After the first few records are created, it becomes easier to create the remaining record structures. Visible Analyst has a search feature that provides lists of the elements contained in the design.

"I think that we've designed a complete set of elements," Chip says at a checkpoint meeting.

"Yes," replies Anna. "There are reports that will show us the details of the data structures and help us to spot duplications and omissions. Let's put Visible Analyst to work producing record layouts for us."

The **Reports** feature was used to print record layouts for all master data stores.

RECORD AND ELEMENT ANALYSIS

"Now let's really put the power of Visible Analyst to use," Anna says. "Let's see how well we've really designed our data."

"What do you mean?" Chip asks.

"I've been studying the analysis features contained in Visible Analyst, and there's a wealth of options for checking our design for consistency and correctness," Anna replies. "The first step is to use the **Reports** feature to produce a summary report of the elements we've added. Then we can examine the list for duplications and redundancy."

Figure E8.4 is an example of a portion of the element summary report displayed using Microsoft Internet Explorer. Analysts would examine the contents carefully and look for redundancy, or elements defined more than once. These redundancies are usually easy to spot because the list is sorted by element name. The elements HARDWARE INVENTORY NUMBER and HARDWARE NUMBER and the elements SOFTWARE INVENTORY NUMBER and SOFTWARE NUM appear to be duplicate elements. Other duplicates, such as ROOM LOCATION and LOCATION, are harder to spot.

"Next we should use the **No Location References** option, which shows all the elements that are not included on any record," says Anna.

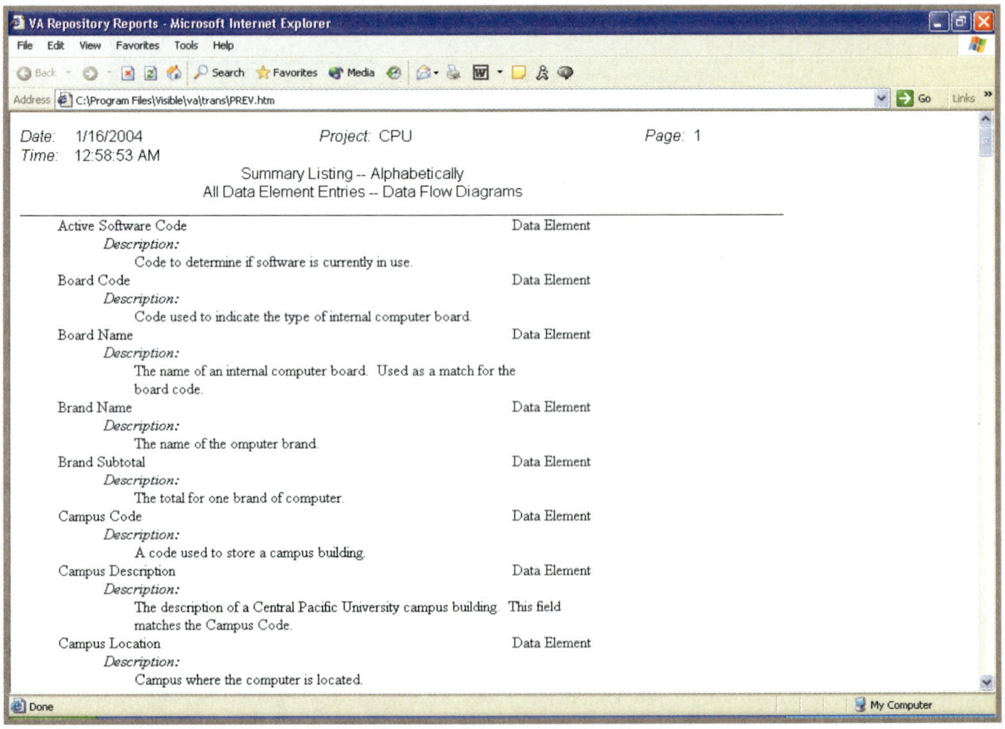
VA Repository Reports - Microsoft Internet Explorer

Address C:\Program Files\Visible\va\trans\PREV.htm

Date: 1/16/2004 *Project:* CPU *Page:* 1
Time: 12:58:53 AM

Summary Listing -- Alphabetically
All Data Element Entries -- Data Flow Diagrams

Active Software Code — Data Element
Description:
Code to determine if software is currently in use.

Board Code — Data Element
Description:
Code used to indicate the type of internal computer board.

Board Name — Data Element
Description:
The name of an internal computer board. Used as a match for the board code.

Brand Name — Data Element
Description:
The name of the omputer brand.

Brand Subtotal — Data Element
Description:
The total for one brand of computer.

Campus Code — Data Element
Description:
A code used to store a campus building.

Campus Description — Data Element
Description:
The description of a Central Pacific University campus building. This field matches the Campus Code.

Campus Location — Data Element
Description:
Campus where the computer is located.

FIGURE E8.4
Element summary preview.

"This is terrific!" exclaims Chip. "This **No Location References** shows design work that needs to be completed. We should produce this report for all the design components."

The elements were either added to other structures or deleted as duplicates. Producing the **No Location References** report a second time revealed no further isolated elements.

"Well, I guess that wraps up the data portion of the system design," Chip says.

"Guess again," replies Anna. "We've only begun to analyze. The **Report Query** feature will provide us with a lot of design information, both for analysis and documentation."

The analysts select a report called **Def Entities without Composition** as their first choice. The report shows entries that are a data store or data structure and do have a composition entry. The output shows that there are no records in error. The next report query is **Elements without Pictures,** and it shows all elements that do not have pictures defined for them. A last report that Chip and Anna create is called **Undefined Elements,** indicating all elements that have not been defined; that is, they exist in the repository as a name only, but with no physical characteristics.

"I'm really impressed with this analysis," Chip says. "Since correcting the errors in our design, I've come to realize how easy it is to feel confident that the design has been completed when there are discrepancies and omissions still needing our attention."

"We're not finished yet. There are some useful matrices that will provide documentation for any changes that may be made in the future. Let's produce the **Data Elements versus Data Structures** matrix, which shows records and their elements," Anna suggests.

The **Report** feature has the ability to produce reports as well as matrices in a grid representation. It shows all elements and the data structures in which they are contained. This matrix is used to access the effect of changing an element by showing which corresponding data structures must be changed.

The next matrix created is the **Diagram Location Matrix,** showing all data stores and the diagrams in which they are located. This information is useful if a change needs to be made to the data store, because it will indicate where programs and documentation need to be changed.

A final matrix is the **Composition Matrix,** showing all data elements and the data stores in which they are contained. This matrix gives Chip and Anna a picture of which elements may be stored redundantly, that is, in several data stores rather than one.

"There are many other reports and matrices that would be useful for us to produce," Anna says. "Some of these should be used later for documentation and tracking any proposed changes. I'm really pleased with what we've accomplished."

EXERCISES

E-1. Use Visible Analyst to view the COMPUTER MASTER data store. Jump to the data structure and browse the elements and structural records.

E-2. Print the SOFTWARE MASTER record using the **Report** feature.

The exercises preceded by a web icon indicate value-added material is available from the Web site at www.prenhall.com/kendall. Students can download a sample Visible Analyst Project and a Microsoft Access database that can be used to complete the exercises. Visible Analyst software can be packaged with this text for an additional fee.

E-3. Use the **Jump** button to move to the **Software Record Structure.** Delete the following elements:

ACTIVE SOFTWARE CODE
INSTALLATION COMPUTER
SOFTWARE EXPERT

E-4. Modify the SOFTWARE CHANGES record, supplying changes to the SOFTWARE MASTER record. The modifications are as follows:

a. Add a [pk], for primary key, in front of the SOFTWARE INVENTORY NUMBER.
b. Add the following elements: COMPUTER BRAND, COMPUTER MODEL, MEMORY REQUIRED, MONITOR REQUIRED, PRINTER REQUIRED, SITE LICENSE, and NUMBER OF COPIES.

E-5. Modify the COMPUTER ADD TRANSACTION record, which contains new computer records to be placed on the COMPUTER MASTER data store.

a. Insert the BRAND NAME and MODEL above the SERIAL NUMBER.
b. Place the CAMPUS LOCATION and ROOM LOCATION after the SERIAL NUMBER.
c. Add the following elements at the bottom of the list: HARD DRIVE 1, HARD DRIVE 2, and CD-RW.
d. Delete the INTERNAL BOARDS element, which will be determined after the computer installation.

E-6. Modify the INSTALLED SOFTWARE TRANSACTION, which is used to update the SOFTWARE MASTER and to produce the SOFTWARE INSTALLATION LISTING. Delete the TITLE and VERSION NUMBER, because they may be obtained from the SOFTWARE MASTER and are redundant keying. Add the HARDWARE INVENTORY NUMBER, specifying the installation computer. Delete the CAMPUS LOCATION and ROOM LOCATION, because they are elements of the installation computer.

E-7. View the alias entry for the SOFTWARE MASTER TABLE.

E-8. Modify the INSTALLED SOFTWARE data store. Add the composition record INSTALLED SOFTWARE TRANSACTION. The index elements are SOFTWARE INVENTORY NUMBER and HARDWARE INVENTORY NUMBER.

E-9. Define the data store SOFTWARE LOG FILE. This file is used to store information on the new software records, plus the date, time, and user ID of the person entering the record. Index elements are SOFTWARE INVENTORY NUMBER, TITLE, VERSION (a concatenated key), and SOFTWARE CATEGORY.

E-10. Define the data store PENDING COMPUTER ORDERS. This file is created when a purchase order is made for ordering new computers, and it is updated by the computer system. Place a comment in the **Notes** area stating that the average number of records is 100. Index elements are PURCHASE ORDER NUMBER and a concatenated key consisting of BRAND NAME and MODEL.

E-11. View the entry for the SOFTWARE RECORD data flow. Click **Jump** with the cursor in the **Composition** area and examine the SOFTWARE MASTER record. Click **Back** to return to the data flow description screen.

E-12. Modify the SOFTWARE UPGRADE INFORMATION data flow. The composition record is SOFTWARE UPGRADE INFORMATION.

E-13. Modify the SOFTWARE CROSS-REFERENCE REPORT data flow. The composition record is SOFTWARE CROSS-REFERENCE REPORT.

E-14. Modify the data flow entity for INSTALL UPDATE. This flow updates the COMPUTER MASTER record with installation information. Its data structure is INSTALL UPDATE RECORD. Include a comment that it processes about 50 records per month in updating the COMPUTER MASTER.

E-15. Use the INSTALL UPDATE data flow to jump to (and create) the INSTALL UPDATE RECORD. Provide a definition based on information supplied in the previous problem. Enter the following elements:

HARDWARE INVENTORY NUMBER (primary key)
CAMPUS LOCATION
ROOM
INTERNAL BOARDS (occurs 5 times)
HARD DRIVE 2
PRINTER
MAINTENANCE INTERVAL
DATE INSTALLED

E-16. Create the data flow description for the SOFTWARE INSTALLATION LIST. This flow contains information on specific software packages and the machines on which the software should be installed. The composition should include the SOFTWARE INSTALLATION LISTING, a data structure.

E-17. Use the SOFTWARE INSTALL LIST to jump to (and therefore create) the SOFTWARE INSTALLATION LISTING. The elements on the listing are as follows:

SOFTWARE INVENTORY NUMBER
TITLE
VERSION NUMBER
HARDWARE INVENTORY NUMBER
CAMPUS LOCATION
ROOM LOCATION

E-18. Modify and print the element HARDWARE SUBTOTAL. Change the type to Numeric, the length to 6,2, and the picture to Z, ZZZ, ZZ9.99.

E-19. Modify and print the MONITOR NAME element, the result of a table lookup using a monitor code. The type should be Character, the length 30, and the Picture X(30).

E-20. Modify and print the DEPARTMENT NAME element. Create an alias of STAFF DEPARTMENT NAME. In the **Notes** area, enter the following comment: Table of codes: Department Table. The type should be Character, the length 25, and the picture X(25).

E-21. Create the following element descriptions. Use the values supplied in the table. Create any alternate names and definitions based on your understanding of the element.

Name	PURCHASE ORDER NUMBER	PROBLEM DESCRIPTION
Type	Character	Character
Length	7	70
Picture	9999999	X(70)
Name	TOTAL COMPUTER COST	NEXT PREVENTIVE MAINTENANCE DATE

Type	Numeric	Date
Length	7,2	8
Picture	Z, ZZZ, ZZ9.99	Z9/99/9999
Notes		The NEXT PREVENTIVE MAINTENANCE DATE is calculated by adding the MAINTENANCE INTERVAL to the LAST PREVENTIVE MAINTENANCE DATE.
Name	PHONE NUMBER	REPAIR STATUS
Type	Character	Character
Length	7	1
Picture	999-9999	X
Notes		Table of codes: Repair Table
Default		C

E-22. Use the **Repository Reports** feature to produce the following reports and matrices, either by printing the reports or by previewing them using your Web browser. The selection criteria from the **Repository Reports** dialogue box are listed, separated with a slash (/). Explain in a paragraph where the information produced may be effectively used.

a. Data Flow/Cross-Reference Listing/Data Element/Entire Project
b. Data Flow/Cross-Reference Listing/Data Structure/Entire Project
c. Record Contains Element (One Level) Matrix
d. Data Flow/Single-Entry Listing/Software Master—Normalized
e. Data Flow/Diagram Location Matrix/Data Stores versus Diagrams
f. Data Flow/Composition Matrix/Data Elements versus Data Flows
g. Data Flow/Composition Matrix/Data Elements versus Data Structures
h. Data Flow/Composition Matrix/Data Element versus Data Stores

E-23. Use the **Report Query** feature to produce the following reports. Explain in a sentence what information the report is providing you with.

a. The **Undefined Elements** report
b. The **Elements without Pictures** report
c. The **Coded Elements** report
d. The **Any Item with Components** report

E-24. Print a summary report for all data flow components that do not have a description. (*Hint:* Click the **No Descriptive Info.** radio button.)

E-25. Print a summary report for all data flow components that are not on a diagram. (*Hint:* Click the **No Location References** radio button.)

E-26. Print a detailed report for all elements. Include only the physical information and the values and meanings. (*Hint:* Click the **Fields** button and then the **Invert** button and select the fields that you want printed.) Why would this report be useful to the analyst?

DESCRIBING PROCESS SPECIFICATIONS AND STRUCTURED DECISIONS

9

Learning Objectives

Once you have mastered the material in this chapter you will be able to:

1. **Understand the purpose of process specifications.**
2. **Recognize the difference between structured and semistructured decisions.**
3. **Use structured English, decision tables, and decision trees to analyze, describe, and document structured decisions.**
4. **Choose an appropriate decision analysis method for analyzing structured decisions and creating process specifications.**

The systems analyst approaching process specifications and structured decisions has many options for documenting and analyzing them. In Chapters 7 and 8 you noted processes such as VERIFY AND COMPUTE FEES, but you did not explain the logic necessary to execute these tasks. The methods available for documenting and analyzing the logic of decisions include structured English, decision tables, and decision trees. It is important to be able to recognize logic and structured decisions that occur in a business and how they are distinguishable from semistructured decisions that tend to involve human judgment. Then it is critical to recognize that structured decisions lend themselves particularly well to analysis with systematic methods that promote completeness, accuracy, and communication.

OVERVIEW OF PROCESS SPECIFICATIONS

To determine the human information requirements of a decision analysis strategy, the systems analyst must first determine the users' objectives, along with the organization's objectives, using either a top-down approach or an object-oriented approach. The systems analyst must understand the principles of organizations and have a working knowledge of data gathering techniques. The top-down approach is critical because all human decisions in the organization should be related, at least indirectly, to the broad objectives of the entire organization.

Process specifications—sometimes called *minispecs,* because they are a small portion of the total project specifications—are created for primitive processes on a data flow diagram as well as for some higher-level processes that explode to a child diagram. They also may be created for class methods in object-oriented design, and, in a more general sense, for the steps in a use case (as discussed in Chapters 2 and 18). These specifications explain the decision-making logic and formulas that will transform process input data into output. Each derived element must have process logic to show how it is produced from the base elements or other previously created derived elements that are input to the primitive process.

The three goals of producing process specifications are as follows:

1. To reduce the ambiguity of the process. This goal compels the analyst to learn details about how the process works. Any vague areas should be noted, written down, and consolidated for all process specifications. These observations form a basis and provide the questions for follow-up interviews with the user community.
2. To obtain a precise description of what is accomplished, which is usually included in a packet of specifications for the programmer.
3. To validate the system design. This goal includes ensuring that a process has all the input data flow necessary for producing the output. In addition, all input and output must be represented on the data flow diagram.

You will find many situations in which process specifications are not created. Sometimes the process is very simple or the computer code already exists. This eventuality would be noted in the process description, and no further design would be required. Categories of processes that generally *do not* require specifications are as follows:

1. Processes that represent physical input or output, such as read and write. These processes usually require only simple logic.
2. Processes that represent simple data validation, which is usually fairly easy to accomplish. The edit criteria are included in the data dictionary and incorporated into the computer source code. Process specifications may be produced for complex editing.
3. Processes that use prewritten code. These processes are generally included in a system as subprograms and functions.

Subprograms are computer programs that are written, tested, and stored on the computer system. They usually perform a general system function, such as validating a date or a check digit. These general-purpose subprograms are written and documented only once but form a series of building blocks that may be used in many systems throughout the organization. Thus, these subprograms appear as processes on many data flow diagrams. Functions are similar to subprograms but are coded differently.

PROCESS SPECIFICATION FORMAT

Process specifications link the process to the data flow diagram, and hence the data dictionary, as illustrated in Figure 9.1. Each process specification should be entered on a separate form or into a CASE tool screen such as the one used for Visible Analyst and shown in the CPU case at the end of this chapter. Enter the following information:

1. The process number, which must match the process ID on the data flow diagram. This specification allows an analyst to work on or review any process, and to locate the data flow diagram containing the process easily.
2. The process name, which again must be the same as the name displayed in the process symbol on the data flow diagram.
3. A brief description of what the process accomplishes.

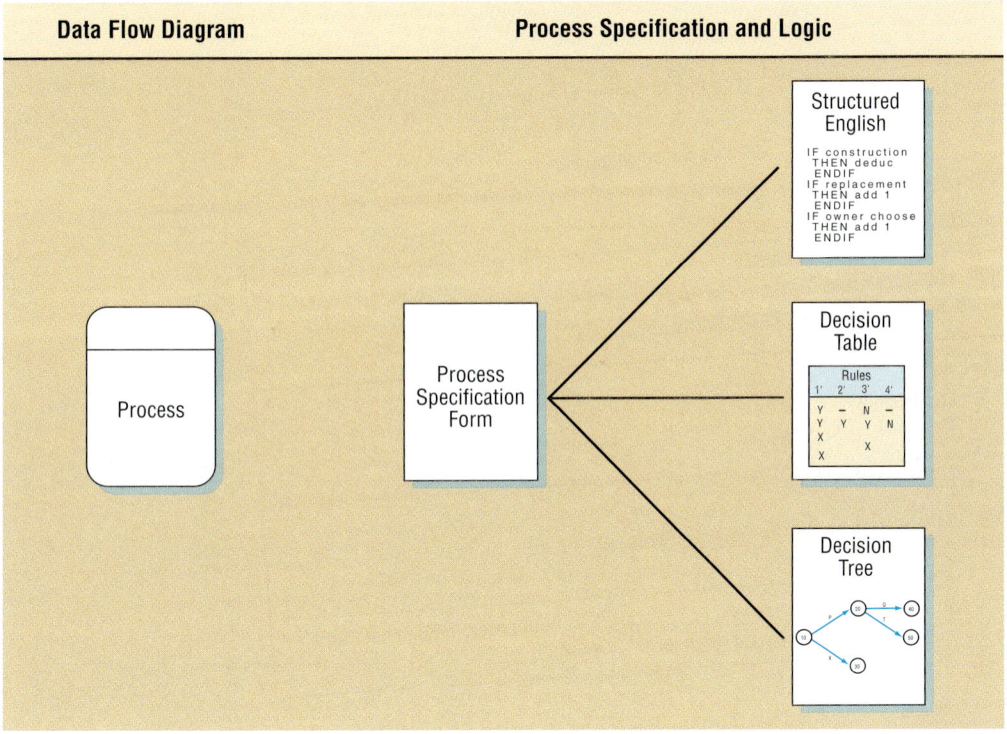

FIGURE 9.1

How process specifications relate to the data flow diagram.

4. A list of input data flows, using the names found on the data flow diagram. Data names used in the formula or logic should match those in the data dictionary to ensure consistency and good communication.
5. The output data flows, also using data flow diagram and data dictionary names.
6. An indication of the type of process: batch, online, or manual. All online processes require screen designs, and all manual processes should have well-defined procedures for employees performing the process tasks.
7. If the process uses prewritten code, include the name of the subprogram or function containing that code.
8. A description of the process logic that states policy and business rules in everyday language, not computer language pseudocode. Business rules are the procedures, or perhaps a set of conditions or formulas, that allow a corporation to run its business. The early problem definition (as explained in Chapter 3) that you completed initially may provide a starting place for this description. Common business rule formats include the following:
   - Definitions of business terms.
   - Business conditions and actions.
   - Data integrity constraints.
   - Mathematical and functional derivations.
   - Logical inferences.
   - Processing sequences.
   - Relationships among facts about the business.
9. If there is not enough room on the form for a complete structured English description, or if there is a decision table or tree depicting the logic, include the corresponding table or tree name.
10. List any unresolved issues, incomplete portions of logic, or other concerns. These issues form the basis of the questions used for follow-up interviews with users or business experts you have added to your project team.

The above items should be entered to complete a process specification form, which includes a process number, process name, or both from the data flow

Process Specification Form

Number 1.3

Name Determine Quantity Available

Description Determine if an item is available for sale. If it is not available, create a backordered item record. Determine the quantity available.

Input Data Flow

Valid item from Process 1.2
Quantity on Hand from Item Record

Output Data Flow

Available Item (Item Number + Quantity Sold) to Processes 1.4 & 1.5
Backordered item to Inventory Control

Type of Process

☑ Online ☐ Batch ☐ Manual

Subprogram/Function Name

Process Logic:

```
IF the Order Item Quantity is greater than Quantity on Hand
   Then Move Order Item Quantity to Available Item Quantity
        Move Order Item Number to Available Item Number
ELSE
   Subtract Quantity on Hand from Order Item Quantity
        giving Quantity Backordered
   Move Quantity Backordered to Backordered Item Record
   Move Item Number to Backordered Item Record
   DO write Backordered Record
   Move Quantity on Hand to Available Item Quantity
   Move Order Item Number to Available Item Number
ENDIF
```

Refer to: Name:

☐ Structured English ☐ Decision Table ☐ Decision Tree

Unresolved Issues: Should the amount that is on order for this item be taken into account? Would this, combined with the expected arrival date of goods on order, change how the quantity available is calculated?

FIGURE 9.2

An example of a completed process specification form for determining whether an item is available.

diagram, as well as the eight other items shown in the World's Trend example (Figure 9.2). Notice that completing this form thoroughly facilitates linking the process to the data flow diagram and the data dictionary.

STRUCTURED ENGLISH

When the process logic involves formulas or iteration, or when structured decisions are not complex, an appropriate technique for analyzing the decision process is the use of structured English. As the name implies, structured English is based on (1) structured logic, or instructions organized into nested and grouped procedures, and (2) simple English statements such as add, multiply, and move.

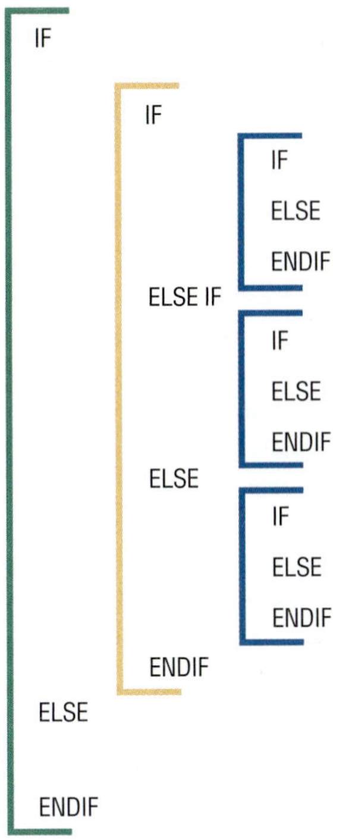

FIGURE 9.3

Proper use of structured English will involve nesting blocks of instructions within others.

A word problem can be transformed into structured English, by putting the decision rules into their proper sequence and using the convention of IF-THEN-ELSE statements throughout. Structured English can be more complex if blocks of instructions are nested within other blocks of instructions, as shown in Figure 9.3.

WRITING STRUCTURED ENGLISH

To write structured English, you may want to use the following conventions:

1. Express all logic in terms of one of these four types: sequential structures, decision structures, case structures, or iterations (see Figure 9.4 for examples).
2. Use and capitalize accepted key words such as IF, THEN, ELSE, DO, DO WHILE, DO UNTIL, and PERFORM.
3. Indent blocks of statements to show their hierarchy (nesting) clearly.
4. When words or phrases have been defined in a data dictionary (as in Chapter 8), underline those words or phrases to signify that they have a specialized, reserved meaning.
5. Be careful when using "and" and "or," and avoid confusion when distinguishing between "greater than" and "greater than or equal to" and like relationships. "A and B" means both A and B; "A or B" means either A or B, but not both. Clarify the logical statements now rather than waiting until the program coding stage.

A Structured English Example The following example demonstrates how a spoken procedure for processing medical claims is transformed into structured English:

> We process all our claims in this manner. First, we determine whether the claimant has ever sent in a claim before; if not, we set up a new record. The claim totals for the year are then updated. Next, we determine if a claimant has policy A or policy B, which differ in deductibles and copayments (the percentage of the claim claimants pay themselves). For both policies, we check to see if the deductible has been met ($100 for plan A and $50 for plan B). If the deductible has not been met, we apply the

CONSULTING OPPORTUNITY 9.1

KIT CHEN KABOODLE, INC.

"I don't want to get anyone stirred up, but I think we need to sift through our unfilled order policies," says Kit Chen. "I wouldn't want to put a strain on our customers. As you know already, Kit Chen Kaboodle is a Web and mail-order cookware business specializing in 'klassy kitsch for kitchens,' as our latest catalog says. I mean, we've got everything you need to do gourmet cooking and entertaining: nutmeg grinders, potato whisks, egg separators, turkey basters, placemats with cats on 'em, ice cube trays in shamrock shapes, and more.

"Here's how we've been handling unfilled orders. We search our unfilled orders file from the Internet as well as mail-order sales once a week. If the order was filled this week, we delete the record, and the rest is gravy. If we haven't written to the customer in four weeks, we send 'em this cute card with a chef peeking into the oven, saying, 'Not ready yet.' (It's a notification that their item is still on backorder.)

"If the backorder date changed to greater than 45 days from now, we send out a notice. If the merchandise is seasonal (as with Halloween treat bags, Christmas cookie cutters, or Valentine's Day cake molds) and the backorder date is 30 days or more, though, we send out a notice with a chef glaring at his egg timer.

"If the backorder date changed at all and we haven't sent out a card in the last two weeks, we send out a card with a chef checking his recipe. If the merchandise is no longer available, we send a notice (complete with chef crying in the corner) and delete the record. We haven't begun to use email in place of mailed cards, but I'd like to.

"Thanks for listening to all this. I think we've got the right ingredients for a good policy; we just need to blend them together and cook up something special."

Because you are the systems analyst whom Kit hired, go through the narrative of how Kit Chen Kaboodle, Inc., handles unfilled orders, drawing boxes around each action Kit mentions and circling each condition brought up. Make a list of any ambiguities you would like to clarify in a later interview, and then write five questions to address them.

claim to the deductible. Another step adjusts for the copayment; we subtract the percentage the claimant pays (40 percent for plan A and 60 percent for plan B) from the claim. Then we issue a check if there is money coming to the claimant, print a summary of the transaction, and update our accounts. We do this until all claims for that day are processed.

In examining the foregoing statements, one notices some simple sequence structures, particularly at the beginning and end. There are a couple of decision structures, and

FIGURE 9.4
Examples of logic expressed in a sequential structure, a decision structure, a case structure, and an iteration.

Structured English Type	Example
Sequential Structure A block of instructions in which no branching occurs	Action #1 Action #2 Action #3
Decision Structure Only IF a condition is true, complete the following statements; otherwise, jump to the ELSE	IF Condition A is True THEN implement Action A ELSE implement Action B ENDIF
Case Structure A special type of decision structure in which the cases are mutually exclusive (if one occurs, the others cannot)	IF Case #1 implement Action #1 ELSE IF Case #2 Implement Action #2 ELSE IF Case #3 Implement Action #3 ELSE IF Case #4 Implement Action #4 ELSE print error ENDIF
Iteration Blocks of statements that are repeated until done	DO WHILE there are customers. Action #1 ENDDO

CONSULTING OPPORTUNITY 9.2

KNEADING STRUCTURE

Kit Chen has risen to the occasion and answered your questions concerning the policy for handling unfilled orders at Kit Chen Kaboodle, Inc. Based on those answers and any assumptions you need to make, pour Kit's narrative (from Consulting Opportunity 9.1) into a new mold by rewriting the recipe for handling unfilled orders in structured English. In a paragraph, describe how this process might change if you used email for notification rather than regular mail.

it is most appropriate to nest them, first by determining which plan (A or B) to use and then by subtracting the correct deductibles and copayments. The last sentence points to an iteration: Either DO UNTIL all the claims are processed or DO WHILE there are claims remaining.

Realizing that it is possible to nest the decision structures according to policy plans, we can write the structured English for the foregoing example (see Figure 9.5). As one begins to work on the structured English, one finds that some logic and relationships that seemed clear at one time are actually ambiguous. For example, do we add the claim to the year-to-date (YTD) claim before or after updating the

```
DO WHILE there are claims remaining
  IF claimant has not sent in a claim
    THEN set up new claimant record
  ELSE continue
Add claim to YTD Claim
  IF claimant has policy-plan A
    THEN IF deductible of $100.00 has not been met
      THEN subtract deductible-not-met from claim
      Update deductible
    ELSE continue
    ENDIF
    Subtract copayment of 40% of claim from claim
  ELSE IF claimant has policy-plan B.
    THEN IF deductible of $50.00 has not been met
      THEN subtract deductible-not-met from claim
      Update deductible
    ELSE continue
    ENDIF
    Subtract copayment of 60% of claim from claim
  ELSE continue
  ELSE write plan-error-message
  ENDIF
ENDIF
IF claim is greater than zero
  THEN print check
ENDIF
Print summary for claimant
Update accounts
ENDDO
```

FIGURE 9.5
Structured English for the medical-claim processing system. Underlining signifies that the terms have been defined in the data dictionary.

deductible? Is it possible that an error can occur if something other than plan A or B is stored in the claimant's record? We subtract 40 percent of what from the claim? These ambiguities need to be clarified at this point.

Besides the obvious advantage of clarifying the logic and relationships found in human languages, structured English has another important advantage: It is a communication tool. Structured English can be taught to and hence understood by users in the organization, so if communication is important, structured English is a viable alternative for decision analysis.

DATA DICTIONARY AND PROCESS SPECIFICATIONS

All computer programs may be coded using the three basic constructs: sequence, selection (IF . . . THEN . . . ELSE and the case structure), and iteration or looping. The data dictionary indicates which of these constructs must be included in the process specifications.

If the data dictionary for the input and output data flow contains a series of fields without any iteration—{ }—or selection—[ ]—the process specification will contain a simple sequence of statements, such as MOVE, ADD, and SUBTRACT. Refer to the example of a data dictionary for the SHIPPING STATEMENT, illustrated in Figure 9.6. Notice that the data dictionary for the SHIPPING STATEMENT has the ORDER NUMBER, ORDER DATE, and CUSTOMER NUMBER as simple

FIGURE 9.6
Data structure for a shipping statement for World's Trend.

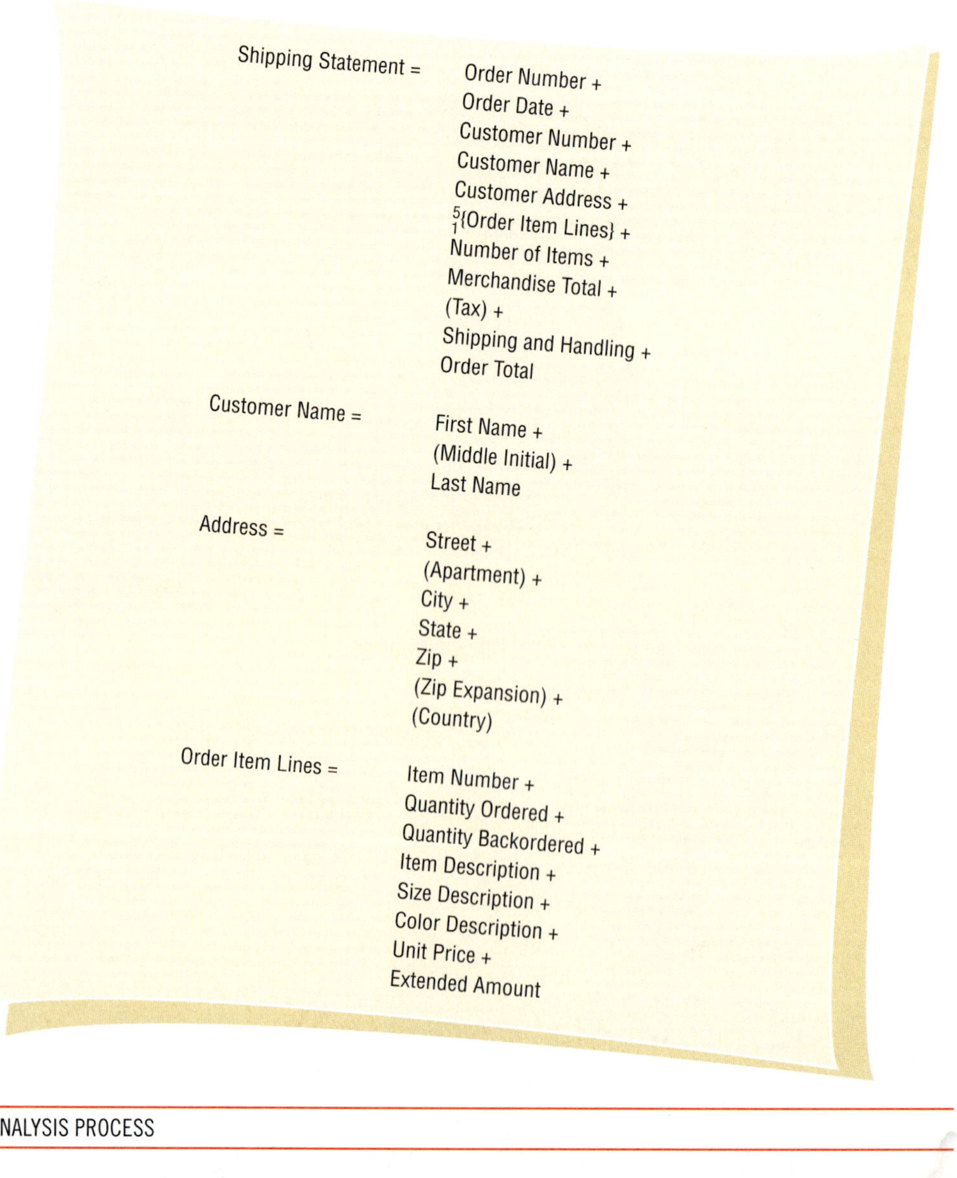
Shipping Statement = Order Number +
Order Date +
Customer Number +
Customer Name +
Customer Address +
$^{5}_{1}${Order Item Lines} +
Number of Items +
Merchandise Total +
(Tax) +
Shipping and Handling +
Order Total

Customer Name = First Name +
(Middle Initial) +
Last Name

Address = Street +
(Apartment) +
City +
State +
Zip +
(Zip Expansion) +
(Country)

Order Item Lines = Item Number +
Quantity Ordered +
Quantity Backordered +
Item Description +
Size Description +
Color Description +
Unit Price +
Extended Amount

```
Structured English

Format the Shipping Statement. After each line of the statement has been
formatted, write the shipping line.

1.  GET Order Record
2.  GET Customer Record
3.  Move Order Number to shipping statement
4.  Move Order Date to Shipping Statement
5.  Move Customer Number to Shipping Statement
6.  DO format Customer Name (leave only one space between First/Middle/Last)
7.  DO format Customer Address lines
8.  DO WHILE there are items for the order
9.       GET Item Record
10.      DO Format Item Line
11.      Multiply Unit Price by Quantity Ordered giving Extended Amount
12.      Move Extended Amount to Order Item Lines
13.      Add Extended Amount to Merchandise Total
14.      IF Quantity Backordered is greater than zero
15.           Move Quantity Backordered to Order Item Lines
16.      ENDIF
17. ENDDO
18. Move Merchandise Total to Shipping Statement
19. Move 0 to Tax
20. IF State is equal to CT
21.      Multiply Merchandise Total by Tax Rate giving Tax
22. ENDIF
23. Move Tax to Shipping Statement
24. DO calculate Shipping and Handling
25. Move Shipping and Handling to Shipping Statement
26. Add Merchandise Total, Tax, and Shipping and Handling giving Order Total
27. Move Order Total to Shipping Statement
```

FIGURE 9.7
Structured English for creating the shipping statement for World's Trend.

sequential fields. The corresponding logic, shown in lines 3 through 5 in the corresponding structured English in Figure 9.7, consists of simple MOVE statements.

A data structure with optional elements contained in parentheses or either/or elements contained in brackets will have a corresponding IF . . . THEN . . . ELSE statement in the process specification. Also, if an amount, such as QUANTITY BACKORDERED, is greater than zero, the underlying logic will be IF . . . THEN . . . ELSE. Iteration, indicated by braces on a data structure, must have a corresponding DO WHILE, DO UNTIL, or PERFORM UNTIL to control looping on the process specification. The data structure for the ORDER ITEM LINES allows up to five items in the loop. Lines 8 through 17 show the statements contained in the DO WHILE through the END DO necessary to produce the multiple ORDER ITEM LINES.

DECISION TABLES

A decision table is a table of rows and columns, separated into four quadrants, as shown in Figure 9.8. The upper left quadrant contains the condition(s); the upper right quadrant contains the condition alternatives. The lower half of the table

FIGURE 9.8

The standard format used for presenting a decision table.

Conditions and Actions	Rules
Conditions	Condition Alternatives
Actions	Action Entries

contains the actions to be taken on the left and the rules for executing the actions on the right. When a decision table is used to determine which action needs to be taken, the logic moves clockwise beginning from the upper left.

Suppose a store wanted to illustrate its policy on noncash customer purchases. The company could do so using a simple decision table as shown in Figure 9.9. Each of the three conditions (sale under $50, pays by check, and uses credit cards) has only two alternatives. The two alternatives are Y (yes, it is true) or N (no, it is not true). Four actions are possible:

1. Complete the sale after verifying the signature.
2. Complete the sale. No signature needed.
3. Call the supervisor for approval.
4. Communicate electronically with the bank for credit card authorization.

The final ingredient that makes the decision table worthwhile is the set of rules for each of the actions. Rules are the combinations of the condition alternatives that precipitate an action. For example, Rule 3 says:

IF N (the total sale is NOT under $50.00)
AND
IF Y (the customer paid by check and had two forms of ID)
AND
IF N (the customer did not use a credit card)
THEN
DO X (call the supervisor for approval).

The foregoing example featured a problem with four sets of rules and four possible actions, but that is only a coincidence. The next example demonstrates that decision tables often become large and involved.

FIGURE 9.9

Using a decision table for illustrating a store's policy of customer checkout with four sets of rules and four possible actions.

Conditions and Actions	Rules 1	2	3	4
Under $50	Y	Y	N	N
Pays by check with two forms of ID	Y	N	Y	N
Uses credit card	N	Y	N	Y
Complete the sale after verifying signature.	X			
Complete the sale. No signature needed.		X		
Call supervisor for approval.			X	
Communicate electronically with bank for credit card authorization.				X

DEVELOPING DECISION TABLES

To build decision tables, the analyst needs to determine the maximum size of the table; eliminate any impossible situations, inconsistencies, or redundancies; and simplify the table as much as possible. The following steps provide the analyst with a systematic method for developing decision tables:

1. Determine the number of conditions that may affect the decision. Combine rows that overlap, such as conditions that are mutually exclusive. The number of conditions becomes the number of rows in the top half of the decision table.
2. Determine the number of possible actions that can be taken. That number becomes the number of rows in the lower half of the decision table.
3. Determine the number of condition alternatives for each condition. In the simplest form of decision table, there would be two alternatives (Y or N) for each condition. In an extended-entry table, there may be many alternatives for each condition. Make sure that all possible values for the condition are included. For example, if a problem statement calculating a customer discount mentions one range of values for an order total from $100 to $1,000 and another range of greater than $1,000, the analyst should realize that the range from 0 up to $100 should also be added as a condition. This is especially true when there are other conditions that may apply to the 0 up to $100 order total.
4. Calculate the maximum number of columns in the decision table by multiplying the number of alternatives for each condition. If there were four conditions and two alternatives (Y or N) for each of the conditions, there would be 16 possibilities as follows:

   Condition 1: × 2 alternatives
   Condition 2: × 2 alternatives
   Condition 3: × 2 alternatives
   Condition 4: × 2 alternatives
   16 possibilities

5. Fill in the condition alternatives. Start with the first condition and divide the number of columns by the number of alternatives for that condition. In the foregoing example, there are 16 columns and two alternatives (Y or N), so 16 divided by 2 is 8. Then choose one of the alternatives, say Y, and write it in the first eight columns. Finish by writing N in the remaining eight columns as follows:

   Condition 1: Y Y Y Y Y Y Y Y N N N N N N N N

   Repeat this step for each condition, using a subset of the table,

   Condition 1: Y Y Y Y Y Y Y Y N N N N N N N N
   Condition 2: Y Y Y Y N N N N
   Condition 3: Y Y N N
   Condition 4: Y N

   and continue the pattern for each condition:

   Condition 1: Y Y Y Y Y Y Y Y N N N N N N N N
   Condition 2: Y Y Y Y N N N N Y Y Y Y N N N N
   Condition 3: Y Y N N Y Y N N Y Y N N Y Y N N
   Condition 4: Y N Y N Y N Y N Y N Y N Y N Y N

CONSULTING OPPORTUNITY 9.3

SAVING A CENT ON CITRON CAR RENTAL

"We feel lucky to be this popular. I think customers feel we have so many options to offer that they ought to rent an auto from us," says Ricardo Limon, who manages several outlets for Citron Car Rental. "Our slogan is, 'You'll never feel squeezed at Citron.' We have five sizes of cars that we list as A through E.

A	Subcompact
B	Compact
C	Midsize
D	Full-size
E	Luxury

"Standard transmission is available only for A, B, and C. Automatic transmission is available for all cars."

"If a customer reserves a subcompact (A) and finds on arriving that we don't have one, that customer gets a free upgrade to the next-sized car, in this case a compact (B). Customers also get a free upgrade from their reserved car size if their company has an account with us. There's a discount for membership in any of the frequent flyer clubs run by cooperating airlines, too. When customers step up to the counter, they tell us what size car they reserved, and then we check to see if we have it in the lot ready to go. They usually bring up any discounts, and we ask them if they want insurance and how long they will use the car. Then we calculate their rate and write out a slip for them to sign right there."

Ricardo has asked you to computerize the billing process for Citron so that customers can get their cars quickly and still be billed correctly. Draw a decision table that represents the conditions, condition alternatives, actions, and action rules you gained from Ricardo's narrative that will guide an automated billing process.

Ricardo wants to expand the ecommerce portion of his business by making it possible to reserve a car over the Web. Draw an updated decision table that shows a 10-percent discount for booking a car over the Web.

6. Complete the table by inserting an X where rules suggest certain actions.
7. Combine rules where it is apparent that an alternative does not make a difference in the outcome. For example,

Condition 1:	Y Y
Condition 2:	Y N
Action 1:	X X

can be expressed as:

Condition 1:	Y
Condition 2:	–
Action 1:	X

The dash [—] signifies that Condition 2 can be either Y or N, and the action will still be taken.

8. Check the table for any impossible situations, contradictions, and redundancies. They are discussed in more detail later.
9. Rearrange the conditions and actions (or even rules) if it makes the decision table more understandable.

A Decision Table Example Figure 9.10 is an illustration of a decision table developed using the steps previously outlined. In this example a company is trying to maintain a meaningful mailing list of customers. The objective is to send out only the catalogs from which customers will buy merchandise.

The managers realize that certain loyal customers order from every catalog and that some people on the mailing list never order. These ordering patterns are easy to observe, but deciding which catalogs to send customers who order only from selected catalogs is more difficult. Once these decisions are made, a decision table is constructed for three conditions (C1: customer ordered from Fall catalog;

Conditions and Actions	Rules 1	2	3	4	5	6	7	8
Customer ordered from Fall catalog.	Y	Y	Y	Y	N	N	N	N
Customer ordered from Christmas catalog.	Y	Y	N	N	Y	Y	N	N
Customer ordered from specialty catalog.	Y	N	Y	N	Y	N	Y	N
Send out this year's Christmas catalog.		X		X		X		X
Send out specialty catalog.			X				X	
Send out both catalogs.	X				X			

FIGURE 9.10

Constructing a decision table for deciding which catalog to send to customers who order only from selected catalogs.

C2: customer ordered from Christmas catalog; and C3: customer ordered from specialty catalog), each having two alternatives (Y or N). Three actions can be taken (A1: send out this year's Christmas catalog; A2: send out the new specialty catalog; and A3: send out both catalogs). The resulting decision table has six rows (three conditions and three actions) and eight columns (two alternatives × two alternatives × two alternatives).

The decision table is now examined to see if it can be reduced. There are no mutually exclusive conditions, so it is not possible to get by with fewer than three condition rows. No rules allow the combination of actions. It is possible, however, to combine some of the rules as shown in Figure 9.11. For instance, Rules 2, 4, 6, and 8 can be combined because they all have two things in common:

1. They instruct us to send out this year's Christmas catalog.
2. The alternative for Condition 3 is always N.

It doesn't matter what the alternatives are for the first two conditions, so it is possible to insert dashes [—] in place of the Y or N.

The remaining rules—Rules 1, 3, 5, and 7—cannot be reduced to a single rule because two different actions remain. Instead, Rules 1 and 5 can be combined; likewise, Rules 3 and 7 can be combined.

Conditions and Actions	Rules 1	2	3	4	5	6	7	8
Customer ordered from Fall catalog.	Y	Y	Y	Y	N	N	N	N
Customer ordered from Christmas catalog.	Y	Y	N	N	Y	Y	N	N
Customer ordered from specialty catalog.	Y	N	Y	N	Y	N	Y	N
Send out this year's Christmas catalog.		X		X		X		X
Send out specialty catalog.			X				X	
Send out both catalogs.	X				X			

Conditions and Actions	Rules 1'	2'	3'
Customer ordered from Fall catalog.	—	—	—
Customer ordered from Christmas catalog.	Y	—	N
Customer ordered from specialty catalog.	Y	N	Y
Send out this year's Christmas catalog.		X	
Send out specialty catalog.			X
Send out both catalogs.	X		

FIGURE 9.11

Combining rules to simplify the customer-catalog decision table.

FIGURE 9.12
Adding a rule to the customer-catalog decision table changes the entire table.

Conditions and Actions	Rules 1'	2'	3'	4'
Customer ordered from Fall catalog.	—	—	—	—
Customer ordered from Christmas catalog.	Y	—	N	—
Customer ordered from specialty catalog.	Y	N	Y	—
Customer ordered $50 or more.	Y	Y	Y	N
Send out this year's Christmas catalog.		X		
Send out specialty catalog.			X	
Send out both catalogs.	X			
Do not send out any catalog.				X

CHECKING FOR COMPLETENESS AND ACCURACY

Checking over your decision tables for completeness and accuracy is essential. Four main problems can occur in developing decision tables: incompleteness, impossible situations, contradictions, and redundancy.

Ensuring that all conditions, condition alternatives, actions, and action rules are complete is of utmost importance. Suppose an important condition—if a customer ordered less than $50—had been left out of the catalog store problem discussed earlier. The whole decision table would change because a new condition, new set of alternatives, new action, and one or more new action rules would have to be added. Suppose the rule is: IF the customer did not order more than $50, THEN do not send any catalogs. A new Rule 4 would be added to the decision table, as shown in Figure 9.12.

When building decision tables as outlined in the foregoing steps, it is sometimes possible to set up impossible situations. An example is shown in Figure 9.13. Rule 1 is not feasible, because a person cannot earn greater than $50,000 per year and less than $2,000 per month at the same time. The other three rules are valid. The problem went unnoticed because the first condition was measured in years and the second condition in months.

Contradictions occur when rules suggest different actions but satisfy the same conditions. The fault could lie with the way the analyst constructed the table or with the information the analyst received. Contradictions often occur if dashes [—] are incorrectly inserted into the table. Redundancy occurs when identical sets of alternatives require the exact same action. Figure 9.14 illustrates a contradiction and a redundancy. The analyst has to determine what is correct and then resolve the contradiction or redundancy.

FIGURE 9.13
Checking the decision table for impossible situations is important.

Conditions and Actions	Rules 1	2	3	4
Salary > $50,000/year	Y	Y	N	N
Salary < $2,000/month	Y	N	Y	N
Action 1				
Action 2				

This is an impossible situation.

Conditions and Actions	Rules 1	2	3	4	5	6	7
Condition 1	Y	Y	Y	Y	Y	N	N
Condition 2	Y	Y	Y	N	N	Y	N
Condition 3	—	N	—	—	—	N	Y
Action 1	X			X	X		
Action 2			X			X	
Action 3		X					X

Contradiction (Rules 1, 2, 3) — Redundancy (Rules 4, 5)

FIGURE 9.14

Checking the decision table for inadvertent contradictions and redundancy is important.

MORE ADVANCED DECISION TABLES

Decision tables can become very burdensome because they grow rapidly as the number of conditions and alternatives increases. A table with only seven conditions with yes or no alternatives would have 128 columns. To reduce the complexity of unwieldy decision tables, use extended entries or the ELSE rule, or construct multiple tables.

Notice in the following Y or N table that the conditions are mutually exclusive.

C1:	Did not order	Y N N N
C2:	Ordered once	N Y N N
C3:	Ordered twice	N N Y N
C4:	Ordered more than twice	N N N N

Therefore, the conditions can be written in extended-entry form as follows:

C1: Number of times customer ordered 0 1 2 >2

The number of required columns and rows decreases and the understandability increases. Instead of using four rows for the number of times a customer orders, only one row is needed.

Decision tables are an important tool in the analysis of structured decisions. One major advantage of using decision tables over other methods is that tables help the analyst ensure completeness. When using decision tables, it is also easy to check for possible errors, such as impossible situations, contradictions, and redundancy. Decision table processors, which take the table as input and provide computer program code as output, are also available.

DECISION TREES

Decision trees are used when complex branching occurs in a structured decision process. Trees are also useful when it is essential to keep a string of decisions in a particular sequence. Although the decision tree derives its name from natural trees, decision trees are most often drawn on their side, with the root of the tree on the left side of the paper; from there, the tree branches out to the right. This orientation allows the analyst to write on the branches to describe conditions and actions.

Unlike the decision tree used in management science, the analyst's tree does not contain probabilities and outcomes, because in systems analysis, trees are used mainly for identifying and organizing conditions and actions in a completely structured decision process.

CONSULTING OPPORTUNITY 9.4

A TREE FOR FREE

"I know you've got a plane to catch, but let me try to explain it once again to you, sir," pleads Glen Curtiss, a marketing manager for Premium Airlines. Curtiss has been attempting (unsuccessfully) to explain the airline's new policy for accumulating miles for awards (such as upgrades to first class and free flights) to a member of Premium's "Flying for Prizes" club.

Glen takes another pass at getting the policy off the ground, saying, "You see, sir, the traveler (that's you, Mr. Icarus) will be awarded the miles actually flown. If the actual mileage for the leg was less than 500 miles, the traveler will get 500 miles credit. If the trip was made on a Saturday, the actual mileage will be multiplied by two. If the trip was made on a Tuesday, the multiplication factor is 1.5. If this is the ninth leg traveled during the calendar month, the mileage is doubled no matter what day, and if it is the seventeenth leg traveled, the mileage is tripled. If the traveler booked the flight on the Web or through a travel service such as Orbitz or Travelocity, 100 miles are added.

"I hope that clears it up for you, Mr. Icarus. Enjoy your flight, and thanks for flying Premium."

Mr. Icarus, whose desire to board the Premium plane has all but melted away during Glen's long explanation, fades into the sea of people wading through the security lanes, without so much as a peep in reply.

Develop a decision tree for Premium Airlines' new policy for accumulating award miles so that the policy becomes clearer, is easier to grasp visually, and hence is easier to explain.

DRAWING DECISION TREES

It is useful to distinguish between conditions and actions when drawing decision trees. This distinction is especially relevant when conditions and actions take place over a period of time and their sequence is important. For this purpose, use a square node to indicate an action and a circle to represent a condition. Using notation makes the decision tree more readable, as does numbering the circles and squares sequentially. Think of a circle as signifying IF, whereas the square means THEN.

When decision tables were discussed in an earlier section, a point-of-sale example was used to determine the purchase approval actions for a department store. Conditions included the amount of the sale (under $50) and whether the customer paid by check or credit card. The four actions possible were to: complete the sale after verifying the signature; complete the sale with no signature needed; call the supervisor for approval; or communicate electronically with the bank for credit card authorization. Figure 9.15 illustrates how this example can be drawn as a decision tree. In drawing the tree:

1. Identify all conditions and actions and their order and timing (if they are critical).
2. Begin building the tree from left to right, making sure you list all possible alternatives before moving to the right.

This simple tree is symmetrical, and the four actions at the end are unique. A tree does not need to be symmetrical. Most decision trees have conditions that have a different number of branches. Also, identical actions may appear more than once.

FIGURE 9.15
Drawing a decision tree to show the noncash purchase approval actions for a department store.

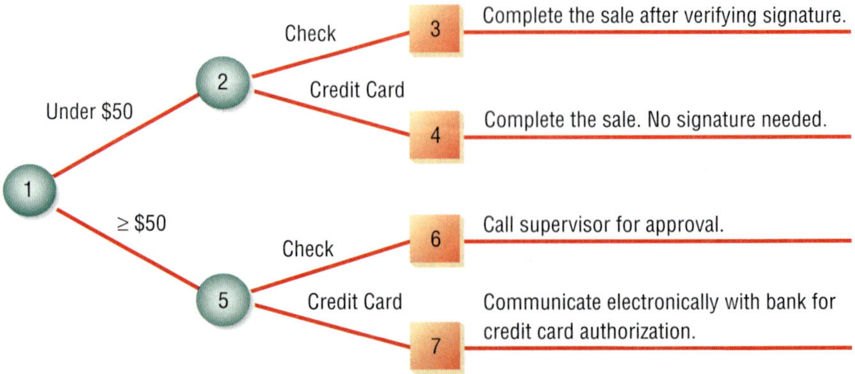

The decision tree has three main advantages over a decision table. First, it takes advantage of the sequential structure of decision tree branches so that the order of checking conditions and executing actions is immediately noticeable. Second, conditions and actions of decision trees are found on some branches but not on others, which contrasts with decision tables, in which they are all part of the same table. Those conditions and actions that are critical are connected directly to other conditions and actions, whereas those conditions that do not matter are absent. In other words, the tree does not have to be symmetrical. Third, compared with decision tables, decision trees are more readily understood by others in the organization. Consequently, they are more appropriate as a communication tool.

CHOOSING A STRUCTURED DECISION ANALYSIS TECHNIQUE

We have examined the three techniques for analysis of structured decisions: structured English, decision tables, and decision trees. Although they need not be used exclusively, it is customary to choose one analysis technique for a decision rather

FIGURE 9.16
Data flow diagram explosion of process 4, RECORD CUSTOMER BID.

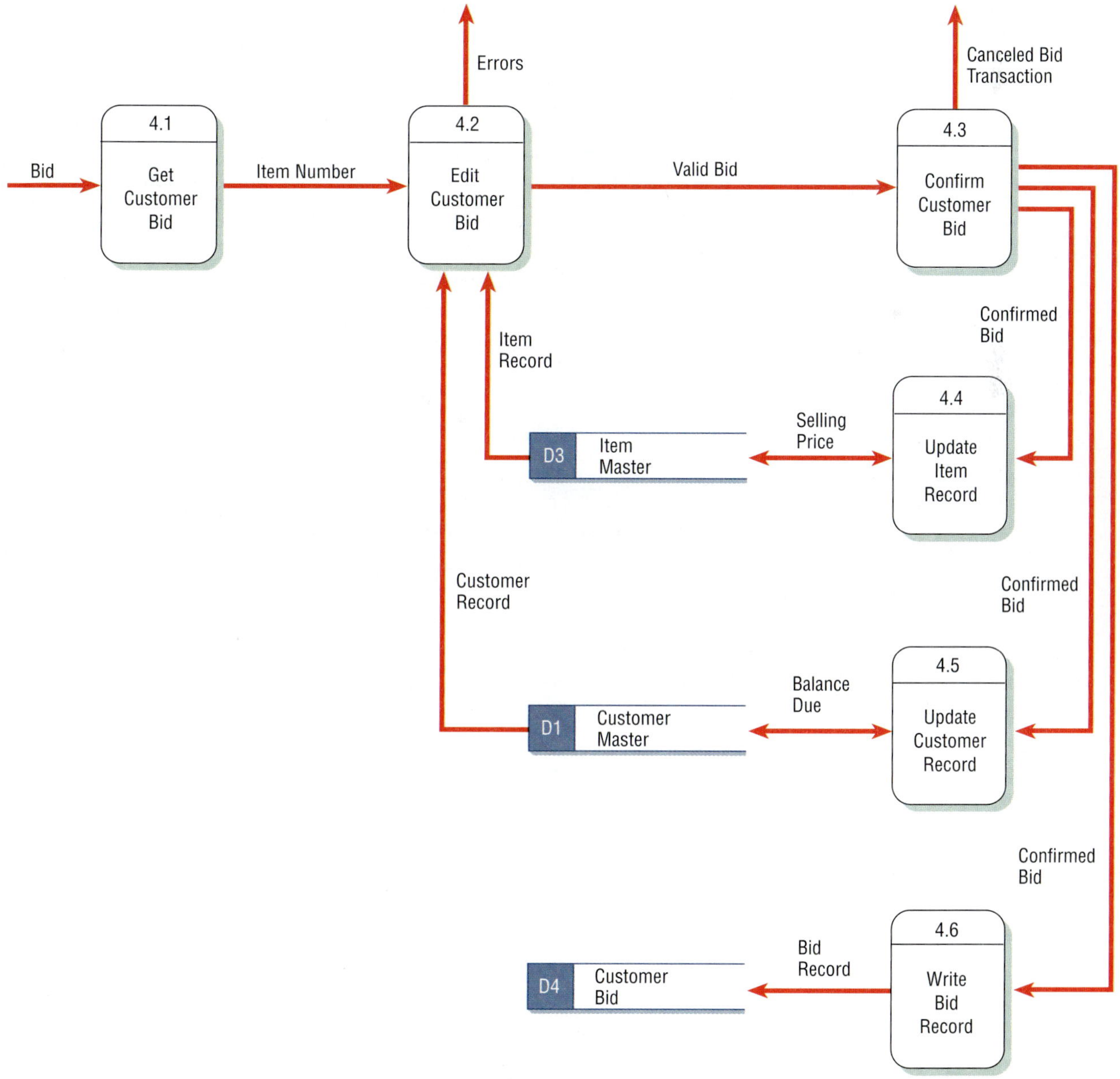

than employing all three. The following guidelines provide you with a way to choose one of the three techniques for a particular case:

1. Use structured English when
   a. There are many repetitious actions,
      OR
   b. Communication to end users is important.
2. Use decision tables when
   a. Complex combinations of conditions, actions, and rules are found,
      OR
   b. You require a method that effectively avoids impossible situations, redundancies, and contradictions.

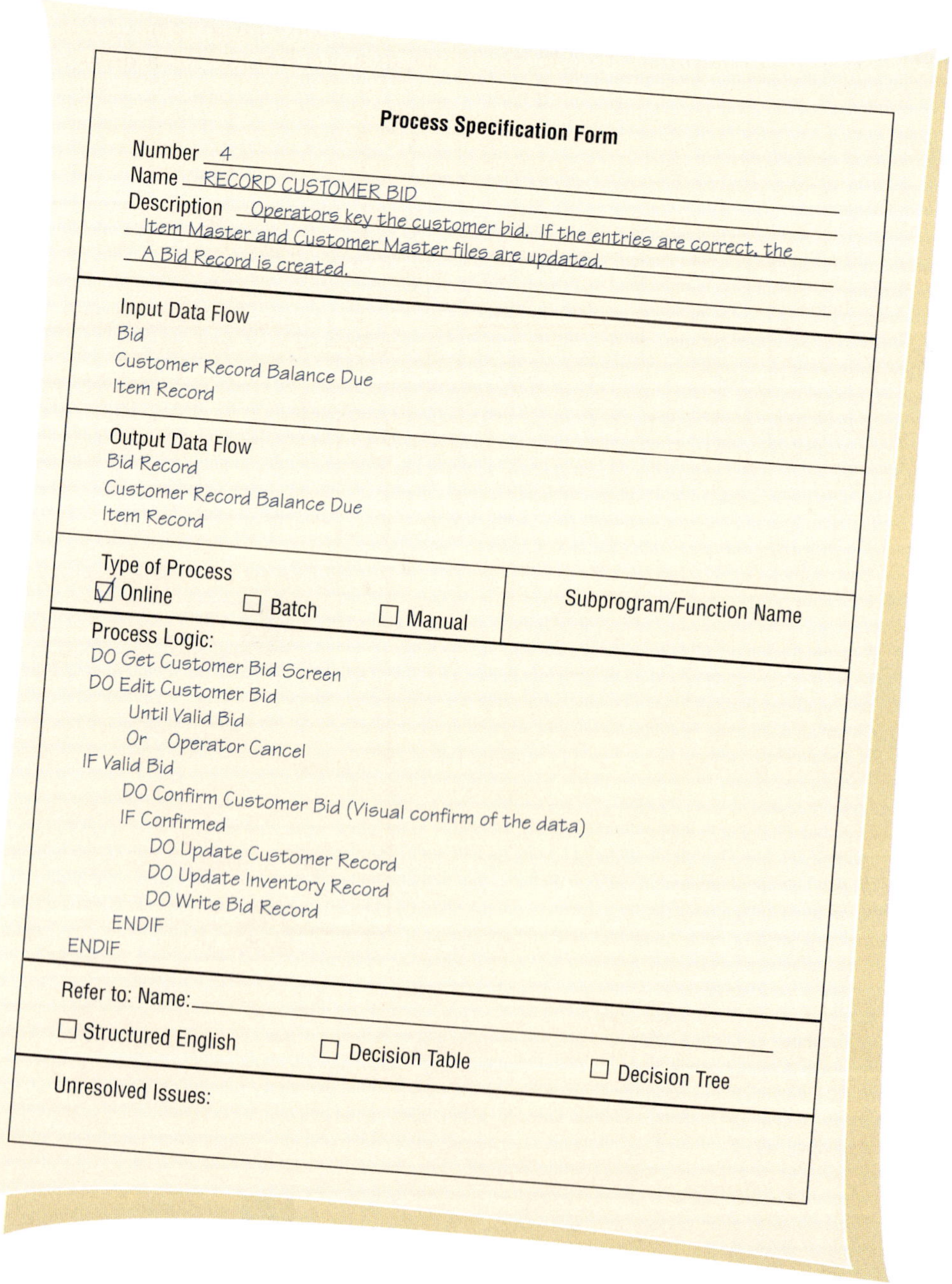

Process Specification Form

Number 4

Name RECORD CUSTOMER BID

Description Operators key the customer bid. If the entries are correct, the Item Master and Customer Master files are updated. A Bid Record is created.

Input Data Flow
Bid
Customer Record Balance Due
Item Record

Output Data Flow
Bid Record
Customer Record Balance Due
Item Record

Type of Process
☑ Online ☐ Batch ☐ Manual

Subprogram/Function Name

Process Logic:

```
DO Get Customer Bid Screen
DO Edit Customer Bid
    Until Valid Bid
    Or  Operator Cancel
IF Valid Bid
    DO Confirm Customer Bid (Visual confirm of the data)
    IF Confirmed
        DO Update Customer Record
        DO Update Inventory Record
        DO Write Bid Record
    ENDIF
ENDIF
```

Refer to: Name:

☐ Structured English ☐ Decision Table ☐ Decision Tree

Unresolved Issues:

FIGURE 9.17
Structured English for a process that explodes to a child diagram.

3. Use decision trees when
   a. The sequence of conditions and actions is critical,
      OR
   b. When not every condition is relevant to every action (the branches are different).

PHYSICAL AND LOGICAL PROCESS SPECIFICATIONS

The remaining sections in this chapter are advanced topics that may be explored further if you wish. The first section shows how a data flow diagram can be transformed into process specifications. The second section explains how process specifications can in turn be used to balance (and correct) a data flow diagram.

Each data flow diagram process expands to a child diagram, a structure chart (discussed in Chapter 16), or process specifications (as structured English). If the process is primitive, the specifications show the logic, arithmetic, or algorithm for transforming the input into output. These specifications are a portion of the logical

FIGURE 9.18
Diagram 3, Produce Supplier Payment Statement (unfinished).

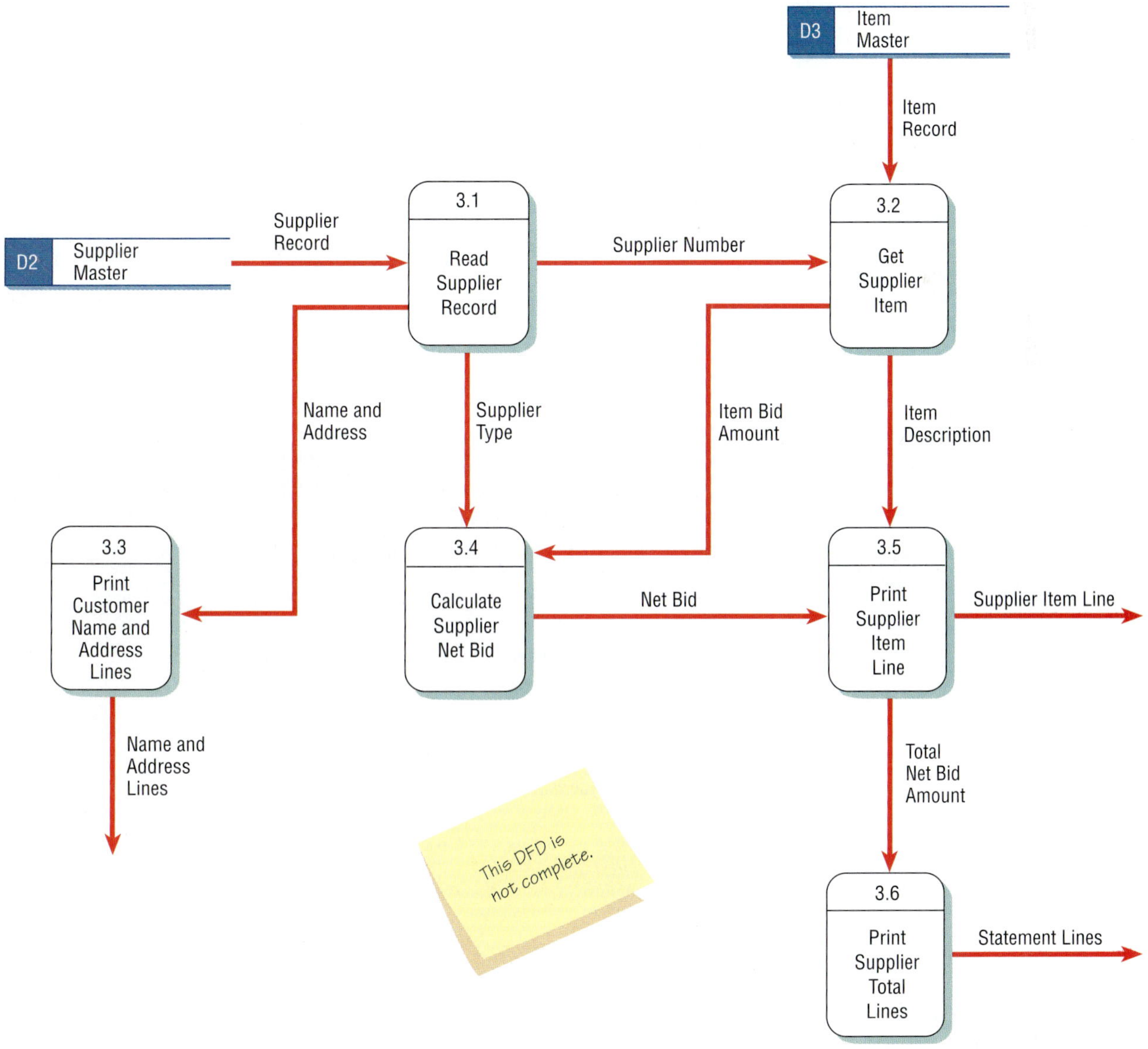

model—the business rules—that would exist regardless of the type of system used to implement the business.

For example, we observe that an auction house has a computer system to keep track of successful customer bids (process 4) and to produce a payment statement for the person supplying the auctioned item (process 3). If the process expands to a child diagram or a structure chart, the process specification describes the order and conditions under which the child diagram processes will execute. This control logic is a part of the physical model and would be created after the method of implementation (either batch or online) for the process has been determined. Figure 9.16 shows the auction system Diagram 4, an explosion of process 4, RECORD CUSTOMER BID. We can take this DFD and express its logic in structured English as shown in the Process Logic box of the Process Specification Form in Figure 9.17.

USING PROCESS SPECIFICATIONS: HORIZONTAL BALANCING

Process specifications, whether on paper or captured using a CASE tool, may be used for generating computer language source code and for analyzing the system design. Computer programs are indicated by partitioning on a data flow diagram. All the individual process specifications for a program are consolidated to become the processing details in a program specification packet.

To attempt to write the specifications for a program without examining each process may lead to omissions and errors. Because process specifications are

FIGURE 9.19
Data dictionary entries for producing the Supplier Sales Receipt.

Supplier Sales Receipt = Current Date +
Supplier Type +
Supplier Name +
Address +
{Supplier Item Line} +
Auction Surcharge +
Total Amount Paid to Supplier

Supplier Item Line = Item Description +
(Item Bid Amount) +
(Net Bid) +
(Date Sold)

Supplier Record = Supplier Number +
Supplier Type +
Supplier Name +
Address

Item Record = Item Number +
Item Description +
(Item Bid Amount) +
(Amount Paid to Supplier) +
(Date Sold) +
Supplier Number

developed on a small scale, one process at a time, each one may be analyzed for complete and correct logic. When the analysis is finished and corrections are made for all processes in a program, the final program specifications should be complete and accurate.

Process specifications may be used to analyze the data flow diagram and data dictionary through a method called horizontal balancing. Horizontal balancing dictates that all output data flow elements must be obtained from the input elements and process logic. Base elements in an output data flow must be present in the input flow, and derived elements on an output flow must be either present on an input data flow or created using the process specifications. Unresolved areas should be posed as questions during follow-up interviews with key users.

We will use these figures to show how structured English can help us complete the data flow diagram. Figure 9.18 illustrates Diagram 3, an unfinished explosion of the AUCTION SYSTEM process 3, PRODUCE SUPPLIER PAYMENT STATEMENT. Figure 9.19 shows the corresponding data dictionary entries. Figure 9.20 is the structured English for process 3.4, CALCULATE

Structured English: Process 3.4, CALCULATE SUPPLIER NET BID

```
BEGIN CASE
IF the Supplier Type is a charitable organization
   THEN Commission Rate = 10%
ELSE IF the Supplier Type is a government unit
   THEN Commission Rate = 15%
ELSE IF the Supplier Type is a bankruptcy
   THEN Commission Rate = 18%
ELSE IF the Supplier Type is an estate
   THEN Commission Rate = 20%
ELSE Commission Rate = 25%
END CASE
Multiply Item Bid Amount by Commission Rate giving Commission
Subtract Commission from Item Bid Amount giving Net Bid
Move Net Bid to the Amount Paid in Supplier on the Item Record
Rewrite the Item Record
Add Net Bid to Year-to-Date Net Bid on the Supplier Record
Rewrite the Supplier Record
```

Structured English: Process 3.5, PRINT BID LINE

```
Move Item Description to Supplier Item Line
Move Date Sold to Supplier Item Line
Move Item Bid Amount to Supplier Item Line
Move Net Bid to the Supplier Item Line
Write Supplier Item Line
Add Net Bid to Total Net Bid Amount
```

FIGURE 9.20
Structured English description for processes 3.4 and 3.5.

FIGURE 9.21
Structured English description for process 3.6.

Structured English: Process 3.6, PRINT SUPPLIER TOTAL DUE LINE

Note: The Auction Surcharge is a one-time cost per auction to cover setup costs.

```
BEGIN CASE
IF the Supplier Type is a charitable organization
   THEN Auction Surcharge = $200
ELSE IF the Supplier Type is a governmental unit
   THEN Auction Surcharge = $500
ELSE IF the Supplier Type is a bankruptcy
   THEN Auction Surcharge = $400
ELSE IF the Supplier Type is an estate
   THEN Auction Surcharge = $300
ELSE Auction Surcharge = $500
END CASE
Multiply Item Bid Amount to Statement Line
Write Statement Line
Move Auction Surcharge to Statement Line
Write Statement Line
Subtract Auction Surcharge from Total Net Bid Amount giving Payment Total
Move Payment Total to Statement Line
Write Statement Line
```

SUPPLIER NET BID, and for process 3.5, PRINT BID LINE. Figure 9.21 is the structured English for process 3.6, PRINT SUPPLIER TOTAL DUE LINE.

The output from process 3.4 is the NET BID for each item, a derived element. The logic for the process requires as input the SUPPLIER TYPE and ITEM BID AMOUNT, both used in the NET BID calculation. Checking the data flow diagram reveals that both these elements are inputs to process 3.4. Only the NET BID is shown as an output from the process, however. The AMOUNT PAID TO SUPPLIER, included in the structured English figure, is not shown on the data flow diagram, nor is the ITEM MASTER data store. The YEAR-TO-DATE NET BID is not included in the data dictionary for the SUPPLIER RECORD, nor is it shown on the data flow diagram. The data flow diagram and data dictionary must be updated to include these missing components. Figure 9.22 shows Diagram 3 with the necessary corrections.

Examine the output from process 3.5. The SUPPLIER ITEM LINE contains four elements: ITEM DESCRIPTION, ITEM BID AMOUNT, NET BID, and DATE SOLD. The ITEM DESCRIPTION and NET BID are input to process 3.5, but DATE SOLD and ITEM BID AMOUNT, which are base elements, are not on any input flow. They must be added to the data flow diagram. To avoid having three input flows (ITEM DESCRIPTION, ITEM BID AMOUNT, and DATE SOLD) traveling from process 3.2 to 3.3, the entire item record is passed between the two processes. The final process to be examined is 3.6. The structured English requires that SUPPLIER TYPE and TOTAL NET BID AMOUNT be present as input flows. Because only the TOTAL NET BID AMOUNT is present, process 3.6 has missing input.

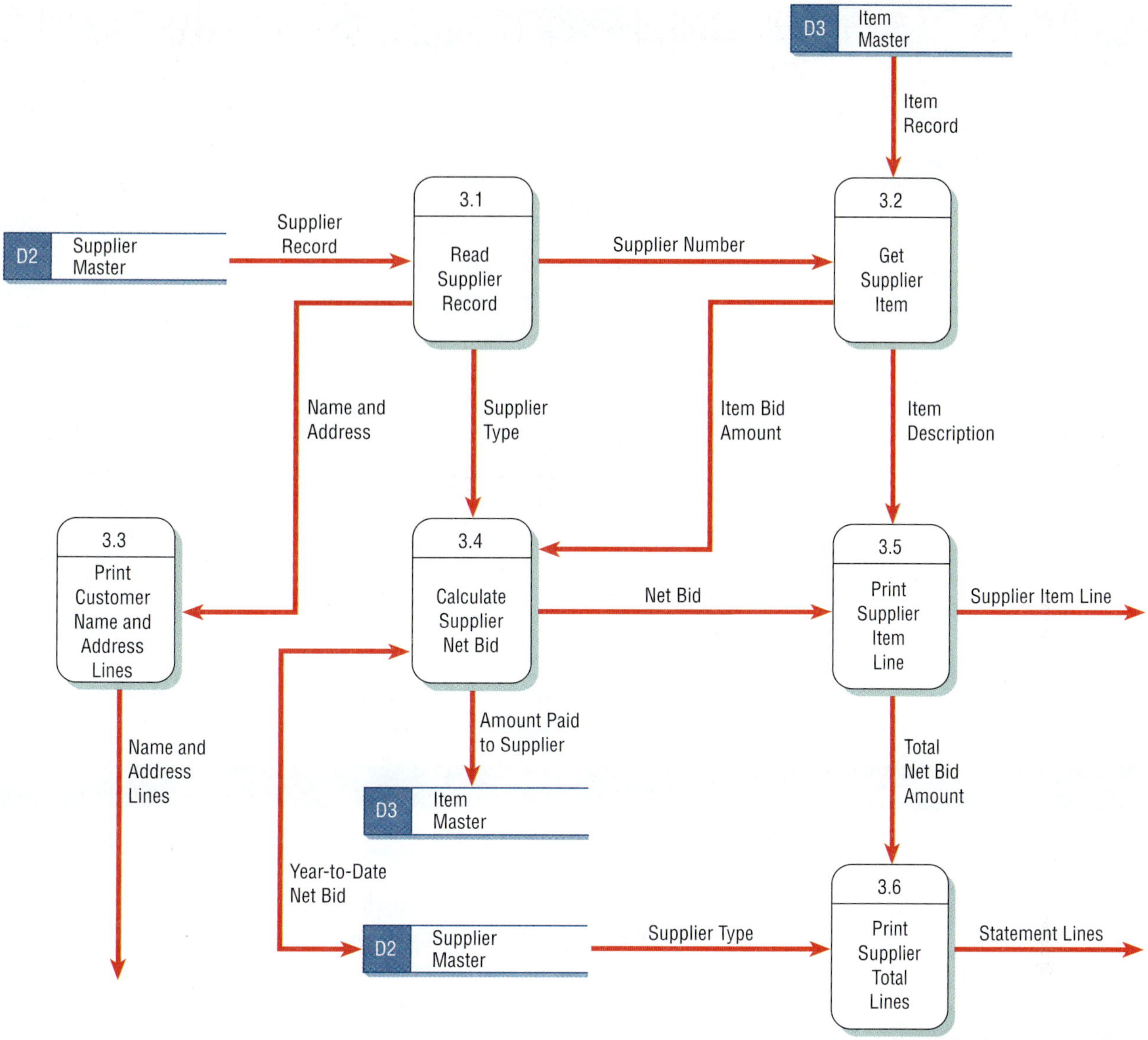

FIGURE 9.22
Corrected data flow diagram, an explosion of process 3, Produce Supplier Payment Statement.

SUMMARY

Once the analyst works with users to identify data flows and begins constructing a data dictionary, it is time to turn to process specification and decision analysis. The three methods for decision analysis and describing process logic discussed in this chapter are structured English, decision tables, and decision trees.

Process specifications (or minispecs) are created for primitive processes on a data flow diagram as well as for some higher-level processes that explode to a child diagram. These specifications explain the decision-making logic and formulas that will transform process input data into output. The three goals of process specification are to reduce the ambiguity of the process, to obtain a precise description of what is accomplished, and to validate the system design.

HYPERCASE® EXPERIENCE 9

"It's really great that you've been able to spend all of this time with us. One thing's for sure, we can use the help. And clearly, from your conversations with Snowden and others, you must realize we all believe that consultants have a role to play in helping companies change. Well, most of us believe it anyway.

"Sometimes structure is good for a person. Or even a company. As you know, Snowden is keen on any kind of structure. That's why some of the Training people can drive him wild sometimes. They're good at structuring things for their clients, but when it comes to organizing their own work, it's another story. Oh well, let me know if there's any way I can help you."

HYPERCASE QUESTION

1. Assume you will create the specifications for an automated project tracking system for the Training employees. One of the system's functions will be to allow project members to update or add names, addresses, and phone/fax numbers of new clients. Using structured English, write a procedure for carrying out the process of entering a new client name, address, and phone/fax number. [*Hint:* The procedure should ask for a client name, check to see if the name is already in an existing client file, and let the user either validate and update the current client address and phone/fax number (if necessary) or add a new client's address and phone/fax number to the client file.]

A large part of a systems analyst's work will involve structured decisions, that is, decisions once made by people that can be safely automated if identified conditions occur. To do that, the analyst needs to define four variables in the decision being examined: conditions, condition alternatives, actions, and action rules.

One way to describe structured decisions is to use the method referred to as structured English, in which logic is expressed in sequential structures, decision structures, case structures, or iterations. Structured English uses accepted key words such as IF, THEN, ELSE, DO, DO WHILE, and DO UNTIL to describe the logic used, and it indents to indicate the hierarchical structure of the decision process.

Decision tables provide another way to examine, describe, and document decisions. Four quadrants (viewed clockwise from the upper left corner) are used to (1) describe the conditions, (2) identify possible decision alternatives (such as Y or N), (3) indicate which actions should be performed, and (4) describe the actions. Decision tables are advantageous because the rules for developing the table itself, as well as the rules for eliminating redundancy, contradictions, and impossible situations, are straightforward and manageable. The use of decision tables promotes completeness and accuracy in analyzing structured decisions.

The third method for decision analysis is the decision tree, consisting of nodes (a square for actions and a circle for conditions) and branches. Decision trees are appropriate when actions must be accomplished in a certain sequence. There is no requirement that the tree be symmetrical, so only those conditions and actions that are critical to the decisions at hand are found on a particular branch.

Each of the decision analysis methods has its own advantages and should be used accordingly. Structured English is useful when many actions are repeated and when communicating with others is important. Decision tables provide a complete analysis of complex situations while limiting the need for change attributable to impossible situations, redundancies, or contradictions. Decision trees are important when proper sequencing of conditions and actions is critical and when each condition is not relevant to each action.

Each data flow diagram process expands to a child diagram, a structure chart, or process specifications (as structured English). If the process is primitive, the specifications show the logic, arithmetic, or algorithm for transforming the input into output. These logical model specifications are part of the business rules (which are often used as the basis for creating procedural language when code generators are used).

If the process expands to a child diagram or a structure chart, the process specification describes the order and conditions under which the child diagram processes will execute. This control logic is part of the physical model.

Process specifications may be used to analyze the data flow diagram and data dictionary through a method called horizontal balancing, which dictates that all data flow output elements must be obtained from the input elements and process logic. Unresolved areas can be posed as questions to users or to business experts you have added to your project management team during follow-up interviews.

KEYWORDS AND PHRASES

- action
- action rule
- condition
- condition alternative
- contradiction
- decision table
- decision tree
- horizontal balancing
- impossible situation
- incompleteness
- minispecs
- process specifications
- redundancy
- structured decision
- structured English

REVIEW QUESTIONS

1. List three reasons for producing process specifications.
2. Define what is meant by a structured decision.
3. What four elements must be known for the systems analyst to design systems for structured decisions?
4. What are the two building blocks of structured English?
5. List five conventions that should be followed when using structured English.
6. What is the advantage of using structured English to communicate with people in the organization?
7. Which quadrant of the decision table is used for conditions? Which is used for condition alternatives?
8. What is the first step to take in developing a decision table?
9. List the four main problems that can occur in developing decision tables.
10. What is one way to reduce the complexity of unwieldy decision tables?
11. What is one of the major advantages of decision tables over other methods of decision analysis?
12. What are the main uses of decision trees in systems analysis?
13. List the four major steps in building decision trees.
14. What three advantages do decision trees have over decision tables?
15. In which two situations should you use structured English?
16. In which two situations do decision tables work best?
17. In which two situations are decision trees preferable?

18. How do data dictionary structures help in determining the type of structured English statements for a process?
19. What is horizontal balancing? Why is it desirable to balance each process?

PROBLEMS

1. Clyde Clerk is reviewing his firm's expense reimbursement policies with the new salesperson, Trav Farr. "Our reimbursement policies depend on the situation. You see, first we determine if it is a local trip. If it is, we only pay mileage of 18.5 cents a mile. If the trip was a one-day trip, we pay mileage and then check the times of departure and return. To be reimbursed for breakfast, you must leave by 7:00 A.M., lunch by 11:00 A.M., and have dinner by 5:00 P.M. To receive reimbursement for breakfast, you must return later than 10:00 A.M., lunch later than 2:00 P.M., and have dinner by 7:00 P.M. On a trip lasting more than one day, we allow hotel, taxi, and airfare, as well as meal allowances. The same times apply for meal expenses." Write structured English for Clyde's narrative of the reimbursement policies.
2. Draw a decision tree depicting the reimbursement policy in Problem 1.
3. Draw a decision table for the reimbursement policy in Problem 1.
4. A computer supplies firm called True Disk has set up accounts for countless businesses in Dosville. True Disk sends out invoices monthly and will give discounts if payments are made within 10 days. The discounting policy is as follows: If the amount of the order for computer supplies is greater than $1,000, subtract 4 percent for the order; if the amount is between $500 and $1,000, subtract a 2-percent discount; if the amount is less than $500, do not apply any discount. All orders made via the Web automatically receive an extra 5-percent discount. Any special order (computer furniture, for example) is exempt from all discounting.

   Develop a decision table for True Disk discounting decisions, for which the condition alternatives are limited to Y and N.
5. Develop an extended-entry decision table for the True Disk company discount policy described in Problem 4.
6. Develop a decision tree for the True Disk company discount policy in Problem 4.
7. Write structured English to solve the True Disk company situation in Problem 4.
8. Premium Airlines has recently offered to settle claims for a class-action suit, which was originated for alleged price fixing of tickets. The proposed settlement is stated as follows:

   > Initially, Premium Airlines will make available to the settlement class a main fund of $25 million in coupons. If the number of valid claims submitted is 1.25 million or fewer, the value of each claim will be the result obtained by dividing $25 million by the total number of valid claims submitted. For example, if there are 500,000 valid claims, each person submitting a valid claim will receive a coupon with a value of $50.
   >
   > The denomination of each coupon distributed will be in a whole dollar amount not to exceed $50. Thus, if there are fewer than 500,000 valid claims, the value of each claim will be divided among two coupons or more. For example, if there are 250,000 valid claims, each person submitting a valid claim will receive two coupons, each having a face value of $50, for a total coupon value of $100.
   >
   > If the number of valid claims submitted is between 1.25 million and 1.5 million, Premium Airlines will make available a supplemental fund of coupons, with a potential value of $5 million. The supplemental fund will

be made available to the extent necessary to provide one $20 coupon for each valid claim.

If there are more than 1.5 million valid claims, the total amount of the main fund and the supplemental fund, $30 million, will be divided evenly to produce one coupon for each valid claim. The value of each such coupon will be $30 million divided by the total number of valid claims.

Draw a decision tree for the Premium Airlines settlement.

9. Write structured English for the Premium Airlines settlement in Problem 8.
10. "Well, it's sort of hard to describe," says Sharon, a counselor at Less Is More Nutrition Center. "I've never had to really tell anybody about the way we charge clients or anything, but here goes.

    "When clients come into Less Is More, we check to see if they've ever used our service before. Unfortunately for them, I guess, we have a lot of repeat clients who keep bouncing back. Repeat clients get a reduced rate (pardon the pun) of $100 for the first visit if they return within a year of the end of their program.

    "Everyone new pays an initial fee, which is $200 for a physical evaluation. The client may bring in a coupon at this time, and then we deduct $50 from the up-front fee. Half of our clients use our coupons and find out about us from them. We just give our repeaters their $100 off, though; they can't use a coupon, too! Clients who transfer in from one of our centers in another city get $75 off their first payment fee, but the coupon doesn't apply. Customers who pay cash get 10 percent off the $200, but they can't use a coupon with that."

    Create a decision table with Y and N conditions for the client charge system at Less Is More Nutrition Center.
11. Reduce the decision table in Figure 9.EX1 to the minimum number of rules.
12. Azure Isle Resort has a pricing structure for vacationers in one of its three dwelling categories: the hotel, villas, and beach bungalows. The base price is for staying in the hotel. Beach bungalows have a 10-percent surcharge and renting a villa has a 15-percent surcharge. The final price includes a discount of 4 percent for returning customers. Further conditions apply to how close the resort is filled to capacity and whether the requested date is within one month from the current date. If the resort is 50-percent full and the time is within one month, there is a 12-percent discount. If the resort is 70-percent full and the time is within one month, there is a 6-percent discount. If the resort is 85-percent full and it is within one month, there is a 4-percent discount.

    Develop an optimized decision table for the Azure Isle Resort pricing structure.

Conditions and Actions	**1**	**2**	**3**	**4**	**5**	**6**	**7**	**8**	**9**	**10**	**11**	**12**	**13**	**14**	**15**	**16**
								Rules								
Sufficient quantity on hand	Y	Y	Y	Y	Y	Y	Y	Y	N	N	N	N	N	N	N	N
Quantity large enough for discount	Y	Y	Y	Y	N	N	N	N	Y	Y	Y	Y	N	N	N	N
Wholesale customer	Y	Y	N	N	Y	Y	N	N	Y	Y	N	N	Y	Y	N	N
Sales tax exemption Filed	Y	N	Y	N	Y	N	Y	N	Y	N	Y	N	Y	N	Y	N
Ship items and prepare invoice	X	X	X	X	X	X	X	X								
Set up backorder									X	X	X	X	X	X	X	X
Deduct discount	X	X														
Add sales tax		X	X	X		X	X	X								

FIGURE 9.EX1
A decision table for a warehouse.

13. Create a decision tree for Problem 12.
14. The base ticket price for Cloudliner Airlines is determined by the distance traveled and the day of the week a passenger is traveling. In addition, the airline adjusts it ticket prices based on a number of categories. If the seats remaining are greater than 50 percent of capacity and the number of days before the flight is less than 7, the price is deeply discounted with a special Web offer for the flight. If the seats remaining are greater than 50 percent and the flight date is from 7 to 21 days in the future, there is a medium price discount. If the seats remaining are greater than 50 percent and the number of days before travel are greater than 21, there is only a small discount.

    If the seats remaining are from 20 to 50 percent and the days before the flight are fewer than 7, the ticket has a medium discount. If the seats remaining are from 20 to 50 percent and the flight date is from 7 to 21 days in the future, there is a low discount for prices. If the seats remaining are from 20 to 50 percent and the number of days before travel are greater than 21, there is no discount.

    If the seats remaining are less than 20 percent and the number of days before the flight is less than 7, the ticket has the highest increase in price. If the seats remaining are less than 20 percent and the flight date is from 7 to 21 days in the future, there is a large increase in price. If the seats remaining are less than 20 percent and number of days before travel are greater than 21, there is a small increase in price.

    Develop an optimized decision table for the Cloudliner Airlines ticket price adjustment policies.
15. Develop a decision tree for the situation in Problem 14.

GROUP PROJECTS

1. Each group member (or each subgroup) should choose to become an "expert" and prepare to explain how and when to use one of the following structured decision techniques: structured English, decision tables, or decision trees. Each group member or subgroup should then make a case for the usefulness of its assigned decision analysis technique for studying the types of structured decisions made by Maverick Transport on dispatching particular trucks to particular destinations. Each group should make a presentation of its preferred technique.
2. After hearing each presentation, the group should reach a consensus on which technique is most appropriate for analyzing the dispatching decisions of Maverick Transport and why that technique is best in this instance.

SELECTED BIBLIOGRAPHY

Adam, E. E., Jr., and R. J. Ebert. *Production and Operations Management*, 3d ed. Englewood Cliffs, NJ: Prentice Hall, 1986.

Anderson, D. R., D. J. Sweeney, and T. A. Williams. *An Introduction to Management Science*, 8th ed. New York: West, 1997.

Evans, J. R. *Applied Production and Operations Management*, 4th ed. St. Paul, MN: West, 1993.

Gane, C., and T. Sarson. *Structured Systems Analysis and Design Tools and Techniques.* Englewood Cliffs, NJ: Prentice Hall, 1979.

ALLEN SCHMIDT, JULIE E. KENDALL, AND KENNETH E. KENDALL

TABLING A DECISION

After doing many follow-up interviews with Dot Matricks, Anna tells Chip, "I've determined the logic needed to update the PENDING COMPUTER ORDERS data store. Because many computers may be ordered on the same purchase order, as each computer is entered, the matching record is located and one is subtracted from the number of outstanding computers per purchase order."

Anna shows Chip the **Process** repository screen print (depicted in Figure E9.1). "The name of the corresponding process, UPDATE PENDING COMPUTER ORDER (process 2.5), links the process specification to the data flow diagram," she explains. Inputs and outputs are listed and should match the data flow into or out of the process. "The VALID COMPUTER TRANSACTION record is input, and the updated PENDING ORDER is the output flow."

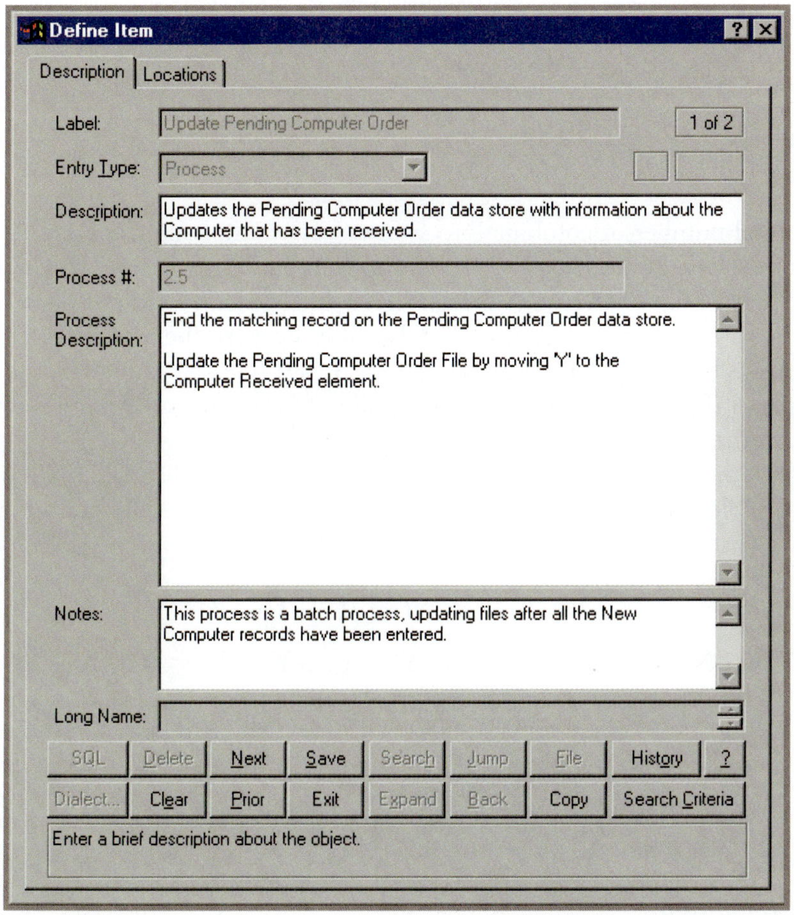

FIGURE E9.1
Process Repository screen, UPDATE PENDING COMPUTER ORDER.

"That will be useful," Chip says, "even though it took a while to untangle it all."

Anna points out, "The **Process Description** area contains the logic, shown in structured English."

When the logic is complete, Anna further enters a few notes on the nature of the process, notes that it is a batch process, and also adds timing information.

A decision table may be created for control or process logic. Before the decision table is keyed, it is a good idea to create it on paper and optimize the table. This way only the essential conditions and actions will be entered.

"I've been busy, too," Chip assures Anna. "I've spoken with Cher Ware several times since you interviewed her. I've finally captured some of the logic for calculating the cost of a software upgrade.

"Cher indicated three different conditions affecting the cost. The site license provides unlimited copies and is used for popular software installed on many computers. An educational discount is provided by many publishers, and a discount for quantity is usually available," he continues.

"First I determined the values for the conditions and the number of combinations," Chip says. He set out the three conditions and their values as follows:

Condition	*Values*	*Number of Values*
SITE LICENSE	Y/N	2
EDUCATIONAL DISCOUNT	Y/N	2
DISCOUNT FOR QUANTITY	Y/N	2

"The total number of combinations is found by multiplying the number of values for each of the conditions, $2 \times 2 \times 2 = 8$. The next step is to decide which conditions should be first." Chip continues, "I reason that a site license would not have a discount for quantity or an additional educational discount, because the actual site license cost already reflects this kind of discount. Therefore, SITE LICENSE should be the first condition. Each of the two other conditions would not have any particular advantage over the other, so the order is unimportant.

"Because the total number of conditions is eight and the SITE LICENSE condition has two possible values, the repeat factor would be 8/2, or 4." Chip continues by noting that the first row of the decision table would be

Condition	*1*	*2*	*3*	*4*	*5*	*6*	*7*	*8*
SITE LICENSE	Y	Y	Y	Y	N	N	N	N

"The next condition is EDUCATIONAL DISCOUNT, which also has two values. Dividing these two into the previous factor of four yields $4/2 = 2$ for the next repeat factor." Chip notes that the decision table now expands to

Condition	*1*	*2*	*3*	*4*	*5*	*6*	*7*	*8*
SITE LICENSE	Y	Y	Y	Y	N	N	N	N
EDUCATIONAL DISCOUNT	Y	Y	N	N	Y	Y	N	N

Chip continues, "The last condition, DISCOUNT FOR QUANTITY, also has two values, and dividing these two into the previous repeat factor of two gives $2/2 = 1$, which should always be the repeat factor for the last row of the conditions." He notes that the completed condition entry is

Condition	*1*	*2*	*3*	*4*	*5*	*6*	*7*	*8*
SITE LICENSE	Y	Y	Y	Y	N	N	N	N
EDUCATIONAL DISCOUNT	Y	Y	N	N	Y	Y	N	N
DISCOUNT FOR QUANTITY	Y	N	Y	N	Y	N	Y	N

Chip points out that when the actions are included, the completed decision table is

Condition	*1*	*2*	*3*	*4*	*5*	*6*	*7*	*8*
SITE LICENSE	Y	Y	Y	Y	N	N	N	N
EDUCATIONAL DISCOUNT	Y	Y	N	N	Y	Y	N	N
DISCOUNT FOR QUANTITY	Y	N	Y	N	Y	N	Y	N
Actions								
COST = SITE LICENSE COST	X	X	X	X				
COST = EDUCATIONAL COST × COPIES						X		
COST = DISCOUNT COST × COPIES							X	
COST = UPGRADE COST × COPIES								X
COST = (EDUC COST – DISC) × COPIES					X			

"I have proceeded to reduce some of the redundant actions, specifically those occurring when a site license has been obtained," Chip continues. "Because the actions are the same for Site License values of Y, the educational and quantity discounts are meaningless to the condition and don't have to be considered. Rules 1 through 4 may be reduced to one rule." Chip concludes by noting that the final, optimized decision table is

Condition	*1*	*2*	*3*	*4*	*5*
SITE LICENSE	Y	N	N	N	N
EDUCATIONAL DISCOUNT	—	Y	Y	N	N
DISCOUNT FOR QUANTITY	—	Y	N	Y	N
Actions					
COST = SITE LICENSE COST	X				
COST = EDUCATIONAL COST × COPIES			X		
COST = DISCOUNT COST × COPIES				X	
COST = UPGRADE COST × COPIES					X
COST = (EDUC COST – DISC) × COPIES		X			

The final decision table, shown in Figure E9.2, contains the optimized decision table. There are three conditions: whether a site license, an educational discount, or a quantity discount is available. The top left quadrant contains the conditions. Directly below it are the actions. The condition alternatives are in the upper right quadrant, and the action entries are in the lower right quadrant. The actions show how the upgrade cost is determined for each condition, indicated by an **X** in the rule columns.

9

Conditions and Actions	1	2	3	4	5
Site license	Y	N	N	N	N
Educational discount		Y	Y	N	N
Discount for quantity		Y	N	Y	N
Upgrade cost = Site license cost	X				
Upgrade cost = Educational cost * Number of copies			X		
Upgrade cost = Discount cost * Number of copies				X	
Upgrade cost = Cost per copy * Number of copies					X
Upgrade cost = (Educational cost – Discount) *Number of copies		X			

FIGURE E9.2
Decision Table, UPGRADE COST.

EXERCISES

E-1. Use Visible Analyst to view the **Process** repository entry for UPDATE PENDING COMPUTER ORDER.

E-2. Modify and print the ACCUMULATIVE HARDWARE SUBTOTALS **Process** entry. Add the **Process Description,** "Accumulate the hardware subtotals. These include the number of machines for each hardware brand."

E-3. Modify and print the CONFIRM COMPUTER DELETION **Process** entry. Add the following **Process Description:**

Use the COMPUTER RECORD to format the **Deletion Confirmation** screen (refer to the **Delete Computer Prototype** screen).

Prompt the user to click the **OK** button to confirm the deletion; otherwise, click the **Cancel** button to cancel the deletion.

If the operator clicks **OK** to delete the record, delete the record and display a "Record Deleted" message; otherwise, display a "Deletion Canceled" message.

E-4. Create **Process** specifications for process 6.6, VALIDATE COMPUTER CHANGES. The **Process Description** for the process is as follows:

Validate the changes to the COMPUTER MASTER. Include a note to use the edit criteria established for each element. Provide the following additional editing criteria:

The ROOM LOCATION must be valid for a particular campus.

The MONITOR must not be a lower grade than the graphics board. An example of this error would be an XGA (higher resolution) graphics board paired with an SVGA (lower resolution) monitor.

There must not be a second hard drive without the first one.

The LAST PREVENTIVE MAINTENANCE DATE must not be greater than the current date.

The exercises preceded by a Web icon indicate value-added material is available from the Web site at www.prenhall.com/kendall. Students can download a sample Visible Analyst Project and a Microsoft Access database that can be used to complete the exercises. Visible Analyst software can be packaged with this text for an additional fee.

The DATE PURCHASED must not be greater than the LAST PREVENTIVE MAINTENANCE DATE or greater than the current date.

The MODEL must conform to the type supported by the BRAND name.

No changes may be made to an inactive record.

E-5. Create process specifications for process 1.4, CREATE SOFTWARE LOG FILE. Use the data flow diagram examples to determine inputs and outputs. Process details are as follows:

Format the SOFTWARE LOG RECORD from the following information:

The confirmed NEW SOFTWARE RECORD elements.

The following system elements: SYSTEM DATE, SYSTEM TIME, USER ID, NETWORK ID.

When the record has been formatted, write to the SOFTWARE LOG FILE.

E-6. Produce process specifications for process 9.7.2, FIND MATCHING HARDWARE RECORD. This process is part of a program producing a report showing all computers on which each software package is located. Use Visible Analyst to view data flow diagram 9.7. Use structured English to depict the following logic: For each SOFTWARE RECORD, loop while there is a matching hardware inventory number. Within the loop, accomplish the following tasks:

Randomly read the COMPUTER MASTER file.

If a record is found, format the MATCHING COMPUTER RECORD information.

If no record is found, format a NO MATCHING error line.

Furthermore, if the found COMPUTER RECORD is inactive, indicating that it has been removed from service, format an INACTIVE MATCHING COMPUTER error line.

E-7. Use paper or any word processor that supports tables to create the CALCULATE SOFTWARE UPGRADE COST decision table, shown in Figure E9.2.

E-8. Create the FIND SOFTWARE LOCATION decision table, representing the logic for an inquiry program for displaying all locations for a given SOFTWARE TITLE and VERSION. The conditions have been created and optimized, resulting in five rules, illustrated in Figure E9.3. Enter the actions that need to be entered and an

Conditions and Actions	1	2	3	4	5
Matching software record found	Y	Y	Y	Y	N
Version of software found	Y	Y	Y	N	
Matching computer record found	Y	Y	N		
Campus code found in table	Y	N			
Display 'No Matching Software Record' error message					X
Display 'Version Not Available' error message				X	
Display 'Machine Not Found' error message			X		
Display 'Campus Code Not Found' error message		X			
Display location information	X				

FIGURE E9.3
Decision Table, FIND SOFTWARE LOCATION.

9

X in the column related to the conditions. If you are using a word processor, print the final decision table. The conditions and actions are represented by the following logic:

The SOFTWARE MASTER file is located for the specified TITLE. If the matching record is not found, an error message is displayed. Because there may be several versions, the VERSION NUMBER on the record is checked for a match to the version entered. If the requested version is not found, further records are read using the alternate index. If all records are read and the version number is not found, an error message, VERSION NOT AVAILABLE, is displayed.

Once the correct software has been located, a matching COMPUTER MASTER record is obtained. If the COMPUTER MASTER is not found, the error message MACHINE NOT FOUND is displayed. For each matching machine, the CAMPUS TABLE is searched for the CAMPUS LOCATION code. If the code is not found, the message CAMPUS CODE NOT FOUND is displayed.

If no errors occur, the requested information is displayed.

www E-9. Create a decision table for a batch update of the COMPUTER MASTER file. There are three types of updates: Add, Delete, and Change.

The COMPUTER MASTER record must be read. If the transaction is an Add and the master is not found, format and write the new COMPUTER MASTER record. Print a valid transaction line on an UPDATE REPORT. For a Change or Delete transaction, print a CHANGE ERROR LINE or a DELETE ERROR LINE if the COMPUTER MASTER record is not found.

If the COMPUTER MASTER record is found, check the active code. If the record is inactive and the transaction is an Add, format and rewrite the new COMPUTER MASTER record. Print a valid transaction line on an UPDATE REPORT. For a Change or Delete transaction, print a CHANGE ERROR LINE or a DELETE ERROR LINE.

If the COMPUTER MASTER record is active and the transaction is an Add, print an ADD ERROR LINE. For a Change transaction, format the changes and rewrite the COMPUTER MASTER record. Print the VALID TRANSACTION LINE. For a Delete transaction, change the ACTIVE CODE to inactive and rewrite the COMPUTER MASTER record. Print the VALID TRANSACTION LINE.

PREPARING THE SYSTEMS PROPOSAL

10

Learning Objectives

Once you have mastered the material in this chapter you will be able to:

1. **Inventory and appraise current and proposed hardware and software and the way it supports human interactions with technology.**
2. **Evaluate software by addressing the trade-offs among creating custom software, purchasing COTS software, and outsourcing to an application service provider.**
3. **Assist decision makers in choosing decision support systems, including recommendation systems and neural nets.**
4. **Forecast tangible and intangible costs and benefits, and perform a cost-benefit analysis using a number of methods.**
5. **Professionally write and present an effective systems proposal, incorporating figures and graphs.**

The systems proposal is a distillation of all that the systems analyst has learned about the users, the business, and what is needed to improve their performance. To address human and systems information requirements adequately, the systems analyst must use systematic methods for acquiring hardware and software, identify and forecast future costs and benefits, and perform a cost-benefit analysis. All these methods are used in preparing the systems proposal.

Information needs of users drive the selection of computer hardware, data storage media, and any commercial off-the-shelf (COTS) software. The hardware and software system that is eventually proposed is the analyst's response to users' information needs and a reflection of the human needs they have communicated thus far. This chapter provides the methods that are needed to project future needs systematically and then to weigh current hardware and software alternatives. Forecasting, guidelines for hardware and software acquisition, and cost-benefit analysis are also considered.

ASCERTAINING HARDWARE AND SOFTWARE NEEDS

In this section, we cover the process of estimating the present and future workloads of a business, and the process involved in evaluating the ability of computer hardware and software to handle workloads adequately. Figure 10.1 shows the

FIGURE 10.1
Steps in choosing hardware and software.

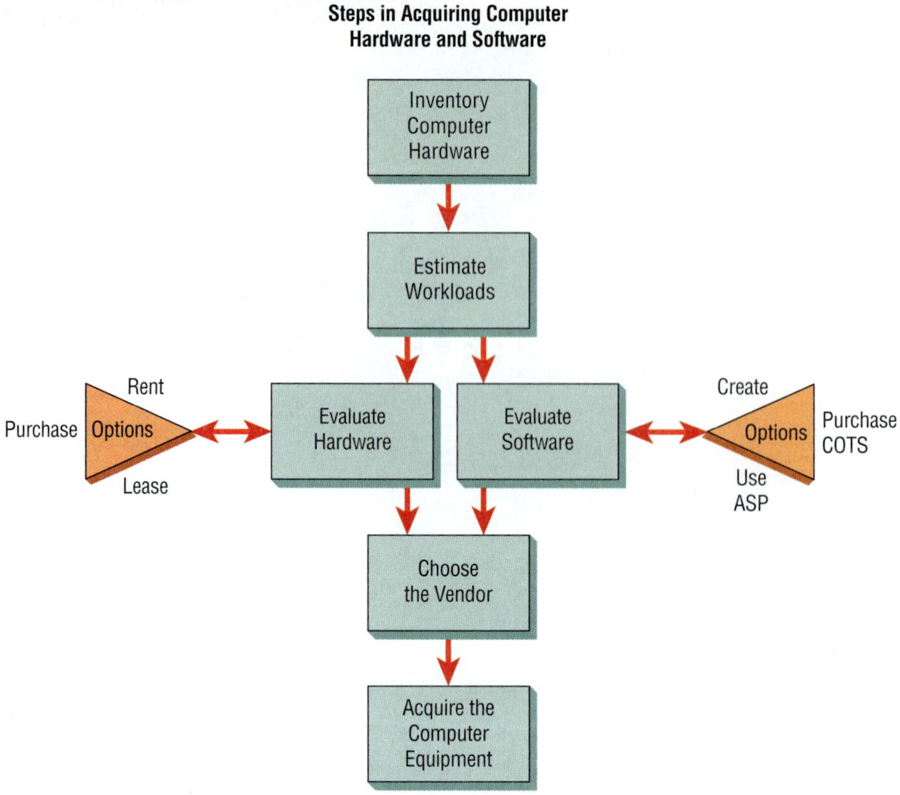

steps the systems analyst takes in ascertaining hardware and software needs. First, all current computer hardware must be inventoried to discover what is on hand and what is usable. Next, current and future system workloads must be estimated. Then an evaluation of available hardware and software is undertaken.

The systems analyst needs to work with users to determine what hardware will be needed. Hardware determinations can come only in conjunction with determining human information requirements. Knowledge of the organizational structure (as discussed in Chapter 2) and how users interact with technologies in an organizational setting can also be helpful in hardware decisions. Only when systems analysts, users, and management have a good grasp of what kinds of tasks must be accomplished can hardware options be considered.

INVENTORYING COMPUTER HARDWARE

Begin by inventorying what computer hardware is already available in the organization. As will become apparent, some of the hardware options involve expanding or recycling current hardware, so it is important to know what is on hand.

If an updated computer hardware inventory is unavailable, the systems analyst needs to set up one quickly and carry through on it. You need to know the following:

1. The type of equipment: model number, manufacturer.
2. The operation status of the equipment: on order, operating, in storage, in need of repair.
3. The estimated age of the equipment.
4. The projected life of the equipment.
5. The physical location of the equipment.
6. The department or person considered responsible for the equipment.
7. The financial arrangement for the equipment: owned, leased, rented.

Ascertaining the current hardware available will result in a sounder decision-making process when hardware decisions are finally made, because much of the guesswork about what exists will be eliminated. Through your earlier interviews with users, questionnaires surveying them, and research of archival data, you will already know the number of people available for data processing as well as their skills and capabilities. Use this information to project how well the staffing needs for new hardware can be met.

ESTIMATING WORKLOADS

The next step in ascertaining hardware needs is to estimate workloads. Thus, systems analysts formulate numbers that represent both current and projected workloads for the system so that any hardware obtained will possess the capability to handle current and future workloads.

If estimates are accomplished properly, the business should not have to replace hardware solely due to unforeseen growth in system use. (Other events, however, such as superior technological innovations, may dictate hardware replacement if the business wants to maintain its competitive edge.)

Out of necessity, workloads are sampled rather than actually put through several computer systems. The guidelines given on sampling in Chapter 5 can be of use here, because in workload sampling, the systems analyst is taking a sample of necessary tasks and the computer resources required to complete them.

Figure 10.2 is a comparison of the times required by an existing and a proposed information system that are supposed to handle a given workload. Notice that the company is currently using a legacy computer system to prepare a summary of shipments to its distribution warehouses, and a Web-based dashboard is being suggested. The workload comparison looks at when and how each process is done, how much human time is required, and how much computer time is needed. Notice that the newly proposed system should cut down the required human and computer time significantly.

EVALUATING COMPUTER HARDWARE

Evaluating computer hardware is the shared responsibility of management, users, and systems analysts. Although vendors will be supplying details about their particular offerings, analysts need to oversee the evaluation process personally because they will have the best interests of the business at heart. In addition, systems analysts may have to educate users and management about the general advantages and disadvantages of hardware before they can capably evaluate it.

Based on the current inventory of computer equipment and adequate estimates of current and forecasted workloads, the next step in the process is to consider the kinds of equipment available that appear to meet projected needs. Information from vendors on possible systems and system configurations becomes more pertinent at this stage and should be reviewed with management and users.

In addition, workloads can be simulated and run on different systems, including those already used in the organization. This process is referred to as benchmarking.

Criteria that the systems analysts and users should use to evaluate performance of different systems hardware include the following:

1. The time required for average transactions (including how long it takes to input data and how long it takes to receive output).
2. The total volume capacity of the system (how much can be processed at the same time before a problem arises).
3. The idle time of the CPU or network.
4. The size of the memory provided.

	Existing System	Proposed System
Task	Compare performance of distribution warehouses by running the summary program.	Compare performance of distribution warehouses on the Web-based dashboard.
Method	Computer programs are run when needed; processing is done from the workstation.	Updates occur immediately; processing is done online.
Personnel	Distribution manager	Distribution manager
When and how	Daily: Enter shipments on Excel spreadsheet; verify accuracy of spreadsheet manually; and then write files to backup media. Monthly: Run program that summarizes daily records and prints report; get report and make evaluations.	Daily: Enter shipments on the Web-based system using drop-down boxes. Data are automatically backed up to remote location. Monthly: Compare warehouses online using the performance dashboard; print only if needed.
Human time requirements	Daily: 20 minutes Monthly: 30 minutes	Daily: 10 minutes Monthly: 10 minutes
Computer time requirements	Daily: 20 minutes Monthly: 30 minutes	Daily: 10 minutes Monthly: 10 minutes

FIGURE 10.2
Comparisons of workloads between existing and proposed systems.

Some criteria will be shown in formal demonstrations; some cannot be simulated and must be gleaned from manufacturers' specifications. It is important to be clear about the required and desired functions before getting too wrapped up in vendors' claims during demonstrations.

Once functional requirements are known and the current products available are comprehended and compared with what already exists in the organization, decisions are made by the systems analysts in conjunction with users and management about whether obtaining new hardware is necessary. Options can be thought of as existing on a continuum from using only equipment already available in the business all the way to obtaining entirely new equipment. In between are options to make minor or major modifications to the existing computer system.

Computer Size and Use The rapid advance of technology dictates that the systems analyst research types of computers available at the particular time that the systems proposal is being written. Computer sizes range all the way from miniature mobile phones to room-sized supercomputers. Each has different attributes that should be considered when deciding how to implement a computer system.

ACQUISITION OF COMPUTER EQUIPMENT

The three main options for acquisition of computer hardware are buying, leasing, or renting it. There are advantages and disadvantages that ought to be weighed for

	Advantages	Disadvantages
Purchasing	• Cheaper than leasing or renting over the long run • Ability to change system • Provides tax advantages of accelerated depreciation • Full control	• Initial cost is high • Risk of obsolescence • Risk of being stuck if choice was wrong • Full responsibility
Leasing	• No capital is tied up • No financing is required • Leases are lower than rental payments	• Company doesn't own the system when lease expires • Usually a heavy penalty for terminating the lease • Leases are more expensive than buying
Renting	• No capital is tied up • No financing is required • Easy to change systems • Maintenance and insurance are usually included	• Company doesn't own the computer • Cost is very high because vendor assumes the risk (most expensive option)

FIGURE 10.3
Comparing the advantages and disadvantages of buying, leasing, and renting computer equipment.

each of the decisions, as shown in Figure 10.3. Some of the more influential factors to consider in deciding which option is best for a particular installation include initial versus long-term costs, whether the business can afford to tie up capital in computer equipment, and whether the business desires full control of and responsibility for the computer equipment.

Buying implies that the business itself will own the equipment. One of the main determinants of whether to buy is the projected life of the system. If the system will be used longer than four to five years (with all other factors held constant), the decision is usually made to buy. Notice in the example in Figure 10.4 that the cost of purchase after three years is lower than that of leasing or renting. As systems become smaller, more powerful, and less expensive, and as distributed systems become more popular, more businesses are deciding to purchase equipment.

Leasing, rather than purchasing, computer hardware is another possibility. Leasing equipment from the vendor or a third-party leasing company is more

FIGURE 10.4
Comparison of alternatives for computer acquisition.

practical when the projected life of the system is less than four years. In addition, if significant change in technology is imminent, leasing is a better choice. Leasing also allows the business to put its money elsewhere, where it can be working for the company rather than be tied up in capital equipment. Over a long period, however, leasing is not an economical way to acquire computer equipment.

Rental of computer hardware is the third main option for computer acquisition. One of the main advantages of renting is that none of the company's capital is tied up, and hence no financing is required. Also, renting computer hardware makes it easier to change system hardware. Finally, maintenance and insurance are usually included in rental agreements. Because of the high costs involved and the fact that the company will not own the rented equipment, however, rental should be contemplated only as a short-term move to handle nonrecurring or limited computer needs or technologically volatile times.

Evaluation of Vendor Support for Computer Hardware Several key areas ought to be evaluated when weighing the support services available to businesses from vendors. Most vendors offer testing of hardware on delivery and a 90-day warranty covering any factory defects, but you must ascertain what else the vendor has to offer. Vendors of comparable quality frequently distinguish themselves from others by the range of support services they offer.

A list of key criteria that ought to be checked when evaluating vendor support is provided in Figure 10.5. Most of the extra vendor support services listed there are negotiated separately from hardware lease or purchase contracts.

Support services include routine and preventive maintenance of hardware, specified response time (within six hours, next working day, etc.) in case of emergency equipment breakdowns, loan of equipment in the event that hardware must be permanently replaced or offsite repair is required, and in-house training or off-site group seminars for users. Peruse the support services documents accompanying the purchase or lease of equipment and remember to involve appropriate legal staff before signing contracts for equipment or services.

Unfortunately, evaluating computer hardware is not as straightforward as simply comparing costs and choosing the least expensive option. Some other eventualities commonly brought up by users and management include (1) the possibility of adding on to the system if the need comes up later; (2) the possibility of interfacing with equipment from other vendors if the system needs to grow; (3) the benefits of buying more memory than is projected as necessary, with the expectation that business will eventually "grow into it"; and (4) the corporate stability of the vendor.

FIGURE 10.5
Guidelines for vendor selection.

Vendor Services	Specifics Vendors Typically Offer
Hardware Support	Full line of hardware Quality products Warranty
Software Support	Complete software needs Custom programming Warranty
Installation and Training	Commitment to schedule In-house training Technical assistance
Maintenance	Routine maintenance procedures Specified response time in emergencies Equipment loan while repair is being done

Competition among vendors has made the idea of producing hardware that is compatible with competitors' hardware important for the vendors' survival. Before becoming convinced that buying cheaper compatibles is the way to endow your system with add-on capability, however, do enough research to feel confident that the original vendor is a stable corporate entity.

SOFTWARE EVALUATION

Analysts and organizations are increasingly faced with a make, buy, or outsource decision when assessing software for information systems projects, particularly when contemplating upgrades to existing or legacy systems.

You have seen the decisions that analysts make when deciding about renting, buying, or leasing hardware. Some of the decision making surrounding purchase of COTS software, "rental" of the software from an application service provider (ASP), or creation of custom software for the project is analogous to the hardware decision process.

It should be noted that regardless of whether you develop software or purchase a COTS product for a particular project, it is imperative to complete a human information requirements analysis of the users and the systems they use first (as discussed in preceding chapters). As an analyst, part of the expertise you are developing is to make sound judgments regarding developing software versus the purchase of COTS software for new and existing systems. The following sections discuss when to create your own software, when to purchase COTS packages, and when to use an ASP. Figure 10.6 summarizes the advantages and disadvantages of each of these options.

	Advantages	Disadvantages
Creating Custom Software	• Specific response to specialized business needs • Innovation may give firm a competitive advantage • In-house staff available to maintain software • Pride of ownership	• May be significantly higher initial cost compared to COTS software or ASP • Necessity of hiring or working with a development team • Ongoing maintenance
Purchasing COTS Packages	• Refined in the commercial world • Increased reliability • Increased functionality • Often lower initial cost • Already in use by other firms • Help and training comes with software	• Programming focused; not business focused • Must live with the existing features • Limited customization • Uncertain financial future of vendor • Less ownership and commitment
Using an ASP	• Organizations that do not specialize in information systems can focus on what they do best (their strategic mission) • There is no need to hire, train, or retain a large IT staff • There is no expenditure of employee time on nonessential IT tasks	• Loss of control of data, systems, IT employees, and schedules • Concern over the financial viability and long-run stability of the ASP • Security, confidentiality, and privacy concerns • Loss of potential strategic corporate advantage regarding innovativeness of applications

FIGURE 10.6
Comparing the advantages and disadvantages of creating custom software, purchasing COTS packages, and outsourcing to an ASP.

When to Create Custom Software There are several situations that call for the creation of original software or software components. The most likely instance is when COTS software does not exist or cannot be identified for the desired application. Alternatively, the software may exist but it is unaffordable or cannot easily be purchased or licensed.

Original software should be created when the organization is attempting to gain a competitive advantage through the leveraged use of information systems. This is often the case when an organization is creating ecommerce or other innovative applications where none existed. It is also possible that the organization is a "first mover" in the use of a particular technology or in its particular industry. Organizations that have highly specialized requirements or exist in niche industries can also benefit from original software.

The advantages of creating your own software include being able to respond to specialized user and business needs, gaining a competitive advantage by creating innovative software, having in-house staff available to maintain the software, and the pride of owning something you have created.

The drawbacks of developing your own software include the potential for a significantly higher initial cost compared to purchasing COTS software or contracting with an ASP, the necessity of hiring or working with a development team, and the fact that you are responsible for the ongoing maintenance because you were the software's creator.

When to Buy COTS Software Commercial off-the-shelf software includes such products as the Microsoft Office suite, which includes Word for word processing, Excel for spreadsheets, Access for building databases, and other applications. Other types of COTS software are for organizational-level systems rather than office or personal use. Some authors include popular (but costly) ERP packages such as Oracle and SAP in their examples of COTS software. These packages differ radically in the amount of customization, support, and maintenance required compared to Microsoft Office. COTS software can also refer to software components or objects (also called building blocks) that can be purchased to provide a particular needed functionality in a system.

Consider using COTS software when you can easily integrate the applications or packages into existing or planned systems, and when you have identified no necessity to immediately or continuously change or customize them for users. Your forecasts should demonstrate that the organization you are designing the system for is unlikely to undergo major changes after the proposed purchase of COTS software, such as a dramatic increase in customers or large physical expansions.

There are some advantages to purchasing COTS software that you should keep in mind as you weigh alternatives. One advantage is that these products have been refined through the process of commercial use and distribution, so that often there are additional functionalities offered. Another advantage is that packaged software is typically extensively tested, and thus extremely reliable.

Increased functionality is often offered with COTS software, because a commercial product is likely to have sister products, add-on features, and upgrades that enhance its attractiveness. Additionally, analysts often find that the initial cost of COTS software is lower than the cost for either in-house software development or the use of an ASP.

Another advantage of purchasing COTS packages includes their use by many other companies, so analysts are not experimenting on their clients with one-of-a-kind software applications. Lastly, COTS software boasts an advantage in the help and training that accompanies the purchase of the packaged software.

One example of the use of COTS software is from a theatre company in the nonprofit sector, in which organizations (particularly in the performing arts) tend to lag behind their for-profit counterparts in adoption of information communication technologies (ICTs). The theatre company was predictably slow to move to the Web. When they desired to create ecommerce applications, they were put in a position of having to hire outside designers to create ecommerce applications for them. In light of the expense and lack of in-house expertise, many nonprofit organizations simply did not move the business portion of their organizations to the Web, waiting instead for COTS packages, such as PC-based, box-office software, or ASPs such as online ticketing agencies with automation already in place, to make these services available to patrons. In-house software development was out of the question for most of these groups, who typically have small or nonexistent IT staffs and budgets, and minimal internal IT expertise.

There is a downside to the use of COTS software. Because it is not meant to be fully customizable, the theatre company lost its ability to change the software to include key features in their donor database that users were reliant on. COTS software may also include errors that could expose an organization to liability issues.

There are other disadvantages to consider with the purchase of COTS software, including the fact that packages are programming, rather than being focused on human users working in a business. Additionally, users must live with whatever features exist in the software, whether they are appropriate or not. A disadvantage that grows out of this is the limited customizability of most packaged software. Other disadvantages to purchasing COTS software include the necessity of investigating the financial stability of the software vendor, and the diminished sense of ownership and commitment that is inevitable when the software is considered a product rather than a process.

To achieve some perspective on systems being developed, you should recognize that over half of the projects are built from scratch (two-thirds using traditional methods like SDLC and prototyping and one-third using agile or object-oriented technologies). Most of these are developed using an internal systems analysis team. Programmers may be in-house or outsourced.

Less than half of all projects are developed from existing applications or components. The great majority are modified, some extensively. Less than 5 percent of software is off-the-shelf software that requires no modifications at all.

When to Outsource Software Services to an Application Service Provider Organizations may realize some benefits from taking an entirely different approach to procuring software. This third option is to outsource some of the organization's software needs to an application service provider that specializes in IT applications.

There are specific benefits to outsourcing applications to an ASP. For example, organizations that desire to retain their strategic focus and do what they're best at may want to outsource the production of information systems applications. Additionally, outsourcing one's software needs means that the organization doing the outsourcing may be able to sidestep the need to hire, train, and retain a large IT staff. This can result in significant savings. When an organization uses an ASP, there is little or no expenditure of valuable employee time on nonessential IT tasks (these are handled professionally by the ASP).

Hiring an application service provider should not be considered a magic formula for addressing software requirements. There are drawbacks to the use of an ASP that must be seriously considered. One disadvantage is a general loss of control over corporate data, information systems, IT employees, and even processing and project schedules. Some companies believe that the heart of their business is their information, so even the thought of relinquishing control over it is distressing.

Another disadvantage is concern over the financial viability of any ASP that is chosen. There might also be concerns about the security of the organization's data and records, along with concern about confidentiality of data and client privacy. Finally, when choosing an ASP, there is a potential loss of strategic corporate advantage that might have been gained though the company's own deployment of innovative applications created by their employees.

Evaluation of Vendor Support for Software and ASPs Whether you purchase a COTS package or contract for ASP services, you will be dealing with vendors who may have their own best interests at heart. You must be willing to evaluate software with users and not be unduly influenced by vendors' sales pitches. Specifically, there are six main categories on which to grade software, as shown in Figure 10.7: performance effectiveness, performance efficiency, ease of use, flexibility, quality of documentation, and manufacturer support.

Evaluate packaged software based on a demonstration with test data from the business considering it and an examination of accompanying documentation. Vendors' descriptions alone will not suffice. Vendors typically certify that software is working when it leaves their supply house, but they will not guarantee that it will be error-free in every instance or that it will not crash when incorrect actions are taken by users. Obviously, they will not guarantee their packaged software if used in conjunction with faulty hardware.

DECISION SUPPORT TOOLS

Although some COTS software may address certain information processing problems, the systems analyst also needs to be able to evaluate, recommend, or

FIGURE 10.7
Guidelines for evaluating software.

Software Requirements	Specific Software Features
Performance Effectiveness	Able to perform all required tasks Able to perform all tasks desired Well-designed display screens Adequate capacity
Performance Efficiency	Fast response time Efficient input Efficient output Efficient storage of data Efficient backup
Ease of use	Satisfactory user interface Help menus available "Read Me" files for last-minute changes Flexible interface Adequate feedback Good error recovery
Flexibility	Options for input Options for output Usable with other software
Quality of Documentation	Good organization Adequate online tutorial Web site with FAQ
Manufacturer Support	Technical support hot line Newsletter/email Web site with downloadable product updates

CONSULTING OPPORTUNITY 10.1

VENI, VIDI, VENDI, OR, I CAME, I SAW, I SOLD

"It's really some choice. I mean, no single package seems to have everything we want. Some of them come darn close, though," says Roman, an advertising executive for *Empire Magazine* with whom you have been working on a systems project. Recently, the two of you have decided that packaged software would probably suit the advertising department's needs and stem its general decline.

"The last guy's demo we saw, you know, the one who worked for Data Coliseum, really had a well-rounded pitch. And I like their brochure. Full-color printing, on card stock. Classic," Roman asserts.

"And what about those people from Vesta Systems? They're really fired up. And their package was easy to use with a minimum of ceremony. Besides, they said they would train all 12 of us, onsite, at no charge. But look at their advertising. They just take things off their printers."

Roman fiddles in his chair as he continues his ad hoc review of software and software vendors. "That one package from Mars, Inc., really sold me all on its own, though. I mean, it had a built-in calendar. And I like the way the menus for the screen displays could all be chosen by Roman numerals. It was easy to follow. And the vendor isn't going to be hard to move on price. I think they're already in a price war."

"Do you want to know my favorite, though?" Roman asks archly. "It's the one put out by Jupiter, Unlimited. I mean, it has everything, doesn't it? It costs a little extra coin, but it does what we need it to do, and the documentation is heavenly. They don't do any training, of course. They think they're above it."

You are already plotting that to answer Roman's burning questions by your March 15 deadline, you need to evaluate the software as well as the vendors, systematically, and then render a decision. Evaluate each vendor and package based on what Roman has said so far (assume you can trust his opinions). What are Roman's apparent biases when evaluating software and vendors? What further information do you need about each company and its software before making a selection? Set up a table to evaluate each vendor. Answer each question in a separate paragraph.

support the use of decision-making tools and decision support systems for users making medium- to long-range decisions at the middle and strategic levels of the organization.

AHP and Other Multiple-Criteria Software Commercial software packages that are based on analytical hierarchy processing (AHP) and other types of multicriteria decision making are widely available. Figure 10.8 lists some of these packages.

Decision support software requires that a decision maker's objectives are well defined, their priorities are known, and decision criteria are explicitly included. The analyst may also help the decision maker by gathering and providing information about each of the alternatives. This information is usually called an attribute.

To illustrate, consider the decision to buy the most suitable car for personal use (the objective). We would first try to identify certain models of cars to consider (our alternatives). We would then determine what we value about a car, including price, fuel mileage, safety, resale value, comfort, and other features (our criteria), then weight these criteria by importance, perhaps giving price a weight (or priority) of .20, fuel mileage a weight of .10, and so on until we assign a total weight of 1.00, or 100 percent.

Finally, we would determine a score for each of the cars we are considering based on each of the criteria. The score could be expressed in many ways, such as on a scale of 1 to 10, with 10 being the best. For example, a Honda may receive a score of 9 out of 10 for safety.

Product	Company	Web Site
Crystal Ball 2000	Decisioneering	www.crystalball.com
Criterium DecisionPlus	Info Harvest	www.infoharvest.com
Expert Choice	ExpertChoice	www.expertchoice.com

FIGURE 10.8
Selected COTS software packages that use either AHP or similar multicriteria techniques.

HYPERCASE® EXPERIENCE

10.1

"So many decisions are made here. You'd be surprised at the types of things even the administrative assistants like me are asked to decide. And at the spur of the moment, not after long hours of analysis. They are not trivial questions by any means. It seems as if the computers could help us decide most things if we would just plan for it. It's all these ad hoc decisions we make that could use some support, however. I think Snowden would be all for it. I can certainly see the benefits."

HYPERCASE QUESTIONS

1. Where might a decision support system fit in at MRE?
2. Who (which MRE employees) would be most likely to benefit from a DSS? Defend your choices.
3. Identify three semistructured, multicriteria decisions that require computer and human judgment and are being made in the Management Systems and Training Unit. Choose one to support with a DSS. Explain your choice.

Some decision tools use AHP, which asks the decision maker to compare one model of car to another, and then another, until all pairwise comparisons are made. AHP, therefore, does not require that the values of attributes be quantified. Other decision models require quantifying attributes, and then use other methods such as goal programming or conjunctive constraints to support the decision maker in a choice.

EXPERT SYSTEMS, NEURAL NETS, AND OTHER DECISION TOOLS

Other decision models available to managers include expert systems and neural nets. Expert systems are rule-based reasoning systems developed around an expert in the field. Gathering expertise is called knowledge acquisition and is the most difficult part of rule set specification. From this point on, you can assume that software tools are widely available in all price categories. One example is Exsys CORVID (www.exsys.com).

Neural nets are developed by solving a number of problems of one type and letting the software get feedback on the decisions, observing what was involved in successful decisions. This process is referred to as training the neural net.

Both these models are often placed in the realm of artificial intelligence. What makes them decision support systems? Typically, it takes a human decision maker to do problem identification, knowledge acquisition, and sensitivity analysis. Rarely are these decisions left solely to the computer. The complexity of the problems solved allows these techniques to be part of the decision support system world.

Recommendation Systems Recommendation systems are software and database systems that allow decision makers to reduce the number of alternatives by ranking, counting, or some other method. A restaurant guide, such as *Zagat's*, is an example of a recommendation system. It surveys diners and reports the results both online and in a book; information for dining in some major cities is available for downloading to wireless handheld devices. A widely used term for the process is *collaborative filtering*.

Type of Service	Product	Web Site
Push technologies	BackWeb BMC Software	www.backweb.com www.bmc.com
Personalized home pages	My Yahoo! Google Home Page	www.my.yahoo.com www.google.com
Online newspapers	CNN Interactive London Times New York Times The Age USA Today	www.cnn.com www.timesonline.co.uk www.nytimes.com www.theage.com.au www.usatoday.com
Intelligent agents	WebQL	www.ql2.com

FIGURE 10.9
Selected sources for external information available on the Web.

More sophisticated recommendation systems are being developed all the time. There are systems that allow users to rate the alternatives by either using a numeric system (such as 1 to 7) or an alphanumeric system (A–F, such as grades). Users can get collaborative filtering of books, cars, current films, and so on.

A recommendation system does not depend on numeric weights. This system counts the number of occurrences, such as how many people bookmarked a certain Web site or how many users mentioned an author. An example of a recommendation system is Net Perceptions (www.netperceptions.com), which is responsible for the collaborative filtering at Amazon.com. Sites that use collaborative filtering are HollywoodVido.com, netflix.com, and TiVo.com.

Getting External Information from the Web At times, decision makers want to filter their own information rather than depend on recommendation systems. We can classify this information as news about the economy, industry competition, and so on. The Web, however, is dynamic, and it is difficult to predict how executives will get their information in the years ahead. Figure 10.9 lists a sampling of various types of services a decision maker can use to obtain external information about things such as the economy, customers, or trends.

Push technologies (the first group) have enormous potential. Executives can configure one of these products to receive news from the Internet directly on their personal computers, or in some cases on wireless Palm computers, cell phones, or pagers that use wireless application protocol. One version of a push product can also serve as a screen saver, with a news ticker crawling across the screen much like a stock ticker. Personalized home pages can be set up to search for specific information. Online newspapers are good for browsing, because the user has control over a broad search. Finally, intelligent agents get to know your personality, learn your behavior, and track the topics they think you want to keep up to date on.

IDENTIFYING AND FORECASTING COSTS AND BENEFITS

Costs and benefits of the proposed computer system must always be considered together, because they are interrelated and often interdependent. Although the systems analyst is trying to propose a system that fulfills various information requirements, decisions to continue with the proposed system will be based on a cost-benefit analysis, not on information requirements. In many ways, benefits are measured by costs, as becomes apparent in the next section.

FORECASTING COSTS AND BENEFITS

Systems analysts are required to predict certain key variables before the proposal is submitted to the client. To some degree, a systems analyst will rely on a what-if analysis, such as, "What if labor costs rise only 5 percent per year for the next three years, rather than 10 percent?" The systems analyst should realize, however, that he or she cannot rely on what-if analysis for everything if the proposal is to be credible, meaningful, and valuable.

The systems analyst has many forecasting models available. The main condition for choosing a model is the availability of historical data. If they are unavailable, the analyst must turn to one of the judgment methods: estimates from the sales force, surveys to estimate customer demand, Delphi studies (a consensus forecast developed independently by a group of experts through a series of iterations), creating scenarios, or drawing historical analogies.

If historical data are available, the next differentiation between classes of techniques involves whether the forecast is conditional or unconditional. Conditional implies that there is an association among variables in the model or that such a causal relationship exists. Common methods in this group include correlation, regression, leading indicators, econometrics, and input/output models.

Unconditional forecasting means the analyst isn't required to find or identify any causal relationships. Consequently, systems analysts find that these methods are low-cost, easy-to-implement alternatives. Included in this group are graphical judgment, moving averages, and analysis of time series data. Because these methods are simple, reliable, and cost effective, the remainder of the section focuses on them.

Estimation of Trends Trends can be estimated in a number of different ways. The most widely used techniques are (1) graphical judgment, (2) the method of least squares, and (3) the moving average method. A brief explanation of these techniques is in order.

Graphical Judgment. The simplest way to identify a trend and forecast future trends is by graphical judgment, which is accomplished by simply looking at a graph and estimating by freehand an extension of a line or curve. An example of graphical judgment is illustrated in Figure 10.10.

The disadvantages of this method are obvious from looking at the graphs in the figure. The extension of the line or curve may depend too much on individual judgment and may not represent the real situation. The graphical judgment method is useful, however, because the ability to perform sensitivity (what-if) analysis has increased with the introduction of electronic spreadsheets.

The Method of Least Squares. When a trend line is constructed, the actual data points will fall on either side of that line. The objective in estimating a trend using the least squares method is to find the best-fitting line by minimizing the

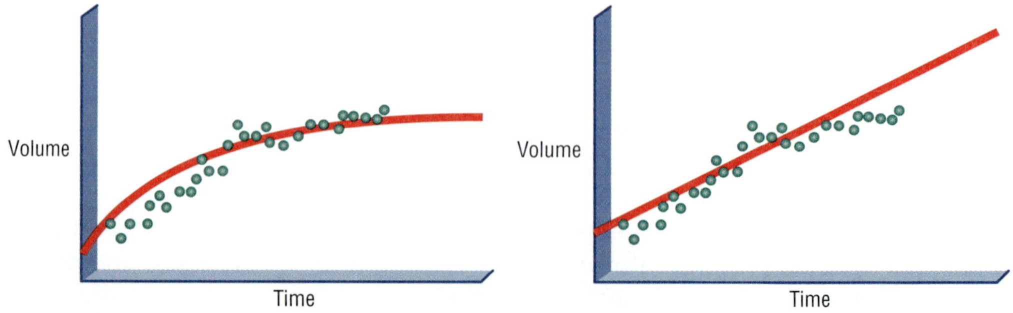

FIGURE 10.10
Different conclusions can easily be drawn from the same set of data.

sum of the deviations from a line. Once the best-fitting line is found, it can be graphed, and the line can then be extended to forecast what will happen.

The best-fitting line, or least square line, is developed from the data points $(X_1, Y_1), (X_2, Y_2), \ldots, (X_N, Y_N)$, where the X coordinates signify the time periods and the Y coordinates represent the variable the systems analyst is trying to predict. The equation for the least square line is expressed in the form

$$Y = m \times X + b$$

where the variable m represents the slope of the line and b represents the Y intercept, the point at which the line intercepts the Y axis.

We recommend a more computationally efficient method to find the least square equation, by calculating the center of gravity of the data by taking $x = X - \overline{X}$ and $y = Y - \overline{Y}$ and then calculating the least square line as

$$y = \left(\frac{\Sigma xy}{\Sigma x^2}\right) \times x$$

finally substituting back the $X - \overline{X}$ for x and $Y - \overline{Y}$ for y.

In Excel, you can calculate the trend based on least squares directly by using the **Trend** function.

Moving Averages. The method of moving averages is useful because some seasonal, cyclical, or random patterns may be smoothed, leaving the trend pattern. The principle behind moving averages is to calculate the arithmetic mean of data from groups or periods, using the equation

$$\frac{Y_1 + Y_2 + \cdots + Y_N}{N}$$

where N equals the number of periods. Then calculate the next arithmetic mean by discarding the oldest period's data and adding data from the next period:

$$\frac{Y_2 + Y_3 + \cdots + Y_{N+1}}{N}$$

Figure 10.11 shows one type of moving average. Here, five years' data are averaged and the resulting figure is indicated. Notice that years 1993 through 1997, inclusive, are averaged to predict 1998, then the years 1994 through 1998 are averaged to predict the amount for 1999, and so on. When the results are graphed, it is easily noticeable that the widely fluctuating data are smoothed.

The moving average method is useful for its smoothing ability, but at the same time it has many disadvantages. Moving averages are more strongly affected by extreme values than the methods of graphical judgment and least squares.

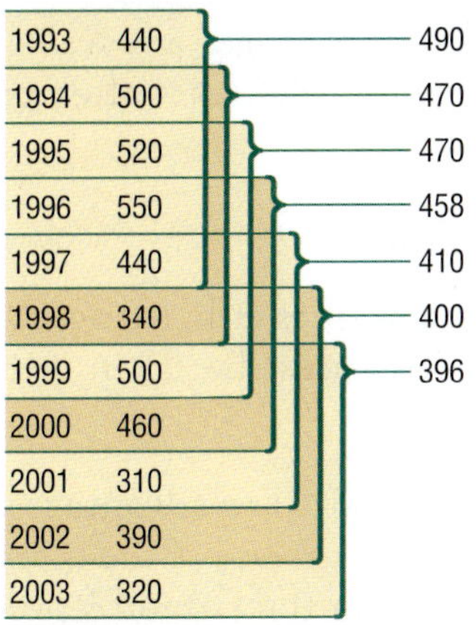

FIGURE 10.11
Calculating a five-year moving average.

CONSULTING OPPORTUNITY 10.2

WE'RE OFF TO SEE THE WIZARDS

Elphaba I. Menzel and Glinda K. Chenoweth are the owners of Emerald City Beautyscapes, a commercial landscaping company. They are trying to decide whether to write their own software, perhaps using Microsoft Access as a basis, adopt a COTS software package such as QuickBooks Pro, or hire a service called Lawn Wizards, Inc., to perform all of their bookkeeping functions.

Elphaba turned to Glinda and asked, "Is it possible for us to create a system of our own?"

Glinda replied, "I suppose we could, but it would take forever. We would need to define all our fields, our queries, and our reports. We would need to know who hasn't paid us yet, and how long it has been since we last billed them."

"Yes," says Elphaba, "and we would also have to create product descriptions, service descriptions, and codes for everything we sell and provide."

"If that was all we needed, we could probably do it," says Glinda. "But we also need to include a scheduling system. We need to know when we can provide the services to our customers and what to do if we fall behind schedule. Maybe it just isn't worth it.

"Still," reflects Glinda, "my mother used to say 'There's no place like home.' Maybe there's no software like home grown."

"You see both sides of everything," remarks Elphaba. "But the path you want to take is too long and risky. We need a software package that is ready for us to use now. I hear that there are products they call commercial off-the-shelf software that we can buy and adapt to our lawn service business. I'll investigate." So, Elphaba sets out to look for software that may be suitable.

"I've found something," cries Elphaba. "I found this software called QuickBooks Pro at www.quickbooks.com and it looks like we can afford it. There are numerous versions of the software already—one for accounting, one for construction, one for health services. Maybe we can find a package that suits us. If not, it looks like we can customize the generic version of QuickBooks Pro to fit our needs.

"Our system could grow, too. QuickBooks Pro is readily scalable. We can add customers, suppliers, or products easily. I just wanted to plant the idea of buying a ready-made package on you."

"That's interesting," says Glinda, "but I've been doing my own research. Some of our competitors have told me they let a company do all the work for them. The company is called Lawn Wizards. They do landscaping, but they also maintain accounts receivable and scheduling packages."

So off they went to see the Wizards.

Joel Green, the owner and creator of Lawn Wizards, is proud of his software. "I spent a great deal of time working with my suppliers, that is, nurseries, in the area, and we have developed a coding system for everything," he brags. "All the trees, sizes of trees, shrubs, flowers, mulch, and even lawn care tools have numbers.

"I started with a small firm, but when customers realized I paid attention to every little detail, my business blossomed." He adds, "My suppliers love my system because it cuts down on confusion.

"I noticed that my competitors were working with the same suppliers, but were getting less preferential treatment because they couldn't communicate about product very effectively. So I decided I would offer my software for hire. I would make money by renting out my software and demand even greater respect from my suppliers. My end user license agreement states that I own the software, product codes, and data generated by the system.

"Using my unique Wizards software, I can customize the package a bit for the customer, but essentially all the lawn services in the state will be using my database, codes, and B2B features. I maintain my software. If you could see the software code, it would look just like a manicured lawn."

Now Glinda and Elphaba are even more confused than before. They have three distinct options: to create a package on their own, buy commercial off-the-shelf software such as QuickBooks Pro, or outsource their needs to Lawn Wizards. Help them learn the true secret of (software) happiness by helping them articulate the pros and cons of each of their alternatives. What would you recommend? In two paragraphs, write a recommendation that grows out of your consideration of their specific business situation.

Many worthwhile forecasting packages are available for PCs and mainframes. The analyst should learn forecasting well, as it often provides information valuable in justifying the entire project.

IDENTIFYING BENEFITS AND COSTS

Benefits and costs can be thought of as either tangible or intangible. Both tangible and intangible benefits and costs must be taken into account when systems are considered.

Tangible Benefits Tangible benefits are advantages measurable in dollars that accrue to the organization through the use of the information system. Examples of tangible benefits are an increase in the speed of processing, access to otherwise inaccessible information, access to information on a more timely basis than was possible before, the advantage of the computer's superior calculating power, and decreases in the amount of employee time needed to complete specific tasks. There are still others. Although measurement is not always easy, tangible benefits can actually be measured in terms of dollars, resources, or time saved.

Intangible Benefits Some benefits that accrue to the organization from the use of the information system are difficult to measure but are important nonetheless. They are known as intangible benefits.

Intangible benefits include improving the decision-making process, enhancing accuracy, becoming more competitive in customer service, maintaining a good business image, and increasing job satisfaction for employees by eliminating tedious tasks. As you can judge from the list given, intangible benefits are extremely important and can have far-reaching implications for the business as it relates to people both outside and within the organization.

Although intangible benefits of an information system are important factors that must be considered when deciding whether to proceed with a system, a system built solely for its intangible benefits will not be successful. You must discuss both tangible and intangible benefits in your proposal, because presenting both will allow decision makers in the business to make a well-informed decision about the proposed system.

Tangible Costs The concepts of tangible and intangible costs present a conceptual parallel to the tangible and intangible benefits discussed already. Tangible costs are those that can be accurately projected by the systems analyst and the business' accounting personnel.

Included in tangible costs are the cost of equipment such as computers and terminals, the cost of resources, the cost of systems analysts' time, the cost of programmers' time, and other employees' salaries. These costs are usually well established or can be discovered quite easily, and are the costs that will require a cash outlay of the business.

Intangible Costs Intangible costs are difficult to estimate and may not be known. They include losing a competitive edge, losing the reputation for being first with an innovation or the leader in a field, declining company image due to increased customer dissatisfaction, and ineffective decision making due to untimely or inaccessible information. As you can imagine, it is next to impossible to project a dollar amount for intangible costs accurately. To aid decision makers who want to weigh the proposed system and all its implications, you must include intangible costs even though they are not quantifiable.

COMPARING COSTS AND BENEFITS

There are many well-known techniques for comparing the costs and benefits of the proposed system. They include break-even analysis, payback, cash-flow analysis, and present value analysis. All these techniques provide straightforward ways of yielding information to decision makers about the worthiness of the proposed system.

BREAK-EVEN ANALYSIS

By comparing costs alone, the systems analyst can use break-even analysis to determine the break-even capacity of the proposed information system. The point at which the total costs of the current system and the proposed system intersect represents the break-even point, the point where it becomes profitable for the business to get the new information system.

FIGURE 10.12
Break-even analysis for the proposed inventory system.

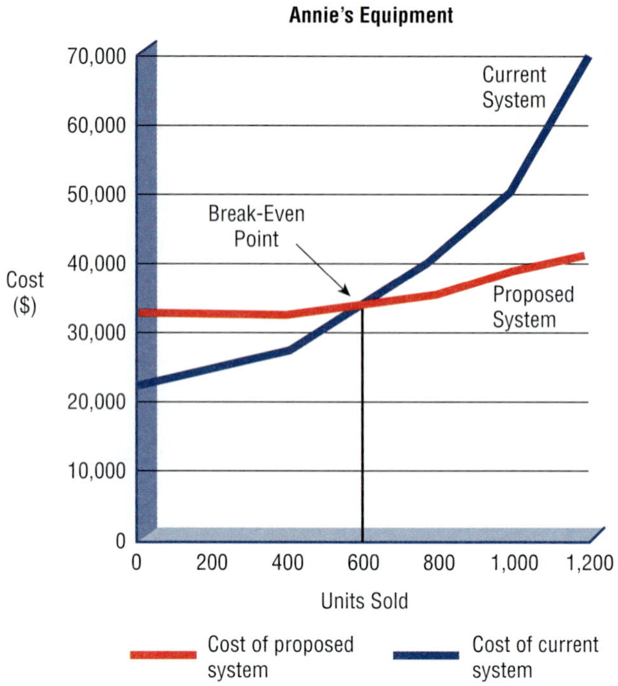

Total costs include the costs that recur during operation of the system plus the developmental costs that occur only once (one-time costs of installing a new system), that is, the tangible costs that were just discussed. Figure 10.12 is an example of a break-even analysis on a small store that maintains inventory using a manual system. As volume rises, the costs of the manual system rise at an increasing rate. A new computer system would cost a substantial sum up front, but the incremental costs for higher volume would be rather small. The graph shows that the computer system would be cost effective if the business sold about 600 units per week.

Break-even analysis is useful when a business is growing and volume is a key variable in costs. One disadvantage of break-even analysis is that benefits are assumed to remain the same, regardless of which system is in place. From our study of tangible and intangible benefits, we know that is clearly not the case.

Break-even analysis can also determine how long it will take for the benefits of the system to pay back the costs of developing it. Figure 10.13 illustrates a system with a payback period of three and a half years.

FIGURE 10.13
Break-even analysis showing a payback period of three and a half years.

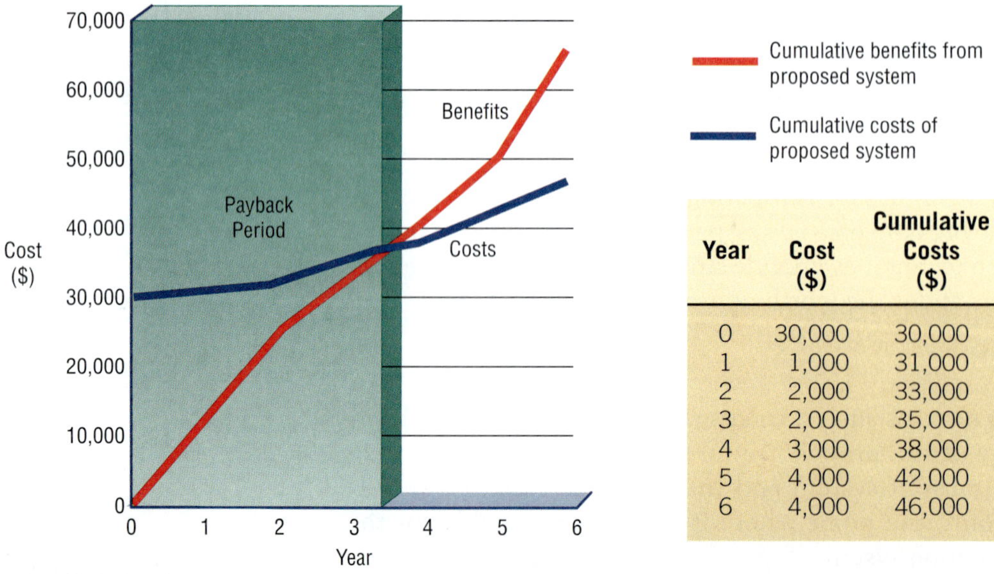

Year	Cost ($)	Cumulative Costs ($)	Benefits ($)	Cumulative Benefits ($)
0	30,000	30,000	0	0
1	1,000	31,000	12,000	12,000
2	2,000	33,000	12,000	24,000
3	2,000	35,000	8,000	32,000
4	3,000	38,000	8,000	40,000
5	4,000	42,000	10,000	50,000
6	4,000	46,000	15,000	65,000

HYPERCASE® EXPERIENCE

10.2

"Sometimes the people who have been here for some time are surprised at how much we have actually grown. Yes, I do admit that it isn't easy to keep track of what each person is up to or even what purchases each department has made in the way of hardware and software. We're working on it, though. Snowden would like to see more accountability for computer purchases. He wants to make sure we know what we have, where it is, why we have it, who's using it, and if it's boosting MRE productivity, or, as he so delicately puts it, 'to see whether it's just an expensive toy' that we can live without."

HYPERCASE QUESTIONS

1. Complete a computer equipment inventory for the Training and Management Systems Unit, describing all of the systems you find. Hint: Create an inventory form to simplify your task.
2. Using the software evaluation guidelines given in the text, do a brief evaluation of GEMS, a software package used by the Management Systems employees. In a paragraph, briefly critique this custom software by comparing it with commercial off-the-shelf software such as Microsoft Project.
3. List the intangible costs and benefits of GEMS as reported by employees of MRE.
4. Briefly describe the two alternatives Snowden is considering for the proposed project tracking and reporting system.
5. What organizational and political factors should Snowden consider in proposing his new system at MRE? (In a brief paragraph, discuss three central conflicts.)

CASH-FLOW ANALYSIS

Cash-flow analysis examines the direction, size, and pattern of cash flow that is associated with the proposed information system. If you are proposing the replacement of an old information system with a new one and if the new information system will not be generating any additional cash for the business, only cash outlays are associated with the project. If that is the case, the new system cannot be justified on the basis of new revenues generated and must be examined closely for other tangible benefits if it is to be pursued further.

Figure 10.14 shows a cash-flow analysis for small company that is providing a mailing service to other small companies in the city. Revenue projections are that only $5,000 will be generated in the first quarter, but after the second quarter, revenue will grow at a steady rate. Costs will be large in the first two quarters and then level off. Cash-flow analysis is used to determine when a company will begin to make a profit (in this case, it is in the third quarter, with a cash flow of $7,590) and when it will be "out of the red," that is, when revenue has made up for the initial investment (in the first quarter of the second year, when accumulated cash flow changes from a negative amount to a positive $10,720).

The proposed system should have increased revenues along with cash outlays. Then the size of the cash flow must be analyzed along with the patterns of cash flow associated with the purchase of the new system. You must ask when cash outlays and revenues will occur, not only for the initial purchase but also over the life of the information system.

FIGURE 10.14
Cash-flow analysis for the computerized mail-addressing system.

	Year 1 Quarter 1	Quarter 2	Quarter 3	Quarter 4	Year 2 Quarter 1
Revenue	$5,000	$20,000	$24,960	$31,270	$39,020
Costs					
Software development	10,000	5,000			
Personnel	8,000	8,400	8,800	9,260	9,700
Training	3,000	6,000			
Equipment lease	4,000	4,000	4,000	4,000	4,000
Supplies	1,000	2,000	2,370	2,990	3,730
Maintenance	0	2,000	2,200	2,420	2,660
Total Costs	26,000	27,400	17,370	18,670	20,090
Cash Flow	–21,000	–7,400	7,590	12,600	18,930
Cumulative Cash Flow	–21,000	–28,400	–20,810	–8,210	10,720

PRESENT VALUE ANALYSIS

Present value analysis helps the systems analyst to present to business decision makers the time value of the investment in the information system as well as the cash flow (as discussed in the previous section). Present value is a way to assess all the economic outlays and revenues of the information system over its economic life, and to compare costs today with future costs and today's benefits with future benefits.

In Figure 10.15, system costs total $272,000 over six years and benefits total $280,700. Therefore, we might conclude that benefits outweigh the costs. Benefits only started to surpass costs after the fourth year, however, and dollars in the sixth year will not be equivalent to dollars in the first year.

For instance, a dollar investment at 7 percent today will be worth $1.07 at the end of the year and will double in approximately 10 years. The present value, therefore, is the cost or benefit measured in today's dollars and depends on the cost of money. The cost of money is the opportunity cost, or the rate that could be obtained if the money invested in the proposed system were invested in another (relatively safe) project.

The present value of $1.00 at a discount rate of i is calculated by determining the factor

$$\frac{1}{(1+i)^n}$$

where n is the number of periods. Then the factor is multiplied by the dollar amount, yielding the present value as shown in Figure 10.16. In this example, the cost of money—the discount rate—is assumed to be .12 (12 percent) for the entire

FIGURE 10.15
Without considering present value, the benefits appear to outweigh the costs.

	Year 1	2	3	4	5	6	Total
Costs	$40,000	42,000	44,100	46,300	48,600	51,000	272,000
Benefits	$25,000	31,200	39,000	48,700	60,800	76,000	280,700

	Year						
	1	2	3	4	5	6	Total
Costs	$40,000	42,000	44,100	46,300	48,600	51,000	
Multiplier	.89	.80	.71	.64	.57	.51	
Present Value of Costs	35,600	33,600	31,311	29,632	27,702	26,010	183,855
Benefits	$25,000	31,200	39,000	48,700	60,800	76,000	
Multiplier	.89	.80	.71	.64	.57	.51	
Present Value of Benefits	22,250	24,960	27,960	31,168	34,656	38,760	179,484

FIGURE 10.16

Taking into account present value, the conclusion is that the costs are greater than the benefits. The discount rate, *i*, is assumed to be .12 in calculating the multipliers in this table.

planning horizon. Multipliers are calculated for each period: $n = 1, n = 2, \ldots, n = 6$. Present values of both costs and benefits are then calculated using these multipliers. When that step is done, the total benefits (measured in today's dollars) are $179,484, and thus less than the costs (also measured in today's dollars). The conclusion to be drawn is that the proposed system is not worthwhile if present value is considered.

Although this example, which used present value factors, is useful in explaining the concept, all electronic spreadsheets have a built-in present value function. The analyst can directly compute present value using this feature.

GUIDELINES FOR ANALYSIS

The use of the methods discussed in the preceding subsections depends on the methods employed and accepted in the organization itself. For general guidelines, however, it is safe to say the following:

1. Use break-even analysis if the project needs to be justified in terms of cost, not benefits, or if benefits do not substantially improve with the proposed system.
2. Use payback when the improved tangible benefits form a convincing argument for the proposed system.
3. Use cash-flow analysis when the project is expensive relative to the size of the company or when the business would be significantly affected by a large drain (even if temporary) on funds.
4. Use present value analysis when the payback period is long or when the cost of borrowing money is high.

Whichever method is chosen, it is important to remember that cost-benefit analysis should be approached systematically, in a way that can be explained and justified to managers, who will eventually decide whether to commit resources to the systems project. Next, we turn to the importance of comparing many systems alternatives.

EXAMINING ALTERNATIVE SYSTEMS

Through the use of break-even analysis, payback, cash-flow analysis, and present value analysis, it is possible to compare alternatives for the information system. As shown previously, it is important to use multiple analyses to cover the shortcomings of each approach adequately. Although you will consider several alternatives, you will recommend only one in the proposal. Thus, you will have done comparative analyses about which system makes better economic sense before the proposal is written. Those analyses can be included to provide support for the system you are recommending.

Do not think there is only one "correct" system solution to help users in a business solve their problems and reach their goals. Different businesses call for different system attributes, and systems analysts themselves differ about the best way to handle a variety of business problems.

The key point is that you want to compare and contrast opinions in as fair a manner as possible so that a true choice is offered to organizational decision makers. The closer their initial identification with and acceptance of the proposed system, the greater the likelihood of its continued use and acceptance once the system is in place. Continue including decision makers in the planning, even though you must in some ways expect to play the role of the systems expert now.

THE SYSTEMS PROPOSAL

ORGANIZING THE SYSTEMS PROPOSAL

Once you have gathered the material to be included in your systems proposal, you need to piece it together in a logical and visually effective way. You need to include 10 main functional sections, use an effective writing style, use figures to supplement your writing, and attend to the visual details of the written proposal.

What to Include in the Systems Proposal Ten main sections comprise the written systems proposal. Each part has a particular function, and the eventual proposal should be arranged in the following order:

1. Cover letter.
2. Title page of project.
3. Table of contents.
4. Executive summary (including recommendations).
5. Outline of systems study with appropriate documentation.
6. Detailed results of the systems study.
7. Systems alternatives (three or four possible solutions).
8. Systems analysts' recommendations.
9. Proposal summary.
10. Appendices (assorted documentation, summary of phases, correspondence, and so on).

A cover letter to managers and the IT task force should accompany the systems proposal. It should list the people who did the study and summarize the objectives of the study. Keep the cover letter concise and friendly.

Include on the title page the name of the project, the names of the systems analysis team members, and the date the proposal is submitted. The proposal title must accurately express the content of the proposal, but it can also exhibit some imagination. The table of contents can be useful to readers of long proposals. If the proposal is less than 10 pages long, omit the table of contents.

The executive summary, in 250 to 375 words, provides the who, what, when, where, why, and how of the proposal, just as would the first paragraph in a news story. It should also include the recommendations of the systems analysts and desired management action, because some people will only have time to read the summary. It should be written last, after the rest of the proposal is complete.

The outline of the systems study provides information about all the methods used in the study and who or what was studied. Any questionnaires, interviews, sampling of archival data, observation, or prototyping used in the systems study should be discussed in this section.

This detailed results section describes what the systems analyst has found out about human and systems needs through all the methods described in the preceding section. Conclusions about problems workers experience when interacting with technologies and systems that have come to the fore through the study should be noted here. This section should raise the problems or suggest opportunities that call forth the alternatives presented in the next section.

In the systems alternatives section of the proposal, the analyst presents two or three alternative solutions that directly address the aforementioned problems. The alternatives you present should include one that recommends keeping the system the same. Each alternative should be explored separately. Describe the costs and benefits of each situation. Because there are usually trade-offs involved in any solution, be sure to include the advantages and disadvantages of each.

Each alternative must clearly indicate what users and managers must do to implement it. The wording should be as clear as possible, such as, "Buy notebook computers for all middle managers," "Purchase packaged software to support users in managing inventory," or "Modify the existing system through funding in-house programming efforts."

After the systems analysis team has weighed the alternatives, it will have a definite professional opinion about which solution is most workable. The systems analysts' recommendations section expresses the *recommended* solution. Include the reasons supporting the team's recommendation so that it is easy to understand why it is being made. The recommendation should flow logically from the preceding analysis of alternative solutions, and it should clearly relate the human–computer interaction findings to the choice offered.

The proposal summary is a brief statement that mirrors the content of the executive summary. It gives the objectives of the study and the recommended solution. The analyst should once more stress the project's importance and feasibility along with the value of the recommendations for reaching the users' goals and improving the business. Conclude the proposal on a positive note.

The appendix is the last part of the systems proposal, and it can include any information that the systems analyst feels may be of interest to specific individuals, but that is not essential for understanding the systems study and what is being proposed.

Once the systems proposal is written, carefully select who should receive the report. Personally hand the report to the people you have selected. Your visibility is important for the acceptance and eventual success of the system.

USING FIGURES FOR EFFECTIVE COMMUNICATION

The emphasis so far in this section has been on considering your audience when composing the systems proposal. Tables and graphs as well as words are important in capturing and communicating the basics of the proposed system.

Integrating figures into your proposal helps demonstrate that you are responsive to the different ways people absorb information. Figures in the report supplement written information and must always be interpreted in words; they should never stand alone.

Effective Use of Tables Although tables are technically not visual aids, they provide a different way of grouping and presenting analyzed data that the analyst wants to communicate to the proposal reader. Tables are more similar to figures than they are to written text and are therefore discussed here.

Tables use labeled columns and rows to present statistical or alphabetical data in an organized way. Each table must be numbered according to the order in which

FIGURE 10.17
Guidelines for creating effective tables.

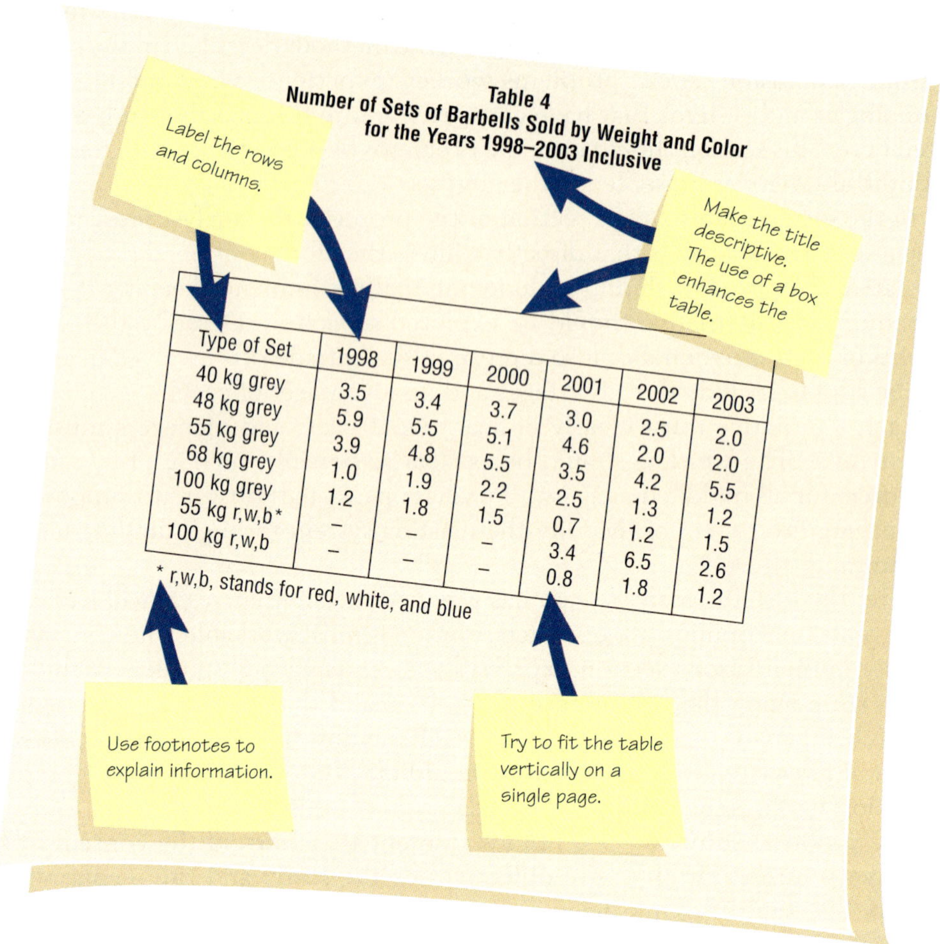

it appears in the proposal and should be meaningfully titled. Figure 10.17 shows appropriate layout and labeling for a table.

Some guidelines for tables are the following:

1. Integrate tables into the body of the proposal. Don't relegate them to the appendices.
2. Try to fit the entire table vertically on a single page if possible.
3. Number and title the table at the top of the page. Make the title descriptive and meaningful.
4. Label each row and column. Use more than one line for a title if necessary.
5. Use a boxed table if room permits. Vertically ruled columns will enhance the readability.
6. Use footnotes if necessary to explain detailed information contained in the table.

Several methods for comparing costs and benefits were presented in previous sections. Tabled results of those comparisons should appear in the systems proposal. If a break-even analysis is done, a table illustrating results of the analysis should be included. Payback can be shown in tables that serve as additional support for graphs. A short table comparing computer systems or options might also be included in the systems proposal.

Effective Use of Graphs This section covers different kinds of graphs: line graphs, column charts, bar charts, and pie charts. Line graphs, column graphs, and bar charts compare variables, whereas pie charts illustrate the composition of 100 percent of an entity.

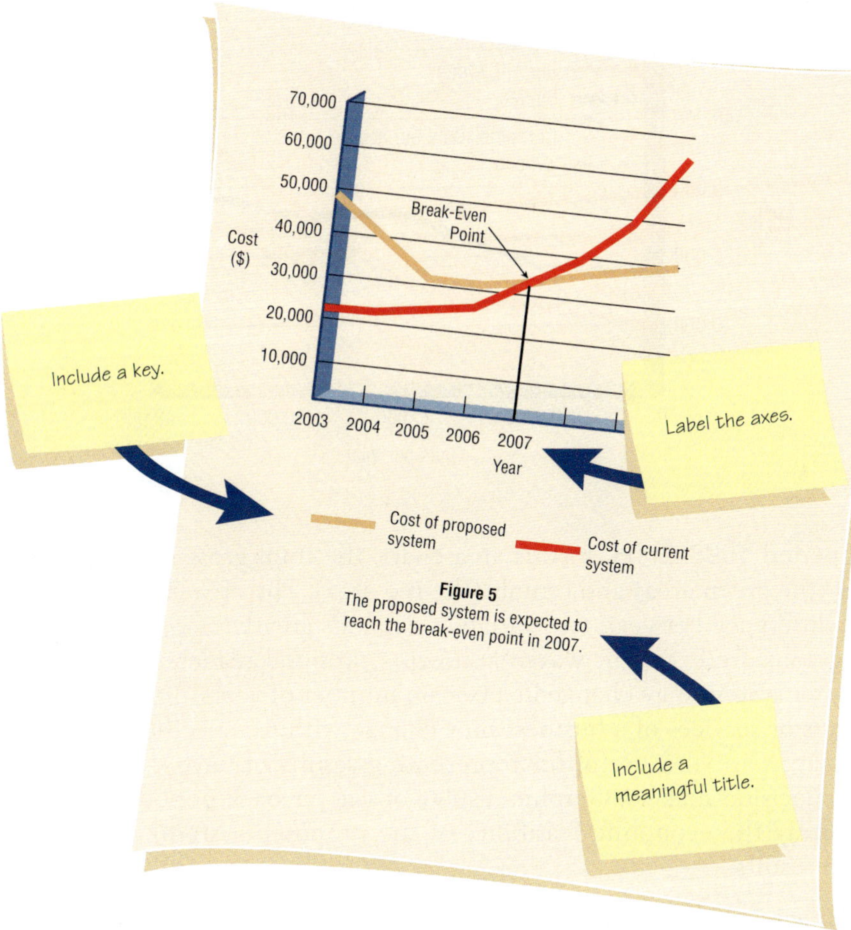

FIGURE 10.18
Guidelines for drawing effective line graphs.

The guidelines for including effective graphs in a proposal are as follows:

1. Choose a style of graph that communicates your intended meaning well.
2. Integrate the graph into the body of the proposal.
3. Give the graph a sequential figure number and a meaningful title.
4. Label each axis and any lines, columns, bars, or pieces of the pie on the graph.
5. Include a key to indicate differently colored lines, shaded bars, or crosshatched areas.

An example of how a graph would appear on a page in a systems proposal is shown in Figure 10.18. Our explanation of graphs begins with the simplest type, called a line graph.

Line Graphs. Line graphs are used primarily to show change over time. No other type of graph shows a trend more clearly than a line graph. Changes in a single variable or up to five variables can be illustrated in a single line graph.

At times, however, a line graph is used to show something other than time on the horizontal axis. This situation occurs when one has to estimate when two or more lines intersect, as shown in Figure 10.19. In this example, the current system is the least expensive until Annie's Equipment grows to approximately 24,000 units per year. Then Computer Data Services offers the least expensive option. Later we find that Syscom becomes the least expensive option if Annie's were to grow to over 28,000 units annually.

A dramatic method of visual comparison, in the same general family as line graphs, is the area chart. Figure 10.20 shows the growth of the DVD industry over

FIGURE 10.19

Depicting each variable with a different kind of line on the line graph.

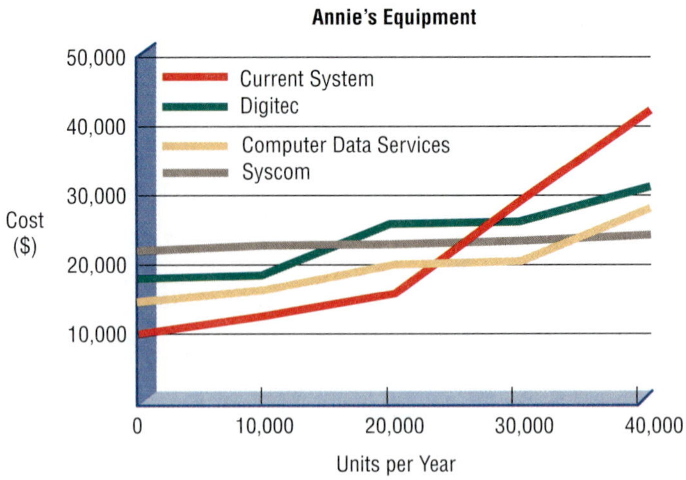

the time period 1998–2003. In this area chart, the total gross receipts consist of both sales (the green area) and rentals (the red area). The area chart is very useful when the difference between two variables expands greatly.

Line graphs are excellent ways of showing proposal readers how demand on the computer system may change in a certain number of years, or how demand for the products or services of a business may change within a specific time period.

Line graphs are also useful for representing results of payback or break-even analysis to decision makers. Graphic display of the payback period is an excellent way to portray the economic feasibility of the proposed system, as is a graph of break-even results.

Column Charts. Another familiar kind of graph is the column chart. Column charts can depict a comparison between two or more variables over time, but they are used more often to compare different variables at a particular point in time. Although they do not show trends as well as line graphs—nor can one easily estimate value between columns using them—many people find column charts easier to understand than line graphs.

Figure 10.21 shows a column chart with more than one variable. In this situation, the columns are drawn in different colors or shades to distinguish between the variables. Notice that there is space between each of the two classes (HQ and Troops A, B, C, D, and E) but no space between the two variables, "current strength" and "minimum required."

FIGURE 10.20

An area chart is a form of line graph that may make more of an impact.

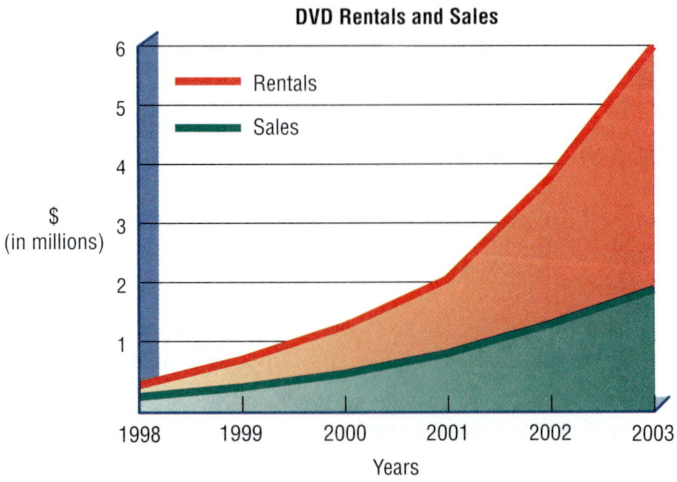

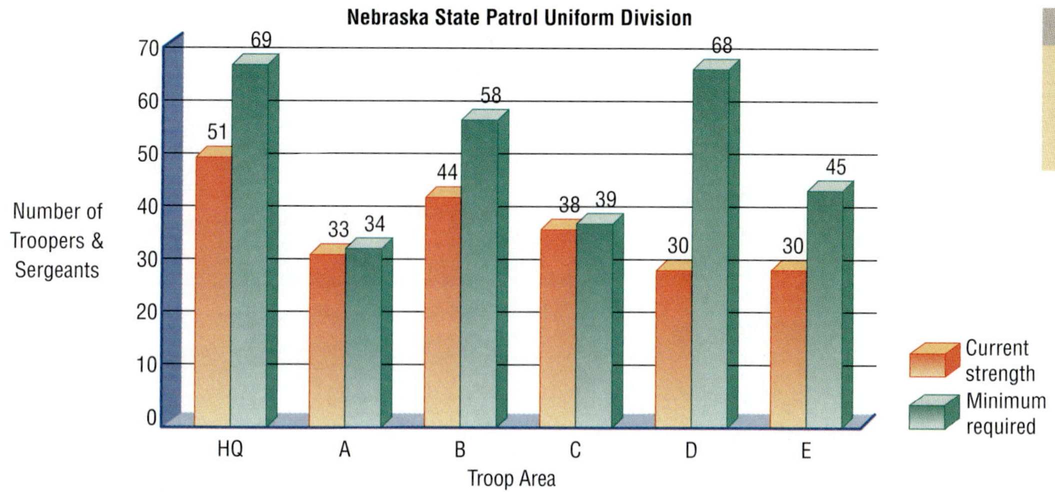

FIGURE 10.21

More than one variable can be displayed on a column chart by shading or coloring the column bars.

There are also special forms of column charts. A 100-percent stacked column chart is shown in Figure 10.22. This type of chart is used to show the relationship between two variables that make up 100 percent of an entity. Here, sporting goods sales are made up of competitive sporting equipment and individual achievement equipment. The chart depicts the individual achievement equipment as shrinking as a percentage of total sales. (It does not, however, show the actual sales, which may indeed be growing even though the percentage is diminishing.)

Another special type of column chart is the deviation column chart. This type of chart is useful for emphasizing years that show a loss, or pointing out the year in which the company intends to break even. Furthermore, the chart can be drawn to show the deviation from an average. An example of a deviation column chart is shown in Figure 10.23, in which the differences in above- and below-average months are emphasized.

Bar Charts. Horizontally drawn, bar charts are similar to column charts, but they are never used to show a relationship over a period of years. Rather, they are used to show one or more variables in certain classes or categories during a specific time period.

The bars themselves may be organized in many different ways. They can be in alphabetical, numerical, geographical, or progressive order, or they can be sorted by magnitude. For instance, in a systems proposal, a bar chart would be useful in

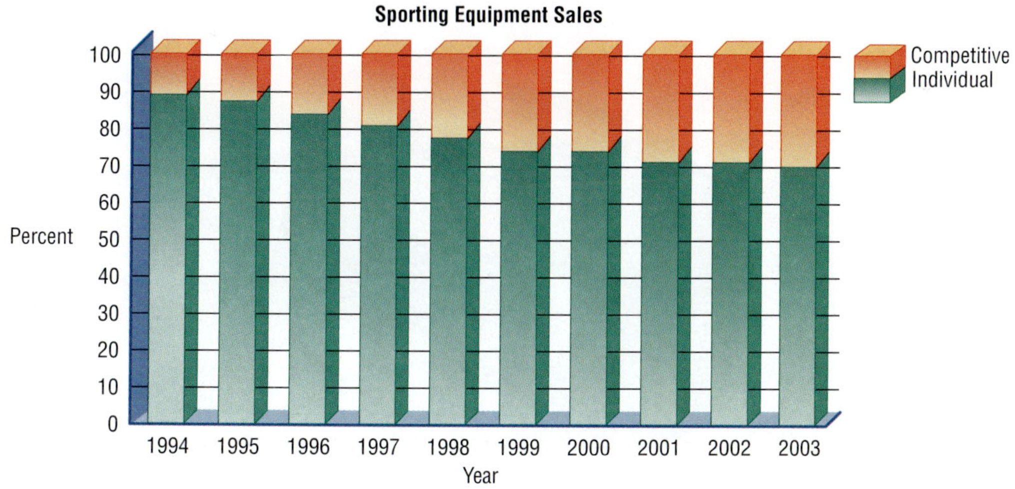

FIGURE 10.22

A 100-percent column chart can be used to show the percentage share over time.

FIGURE 10.23

A deviation column chart can be more effective in showing which months have above-average transactions.

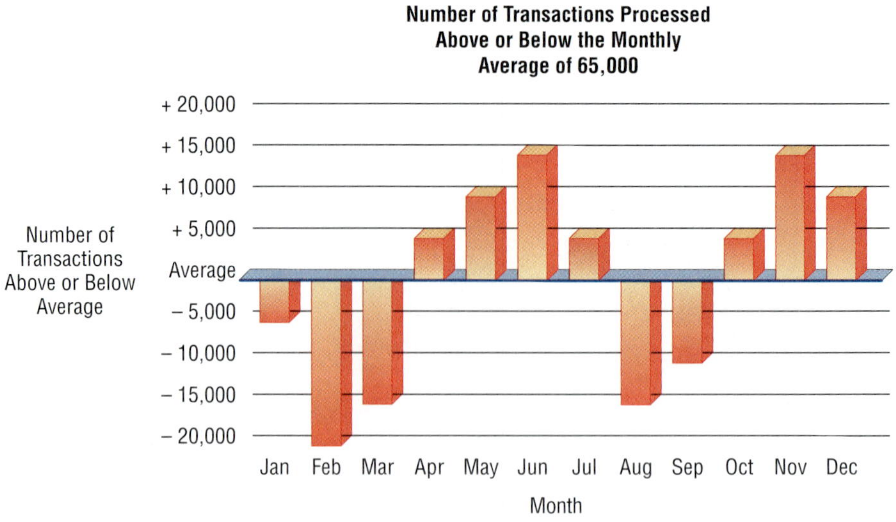

comparing the volumes of shipping invoices, customer accounts, and vendor invoices processed by the computer system during July. A bar chart is one of the most widely known forms of graphs and can make a comparison in a straightforward way.

Pie Charts. Another commonly used type of graph is the circle or pie chart. It is used to show how 100 percent of a commodity is divided at a particular point in time, as in Figure 10.24.

Pie charts are easier to read than 100-percent stacked column charts or 100-percent subdivided bar charts. Their main disadvantage is that they take up a lot of room on a page.

PRESENTING THE SYSTEMS PROPOSAL

As a systems analyst, you should understand your audience and how to organize, support, and deliver the oral presentation.

UNDERSTANDING THE AUDIENCE

Just as the audience for the written proposal helps dictate the writing style, level of detail, and type of figures, the audience for the oral presentation helps the speaker discover how formal to be, what to present, and what types of visual aids to include. It is imperative that you know *whom* you will be addressing.

FIGURE 10.24

A visually appealing way to display how 100 percent of an entity is divided up at a particular time is a pie chart.

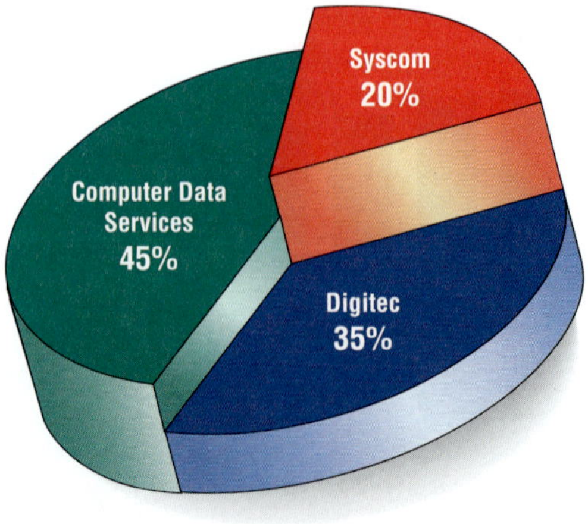

CONSULTING OPPORTUNITY 10.3

SHOULD THIS CHART BE BARRED?

"Gee, I'm glad they hired you guys. I know the Redwings will be better next season because of you. My job'll be a lot easier, too," says Andy Skors, ticket manager for the Kitchener, Ontario, hockey team, the Kitchener Redwings. Andy has been working with your systems analysis team on analyzing the systems requirements for computerizing ticket sales.

Recall that when we last heard from the systems analysis team, consisting of Hy Sticking (your leader), Rip Shinpadd, Fiona Wrink, and you, you were wrestling with whether to expedite the project and set team productivity goals (in Consulting Opportunity 3.3).

Andy is talking with the team about what to include in the systems proposal to make it as persuasive as possible to the Redwings' management. "I know they're going to like this chart," Andy continues. "It's a little something I drew up after you asked me all those questions on past ticket sales, Rip."

Andy hands the bar chart to Rip, who looks at it and suppresses a slight smile. "As long as we have you here, Andy, why don't you explain it to us?"

Like a player fresh out of the penalty box, Andy skates smoothly into his narrative of the graph. "Well, our ticket sales reached an all-time high in 1996. We were real crowd pleasers that year. Could've sold seats on the scoreboard if they let me. Unfortunately, ticket sales were at an all-time low in 1997. I mean, we're talking about a disaster. Tickets moved slower than a glacier. I had to convince the players to give tickets away when they made appearances at the shopping mall. Why, just look at this table, it's terrible.

"I think computerizing the ticket sales will help us pick out who our season supporters are. We've got to figure out who they are and get them back. Get them to stick with us. That would be a good goal to shoot for," Andy concludes.

As Andy's presentation finally winds down, Hy looks as if he thought the 20-minute period would never end. Picking up on his signal, Fiona says, "Thanks for the data, Andy. We'll work on getting them into the report somehow."

As Fiona and Rip head out of the room with Andy, Hy realizes the bench has emptied, so he asks you, the fourth team member, to coach Andy on his bar chart by making a list of the problems you see in it. Hy would also like you to sketch some alternative ways to graph the data on ticket sales so that a correct and persuasive graph of ticket sales can be included in the systems proposal. Draw two alternatives.

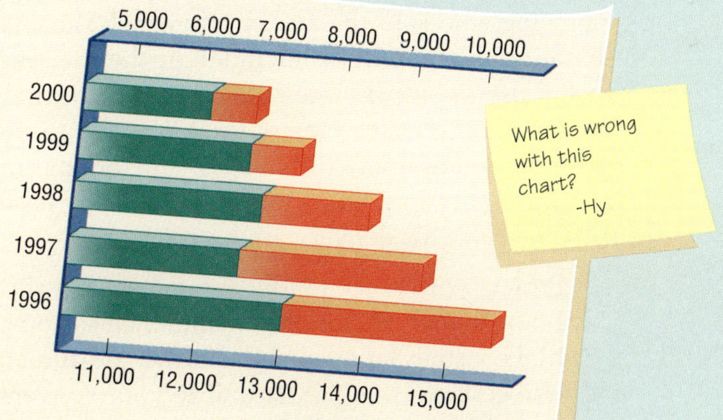

Status	Year	Average tickets sold per game	Season tickets sold per season
Best year	1999	15,643	7,505
	2000	14,880	6,808
	2001	14,100	7,089
	2002	13,254	6,735
Worst year	2003	12,690	6,351

FIGURE 10.C1
An incorrectly drawn graph.

ORGANIZING THE SYSTEMS PROPOSAL PRESENTATION

Page through the data collected from the organization that are summarized in the written proposal. Find four to six main points that capsulize the proposal. In particular, check the executive summary, the recommendations section, and the proposal summary. If the time allotted for the oral presentation is longer than half an hour, main points can be expanded to nine or more.

Once main points and supporting points are worked out, an introduction and conclusion can be written. Notice that writing the introduction comes last, not first, because the introduction should preview the proposal's four to six main points, which are impossible to determine at the outset.

The introduction should also include a "hook," something that will get the audience intrigued with what is coming next. The hook should be a creative approach to the proposal that directly unites the audience's interests with the new material being presented. An anecdote, an analogy, a quotation, poetry, or even a joke can open a presentation successfully. If humor is used, it should be directly relevant to the topic and should make a point about what is coming up.

Conclusions should mirror introductions. The main ideas should be reiterated and a closing thought (similar to the creative hook of the introduction) should be given.

Questions can be taken either during or after the presentation. Answering questions during the presentation makes for a more informal meeting. If there is a serious challenge, however, it could derail the proposal. To maintain control and communicate your points effectively, it is permissible to request that questions be saved until the end.

PRINCIPLES OF DELIVERY

Knowing who is in the audience will tell the analyst how formal to make the presentation. If the CEO is included in the meeting, chances are it will be quite formal. If users comprise the audience, a less formal, workshop-style presentation will be more appropriate. One of the best ways to gauge the formality of presentations is by observing many different organizational meetings prior to the systems proposal presentation. Expectations are usually based on customs and culture.

The rules for delivery are basic:

1. Project your voice loudly enough so that the audience can hear you.
2. Look at each person in the audience as you speak.
3. Make visuals large enough so that the audience can see them.
4. Use gestures that are natural to your conversational style.
5. Introduce and conclude your talk confidently.

The very thought of getting up in front of people can make presenters extremely nervous; in fact, the greatest fear of men is said to be public speaking (it's the second-greatest fear of women). However, by being yourself, being prepared, and speaking naturally, you will be able to communicate your recommendations in a credible way.

SUMMARY

By inventorying equipment already on hand and on order, systems analysts will be able to better determine whether new, modified, or current computer hardware is to be recommended.

HYPERCASE® EXPERIENCE 10.3

"I know it's hard to get your feet wet, but you've been here long enough to know that we're all curious about what you've come up with so far. We're especially interested in what you think of us! Are we one big happy family, or is this a zoo? Seriously, Snowden would like it very much if you gave a brief oral presentation of a preliminary proposal for a new automated project reporting system for the Training Group. Who should we include? Well, Mr. Torrey, Dan Hill, Tom Ketcham, and Snowden, of course, will want to be there. Let's see . . . I've got the executive calendar on the screen here. Everyone we need is free a week from Thursday at 3:00. You can bring your whole team along if you want. That room has multimedia capabilities, if you want to get fancy, but keep it to about 15 minutes at the most. Oh, one more thing, I'm sure Mr. Hyatt will want to come. Have fun!"

HYPERCASE QUESTIONS

1. Prepare an outline of the preliminary proposal for a new automated project reporting system for the Training Group. Include enough detail so that it would be possible to use your outline as speaking notes during a presentation.
2. Use a software package such as Microsoft PowerPoint to create a short (3 to 5 slides) slide show to illustrate the preliminary proposal for the automated project reporting system you outlined in Question 1.
3. Have your teammates role play the parts of Warren Torrey, Dan Hill, Tom Ketcham, and Snowden Evans (the part of Mr. Hyatt is optional). Present your brief preliminary proposal for the new automated project reporting system to them. Use the slide show you have created for Question 2.
4. Write a two-paragraph report based on feedback received on the preliminary proposal during the role playing in Question 3. What questions arose? What changes will you make?

Computer hardware can be acquired through purchase, lease, or rental. Vendors will supply support services such as preventive maintenance and user training that are typically negotiated separately. Software can be created as a custom product, purchased as a commercial off-the shelf (COTS) software package, or outsourced to an application service provider (ASP).

Often systems analysts are required to develop or evaluate higher-level software packages to support decision making with decision support systems. The analyst may help get information necessary for identifying objectives, alternatives, criteria, attributes, and priorities or weights needed for multiple-criteria decision making.

Decision makers can also use expert systems and neural nets to solve problems. They can also seek advice from recommendation systems, which poll user preferences and arrive at results by either numerical weighting or by occurrence. Executives seek external information, and there are many different ways to obtain that information from the Web. These methods include push technologies, personalized home pages, online newspapers, and intelligent agents. Information to support decisions can even be pushed to handheld devices, cell phones, and pagers. Use the methods in the earlier chapters to understand and interpret how useful and usable different technologies are for different workers.

The HCI factors must be weighed alongside the other costs of technology being proposed. Preparing a systems proposal means identifying all the costs and benefits of a number of alternatives. The systems analyst has a number of methods available to forecast future costs, benefits, volumes of transactions, and economic variables that affect costs and benefits. Costs and benefits can be tangible (quantifiable) or intangible (nonquantifiable and resistant to direct comparison).

A systems analyst has many methods for analyzing costs and benefits. Break-even analysis examines the cost of the existing system versus the cost of the proposed system. The payback method determines the length of time it will take before the new system is profitable. Cash-flow analysis is appropriate when it is critical to know the amount of cash outlays, whereas present value analysis takes into consideration the cost of borrowing money. These tools help the analyst examine the alternatives at hand and make a well-researched recommendation in the systems proposal.

The systems analyst has three main steps to follow for putting together an effective systems proposal: effectively organizing the proposal content, writing the proposal in an appropriate business style, and orally presenting an informative systems proposal. To be effective, the proposal should be written in a clear and understandable manner, and its content should be divided into 10 functional sections.

Visual considerations are important when putting together a proposal. Much of what is important in the systems proposal can be enhanced through the correct use of figures, including tables and graphs. Graphs compare two or more variables over time or at a particular point in time. Figures are always accompanied by a written interpretation in the proposal. The graphs and tables used for planning prior to the proposal can be incorporated into it if relevant. The oral presentation of the system is based on the written proposal and is another way of effectively selling the system.

KEYWORDS AND PHRASES

analytic hierarchy processing (AHP)
bar chart
benchmarking
break-even analysis
cash-flow analysis
collaborative filtering
column chart
decision support system (DSS)
expert system
forecasting
graphical judgment
intangible benefits
intangible costs
intelligent agent (re: the Web)
line graph
method of least squares
moving average
neural net
payback
pie chart
present value
push technologies
recommendation systems
systems proposal
tangible benefits
tangible costs
vendor support

REVIEW QUESTIONS

1. List the elements that should be included on a computer hardware inventory form.
2. What is meant by the term *estimated workload*?

3. List four criteria for evaluating system hardware.
4. What are the three main options for the acquisition of computer hardware?
5. Under what conditions is rental of computer hardware appropriate?
6. What does COTS stand for?
7. What does ASP stand for in terms of software delivery?
8. What are the advantages and disadvantages of creating your own software?
9. What are the advantages and disadvantages of purchasing COTS software?
10. What are the advantages and disadvantages of outsourcing software needs to an ASP?
11. List the six main categories on which to grade software.
12. What does AHP stand for?
13. What are recommendation systems?
14. How can decision makers get external information from the Web?
15. What is the difference between push technologies, personalized home pages, online newspapers, and intelligent agents?
16. Why is forecasting a useful tool for the systems analyst?
17. Define unconditional forecasting.
18. What is a disadvantage of graphical judgment?
19. What is the objective in estimating a trend using the least squares method?
20. Why is the method of moving averages a useful one?
21. Define tangible costs and benefits. Give an example of each one.
22. Define intangible costs and benefits. Give an example of each one.
23. List four techniques for comparing the costs and benefits of a proposed system.
24. When is break-even analysis useful?
25. What are the three drawbacks of using the payback method?
26. When is cash-flow analysis used?
27. Define present value analysis.
28. As a general guideline, when should present value analysis be used?
29. What are the three steps the systems analyst must follow to put together an effective systems proposal?
30. List the 10 main sections of the systems proposal.
31. What relationships does a line graph depict?
32. What relationships does a column chart depict?
33. What relationships does a bar chart depict?
34. What relationships does a pie chart depict?
35. List the five guidelines for using figures effectively in the systems proposal.
36. What sort of support material should be included in an oral presentation of the systems proposal to executive audiences?

PROBLEMS

1. Delicato, Inc., a manufacturer of precise measuring instruments for scientific purposes, has presented you with a list of attributes that its managers think are probably important in selecting a vendor for computer hardware and software. The criteria are not listed in order of importance.
    1. Low price.
    2. Precisely written software for engineering applications.
    3. Vendor performs routine maintenance on hardware.
    4. Training for Delicato employees.

    a. Critique the list of attributes in a paragraph.
    b. Using its initial input, help Delicato, Inc., draw up a more suitable list of criteria for selecting computer hardware and software vendors.

2. SoftWear Silhouettes is a rapidly growing mail-order house specializing in all-cotton clothing. Management would like to expand sales to the Web with the creation of an ecommerce site. The company has two full-time system analysts and one programmer. Company offices are located in a small, isolated New England town, and the employees who handle the traditional mail-order business have little computer training.
   a. Considering the company's situation, draw up a list of software attributes that SoftWear Silhouettes should emphasize in its choice of software to create a Web site and integrate the mail-order business with business from the Web site.
   b. Would you recommend COTS software, custom software, or outsourcing to an ASP? State your choice and defend it in a paragraph.
   c. List the variables that contributed to your response in Problem 2b.
3. Below is 12 years' demand for Viking Village, a game now available for handhelds and smartphones.

Year	Demand
1995	20,123
1996	18,999
1997	20,900
1998	31,200
1999	38,000
2000	41,200
2001	49,700
2002	46,400
2003	50,200
2004	52,300
2005	49,200
2006	57,600

   a. Graph the demand data for Viking Village.
   b. Forecast the demand for Viking Village for the next five years using the graphical judgment approach.
4. For the Viking Village problem in Problem 3:
   a. Determine the linear trend for Viking Village demand using the least squares method.
   b. Estimate the demand for Viking Village for the next five years using the trend you determined.
5. Using the data in Problem 3:
   a. Determine the linear trend for Viking Village using a three-year moving average.
   b. Use least squares on the averages in Problem 3a to determine a linear trend.
   c. Estimate demand for Viking Village for the next five years by extending the linear trend found in Problem 4a.
6. Do the data for Viking Village appear to have a cyclical variation? Explain.
7. Interglobal Paper Company has asked for your help in comparing its present computer system with a new one its board of directors would like to see implemented. Proposed system and present system costs are as follows:

Year	Proposed System Costs	Present System Costs
Year 1		
Equipment Lease	$20,000	$11,500
Salaries	30,000	50,000
Overhead	4,000	3,000
Development	30,000	—
Year 2		
Equipment Lease	$20,000	$10,500
Salaries	33,000	55,000
Overhead	4,400	3,300
Development	12,000	—
Year 3		
Equipment Lease	$20,000	$10,500
Salaries	36,000	60,000
Overhead	4,900	3,600
Development	—	—
Year 4		
Equipment Lease	$20,000	$10,500
Salaries	39,000	66,000
Overhead	5,500	4,000
Development	—	—

a. Using break-even analysis, determine the year in which Interglobal Paper will break even.

b. Graph the costs and show the break-even point.

8. Below are system benefits for Interglobal Paper Company (from Problem 7):

Year	Benefits
1	$55,000
2	75,000
3	80,000
4	85,000

a. Use the costs of Interglobal Paper's proposed system from Problem 7 to determine the payback period (use the payback method).

b. Graph the benefits versus the costs and indicate the payback period.

9. Glenn's Electronics, a small company, has set up a computer service. The table below shows the revenue expected for the first five months of operation, in addition to the costs for office remodeling, and so on. Determine the cash flow and accumulated cash flow for the company. When is Glenn's expected to show a profit?

	July	August	September	October	November
REVENUE	$35,000	$36,000	$42,000	$48,000	$57,000
COSTS					
Office Remodeling	$25,000	$8,000			
Salaries	11,000	12,100	$13,300	$14,600	$16,000
Training	6,000	6,000			
Equipment Lease	8,000	8,480	9,000	9,540	10,110
Supplies	3,000	3,150	3,300	3,460	3,630

10. Alamo Foods of San Antonio wants to introduce a new computer system for its perishable products warehouse. The costs and benefits are as follows:

Year	Costs	Benefits
1	$33,000	$21,000
2	34,600	26,200
3	36,300	32,700
4	38,100	40,800
5	40,000	51,000
6	42,000	63,700

a. Given a discount rate of 8 percent (.08), perform present value analysis on the data for Alamo Foods. (*Hint:* Use the formula

$$\frac{1}{(1+i)^n}$$

to find the multipliers for years 1 to 6.)

b. What is your recommendation for Alamo Foods?

11. a. Suppose the discount rate in Problem 10a changes to 13 percent (.13). Perform present value analysis using the new discount rate.

b. What is your recommendation to Alamo Foods now?

c. Explain the difference between Problem 10b and Problem 11b.

12. Solve Problem 7 using an electronic spreadsheet program such as Excel.
13. Use a spreadsheet program to solve Problem 9.
14. Solve Problem 10 using a function for net present value, such as @NPV (*x*, range) in Excel.
15. "I think it's only fair to write up *all* the alternatives you've considered," says Lou Cite, a personnel supervisor for Day-Glow Paints. "After all, you've been working on this systems thing for a while now, and I think my boss and everyone else would be interested to see what you've found out." You are talking with Lou as you prepare to put together the final systems proposal that your team will be presenting to upper management.

a. In a paragraph, explain to Lou why your proposal will not (and should not) contain all the alternatives that your team has considered.

b. In a paragraph, discuss the sorts of alternatives that should appear in the final systems proposal.

16. In going over the data you have collected for your proposal for Linder's Machine Parts of Duluth, Minnesota, you find a forecast of demand for parts for the next five years as well as the forecast of the number of companies purchasing parts. You would like to include the data in your systems proposal to help support the need for a new system, and the numbers currently given in this narrative are as follows: "The columns show that demand of 120,000 will increase to 130,000 in year 2, go up 20,000 in year 3, go up 40,000 in year 4, and level off in year 5. Although demand for parts will be going up, the total number of companies who will be buying will be 700 in year 1 and will be reduced by 50 companies each year through the next five years."

a. Based on the narrative, draw a bar graph to depict demand over the next five years for Linder's.

b. Based on the narrative, draw a column chart to depict demand over the next five years for Linder's.

c. Based on the narrative, draw a bar graph to show the decline in the total number of companies ordering machine parts from Linder's.

d. Based on the narrative, draw a line graph to depict both the increase in demand and the decrease in the total number of companies purchasing parts.

17. "I was thinking of how I'll handle my portion of the presentation to management," says Margaret, a member of your systems analysis team. "Even though some of them told us they 'haven't been keeping up with computers,' I think they need to know the technical aspects of our recommended system inside and out; otherwise they may not accept it. So I'll begin by defining basic terms such as 'byte' and 'program code,' and then I'll turn the meeting into a short tutorial on computing. What do you think?"
    a. In a paragraph, critique Margaret's approach to the systems proposal presentation to the executive audience.
    b. In a paragraph, suggest a different way to approach the executive audience for the systems proposal presentation. Be sure to include types of support—as well as topics—that would be more appropriate than what Margaret has in mind.

GROUP PROJECTS

1. The Weil Smile Clinic is a dental practice run by Drs. Bonnie and Jeff and they need to keep the necessary patient and insurance data safe and secure. They looked into online backup like SOS Online, Spare Backup, Mozy Remote Backup, and Data Deposit Box. Look into the cost of these or other services, then help Drs. Bonnie and Jeff make a decision. What are the intangible costs and benefits of backing up this way? Should they use a backup system or find some other way? Defend your analysis and recommendations.
2. Explore four or five voice-over IP (VoIP) providers. Make a list of costs including the setup fee, monthly cost of the basic plan, monthly cost of the unlimited plan, and cost of an adapter or other fees if required. Then make a list of attributes, such as free in-network calls, international calling, virtual telephone numbers, teleconferencing, support for caller ID, and so on. Explain how a person would use all of the quantitative and qualitative information to make an informed decision about which VoIP provider to select. Are any other variables important? Would you recommend any type of software to help compare these services?
3. Make a choice on a VoIP provider based on the analysis in Group Project 2.

SELECTED BIBLIOGRAPHY

Alter, S. *Information Systems: The Foundation of E-Business,* 4th ed. Upper Saddle River, NJ: Prentice Hall, 2002.

Carey, P., and J. Carey. *Microsoft PowerPoint 97 at a Glance.* Redmond, WA: Microsoft Press, 1997.

Carnegie-Mellon Software Engineering Institute, "CBS Overview." Available at: www.sei.cmu.edu/cbs/overview.html. Last accessed May 25, 2003.

Levine, D. M., P. R. Ramsey, and M. L. Berenson. *Business Statistics for Quality and Productivity.* Upper Saddle River, NJ: Prentice Hall, 1995.

Stefik, M., G. Foster, D. G. Bobrow, K. Kahn, S. Lanning, and L. Suchman. "Beyond the Chalkboard: Computer Support for Collaboration and Problem Solving in Meetings." *Communications of the ACM,* Vol. 30, No. 1, January 1987, pp. 32–47.

Vigder, M. R., W. M. Gentleman, and J. C. Dean, "Using COTS Software in Systems Development." Available at: http://iit-iti.nrc-cnrc.gc.ca/projects-projets/cots-lc_e.html. Last accessed May 25, 2003.

10

ALLEN SCHMIDT, JULIE E. KENDALL, AND KENNETH E. KENDALL

CPU

PROPOSING TO GO FORTH

"Because we chose to design and implement the new computer system using PCs linked with a local area network, we should work on preparing the systems proposal," Anna begins. She and Chip are meeting to plan the next phase of the design.

"Yes," replies Chip. "We need to make some hardware and software decisions as well as ensure that the users are aware of the benefits the new system will provide."

"We should determine which software will be required to implement the system and the hardware requirements for each user of the system," notes Anna. "Why don't you work on the hardware portion, and I'll investigate software?"

"Sure," Chip replies. "I plan to meet with each of the users again. When I have all of the information, I'll produce a summary report."

Chip proceeds to work with each user to determine what equipment would be required. Some of his findings are as follows:

Mike Crowe has a 3.2 GHz Pentium D mini-tower. This computer is more than adequate for serving the needs of the new system. Additional, necessary equipment is a laptop computer for creating transactions when performing physical inventory and preventive maintenance work.

Dot Matricks has a 3.0 GHz Pentium 4 desktop computer with mainframe terminal emulation. This computer is adequate for the new system.

Hy Perteks has a 2.8 GHz Pentium 4 notebook with a wireless network card on his desk. This computer is adequate for the new system.

Paige Prynter has a 1.80 GHz Celeron desktop computer. Recommend replacing it with a 3.0 GHz Pentium computer. Add software to run terminal emulation on the new computer.

Cher Ware has an older 1.20 GHz Celeron computer. Recommend that it be upgraded a 3.0 GHz Pentium computer.

Other equipment and supplies: a server computer to manage the network should be a 3.0 GHz Pentium or better, one fitted with communication boards. A high-speed laser printer attached directly to the server and smaller inkjet or laser printers attached to each computer should be provided. In addition, cable must be purchased to connect each user to the network.

Meanwhile, Anna is determining the software that would be needed to implement the system. Because each of the users will be receiving software developed by programmers, the major task is to decide what software will be needed for system development and to network the computers. After researching software options, Anna makes the following recommendations:

1. Development software to create the system. Three options are available:
   a. Use C++ to write the application software. The advantage of C++ is that it is currently being used by a few members of the programming staff and is object oriented.
   b. Use a database package and write object-oriented code. Compile the database programs into executable code. Currently, Access is available in the student labs. Other database packages should be evaluated.

c. Build a Web solution. PHP, Visual Basic, .NET, Ruby on Rails, and Java are very powerful, and they work with many different databases.

2. Network software is required to establish and make the local area network user friendly with graphical user interface screens.

Chip and Anna sit at a work table and examine each other's findings.

"I suppose the next task is to obtain some cost figures for the hardware and software selection," Anna says. "What do you think is our best source of cost information?"

"There are several sources of information," Chip replies. "We could search the Web or examine trade journals for prices. There are many ecommerce companies that have online catalogs with excellent pricing, often with an online discount. We should also call or visit dealers and obtain quotes, especially with educational discounts. The manufacturers may have special programs available. We'll check with the university purchasing officer, too. Once we have all the cost information, we can produce a document as part of the systems proposal."

EXERCISES

E-1. Use computer periodicals in your library to investigate costs for each of the machines and peripheral devices to be purchased. Make a comparison list for each machine.

E-2. Visit a local computer retail store and obtain cost information for each computer listed in this episode. Include printers and high-quality (minimum of 17-inch) flat panel monitors. Make a comparison list for each machine.

E-3. Search the Web for Internet stores or computer retailers and obtain cost information for each computer listed in this episode. Include printers and high-quality monitors. Make a comparison list for each machine.

E-4. Scan trade journals and summarize your findings, comparing three different database packages, their features, and costs.

E-5. Investigate the features and prices for C++ packages. Make a summary list of your findings.

E-6. Investigate the features and prices for database packages. Make a summary list of your findings.

E-7. Investigate the features and prices for PHP, Visual Basic, .NET, Ruby on Rails, and Java. Make a summary list of your findings. What are the advantages of purchasing off-the-shelf software versus obtaining freeware or open source software?

E-8. Use the Web to find out information about the features of three of the software packages mentioned above. Make a summary list of your findings.

E-9. Using the information gathered in the exercises above, calculate the total cost for three unique solutions.

11

DESIGNING EFFECTIVE OUTPUT

LEARNING OBJECTIVES

Once you have mastered the material in this chapter you will be able to:

1. **Understand the objectives for effective output design.**
2. **Relate output content to output methods inside and outside the organizational context.**
3. **Realize how output bias affects users.**
4. **Design display output.**
5. **Design tabular and graphic output for users interacting with decision support systems.**
6. **Design a Web site for ecommerce.**

Output is information delivered to users through the information system by way of intranets, extranets, or the World Wide Web. Some data require extensive processing before they become suitable output; other data are stored, and when they are retrieved, they are considered output with little or no processing. Output can take many forms: the traditional hard copy of printed reports, and soft copy such as computer screens, microforms, and audio output. Users rely on output to accomplish their tasks, and they often judge the merit of the system solely by its output. To create the most useful output possible, the systems analyst works closely with the user through an interactive process until the result is considered to be satisfactory.

OUTPUT DESIGN OBJECTIVES

Because useful output is essential to ensuring the use and acceptance of the information system, there are several objectives that the systems analyst tries to attain when designing output. There are six objectives for output:

1. Designing output to serve a specific user or organizational purpose.
2. Making output meaningful to the user.
3. Delivering the appropriate quantity of output.
4. Providing appropriate output distribution.
5. Providing output on time.
6. Choosing the most effective output method.

DESIGNING OUTPUT TO SERVE THE INTENDED PURPOSE

All output should have a purpose. It is not enough to make a report, screen, or Web page available to users because it is technologically possible to do so. During the information requirements determination phase of analysis, the systems analyst finds out what user and organizational purposes must be served. Output is then designed based on those purposes.

You will see that you have numerous opportunities to supply output simply because the application permits you to do so. Remember the rule of purposiveness, however. If the output is not functional, it should not be created, because there are costs of time and materials associated with all output from the system.

DESIGNING OUTPUT TO FIT THE USER

With a large information system serving many users for many different purposes, it is often difficult to personalize output. On the basis of interviews, observations, cost considerations, and perhaps prototypes, it will be possible to design output that addresses what many, if not all, users need and prefer.

Generally speaking, it is more practical to create user-specific or user-customizable output when designing for a decision support system or other highly interactive applications such as those mounted on the Web. It is still possible, however, to design output to fit a user's tasks and function in the organization, which leads us to the next objective.

DELIVERING THE APPROPRIATE QUANTITY OF OUTPUT

More is not always better, especially where the amount of output is concerned. Part of the task of designing output is deciding what quantity of output is correct for users.

A useful heuristic is that the system must provide what each person needs to complete his or her work. This answer, however, is still far from a total solution, because it may be appropriate to display a subset of that information at first and then provide a way for the user to access additional information easily.

The problem of information overload is so prevalent as to have become a cliché, but it remains a valid concern. No one is served if excess information is given only to flaunt the capabilities of the system. Always keep the decision makers in mind. Often they will not need great amounts of output, especially if there is an easy way to access more via a hyperlink or drill-down capability.

MAKING SURE THE OUTPUT IS WHERE IT IS NEEDED

Output is often produced at one location (for example, in the data processing department) and then distributed to the user. The increase in online, screen-displayed output that is personally accessible has cut down somewhat on the problem of distribution, but appropriate distribution is still an important objective for the systems analyst. To be used and useful, output must be presented to the right user. No matter how well designed reports are, if they are not seen by the pertinent decision makers, they have no value.

PROVIDING THE OUTPUT ON TIME

One of the most common complaints of users is that they do not receive information in time to make necessary decisions. Although timing isn't everything, it does play a large part in how useful output will be to decision makers. Many reports are required on a daily basis, some only monthly, others annually, and others only by exception. Using well-publicized, Web-based output can alleviate some problems with the timing of output distribution as well. Accurate timing of output can be critical to business operations.

CHOOSING THE RIGHT OUTPUT METHOD

As mentioned earlier, output can take many forms, including printed paper reports, information on screens, audio with digitized sounds that simulate the human voice, microforms, and Web documents. Choosing the right output method for each user is another objective in designing output.

Much output now appears on display screens, and users have the option of printing it out with their own printer. The analyst needs to recognize the trade-offs involved in choosing an output method. Costs differ; for the user, there are also differences in the accessibility, flexibility, durability, distribution, storage and retrieval possibilities, transportability, and overall impact of the data. The choice of output methods is not trivial, nor is it usually a foregone conclusion.

RELATING OUTPUT CONTENT TO OUTPUT METHOD

The content of output from information systems must be considered as interrelated to the output method. Whenever you design output, you need to think of how function influences form and how the intended purpose will influence the output method that you choose.

Output should be thought of in a general way so that any information put out by the computer system that is useful to people in some way can be considered output. It is possible to conceptualize output as either external (going outside the business), such as information that appears to the public on the Web, or internal (staying within the business), such as material available on an intranet.

External output is familiar to you through utility bills, advertisements, paychecks, annual reports, and myriad other communications that organizations have with their customers, vendors, suppliers, industry, and competitors. Some of this output, such as utility bills, is designed by the systems analyst to serve double duty as a turnaround document. Figure 11.1 is a gas bill that is a turnaround document for a gas company's data processing. The output for one stage of processing becomes the input for the next. When the customer returns the designated portion of the document, it is optically scanned and used as computer input.

External output differs from internal output in its distribution, design, and appearance. Many external documents must include instructions to the recipient if they are to be used correctly. Many external outputs are placed on preprinted forms or Web sites bearing the company logo and corporate colors.

Internal outputs include various reports to decision makers. They range from short summary reports to lengthy, detailed reports. An example of a summary report is a report summarizing monthly sales totals. A detailed report might give weekly sales by salesperson.

Other kinds of internal reports include historical reports and exception reports that are output only at the time an exception occurs. Examples of exception reports are a listing of all employees with no absences for the year, a listing of all salespeople who did *not* meet their monthly sales quota, or a report on consumer complaints made in the last six months.

OUTPUT TECHNOLOGIES

Producing different types of output requires different technologies. For printed output, the options include a variety of printers. For screen output, the options

FIGURE 11.1

A turnaround document for Minigasco's data processing.

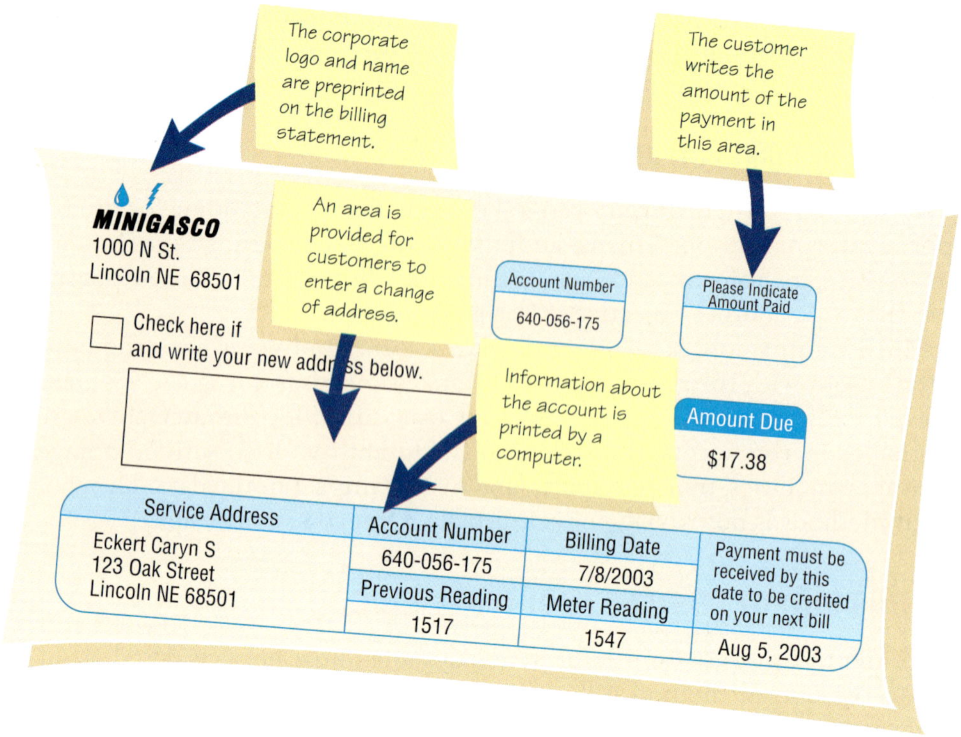

include attached or stand-alone displays. Audio output can be amplified over a loudspeaker or listened to on a variety of speakers, ranging from small to surround sound–capable on a PC. Audio output may also be designed for mobile phones. Electronic output is created with special software tools. As you can see, the choices are numerous. Figure 11.2 is a comparison of output methods.

Printers Because printed reports are such a common kind of output, it is logical to assume that in any large organization printers are ubiquitous. Although other types of output are gaining popularity, it is likely that businesses will still desire printed output, or will want to design output that will look good if customers, suppliers, or vendors print it out using their own software and hardware.

The trend in printers is toward increased flexibility. This trend translates into expanding the options for the location of the printing site itself, accommodating different numbers of characters per page, including numerous type styles and type fonts, changing the position of print on the page, including more graphics capability and color, producing quieter printing, reducing the number of preprinted forms in inventory, simplifying operator tasks, and reducing the amount of overall operator intervention.

Together with users, the systems analyst must determine the purpose for the printer. Once that is established, three key factors of printers to keep in mind are:

1. Reliability.
2. Compatibility with software and hardware.
3. Manufacturer support.

Displays as Output Display screens are an increasingly popular output technology. Once used mostly for data entry, screens are also becoming a feasible technology for many other uses as their size and price decrease and as their compatibility with other system components increases.

Screens have distinct advantages over printers because of their quietness and potential for interactive user participation. In the latter regard, screen output can

Output Method	Advantages	Disadvantages
Printer	• Affordable for most organizations • Flexible in types of output, location, and capabilities • Handles large volumes of output • Highly reliable with little down time	• Still requires some operator intervention • Compatibility problems with computer software • May require special, expensive supplies • Depending on model, may be slow • Environmentally unfriendly
Display screen	• Interactive • Online, real-time transmission • Quiet • Takes advantage of computer capabilities for movement within databases and files • Good for frequently accessed, ephemeral messages	• May require cabling and setup space • Still may require printed documentation
Audio output and podcasts	• Good for individual user • Good for transient messages • Good where worker needs hands free • Good if output needs to be widely distributed	• Is expensive to develop • Needs earbuds where output will not interfere with other tasks • Has limited application
DVD, CD-ROM, and CD-RW	• Has large capacity • Allows multimedia output	• Requires a computer for reading data
Electronic output (email, Web sites, blogs, and RSS feeds)	• Reduces paper • Can be updated very easily • Can be "broadcast" • Can be made interactive	• Is not conducive to formatting (email) • Is difficult to convey context of messages (email) • Web sites need diligent maintenance

FIGURE 11.2
A comparison of output methods.

afford flexibility in allowing the user to change output information in real time either through deletion, addition, or modification. Screens also permit the review of stored output through access to and the display of items from a relevant database, permitting individual decision makers to move away from storing redundant printouts.

Display screens as output result in cost savings. If users can complete their tasks by interacting with a screen, they may not need paper, thereby eliminating the cost of printing, filing, and physical storage. Furthermore, if a report was previously sent out by post, convincing users to view the documents on screen can save mailing, as well as printing costs. Stockbrokers, phone companies, utilities, and banks are all offering electronic delivery to their customers.

Electronic display may also be desirable from the user's standpoint. A user may want just to glance briefly at a monthly statement to verify its accuracy. The user needs, however, to file the statement away for tax reasons. If the statement is delivered via email, the electronic copy may be all that the user wants. This will help recordkeeping and consequently encourage the user to prefer the electronic statement over the paper statement.

Another reason for preferring display output over paper output is that it is easier to keep the electronic version up-to-date. Printing and mailing may take a couple of days to a week, but displays can update output immediately.

One potential drawback is showing output on a variety of display screens using different screen resolutions. If the screen displayed is from a Web page, the Web page programmer needs a plan for checking images at each resolution (for example, 800 × 600, 1600 × 1200, and so on), using different browsers, to make sure that the pages look similar. If users need access to handheld computers or mobile phones to complete their work, special Web pages may need to be developed as well.

If the output is a report other than a Web page, the analyst is faced with solving other problems. Users may not have the necessary fonts on their computers, and their Microsoft Word documents may be customized with unusual margins. If a Word document is sent by email, a beautifully formatted document on a sender's computer may end up looking poorly formatted on a receiver's computer. An increasingly popular way to deliver these documents is to convert them to pdf files using Adobe Acrobat. This allows unusual fonts to be embedded and all of the margins to be set properly no matter what computer or screen resolution the receiving party has.

Video, Audio, and Animation Many of the tools and application packages you will be working with facilitate the inclusion of video in the output options. Video is a complex form of output, as it combines the strength and potential emotional impact of audio (including sound effects, voice, and music) with a visual channel. Some familiar applications are those that are Web-based. Examine Figure 11.3 to see a Web page that provides a series of six brief video clips of an actual event, the Decision Sciences Institute (DSI) Knowledge Bowl. Video output is useful here, because the event was held to commemorate an important anniversary in the organization's history.

There are many uses for including video output in your users' displays. Video clips make useful output for:

1. Supplementing static, printed output.
2. Distance collaboration that connects people who do not often get to see each other. For example, this can be helpful for virtual project team members who must work together, but who do not typically meet face to face.
3. Showing how to perform an action, such as demonstrating how a form should be filled out, how software should be installed, or how a product should be assembled.
4. Providing brief training episodes that are job specific or task specific in order to emphasize a new or unfamiliar skill.

FIGURE 11.3

Streaming video can be used effectively for telling a story or sharing an event. This Web page chronicles an event called the DSI Knowledge Bowl (www.thekendalls.org/dsi-bowl).

5. Shifting the time of an actual event by recording it for later output.
6. Preserving an important occasion for addition to an organization's archives.

In a way, audio output can be thought of as the opposite of printed output. Audio output is transient, whereas the printed word is permanent. Audio output is usually output for the benefit of one user, whereas printed output is often widely distributed. Audio output can be interpreted by the human ear as speech, although it is actually produced by discrete digital sounds that are then put together in such a way as to be perceived as continuous words. Telephone companies were among the first businesses to produce systems using audio output for customers.

Sound can also enhance a presentation. Public domain music and sound effects are readily available. Presentation packages such as Microsoft PowerPoint allow users to insert sound, music, and even videos. Sound files come in various formats, but some of the most common for PCs are MP3, .WMP (Windows Media Player), .aac (iTunes), and .WAV files.

Audio output is being used to "staff" toll-free catalog numbers 24 hours a day, seven days a week. By using a digital phone, consumers can call the number and, in response to instructions via audio output, enter the item number, quantity, price, and their credit card number. Stores are capturing sales that would otherwise be missed, because hiring actual employees might be too expensive to justify offering a 24-hour number.

When using audio and telephone systems to enter data, be sure to provide proper user feedback, such as, "You have entered thirty three dollars. Press one if this is correct. Press two to change." Audio input must be scripted into a well designed and clear sequence. Keep audio instructions brief so that people remember the beginning segments.

Podcasting is the technique of putting downloadable voice files on the Web. These voice files may be used to inform customers about new products or the product of the week, to provide a walking tour of a city or other tourist destination, to deliver a newscast, and many other applications. Capability to download audio and video files has been available for some time on the Web, but podcasting uses a small RSS file (an XML file) to store the latest version of a podcast (if they are updated frequently). The steps to making a podcast are:

1. Make a script of the podcast.
2. Record and produce your show. If the podcast is audio only, free tools include Audacity (audacity.sourceforge.net) and PodProducer (www.podproducer.net). If the podcast is lengthy, split it into multiple tracks at a good breaking point. Try to keep roughly the same length for each track if possible.
3. Publish the show to a Web server.
4. Optionally, create an RSS file and publish it to the Web server.

Animation is another form of output that can be used to enhance a Web site or presentation. Animation is the presentation of different images in a series, one at a time. Animation images are composed of several basic elements. Elemental symbols can be abstract objects or real photos, and they can take on different colors, forms, and textures. Spatial orientation helps the user grasp whether symbols are closely related to one another. Transition effects are either gradual or abrupt, just as with PowerPoint slide transitions. Alteration effects include changing the color, size, or texture, and can also include transforming the image through morphing.

If animation is used to support decision making, experiments have shown that the use of realistic, rather than abstract, images results in better quality of decisions. Experimental subjects who viewed gradual, rather than abrupt, animated transitions made better decisions. When using animation on Web pages, use caution to keep sequences streamlined, and not busy.

CONSULTING OPPORTUNITY 11.1

YOUR CAGE OR MINE?

"Why can't they get this right? It's driving me to distraction. The zoo in Colombia is writing to me about a tiger that has been on loan from our place since 2002. They should be writing to Tulsa," trumpets Ella Fant, waving a letter in the air. Ella is general curator in charge of the animal breeding program at the Gotham Zoo.

She is talking with members of the zoo's five-person committee about the proposals before them. The committee meets every month to decide which animals to loan to other zoos and which animals to get on loan so as to breed them. The committee is composed of Ella Fant, the general curator; Ty Garr, the zoo's director; two zoo employees, Annie Malle and Mona Key; and a layperson, Rex Lyon, who is in business in the community.

Ty paces in front of the group and continues the meeting, saying, "We have the possibility of loaning out two of our golden tamarins, and we have the opportunity to play matchmaker for two lesser pandas. Because three of you are new to the committee, I'll briefly discuss your responsibilities. As you know, Ella and I would pounce on any chance to lure animals in for the breeding program. Your duties are to assess the zoo's financial resources and to look at our zoo's immediate demands. You also must consider the season and our shipping capability, as well as that of the zoos we're considering. The other zoos charge us nothing for the loan of their animals for the breeding program. We pay the shipping for any animal being loaned to us and then maintain them, and that gets expensive."

"We are linked, via the Internet, to a database of selected species with 164 other zoos," says Ella as she picks up the story from Ty. "My office has a computer equipped with a display. I can access the records of all captive animals in the system, including those from the two zoos we are negotiating with right now."

As the committee members work, they begin asking questions. "I need to read some information, get some meat to sink my teeth into, before I'm ready to decide whether the loan of the lesser pandas is a good idea. Where are the data on the animals we're considering?" growls Rex.

Annie replies, "We have to go to Ella's office to get to it. Mostly, the other employees who need to know just use her computer.

Mona gets into the swing of the discussion and says, "Some information on the current state of the budget would be divine, too. I'll go bananas with new expenditures until we at least have a summary of what we're spending. I bet it's a bunch."

Ty answers, "We don't mean to monkey around, but frankly we feel trapped. Costs of reproducing all the financial data seem high to us. We'd rather put our money into reproducing rare and endangered species! Paperwork multiplies on its own."

The group laughs nervously together, but there is an air of expectancy in the room. The consensus is that the committee members need more internal information about the zoo's financial status and the prospective loan animals.

Ella, aware that the group cannot be tamed in the way the previous one was, says, "The old committee preferred to get their information informally, through chattering with us. Let's spend this first meeting discovering what kinds of documents you think you need to do your work as a committee. Financial data are on a stand-alone PC that our financial director uses. It's his baby, of course."

What are some of the problems related to output that the committee is experiencing? What suggestions do you have for improving output to the committee? How can the budget constraints of the zoo be met while still allowing the committee to receive the output it needs to function? Comment on the adequacy of the output technology that is currently in use at the zoo. Suggest alternatives or modifications to output and output technology that would enhance what is being done. (*Hint:* Consider ways in which the committee can leverage its use of the Internet—say, more use of the Web—to get the output that it needs and that it needs to share.) Analyze both internal and external output requirements.

CD-ROMs and DVDs With the demand for multimedia output growing, the display of material on CD-ROMs has become widespread. CD-ROMs are less vulnerable to damage from human handling than other output. CD-ROMs can include full-color text and graphics, as well as music and full-motion video, so as an output medium they provide a designer maximum creativity. The DVD (digital versatile disc) is also a useful output technology. Not only are DVDs used for output, but they also are used for backup storage.

Electronic Output Many of the new Web-based systems you design will have the capability of sending electronic output in the form of email, faxes, and bulletin board messages that can be sent from one computer to another without the need for hard copy.

Email can be set up and run internally in the organization through an intranet, or that can be set up through communication companies or online service providers. By designing email systems, you can support communication throughout the organization. A useful and flexible email system can form the basis of support for workgroups.

Two newer groups of technologies that allow users to pull information from the Web and also allow organizations to send information to them periodically are being designed for organizations. These output technologies are called pull and push technologies, reflecting the way users and organizations look for information on the Web and either "pull" it in downloads or have it sent, or "pushed," to them.

RSS (really simple syndication) feeds are XML documents that users can obtain from links on Web pages or to which they can subscribe. They contain a title, usually the same name as the Web site of the RSS feed; a link, often the same link as the Web page; a short description; copyright; the language the text is written in, using a standard code such as en-us (for English—United States); pubDate (the published date); lastBuildDate (the date that the RSS feed was last modified); images; text; and other information. RSS feeds are usually marked on a Web page by white XML or RSS text on an orange button. Recently an orange square with three white lines depicting radio waves was introduced in Firefox as a secondary button symbol and it is gaining in popularity.

RSS is supposed to be really simple. It is made up of a feed (also known as a channel), which has a title, link, and description, followed by a number of news items, each with its own title, link, and description. An example of RSS feed code can be found in Figure 11.4. Although it is supposed to be simple, you should realize that there are over a half a dozen different versions of RSS and a similar syndication format called Atom. Developers can provide RSS feeds on their company's Web site or develop them for clients.

```
<?xml version="1.0"?>
<rss version="2.0">
  <channel>
    <title>CPU News</title>
    <link>http://CPU_news.cpuweb.edu/</link>
    <description>Central Pacific University's Newsletter</description>
    <language>en-us</language>
    <pubDate>Tue, 10 Jun 2006 04:00:00 GMT</pubDate>
    <lastBuildDate>Tue, 10 Jun 2006 09:41:01 GMT</lastBuildDate>
    <webMaster>webmaster@cpuweb.edu</webMaster>
    <item>
      <title>Mike Crowe speech</title>
      <link>http://CPU_news.cpuweb.edu/news/2006/news-Crowe.asp</link>
      <description>Mike Crowe delivers presentation at Decision Sciences Institute
            Annual Meeting to standing ovation.</description>
      <pubDate>Tue, 04 Jun 2006 09:41:22 GMT</pubDate>
      <guid>http://CPU_news.cpuweb.edu/2006/06/04.html#item523</guid>
    </item>
    <item>
      <title>Soccer team wins</title>
      <link>http://CPU_news.cpuweb.edu/news/2006/news-soccer.asp</link>
      <description>Big Blue wins again. CPU's soccer team still
            undefeated.</description>
      <pubDate>Fri, 29 May 2006 10:07:42 GMT</pubDate>
      <guid>http://CPU_news.cpuweb.edu/2006/05/29.html#item522</guid>
    </item>
  </channel>
</rss>
```

FIGURE 11.4

An example of RSS feed code for a newsletter delivered via RSS on a university Web site.

The RSS feed is read using RSS reader software, often a free program. These readers, sometimes called news aggregators, are programs that track updates, download, categorize, and display RSS feeds. RSS is a way of gathering and distributing news and other content from multiple sources. RSS news readers can either stand alone or be integrated with your browser as plug-ins. At the time this book is being written, popular news readers are Bloglines, BottomFeeder, FeedDEMON, MY MSN, My Yahoo!, NewsIsFree, NEWSMONSTER, Pluck, RSSBANDIT, SHARPREADER, and Wizz RSS (for Firefox browsers). Soon the market for RSS readers will shake out and only a few RSS readers will survive. Feedster and Blogdigger are search engines for RSS feeds.

RSS has the advantage of efficiently organizing news and other information from a variety of sources chosen by the user. It is also timely, with the latest news displayed first. RSS is not limited to news but can be used to keep track of the latest revision of a book or manuscript, check new movie or theatre reviews, gain early knowledge of new software for your mobile phone, and keep abreast of what other people from your graduating class are doing now.

Pull Technology An important output technology made possible by the Web is pull technology. If you have tried to pull information from the Web by clicking on links, you have used the most basic type of pull technology. Figure 11.5 shows a Web page for an international IS research organization. When each issue is complete, *OASIS*, the organization's newsletter, is mounted on the organization's Web site, and members of the association can pull it off the Web by viewing it as an Adobe Acrobat document.

This type of pull technology has several advantages compared with sending output as a simple paper newsletter. For example, whenever the newsletter is complete, it can be mounted on the Web; there is no delay in delivery. In addition, if the user has a color printer, color copies can be obtained, whereas reproducing the newsletter in color on paper and posting it worldwide for all members is prohibitively expensive for a nonprofit organization.

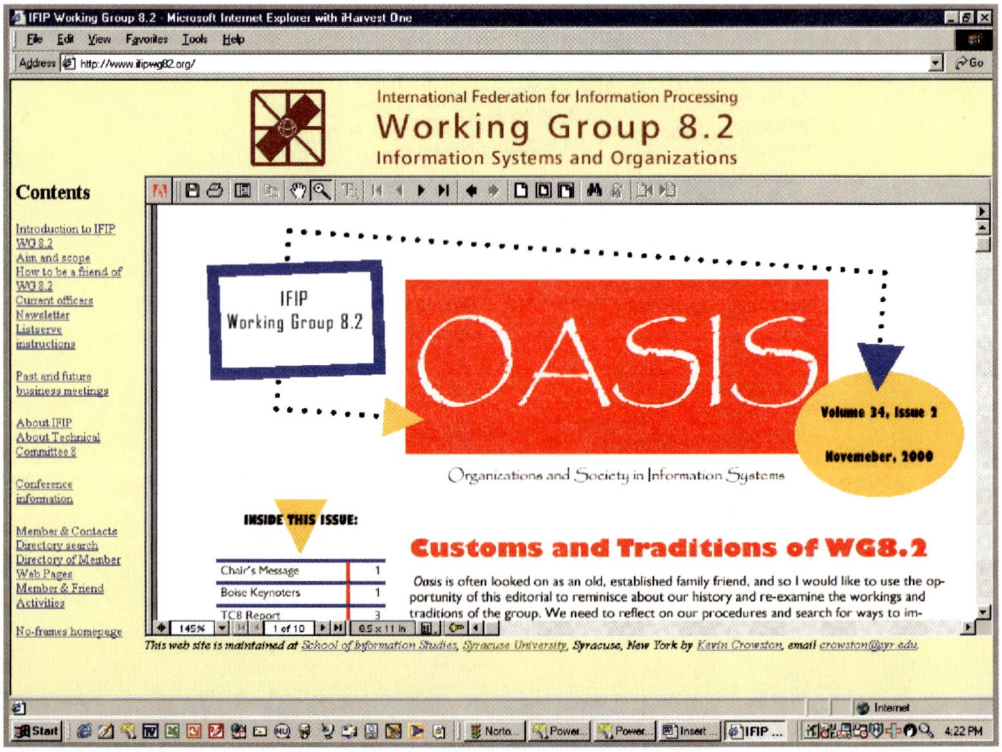

FIGURE 11.5

Pull technology refers to a user pulling information from a Web site. In this example, the newsletter OASIS can be accessed from the IFIP WG 8.2 Web site (www.ifipwg82.org).

In the future, evolutionary agents (programmed using intelligent agent software) may be used to help organizational members find what they need on the Web. These agents will relieve some of the users' typical burden of searching the Web, because the agents will observe and understand users' behavior as they interact with a variety of material on the Web, and then can be programmed to seek out the information users want. In this way, Web searches will be more efficient and more effective for users.

Push Technology Another type of output analysts design is Web and wireless content delivered via push technology. Push technology can be used for external communication to push (electronically send) solicited or unsolicited information to a customer or client. It can also be used within the organization to focus the immediate attention of an employee or a decision maker who is facing a critical deadline, to critical items. The term *push technology* can be described as any content sent to users at specified times, from basic Webcasting to selective content delivery using sophisticated evolutionary filtering agents.

Many traditional as well as Internet-based businesses are experimenting with push technology. One example is pushing an electronic newsletter to subscribers via email. The page design, including a variety of fonts, strategic use of color, and engaging writing, intentionally emulates the look of a Web page even though it is delivered via email.

Push technology can also get the information to the person who needs it. Broadcasting information to all employees is less expensive than printing out information and then distributing it to a select few. Although in this instance managers do not need to be concerned whether or not a particular employee should get a report, the analyst needs to guard against flooding employees with meaningless pushed information.

When working with push technologies, you will be struck by their flexibility compared with paper output. When data are delivered over an intranet to a PC, the user is able to take it and customize it in many ways. For instance, an employee may decide to look at a single product or may want to generate a graph of sales over time.

Many organizations are experimenting with push technology. National Semiconductor added its own channel to a Webcaster that includes three types of product-related information. Wheat First Securities used a different Webcaster to deliver information to its brokers. MCI's network operations group uses another commercial Webcaster to send information about outage alerts to the 7,000 employees who run its long-distance network.

FACTORS TO CONSIDER WHEN CHOOSING OUTPUT TECHNOLOGY

As you can determine from this brief discussion of output technology, there are several factors to consider when choosing it. Although the technology changes rapidly, certain usage factors remain fairly constant in relation to technological breakthroughs. These factors, some of which present trade-offs, must be considered. They include the following:

1. Who will use (see) the output (requisite quality)?
2. How many people need the output?
3. Where is the output needed (distribution, logistics)?
4. What is the purpose of the output? What user and organizational tasks are supported?
5. What is the speed with which output is needed?
6. How frequently will the output be accessed?
7. How long will (or must) the output be stored?

8. Under what special regulations is the output produced, stored, and distributed?
9. What are the initial and ongoing costs of maintenance and supplies?
10. What are the human and environmental requirements (accessibility, noise absorption, controlled temperature, space for equipment, cabling, and proximity to Wi-Fi transmitters or access points ("hot spots")) for output technologies?

Examining each factor separately will allow you to see the interrelationships and how they may be traded off for one another in a particular system.

Who Will Use (See) the Output? Discovering who will use the output is important because job requirements help dictate what output method is appropriate. For example, when district managers must be away from their desks for extended periods, they need printed output that can travel with them or technology that can access appropriate Web sites and databases as they visit the managers in their region. Screen output or interactive Web documents are excellent for people such as truck dispatchers who are deskbound for long periods.

External recipients of output (clients and customers, vendors and suppliers, shareholders, and regulatory agencies) and users within the business will require different output. Clients, vendors, and suppliers can be part of several extranets, which are networks of computers built by the organization, providing applications, processing, and information to users on the network.

Examine the Web site shown in Figure 11.6 for an ecommerce company called Merchants Bay. The Web designer is clearly attuned to the intended users of the wholesale gift site. The ecommerce company's Web site is powered by a patented negotiating algorithm in which users submit bids (for one item or 400) on an array of merchandise, dubbed "good stuff" by the company president. The company's strategy is based on the president's personal experience with flea markets and the observation that people are powerfully attracted to bargaining for a deal.

The Web site has intentionally invoked a cluttered feel, similar to what one gets walking through a flea market. The site is intended for customers who would frequent flea markets in person: they are known to be collectors, gregarious and

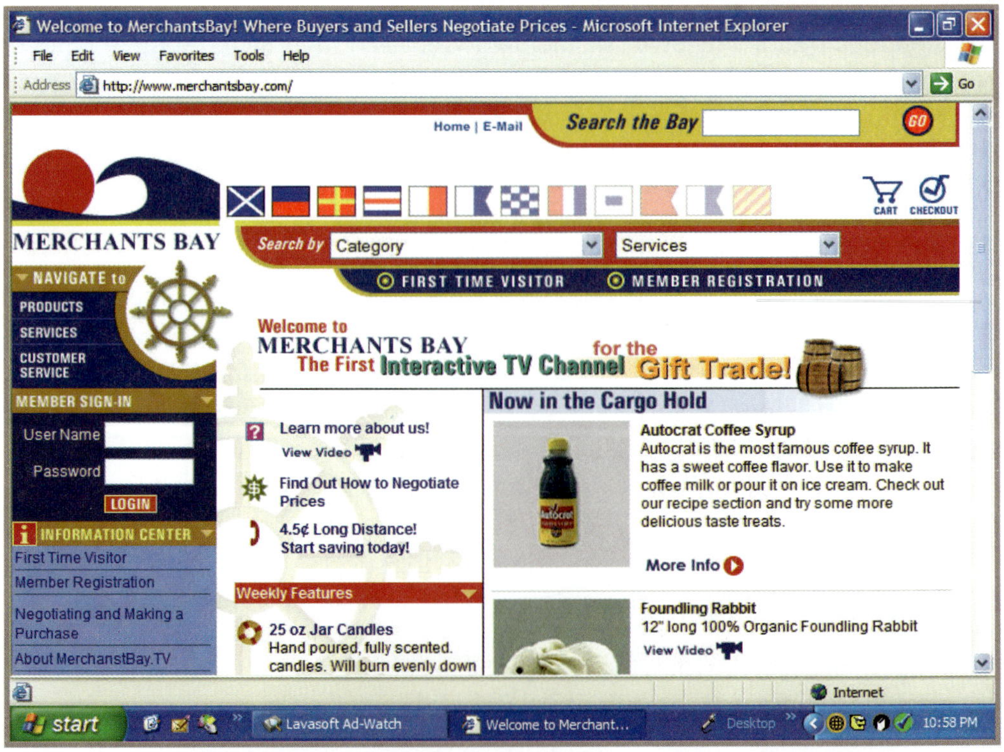

FIGURE 11.6

When designing a Web site it is important to choose a metaphor that can be used throughout the site. This example from Merchants Bay (www.merchantsbay.com) employs a nautical theme.

"Spam overload."

Source: © 2003 Mick Stevens from cartoonbank.com. All Rights Reserved.

curious by nature. The Web site is a profusion of colors, includes a variety of sale signs in a mixture of lettering, and even incorporates a video that provides new layers of color and action. Colloquial language is used throughout the site.

Notice that the company's catchphrase is "purveyor of good stuff." The Web designer has successfully carried out a nautical metaphor throughout the site. For instance, the user is invited to "search the Bay" for merchandise. In addition, the company's logo includes a wave and a sun on the horizon, and an icon of a ship's steering wheel is placed above a column that invites the user to "navigate" for products, services, and customer service.

To complete a transaction on the site, a customer has an opportunity to accept the "Captain's price" as posted or to submit a bid. If the bid submitted is too low according to the stored negotiation algorithm, a natural language response is returned in a pop-up window stating: "Thanks for your offer, mate. You don't like to part with your money if you don't have to, heh? Yet hey, I like ya, mate. Please try again by offering a better price or by ordering a larger quantity." In this way, the bid is rejected in a friendly, humorous way, and bidders are even given two hints on how to improve the chances that their next bids will be successful. It is clear that the Web designer had a solid profile of the intended customer in mind when designing the site.

How Many People Need the Output? Choice of output technology is also influenced by how many users need the output. If many people need output, Web-based documents with a print option or printed copies are probably justified. Some external customers may want a printed copy of specific documents, such as a stockholder report or a monthly billing statement, but others may prefer Web-based documents with an email notification. If only one user needs the output, a screen or audio may be more suitable.

If many users in the business need different output at different times for short periods and they need it quickly, Web documents or screens connected to online terminals that are able to access database contents are a viable option.

Where Is the Output Needed (Distribution, Logistics)? Another factor influencing the choice of output technology is the physical destination of the output. Information that will remain close to its point of origin, that will be used by only a few users in the business, and that may be stored or referred to frequently, can safely be printed or mounted on an intranet. An abundance of information that must be transmitted to users at great distances in branch operations may be better distributed electronically, via the Web or extranets, with the recipient deciding whether to customize and print output, display it, or store it.

Sometimes federal or state regulations dictate that a printed form remain on file at a particular location for a specified period of time. In those instances, it is the responsibility of the systems analyst to see that the regulation is observed for any new or modified output that is designed.

What Is the Purpose of the Output? What user and organizational tasks are supported? The purpose of the output is another factor to consider when choosing output technology. If the output is intended to be a report created to attract shareholders to the business by allowing them to peruse corporate finances at their leisure, well-designed, printed output such as an annual report is desirable. A variety of media may also be used so that the annual report is available on the Web as well as in printed form. If the purpose of the output is to provide 15-minute updates on stock market quotations, and if the material is highly encoded and changeable, screen crawls, Web pages, or audio presentations are preferable. Output must support user tasks, such as performing analysis, or determining ratios, so software tools, including calculators and embedded formulae, could be part of output. It must also support organizational tasks such as tracking, scheduling, and monitoring, where interactive, real-time screens provide useful insights.

What Is the Speed with Which Output Is Needed? As we go through the three levels of strategic, middle, and operations management in the organization, we find that decision makers at the lowest level of operations management need output rapidly so that they can quickly adjust to events, such as a stopped assembly line, raw materials that have not arrived on time, or a worker who is absent unexpectedly. Online screen output may be useful here.

As we ascend the management levels, we observe that strategic managers are more in need of output for a specific time period, which helps in forecasting business cycles and trends.

How Frequently Will the Output Be Accessed? The more frequently output is accessed, the more important is the capability to view it on a display connected to local area networks or the Web. Infrequently accessed output that is needed by only a few users is well suited to a CD ROM archive.

Output that is accessed frequently is a good candidate for incorporation into Web-based or other online systems or networks with displays. Adopting this type of technology allows users easy access and alleviates physical wear and tear that cause frequently handled printed output to deteriorate.

How Long Will (or Must) the Output Be Stored? Output printed on paper deteriorates rapidly with age. Output preserved on microforms or digitized in archives is not as prone to succumb to environmental disturbances such as light, humidity, and human handling. However, if hardware to access the archived material becomes hard to acquire or obsolete, this output method can become problematic.

CONSULTING OPPORTUNITY 11.2

A RIGHT WAY, A WRONG WAY, AND A SUBWAY

"So far so good. Sure, there have been some complaints, but any new subway will have those. The 'free ride' gimmick has helped attract some people who never would have ridden otherwise. I think there are more people than ever before interested in riding the subway," says Bart Rayl. "What we need is an accurate fix on what ridership has been so far so we can make some adjustments on our fare decisions and scheduling of trains."

Rayl is an operations manager for S.W.I.F.T., the newly built subway for Western Ipswich and Fremont Transport that serves a major northeastern city in the United States. He is speaking with Benton Turnstile, who reports to him as operations supervisor of S.W.I.F.T. The subway system is in its first month of operation, offering limited lines. Marketing people have been giving away free rides on the subway to increase public awareness of S.W.I.F.T.

"I think that's a good idea," says Turnstile. "It's not just a token effort. We'll show them we're really on the right track. I'll get back to you with ridership information soon," he says.

A month later, Rayl and Turnstile meet to compare the projected ridership with the new data. Turnstile proudly presents a two-inch-high stack of computer printouts to Rayl. Rayl looks a little surprised but proceeds to go through it with Turnstile. "What all is in here?" Rayl asks, fingering the top page of the stack hesitantly.

"Well," says Turnstile, training his eyes on the printout, "it's a list of all the tickets that were sold from the computerized machines. It tells us how many tickets were bought and what kinds of tickets were bought. The guys from Systems That Think, Inc., told me this report would be the most helpful for us, just like it was for the operations people in Buffalo and Pittsburgh," says Turnstile, turning quickly to the next page.

"Maybe, but remember those subway systems began with really limited service. We're bigger. And what about the sales from the three manned ticket booths in the Main Street Terminal?" asks Rayl.

"The clerks in the booth can get information summarizing ticket sales onscreen any time they want it, but it's not included here. Remember that we projected that only 10 percent of our sales would be from the booths anyway. Let's go with our original idea and add that to the printout," suggests Turnstile.

Rayl replies, "But I've been observing riders. Half of them seem to be afraid of the computerized ticket machines. Others start using them, get frustrated reading the directions, or don't know what to do with the ticket that comes out, and they wind up at the ticket booth blowing off steam. Furthermore, they can't understand the routine information posted on the kiosks, which is all in graphics. They wind up asking clerks what train goes where." Rayl pushes the printout holding the ticket sales to one side of the conference table and says, "I don't have much confidence in this report. I feel as if we're sitting here trying to operate the most sophisticated subway system in the United States by peering down a tunnel instead of at the information as we should be. I think we need to think seriously about capturing journey information on magnetically stripped cards like the New York Transit Authority is doing. Every time you insert the card to take a ride, the information is stored."

What are some of the specific problems with the output that the systems consultants and Benton Turnstile gave to Bart Rayl? Evaluate the media that are being used for output as well as the timing of its distribution. Comment on the external output that users of the computerized ticket machines are apparently receiving. Suggest some changes in output to help Rayl get the information he needs to make decisions on fares and scheduling of trains, and to help users of the subway system get the information they need. What are some decisions facing organizations like the New York Transit Authority if they collect and store input concerning an individual's destinations each time a trip is taken? What changes would S.W.I.F.T. have to make to its output and its tickets if it adopted this technology?

A business may be subject to governmental regulations on local, state, or federal levels, that dictate how long output must be kept. As long as the corporation is willing to maintain it and it is nonproprietary, archival information, it can be maintained in Web documents as part of the organization's Web site. Organizations themselves also enact policies about how long output must be retained.

Under What Special Regulations Is the Output Produced, Stored, and Distributed? The appropriate format for some output is actually regulated by the government. For example, in the United States, the statement of an employee's wages and tax withholding, called a W-2 form, must be printed; its final form cannot be a screen or microform output. Each business in each country exists within a different complex of regulations under which it produces output. To that extent, appropriate technology for some functions may be dictated by law.

Much of this regulation, however, is industry-dependent. For example, in the United States a regional blood system is required by federal law to keep a medical history of a blood donor—as well as his or her name—on file. The exact output form is not specified, but the content is strictly spelled out.

What Are the Initial and Ongoing Costs of Maintenance and Supplies? The initial costs of purchasing or leasing equipment must be considered as yet another factor that enters into the choice of output technology. Most vendors will help you estimate the initial purchase or lease costs of computer hardware, including the cost of printers and displays, the cost of access to online service providers (Internet access), or the costs of building intranets and extranets. Many vendors, however, do not provide information about how much it costs to keep a printer or other technologies working. Therefore, it falls to the analyst to research the costs of operating different output technologies or of maintaining a corporate Web site over time.

What Are the Human Environmental Requirements (accessibility, noise absorption, controlled temperature, space for equipment, cabling, and proximity to Wi-Fi transmitters or access points ["hot spots"]) for Output Technologies? When humans interact with technologies, specific environments help systems run more effectively and efficiently. Users need accessibility and support in accessing Web pages as well as other output.

Printers require a dry, cool environment to operate properly. Displays require space for setup and viewing. Audio and video output require a quiet environment if they are to be heard, and they should not be audible to employees (or customers) who are not using it. Thus, the analyst should not specify audio output for a work situation in which many employees are engaged in a variety of tasks unrelated to the output.

In order to set up wireless local area networks so users can access the Web wirelessly, Wi-Fi access points need to be made available. These work when PCs are within a few hundred feet of transmitters, but can be subject to interference by other devices.

Some output technologies are prized for their unobtrusiveness. Libraries, which emphasize silence in the workplace, make extensive use of displays for Web documents and other networked database information, but printers might be scarce.

REALIZING HOW OUTPUT BIAS AFFECTS USERS

Whatever form it takes, output is not just a neutral product that is subsequently analyzed and acted on by decision makers. Output affects users in many different ways. The significance of this fact for the systems analyst is that great thought and care must be put into designing the output so as to avoid biasing it.

RECOGNIZING BIAS IN THE WAY OUTPUT IS USED

It is a common error to assume that once the systems analyst has signed off on a system project, his or her impact is ended. Actually, the analyst's influence is long-lasting. Much of the information on which organizational members base their decisions is determined by what analysts perceive is important to the business.

Bias is present in everything that humans create. This statement is not to judge bias as bad, but to make the point that it is inseparable from what we (and consequently our systems) produce. The concerns of systems analysts are to avoid unnecessarily biasing output and to make users aware of the possible biases in the output they receive, even if they helped design it.

Presentations of output are unintentionally biased in three main ways:

1. How information is sorted.
2. Setting of acceptable limits.
3. Choice of graphics.

Each source of bias is discussed separately in the following subsections.

Introducing Bias When Information Is Sorted Bias is introduced to output when the analyst and users make choices about how information is sorted for a report. Common sorts include alphabetical, chronological, and cost.

Information presented alphabetically may overemphasize the items that begin with the letters A and B, because users tend to pay more attention to information presented first. For example, if past suppliers are listed alphabetically, companies such as Aardvark Printers, Advent Supplies, and Barkley Office Equipment are shown to the purchasing manager first. When certain airlines created the SABRE and APOLLO reservations systems, they listed their own flights first, until the other airlines complained that this type of sorting was biased.

Introducing Bias by Setting Limits A second major source of bias in output is the predefinition of limits for particular values being reported. Many reports are generated on an exception basis only, which means that when limits on values are set beforehand, only exceptions to those values will be output. Exception reports make the decision maker aware of deviations from satisfactory values.

For example, limits that are set too low for exception reports can bias the user's perception. An insurance company that generates exception reports on all accounts one week overdue has set too low a limit on overdue payments. The decision maker receiving the output will be overwhelmed with "exceptions" that are not really cause for concern. The one-week overdue exception report leads to the user's misperception that there are a great many overdue accounts. A more appropriate limit for generating an exception report would be accounts 30 days or more overdue.

Introducing Bias Through Graphics Output is subject to a third type of presentation bias, which is brought about by the analyst's (or users') choice of graphics for output display. Bias can occur in the selection of the graph size, its color, the scale used, and even the type of graphic.

Graph size must be proportional so that the user is not biased as to the importance of the variables that are presented. For example, Figure 11.7 shows a column chart comparing the number of no-shows for hotel bookings in 2002 with no-shows for hotel bookings in 2003. Notice that the vertical axis is broken, and it appears

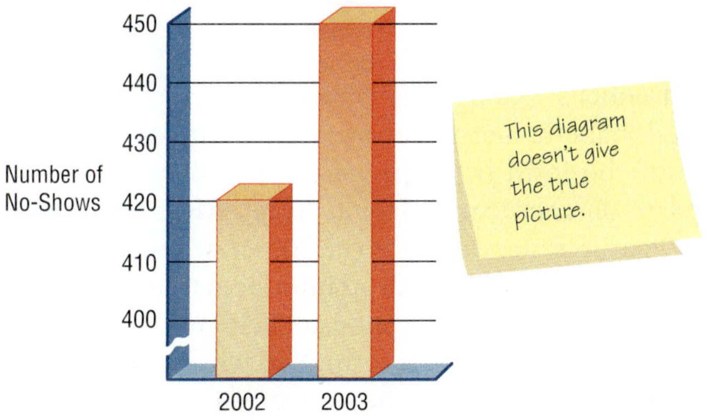

FIGURE 11.7
A misleading graph will most likely bias the user.

that the number of no-shows for 2003 is twice as much as the number of no-shows in 2002, although the number of no-shows has actually gone up only slightly.

AVOIDING BIAS IN THE DESIGN OF OUTPUT

Systems analysts can use specific strategies to avoid biasing the output they and others design:

1. Be aware of the sources of bias.
2. Create an interactive design of output during prototyping that includes users and a variety of differently configured systems during the testing of Web document appearance.
3. Work with users so that they are informed of the output's biases and can recognize the implications of customizing their displays.
4. Create output that is flexible and that allows users to modify limits and ranges.
5. Train users to rely on multiple outputs for conducting "reality tests" on system output.

All these strategies (except the first) focus on the relationship between the systems analyst and the user as it involves output. Systems analysts first need to recognize the potential impact of output and be aware of the possible ways in which output is unintentionally biased. They then need to be proactive in helping users design output with minimal, but identifiable, biases.

DESIGNING PRINTED OUTPUT

The source of information to be included in reports is the data dictionary, the compilation of which was covered in Chapter 8. Recall that the data dictionary includes names of data elements as well as the required field length of each entry.

Reports fall into three categories: detailed, exception, and summary. Detailed reports print a report line for every record on the master file. They are used for mailing to customers, sending student grade reports, printing catalogs, and so on. Inquiry screens have replaced many detailed reports.

Exception reports print a line for all records that match a set of conditions, such as which DVDs are overdue at a video store or which students are on the dean's list. They are usually used to help operational managers and clerical staff run a business. Summary reports print one line for a group of records and are used to make decisions, such as which items are not selling and which are hot selling.

GUIDELINES FOR PRINTED REPORT DESIGN

Figure 11.8 is an output report that is intended for divisional managers of a food wholesaler that supplies a number of franchise grocery stores. We will focus on different aspects of the report as we cover the tools, conventions, and functional and stylistic design attributes of printed output reports.

Report Design Conventions Conventions to follow when designing a form include the type of data (alphabetic, special, or numeric) that will appear in each position, showing the size of the form being prepared, and showing the way to indicate a continuation of data on consecutive layout forms. Most form design software that analysts now use features standard conventions for designing forms onscreen. In addition, it features familiar drag and drop interfaces that allow you to select attributes such as an address block with a mouse click and then drop it on the screen where you want to position it on your form. You will be using WYSIWYG or "what you see is what you get," so it makes the design of forms a very visual exercise.

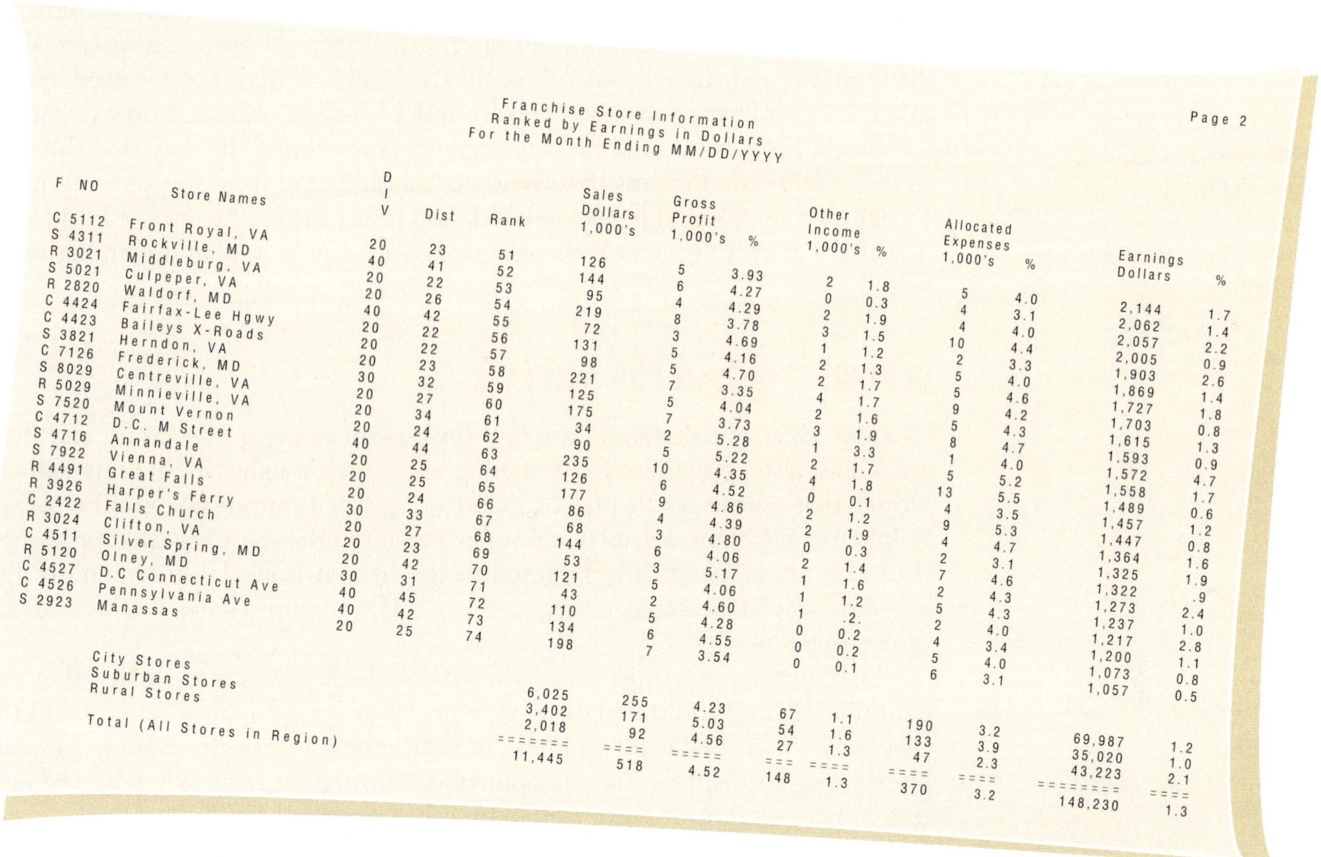

Franchise Store Information
Ranked by Earnings in Dollars
For the Month Ending MM/DD/YYYY

Page 2

F NO	Store Names	DIV	Dist	Rank	Sales Dollars 1,000's	Gross Profit 1,000's	%	Other Income 1,000's	%	Allocated Expenses 1,000's	%	Earnings Dollars	%
C 5112	Front Royal, VA	20	23	51	126	5	3.93	2	1.8	5	4.0	2,144	1.7
S 4311	Rockville, MD	40	41	52	144	6	4.27	0	0.3	4	3.1	2,062	1.4
R 3021	Middleburg, VA	20	22	53	95	4	4.29	2	1.9	4	4.0	2,057	2.2
S 5021	Culpeper, VA	20	26	54	219	8	3.78	3	1.5	10	4.4	2,005	0.9
R 2820	Waldorf, MD	40	42	55	72	3	4.69	1	1.2	2	3.3	1,903	2.6
C 4424	Fairfax-Lee Hgwy	20	22	56	131	5	4.16	2	1.3	5	4.0	1,869	1.4
C 4423	Baileys X-Roads	20	22	57	98	5	4.70	2	1.7	5	4.6	1,727	1.8
S 3821	Herndon, VA	20	23	58	221	7	3.35	4	1.7	9	4.2	1,703	0.8
C 7126	Frederick, MD	30	32	59	125	5	4.04	2	1.6	5	4.3	1,615	1.3
S 8029	Centreville, VA	20	27	60	175	7	3.73	3	1.9	8	4.7	1,593	0.9
R 5029	Minnieville, VA	20	34	61	34	2	5.28	1	3.3	1	4.0	1,572	4.7
S 7520	Mount Vernon	20	24	62	90	5	5.22	2	1.7	5	5.2	1,558	1.7
C 4712	D.C. M Street	40	44	63	235	10	4.35	4	1.8	13	5.5	1,489	0.6
S 4716	Annandale	20	25	64	126	6	4.52	0	0.1	4	3.5	1,457	1.2
S 7922	Vienna, VA	20	25	65	177	9	4.86	2	1.2	9	5.3	1,447	0.8
R 4491	Great Falls	20	24	66	86	4	4.39	2	1.9	4	4.7	1,364	1.6
R 3926	Harper's Ferry	30	33	67	68	3	4.80	0	0.3	2	3.1	1,325	1.9
C 2422	Falls Church	20	27	68	144	6	4.06	2	1.4	7	4.6	1,322	.9
R 3024	Clifton, VA	20	23	69	53	3	5.17	1	1.6	2	4.3	1,273	2.4
C 4511	Silver Spring, MD	20	42	70	121	5	4.06	1	1.2	5	4.3	1,237	1.0
R 5120	Olney, MD	30	31	71	43	2	4.60	1	.2.	2	4.0	1,217	2.8
C 4527	D.C Connecticut Ave	40	45	72	110	5	4.28	0	0.2	4	3.4	1,200	1.1
C 4526	Pennsylvania Ave	40	42	73	134	6	4.55	0	0.2	5	4.0	1,073	0.8
S 2923	Manassas	20	25	74	198	7	3.54	0	0.1	6	3.1	1,057	0.5
	City Stores				6,025	255	4.23	67	1.1	190	3.2	69,987	1.2
	Suburban Stores				3,402	171	5.03	54	1.6	133	3.9	35,020	1.0
	Rural Stores				2,018	92	4.56	27	1.3	47	2.3	43,223	2.1
					=======	====	=====	===	====	====	====	========	====
	Total (All Stores in Region)				11,445	518	4.52	148	1.3	370	3.2	148,230	1.3

FIGURE 11.8

A printed output report for divisional managers of a food wholesaler.

Constant information is information that remains the same whenever the report is printed. The title of the report and all of the column headings are written as constant information. *Variable information* is information that can vary each time the report is printed out. In our example, the sales figures in thousands of dollars will change; hence, they are indicated as variable information.

Paper Quality, Type, and Size Output can be printed on innumerable kinds of paper. The overriding constraint is usually cost. One example is the use of security paper for checks and check envelopes, as well as for documents that must bear official, inalterable seals or holograms, such as passports.

Preprinted forms can easily convey a distinctive corporate image through the use of corporate colors and design. Using innovative shapes, colors, and layouts is also a dramatic way of drawing users' attention to the report contained on the preprinted form.

Design Considerations In designing the printed report, the systems analyst works with users to incorporate both functional and stylistic or aesthetic considerations so that the report supplies the user with necessary information in a readable and pleasing format. Because function and form reinforce each other, one should not be emphasized at the expense of the other.

Functional Attributes. The functional attributes of a printed report include (1) the heading or title of the report, (2) the page number, (3) the date of preparation, (4) the column headings, (5) the grouping of related data items together, and (6) the use of control breaks. Each of these serves a distinctive purpose for the user.

There are several stylistic or aesthetic considerations for the systems analyst to observe when designing a printed report. If printed output is unappealing and difficult to read, it will not be used effectively or may not be used at all. The upshot is uninformed decision makers and a waste of organizational resources.

Printed reports should be well organized, reflecting the way that the eye sees. In this culture, that means that the report should read from top to bottom and left to right. As mentioned before, related data items should be grouped together. The aesthetics of Web site and Web page design are covered in an upcoming section of this chapter.

DESIGNING OUTPUT FOR DISPLAYS

Chapter 12 covers designing displays for human or computer input, and the same guidelines also apply here for designing output, although the contents will change. Notice that output for displays differs from printed output in a number of ways. It is ephemeral (that is, a display is not permanent in the same way that printouts are), it can be more specifically targeted to the user, it is available on a more flexible schedule, it is *not* portable in the same way, and sometimes it can be changed through direct interaction.

In addition, users must be instructed on which keys to press when they want to continue reading additional displays, when they want to know how to end the display, and when they want to know how to interact with the display (if possible). User access to displays may be controlled through a password, whereas distribution of printed output is controlled by other means.

GUIDELINES FOR DISPLAY DESIGN

Four guidelines facilitate the design of displays:

1. Keep the display simple.
2. Keep the presentation consistent.
3. Facilitate user movement among displayed output.
4. Create an attractive and pleasing display.

Just as with printed output, good displays are not created in isolation. Systems analysts need the feedback of users to design worthwhile displays. Once approved by users after successive prototypes and refinements, the display layout can be finalized.

The output produced from the design display is pictured in Figure 11.9. Notice that it is uncluttered, but it still gives a basic summary of the shipping status. The display orients users as to what they are looking at with the use of a heading. Instructions at the bottom of the display provide users with several options, including continuing the present display, ending the display, getting help, or getting more detail. This display provides context for users attempting to complete a task such as checking on the status of an order.

Output displays in an application should show information consistently from page to page. Figure 11.10 shows the display that results when the user positions the cursor over the order number for a particular retailer. The new display presents more details on Bear Bizarre. In the body of the display, the user can see the retailer's order number, complete address, the order date, and the status. In addition, a detailed breakdown of the shipment and a detailed status of each part of the shipment are given. A contact name and phone number are supplied, along with the account balance, credit rating, and shipment history. Notice that the bottom portion of the display advises the user of options, including more details, ending

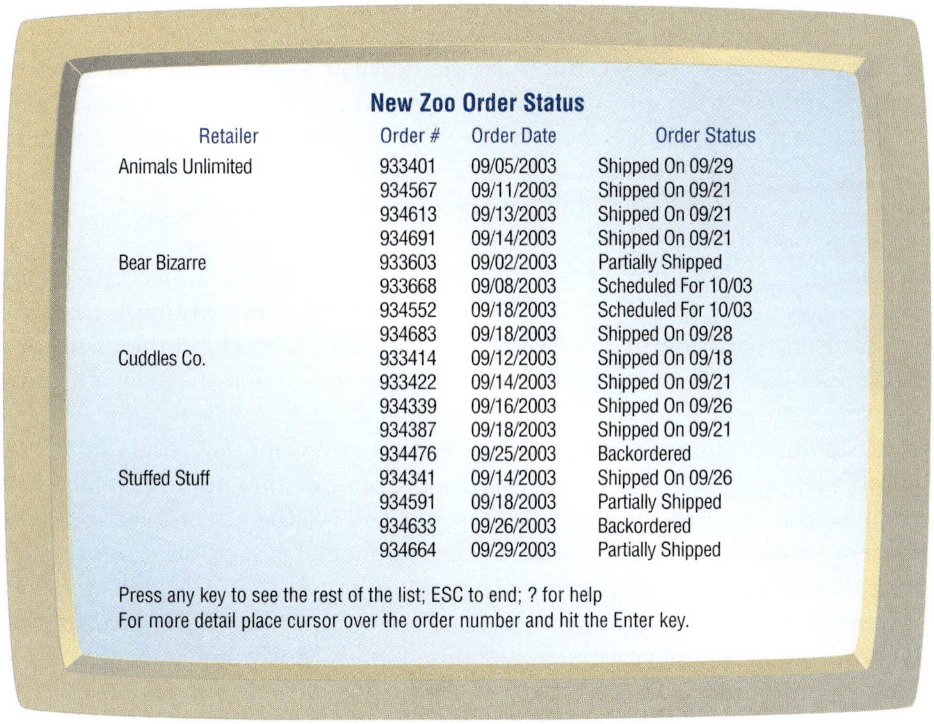

New Zoo Order Status

Retailer	Order #	Order Date	Order Status
Animals Unlimited	933401	09/05/2003	Shipped On 09/29
	934567	09/11/2003	Shipped On 09/21
	934613	09/13/2003	Shipped On 09/21
	934691	09/14/2003	Shipped On 09/21
Bear Bizarre	933603	09/02/2003	Partially Shipped
	933668	09/08/2003	Scheduled For 10/03
	934552	09/18/2003	Scheduled For 10/03
	934683	09/18/2003	Shipped On 09/28
Cuddles Co.	933414	09/12/2003	Shipped On 09/18
	933422	09/14/2003	Shipped On 09/21
	934339	09/16/2003	Shipped On 09/26
	934387	09/18/2003	Shipped On 09/21
	934476	09/25/2003	Backordered
Stuffed Stuff	934341	09/14/2003	Shipped On 09/26
	934591	09/18/2003	Partially Shipped
	934633	09/26/2003	Backordered
	934664	09/29/2003	Partially Shipped

Press any key to see the rest of the list; ESC to end; ? for help
For more detail place cursor over the order number and hit the Enter key.

FIGURE 11.9
The New Zoo output display screen is uncluttered and orients users well.

the display, or getting help. Users are provided control over what they might do next while viewing the display.

Rather than crowding all retailer information onto one page, the analyst has made it possible for the user to bring up a particular retailer if a problem or question arises. If, for example, the summary indicates that an order was only partially shipped, the user can check further on the order by calling up a detailed retailer display and then following up with appropriate action.

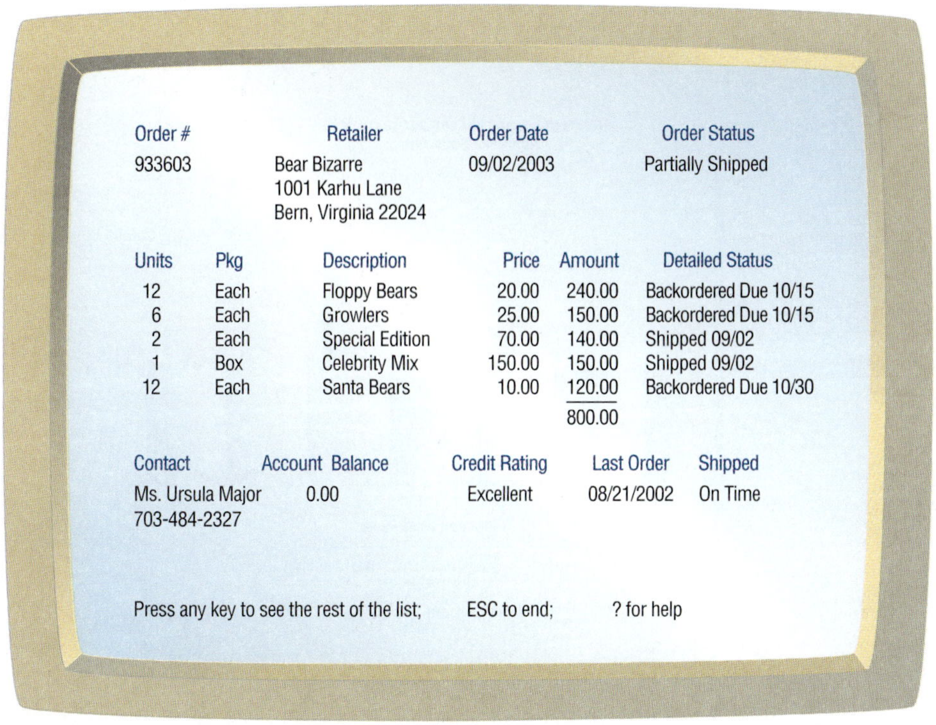

Order #	Retailer	Order Date	Order Status
933603	Bear Bizarre 1001 Karhu Lane Bern, Virginia 22024	09/02/2003	Partially Shipped

Units	Pkg	Description	Price	Amount	Detailed Status
12	Each	Floppy Bears	20.00	240.00	Backordered Due 10/15
6	Each	Growlers	25.00	150.00	Backordered Due 10/15
2	Each	Special Edition	70.00	140.00	Shipped 09/02
1	Box	Celebrity Mix	150.00	150.00	Shipped 09/02
12	Each	Santa Bears	10.00	120.00	Backordered Due 10/30
				800.00	

Contact	Account Balance	Credit Rating	Last Order	Shipped
Ms. Ursula Major 703-484-2327	0.00	Excellent	08/21/2002	On Time

Press any key to see the rest of the list; ESC to end; ? for help

FIGURE 11.10
If users want more details regarding the shipping status, they can call up a separate screen.

USING GRAPHICAL OUTPUT IN SCREEN DESIGN

Graphical output can be powerful. It is much easier to identify a trend or notice a pattern when the right graph is displayed. Most people notice differences in graphs more easily than they notice differences in tables. It is important to collaborate with users in choosing the correct style of graph to communicate your meaning. You may want to review the section on graphing in Chapter 10 to familiarize yourself with the options.

As with the presentation of tabular output, graphical output needs to be accurate and easy to understand and use if it is to be effective in communicating information to users. Decision makers using the graphs need to know the assumptions (biases) under which the graphs are being constructed so that they can adjust to or compensate for them.

In designing graphical output, the systems analyst and any users involved in design prototyping must determine (1) the purpose of the graph, (2) the kind of data that need to be displayed, (3) its audience, and (4) the effects on the audience of different kinds of graphical output. In the instance of a decision support system, the purposes of graphical displays are to support any of the three phases of problem solving a user experiences: intelligence, design, or choice. An example from the Nebraska State Patrol workforce planning DSS is shown in Figure 11.11. Here, current response times, forecasted response times, and minimum requirements are graphed as differently shaded bars.

DASHBOARDS

Decision makers need output that helps them make decisions effectively and quickly. It helps executives and other decision makers if all of the information they need to make decisions is displayed in front of them. When given a written report, a decision maker would prefer all the information to be contained in that one report rather than searching for information in other places. The same principle applies to screen design.

FIGURE 11.11
A bar chart display for onscreen inspection of troop time response.

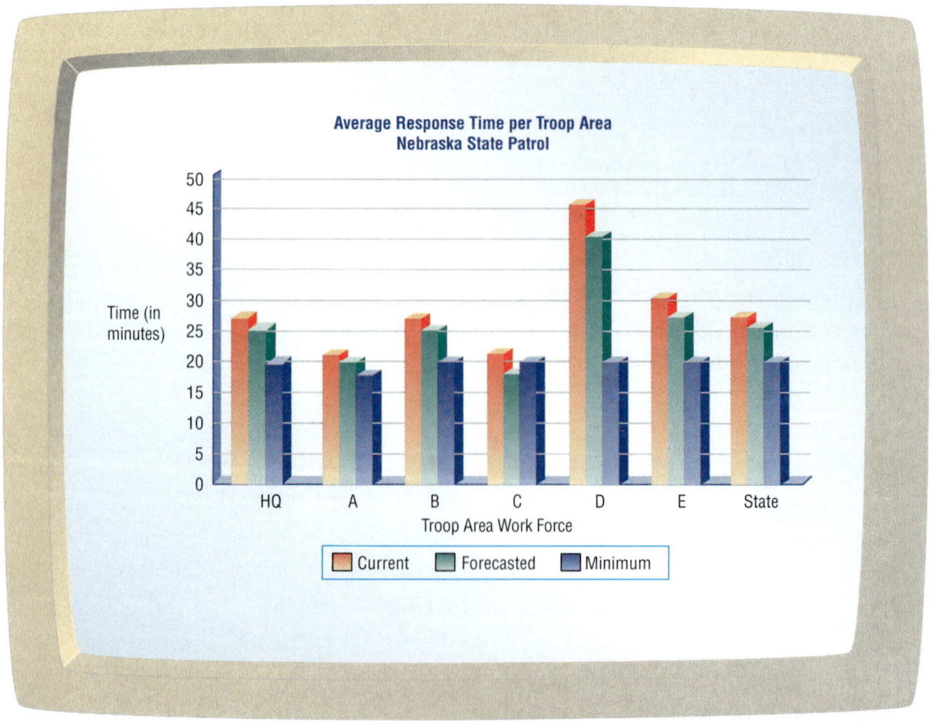

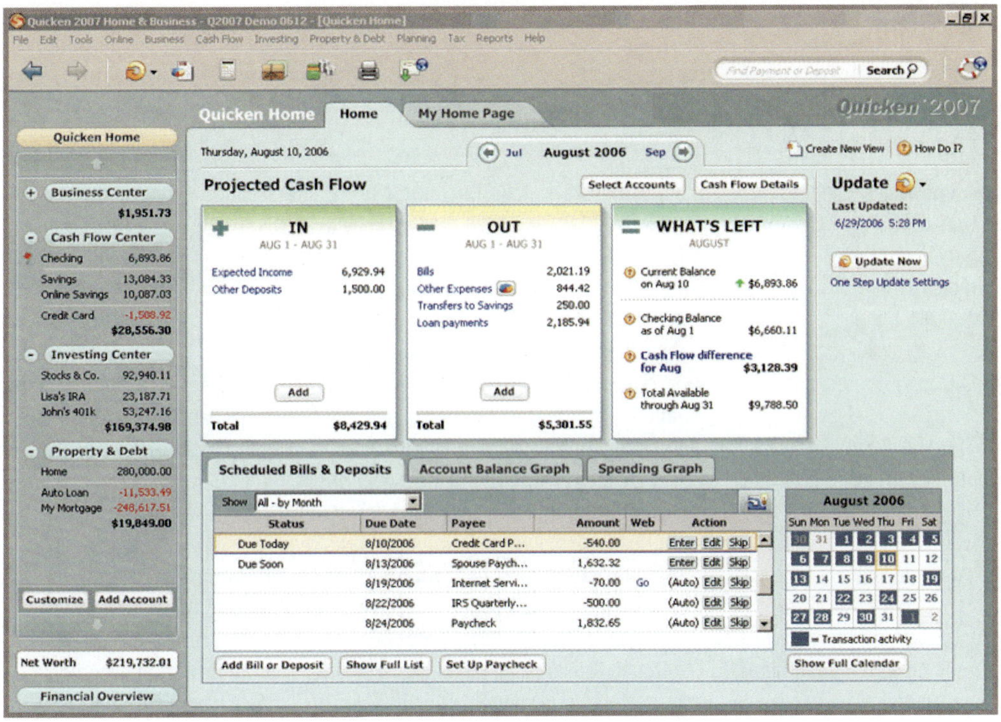

FIGURE 11.12
This dashboard designed for Quicken Premier has a variety of displays depicting performance measurements to help make decisions. (Courtesy of Intuit, www.intuit.com.)

A dashboard, similar to the dashboard in a car, has many different gauges. Each gauge can display a graph (similar to the speed in miles or kilometers per hour), a problem light (similar to a light showing that the automatic braking system is not functioning), or even text (like an odometer that simply counts the miles traveled).

An executive can find a dashboard to be extremely useful in making decisions, but only if the dashboard is designed properly. The dashboard in Figure 11.12 shows that a considerable amount of information can be included on a single screen.

Dashboards are all about communicating measurements to the user. An executive uses a dashboard to review performance measures and to take action if the information on the screen calls for it. Here are some rules of thumb that can be used to make the dashboard you design more attractive and more effective:

1. Make sure the data have context. If you design a screen stating that sales last month were $851,235, what does that mean? Are sales above or below average?
2. Display the proper amount of summarization and precision. It will clutter the screen if you display last month's sales as $851,235.32 instead of $851,235 or even $851K.
3. Choose appropriate performance measures for display. For example, plotting the difference in actual versus expected sales in a deviation chart (see Chapter 10) is much more meaningful than using a line chart to plot actual and expected sales.
4. Present data fairly. If you introduce bias into the dashboard (see Chapter 10), it will hinder rather than support good decisions.
5. Choose the correct style of graph or chart for display. Using the correct chart is important. In Chapter 10 we discussed the types of graphs and their benefits for certain uses. While a pie chart may be an excellent graph to persuade someone, it may not be a good way for an executive to watch the performance of regional offices, for example.
6. Use well designed display media. Even if you choose the very best type of graph, you still need to draw, size, color, and label the graph in a meaningful and pleasing way.

CONSULTING OPPORTUNITY 11.3

IS YOUR WORK A GRIND?

"I want everything I can get my hands on, and the tighter the information is packed, the better. Forget that stuff you hear about information overload. It's not in my vocabulary. I want it all, and not in a bunch of pretty-looking, half-page reports either. I want it all together, packed on one sheet that I can take into a meeting in case I need to look something up. And I need it every week," proclaims Stephen Links, vice president of a large, family-owned sausage company.

During an interview, Links has been grilling Paul Plishka, who is part of the systems analysis team that is busy designing an information system for Links Meats. Although Paul is hesitant about what Links has told him, he proceeds to design a printed report that includes all the important items the team has settled on during the analysis phase.

When a prototype of the new report, designed to his specifications, is handed to Stephen, however, there appears to be a change of heart. Links says in no uncertain terms that he can't find what he needs.

"This stuff looks terrible. It looks like scraps. My kindergartner makes better reports in crayon. Look at it. It's all ground up together. I can't find anything. Where's the summary of the number of pork items sold in each outlet? Where is the total volume of items sold for *all* outlets? How about the information on our own shop downtown?" says Links, slicing at the report.

The report clearly needs to be redesigned. Design a report (or reports) that better suits Stephen Links. What tack can the analyst take in suggesting more reports with a less-crowded format? Comment on the difficulty of implementing user suggestions that go against your design training. What are the trade-offs involved (as far as information overload goes) in generating numerous reports as opposed to generating one large report containing all the information Stephen wants? Devise a heuristic concerning the display of report information on one report in contrast to the generation of numerous reports. Consider advocating a Web-based or dashboard solution that would permit hyperlinks to all the information Stephen desires. How feasible is that?

7. Limit the variety of item types. Keep the number of graph, chart, and table styles to a minimum so that the information can be communicated quickly and accurately.
8. Highlight important data. Use bright colors and bold fonts only for important data. You can highlight key performance measures or important exceptions that are occurring but not both. Choose what to emphasize.
9. Arrange the data in meaningful groups. Performance measures are almost always associated with other performance measures because of the data displayed or the type of graph. Learn how to group associated items together.
10. Keep the screen uncluttered. Avoid photographs, ornate logos, or themes that can distract users from the data.
11. Keep the entire dashboard on a single screen. All of the performance measures are meant to be on the same screen. If forced to switch screens, a user will not see two relevant measures at the same time.
12. Allow flexibility. If an executive wants a different graph or chart, consider replacing it. Prototyping the dashboard and refining it based on the user's feedback makes sense. Decision makers often know best when it comes to getting the right information in the most appropriate form for their decision style.

WIDGETS AND GADGETS—CHANGING THE DESKTOP METAPHOR

Related to dashboards are new, user-designed desktops. Systems designers who develop software for personal computers should be aware of a trend to encourage users to personalize their desktops with widgets and gadgets. These items are small programs, usually written in JavaScript and VBScript, that reside either in a sidebar attached to a browser or program or even reside in a special layer on the desktop itself.

Widgets (as they are called by Yahoo), Dashboard Widgets (as named by Apple), and Gadgets (as they are called by Google and Microsoft) can be any type of program that may be useful to anyone interacting with a computer. Clocks, calculators, bookmark helpers, translators, search engines, easy access to utilities, quick launch panels, and sticky notes are popular productivity widgets.

Stock tickers, weather reports, and RSS feeds are also useful widgets. Gadgets allow users to track packages and check schedules. The user can put amusements like games, music podcasts, and hobbies on their desktop as well. Widgets and gadgets possess dual, almost paradoxical natures. They can empower users to take part in the design of their own desktop, and designers who are observant can learn a lot about what users prefer when they study user-designed desktops. But widgets and gadgets can also distract people from system-supported tasks. Designers need to work with users to support them in achieving a balance. One possibility is to add user-specific performance measures as widgets and gadgets that are helpful to decision makers.

DESIGNING A WEB SITE

You can borrow some of the design principles from designing displays when you design a Web site. Remember, though, that the key word here is *site*. The first documents displayed on the Internet using the http protocol were called home pages, but it became apparent very quickly that companies, universities, governments, and people were not going to be displaying just one page. The term *Web site* replaced *home page*, indicating that the array of pages would have to be organized, coordinated, designed, developed, and maintained in an orderly process.

Printing is a highly controlled medium, and the analyst has a very good idea of what the output will look like. GUI and character-based (CHUI, character-based user interface) screens are also highly controlled. The Web, however, is a very uncontrolled environment for output.

Different browsers display images differently, and screen resolution has a large impact on the look and feel of a Web site. The standard resolutions are 1024 × 768 pixels or 1600 × 1200 pixels. The issue is further complicated by the use of handheld devices, such as mobile phones, that are used to browse the Web. The complexity deepens when you realize that each person may set a browser to use different fonts and may disable the use of JavaScript, cookies, and other Web programming elements. Clearly, analysts and users face many decisions when designing a Web site.

In addition to the general design elements discussed earlier in this chapter, there are specific guidelines appropriate for the design of professional-quality Web sites. Web terms are defined in Figure 11.13. The following subsections address these guidelines.

GENERAL GUIDELINES FOR DESIGNING WEB SITES

There are many tools as well as examples that can guide you in designing Web sites.

Use Professional Tools Use software called a Web editor such as Macromedia Dreamweaver or Microsoft FrontPage. These tools are definitely worth the price. You will be more creative and you'll get the Web site finished much faster than working directly with HTML (hypertext markup language).

Study Other Web Sites Look at Web sites you and other users think are engaging. Analyze what design elements are being used and see how they are functioning, then try to emulate what you see by creating prototype pages. (It is not ethical or legal to cut and paste pictures or code, but you still can learn from the other sites.)

Web Term	Meaning
Ajax	A method using JavaScript and XML to dynamically change Web pages without displaying a new page by obtaining small amounts of data from the server.
CSS	Cascading style sheets, a set of styles that control the formatting of a Web page. CSS may be stored in a file and used to format a number of Web pages, or may be defined within a Web page.
DHTML	Dynamic HTML, a way of combining JavaScript and perhaps cascading style sheets to have the Web page change with user actions.
FAQ	Frequently Asked Questions. Web sites often have a page devoted to these so that the company sales force or tech support is not inundated with the same questions over and over again and users can have 24-hour access to answers.
FTP	File transfer protocol, currently the most common way to move files between computer systems.
GIF	Graphic interchange format, a popular compressed image format best suited for artwork.
Java	An object-oriented language that allows dynamic applications to be run on the Internet. Nonprogrammers can use software packages such as Symantec's Visual Café for Java.
JPEG	Joint Photographic Expert Group, the acronym for a popular compressed image format best suited for photographs, whose quality can be adjusted by the designer.
HTML	Hypertext markup language, the language behind the appearance of documents on the Web. It is actually a set of conventions that mark the portions of a document, telling a browser what distinctive format should appear on each portion of a page.
http://	Hypertext transfer protocol, used to move Web pages between computers, such as from a Web site on a computer in another country to your personal computer.
PHP	An open source programming language, often used with MySQL, a database management system.
plug-ins	Additional software (often developed by a third party) that can be used with another program; for example, RealNetworks' Real Player or Macromedia Flash are used as plug-ins in Web browsers to play streaming audio or video and view vector-based animation.
URL	Uniform resource locator, the address of a document or program on the Internet. Familiar extensions are .com for commercial, .edu for educational institution, .gov for government, .org for organization, and so on.
VB .NET	Visual Basic .NET, a Microsoft programming environment.
Webmaster	The person responsible for maintaining the Web site.
WMP	Windows media photo, a Microsoft-developed alternative to JPEG.

FIGURE 11.13
Web vocabulary terms.

Firefox, which is part of the open source software movement, is a wonderful browser for studying other Web sites. It has a number of extensions created by third-party developers that are available as free downloads. Run Firefox and click "Tools/Extensions" and "Get More Extensions." There are pages of extensions but one called Web Developer is very useful to designers and Webmasters. It allows the analyst to outline tables and styles and to view JavaScript and cookies; it provides form information as well as a wealth of other useful items from which to choose. Palette Grabber is another extension that allows Web developers to see a display of color codes just by picking any color on a Web site. There are also tools for working with XML. Figure 11.14 is an example of the Web Developer toolbar used to highlight table cells. Notice the red border around each individual cell.

Use the Resources That the Web Has to Offer Look at Web sites that give hints on design. One such site is useit.com.

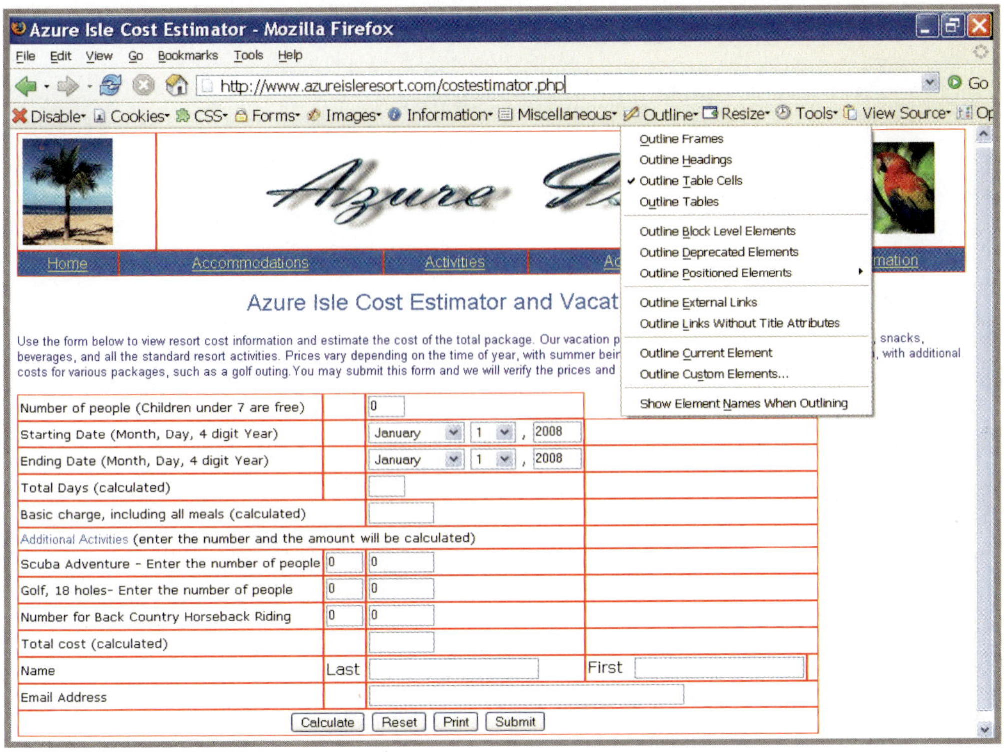

FIGURE 11.14
A Web developer can outline table cells when designing a Web page, as shown in this example.

Examine the Web Sites of Professional Designers Some design houses are listed in Figure 11.15, along with some of the often-visited and praised Web sites they developed. As you look at these pages, ask yourself, "What works? What doesn't work? In what ways can users interact with the site?" For example, does the site have hot links to email addresses, interactive forms to fill in, consumer surveys, games, quizzes, chat rooms, and so on?

Use the Tools You've Learned Figure 11.16 provides a form that has been used successfully by Web designers to evaluate Web pages systematically. You might want to use copies of the form to help you compare and contrast the many Web sites you will visit as you go about learning Web page design.

Consult the Books Something that can add to your expertise in this new field is to read about Web design. Some books on Web site design are:

Flanders, V., and D. Peters. *Son of Web Pages That Suck: Learn Good Design by Looking at Bad Design*. Alameda, CA: Sybex, 2002.

Pring, R. *www.type: Effective Typographic Design for the World Wide Web*. New York: Watson-Guptill, 2000.

Weinman, L. *Designing Web Graphics 4: How to Prepare Images and Media for the Web*, 4th ed. Indianapolis, IN: NRP, 2002.

Design House	Web Address	Sites It Designed
Organic	www.organic.com	www.hp.com www.potterybarn.com www.sirius.com
Modem media	modemmedia.com	www.delta.com www.michelinman.com www.flysong.com

FIGURE 11.15
Selected Web site designer houses.

FIGURE 11.16
A Web site evaluation form.

Web Site Critique

Date Visited: __ / __ / __
Time Visited: ________

Analyst's Name ________
URL Visited ________

DESIGN	**Needs Improvement**				**Excellent**
Overall Appearance	1	2	3	4	5
Use of Graphics	1	2	3	4	5
Use of Color	1	2	3	4	5
Use of Sound/Video (Multimedia)	1	2	3	4	5
Use of New Technology and Products	1	2	3	4	5
CONTENT & INTERACTIVITY					
Content	1	2	3	4	5
Navigability	1	2	3	4	5
Site Management and Communications	1	2	3	4	5

SCORE /40

COMMENTS:

Look at Some Poor Examples of Web Pages, Too Critique poor Web pages and remember to avoid those mistakes. Examine the Web site found at www.webpagesthatsuck.com. Despite its "counterculture" name, this is a wonderful site that provides links to many poorly designed sites, and points out the errors that designers have made on them. However, the site also provides links to material that takes the reader through creating a Web site, improving site navigation, learning JavaScript, and much more. The authors are humorous, and vigilant at identifying Web sites both good and bad, and they provide a wealth of useful information.

Create Templates of Your Own If you adopt a standard-looking page for most of the pages you create, you'll get the Web site up and running quickly and it will consistently look good. Web sites may be made using cascading style sheets that allow the designer to specify the color, font size, font type, and many other attributes only once. These attributes are stored in a style sheet file and then are applied to many Web pages. If a designer changes a specification in the style sheet file, all the Web pages using that style sheet will be updated to reflect the new style.

Use Plug-Ins, Audio, and Video Very Sparingly It is wonderful to have features that the professional pages have, but remember that everyone looking at your site doesn't have every new plug-in. Don't discourage visitors to your page.

Plan Ahead Good Web sites are well thought out. Pay attention to the following:

1. Structure.
2. Content.
3. Text.
4. Graphics.
5. Presentation style.
6. Navigation.
7. Promotion.

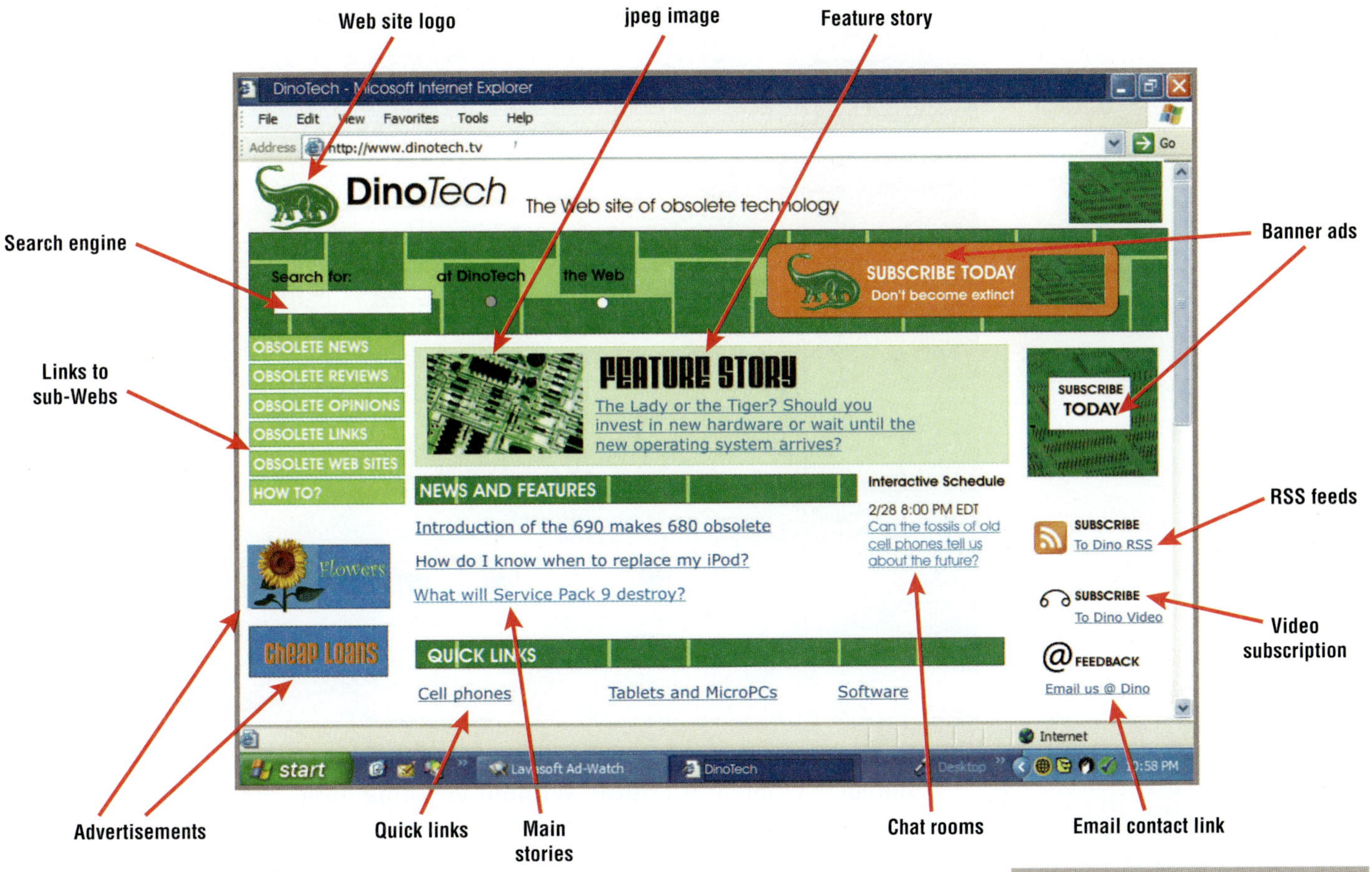

FIGURE 11.17
The DinoTech Web site makes the most of links, RSS feeds, video subscriptions, and banner ads.

Each of these items is described in more detail below.

Structure. Planning the structure of a Web site is one of the most important steps in developing a professional Web site. Think about your goals and objectives. Each page in the overall Web structure should have a distinct message or other related information. Sometimes it is useful to examine professional sites to analyze them for content and features. Figure 11.17 is a screen capture from the DinoTech Web site. The purpose for the site and the Web medium work exceptionally well together. Notice that there is great attention to supporting users on the site. There are words, graphics, JPEG images, and icons. In addition, there are many kinds of links: to RSS feeds, video, sub-Webs, chat rooms, a search engine, and many other features.

To help plan and maintain a solid structure, a Webmaster can benefit from using one of the many Web site diagramming and mapping tools available. Many software packages, including Microsoft Visio, have Web charting options built into the software. Although helpful for development, these tools become even more important when maintaining a Web site. Given the dynamic nature of the Web, sites that are linked to your site may move at any time, requiring you or your Webmaster to update the links.

In Figure 11.18, a map of a section of the authors' Web site is shown in the Visio window. In this example, we explore the Web site down to all the existing levels. Notice the links to HTML pages, documents, images (GIF or JPEG files), and mail-tos (a way to send email to a designated person). The links can be either internal or external. If a link is broken, a red **X** appears and the analyst can investigate further. This Visio file can be printed out in sections and posted on the wall to get an overall picture of the Web site.

FIGURE 11.18

A Web site can be evaluated for broken links by using a package such as Microsoft Visio.

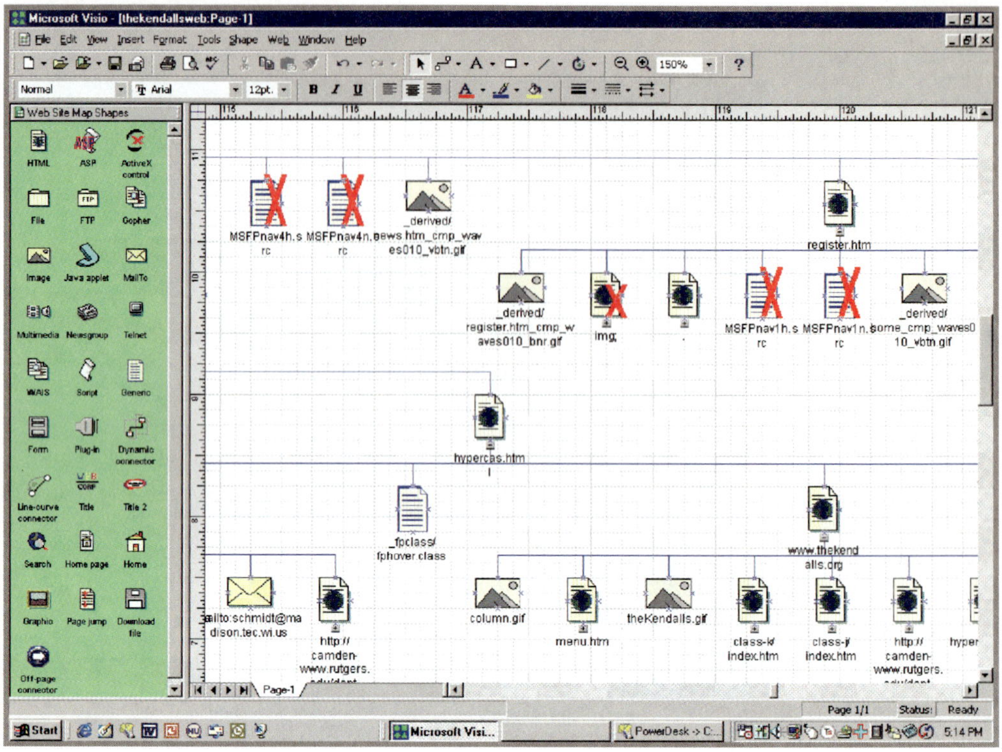

Content. Content is critical. Without anything to say, your Web site will fail. A 12-year-old friend of ours, wise beyond his age, confided, "I could make my own Web site, but what's the point? I have nothing to say!" Exciting animation, movies, and sounds are fun, but you have to include appropriate content to keep the user interested.

Provide something important to Web site users. Supply some timely advice, important information, a free offer, or any activity that you can provide that is interactive and moves users away from a browsing mode and into an interactive one.

"Stickiness" is a quality a Web site can possess. If a user stays at your site for a long period of time, your site has a high degree of stickiness. That is why a merchant includes many items of interest on a site. A wine merchant, for example, may put lessons on how to uncork a bottle, taste the wine, or choose a proper glass.

Use a metaphor or images that provide a metaphor for your site. You can use a theme, such as a storefront, with additional pages having various metaphors related to the storefront, such as a deli. Avoid the overuse of cartoons, and don't be repetitive. An example of the use of metaphors can be found in the Web site www.javaranch.com, which is used as a resource for those learning and using the Java programming language. Refer to Figure 11.19. Notice the use of ranch terms throughout. The Big Moose Saloon is a discussion area, the Cattle Drive gives actual experience writing Java code, and so on.

Every Web site should include an FAQ page. Often these are created based on the experiences of users and technical support people who identify the topics of continuing concern. By having answers readily available, 24 hours a day, you will save valuable employee time and also save user time. FAQ pages also demonstrate to users of your site that you are in concert with them and have a good idea of what they would like to know.

On the Web, COTS software takes on another meaning. A Web site may take advantage of prewritten software. Examples include search engines (such as Google), mapping software (such as MapQuest), weather information, and news and stock tickers. Web site designers value these packages because they can

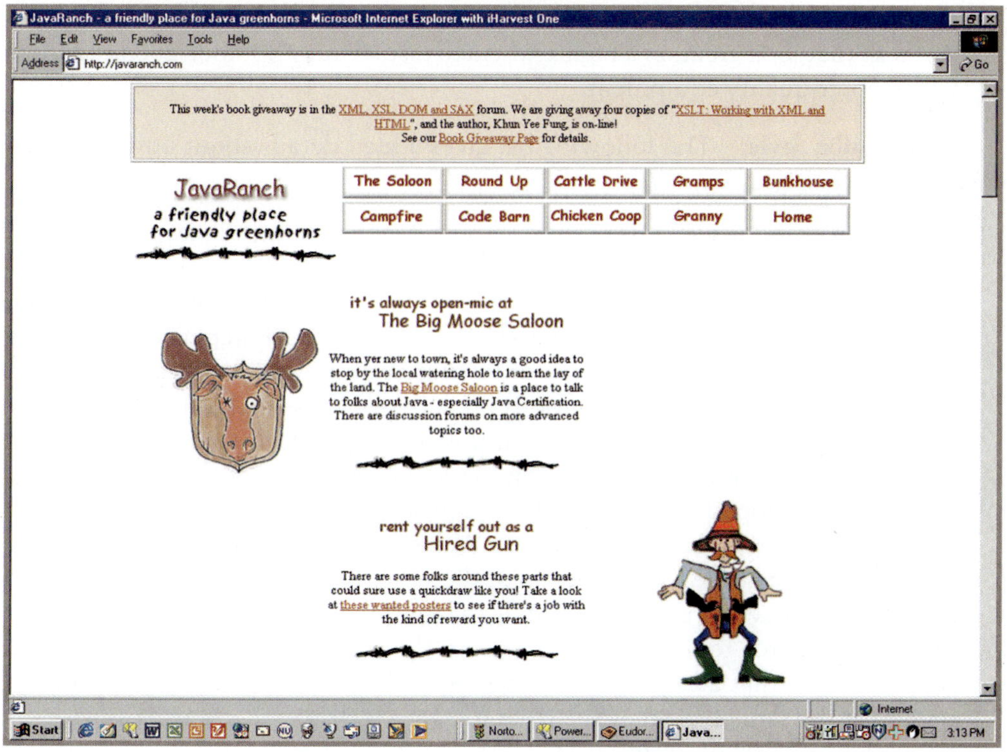

FIGURE 11.19

A good Web site will use a main metaphor as an organizing principle.

increase the functionality of the site, and the additional features encourage users to bookmark their clients' Web sites because they provide valuable bonus content.

Text. Don't forget that text is important, too. Each Web page should have a title. Place meaningful words in the first sentence appearing on your Web page. Let people know that they have indeed navigated to the right Web site. Clear writing is especially important.

Graphics. The following list provides details about creating effective graphics for Web sites:

1. Use one of the most commonly used image formats, JPEG or GIF. JPEGs are best for photographs, and GIFs are best for artwork images. GIFs are limited to 256 colors but may include a transparent background, pixels that allow the background to show through the GIF image. GIF images may also be interlaced, meaning that the Web browser will show the image in successive stages, presenting a clearer image with each stage.

   Microsoft is introducing a format called Windows Media Player (WMP), which it would like to see replace JPEG in the future.
2. Keep the background simple and make sure users can read the text clearly. When using a background pattern, make sure that you can see the text clearly on top of it.
3. Create a few professional-looking graphics for use on your pages.
4. Keep graphic images small, and reuse bullet or navigational buttons such as BACK, TOP, EMAIL, and NEXT. These images are stored in a cache, an area on the browsing computer's hard drive. Once an image has been received, it will be taken from the cache whenever it is used again. Using cached images improves the speed with which a browser can load a Web page.
5. Include text in what is called an ALT attribute for images and image hot spots. The text displays when the user moves the mouse over the image and is essential to support Web accessibility for visually impaired site visitors.

6. Examine your Web site on a variety of displays and screen resolutions. Scenes and text that look great on a high-end video display may not look good to others with poorer-quality equipment.

Presentation Style. The following list gives added details about how to design engaging entry displays for Web sites:

1. Provide an entry display (also called a home page) that introduces the visitor to the Web site. The page must be designed to load quickly. A useful rule of thumb is to design a page that will load in 14 seconds. Many users, especially in rural areas, have at best a 56K modem. (Although you may be designing the page on a workstation at the university, a visitor to your Web site may be accessing it from home.) This entry display should be 100 kilobytes or less, including all graphics.

   The entry page should contain a number of choices, much like a menu. An easy way to accomplish that is to design a set of buttons and position them on the left side or the top of the screen. These buttons can be linked to other pages on the same Web site or linked to different Web sites. A text menu may be included in a smaller font at the top or bottom of the page. An example of this is shown in Figure 11.20, an entry page that contains a large image and some content but that directs the visitor to journey elsewhere in the site. This page was constructed with software that allows designers to see HTML code (at the bottom of the screen) at the same time they see what the page would look like in a browser.
2. Keep the number of graphics to a reasonable minimum. It takes additional download time to transfer a graphics-intensive site.
3. Use large and colorful fonts for headings.
4. Use interesting images and buttons for links. A group of images combined into a single image is called an image map, which contains various hot spots that act as links to other pages.
5. Use cascading style sheets (CSS) to control the formatting and layout of the Web page. CSS separates the content (the text and images) from how they look (the presentation). Cascading style sheets are commonly stored in a file

FIGURE 11.20

Using a visual HTML editor (in this example, Visual Page), a Web site designer can see what a page looks like in a browser and the HTML Code (see bottom of screen) at the same time.

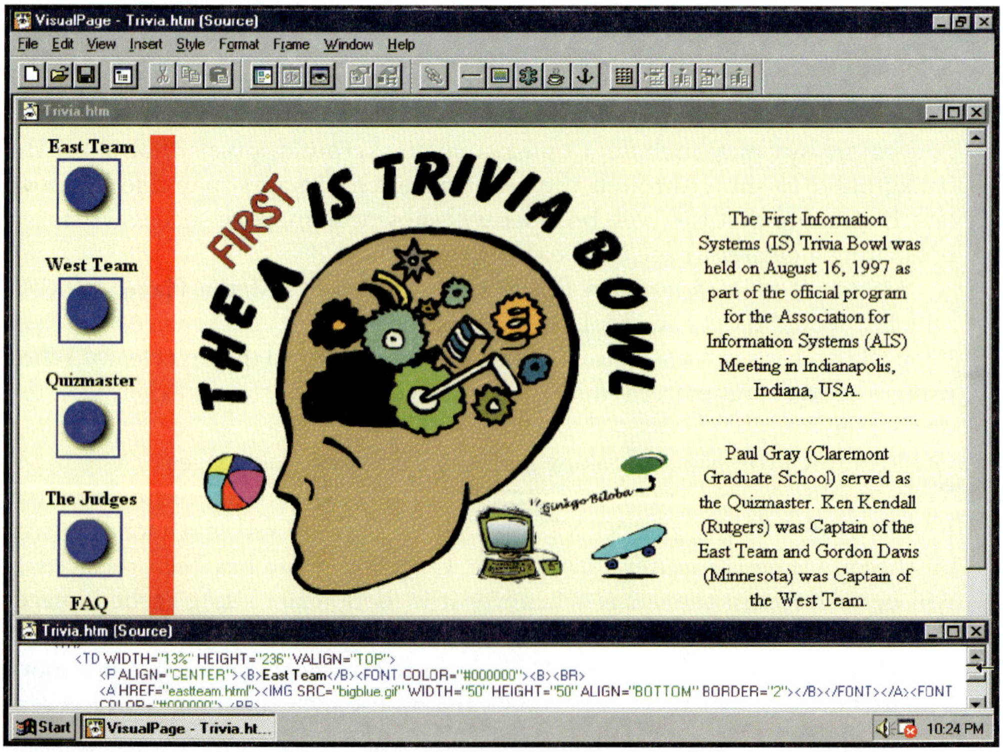

external to the Web page, and one style sheet may control the formatting of many pages. An advantage of using external style sheets is making a change in the style sheet, for example, changing the color of bold text will change the formatting of all the Web pages that use the style sheet. Cascading style sheets may also be used in a single Web page, and any duplicate styles will override an external style sheet if one is used. This allows the designer to vary from the standard look and feel of a Web site, perhaps for a "special sale" Web page or some other exception. Styles may be added to individual items on a Web page, overriding any other style sheets.

6. Use divisions and cascading styles or tables to enhance a layout. Tables are easy to use and provide adequate layout. However, tables are not well suited for visually impaired visitors. Screen reading software reads across the page, not necessarily in a table column. Divisions control the layout by providing blocks of text on the Web page. Each block may be defined with a position from the top and left of the screen or a larger block, and it may have a width and height, as well as border style and background color. Divisions eliminate the need for tables within tables and simplify design; screen reading software will read all the text in the division, making the site accessible for visually impaired viewers.
7. Use the same graphics image on several Web pages. Consistency will be improved, and the pages will load more quickly because the computer stores the image in a cache and doesn't have to load it again.
8. Use JavaScript to enhance the Web page layout by having images that change when a mouse is moved over them, having menus expand, and so on. JavaScript may be used to reformat the Web page based on the height and width of the screen. If the Web site is multinational, JavaScript can detect the language being used (a browser setting) and redirect the viewer to a different Web page in a different language.
9. Avoid overusing animation, sound, and other elements.

Navigation. Is it fun for you to follow links on the Web? The answer most likely is that it depends. When you discover a Web site that loads easily, has meaningful links, and allows you to easily return to the places you want to go back to, then chances are you think it is fun. Fun is not just play; it can be an important part of work too. Recent research shows that fun can have a powerful effect on making computer training effective.

If, on the other hand, you can't decide which button or hot spot to push, and you are afraid to choose the wrong one because you might get into the wrong page that takes a long time to load, navigation is more painful than fun. An example is visiting a software company's page to find information about the features of the latest version of a product. You have choices such as products, download, FAQ, and tech support. Which button will lead to the answers you're looking for?

Most importantly, observe the three-clicks rule. A user should be able to move from the page they are currently on to the page containing the information they want in three clicks of the mouse button.

Promotion. Promote your site. Don't assume that search engines will find you right away. Submit your site every few months to various search engines. Include key words, called metatags that search engines will use to link search requests to your site. General information about metatags may be found at searchenginewatch.com/showPage.html?page=2167931. Free metatag generating software may be downloaded at www.siteup.com/meta.html, and a metatag builder may be found at vancouver-webpages.com/META/mk-metas.html. You can also purchase software to make this process easier. If you try to use email to promote your site, others will consider it junk email or spam.

CONSULTING OPPORTUNITY 11.4

A FIELD DAY

"The thing of it is, I get impatient," says Seymour Fields, owner of a chain of 15 highly successful florist shops/indoor floral markets called Fields that are located in three Midwestern cities. "See this thing here?" He taps his PC display irritatedly. "We do all the payroll and all the accounting with these things, but I don't use it like I should. I actually feel a little guilty about it. See?" he says, as he makes a streak on the display with his finger. "It's even got dust on it. I'm a practical person, though. If it's sitting here, taking up space, I want to use it. Or smell it, or at least enjoy looking at it, like flowers, right? Or weed it out, that's what I say. The one time I tried something with it, it was a real disaster. Well, look, I can show you if I still remember how." Seymour proceeds to try to boot a program, but can't seem to get it working.

Clay Potts, a systems analyst, has been working on a systems project for the entire Fields chain. Part of the original proposal was to provide Seymour and his vice presidents with a group decision support system that would help them devise a strategy to determine which European markets to visit to purchase fresh flowers, which outlets to ship particular kinds of flowers to, and how much general merchandise, such as planters, vases, note cards, and knickknacks, to stock in each outlet.

Seymour continues, "I can tell you what we disliked about the program I worked with. There were too many darn layers, too much foliage, or whatever you call it, to go through. Even with a screen in front of me, it was like paging through a thick report. What do you call that?"

"Menus?" Potts suggests helpfully. "The main point is that you didn't like having to go through lots of information to get to the display you needed."

Seymour Fields looks happily at Potts and says, "You've got it. I want to see more fields on each screen."

How should Potts design screen output so that Fields and his group can get what they want on each screen while observing the guidelines for good display design? Remember that the group members are busy and that they are infrequent computer users. Design a hyperlinked page that would work well in a DSS for the vice presidents. What should be included in the first display, and what should be stored in hyperlinks? List elements for each and explain in a paragraph why you have decided on this strategy.

Encourage your readers to bookmark your Web site. If you link to and suggest that they go to affiliated Web sites that feature the "best movie review page in the world" or to the "get music for free" Web site, don't assume they'll be coming back to your site in the near future. You will encourage them to revisit if they bookmark your site (bookmarks are called "favorites" on Microsoft Internet Explorer). You may add a **Click here to bookmark this page** link to your Web page to automate the process. You may also want to design a "favicon," or favorite icon, so that users can identify your site in their lists of favorites.

CREATING BLOGS (WEB LOGS)

Blogs, also called Web logs, are being written by corporate users for both internal and external communication. Blogs are informal and personal, and they often invite comments and feedback. They are easy to create and update and are designed to change daily. Companies are using blogs for advertising and to build social networks for consumers, clients, and vendors around their products, building trust and customer relationships.

Corporate blogs are monitored out of a sense of responsibility for the participants. Guidelines, policies, and laws that shape monitoring practices include shared cultural, ethical, and legal values such as respecting other employees and customers; not publishing any sensitive or secret corporate information or anything protected by copyright (without permission); and excluding anything that is hateful or profane or that violates anyone's privacy.

Even with all of the preceding guidelines, you still need to ensure that blog posts are written in a human voice, not immersed in legal language. The latest entry should be at the start of the blog. It should contain the following elements:

1. The permalink, or permanent link, specific for the blog post. The permalink should never change.
2. The headline or title of the post.
3. The primary link, which connects the reader to the subject under discussion.
4. An optional summary, often appearing after the link.
5. The blog text or commentary.
6. An optional image.
7. A block quote containing quotations or other material from other sources that contributes to the discussion (often indented or in a different font to set it apart from the main text).
8. Links for comments by other people.
9. Other blog software features, such as a calendar, search form, and other universal features.

OUTPUT PRODUCTION AND XML

Output production varies depending on the platform used to produce it. There are many different ways to create output, ranging from simple database software, such as Microsoft Access, to programs such as SAS, Crystal Reports, and Adobe Acrobat's PDF files.

We discussed XML in Chapter 8. One of the advantages of using XML is that the XML document may be transformed into different output media types. This is done using cascading style sheets (CSSs) or extensible style language transformations (XSLTs). These methods reinforce the idea that data should be defined once and used many times in different formats.

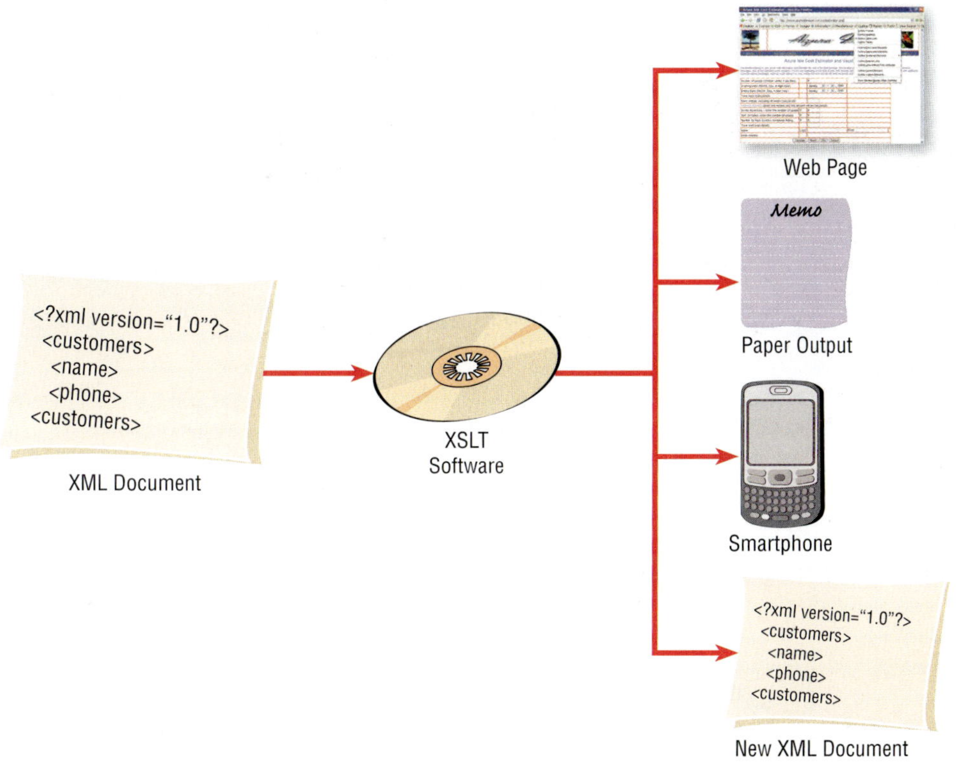

FIGURE 11.21
Extensible style language transformation (XSLT) software can be used to make XML documents and transform them into many different formats for a variety of platforms.

Cascading style sheets are an easy way to transform an XML document. The style sheet provides a series of styles, such as font family, size, color, border, and so on, that are linked to the elements of the XML document. These styles may vary for different media, such as a screen, printed output, or a handheld device. The transforming software detects the type of device and applies the correct styles to control the output.

For example, a style used for a flat-panel display might use a rich palette of colors and a sans serif font, which is easier to read on a screen. A different style using a serif font and black or gray color may be used to define a printed report for the same data. A smaller font size might be used for a handheld device or mobile phone.

The drawback of using cascading style sheets is that they do not allow the analyst to manipulate the data, such as rearranging the order of the elements or sorting, and only a limited amount of identifying text, such as captions, may be added. They are basically used for formatting.

FIGURE 11.22

An XML transformation with XML, on the left and the result of the transformation on the right. Only data between the tags are included in the output on the right.

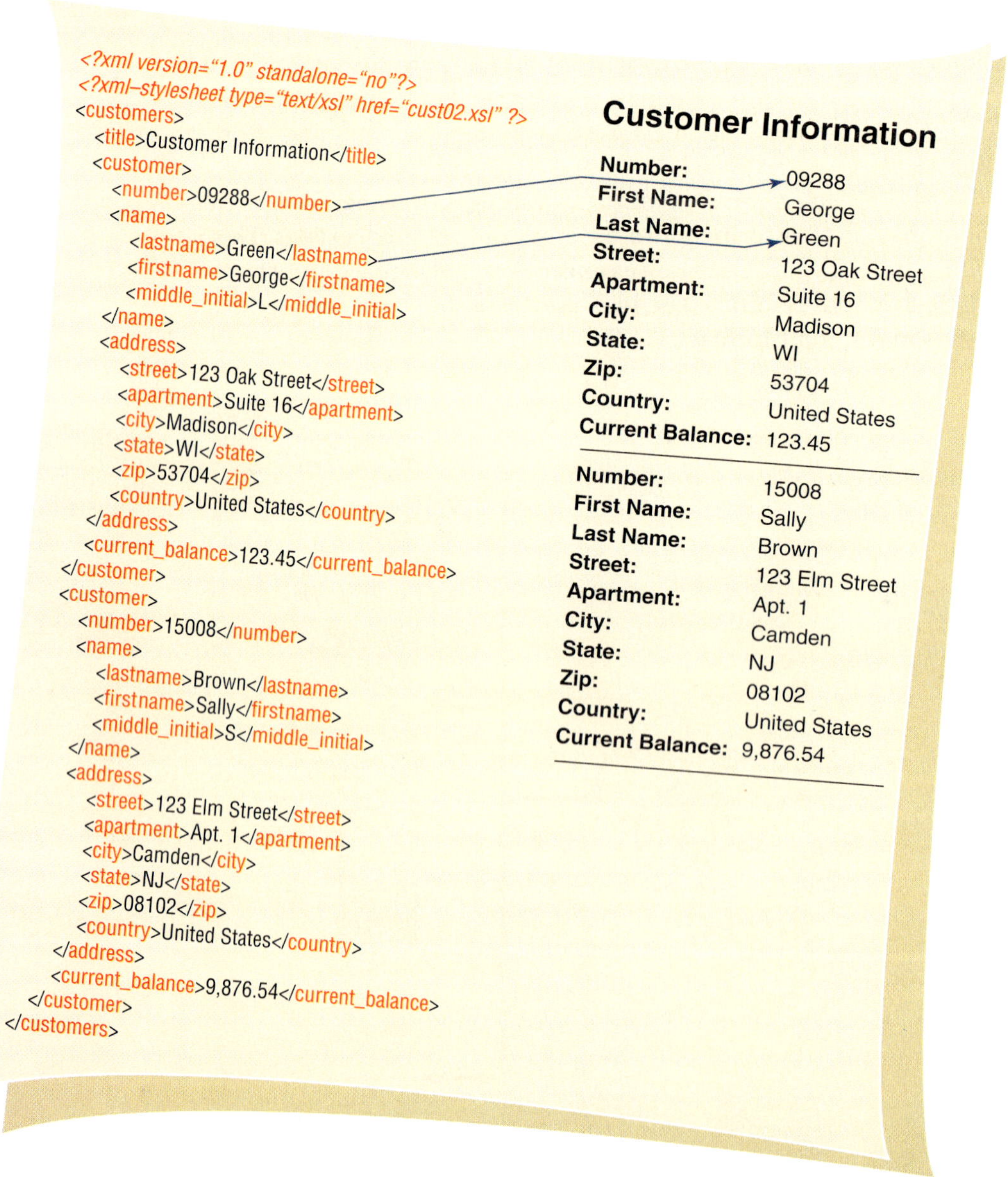

Extensible style language transformations (XSLT) are a more powerful means of transforming an XML document. They allow the analyst to select the elements and insert them into a Web page or another output medium. Figure 11.21 illustrates the transformation process. XSLT is not a programming language, but uses a series of statements to define which elements should be output, the sort sequence, the selection of data, and so on. An example of an XML transformation is illustrated in Figure 11.22. The XML is shown on the left, and the result of the transformation is shown on the right. Notice that only the data between the tags (the tags are the less than [<] and greater than [>] symbols) are included in the output.

AJAX

Another technique, called Ajax, uses both JavaScript and XML to obtain small amounts of data, either plain text or XML, from a server without leaving the Web page. This is a big advantage because it means that the entire Web page does not need to be reloaded. It works by allowing the Web page to reformat itself based on choices that a user inputs. Since Ajax is related to user input as well, it will be explained in more detail in Chapter 12.

Ajax is discussed here because the output implications are important as well. It is up to the analyst and designer to determine when data should be added or changed on a Web page and to identify the conditions that cause the change. The order in which the questions are asked plays into this design as well.

An example of a Web page using Ajax is shown in Figure 11.23, which demonstrates that Ajax makes it possible to display much less data on a page, thereby making the output less cluttered and less confusing. In this example, the user entered one of four ways to narrow down the search to view a list of current customers. The options the user had available were (1) enter the first three digits of a zip code (postal code), (2) enter a telephone area code, (3) select the

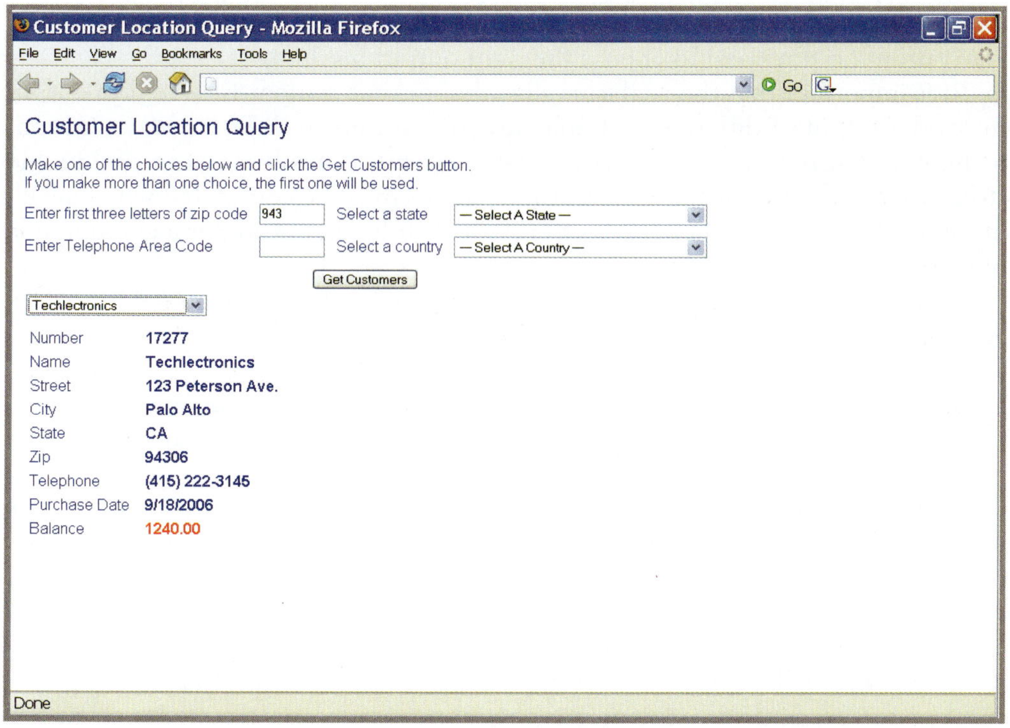

FIGURE 11.23
A Web page using Ajax makes it possible to display much less data on a page, allowing an uncluttered display.

state, or (4) select a country. The user may not know the postal code or area code and may therefore need to search by state or country, so the options are very useful.

After entering one of the location choices, in this case the first three digits of the postal code, the user clicked on the **Get Customers** button. The value of the postal code is sent to the server along with data indicating it was a postal code. The server then finds all customer records for the selected location, creates an XML document, and sends it to the same Web page.

When designing output, the systems analyst has many different options regarding how to display this data on the Web page. In this case, the systems analyst specified that the XML document would be used to create a drop-down list containing all current customers for the desired location. Once a user selects a customer from the drop-down list, more information about the particular customer is displayed, as shown in the example.

The advantage of using Ajax for displaying data is that the user does not have to wait for a new Web page to display after making a selection. The Ajax philosophy is to display limited questions for the user to answer on an incremental basis. This eliminates screen clutter. Once the user responds to an answer by making a choice, a new question may be generated. Because Ajax involves input as well as output, you can learn more about Ajax in Chapter 12.

SUMMARY

Output is any useful information or data delivered by the information system or decision support system to the user. Output can take virtually any form, including print, display, audio, microforms, CD-ROMs or DVDs, and Web-based documents.

The systems analyst has six main objectives in designing output. They are to design output to serve the intended human and organizational purpose, to fit the user, to deliver the right quantity of output, to deliver it to the right place, to provide output on time, and to choose the right output method.

It is important that the analyst realize that output content is related to output method. Output of different technologies affects users in different ways. Output technologies also differ in their speed, cost, portability, flexibility, accessibility, and storage and retrieval possibilities. All these factors must be considered when deciding among print, display, audio, electronic, or Web-based output, or a combination of these.

The presentation of output can bias users in their interpretation of it. Analysts and users must be aware of the sources of bias; Analysts must interact with users to design and customize output; must inform users of the possibilities of bias in output, must create flexible and modifiable output; and must train users to use multiple outputs to help verify the accuracy of any particular report.

Printed reports are designed with the use of computer-aided software design tools that feature form design templates and drag and drop interfaces. The data dictionary serves as the source for necessary data on each report.

Designing output for user displays is important, especially for decision support systems, as well as the Web. Once again, aesthetics and usefulness are important when creating well-designed output for displays. It is important to produce prototypes of screens and Web documents that allow users to interact with them and make changes where desired.

"I'd say the reception you received, or should I say your team received, for your proposal presentation was quite warm. How did you like meeting Mr. Hyatt? What? He didn't come? Oh [*laughing*], he's his own man. Anyway, don't worry about that too much. The reports I got from Snowden were encouraging. In fact, now he wants to see some preliminary designs from you all. Can you have something on his desk or his computer display in two weeks? He'll be in Singapore on business next week, but then when he recovers from the jet lag, he'll be looking for those designs. Thanks."

HYPERCASE QUESTIONS

1. Consider the reports from the Training Unit. What are Snowden's complaints about these reports? Explain in a paragraph.
2. Using either a layout paper form or a CASE tool, design a prototype output display based on the Training Unit's reports that will summarize the following information for Snowden:
   Number of accepted projects in the Training Unit.
   Number of projects currently being reevaluated.
   Training subject areas for which a consultant is being requested.
3. Design an additional output display that you think will support Snowden in the kind of decision making he does frequently.
4. Show your designs to three classmates. Get written feedback from them about how to improve the output displays you have designed.
5. Redesign the displays to capture the improvements suggested by your classmates. In a paragraph, explain how you have addressed each of their concerns.

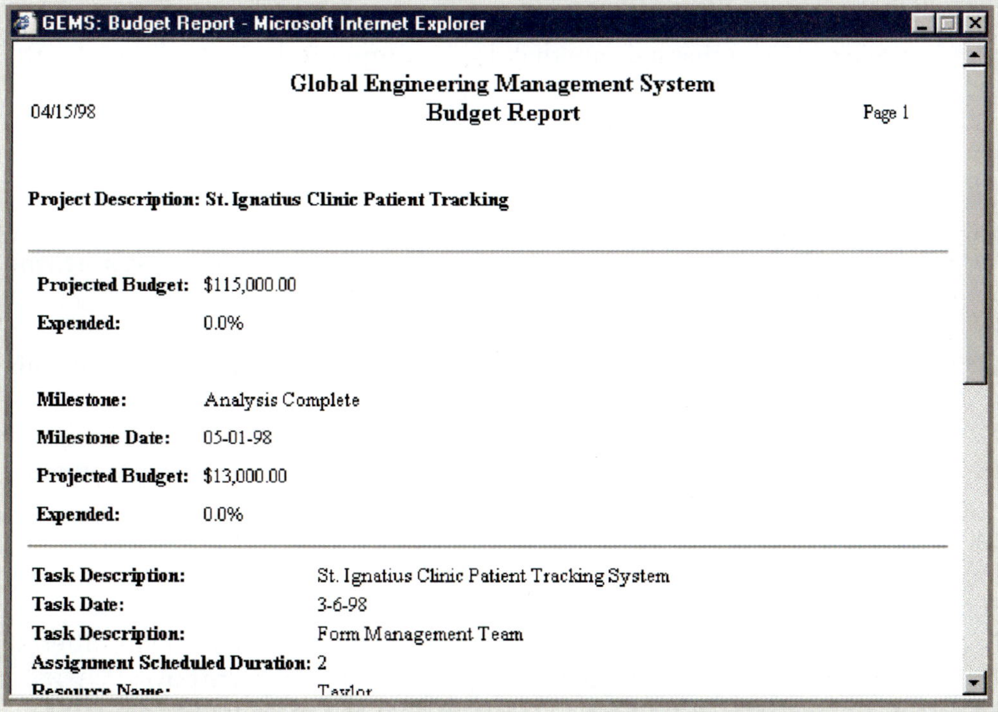
GEMS: Budget Report - Microsoft Internet Explorer

Global Engineering Management System
Budget Report

04/15/98 Page 1

Project Description: St. Ignatius Clinic Patient Tracking

Projected Budget: $115,000.00
Expended: 0.0%

Milestone: Analysis Complete
Milestone Date: 05-01-98
Projected Budget: $13,000.00
Expended: 0.0%

Task Description: St. Ignatius Clinic Patient Tracking System
Task Date: 3-6-98
Task Description: Form Management Team
Assignment Scheduled Duration: 2
Resource Name: Taylor

FIGURE 11.HC1
You have the ability to view and critique output screens in HyperCase.

KEYWORDS AND PHRASES

- Ajax
- audio output
- bookmark
- browser
- cascading style sheet (CSS)
- CD-ROM
- constant information
- dashboard
- display screen
- DVD
- electronic bulletin board
- electronic output
- email
- extensible style language transformation (XSLT)
- external output
- FAQ
- hyperlink
- hypertext
- internal output
- Java
- output bias
- output design
- plug-in
- podcasting
- RSS feeds
- stickiness
- uniform resource locator (URL)
- variable information
- Web/logs (blogs)
- Webmaster
- Web page
- Web site
- World Wide Web (WWW)

REVIEW QUESTIONS

1. List six objectives the analyst pursues in designing system output.
2. Contrast external outputs with internal outputs produced by the system. Remember to consider differences in external and internal users.
3. What are three situations that point to printers as the best choice for output technology?
4. Give two instances that indicate that display output is the best solution for the choice of output technology.
5. List potential electronic output methods for users.
6. What are the drawbacks of electronic and Web-based output?
7. List 10 factors that must be considered when choosing output technology.
8. What output type is best if frequent updates are a necessity?
9. What kind of output is desirable if many readers will be reading, storing, and reviewing output over a period of years?
10. What are two of the drawbacks to audio output?
11. List three main ways in which presentations of output are unintentionally biased.
12. What are five ways the analyst can avoid biasing output?
13. What is the difference between constant and variable information presented on a report?
14. Why is it important to show users a prototype output report or display?
15. List six functional elements of printed reports.
16. List five stylistic or aesthetic elements of printed reports.
17. In what ways do displays, printed output, and Web-based documents differ?
18. List four guidelines to facilitate the design of good display output.
19. What differentiates output for a DSS from that of a more traditional MIS?
20. What are the four primary considerations the analyst has when designing graphical output for decision support systems?
21. Define stickiness.
22. List seven guidelines for creating good Web sites.
23. List five guidelines for using graphics in designing Web sites.

24. List seven ideas for improving the presentation of corporate Web sites that you design.
25. What is the "three-clicks" rule?
26. In what ways can you encourage companies to promote their Web sites that you have developed?
27. How does a cascading style sheet allow the analyst to produce output?
28. What are the advantages of using XSLT instead of a cascading style sheet?
29. What are RSS feeds?
30. How can the Web administrator use RSS feeds?
31. What are dashboards mainly used for?
32. What are widgets (or gadgets)?
33. Why should a systems designer be aware of the popularity of widgets (or gadgets)?
34. How does a cascading style sheet allow the analyst to produce output?
35. What are the advantages of using an extensible style language transformation instead of a cascading style sheet?
36. How does Ajax help to build effective Web pages?

PROBLEMS

1. "I'm sure they won't mind if we start sending them the report on these oversized computer sheets. All this time we've been condensing it, retyping it, and sending it to our biggest accounts, but we just can't now. We're so understaffed, we don't have the time," says Otto Breth. "I'll just write a comment here telling them how to respond to this report, and then we can send it out."
    a. What potential problems do you see in casually changing external output? List them.
    b. Discuss in a paragraph how internal and external output can differ in appearance and function.
2. "I don't need to see it very often, but when I do, I have to be able to get at it quickly. I think we lost the last contract because the information I needed was buried in a stack of paper on someone's desk somewhere," says Luke Alover, an architect describing the company's problems to one of the analysts assigned to the new systems project. "What I need is instant information about how much a building of that square footage cost the last time we bid it; what the basic materials such as steel, glass, and concrete now cost from our three top suppliers; who our likely competition on this type of building might be; and who comprises the committee that will be making the final decision on who gets the bid. Right now, though, it's in a hundred reports somewhere. I have to look all over for it."
    a. Given the limited details you have here, write a paragraph to suggest an output method for Luke's use that will solve some of his current problems. In a second paragraph, explain your reasons for choosing the output method you did. (*Hint:* Be sure to relate output method to output content in your answer.)
    b. Luke's current thinking is that no paper record of the output discussed need be kept. In a paragraph, discuss what factors should be weighed before displayed output is used to the exclusion of printed reports.
    c. Make a list of five to seven questions concerning the output's function in the organization that you would ask Luke and others before deciding to do away with any printed reports currently being used.

3. Here are several situations calling for decisions about output content, output methodology, distribution, and so on. For each situation, note the appropriate output decision.
   a. A large, well-regarded supplier of key raw materials to your company's production process requires a year-end summary report of totals purchased from it.
   b. Internal brainstorming memos are circulated through the staff regarding plans for a company picnic and fundraiser.
   c. A summary report of the company's financial situation is needed by a key decision maker, who will use it when presenting a proposal to potential external backers.
   d. A listing of the current night's hotel room reservations is needed for front desk personnel.
   e. A listing of the current night's hotel room reservations is needed by the local police.
   f. A real-time count of people passing through the gates of Wallaby World (an Australian theme park) will be used by parking lot patrols.
   g. An inventory system must register an item each time it has been scanned by a wand.
   h. A summary report of merit pay increases allotted to each of 120 employees will be used by 22 supervisors during a joint supervisors' meeting, and subsequently when explaining merit pay increases to the supervisors' own departmental employees.
   i. Competitive information is needed by three strategic planners in the organization, but it is industrially sensitive if widely distributed.
   j. A casual style of conversation is needed to inform customers about powerful but seldom used features of a product.
   k. A historic district of a city wants to let visitors know about historical buildings and events.
   l. Storm warnings must be delivered to subscribers in a large geographical area.
4. "I think I see now where that guy was coming from, but he had me going for a minute there," says Miss deLimit. She is discussing a prototype of display output, one designed by the systems analyst, that she has just seen. "I mean, I never considered it a problem before if even as much as 20 percent of the total class size couldn't be fit into a class," she says. "We know our classes are in demand, and because we can't hire more faculty to cover the areas we need, the adjustment has to come in the student demand. He's got it highlighted as a problem if only 5 percent of the students who want a class can't get in, but that's okay. Now that I know what he means, I'll just ignore it when the computer beeps."
   a. In a sentence or two, describe the problem Miss deLimit is experiencing with the display output.
   b. Is her solution to "ignore the beeps" a reasonable one given that output is in the prototype stage?
   c. In a paragraph, explain how the display output for this particular problem can be changed so that it better reflects the rules of the system Miss deLimit is using.
5. Following is a log sheet for a patient information system used by nurses at a convalescent home to record patient visitors and activities during their shifts. Design a printed report using form design software that provides a summary for the charge nurse of each shift and a report for the activities coordinator at the end of a week. Be sure to use proper conventions to indicate constant data, variable data, and so on. These reports will be used to determine staffing patterns and future activities offerings.

Date	Patient	Visitors	Relationship	Activities
2/14	Clarke	2	Mother, father	Walked about halls, attended chapel, meals in cafeteria
	Coffey	6	Coworkers	Played games, party in room
	Martine	0	—	Meals in room
	Laury	4	Husband and friends	Games in sunroom, watched TV
	Finney	2	Parents	Conversation, meals in cafeteria
	Cartwright	1	Sister	Conversation, crafts room
	Goldstein	2	Sister, brother	Conversation, games out of room, whirlpool

6. Design display output for Problem 5 using form design software. Make any assumptions about system capability necessary and follow display design conventions for onscreen instructions. (*Hint:* You can use more than one display screen if you wish.)
   a. In a paragraph, discuss why you designed each report as you did in Problems 5 and 6. What are the major differences in your approach to each one? Can the printed reports be successfully transplanted to displays without changes? Why or why not?
   b. Some of the nurses are interested in a Web-based system that patients' families can access from home with a password. Design an output screen for the Web. In a paragraph, describe how your report had to be altered so that it could be viewed by one patient's family.
7. Clancy Corporation manufactures uniforms for police departments worldwide. Its uniforms are chosen by many groups because of their low cost and simple but dignified design. You are helping to design a DSS for Clancy Corporation, and it has asked for tabular output that will help it in making various decisions about what designers to use, where to market its uniforms, and what changes to make to uniforms to keep them looking up to date. The following table lists some of the data the company would like to see in tables, including uniform style names, an example of a buyer group for each style, and which designers design which uniform styles. Prepare an example of tabular output for display that incorporates these data about Clancy's. Follow proper conventions for tabular output displays. Use codes and a key where appropriate.

Style Name	Example Buyer	Designers
Full military	NYPD	Claudio, Rialtto, Melvin Mine
Half military	LAPD	Rialtto, Calvetti, Duran, Melvin Mine
Formal dress	Australian Armed Forces	Claudio, Dundee, Melvin Mine
Casual dress	"Miami Vice"	Johnson, Melvin Mine

8. Clancy's is interested in graphical output for its DSS. It wants to see a graphical comparison of how many of each style of uniform are being sold each year.
   a. Choose an appropriate graph style and design a graph for display that incorporates the following data:

	Full Military (percent of total)	Half Military	Formal Dress	Casual Dress
2002	50	20	20	10
2003	55	15	20	10
2004	60	15	15	10
2005	62	15	15	8
2006	65	10	15	10

   Be sure to follow proper design conventions for displays. Use codes and a key if necessary.
   b. Chose a second method of graphing that might allow the decision makers at Clancy's to see a trend in the purchase of particular uniform styles over time. Draw a graph for display as part of the output for Clancy's DSS. Be sure to follow proper design conventions for displays. Use codes and a key if necessary.
   c. In a paragraph, discuss the differences in the two onscreen graphs you have chosen. Defend your choices.
9. Derek Collard owns a number of cars used for racing. What performance measures does he need to develop to keep track of the performance of his driver, pit crews, and support staff?
10. Design a dashboard for Derek (Problem 9). Use appropriate types of charts and graphs to illustrate performance.
11. Design a dashboard for keeping track of a person's stock and portfolio. Think about how the dashboard could be used to make decisions about buying and selling stock. Remember that a client can have more than one stockbroker.
12. Gabriel Shanks runs a nonprofit theatre that produces seven plays per year in three theatres. Each play lasts eight weeks but can be extended four weeks if the show is a success. Design a dashboard for Gabriel, taking into consideration the different phases of putting on a performance as well as the need to sell as many tickets as possible. Don't forget that Gabriel is involved in theatre and is very visual. He doesn't like tables, however.
13. While Gabriel (from the previous problem) is taking care of various details during an ordinary day, he would like to keep up on theatre news in Manhattan, at the same time having some simple tools around to help him with his computer-related activities. What sort of widgets and gadgets would Gabriel need to do his job while having some simple computer-based tools always available?
14. Browse the Web to view well designed and poorly designed Web sites. Choose three examples of each. Comment on what makes the sites excellent or poor, using the critique form presented earlier in the chapter to compare and contrast them.
15. Propose a Web site for Clancy's, the uniform company described in Problems 7 and 8. Sketch by hand or use form design software to create a prototype of a Clancy's home page. Indicate hyperlinks, and include a sketch of one hyperlink document. Remember to include graphics, icons, and even sound or other media if appropriate. In a paragraph, describe who the intended users of the Web site are and state why it makes sense for Clancy's to have a Web presence.

16. Elonzo's Department Stores is a chain of about 50 retail stores, specializing in kitchen, bath, and other household items, including many decorative and fashionable items. Recently Elonzo's decided to automate its gift registry to allow wedding and other event guests to be able to browse for items that were selected by the wedding couple or others.
    a. Design a Web page that would allow customers to enter a zip code and find the nearest store.
    b. Design a Web page for customers to browse gifts and order them online. Do not include the actual ordering forms, simply the products. What sort of options should be available for customers? Include buttons or links to change the sort sequence in your design.
    c. Design a printed list that customers could request when they go to one of the stores. What sequences would be optimal for a customer trying to find items? Would all items requested by the wedding couple be included on the list? (*Hint:* Some may have been purchased already.)
17. Design an outline of a podcast for someone touring your university, college, or business. What sequence would you place the topics in? How much time would you allow for each campus or building location? Assume the party will arrive in the morning and sequence lunch into the podcast.
18. Design an airline flight reminder screen for a cell phone or other handheld device.
19. Design an Ajax style of Web page that would allow a dean at a community college to select part-time instructors. The dean should be able to select a discipline or a course and have the server send an XML document containing all the potential part-time instructors for the selection. The XML document should be used to populate a drop-down list of the instructor names. Clicking an instructor's name would display information about the potential instructor. Decide what information to include that would help the dean make a decision on whom to hire. (*Hint:* Part-time instructors may be able to teach only on certain days or only in the morning, afternoon, or evening.)

GROUP PROJECTS

1. Brainstorm with your team members about what types of output are most appropriate for a variety of executives and high-level managers of Dizzyland, a large theme park in Florida. Include a list of environments or decision-making situations and types of output. In a paragraph, discuss why the group suggested particular options for output.
2. Have each group member design an output display or form for the output situations you listed in Group Project 1. (Use either a CASE tool or paper layout form to complete each display or form.)
3. Create a dashboard for Dizzyland in Group Project 1.
4. Design a Web site, either on paper or using software with which you are familiar, for Dizzyland in Group Project 1. Although you may sketch documents or graphics for three levels of pages and required hyperlinks on paper, create a prototype home page for Dizzyland, indicating hyperlinks where appropriate. Obtain feedback from other groups in your class and modify your design accordingly. In a paragraph, discuss how designing a Web site is different from designing displays for other online systems.
5. Use brainstorming to develop a new set of widgets (gadgets) to be more productive. Come up with a list of your top five bright ideas for new widgets.

SELECTED BIBLIOGRAPHY

Davenport, T. H. "Saving IT's Soul: Human-Centered Information Management." *Harvard Business Review*, March–April 1994, pp. 119–131.

Davis, G. B., and H. M. Olson. *Management Information Systems, Conceptual Foundations, Structure, and Development*, 2d ed. New York: McGraw-Hill, 1985.

Fahey, M. J. *Web Publishers Design Guide for Windows.* Scottsdale, AZ: Coriolis Group, 1997.

Jarvenpaa, S. L., and G. W. Dickson. "Myth vs. Facts about Graphics in Decision Making." *Spectrum*, Vol. 3, No. 1, February 1986, pp. 1–3.

Laudon, K. C., and J. P. Laudon. *Management Information Systems*, 9th ed. Upper Saddle River, NJ: Prentice Hall, 2006.

McCombie, K. "Connecting Your Enterprise LAN to the Internet." *Internet World*, June 1994.

Merholz, P. "10 Hottest Web Designers and Design Houses." *The Net*, Vol. 2, Issue 1, No. 6, 1996, p. 46.

Pring, R. *www.type: Effective Typographic Design for the Worldwide Web.* New York: Watson-Guptill, 2000.

Quarterman, J. S. "What Can Businesses Get Out of Internet." *Computerworld*, February 22, 1993.

Siegel, D. *Creating Killer Web Sites*, 2d ed. New York: Hayden, 2001.

Weinman, L. *Designing Web Graphics 4: How to Prepare Images and Media for the Web*, 4th ed. Indianapolis, IN: New Riders Publication, 2002.

ALLEN SCHMIDT, JULIE E. KENDALL, AND KENNETH E. KENDALL

REPORTING ON OUTPUTS

"Let's create output specifications and then work backward through the data flow to determine the corresponding input data," says Anna during her next meeting with Chip.

"Of course," Chip agrees.

Output was separated into two categories: reports and displays. Reports were further defined as external reports such as the USER SOFTWARE NOTIFICATION or internal reports such as the HARDWARE INVENTORY LISTING. Each report was further classified as a detailed, exception, or summary report.

Based on conversations with Paige Prynter, the analysts think the HARDWARE INVESTMENT REPORT has the highest priority. It is needed as soon as possible because the budget process will soon reach a critical phase and there are many requests for new hardware as well as upgrades for existing equipment.

The process used for creating the HARDWARE INVESTMENT REPORT is similar to the process for creating all reports. Chip examines the data flow diagrams for the new system and locates the data flow labeled HARDWARE INVESTMENT REPORT. Double clicking on the data flow line brings up the repository entry for this report.

"I'm really glad we took the time to document the prototype reports and displays when creating the data flow diagrams," remarks Chip. "I can easily identify the elements required to produce the report."

Chip places the cursor in a composition element and clicks the **Jump** key to display the details for each element.

"This is great," exclaims Chip. "It was a good idea to define all the elements as we learned about them."

Chip then proceeds to create a sample report using Access. After the first draft, Chip uses the **Print Preview** feature to preview the report.

"Hmmm," murmers Chip. "Some of the fields need rearranging, and the horizontal spacing needs some work."

The report design is modified and reviewed again. By the third try, the report is in its final form. The next step is crucial: Chip asks Paige to review the report and make any changes she likes. Chip asks, "Are there any additional columns or other data missing that would make for a more useful report? Are all the data on the report necessary?"

Paige studies the output for a few minutes and remarks, "Subtotals for each BRAND, including the NUMBER OF MACHINES and grand totals, are necessary. We receive requests for different types of machines, and knowing how many of each machine may help determine what is purchased."

Chip returns to his computer and makes the necessary changes. The final HARDWARE INVESTMENT REPORT sample is shown in Figure E11.1. This version is again reviewed by Paige, and she signs off on the layout as complete.

The logic for this summary report is outlined in a process specification. The COMPUTER MASTER file is sorted by MODEL within BRAND. Records are read from the COMPUTER MASTER file, and totals for each BRAND and MODEL are accumulated. When either BRAND or MODEL changes, a report line is printed. When a change in BRAND occurs, BRAND SUBTOTALS are printed. GRAND TOTALS are printed after all records are processed.

11

1/12/04 Hardware Investment Report Page 1 of 1

Brand Name	Model		Number of Machines	Total Invested
Xxxxxxxxxxxx	Xxxxxxxxxxxxxxxxxx		3	$29,997.00
		Brand Subtotal	3	$29,997.00
Xxxxxxxxxxxxxx	Xxxxxxxxxxxxxxxx		4	$39,996.00
Xxxxxxxxxxxxxx	Xxxxxxxxxxxxxxxxxx		2	$19,998.00
		Brand Subtotal	6	$59,994.00
Xxxxxxxxxxxxxxxx	Xxxxxxxxxxxxxxxx		3	$29,997.00
Xxxxxxxxxxxxxxxx	Xxxxxxxxxxxxxxxxxxxx		8	$79,992.00
		Brand Subtotal	11	$109,989.00
		Grand Total	20	$199,980.00

FIGURE E11.1
HARDWARE INVESTMENT REPORT sample output.

Anna spends some time speaking with Cher Ware about her report needs. Several printed reports are outlined when Cher asks the question, "Will I get reports on the computer display, ones that I can quickly view, that have the latest information?"

The discussion that follows results in the creation of several reports for display.

"How would you like to view the software categories?" asks Anna. "Would you like to see all the software on one large scrolling display?"

"Well, I would like to have some way of finding one category and then displaying all the software available for that category," replies Cher. "It would also be useful to be able to move to subsequent and previous categories."

Anna creates the SOFTWARE BY CATEGORY display by creating an Access form, shown in Figure E11.2. There is a button for finding records as well as buttons to move to the previous and next categories. In the lower area of the screen is an area to display multiple software packages for the category. The OPERATING SYSTEM field is stored as a code on the corresponding database table and is converted to the code description on the display.

Anna shows both Chip and Cher the completed display. "I'm impressed," exclaims Cher. "That's exactly what I need!"

At that moment, Hy Perteks saunters in. "What's going on?" he asks. After viewing the display, he remarks, "I've been involved in the intranet project underway. Is their any chance of getting some information posted to a Web page?"

"What do you have in mind?" inquires Chip.

"Well, I have been giving it some thought," replies Hy. "I envision that it would be useful for the faculty and staff to be able to look up information about the software courses we are planning to offer. Later we could add an intranet form for them to enroll in the courses."

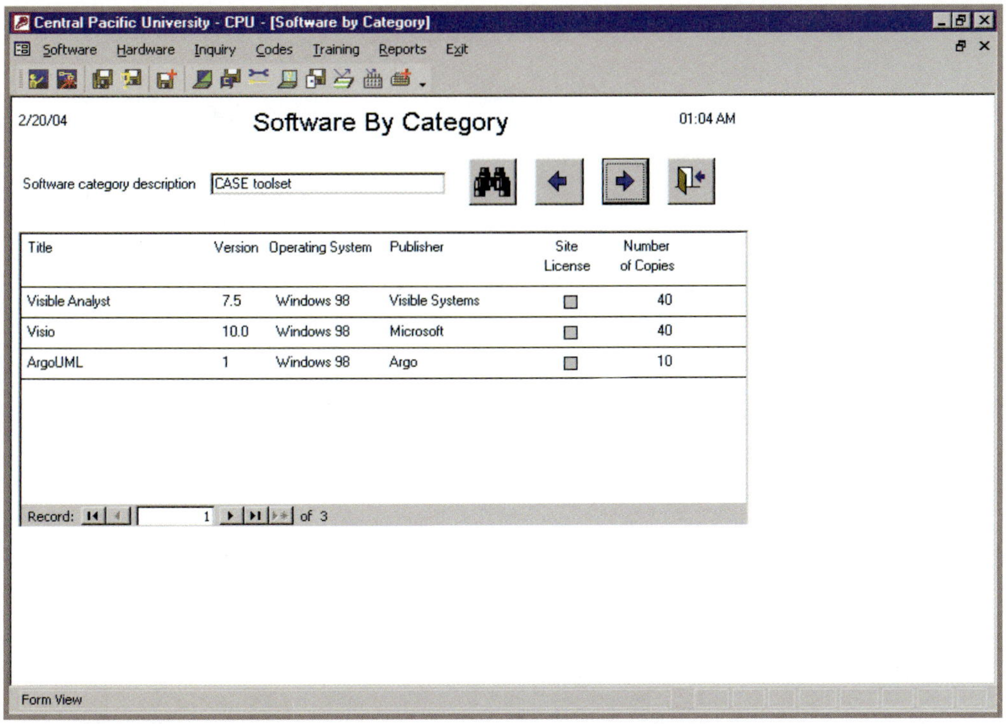

FIGURE E11.2
SOFTWARE BY CATEGORY Access display screen.

"I've heard a lot about the intranet and have created some prototypes for it," remarks Chip. "That would be a fun project to work on! We could include a link to the page from our Technology Support menus."

"Count me in on it," replies Anna. "I've been creating some Web pages myself. What would you like on the page?"

"I would like to create a main page that lists the courses, followed by other pages that list the level, such as beginning or intermediate, for the course and the dates that the courses start," replies Hy.

Chip and Anna set to work on the Web page. The fields are identified and grouped onto the TRAINING CLASSES OFFERED data flow, illustrated in Figure E11.3. Note that the Web address is included as an alias. Anna creates the final intranet Web page, illustrated in Figure E11.4. Chip and Hy review the page.

"I like the menus on the top of the page and the submenu that displays below it for specific features," remarks Chip.

"The calendar makes it very useful for the staff to view the currently scheduled courses by date, with buttons to change the month and year," comments Hy.

"Yes, and I think allowing the staff to change how the data are displayed is also very good. Many staff members like to view courses offered at their campus," remarks Chip.

"It would add some pizzazz if we include an image for the mascot," adds Hy, "and the university motto."

"I'll get right on it," replies Anna. "These are really good suggestions."

The final intranet display is finished and approved by Hy.

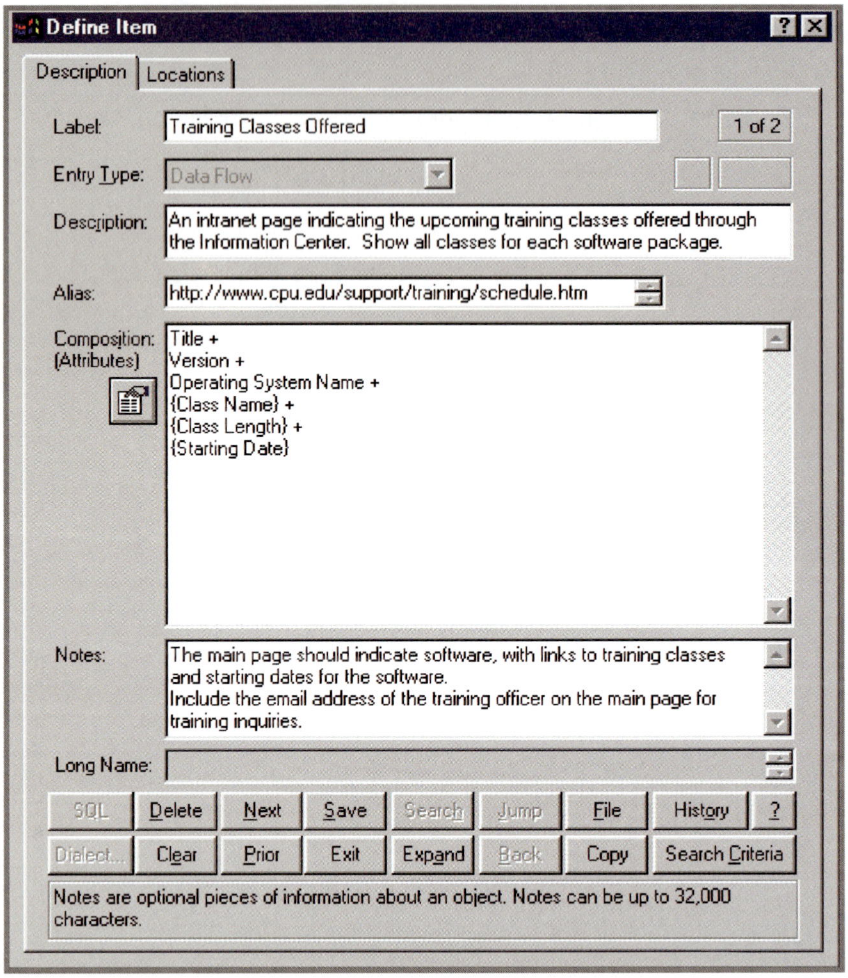

FIGURE E11.3
TRAINING CLASSES OFFERED data flow display screen.

"I'll put out an email to all the faculty and staff on the listserv," remarks Hy. "Thanks for including my email address. It should help to facilitate registering for courses and answering any questions. I think we are really making progress!"

The following exercises may be done by designing the report or display using layout forms, or they may be created using any word processor with which you are familiar. The fields and other related information for the reports are contained in Visible Analyst data flow repository entries. The names for the data flow are listed for each exercise.

Corresponding reports and displays (called forms in Microsoft Access) have been created. All the information is present in the Microsoft Access database; you only have to modify the existing reports and screens to produce the final versions. Modifications are made by clicking on the desired report or screen and then clicking the **Design** button. The following modifications may be made. The **Page Header** contains column headings. The **Detail** area contains the print fields for the report.

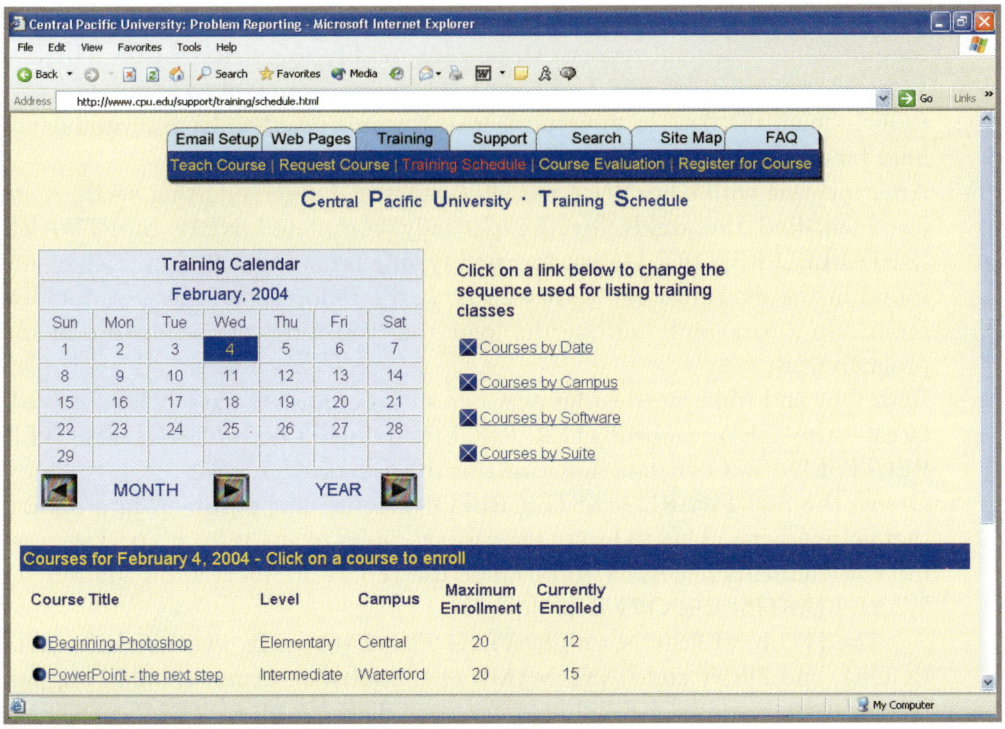

FIGURE E11.4

An intranet Web page for Central Pacific University.

Click in a field to select it. Click on several fields while holding the shift key to select them.

Drag a selected field (or fields) to move them.

Click on one of the small boxes surrounding the field to change the field size.

Select several fields and click **Format** and one of the following:

- **Align,** to align all fields with the top, left, and so forth field.
- **Size,** to make fields equal to the widest, tallest, and so forth field.
- **Horizontal Spacing,** to make horizontal spacing equal or to increase or decrease the spacing.
- **Vertical Spacing,** to make vertical spacing equal or to increase or decrease the spacing.

EXERCISES

E-1. Use Access to view the HARDWARE INVESTMENT REPORT. If you are familiar with Access, use the **File/Export . . .** menu option to save the report as a Web page. When the **Export** dialogue box opens, click in the **Save As Type** drop-down list and select **HTML Documents.**

The exercises preceded by a Web icon indicate value-added material is available from the Web site at www.prenhall.com/kendall. Students can download a sample Visible Analyst Project and a Microsoft Access database that can be used to complete the exercises. Visible Analyst software can be packaged with this text for an additional fee.

E-2. Chip, Dot, and Mike participated in several brainstorming sessions resulting in the outlining of several reports. Design (or modify using Access) the HARDWARE MASTER REPORT. This report is large, and you will have to be careful to include all the data in the report area. You may want to have several detail lines for each record. Print the completed report.

E-3. After meeting with Cher Ware and Hy Perteks to discuss reporting needs, Anna has identified the fields for the partially completed NEW SOFTWARE INSTALLED REPORT. Design (or modify) the report to include the elements found in the data flow repository entry. Is the report a summary or detailed report? In a paragraph, outline the logic that you think the report-producing program must use.

E-4. Both Dot and Mike need to know when new computers have been received. Create the NEW COMPUTER RECEIVED REPORT. The COMPUTER RECEIVED REPORT data flow contains the necessary elements.

E-5. Design the SOFTWARE MASTER REPORT containing pertinent information that helps Cher and Hy to locate the various copies of any software package easily. The elements necessary to produce the report are located on the SOFTWARE MASTER REPORT data flow.

The TITLE, VERSION, OPERATING SYSTEM NAME, PUBLISHER, CATEGORY, and FIRST and LAST NAME of the software expert should be group printed. Totals are to be included for each TITLE/OPERATING SYSTEM/VERSION combination. Print the completed report design.

E-6. Design the HARDWARE INVENTORY LISTING, showing the software available in each room at each campus. The CAMPUS field should be the CAMPUS DESCRIPTION, not the code representing the campus.

E-7. Design the INSTALLED COMPUTER REPORT, showing personal computers that have been installed in each room. Use the CAMPUS DESCRIPTION and group print by CAMPUS DESCRIPTION and ROOM LOCATION. The INSTALLED BOARDS is a repeating group, with up to five entries per computer.

E-8. Use Access to view the SOFTWARE BY CATEGORY screen report. Click the **Find** button and locate **CASE toolset.** Click the **Next** and **Previous** buttons to view next and previous **Software Categories.**

E-9. Design the SOFTWARE BY MACHINE screen report. Refer to the data flow repository entry for elements.

E-10. Design the COMPUTER PROBLEM REPORT. This report shows all computers that have a large number of repairs or a large repair cost. Refer to the repository description for the data flow for the elements or modify the Access report.

E-11. Design or modify the INSTALLATION REPORT. Refer to the repository entry for the data flow for the elements. This report shows which computers have been recently received and are available for installation.

E-12. Design the NEW COMPUTER RECEIVED REPORT. Refer to the repository description for the data flow for the elements or modify the Access report. This summary report shows the number of computers of each brand and model. These computers need to be unpacked and have component boards and other hardware installed in them before they may be installed in rooms.

E-13. Design or modify the PREVENTIVE MAINTENANCE REPORT. Refer to the repository entry for the data flow for the elements. This report shows which computers need to have preventive maintenance performed on them.

E-14. Design the SOFTWARE CROSS REFERENCE REPORT. Refer to the repository description for the data flow for the elements or modify the Access report. This report shows the computer in which each software package is installed. The TITLE, VERSION, OPERATING SYSTEM MEANING, and PUBLISHER are group printed. The detail lines under the group contain data showing the machine, installation campus, and room.

E-15. Design or modify the OUTSTANDING COMPUTER PURCHASE ORDERS REPORT. Refer to the repository entry for the data flow for the elements. This report would be produced for all PURCHASE ORDER records that have a purchase order code of M101, representing computers, with the additional condition that the QUANTITY ORDERED on the record must be greater than the QUANTITY RECEIVED. In a paragraph, state whether this report is a summary, exception, or detailed report. Explain.

E-16. Design the SOFTWARE INVESTMENT REPORT. Refer to the repository description for the data flow for the elements or modify the Access report.

DESIGNING EFFECTIVE INPUT

12

Learning Objectives

Once you have mastered the material in this chapter you will be able to:

1. **Design functional input forms for users of business systems.**
2. **Design engaging input displays for users of information systems.**
3. **Design useful input forms for people interacting on the Web.**
4. **Design useful input pages for users of intranets and the Internet.**

Users deserve quality output. The quality of system input determines the quality of system output. It is vital that input forms, displays, and interactive Web documents be designed with this critical relationship in mind.

Well-designed input forms, displays, and interactive Web fill-in forms should meet the objectives of effectiveness, accuracy, ease of use, consistency, simplicity, and attractiveness. All these objectives are attainable through the use of basic design principles, the knowledge of what is needed as input for the system, and an understanding of how users respond to different elements of forms and displays.

Effectiveness means that input forms, input displays, and fill-in forms on the Web all serve specific purposes for users of the information system, whereas accuracy refers to design that ensures proper completion. Ease of use means that forms and displays are straightforward and require no extra time for users to decipher. Consistency means that all input forms, whether they are input displays or fill-in forms on the Web, group data similarly from one application to the next, whereas simplicity refers to keeping those same designs uncluttered in a manner that focuses the user's attention. Attractiveness implies that users will enjoy using input forms because of their appealing design.

GOOD FORM DESIGN

The systems analyst should be capable of designing a complete and useful form. Unnecessary forms that waste an organization's resources should be eliminated.

Forms are important instruments for steering the course of work. They are preprinted papers that require people to fill in responses in a standardized way. Forms elicit and capture information required by organizational members that will often be input to the computer. Through this process, forms often serve as source documents for users or for input to ecommerce applications that humans must enter.

To design forms that people find useful, four guidelines for form design should be observed:

1. Make forms easy to fill in.
2. Ensure that forms meet the purpose for which they are designed.
3. Design forms to ensure accurate completion.
4. Keep forms attractive.

Each of the four guidelines is considered separately in the following sections.

MAKING FORMS EASY TO FILL IN

To reduce error, speed completion, and facilitate the entry of data, it is essential that forms be easy to fill in. The cost of the forms is minimal compared with the cost of the time employees spend filling them in and then entering data into the information system. It is often possible to eliminate the process of transcribing data that are entered on a form into the system by using electronic submission. That method often features data keyed in by users themselves, who visit Web sites set up for informational or ecommerce transactions.

Form Flow Designing a form with proper flow can minimize the time and effort expended by employees in form completion. Forms should flow from left to right and top to bottom. Illogical flow takes extra time and is frustrating. A form that requires people to go directly to the bottom of the form and then skip back up to the top for completion exhibits poor flow.

Seven Sections of a Form A second method that makes it easy for people to fill out forms correctly is logical grouping of information. The seven main sections of a form are the following:

1. Heading.
2. Identification and access.
3. Instructions.
4. Body.
5. Signature and verification.
6. Totals.
7. Comments.

Ideally, these sections should appear on a page grouped as they are in Figure 12.1. Notice that the seven sections cover the basic information required on most forms. The top quarter of the form is devoted to three sections: the heading, the identification and access section, and the instructions section.

The heading section usually includes the name and address of the business originating the form. The identification and access section includes codes that may be used to file the report and gain access to it at a later date. (In Chapter 13, we discuss in detail how to access specially keyed information in a database.) This information is very important when an organization is required to keep the document for a specified number of years. The instructions section tells how the form should be filled out and where it should be routed when complete.

The middle of the form is its body, which composes approximately half of the form. This part of the form requires the most detail and development from the person completing it. The body is the part of the form most likely to contain explicit, variable data.

The bottom quarter of the form is composed of three sections: signature and verification, totals, and comments. Requiring ending totals and a summary of comments is a logical way to provide closure for the person filling out the form.

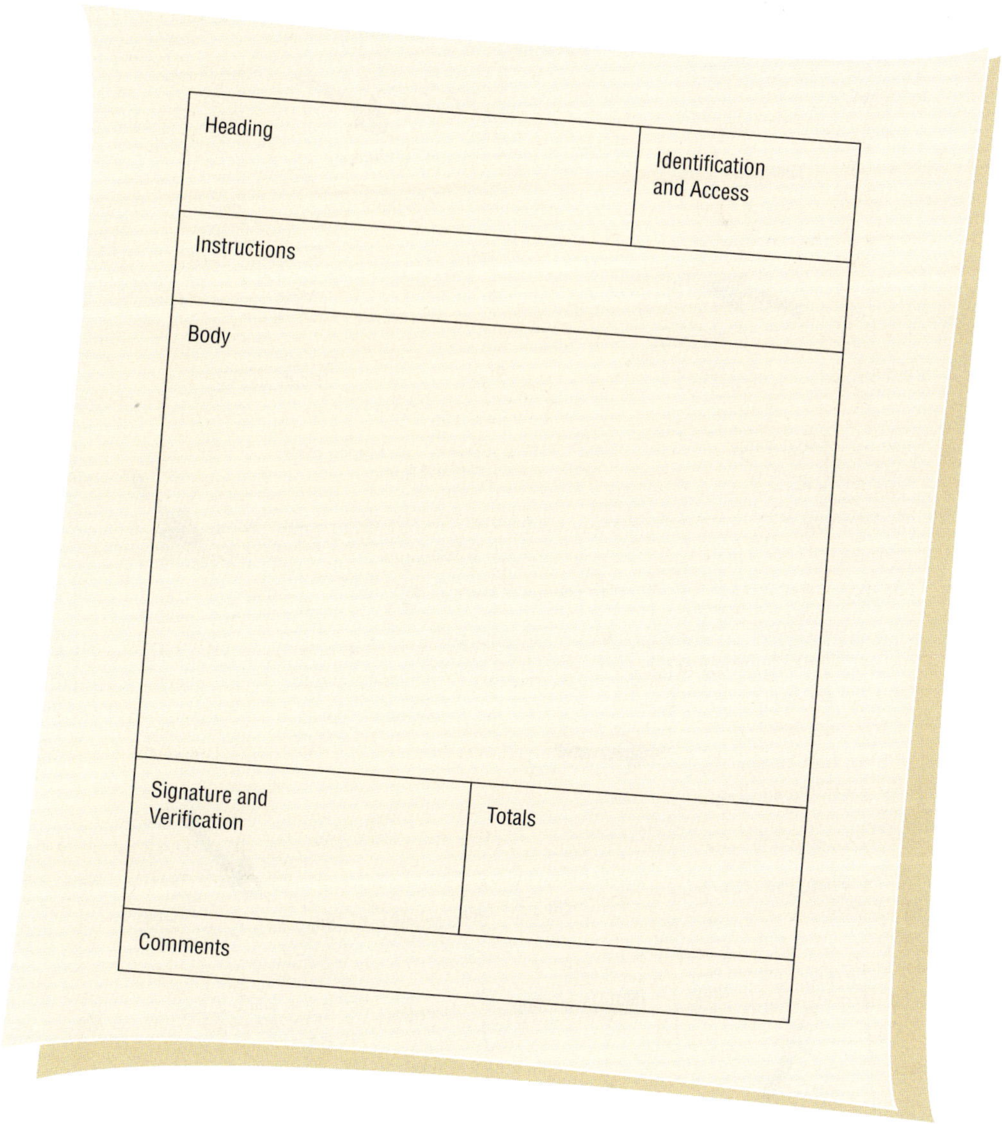

FIGURE 12.1

Seven sections found in well-designed forms.

Captioning Clear captioning is another technique that can make easy work of filling out a form. Captions tell the person completing the form what to put in a blank line, space, or box. Several options for captioning are shown in Figure 12.2. Two types of line captions, two types of check-off captions, and examples of a boxed caption and table caption are shown.

The advantage of putting the caption below the line is that there is more room on the line itself for data. The disadvantage is that it is sometimes unclear which line is associated with the caption: the line above or below the caption.

Line captions can be to the left of blanks and on the same line, or they can be printed below the line on which data will be entered.

Another way to caption is to provide a box for data instead of a line. Captions can be placed inside, above, or below the box. Boxes on forms help people enter data in the correct place, and they also make reading the form easier for the form's recipient. The caption should use a small type size so that it does not dominate the entry area. Small vertical tick marks may be included in the box if the data is intended for entry into a computer system. If there is not enough room on a record for the data, the person filling out the form, rather than the data entry operator, has the freedom to determine how the data should be abbreviated. Captions may also include small clarification notes to help the

FIGURE 12.2

Major captioning alternatives.

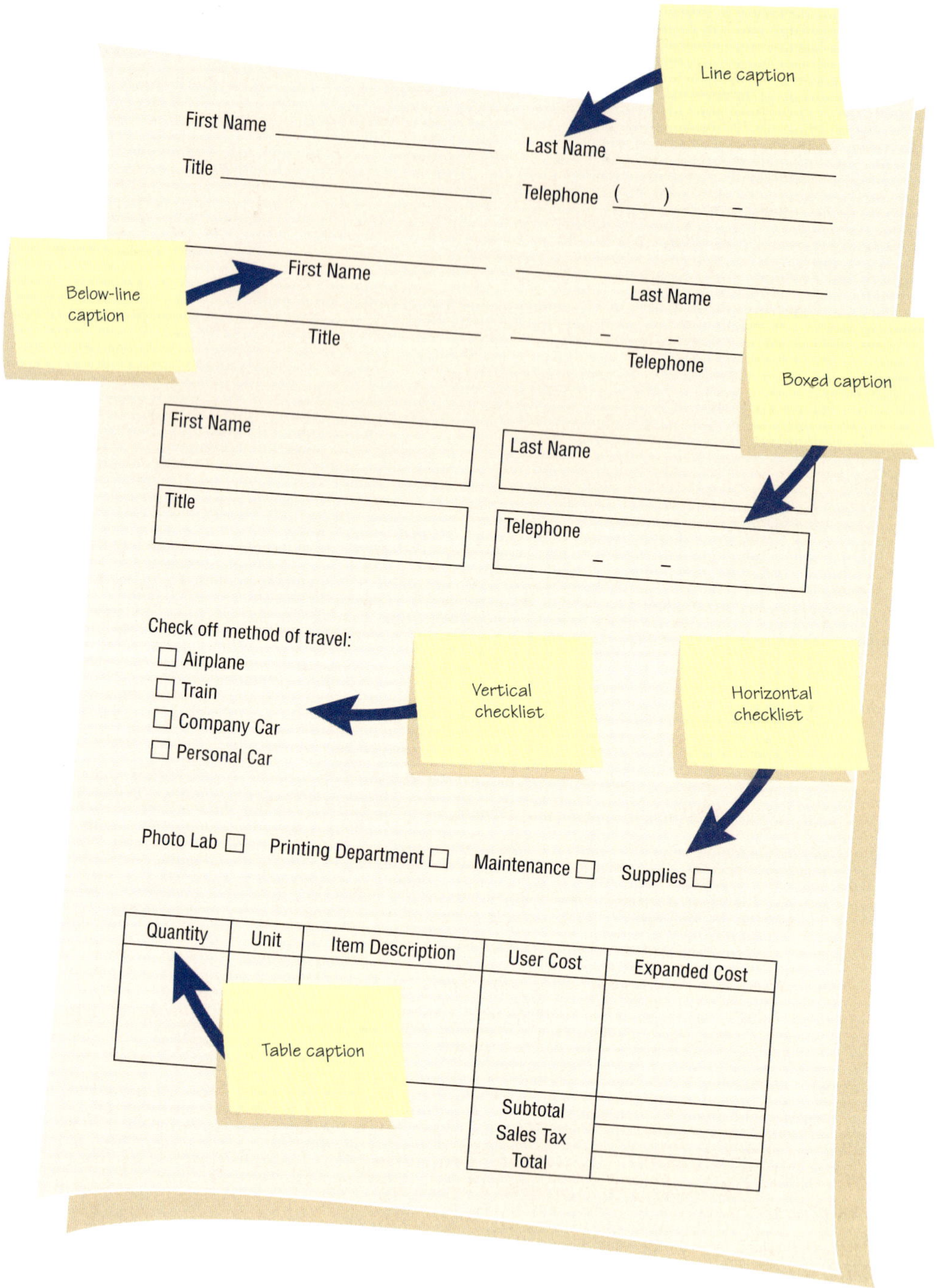

user correctly enter the information, such as Date (MM/DD/YYYY) or Name (Last, First, Middle Initial).

Whatever styles of line caption are chosen, it is important to employ them consistently. For instance, it is confusing to fill out a form that has both above- and below-line captions.

Check-off captions are superior when response options are necessarily restricted. Notice the list of travel methods shown for the vertical check-off example in the previous figure. If employee expenses for business travel are reimbursed only for those travel methods listed, a check-off system is more expedient than a blank line. This method has the added advantage of reminding the person who is verifying the data to look for an airline ticket stub or other receipt.

A horizontal check-off caption is also superior to a line caption when information required is routine and constant. An example is a form that would request services from one of the following departments: Photo Lab, Printing Department, Maintenance, or Supplies. The departments routinely provide services to others in the organization and are not likely to change quickly.

Table captions work well in the body of a form on which details are required. When an employee properly fills out a form with table captions, he or she is creating a table for the next person receiving the form, thereby helping to organize data coherently.

A combination of captions can also be used effectively. For example, table captions can be used to specify categories such as quantity, and line captions can be used to indicate where the subtotal, sales tax, and total should be. Because different captions serve different purposes, it is generally necessary to employ several caption styles in each form.

MEETING THE INTENDED PURPOSE

Forms are created to serve one or more purposes in the recording, processing, storing, and retrieving of information for businesses. Sometimes it is desirable to provide different information to different departments or users but still share some basic information. This situation is where specialty forms are useful.

The term *specialty form* can also refer solely to the way forms are prepared by the stationer. Examples of stationers' specialty forms are multiple-part forms that are used to create instant triplicates of data, continuous-feed forms that run through the printer without intervention, and perforated forms that leave a stub behind as a record when they are separated.

ENSURING ACCURATE COMPLETION

Error rates typically associated with collecting data will drop sharply when forms are designed to ensure accurate completion. Design is important for ensuring that people do the right thing with the form whenever they use it. When service employees such as meter readers or inventory takers use handheld devices to scan or otherwise key in data at the appropriate site, the extra step of transcription during data entry is avoided. Handheld devices use wireless transmission, or are plugged back into larger computer systems so they can upload the data that the service worker has stored. No further transcription of what has occurred in the field is necessary.

The Bakerloo Brothers employee expense voucher, shown in Figure 12.3, goes a long way toward securing accurate form completion by users. Many of the form design techniques we have discussed are used in this sample expense voucher. The form design implements the correct flow: top to bottom and left to right. It also observes the idea of seven main sections or information categories. In addition, the employee expense voucher uses a combination of clear captions and instructions.

Because Bakerloo Brothers employees are reimbursed only for actual expenses, getting a correct total expenditure is essential. The form design provides an internal double check, with column totals and row totals expected to add up to the same number. If the row and column totals don't add up to the same number, the employee filling out the form knows there is a problem and can correct it on the spot. An error is prevented, and the employee can be reimbursed the amount due; both outcomes are attributable to a suitable form design.

KEEPING FORMS ATTRACTIVE

Although attractiveness of forms is dealt with last, its order of appearance is not meant to diminish its importance. Rather, it is addressed last because making forms

FIGURE 12.3

A form that encourages accurate completion.

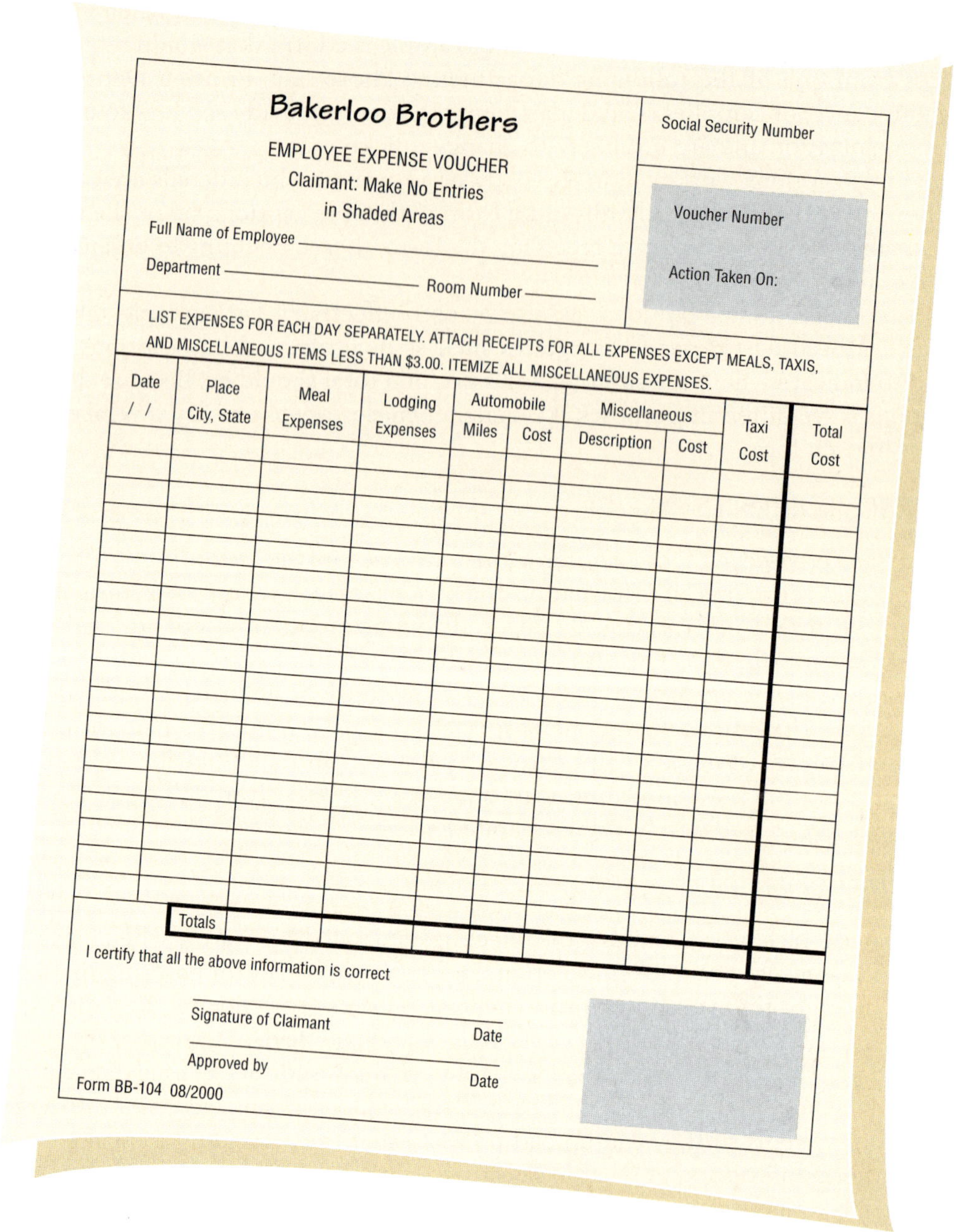

Bakerloo Brothers

EMPLOYEE EXPENSE VOUCHER

Claimant: Make No Entries in Shaded Areas

Social Security Number

Voucher Number

Action Taken On:

Full Name of Employee ____

Department ____ Room Number ____

LIST EXPENSES FOR EACH DAY SEPARATELY. ATTACH RECEIPTS FOR ALL EXPENSES EXCEPT MEALS, TAXIS, AND MISCELLANEOUS ITEMS LESS THAN $3.00. ITEMIZE ALL MISCELLANEOUS EXPENSES.

Date / /	Place City, State	Meal Expenses	Lodging Expenses	Automobile		Miscellaneous		Taxi Cost	Total Cost
				Miles	Cost	Description	Cost		
	Totals								

I certify that all the above information is correct

Signature of Claimant ____ Date

Approved by ____ Date

Form BB-104 08/2000

appealing is accomplished by applying the techniques discussed in the preceding sections. Aesthetic forms draw people into them and encourage completion.

Forms should look uncluttered. To be attractive, forms should elicit information in the expected order: convention dictates asking for name, street address, city, state, and zip or postal code (and country, if necessary). Proper layout and flow contribute to a form's attractiveness.

Using different type fonts in the same form can help make it appealing for users to fill in. Separating categories and subcategories with thick and thin lines can also encourage interest in the form. Type fonts and line weights are useful design elements for capturing attention and making people feel secure that they are filling in the form correctly.

COMPUTER-ASSISTED FORM DESIGN

Numerous form design packages are available for PCs. Some of the features of paper and electronic forms design software are given in Figure 12.4.

Features of Electronic Form Design Software

- Gives the ability to design paper forms, electronic forms, or Web-based forms using one integrated package
- Allows form design using form templates
- Enables form design by cutting and pasting familiar shapes and objects
- Facilitates electronic form completion through use of a companion data entry software package
- Permits customization of electronic form completion with the capability to customize menus, toolbars, keyboards, and macros
- Supports integration with popular databases
- Enables the sending and broadcasting of electronic forms
- Permits sequential routing of forms
- Assists tracking of routed forms
- Encourages automatic delivery and processing (push technology for forms)
- Allows the development of roles databases (that show relationships between people and types of information)
- Establishes security protection for electronic forms
- Takes scanned paper forms and permits publishing them to the Web
- Creates electronic fields automatically from scanned paper forms
- Permits form fill-in on the Web
- Allows calculations to be accomplished automatically

FIGURE 12.4
Software for electronic form design has many dynamic features.

Figure 12.5 is an example of a display created by OmniForm by ScanSoft. This software is enormously useful to an analyst seeking to automate quickly business processes for which paper forms are already in existence. Paper forms can be scanned in and then published to the Web. The analyst can use a set of tools to set up fields, check boxes, lines, boxes, and many other features.

Figure 12.6 shows the scanning process. The bottom of the split screen shows the form as it was scanned in, and the top portion of the screen shows an enlarged view of some of the fields automatically identified by the software. After scanning in a form, the analyst used a wizard to proofread, enhance, identify fields, and change the tab order so that the form could be used electronically.

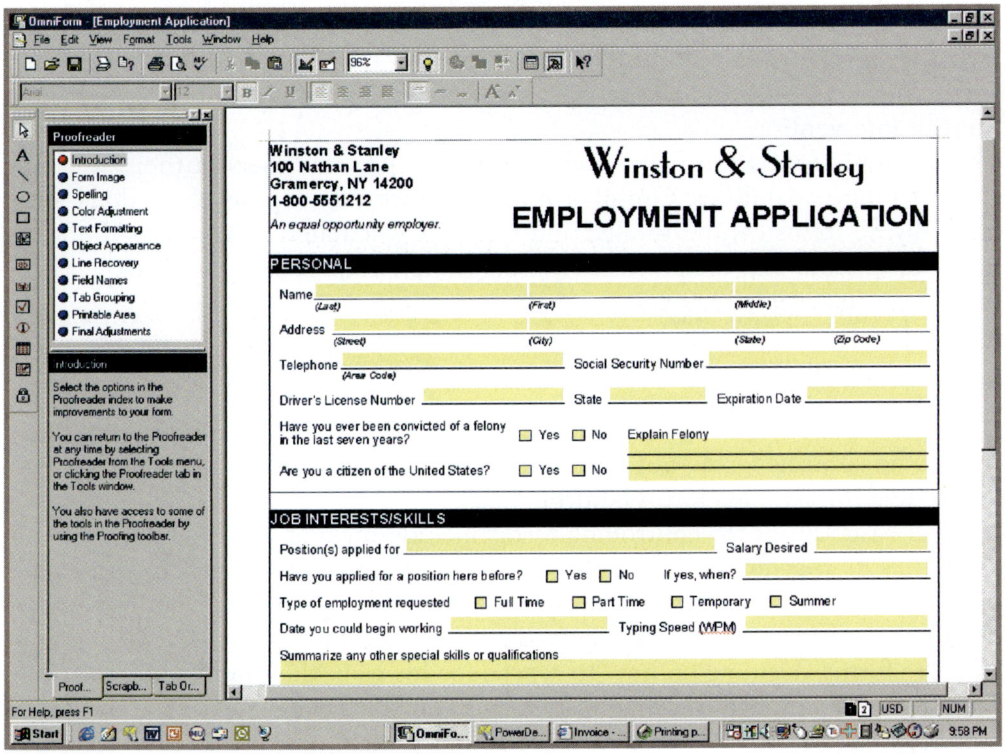

FIGURE 12.5
OmniForm from ScanSoft allows the user to take an existing form, scan it into the computer, and define fields so that the form can be easily filled out on a PC.

FIGURE 12.6

An example from OmniForm by ScanSoft of the scanning process, where fields are automatically generated by the software.

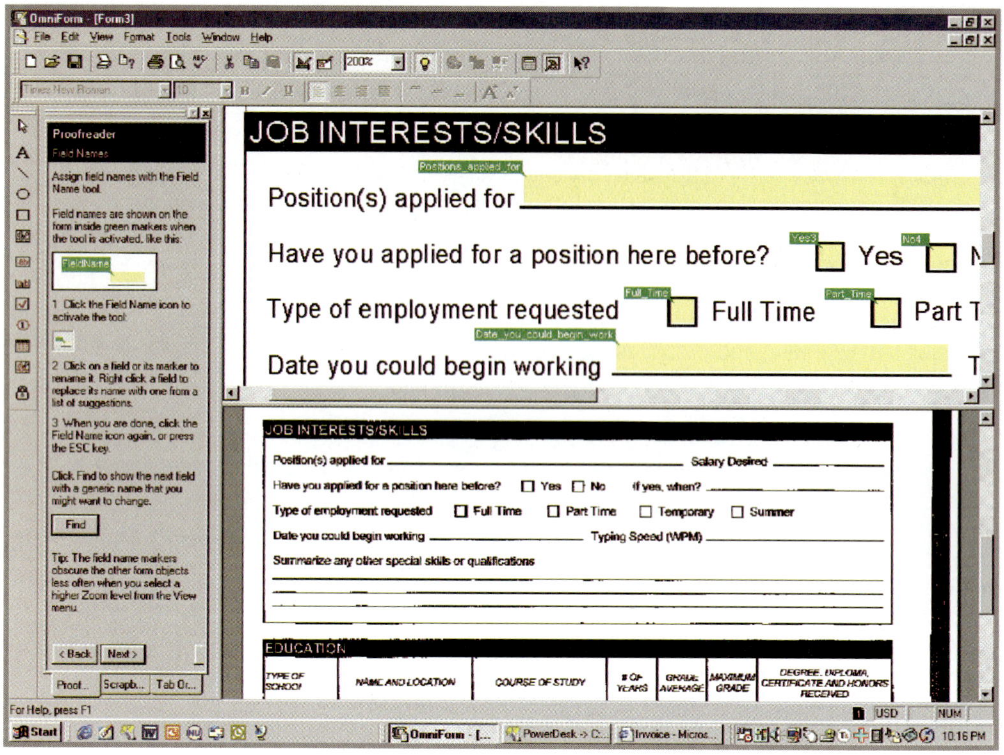

The functionality of the form is extended because OmniForm automatically creates field names for fields in forms that are scanned. Notice that when it is activated in this mode, the software displays the created fields in green. On the left side of the screen is a description of the field creation feature in this software. This description can dramatically speed up the automating of standard processes for cases in which time is limited and the desire for innovation may also be limited.

Once a form is scanned, it can be easily modified and published to the Web. ScanSoft currently offers a form hosting service called eOmniForm.com, at which you can store up to 10,000 filled records on the Web site. This service is an advantage not only in B2C ecommerce applications, but also in B2B applications. Furthermore, employees have easy access to company forms without extra administrative intervention.

Electronic forms can have intelligence that supports users in their tasks and extends their capabilities. OmniForm also enables calculations to be done automatically, so items can be totaled and sales tax calculated. It can also check the field and validate that the data are entered properly. An example is checking that a date is entered as 99/99/9999.

CONTROLLING BUSINESS FORMS

Controlling business forms is an important task. Businesses often have a forms specialist who controls forms, but sometimes this job falls to the systems analyst, who sets up and implements forms control.

The basic duties for controlling forms include making sure that each form in use fulfills its specific purpose in helping workers accomplish their tasks and that the specified purpose is integral to organizational functioning, preventing duplication of the information that is collected and of the forms that collect it, designing effective forms, deciding on how to reproduce forms in the most economical way, and establishing procedures that make forms available (when needed) at the lowest possible cost. Often this entails making forms available on the Web for printout.

A unique form number and revision date (month/year) should be included on each form, regardless of whether it is completed and submitted manually or electronically. This helps users be organized and efficient. Adobe LifeCycle Form Manager offers a custom portal to manage forms and a central repository to ensure that corporate employees will have access to correct versions of each form they need.

GOOD DISPLAY AND WEB FORMS DESIGN

Much of what we have already said about good form design is transferable to display design and the design of Web sites and Web pages. Once again, the user must remain foremost in the analyst's thoughts during the design of displays.

There are differences, however, and systems analysts should strive to realize the unique qualities of displays rather than to adopt blindly the conventions of paper forms. One big difference is the constant presence of a cursor on the display, which orients the user to the current data entry position. As data are entered onscreen, the cursor moves one character ahead, pointing the way.

Another major difference among electronic, Web, and static forms is that designers can include context-sensitive user help in any electronic fill-in form. This practice can reduce the need for instructions being shown for each line, thus reducing the clutter of the form and cutting down on calls to Technical Support. Using a Web-based approach also permits the designer to take advantage of hyperlinks, thus ensuring that the forms are filled out correctly by providing users with hyperlinked examples of correctly completed forms.

In this section, we present guidelines for effective display design. They are presented in order to aid the attainment of the overall input design goals of effectiveness, accuracy, ease of use, simplicity, consistency, and attractiveness.

The four guidelines for display design are important but not exhaustive. As noted in Chapter 11, they include the following:

1. Keep the display simple.
2. Keep the display presentation consistent.
3. Facilitate user movement among display screens and pages.
4. Create an attractive and pleasing display.

In the next subsections, we develop each of these guidelines, and we present many design techniques for observing the four guidelines.

KEEPING THE DISPLAY SIMPLE

The first guideline for good display design is to keep the display simple. The display should show only that which is necessary for the particular action being undertaken. For the occasional user, 50 percent of the display area should contain useful information.

Three Screen Sections Display output should be divided into three sections. The top of the screen features a "heading" section. The heading contains titles of software and open files, pull-down menus, and icons that do certain tasks.

The middle section is called the "body" of the display. The body can be used for data entry and is organized from left to right and top to bottom, because people in Western cultures move their eyes on a page in this way. Captions and instructions should be supplied in this section to help the user enter the pertinent data in the right place. Context-sensitive help can also be made available by having the user click the right mouse button in the body section of the display.

The third section of the display is the "comments and instructions" section. This section may display a short menu of commands that remind the user of basics such

CONSULTING OPPORTUNITY 12.1

THIS FORM MAY BE HAZARDOUS TO YOUR HEALTH

Figure 12.C1 is a printed medical history form that Dr. Mike Robe, a family practitioner, has his receptionist give to all new patients. All patients must fill it out before they see the doctor.

The receptionist is getting back many incomplete or confusing responses, which makes it difficult for Dr. Robe to review the forms and understand why the new patient is there. In addition, the poor responses make it time consuming for the receptionist to enter new patients into the files.

Redesign the form on 8½″ × 11″ paper so that pertinent new patient data can be collected in a logical and inoffensive way. Make sure the form is self-explanatory to new patients. It should also be easy for Dr. Robe to read and easy for the receptionist to enter into the patient database, which is sorted by patient name and Social Security number. The office uses PCs connected by a LAN. How would you redesign the form so that it can be electronically submitted by the receptionist? Which office procedures would you have to change?

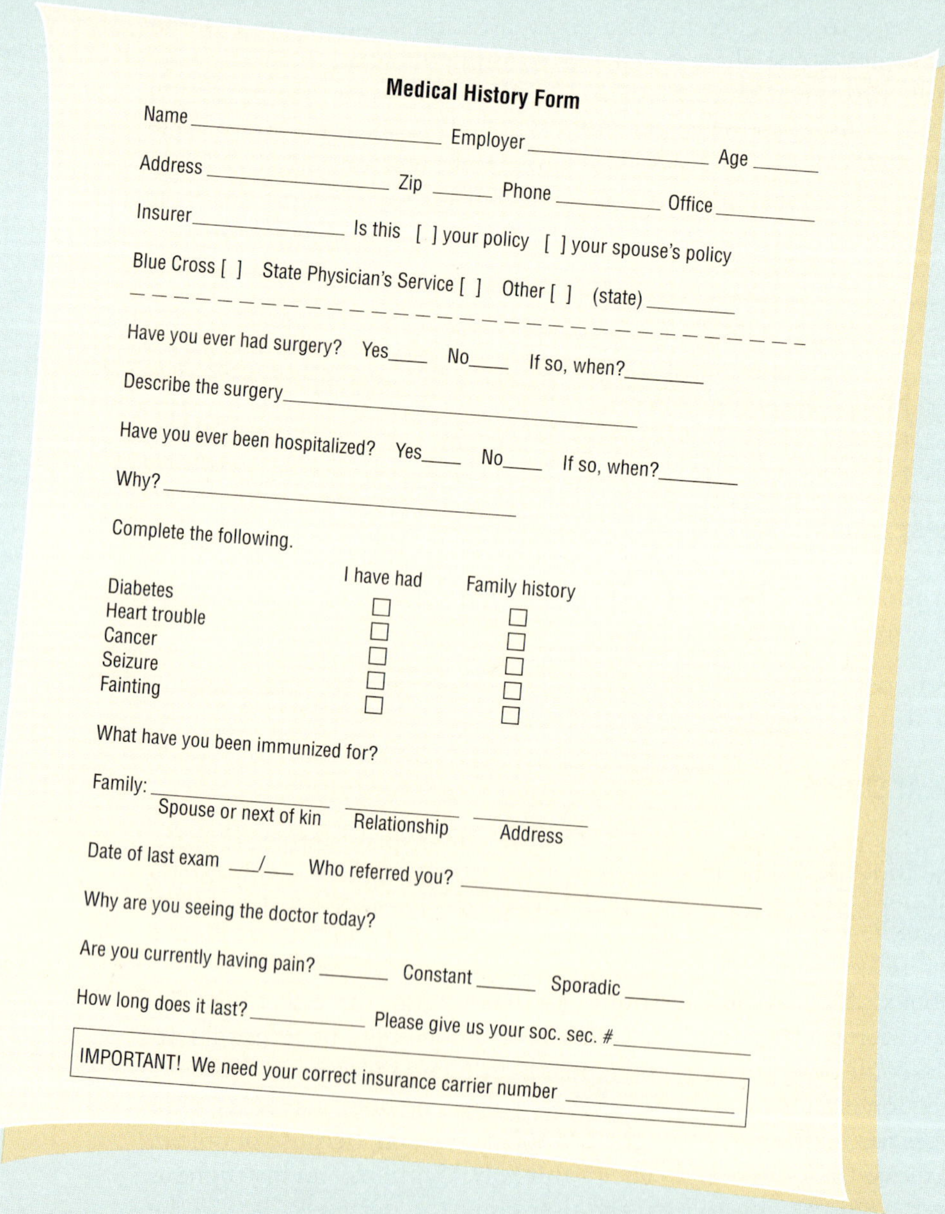

Medical History Form

Name ______________________ Employer ________________ Age ______

Address ________________ Zip _____ Phone _________ Office _________

Insurer_____________ Is this [ ] your policy [ ] your spouse's policy

Blue Cross [ ] State Physician's Service [ ] Other [ ] (state) ________

– –

Have you ever had surgery? Yes____ No____ If so, when?_______

Describe the surgery_______________________________

Have you ever been hospitalized? Yes____ No____ If so, when?_______

Why? _______________________________

Complete the following.

	I have had	Family history
Diabetes	☐	☐
Heart trouble	☐	☐
Cancer	☐	☐
Seizure	☐	☐
Fainting	☐	☐

What have you been immunized for?

Family: ________________ ____________ __________

Spouse or next of kin Relationship Address

Date of last exam ___/___ Who referred you? ____________________

Why are you seeing the doctor today?

Are you currently having pain? ______ Constant _____ Sporadic _____

How long does it last?__________ Please give us your soc. sec. #__________

IMPORTANT! We need your correct insurance carrier number ____________

FIGURE 12.C1

Your help in improving this form is greatly appreciated.

as how to change pages or functions, save the file, or terminate entry. Inclusion of such basics can make inexperienced users feel infinitely more secure about their ability to complete their task.

Another way to keep the display simple is to use context-sensitive help and other pop-up windows. Users can minimize or maximize the size of windows as needed. In this way, users start with a simple, well-designed display that they can customize and control through the use of multiple windows. Hyperlinks on a Web-based fill-in form serve a similar purpose.

KEEPING THE DISPLAY CONSISTENT

The second guideline for good display design is to keep the display consistent. If users are working from paper forms, displays should follow what is shown on paper. Displays can be kept consistent by locating information in the same area each time a new display is accessed. Also, information that logically belongs together should be consistently grouped together: Name and address go together, not name and zip code. Although the display should have a natural movement from one region to another, information should not overlap from one group to another. You would not want name and address in one area and zip code in another.

FACILITATING MOVEMENT

The third guideline for good display design is to make it easy to move from one page to another. The "three-clicks" rule says that users should be able to get to the pages they need within three mouse or keyboard clicks. Web-based forms facilitate movement with the use of hyperlinks to other relevant Web pages. Another common method for movement is to have users feel as if they are physically moving to a new page. There are at least three ways this illusion of physical movement among screens is developed. They are:

1. Scrolling by using arrows or PgDn keys.
2. Context-sensitive pop-up windows.
3. Onscreen dialog.

An example of a context-sensitive pop-up window is shown in Figure 12.7.

DESIGNING AN ATTRACTIVE AND PLEASING DISPLAY

The fourth guideline for good display design is to create an attractive display for the user. If users find displays appealing, they are likely to be more productive, need less supervision, and make fewer errors. Some of the design principles used for forms apply here, too, and some aesthetic principles have already come up in a slightly different context.

Displays should draw users into them and hold their attention. This goal is accomplished with the use of plenty of open area surrounding data entry fields so that the display achieves an uncluttered appearance. You would never crowd a form; similarly, you should never crowd a display. You are far better off using multiple windows or hyperlinks than jamming everything onto one page. By creating displays that are easy to grasp at first glance, you appeal to both inexperienced and experienced users.

Use logical flows in the plan to your display pages. Organize material to take advantage of the way people conceptualize their work so that they can easily find their way around. Also, consistently partition information into the three smaller sections detailed earlier.

FIGURE 12.7
Calling up more detail on an employee's meal expenses (screen designed using FormFlow Filler by JetForm).

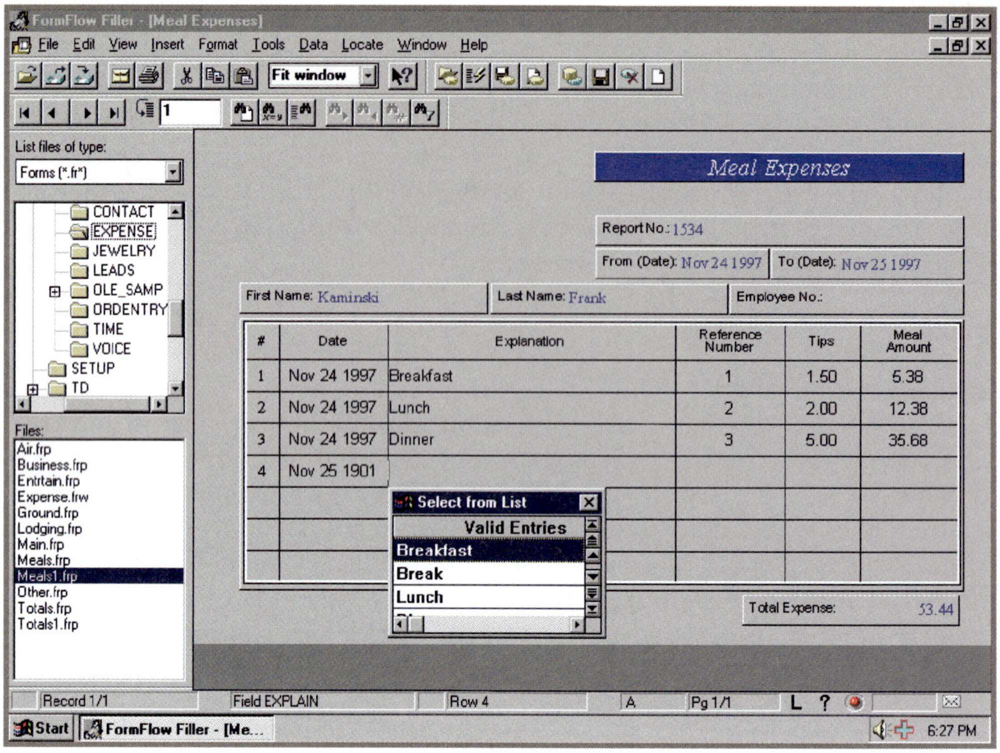

If the display is necessarily complex, thickness of separation lines between subcategories can be varied to add further distinctions. Variety helps the user to see quickly both the purpose of the screen and what data items are required.

With the advent of GUIs, it is possible to make input displays very attractive. By using color or shaded boxes and creating three-dimensional boxes and arrows, you can make forms user friendly and fun to use. Figure 12.8 shows an example of

FIGURE 12.8
You can design an attractive data entry screen with a three-dimensional effect using JetForm's FormFlow.

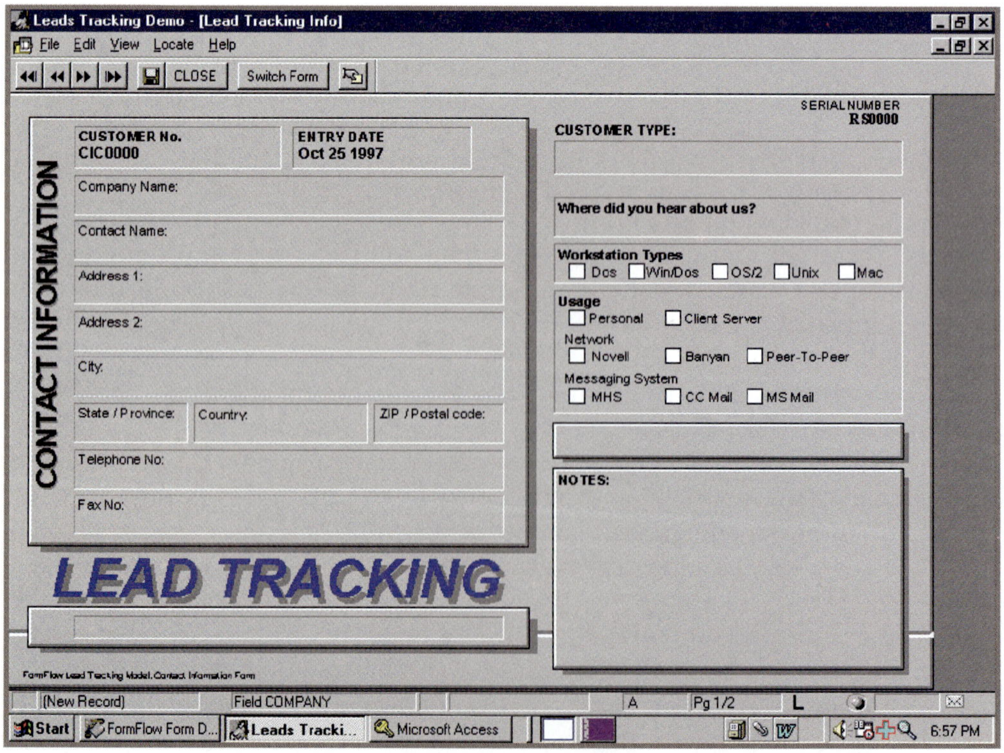

CONSULTING OPPORTUNITY 12.2

SQUEEZIN' ISN'T PLEASIN'

The Audiology Department in a large veteran's hospital is using a PC and monitor so that audiology technicians can enter data directly into the patient records system. After talking with Earl Lobes, one of the technicians, you determine that the screen design is a major problem.

"We used a form at one time, and that was decent," said Mr. Lobes. "The display doesn't make sense, though. I guess they had to squeeze everything on there, and that ruined it."

You have been asked to redesign the display (see Figure 12.C2) to capture the same information but simplify it, and by doing so reduce the errors that have been plaguing the technicians. You realize that squeezing isn't the only problem with the display.

Explain your reasons for changing the display as you did. You may use more than one display page if you think it is necessary.

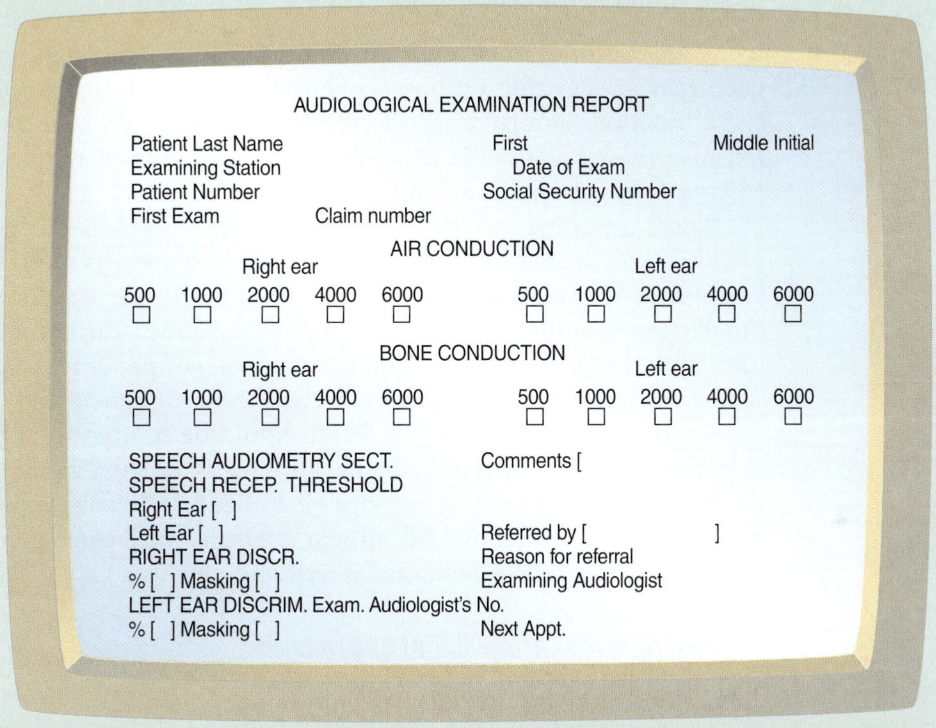

FIGURE 12.C2
This screen can be designed to be more user friendly.

an order entry display that is effective. These features are also available for Web-based fill-in forms.

Inverse Video and Blinking Cursors Other techniques can also effectively enhance the attractiveness of displays for users, but only if they are used sparingly. They include inverse video, a blinking cursor or fields, and font types in various styles and sizes.

When you are considering the use of these techniques, simplicity is still the watchword. Design a basic display that will include basic information first. Then, if greater differentiation is still needed, the basics can be embellished.

Using Different Font Types State-of-the-art computer systems and software allow font types of different styles and sizes. Font types are another way to make displays attractive to users. Different styles enhance differentiation among categories. For instance, bold, sans serif font styles can be used to denote main categories and to give displays a highly legible and modern look. Larger fonts can indicate captions for data entry fields.

When contemplating the use of different font styles and sizes, ask yourself if they truly assist the user in understanding and approving of the display. If they draw undue attention to the art of display design or if they serve as a distraction, leave them out. Be aware that not all Web pages are viewed identically by different browsers. Test your prototype forms with a variety of combinations to see if users declare preferences for combinations or whether they are distressing to the majority of users. For Web fonts use Verdana or Arial.

USING ICONS IN DISPLAY DESIGN

Icons are pictorial, onscreen representations symbolizing computer actions that users may select using a mouse, keyboard, lightpen, touch screen, or joystick. Icons serve functions similar to those of words and may replace them in many menus, because their meaning is more quickly grasped than words. Icons designed for Microsoft Excel are shown in Figure 12.9.

There are some guidelines for the design of effective icons. Shapes should be readily recognizable so that the user is not required to master a new vocabulary. Numerous icons are already known to most users. Use of standard icons can quickly tap into this reservoir of common meaning. A user may point to a file cabinet, "pull out" a file folder icon, "grab" a piece of paper icon, and "throw" it in the wastebasket icon. By employing standard icons, designers and users all save time.

Icons for a particular application should be limited to approximately 20 recognizable shapes, so that icon vocabulary is not overwhelming and so that a worthwhile coding scheme can still be realized. Use icons consistently throughout applications where they will appear together to ensure continuity and understandability. Generally, icons are worthwhile for users if they are meaningful.

GRAPHICAL USER INTERFACE DESIGN

A graphical user interface (GUI, pronounced "goo'ē") is the way that users interface with the Windows and Macintosh operating systems. This is also referred to as a point-and-click interface. Users can use a mouse to click on an object and drag it into position. Graphical user interfaces take advantage of additional features in display design such as text boxes, check boxes, option buttons, list and drop-down list boxes, sliders and spin buttons, image maps, and tab control dialog boxes. Figure 12.10 is a Microsoft Access input display showing a variety of GUI controls.

FIGURE 12.9
Icons from Microsoft Excel.

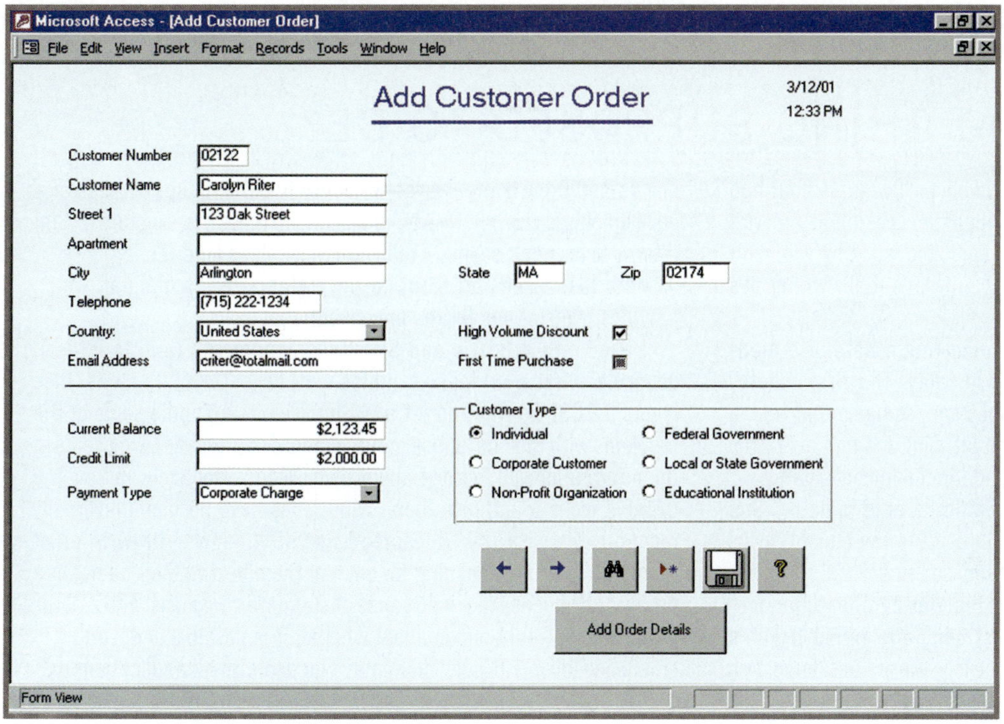

FIGURE 12.10

The designer has many GUI components that allow flexibility in designing input screens for the Web or other software packages. This example is from Microsoft Access.

Text Boxes A rectangle represents a text box, as mentioned previously, and is used to outline data entry and display fields. Care must be taken to ensure that the text box is large enough to accommodate all the characters that must be entered. Each text box should have a caption to the left, identifying what is to be entered or what is displayed in the box. In Microsoft Access, character data are aligned on the left, and numeric data are aligned on the right.

Check Boxes In the GUI controls example, a check box is used to indicate a new customer. Check boxes contain an X or are empty, corresponding to whether or not the user selected the option; they are used for nonexclusive choices in which one or more of the options may be checked. An alternative notation is to use a square button with a check mark (√) to indicate that the option has been selected. Note that check box text, or label, is usually placed to the right of the box. If there is more than one check box, the labels should have some order to them, either alphabetic or with the most commonly checked item appearing first in a list. If there are more than 10 check boxes, group them together in a bordered box.

Option Buttons A circle, called an option button or a radio button, is used to select exclusive choices. Only one of several options can be chosen. In this way you can make it clear to users that they must decide among options. Choices are again listed to the right of the button, usually in some sequence. If there is a commonly selected option, it is usually selected as a default when the page first displays. Often there is a rectangle, called an option group, surrounding the radio buttons. If there are more than six option buttons, consider using a list box or a drop-down list box.

List and Drop-Down List Boxes A list box displays several options that may be selected with the mouse. A drop-down list box is used when there is little room available on the page. A single rectangle with an arrow points down toward a line located on the right side of the rectangle. Selecting this arrow causes a list box to be displayed. Once a user makes a choice, it is displayed in the drop-down selection

CONSULTING OPPORTUNITY 12.3

WHAT'S THAT THING SUPPOSED TO BE?

Art Istik flips off his display with a loud click. "I've just about had it," he says, turning impatiently to his colleague. Looking at Art with mock sympathy, Sim Ball says, "New system is too much for you, isn't it?" Art replies, "No, it's not, but I'll tell you what's really wrong. It's these silly pictures."

Art turns on his newly installed PC, rebooting a database management program that appears on his display. The first display shows icons shaped like a Sherlock Holmes cap, some kind of tree, a pair of socks, an apple, a door, and a rabbit. Sim, leaning over Art's shoulder, takes one look at the display and laughs uncontrollably.

Art says sarcastically, "I knew you would be able to help." Sim manages to stop laughing long enough to point to the pair-of-socks icon and demands, "What's that thing supposed to be?"

Art replies, "I have no idea. All I know is that this database management package is from some West Coast company called Organic Outputs. The software is called DATAPIX: The Icon-Based Database, by a guy named Drew Ikahn. Maybe we ought to call him up. His idea of a good display is way out. No way can I learn all these crazy pictures." Sim returns to his desk, saying, "Yeah, but at least it's entertaining."

As a last resort, Art turns to the DATAPIX user's manual, which provides translations for the unconventional icons.

Based on Art Istik's and Sim Ball's comments (and laughter), describe what you feel is amiss with the DATAPIX icons (see Figure 12.C3). To what do Art and Sim seem to attribute some of the problems with their database management program? Applying some of the information you learned about using icons effectively, redraw the DATAPIX icons to improve them. What icons have become universally recognizable with the widespread use of Windows? Draw three of them and write the meaning for each of them next to their name. In a paragraph, discuss the importance of standardizing icons. Add a paragraph voicing your opinion about whether it is possible or desirable to create one universal icon "dictionary" for use with all applications.

Description	Icon	Meaning
Apple		**Create** a file (as in Adam and Eve)
Door		**Enter** data (as you would a door)
Sherlock's Cap		**Find** (after Holmes's famous investigative powers)
Pair of Socks		**Sort** (as in laundry)
Tree		**Print** (a gentle reminder that printing destroys the trees)
Rabbit		**Copy** a file (for making multiple copies)

FIGURE 12.C3
These DATAPIX icons can be improved.

rectangle and the list box disappears. If there is a commonly selected choice, it is usually displayed in the drop-down list by default.

Sliders and Spin Buttons Sliders and spin buttons are used to change data that have a continuous range of values, giving users more control when choosing values. Moving the slider in one direction or the other (either left/right or up/down) increases or decreases the values. Figure 12.11 illustrates the use of sliders to

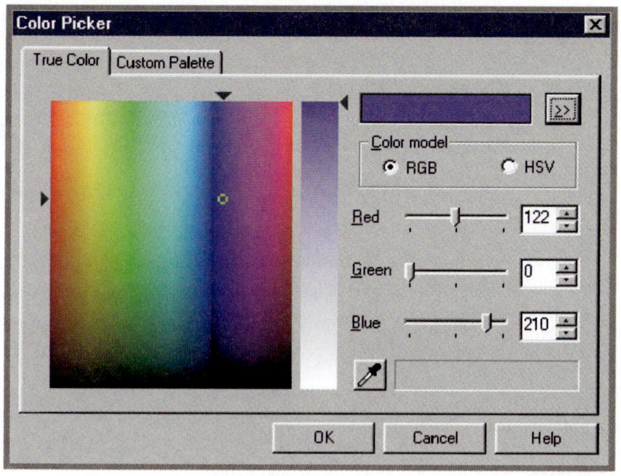

FIGURE 12.11

Sliders and spin buttons are two additional GUI components the analyst can use to design input screens.

change the amount of red, green, and blue when selecting a new color. Spin buttons are also used to change a continuous value and are shown to the right of the sliders.

Image Maps Image map fields are used to select values within an image. The user clicks on a point within an image and the corresponding x and y coordinates are sent to the program. Image maps are used when creating Web pages containing maps with instructions to click in a certain area in order to view a detailed map of the region.

Text Areas A text area is used for entering a larger amount of text. These areas include a number of rows, columns, and scroll bars that allow the user to enter and view text greater than the size of the box area. There are two ways to handle this text. One is to avoid the use of word wrap, forcing the user to press the **Enter** key to move to the next line; the text will scroll to the right if it exceeds the width of the text area. The other option is to allow word wrap.

Message Boxes Message boxes are used to warn users and provide other feedback messages in a dialog box, often overlapping the display. These message boxes have different formats. Each should appear in a rectangular window and should clearly spell out the message so that the user knows precisely what is happening and what actions are possible.

Command Buttons A command button performs an action when the user selects it with the mouse. Calculate Total, Add Order, and OK are all examples. The text is centered inside the button, which has a rectangular shape. If there is a default action, the text is surrounded with a dashed line. The button may also be shaded to indicate that it is the default. Users press the Enter key to select the default button.

FORM CONTROLS AND VALUES

Each of the controls included in a GUI interface must have some way of storing the data associated with the control. On a Web page this is done using a name and a value pair that are transmitted to the server or in an email sent along with the form, such as a name of city and a value of Paris. The name is defined on the Web page form and the server software must recognize the name to understand what to do with the value or data sent with the Web form.

How the value is obtained differs for each Web form control. In text boxes or text areas, the value consists of the characters keyed into the boxes. In radio buttons

FIGURE 12.12

A Web-based input form for users to register for a cruise.

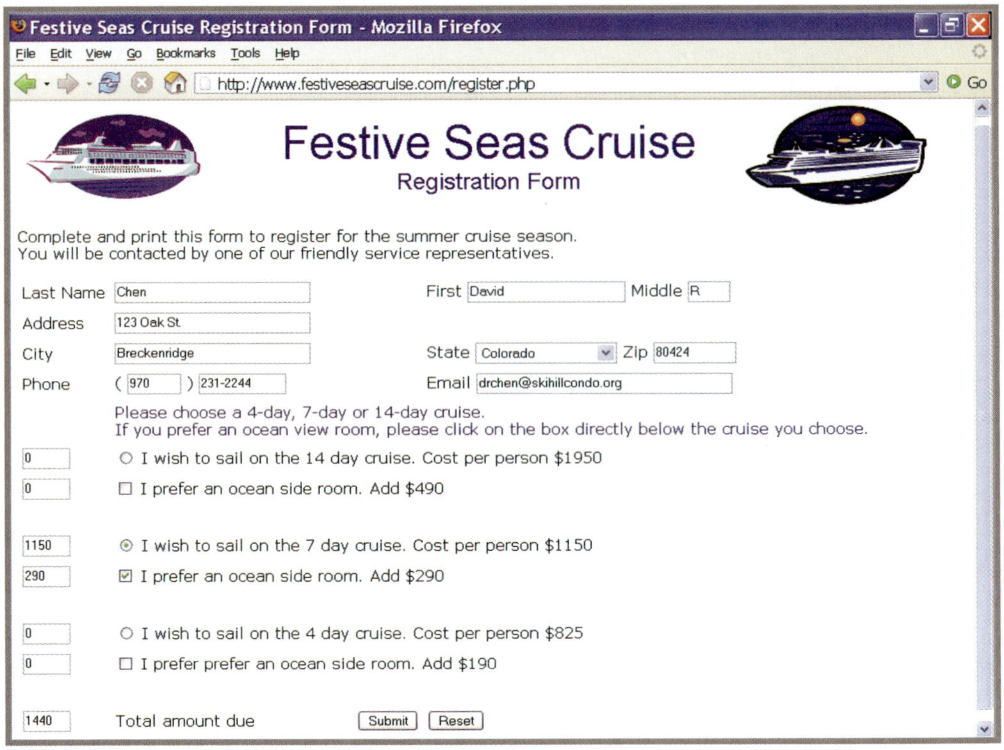

and check boxes, the text that displays to the right of each radio button or check box is for human use only. The value is defined in the Web form and is transmitted when the form is sent. If these data are used to update a database, the values are often codes that are sent and then stored at the server, and the analyst must decide what the appropriate values should be when each radio button or check box is clicked. Drop-down lists are somewhat different from radio buttons or check boxes in that there are many options for a given drop-down list. Values must be decided for each of the drop-down list options and, when an option is chosen, the selected value is sent with the form. Form values may also be used in calculations that are performed using JavaScript on the browser. These may be used to multiply, add, and make decisions.

Figure 12.12 is an example of a form used to obtain prices and to register for a cruise. The text in the Name, Address, City, State, Zip, Phone, and Email areas is sent to the server when the form is submitted. Only one of the radio buttons for the four-day, seven-day, or 14-day cruise may be selected. The values sent are S for short if the four-day cruise is selected, A for average length if seven days has been selected, and L for a long cruise if the 14-day cruise is selected. In addition, when one of these cruises is selected, the dollar amount is inserted into one of the text boxes on the left side of the Web form, and any previously selected radio buttons and amounts are cleared. If the ocean side room check box is checked, a value of Y for yes is transmitted to the server, the amount is inserted into the left-side text box, and the total is updated. If the customer tries to change the amounts in the calculated text boxes, they are reset. When the submit button is clicked, the amounts are sent to the server along with all the other data.

HIDDEN FIELDS

Another type of control found on Web forms is a hidden field. These are not visible to the viewer, do not take up any space on the Web page, and can contain only a name and a value. Often hidden fields are used to store values sent from one Web form to the server. These typically need to be included on a second form when multiple forms are required to capture all the transaction data. Sometimes they are used to retain information about the type of browser being used, the viewer's operating system, and so on. Sometimes a hidden field will contain a key field used to locate a record for the customer or the browsing session.

EVENT-RESPONSE CHARTS

When there are complicated interactions on a Web form (or any other GUI form), an event-response chart may be used to list the variety of events that can occur. Event-response charts may be used at a high level to model business events and responses (covered in Chapter 7), but the events that occur on a Web form or other display are usually limited to user actions. These events may be clicking a button, changing a value, focusing the field (moving the cursor inside the field or to a radio button, check box, or other control), blurring a field (the user moves the cursor out of the field), loading the Web page, detecting keystrokes, and many other events. The response lists how the Web page should react when the event occurs. Events are for a particular object, such as a button, a text field, the whole Web page, and so on.

Figure 12.13 is a Web site used to estimate the cost of staying at Azure Islé Resort. The user can enter the number of people, change the starting and ending dates, and enter the number of people for a variety of extra activities, such as scuba diving or golf.

The event-response chart is shown in Figure 12.14. Notice that there may be a number of events for each Web form control. Since the user may do any number of actions in any order, the event-response chart is useful to show what should happen. For example, the user may click the Calculate button first, change the starting and ending dates, or change the number of people. The event-response chart is also useful for building a Web form that requires minimal action from the user. An example of this is when the user changes the starting month or day, the ending month or day is then changed to match the starting month or day. The

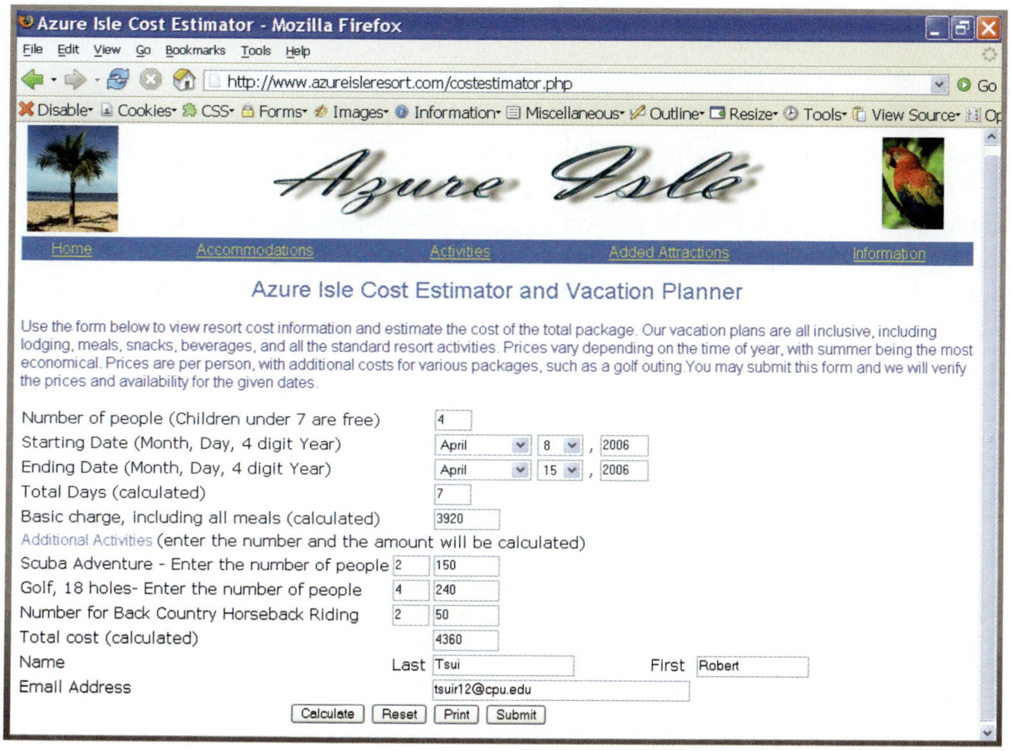

FIGURE 12.13

A Web site permitting users to estimate the cost of staying at Azure Islé Resort. Cost changes depending on the number of people included, length of stay, and extra activities added.

Form Control	Event	Response
Web Page	Page loads	Place the current year in the **Starting Year** and **Ending Year** fields. Place the cursor in the **Number of People** field.
Number of People	Value changes	Verify that **Number of People** contains a number greater than zero.
Starting Month	Selection changes	Set the **Ending Month** in the drop-down list to the **Starting Month**. If the month is less than the current month, change the **Starting Year** and **Ending Year** values to the next year.
Starting Day	Selection changes	Set the **Ending Day** in the drop-down list to the **Starting Day**. Use the **Starting Month** value to set the **Starting Year** and **Ending Year** values.
Starting Year	Receives focus	Use the **Starting Month** value to calculate the **Starting Year** and **Ending Year** values.
Number of Days	Receives focus; value changes	Calculate the **Number of Days** that the customer is staying. If the number is less than or equal to zero, display an error message.
Basic Charge	Receives focus	Calculate the **Basic Charge** and put the cursor in the **Scuba Adventure Number of People** field.
Scuba Adventure Number of People	Receives focus	Select the current amount displayed (zero) so the customer may replace it.
Scuba Adventure Number of People	Value changes	Calculate the **Scuba Cost** based on the value of **Scuba Adventure Number of People** and put the cursor in the **Golf Number of People** field.
Scuba Cost	Value changes	Recalculate the **Scuba Cost** and put the cursor in the **Golf Number of People** field.
Golf Number of People	Receives focus	Select the current amount (zero) so the customer may replace it.
Golf Number of People	Value changes	Calculate the **Golf Cost** and put the cursor in the **Horseback Riding Number of People** field.
Golf Cost	Value changes	Recalculate the **Golf Cost** and put the cursor in the **Horseback Riding Number of People** field.
Horseback Riding Number of People	Receives focus	Select the current amount displayed (zero) so the customer may replace it.
Horseback Riding Number of People	Value changes	Calculate the **Horseback Riding Cost** based on the value of **Horseback Riding Number of People** and put the cursor in the **Last Name** field.
Horseback Riding Cost	Value changes	Recalculate the **Horseback Riding Cost** and put the cursor in the **Last Name** field.
Total Cost	Value changes	Calculate the total cost and put the cursor in the **Last Name** field.
Calculate Button	Button clicked	Validate the form data and display an error message if any errors occur. Calculate the **Total Cost** if there are no errors.
Reset Button	Button clicked	Clear the form and place the current year in the **Starting Year** and **Ending Year** fields. Place the cursor in the **Number of People** field.
Print Button	Button clicked	Validate the form data and display an error message if any errors occur. Calculate **Total Cost** if there are no errors. Use a Web cookie to pass the data to a confirmation page that does not allow the users to change any data.
Submit Button	Button clicked	Validate the form data and display an error message if any errors occur. Calculate **Total Cost** if there are no errors. Send the form to the server and send confirmation to the user.

FIGURE 12.14

An event response chart that lists the form control, event, and response for a number of events that can occur as a user interacts with the Azure Islé Resort cost estimator screen.

year changes when the month is earlier than the current month, since people cannot stay at the resort prior to the current day in the same year.

Sometimes the event-response chart may be used to explore improvements to the Web page. Suppose that Azure Islé Resort determined that most of its customers stayed for seven days. When the starting month or day changes, the ending date could be set for seven days in the future as a default. It might also be a good idea to have radio buttons that allow the customer to select a stay of four, seven, or 14 days and calculate the ending date. Other improvements to a Web page might be detecting when a number of characters have been entered, for example the three digits that comprise a U.S. telephone area code, and then moving the cursor into the next field.

Events are not limited to working within a single Web page. They may also be used to control navigation among Web pages. This can happen when changing a selection in a drop-down list or clicking a radio button. Events may also be used to change the contents of drop-down lists. For example, on a job search page, by selecting one category of job, detailed positions for that job appear in a second drop-down list.

DYNAMIC WEB PAGES

Dynamic Web pages change themselves as the result of user action. They often use JavaScript to modify some part of the Web page or a style. Changing an image when the mouse moves over it or rotating random images at a given time interval are common examples of dynamic Web pages. The Web page may detect the width of the browser window and modify the page accordingly. Menus that expand when the user clicks a small plus sign to the left of the menu or when the mouse moves over a menu are other examples of dynamic Web pages.

The power of dynamic Web pages has been greatly expanded in recent Web browsers (typically version 6 or better of Internet Explorer, or Firefox 1.0 or better). By using JavaScript, a Web form may morph or change itself to add new fields or remove old fields, or change field attributes, such as the length of a field or a radio button changing into a check box. This makes the Web page more responsive to user actions and often will eliminate the need to load new Web pages based on user choices.

Dynamic Web pages may also be used to temporarily display information, such as a block of help information, a calendar with clickable dates used to assist date entry fields, airport codes, and other information. This information may be stored by using a series of stacked layers in the Web page design, each on top of another. The main Web page is the standard layer, while others below the page are not visible. When help is requested or the user clicks in the date field, the layer is moved to the top and becomes visible. The position of the layer is determined by the designer or analyst, such as a calendar appearing on the right side of a date field. When a date is selected, the layer then moves below the surface of the Web page. Using layers is an effective way to build Web sites since it does not require any pop-up pages (which may be blocked by Internet security software). Furthermore, a new Web page does not have to load, and, because the information is contained in a layer, it does not take up any space on the main Web page.

Figure 12.15 is an example of a Web form used by an insurance company to change client information; to add a new location for a client, such as a new store or restaurant for an existing client; or to remove a store for the client. If the **Corporate** check box is checked, the **Last Name, First Name** and **Middle** are changed to a **Company** name field, with the caption text changing as well. If the **Add New Property** button is clicked, a new set of fields for the third property is added. Care

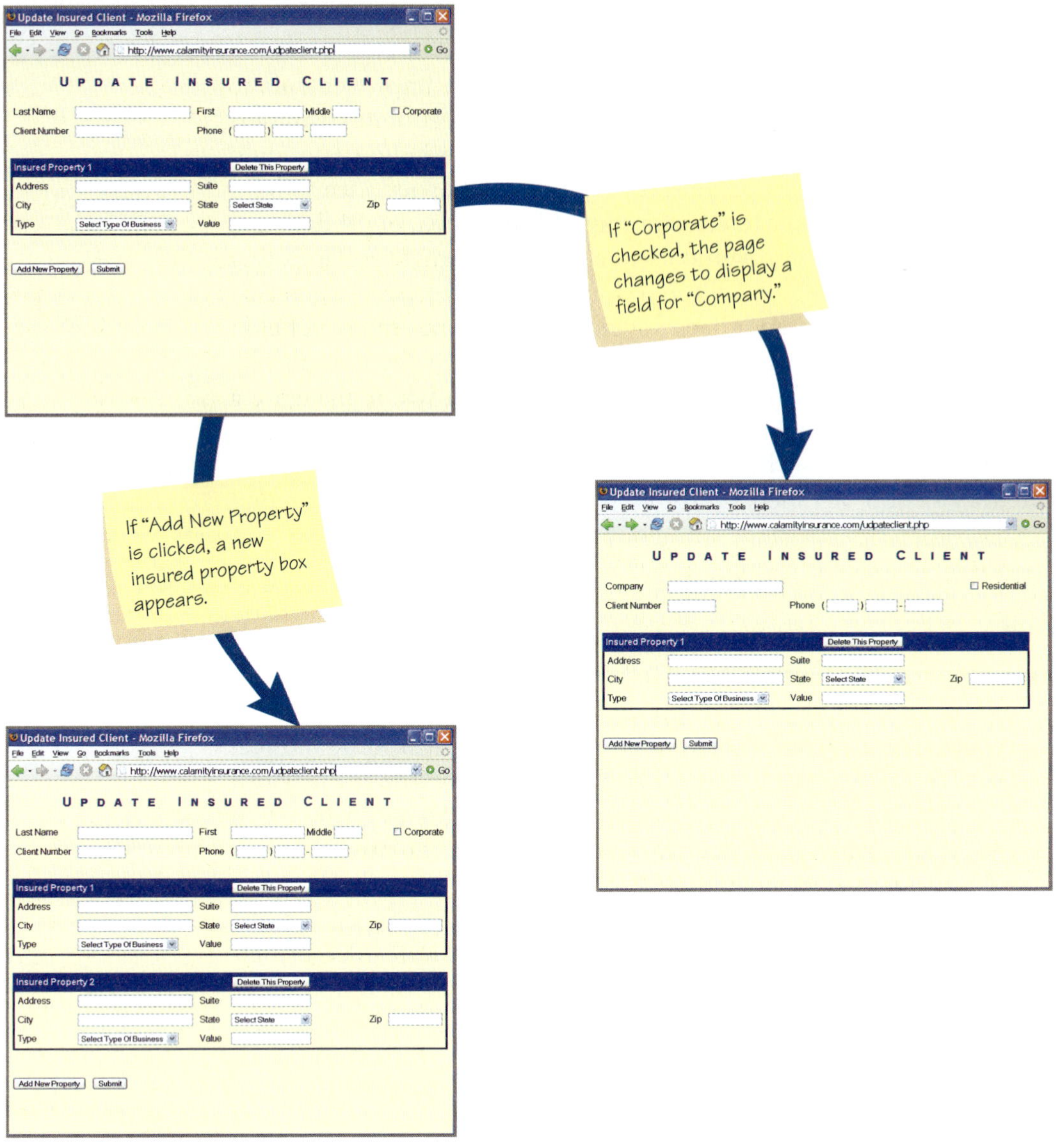

FIGURE 12.15

An example of a dynamic Web page from an insurance company. If a user clicks on "Add New Property," a new insured property box appears.

must be taken to generate unique names that the server will recognize for the additional fields. When the form is submitted, the server updates the database tables for the additional fields.

The analyst must decide when use of dynamic Web pages is appropriate. If the data change when other parts of the Web page change (such as clicking a radio button or selecting an item from a drop-down list), it may be good policy to design the Web pages as a dynamic form. If, however, some parts of the Web form are unsecured and other parts require encryption, it is probably best not to use dynamic forms.

A good example of a form that modifies itself may be found at Expedia.com (www.expedia.com). Clicking radio buttons for a flight, hotel, car, or cruise causes the form to change to gather the data appropriate to reserving a flight, hotel, and so on.

Dynamic Web pages have the advantage of modifying themselves quickly, with fewer interruptions to send and receive data from the server. However, there are several disadvantages when creating dynamic Web pages. One is that they will not work if JavaScript is turned off. The analyst must decide what to do in this situation.

If the person must use the Web site (as in a corporate intranet environment, in a site used to obtain student loans, or in the case of processing government or other transactions), the Web page can state clearly that it will not function if JavaScript is turned off and then direct the user on how to turn it on. Most commerce Web sites will not require JavaScript to be turned on and will have an alternate Web site for customers.

A second disadvantage when using dynamic Web pages is that they may not be compliant with the American Disabilities Act. (For more on Web accessibility for all users, please see Chapter 14 on designing human–computer interaction.)

AJAX (ASYNCHRONOUS JAVASCRIPT AND XML)

Ajax is a technique that works in more recent Web browsers. It involves the use of JavaScript and extensible markup language (XML). Traditionally, each time a Web page needed data from a different database table, a request was sent to the server and a whole new page was loaded. This is effective but slow, because an entire page must be loaded just to provide additional data for a drop-down list or some other Web form control based on the one selected previously.

Ajax allows Web developers to build a Web page that works more like a traditional desktop program. As new data are needed, the browser sends a request to the server, and the server sends a small amount of data back to the browser, which updates the current page. This means that the viewer does not experience an interruption of work and the Web page does not reload. The page is dynamically updated with the new data.

The data may be either a small text file or an XML document containing many customers or other repeating data. If the data is an XML file, each customer element is called a node, and each node is numbered (starting with zero) from the beginning of the XML document. This allows the Web page to go to the first or last customer or to loop through all the customers one by one with a button click.

Let's say a systems analyst was designing a traditional Web site, without Ajax, for making a reservation for a European ferry. The resultant Web site might contain several pages. The first page would ask the customer about the origin and destination of the journey, the date of the planned trip, and the number of passengers. Since pricing is determined by the number and ages of the passengers, a second Web page would display asking for the ages of the passengers. A third would ask the type of vehicle desired for land transportation, and so on.

The same information may be obtained using Ajax techniques, illustrated in Figure 12.16. The same starting and ending destinations, as well as dates, are entered on the top of the Web form. The Web page uses the destinations and dates to determine whether there is any available space on the ferry. After the customer changes the number of passengers, the form dynamically changes to add the three drop-down lists for each passenger, along with instructions on the side—without reloading the entire page. When the type of vehicle changes, in this example to **Car,** the selected vehicle type is sent to the server. The caption on the form changes the text from vehicle to **Car Make.** The server sends the possible car makes, and the **Car Make** drop-down list is populated with the data. When the car make is selected, the chosen value is sent to the server and the **Car Model** drop-down list is populated, and so on.

The Web page used in this example responds much faster than the alternative, which is having several different pages displayed, and it is easier for the user to work with. There is still a need to have a confirmation Web page (although the page could dynamically change to remove form fields and replace them with text), and another Web page for name, address, and credit card information. The analyst must decide how to partition the transaction into a series of pages, some using Ajax and some not. If small amounts of data need to be obtained to continue the transaction, and the data logically fits on a single Web form or page, then Ajax may be the best

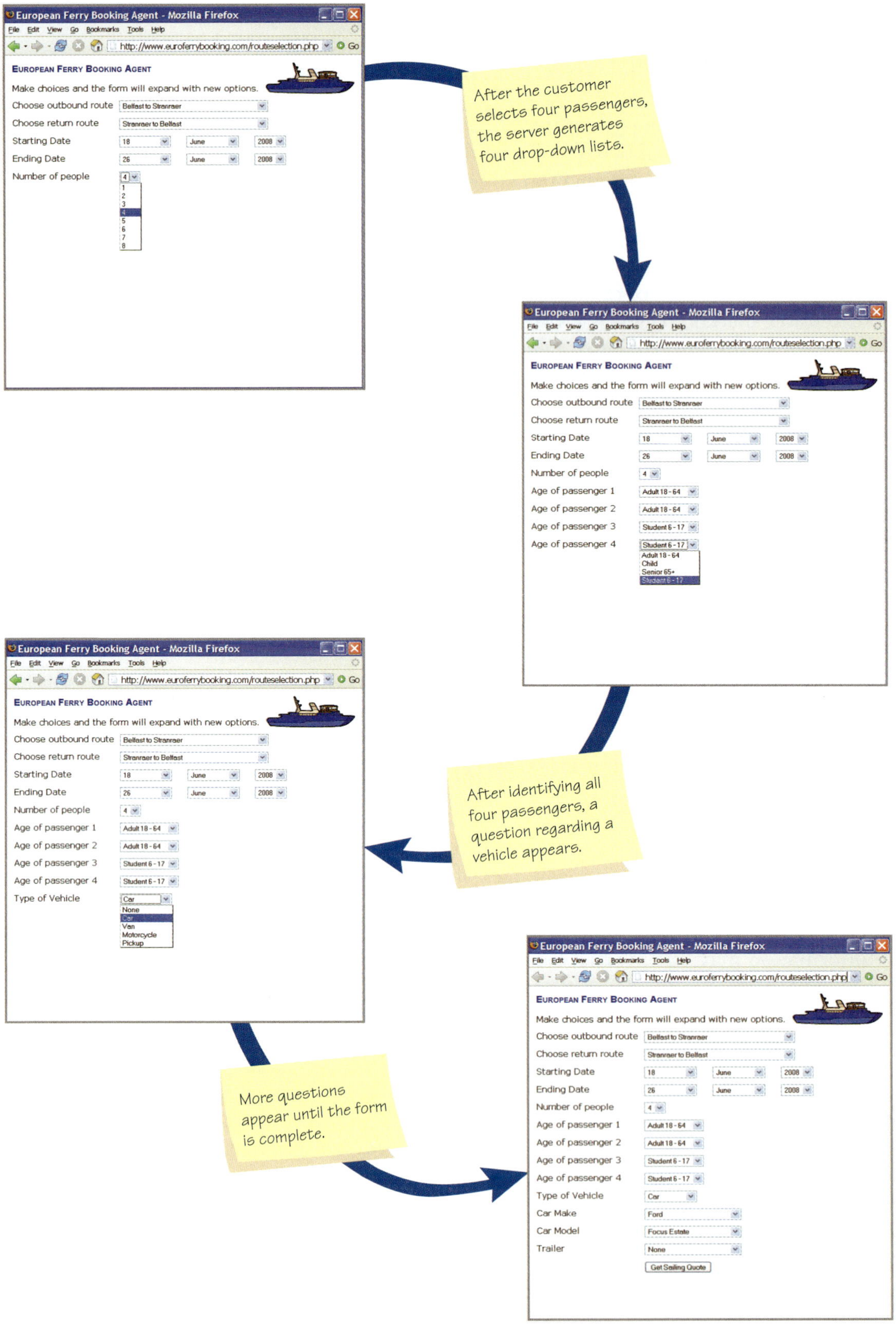

FIGURE 12.16

When analysts use Ajax techniques, a dynamic Web page responds more rapidly to short user input than it would if several different pages were required for display.

approach. At times it is better to have several pages, such as when making an airline reservation. One Web form would obtain all the flight information, and another page would be used to display the flights. A third page might be used to obtain passenger information, and a fourth page might use Ajax to select seat locations, meals, and other individual needs for each passenger.

Ajax has the advantage of making the Web work faster and of providing a smoother viewing experience for users. The disadvantages are that JavaScript must be enabled and that the Web page may violate the American Disability Act. Security must be taken into consideration if needed. There are numerous examples of Ajax Web sites. Some notable ones include Google Earth (earth.google.com), and Google Suggest, which responds to the viewer's keystrokes by providing a drop-down list of possible search terms. Ajax Write (www.ajaxlaunch.com/ajaxwrite/) is a Web-based word processor. There is also an Ajax spreadsheet and a sketching tool (visit www.Ajaxlaunch.com/).

TAB CONTROL DIALOG BOXES

Tab control dialog boxes are another part of graphical user interfaces and another way to get users organized and into system material efficiently. Figure 12.17 provides an example of a tab control dialog box. Guidelines for designing the control dialog boxes include:

1. Create a separate tab for each unique feature (for example, a tab to select color and another to select text, background, grid, or other font characteristics).
2. Place the most commonly used tabs in front and display them first.
3. Consider including three basic buttons in your design: OK, Cancel, and Help.

Microsoft Office 2000 first introduced a type of dialog box that has the look and feel of a Web page, as can be seen in Figure 12.18. On the left side are buttons

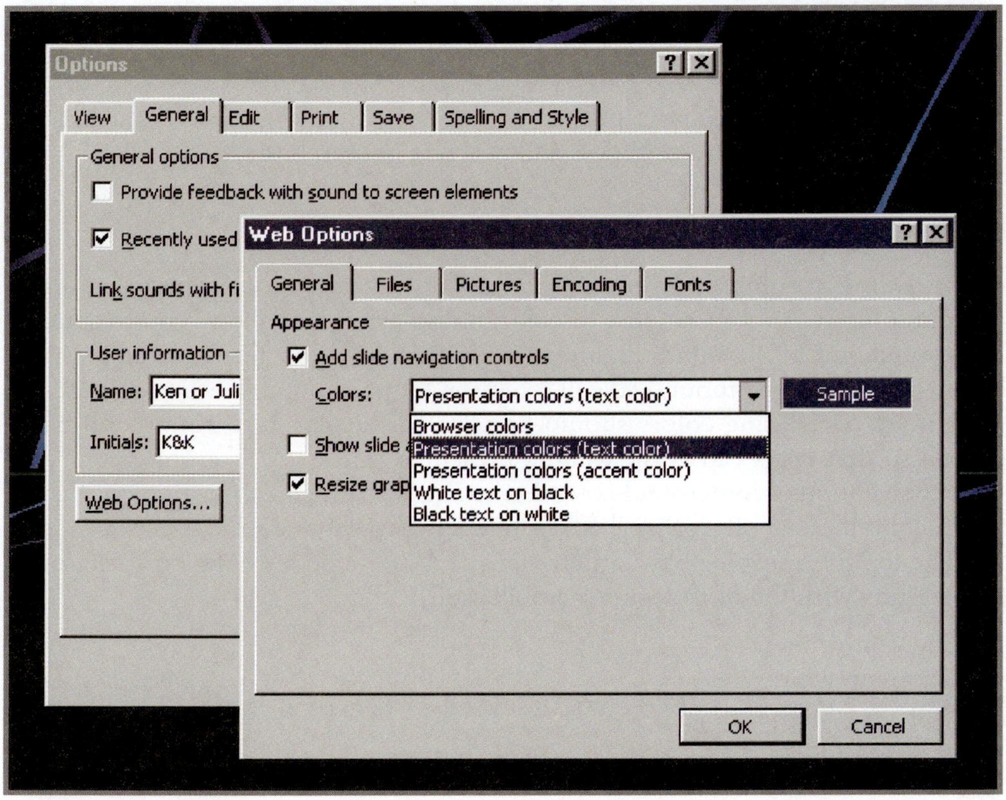

FIGURE 12.17
A tab control dialog box from Microsoft PowerPoint showing drop-down lists and check boxes.

FIGURE 12.18

A new dialog box with the look and feel of a Web page was introduced by Microsoft in Office 2000.

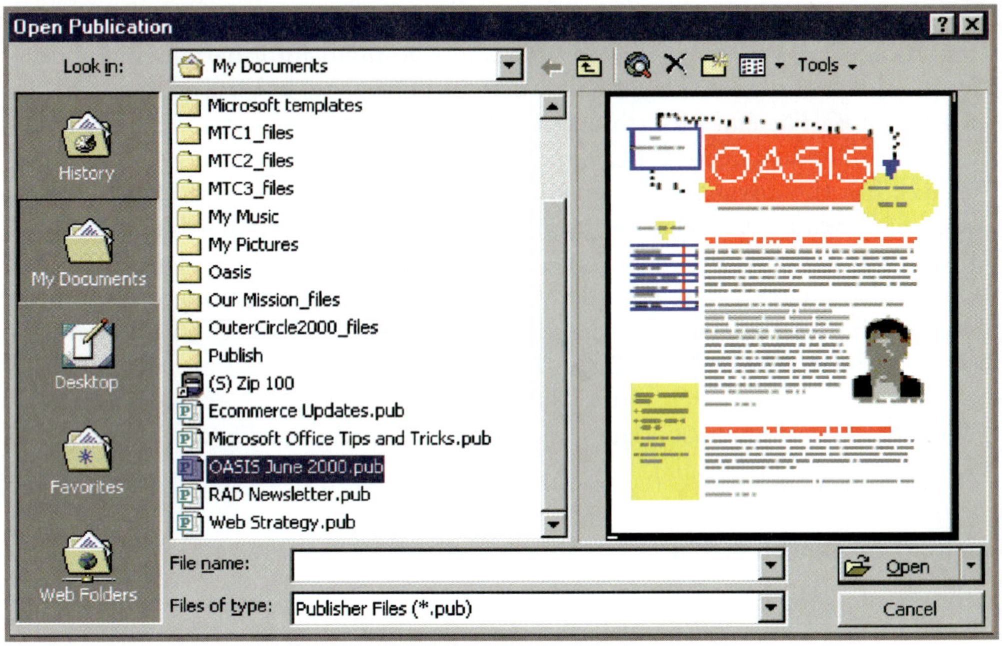

called places. These buttons are hyperlinked to items a user would want to access frequently. The default places are "History," which pulls up a list of the most recent files used; "My Documents," which is the default location for saving files; "Desktop"; "Favorites," which are the Web sites the user bookmarked in their browser; and "Web Folders," which are Web sites the user constructed. These places can be customized using special software such as the WOPR Placebar Customizer so that users can construct their own shortcut buttons.

In the center of the dialog box is the current directory; any files or folders in the current directory are displayed there. The box to the right is called the viewing area. By clicking on an icon, a user can see details about the files, properties of a single file, or a preview of the current file. In this example, the Microsoft Publisher document "OASIS June 2000.pub" is previewed.

This dialog box also has a pull-down box for easy navigation, and icons that allow the user to create new folders and navigate or search the Web.

USING COLOR IN DISPLAY DESIGN

Color is an appealing and proven way to facilitate users with tasks requiring computer input. Appropriate use of color in display screens allows you to contrast foreground and background, highlight important fields on forms, feature errors, highlight special code input, and call attention to many other special attributes.

Highly contrasting colors should be used for display foreground and background so that users can grasp what is presented quickly. Background color will affect perception of foreground color. For example, dark green may look like a different color if taken off a white background and placed on a yellow one.

The top five most legible combinations of foreground lettering on background are (starting with the most legible combination):

1. Black on yellow.
2. Green on white.
3. Blue on white.
4. White on blue.
5. Yellow on black.

CONSULTING OPPORTUNITY 12.4

IT'S ONLY SKIN DEEP

When contemplating upgrading the design of the ecommerce Web site for Marathon Vitamin Shops, Bill Berry, the owner, realized that his customers were diverse.

"We've worked hard to attract many different types of customers. As far as the store goes, we are succeeding. People with many different interests come in. I've met sports enthusiasts who want high-energy vitamins to boost their power. Other customers want to lose weight with the help of vitamin supplements. Some of our customers are health conscious and believe that a vitamin a day keeps the doctor away. Some even embrace the lifestyle first cultivated in the 1970s. By the way the store is set up, you can see that we're trying to segment the space so that each kind of consumer feels welcome. It's hard to translate that to the Web, though."

Bill turns to one of his employees, Jin Singh, and asks her, "Is there anything we can do to transform the online catalog so that it attracts different customers? And what about being responsive to the different people who visit the site?"

Jin, who just happens to be an Internet Webcast enthusiast, says, "I have just the thing," as she turns to her computer and brings up her Windows Media Player. "Personally, I like to get into a frame of mind that matches the music or videos I am experiencing on the Web."

Jin shows Bill examples of some "skins" on the screen. You can see a variety of skins for the Microsoft Windows Media Player displayed in Figure 12.C4.

Jin continues, "Skins allow me to customize the appearance of my Media Player. When I play oldies, I choose a rusty skin. When I am playing something new age, I opt for a skin that has a rainbow of colors, and so on."

Peering at the screen, Bill exclaims, "I think you're on to something. What did you call those things again?"

Jin laughs and explains, "They're called skins, but they're just fun overlays that customers can add to whatever it is they're viewing. I can envision that eventually the Web site can take on an entirely new appearance depending on customer preferences for a particular kind of skin."

Based on your assessment of the different types of customers Marathon would like to attract to its Web site, design, draw, and describe a series of skins that would be appropriate for the company's purposes. Explain in two paragraphs how the inclusion of user-controlled skins on a Web site can further the analyst's design objectives of attractiveness and ease of use for input.

FIGURE 12.C4
Six skins from Microsoft's Windows Media Player allow users to customize their players to fit their moods.

The least legible are red on green and blue on red. As can be gathered from these foreground and background combinations, bright colors should be used for foregrounds, with less bright colors for the background. Strongly contrasting colors should be assigned first to fields that must be differentiated; then other colors can be assigned.

Use color to highlight important fields on displays. Fields that are important can be colored differently than the rest. Take into consideration cultural norms. Red usually means danger, but "in the red" also means a company is losing money. Green means "go" and is a safe color in Western countries.

By observing Web accessibility guidelines, you will also want to take into consideration that 8–10 percent of the male population has color blindness, but less than 1 percent of females suffer from it. Use other indicators in addition to color to support users in completing their tasks.

As with any enhancement, designers need to question the added value of using color. Use of color can be overdone; a useful heuristic is no more than four colors for new users and only up to seven for experienced ones. Irrelevant colors distract users and detract from their performance. In numerous instances, however, color has been shown to facilitate use in very specific ways. Color should be considered an important way to contrast foreground and background, highlight important fields and data, point out errors, and allow special coding of input.

INTRANET AND INTERNET PAGE DESIGN

In Chapter 11, the rudiments of designing Web sites were discussed. There are more hints about designing a good Internet or intranet fill-in form that should be noted now that you have learned some of the elementary aspects of input form and display design. Figure 12.19 shows a fill-in form order page that shows many elements of good design for the Web. Guidelines include the following:

1. Provide clear instructions, because Web users may not be familiar with computer terminology.

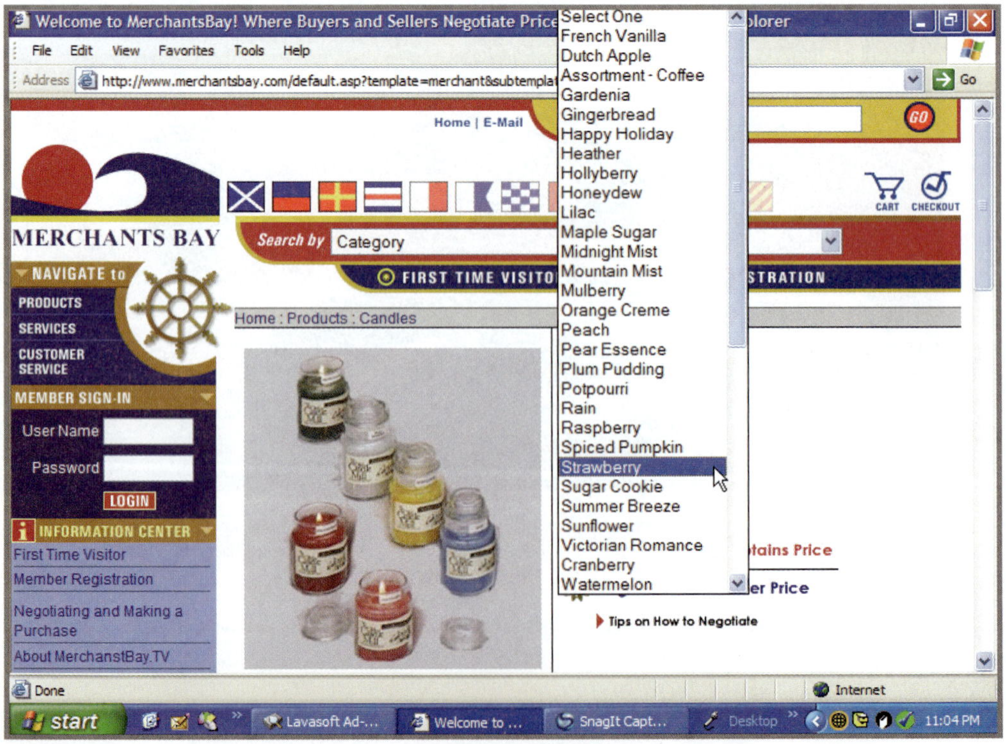

FIGURE 12.19
The order screen from the Merchants Bay Web site (www.merchantsbay.com) is a good example of how to design an input form that is clear, easy to use, and functional.

2. Demonstrate a logical entry sequence for fill-in forms, especially because the users may have to scroll down to a region of the page that is not visible at first.
3. Use a variety of text boxes, push buttons, drop-down menus, check boxes, and radio buttons to serve specific functions and to create interest in the form.
4. Provide a scrolling text box if you are uncertain about how much space users will need to respond to a question, or about what language, structure, or form users will use to enter data.
5. Prepare two basic buttons on every Web fill-in form: Submit and Clear Form.
6. If the form is lengthy and the users must scroll excessively, divide the form into several simpler forms on separate pages.
7. Create a feedback screen that refuses submission of a form unless mandatory fields are filled in correctly. The returned form screen can provide detailed feedback to the user in a different color. Red is appropriate here. For example, a user may be required to fill in a country in the country field, or indicate a credit card number if that type of payment has been checked off. Often a required field is denoted on an initial screen with a red asterisk.

Ecommerce applications involve more than just good design of Web sites. Customers need to feel confident that they are buying the correct quantity, that they are getting the right price, and that the total cost of an Internet purchase, including shipping charges, is what they expect. The most common way to establish this confidence is to use the metaphor of a shopping cart or shopping bag. Figure 12.20 shows the contents of a shopping cart for a customer making a purchase. An important feature of the shopping cart is that the customer can edit the quantity of the item ordered or can remove the item entirely.

Ecommerce applications add more demands to the analyst who must design Web sites to meet several user and business objectives, including setting forth the corporate mission and values regarding confidentiality, preserving user privacy, and easy and rapid product returns; the efficient processing of transactions; and building good customer relationships.

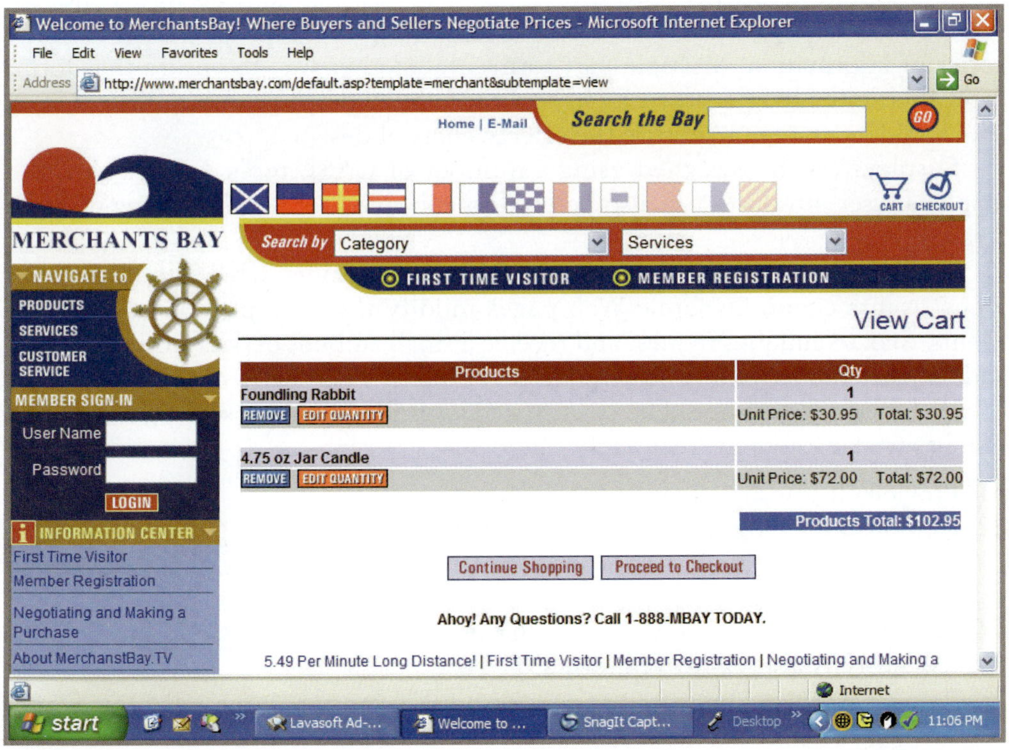

FIGURE 12.20

The Merchants Bay Web site (www.merchantsbay.com) is a good example of a shopping cart.

SUMMARY

This chapter has covered elements of input design for forms, displays, and Web fill-in forms. Well-designed input should meet the goals of effectiveness, accuracy, ease of use, simplicity, consistency, and attractiveness. Knowledge of many different design elements will allow the systems analyst to reach these goals.

The four guidelines for well-designed input forms are the following:

1. Forms must be easy to fill out.
2. Forms must meet the purpose for which they are designed.
3. Forms must be designed to ensure accurate completion.
4. Forms must be pleasing and attractive.

Design of useful forms, displays, and Web fill-in forms overlaps in many important ways, but there are some distinctions. Displays show a cursor that continually orients the user. Displays often provide assistance with input, whereas with the exception of preprinted instructions, it may be difficult to get additional assistance with a form. Web-based documents have additional capabilities, such as embedded hyperlinks, context-sensitive help functions, and feedback forms, to correct input before final submission. Skins can be added as an option to personalize a Web site.

The four guidelines for well-designed displays are as follows:

1. Displays must be kept simple.
2. Displays must be consistent in presentation.
3. Design must facilitate movement between pages.
4. Displays must be attractive.

Many different design elements allow the systems analyst to meet these guidelines.

The proper flow of paper forms, display screens, and fill-in forms on the Web is important. Forms should group information logically into seven categories, and displays should be divided into three main sections. Captions on forms and displays can be varied, as can font types and the weights of lines dividing subcategories of information. Multiple-part forms are another way to ensure that forms meet their intended purposes. Designers can use windows, prompts, dialog boxes, and defaults onscreen to ensure the effectiveness of design.

Displays can be designed using a number of CASE tools. Icons, color, and graphical user interfaces can also be used to enhance user understanding of input screens.

Event-response charts help the analyst to document what should happen when events occur. Dynamic Web pages modify the Web page in response to events. Ajax techniques request and receive a small amount of data from the server and use the data to modify the Web page on the fly.

Web fill-in forms should be constructed with the following seven guidelines in mind as well as those in Chapter 11:

1. Provide clear instructions.
2. Demonstrate a logical entry sequence for fill-in forms.
3. Use a variety of text boxes, push buttons, drop-down menus, check boxes, and radio buttons.
4. Provide a scrolling text box if you are uncertain about how much space users will need to respond to a question.
5. Prepare two basic buttons on every Web fill-in form: Submit and Clear Form.

"Isn't spring the most beautiful season here? The architect really captured the essence of the landscape, didn't he? I mean, you can't go anywhere in the building without seeing another beautiful vista through those huge windows. When Snowden came back, he looked at your output displays. The good news is that he thinks they'll work. The project is blossoming, just like the flowers and trees. When Snowden returns from Finland, would you have some input display screens ready to demonstrate? He doesn't want things to slow down just because he's out of the country. By the way, the Singapore trip was very successful. Maybe MRE will be worldwide someday."

HYPERCASE QUESTIONS

1. Using either a paper layout form or software such as JetForm's FormFlow, design a prototype paper form that captures client information for the Training Unit.
2. Test your form on three classmates by having each of them fill it out. Ask them for a written critique of the form.
3. Redesign your input form to reflect your classmates' comments.
4. Using either a paper layout form or a CASE tool, design a prototype display form that captures client information for the Training Unit.
5. Test your input display on three classmates by having each of them try it out. Ask them for a written critique of the display's design.
6. Redesign the input display based on the comments you receive. In a paragraph, explain how you have addressed each comment.

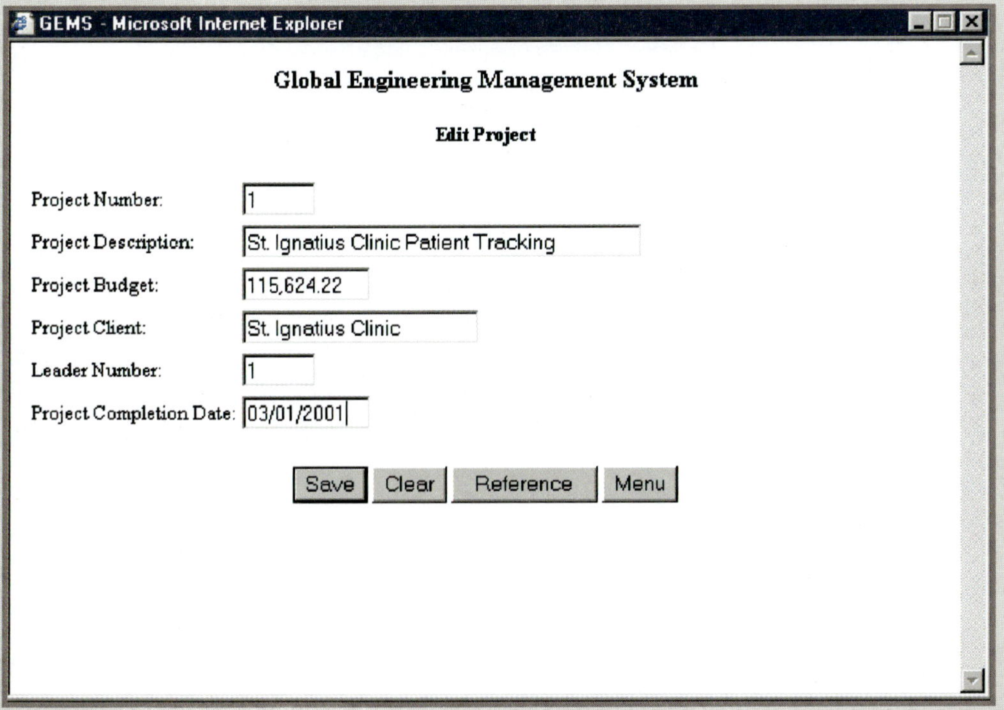

FIGURE 12.HC1
Take a look at some of the input screens in HyperCase. You may want to redesign some of the electronic forms.

6. If the form is lengthy and the users must scroll extensively, divide the form into several simpler forms on separate pages.
7. Create a feedback screen that highlights errors in an appropriate color and refuses submission of the form until mandatory fields are correctly filled in.

KEYWORDS AND PHRASES

- Ajax
- blinking cursor
- box caption
- check box
- command button
- control of business forms
- cursor
- display color combinations
- drop-down list box
- dynamic Web pages
- event-response chart
- facilitating movement on pages
- form flow
- form values
- hidden field
- horizontal check-off caption
- image map
- Internet/intranet fill-in form
- inverse video
- line caption
- list box
- message box
- onscreen color
- onscreen dialog
- onscreen icon
- option button
- prompt
- radio button
- response time
- seven sections of a form
- skins
- slider
- specialty form
- spin button
- tab control dialog box
- table caption
- text box
- three sections of a display
- vertical check-off caption

REVIEW QUESTIONS

1. What are the design objectives for paper input forms, input screens, or Web-based fill-in forms?
2. List the four guidelines for good form design.
3. What is proper form flow?
4. What are the seven sections of a good form?
5. List four types of captioning for use on forms.
6. What is a specialty form? What are some disadvantages of using specialty forms?
7. What are the basic duties involved in controlling forms?
8. List the four guidelines for good display design.
9. What are the three sections useful for simplifying a display?
10. What are the advantages of using onscreen windows?
11. What are the disadvantages of using onscreen windows?
12. List two ways display screens can be kept consistent.
13. Give three ways to facilitate movement between display pages.
14. List four graphical interface design elements. Alongside each one, describe when it would be appropriate to incorporate each of them in a display design or on a Web-based fill-in form.
15. When should check boxes be used?
16. When should option buttons be used?
17. What are two different ways that form values are used?
18. What are hidden fields used for on a Web form?

19. List four different types of events.
20. What are dynamic Web pages?
21. How does Ajax improve a Web page that changes based on user actions?
22. List the five most legible foreground and background color combinations for display use.
23. Define what is meant by the term *skins* when used in Web design.
24. What three buttons should be included with a tab control dialog box?
25. What are four situations in which color may be useful for display and Web-based fill-in form design?
26. List seven design guidelines for a Web-based fill-in form.

PROBLEMS

1. Here are captions used for a state census form:

   Name
   ....
   Occupation
   ....
   Address
   ....
   Zip code
   ....
   Number of people in household
   ....
   Age of head of household
   ....

   a. Redo the captions so that the state census bureau can capture the same information requested on the old form without confusing respondents.
   b. Redesign the form so that it exhibits proper flow. (*Hint:* Make sure to provide an access and identification section so that the information can be stored in the state's computers.)
   c. Redesign the form so it can be filled in by citizens who visit the state's Web site. What changes were necessary in moving from a paper form to one that will be submitted electronically?
2. Elkhorn College needs to keep better track of the books checked out from its Buck Memorial Library.
   a. Design and draw a form on 4½″ × 5½″ paper to use for checking out library books. Label the seven sections of a form that you included.
   b. Design and draw a representation of a display screen to accomplish the same thing. Label the three sections of a display that you included.
3. Refer to Figure 12.9, which shows the icons from Microsoft Excel, and try to explain what each icon means. Propose new icons if the actual ones are confusing.
4. Take a look at Figure 12.EX1. These icons are from Freelance Graphics. Try to guess what each icon means. Does the lightbulb have the same meaning as the lightbulb in the Excel application in Problem 3? Explain. Suggest other icons that are better.
5. Speedy Spuds is a fast-food restaurant offering all kinds of potatoes. The manager has a 30-second rule for serving customers. Servers at the counter say they could achieve that rule if the form they must fill out and give to the kitchen crew were simplified. The information from the completed form is keyed into the computer system at the end of the day, when the data entry person needs to enter the kind of potato purchased, additional toppings purchased, the

FIGURE 12.EX1
Icons from a popular graphics package.

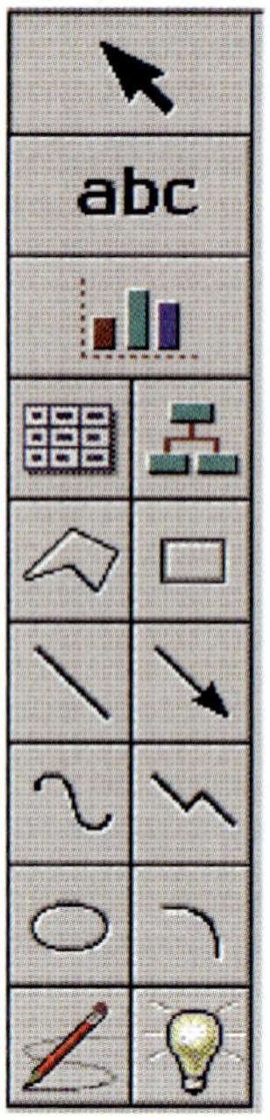

quantity, and the price charged. The current form is difficult for servers to scan and fill out quickly.

a. Design and draw a form (you choose the size, but be sensible) that lists possible potatoes and toppings in a manner that is easy for counter servers and kitchen crew to scan, and can also be used as input for the inventory/reorder system that is on the extranet connecting Speedy Spuds and Idaho potato growers. (*Hint:* Remember to observe *all* the guidelines for good form design.)

b. Design and draw a representation of a display screen that can be used by the servers and clerks to fill in the information captured on the form.

c. Design a display screen based on the display you designed in Problem 5b. This time, it should function as a display that shows a kitchen crew member what to prepare for each Spuds order. List three changes to the existing display that you made to adapt it to function as an output display.

6. Sherry's Meats, a regional meat wholesaler and retailer, needs to collect up-to-date information on how much of each meat product it has in each store. It will then use that information to schedule deliveries from its central warehouse. Currently, customers entering the store fill out a detailed form specifying their individual orders. The form lists over 150 items; it includes meat and meat products available in different amounts. At the end of the day, between 250 and 400 customer orders are tabulated and deducted from the store's inventory. Then the office worker in each store phones in an order for the next day. Store employees have a difficult time tabulating sales because of the mistakes customers make in filling out their forms.

   a. It is not possible to have the solitary office worker in each store fill out the numerous customer order forms. Change the form (3½″ × 6″ *either* horizontal *or* vertical) and draw it so that it is easier for customers to fill out correctly and for office workers to tabulate.

   b. Design and draw a specialty form of the same size that will meet the needs of Sherry's customers, office workers, and warehouse workers.

   c. Design and draw two different forms of the same size to meet the purposes in Problem 6b, because Sherry's carries both poultry and beef products. (*Hint:* Think about ways to make forms easy to distinguish visually.)

d. Design a fill-in form for onscreen display. When a customer submits an order, it is entered into Sherry's inventory system by any person who is serving customers at the counter. This information will be captured and sent to the central warehouse computer to help control inventory.
e. In a paragraph, describe the drawbacks of having lots of different people at different locations enter data. In a paragraph, list steps you can take as the designer so that the fill-in form is designed to ensure accuracy of entry.
f. Design a Web page used by a customer to enter an order directly to Sherry's.
g. Design a Web page to obtain credit card information for a Web order. Partition the data onto two Web pages for additional security.
h. Design a dynamic Web page that allows Sherry's to customize certain products, such as a meatloaf or a salad. When the customer selects a product from a drop-down list, the ingredients must be displayed with a means of selecting which ones should be included in the product.

7. R. George's, a fashionable clothing store that also has a mail-order business, would like to keep track of the customers coming into the store so as to expand its mailing list.
   a. Design and draw a simple form that can be printed on 3″ × 5″ cards and given to in-store customers to fill out. (*Hint:* The form must be aesthetically appealing to encourage R. George's upscale clientele to complete it.)
   b. Design and draw a representation of a display screen that captures in-store customer information from the cards in Problem 7a.
   c. Design and draw an onscreen tab control dialog box that can be used with the display in Problem 7b, one that allows a comparison between in-store customer information and a listing of customers who hold R. George's credit cards.
   d. Design and draw a second onscreen tab control dialog box that compares in-store customers with mail-order customers.
   e. The owner is having you help set up an ecommerce site. Design a Web-based form to capture visitor information to the Web site. In a paragraph, explain how it will differ from the printed form.
8. Figure 12.EX2 depicts the icons from the personal information manager (PIM) called Organizer. See if you can guess what each icon means. Why do you think that good icon design is important? Explain in a paragraph why you think (or do not think) these icons conform to the principles of good design.
9. Design a system of onscreen display icons with readily recognizable shapes that allows account executives in brokerage houses to determine at a glance what actions (if any) need to be taken on a client's account. (*Hint:* Use color coding as well as icons to facilitate quick identification of extreme conditions.)
   a. Design and draw icons that correspond to the following:
      i. Transaction completed on the same day.
      ii. Account needs updating.

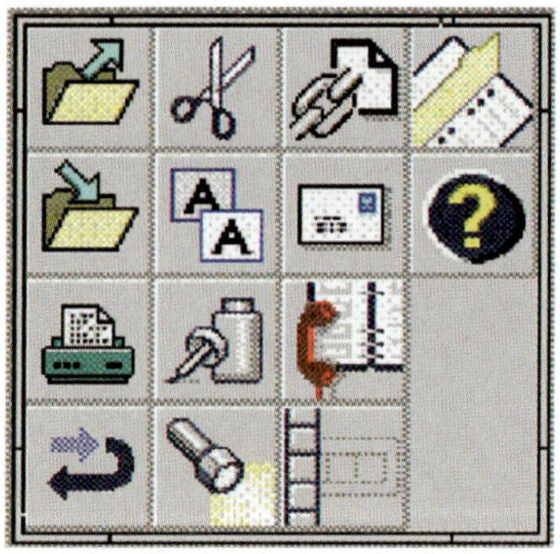

FIGURE 12.EX2
Icons from a popular organizer.

   iii. Client has requested information.
   iv. Account in error.
   v. Account inactive for two months.
   vi. Account closed.

   b. Recently, an up-and-coming discount brokerage house expressed an interest in developing its own Web-based portfolio management software that clients could use at home on their PCs to make trades, get real-time stock quotes, and so on. Design two input displays that make data entry easy for the client. The first display should allow users to enter stock symbols for the stocks they want to track on a daily basis. The second display should allow the client to use an icon-based system to design a customized report showing stock price trends in a variety of graphs or text.
   c. Suggest two other input displays that should be included in this new portfolio management software.

10. My Belle Cosmetics is a large business that has sales well ahead of any other regional cosmetics firm. As an organization, it is very sensitive to color, because it introduces new color lines in its products every fall and spring. The company has recently begun using technology to electronically show in-store customers how they appear in different shades of cosmetics without requiring them to actually apply the cosmetics.
    a. Design and draw a representation of a display screen that can be used by sales clerks at a counter to try many shades of lipstick and makeup on an individual customer very quickly and with a high degree of accuracy. Input from customers should be their hair color, the color of their favorite clothing, and their typical environmental lighting (fluorescent, incandescent, outdoor, and so on).
    b. Design and draw a representation of a display screen that is equivalent to the one in Problem 10a but that vividly demonstrates to decision makers in My Belle how color improves the understandability of the screen.
    c. One of the affiliates My Belle has on the Web is a large department store chain. In a paragraph, describe how the display screen in Problem 10a can be altered so that an individual can use it and My Belle can put it on the department store's ecommerce site to attract customers.
11. The Home Finders Realty Corporation specializes in locating homes for prospective buyers. Home information is stored in a database and is to be shown on an inquiry display screen. Design a GUI interface, Web-based display to enter the following data fields, which are used to select and display homes matching the criteria. Keep in mind the features available for a GUI display. The design elements (which are not in any particular sequence) are as follows:
    a. Minimum size (in square feet).
    b. Maximum size (in square feet, optional).
    c. Minimum number of bedrooms.
    d. Minimum number of bathrooms.
    e. Garage size (number of cars, optional).
    f. School district (a limited number of school districts are available for each area).
    g. Swimming pool (yes/no, optional).
    h. Setting (either city, suburban, or rural).
    i. Fireplace (yes/no, optional).
    j. Energy efficient (yes/no).

    In addition, describe the hyperlinks necessary to achieve this type of interaction.

12. Use index cards to design a tab control dialog box that changes the following database display settings. Use one card for each tab. Be sure to group each tab by function.
    a. Change the background color.
    b. Change the font.
    c. Change the object border to a raised look.
    d. Set the foreground color.
    e. Change the object border to a sunken look.
    f. Set the border color.
    g. Change the font size.
    h. Set the text to bold.
    i. Change the object border to a flat look.
    j. Set the text to underline.
    k. Change the object background color.
13. Design a Web entry page for the Home Finders Realty Corporation display screen created in Problem 11.
14. The five-year-old TowerWood hotel chain needs help designing its Web site. The company maintains properties in all the large U.S. tourist communities such as Orlando, Florida (near Disney World); Maui, Hawaii; Anaheim, California (near Disneyland); Las Vegas, Nevada; and New Orleans, Louisiana. Their properties feature a variety of rooms in all these locations.
    a. In a paragraph, discuss how the company can use skins on its Web site to attract different types of clientele, including families with small children, young couples on their honeymoon, retired couples who want to travel on a budget, and business travelers who need business services.
    b. Design and draw a series of skins that would appeal to the different types of hotel clientele listed in Problem 14a. (*Hint:* Use a graphics package or drawing program to help design the skins.)
    c. Add a group of potential Web site users for the TowerWood hotel chain who were *not* mentioned in Problem 14a and design and draw additional skins for them. Then create a table that matches each client group with a particular skin you designed.
15. Sludge's Auto is an auto parts recycling center, including classic and antique cars. Rhode Wheeler, the owner, would like to get his bearings on a Web site for customers to browse for parts. Design an Ajax Web page used to find parts. The customer needs to know the make, model, and year of a car as well as the part. If the part is in stock, the description, condition of the part, price, and shipping cost are displayed, with the quantity available for each condition of the part, along with a picture of the part. Provide a button for each part that may be clicked to purchase the part.
16. Design the Add Customer Web page for Sludge's auto. Include a profile that would allow Sludge's to send the customer an email if a certain part becomes available.
17. Design the Purchase Web page for Sludge's Auto. Assume that the customer has been added and has been logged on. Display some information about the customer. Split credit card information (type of credit card, credit card number, expiration date, and the security code found on the back of the card) between two Web pages.
18. Design a Web page using Ajax for registering an electronic product, either hardware or software. The form should have the purchaser's name and address, telephone number, email address, and a drop-down list of product categories. When the category is changed, send the category value to the server, which

returns an XML document containing the products for the category, used to create a drop-down list of products. When the customer selects a product, the product value is sent to the server, which returns an XML document used to create a model or version of the product.

GROUP PROJECTS

1. Maverick Transport is considering updating its input display screens. With your team, brainstorm about what should appear on input screens of computer operators who are entering delivery load data as loads are approved. Fields will include date of delivery, contents, weight, special requirements (for example, whether contents are perishable), and so on.
2. Each team member should design an appropriate input display using either a CASE tool or paper and pencil. Share your results with your team members.
3. Make a list of other input displays that Maverick Transport should develop. Remember to include dispatcher screens as well as screens to be accessed by customers and drivers. Indicate which should be PC screens or displays on wireless handheld devices.
4. Design a Web-based screen that will allow Maverick Transport customers to track the progress of a shipment. Brainstorm with team members for a list of elements, or perform an interview with a local trucking company to find out its requirements. List what hyperlinks will be essential. How will you control access so that customers can track only their own shipments?

SELECTED BIBLIOGRAPHY

Dahlboom, B., and L. Mathiassen. *Computers in Context.* Cambridge, MA: NCC Blackwell, 1993.

Direct Ferries. Web site uses Ajax in their application. Available at: www.directferries.co.uk/poirishsea.htm. Last accessed September 16, 2006.

Garrett, J. J. "Ajax: A New Approach to Web Applications" February 18, 2005. Available at: www.adpativepath.com. Last accessed December 20, 2006.

Google Suggest. Web site that uses Ajax. Available at: www.google.com/webhp?complete=1&hl=en. Last accessed September 16, 2006.

Ives, B. "Graphical User Interfaces for Business Information Systems." *MIS Quarterly* (Special Issue), December 1982, pp. 15–48.

Nielsen, J. R. Molich, C. Snyder, and S. Farrell. *E-Commerce User Experience*. Fremont, CA: Nielsen Norman Group, 2001.

Reisner, P. "Human Factors Studies of Data Base Query Languages: A Survey and Assessment." *Computing Surveys,* Vol. 4, No. 1, 1981.

Schmidt, A., and K. E. Kendall. "Using Ajax to Clean Up a Web Site: A New Programming Technique for Web Site Development." *Decision Line,* October 2006, pp. 11–13.

ALLEN SCHMIDT, JULIE E. KENDALL, AND KENNETH E. KENDALL

FORMING SCREENS AND SCREENING FORMS

Pooling information from the output design and reviewing their progress, Chip and Anna proceed to the next stage, the design of input. "Forms and displays must be designed to capture input information easily and accurately," remarks Anna.

Chip replies, "Special attention should be placed on creating input displays that are easy to use and require minimal operator entry."

Chip loads Visible Analyst and examines Diagram 0. "Perhaps the first form that we should create is the NEW COMPUTER RECORD, flowing from the SHIPPING/ RECEIVING DEPARTMENT into process 2, ADD NEW COMPUTER." Chip double clicks on the data flow representing the form to bring up its repository record. Its Composition area contains a data structure called NEW COMPUTER FORM RECORD. "I decided to create a separate structure for the form, because the elements are used both on the form and on the matching display screen," muses Chip. He clicks in the area and then clicks the Jump button. The elements contained on the form are included in the structure's Composition area. The Notes area contains information about which fields should be implemented as drop-down lists and check boxes.

Chip goes to work at designing the form. It is zoned to group logically related elements, which are arranged in a manner that would allow the user to complete the form easily. Because a prototype of the data entry display was previously approved, the task of designing the form is considerably simplified.

Chip schedules a meeting with Dot to review the form. She looks thoughtfully at the document for a few minutes and remarks, "It looks very good. I can see you've considered our viewpoint when designing the form. The only change I would recommend is to separate the initial information we have when the computer is received from the data supplied as we make decisions on which printer and monitor to attach."

Chip revises the form with the suggested changes and obtains final approval from Dot. The completed form is shown in Figure E12.1. Notice the zoning and the use of tick marks indicating the number of characters to be keyed. These help the user decide how to abbreviate data that would not fit in the file or database field length.

With the form complete, Chip starts working on modifying the display used to enter the form data. The ADD NEW COMPUTER entry display is shown in Figure E12.2.

One of the considerations of the entry display is ease of entering data, and another is accuracy. Still another consideration is the availability of help. New employees would not be familiar with the operation of the system or with what is required for a particular field entry. To achieve these goals, Chip includes pull-down lists for the MONITOR, PRINTER, NETWORK CONNECTION, and COMPUTER BOARDS. "I like the way these pull-down lists work," he remarks to Anna. "The users can easily select the codes that should be stored in the database."

"Why have the users select codes?" replies Anna. "There must be a way for them to select descriptive code meanings, such as the name of the printer, and have the computer store the codes."

"That's an excellent idea," exclaims Chip. A short time later, the modifications have been implemented.

EPISODE *CPU CASE*

12

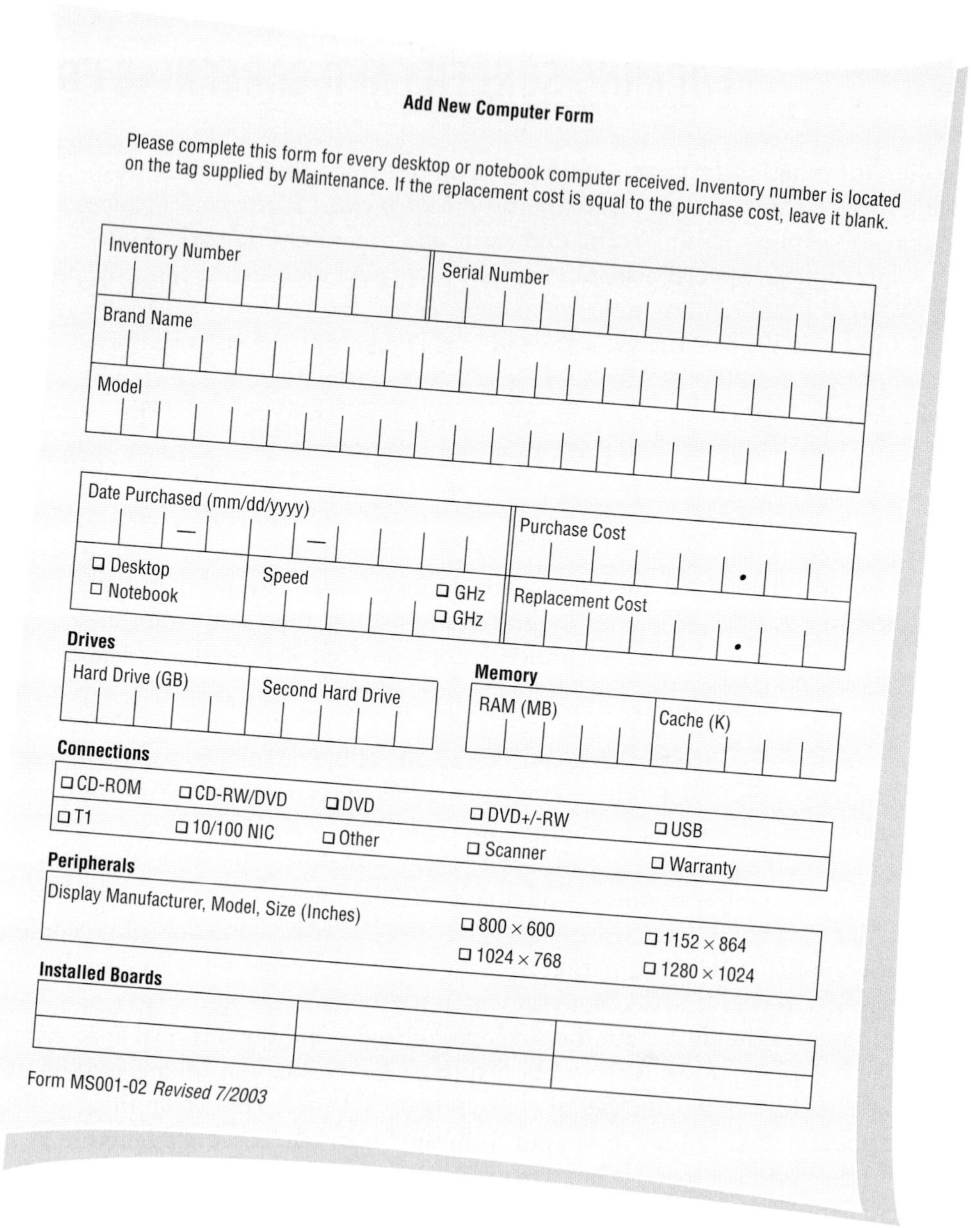

Add New Computer Form

Please complete this form for every desktop or notebook computer received. Inventory number is located on the tag supplied by Maintenance. If the replacement cost is equal to the purchase cost, leave it blank.

Inventory Number | Serial Number

Brand Name

Model

Date Purchased (mm/dd/yyyy) — — | Purchase Cost .

☐ Desktop ☐ Notebook | Speed ☐ GHz ☐ GHz | Replacement Cost .

Drives

Hard Drive (GB) | Second Hard Drive

Memory

RAM (MB) | Cache (K)

Connections

☐ CD-ROM ☐ CD-RW/DVD ☐ DVD ☐ DVD+/-RW ☐ USB

☐ T1 ☐ 10/100 NIC ☐ Other ☐ Scanner ☐ Warranty

Peripherals

Display Manufacturer, Model, Size (Inches) ☐ 800 × 600 ☐ 1024 × 768 ☐ 1152 × 864 ☐ 1280 × 1024

Installed Boards

Form MS001-02 *Revised 7/2003*

FIGURE E12.1
NEW COMPUTER FORM RECORD data structure screen showing elements.

Anna reviews the display screen and remarks, "This looks terrific! I like the grouping of the check boxes and descriptive information contained in the drop-down lists."

"Watch this one in action," replies Chip. "I've added a button for the users to click when they have entered all the data and made all the selections. They can also print the completed form."

"What about help?" asks Anna.

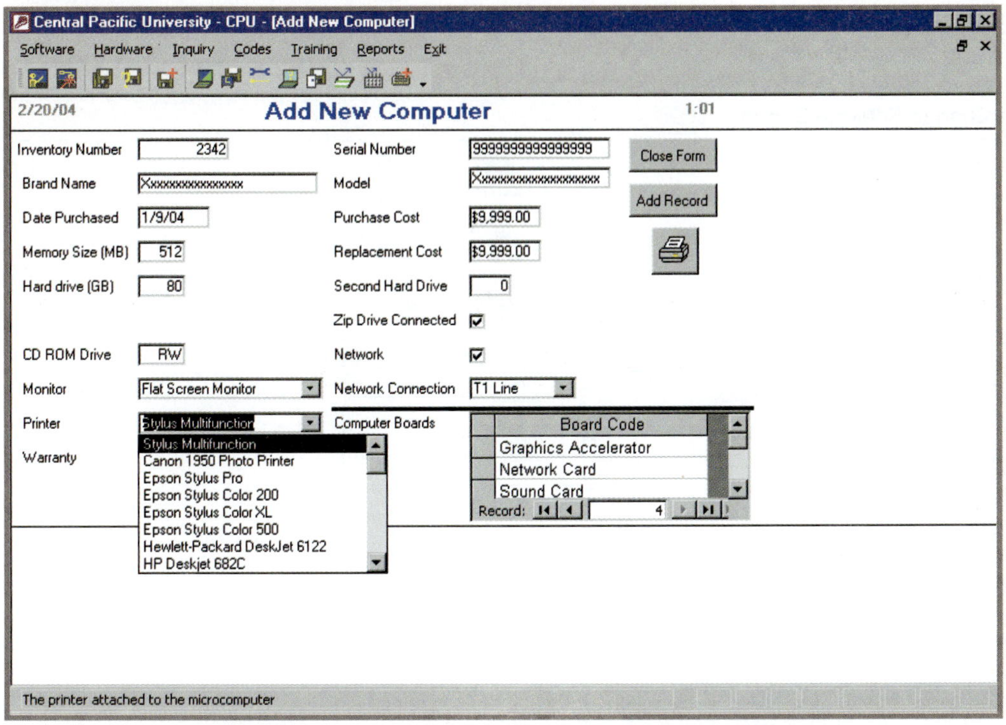

FIGURE E12.2

Pull-down lists on the ADD NEW COMPUTER Microsoft Access screen.

"I've thought about that also," answers Chip. "As the cursor moves from field to field, the status line on the bottom of the screen displays one line of help appropriate for that field. I can also add tool-tip help, a small box of help options that appears when the mouse cursor remains over one entry area for a short amount of time." Notice that the pull-down lists have meaningful names in the data areas. There is room for three internal computer boards in the BOARD CODE entry area. Scroll bars provide additional entry areas if needed. Help is shown in the status line at the bottom of the display.

Dot reviews the completed display and enters some test data. "I'm really impressed!" she exclaims. "It is much smoother than I ever expected. When can we expect the rest of the system?" Chip smiles with appreciation and remarks that great progress is being made. "I do hope that the rest of the system is as clear to use and easy to operate!" Dot says appreciatively.

Meanwhile, Anna is meeting with Hy Perteks, who is desperately seeking help. "I'm swamped with requests for help on software packages! Is there any way to design a portion of the system for maintaining information on the available software experts?" asks Hy. "I have names written on scraps of paper and I keep misplacing them. Often I find out who these experts are only after someone else finds them first."

Anna asks some questions about what information would be required and how Hy would like to maintain and display the records. Hy replies, "There is so much expertise available, but the only way I have of locating the person's information is by using their name as an index. And, I confess, I'm awful at remembering the correct spelling of the

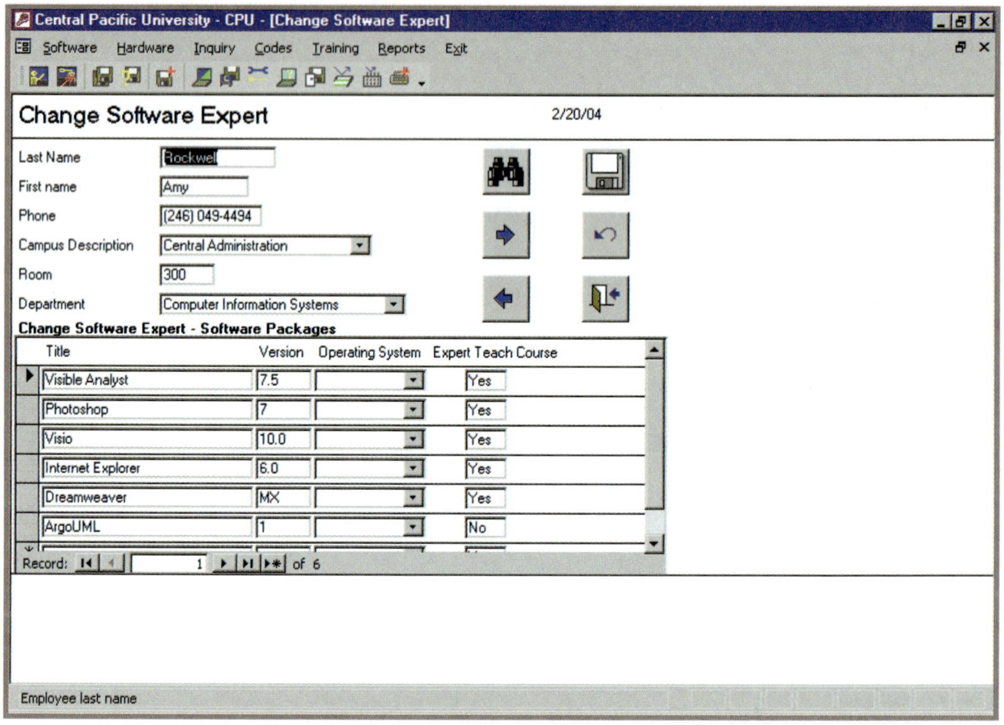

FIGURE E12.3
The CHANGE SOFTWARE EXPERT Microsoft Access screen.

first name, let alone the last name." Anna assures him that there will be an easy-to-use system available soon.

Back at her desk, Anna thinks about the problem. "The ADD display screen would be easy to create, but what about the CHANGE one?" She wonders, "How can I?" and then thinks, "Ah ha!" as she snaps her fingers. The design becomes clear. There would be a display with two distinct regions on it. The first region would contain the last and first name of the software expert. Included with the display is a Find button as well as buttons for scrolling back and forth through records. If the users make a mistake entering data, there is an Undo button, and there is also a button to save the changes. The completed display screen is illustrated in Figure E12.3.

"Great-looking display," grins Chip. "I want to be here when you show it to Hy."

The problem of deleting software course records for software that is no longer in use requires a different approach. Anna reasons that it would be easy if she used the **Find** feature to locate a record and then used a Find Next button to locate the next record that matches the criteria. There would also be buttons that allow her to move to the next or previous records. (See the DELETE SOFTWARE COURSE form on the disk.)

After the record is located, the DELETE SOFTWARE COURSE program would display pertinent information. All codes on the file, such as COURSE LEVEL and OPERATING SYSTEM, would be replaced with the full code meaning. None of the data would be able to be modified at this time. The operator would have the opportunity to review the record and then choose to either delete or not delete the record.

When the delete button is clicked, a dialog box is displayed asking the users if they really want to delete the record. They may choose to cancel the delete at that time.

Hy is delighted with the prototype display screens. As he tests each of them, he remarks, "You don't know how easy it's going to be for me to answer help requests. These are fabulous!" He pauses for a long moment and then asks, "I have a lot of requests about providing periodically scheduled training courses. Do you think we could work on a system to register for courses?"

Anna purses her lips for a moment and remarks, "Did you ever hear of a project having scope creep, always adding little things and the project never ends? The university does, however, have an intranet initiative going, and it is looking for volunteers. Perhaps we can design a Web page for registering courses."

"That's great!" replies Hy. "That's more than I ever hoped for."

Anna starts to design the Web page, including the users' first and last names as well as their Internet addresses and office phones. Additional areas are used to enter the campus where they are located, the software they use, and their class level. Chip reviews the form and remarks, "Rather than have them type in the campus and software information, why not have them select options from a pull-down list? And what about allowing them to select convenient times for training?"

"Good idea," replies Anna. "And I think the levels of training should be a group of radio buttons." The completed intranet Web page is illustrated in Figure E12.4. Notice that there are buttons to submit the query or reset it to spaces and pull-down list default values. There is also a link for submitting email questions to the training officer.

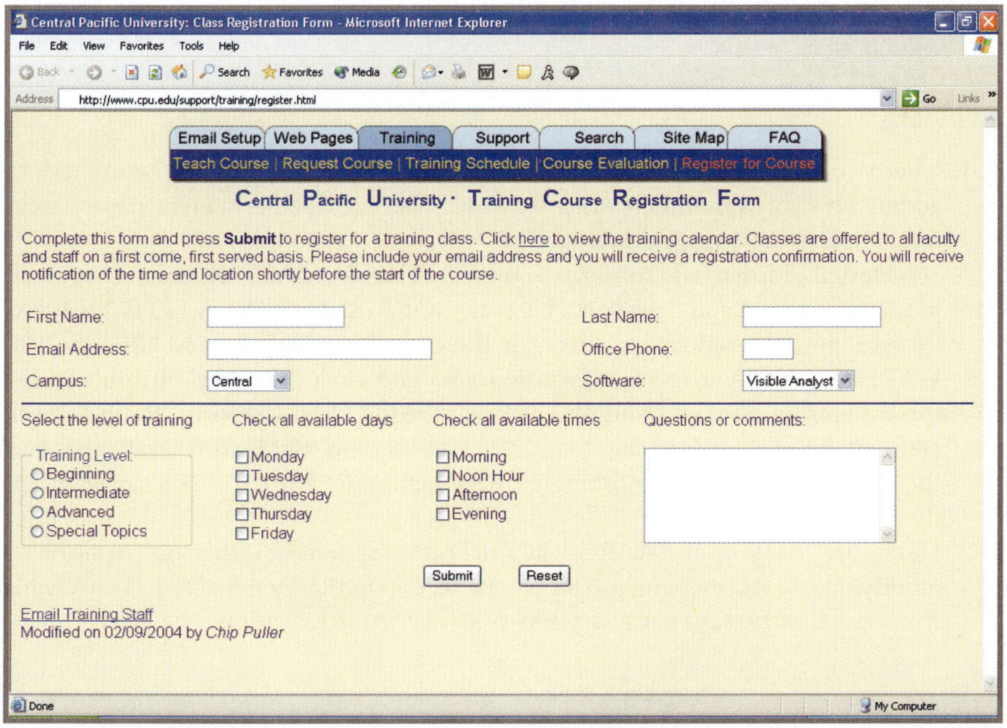

FIGURE E12.4

An intranet Web form for Training Registration on the CPU Web site.

12

Hy is thrilled. "This form is better than I ever imagined. I think we are really providing effective training registration, and I know that my phone will not be ringing as much. I've got another great idea!"

The following exercises may be done by designing the report or display screen using printer or display screen layout forms, or they may be created using any word processor with which you are familiar. The fields and other related information for the reports are contained in Visible Analyst data flow repository entries. The names for the data flow are listed for each exercise.

Corresponding reports and displays (called forms in Access) have been created. All the information is present in the Access database; you only have to modify the existing reports and display screens to produce the final versions. Modifications are made by clicking on the desired report or screen and then clicking the Design button. The following modifications may be made. The Page Header contains column headings. The Detail area contains the print fields for the report.

Click in a field to select it. Click on several fields while holding the Shift key to select them.
Drag a selected field (or fields) to move them.
Click on one of the small boxes surrounding the field to change the field size.
Select several fields and click Format and either:
  Align, to align all fields with the top, left, and so on field.
  Size, to make fields equal to the widest, tallest, and so on field.
  Horizontal spacing, to make horizontal spacing equal, or to increase or decrease the spacing.
  Vertical spacing, to make vertical spacing equal, or to increase or decrease the spacing.

EXERCISES

E-1. Cher Ware has remarked several times that a good form would make the task of adding new software much easier. It would also provide permanent paper documentation for software additions.

Design a form to add software to the SOFTWARE MASTER. Open Diagram 0 in Visible Analyst and double click on the SOFTWARE RECEIVED FORM data flow to view the repository entry for the data flow. Click on the NEW SOFTWARE RECORD in the Composition area and click the Jump button to view the data structure containing the elements required on the form. Jump to each element to determine the length of the screen field. You may also use the Repository Reports and Single Entry Listing to print a list of elements for the form.

E-2. Design the ADD SOFTWARE RECORD display screen, either on paper or by modifying the Access screen. Use the fields created in Exercise E-1. The Visible Analyst data structure name is NEW SOFTWARE RECORD.

The exercises preceded by a Web icon indicate value-added material is available from the Web site at www.prenhall.com/kendall. Students can download a sample Visible Analyst Project and a Microsoft Access database that can be used to complete the exercises. Visible Analyst software can be packaged with this text for an additional fee.

E-3. Hy Perteks would like a form to fill in as he learns about new software experts. Use the Visible Analyst ADD SOFTWARE EXPERT data structure to determine the fields required for the form.

E-4. Create the ADD SOFTWARE EXPERT display on paper, using a word processor, or by modifying the Access form. Test the ADD SOFTWARE EXPERT display, using the drop-down lists and observing the status bar on the bottom of the screen.

E-5. Design or modify the Access form for the DELETE SOFTWARE EXPERT display. Which fields are drop-down lists? Use the Visible Analyst DELETE SOFTWARE EXPERT data structure.

E-6. Design or modify the Access form for the DELETE COMPUTER RECORD display. The Visible Analyst structure is called DELETE COMPUTER RECORD.

E-7. Cher Ware and Anna spent the better part of a morning working out the details on the software portion of the system. Plagued by the problem of providing consistent software upgrades for all machines, Cher would like an easy method of upgrading. A few older versions of software may also be retained for special needs.

Part of the solution is to produce a report, sorted by location, of all machines containing the software to be upgraded. As the new software is installed, a check mark is placed on the report after each machine.

Design the UPGRADE SOFTWARE display design. Add a **Find** button to locate the title and to provide a field that can be used to enter the new VERSION NUMBER. The update program will display a line for each machine containing the old version of the installed software. These lines are sorted by CAMPUS LOCATION and ROOM LOCATION.

Columns are CAMPUS LOCATION, ROOM LOCATION, INVENTORY NUMBER, BRAND NAME, MODEL, UPGRADE, and RETAIN OLD VERSION. The UPGRADE column contains a check box that is to be checked if the software is to be upgraded. The RETAIN OLD VERSION is also a check box, unchecked by default. The users would check the box for a specific machine that must retain the old and new versions of the software.

Look in the Visible Analyst SOFTWARE UPGRADE data structure for the elements contained on the screen.

E-8. Explain why the UPGRADE SOFTWARE display screen would display machines rather than have Cher enter the machine IDs. In a paragraph, discuss why the display shows records in a CAMPUS/ROOM sequence.

E-9. Design the CHANGE SOFTWARE display screen. This allows Cher Ware to modify data that have been entered incorrectly, as well as information that routinely changes, such as SOFTWARE EXPERT and NUMBER OF COPIES. The SOFTWARE INVENTORY NUMBER is the primary key and may not be changed. The other SOFTWARE MASTER fields that should be included on the screen are found in the Visible Analyst SOFTWARE CHANGES data structure. Use these fields to design the display screen. A limited display screen, CHANGE SOFTWARE RECORD, has been created in Access. Use the Access Field List to add fields to it. Include the following buttons: Find, Find Next, Previous Record, Next Record, Save Record, and Cancel Changes.

E-10. Hy Perteks is concerned that old courses for obsolete versions of software are cluttering the drives. Create and print the DELETE SOFTWARE COURSE display.

Entry fields are the SOFTWARE TITLE, OPERATING SYSTEM, and VERSION NUMBER. The program displays a line for each course taught for the software version. The first column contains an entry field with a D (for delete) presented as a default. Placing a space in the field will prevent the record from being deleted. The other columns for each line are COURSE TITLE, LEVEL, and CLASS LENGTH. Add a meaningful operator message.

E-11. Design the UPDATE MAINTENANCE INFORMATION display screen. It contains entry fields that allow Mike Crowe to change maintenance information as computers are repaired or as routine maintenance is performed on them. The Visible Analyst data structure is UPDATE MAINTENANCE INFORMATION.

DESIGNING DATABASES

13

Learning Objectives

Once you have mastered the material in this chapter you will be able to:

1. **Understand database concepts.**
2. **Use normalization to efficiently store data in a database.**
3. **Use databases for presenting data.**
4. **Understand the concept of data warehouses.**
5. **Comprehend the usefulness of publishing databases to the Web.**

Data storage is considered by some to be the heart of an information system. First, the data have to be available when the user wants to use them. Second, the data must be accurate and consistent (they must possess integrity). Beyond this requirement, the objectives of database design include efficient storage of data as well as efficient updating and retrieval. Finally, it is necessary that information retrieval be purposeful. The information obtained from the stored data must be in a form useful for managing, planning, controlling, or decision making.

There are two approaches to the storage of data in a computer-based system. The first is to store the data in individual files, each unique to a particular application. The second approach involves building a database. A database is a formally defined and centrally controlled store of data intended for use in many different applications.

Conventional files will remain a practical way to store data for some (but not all) applications. A file can be designed and built quite rapidly, and any concerns about data availability and security are minimized. When file designs are carefully thought out, all the necessary information can be included and the risk of unintentionally omitting data will be low.

The use of individual files has many consequences. Files are often designed only with immediate needs in mind. When it becomes important to query the system for a combination of some of the attributes, these attributes may be contained in separate files or may not even exist. Redesigning files often implies that programs that access the files must be rewritten accordingly, which translates into expensive programming time for file and program development and maintenance.

A system using conventional files implies that stored data will be redundant. Furthermore, updating files is more time consuming. Finally, data integrity is a concern, because a change in one file will also require modification of the same data in other files.

DATABASES

Databases are not merely a collection of files. Rather, a database is a central source of data meant to be shared by many users for a variety of applications. The heart of a database is the database management system (DBMS), which allows the creation, modification, and updating of the database; the retrieval of data; and the generation of reports and displays. The person who ensures that the database meets its objectives is called the database administrator.

The effectiveness objectives of the database include the following:

1. Ensuring that data can be shared among users for a variety of applications.
2. Maintaining data that are both accurate and consistent.
3. Ensuring that all data required for current and future applications will be readily available.
4. Allowing the database to evolve as the needs of the users grow.
5. Allowing users to construct their personal view of the data without concern for the way the data are physically stored.

The foregoing list of objectives provides us with a reminder of the advantages and disadvantages of the database approach. First, the sharing of the data means that data need to be stored only once. That in turn helps achieve data integrity, because changes to data are accomplished more easily and reliably if the data appear once rather than in many different files.

When a user needs particular data, a well-designed database anticipates the need for such data (or perhaps it has already been used for another application). Consequently, the data have a higher probability of being available in a database than in a conventional file system. A well-designed database can also be more flexible than separate files; that is, a database can evolve as the needs of users and applications change.

Finally, the database approach has the advantage of allowing users to have their own view of the data. Users need not be concerned with the actual structure of the database or its physical storage.

Many users are extracting parts of the central database from mainframes and downloading them onto PCs or handheld devices. These smaller databases are then used to generate reports or answer queries specific to the end user.

Relational databases for PCs have improved dramatically over the last few years. One major technological change has been the design of database software that takes advantage of the GUI. With the advent of programs such as Microsoft Access, users can drag and drop fields between two or more tables. Developing relational databases with these tools has been made relatively easy.

DATA CONCEPTS

It is important to understand how data are represented before considering the use of files or the database approach. In this section, critical definitions are covered, including the abstraction of data from the real world to the storage of data in tables and database relations.

CONSULTING OPPORTUNITY 13.1

HITCH YOUR CLEANING CART TO A STAR

The Marc Schnieder Janitorial Supply Company has asked for your assistance in cleaning up its data storage. As soon as you begin asking Marc Schnieder detailed questions about his database, his face gets flushed. "We don't really have a database as you describe it," he says with some embarrassment. "I've always wanted to clean up our records, but I couldn't find a capable person to head the effort."

After talking with Mr. Schnieder, you walk down the hall to the closet-sized office of Stan Lessink, the chief programmer. Stan fills you in on the historical development of the current information system. "The Marc Schnieder Janitorial Supply Company is a rags-to-riches story," Stan remarks. "Mr. Schnieder's first job was as a janitor in a bowling alley. He saved enough money to buy some products and started selling them to other alleys. Soon he decided to expand the janitorial supply business. He found out that as his business grew, he had more product lines and types of customers. Salespeople in the company are assigned to different major product lines (stores, offices, and so on); some are in-house sales, and some specialize in heavy equipment, such as floor strippers and waxers. Records were kept in separate files."

You recall Mr. Schnieder saying, "The problem is that we have no way to compare the profits of each division. We would like to set up incentive programs for salespeople and provide better balance in allocating salespeople to each product line."

When you talk with Stan, however, he adds, "Each division has its own incentive system. Commissions vary. I don't see how we can have a common system. Besides, I can get our reports out quickly because our files are set up the way we want them. We have never issued a paycheck late."

Describe how you would go about analyzing the data storage needs of the Marc Schnieder Janitorial Supply Company. Would you trash the old system or just polish it up a bit? Discuss the implications of your decision in two paragraphs.

REALITY, DATA, AND METADATA

The real world will be referred to as reality. Data collected about people, places, or events in reality will eventually be stored in a file or database. To understand the form and structure of the data, information about the data itself is required. The information that describes data is referred to as metadata.

The relationship between reality, data, and metadata is pictured in Figure 13.1. Within the realm of reality are entities and attributes; within the realm of actual data are record occurrences and data item occurrences; and within the realm of metadata are record definitions and data item definitions. The meanings of these terms are discussed in the following subsections.

Entities Any object or event about which someone chooses to collect data is an entity. An entity may be a person, place, or thing (for example, a salesperson, a city, or a product). Any entity can also be an event or unit of time such as a machine breakdown, a sale, or a month or year. In addition to the entities discussed in Chapter 2 is an additional minor entity called an entity subtype. Its symbol is a smaller rectangle within the entity rectangle.

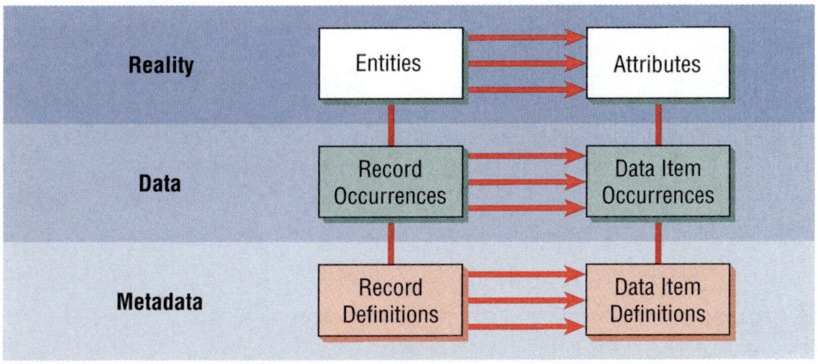

FIGURE 13.1
Reality, data, and metadata.

An entity subtype is a special one-to-one relationship used to represent additional attributes (fields) of another entity that may not be present on every record of the first entity. Entity subtypes eliminate the situation in which an entity may have null fields stored on database tables.

An example is the primary entity of a customer. Preferred customers may have special fields containing discount information, and this information would be in an entity subtype. Another example is students who have internships. The STUDENT MASTER should not have to contain information about internships for each student, because perhaps only a small number of students have internships.

FIGURE 13.2
Entity-relationship (E-R) diagrams can show one-to-one, one-to-many, many-to-one, or many-to-many associations.

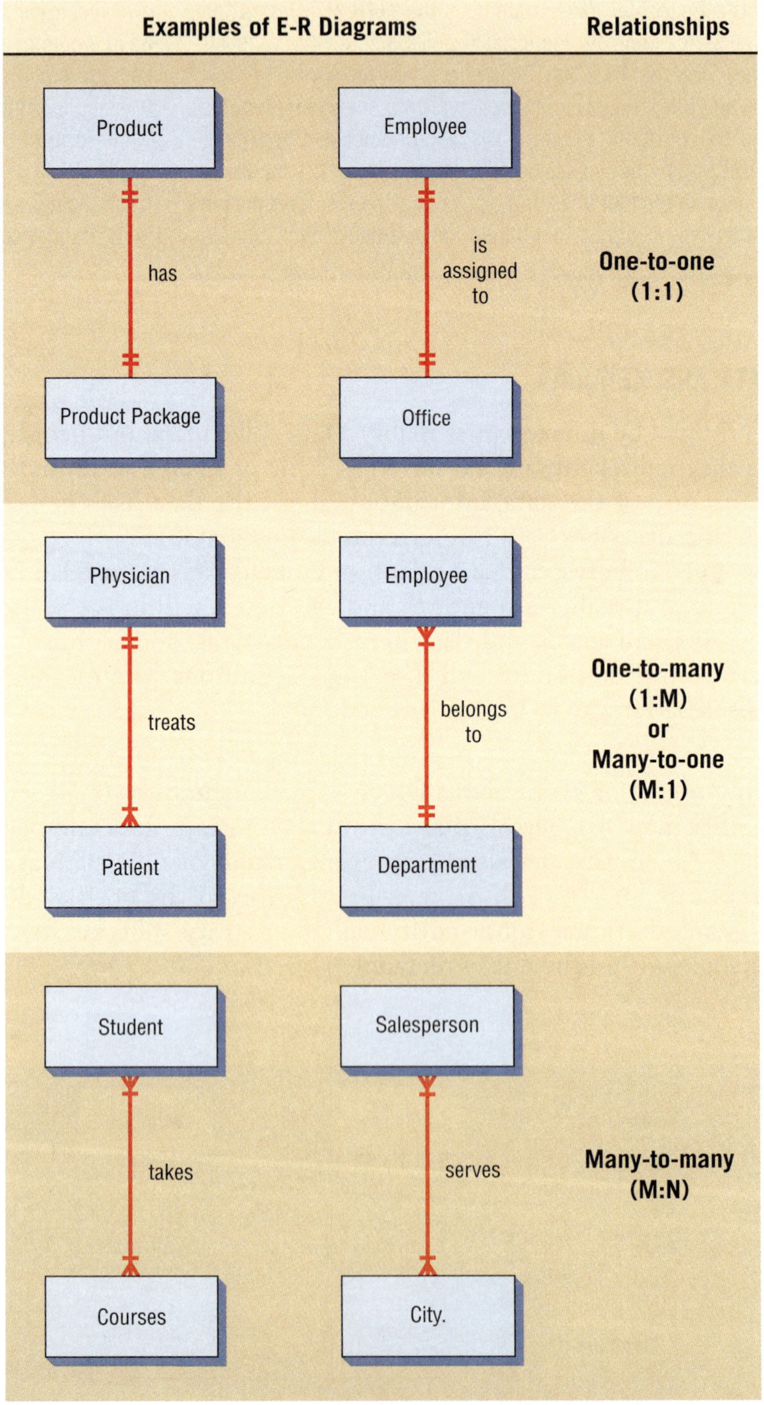

Relationships Relationships are associations between entities (sometimes they are referred to as data associations). Figure 13.2 is an entity-relationship (E-R) diagram that shows various types of relationships.

The first type of relationship is a one-to-one relationship (designated as 1:1). The diagram shows that there is only one PRODUCT PACKAGE for each PRODUCT. The second one-to-one relationship shows that each EMPLOYEE has a unique OFFICE. Notice that all these entities can be described further (a product price would not be an entity, nor would a phone extension).

Another type of relationship is a one-to-many (1:M) or a many-to-one association. As shown in the figure, a PHYSICIAN in a health maintenance organization is assigned many PATIENTS, but a PATIENT is assigned only one PHYSICIAN. Another example shows that an EMPLOYEE is a member of only one DEPARTMENT, but each DEPARTMENT has many EMPLOYEE(s).

Finally, a many-to-many relationship (designated as M:N) describes the possibility that entities may have many associations in either direction. For example, a STUDENT can have many COURSE(s), and at the same time a COURSE may have many STUDENT(s) enrolled in it. The second example shows that a SALESPERSON can call on many CITY(s) and a CITY can be a sales area for many SALESPERSON(s).

The standard symbols for crow's foot notation, the official explanation of the symbols, and what they actually mean, are all given in Figure 13.3. Notice that the symbol for an entity is a rectangle. An entity is defined as a class of a person, place, or thing. A rectangle with a diamond inside stands for an associative entity,

Symbol	Official Explanation	What It Really Means
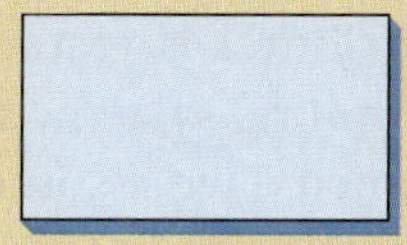	Entity	A class of persons, places, or things
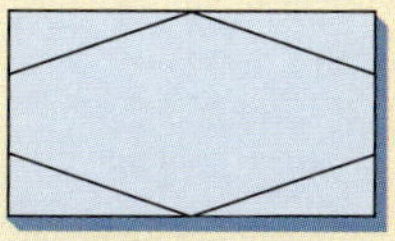	Associative entity	Used to join two entities
	Attributive entity	Used for repeating groups
	To 1 relationship	Exactly one
	To many relationship	One or more
	To 0 or 1 relationship	Only zero or one
	To 0 or more relationship	Can be zero, one, or more
	To more than 1 relationship	Greater than one

FIGURE 13.3
The entity-relationship symbols and their meanings.

which is used to join two entities. A rectangle with an oval in it stands for an attributive entity, which is used for repeating groups.

The other notations necessary to draw E-R diagrams are the connections, of which there are five different types. In the lower portion of the figure, the meaning of the notation is explained. When a straight line connects two plain entities and the ends of the line are both marked with two short marks (||), a one-to-one relationship exists. Following that you will notice a crow's foot with a short mark (|); when this notation links entities, it indicates a relationship of one-to-one or one-to-many (to one or more).

Entities linked with a straight line plus a short mark (|) and a zero (which looks more like a circle, O) are depicting a relationship of one-to-zero or one-to-one (only zero or one). A fourth type of link for relating entities is drawn with a straight line marked on the end with a zero (O) followed by a crow's foot. This type shows a zero-to-zero, zero-to-one, or zero-to-many relationship. Finally, a straight line linking entities with a crow's foot at the end depicts a relationship to more than one.

An entity may have a relationship connecting it to itself. This type of relationship is called a self-join relationship; the implication is that there must be a way to link one record in a file to another record in the same file. An example of a self-join relationship can be found in the HyperCase simulations found throughout these chapters. A task may have a precedent task (that is, one that must be completed before starting the current task). In this situation, one record (the current task) points to another record (the precedent task) in the same file.

The relationships in words can be written along the top or the side of each connecting line. In practice, you see the relationship in one direction, although you can write relationships on both sides of the line, each representing the point of view of one of the two entities. (See Chapter 2 for more details about drawing E-R diagrams.)

An Entity-Relationship Example An entity-relationship diagram containing many entities, many different types of relations, and numerous attributes is featured in Figure 13.4. In this E-R diagram, we are concerned about a billing system, and in particular with the prescription part of the system. (For simplicity, we assume that office visits are handled differently and are outside the scope of this system.)

FIGURE 13.4

The entity-relationship diagram for patient treatment. Attributes can be listed alongside the entities. In each case, the key is underlined.

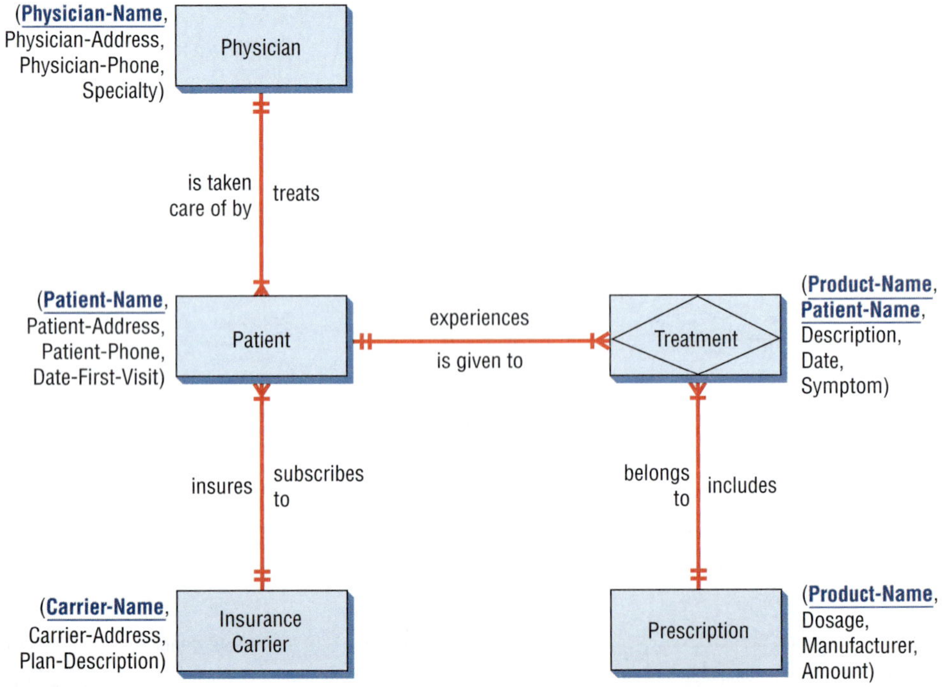

The entities are PRESCRIPTION, PHYSICIAN, PATIENT, and INSURANCE CARRIER. The entity TREATMENT is not important for the billing system, but it is part of the E-R diagram because it is used to bridge the gap between PRESCRIPTION and PATIENT. We therefore drew it as an associative entity in the figure.

Here, a PHYSICIAN treats many PATIENT(s) (1:M), who each subscribe to an individual INSURANCE CARRIER. Of course, the PATIENT is only one of many patients that subscribe to that particular INSURANCE CARRIER (M:1).

To complete the PHYSICIAN's records, the physician needs to keep information about the treatments a PATIENT has. Many PATIENT(s) experience many TREATMENT(s), making it a many-to-many (M:N) relationship. TREATMENT is represented as an associative entity because it is not important in our billing system by itself. TREATMENT(s) can include the taking of PRESCRIPTION(s), and thus is also an M:N relationship, because many treatments may call for combinations of pharmaceuticals and many drugs may work for many treatments.

Some detail is then filled in for the attributes. The attributes are listed next to each of the entities, and the key is underlined. For example, the entity PRESCRIPTION has a <u>PRODUCT-NAME</u>, DOSAGE, MANUFACTURER, and AMOUNT. Ideally, it would be beneficial to design a database in this fashion, using entity-relationship diagrams and then filling in the details concerning attributes. This top-down approach is desirable, but it is sometimes very difficult to achieve.

Attributes An attribute is some characteristic of an entity. There can be many attributes for each entity. For example, a patient (entity) can have many attributes, such as last name, first name, street address, city, state, and so on. The date of the patient's last visit as well as the prescription details are also attributes. When the data dictionary was constructed in Chapter 8, the smallest particular described was called a data element. When files and databases are discussed, these data elements are generally referred to as data items. Data items are in fact the smallest units in a file or database. The term *data item* is also used interchangeably with the word *attribute.*

Data items can have values. These values can be of fixed or variable length; they can be alphabetic, numeric, special characters, or alphanumeric. Examples of data items and their values can be found in Figure 13.5.

Sometimes a data item is also referred to as a field. A field, however, represents something physical, not logical. Therefore, many data items can be packed into a field; the field can be read and converted to a number of data items. A common example of this is to store the date in a single field as MM/DD/YYYY. To sort the file in order by date, three separate data items are extracted from the field and sorted first by YYYY, then by MM, and finally by DD.

Records A record is a collection of data items that have something in common with the entity described. Figure 13.6 is an illustration of a record with many related data items. The record shown is for an order placed with a mail-order company. The <u>ORDER-#</u>, LAST NAME, INITIAL, STREET ADDRESS, CITY, STATE, and CREDIT CARD are all attributes. Most records are of fixed length, so there is no need to determine the length of the record each time.

Under certain circumstances (for instance, when space is at a premium), variable-length records are used. A variable-length record is used as an alternative to reserving a large amount of space for the longest possible record, such as the maximum number of visits a patient has made to a physician. Each visit would contain many data items that would be part of the patient's full record (or file folder in a manual system). Later in this chapter, normalization of a relation is discussed. Normalization is a process that eliminates repeating groups found in variable-length records.

FIGURE 13.5
Typical values assigned to data items may be numbers, alphabetic characters, special characters, and combinations of all three.

Entity	Data Item	Value
Salesperson	Salesperson Number	87254
	Salesperson Name	Kaytell
	Company Name	Music Unlimited
	Address	45 Arpeum Circle
	Sales	$20,765
Package	Width	2
	Height	16
	Length	16
	Weight	3
	Mailing Address	765 Dulcinea Drive
	Return Address	P.O. Box 341, Spring Valley, MN
Order	Product(s)	B521
	Description(s)	"My Fair Lady" compact disc
	Quantity Ordered	1
	Last Name of Customer	Kiley
	First Initial	R.
	Street Address	765 Dulcinea Drive
	City	La Mancha
	State	CA
	Zip Code	93407
	Credit Card Number	65-8798-87
	Date Order Was Placed	05/01/2003
	Amount	$6.99
	Status	Backordered

Keys A key is one of the data items in a record that is used to identify a record. When a key uniquely identifies a record, it is called a primary key. For example, ORDER-# can be a primary key because only one number is assigned to each customer order. In this way, the primary key identifies the real-world entity (customer order).

Special care must be taken when designing the primary key. Often it is a sequential number or a sequential number with a self-checking number (called a check digit) at the end of the digits. At times there is some meaning built into the primary key, but defining a primary key based on an attribute is considered a risk. If the attribute changes, the primary key will also change, creating a dependency between the primary key and the data.

An example of a primary key based on data is using a state abbreviation for the state name or an airline luggage code for an airport name. An attribute or a collection of attributes that can serve as a primary key is called a candidate key. A primary key should also be minimal and contain no extra attributes than are necessary to identify a record.

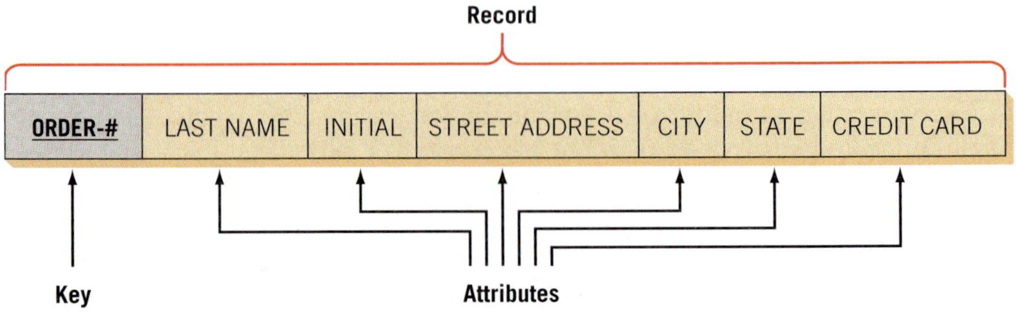

FIGURE 13.6
A record has a primary key and may have many attributes.

A key is called a secondary key if it cannot uniquely identify a record. Secondary keys either may be unique or may identify multiple records in a database. Secondary keys can be used to select a group of records that belong to a set (for example, orders from the state of Virginia).

When it is not possible to identify a record uniquely by using one of the data items found in a record, a key can be constructed by choosing two or more data items and combining them. This key is called a concatenated, or composite, key. When a data item is used as a key in a record, the description is underlined. Therefore, in the ORDER record (ORDER-#, LAST NAME, INITIAL, STREET ADDRESS, CITY, STATE, CREDIT CARD), the key is ORDER-#. If an attribute is a key in another file, it should be underlined with a dashed line.

Some databases allow the developer to use an object identifier (OID), which is a unique key for each record in the database, not just in a table. Given an object identifier, one record will be obtained regardless of the table on which exists. This may be included with an order or a payment confirmation, along with a message like, "This is your confirmation number."

Metadata Metadata are data about the data in the file or database. Metadata describe the name given and the length assigned each data item. Metadata also describe the length and composition of each of the records.

Figure 13.7 is an example of metadata for a database for some generic software. The length of each data item is indicated according to a convention, where

Data Item	Value		
Salesperson Number	N	5	
Salesperson Name	A	20	
Company Name	A	26	
Address	A	36	
Sales	N	9.2	
Width	N	2	
Height	N	2	
Length	N	2	
Weight	N	2	
Mailing Address	A	36	
Return Address	A	36	
Product(s)	A	4	
Description(s)	A	30	
Quantity Ordered	N	2	
Last Name of Customer	A	24	
First Initial	A	1	
Street Address	A	28	
City	A	12	
State	A	2	
Zip Code	N	9	
Credit Card Number	N	10	
Date Order Was Placed	D	8	MM/DD/YYYY
Amount	$	7.2	
Status	A	22	

Fields

N	Numeric
A	Alphanumeric or text
D	Date MM/DD/YYYY
$	Currency
M	Memo

7.2 means that the field takes up 7 digits, two of which are right of the decimal.

Special formats for fields may be specified.

FIGURE 13.7

Metadata includes a description of what the value of each data item looks like.

7.2 means that seven spaces are reserved for the number, two of which are to the right of the decimal point. The letter N signifies "numeric," and the A stands for "alphanumeric." The D stands for "date" and is automatically in the form MM/DD/YYYY. Some programs, such as Microsoft Access, use plain English for metadata, so words such as *text*, *currency*, and *number* are used. Microsoft Access provides a default of 50 characters as the field length for names, which is fine when working with small systems. If, however, you are working with a large database for a bank or a utility company, for example, you do not want to devote that much space to that field. Otherwise, the database would become quite large and filled with wasted space. That is when you can use metadata to plan ahead and design a more efficient database.

FILE ORGANIZATION

A file contains groups of records used to provide information for operations, planning, management, and decision making. The types of files used are discussed first, followed by a description of the many ways conventional files can be organized.

File Types Files can be used for storing data for an indefinite period of time, or they can be used to store data temporarily for a specific purpose. Master files and table files are used to store data for a long period. The temporary files are usually called transaction files, work files, or report files.

Master Files. Master files contain records for a group of entities. The attributes may be updated often, but the records themselves are relatively permanent. These files tend to have large records containing all the information about a data entity. Each record usually contains a primary key and several secondary keys.

Although the analyst is free to arrange the data elements in a master file in any order, a standard arrangement is to place the primary key field first, followed by descriptive elements, and finally by elements that change frequently with business activities. Examples of a master file include patient records, customer records, a personnel file, and a parts inventory file.

Table Files. A table file contains data used to calculate more data or performance measures. One example is a table of postage rates used to determine the shipping costs of a package. Another example is a tax table. Table files usually are read only by a program.

Transaction Files. A transaction file is used to enter changes that update the master file and produce reports. Suppose a newspaper subscriber master file needs to be updated; the transaction file would contain the subscriber number, and a transaction code such as E for extending the subscription, C for canceling the subscription, or A for address change. Then only information relevant to the updating needs to be entered; that is, the length of renewal if E, and the address if A. No additional information would be needed if the subscription were canceled. The rest of the information already exists in the master file. Transaction files may contain several different types of records, such as the three used for updating the newspaper subscription master, with a code on the transaction file indicating the type of transaction.

Report Files. When it is necessary to print a report when no printer is available (e.g., when the printer is busy printing other jobs), a report file is used. Sending the output to a file rather than a printer is called spooling. Later, when the device is ready, the document can be printed. Report files are very useful, because users can take files to other computer systems and output to specialty devices.

	ORDER-#	LAST NAME	I	STREET ADDRESS	CITY	ST	CREDIT CARD
1	10784	MacRae	G	2314 Curly Circle	Lincoln	NE	45-4654-76
2	10796	Jones	S	34 Dream Lane	Oklahoma City	OK	45-9876-74
3	11821	Preston	R	1008 Madison Ave.	River City	IA	34-7642-64
4	11845	Channing	C	454 Harmonia St.	New York	NY	34-0876-87
5	11872	Kiley	R	765 Dulcinea Drive	La Mancha	CA	65-8798-87
6	11976	Verdon	G	7564 K Street	Chicago	IL	67-8453-18
7	11998	Rivera	C	4342 West Street	Chicago	IL	12-2312-54
8	12765	Orbach	J	1345 Michigan Ave.	Chicago	IL	23-4545-65
9	12769	Steele	T	3498 Burton Lane	Finnian	NJ	65-7687-09
10	12965	Crawford	M	1986 Barnum Cir.	London	NH	23-0098-23
11	13432	Cullum	J	354 River Road	Shenandoah	VT	45-8734-33
12	13542	Mostel	Z	65 Fiddler Street	Anatevka	ND	34-6723-98

FIGURE 13.8

A sequential file sorted by ORDER-#.

Sequential Organization When records are physically in order in a file, the file is said to be a sequential file. When a sequential file is updated, it is necessary to go through the entire file. Because records cannot be inserted in the middle of the file, a sequential file is usually copied over during the updating process.

Figure 13.8 illustrates a file of current orders for a mail-order company that sells music CDs. The file contains 12 records and is stored sequentially according to the ORDER-#. If we want to look up order 13432, we would start at the beginning and read through the file until we arrived at order 13432.

Sequential master files are used when the hardware requires it (remember that a magnetic tape is a sequential device) or when the normal access requires that most of the records be accessed. In other words, when we need to read or update only a few records, it is inefficient to use a sequential structure, but when many records need to be read or modified, sequential organization would make sense. Sequential organization is normally used for all types of files except master files.

Linked Lists When files are stored on direct-access devices such as a disk, the options are expanded. Records can be sorted logically, rather than physically, using linked lists. Linked lists are achieved by using a set of pointers to direct you to the next logical record located anywhere in the file.

Figure 13.9 shows the music CD ordering file with an additional attribute used to store the pointer. Because the file is already stored in sequential order

ORDER START = 4

	ORDER-#	LAST NAME	I	STREET ADDRESS	CITY	ST	CREDIT CARD	POINTER
1	10784	MacRae	G	2314 Curly Circle	Lincoln	NE	45-4654-76	12
2	10796	Jones	S	34 Dream Lane	Oklahoma City	OK	45-9876-74	5
3	11821	Preston	R	1008 Madison Ave.	River City	IA	34-7642-64	7
4	11845	Channing	C	454 Harmonia St.	New York	NY	34-0876-87	10
5	11872	Kiley	R	765 Dulcinea Drive	La Mancha	CA	65-8798-87	1
6	11976	Verdon	G	7564 K Street	Chicago	IL	67-8453-18	END
7	11998	Rivera	C	4342 West Street	Chicago	IL	12-2312-54	9
8	12765	Orbach	J	1345 Michigan Ave.	Chicago	IL	23-4545-65	3
9	12769	Steele	T	3498 Burton Lane	Finnian	NJ	65-7687-09	6
10	12965	Crawford	M	1986 Barnum Cir.	London	NH	23-0098-23	11
11	13432	Cullum	J	354 River Road	Shenandoah	VT	45-8734-33	2
12	13542	Mostel	Z	65 Fiddler Street	Anatevka	ND	34-6723-98	8

FIGURE 13.9

A linked list uses pointers to designate the logical order of the records.

according to ORDER-#, the pointer is used to point to records in logical (alphabetical) order by LAST NAME. This example shows an obvious advantage of using linked lists: Files can be sorted logically in many different ways by using a variety of pointers.

Hashed File Organization Direct access devices also permit access to a given record by going directly to its address. Because it is not feasible to reserve a physical address for each possible record, a method called hashing is used. Hashing is the process of calculating an address from the record key.

Suppose there were 500 employees in an organization and we wanted to use Social Security number as a key. It would be inefficient to reserve 999,999,999 addresses, one for each Social Security number. Therefore, we could take the Social Security number and use it to derive the address of the record.

There are many hashing techniques. A common one is to divide the original number by a prime number that approximates the storage locations and then to use the remainder as the address, as follows: Begin with the Social Security number 053-46-8942. Then divide by 509, yielding 105,047. Note that 105,047 multiplied by 509 does not equal the original number; it equals 53,468,923 instead. The difference between the original number, 53,468,942, and the dividend, 53,468,923, is the remainder, and it equals 19. The storage location of the record for an employee whose Social Security number is 053-46-8942 would thus be 19.

A problem arises, however, when a person with a different Social Security number (say, 472-38-4086) has the same remainder. When this occurs, the second person's record has to be placed in a special overflow area.

RELATIONAL DATABASES

Databases can be organized in several ways. Here we will consider the most common approach, the relational database.

Logical and Physical Views of Data A database, unlike a file, is intended to be shared by many users. It is clear that the users all see the data in different ways. We refer to the way a user pictures and describes the data as a user view. The problem, however, is that different users have different user views. These views need to be examined by the systems analyst, and an overall logical model of the database developed. Finally, the logical model of the database must be transformed into a corresponding physical database design. Physical design is involved with how data are stored and related, as well as how they are accessed.

In database literature, the views are referred to as schema. Figure 13.10 shows how the user reports and user views (user schema) are related to the logical model (conceptual schema) and physical design (internal schema).

There are three main types of logically structured databases: hierarchical, network, and relational. The first two types may be found in legacy (older) systems. An analyst today would typically design a relational database.

Relational Data Structures A relational data structure consists of one or more two-dimensional tables, which are referred to as relations. The rows of the table represent the records, and the columns contain attributes.

The music CD ordering database described earlier in this chapter is depicted as a relational structure in Figure 13.11. Here, three tables are needed to

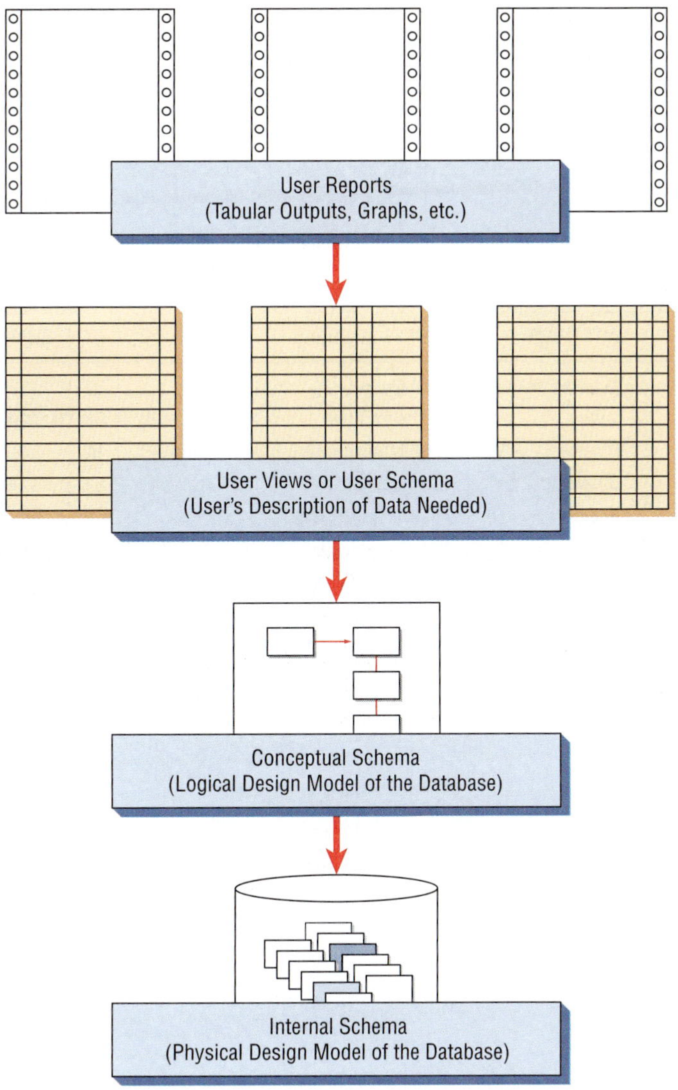

FIGURE 13.10
Database design includes synthesizing user reports, user views, and logical and physical designs.

(1) describe the items and keep track of the current price of CDs (ITEM PRICE), (2) describe the details of the order (ORDER), and (3) identify the status of the order (ITEM STATUS).

To determine the price of an item, we need to know the item number to be able to find it in the relation ITEM PRICE. To update G. MacRae's credit card number, we can search the ORDER relation for MacRae and correct it only once, even though he ordered many CDs. To find out the status of part of an order, however, we must know the ITEM-# and ORDER-#, and then we must locate that information in the relation ITEM STATUS.

Maintaining the tables in a relational structure is usually quite simple when compared with maintaining a hierarchical or network structure. One of the primary advantages of relational structures is that ad hoc queries are handled efficiently.

When relational structures are discussed in database literature, different terminology is often used. A file is called either a table or relation, a record is usually referred to as a tuple, and the attribute value set is called a domain.

For relational structures to be useful and manageable, the relational tables must first be normalized. Normalization is detailed in the following section.

FIGURE 13.11
In a relational data structure, data are stored in many tables.

ITEM PRICE

ITEM-#	TITLE	PRICE
B235	Guys and Dolls	8.99
B521	My Fair Lady	6.99
B894	42nd Street	10.99
B992	A Chorus Line	10.99

ORDER

ORDER-#	LAST NAME	I	STREET ADDRESS	CITY	ST	CHARGE ACCT
10784	MacRae	G	2314 Curly Circle	Lincoln	NE	45-4654-76
10796	Jones	S	34 Dream Lane	Oklahoma City	OK	44-9876-74
11821	Preston	R	1008 Madison Ave.	River City	IA	34-7642-64
11845	Channing	C	454 Harmonia St.	New York	NY	34-0876-87
11872	Kiley	R	765 Dulcinea Drive	La Mancha	CA	65-8798-87

ITEM STATUS

ITEM-#	ORDER-#	STATUS
B235	10784	Shipped 5/12
B235	19796	Shipped 5/14
B235	11872	In Process
B521	11821	In Process
B894	11845	Backordered
B894	11872	Shipped 5/12
B992	10784	Shipped 5/12

NORMALIZATION

Normalization is the transformation of complex user views and data stores to a set of smaller, stable data structures. In addition to being simpler and more stable, normalized data structures are more easily maintained than other data structures.

THE THREE STEPS OF NORMALIZATION

Beginning with either a user view or a data store developed for a data dictionary (see Chapter 8), the analyst normalizes a data structure in three steps, as shown in Figure 13.12. Each step involves an important procedure, one that simplifies the data structure.

The relation derived from the user view or data store will most likely be unnormalized. The first stage of the process includes removing all repeating groups and identifying the primary key. To do so, the relation needs to be broken up into two or more relations. At this point, the relations may already be of the third normal form, but it is likely more steps will be needed to transform the relations to the third normal form.

The second step ensures that all nonkey attributes are fully dependent on the primary key. All partial dependencies are removed and placed in another relation.

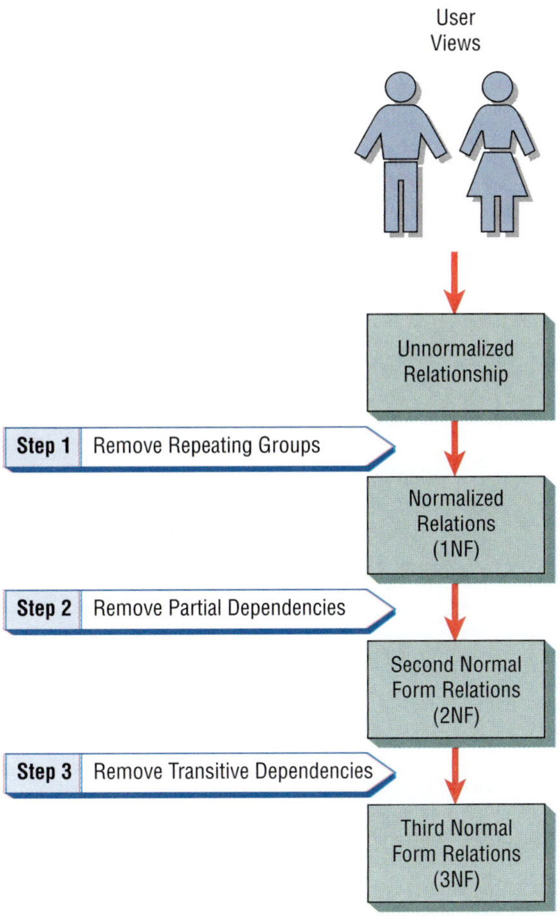

FIGURE 13.12
Normalization of a relation is accomplished in three major steps.

The third step removes any transitive dependencies. A transitive dependency is one in which nonkey attributes are dependent on other nonkey attributes.

A NORMALIZATION EXAMPLE

Figure 13.13 is a user view for the Al S. Well Hydraulic Equipment Company. The report shows the (1) SALESPERSON-NUMBER, (2) SALESPERSON-NAME, and (3) SALES-AREA. The body of the report shows the (4) CUSTOMER-NUMBER and (5) CUSTOMER-NAME. Next is the (6) WAREHOUSE-NUMBER that will service the customer, followed by the (7) WAREHOUSE-LOCATION, which is the city in which the company is located. The final information contained in the user view is the (8) SALES-AMOUNT. The rows (one for each customer) on the user view show that items 4 through 8 form a repeating group.

If the analyst was using a data flow/data dictionary approach, the same information in the user view would appear in a data structure. Figure 13.14 shows how the data structure would appear at the data dictionary stage of analysis. The repeating group is also indicated in the data structure by an asterisk (*) and indentation.

Before proceeding, note the data associations of the data elements in Figure 13.15. This type of illustration is called a bubble diagram or data model diagram. Each entity is enclosed in an ellipse, and arrows are used to show the relationships. Although it is possible to draw these relationships with an E-R diagram, it is sometimes easier to use the simpler bubble diagram to model the data.

FIGURE 13.13

A user report for the Al S. Well Hydraulic Equipment Company.

Al S. Well
Hydraulic Equipment Company
Spring Valley, Minnesota

Salesperson #: 3462
Name: Waters
Sales Area: West

CUSTOMER NUMBER	CUSTOMER NAME	WAREHOUSE NUMBER	WAREHOUSE LOCATION	SALES
18765	Delta Services	4	Fargo	13,540
18830	M. Levy and Sons	3	Bismarck	10,600

In this example, there is only one SALESPERSON-NUMBER assigned to each SALESPERSON-NAME, and that person will cover only one SALES-AREA, but each SALES-AREA may be assigned to many salespeople: hence, the double arrow notation from SALES-AREA to SALESPERSON-NUMBER. For each SALESPERSON-NUMBER, there may be many CUSTOMER-NUMBER(s).

Furthermore, there would be a one-to-one correspondence between CUSTOMER-NUMBER and CUSTOMER-NAME; the same is true for WAREHOUSE-NUMBER and WAREHOUSE-LOCATION. CUSTOMER-NUMBER will have only one WAREHOUSE-NUMBER and WAREHOUSE-LOCATION, but each WAREHOUSE-NUMBER or WAREHOUSE-LOCATION may service many CUSTOMER-NUMBER(s). Finally, to determine the SALES-AMOUNT for one salesperson's calls to a particular company, it is necessary to know both the SALESPERSON-NUMBER and the CUSTOMER-NUMBER.

FIGURE 13.14

The analyst would find a data structure (from a data dictionary) useful in developing a database.

SALESPERSON-NUMBER
SALESPERSON-NAME
SALES-AREA
CUSTOMER-NUMBER* (1-)
    CUSTOMER-NAME
    WAREHOUSE-NUMBER
    WAREHOUSE-LOCATION
    SALES-AMOUNT

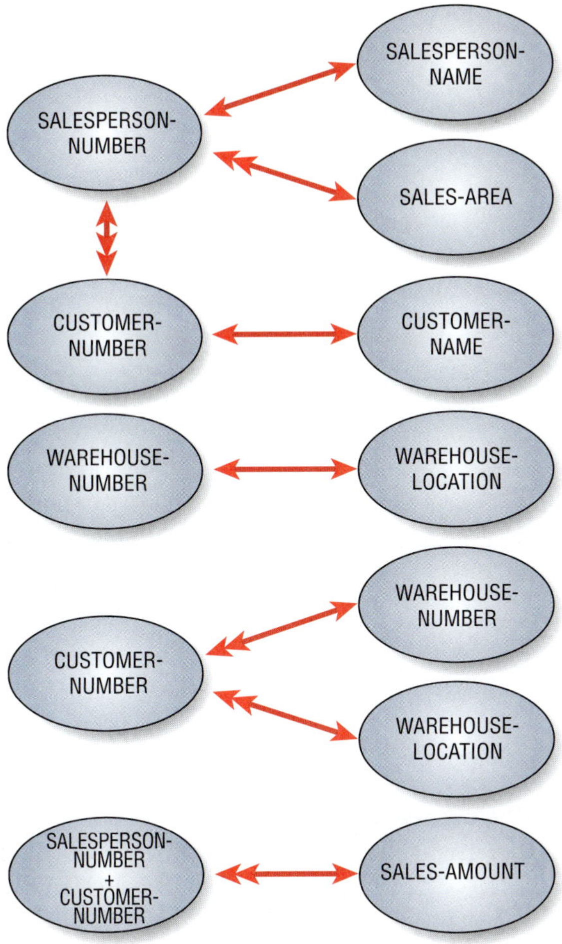

FIGURE 13.15

Drawing data model diagrams for data associations sometimes helps analysts appreciate the complexity of data storage.

The main objective of the normalization process is to simplify all the complex data items that are often found in user views. For example, if the analyst were to take the user view discussed above and attempt to make a relational table out of it, the table would look like Figure 13.16. Because this relation is based on our initial user view, we refer to it as SALES-REPORT.

SALES-REPORT is an unnormalized relation, because it has repeating groups. It is also important to observe that a single attribute such as SALESPERSON-NUMBER cannot serve as the key. The reason is clear when one examines the relationships between SALESPERSON-NUMBER and the other attributes in Figure 13.17. Although there is a one-to-one correspondence between SALESPERSON-NUMBER and two attributes (SALESPERSON-NAME and

SALESPERSON NUMBER	SALESPERSON NAME	SALES AREA	CUSTOMER NUMBER	CUSTOMER NAME	WAREHOUSE NUMBER	WAREHOUSE LOCATION	SALES AMOUNT
3462	Waters	West	18765	Delta Systems	4	Fargo	13540
			18830	A. Levy and Sons	3	Bismarck	10600
			19242	Ranier Company	3	Bismarck	9700
3593	Dryne	East	18841	R. W. Flood Inc.	2	Superior	11560
			18899	Seward Systems	2	Superior	2590
			19565	Stodola's Inc.	1	Plymouth	8800
etc.							

FIGURE 13.16

If the data were listed in an unnormalized table, there could be repeating groups.

FIGURE 13.17

A data model diagram shows that in the unnormalized relation, the SALESPERSON-NUMBER has a one-to-many association with some attributes.

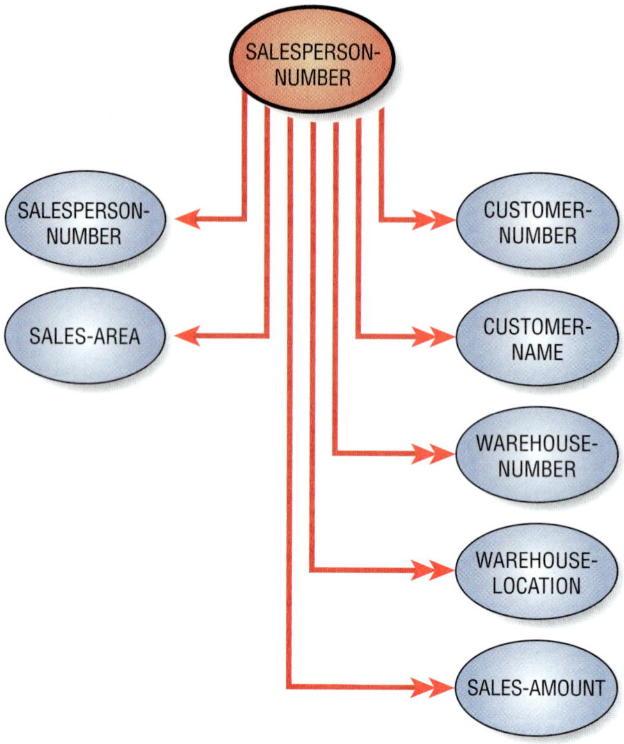

SALES-AREA), there is a one-to-many relationship between SALESPERSON-NUMBER and the other five attributes (CUSTOMER-NUMBER, CUSTOMER-NAME, WAREHOUSE-NUMBER, WAREHOUSE-LOCATION, and SALES-AMOUNT).

SALES-REPORT can be expressed in the following shorthand notation:

SALES REPORT (SALESPERSON-NUMBER,
SALESPERSON-NAME, SALES-AREA,
(CUSTOMER-NUMBER,
CUSTOMER-NAME,
WAREHOUSE-NUMBER,
WAREHOUSE-LOCATION,
SALES-AMOUNT))

where the inner set of parentheses represents the repeated group.

First Normal Form (1NF) The first step in normalizing a relation is to remove the repeating groups. In our example, the unnormalized relation SALES-REPORT will be broken into two separate relations. These new relations will be named SALESPERSON and SALESPERSON-CUSTOMER.

Figure 13.18 shows how the original, unnormalized relation SALES-REPORT is normalized by separating the relation into two new relations. Notice that the relation SALESPERSON contains the primary key <u>SALESPERSON-NUMBER</u> and all the attributes that were not repeating (SALESPERSON-NAME and SALES-AREA).

The second relation, SALESPERSON-CUSTOMER, contains the primary key from the relation SALESPERSON (the primary key of SALESPERSON is <u>SALESPERSON-NUMBER</u>), as well as all the attributes that were part of the repeating group (CUSTOMER-NUMBER, CUSTOMER-NAME, WAREHOUSE-NUMBER, WAREHOUSE-LOCATION, and SALES-AMOUNT). Knowing the

SALES-REPORT

SALESPERSON NUMBER	SALESPERSON NAME	SALES AREA	CUSTOMER NUMBER	CUSTOMER NAME	WAREHOUSE NUMBER	WAREHOUSE LOCATION	SALES AMOUNT

SALESPERSON

SALESPERSON NUMBER	SALESPERSON NAME	SALES AREA
3462	Waters	West
3593	Dryne	East
etc.		

SALESPERSON-CUSTOMER

SALESPERSON NUMBER	CUSTOMER NUMBER	CUSTOMER NAME	WAREHOUSE NUMBER	WAREHOUSE LOCATION	SALES AMOUNT
3462	18765	Delta Systems	4	Fargo	13540
3462	18830	A. Levy and Sons	3	Bismarck	10600
3462	19242	Ranier Company	3	Bismarck	9700
3593	18841	R. W. Flood Inc.	2	Superior	11560
3593	18899	Seward Systems	2	Superior	2590
3593	19565	Stodola's Inc.	1	Plymouth	8800
etc.					

FIGURE 13.18
The original unnormalized relation SALES-REPORT is separated into two relations, SALESPERSON (3NF) and SALESPERSON-CUSTOMER (1NF).

SALESPERSON-NUMBER, however, does not automatically mean that you will know the CUSTOMER-NAME, SALES-AMOUNT, WAREHOUSE-LOCATION, and so on. In this relation, one must use a concatenated key (both SALESPERSON-NUMBER and CUSTOMER-NUMBER) to access the rest of the information. It is possible to write the relations in shorthand notation as follows:

SALESPERSON (SALESPERSON-NUMBER,
SALESPERSON-NAME, SALES-AREA)

and

SALESPERSON-CUSTOMER (SALESPERSON-NUMBER,
CUSTOMER-NUMBER,
CUSTOMER-NAME,
WAREHOUSE-NUMBER,
WAREHOUSE-LOCATION,
SALES-AMOUNT)

The relation SALESPERSON-CUSTOMER is a first normal relation, but it is not in its ideal form. Problems arise because some of the attributes are not functionally dependent on the primary key (that is, SALESPERSON-NUMBER, CUSTOMER-NUMBER). In other words, some of the nonkey attributes are dependent only on CUSTOMER NUMBER and not on the concatenated key. The data model

FIGURE 13.19

A data model diagram shows that three attributes are dependent on CUSTOMER-NUMBER, so the relation is not yet normalized. Both SALESPERSON-NUMBER and CUSTOMER-NUMBER are required to look up SALES-AMOUNT.

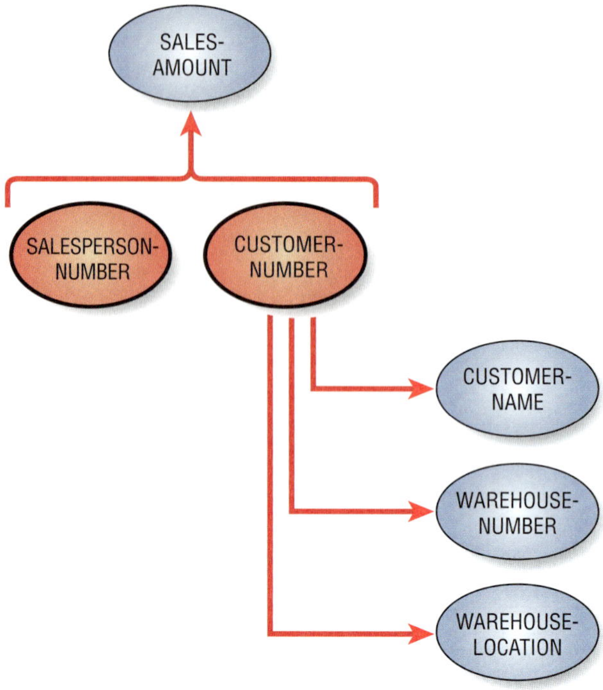

diagram in Figure 13.19 shows that SALES-AMOUNT is dependent on both SALESPERSON-NUMBER and CUSTOMER-NUMBER, but the other three attributes are dependent only on CUSTOMER-NUMBER.

Second Normal Form (2NF) In the second normal form, all the attributes will be functionally dependent on the primary key. Therefore, the next step is to remove all the partially dependent attributes and place them in another relation. Figure 13.20 shows how the relation SALESPERSON-CUSTOMER is split into two new relations: SALES and CUSTOMER-WAREHOUSE. These relations can also be expressed as follows:

SALES (SALESPERSON-NUMBER, CUSTOMER-NUMBER, SALES-AMOUNT)

and

CUSTOMER-WAREHOUSE (CUSTOMER-NUMBER, CUSTOMER-NAME, WAREHOUSE-NUMBER, WAREHOUSE-LOCATION)

The relation CUSTOMER-WAREHOUSE is in the second normal form. It can still be simplified further because there are additional dependencies in the relation. Some of the nonkey attributes are dependent not only on the primary key, but also on a nonkey attribute. This dependency is referred to as a transitive dependency.

Figure 13.21 shows the dependencies in the relation CUSTOMER-WAREHOUSE. For the relation to be a second normal form, all the attributes must be dependent on the primary key CUSTOMER-NUMBER, as shown in the diagram. WAREHOUSE-LOCATION, however, is obviously dependent on WAREHOUSE-NUMBER also. To simplify this relation, another step is required.

SALESPERSON-CUSTOMER

SALESPERSON NUMBER	CUSTOMER NUMBER	CUSTOMER NAME	WAREHOUSE NUMBER	WAREHOUSE LOCATION	SALES AMOUNT

CUSTOMER-WAREHOUSE

CUSTOMER NUMBER	CUSTOMER NAME	WAREHOUSE NUMBER	WAREHOUSE LOCATION
18765	Delta Systems	4	Fargo
18830	A. Levy and Sons	3	Bismarck
19242	Ranier Company	3	Bismarck
18841	R. W. Flood Inc.	2	Superior
18899	Seward Systems	2	Superior
19565	Stodola's Inc.	1	Plymouth
etc.			

SALES

SALESPERSON NUMBER	CUSTOMER NUMBER	SALES AMOUNT
3462	18765	13540
3462	18830	10600
3462	19242	9700
3593	18841	11560
3593	18899	2590
3593	19565	8800
etc.		

FIGURE 13.20

The relation SALESPERSON-CUSTOMER is separated into a relation called CUSTOMER-WAREHOUSE (2NF) and a relation called SALES (1NF).

Third Normal Form (3NF) A normalized relation is in the third normal form if all the nonkey attributes are fully functionally dependent on the primary key and there are no transitive (nonkey) dependencies. In a manner similar to the previous steps, it is possible to break apart the relation CUSTOMER-WAREHOUSE into two relations, as shown in Figure 13.22.

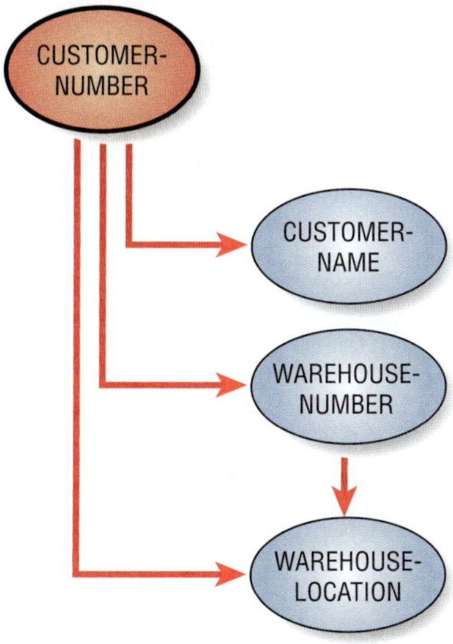

FIGURE 13.21

A data model diagram shows that a transitive dependency exists between WAREHOUSE-NUMBER and WAREHOUSE-LOCATION.

FIGURE 13.22

The relation CUSTOMER-WAREHOUSE is separated into two relations called CUSTOMER (1NF) and WAREHOUSE (1NF).

CUSTOMER-WAREHOUSE

CUSTOMER NUMBER	CUSTOMER NAME	WAREHOUSE NUMBER	WAREHOUSE LOCATION

CUSTOMER

CUSTOMER NUMBER	CUSTOMER NAME	WAREHOUSE NUMBER
18765	Delta Systems	4
18830	A. Levy and Sons	3
19242	Ranier Company	3
18841	R. W. Flood Inc.	2
18899	Seward Systems	2
19565	Stodola's Inc.	1
etc.		

WAREHOUSE

WAREHOUSE NUMBER	WAREHOUSE LOCATION
4	Fargo
3	Bismarck
2	Superior
1	Plymouth
etc.	

The two new relations are called CUSTOMER and WAREHOUSE, and can be written as follows:

CUSTOMER (CUSTOMER-NUMBER, CUSTOMER-NAME, WAREHOUSE-NUMBER)

and

WAREHOUSE (WAREHOUSE-NUMBER, WAREHOUSE-LOCATION)

The primary key for the relation CUSTOMER is CUSTOMER-NUMBER, and the primary key for the relation WAREHOUSE is WAREHOUSE-NUMBER.

In addition to these primary keys, we can identify WAREHOUSE-NUMBER to be a foreign key in the relation CUSTOMER. A foreign key is any attribute that is nonkey in one relation but a primary key in another relation. We designated WAREHOUSE-NUMBER as a foreign key in the previous notation and in the figures by underscoring it with a dashed line: _ _ _ _ _ _ _ _ _ _ _ _ _.

Finally, the original, unnormalized relation SALES-REPORT has been transformed into four third normal form (3NF) relations. In reviewing the relations shown in Figure 13.23, one can see that the single relation SALES-REPORT was transformed into the following four relations:

SALESPERSON (SALESPERSON-NUMBER, SALESPERSON-NAME, SALES-AREA)
SALES (SALESPERSON-NUMBER, CUSTOMER-NUMBER, SALES-AMOUNT)
CUSTOMER (CUSTOMER-NUMBER, CUSTOMER-NAME, WAREHOUSE-NUMBER)

and

WAREHOUSE (WAREHOUSE-NUMBER, WAREHOUSE-LOCATION)

The third normal form is adequate for most database design problems. The simplification gained from transforming an unnormalized relation into a set of 3NF

SALESPERSON

SALESPERSON NUMBER	SALESPERSON NAME	SALES AREA
3462	Waters	West
3593	Dryne	East
etc.		

SALES

SALESPERSON NUMBER	CUSTOMER NUMBER	SALES AMOUNT
3462	18765	13540
3462	18830	10600
3462	19242	9700
3593	18841	11560
3593	18899	2590
3593	19565	8800
etc.		

CUSTOMER

CUSTOMER NUMBER	CUSTOMER NAME	WAREHOUSE NUMBER
18765	Delta Systems	4
18830	A. Levy and Sons	3
19242	Ranier Company	3
18841	R. W. Flood Inc.	2
18899	Seward Systems	2
19565	Stodola's Inc.	1
etc.		

WAREHOUSE

WAREHOUSE NUMBER	WAREHOUSE LOCATION
4	Fargo
3	Bismarck
2	Superior
1	Plymouth
etc.	

FIGURE 13.23
The complete database consists of four 1NF relations called SALESPERSON, SALES, CUSTOMER, and WAREHOUSE.

relations is a tremendous benefit when it comes time to insert, delete, and update information in the database.

An entity-relationship diagram for the database is shown in Figure 13.24. One SALESPERSON serves many CUSTOMER(s), who generate SALES and receive their items from one WAREHOUSE (the closest WAREHOUSE to their location). Take the time to notice how the entities and attributes relate to the database.

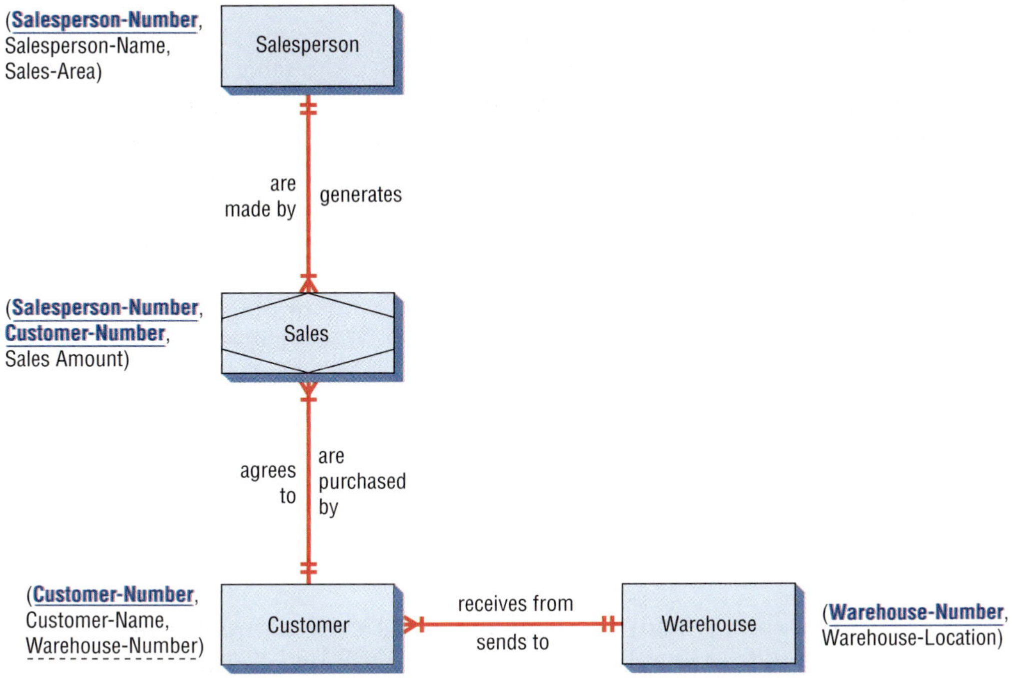

FIGURE 13.24
An entity-relationship diagram for the Al S. Well Hydraulic Company database.

FIGURE 13.25

An entity-relationship diagram for customer orders.

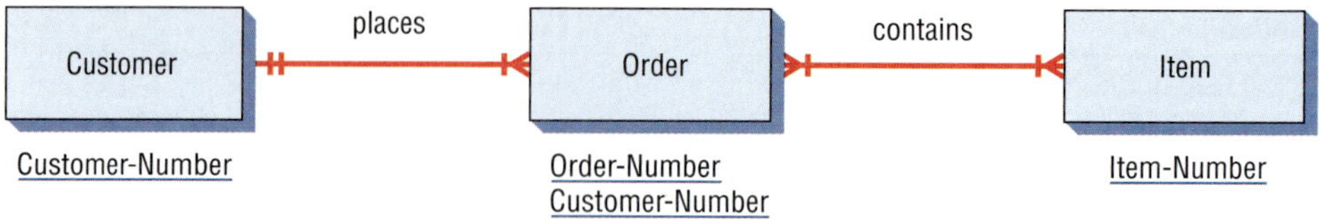

USING THE ENTITY-RELATIONSHIP DIAGRAM TO DETERMINE RECORD KEYS

The entity-relationship diagram may be used to determine the keys required for a record or a database relation. The first step is to construct the entity-relationship diagram and label a unique (primary) key for each data entity. Figure 13.25 shows an entity-relationship diagram for a customer order system. There are three data entities: CUSTOMER, with a primary key of CUSTOMER-NUMBER; ORDER, with a primary key of ORDER-NUMBER; and ITEM, with ITEM-NUMBER as the primary key. One CUSTOMER may place many orders, but each ORDER can be placed by one CUSTOMER only, so the relationship is one-to-many. Each ORDER may contain many ITEM(s), and each ITEM may be contained in many ORDER(s), so the ORDER-ITEM relationship is many-to-many.

A foreign key, however, is a data field on a given file that is the primary key of a different master file. For example, a DEPARTMENT-NUMBER indicating a student's major may exist on the STUDENT MASTER table. DEPARTMENT-NUMBER could also be the unique key for the DEPARTMENT MASTER table.

ONE-TO-MANY RELATIONSHIP

A one-to-many relationship is the most common type of relationship, since all many-to-many relationships must be broken down into two one-to-many relationships. When a one-to-many relationship occurs, place the primary key on the table at the one end of the relationship as a foreign key on the table on the many end of the relationship. For example, since one customer may have many orders, place the customer number on the order record.

The design of Web pages, displays, or reports that include information from only one record of the many relationship, along with information from the one end of the relationship, is easy to construct. The display will not have any repeating information. An example is an order inquiry using an order number to look up a single order. Since the order is for one customer, the result would be fields from the order and a single customer.

Designing the reverse is more complicated, since the table at the one end of the relationship may have many records for the many end. These are implemented in a variety of ways. For a simple display screen, the information from the one end is displayed with a repeating number of groups of information from the many end of the relationship. In Access, this might be a form with a subform, such as a customer with a subform of all the customer's orders. If there was a large number of records from the many end, scroll bars would appear.

In simple situations, the relationship might also be implemented by using a drop-down list, with each record from the many end becoming one entry in the one end; an example is the display of a car along with a drop-down list containing all the models for the car. When designing Web sites, the information from the one end might be at the top of the page, with multiple groups of data below it or multiple links to the data. An example is one search engine topic resulting in many matching links or one genre of music and many artists that match the genre.

MANY-TO-MANY RELATIONSHIP

When the relationship is many-to-many, three tables are necessary: one for each data entity and one for the relationship. The ORDER and ITEM entities in our

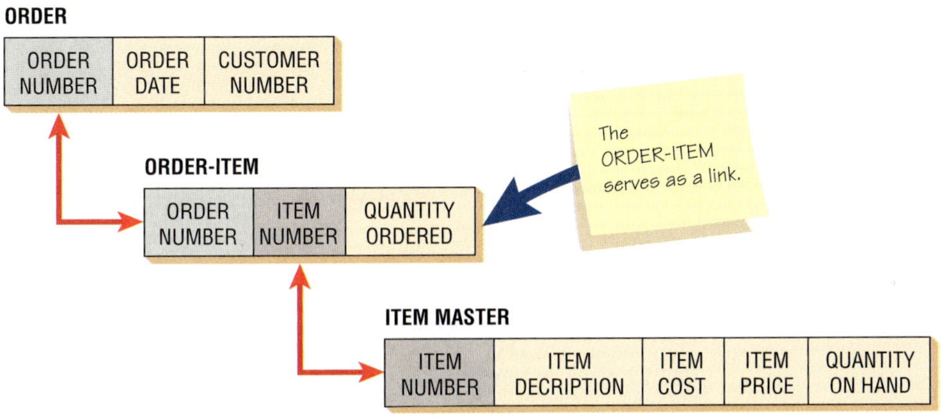

FIGURE 13.26
When the relationship is many-to-many, three files are necessary.

example have a many-to-many relationship. The primary key of each data entity is stored as a foreign key of the relational table. The relational table may simply contain the primary keys for each data entity or may contain additional data, such as the grade received for a course or the quantity of an item ordered. Refer to the table layout illustrated in Figure 13.26. The ORDER ITEM table contains information about which order contains which items, and provides a link between the ORDER table and the ITEM MASTER table.

The relationship table should be indexed on each foreign key—one for each of the tables in the relationship—and may have a primary key consisting of a combination of the two foreign keys. Often corporations will use a unique key, such as sequence number, as the primary key for the relational table. To find many records from a second table given the first table, directly read the relational table for the desired key. Locate the matching record in the second *many* table. Continue to loop through the relational table until the desired key is no longer found. For example, to find records in the ITEM MASTER for a specific record in the ORDER table, directly read the ORDER ITEM table using the ORDER-NUMBER as the index. Records are logically sequenced based on the data in the index, so all records for the same ORDER-NUMBER are grouped together. For each ORDER ITEM record that matches the desired ORDER-NUMBER, directly read the ITEM MASTER table using the ITEM-NUMBER as an index.

The logic is the same for the reverse situation, such as finding all the orders for a backordered item that has been received. Use the desired ITEM-NUMBER to read the ORDER-ITEM table directly. The ORDER ITEM index is set to the ITEM-NUMBER. For all matching ORDER ITEM records, use the ORDER-NUMBER to read the ORDER table directly. Finally, read the CUSTOMER MASTER table directly to obtain the CUSTOMER-NAME and ADDRESS using the CUSTOMER-NUMBER on the ORDER table.

Relational tables may have relationships to more tables in the database than just the two to which they directly connect. For example, there might be a relational table called Class or Section to link students and courses, since each student may take many courses and each course may have many students. The Section table may have a relationship to the Textbook or to the Instructor for that section.

GUIDELINES FOR MASTER FILE/DATABASE RELATION DESIGN

The following guidelines should be taken into account when designing master files or database relations:

1. Each separate data entity should create a master database table. Do not combine two distinct entities on one file. For example, items are purchased from vendors.

FIGURE 13.27
The improved item and vendor master files.

```
Item Record =      Item Number +
                   Item Description +
                   Item Category +
                   Unit Cost +
                   Unit Price +
                   Reorder Point +
                   Reorder Quantity +
                   Month Sales +
                   Month Backordered +
                   Year-To-Date Sales +
                   Year-To-Date Backordered +
                   Vendor Number

Vendor Record =    Vendor Number +
                   Vendor Name +
                   Vendor Street +
                   Vendor City +
                   Vendor State +
                   Vendor Zip +
                   Vendor Contact Person
```

The ITEM MASTER table should contain only item information, and the VENDOR MASTER table should contain only vendor information. Figure 13.27 illustrates the data dictionary for ITEM MASTER table and VENDOR MASTER table.

2. A specific data field should exist only on one master table. For example, the CUSTOMER NAME should exist only on the CUSTOMER MASTER table, not on the ORDER table or any other master table. The exceptions to this guideline are the key or index fields, which may be on as many tables as necessary. If a report or screen needs information from many tables, the indexes should provide the linkage for obtaining the required records.
3. Each master table or database relation should have programs to **C**reate, **R**ead, **U**pdate, and **D**elete (abbreviated CRUD) the records. Ideally, only one program should add new records and only one program should delete specified records. Many programs, however, may be responsible for changing data fields in the course of normal business activities. For example, a CUSTOMER MASTER file may have a CURRENT BALANCE field that is increased by the ORDER TOTAL in the order processing program and decreased by a PAYMENT AMOUNT or an AMOUNT RETURNED from two additional programs.

INTEGRITY CONSTRAINTS

Integrity constraints are rules that govern changing and deleting records, and that help keep the data in the database accurate. Three types of integrity constraints apply to a database:

1. Entity integrity.
2. Referential integrity.
3. Domain integrity.

Entity integrity constraints are rules that govern the composition of primary keys. The primary key cannot have a null value, and if the primary key is a composite key, none of the component fields in the key can contain a null value. Some databases allow you to define a unique constraint or a unique key. This unique key identifies only one record, which is not a primary key. The difference between a unique key and a primary key is that a unique key may contain a null value.

Referential integrity governs the nature of records in a one-to-many relationship. The table that is connected to the one end of the relationship is called the parent. The table connected to the many end of the relationship is called the child table. Referential integrity means that all foreign keys in the many table (the child table) must have a matching record in the parent table. Hence, you cannot add a record in the child (many) table without a matching record in the parent table.

A second implication is that you cannot change a primary key that has matching child table records. If you could change the parent record, the result would be a child record that would have a different parent record or an orphan record, or a child record without a parent record. Examples are a GRADE record for a student that would not be on the STUDENT MASTER table and an ORDER record for a CUSTOMER NUMBER that did not exist. The last implication of referential integrity is that you cannot delete a parent record that has child records. That would also lead to the orphan records mentioned earlier.

Referential integrity is implemented in two different ways. One way is to have a restricted database, in which the system can update or delete a parent record only if there are no matching child records. A cascaded database will delete or update all child records when a parent record is deleted or changed (the parent triggers the changes).

A restricted relationship is better when deleting records. You would not want to delete a customer record and have all the outstanding invoices deleted as well! The cascaded approach is better when changing records. If the primary key of a student record is changed, all the course records for that student would have their foreign keys (the STUDENT NUMBER on the COURSE MASTER) changed as well.

Domain integrity rules are used to validate the data, such as table, limit, range, and other validation checks. They are further explained in Chapter 15. The domain integrity rules are usually stored in the database structure in one of two forms. Check constraints are defined at the table level and can refer to one or more fields in the table. An example is that the DATE OF PURCHASE is always less than or equal to the current date. Rules are defined at the database level as separate objects and can be used with a number of fields. An example is a value that is greater than zero, used to validate a number of elements.

ANOMALIES

Four anomalies may occur when creating database tables:

1. Data redundancy.
2. Insert anomaly.
3. Deletion anomaly.
4. Update anomaly.

Data redundancy occurs when the same data are stored in more than one place in the database (except for primary keys stored as foreign keys). This problem is solved by creating tables that are in the third normal form.

An insert anomaly occurs when the entire primary key is not known and the database cannot insert a new record, which would violate entity integrity. This problem usually occurs when the primary key is a composite key containing several smaller attributes. An insert anomaly may be avoided by using a sequence number for the primary key.

A deletion anomaly happens when a record is deleted, resulting in the loss of other related data. An example is an item that has a vendor number and a particular item is the only reference to a certain vendor. If that item is deleted, there would be no reference to the vendor record.

An update anomaly results when a change to one attribute value either causes the database to contain inconsistent data or causes multiple records to need changing. An example is when a street name changes in a city. You might change some of the street names and not others, or you will have to ensure that all street names have been changed. This can occur when you have transitive dependencies and may be prevented by creating tables that are in the third normal form (although in the street example, the data may be in the third normal form).

MAKING USE OF THE DATABASE

There are several steps you must take in sequential order to assure that the database will be useful for presenting data.

STEPS IN RETRIEVING AND PRESENTING DATA

There are eight steps in the retrieval and presentation of data:

1. Choose a relation from the database.
2. Join two relations together.
3. Project columns from the relation.
4. Select rows from the relation.
5. Derive new attributes.
6. Index or sort rows.
7. Calculate totals and performance measures.
8. Present data.

The first and last steps are mandatory, but the six steps in between are optional, depending on how data are to be used. Figure 13.28 is a visual guide to the steps, which are described in the following subsections.

Choose a Relation from the Database The first and obvious step is to choose a relation from the database. A good way to accomplish this step is to keep a directory of user views as a memory aid. Even if the user wants an ad hoc query, it is useful to have similar views available.

Join Two Relations Together The operation join is intended to take two relations and put them together to make a larger relation. For two relations to be joined, they must have a common attribute. For instance, take two relations from our example:

CUSTOMER (CUSTOMER-NUMBER, CUSTOMER-NAME, WAREHOUSE-NUMBER)

and

WAREHOUSE (WAREHOUSE-NUMBER, WAREHOUSE-LOCATION)

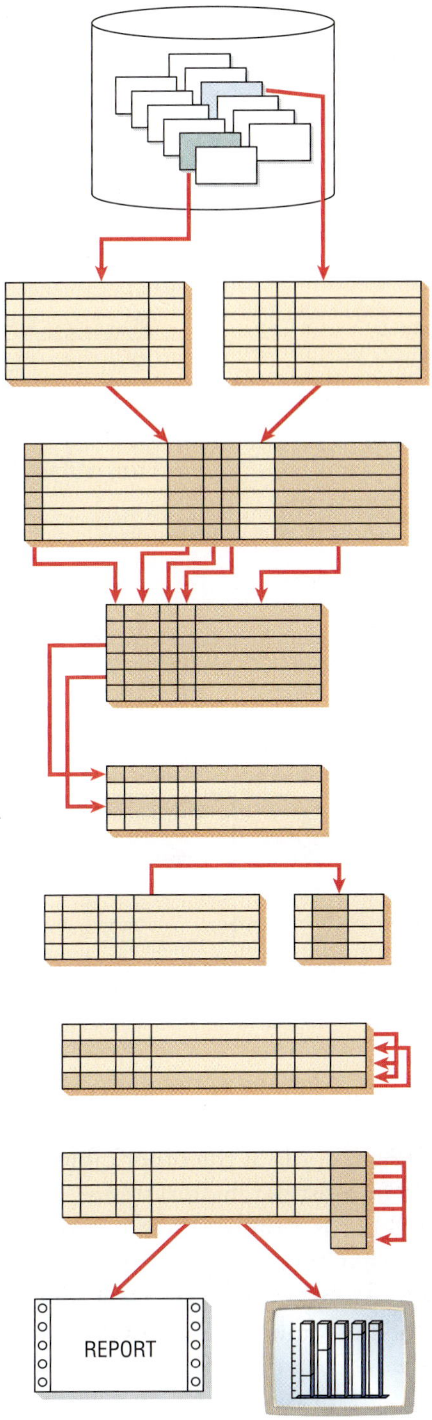

FIGURE 13.28

Data are retrieved and presented in eight distinct steps.

Suppose we join these relations over WAREHOUSE-NUMBER to get a new relation, CUSTOMER-WAREHOUSE-LOCATION. The joining of these relations is illustrated in Figure 13.29. Also note that the new relation is not 3NF.

The operation join may also go one step further; that is, it may combine files for rows that have an attribute that meets a certain condition. Figure 13.30 shows an example in which two relations, SALES and QUOTA, are joined by satisfying the condition that a salesperson has met or exceeded predetermined quotas.

Join is an important operation because it can take many 3NF relations and combine them to make a more useful relation. Together with the operations following, join is a powerful operation.

FIGURE 13.29
The operation join takes two relations and puts them together to form a single relation.

CUSTOMER

CUSTOMER NUMBER	CUSTOMER NAME	WAREHOUSE NUMBER
18765	Delta Systems	4
18830	A. Levy and Sons	3
19242	Ranier Company	3
18841	R. W. Flood Inc.	2
18899	Seward Systems	2
19565	Stodola's Inc.	1
etc.		

WAREHOUSE

WAREHOUSE NUMBER	WAREHOUSE LOCATION
4	Fargo
3	Bismarck
2	Superior
1	Plymouth
etc.	

Join

CUSTOMER-WAREHOUSE-LOCATION

CUSTOMER NUMBER	CUSTOMER NAME	WAREHOUSE NUMBER	WAREHOUSE LOCATION
18765	Delta Systems	4	Fargo
18830	A. Levy and Sons	3	Bismarck
19242	Ranier Company	3	Bismarck
18841	R. W. Flood Inc.	2	Superior
18899	Seward Systems	2	Superior
19565	Stodola's Inc.	1	Plymouth
etc.			

The most common type of join, an inner join, is the intersection of both tables. This join includes records that have matching records in both of the tables being joined. Records that have no matching records in the other tables are not included. This is the default type of join form in most database systems.

An outer join contains all the records from one table and matching records from the other table. The result is that there may be null or blank data in the joined table for some of the records. An example is an outer join of the customer and order tables, which would list all customers and orders for some customers. A left outer join includes all the records from the left or first table mentioned and only the records from the right (or last table mentioned) when they match the left table. A right outer join is the reverse. A full outer join includes all records from both tables but with nulls or spaces where there are no matching records.

A self-join is when a table is joined to itself. One of the attributes must contain data that link to the primary key of the table. An example is an Employee table with a primary key of employee number and another attribute or column containing the employee number of their supervisor. The Supervisor column would be joined to the Employee Number column in the same database table.

Project Columns from the Relation Projection is the process of building a smaller relation by choosing only relevant attributes from an existing relation. In other words, projection is the extraction of certain columns from a relational table.

FIGURE 13.30
Relations can be joined subject to certain conditions.

SALES

SALESPERSON NUMBER	CUSTOMER NUMBER	SALES AMOUNT
3462	18765	13540
3462	18830	10600
3462	19242	9700
3593	18841	11560
3593	18899	2590
3593	19565	8800
etc.		

QUOTA

AWARD LEVEL	AMOUNT
Certificate	9000
Medal	12000

Join

SALES-QUOTA

SALESPERSON NUMBER	CUSTOMER NUMBER	SALES AMOUNT	AWARD LEVEL	AMOUNT
3462	18765	13540	Certificate	9000
3462	18765	13540	Medal	12000
3462	18830	10600	Certificate	9000
3462	18830	10600	Medal	12000
3462	19242	9700	Certificate	9000
3593	18841	11560	Certificate	12000
etc.				

An example of projection is featured in Figure 13.31. The relation

CUSTOMER-WAREHOUSE-LOCATION (CUSTOMER-NUMBER,
CUSTOMER-NAME,
WAREHOUSE-NUMBER),
WAREHOUSE-LOCATION

is projected over CUSTOMER-NUMBER and WAREHOUSE-LOCATION, and during the projection process, duplicate records are removed.

Select Rows from the Relation The operation referred to as selection is similar to projection, but instead of extracting columns it extracts rows. Selection creates a new (smaller) relation by extracting records that contain an attribute meeting a certain condition.

Figure 13.32 illustrates how the selection operation works. Selection is performed on the relation PERSONNEL to extract salaried employees only. There is no need to remove duplicate records here, as there was in the previous illustration of projection.

Selection may also be performed for a more complex set of conditions, such as select all the employees who are salaried *and* who make more than $40,000 annually, or select employees who are hourly *and* make more than $15.00 per hour. Selection is an important operation for ad hoc queries.

FIGURE 13.31

Projection creates a smaller relation by choosing only relevant attributes (columns) from the relation.

CUSTOMER-WAREHOUSE-LOCATION

CUSTOMER NUMBER	CUSTOMER NAME	WAREHOUSE NUMBER	WAREHOUSE LOCATION
18765	Delta Systems	4	Fargo
18830	A. Levy and Sons	3	Bismarck
19242	Ranier Company	3	Bismarck
18841	R. W. Flood Inc.	2	Superior
18899	Seward Systems	2	Superior
19565	Stodola's Inc.	1	Plymouth
etc.			

Projection

CUSTOMER-LOCATION

CUSTOMER NUMBER	WAREHOUSE LOCATION
18765	Fargo
18830	Bismarck
19242	Bismarck
18841	Superior
18899	Superior
19565	Plymouth
etc.	

Derive New Attributes The fifth step involves the manipulation of the existing data plus some additional parameters (if necessary) to derive new data. New columns are created for the resulting relation. An example of derivation of new attributes can be found in Figure 13.33. Here, two new attributes are determined: (1) GIRTH (by multiplying the sum of width and height by 2 and adding it to length), and (2) SHIPPING-WEIGHT (which depends on the girth).

Index or Sort Rows People require that data be organized in a certain order so that they can either locate items in a list more easily or group and subtotal items more easily. Two options for ordering data are available: indexing and sorting.

Indexing is the logical ordering of rows in a relation according to some key. As discussed in the previous section, the logical pointer takes up space, and listing the relation by using an index is slower than if the relation were in the proper physical order. The index, however, takes up far less space than a duplicate file.

Sorting is the physical ordering of a relation. The result of physical sorting is a sequential file as discussed earlier in the chapter. Figure 13.34 illustrates indexing and sorting of the relation PERSONNEL by employee name in alphabetical order.

Calculate Totals and Performance Measures Once the appropriate subset of data is defined and the rows of the relation are ordered in the required manner, totals and performance measures can be calculated. Figure 13.35 shows how calculation is performed.

PERSONNEL

NUMBER	EMPLOYEE NAME	DEPARTMENT	S/H	GROSS
72845	Waters	Outside Sales	S	48960
72888	Dryne	Outside Sales	S	37200
73712	Fawcett	Distribution	H	23500
80345	Well, Jr.	Marketing	S	65000
84672	Piper	Maintenance	H	20560
89760	Acquia	Accounting	H	18755
etc.				

Selection

SALARIED-EMPLOYEES

NUMBER	EMPLOYEE NAME	DEPARTMENT	S/H	GROSS
72845	Waters	Outside Sales	S	48960
72888	Dryne	Outside Sales	S	37200
80345	Well, Jr.	Marketing	S	65000
etc.				

FIGURE 13.32

Selection extracts the relevant records (rows) from the relation.

Present Data to the User The final step in the retrieval of data is presentation. Presentation of the data abstracted from the database can take many forms. Sometimes the data will be presented in tabular form, sometimes in graphs, and other times as a single-word answer on a screen. Output design, as covered in Chapter 11, provides a more detailed look at presentation objectives, forms, and methods.

DENORMALIZATION

One of the main reasons for normalization is to organize data so as to reduce redundant data. If you are not required to store the same data over and over again, you can save a great deal of space. Such organization allows the analyst to reduce the amount of storage needed, something that was very important when storage was expensive.

We learned in the last section that to use normalized data we had to progress through a series of steps that involved joining, sorting, and summarizing. When speed of querying the database (that is, asking a question and requiring a rapid response) is critical, it may be important to store data in other ways.

Denormalization is the process of taking the logical data model and transforming it into a physical model that is efficient for the most often needed tasks. These tasks can include report generation, but they can also mean more efficient queries. Complex queries such as online analytic processing (OLAP), as well as data mining and knowledge data discovery (KDD) processes, can also make use of databases that are denormalized.

Denormalization can be accomplished in a number of different ways. Figure 13.36 depicts some of these approaches. First, we can take a many-to-many relationship, such as that of SALESPERSON and CUSTOMER, which share the associative entity SALES. By combining the attributes from SALESPERSON

FIGURE 13.33

Derivation creates new attributes (columns) in the relation by manipulating the data contained in existing attributes.

PACKAGE-INFO

PACKAGE NUMBER	WIDTH	HEIGHT	LENGTH	WEIGHT
A3456	4	3	26	4
A3457	12	12	20	10
A3458	10	20	34	20
A3459	15	15	22	18
A3460	10	10	40	40
A3461	10	20	34	22
A3462	5	10	15	30
A3463	8	14	44	35

GIRTH = 2 (WIDTH + HEIGHT) + LENGTH

Derivation

IF GIRTH > 84 AND WEIGHT < 25
THEN SHIPPING WEIGHT = 25
ELSE SHIPPING WEIGHT = WEIGHT

PACKAGE-SHIP-INFO

PACKAGE NUMBER	WIDTH	HEIGHT	LENGTH	WEIGHT	GIRTH	SHIPPING WEIGHT
A3456	4	3	26	4	50	4
A3457	12	12	20	10	68	10
A3458	10	20	34	20	94	25
A3459	15	15	22	18	82	18
A3460	10	10	40	40	80	40
A3461	10	20	34	22	90	25
A3462	5	10	15	30	45	30
A3463	8	14	44	35	88	35

and SALES we can avoid one of the join processes. This may result in a considerable amount of data duplication, but it makes the queries about sales patterns more efficient.

Another reason for denormalization is to avoid repeated reference to a lookup table. It may be more efficient to repeat the same information—for example, the city, state, and zip code—even though this information can usually be stored as a zip code only. Hence, in the sales example, CUSTOMER and WAREHOUSE may be combined.

Finally, we look at one-to-one relationships because they are very likely to be combined for practical reasons. If we learn that many of the queries regarding orders also are interested in how the order was shipped, it would make sense to combine, or denormalize. Hence, in the example, some of the details can appear in both ORDER-DETAILS and SHIPPING-DETAILS when we go through denormalization.

DATA WAREHOUSES

Data warehouses differ from traditional databases. The purpose of a data warehouse is to organize information for quick and effective queries. In effect, they store denormalized data, but they go one step farther. They organize data around

PERSONNEL

NUMBER	EMPLOYEE NAME	DEPARTMENT	S/H	GROSS
72845	Waters	Outside Sales	S	48960
72888	Dryne	Outside Sales	S	37200
73712	Fawcett	Distribution	H	23500
80345	Well, Jr.	Marketing	S	65000
84672	Piper	Maintenance	H	20560
89760	Acquia	Accounting	H	18755

↓ **Sort** ↓

EMPLOYEES-BY-NAME

NUMBER	EMPLOYEE NAME	DEPARTMENT	S/H	GROSS
89760	Acquia	Accounting	H	18755
72888	Dryne	Outside Sales	S	37200
73712	Fawcett	Distribution	H	23500
84672	Piper	Maintenance	H	20560
72845	Waters	Outside Sales	S	48960
80345	Well, Jr.	Marketing	S	65000

FIGURE 13.34

The operation sort orders the records (rows) in the relation so that records can be displayed in order and can be grouped for subtotals. Here the PERSONNEL relation is sorted alphabetically according to EMPLOYEE NAME.

subjects. Most often, a data warehouse is more than one database processed so that data are represented in uniform ways. Therefore, the data stored in data warehouses comes from different sources, usually databases that were set up for different purposes.

The data warehouse concept is unique. Differences between data warehouses and traditional databases include the following:

1. In a data warehouse, data are organized around major subjects rather than individual transactions.
2. Data in a data warehouse are typically stored as summarized data rather than the detailed, raw data found in a transaction-oriented database.
3. Data in a data warehouse cover a much longer time frame than data in traditional transaction-oriented databases because queries usually concern longer-term decision making rather than daily transaction details.
4. Most data warehouses are organized for fast queries, whereas the more traditional databases are normalized and structured in such a way as to provide efficient storage of information.
5. Data warehouses are usually optimized for answering complex queries, known as OLAP, from managers and analysts, rather than simple, repeatedly asked queries.
6. Data warehouses allow easy access via data mining software (called siftware) that searches for patterns and is able to identify relationships not imagined by human decision makers.
7. Data warehouses include not just one but multiple databases that have been processed so that the warehouse's data are defined uniformly. These databases are referred to as clean data.

FIGURE 13.35
Calculation provides subtotals, totals, and other performance measures.

SHIPPING-WEIGHT

PACKAGE NUMBER	WIDTH	HEIGHT	LENGTH	WEIGHT	GIRTH	SHIPPING WEIGHT
A3456	4	3	26	4	50	4
A3457	12	12	20	10	68	10
A3458	10	20	34	20	94	25
A3459	15	15	22	18	82	18
A3460	10	10	40	40	80	40
A3461	10	20	34	22	90	25
A3462	5	10	15	30	45	30
A3463	8	14	44	35	88	35

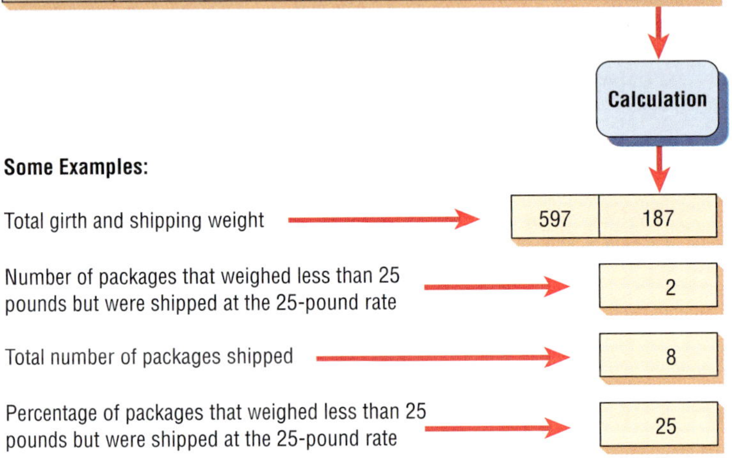

8. Data warehouses usually include data from outside sources (such as an industry report, the company's Security and Exchange Commission filing, or even information about competitors' products), as well as data generated for internal use.

Building a data warehouse is a monumental task. The analyst needs to gather data from a variety of sources and translate that data into a common form. For example, one database may store information about gender as "Male" and "Female," another may store it as "M" and "F," and a third may store it as "1" and "0." The analyst needs to set a standard and convert all the data to the same format.

Once the data are clean, the analyst has to decide how to summarize the data. Once summarized, the detail is lost, so an analyst has to predict the type of queries that might be asked.

Then, the analyst needs to design the data warehouse by logically organizing, and perhaps even physically clustering, the data by subject, requiring much analysis and design. The analyst needs to know a substantial amount about the business.

Typical data warehouses tend to be from 50 gigabytes to tens of terabytes in size. Because they are large, they are also expensive. Most data warehouses cost millions of dollars.

ONLINE ANALYTIC PROCESSING

First introduced in 1993 by E. F. Codd, online analytic processing (OLAP) was meant to answer decision makers' complex questions. Codd concluded that a decision maker had to look at data in a number of different ways. Therefore, the database itself had to be multidimensional. Many people picture OLAP as a

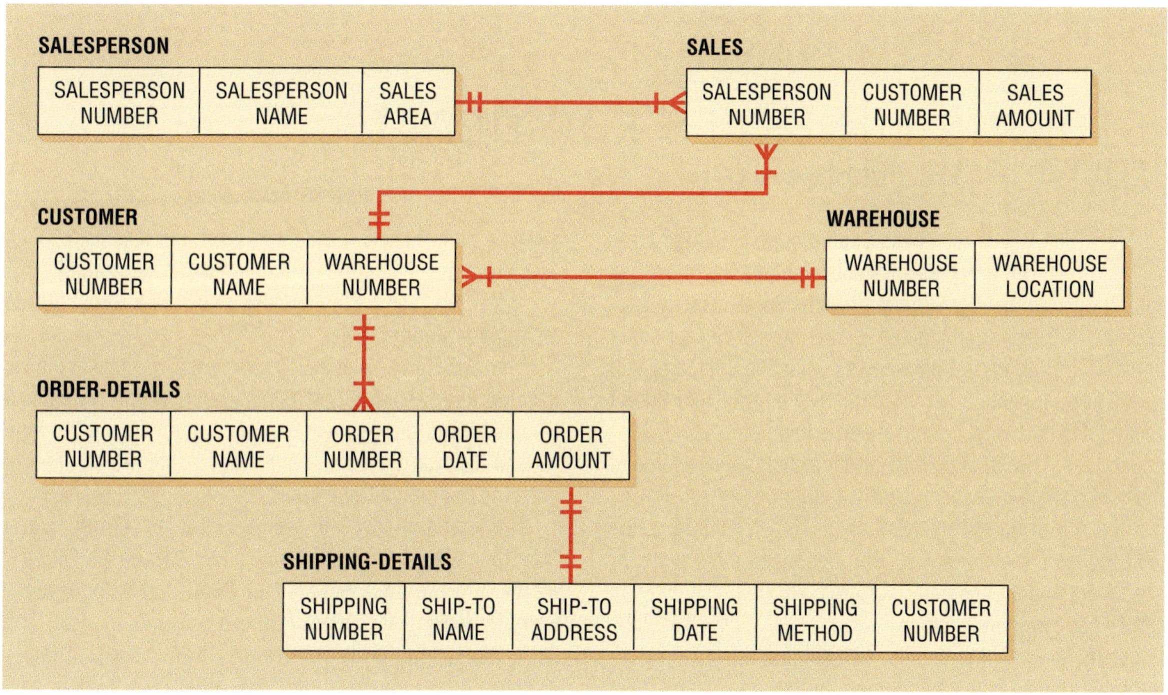

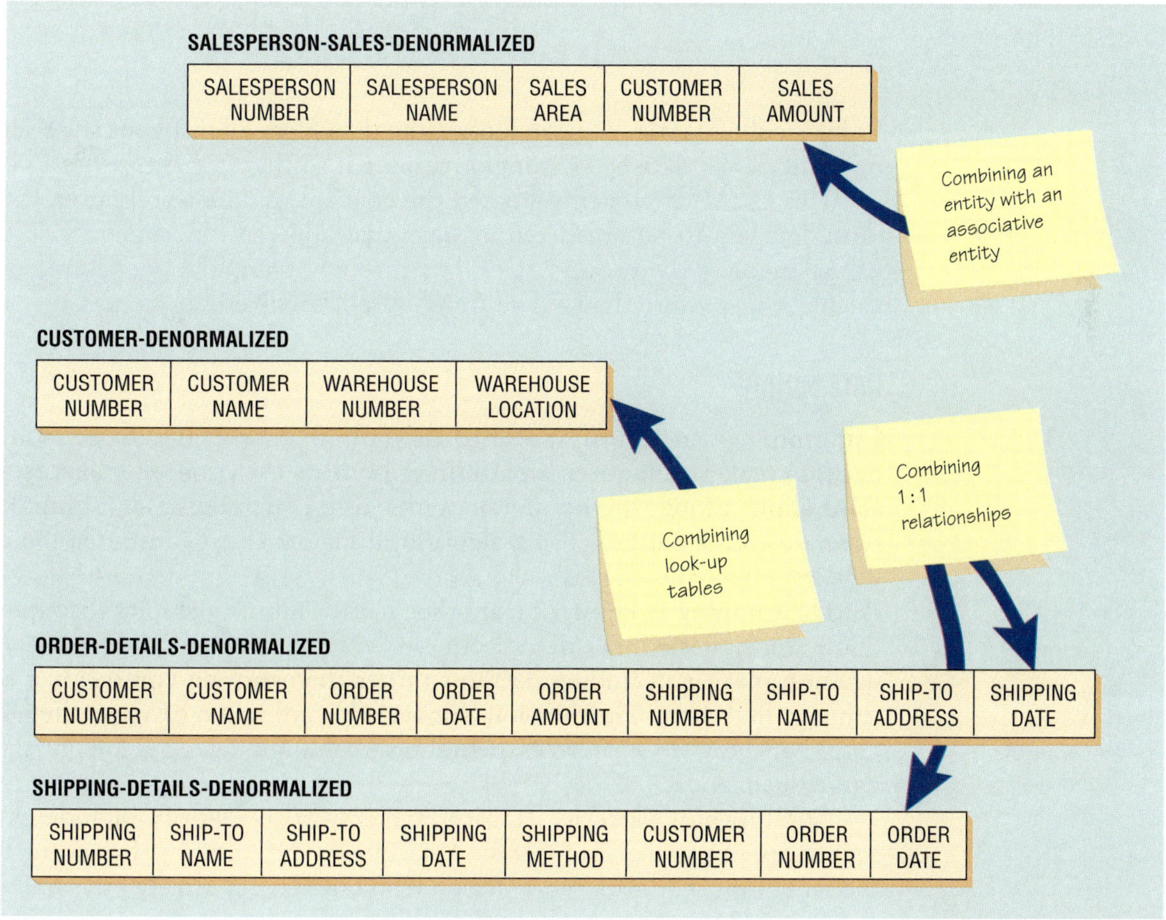

FIGURE 13.36

Three examples of denormalization in order to make access more efficient.

CONSULTING OPPORTUNITY 13.2

STORING MINERALS FOR HEALTH, DATA FOR MINING

One of Marathon Vitamin Shops's employees, Esther See, approaches the owner, Bill Berry, about an observation she had. "I've noticed that our customers have different habits. Some come in regularly, and others are less predictable," Esther says. "When I see a regular customer, I pride myself on knowing what the customer will buy and maybe even suggest other vitamins they might like. I think I generate more sales that way. The customer is happier, too."

Esther continues, "I wish I could be better at helping out some of the customers who come in less frequently, though."

"That's a very nurturing attitude, Esther, and it helps out our store as well," Bill replies. "I know that we can benefit in other ways by getting a better handle on customer patterns. For instance, we can be sure that we have an item in stock."

Esther nods in agreement and adds, "It's not just the type of vitamin I'm talking about. Some customers prefer one brand over another. I don't know if it depends on their income level or the interests they have in leisure activities. Sports, for example."

"I see, Ms. See," Bill chuckles at his own joke, "but do you have anything in mind?"

"Yes, Mr. Berry," she says more formally. "We should organize the data we have about our customers using a data warehouse concept. We can merge the data we have with data from other sources. Then we can look for patterns in our data. Maybe we can identify existing patterns and predict new trends."

Think about how you would organize a data warehouse for Marathon Vitamin Shops. What other databases would you like to merge into the data warehouse? What sort of patterns should Bill Berry be looking for? Identify these patterns by type (associations, sequences, clustering, or trends) and discuss them in a page or two.

Rubik's cube of data. You can look at the data from all different sides, and can also manipulate the data by twisting or turning it so that it makes sense.

This OLAP approach validated the concept of data warehouses. It then made sense for data to be organized in ways that allowed efficient queries. Of course, OLAP involves the processing of data through manipulation, summarization, and calculation, so more than a data warehouse is involved.

DATA MINING

Data mining can identify patterns that a human is unable to detect. Either the decision maker cannot see a pattern, or perhaps the decision maker is not able to think about asking whether that pattern exists. Data mining algorithms search data warehouses for patterns using algorithms. Figure 13.37 illustrates the concept of data mining.

Data mining is known by another name, knowledge data discovery (KDD). Some think that KDD differs from data mining because KDD is meant to assist decision makers in finding patterns rather than turning control over to an algorithm to find them. The decision aids available are called siftware; they include statistical analysis, decision trees, neural networks, intelligent agents, fuzzy logic, and data visualization.

The types of patterns decision makers try to identify include associations, sequences, clustering, and trends. Associations are patterns that occur together at the same time. For example, a person who buys cereal usually buys milk to go with the cereal. Sequences, on the other hand, are patterns of actions that take place over a period of time. For example, if a family buys a house this year, they will most likely buy durables (a refrigerator, or washer and dryer) next year. Clustering is the pattern that develops among a group of people. For example, customers who live in a particular zip code may tend to buy a particular car. Finally, trends are patterns

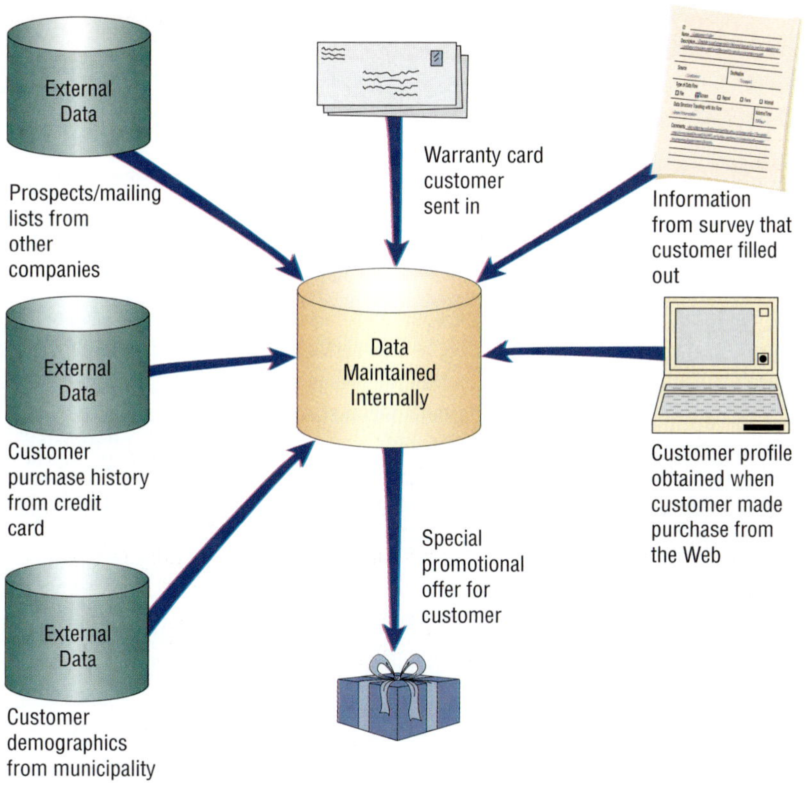

FIGURE 13.37

Data mining collects personal information about customers in an effort to be more specific in interpreting and anticipating their preferences.

that are noticed over a period of time. For example, consumers may move from buying generic goods to premium products.

The concept of data mining came from the desire to use a database for a more selective targeting of customers. Early approaches to direct mail included using zip code information as a way to determine what a family's income might be (assuming a family must generate sufficient income to afford to live in the prestigious Beverly Hills zip code 90210 or some other affluent neighborhood). It was a way (not perfect, of course) to limit the number of catalogs sent.

Data mining takes this concept one step further. Assuming past behavior is a good predictor for future purchases, a large amount of data is gathered on a particular person from credit card purchases. The company can identify what stores we shop in, what we have purchased, how much we paid for an item, and when and how frequently we travel. Data are also entered, stored, and used for a variety of purposes when we fill out warranties, apply for a driver's license, respond to a free offer, or apply for a membership card at a video rental store. Moreover, companies share these data and often make money on the sale of them as well.

American Express has been a leader in data mining for marketing purposes. American Express will send you discount coupons for new stores or entertainment when it sends you a credit card bill, having determined that you have shopped in similar stores or attended similar events. General Motors offers a MasterCard that allows customers to accumulate bonus points toward the purchase of a new car, and then sends out information about new vehicles at the most likely time that a consumer would be interested in purchasing a new car.

The data mining approach is not without problems, however. First, the costs may be too high to justify data mining, something that may only be discovered after huge setup costs have been accrued. Second, data mining has to be coordinated so that various departments or subsidiaries do not all try to reach the customer at the

CONSULTING OPPORTUNITY 13.3

LOSING PROSPECTS

"Market share can be a real problem," says Ryan Taylor, Director of Marketing Systems for a large East Coast health insurer. "One of the greatest challenges we face is how to identify good leads for our salespeople. With over 50-percent market share, we must eliminate the names of most of the prospects we buy before populating our marketing database. It is critical that we get it right because our marketing database is a critical part of our company's arsenal of strategic information tools."

Ryan explains to Chandler, one of your systems analysis team members, "A marketing database, or MDB for short, is a powerful, relational database that is the heart of marketing systems. Our marketing database is used to provide information for all marketing systems. They include productivity tools, such as our Sales Force Automation and our Mass Mailing Systems, which are designed to aid our salespeople in managing the sales cycle. They also include analytical tools, such as our geographic information systems (GIS) or graphical query language (GQL) tools, which are designed to provide decision support.

"The primary function of a marketing database, though, is to track information on our customers and prospects. We currently track geographic information, demographic information, and psychographic information, or, as I like to say, where they live, who they are, and how they think.

"The simplest marketing databases can be made up of just three files: Prospect Profile, Customer Profile, and Purchase and Payment History.

"Once you have designed your marketing database, the next challenge is deciding how to populate it. We currently purchase our prospect information from a list vendor. Because our company's marketing strategy is based on mass marketing, we buy every business in our area. Because of this volume, we pay less than a dime for each prospect. If, however, a company is practicing product differentiation, their prospect base will likely be more defined. This company would likely pay a premium for more detailed data that have been carefully validated," explains Ryan.

"We face a real challenge. If I had a dollar for every time a rep complained to me about the address on a prospect being wrong, I could retire and move to Florida," Ryan quips. "I'm expected to identify which prospects are bad. That's not too hard if you only have a thousand of them, but what do you do when you have over a quarter of a million?"

Ryan continues, "Because we use these data frequently for large mailings, it is very important for us to ensure that the names and addresses on that file are as accurate as possible. For example, they should conform to postal standards and should not be duplicates.

"We achieve this through a technique called data hygiene. How's that for a geeky term? Data hygiene is usually accomplished with specialized software, which is used to determine the validity of an address. This software matches the database address to its own internal database of valid streets and number ranges in a given city or zip code."

Ryan resumes, "One of the other data challenges faced by marketers is eliminating duplicate records in the marketing database. There are two types of duplicates we look for: internal duplicates, which are the existence of multiple records of the same customer or prospect, and external duplicates, which represent our inability to eliminate customers from our prospect data.

"Internal duplicates create reporting problems and increase mailing costs. External duplicates are even worse; they are both costly and embarrassing," Ryan explains. "One of the most embarrassing things for a sales representative is to make a prospecting call only to find out that the business is already our customer. The customer is generally left feeling like only a number in one of our computers. It creates a poor impression and wastes valuable time and resources."

In two paragraphs, describe some techniques Ryan could use to help identify internal and external duplicates in his company's marketing database. Describe how you would build a marketing database to minimize duplicates (use a paragraph). Are there operational methods that might cut down on this problem? List them. Who else in the organization could help with this process? Provide a brief list. In a paragraph, recommend methods to Chandler and your other systems analysis team members that can be used to help enlist and secure the assistance of other relevant organizational members.

same time. In addition, customers may think their privacy has been invaded and resent the offers that are coming their way. Finally, customers may think profiles created solely on the basis of their credit card purchases present a highly distorted image of who they are.

Analysts should take responsibility for considering the ethical aspects of any data mining projects that are proposed. Questions about the length of time profile material is kept, the confidentiality of it, the privacy safeguards included, and the uses to which inferences are put should all be asked and considered with the client. The opportunities for abuse are apparent and must be guarded against. For consumers, data mining is another push technology, and if consumers do not want to be pushed, the data mining efforts will backfire.

SUMMARY

How to store data is often an important decision in the design of an information system. There are two approaches to storing data. The first approach is to store data in individual files, one file for each application. The second approach is to develop a database that can be shared by many users for a variety of applications as the need arises. Dramatic improvements have been made in the design of database software to take advantage of the graphical user interface.

The conventional file approach may at times be a more efficient approach, because the file can be application-specific. On the other hand, the database approach may be more appropriate because the same data need to be entered, stored, and updated only once.

An understanding of data storage requires a grasp of three realms: reality, data, and metadata. An entity is any object or event for which we are willing to collect and store data. Attributes are the actual characteristics of these entities. Data items can have values and can be organized into records that can be accessed by a key. Metadata describe the data and can contain restrictions about the value of a data item (such as numeric only).

Examples of conventional files include master files, table files, transaction files, work files, and report files. They can have a sequential organization, linked lists, or hashed file organization. Databases typically are constructed with a relational structure. Legacy systems can have hierarchical or network structures, however.

Normalization is the process that takes user views and transforms them into less complex structures called normalized relations. There are three steps in the normalization process. First, all repeating groups are removed. Second, all partial dependencies are removed. Finally, the transitive dependencies are taken out. After these three steps are completed, the result is the creation of numerous relations that are of third normal form (3NF).

The entity-relationship diagram may be used to determine the keys required for a record or a database relation. The three guidelines to follow when designing master tables or database relations are that (1) each separate data entity should create a master table (do not combine two distinct entities within one table); (2) a specific data field should exist only on one master table; and (3) each master table or database relation should have programs to Create, Read, Update, and Delete.

Four anomalies may occur when creating database tables: (1) data redundancy, (2) an insert anomaly, (3) a deletion anomaly, and (4) an update anomaly. There are prescribed ways to avoid each of these.

The process of retrieving data may involve as many as eight steps: (1) a relation or relations are chosen and (2) joined, (3) projection and (4) selection are performed on the relation to extract the relevant rows and columns, (5) new attributes may be derived, (6) rows are sorted or indexed, (7) totals and performance measures are calculated, and finally (8) the results are presented to the user.

Denormalization is a process that takes the logical data model and transforms it into a physical model that is efficient for tasks that are most needed. Data warehouses differ from traditional databases in many ways; one is that they store denormalized data, which is organized around subjects. Data warehouses allow easy access via data mining software, called siftware, that searches for patterns and identifies relationships not imagined by human decision makers.

Extensible markup language (XML) is a nonproprietary standard language that serves as a mechanism to take raw data and translate it into a universal language

HYPERCASE® EXPERIENCE 13

"I hear very good things about your team from the people in Management Systems. You even got some hard-earned praise from Training people. You know, Tom Ketcham isn't easy to please these days. Even *he* is seeing some possibilities. I think you'll pull us together yet . . . unless we all go off in different directions again. I'm just teasing you. I told you to think about whether we are a family, a zoo, or a war zone. Now's the time to start designing systems for us that fit us. You've been here long enough now to form those opinions. I hope they're favorable. I think our famous Southern hospitality should help influence you, don't you? I was so busy persuading you that we're worth the effort that I almost forgot to tell you: Tom and Snowden have agreed to think about moving toward a database of some sort. Would you have this ready in the next two weeks? Tom is at a conference in Minneapolis, but when he returns you should have some database ideas worked up for Snowden and him to discuss. Keep at it."

HYPERCASE QUESTIONS

1. Assume your team members have used the Training Unit Client Characteristics Report to design a database table to store the relevant information contained on this report, with the following result:

   Table name: CLIENT TABLE

COLUMN NAME	DESCRIPTION
CLIENT ID (primary key)	Mnemonic made up by users, such as STHSP for State Hospital
CLIENT NAME	The actual, full client name
ADDRESS	The client's address
CONTACT	The name of contact person
PHONE NUMBER	The phone number of contact person
CLASS	The type of institution (Veteran's Administration hospital, clinic, other)
STAFF-SIZE	Size of client staff (number)
TRAINING LEVEL	Minimum required expertise level of the staff (as defined by the class)
EQUIP-QTY	The number of medical machines that the client has
EQUIP TYPE	The type of medical machines (e.g., X-ray, MRI, CAT)
EQUIP MODEL-YR	The model and year of each medical machine

2. Apply normalization to the table your team has developed to remove repeating groups. Display your results.
3. Remove transitive dependencies from your table and show your resulting database table.

that can be read by anyone with the appropriate translation tools. It is used primarily for business data exchange.

Data mining involves using a database for more selective targeting of customers. Assuming that past behavior is a good predictor for future purchases, companies collect data about a person from past credit card purchases, driver's license applications, warranty cards, and so on. Data mining can be powerful, but it may be costly and it needs to be coordinated. In addition, it may infringe on consumer privacy or even a person's civil rights.

KEYWORDS AND PHRASES

- anomaly
- attribute
- bubble diagram
- clean data
- concatenated key
- conventional file
- CRUD (Create, Read, Update, and Delete)
- data element
- data item
- data mining
- data model diagram
- data storage
- data warehouse
- database
- database administrator
- database management system (DBMS)
- delete anomaly
- denormalization
- domain integrity
- entity
- entity integrity constraint
- entity-relationship (E-R) diagram
- entity subtype
- extensible markup language (XML)
- first normal form (1NF)
- hashed file organization
- hierarchical data structure
- inner join
- insert anomaly
- key
- linked list
- logical view
- master file
- network data structure
- normalization
- object identifier (OID)
- online analytical processing (OLAP)
- outer join
- partial dependencies
- patterns
  - associations
  - sequences
  - clustering
  - trends
- physical view
- primary key
- reality, data, and metadata
- record
- referential integrity
- relational data structure
- relationship
- repeating group
- report file
- retrieval
- second normal form (2NF)
- secondary key
- self-join
- siftware
- special characters
- steps in information retrieval
  - choose
  - join
  - project
  - select
  - derive
  - index or sort
  - calculate
  - present
- table file
- third normal form (3NF)
- transaction file
- transitive dependencies
- unnormalized relation
- update anomaly
- work file

REVIEW QUESTIONS

1. What are the advantages of organizing data storage as separate files?
2. What are the advantages of organizing data storage using a database approach?
3. What are the effectiveness measures of database design?
4. List some examples of entities and their attributes.
5. What is the difference between a primary key and an object identifier?
6. Define the term *metadata*. What is the purpose of metadata?
7. List types of commonly used conventional files. Which of these are temporary files?
8. What is a linked list?

9. What often occurs when a hashed file organization is used?
10. Name the three main types of database organization.
11. Define the term *normalization*.
12. What is removed when a relation is converted to the first normal form?
13. What is removed when a relation is converted from 1NF to 2NF?
14. What is removed when a relation is converted from 2NF to 3NF?
15. List the three entity constraints. In a sentence, describe the meaning of each entity constraint.
16. Describe the four anomalies that may occur when creating database tables.
17. List the eight steps for retrieving, presorting, and presenting data.
18. What does join do? What is projection? What is selection?
19. How does an outer join differ from an inner join?
20. What must be present on a table to implement a self-join?
21. State the differences between sort and index.
22. What are the two different foreign keys that must be present on a relational table?
23. Define denormalization.
24. Explain the differences between traditional databases and data warehouses.
25. Define what siftware does when used in data mining.
26. Explain how XML works to facilitate business data exchange.

PROBLEMS

1. Given the following file of renters:

Record Number	Last Name	Apartment Number	Rent	Lease Expires
41	Warkentin	102	550	4/30
42	Buffington	204	600	4/30
43	Schuldt	103	550	4/30
44	Tang	209	600	5/31
45	Cho	203	550	5/31
46	Yoo	203	550	6/30
47	Pyle	101	500	6/30

   a. Develop a linked list by apartment number in ascending order.
   b. Develop a linked list according to last name in ascending order.

2. The following is an example of a grade report for two students at the University of Southern New Jersey:

USNJ Grade Report
Spring Semester 2007

Name: I. M. Smarte — *Major: MIS*
Student: 053-6929-24 — *Status: Senior*

Course Number	Course Title	Professor	Professor's Department	Grade
MIS 403	Systems Analysis	Diggs, T.	MIS	A
MIS 411	Conceptual Foundations	Barre, G.	MIS	A
MIS 420	Human Factors in IS	Barre, G.	MIS	B
CIS 412	Database Design	Menzel, I.	CIS	A
DESC 353	Management Models	Murney, J.	MIS	A

USNJ Grade Report Spring Semester 2007 Name: E.Z. Grayed Major: MIS Student: 472-6124-59 Status: Senior				
Course Number	**Course Title**	**Professor**	**Professor's Department**	**Grade**
MIS 403	Systems Analysis	Diggs, T.	MIS	B
MIS 411	Conceptual Foundations	Barre, G.	MIS	A

3. Draw a data model diagram with associations for the user view in Problem 2.
4. Convert the user view in Problem 3 to a 3NF relation. Show each step along the way.
5. What problem might arise when using a primary key of course number for the data in Problem 2? (*Hint:* Think about what would happen if the Department Name [not shown in the data] changes.)
6. Draw an entity-relationship diagram for the following situation: Many students play many different sports. One person, called the head coach, assumes the role of coaching all these sports. Each of the entities has a number and a name. (Make any assumptions necessary to complete a reasonable diagram. List your assumptions.)
7. The entity-relationship diagram you drew in Problem 5 represents the data entities that are needed to implement a system for tracking students and the sports teams that they play. List the tables that are needed to implement the system, along with primary, secondary, and foreign keys that are required to link the tables.
8. Draw an entity-relationship diagram for the following situation: A commercial bakery makes many different products. These products include breads, desserts, specialty cakes, and many other baked goods. Ingredients such as flour, spices, and milk are purchased from vendors. Sometimes an ingredient is purchased from a single vendor, and other times an ingredient is purchased from many vendors. The bakery has commercial customers, such as schools and restaurants, that regularly place orders for baked goods. Each baked good has a specialist that oversees the setup of the bakery operation and inspects the finished product.
9. List the tables and keys that are needed to implement the commercial bakery system.
10. Draw an E-R diagram for the ordering system in Figure 13.26.
11. Draw a data flow diagram for placing an order. Base your data flow diagram on the E-R diagram.
12. Create an entity-relationship diagram for a genealogy software package called "PeopleTree" to keep track of ancestors. Assume that each person will be on a Person table and that one person may have one biological father and mother as well as an adopted mother and father. The mothers and fathers must be stored on the Person table as well. Each person should have only one birthplace, stored on the Place table. Many people may be born in the same place.
13. Define the primary key used for the Person and Place tables.
14. GaiaOrganix is an organic food wholesale co-op linking producers and consumers. GaiaOrganix negotiates purchases by grocery and other stores from farmers who raise a variety of crops, such as fruit, vegetables, and grain. Each farmer may produce a number of crops, and each crop may be produced by a number of farmers. To provide the highest level of fresh products, the produce is shipped directly from the farm to the store. Each store may purchase from

many farms, and each farm may sell to many stores. Draw an entity-relationship diagram in the third normal form showing the relationship between producer (farms) and the retailer (stores).

15. ArticleIndex.com is a company that produces indexes of magazine and periodical articles for a given discipline. A Web user should be able to enter an article topic or authors and receive a detailed list of all the articles and periodicals in which the topic was found. Each article may have many authors, and each author may write many articles. An article may be found in only one periodical, but each periodical will usually contain many articles. Each article may have many topics, and each topic may be in many articles. Draw an entity-relationship diagram in the third normal form for the articles, authors, periodicals, and topics.
16. Identify the primary and foreign keys for the entity-relationship diagram created in Problem 15.

GROUP PROJECT

1. Gregg Baker orders tickets for two concerts over the Web. His orders are processed, exact seat locations are assigned, and the tickets are mailed separately. One of the sets of tickets gets lost in the mail. When he calls the service number, he does not remember the date or the seat numbers, but the ticket agency was able to locate his tickets quickly because the agency denormalized the relation. Describe the ticket ordering system by listing the data elements that are kept on the order form and the shipping form. What information did Gregg give the ticket agency to retrieve the information?

SELECTED BIBLIOGRAPHY

Avison, D. E. *Information Systems Development: A Database Approach*, 2d ed. London: Blackwell Scientific, 1992.

Avison, D. E., and G. Fitzgerald. *Information Systems Development: Methodologies, Techniques, and Tools*, 2d ed. New York: McGraw-Hill, 1995.

Codd, E. F. "Twelve Rules for On-Line Analytic Processing." *Computerworld*, April 13, 1995.

Dietel, H. M., P. J. Dietel, and T. R. Nieto. *E-Business and e-Commerce: How to Program*. Upper Saddle River, NJ: Prentice-Hall, 2001.

Everest, G. C. *Database Management: Objectives, System Functions, and Administration*. New York: McGraw-Hill, 1985.

Gane, C., and T. Sarson. *Structured Systems Analysis: Tools and Techniques.* Englewood Cliffs, NJ: Prentice-Hall, 1979.

Gray, P. "Data Warehousing: Three Major Applications and Their Significance." In *Emerging Information Technologies, Improving Decision, Cooperation, and Infrastructure.* Edited by K. E. Kendall. Thousand Oaks, CA: Sage Publications, 1999.

McFadden, F., and J. A. Hoffer. *Modern Database Management*, 4th ed. Redwood City, CA: Benjamin-Cummings, 1994.

Sanders, G. L. *Data Modeling.* New York: Boyd and Fraser, 1995.

"XML." Available at: <www.xml.com>. Last accessed February 9, 2001.

Allen Schmidt, Julie E. Kendall, and Kenneth E. Kendall

BACK TO DATA BASICS

After numerous interviews, prototypes, data flow diagrams, and data dictionary entries have been completed, Anna and Chip both start work on the entity-relationship model. "I'll be responsible for creating the Microsoft Access table relationships," Anna promises. Chip volunteers to complete an entity-relationship diagram. "Let's compare the two diagrams for accuracy and consistency when we're done," Anna suggests, and so they do.

Figure E13.1 shows the entity-relationship diagram for the computer inventory system. Visible Analyst calls each of the rectangles an entity. Each entity represents a file of information stored in the system, corresponding to a data store on the data flow diagram. Each of the diamond rectangles represents a relationship between the data entities. A rectangle with an oval in it represents an entity that cannot exist without the connecting entity, such as a table of codes.

"I've created the entity-relationship diagram, starting with the simplest portions of the system," Chip tells Anna. "The first data entities created are SOFTWARE and COMPUTER. The relationship is that software is installed on the computer. Next I determined the cardinality of the relationship. Because one software package could be installed on many computers, this relationship is one-to-many. Each computer may also have many different software packages installed on it so that it also provides a one-to-many relationship. Because there is a one-to-many relationship for each of the

Computer	Software
Hardware Inventory Number +	Software Inventory Number +
Brand Name +	Title +
Model +	Operating System Name +
Serial Number +	Version Number +
Date Purchased +	Publisher +
Purchase Cost +	Software Category Description +
Replacement Cost +	Number of Media +
Memory Size +	Computer Brand +
Hard Disk Capacity +	Computer Model +
Second Hard Disk Capacity +	Memory Required +
Floppy Drive +	Display Name +
CD-ROM Drive +	Printer Description +
Zip Drive +	Type of Media +
Network +	Site License +
Network Connection Name +	Number of Copies +
Display Name +	Expert Last Name +
Printer Description +	Expert First Name +
Warranty +	Office Phone
Campus Description +	
Room Location	
{Board Code} +	
{Software Inventory Number}	

FIGURE E13.1
Unnormalized entity-relationship diagram for the computer system.

data entities, the full relationship between them becomes many-to-many." The unnormalized entity-relationship diagram is shown in Figure E13.2, along with the data dictionary entries for the tables.

Chip continues by saying, "This first view is far from normalized. Notice that the BOARD CODE and SOFTWARE INVENTORY NUMBER are repeating elements on the HARDWARE entity. I will have to create several entities for each of them." A bit later Chip reviews his work with Anna. The BOARD CODE has become a separate entity, linked by a relational entity, and the SOFTWARE INVENTORY NUMBER has been removed and placed in a relational entity. Refer to the entity-relationship diagram illustrated in Figure E13.2. "This places the data in the first normal form," remarks Chip. "Also, there are no elements that are dependent on only a part of the key, so the data are also in the second normal form. There are, however, elements that are not part of the entity that is represented on the diagram, and they will have to be removed. For example, look at the DISPLAY NAME and PRINTER DESCRIPTION. These elements are not a part of the computer but are connected to it. They should have their own entity. That makes it easier to change the spelling of, say, a printer. Rather than having to change the spelling of the printer on many of the COMPUTER records, it would only have to be changed once."

Anna agrees, remarking, "That's really a good assessment of the situation. It will make implementing the Microsoft Access tables easier."

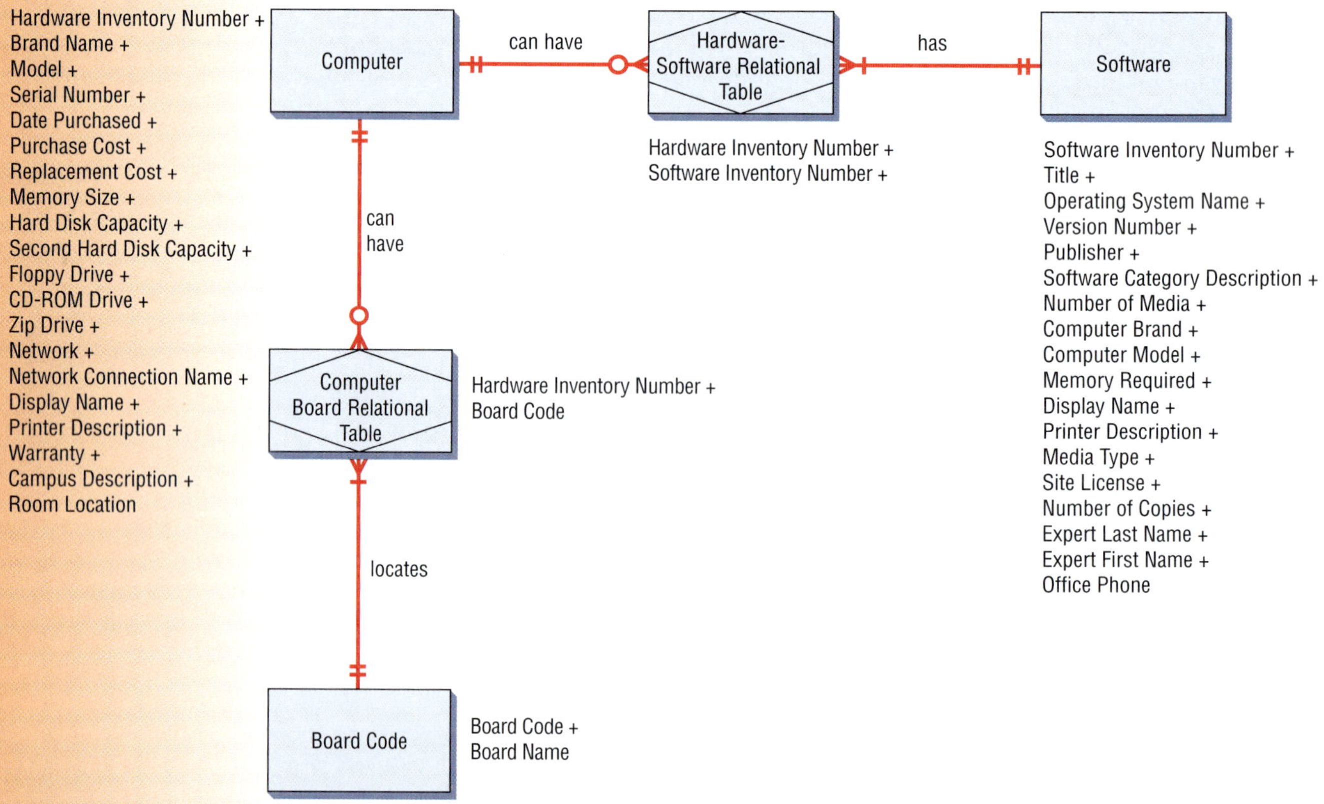

FIGURE E13.2

The computer system's entity-relationship diagram in the first normal form.

Chip continues to work on the entity-relationship diagram. After a few hours he exclaims, "I think it's done. Would you take a look at the final version?" The final version is shown in Figure E13.3. All the entities and relationships have been described in the repository.

Anna reviews the final version and exclaims, "It looks great! You are right in moving the PRINTER and DISPLAY to their own entities. I see that the CAMPUS BUILDING has been moved to its own entity. Good idea, as the building is not a part of the computer. Also, the SOFTWARE EXPERT is definitely not a part of the SOFTWARE entity. How about the SOFTWARE CATEGORY?"

"I moved the SOFTWARE CATEGORY into its own entity to save room on the master files when they are constructed," Chip answers. "It is really a table of codes, and we can store a small code, rather than a lengthy description. Why don't you double check the various keys on the diagram? Each related entity, on the many end, should have a foreign key that matches the primary key of the entity on the one end."

Anna examines the diagram for a while and remarks, "It looks good to me, but why don't you run some of the Visible Analyst reports for the entity-relationship diagram?"

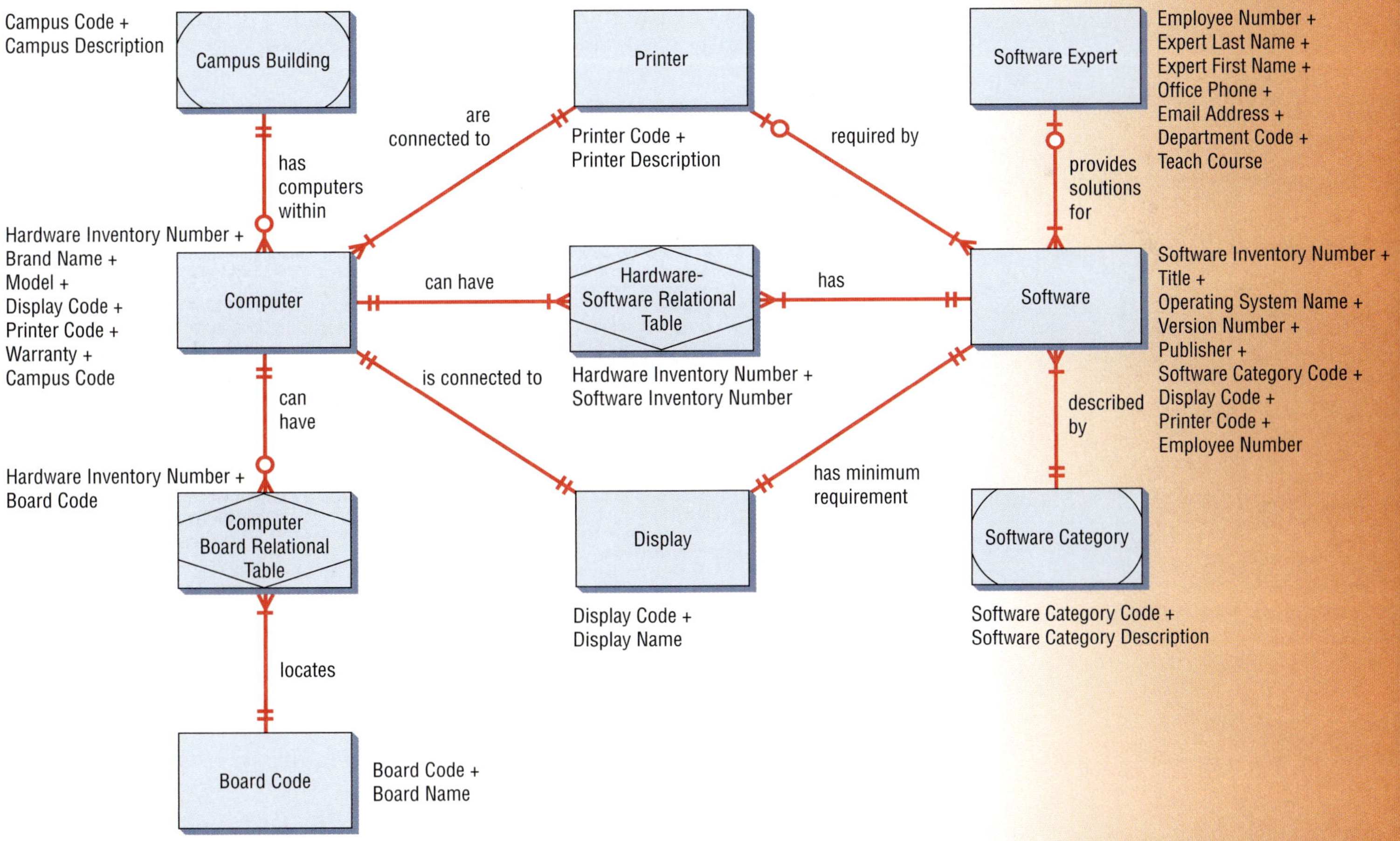

FIGURE E13.3

Final entity-relationship diagram for the computer system.

13

"That's an excellent idea!" exclaims Chip. The first step in the diagram is to run the Visible Analyst Syntax Check for the final entity-relationship diagram. This option checks for entities and relationships that have not been named, and it produces no errors when Chip runs it. Next, Chip runs the Normalization Analysis option, which displays a series of warning error messages. These messages inform Chip that some of the relationships have a one-to-one cardinality, which is acceptable. The other warning messages let Chip know that the SOFTWARE CATEGORY and CAMPUS BUILDING do not have identifying relationships. Hence, the record keys have not been defined in the repository.

The next analysis that Chip runs is **Key Analysis Errors** report. This option performs syntax and normalization analysis as well as reporting problems with primary and foreign keys. The analysis report, which shows that the SOFTWARE CATEGORY has no primary key and that the entity PRINTER has no identifying relationship, is illustrated in Figure E13.4. The final analysis report that Chip runs is the **Model Balancing** report, showing some of the errors detected by previous reports, but, in addition, it shows all elements that are contained in the **Composition** area of the entities and are not used by a data flow diagram process.

"Now that we've done the analysis, watch this feature in action," remarks Chip. "I'm going to run Key Synchronization."

"I thought we were finished with the reports," replies Anna.

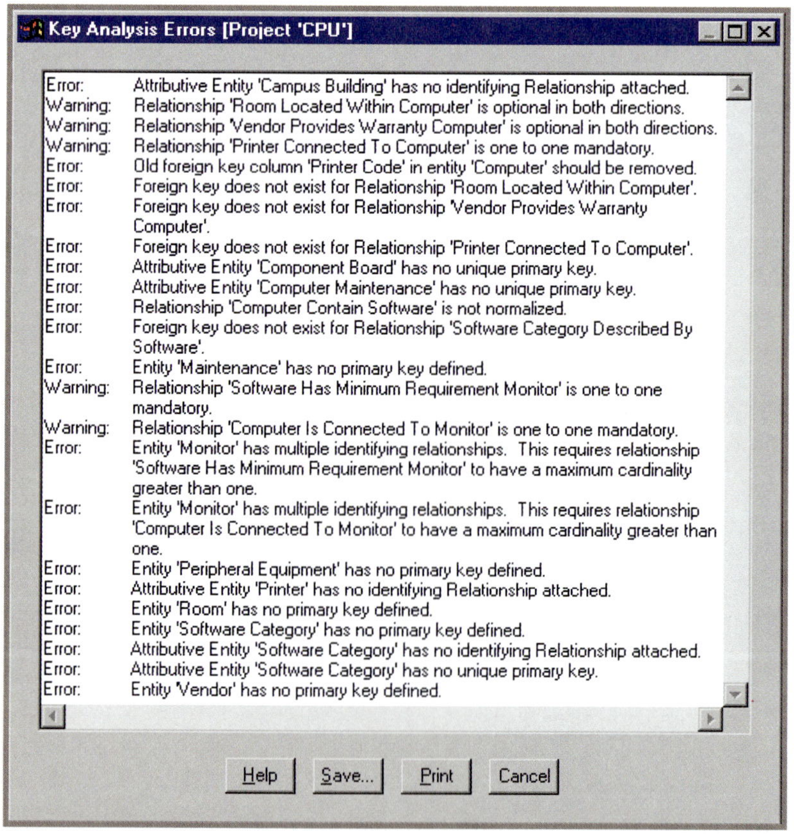

FIGURE E13.4

The KEY ANALYSIS ERRORS output display.

"Key Synchronization is more than a report," answers Chip. "It will define all the foreign keys for the project."

"This I've got to see!" exclaims Anna, as she slides a chair next to Chip.

"First, we have to draw the entity-relationship diagram and define the primary keys, which we've done," explains Chip. "Take a look at this repository entry." Chip opens the entity-relationship diagram and double clicks on the COMPUTERS entity, displaying its repository entry. The primary key (the [pk] notation in front of the HARDWARE INVENTORY NUMBER element in the composition area) and several alternate keys ([Ak1], [Ak2], and [Ak3]) have been defined. Chip clicks Repository and Key Synchronization. A report informing the analysts of the changes made to tables as well as any remaining errors is produced.

After spending time examining the diagram as well as the repository entries and analysis reports, both Anna and Chip are satisfied that the relationships between the data have been accurately portrayed. Next they decide how to design the files or database from the diagrams.

Anna says, "The system should be implemented using Microsoft Access, because a database structure would easily accommodate the many relationships."

The HARDWARE/SOFTWARE relation is analyzed first. Because there is a many-to-many relationship between these two data entities, it may be implemented by using three database tables:

1. A HARDWARE MASTER table.
2. A SOFTWARE MASTER table.
3. A HARDWARE/SOFTWARE RELATIONSHIP table, which would contain the key fields for the HARDWARE and SOFTWARE master tables for all software installed on all machines.

"I guess it's my turn to work on the relationships," says Anna as she takes a copy of the entity-relationship diagram. "I'll modify the Microsoft Access tables from the prototyping sessions."

Anna starts by setting up the primary keys for each of the tables. When the tables are in their final form, she creates the relationships between them. The Microsoft Access relationships diagram is illustrated in Figure E13.5. Rectangles on the diagram represent the database tables and correspond to the various entity types found on the entity-relationships diagram. Notice that the cardinality is represented by "1" and the infinity symbol. The primary key fields are listed as the first field of each rectangle; they are also displayed in boldface type. Foreign keys are shown attached to the other end of the relationship line, if the foreign key is visible in the table rectangle. Keys are dragged from one table to another to establish a relationship, and a dialog box appears to determine properties of the relationship. For example, the property called Enforce Referential Integrity means that you cannot create a record in the many end table without first creating it in the one end (containing the primary key). Figure E13.6 illustrates setting referential integrity for the relationship between SOFTWARE CATEGORY CODE and the SOFTWARE MASTER. Note that **Cascade Update Related Fields** is checked. If you change a SOFTWARE CATEGORY CODE value, the same code will be updated on the SOFTWARE MASTER. **Cascade Delete Related Records,** however, is not checked. You would not want the system to delete a SOFTWARE CATEGORY CODE and have all the related SOFTWARE MASTER records also deleted.

13

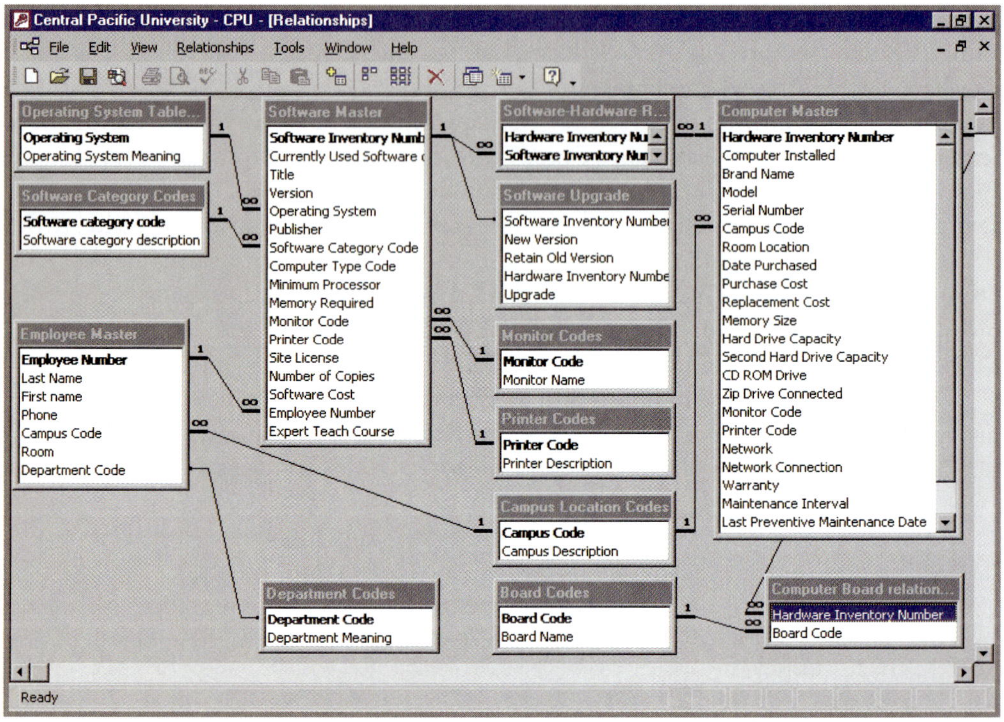

FIGURE E13.5
A Microsoft Access RELATIONSHIPS diagram.

"I would like to produce some documentation for the system," remarks Anna. "It would help when we need to modify the design as well as the Microsoft Access objects and code." There are several matrices found in the **Repository Reports** feature that are useful to produce. The first is the **Entities versus Data Stores Matrix.** It shows the entities found on all the entity-relationship diagrams and data stores that contain similar

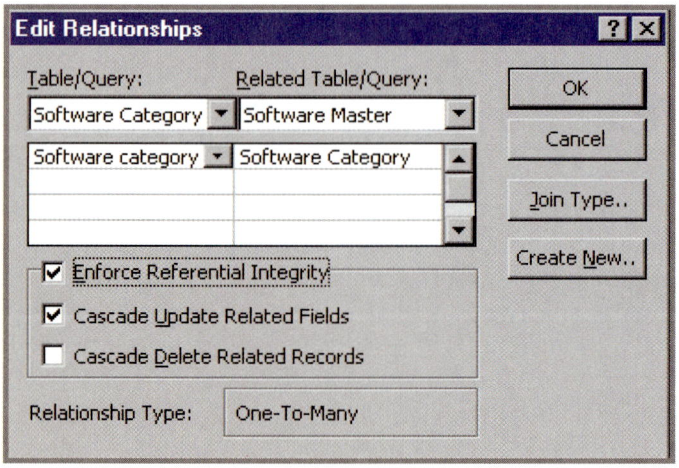

FIGURE E13.6
An example that shows setting referential integrity for the relationship between SOFTWARE CATEGORY CODES and SOFTWARE MASTER.

elements. This matrix is useful for mapping the entity-relationship diagram into a data flow diagram.

The **Composition Matrix** is produced next. It provides a cross-reference grid of elements and the entities in which they are contained. This matrix is useful for determining which entities will need to be modified (or which tables in Microsoft Access) if the element size or any other characteristic of the element changes. A last matrix that is useful in assessing changes to the entire system is the **Diagram Location Matrix.**

EXERCISES

E-1. Use Visible Analyst to view the unnormalized and first normal form entity-relationship diagrams for the computer system.

E-2. Use Visible Analyst to view the entity-relationship diagram for the computer system.

E-3. Add the VENDOR entity to the diagram. The vendor warrants the computers, and the relationship between VENDOR and COMPUTER is that one VENDOR can warrant many COMPUTER(s).

E-4. Add the MAINTENANCE entity to the diagram. Maintenance repairs are performed on computers, and the relationship between MAINTENANCE and COMPUTER(s) is such that one COMPUTER may have many MAINTENANCE records.

E-5. Describe the SOFTWARE CATEGORY entity in the repository. Include the elements found on the entity-relationship diagram below SOFTWARE CATEGORY in the **Composition** area.

E-6. Describe the MAINTENANCE entity in the repository. The elements are as follows:

a. MAINTENANCE ORDER NUMBER.
b. HARDWARE INVENTORY NUMBER.
c. MAINTENANCE DATE.
d. TYPE OF MAINTENANCE.
e. COST OF MAINTENANCE.
f. MAINTENANCE COVERED BY WARRANTY.

E-7. Describe the VENDOR entity. The elements are as follows:

a. VENDOR NUMBER.
b. VENDOR NAME.
c. STREET.
d. CITY.
e. STATE.
f. ZIP CODE.
g. TELEPHONE NUMBER.
h. DATE LAST ORDER SENT.
i. TOTAL AMOUNT PURCHASED FROM VENDOR.
j. TOTAL NUMBER OF ORDERS SENT TO VENDOR.

The exercises preceded by a Web icon indicate value-added material is available from the Web site at www.prenhall.com/kendall. Students can download a sample Visible Analyst Project and a Microsoft Access database that can be used to complete the exercises. Visible Analyst software can be packaged with this text for an additional fee.

E-8. Produce the following reports using Visible Analyst:

a. Open the computer system entity-relationship diagram; then **Syntax Check** the diagram (**Diagram/Analyze/Syntax Check**).

b. Run the **Normalization Analysis** report for the computer system entity-relationship diagram (**Diagram/Analyze/Normalization**).

c. The **Key Analysis Report.**

d. The **Key Synchronization Report.** What has changed in the **Composition** area for each of the entities?

e. The **Model Balancing Report.**

f. The **Entities versus Data Stores Matrix.**

g. The **Composition Matrix.**

h. The **Diagram Location Matrix.**

E-9. Explain in a paragraph the relationship between a foreign key and a primary key, and why it is necessary to have them on separate entities when there is a relationship between the entities.

14

HUMAN–COMPUTER INTERACTION

Learning Objectives

Once you have mastered the material in this chapter you will be able to:

1. **Understand human–computer interaction.**
2. **Know how fit affects performance and well-being.**
3. **Understand the technology acceptance model (TAM) and usability.**
4. **Know how to design for the cognitive styles of individuals and for persons with disabilities.**
5. **Understand the different types of, and reasons for, using alternative user interfaces.**
6. **Design effective dialog for HCI.**
7. **Understand the importance of user feedback.**
8. **Articulate HCI implications for designing ecommerce Web sites.**
9. **Formulate queries that permit users to search the Web.**

Throughout the book your awareness of human–computer interaction (HCI) and its importance to your task as a systems analyst has grown. Your attentiveness to the surrounding issues of HCI and its existence in organizational settings should have been heightened. While awareness is important, by now you recognize that you need to master the concepts surrounding HCI as well as become proficient at assessing human information requirements and incorporating your findings into your designs. Furthermore, the European Union (EU) and the United States have come forth with specific guidelines for usability. These guidelines mandate making Web sites and electronic services accessible to the disabled.

This chapter fills in some of the details about HCI and working with users. It also gives you some experience in applying HCI concepts that you have been learning to help in your design of human–computer interfaces; feedback, ecommerce Web sites, and Web queries.

UNDERSTANDING HUMAN–COMPUTER INTERACTION

Designing for HCI means "Ensuring system functionality and usability, providing effective user interaction support, and enhancing a pleasant user experience." Furthermore, "The overarching goal is to achieve both organizational and individual user effectiveness and efficiency. To reach these goals, managers and developers need to be knowledgeable about the interplay among users, tasks, task contexts, information technology (IT), and the environments in which systems are used," (Carey et al., 2004, p. 358).

How do we ensure that our systems are user centered, so that they appropriately include users' needs as well as organizational needs? One way is to understand HCI concepts, another is to consider interfaces in the light of HCI issues, and another is to apply standard design concepts to computers in new ways because of an HCI approach.

Knowledge about the interplay among users, tasks, task contexts, IT, and the environments in which the systems are used comprises the basis of human–computer interaction. The main tactic of HCI in systems analysis and design is to repeatedly elicit feedback from users about their experiences with prototyped designs (which could be screens, forms, interfaces, and the like), refining the design based on the suggested changes, trying them with users again until the design is acceptable, and until it is frozen by the analyst.

HOW FIT AFFECTS PERFORMANCE AND WELL-BEING

Let's begin our exploration of human–computer interaction with some useful definitions that are commonly shared among those working in the field.

Fit A good fit between the HCI elements of the human, the computer, and the task that needs to be performed leads to performance and well-being, as shown in Figure 14.1. Just as it is important that new shoes comfortably fit the shape of your foot, hold up during the activity you will be doing (such as running), and are made of a material (such as leather) that is durable and cost-effective, so too is it important that the fit among the user, computer, and task all correspond.

Analysts want the best fit in their design. You want to make the best possible use of people in designing a computerized task that is intended to meet an organizational objective. Better fit is meant to result in better performance and greater overall well-being for the human involved in the system.

Fortunately, humans' capacity to learn better ways to work also influences the fit. We would never try running a marathon with a shoe right out of the box, without first getting our foot used to it by breaking it in. By the same token, users can be trained to develop a better fit by learning their tasks and computers thoroughly. Training continues to be an important way to improve fit. Chapter 17 contains more specifics about how the analyst can facilitate user training for new systems and software.

Task In the foregoing chapters you have learned many methods to help you thoroughly understand, document, and graphically depict the tasks that people currently perform in the organization. You have also learned methods to help you design new tasks that will help them reach their objectives with the new systems you are creating. As you recall, tasks can be structured and routine, or they can be ill defined and without apparent structure. Complex tasks that require human, system, and task interaction are supported by ecommerce and Web systems, ERP systems, and wireless systems inside and outside the organization.

Performance The definition of the word *performance* in the HCI context is also key. In this case, "performance" refers to a combination of the efficiency involved in

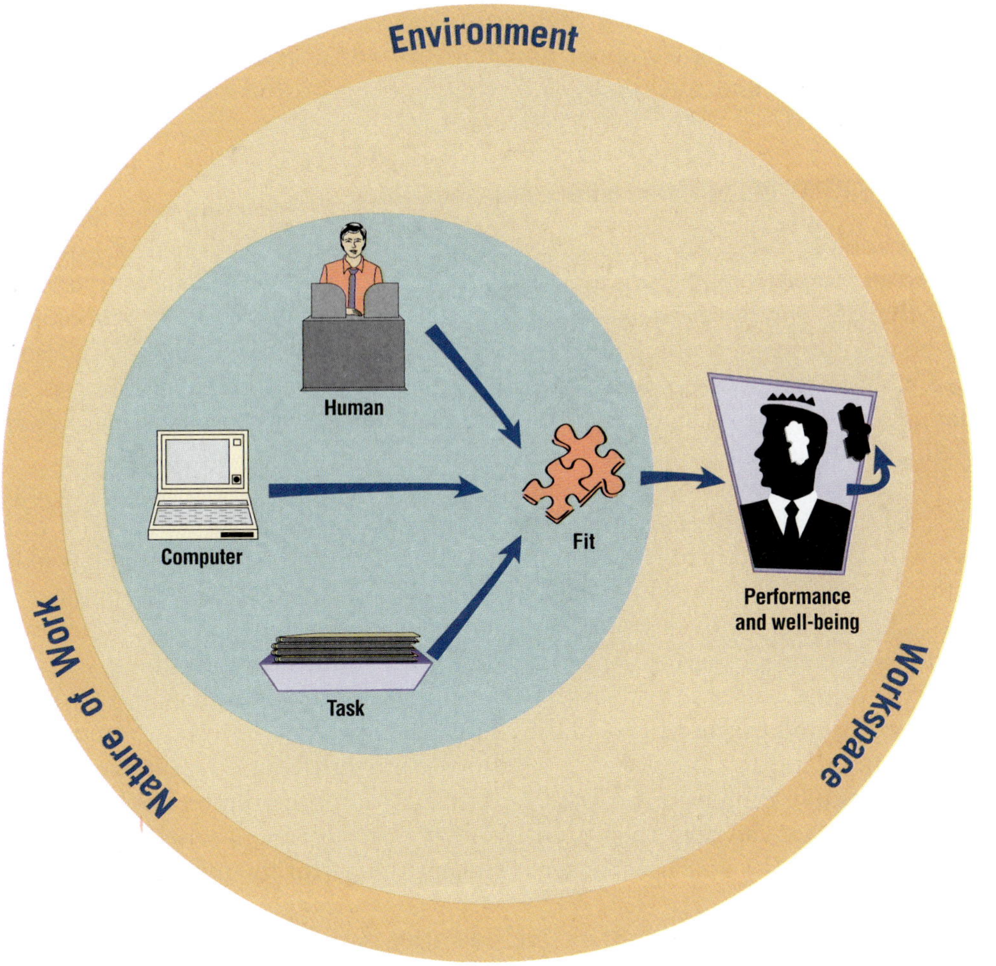

FIGURE 14.1
The "fit" among the human, computer, and task affects performance and well-being.

performing a task and the quality of the work that is produced by the task. For example, if analysts are using a high-level software or CASE tool to create data flow diagrams in which they are proficient, we would predict that the quality of the data flow diagrams produced would be high. The performance is also efficient, because the analysts are using an automated tool with which they are familiar. They can work rapidly, with good results. The task fits the objective, which is to create high-quality data flow diagrams to document a system. The efficiency of producing such diagrams with a CASE tool, which can then be used to store, retrieve, communicate, and modify the DFD diagrams, is excellent, compared to alternatives such as using a drawing tool unrelated to a data dictionary or drafting diagrams by hand, neither of which offer such features.

Well-Being At this point, we can introduce the concept of well-being, which is a concern for a human's overall comfort, safety, and health; in sum it is their physical as well as psychological state. Does using a CASE tool for producing DFDs on a computer serve the analyst's well-being? Yes, because the task fits well with the analyst, the software, the objective, and the computer. Notice that the analyst is working in an environment where they are physically comfortable, are psychologically stimulated to be creative, and can be productive; also, the analyst's work is valued by peers and clients, as well as valued monetarily by the employing organization.

Psychological attitudes (the affective component) are also important. How users feel about themselves, their identities, their work life, and performance can all be gauged through assessing their attitudes. As an analyst taking an HCI perspective, you are concerned about how humans' attitudes color the way they feel about technology and their tasks, and whether their attitudes hinder or enhance their experience.

THE TECHNOLOGY ACCEPTANCE MODEL AND ATTITUDE

The technology acceptance model (TAM), as proposed by Davis in 1989 and later refined and improved by Davis and others, basically is a way for analysts to organize their thinking about whether users will accept and use information technology. It can be used to shape training after a system has been developed, but it can also be used early in the development process to garner user reactions to prototypes so that systems can be changed early on in the development process to increase the likelihood of their adoption and use.

There are many theoretical components and a good deal of research to argue the intricacies of TAM. However, from a practical point of view, you need to be aware that a large body of research on the acceptance and use of technology exists in the information systems literature and that TAM is one of the most popular subjects. TAM draws its power from examining the perceived usefulness of the system to increase one's job performance and the belief about how easy the system will be to use when a user sits down to accomplish a task. So we have the two keys: **perceived usefulness** and **perceived ease of use.** Both can be used to understand how users intend to interact with a proposed system. Some researchers add an explicit attitude dimension to their conceptualization of the technology acceptance model that can help them think more specifically about what psychological states will shape the way users accept or reject the use of the information systems they design.

Attitudes toward computers include user satisfaction with the human–computer interface, as well as users' overall satisfaction with the system. These are generally ascertained through special user satisfaction surveys and are often used following implementation to estimate the overall success or failure of a systems project. (See Chapter 17 for some examples.) When you attempt to characterize attitudes toward computers, you may be surprised by all of the possible human responses that are conveyed. Most of the literature that we are examining for HCI will look at a variety of user attitudes, including satisfaction, anxiety, enjoyment, and playfulness in approaching technology.

The technology acceptance model also points out the importance of whether users find a system useful and are thus motivated to use it. Since this is an important HCI concern, we can measure whether the information technology is found to be useful by examining whether the system provides support for an organizational member's individual tasks. We can also measure whether there are important tasks that a user of the new system could not perform prior to its implementation. Our measurements can also determine whether the system extends a user's capabilities (for example, increasing the ability to perform higher-level analysis quickly or performing an on-the-spot translation of a financial report into another language complete with currency conversions). Part of the usefulness criterion in HCI can also be measured by ascertaining whether users find it rewarding to use the system through postimplementation interviews and observations.

USABILITY

Usability is a term that is defined differently depending on the branch of science in which one first encounters it. For our purposes in exploring usability through an

HCI lens, we will try to focus on usability as a way for designers to evaluate the systems and interfaces they create with an eye toward addressing as many HCI concerns as thoroughly as possible. Usability studies (according to www.useit.com) are all about finding out what works in the world and what doesn't. The ISO has created usability standards that you can explore on http://www.usabilitynet.org/tools/r_international.htm. The standards cover the use of the product (effectiveness, efficiency, and satisfaction in a particular context of use), the user interface and interaction, the process used to develop the product, and the capability of an organization to apply user-centered design.

Nielsen and Mack (1994) and Nielsen, Molich, Snyder, and Farrell (2001) have published usability heuristics (or rules of thumb) based on their thousands of usability tests of interfaces and, later, tests of ecommerce Web sites. They include visibility of system status, match between the system and the real world, user control and freedom, consistency and standards, error prevention, reconnection rather than recall, flexibility and efficiency of use, aesthetic and minimalist design, help that users recognize, diagnosis and recovery from errors, and help and documentation. Some of these are already familiar to you from the input and output design chapters.

Figure 14.2 is a usability survey to give directly to users who have personally interacted with a prototype. It asks users outright about some key usability and ergonomic questions. Another approach is to write up use case scenarios for the system. These are helpful in examining usability concerns.

DESIGNING FOR THE COGNITIVE STYLES OF INDIVIDUAL USERS

One important consideration is that data, particularly data used for decision making, are made available in different forms so that users with different cognitive abilities can make sense of them. Some users may prefer to examine tables and make decisions, some prefer graphs, and others want to read text.

It is even possible for the same person to want different types of presentations at different times. For example, suppose a manager wants to compare inventory held at different stores in a region. A graph can present the data very effectively. A column chart can use colors to show when a store is near its stockout level, and it can also show the relative amount of stock by allowing the user to visually compare the height of the bars directly.

Suppose now the same decision maker wants information about a particular store in a given month. The graphical depiction may have been set up to show the stores from highest to lowest inventory on a month-by-month basis. The user may prefer to return to the table that lists stores alphabetically, with the months listed chronologically. As you can see, the same person may want to see the same data in two very different ways.

Pivot Tables Pivot tables allow users to arrange data in a table in any way they choose. An example of a pivot table template created in Microsoft Excel is shown in Figure 14.3. The user would take an item from the pop-up box called "Pivot Table Field List," such as **Product,** drag it over to the table template, and drop it in one of the blank areas. In this example, the user drags and drops **Product** into the area on the left entitled "Drop Row Fields Here." The user drops **Sales** into the largest area that says "Drop Data Items Here."

Finally the user takes the item called **Quarter** and drops it into the area called "Drop Column Fields Here." The result is a table that shows each of the products in alphabetical order and its sales for each of the four quarters we have data for, followed by the grand total for the year. This table is shown in Figure 14.4.

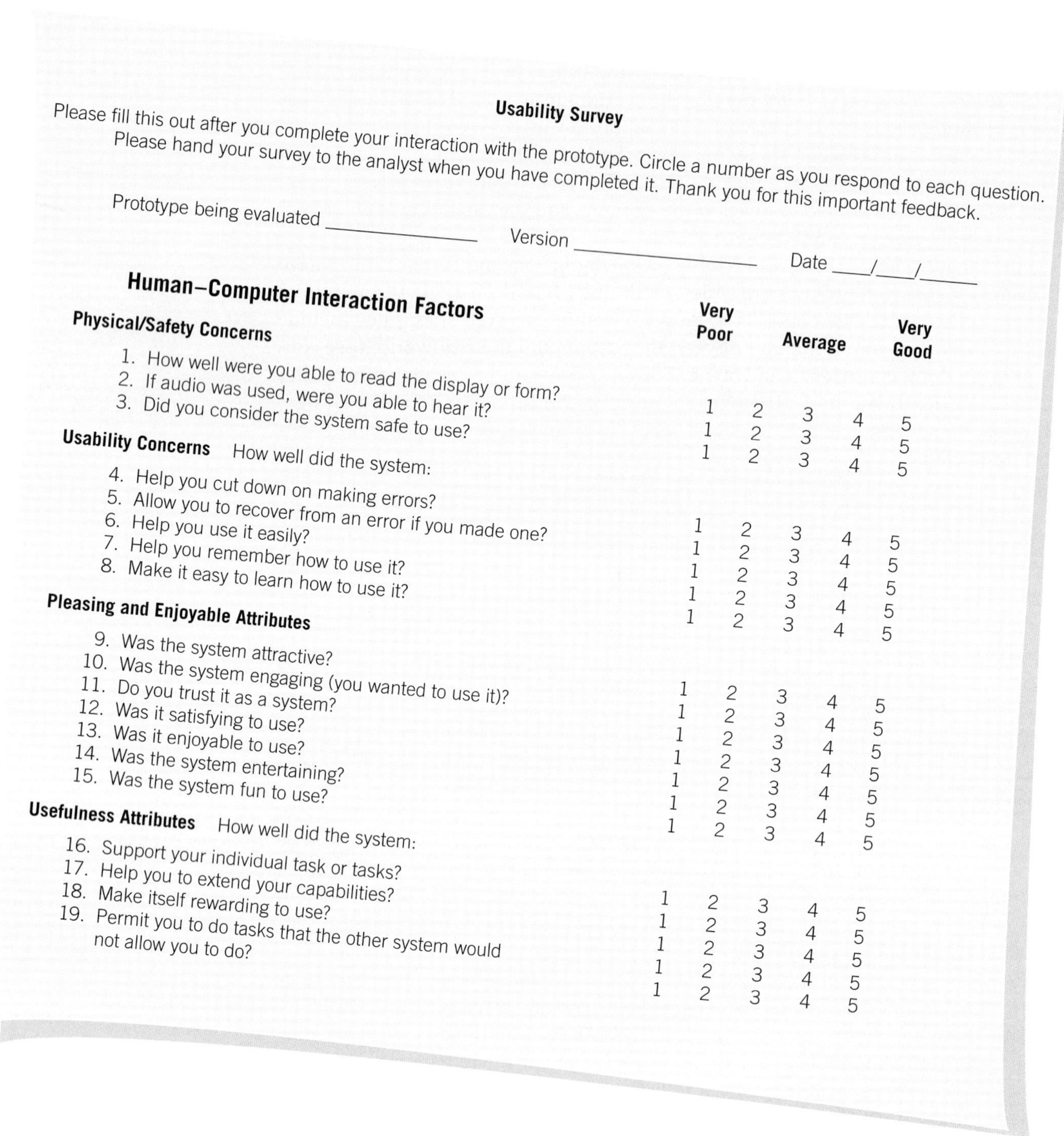

Usability Survey

Please fill this out after you complete your interaction with the prototype. Circle a number as you respond to each question. Please hand your survey to the analyst when you have completed it. Thank you for this important feedback.

Prototype being evaluated ____________ Version ____________ Date ___/___/___

Human–Computer Interaction Factors

	Very Poor		Average		Very Good
Physical/Safety Concerns					
1. How well were you able to read the display or form?	1	2	3	4	5
2. If audio was used, were you able to hear it?	1	2	3	4	5
3. Did you consider the system safe to use?	1	2	3	4	5
Usability Concerns How well did the system:					
4. Help you cut down on making errors?	1	2	3	4	5
5. Allow you to recover from an error if you made one?	1	2	3	4	5
6. Help you use it easily?	1	2	3	4	5
7. Help you remember how to use it?	1	2	3	4	5
8. Make it easy to learn how to use it?	1	2	3	4	5
Pleasing and Enjoyable Attributes					
9. Was the system attractive?	1	2	3	4	5
10. Was the system engaging (you wanted to use it)?	1	2	3	4	5
11. Do you trust it as a system?	1	2	3	4	5
12. Was it satisfying to use?	1	2	3	4	5
13. Was it enjoyable to use?	1	2	3	4	5
14. Was the system entertaining?	1	2	3	4	5
15. Was the system fun to use?	1	2	3	4	5
Usefulness Attributes How well did the system:					
16. Support your individual task or tasks?	1	2	3	4	5
17. Help you to extend your capabilities?	1	2	3	4	5
18. Make itself rewarding to use?	1	2	3	4	5
19. Permit you to do tasks that the other system would not allow you to do?	1	2	3	4	5

FIGURE 14.2

A form may be used to survey users of prototypes on key usability and ergonomic factors. (Categories based on Zhang, Carey, Te'eni, and Tremaine, 2005, table of HCI concerns, p. 522.)

Of course, the user could have done the opposite, that is, drag the item **Quarter** to the leftmost column and the **Product** to the area that says "Drop Column Fields Here." That operation, however, would have produced a table with many columns (one for each product) and only five rows (one for each quarter plus a row for the total). The resulting table would have been difficult to read.

Many different tables can be displayed by just rearranging these four variables. If the user dragged the variable **Category** over to the area that says "Drop Column Fields Here," the columns would have been categories of products, rather than the quarters, and the resulting table would have clearly shown which of the items belonged in each category and produced subtotals for each category. If **Category** was

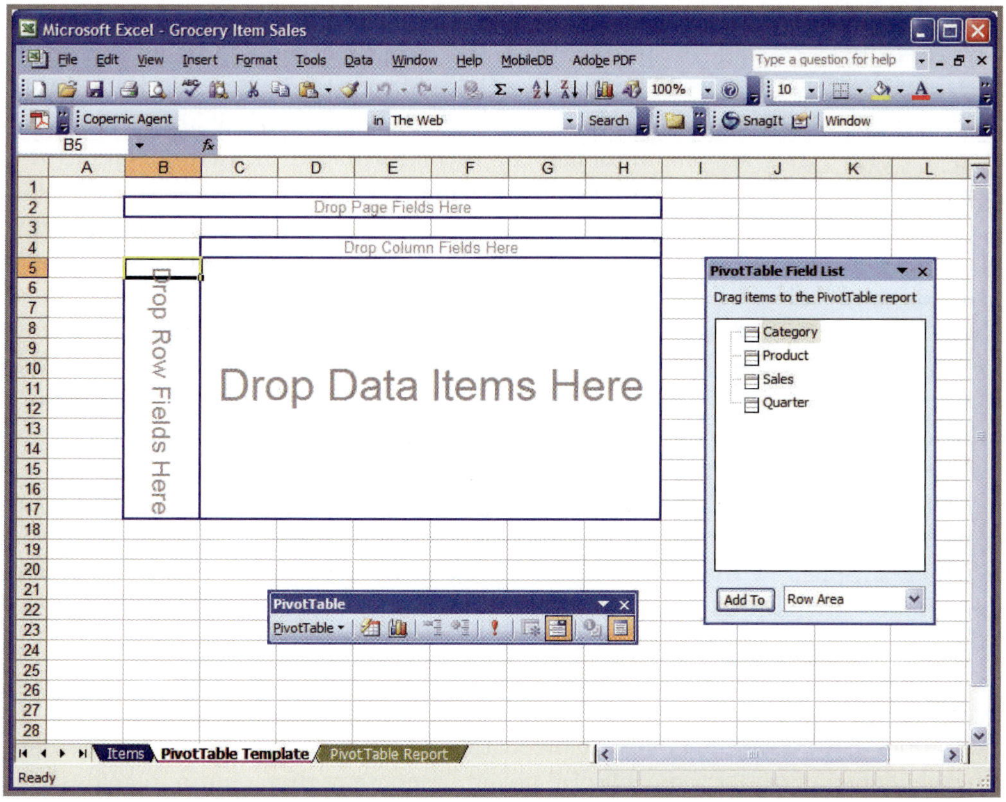

FIGURE 14.3
A pivot table template can make it easier for users to see information displayed in different ways.

dragged to the area at the very top of the template that says "Drop Page Fields Here," then each category would have a table of its own beginning on a separate page.

The idea of a pivot table is useful because it gives users greater control over how they look at data in different ways within a table. We can examine this same concept for graphs in the next section.

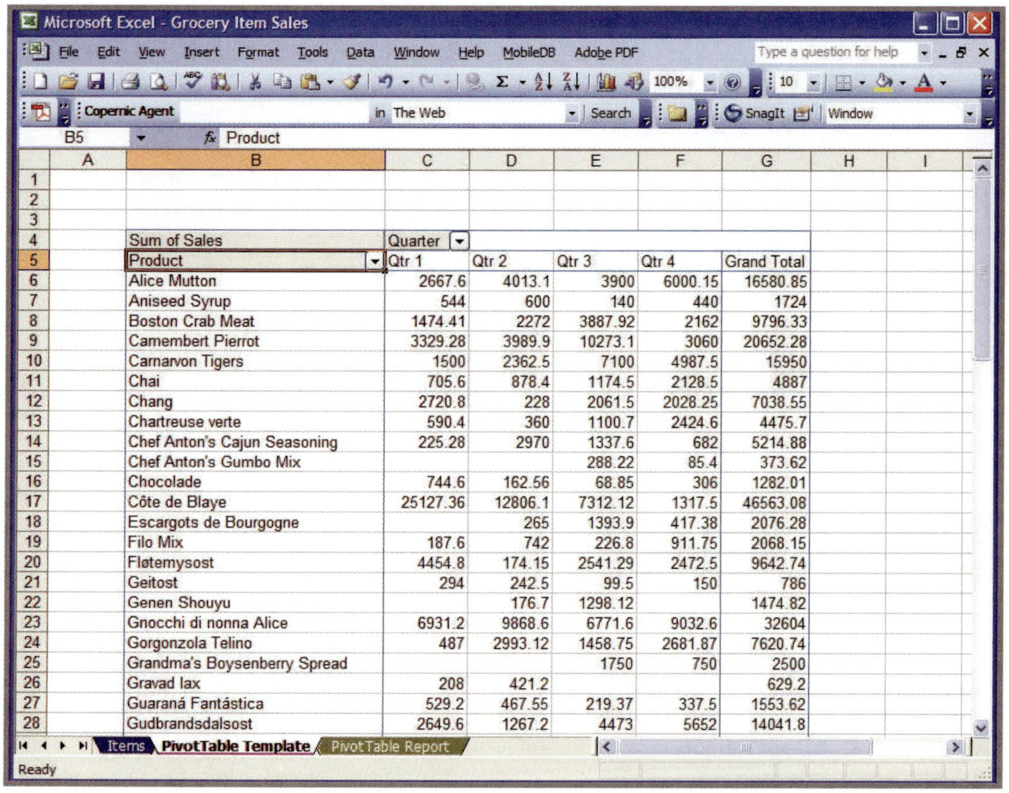

Sum of Sales	Quarter				
Product	Qtr 1	Qtr 2	Qtr 3	Qtr 4	Grand Total
Alice Mutton	2667.6	4013.1	3900	6000.15	16580.85
Aniseed Syrup	544	600	140	440	1724
Boston Crab Meat	1474.41	2272	3887.92	2162	9796.33
Camembert Pierrot	3329.28	3989.9	10273.1	3060	20652.28
Carnarvon Tigers	1500	2362.5	7100	4987.5	15950
Chai	705.6	878.4	1174.5	2128.5	4887
Chang	2720.8	228	2061.5	2028.25	7038.55
Chartreuse verte	590.4	360	1100.7	2424.6	4475.7
Chef Anton's Cajun Seasoning	225.28	2970	1337.6	682	5214.88
Chef Anton's Gumbo Mix			288.22	85.4	373.62
Chocolade	744.6	162.56	68.85	306	1282.01
Côte de Blaye	25127.36	12806.1	7312.12	1317.5	46563.08
Escargots de Bourgogne		265	1393.9	417.38	2076.28
Filo Mix	187.6	742	226.8	911.75	2068.15
Fløtemysost	4454.8	174.15	2541.29	2472.5	9642.74
Geitost	294	242.5	99.5	150	786
Genen Shouyu		176.7	1298.12		1474.82
Gnocchi di nonna Alice	6931.2	9868.6	6771.6	9032.6	32604
Gorgonzola Telino	487	2993.12	1458.75	2681.87	7620.74
Grandma's Boysenberry Spread			1750	750	2500
Gravad lax	208	421.2			629.2
Guaraná Fantástica	529.2	467.55	219.37	337.5	1553.62
Gudbrandsdalsost	2649.6	1267.2	4473	5652	14041.8

FIGURE 14.4
After the user drags the items Product, Quarter, and Sales to the template, the table looks like this.

Visual Analysis of Databases You might be surprised to learn that innovative visual displays of data existed for quite some time, as early as the eighteenth century. Barriers to widely using visual displays included lack of imagination, the inability to draw graphs and charts in a cost-effective manner, and a lack of appreciation for such displays. After all, the audience for the information must understand the information in the diagram or it adds little value.

Software that enables the user to visually examine a database or spreadsheet is available. One example is Tableau Software's product (www.tableausoftware.com). Using an approach similar to the pivot tables we saw in Microsoft Excel, Tableau allows the user to drag and drop variables onto either a row or a column, and they appear on a graph. In Figure 14.5, the **Region** and **Weekday** were designated as columns and the **SUM (Sales Total)** was designated as a row. Each **Product Category** was then graphed (with "furniture" in blue, "office supplies" in orange, and "technology" in green).

The graph demonstrates that technology sales were higher than the other categories, but in particular technology sales were much higher than either furniture or office supplies in the East. The user was easily able to see this because the **Region** was singled out as one of the separators by dragging it to the area as a column.

Tableau is a well designed software package because it goes much further in extending user capabilities to perform their tasks through the use of pivot table techniques. The developers also realized that users may want to group the data into what they consider a meaningful group. Users may then continue analysis by examining one of the groups further.

Figure 14.6 examines the **SUM (Gross Profit)** from each **Product Category** from our example. This graph uses color to indicate a profit (green) or a loss (red). In fact, the intensity of the color indicates the amount of profit or loss.

This graph can be used to explore the situation more deeply by selecting the three clusters of circles that are bright red, isolating them, and then looking at the data for those observations in more detail. Users can examine graphs or simply

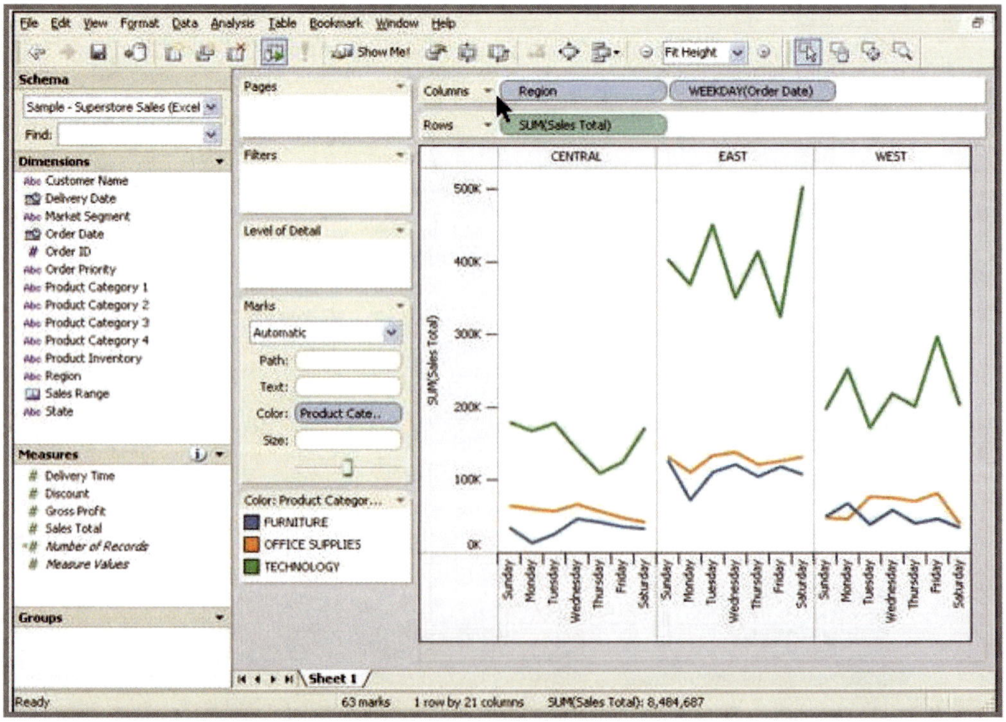

FIGURE 14.5
This table, showing the daily sales by category and by region, was produced using Tableau. (Courtesy of www.tableausoftware.com.)

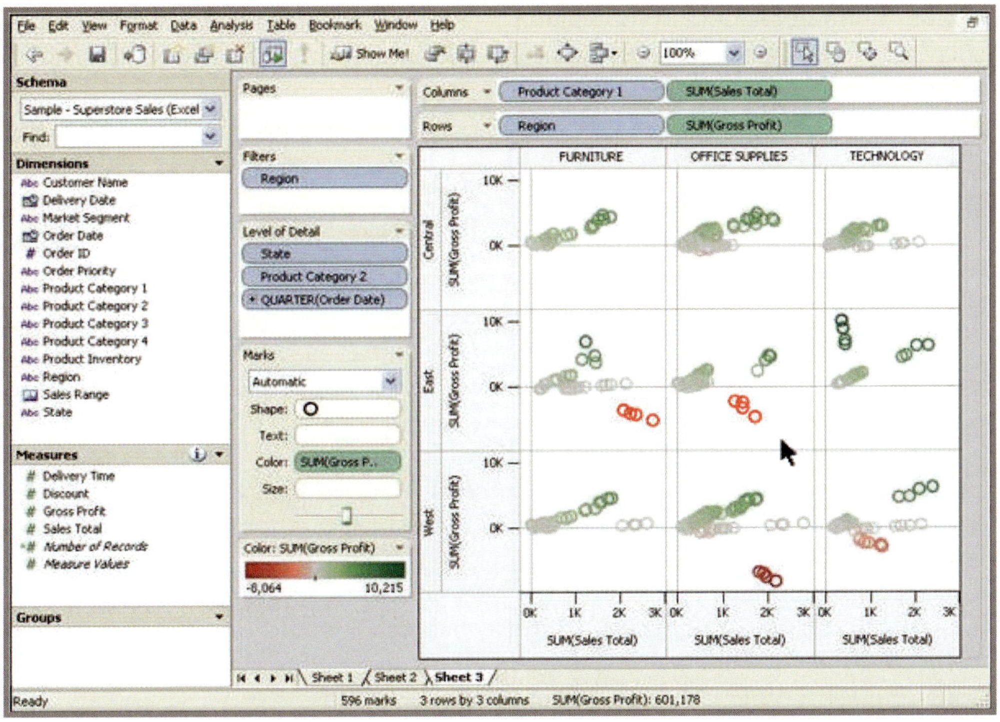

FIGURE 14.6 Products yielding losses are highlighted in bright red on this scatter plot, created using Tableau. (Courtesy of www.tableausoftware.com.)

look at the observations in a table. Once again, they have control over how the information is presented and thus control their task for best cognitive fit.

Another example from Tableau, presented in Figure 14.7 shows that this software can also create a dashboard (explained in Chapter 11). Here a table, a scatter plot, and a column chart are all shown on the same page. Visual analysis tools like this support visual thinking and extend the user's cognitive capabilities to do so. An appropriate visual display will increase the chances of making an appropriate decision.

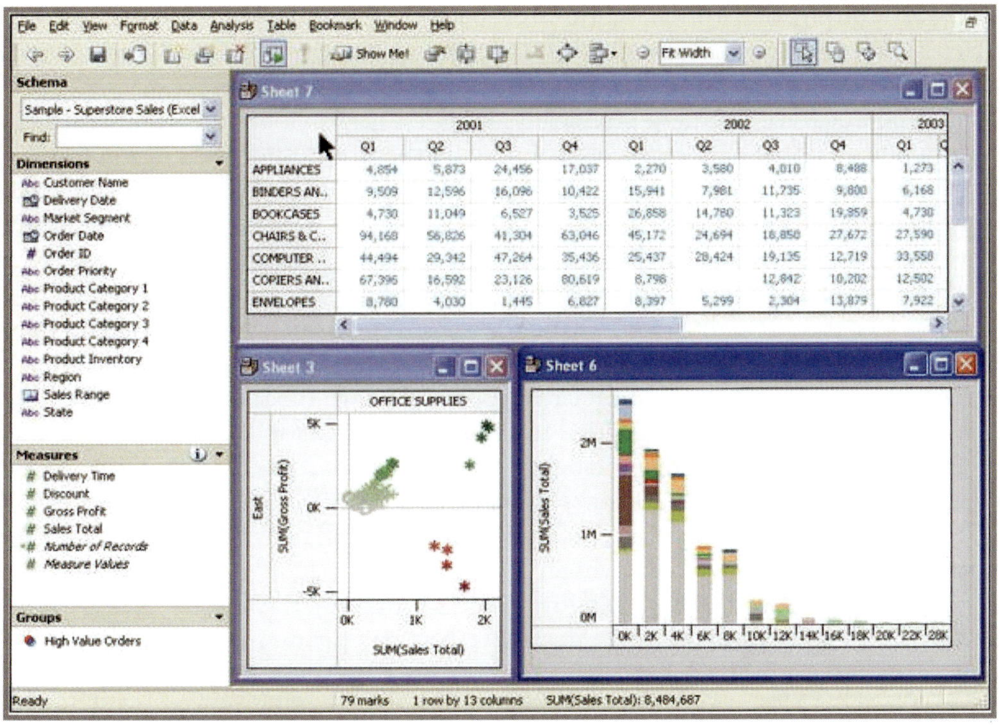

FIGURE 14.7 When different graphs or tables can be displayed on the same page, the page resembles a dashboard. (Courtesy of www.tableausoftware.com.)

PHYSICAL CONSIDERATIONS IN HCI DESIGN

In Chapters 11, 12, and 13 you learned the basis for sound design of screens, forms, Web sites, and databases. This included the special use of fonts, color, and layout design to communicate to users and to help them do the right thing with the input and output they encountered. To examine the underlying reasons for much of the design you learned, it is useful to look at human sensory capabilities and limitations that will inform our design. In keeping with the HCI philosophy, an analyst should be able to compensate, overcome, or replace human senses to a varying extent.

Vision As you learn to become a systems analyst, you are becoming accustomed to designing screens and reports for sighted people. The use of color, fonts, graphics, software, and PowerPoint presentations for displays and printed reports as input and output were detailed in Chapters 11 and 12. However, from an HCI perspective, you will also want to think in terms of limitations on human vision. Factors such as length of the distance from display to the person performing a task; the angle of the display in relation to the person viewing it; the size and uniformity of the characters; the brightness, contrast, balance, and glare of the screen; and whether a display is blinking or stable can all be designed to standards established through ISO and other national and international groups.

Hearing Humans also have limits to the amount of stress their senses can withstand. Noisy laser printers and phone conversations can lead to overload on human hearing. Office workers can wear noise-canceling headphones or get a personal music player like an iPod, but these solutions may have the effect of isolating a person from the organizational setting and may even diminish their capability to perform the task at hand. As an analyst you will need to consider noise when you design office systems.

Touch When using an HCI perspective to evaluate the usefulness of keyboards and other input devices, we can rate the human–computer fit as well as the dimensions examining the human–computer–task fit. Later in this chapter we will discuss the choices of human–computer interfaces, such as keyboards, direct manipulation, using a stylus, a mouse, and touch screens.

Keyboards have been ergonomically designed to provide the correct feedback for the person doing data entry. Users know by the firmness of the key under their finger that the keystroke has been entered. Although keyboards can be silenced, they are often designed with a click of feedback that is emitted when a key is hit. Keyboards also include slightly raised bumps on what are called home keys, often the *f* and the *j* keys, which orients users to where their fingers are positioned on the keyboard, enabling them to look at the screen or type from a printed page on their desk without continually glancing at the keyboard.

Although the popular QWERTY keyboard that we most often use with computers today was originally designed to slow down typists so that mechanical keys of the day would not become entangled, this layout has proved to be quite an efficient way to enter data. In fact, since users do so well with this familiar interface, it is difficult to conduct experiments comparing the efficiency of QWERTY keyboards with other innovative keyboards.

Designing for data entry using numeric keypads as the human entry device also provides a decision point for designers. Notice that numbers on your mobile phone are ordered differently than numbers on a numeric keypad or calculator. Your phone may be arranged with the numbers 1, 2, 3 on the top row. When you look at a calculator layout or a numeric keypad on your keyboard, you will see 7, 8, and 9 on the top row instead. Research now points to the superiority of the calculator layout when the user is doing a lot of data entry. However, the phone digit layout is supposed to be better for locating a number. As a designer, you are constantly examining the fit between the human, the computer, and the tasks set by the organization.

Microsoft is currently developing touch screens featuring familiar icons that will help illiterate workers find domestic jobs through a touch screen interface that does not require reading, yet still allows unemployed workers power over choosing new employers. While illiteracy can be remedied through education, some limitations cannot.

CONSIDERING HUMAN LIMITATIONS, DISABILITIES, AND DESIGN

All humans have limitations in their physical capabilities. Some are immediately visible, others are not. When designing from an HCI perspective, you start realizing that limitations are often discussed in terms of disabilities. The application of HCI to supporting and enhancing the physical capabilities of humans is one of the most promising application areas. Strides in biomedical engineering mean that there is research to support the blind or those with low vision, those who are deaf or have impaired hearing, and people with limited mobility.

There are also improvements in the technical supports available to those who face difficulties in cognitive processing, including persons suffering with symptoms of autism, dyslexia, and attention deficit disorder. As a systems analyst you will be working under the legal provisions of the country in which you are working. For instance, if you are designing for workplaces in the United States, you may want to access the obligations of an employer under the Americans with Disabilities Act at www.eeoc.gov/types/ada.html. There you will find definitions of who is considered disabled, which states in part, "An individual with a disability is a person who: has a physical or mental impairment that substantially limits one or more major life activities; has a record of such impairment; or is regarded as having such an impairment."

An employer in the United States is expected to make reasonable accommodation to employ a disabled person, which includes "Making existing facilities used by employees readily accessible to and usable by persons with disabilities; job restructuring, modifying work schedules, reassignment to a vacant position; acquiring or modifying equipment or devices, adjusting or modifying examinations, training materials, or policies, and providing qualified readers or interpreters."

A qualified employee or application is an individual who, "with or without reasonable accommodation, can perform the essential functions of the job in question." An employer is required to make reasonable accommodation to the known disability of a qualified applicant or employee if it would not impose an undue hardship on the operation of the business. Undue hardship is defined as "an action requiring significant difficulty or expense when considered in light of factors such as an employer's size, financial resources, and the nature and structure of its operation. An employer is not required to lower quality or production standards to make an accommodation."

One of the best ways to ensure the broadest possible accommodation is to begin designing from an HCI perspective. That way, your foremost concern will always be assisting a user in accomplishing a task, set by the organization, with the use of technology. However, when accommodations for disabled people are necessary, there are many sources to examine and many assistive devices to consider.

CONSULTING OPPORTUNITY 14.1

SCHOOL SPIRIT COMES IN MANY SIZES

Matt Scott manages the student-alumni clothing department for a large bookstore in Saratoga Springs.

"Our clothing sales depend not only on whether our sports teams win or lose, but the overall well-being of our students and alums. If they are proud of their university, and want to show their school spirit, they'll buy up everything on our racks," exclaims Matt. "But don't underestimate the weather as a factor," he adds. "If the weather turns cold in October, you'll see a surge in people buying warm sweaters, pullovers, and gloves."

"Our store serves the major three universities in our area," Matt goes on to state. "First, there is Hyde Park, what we call 'the football school.' They have about 17,000 students going there. They have high demand for school-branded clothing, particularly in the fall. Then, of course, there's Pierce University. Pierce thinks it's part of the Ivy League, so the students like to buy crew and Lacrosse shirts. They have about 7,500 students. Then there is St. David's, with about 3,000 students. They are devoted to their basketball team. They really have faith in them. You'll see sales pick up in the second semester, particularly during 'March Madness.'"

Mr. Scott continues, admitting, "I thought about asking the students what to stock, but an email survey is out of the question. I get spammed a lot, so I mostly don't bother with email. Unfortunately, the lead time for getting official branded sportswear into the store is really long, and we run the risk of stocking out. But we try to never run out."

You've been asked to design a set of tables and graphs that will help analyze the sales of Matt Scott's school clothing. Start by listing about 20 different items of school-branded clothing for men and women fans, including items such as hooded sweatshirts, T-shirts, baseball caps, sweatbands, running shorts, and so on. Many of them feature fanciful embroidered designs depicting their mascots in menacing or endearing poses. Hyde Park has their Golden Retrievers; Pierce has their much beloved birds, the Puffins; and St. David's cheers with their Dragons.

Put the items into categories. Then think about what the data would look like. Does it make sense for Matt to look at the data weekly, monthly, or by semester? Will he want to look back five years to see if there were any trends? Set up tables identifying the rows and columns and the content of the main cells. Suggest several tables so that Matt can analyze them in different ways.

Now construct graphs that analyze the same data. Using some of the examples found in this book, suggest the type of graphs and show the data so that different users with different styles can make some decisions regarding the trend of sales over the last few years. Remember to compare the schools as well. Suggest the appropriate graphs from column, line, scatter plots, or even pie charts.

Also suggest three or four specific changes you would make to allow someone who has low vision to be able to read the graphs more easily. Magnification is one way to change a graph, but may not be the best approach.

Consider the size of the schools since this may become the most important factor when determining how Matt Scott should adjust his ordering for David's, Hyde, and Pierce.

For people who are blind or who have low vision, there are braille keyboards as well as special speech software that reads Web pages and other documents aloud. There are also screen magnifiers that fit over a display to magnify the entire screen.

For people who lack certain perceptual sensitivity (incorrectly called color blindness), you can work at testing the colors you are choosing to make certain that they can be easily distinguished from each other. Particular problems occur telling the difference between red and green for instance. Always design the screen or form with alternative cues, such as icons, written text, or audio cues that reinforce the content. For instance if a hyperlink that has been clicked on turns blue to show it has been followed, you can also add another icon to the display to indicate that it has been followed or create a separate sidebar list that shows which Web sites have been visited. These are better alternatives than relying solely on color to convey your message.

For users who experience impaired hearing, you can make sure that the documents and screens you design include access to written versions of the audio material. Alternatively, you might design tasks where headphones can be successfully used.

If you are designing computer tasks for those with limited mobility, you can think of speech input rather than keyboarding. Additionally, new advances in biomedical engineering permit mobility-impaired users to move the cursor on the screen by breathing into a tube or by directing the cursor to the desired spot on the

Guidelines for the HCI Approach to Systems Design

- Examine the task to be done and consider the fit among the human, computer, and task.
- Identify what obstacles exist for users in their attempts to accomplish their assigned tasks.
- Keep in mind the perceived usefulness and perceived ease of use from TAM.
- Consider usability. Examine the usage environment by creating use case scenarios that depict what is going on between users and the technology.
- Use the information you have gained beforehand to figure out the physical and organizational environmental characteristics. Design with prototyping to accommodate diverse users and users with disabilities.

FIGURE 14.8
The HCI approach to systems design emphasizes the fit among the human, computer, and task.

screen by looking at that spot or even, in some highly specialized interfaces, by thinking about where the cursor should move.

IMPLEMENTING GOOD HCI PRACTICES

The ideal is to invite a usability specialist to serve on the systems development team with the other team members. However, many systems groups are quite small, and not many professionals are available who are involved in the practice of usability per se; so even if you make this recommended change to your project, the odds are that the position will go unstaffed or understaffed. However, don't let that discourage you. You can take some simple steps that will positively influence the outcome of your systems project. Figure 14.8 provides a list of guidelines for taking an HCI approach to systems design. As systems designers, we can become aware of important HCI dimensions, knowledgeably linking them to systems designs, and we should attempt to measure how we are meeting each of these concerns for users and organizations.

Although we have been discussing the system in the abstract, it is important to recognize that the interface *is* the system for most users. However well or poorly designed, it stands as the representation of the system and, by reflection, your competence as a systems analyst. A well designed interface improves the fit among the task, the technology, and the user.

Your goal must be to design interfaces that help users and businesses get the information they need in and out of the system by addressing the following objectives:

1. Matching the user interface to the task.
2. Making the user interface efficient.
3. Providing appropriate feedback to users.
4. Generating usable queries.
5. Improving the productivity of computer users.

With these goals in mind, we move to more detailed discussions of how each of the objectives can be met.

TYPES OF USER INTERFACE

In this section, several different kinds of user interfaces are described, including natural-language interfaces, question-and-answer interfaces, menus, form-fill interfaces, command-language interfaces, graphical user interfaces (GUIs), and a variety of Web interfaces for use on the Internet. The user interface has two main components: presentation language, which is the computer-to-human part of the transaction, and action language, which characterizes the human-to-computer portion. Together, both concepts cover the form and content of the term *user interface.*

FIGURE 14.9
Natural-language interfaces.

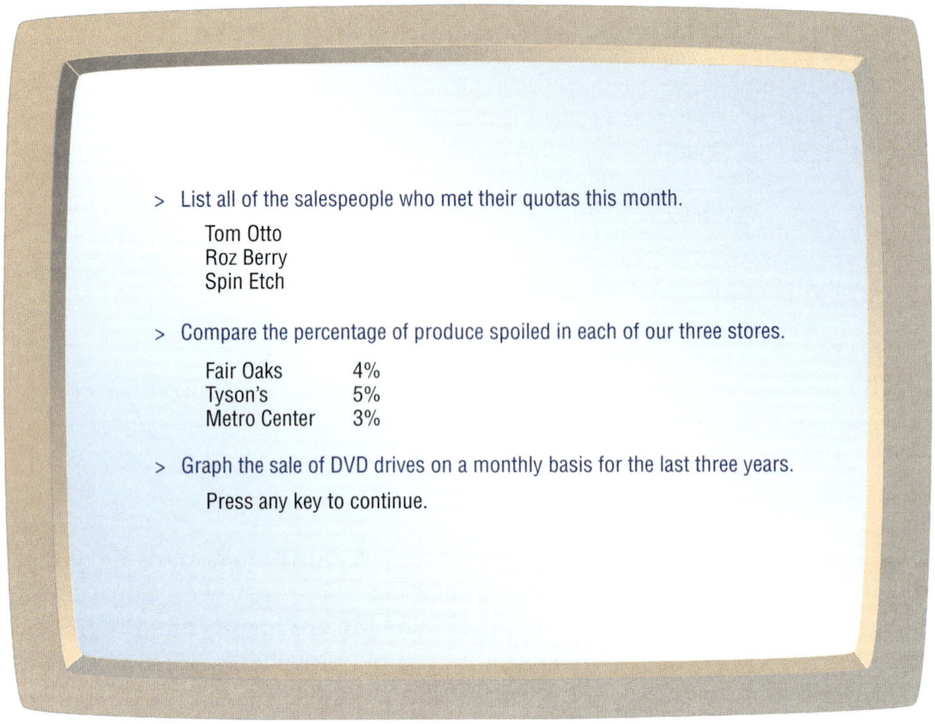

NATURAL-LANGUAGE INTERFACES

Natural-language interfaces are perhaps the dream and ideal of inexperienced users, because they permit users to interact with the computer in their everyday, or natural, language. No special skills are required of the user, who interfaces with the computer using natural language.

The display depicted in Figure 14.9 lists three natural-language questions from three different applications. Notice that interaction with each seems very easy. For instance, the first sentence seems straightforward: "List all of the salespeople who met their quotas this month."

The subtleties and irregularities residing in the ambiguities of English produce an extremely exacting and complex programming problem. Attempts at natural-language interfacing for particular applications in which any other type of interface is infeasible (say, in the case of a user who is disabled) are meeting with some success; however, these interfaces are typically expensive. Implementation problems and extraordinary demand on computing resources have so far kept natural-language interfaces to a minimum. The demand exists, though, and many programmers and researchers are working diligently on such interfaces. It is a growth area, and it therefore merits continued monitoring. Some Web sites, such as Ask.com, use a natural interface for users to enter their search query. When the query is entered, Ask.com responds with a list of responses that match the question entered by the user.

QUESTION-AND-ANSWER INTERFACES

In a question-and-answer interface, the computer displays a question to the user on the display. To interact, the user enters an answer (via a keyboard stroke or a mouse click), and the computer then acts on that input information in a preprogrammed manner, typically by moving to the next question.

A type of question-and-answer interface called a dialog box is shown in Figure 14.10. A dialog box acts as a question-and-answer interface within another

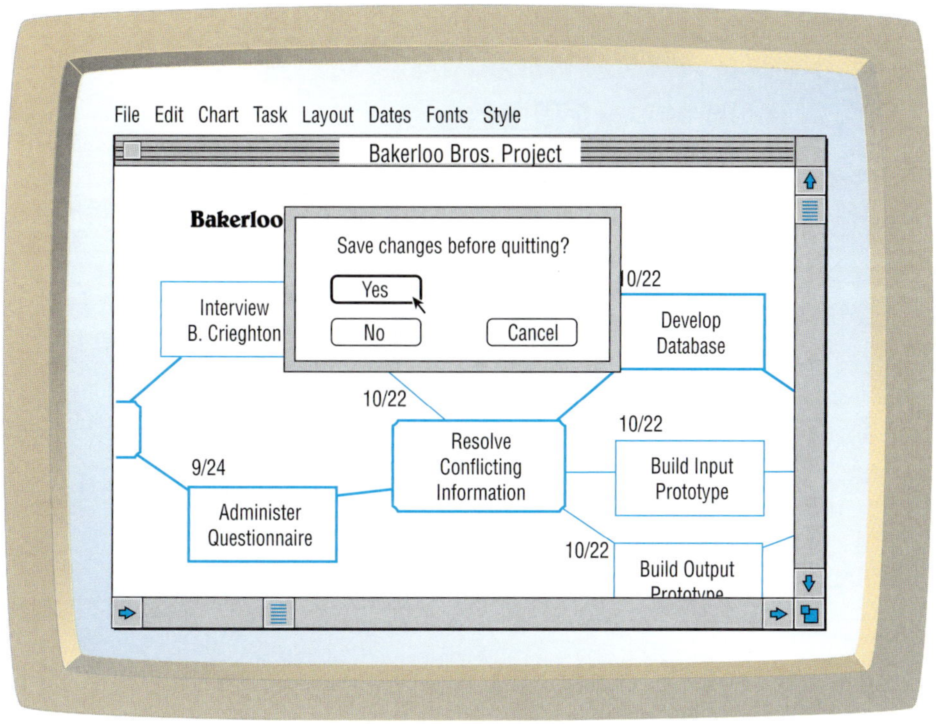

FIGURE 14.10
A dialog box: one type of question-and-answer interface.

application, in this case a PERT chart for a systems analysis project for the Bakerloo Brothers. Notice that the rounded rectangle for "Yes" is highlighted, indicating that it is the most likely answer for this situation. The main interface for this application need not necessarily be question and answer. Rather, by incorporating a dialog box, the programmer has included an easy-to-use interface within a more complicated one.

Wizards used to install software are a common example of a question-and-answer interface. The user responds to questions about the installation process, such as where to install the software or features. Another common example is the use of the Office Assistant with Microsoft products. When the user needs help, the Office Assistant asks questions and responds to the answers with additional questions designed to narrow the scope of the problem. Users unfamiliar with particular applications or not knowledgeable about a topic may find question-and-answer interfaces the most comfortable, quickly gaining confidence through their success.

MENUS

A menu interface appropriately borrows its name from the list of dishes that can be selected in a restaurant. Similarly, a menu interface provides the user with an onscreen list of available selections.

In responding to the menu, a user is limited to the options displayed. The user need not know the system but does need to know what task should be accomplished. For example, with a typical word processing menu, users can choose from the Edit, Copy, or Print options. To utilize the menu best, however, users must know which task they desire to perform.

Menus are not hardware dependent. Variations abound. Menus can be set up to use keyboard entry, light pen, or mouse. Selections can be identified with a number, letter, or keyword, or users can click on a selection with a mouse. Consistency is important in designing a menu interface.

FIGURE 14.11
A pull-down menu is there when the user needs it.

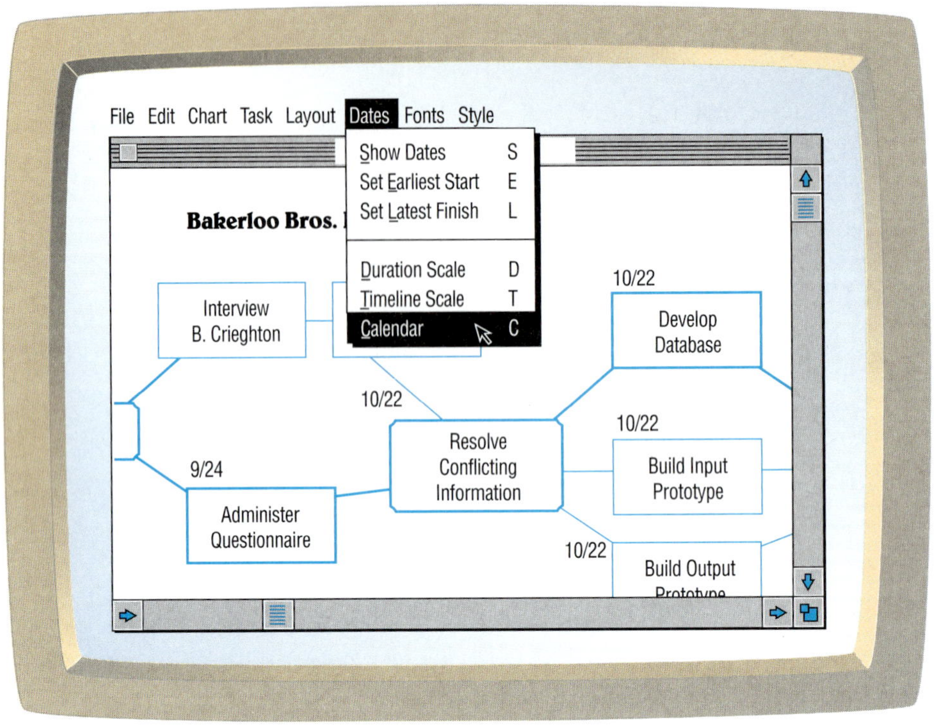

Menus can also be put aside until the user wants to employ them. Figure 14.11 shows how a pull-down menu is used while constructing a PERT diagram for a systems analysis project being completed for the Bakerloo Brothers. The user puts the pointer on **Dates** and pulls it down. Then the user puts the pointer on **Calendar,** selecting the option to display the project on a conventional monthly calendar.

Menus can be nested within one another to lead a user through options in a program. Nested menus allow the screen to appear less cluttered, which is consistent with good design. They also allow users to avoid seeing menu options in which they have no interest. Nested menus can also move users quickly through the program.

GUI menus are used to control PC software and have the following guidelines:

1. The main menu bar is always displayed.
2. The main menu uses single words for menu items. Main menu options always display secondary pull-down menus.
3. The main menu should have secondary options grouped into similar sets of features.
4. The drop-down menus that display when a main menu item is clicked often consist of more than one word.
5. These secondary options perform actions or display additional menu items.
6. Menu items in grey are unavailable for the current activity.

An object menu, also called a pop-up menu, is displayed when the user clicks on a GUI object with the right mouse button. These menus contain items specific for the current activity, and most are duplicate functions of main menu items.

Experienced users may be irritated by nested menus. They may prefer to use a single-line command entry to speed things up. Other users might use the shortcut abbreviations or key combinations such as Alt > I > P > C, which inserts a picture that is clip art in a Microsoft Office document.

CONSULTING OPPORTUNITY 14.2

I'D RATHER DO IT MYSELF

"I can get Mickey to download any data I need from the Web or our server to my PC," DeWitt Miwaye, an upper-level manager for Yumtime Foods (a Midwest food wholesaler) tells you. "Getting data is no problem. What I don't want are a lot of reports. I'd rather play with the data myself."

Miwaye goes on to tell you that as an executive, he doesn't use his PC as often as he'd like, maybe only three times a month, but he has some very specific ideas about what he'd like to do with it.

"I'd like to be able to make some comparisons myself. I could compare the turnover rate for all 12 of our warehouses. I'd also like to see how effectively the capacity of each of our warehouses is being used. Sometimes I'd like to be able to graph the comparisons or see a chart of them over time."

In three paragraphs, compare three different types of interfaces that Miwaye could use. Then recommend one interface for his use that takes into account his infrequent use of the PC, his enjoyment of working with raw data, and his desire to see data displayed in a variety of ways.

FORM-FILL INTERFACES (INPUT/OUTPUT FORMS)

Form-fill interfaces consist of onscreen forms or Web-based forms displaying fields containing data items or parameters that need to be communicated to the user. The form often is a facsimile of a paper form already familiar to the user. This interface technique is also known as a form-based method and input/output forms.

Figure 14.12 shows a form-fill interface. A pull-down menu for **Part No.** automatically enters a **Description** and **Unit Price** for the item. When the user tabs to the **Quantity** field and enters the number of items being purchased, the software automatically calculates the **Extended Price** by multiplying **Quantity** by **Unit Price.**

Forms for display screens are set up to show what information should be input and where. Blank fields requiring information can be highlighted with inverse or flashing characters. The cursor is moved by the user from field to field by a single stroke of an arrow key, for instance. This arrangement allows movement one field backward or one field forward by clicking the appropriate arrow key. It provides the user good control over data entry. Web-based forms afford the opportunity to

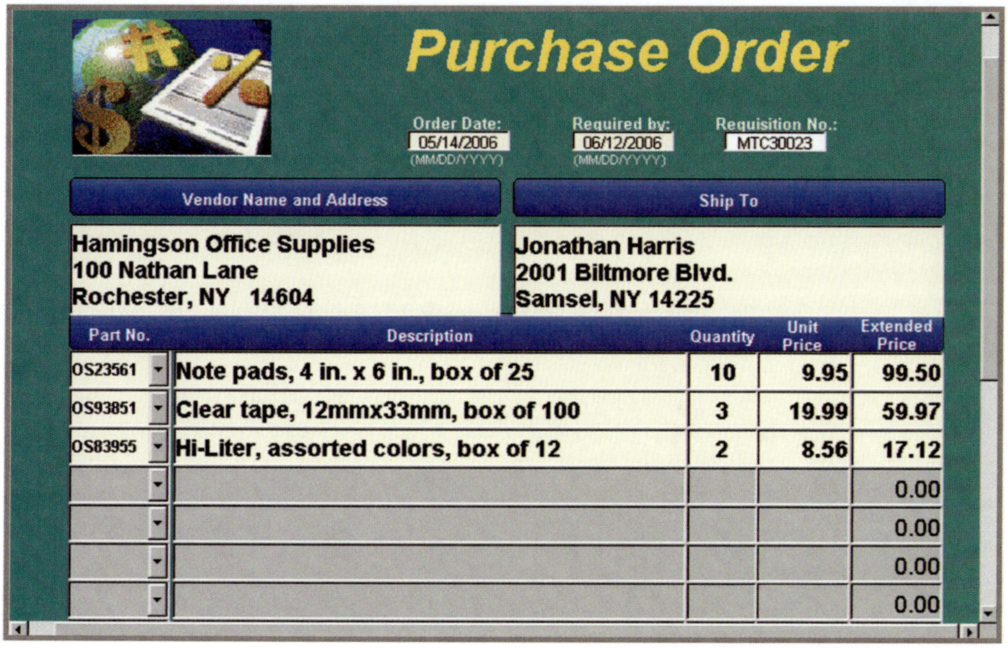

FIGURE 14.12
An example of the form-fill interface from Form Flow by JetForm.

include hyperlinks to examples of correctly filled-out forms or to further help and examples.

Form input for displays can be simplified by supplying default values for fields and then allowing users to modify default information if necessary. For example, a database management system designed to show a form for inputting checks may supply the next sequential check number as a default when a new check form is exhibited. If checks are missing, the user changes the check number to reflect the actual check being input.

Input for display screen fields can be alphanumerically restricted so that, for example, users can enter only numbers in a field requesting a Social Security number, or they can input only letters where a person's name is required. If numbers are input where only letters are allowed, the computer may alert the user via audio output that the field was filled out incorrectly.

The chief advantage of the input/output form interface is that the printed version of the filled-in form provides excellent documentation. It shows field labels as well as the context for entries. In addition, Web forms can return incomplete forms to the user with an explanation of what data must be entered to complete the transaction. Often, fields with missing data are marked with a red asterisk. Web-based documents can be sent directly to billing if a transaction is involved, or they can go directly to a consumer database if a survey is being submitted. Web-based forms push the responsibility for accuracy to the user and make the form available for completion and submission on a 24-hour, 7-day-a-week, worldwide basis.

There are few disadvantages to input/output forms. The main drawback is that users experienced with the system or appplication may become impatient with input/output forms and may want more efficient ways to enter data.

COMMAND-LANGUAGE INTERFACES

A command-language interface allows the user to control the application with a series of keystrokes, commands, phrases, or some sequence of these three methods. It is a popular interface that is more refined than those previously discussed.

FIGURE 14.13
Command-language interfaces.

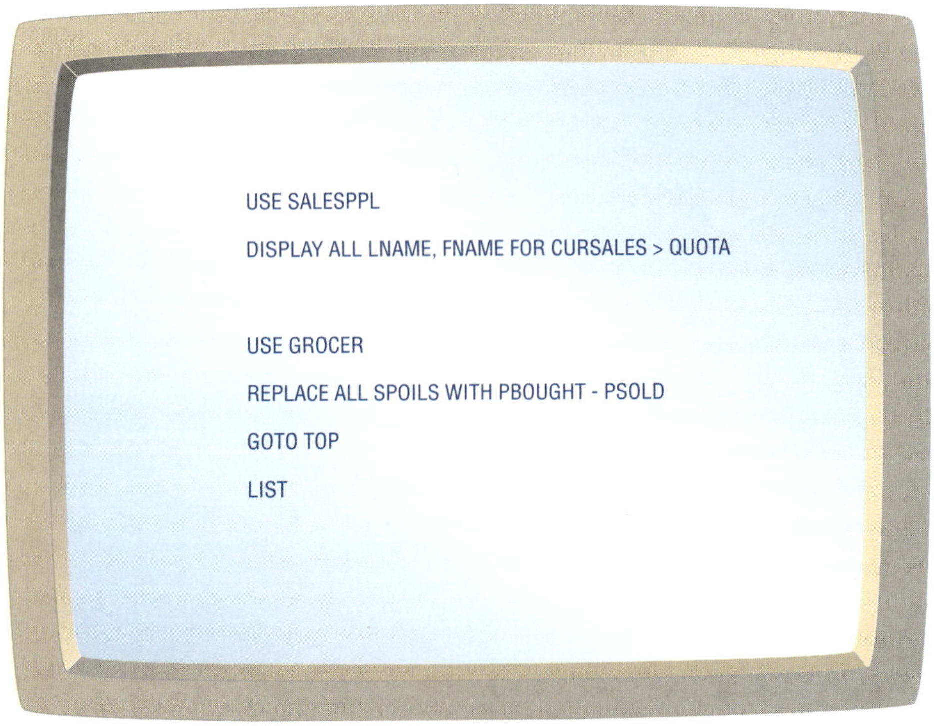

CONSULTING OPPORTUNITY 14.3

DON'T SLOW ME DOWN

"I've seen 'em all," Carrie Moore tells you. "I was here when they got their first computer. I guess I've sort of made a career of this," she says cheerfully, pointing to the large stack of medical insurance claim forms she has been entering into the computer system. As a systems analyst, you are interviewing Carrie, a data entry operator for AbundaCare (a large medical insurance company), about changes being contemplated in the computer system.

"I'm really fast compared with the others," she states as she nods toward the six other operators in the room. "I know, because we have little contests all the time to see who's the fastest, with the fewest errors. See that chart on the wall? That shows how much we enter and how quickly. The gold stars show who's the best each week. Performance measures are my friends."

"I don't really mind if you change computers. Like I say, 'I've seen 'em all.'" She resumes typing on her keyboard as she continues the interview. "Whatever you do, though, don't slow me down. One of the things I'm most proud of is that I can still beat the other operators. They're good too, though," Carrie adds.

Based on this partial interview with Carrie Moore, what type of user interface will you design for her and the other operators? Assume the new system will still require massive amounts of data entry from a variety of medical insurance forms sent in by claimants.

Compare and contrast interfaces such as natural language, question and answer, menus, input/output forms, and Web-based form-fill documents. Then choose and defend one alternative. What qualities possessed by Carrie and the other operators—and the data they will be entering—shaped your choice? Make a list of them. Is there more than one feasible choice? Why or why not? Respond in a paragraph.

Two application examples of command language are shown in Figure 14.13. The first shows a user who asks to use a file containing data on all salespeople, then asks the computer to display all last names and first names for all salespeople whose current sales (CURSALES) are greater than their quotas. In the second example, a user asks to use a file called GROCER, then directs the computer to calculate the spoilage (SPOILS) by subtracting produce sold from produce bought. After that is done, the user asks to go back to the top of the file and to print out (LIST) the file.

The command language has no inherent meaning for the user, and that fact makes it dissimilar to the other interfaces discussed so far. Command languages manipulate the computer as a tool by allowing the user to control the dialog. Command language affords the user more flexibility and control. When the user employs command language, the command is executed by the system immediately. Then the user may proceed to give it another command.

Command languages require memorization of syntax rules that may prove to be obstacles for inexperienced users. Experienced users tend to prefer command languages, possibly because of their faster completion time.

GRAPHICAL USER INTERFACES

The key to graphical user interfaces (GUIs) is the constant feedback on task accomplishment that they provide to users. Continuous feedback on the manipulated object means that changes or reversals in operations can be made quickly, without incurring error messages. The concept of feedback for users is discussed thoroughly in a later section.

The creation of GUIs poses a challenge, because an appropriate model of reality or an acceptable conceptual model of the representation must be invented. Designing GUIs for use on intranets, extranets, and, more pressingly, on the Web requires even more careful planning (see Chapter 12 on Web site design). By and large, the users of Web sites are unknown to the developer, so a design must be clear-cut. The choice of icons, language, and hyperlinks becomes an entire set of

CONSULTING OPPORTUNITY 14.4

THAT'S NOT A LIGHTBULB

From your preliminary analysis, it appears that a substantial reduction in errors will be realized if sales clerks at Bright's Electric (which sells electrical parts, bulbs, and fixtures to wholesale customers) adopt an online system. The new system would allow sales clerks to withdraw a part from inventory (and thereby update inventory), return a part to inventory, check on the inventory status, and check on whether a part is backordered. Currently, to update inventory, sales clerks fill out a three-part form by hand. The customer gets one, inventory keeps one, and at the end of the day the originals are deposited in the front office.

The next morning, the first thing the lone office worker does is enter the data from the forms into the computer. Errors occur when she enters the wrong part numbers or quantities. Additional time is consumed when inventory workers hunt for a part they think might be in stock but is not. Updated inventory sheets are available to the sales clerks around noon, but by that time they have already taken from inventory twice the number of parts that will be taken out after noon. Clearly, a well designed online system would help reduce these errors and also help with inventory control.

The owner, Mr. Bright, has entertained the idea of an online system and dropped it several times over the last five years. The chief reason is that the sales clerks, who would be the heaviest users of the system, do not think the systems analysts they've talked to can fulfill their needs.

M. T. Sockette, the sales clerk who has been with Bright's the longest, is the most vocal, telling you, "We know the parts, we know our customers. What we could do with a computer here would be great. The guys they've brought in here to get it going, though… I mean, they say things like, 'You can step right up and type one 60-watt General Electric lightbulb into the computer.'

"To us, that's not a lightbulb, it's a GE60WSB. All of us know the part numbers here. We pride ourselves on it. Typing in all that junk will take all day."

After talking to Mr. Bright, you decide to implement an online system. You have talked to M. T. and the others and reassured them that the system will use the part numbers they're familiar with and will save them time. Although they're skeptical, you've persuaded them to give it a try.

What type of user interface will you design for the sales clerks? Before you come to your solution, do a careful analysis in three paragraphs that compares and contrasts various user interfaces—natural language, question and answer, menus, input/output forms, command language, and Web-based form-fill documents—for their suitability at Bright's. Then choose one interface and explain in a paragraph why you find this one the most appropriate based on what you know about Bright's sales clerks and their current system. Draw a prototype of a display that will be part of your solution. Describe in a paragraph how you will test its usability with the sales clerks.

decisions and assumptions about what kinds of users the Web site is hoping to attract. The designer must also adhere to conventions that users now expect to encounter on Web sites.

OTHER USER INTERFACES

Other less common user interfaces are growing in popularity. These interfaces include pointing devices such as the stylus, touch-sensitive screens, and speech recognition and synthesis. Each of these interfaces has its own special attributes that uniquely suit it to particular applications.

The stylus (a small pointed stick that resembles a pen) is becoming popular because of new handwriting recognition software for personal digital assistants (PDAs) and mobile phones. Palms, combination mobile phones and PDAs, and Pocket/PC devices have been a success because they have are useful and easy to use. Additionally, they are portable and sell for a comparatively low price. There has been an explosion of fun and useful applications written for these mobile devices, including popular programs for restaurant reviews such as Zagats and for popular games such as Sudoku. Data entry is also facilitated with a docking cradle so that you can synchronize data with your PC.

A tablet PC is a notebook computer with a stylus- or touch-sensitive display. It is much more powerful than a handheld computer but weighs considerably more. Both handhelds and tablet PCs can be equipped with built-in Wi-Fi or Bluetooth® communication.

Touch-sensitive displays allow a user to use a finger to activate the display. Touch-sensitive displays are useful in public information displays, such as maps of cities and their sights posted in hotel lobbies or car rental facilities. They can also be used to explain dioramas in museums and to locate camping facilities in state parks. Touch-sensitive displays require no special expertise from users, and the screen is self-contained, requiring no special input device that might be broken or stolen.

With voice recognition, the user speaks to the computer, and the system is able to recognize an individual's vocal signals, convert them, and store the input. Voice recognition inventory systems are already in operation, and automobiles now feature voice input systems that respond to a driver's voice commands to navigate or to change the radio station.

An advantage of voice recognition systems is that they can speed data entry enormously, and free the user's hands for other tasks (for example, driving). Speech input adds still another dimension to the PC. It is now possible to add equipment and software that allows a PC user to speak commands such as "open file" or "save file" to avoid using the keyboard or mouse. Users with limited mobility or impaired sight can benefit from voice recognition systems. In the example shown in Figure 14.14, the user corrects a word by pulling down a menu of alternative words that sound the same.

When evaluating the interfaces you have chosen, keep some standards in mind:

1. The necessary training period for users should be acceptably short.
2. Early in their training, users should be able to enter commands without thinking about them or without referring to a help menu or manual. Keeping interfaces consistent throughout applications can help in this regard.
3. The interface should be seamless so that errors are few and those that do occur are not occurring because of poor design.
4. The time that users and the system need to bounce back from errors should be short.
5. Infrequent users should be able to relearn the system quickly.

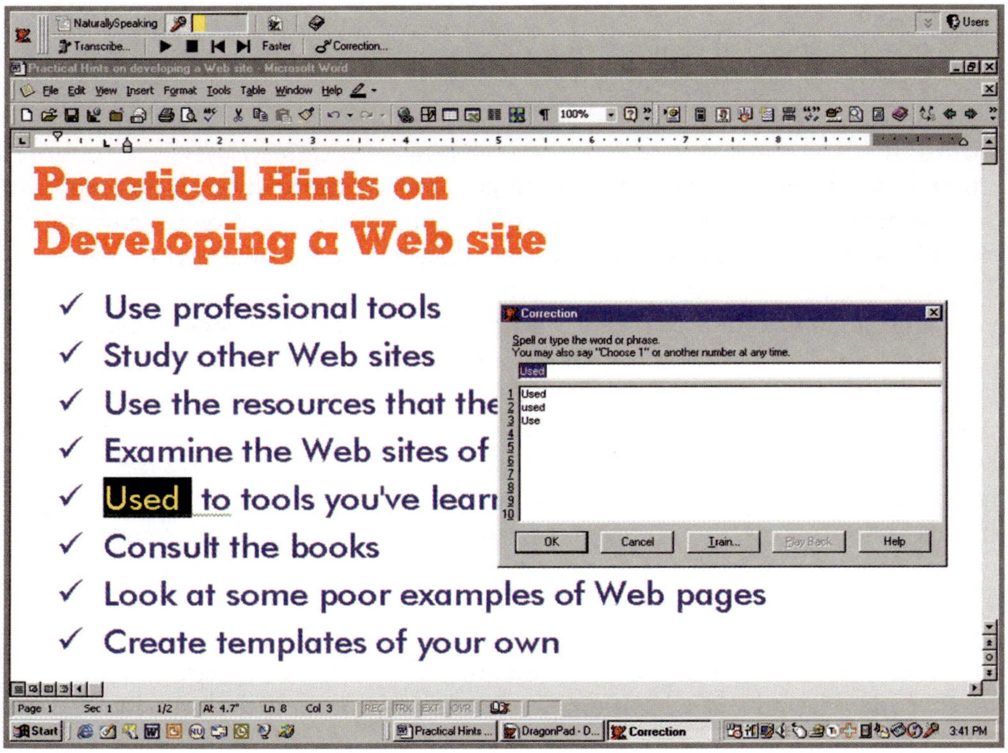

FIGURE 14.14

Using software such as Dragon NaturallySpeaking by Nuance, a user can speak commands to their computer. In this example, the user corrects a word by pulling up a menu of alternative words that sound the same.

Many different interfaces are available, and it is important to realize that an effective interface goes a long way toward addressing key HCI concerns. Users should want to use the system, and they should find it attractive and pleasing to use. In the next section, we discuss the importance of providing feedback for users to support and sustain their involvement with the system, so that they will be able to accomplish their tasks.

GUIDELINES FOR DIALOG DESIGN

Dialog is the communication between the computer and a person. Well designed dialog makes it easier for people to use a computer and lessens their frustration with the computer system. Recall the elements of the TAM (technology acceptance model) indicating that perceived usefulness and perceived ease of use will lead first to an intention to use the system and eventually to using it. There are several key points for designing good dialog. Some of them were mentioned in Chapter 12. They include the following:

1. Meaningful communication, so that the computer understands what people are entering and people understand what the computer is presenting or requesting.
2. Minimal user action.
3. Standard operation and consistency.

MEANINGFUL COMMUNICATION

The system should present information clearly to the user. This means having an appropriate title for each display, minimizing the use of abbreviations, and providing clear user feedback. Inquiry programs should display code meanings as well as data in an edited format, such as displaying slashes between the month, day, and year in a date field or commas and decimal points in an amount field. User instructions should be supplied regarding details, such as available function key assignments. In a graphical interface, the cursor may change shape depending on the work being performed.

Users with less skill in using the computer or doing their tasks with a computer require more communication. Web sites must display more text and instructions to guide the user through the site. Intranet sites may have less dialog, because there is a measure of control over how well trained users are. Internet graphics should have pop-up text or roll-over descriptions when images are used as hyperlinks, because there may be uncertainty in interpreting their meaning, especially if the site is used internationally. Notice that EU guidelines for the display of Web graphics requires that all images be labeled, so that visually impaired users will be able to hear written descriptions announced through special software. Status line information for GUI screens is another way of providing instructions for users.

Easy-to-use help screens should be provided. Many PC help screens have additional topics that may be directly selected using highlighted text displayed on the first help screen. These hyperlinks are usually in a different color, which makes them stand out in contrast to the rest of the help text. Remember to use icons or text in addition to color coding in order to reach the largest number of users. Many of the newer GUIs often incorporate tool tip help, displaying a small help message identifying the function of a command button when the cursor is placed over it. The other side of communication is that the computer should understand what the user has entered. Hence, all data entered on the screen should be edited for validity.

Source: © 2003 Joe Dater from cartoonbank.com. All Rights Reserved.

MINIMAL USER ACTION

Keying is often the slowest part of a computer system, and good dialog will minimize the number of keystrokes required. You can accomplish this goal in a number of different ways:

1. **Keying codes, such as airport codes when making a flight reservation, instead of whole words on entry screens.** Codes are also keyed when using a command-language interface, such as a two-letter state postal abbreviation. On a GUI screen, the codes may be entered by selecting descriptions of the codes from a pull-down list of available options. This helps to ensure accuracy, since the code is stored as a value of the drop-down list, as well as helping to provide meaningful communication since descriptions that are familiar to the user are selected. An example would be selecting a Canadian province and having the two-character postal code stored.
2. **Entering only data that are not already stored on files.** For example, when changing or deleting item records, only the item number should be entered. The computer responds by displaying descriptive information that is currently stored on the item file. Another example is when a user logs on to a Web site, the userID is used to find related records, such as a customer record, outstanding bills, orders, and so on.
3. **Supplying the editing characters (for example, slashes as date field separators).** Users should not have to enter formatting characters such as leading zeros, commas, or a decimal point when entering a dollar amount; nor should they have to enter slashes or hyphens when entering a date. In general, Web sites are an exception to this rule, since Web forms do not include slashes or decimal points. Some Web forms use a series of entry fields with editing characters between them, such as parentheses around an area code.
4. **Using default values for fields on entry screens.** Defaults are used when a user enters the same value in a screen field for the majority of the records being processed. The value is displayed, and the user may press the Enter key to

accept the default or overtype the default value with a new one. GUIs may contain check boxes and radio buttons that are selected when a Web form or dialog box opens. Context-sensitive menus appear when an object is clicked with the right mouse button. These menus contain options specific for the object under the mouse.

5. **Designing an inquiry (or change or delete) program so that the user needs to enter only the first few characters of a name or item description.** The program displays a list of all matching names, and, when the user chooses one, the matching record is displayed.
6. **Providing keystrokes for selecting pull-down menu options.** Often, these options are selected using a mouse, followed by keying. Users must move their hands from the keyboard to the mouse and back. As users become familiar with the system, shortcut keystrokes provide a faster method for manipulating the pull-down menus, because both hands remain on the keyboard. This helps users become efficient at their tasks. On a PC, keystrokes usually involve pressing a function key or the Alt key followed by a letter. Figure 14.15 is an example of nested pull-down menus with shortcut keys from Microsoft Visio Professional. Notice that the user, who is creating a structure chart, can get into a series of ever more specific menus.
7. **Use radio buttons and drop-down lists to control displays of new Web pages or to change Web forms.** For example, when a radio button is clicked, a drop-down list may change to reflect the radio button choice. A radio button may be clicked and a form may change according to the choice. A drop-down list may change or a radio button may be clicked to move to a new Web page. Drop-down lists are often provided on a Web page for quick navigation, selecting a new Web page from the drop-down list takes the viewer to that page.
8. **Provide cursor control for Web forms and other displays so that the cursor moves to the next field when the right number of characters has been entered.** An example would be when a user enters an area code for a telephone number, and, following the entry of three characters, the cursor then moves to the

FIGURE 14.15

Example of nested pull-down menus with shortcut keys from Microsoft Visio Professional.

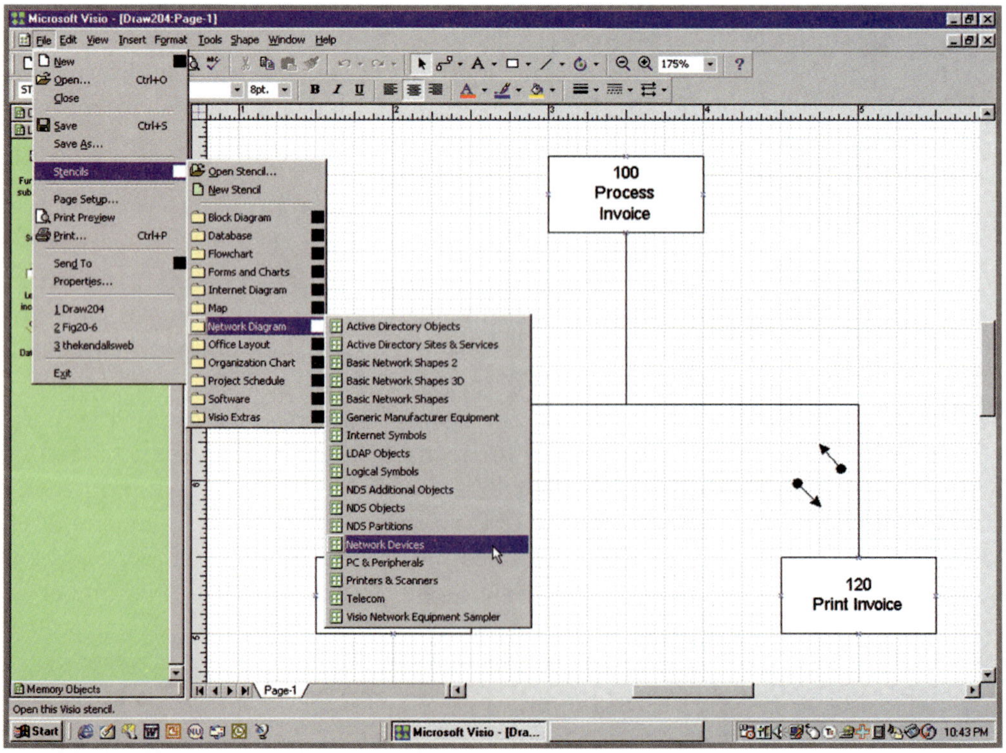

local phone number field. Entering software registration key codes is another example. The codes are often in groups of four or five letters and, when the first field is filled, the cursor moves to the next field and so on. The analyst should examine every field to see if automatic cursor control should occur.

Any combination of these eight approaches can help the analyst decrease the number of keystrokes required by the user, thereby speeding up data entry and minimizing errors.

STANDARD OPERATION AND CONSISTENCY

The system should be consistent throughout its set of different displays and in the mechanisms for controlling the operation of the displays throughout different applications. Consistency makes it easier for users to learn how to use new portions of the system once they are familiar with one component. You can achieve consistency by:

1. Locating titles, date, time, and operator and feedback messages in the same places on all displays.
2. Exiting each program by the same key or menu option. On Web pages there is often a logout image. When using programs such as Microsoft Access, use a common icon to exit the display screen. When using function keys to exit, it would be a poor design that used function key 4 (F4) to exit the ADD CUSTOMER program and function key 6 (F6) to exit the CHANGE CUSTOMER program.
3. Canceling a transaction in a consistent way, usually by pressing the **Esc** key on a PC or by using a function key (usually F12) on a mainframe.
4. Obtaining help in a standardized way. The industry standard for help is function key 1 (F1), and most software developers for the PC are adopting this convention.
5. Standardizing the colors used for all displays or Web pages. Error messages are typically displayed in red. Use a standard combination of a color and an icon to denote an error. Remember to keep the background screen color the same for all applications.
6. Standardizing the use of icons for similar operations when using a graphical user interface. For example, a small piece of paper with a bent upper corner often represents a document. Use standard images on a Web page.
7. Using consistent terminology in a display screen or Web site.
8. Providing a consistent way to navigate through the dialog. For example, find a consistent way to add records or to work with a Web site, such as using the same buttons for **Back** and **Next.**
9. Using consistent font alignment, size, and color on a Web page.

An example of good GUI design is the tab control dialog box shown in Figure 14.16. Currently, the user is choosing HP LaserJet print options, and he or she is in the **Paper** tab but also has the choice of six other tabs, including **Fonts** and **Graphics.** This display shows the options that a user can select by clicking on the left or right arrows on the horizontal sliding bar that runs along the bottom of the **Paper** size window: Com-10 Env, Monarch E, DL Env, C5 Env, and so on. The dark highlight indicates that the user has chosen to print a C5 envelope. Notice that the designer of this interface has used option buttons for both **Layout** and **Orientation.** The user has clicked on a choice of Portrait for orientation. A drop-down menu is also used to select the **Paper** source. In this instance, the user has chosen AutoSelect Tray. The designer has also used push buttons at the very bottom of the display that allow users to enter **OK, Cancel,** or **Apply** in regard to the options they have just chosen.

FIGURE 14.16

This tab control dialog box has seven tabs. The chosen tab "Paper" appears as if it is in front of the other tabs.

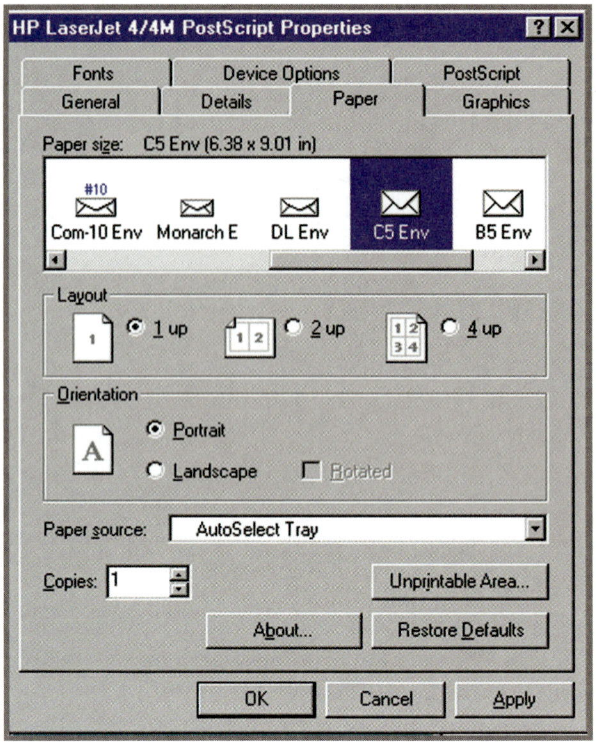

FEEDBACK FOR USERS

All systems require feedback to monitor and change behavior, as discussed in Chapter 2. Feedback usually compares current behavior with predetermined goals and gives back information describing the gap between actual and intended performance.

Because humans themselves are complex systems, they require feedback from others to meet psychological and cognitive processing needs discussed earlier in this chapter. Feedback also increases human confidence. How much feedback is required is an individual characteristic.

When users interface with machines, they still need feedback about how their work is progressing. As designers of user interfaces, systems analysts need to be aware of the human need for feedback and build it into the system. In addition to text messages, icons can often be used. For example, displaying an hourglass while the system is processing encourages the user to wait a while rather than repeatedly hitting keys to get a response.

Feedback to the user from the system is necessary in seven distinct situations, as shown in Figure 14.17. Feedback that is ill timed or too plentiful is not helpful, because humans possess a limited capacity to process information. Each of the seven situations in which feedback is appropriate is explained in the upcoming

FIGURE 14.17

Feedback is used in many ways.

Feedback Is Needed to Tell the User That:

- The computer has accepted the input.
- The input is in the correct form.
- The input is not in the correct form.
- There will be a delay in the processing.
- The request has been completed.
- The computer is unable to complete the request.
- More detailed feedback is available (and how to get it).

CONSULTING OPPORTUNITY 14.5

WAITING TO BE FED

"Yeah, we were sold a package all right. This one right here. Don't get me wrong, it gets the work done. We just don't know when."

You are talking with Owen Itt, who is telling you about the sales unit's recent purchase of new software for its networked PCs that allows the input of sales data for each of its 16 salespeople, provides output showing comparison data for them, and projects future sales based on past sales records.

"We've had some odd experiences with this program, though," Owen continues. "It seems slow or something. For instance, we're never sure when it's done. I type in a command to get a file and nothing happens. About half a minute later, if I'm lucky, the display I want might come up, but I'm never sure. If I ask it to save sales data, I just get a whirring sound. If it works, I'm returned to where I was before. If it doesn't save data, I'm still returned to where I was before. It's confusing, and I never know what to do. There's nothing on the display screen that tells me what to do next. See the little manual that came with it? It's dog-eared because we have to keep thumbing through trying to figure out what to do next. Or we go online to try to get some help, but their technical assistance is just about nonexistent. It takes way too much time, too."

Based on what you've heard in the interview, take this opportunity to supplement the software by designing some onscreen feedback for Owen and his sales team. The feedback should address all of Owen's concerns, and follow the guidelines for giving feedback to users, and the guidelines for designing good displays. Draw a prototype of the displays you think are necessary to address the problems Owen lists.

subsections. Web sites should display a status message or some other way of notifying the user that the site is responding and that input is either correct or in need of further information.

TYPES OF FEEDBACK

Acknowledging Acceptance of Input The first situation in which users need feedback is to learn that the computer has accepted the input. For example, when a user enters a name on a line, the computer provides feedback to the user by advancing the cursor one character at a time when the letters are entered correctly. A Web example would be a Web page displaying a message that "Your payment has been processed. Your confirmation number is 1234567. Thank you for using our services."

Recognizing That Input Is in the Correct Form Users need feedback to tell them that the input is in the correct form. For example, a user inputs a command, and the feedback states "READY" as the program progresses to a new point. A poor example of feedback that tells the user that input is in the correct form is the message "INPUT OK," because that message takes extra space, is cryptic, and does nothing to encourage the input of more data. When placing an order on the Web or making a payment, a confirmation page often displays, requesting that the user review the information and click a button or image to confirm the order or payment.

Notifying That Input Is Not in the Correct Form Feedback is necessary to warn users that input is not in the correct form. When data are incorrect, one way to inform the user is to generate a window that briefly describes the problem with the input and tells how the user can correct it, as shown in Figure 14.18.

Notice that the message concerning an error in inputting the subscription length is polite and concise but not cryptic, so that even inexperienced users will be able to understand it. The subscription length entered is wrong, but the feedback given does not dwell on the user's mistake. Rather, it offers options (13, 26, or 52 weeks) so that the error can be corrected easily. On a GUI screen, feedback is often in the form of a message box with an **OK** button on it.

FIGURE 14.18

Feedback informs the user that input was not in the correct form and lists options.

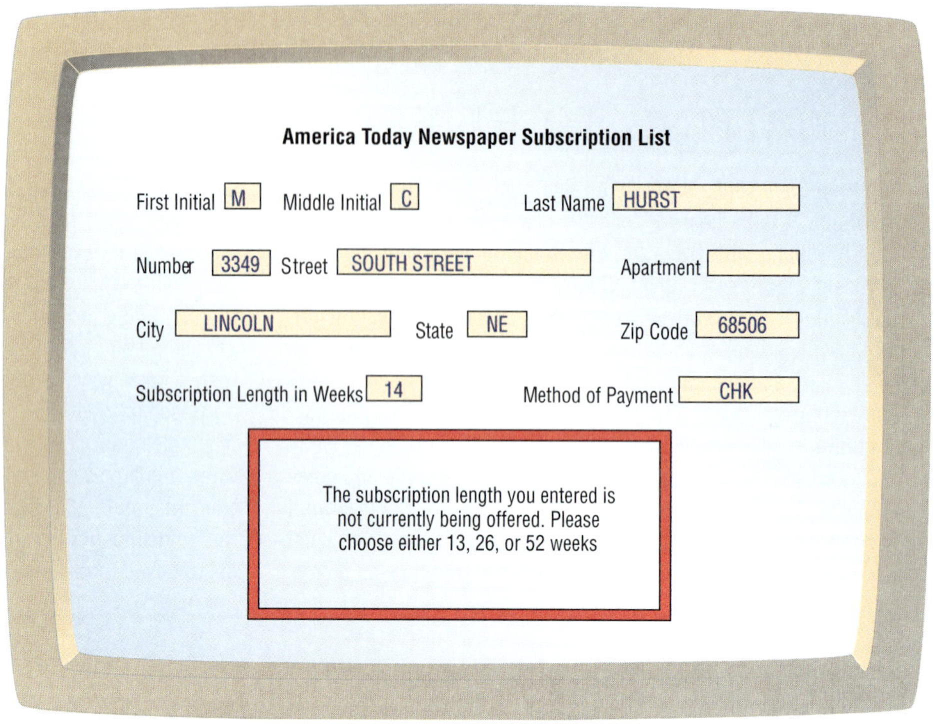

Web messages have a variety of formats. One method is to return a new page with the message on the side of the field containing the error. The new Web page may have a link for additional help. This method works for all Web sites, and the error detection and formatting of the new page are controlled by the server. Another method uses JavaScript to detect the error and display a message box on the current screen with details about the specific error. An advantage of this method is that the Web page does not have to be sent to the server, and the page is more responsive. Disadvantages are that, if JavaScript is turned off, the error will not be detected, and only one error is displayed at a time. There must also be a way of detecting the error on the server. A second disadvantage is that JavaScript may not detect errors that involve reading database tables, such as verifying a credit card number. This may be offset by using Ajax, which can send the number to the server and return an error to the Web page. Remember, however, that as many as 25 percent of users intentionally turn off their JavaScript capability; so analysts need to follow a variety of tactics when communicating errors.

Web pages may also use JavaScript to detect multiple errors and display text messages on the page. Caution must be used so that the error messages are bold enough for the user to notice. A small red line of text may go unnoticed. A message box or audible beeps may be used to alert the users that one or more errors have occurred.

The analyst must decide whether to detect and report errors when a Submit button or link is clicked, called batch validation, or detect errors one at a time, such as when a user enters a month of 14 and leaves the field. The second method is a riskier approach since poor coding may put the browser into a loop, and the user will have to shut down the browser.

So far, we have discussed visual feedback in text or iconic form, but many systems have audio feedback capabilities as well. When a user inputs data in the incorrect form, the system might beep instead of providing a window. But audio feedback alone is not descriptive, so it is not as helpful to users as onscreen instructions. Use audio feedback sparingly, perhaps to denote urgent situations. The same

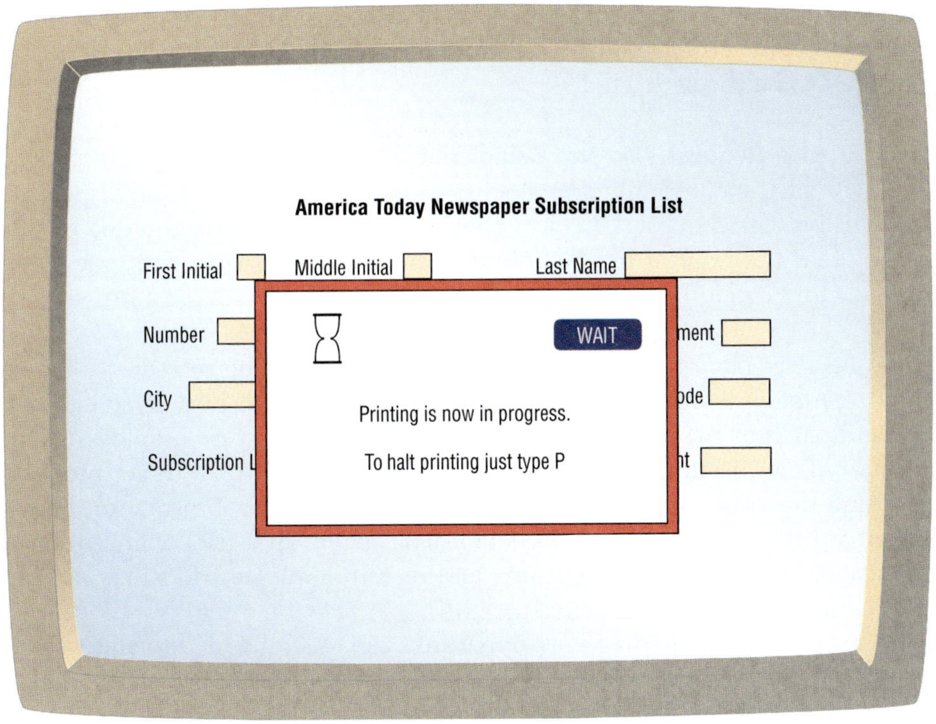

FIGURE 14.19
Feedback tells the user that there will be a delay during printing.

advice also applies to the design of Web sites, which may be viewed in an open office, where sounds carry and a coworker's desktop speakers are within earshot of several other people.

Explaining a Delay in Processing One of the most important kinds of feedback informs the user that there will be a delay in processing his or her request. Delays longer than 10 seconds or so require feedback so that the user knows the system is still working.

Figure 14.19 shows a display providing feedback in a window for a user who has just requested a printout of the newspaper's subscription list. The display shows a sentence reassuring the user that the request is being processed, as well as a sign in the upper right corner instructing the user to "WAIT" until the current command has been executed. The display also provides a way to stop the operation if necessary.

Sometimes during delays, while new software is being installed, a short tutorial on the new application is run, which is meant to serve as a distraction rather than feedback about the installation. Often, a list of files that are being copied and a status bar are used to reassure the user that the system is functioning properly. Web browsers usually display the Web pages that are being loaded and the time remaining.

It is critical to include feedback when using Ajax to update Web forms. Because a new Web page does not load, the user may not be aware that data are being retrieved from the server that will change the current Web page. When a drop-down list is changing, a message, such as "Please wait while the list is being populated" informs the user that the Web page is changing.

Timing feedback of this sort is critical. Too slow a system response could cause the user to input commands that impede or disrupt processing.

Acknowledging That a Request Is Completed Users need to know when their request has been completed and new requests may be input. Often a specific feedback message is displayed when an action has been completed by a user, such as "Employee record has been added," "Customer record has been changed," or "Item number 12345 has been deleted."

Notifying That a Request Was Not Completed Feedback is also needed to let the user know that the computer is unable to complete a request. If the display reads "Unable to process request. Check request again," the user can then go back and check to see if the request has been input correctly rather than continue to enter commands that cannot be executed.

Offering the User More Detailed Feedback Users need to be reassured that more detailed feedback is available, and they should be shown how they can get it. Commands such as Assist, Instruct, Explain, and More may be employed. Or the user may type a question mark or point to an appropriate icon to get more feedback. Using the command Help as a way to obtain further information has been questioned, because users may feel helpless or caught in a trap from which they must escape. This convention is in use, and its familiarity to users may overcome this concern.

When designing Web interfaces, hyperlinks can be embedded to allow the user to jump to the relevant help screens or to view more information. Hyperlinks are typically highlighted with underlining, italics, or a different color. Hyperlinks can be graphics, text, or icons.

INCLUDING FEEDBACK IN DESIGN

It is well worth the systems analyst's time to provide user feedback. If used correctly, feedback can be a powerful reinforcer of users' learning processes, serve to improve user performance with the system, increase motivation to produce, and improve the fit among the user, the task, and the technology.

A Variety of Help Options Feedback on personal computers has developed over the years. "Help" originally started as a response to the user who pressed a function key, such as F1; the GUI alternative is the pull-down help menu. This approach was cumbersome, because end users had to navigate through a table of contents or search via an index. Next came context-sensitive help. Users could simply click on the right mouse button, and topics or explanations about the current screen or area of the screen would be revealed. Some COTS software manufacturers call these cue cards. A third type of help on personal computers occurs when the user places the arrow over an icon and leaves it there for a couple of seconds. At this point, some programs pop up a balloon similar to those found in comic strips. This balloon explains a little bit about the icon function.

The fourth type of help is a wizard, which asks the user a series of questions and then takes action accordingly. Wizards help users through complicated or unfamiliar processes such as setting up network connections or booking an airline seat online. Most users are familiar with wizards through creating a PowerPoint presentation or choosing a style for a word processing memo.

Besides building help into an application, software manufacturers offer online help (either automated or personalized with live chat) or help lines (most customer service telephone lines are not toll free, however). Some COTS software manufacturers offer a fax-back system. A user can request a catalog of various help documents to be sent by fax, and then can order from the catalog by entering the item number with a touch-tone phone.

Finally, users can seek and find support from other users through software forums. This type of support is, of course, unofficial, and the information thus obtained may be true, partially true, or misleading. The principles regarding the use of software forums are the same for those mentioned in Chapter 16, where folklore and recommendation systems are discussed. Beware! Read this section before you accept what is said on bulletin boards.

Besides informal help on software, vendor Web sites are extremely useful for updating drivers, viewers, and the software itself. Most computer magazines have some sort of "driver watch" or "bug report" that monitors the bulletin boards and Web sites for useful programs that can be downloaded. Programs will forage vendor Web sites for the latest updates, inform the user of them, assist with the downloads, and actually upgrade user applications.

SPECIAL DESIGN CONSIDERATIONS FOR ECOMMERCE

Many of the user interface design principles you have learned concerning feedback also extend to designing ecommerce Web sites. A few extra considerations shown in this section can give your Web interface designs improved functionality. They include learning to incorporate methods for eliciting feedback on the Web site from ecommerce customers and four ways to provide one-click navigation on ecommerce sites to ensure that customers can easily navigate the site and that they can readily return to it.

SOLICITING FEEDBACK FROM ECOMMERCE WEB SITE CUSTOMERS

Not only do you need to give users feedback about what is happening with an order, but you need to elicit feedback as well. Most ecommerce Web sites have a **Feedback** button. There are two standard ways to design what users will experience when they click on the **Feedback** button.

The first way is to launch the user's email program with the email address of the company's contact automatically entered into the **To:** field. This method prevents typing errors and facilitates ease in contacting the organization. The user does not need to leave the site to communicate with it. These messages, however, raise expectations that they will be answered just as regular mail or phone calls are. Research indicates that 60 percent of organizations with this type of email contact feature on their sites do not have anyone assigned to reply to the email messages received. Thus, the business is losing valuable feedback, allowing customers to harbor the impression that they are communicating, and engendering ill will when no response is received. If you design this type of feedback opportunity, you also need to design procedures for the organization to reply to email from the Web site. Some designers handle this problem by creating systems to automatically return an email reply, which generates a unique case or incident number, provides further instructions on how to proceed (hyperlinks to FAQ pages perhaps), or offers phone numbers to help lines that are unavailable to the general public.

The second type of design for garnering feedback from customers using an ecommerce Web site is to take users to a blank message template when they click on **Feedback.** Even a familiar tool such as Microsoft FrontPage permits you to create and insert a feedback form into your site easily. This form might begin with a header that states "Company X Feedback" and then "You can use the form below to send suggestions, comments, and questions about the X site to our Customer Service team."

CONSULTING OPPORTUNITY 14.6

WHEN YOU RUN A MARATHON, IT HELPS TO KNOW WHERE YOU'RE GOING

Marathon Vitamin Shops was successful in getting its Web site up and running. The Web developers put the company's entire catalog online and included a choice of skins so that each type of customer would enjoy using the Web site. (See Consulting Opportunities 1.1 and 12.4 for more details.)

The analysts are meeting with owner Bill Berry and some employees to evaluate customer feedback as well as give their own reactions to the new Web site. They are meeting in a large conference room, where they have a computer with Internet access and a projector. As they sit down at the table, the entry screen for the Web site is projected at the front of the room. "The Web site has attracted lots of attention, but we want to give the customers even more so that they keep coming back," says Bill, gesturing to the screen.

He continues, "It's not like we're closing our retail stores or anything. In fact, it's just the opposite. When customers notice we're on the Web, they're eager to locate the store in their community. They want to be able to walk into a store and talk to a trained expert rather than buying everything over the Internet. We need to tell people how to get there."

"We think we can improve the site by adding special enhancements and features," says Al Falfa, a member of the systems team who originally developed and implemented the ecommerce Web site.

"Yes," says Ginger Rute, one of the other members of the systems development team, as she nods in agreement. "Blockbuster and Borders use a mapping facility from MapQuest, and Home Depot uses maps from Microsoft Vicinity, which also produces MapBlast!"

Vita Minn, another member of the original systems development team, speaks up enthusiastically, saying, "We know of a couple good message board services and chat rooms we can build into our Web site. We think they can improve the stickiness of the site, making people stay on the site longer and also making them want to return."

"That's a great idea," says Jin Singh, one of the technologically savvy Marathon employees. "We can let customers talk with one another, tell each other about a product they liked, and so on. We could even let them start their own blogs."

Vita continues by moving to the computer keyboard and saying, "Let me show you the sites at www.planetgov.com and www.worldviewer.com." As she types in the first URL, the group sees the site projected. "They use chat systems from ichat and Multicity.com, respectively," she continues.

"Customers also need to search for more information about a product or manufacturer," Al adds. "Let's make it easier for them. Let's look at www.Cincinnati.com for an example. They use Atomz to search for information."

After listening intently, Bill speaks up. "Medical information could also be useful" he says. "I've notice that www.medpool.com has medical news from NewsEdge. I've seen people on the treadmills at my health and fitness center watching the financial channels while they exercise."

"While we're at it, why don't we add news and financial information to the Web site?" Ginger asks. "I notice that www.nmm.com has market news from a company called Moreover.com."

Think about the conversation between the systems development team and the people from Marathon Vitamin shops. Some of the enhancement suggestions involved taking advantage of free services; others required payments ranging from $1,000 to $5,000 annually. Although some were good ideas, others may not be practical or feasible. Perhaps some of the ideas just do not make sense for the company.

For each of the following, review what you know about the mission and business activities of Marathon Vitamin Shops. Then make a recommendation regarding each option the analysts and clients have made and defend it:

- Mashups using Google Maps.
- Chat rooms and message boards.
- Blogs.
- Search engines.
- Medical information.
- News feeds and financial markets information.

Fields can include First Name, Last Name, Email Address, Regarding (a subject field that supplies a drop-down menu of the company's product or service selections, asking the user to "Please make a selection"), an "Enter Your Message Here:" section (a free-form space where users can type in their message), and the standard **Submit** and **Clear** buttons at the bottom of the form. Using this type of form permits the analyst to have the user data already formatted correctly for storage in a database. Consequently, it makes the data entered into a feedback form easier to analyze in the aggregate.

Thus, the analyst does more than just design a response to individual email. The analyst helps the organization capture, store, process, and analyze valuable customer information in a manner that makes it more likely that the company will be capable of spotting important trends in customer response, rather than simply reacting to individual queries.

EASY NAVIGATION FOR ECOMMERCE WEB SITES

Many authors speak of what is known as "intuitive navigation" for ecommerce Web sites. Users need to know how to navigate the site without having to learn a new interface and without having to explore every inch of the Web site before they can find what they want. The standard for this type of navigational approach is called one-click navigation.

There are four ways to design easy, one-click navigation for an ecommerce site: (1) creating a rollover menu, (2) building a collection of hierarchical links so that the home page becomes an outline of the key topic headings associated with the Web site, (3) placing a site map on the home page and emphasizing the link to it (this would also be placed on every other page on the site), and (4) placing a navigational bar on every inside page (usually at the top or on the left side of the page) that repeats the categories used on the entry screen.

A rollover menu can be created with a Java applet or with JavaScript and HTML layers, if you do not want to make users run a Java applet. The rollover menu appears when the customer using the Web site pauses the pointer over a link.

Creating an outline of the content of the site through the presentation of a table of contents on the home page is another way to speed navigation of the site. This design, however, imposes severe constraints on the designer's creativity, and sometimes simply presenting a list of topics does not adequately convey the strategic mission of the organization to the user.

Designing and then prominently displaying the link to a site map is a third way to improve navigational efficiency. Remember to include the link to the site map on the home page and on every other page as well.

Finally, you can design navigation bars that are consistently displayed on the home page as well as at the top and on the left of all other pages that comprise the site. Once you have established (during the information requirements phase) the most useful and most used categories (usually categories such as "Our Company" "Our Products," "Buy Now," "Contact Us," "Site Map," and "Search"), remember to include them on all pages.

Including a search function is another option. Microsoft FrontPage extensions and other software have search capabilities built in; other possibilities include adding a search engine such as Google to your site. Simple search functions work well for small, manageable sites, but as a site grows large, advanced search functions that include Boolean logic (discussed later in this chapter) are needed.

Creating flexibility in the way users navigate the Web is also important. An expert Web site designer would try to incorporate many different ways to look up information on a particular subject. Figure 14.20 shows a Web page from DinoTech. For example, a user interested in an international IT career can find out information from the DinoTech Web site in three different ways. If they are interested in working in Argentina, they can click on the Argentine flag, click on the name of the country, or click on the map representing Argentina.

Designing a Web site with navigation for users with different cognitive processing or interests is desirable. It is even possible that the same user may use all three of these methods at different times. All of these add to the usability of a Web site.

The main priority in navigation is, however, that, whatever you do, you must make it extremely easy for users to return to a previous page and make it somewhat

FIGURE 14.20

An example of a Web page that allows users to navigate to the desired page in different ways.

easy to return to the place where they entered the client's site. Your main concern is keeping customers on the Web site. The longer customers are on the site, the greater the chance is that they will purchase something. So make sure that, if users navigate to a link in your client's Web site, they can easily find their way back. Doing these things will ensure the stickiness of the Web site. Do not create any barriers to the customer who wants to return to the client's Web site.

MASHUPS

An application programming interface (API) is a set of small programs and protocols used like building blocks for building software applications. When two or more APIs are used together they form a mashup. Many mashups are open source, so developers can use an API from a site like Google maps and combine it with an API that contains other data, resulting in a new Web site that creates an entirely new application.

Bogozo Real Estate (www.bogozo.com), for example, combines CraigsList real estate data with Google Maps. This new applications allows a user to see properties displayed on a map, view the location of neighborhood schools, and in the specific case of New York City, see an overlay of a New York City subway map to help buyers find a place convenient to the subway system.

A large corporation that has many retail outlets in a region may want to make it easier for customers to find their retail stores. They may want to hire a company like Blipstar which provides a service that allows companies to upload information about retail stores. Blipstar geocodes them and places them on a Google map. The company then puts a link to this information on its own Web site, so customers can simply enter their ZIP or postal code and let the mashup display the location of the nearest retail store.

Mashups are becoming a new way to present information. Expect to see many useful mashup applications soon. Look for them at www.programmableweb.com.

DESIGNING QUERIES

When users ask questions of or communicate with the database, they are said to query it. Six different types of queries are among the most common. Your careful attention to query design can help reduce users' time spent in querying the database, help them find the data they want, and result in a smoother user experience overall.

QUERY TYPES

The questions we pose concerning data from our database are referred to as queries. There are six basic query types. Each query involves three items: an entity, an attribute, and a value. In each case, two of these are given, and the intent of the query is to find the remaining item. Figure 14.21 will be used to illustrate all of the query examples.

Query Type 1 The entity and one of the entity's attributes are given. The purpose of the query is to find the value. The query can be expressed as follows:

What is the value of a specified attribute for a particular entity?

Sometimes it is more convenient to use notation to formulate the query. This query can be written as

$$V \longleftarrow (E, A)$$

where V stands for the value, E for entity, and A for attribute, and the variables in parentheses are given.

The question

What did employee number 73712 make in year 2003?

can be stated more specifically as

What is the value of the attribute YEAR-2003 for the entity EMPLOYEE NUMBER 73712?

The record containing employee number 73712 will be found, and the answer to the query will be $47,100.

The years are the attributes.

EARNINGS-HISTORY

EMPLOYEE NUMBER	EMPLOYEE NAME	DEPARTMENT	S/H	YEAR-2000	YEAR-2001	YEAR-2002	YEAR-2003
72845	Waters	Outside Sales	S	48,960	51,400	49,050	52,900
72888	Dryne	Outside Sales	S	42,200	44,700	48,020	50,580
73712	Fawcett	Distribution	H	43,500	45,500	46,780	47,100
80345	Well, Jr.	Marketing	S	65,000	71,000	75,000	78,000
84672	Piper	Maintenance	H	40,560	42,340	43,520	44,910
60	Acquia	Accounting	H	38,755	40,040	41,380	42,540

The employee numbers are the entities.

The salaries are the values.

FIGURE 14.21
It is possible to perform six basic types of queries on a table that contains entities, attributes, and values.

Query Type 2 The intent of the second query type is to find an entity or entities when an attribute and value are given. Query type 2 can be stated as follows:

What entity has a specified value for a particular attribute?

Because values can also be numeric, it is possible to search for a value equal to, greater than, less than, not equal to, greater than or equal to, and so on. An example of this type of query is as follows:

What employee(s) earned more than $50,000 in 2003?

The notation for query type 2 is

$$E \longleftarrow (V, A)$$

In this case, three employees made more than $50,000, so the response will be a listing of the employee numbers for the three employees: 72845, 72888, and 80345.

Query Type 3 The purpose of this query type is to determine which attributes fit the description provided when the entity and value are given. Query type 3 can be stated as follows:

What attribute(s) has a specified value for a particular entity?

This query is useful when many similar attributes have the same property. The following example has similar attributes (specific years) that contain the annual salaries for the employees of the company:

What years did employee number 72845 make over $50,000?

or, more precisely,

What attributes {YEAR-2000, YEAR-2001, YEAR-2002, YEAR-2003} have a value > 50,000 for the entity EMPLOYEE-NUMBER = 72845?

where the optional list in braces ({ }) is the set of eligible attributes.

The notation for query type 3 is

$$A \longleftarrow (V, E)$$

In this example, Waters (employee number 72845) made over $50,000 for two years. Therefore, the response will be year 2001 and year 2003. Query type 3 is rarer than the preceding two types due to the requirement of having similar attributes exhibiting the same properties.

Query Type 4 Query type 4 is similar to query type 1. The difference is that the values of all attributes are desired. Query 4 can be expressed as follows:

List all the values for all the attributes for a particular entity.

An example of query type 4 is:

List all the details in the earnings history file for employee number 72888.

The notation for query type 4 is

$$\text{all } V \longleftarrow (E, \text{all } A)$$

The response for this query will be the entire record for the employee named Dryne (employee number 72888).

Query Type 5 The fifth type of query is another global query, but it is similar in form to query type 2. Query type 5 can be stated as follows:

> List all entities that have a specified value for all attributes.

An example of query type 5 is:

> List all the employees whose earnings exceeded \$50,000 in any of the years available.

The notation for query type 5 is

$$\text{all } E \longleftarrow (V, \text{all } A)$$

The response to this query will be 72845, 72888, and 80345.

Query Type 6 The sixth query type is similar to query type 3. The difference is that query type 6 requests a listing of the attributes for all entities rather than a particular entity. Query type 6 can be stated as follows:

> List all the attributes that have a specified value for all entities.

The following is an example of query type 6:

> List all the years for which earnings exceeded \$40,000 for all employees in the company.

The notation for query type 6 is

$$\text{all } A \longleftarrow (V, \text{all } E)$$

The response will be YEAR-2001, YEAR-2002, and YEAR-2003. As with query type 3, query type 6 is not used as much as other types.

Building More Complex Queries The preceding six query types are only building blocks for more complex queries. Expressions, referred to as Boolean expressions, can be formed for queries. An example of a Boolean expression is:

> List all the customers who have Zip codes greater than or equal to 60001 and less than 70000, and who have ordered more than \$500 from our catalogs or have ordered at least five times in the past year.

One difficulty with this statement is determining which operator (for example, AND) belongs with which condition; it is also difficult to determine the sequence in which the parts of the expression should be carried out. The following may help to clarify this problem:

> LIST ALL CUSTOMERS HAVING (ZIP-CODE GE 60001 AND ZIP-CODE LT 70000) AND (AMOUNT-ORDERED GT 500 OR TIMES-ORDERED GE 5)

Now some of the confusion is eliminated. The first improvement is that the operators are expressed more clearly as GE, GT, and LT than as English phrases, such as "at least." Second, the attributes are given distinct names, such as AMOUNT-ORDERED and TIMES-ORDERED. In the earlier sentence, these attributes were both referred to as "have ordered." Finally, parentheses are used to indicate the order in which the logic is to be performed. Whatever is in parentheses is done first.

Operations are generally performed in a predetermined order of precedence. Arithmetic operations are usually performed first (exponentiation, then either multiplication or division, and then addition or subtraction). Next, comparative operations are performed. These operations are GT (greater than), LT (less than),

CONSULTING OPPORTUNITY 14.7

HEY, LOOK ME OVER (REPRISE)

You have been called back to take another look at Merman's Costume Rentals. Here is part of the database created for Annie Oaklea of Merman's (with whom you last worked in Consulting Opportunities 7.1 and 8.1). The database contains information, such as the cost of the rental, the date checked out, the date due back, and the number of days the costume has been rented since the beginning of the year (YTD DAYS OUT) (see Figure 14.C1).

Analyzing Annie's typical day in the costume rental business, you realize there are several requests she must make of the database so that she can make decisions on when to replace frequently used costumes or even when to buy more costumes of a particular type. She also needs to remember to keep in the good graces of customers she has previously turned down for a particular costume rental, to know when to recall an overdue costume, and so on.

Formulate several queries that will help her get the information she needs from the database. (*Hint:* Make any assumptions necessary about the types of information she needs to make decisions and use as many of the different query types discussed in this chapter as you can.) In a paragraph, describe how Annie's queries would be different if she were working with a Web-based or hyperlinked system.

COSTUME-RENTAL

COSTUME NUMBER	DESCRIPTION	SUIT NUMBER	COLOR	COST OF	DATE CHECKED OUT	DUE DATE	YTD DAYS OUT	TYPE OF COSTUME	REQUESTS TURNED DOWN
0003	Lady MacBeth F, SM	01	Blue	15.00	10/15	11/30	150	Standard	2
1342	Bear F, MED	01	Dk. Brown	12.50	10/24	11/09	26	Standard	0
1344	Bear F, MED	02	Dk. Brown	12.50	10/24	11/09	115	Standard	0
1347	Bear F, LG	01	Black	12.50	10/24	11/09	22	Standard	0
1348	Bear F, LG	02	Black	12.50	11/01	11/08	10	Standard	0
1400	Goldilocks F, MED	01	Light Blue	7.00	10/24	11/09	140	Standard	0
1402	Goldilocks F, MED	02	Light Blue	7.00	10/28	11/09	10	Standard	0
1852	Hamlet M, MED	01	Dark Green	15.00	11/02	11/23	115	Standard	3
1853	Ophelia F, SM	01	Light Blue	15.00	11/02	11/23	22	Standard	0
4715	Prince M, LG	01	White/purple	10.00	11/04	11/21	145	Standard	5
4730	Frog M, SM	01	Green	7.00	11/04	11/21	175	Standard	2
7822	Jester M, MED	01	Multi	7.50	11/10	12/08	12	Standard	0
7824	Jester M, MED	02	Multi	7.50	11/09	11/15	10	Standard	0
7823	Executioner M, LG	01	Black	7.00	11/19	12/05	21	Standard	0
8645	Mr. Spock N, LG	01	Orange	18.00	09/07	09/12	150	Trendy	4
9000	Pantomime F, LG	01	Red	7.00	08/25	09/15	56	Standard	0
9001	Pantomime M, MED	01	Blue	7.00	08/25	09/15	72	Standard	0
9121	Juggler M, MED	01	Multi	7.00	11/05	11/19	14	Standard	0
9156	Napoleon M, SM	01	Blue/white	15.00	10/26	11/23	56	Standard	1

FIGURE 14.C1
A portion of the database from Merman's Costume Rental shop.

and others. Finally, the Boolean operations are performed (first AND and then OR). Within the same level, the order generally goes from left to right. The precedence is summarized in Figure 14.22.

QUERY METHODS

Two popular query methods are query by example and structured query language.

Query by Example Query by example (QBE) is a simple but powerful method for implementing queries in database systems, such as Microsoft Access. The database

Type	Level	Symbol
Arithmetic Operators	1	* *
	2	* /
	3	+ −
Comparative Operators	4	GT LT
		EQ NE
		GE LE
Boolean Operators	5	AND
	6	OR

FIGURE 14.22

Arithmetic, comparative, and Boolean operators are processed in a hierarchical order of precedence unless parentheses are used.

fields are selected and displayed in a grid, and the requested query values are either entered in the field area or below the field. The query should be able to select both rows from the table that match conditions as well as specific columns (fields). Complex conditions may be set to select records, and the user may easily specify the columns to be sorted. Figure 14.23 is an example of query by example using Microsoft Access. The query design screen is divided into two portions. The top portion contains the tables selected for the query and their relationships, and the bottom portion contains the query selection grid. Fields from the database tables are dragged to the grid.

The first two rows contain the field and the table in which the field is located. The next row contains sorting information. In this example, the results will be sorted by CUSTOMER NAME. A check mark in the Show box (fourth row down) indicates that the field is to be displayed in the results. Notice that the CUSTOMER NUMBER, CUSTOMER NAME, and STATUS CODE MEANING are selected for the resulting display (other fields are displayed as well, but they do not show in the display). Notice that the ACCOUNT STATUS CODE and ACCOUNT TYPE CODE are not checked and therefore will not be in the final results. In the criteria rows, there is a *1* in the ACCOUNT STATUS CODE (indicating an active record) and a *C* and *D* (selecting a General Customer or a Discount Customer) in the

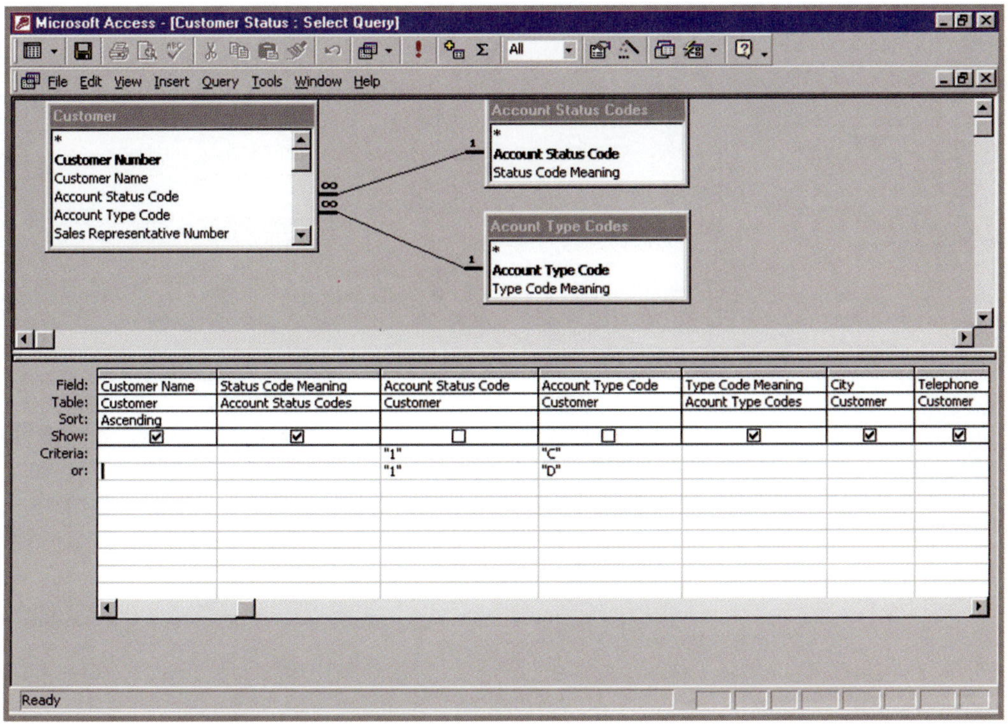

FIGURE 14.23

Query by example using Microsoft Access.

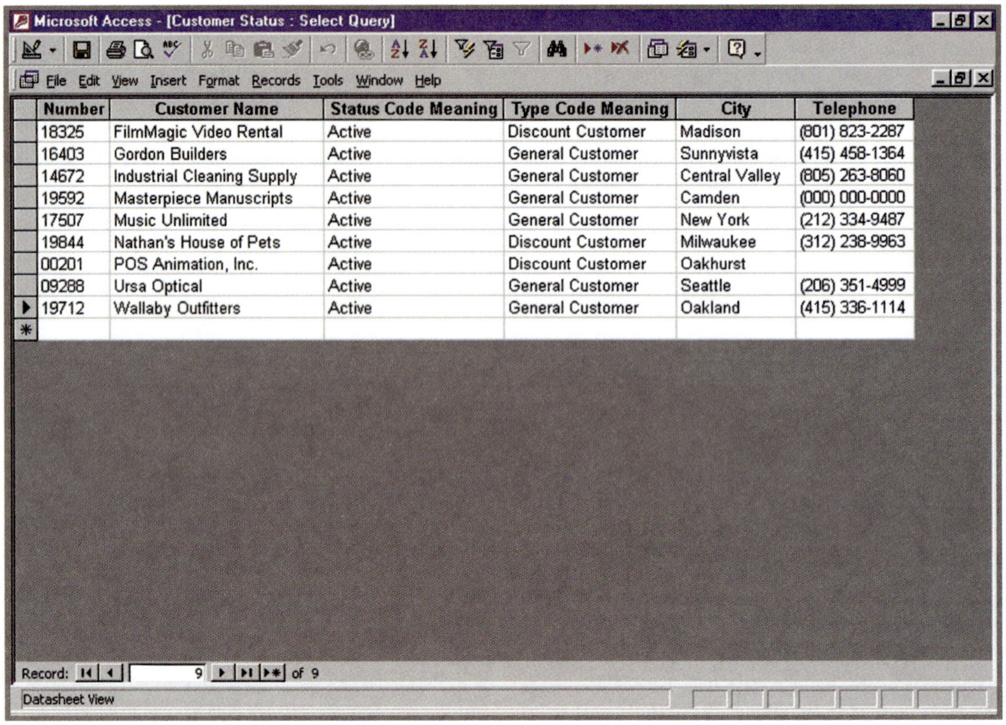

FIGURE 14.24
A query by example for CUSTOMER STATUS yields these results.

ACCOUNT TYPE CODE columns. Two conditions in the same row indicate an AND condition, and two conditions in different rows represent an OR condition. This query specifies that the user should select both an Active Customer and either a General or Discount Customer.

The results of a query are displayed in a table, illustrated in Figure 14.24. Notice that the ACCOUNT STATUS CODE and ACCOUNT TYPE CODE do not display. They are not checked and are included in the query for selection purposes only. Instead, the code meanings are displayed, which are more useful to the user. The customer names are sequenced alphabetically.

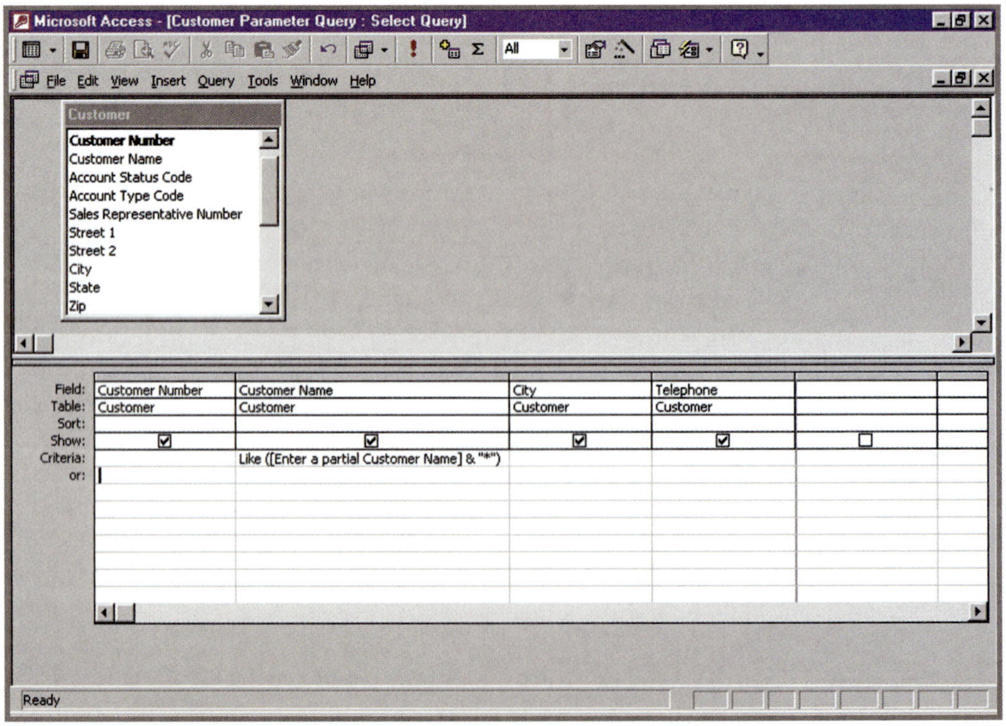

FIGURE 14.25
A parameter query design screen.

```
SELECT DISTINCTROW
        Customer.[Customer Number],
        Customer.[Customer Name],
        Customer.City,
        Customer.Telephone
FROM Customer
WHERE (((Customer.[Customer Name])
Like ([Enter a partial Customer Name] & "*")));
```

FIGURE 14.26
Structured Query Language (SQL) for the CUSTOMER NAME parameter query.

One of the problems encountered when designing queries is that either the user must modify the query parameters or the same conditions are selected each time the query is executed. A solution to this problem is to use a parameter query. This type of query allows the user to enter the conditions in a dialog box each time the query is run. Figure 14.25 illustrates a parameter query. Notice that the Criteria row has the message "Enter a partial Customer Name" included inside brackets. Preceding the message is the word "Like," and following the message is an ampersand (&), indicating that an exact match is not required. When the query is executed, a dialog box opens with the query message on the top. If the value "ma" is entered in the box requesting a partial customer name, then only customers whose names begin with the letters "Ma" are selected and displayed.

Structured Query Language Structured query language (SQL) is another popular way to implement queries. It uses a series of words and commands to select the rows and columns that should be displayed in the resulting table. Figure 14.26 illustrates the SQL code that is equivalent to the preceding parameter query. The SELECT DISTINCTROW keyword determines which rows are to be selected. The WHERE keyword specifies the condition that the CUSTOMER NAME should be used to select the data entered in the LIKE parameter.

SUMMARY

In this chapter we have examined human–computer interaction (HCI), a variety of interfaces, designing the user interface, designing user feedback, and designing ecommerce Web site feedback and navigation. We have focused on understanding HCI to ensure the functionality and usability of computer systems we design. By doing so we intend to provide effective support for user interaction with technology, making system use a pleasant user experience that serves the well-being of the individual and the objectives of the organization. When analysts create a proper fit among the HCI elements of the human, the computer, and the task, it leads to improved performance and overall psychological and physical well-being of the individual.

Designs focus on such a fit, with one of the main concerns of the HCI designer being the overall psychological and physical well-being of the user. Analysts can use the TAM (Technology Acceptance Model) to organize their thinking about whether users will accept technology and eventually use it, by examining perceived usefulness and perceived ease of use experienced by users. This model has been used to predict the likelihood of acceptance and use, as well as to judge acceptance after implementation.

"I have no problem with using a mouse or any other rodent you throw my way. Really, though, whatever Snowden needs is what I try to do. Everyone is different, however. I've seen people here go out of their way to avoid using a computer altogether. Other people would prefer not to talk with a human. In fact, they would be as happy as a puppy chewing on a new bedroom slipper if they could use command language to interact. I have a hunch they would prefer not talking to people at all, but that's just an impression. Most of the folks we have here are open to new things. Otherwise, they wouldn't be here at MRE. We do pride ourselves on our creativity. I have you signed up for a meeting with people from the training group, including Tom Ketchem, Melissa Smith, and Kathy Blandford. You can invite anyone else you think should be included. Snowden may sit in as well, if he has time. That's why he asked me to relay the message, I guess. They'll be very curious to see what kind of interface you are suggesting for them on the new project reporting system."

HYPERCASE QUESTIONS

1. Write a short proposal describing what type of user interface would be appropriate for the users of the project reporting system who are in the training group. Include reasons for your decision.
2. Design a user interface using a CASE tool, such as Visible Analyst, a software package such as Microsoft Access, or paper layout forms. What are the key features that address the needs of the people in the training group?
3. Demonstrate your interface to a group of students who can role-play as members of the training group. Ask for reactions.
4. Redesign the interface based on the feedback you have received. Write a paragraph to say how your new design addresses any comments you have received.

FIGURE 14.HC1

In HyperCase, you can see how users process information in order to create a more effective user interface.

Usability is all about finding out what works for users and what does not. Usability heuristics for judging the usability of computer systems and ecommerce sites include the visibility of system status, the match between the system and the real world, user control and freedom, consistency and standards, error prevention, reconnection rather than recall, flexibility and efficiency of use, aesthetic and minimalist design, help that users recognize, diagnosis and recovery from errors, and help and documentation. It is possible to extend the cognitive capabilities of individuals by creating systems that offer elements such as pivot tables and visual analysis.

Physical considerations of HCI design include vision, hearing, and touch. Physical disabilities and limitations should be taken into consideration during task and interface design. The guidelines for taking an HCI approach to systems design are as follows: (1) Examine the task to be done and consider the fit among the human, computer, and task. (2) Identify what obstacles exist for users in their attempts to accomplish their assigned tasks (keeping in mind the perceived usefulness and perceived ease of use from TAM). (3) Consider usability; examine the usage environment by creating use case scenarios that depict what is going on between users and the technology. (4) Use the information you have gained beforehand to figure out the physical and organizational environmental characteristics. Design with prototyping to accommodate diverse users and users with disabilities. The success of the systems you design depends on user involvement and acceptance. Therefore, thinking about users in systematic and empathic ways is of utmost importance and is not a peripheral issue for systems analysts.

A variety of user interfaces and input devices were covered. Some interfaces are particularly well suited to inexperienced users, such as natural language, question and answer, menus, form-fill and Web-based form-fill, graphical user interfaces (especially on Web pages), the mouse, light pens, the stylus, touch-sensitive screens, and voice recognition systems. Command language is better suited to experienced users.

Combinations of interfaces can be extremely effective. For example, using pull-down menus with graphical user interfaces or employing nested menus in question-and-answer interfaces yields interesting combinations. The Web has posed new challenges for designers, because the user is not known. Web design takes advantage of hyperlinks to allow users to take numerous paths as they interact with the Web site.

Users' need for feedback from the system is also an important consideration. System feedback is necessary to let users know if their input is being accepted, if input is or is not in the correct form, if processing is going on, if requests can or cannot be processed, and if more detailed information is available and how to get it. Feedback is most often visual, with text, graphics, or icons being used. Audio feedback can also be effective.

Special considerations apply to designing ecommerce Web sites. Build improved functionality into the application by eliciting customer feedback through automatic email feedback buttons or by including blank feedback forms on the Web site. In addition, four important navigation design strategies improve the stickiness of ecommerce Web sites: (1) rollover menus, (2) hierarchical displays of links on the entry screen, (3) site maps, and (4) navigation bars that provide one-click navigation, making getting around the site and returning to it as easy as possible for the customer.

Queries are designed to allow users to extract meaningful data from the database. There are six basic types of queries, and they can be combined using Boolean logic to form more complex queries.

KEYWORDS AND PHRASES

- application programming interface (API)
- Boolean operators
- cognitive considerations of HCI
- command-language interface
- continuous speech system
- cue cards
- dialog box
- disabilities and design
- feedback
- feedback for users
- fit
- form-fill (input/output form) interfaces
- graphical user interface (GUI)
- intuitive navigation
- mashup
- menu
- natural-language interface
- navigation bar
- nested menus
- one-click navigation
- performance
- physical considerations of HCI
- psychological considerations of HCI
- pull-down menu
- query
- question-and-answer interface
- rollover menu
- site map
- speech recognition and synthesis
- stickiness
- structured query language (SQL)
- stylus
- task
- technology acceptance model (TAM)
- template
- touch-sensitive screen
- usability
- Web-based form-fill interface
- wizard

REVIEW QUESTIONS

1. Define HCI.
2. Explain how fit among the HCI elements of the human, the computer, and the tasks to be performed leads to performance and well-being.
3. What are the components of the term *performance* in the HCI context?
4. What is meant by the word *well-being* when used using an HCI approach?
5. What are the two variables of the Technology Acceptance Model (TAM)?
6. List five of the eleven usability heuristics for judging the usability of computer systems and ecommerce Web sites provided by Nielsen and others.
7. Describe some of the ways that a pivot table allows a user to arrange data.
8. List three physical considerations that HCI design addresses.
9. List three ways that analysts can improve task or interface design to help, respectively, a person who is visually impaired, hearing impaired, or mobility impaired.
10. What are the five objectives for designing user interfaces?
11. Define natural-language interfaces. What is their major drawback?
12. Explain what is meant by question-and-answer interfaces. To what kind of users are they best suited?
13. Describe how users use onscreen menus.
14. What is a nested menu? What are its advantages?
15. Define onscreen input/output forms. What is their chief advantage?
16. What are the advantages of Web-based fill-in forms?
17. What are the drawbacks of Web-based form-fill interfaces?
18. Explain what command-language interfaces are. To what types of users are they best suited?
19. Define graphical user interfaces. What is the key difficulty they present for programmers?
20. For what type of user is a GUI particularly effective?
21. What are the three guidelines for designing good screen dialog?

22. What are the roles of icons, graphics, and color in providing feedback?
23. List eight ways for achieving the goal of minimal operator action when designing a user interface.
24. List five standards that can aid in evaluating user interfaces.
25. What are the seven situations that require feedback for users?
26. What is an acceptable way of telling the user that input was accepted?
27. When a user is informed that his or her input is not in the correct form, what additional feedback should be given at the same time?
28. List three ways to notify a Web user that the input is not in the correct form.
29. Why is it unacceptable to notify the user that input is not correct solely through the use of beeping or buzzing?
30. When a request is not completed, what feedback should be provided to the user?
31. Describe two types of Web site designs for eliciting feedback from customers.
32. List four practical ways that an analyst can improve the ease of user navigation and the stickiness of an ecommerce Web site.
33. What are hypertext links? Where should they be used?
34. Describe what a mashup is.
35. List in shorthand notation the six basic query types.

PROBLEMS

1. Manu Narayan owns several first-class hotels worldwide, including properties in Manhattan, Bombay, and even some in suburbia. He wants to make sure that the human–computer interface is appropriate to each culture but wants to be able to share the software among all of his hotel reservations departments. Design a nested menus interface for a check-in and checkout hotel reservation system that can be used internationally. Use numbers to select a menu item. Show how each menu would look on a standard PC display.
2. Stefan Lano needs displays that will show the musical instrument inventory in his chain of music stores that caters to musicians playing in world-class symphony orchestras in Basel, Switzerland; Buenos Aires, Argentina; Philadelphia, USA; and New York. Design a form-fill interface for the inventory control of musical instruments in all four stores that could be used on a PC display screen. Assume that English will be the interface language.
3. Design a Web-based form-fill interface to accomplish the same task as in Problem 2.
   a. What difficulties did you encounter? Discuss them in a paragraph.
   b. Of the two designs you did, which would you say is better suited to Mr. Lano's task? Why? List three reasons for your choice. How would you test their usability?
4. A U.K.-based travel agent, Euan Morton, LLC, would like your systems team to design a command-language interface he can use to book seats for airlines to which his firm has solid business ties, such as British Air, RyanAir, and Virgin-Atlantic.
   a. Show what the interface would look like on a standard display.
   b. Make a list of commands needed to book an airline seat and write down what each command means.
5. An IT executive, Felicia Finley, from Jersey IT Innovators, Inc., has asked that you design a graphical user interface for an executive desktop to help her in her work. Use icons for file cabinets, a wastebasket, a telephone, and so on. Show how they would appear on the computer display.

6. Nick, a celebrity chef/restaurant owner from Williamsburg, New York, wants to be able to receive clear feedback on the systems used to manage his many "show place" restaurants. Design a display that provides appropriate feedback for a user whose command cannot be executed.
7. Design a screen for a payroll software package that displays information telling Nick from Problem 6 how to get more detailed feedback.
8. Design a Web-based display that shows an acceptable way to tell Nick that input to his system was accepted.
9. Design a feedback form for Nick's restaurant customers using an ecommerce Web site.
10. Write six different queries for the file in Problem 1 in Chapter 13.
11. Write six different queries for the 3NF relation in Problem 6 in Chapter 13.
12. Design a search that will find potential competitors of a company such as World's Trend on the Web. Assume you are the customer.
13. Search for World's Trend's potential competitors on the Web. (You won't find World's Trend itself on the Web. It is a fictional company.) Make a list of those you've found.

GROUP PROJECTS

1. With your group members, create a pull-down menu for an employment agency that matches professional candidates to position openings. Include a list of keystrokes that would directly invoke the menu options using the Alt-X format. The menu has the following options:

   Add employee
   Change employee
   Delete employee
   Employee inquiry
   Position inquiry
   Employer inquiry
   Add employer
   Change employer
   Delete employer
   Match employee to opening
   Print open positions report
   Print successful matches report
   Add position
   Change position
   Delete position

2. In a paragraph, describe the problems your group faced in creating this menu.
3. The drag-and-drop feature is used in GUIs and allows the user to move sentences around in a word processing package. As a group, suggest how drag and drop can be used to its fullest potential in the following applications:
   a. Project management software (Chapter 3).
   b. Relational database program (Chapter 13).
   c. Display or forms designer (Chapter 12).
   d. Spreadsheet program (Chapter 10).
   e. CASE tool for drawing data flow diagrams (Chapter 7).
   f. Fax program (Chapter 11).
   g. File management program (Chapter 14).
   h. Personal digital assistant (PDA) calendar (Chapter 3).
   i. Illustration in a drawing package (Chapter 10).
   j. CASE tool for developing data dictionaries (Chapter 8).
   k. Decision tree drawing program (Chapter 9).
   l. Web site for collecting consumer opinions on new products (Chapter 11).
   m. Organizing bookmarks for Web sites.

   For each solution your group designs, draw the display and show movement by using an arrow.

4. Ask all the members of your group to request a search based on their leisure activities. If there are four people in your group, there will be four unique searches to perform. Now go ahead and do all the searches. Compare your results. Does the person who is involved with the activity have an advantage over the people who know less about it? Explain.
5. Look at the following mashup Web sites and describe how each of them adds value by providing a service.
   a. Aboutairportparking.com, http://www.aboutairportparking.com/
   b. Baebo, http://baebo.francisshanahan.com/
   c. Bogozo, http://www.bogozo.com/house/?new+york.
   d. Global Incident Map, http://www.globalincidentmap.com/home.php
   e. Hawkee Social Price Comparison, http://www.hawkee.com/
   f. Homethinking, http://www.homethinking.com/
   g. mpire, http://www.mpire.com/buyer/search.page
   h. Streeteasy, http://www.streeteasy.com/
6. The following two mashups have political agendas. Suggest three other mashups that attempt to change something by appealing to the public. Health Care That Works, http://www.healthcarethatworks.org/maps/nyc/ On NY Turf, http://www.onnyturf.com/citycouncil/freedomzones/
7. Try these mashups just for fun.
   a. The Geography of Seinfeld, http://www.stolasgeospatial.com/seinfeld.htm
   b. HBO: The Sopranos, http://www.hbo.com/sopranos/map/
   c. Dig to the Other Side, http://map.pequenopolis.com/
   d. PlotShot, http://www.plotshot.com/
   e. Flickr Sudoku, http://flickrsudoku.com/
   f. liveplasma.com, http://www.liveplasma.com
   g. Ms. Dewey http://www.msdewey.com/

SELECTED BIBLIOGRAPHY

Adam, A., and D. Kreps. "Web Accessibility: A Digital Divide for Disabled People?" In *Societal and Organizational Implications for Information Systems,* IFIP International Federation for Information Processing, Vol. 208, edited by E. Trauth, D. Howcraft, T. Butler, B. Fitzgerald, and J. DeGross, pp. 217–228. Boston: Springer, 2006.

Barki, H., and J. Hartwick. "Measuring User Participation, User Involvement, and User Attitude." *MIS Quarterly,* Vol. 18, No. 1, 1994, pp. 59–82.

Berstel, J., S. C. Reghizzi, G. Roussel, and P. San Pietro. "A Scalable Formal Method for Design and Automatic Checking of User Interfaces." *ACM Transactions on Software Engineering and Methodology,* Vol. 14, No. 2, April 2005, pp. 124–167.

Bort, J. "Navigation: An Art for E-Com Sites." Microtimes.com, Issue 201, December 1999. Available at <microtimes.com/201/ecombort201a.html>. Last accessed February 9, 2001.

Butler, T., and B. Fitzgerald. "A Case Study of User Participation in the Information Systems Development Process." In *Proceedings of the Eighteenth International Conference on Information Systems,* pp. 411–426. Atlanta, GA: ICIS, 1997.

Carey, J., D. Galletta, J. Kim, D. Te'eni, B. Wildemuth, and P. Zhang. "The Role of Human–Computer Interaction in Management Information Systems Curicula: A Call to Action." *Communications of the Association for Information Systems,* Vol. 13, 2004, pp. 357–379.

Davis, F. "Perceived Usefulness, Perceived Ease of Use, and User Acceptance of Information Technology." *MIS Quarterly,* Vol. 13, No. 3, 1989, pp. 319–340.

Davis, G. B., and M. H. Olson. *Management Information Systems: Conceptual Foundations, Structure, and Development.* New York: McGraw-Hill, 1985.

Hornbaek, K., and E. Frokjaer. "Comparing Usability Problems and Redesign Proposals as Input to Practical Systems Development." *CHI 2005*, April 2–7, 2005, pp. 391–400.

Laudon, K. C., and J. P. Laudon. *Management Information Systems*, 9th ed. Upper Saddle River, NJ: Prentice-Hall, 2005.

Mantei, M. M., and Teorey, T. J. "Incorporating Behavioral Techniques in the System Development Lifecycle." *MIS Quarterly*, Vol. 13, No. 3, September 1989. pp. 257–267.

Nielsen, J., R. Molich, C. Snyder, and S. Farrell. *E-Commerce User Experience.* Fremont, CA: Norman Nielsen Group, 2001.

Nielsen, J., and R. L. Mack. *Usability Inspection Methods.* New York: John Wiley, 1994.

Rubin, J. *Handbook of Usability Testing.* New York: John Wiley, 1994.

Sano, D. *Designing Large-Scale Web Sites: A Visual Design Methodology.* New York: John Wiley, 1996.

Schneiderman, B., and C. Plaisant. *Designing the User Interface: Strategies for Effective Human–Computer Interaction.* New York: Addison-Wesley, 2005.

Te'eni, D., J. Carey, and P. Zhang. *Human Computer Interaction: Developing Effective Organizational Systems.* New York: John Wiley, 2007.

U.S. Department of Health and Human Services. "Usability Guide" (for developing Web sites). Available at www.usability.gov. Last accessed August 7, 2006.

U.S. Equal Employment Opportunity Commission Web site listing employer obligations under the Americans with Disabilities Act. Available at www.eeoc.gov/types/ada.html. Last accessed September 24, 2006.

UsabilityNet. "Overview of the User Centred Design Process." Available at: http://www.usabilitynet.org/management/b_overview.htm. Last accessed August 6, 2006.

Venkatesh, V., M. G. Morris, G. B. Davis, and F. D. Davis. "User Acceptance of Information Technology: Toward a Unified View." *MIS Quarterly*, Vol. 27, No. 3, pp. 425–478.

Zhang, P., J. Carey, D. Te'eni, and M. Tremeaine. "Integrating Human–Computer Interaction Development into the Systems Development Life Cycle: A Methodology." *Communications of the Association for Information Systems*, Vol. 15, 2005, pp. 512–543.

ALLEN SCHMIDT, JULIE E. KENDALL, AND KENNETH E. KENDALL

UP TO THE USERS

"Let's take our prototypes and some new displays, reports, and forms to create the final user interface," Anna says to Chip.

"It's about time, isn't it?" replies Chip. He was all too aware of the importance of designing a good interface.

After talking, they set up the following display dialog guidelines:

1. Well-designed displays should:
    - Communicate actions and intentions clearly to users.
    - Show options available to operators. Examples are:
        - MAKE CORRECTIONS OR PRESS ESC TO CANCEL
        - ENTER HARDWARE INVENTORY NUMBER
        - PRESS ENTER KEY
        - PRESS ENTER TO CONFIRM DELETE, ESC TO CANCEL
        - Buttons that say OK or Cancel
    - Standardize use of any abbreviations.
    - Avoid the use of codes, substituting the code meaning.
    - Provide help screens for complicated portions of the dialog.
    - Provide tool-tip help for toolbar icons.
2. Feedback should be provided to the users. Feedback includes:
    - Titles to show the current page.
    - Actions successfully completed messages, such as:
        - RECORD HAS BEEN ADDED
        - RECORD HAS BEEN CHANGED
    - Error messages. Examples are:
        - INVALID DATE
        - CHECKDIGIT IS INVALID
        - SOFTWARE IS NOT ON FILE
    - An invalid data dialog box, with an OK button on a graphical user interface display.
    - Processing delay messages similar to:
        - PLEASE WAIT—REPORT IS BEING PRODUCED
    - An hourglass turning upside down on a graphical user interface.
3. There should be consistency in the design, including:
    - Location of the OPERATOR MESSAGE or FEEDBACK MESSAGE on the bottom of the display or in the status line area.
    - Date, time, system name, and display reference number appearing in heading lines.
    - Consistent exit of all displays, such as through the use of the same function key.
    - Standard use of keys, such as PgDn and PgUp, to display a next or previous page in a multiple-page display.
    - Consistent method of canceling an operation, such as through the use of the Escape key (Esc).
    - Standardized use of color and high-intensity display, such as all error messages appearing in red.
    - Standardized use of icons on a GUI display.
    - Standardized pull-down menus on a GUI display.

4. Minimum operator actions should be required to use the system. Some examples are:
   The use of Y and N as yes and no replies. The use of the plus (+) and minus (−) signs on the number pad as a substitute for Y and N.
   When changing or deleting records, only the record key need be specified. The system would obtain the record and display pertinent information.
   When names are required as key entries, only the first few letters of the name need be entered. The program should find all matching record key names and present them for selection by the operator.
   Data entry displays should allow the entry of codes.
   All numeric entries may omit leading zeros, commas, or a decimal point.
   As each data field is completed, the cursor should advance to the next entry field.
   After each option is completed, the same display, with blank entry areas, should be redisplayed until the Exit key is pressed.
   When an option is exited, the previous menu should be displayed.
   Drop-down list boxes should be used whenever possible on GUI displays.
   Check boxes and radio buttons should be used to make selections whenever possible.
   Default buttons should be outlined so that the user can press the Enter key to select them.
5. Data entering the system should be validated. Guidelines are:
   Specific fields should be verified according to edit criteria.
   As errors are detected, operators should be given a chance either to correct the error or to cancel the transaction.
   When no errors have been detected in a transaction, the entry should be presented to the operator for visual confirmation. The operator should have the opportunity either to accept it or to make corrections to the data entered.

Upon examining the many displays and reports (over 30 in all), Chip and Anna decide to split the menu into several functions. "How do we divide these various functions into a set of menus?" asked Chip.

"Why don't we use a decomposition diagram to organize the functions into a hierarchy," replied Anna. Chip and Anna begin working on the diagram. The menu interactions will be represented in a hierarchical structure, with options shown as rectangles and the overall menu represented by the rectangle on the top. Each secondary menu will be shown beneath the primary menu, with screen programs at the lowest level. The main menu will have six main choices, as illustrated in Figure E14.1: (1) **Update Software,** (2) **Update Hardware,** (3) **Inquiry,** (4) **Modify Codes,** (5) **Training,** and (6) **Report.** Each of these options is further subdivided into smaller menus or individual functions. The Inquiry Menu is subdivided into two smaller menus, **Software Options** and Hardware **Options,** as well as options for running the **Software Expert Inquiry** and the **Printer Location Inquiry.**

The rectangles on the functional decomposition diagram are implemented using a series of pull-down menu lists, which are shown in Figure E14.2. Notice that the Inquiry menu has functions corresponding to the rectangles on the previous figure. A row of buttons for common functions is included below the menus. The menu functions are included as a set of buttons in the main area of the screen, and these buttons may be clicked to run corresponding programs. It was decided that the **Add Computer,**

14

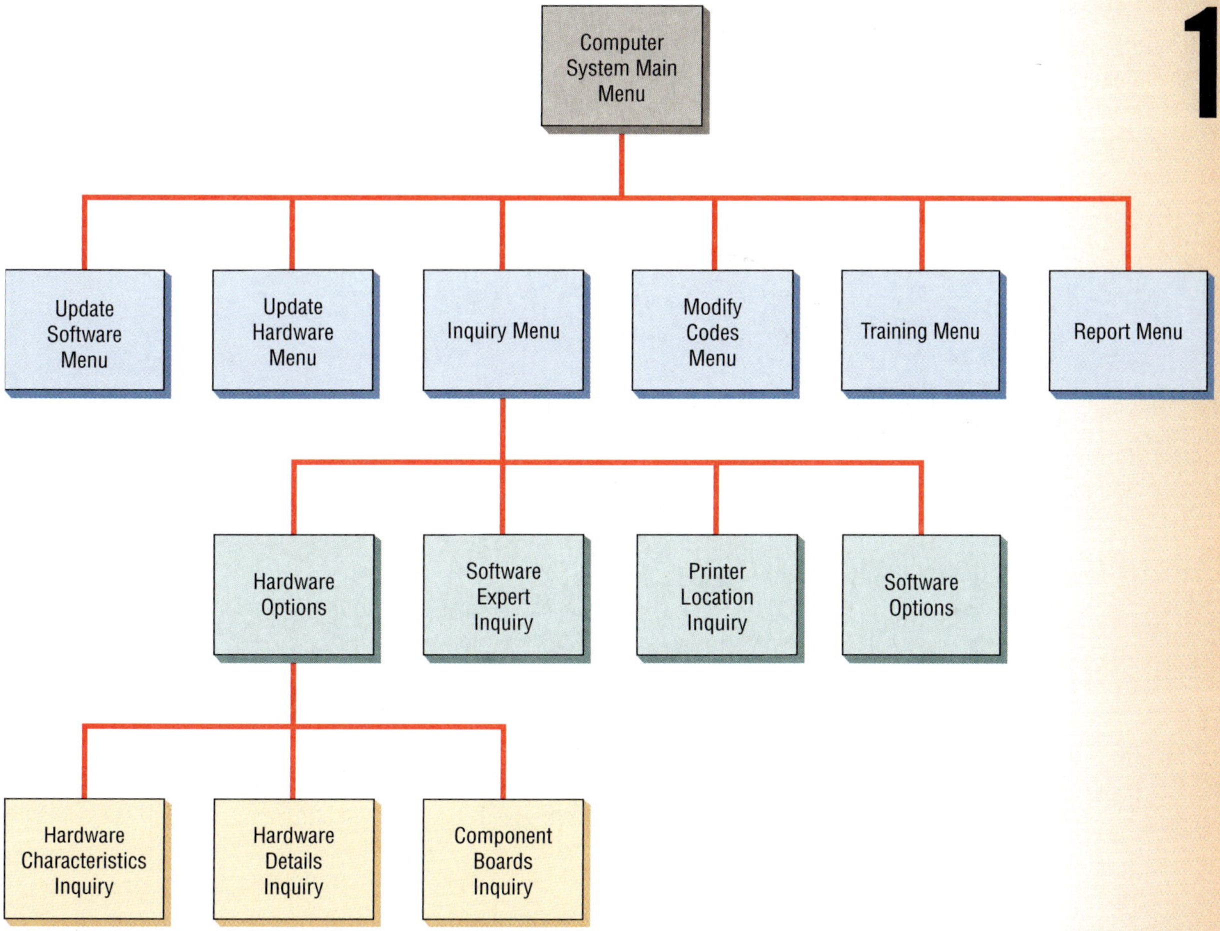

FIGURE E14.1
Screen hierarchy for the computer system.

Add Software Package, and **Change Computer** programs would be run directly from the main menu. Clicking the other buttons causes selection dialog boxes to display, with choices for selecting programs. Figure E14.3 shows the dialog box for the **Reports** option. All the reports are listed, with **Print Preview, Print,** and **Close Form** buttons for selecting actions.

"Here's what I think the guidelines for the update programs should be," Anna tells Chip. "The key focus is on accuracy, with comprehensive editing for each data field. Add programs will display an entry page and allow either hardware or software records to be created. After all entries are complete, a user should double-check the data and click the **Add Software Record** button. Any data that are already in the system should be implemented using drop-down lists. There are also buttons to undo changes, move to different records, print the record, save the changes, and exit the page. A record could be added only if the primary key for the record does not already exist.

"Delete displays must have a simple, primary key entry, such as the COURSE DESCRIPTION in the DELETE SOFTWARE COURSE display," Anna continues.

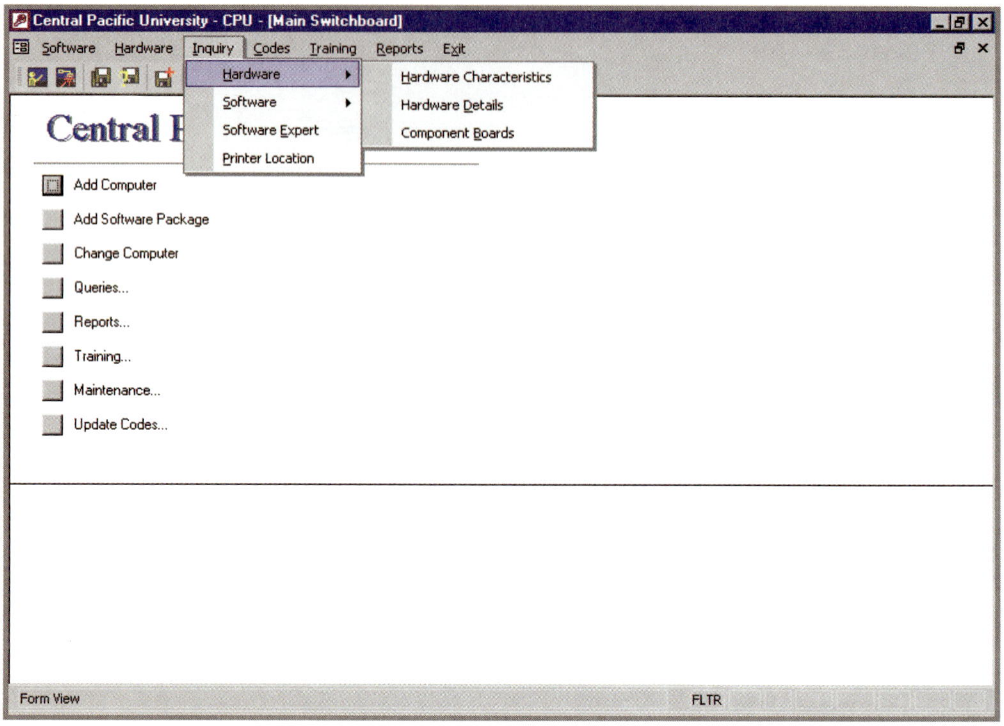

FIGURE E14.2
The main menu for the computer system.

The DELETE SOFTWARE COURSE display uses a Find button (the binoculars) to help locate the desired record. The corresponding record is read and the information is displayed. Users click the Delete button and are prompted to confirm the delete. If the user clicks Cancel, the delete action is canceled. How does all that sound?" she asks Chip.

"So far, so good," he replies. "Anything about onscreen change displays?"

"Yes. They have a primary key for the record entered and the matching record read. Record information is to be displayed that allows the operator to overtype the data with changes. All changes are to be validated with full editing. When all change fields are valid, the user must click a button to save the changes. Is that clear enough for the user?" Anna asks.

"I think it's very good," Chip acknowledges.

Chip is responsible for the inquiry portion of the system. The focus on these programs is speed. A short entry is obtained from the user, and the corresponding records are read. Information is formatted for maximum communication and displayed. "I've met with various users," he tells Anna. "Here's a list of inquiry programs." Each of the inquiry displays is designed, along with the database tables needed and possible errors that could occur.

"The first display I designed was the HARDWARE INQUIRY," Chip continues. "I used the description of the display that we had put into the Visible Analyst repository after the prototypes had been created." The **Notes** area contains information about how it should operate. An INVENTORY NUMBER or partial INVENTORY

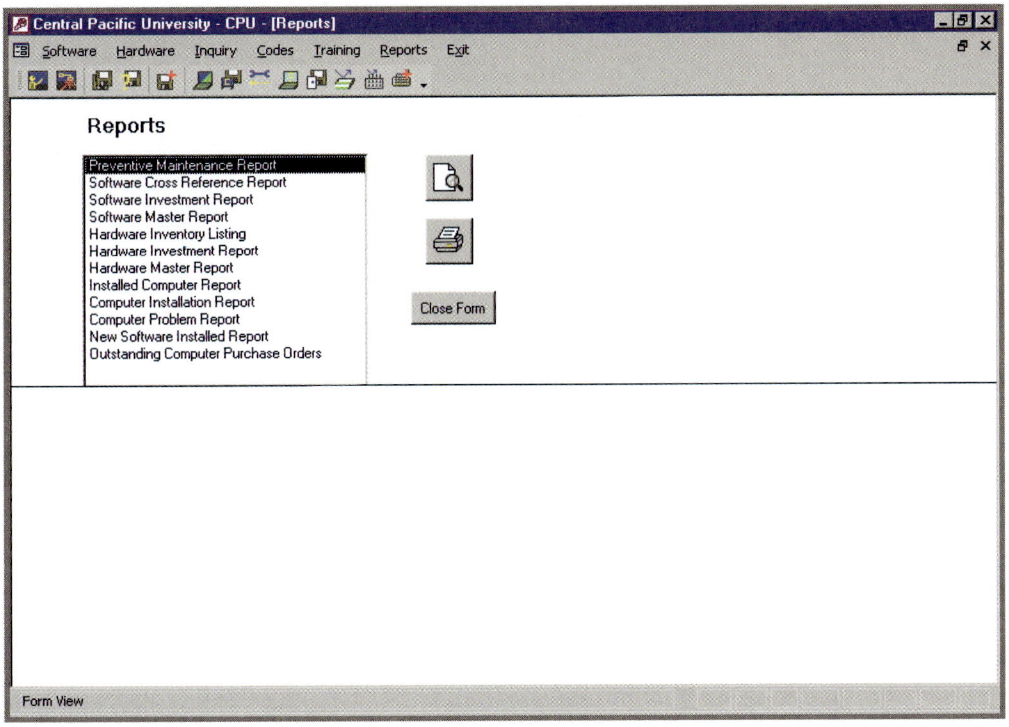

FIGURE E14.3
A dialog box for the computer system report menu.

NUMBER should be entered. The first matching record is read (in the case of a partial INVENTORY NUMBER), and the user can scroll to the next record or to previous records.

"I produced a rough layout and met with Dot to obtain feedback on the design," Chip says. "After pointing out some minor corrections, she mentioned that the maintenance details should be included, providing complete information for each computer."

The program logic is to use the HARDWARE INVENTORY NUMBER as the entry field of a **Parameter Value** dialog box (illustrated in Figure E14.4), with the starting number of 3 entered. The record is searched for in the database. If it is not found, a message is displayed. Once the record is located, the matching board records are read. Board records contain a code for the type of board, and the BOARD CODE TABLE is searched for the matching code. The meaning of the code is formatted on the screen. The resulting display is shown in Figure E14.5. Notice that there are buttons for printing the current record on the form and closing the form. The **New Inventory Number** button redisplays the **Parameter Entry** dialog box, and it allows the user to choose a new record.

"I selected the SOFTWARE LOCATION inquiry as the next display to develop," Chip tells Anna. "After talking at length with Cher, I produced the details and documented them in the Visible Analyst repository. The entry field is a partial software TITLE, entered in a Parameter Value dialog box. The first record matching the partial TITLE is displayed, and, because there are different operating systems and versions of

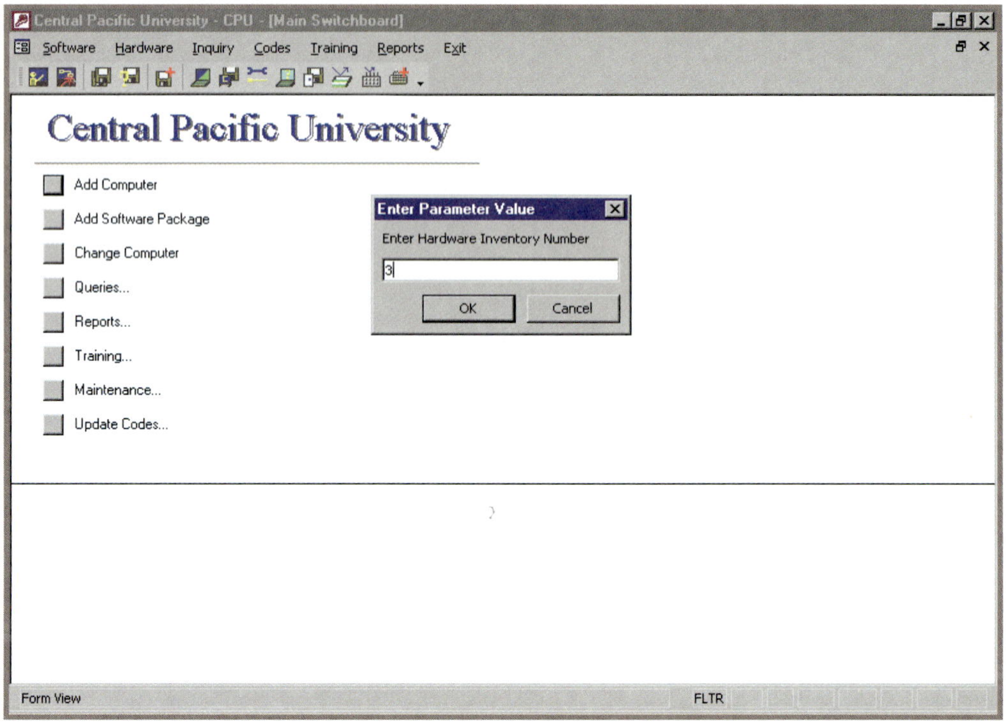

FIGURE E14.4

HARDWARE INVENTORY NUMBER parameter value dialog box.

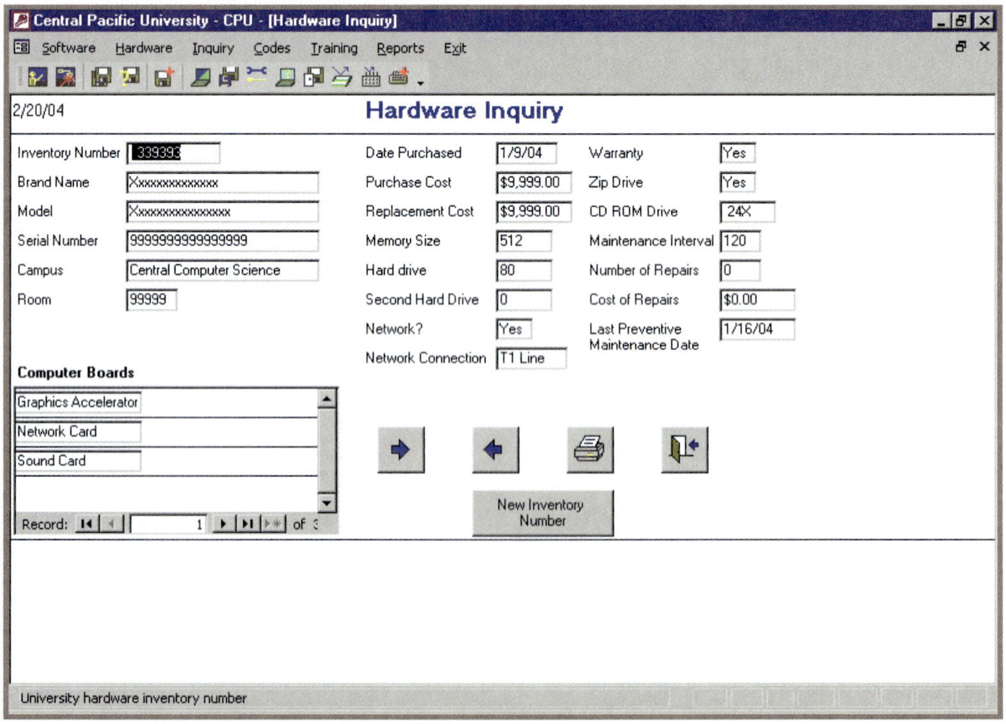

FIGURE E14.5

HARDWARE INVENTORY NUMBER inquiry screen as represented in Microsoft Access.

the software, the user can click buttons to advance to the next (or previous) record. Five columns of information are displayed: HARDWARE INVENTORY NUMBER, BRAND NAME, MODEL, CAMPUS, and ROOM. Cher can quickly locate a machine containing the desired software. She seems to be happy with this idea so far," Chip adds.

The program locates the SOFTWARE MASTER record using the alternate key TITLE. If the matching record is not found, an error message is displayed. Because there may be several versions, the Next Record button may be clicked until the correct OPERATING SYSTEM and VERSION NUMBER are obtained.

Once the correct software has been obtained, the relational file is used to find the matching SOFTWARE INVENTORY NUMBER. This relational file contains the SOFTWARE INVENTORY NUMBER and the matching HARDWARE INVENTORY NUMBER, which is used to locate the matching record in the COMPUTER MASTER. For each matching machine, the CAMPUS table is used to locate the CAMPUS LOCATION code and to display the matching CAMPUS DESCRIPTION. The area for displaying the machines containing the software is a scroll region, because it may contain more machines than will fit on a single screen.

"I think we've got a good start on designing our user interfaces," Anna comments. Chip nods in agreement.

EXERCISES

E-1. Use Microsoft Access to view the menu options for the computer system.

E-2. Examine the HARDWARE INQUIRY. Explain the inquiry type using the value, entity, and attribute (*V*, *E*, *A*) notation.

E-3. In a paragraph, explain why a data entry display should emphasize accuracy, whereas an inquiry display emphasizes how fast results may be displayed.

E-4. Modify and print the hierarchy chart representing the **Update Hardware** menu. Add rectangles to represent the following menu options:

CHANGE COMPUTER
DELETE COMPUTER RECORD
UPDATE INSTALLED COMPUTER

E-5. Use the **Functional Decomposition** feature of Visible Analyst to draw a hierarchy chart representing the options found on the **Update Software** menu. Start with the top rectangle representing the **Update Software** menu.

ADD SOFTWARE PACKAGE
CHANGE SOFTWARE RECORD
DELETE SOFTWARE RECORD
UPGRADE SOFTWARE PACKAGE

E-6. Chip and Anna realize that the menu that has been designed is for the users involved in the installation and maintenance of computer hardware and software. This menu would not be suitable for general faculty and staff members, because they should not have the ability to update the records. Design a menu, either on paper or using software with which you are familiar, that would provide the general user with the ability to perform inquiries and reports.

The exercises preceded by a Web icon indicate value-added material is available from the Web site at www.prenhall.com/kendall. Students can download a sample Visible Analyst Project and a Microsoft Access database that can be used to complete the exercises. Visible Analyst software can be packaged with this text for an additional fee.

E-7. Discuss in a paragraph why the users would need to move to another page (by pressing the **Next Record** button) to display the correct record for the SOFTWARE LOCATION inquiry.

E-8. Design the SOFTWARE DETAILS inquiry display. The entry field is SOFTWARE INVENTORY NUMBER, and all software information, with the exception of EXPERT and MACHINES INSTALLED ON, should be displayed. Refer to the Visible Analyst SOFTWARE DETAILS data flow repository entry.

E-9. When scheduling classrooms for student use, Cher Ware needs to know all the software packages in a given room. She would like to enter the CAMPUS LOCATION and the ROOM on an inquiry display. The fields would be TITLE, VERSION, SITE LICENSE, and NUMBER OF COPIES.

Design the SOFTWARE BY ROOM inquiry, which is described as a data flow in the Visible Analyst repository.

E-10. Mike Crowe needs to know which component boards are installed in each machine. Use Visible Analyst to view the data flow entry for COMPONENT BOARD and to design the COMPONENT BOARD inquiry. The input field is the HARDWARE INVENTORY NUMBER. Output fields are BRAND NAME, MODEL, and a scroll region for BOARD. The logic is to read the COMPUTER MASTER using the HARDWARE INVENTORY NUMBER. If the record is not found, display an error message to that effect. Find the matching BOARD records. Use value, entity, and attribute (*V*, *E*, *A*) notation for the type of inquiry.

E-11. Every so often, Hy Perteks receives a request for help concerning a given software package. Staff members and students need to perform advanced options or transfer data to and from different packages, and they are having difficulties. Hy would like to enter the software TITLE and VERSION NUMBER. The resulting display would show the SOFTWARE EXPERT NAME and his or her CAMPUS LOCATION and ROOM NUMBER. Design the screen for the LOCATE SOFTWARE EXPERT inquiry. Describe the logic and files needed to produce the inquiry. Use value, entity, and attribute (*V*, *E*, *A*) notation for this inquiry. The details for this inquiry are included in the Visible Analyst SOFTWARE EXPERT data flow repository entry.

E-12. In a follow-up interview with Cher Ware, it was determined that she needs to know what machines are available to install any software package, given the package's graphics requirements. Produce an inquiry that would allow Cher to enter the DISPLAY CODE and, optionally, a GRAPHICS BOARD and CAMPUS LOCATION for the software. Four columns should be displayed:

HARDWARE INVENTORY NUMBER
CAMPUS LOCATION
ROOM LOCATION
GRAPHICS BOARD

Refer to the Visible Analyst MONITOR REQUIRED data flow. Write a paragraph describing the logic involved in obtaining the results. Include the type of inquiry using value, entity, and attribute (*V*, *E*, *A*) notation.

E-13. Both Cher and Hy expressed an interest in finding machines of a specified brand connected to different printers. Sometimes the engineering students need a plotter, whereas other situations demand a color laser or portable printer.

Design an inquiry that would have the PRINTER and BRAND NAME of the computer as input fields. Output would be two columns: CAMPUS LOCATION (full name, not a code) and ROOM LOCATION. Refer to the Visible Analyst PRINTER LOCATION data flow.

Briefly describe the logic used in producing the output. Would this inquiry need a scroll region to display all the information? Why or why not? Use a paragraph to describe the type of inquiry using value, entity, and attribute (*V*, *E*, *A*) notation.

E-14. Hy receives a number of requests for training classes. He would like to plan training and place the upcoming classes on the intranet so that faculty would have an adequate amount of lead time to schedule a class. Design the SOFTWARE TRAINING CLASSES inquiry. The details may be found in the Visible Analyst data flow repository entry called SOFTWARE TRAINING CLASSES.

15

DESIGNING ACCURATE DATA ENTRY PROCEDURES

LEARNING OBJECTIVES

Once you have mastered the material in this chapter you will be able to:

1. **Understand the uses of effective coding to support users in acomplishing their tasks.**
2. **Design effective and efficient data capture approaches for people and systems.**
3. **Recognize how to ensure data quality through validation.**
4. **Articulate accuracy advantages of user input on ecommerce Web sites.**

Making sure that users are able to enter data into the system accurately is of utmost importance. It is by now axiomatic that the quality of data input determines the quality of information output. The systems analyst can support accurate data entry through the achievement of four broad objectives: (1) creating meaningful coding for data, (2) designing efficient data capture approaches, (3) assuring complete and effective data capture, and (4) assuring data quality through validation.

The quality of data is a measurement of how consistently correct the data are within certain preset limits. Effectively coded data facilitate accurate data entry by humans through cutting down on the sheer quantity of data, and thus the time required to enter the information.

When users enter data efficiently, data entry is meeting predetermined performance measures that give the relationship between the time spent on entry and the number of data items entered. Effective coding, effective and efficient data capture and entry, and ensuring data quality through validation procedures are all data entry objectives covered in this chapter.

EFFECTIVE CODING

One of the ways that data can be entered more accurately and efficiently is through the knowledgeable employment of various codes. The process of putting ambiguous or cumbersome data into short, easily entered digits or letters is called coding (not to be confused with program coding).

Coding aids the systems analyst in reaching the objective of efficiency, because data that are coded require less time for people to enter, and thus reduce the number of items entered. Coding can also help in the appropriate sorting of data at a later point in the data transformation process. In addition, coded data can save valuable memory and storage space. In sum, coding is a way of being eloquent but succinct in capturing data. Besides providing accuracy and efficiency, codes should have a purpose that supports users. Specific types of codes allow us to treat data in a particular manner. Human purposes for coding include the following:

1. Keeping track of something.
2. Classifying information.
3. Concealing information.
4. Revealing information.
5. Requesting appropriate action.

Each of these purposes for coding is discussed in the following sections, along with some example of codes.

KEEPING TRACK OF SOMETHING

Sometimes we want merely to identify a person, place, or thing just to keep track of it. For example, a shop that manufactures custom-made upholstered furniture needs to assign a job number to a project. The salesperson needs to know the name and address of the customer, but the job shop manager or the workers who assemble the furniture need not know who the customer is. Consequently, an arbitrary number is assigned to the job. The number can be either random or sequential, as described in the following subsection.

Simple Sequence Codes The simple sequence code is a number that is assigned to something if it needs to be numbered. It therefore has no relation to the data themselves. Figure 15.1 shows how a furniture manufacturer's orders are assigned an order number. With this easy reference number, the company can keep track of the order in process. It is more efficient to enter job "5676" than "that brown and black rocking chair with the leather seat for Arthur Hook, Jr."

Using a sequence code rather than a random number has some advantages. First, it eliminates the possibility of assigning the same number. Second, it gives users an approximation of when the order was received.

Sequence codes should be used when the order of processing requires knowledge of the sequence in which items enter the system or the order in which events unfold. An example is found in the situation of a bank running a special promotion that makes it important to know when a person applied for a special, low-interest home loan, because (all other things being equal) the special mortgage loans will be granted on a first-come, first-served basis. In this case, assigning a correct sequence code to each applicant is important.

Alphabetic Derivation Codes At times it is undesirable to use sequence codes. The most obvious instance is when you do *not* wish to have someone read the code to figure out how many numbers have been assigned. Another situation in which sequence codes may not be useful is when a more complex code is desirable to avoid

FIGURE 15.1
Using a simple sequence code to indicate the sequence in which orders enter a custom furniture shop.

Order #	Product	Customer
5676	Rocking Chair/with Leather	Arthur Hook, Jr.
5677	Dining Room Chair/Upholstered	Millie Monice
5678	Love Seat/Upholstered	J. & D. Pare
5679	Child's Rocking Chair/Decals	Lucinda Morely

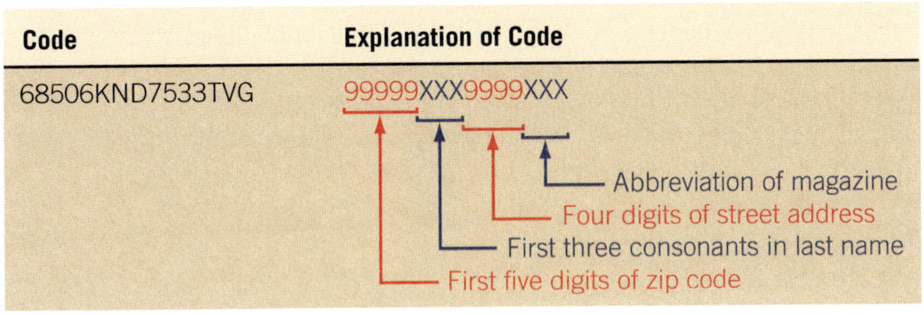

FIGURE 15.2
Identifying the account of a magazine subscriber with an alphabetic derivation code.

a costly mistake. One possible error would be to add a payment to account 223 when you meant to add it to account 224, because you entered an incorrect digit.

The alphabetic derivation code is a commonly used approach in identifying an account number. The example in Figure 15.2 comes from a mailing label for a magazine. The code becomes the account number. The first five digits come from the first five digits of the subscriber's zip code, the next three are the first three consonants in the subscriber's name, the next four numbers are from the street address, and the last three make up the code for the magazine. The main purpose of this code is to identify an account.

A secondary purpose is to print mailing labels. When designing this code, the zip code is the first part of the account number. The subscriber records are usually updated only once a year, but the primary purpose of the records is to print mailing labels once a month or once per week. Having the zip code as the first part of a primary key field means that the records do not have to be sorted by zip code for bulk mailing, because records on a file are stored in primary key sequence. Notice that the expiration date is not part of the account number, because that number can change more frequently than the other data.

One disadvantage of an alphabetic derivation code occurs when the alphabetic portion is small (for example, the name Po) or when the name contains fewer consonants than the code requires. The name Roe has only one consonant and would have to be derived as RXX, or derived using some other scheme. Another disadvantage is that some of the data may change. Changing one's address or name would change the primary key for the file.

CLASSIFYING INFORMATION

Classification affords the ability to distinguish among classes of items. Classifications are necessary for many purposes, such as reflecting what parts of a medical insurance plan an employee carries, or showing which student has completed the core requirements of his or her coursework.

To be useful, classes must be mutually exclusive. For example, if a student is in class F, meaning freshman, having completed 0 to 36 credit hours, he or she should not also be classifiable as a sophomore (S). Overlapping classes would be F = 0 – 36 credit hours, S = 32 – 64 credit hours, and so on. Data are unclear and not as readily interpretable when coding classes are not mutually exclusive.

Classification Codes Classification codes are used to distinguish one group of data with special characteristics from another. Classification codes can consist of either a single letter or a number. They are a shorthand way of describing a person, place, thing, or event.

Classification codes are listed in manuals or posted so that users can locate them easily. Many times, users become so familiar with frequently used codes that they memorize them. A user classifies an item and then enters its code directly into the terminal of an online system or onto a source document of a batch system.

FIGURE 15.3

Grouping tax-deductible items through the use of a one-letter classification code.

Code	Tax-Deductible Item
I	Interest Payments
M	Medical Payments
T	Taxes
C	Contributions
D	Dues
S	Supplies

An example of classification coding is the way you may wish to group tax-deductible items for the purpose of completing your income taxes. Figure 15.3 shows how codes are developed for items such as interest, medical payments, contributions, and so on. The coding system is simple: Take the first letter of each of the categories; contributions are C, interest payments are I, and supplies are S.

All goes well until we get to other categories (such as computer items, insurance payments, and subscriptions) that begin with the same letters we used previously. Figure 15.4 demonstrates what happens in this case. The coding was stretched so that we could use P for "comPuter," N for "iNsurance," and B for "suBscriptions." Obviously, this situation is far from perfect. One way to avoid this type of confusion is to allow for codes longer than one letter, discussed later in this chapter under the subheading of mnemonic codes. Pull-down menus in a GUI system often use classification codes as a shortcut for running menu features, such as **Alt-F** for the **File** menu.

Block Sequence Codes Earlier we discussed sequence codes. The block sequence code is an extension of the sequence code. Figure 15.5 shows how a business user assigns numbers to computer software. Main categories of software are browser packages, database packages, word processing packages, and presentation packages. These were assigned sequential numbers in the following "blocks," or ranges: browser, 100–199; database, 200–299; and so forth. The advantage of the block sequence code is that the data are grouped according to common characteristics, but still take advantage of the simplicity of assigning the next available number (within the block, of course) to the next item needing identification.

FIGURE 15.4

Problems in using a one-letter classification code occur when categories share the same letter.

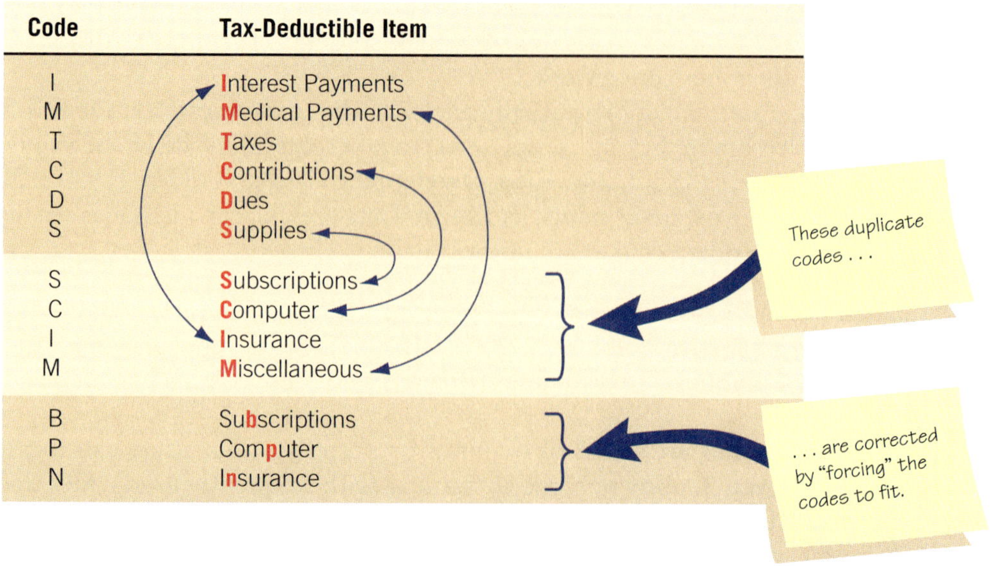

Code	Name of Software Package	Type
100	Netscape	Browser
101	Internet Explorer	
102	Lynx	
⋮	⋮	
200	Access	Database
201	Paradox	
202	Oracle	
⋮	⋮	
300	Microsoft Word	Word Processing
301	WordPerfect	
⋮	⋮	
400	Astound	Presentation
401	Micrografx Designer	
402	PowerPoint	

FIGURE 15.5
Using a block sequence code to group similar software packages.

CONCEALING INFORMATION

Codes may be used to conceal or disguise information we do not wish others to know. There are many reasons why a business user may want to do that. For example, a corporation may not want information in a personnel file to be accessed by data entry workers. A store may want its salespeople to know the wholesale price to show them how low a price they can negotiate, but they may encode it on price tickets to prevent customers from finding that out. A restaurant may want to capture information about the service without letting the customer know the name of the server. Concealing information and security have become very important in the last few years. Corporations have started to allow vendors and customers to access their databases directly, and handling business transactions over the Internet has made it necessary to develop tight encryption schemes. The following subsection describes an example of concealing information through codes.

Cipher Codes Perhaps the simplest coding method is the direct substitution of one letter for another, one number for another, or one letter for a number. A popular type of puzzle called a cryptogram is an example of letter substitution. Figure 15.6 is an example of a cipher code taken from a Buffalo, New York, department store that coded all markdown prices with the words BLEACH MIND. No

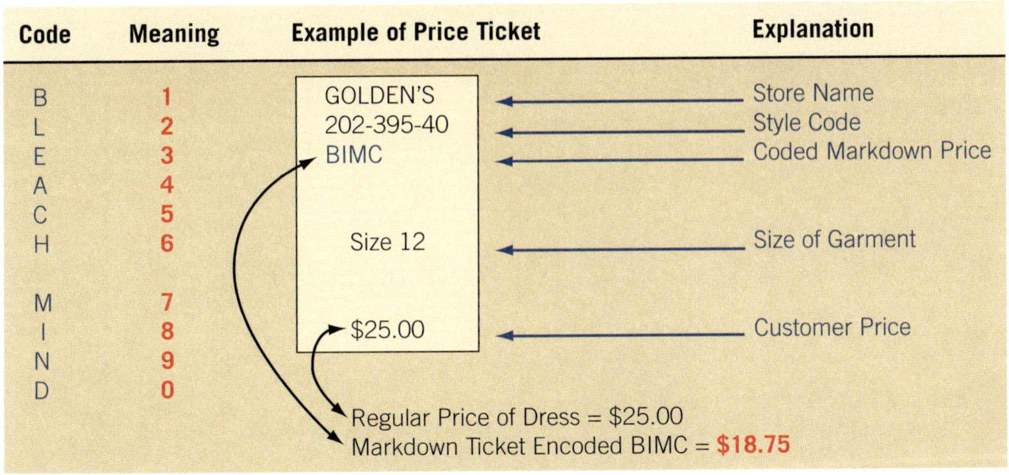

FIGURE 15.6
Encoding markdown prices with a cipher code is a way of concealing price information from customers.

one really remembered why whose words were chosen, but all the employees knew them by heart, and so the cipher code was successful. Notice in this figure that an item with a retail price of $25.00 would have a markdown price of BIMC, or $18.75 when decoded letter by letter.

REVEALING INFORMATION

Sometimes it is desirable to reveal information to specific users through a code. In a clothing store, information about the department, product, color, and size is printed along with the price on the ticket for each item. This information helps the salespeople and stockpeople locate the place for the merchandise.

Another reason for revealing information through codes is to make the data entry more meaningful for humans. A familiar part number, name, or description supports more accurate data entry. The examples of codes in the following subsection explain how these concepts can be realized.

Significant-Digit Subset Codes When it is possible to describe a product by virtue of its membership in many subgroups, we can use a significant-digit subset code to help describe it. The clothing store price ticket example in Figure 15.7 is an example of an effective significant-digit subset code.

To the casual observer or customer, the item description appears to be one long number. To one of the salespeople, however, the number is made up of a few smaller numbers, each one having a meaning of its own. The first three digits represent the department, the next three the product, the next two the color, and the last two the size.

FIGURE 15.7
Using a significant-digit subset code helps employees locate items belonging to a particular department.

Code	Merchandise Described	Explanation of Code
2023954010	Red maternity dress, style 395, size 10	202 — 395 — 40 — 10 202: Department (Maternity) 395: Product (Dress Style 395) 40: Color (Red) 10: Size (Size 10)
4142191912	Beige winter coat, style 219, size 12	414 — 219 — 19 — 12 414: Department (Winter Coats) 219: Product (Coat Style 219) 19: Color (Beige) 12: Size (Size 12)

Significant-digit subset codes may consist of either information that actually describes the product (for example, the number 10 means size 10), or numbers that are arbitrarily assigned (for instance, 202 is assigned to mean the maternity department). In this case, the advantage of using a significant-digit subset code is that it makes it possible to locate items that belong to a certain group or class. For example, if the store's manager decided to mark down all winter merchandise for an upcoming sale, salespeople could locate all items belonging to departments 310 through 449, the block of codes used to designate "winter" in general.

Another advantage of using significant-digit subset codes is that inquiries may be performed on a portion of the code. Using the example illustrated in Figure 15.7, a salesperson might look for other matching red items, for other items in size 10, for other maternity items, or for similar dresses with the same style. This code is also very useful for marketing a product. Internet businesses often recommend products that they think a customer might like. For example, if a customer purchased a certain type of music, a Web site might recommend other music in the genre. When a customer purchases a certain type of book, a Web site might recommend other titles that have the same author, or similar content or style.

Mnemonic Codes A mnemonic (pronounced nî-môn′-ĭk) is a human memory aid. Any code that helps either the data entry person remember how to enter the data or the user remember how to use the information can be considered a mnemonic. Using a combination of letters and symbols affords a strikingly clear way to code a product so that the code is easily seen and understood.

The city hospital codes formerly used by the Buffalo Regional Blood Center were mnemonic, as shown in Figure 15.8. The simple codes were invented precisely because the blood center administrators and systems analysts wanted to ensure that hospital codes were easy to memorize and recall. Mnemonic codes for the hospitals helped lessen the possibility of blood being shipped to the wrong hospital.

UNICODE

Codes allow us to reveal characters that we normally cannot input or view. Traditional keyboards support character sets that are familiar to people using Western alphabetic characters (referred to as Latin characters), but many languages, such as Greek, Japanese, Chinese, or Hebrew, do not use the Western alphabet. These languages may use Greek letters, or glyphs or symbols representing syllables or whole words. The International Standards Organization (ISO) has defined the Unicode character set, which includes all standard language symbols, and has room for 65,535 characters. You can display Web pages written in other alphabets by downloading an input method editor from Microsoft.

Code	City Hospitals
BGH	**B**uffalo **G**eneral **H**ospital
ROS	**Ros**well Park Memorial Institute
KEN	**Ken**more Mercy
DEA	**Dea**coness Hospital
SIS	**Sis**ters of Charity
STF	**S**ain**t** **F**rancis Hospital
STJ	**S**ain**t** **J**oseph's Hospital
OLV	**O**ur **L**ady of **V**ictory Hospital

FIGURE 15.8
Mnemonic codes function as memory aids by using a meaningful combination of letters and numbers.

Glyph symbols are represented using an "&#xnnnn;" notation, in which nnnn represents a specific letter or symbol, and x means that hexadecimal notation, or base 16 numbering, is used to represent the Unicode characters. For example, &#30B3 represents the Japanese Katakana symbol *ko*. The code used for the Japanese word for hello, konichiwa, is こにち&#x308F. In Japanese, the word looks like:

こ に ち わ
ko ni chi wa
hello

The full set of Unicode characters are grouped by language and may be found at www.unicode.org.

REQUESTING APPROPRIATE ACTION

Codes are often needed to instruct either the computer or the decision maker about what action to take. Such codes are generally referred to as function codes, and they typically take the form of either sequence or mnemonic codes.

Function Codes The functions that the analyst or programmer desires the computer to perform with data are captured in function codes. Spelling out precisely what activities are to be accomplished is translated into a short numeric or alphanumeric code.

Figure 15.9 shows examples of a function code for updating inventory. Suppose you managed a dairy department; if a case of yogurt spoiled, you would use the code 3 to indicate this event. Of course, data required for input vary depending on what function is needed. For example, appending or updating a record would require only the record key and function code, whereas adding a new record would require all data elements to be input, including the function code.

GENERAL GUIDELINES FOR CODING

In the previous sections, we examined the purposes for using different types of codes when humans and machines enter and store data. Next, we examine a few heuristics for establishing a coding system. These rules are highlighted in Figure 15.10.

Be Concise Codes should be concise. Overly long codes mean more keystrokes and consequently more errors. Long codes also mean that storing the information in a database will require more memory.

Short codes are easier for people to remember and easier to enter than long codes. If codes must be long, they should be broken up into subcodes. For example, 5678923453127 could be broken up with hyphens as follows: 5678-923-453-127.

FIGURE 15.9
Function codes compactly capture functions that the computer must perform.

Code	Function
1	Delivered
2	Sold
3	Spoiled
4	Lost or Stolen
5	Returned
6	Transferred Out
7	Transferred In
8	Journal Entry (Add)
9	Journal Entry (Subtract)

CONSULTING OPPORTUNITY 15.1

IT'S A WILDERNESS IN HERE

"I can't stand this. I've been looking for this hat for the last 45 minutes," complains Davey, as he swings a coonskin cap by its tail above his head. He is one of the new warehouse workers for Crockett's, a large catalog sales firm. "The catalog slip calls it a 'Coo m5–9w/tl.' Good thing you told me 'Coo' stands for coonskin. Then, of course, I thought about caps and looked over here. I found it here in this bin labeled BOYS/CAP. Wouldn't it be easier if the catalog matched the bins? To me, this invoice says, 'Cookware, metallic, 5–9-piece set with Teflon.' I've been stranded in the cookware sets the whole time."

Daniel, Davey's coworker, barely listens as he hurriedly pulls items out of bins to fill another order. "You'll get used to it. They've got to have it this way so that the computers can understand the bill later. Mostly, I look at the catalog page number on the invoice, then I look it up in the book and sort of translate it to back here . . . unless I remember it from finding it before," Daniel explains.

Davey persists, saying, "Computers are smart, though, and we have to fill so many orders. We should tell the people up in billing the names we've got on our bins."

Daniel replies cynically, "Oh, sure. They're dying to know what we think." Then he continues in a quieter tone. "You know, we used to have it like that, but when they got all the new computers and went to 24-hour phone and Internet orders, it all changed. They said the operators (and users) had to know more about what they were selling (or buying), so they changed their codes to be more like a story."

Davey, surprised at Daniel's revelation, asks, "What's the story for the one I was working on?"

Inspecting the code on the cap's invoice, Daniel replies, "The one you were working on was 'Coo m5–9w/tl.' After looking it up real fast on her computer the operator can tell the customer, 'It's a coonskin (Coo) cap for boys (m for male) ages 5–9 with a real tail (w/tl).' We can't see the forest for the trees because of their codes, but you know Crockett's. They've got to make the sale."

How important is it that the warehouse bins and invoices are coded inconsistently? Respond in a paragraph. What are some of the problems created when a code appears to be mnemonic but employees are never given an appropriate "key" to decode it? Discuss your response in two paragraphs. What changes would you make to invoice/warehouse coding for Crockett's? Document your changes, identify the type of code you would use, and use the code in an example of a product that Crockett's might sell. Remember to decipher it as well.

This approach is much more manageable and takes advantage of the way people are known to process information in short chunks. Sometimes codes are made longer than necessary for a reason. Credit card numbers are often long to prevent people from guessing a credit card number. Visa and MasterCard use 16-digit numbers, which would accommodate nine trillion customers. Because the numbers are not assigned sequentially, chances of guessing a credit card number are very slight.

Keep the Codes Stable Stability means that the identification code for a customer should not change each time new data are received. Earlier, we presented an alphabetic derivation code for a magazine subscription list. The expiration date was not part of the subscriber identification code because it was likely to change.

Don't change the code abbreviations in a mnemonic system. Once you have chosen the code abbreviations, do not try to revise them, because that makes it extremely difficult for data entry personnel to adapt.

In Establishing a Coding System, the Analyst Should:
Keep codes concise
Keep codes stable
Make codes that are unique
Allow codes to be sortable
Avoid confusing codes
Keep codes uniform
Allow for modification of codes
Make codes meaningful

FIGURE 15.10
There are eight general guidelines for establishing a coding system.

FIGURE 15.11

Plan ahead in order to be able to do something useful with data that have been entered. In this example, the person creating the codes did not realize the data would have to be sorted.

Incorrect Sorting Using MMM-DD-YYYY	Incorrect Sorting Using MM-DD-YYYY	Incorrect Sorting (Year 2000 Problem) YY-MM-DD	Correct Sorting Using YYYY-MM-DD
Dec-25-1998	06-04-1998	00-06-11	1997-06-12
Dec-31-1997	06-11-2000	97-06-12	1997-12-31
Jul-04-1999	06-12-1997	97-12-31	1998-06-04
Jun-04-1998	07-04-1999	98-06-04	1998-10-24
Jun-11-2000	10-24-1998	98-10-24	1998-12-25
Jun-12-1997	12-25-1998	98-12-25	1999-07-04
Oct-24-1998	12-31-1997	99-07-04	2000-06-11

Ensure That Codes Are Unique For codes to work, they must be unique. Make a note of all codes used in the system to ensure that you are not assigning the same code number or name to the same items. Code numbers and names are an essential part of the entries in data dictionaries, discussed in Chapter 8.

Allow Codes to Be Sortable If you are going to manipulate the data usefully, the codes must be sortable. For example, if you were to perform a text search on the months of the year in ascending order, the "J" months would be out of order (January, July, and then June). Dictionaries are sorted in this way, one letter at a time from left to right. So, if you sorted MMMDDYYYY where the MMM stood for the abbreviation for the month, DD for the day, and YYYY for the year, the result would be in error.

Figure 15.11 shows what would happen if a text search were performed on different forms of the date. The third column shows a problem that was part of the year 2000 (Y2K) crisis that caused some alarm and even made the cover of *Time* magazine.

One of the lessons learned is to make sure that users can do what you intend them to do with the codes you create. Numeric codes are much easier to sort than alphanumerics; therefore, consider converting to numerics wherever practical.

Avoid Confusing Codes Try to avoid using coding characters that look or sound alike. The characters O (the letter oh) and 0 (the number zero) are easily confused, as are the letter I and the number 1, and the letter Z and the number 2. Therefore, codes such as B1C and 280Z are unsatisfactory.

One example of a potentially confusing code is the Canadian Postal Code, as shown in Figure 15.12. The code format is X9X 9X9, where X stands for a letter and 9 stands for a number. One advantage to using letters in the code is to allow more data in a six-digit code (there are 26 letters, but only 10 numbers). Because the code is used on a regular basis by Canadians, the code makes perfectly good sense to them. To foreigners sending mail to Canada, however, it may be difficult to tell if the second-to-last symbol is a Z or a 2.

FIGURE 15.12

Combining look-alike characters in codes can result in errors.

Code Format for Canadian Postal Code X9X 9X9

Handwritten Code	Actual Code	City, Province	Problem
L8S 4M4	L8S 4M4	Hamilton, Ontario	S looks like a 5
T3A ZE5	T3A 2E5	Calgary, Alberta	2 looks like a Z 5 looks like an S
LOS 1JO	LOS 1JO	Niagara-on-the-Lake, Ontario	Zero and Oh look alike S looks like a 5 1 looks like an I

Keep the Codes Uniform To be effective and efficient for humans, codes need to follow readily perceived forms most of the time. Codes used together, such as BUF-234 and KU-3456, are poor because the first contains three letters and three numbers, whereas the second has only two letters followed by four numbers.

When you are required to add dates, try to avoid using the codes MMDDYYYY in one application, YYYYDDMM in a second, and MMDDYY in a third. It is important to keep codes uniform among as well as within programs.

In the past, uniformity meant that all codes be kept the same length. With the introduction of online systems, the length is not as important as it once was. With online systems, the **Enter** key is pressed after data entry is verified by the operator as correct, so it doesn't make much difference if the code is three characters or four characters long.

Allow for Modification of Codes Adaptability is a key feature of a good code. The analyst must keep in mind that the system will evolve over time, and the coding system should be able to encompass change. The number of customers should grow, customers will change names, and suppliers will modify the way they number their products. The analyst needs to be able to forecast the predictable changes that business users will desire and anticipate a wide range of future needs when designing codes.

Make Codes Meaningful Unless the analyst wants to hide information intentionally, codes should be meaningful. Effective codes not only contain information, but they also make sense to the people using them. Meaningful codes are easy to understand, work with, and recall. The job of data entry becomes more interesting when working with meaningful codes instead of just entering a series of meaningless numbers.

Using Codes Codes are used in a number of ways. In validation programs, input data is checked against a list of codes to ensure that only valid codes have been entered. In report and inquiry programs, a code stored on a file is transformed into the meaning of the code. Reports and displays should not show or print the actual code. If they did, the user would have to memorize code meanings or look them up in a manual. Codes are used in GUI programs to create drop-down lists.

EFFECTIVE AND EFFICIENT DATA CAPTURE

To ensure the quality of data users enter into the system, it is important to capture data effectively. Data capture has received increasingly greater attention as the point in information processing at which excellent productivity gains can be made. Great progress in improving data capture has been made since the 1970s, as we have moved from multiple-step, slow, and error-prone systems such as keypunching to using sophisticated systems including such things as optical character recognition (OCR), bar codes, point-of-sale terminals, and scanning special characters in magazines and catalogs to access a Web site directly.

DECIDING WHAT TO CAPTURE

The decision about what to capture precedes user interaction with the system. Indeed, it is vital in making the eventual interface worthwhile, for the adage "garbage in, garbage out" is still true.

Decisions about what data to capture for system input are made among systems analysts and systems users. Much of what will be captured is specific to the particular business. Capturing data, inputting them, storing them, and retrieving

CONSULTING OPPORTUNITY 15.2

CATCHING A SUMMER CODE

Vicky takes her fingers off her keyboard and bends over her workstation to verify the letters on the invoices stacked in front of her. "What on earth?" Vicky asks aloud as she further scrutinizes the letters that encode cities where orders are to be shipped.

Shelly Overseer, her supervisor, who usually sits a couple of workstations away, is passing by and sees Vickie's consternation. "What's the matter? Did the sales rep forget to write in the city code again?"

Vicky swings around in her chair to face Shelly. "No, there are codes here, but they're weird. We usually use a three-letter code, right? Like CIN for Cincinnati, SEA for Seattle, MIN for Minneapolis, BUF for Buffalo. They're all *five*-letter codes here, though."

"Look," Vicky says, lifting the invoice to show Shelly. "CINNC, SEATT, MINNE. It'll take me all day to enter these. No kidding, it's really slowing me down. Maybe there's a mistake. Can't I just use the standard?"

Shelly backs away from Vicky's workstation as if the problem were contagious. Excusing herself apologetically, Shelly says, "It's the part-timers. They are learning sales now, and management was worried that they'd get messed up on their cities. I think it has something to do with mixing up Newark and New Orleans on the last orders. So, a committee decided to make the cities more recognizable by having them add two letters. Those kids can't learn everything we know overnight, even though they try. It's just until August 19, though, when the part-timers go back to school."

As Vicky glumly turns back to her keyboard, Shelly puts her hand sympathetically on Vicky's shoulder and says, "I know it's a strain and it's making you feel miserable, but don't worry. You'll get over it. It's just a summer code."

What general guidelines of coding has management overlooked in its decision to use a summer code for cities? Make a list of them. What is the effect on full-time data entry personnel of changing codes for the ease of temporary help? Respond in two paragraphs. What future impact could the temporary change in codes have on sorting and retrieving data entered during the summer period? Take two paragraphs to discuss these implications. What changes can you suggest so that the part-timers don't get mixed up on codes in the short term? In a memo to the supervisor of this work group, make a list of five to seven changes in the data capture or data entry procedures that can be made to accommodate short-term hires without disrupting normal business. In a paragraph, indicate how this goal can be accomplished without marring the productivity of data entry personnel.

them are all costly endeavors. With all these factors in mind, determining what to capture becomes an important decision.

There are two types of data to enter: data that *change* or *vary* with every transaction, and data that concisely *differentiate* the particular item being processed from all other items.

An example of changeable data is the quantity of supplies purchased each time an advertising firm places an order with the office supply wholesaler. Because quantities change depending on the number of employees at the advertising firm and on how many accounts they are servicing, quantity data must be entered each time an order is placed.

An example of differentiation data is the inclusion on a patient record of the patient's Social Security number and the first three letters of his or her last name. In this way, the patient is uniquely differentiated from other patients in the same system.

LETTING THE COMPUTER DO THE REST

When considering what data to capture for each transaction and what data to leave to the system to enter, the systems analyst must take advantage of what computers do best. In the preceding example of the advertising agency ordering office supplies, it is not necessary for the operator entering the stationery order to reenter each item description each time an order is received. The computer can store and access this information easily.

Computers can automatically handle repetitive tasks, such as recording the time of the transaction, calculating new values from input, and storing and retrieving data on demand. By employing the best features of computers, efficient data

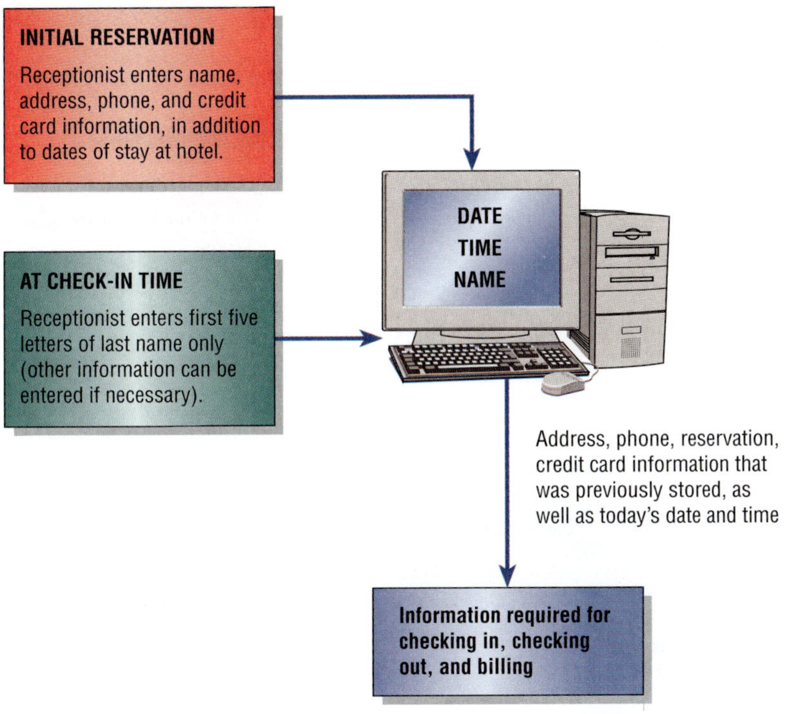

FIGURE 15.13

Automatically recording the date and time in a hotel reservation system eliminates unnecessary data entry.

capture design avoids needless data entry, which in turn alleviates much human error and boredom, and permits people to focus on higher-level or creative tasks.

Software can be written to ask the user to enter today's date or capture the date from the computer's internal clock. Once entered, the system proceeds to use that date on all transactions processed in that data entry session.

Part of a display screen for hotel reservations and guest check-ins is shown in Figure 15.13. Notice that when a reservation is made initially, the guest's name and credit card number are entered. When the guest checks in, the desk clerk calls up the record without having to entirely reenter the name or number. The system also automatically records the date and time, saving further data entry.

A prime example of reusing data entered once is that of the online computer library center (OCLC) used by thousands of libraries in the United States. OCLC was built on the idea that each item bought by a library should only have to be cataloged once for all time. Once an item is entered, cataloging information goes into the huge OCLC database and is shared with participating libraries. In this case, implementation of the simple concept of entering data only once has saved enormous data entry time.

The calculating power of the computer should also be taken into account when deciding what *not* to reenter. Computers are adept at long calculations, using data already entered.

For example, the person doing data entry may enter the flight numbers and account number of an air trip taken by a customer belonging to a frequent flyer incentive program. The computer then calculates the number of miles accrued for each flight, adds it to the miles already in the customer's account, and updates the total miles accrued to the account. The computer may also flag an account that, by virtue of the large number of miles flown, is now eligible for an award. Although all this information may appear on the customer's updated account, the only new data entered were the flight numbers of the flights flown.

In systems that use a graphical user interface (GUI), codes are often stored either as a function or as a separate table in the database. There is a trade-off on

FIGURE 15.14

A table of codes used in drop-down list. This list is used to select a code for adding or changing an item in a record.

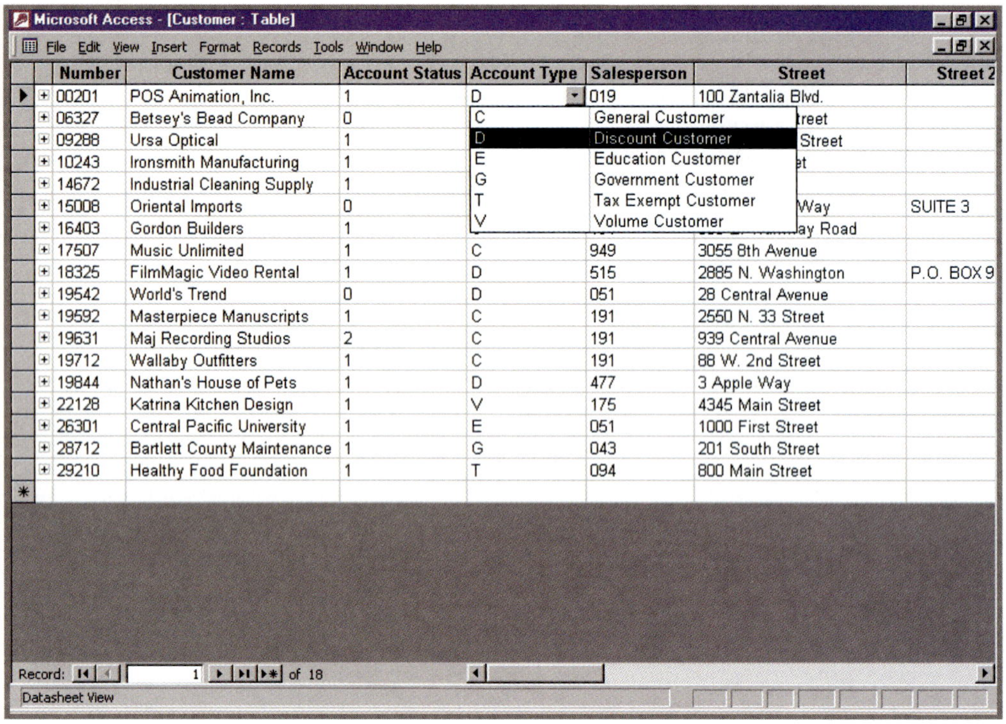

creating too many tables, because the software must find matching records from each table, which may lead to slow access. If the codes are relatively stable and rarely change, they may be stored as a database function. If the codes change frequently, they are stored on a table so that they may be easily updated.

Figure 15.14 shows how a drop-down list is used to select the codes for adding or changing a record in the CUSTOMER table. Notice that the code is stored, but the drop-down list displays both the code and the code meaning. This method helps to ensure accuracy, because the user does not have to guess at the meaning of the code and there is no chance of typing an invalid code.

AVOIDING BOTTLENECKS AND EXTRA STEPS

A bottleneck in data entry is an apt allusion to the physical appearance of a bottle. Data are poured rapidly into the wide mouth of the system only to be slowed in its "neck" because of an artificially created instance of insufficient processing for the volume or detail of the data being entered. One way a bottleneck can be avoided is by ensuring that there is enough capacity to handle the data that are being entered.

Ways to avoid extra steps are determined not only at the time of analysis, but also when users begin to interact with prototypes of the system. The fewer steps involved in inputting data, the fewer chances there are for the introduction of errors. So, beyond the obvious consideration of saved labor, avoiding extra steps is also a way to preserve the quality of data. Once again, use of an online, real-time system that captures customer data without necessitating the completion of a form is an excellent example of saving steps in data entry.

STARTING WITH A GOOD FORM

Effective data capture is achievable only if prior thought is given to what the source document should contain. The data entry operator inputs data from the source document (usually some kind of form); this document is the source of a large amount of all system data. Online systems (or special data entry methods such as bar codes) may circumvent the need for a source document, but often some kind of paper form, such as a receipt, is created anyway.

With effective forms, it is not necessary to reenter information that the computer has already stored, or data such as time or date of entry that the computer can determine automatically. Chapter 11 discussed in detail how a form or source document should be designed to maximize its usefulness for capturing data and to minimize the time users need to spend entering data from it.

CHOOSING A DATA ENTRY METHOD

Several efficient data entry methods are available, and choosing one of them is shaped by many factors, including the need for speed, accuracy, and user training; the cost of the data entry method (whether it is materials- or labor-intensive); and the methods currently in use in the organization.

Keyboards Keyboarding is the oldest method of data entry, and certainly it is the one with which organizational members are the most familiar. Some improvements have been made over the years to improve keyboards. Features include special function keys to open programs, keys used to scroll and explore the Web, and keys that can be programmed with macros to reduce the number of keystrokes required. Ergonomic keyboards and infrared or Bluetooth-enabled keyboards and mice are big improvements, as well.

Optical Character Recognition Optical character recognition (OCR) lets a user read input from a source document with an optical scanner rather than off the magnetic media we have been discussing so far. Using OCR devices can speed data input from 60 to 90 percent over some keying methods.

What is needed is a source document that can be optically scanned when it is filled out, either through special block printing or by hand, as shown in Figure 15.15.

The increased speed of OCR comes through not having to encode or key in data from source documents. It eliminates many of the time-consuming and error-fraught steps of other input devices. In doing so, OCR demands few employee skills and commensurately less training, resulting in fewer errors and less time spent by employees in redundant efforts. It also decentralizes responsibility for quality data directly to the unit that is generating it. OCR, which has become available to all, has one additional, highly practical use: the transformation of faxes into documents that can be edited.

Other Methods of Data Entry Other methods of data entry are also becoming more widely employed. Most of these methods reduce labor costs by requiring few

FIGURE 15.15
Optical character recognition (OCR) of special-character source documents facilitates data entry.

operator skills or little training, they move data entry closer to the source of data, and they eliminate the need for a source document. In doing so, they have become fast and highly reliable data entry methods. The data entry methods discussed in the following subsections include magnetic ink character recognition, mark-sense forms, punch-out forms, bar codes, and data strips.

Magnetic Ink Character Recognition Magnetic ink characters are found on the bottom of bank checks and some credit card bills. This method is akin to OCR in that special characters are read, but its use is limited. Data entry through magnetic ink character recognition (MICR) is done through a machine that reads and interprets a single line of material encoded with ink that is made up of magnetic particles.

Some advantages of using MICR are (1) it is a reliable and high-speed method that is not susceptible to accepting stray marks (because they are not encoded

FIGURE 15.16

A mark-sense form that can be read by a scanner speeds data entry.

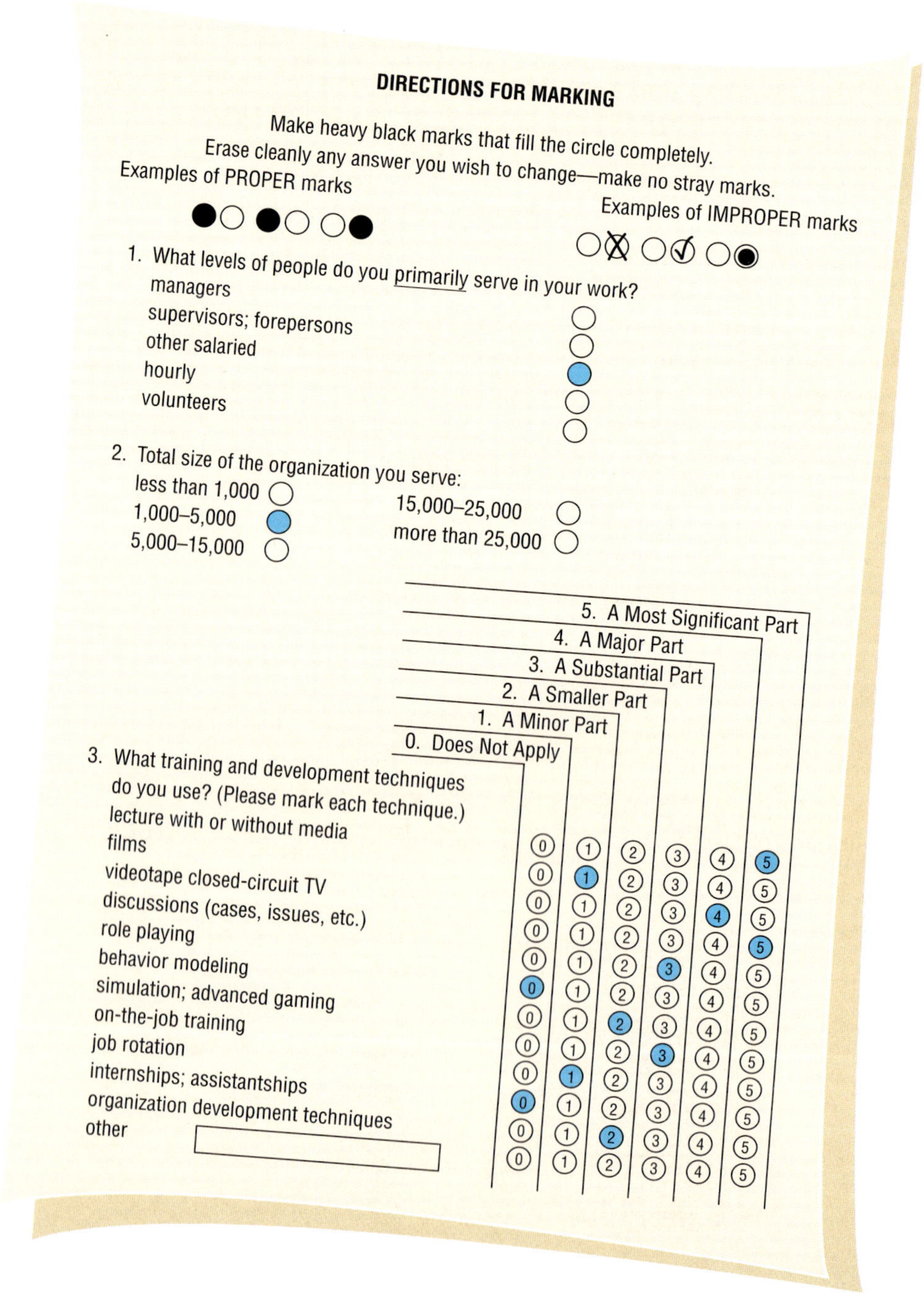

magnetically); (2) if it is required on all withdrawal checks, it serves as a security measure against bad checks; and (3) data entry personnel can see the numbers making up the code if it is necessary to verify it.

Mark-Sense Forms Mark-sense forms allow data entry through the use of a scanner that senses where marks have been made on special forms. A common usage is for scoring answer sheets for survey questionnaires, as shown in Figure 15.16. Little training of entry personnel is necessary, and a high volume of forms can be processed quickly.

One drawback of mark-sense forms is that although the readers can determine whether a mark has been made, they cannot interpret the mark in the way that optical character readers do. Stray marks on forms can thus be entered as incorrect data. In addition, choices are limited to the answers provided on the mark-sense form, forms have difficulty in capturing alphanumeric data because of the space required for a complete set of letters and numbers, and it is easy for those filling out mark-sense forms to get confused and put a mark in an incorrect position.

Bar Codes Bar codes typically appear on product labels, but they also appear on patient identification bracelets in hospitals and in almost any context in which a person or object needs to be checked into and out of any kind of inventory system. Bar codes can be thought of as metacodes, or codes encoding codes, because they appear as a series of narrow and wide bands on a label that encodes numbers or letters. These symbols in turn have access to product data stored in computer memory. A beam of light from a scanner or lightpen is drawn across the bands on the label either to confirm or record data about the product being scanned.

A bar-coded label, such as the one shown in Figure 15.17, includes the following elements of coding for a particular grocery product: the manufacturer identification number, the product identification number, a code to verify the scan's accuracy, and codes to mark the beginning and end of the scan.

Bar coding affords an extraordinarily high degree of accuracy for data entry. It saves labor costs for retailers because each item does not have to be individually price-marked. In addition, bar coding allows the automatic capturing of data that can be used for reordering, more accurate inventory tracking, and the forecasting of future needs. Sale prices or other changes in the meaning of the bar codes are entered into the central processor, thus saving the trouble of marking down numerous items.

One new use of bar coding is the tracking of an individual's credit card purchases for the purpose of building a consumer profile that can then in turn be used to refine marketing to that individual or type of consumer. New input devices are constantly being developed. Of course, it has been possible to transfer photographic images for

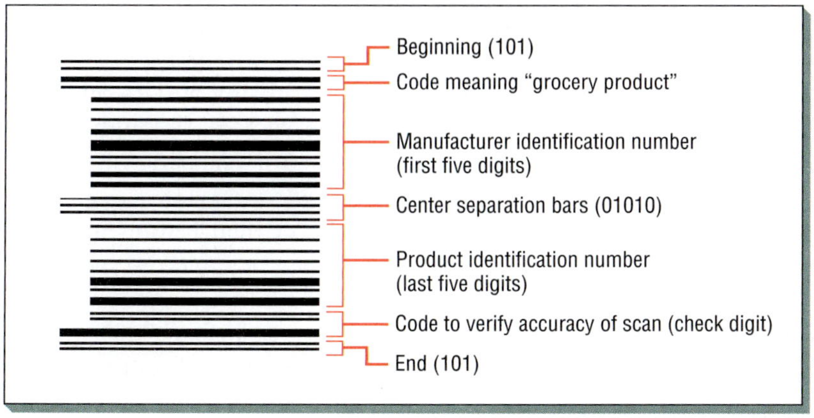

FIGURE 15.17
Bar coding, as shown in this label for a grocery product, affords highly accurate data entry. Used with the permission of the Uniform Code Council, Dayton, Ohio.

some time now using systems such as the Kodak Photo CD process, but using a digital camera eliminates the middle step of users needing to digitize their own photographs.

RFID. Commonly known as RFID, radio frequency identification allows the automatic collection of data using RFID tags or transponders that contain a chip and an antenna. An RFID tag may or may not have its own power source. If it does not have its own power, the antenna provides just enough power from an incoming signal to power the chip and transmit a response. RFID tags can be attached to products, packages, animals, or even humans so that the item or person can be identified using a radio frequency.

RFID tags, also called proximity cards because of their limited range, can be passive or active. Passive RFID tags have no internal power source; active tags do. Passive tags are inexpensive (less than 5¢ per tag) and are typically the size of a postage stamp. They are used in large retail stores, including Wal-Mart and Target. Wal-Mart has been actively pursuing RFID technology in improving its inventory management and supply chain processes.

Active tags are much more reliable because they have their own power supply. The U.S. Department of Defense has used these tags to minimize the costs related to logistics and increase supply chain visibility. Active tags cost only a few dollars each.

To capture the data on an RFID tag, a reader is required. The reader activates the tag so that it can be read. The reader decodes the data and the unique product code on the chip inside the tag, then passes it along to a host computer that processes the data.

One example is an electronic toll pass used in vehicles traversing toll roads. An RFID transponder can be attached to the windshield and read every time the vehicle passes through a toll booth. The toll booth's RFID reader can also act as a writer, so a balance can be stored on the RFID chip.

The Moscow Metro was the first transportation system to use RFID smartcards in 1998. Other applications include the tracking of cattle to identify the herd of origin, which enables better tracking of mad cow disease, as well as RFID tracking in bookstores, airline baggage services, pharmaceuticals, and even patients or inmates.

RFID tags have found common use in most shipping applications. The technology will soon be used in general electronic cash transactions. They may even replace UPC codes since their advantages include security (by reducing the number of items stolen) and not requiring scanning (they can simply pass through the reader zone).

RFID is not without controversy. Privacy is a concern. An individual who pays for a tagged item by a credit card or a shoppers' card could be identified.

The systems analyst needs to think of the users involved and their rights when considering whether this technology is suited for the application being designed.

ENSURING DATA QUALITY THROUGH INPUT VALIDATION

So far, we have discussed ensuring the effective capturing of data onto source documents and the data's efficient entry into the system through various input devices. Although these conditions are necessary for ensuring quality data, they alone are not sufficient.

Errors cannot be ruled out entirely, and the critical importance of catching errors during input, *prior* to processing and storage, cannot be overemphasized. The snarl of problems created by incorrect input can be a nightmare, not the least of which is that many problems take a long time to surface. The systems analyst must assume that errors in data *will* occur and must work with users to design

This Type of Validation	Can Prevent These Problems
Validating Input Transactions	Submitting the wrong data Data submitted by an unauthorized person Asking the system to perform an unacceptable function
Validating Input Data	Missing data Incorrect field length Data have unacceptable composition Data are out of range Data are invalid Data do not match with stored data

FIGURE 15.18

Validating input is important to ensure that most potential problems with data are eliminated early.

input validation tests to prevent erroneous data from being processed and stored, because initial errors that go undiscovered for long periods are expensive and time consuming to correct.

You cannot imagine everything that will go awry with input, but you must cover the kinds of errors that give rise to the largest percentage of problems. A summary of potential problems that must be considered when validating input is given in Figure 15.18.

VALIDATING INPUT TRANSACTIONS

Validating input transactions is largely done through software, which is the programmer's responsibility, but it is important that the systems analyst know what common problems might invalidate a transaction. Businesses committed to quality will include validity checks as part of their routine software.

Three main problems can occur with input transactions: submitting the wrong data to the system, the submitting of data by an unauthorized person, or asking the system to perform an unacceptable function.

Submitting the Wrong Data An example of submitting the wrong data to the system is the attempt to input a patient's Social Security number into a hospital's payroll system. This error is usually an accidental one, but it should be flagged before data are processed.

Submitting of Data by an Unauthorized Person The system should also be able to discover if otherwise correct data are submitted by an unauthorized person. For instance, only the supervising pharmacist should be able to enter inventory totals for controlled substances in the pharmacy. Invalidation of transactions submitted by an unauthorized individual applies to privacy and security concerns surrounding payroll systems and employee evaluation records that determine pay levels, promotions, or discipline; files containing trade secrets; and files holding classified information, such as national defense data.

Asking the System to Perform an Unacceptable Function The third error that invalidates input transactions is asking the system to perform an unacceptable function. For instance, it would be logical for a human resources manager to update the existing record of a current employee, but it would be invalid to ask the system to create a new file rather than merely to update an existing record.

CONSULTING OPPORTUNITY 15.3

TO ENTER OR NOT TO ENTER: THAT IS THE QUESTION

"I've just taken on the presidency of Elsinore Industries," says Rose N. Krantz. "We're actually part of a small cottage industry that manufactures toy villages for children seven years old and up. Our tiny hamlets consist of various kits that will build what children want from interlocking plastic cubes, essentials such as city hall, the police station, the gas station, and a hot dog stand. Each kit has a unique part number from 200 to 800, but not every number is used. The wholesale prices vary from $54.95 for the city hall to $1.79 for a hot dog stand.

"I've been melancholy over what I've found out since signing on at Elsinore. 'Something is rotten' here, to quote a famous playwright. In fact, the invoicing system was so out of control that I've been working around the clock with our bookkeeper, Gilda Stern," Krantz soliloquizes.

"I would like you to help straighten things out," Rose continues. "We ship to 12 distribution warehouses around the country. Each invoice we write out includes the warehouse number, 1 through 12, its street address, and the U.S. postal code (zip code). We also put on each invoice the date we fill the order, code numbers for the hamlet kits they order, a description of each kit, the price per item, and the quantity of each kit ordered. Of course, we also include the subtotals of kit charges, shipping charges, and the total that the warehouse owes us. No sales tax is added, because they resell what we send them to toy stores in all 50 states. I want you to help us design a computerized order entry system that will be part of the invoicing system for Elsinore Industries."

For your design of a data entry system for Elsinore, take into consideration all the objectives for data entry discussed throughout this chapter. Draw any displays necessary to illustrate your design. How can you make the order entry system efficient? Respond in a paragraph. Specify what data can be stored and retrieved and what data must be entered anew for each order. How can unnecessary work be avoided? Write a paragraph to explain why the system you propose is more efficient than the old one. How can data accuracy be ensured? List three strategies that will work with the type of data that are being entered for Elsinore Industries.

VALIDATING INPUT DATA

It is essential that the input data themselves, along with the transactions requested, are valid. Several tests can be incorporated into software to ensure this validity. We consider eight possible ways to validate input.

Test for Missing Data The first kind of validity test examines data to see if there are any missing items. For some situations, *all* data items must be present. For example, a Social Security file for paying out retirement or disability benefits would be invalid if it did not include the payee's Social Security number.

In addition, the record should include both the key data that distinguish one record from all others and the function code telling the computer what to do with the data. The systems analyst needs to interact with users to determine what data items are essential and to find out whether exceptional cases ever occur that would allow data to be considered valid even if some data items were missing. For example, a second address line containing an apartment number or a person's middle initial may not be a required entry.

Test for Correct Field Length A second kind of validity test checks input to ensure it is of the correct length for the field. For example, if the Omaha, Nebraska, weather station reports into the national weather service computer but mistakenly provides a two-letter city code (OM) instead of the national three-letter city code (OMA), the input data might be deemed invalid, and hence would not be processed.

Test for Class or Composition The test for class or composition validity checks to see that data fields that are supposed to be exclusively composed of numbers do not include letters, and vice versa. For example, a credit card account number for American Express should not include any letters. Using a composition test, the program should not accept an American Express account number that includes both letters and numbers.

Test for Range or Reasonableness Validity tests for range or reasonableness are really common-sense measures of input that answer the question of whether data fall within an acceptable range or whether they are reasonable within predetermined parameters. For instance, if a user was trying to verify a proposed shipment date, the range test would neither permit a shipping date on the 32nd day of October nor accept shipment in the 13th month, the respective ranges being 1 to 31 days and 1 to 12 months.

A reasonableness test ascertains whether the item makes sense for the transaction. For example, when adding a new employee to the payroll, entering an age of 120 years would not be reasonable. Reasonableness tests are used for data that are continuous, that is, data that have a smooth range of values. These tests can include a lower limit, an upper limit, or both a lower and an upper limit.

Test for Invalid Values Checking input for invalid values works if there are only a few valid values. This test is not feasible for situations in which values are neither restricted nor predictable. This kind of test is useful for checking responses where data are divided into a limited number of classes. For example, a brokerage firm divides accounts into three classes only: class 1 = active account, class 2 = inactive account, and class 3 = closed account. If data are assigned to any other class through an error, the values are invalid. Value checks are usually performed for discrete data, which are data that have only certain values. If there are many values, they are usually stored in a table of codes file. Having the values in a file provides an easy way to add or change values.

Cross-Reference Checks Cross-reference checks are used when one element has a relationship with another one. To perform a cross-reference check, each field must be correct in itself. For example, the price for which an item is sold should be greater than the cost paid for the item. Price must be entered, numeric, and greater than zero. The same criterion is used to validate cost. When both price and cost are valid, they may be compared.

A geographical check is another type of cross-reference check. In the United States, the state abbreviation may be used to ensure that a telephone area code is valid for that state and that the first two digits of the zip code are valid for the state.

Test for Comparison with Stored Data The next test for validity of input data that we consider is one comparing it with data that the computer has already stored. For example, a newly entered part number can be compared with the complete parts inventory to ensure that the number exists and is being entered correctly.

Setting Up Self-Validating Codes (Check Digits) Another method for ensuring the accuracy of data, particularly identification numbers, is to use a check digit in the code itself. This procedure involves beginning with an original numeric code, performing some mathematics to arrive at a derived check digit, and then adding the check digit to the original code. The mathematical process involves multiplying each of the digits in the original code by some predetermined weights, summing these results, and then dividing this sum by a modulus number. The modulus number is needed because the sum usually is a large number, and we need to reduce the result to a single digit. Finally, the remainder is subtracted from the modulus number, giving us the check digit.

FIGURE 15.19

Steps in converting a five-digit part number to a six-digit number containing a check digit.

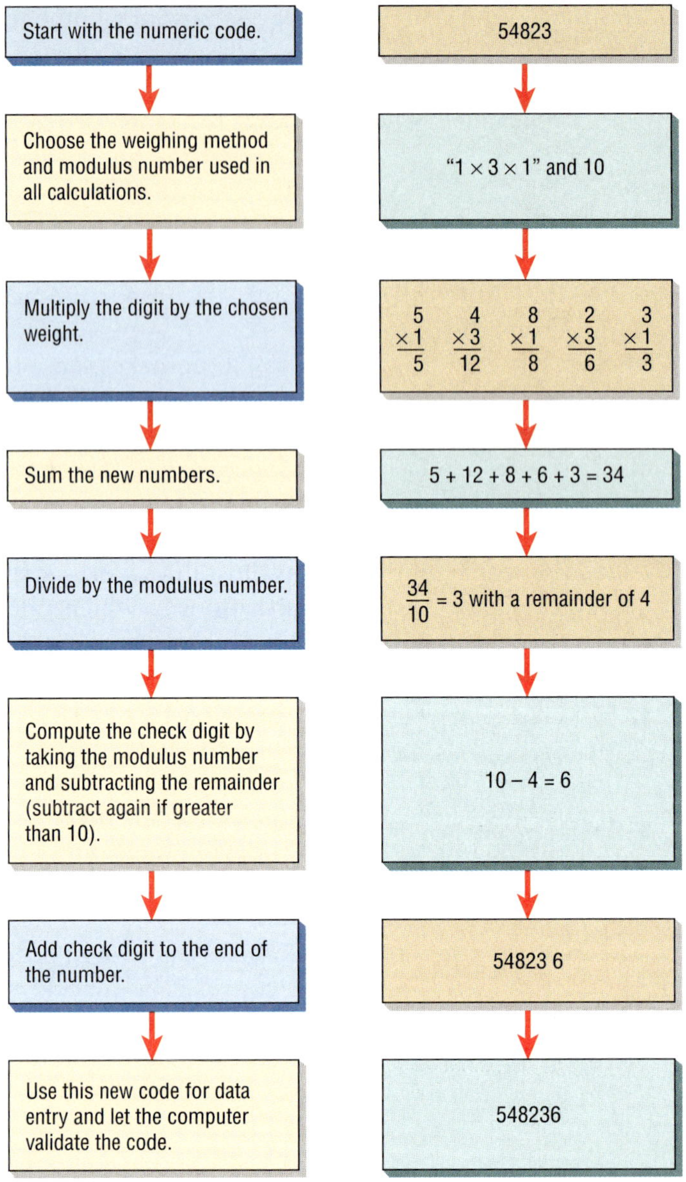

Figure 15.19 shows how a five-digit part number for a radiator hose (54823) is converted to a six-digit number containing a check digit. In this example, the weights chosen were the "1-3-1" system; in other words, the weights alternate between 1 and 3. After the digits 5, 4, 8, 2, and 3 were multiplied by 1, 3, 1, 3, and 1, they became 5, 12, 8, 6, and 3. These new digits sum to 34. Next, 34 is divided by the chosen modulus number, 10, with the result of 3 and a remainder of 4. The remainder, 4, is subtracted from the modulus number, 10, giving a check digit of 6. The digit 6 is now tacked onto the end of the original number, giving the official product code for the radiator hose (548236).

Using Check Digits. The check digit system works in the following way. Suppose we had the part number 53411. This number has to be typed into the system, and while that is being done, different types of errors can occur. One possible error is the single-digit miskey; for example, the clerk types in 54411 instead of 53411. Only the digit in the thousands place is incorrect, but this error may result in the wrong part being shipped.

A second type of error is transposed digits. It commonly occurs that the intended number 53411 gets typed in as number 54311 instead, just because two

Status	Original Code	Check Digit	New Code
Correct	5 3 4 1 1	8	534118
Single-digit miskey	5 4 4 1 1	5	544115
Transpose	5 4 3 1 1	6	543116

FIGURE 15.20
Avoiding common data-entry errors through the use of a check digit.

keys are pressed in reverse order. Transposition errors are also difficult for humans to detect.

These errors are avoidable through the use of a check digit because each of these numbers—the correct one and the error—would have a different check digit number, as shown in Figure 15.20. If part number 53411 was modified to 534118 (including the check digit 8) and either of the two errors just described occurred, the mistake would be caught. If the second digit was miskeyed as a 4, the computer would not accept 544118 as a valid number, because the check digit for 54411 would be 5, not 8. Similarly, if the second and third digits were transposed, as in 543118, the computer would also reject the number because the check digit for 54311 would be 6, not 8.

The systems analyst chooses the weights and the modulus number, but once chosen, they must not change. Some examples of weighting methods and modulus numbers can be found in Figure 15.21.

Verifying Credit Cards When credit cards are entered into a Web site or computer program, the first check is the length of the number. Credit card companies designed their cards to include a different number of digits. For example,

Check Digit Method	Calculations for Check Digit to Be Added to the Original Number 29645
Modulus 10 "2-1-2"	2 × 2 = 4; 9 × 1 = 9; 6 × 2 = 12; 4 × 1 = 4; 5 × 2 = 10 4 + 9 + 12 + 4 + 10 = 39/10 = 3 remainder (9) 10 − (9) = 1 Check digit equals 1 Code with check digit is 296451.
Modulus 10 "3-1-3"	2 × 3 = 6; 9 × 1 = 9; 6 × 3 = 18; 4 × 1 = 4; 5 × 3 = 15 6 + 9 + 18 + 4 + 15 = 52/10 = 5 remainder (2) 10 − (2) = 8 Check digit equals 8 Code with check digit is 296458.
Modulus 11 "Arithmetic"	2 × 6 = 12; 9 × 5 = 45; 6 × 4 = 24; 4 × 3 = 12; 5 × 2 = 10 12 + 45 + 24 + 12 + 10 = 103/11 = 9 remainder (4) 11 − (4) = 7 Check digit equals 7 Code with check digit is 296457.
Modulus 10 "Geometric"	2 × 32 = 64; 9 × 16 = 144; 6 × 8 = 48; 4 × 4 = 16; 5 × 2 = 10 64 + 144 + 48 + 16 + 10 = 282/11 = 25 remainder (7) 11 − (7) = 4 Check digit equals 4 Code with check digit is 296454.

FIGURE 15.21
Examples of weighting methods and modulus numbers.

Visa cards are 16 digits long while American Express card numbers are 15 digits in length.

Another test is to match the credit card company and bank to verify that it is indeed a card issued by that company. The first four digits usually signify the type of card. The middle digits usually represent the bank and the customer. The last digit is a check digit.

In addition to these verification methods, credit card processing uses a check digit formula called the Luhn formula, created in the 1960s. Suppose we are given a number 7-7-7-8-8-8, where the first five numbers is a bank account number and the last digit is a check digit. Let's apply the Luhn formula to see if this is a valid number.

1. Double the second last digit, then double every other digit (i.e., skip a digit, double the next, skip a digit, double the next, etc.). For example, the number 7-7-7-8-8-8 becomes 14-7-14-8-16-8.
2. If doubling any digit results in number that is larger than 10, reduce this two-digit number to a single digit by adding the numbers together. In our example, the 14 becomes $1 + 4 = 5$ and the 16 becomes $1 + 6 = 7$. In doing so, our original number, 7-7-7-8-8-8 has been transformed into a new number, 5-7-5-8-7-8.
3. Now add all of the digits in the new number together. So, $5 + 7 + 5 + 8 + 7 + 8 = 40$.
4. Look at the total. If it ends in zero, the number is valid according to the Luhn formula. Since 40 ends in zero, we can say that it passes the Luhn formula test.

The Luhn formula can be used to identify mistakes in entering an incorrect credit card. For example, the credit card number 1334-1334-1334-1334 is assumed to be valid because the digits of the transformed number 2364-2364-2364-2364 will add up to 60, a number ending in zero. If a user incorrectly enters a wrong digit, the total would not be a multiple of zero.

The Luhn formula does not catch every error, however. If a user makes mistakes in entering more than one digit, for example entering 1334-1334-1334-3314, the total of the transformed number, 2364-2364-2364-6324, is still 60. This transposition error (flipping the second last and fourth last digit) will not be caught.

Credit card companies also use the expiration date and a three- or four-digit verification code, often written on the reverse side of the card for more security.

The seven tests for checking on validity of input can go a long way toward protecting the system from the entry and storage of erroneous data. Always assume human errors in input are more likely than not to occur. It is your responsibility to understand which errors will invalidate data, and how to use the computer to guard against those human errors and thus limit their intrusion into system data.

THE PROCESS OF VALIDATION

It is important to validate each field until it is either valid or an error has been detected. The order of testing data is to first check for missing data. Then a syntax test can check the length of the data entered and check for proper class and composition. Only after the syntax is correct are the semantics, or meaning, of the data validated. This includes a range, reasonable, or value test, followed by a check digit test.

GUI screens help to reduce the number of human input errors when they incorporate radio buttons, check boxes, and drop-down lists. When radio buttons are used, one should be set as the default, and the only way it would be unchecked is if the user clicks a different radio button. In the case of drop-down lists, the first choice should contain a message informing the user to change the list. If the first choice is still selected when the form is submitted, a message should inform the user to select a different option.

Usually validating a single field is done with a series of IF . . . ELSE statements, but there are also pattern validation methods. Usually these patterns are found in the database design (as in Microsoft Access) but may be included in programming languages, such as Perl, JavaScript, and XML schemas. The patterns are called regular expressions and contain symbols that represent the type of data that must be present in a field. Figure 15.22 illustrates characters used in JavaScript regular expressions.

An example of pattern validation used to test an email address is

[A-Za-z0-9]\w{2,}@[A-Za-z0-9]{3,}\.[A-Za-z]{3}/

The meaning of this pattern is as follows: The first letter must be any uppercase letter, lowercase letter, or number ([A-Za-z0-9]). This is followed by two or more characters that are any letter, number, or an underscore (\w{2,}). There must then be an @ symbol, followed by at least three letters or numbers, a period, and exactly three characters after the period.

A cross-reference check assumes that the validity of one field may depend on the value of another field. An example of a cross-reference check is checking for a valid date. In one very special case, the validity of the day of the month depends on the year. That is, February 29 is only valid during leap years. Once single fields have been checked, you can perform cross-reference checks. Obviously, if one of the fields is incorrect, the cross-reference check is meaningless and should not be performed.

Character Code	Meaning Used in Regular Expression Validation
\d	Any digit 0–9
\D	Any nondigit character
\w	Any letter, number, or underscore
\W	Any character other than a letter, number, or underscore
.	Matches any character
[characters]	Matches the characters in the brackets
[char-char]	Matches the range of characters
[a–z][A–Z][0–9]	Will accept any letter or digit
[^characters]	Match anything other than the characters
[^char-char]	Match anything outside the range of characters
[^a–z]	Will accept anything except lowercase letters
{n}	Match exactly n occurrences of the preceding character
{n,}	Match at least n occurrences of the character
\s	Any white space formatting character (tab, new line, return, etc.)
\S	Any non-white space character

FIGURE 15.22
These characters are used in regular expression (pattern) validation.

CONSULTING OPPORTUNITY 15.4

DO YOU VALIDATE PARKING?

"What are we going to do, Mercedes?" Edsel asks wearily. Together, Mercedes and Edsel are reviewing the latest billing printout for their firm, Denton and Denton Parking Garages. They have been purchasing batch billing services from a small, local computer services company since they acquired three parking garages in a medium-sized metropolitan area. Denton and Denton Parking Garages rents daily, monthly, and yearly parking places to corporations and individuals.

Mercedes replies, "I'm not sure what our next move is, but the billing is all wrong. Maybe we should try to talk to the computer people."

"They said they could figure out how to compute these charges from looking at what the old owners did by hand before, and they said they didn't want to run the old and new systems in parallel," Edsel remarks, shaking his head. "That isn't right, though. At least I can't figure it out. Maybe you can."

Mercedes accepts the notion of chasing the suspect output and starts looking at the report in detail. "Well, for one thing, they don't realize we get cars from all over in here. Wherever we've got a car with plates that aren't in-state, it seems as if the computer stops figuring. Look, our plates start with a number and then a letter, right? Well this one from New York begins with three letters. The computer can't handle it," she says.

Edsel catches on and starts to think about the business as he looks at the printout. "Yeah, and look here. This person doesn't have a yearly account number, just a monthly one, so no bill came out," he says. "We've got monthlies, too, and the computer doesn't know it?"

"And look at this. It still made daily charges for the three days in November when we told them right out there weren't any vacancies for daily customers. It isn't reasonable," Mercedes asserts.

Edsel continues paging through the printout, but Mercedes stops him, saying, "Don't look any further. I'm calling the computer people so we can get this mess straightened out."

How would you characterize the problems being encountered with the current garage billing system? Use a paragraph to formulate a response. What are some tests for validity of data that could be included in the software for a revised billing system for the parking garages? List them. What could the programmer and analysts for the computer services company have done differently so that the customer was not faced with correcting the poor-quality output? Use three paragraphs to do a critical analysis of what was done and what *should* have been done.

XML documents may be validated by comparing them to a document type definition (DTD) or a schema (refer to Chapter 8). The DTD will check to see whether the format of the document is valid, but a schema is much more powerful and will check the type of data, such as a short or long integer, a decimal number, or date. A schema will also check a range of values, the number of digits to the left and right of a decimal point, and the values of codes. There are free tools to validate a DTD or schema. IEXMLTLS is a Microsoft extension to Internet Explorer that adds new menu options when the user right-clicks in an XML document. XML Spy from Altova has a free product for home use that may be downloaded from www.altova.com/support_freexmlspyhome.asp.

ACCURACY ADVANTAGES IN ECOMMERCE ENVIRONMENTS

One of the many bonuses of ecommerce transactions is increased accuracy of data, due to four reasons:

1. Customers generally key or enter data themselves.
2. Data entered by customers are stored for later use.
3. Data entered at the point of sale are reused throughout the entire order fulfillment process.
4. Information is used as feedback to customers.

An analyst needs to be aware of the advantages that have resulted from ecommerce and the electronic capture and use of information.

CUSTOMERS KEYING THEIR OWN DATA

First, customers know their own information better than anyone else. They know how to spell their street address, they know whether they live on a "Drive" or a "Street," and they know their own area code. If this information is transmitted by phone, it is easier to make a mistake spelling the address; if it is entered by using a faxed paper form, mistakes can occur if the fax transmission is difficult to read. If users enter their own information, however, accuracy increases.

STORING DATA FOR LATER USE

After customers enter information, it may be stored on their own personal computers. If they return to that ecommerce site and fill out the same form to complete a second transaction, they will witness the advantage of storing this information. As they begin to type their name, drop-down lists will prompt them with their full name even though only a couple of characters were entered. By clicking on this prompt, the full name is entered and no further typing is necessary for this field. This autocomplete feature can suggest matches for credit card and password information as well, and this information is encrypted so that Web sites cannot read the information stored on the user's computer.

Companies that want to store information to enable faster and more accurate transactions do so in small files called cookies. Specific credit card and other personal information can only be accessed by the company that placed the cookie on the user's computer.

USING DATA THROUGH THE ORDER FULFILLMENT PROCESS

When companies capture information from a customer order, they can use and reuse that information throughout the entire order fulfillment process. Hence, the information gathered to complete an order can also be used to send an invoice to a customer, obtain the product from the warehouse, ship the product, send feedback to the customer, and restock the product by notifying the manufacturer. It can also be used again to send a paper catalog to the customer or send a special offer by email.

These ecommerce enhancements replace the traditional approach, which used a paper-based procurement process with purchase orders sent via fax or mail. This electronic process not only speeds up the delivery of the product, but also increases the accuracy so that the product is delivered to the correct address. Rather than reading a fax or a mailed-in form, a shipper uses the more accurate electronic version of the data. Electronic information allows better supply chain management, including checking product and resource availability electronically, and automating planning, scheduling, and forecasting.

PROVIDING FEEDBACK TO CUSTOMERS

Confirmations and order status updates are ways to enhance feedback to customers. If a customer receives confirmation of a mistake in an order just placed, the order can be corrected immediately. For example, suppose a customer mistakenly submits an order for two copies of a DVD rather than one. After submitting the order, the customer receives an email confirming the order. The customer notices the mistake, immediately contacts the company, and has the order corrected, thereby avoiding having to return the extra copy of the DVD. Accuracy is improved by better feedback.

SUMMARY

Ensuring the quality of the data input to the information system is critical to ensuring quality output. The quality of data entered can be improved through the attainment of the three major data entry objectives: effective coding, effective and efficient data capture, and the validation of data.

One of the best ways to speed data entry by humans is through effective use of coding, which puts data into short sequences of digits and/or letters. Both simple sequence codes and alphabetic derivation codes can be used to follow the progress of a given item through a system. Classification codes and block sequence codes are useful for distinguishing classes of items from each other. Codes such as the cipher code are also useful because they can conceal information that is sensitive or is restricted to personnel within the business.

Revealing information to specific users is also a worthwhile use of codes, because it can enable business employees to locate items in stock and can also make data entry more meaningful. Significant-digit subset codes use subgroups of digits to describe a product. Mnemonic codes also reveal information by serving as human memory aids that can help a data entry operator enter data correctly or help the end user in using information. The Unicode character set includes all standard language symbols. You can display Web pages written in other alphabets (Greek, Japanese, Chinese, or Hebrew, for example) by downloading an input method editor from Microsoft. Codes that are useful for informing computers or people about what functions to perform or what actions to take are called function codes; they circumvent having to spell out in detail what actions are necessary.

Another part of assuring effective data entry is attention to the input devices being used. A well-designed, effective form that serves as a source document (where needed) is the first step. Data can be input through many different methods, each with varying speed and reliability. Keyboards have been redesigned for efficiency and improved ergonomics. Optical character recognition (OCR) allows the reading of input data through the use of special software, which eliminates some steps and also requires fewer employee skills.

Other data entry methods include magnetic ink character recognition (MICR), which is used by banks to encode customer account numbers, and mark-sense forms, which are used for high-volume data entry. Bar codes (applied to products or human identification, and then scanned) also speed data entry and improve data accuracy and reliability. New input technologies such as digital cameras expand the ease of use and the range of functions available. Intelligent terminals are input devices (often microprocessor based) with a display and keyboard, and they can be networked to the CPU. They permit transactions to be entered and completed in real time. RFID (radio frequency identification) allows the automatic collection of data using RFID tags on products, people, or anything in between. They can improve inventory management and supply chain processes.

Along with appropriate coding, data capture, and input devices, accurate data entry can be enhanced through the use of input validation. The systems analyst must assume that errors in data *will* occur and must work with users to design input validation tests to prevent erroneous data from being processed and stored, because initial errors that go undiscovered for long periods are expensive and time consuming to correct.

Input transactions should be checked to ensure that the transaction requested is acceptable, authorized, and correct. Input data can be validated through the inclusion in the software of several types of tests that check for missing data,

HYPERCASE® EXPERIENCE 15

"Sometimes I think I'm the luckiest person on Earth. Even though I've been here five years, I still enjoy the people I meet and what I do. Yes, I know Snowden's demanding. You've experienced some of that, haven't you? He, for one, loves codes. I think they are a pain. I always forget them or try to make up new ones or something. Some of the physicians, though, think they're great. It must be all those Latin abbreviations they studied in med school. I hear that your most pressing assignment this week has to do with actually getting the information into the project reporting system. The Training Unit wants your ideas, and it wants them fast. Good luck with it. Oh, and when Snowden gets back from Thailand, I'm certain he'll want to take a peek at what your team has been up to."

HYPERCASE QUESTIONS

1. Using a CASE tool, a software package such as Microsoft Access, or a paper layout form, design a data entry procedure for the proposed project reporting system for the Training Unit. Assume we are particularly concerned about the consulting physicians staff, who don't want to spend a great deal of time keying in large amounts of data when using the system.
2. Test your data entry procedure on three teammates. Ask for feedback concerning the appropriateness of the procedure, given the type of users the system will have.
3. Redesign the data entry procedure to include the feedback you have received. Explain in a paragraph how your changes reflect the comments you were given.

length of data items, range and reasonableness of data, and invalid values for data. Input data can also be compared with stored data for validation purposes. Once numerical data are input, they can be checked and corrected automatically through the use of check digits. Credit card processing uses a check digit called the Luhn formula, created in the 1960s.

There is a set order for the testing of data to validate each field. There are also pattern validation methods found in the database design or included in programming languages. The patterns are called regular expressions and contain symbols that represent the type of data that must be present in a field.

Ecommerce environments afford the opportunity for increasing accuracy of data. With proper emphasis on user-centered design elements, customers can enter their own data, store data for later use, use the same stored data throughout the order fulfillment process, and receive feedback regarding order confirmations and updates.

KEYWORDS AND PHRASES

- alphabetic derivation code
- autocomplete feature
- bar code
- block sequence code
- bottleneck
- changeable
- check digit
- cipher code
- classification code
- coding
- cookies
- cross-reference test

differentiated
function code
intelligent terminal
keyboarding
Luhn formula
magnetic ink character recognition (MICR)
mark-sense form
mnemonic code
optical character recognition (OCR)
radio frequency identification (RFID)
redundancy in input data
regular expression
self-validating code
significant-digit subset code
simple sequence code
supply chain management
test for class or composition
test for comparison with stored data
test for correct field length
test for invalid values
test for missing data
test for range or reasonableness
Unicode
validating input

REVIEW QUESTIONS

1. What are the four primary objectives of data entry?
2. List the five general purposes for coding data.
3. Define the term *simple sequence code.*
4. When is an alphabetic derivation code useful?
5. Explain what is accomplished with a classification code.
6. Define the term *block sequence code.*
7. What is the simplest type of code for concealing information?
8. What are the benefits of using a significant-digit subset code?
9. What is the purpose of using a mnemonic code for data?
10. Define the term *function code.*
11. List the eight general guidelines for proper coding.
12. What are changeable data?
13. What are differentiation data?
14. What is one specific way to reduce the redundancy of data being entered?
15. Define the term *bottleneck* as it applies to data entry.
16. What three repetitive functions of data entry can be done more efficiently by a computer than by a data entry operator?
17. List six data entry methods.
18. List the three main problems that can occur with input transactions.
19. Define RFID. What are the differences between active and passive RFID tags?
20. Give two examples of the use of RFID tags in process or inventory management in retail or health care environments.
21. What are the eight tests for validating input data?
22. Which test checks to see whether data fields are correctly filled in with either numbers or letters?
23. What common error is missed by the Luhn formula?
24. Which test would not permit a user to input a date such as October 32?
25. Which test ensures data accuracy by the incorporation of a number in the code itself?
26. List four improvements to data accuracy that transactions conducted over ecommerce Web sites can offer.
27. What is Unicode, and how is it used?
28. What is the process for validating data entered into fields?
29. What is a regular expression?

PROBLEMS

1. A small, private university specializing in graduate programs needs to keep track of the list of students who (a) apply, (b) are accepted, and (c) actually enroll in the university. For security purposes the university also must send a report to the government with a list a foreign students who enroll but fail to register. Suggest a kind of code for this purpose, and give an example of its use in the university that demonstrates its appropriateness. What are its advantages?
2. The Central Pacific University Chipmunks have been using a simple sequence code to keep track of season ticket holders and fans who are not season ticket holders for all of its sports programs. There have been some upsetting mixups.

   In a paragraph, suggest a different coding scheme that will help uniquely identify each ticket holder and explain how it will prevent mixups.
3. A code used by an ice cream store to order its products is 12DRM215-220. This code is deciphered in this manner: 12 stands for the count of items in the box, DRM stands for Dreamcicles (a particular kind of ice cream novelty), and 215-220 indicates the entire class of low-fat products carried by the distributor.
   a. What kind of code is used? Describe the purpose behind each part (12, DRM, 215-220) of the code.
   b. Construct a coded entry using the same format and logic for an ice cream novelty called Pigeon Bars, which come in a six-count package and are *not* low-fat.
   c. Construct a coded entry using the same format and logic for an ice cream novelty called Airwhips, which come in a 24-count package and are low-fat.
4. The data entry operators at Michael Mulheren Construction have been making errors when entering the codes for residential siding products, which are as follows: U = stUcco, A = Aluminum, R = bRick, M = Masonite, EZ = EZ color-lok enameled masonite, N = Natural wood siding, AI = pAInted finish, SH = SHake SHingles. Only one code per address is permitted.
   a. List the possible problems with the coding system that could be contributing to erroneous entries. (*Hint:* Are the classes mutually exclusive?)
   b. Devise a mnemonic code that will help the operators understand what they are entering and subsequently help their accuracy.
   c. How would you redesign the classes for siding materials? Respond in a paragraph.
5. The following is a code for one product in an extensive cosmetic line: L02002Z621289. L means that it is a lipstick, 0 means it was introduced without matching nail polish, 2002 is a sequence code indicating in what order it was produced, Z is a classification code indicating that the product is hypoallergenic, and 621289 is the number of the plant (there are 15 plants) where the product is produced.
   a. Critique the code by listing the features that might lead to inaccurate data entry.
   b. Designer Brian d'Arcy James owns the cosmetic firm that uses this coding scheme. Always interested in new design, Brian is willing to look at a more elegant code that encodes the *same* information in a better way. Redesign the coding scheme and provide a key for your work.
   c. Write a sentence for each change you have suggested, indicating what data entry problem (from Problem 5a) the change will eliminate.
6. The d'Arcy James cosmetic firm requires its salespeople to use notebooks to enter orders from retail department stores (their biggest customers). This

information is then relayed to warehouses, and orders are shipped on a first-come, first-served basis. Unfortunately, the stores are aware of this policy and are extremely competitive about which one of them will offer a new d'Arcy James product first. Many retailers have taken the low road and persuaded salespeople to falsify their order dates on sales forms by making them earlier than they actually were.

a. This problem is creating havoc at the warehouse. Disciplining any of the personnel involved is not feasible. How can the warehouse computer be used to certify when orders are actually placed? Explain in a paragraph.

b. Salespeople are complaining that they have to ignore their true job of selling so that they can key in order data. List the data items relating to sales of cosmetics to retailers that should be stored in and retrieved from the central computer rather than keyed in for every order.

c. Describe in a paragraph or two how bar coding might help solve the problem in Problem 6b.

7. List the best data entry method and your reason for choosing it for each of the five situations listed below:

a. Turnaround document for a utility company that wants notification of a change in the customer address.

b. Data retrieval allowed only if there is positive machine identification of the party requesting data.

c. Not enough trained personnel available to interpret long, written responses; many forms submitted that capture answers to multiple-choice examinations; high reliability necessary; fast turnaround not required.

d. Warehouse set up for a discount compact disc operation; bins are labeled with price information, but individual discs are not; and few skilled operators are available to enter price data.

e. Poison control center that maintains a large database of poisons and antidotes; needs a way to enter data on the poison taken; also enter weight, age, and general physical condition of the victim when a person calls the center's toll-free number for emergency advice.

f. Online purchase of a CD by a consumer with a credit card.

8. Ben Coleman, one of your systems analysis team members, surprises you by asserting that when a system uses a test for correct field length, it is redundant also to include a test for range or reasonableness. In a paragraph, give an example that demonstrates that Ben is mistaken on this one.

9. Several retailers have gotten together and begun issuing a "state" credit card that is good only in stores in their state. As a courtesy, sales clerks are permitted to transcribe the 15-digit account number by hand (after getting it from the accounting office) if the customer is not carrying the card. The only problem with accounts that retailers have noticed so far is that sometimes erroneous account numbers are accepted into the computer system, resulting in a bill being issued to a nonexistent account.

a. What sort of validity test would clear up the problem? How? Respond in a paragraph.

b. Suggest an alternative data entry method that might alleviate this problem altogether.

10. The following are part numbers: 238902, 238933, 239402, 235693, 235405, 239204, 240965. Develop a check digit for them using 1-3-1-3-1 multipliers and modulus 11. Use the method presented in this chapter. Why do some numbers have the same check digit?

11. Develop a check digit system for the part numbers in Problem 10 using 5-4-3-2-1 multipliers and modulus 11.

12. Develop a check digit system for the part numbers in Problem 10 using the Luhn formula.
13. Why would a check digit system such as 1-1-1-1-1 not work as well as other methods? What errors would it miss?
14. Define a regular expression for validating each of the following:
    a. A United States zip code, which must have five digits, followed by an optional hyphen and four digits.
    b. A telephone number in the format (aaa) nnn-nnnn, where aaa represents the area code and the *n*s represent digits.
    c. A date in the form of day-month-year, where the month is a three-letter code and the year is four digits. Hyphen must separate the day and month and year and month.
    d. The alphabetic derivation code illustrated in this chapter for a magazine subscriber. The format is 99999XXX9999XXX, where X represents a letter and 9 represents a number.
15. For the following codes, define the validation criteria (there may be multiple checks for each field) and the order that you would test each of the conditions.
    a. **A credit card number entered on a Web form:** The customer has selected the type of credit card from a drop-down list.
    b. **A part number in a hardware store:** The part number is a complex code, where the first digit represents the department (such as housewares, automotive, and so on), and the number should be self-checking. There are seven different departments.
    c. **The date that a book was postmarked when returned to an online bookstore:** A copy of the customer receipt must be included with the book. Returned books must be postmarked within 30 days of the purchase date.
    d. **A language spoken code used on a Web site:** *Hint:* Search the Web for standard language codes.
    e. **A driver's license number, composed of several parts:** The person's birth month, the birthday, and birth year, not necessarily together; a code representing eye color; and a sequence number. The driver's license contains the date of birth, the eye and hair color, as well as the person's name and address.
    f. **The Canadian postal code:** The format is X9X 9X9 (X is any letter, 9 is any number).
    g. **Airline luggage codes,** such as LAX for Los Angeles or DUB for Dublin.
    h. **A product key used to unlock purchased software:** The key consists of four groups of five characters each. The first group must have two letters followed by three numbers; the second group must contain two numbers followed by three letters; the third group must contain two letters, each from A through G followed by three numbers from one through four; and the last group must contain a letter, either an E, G, or C, two digits with values from four through seven and two letters, either an A, B, or C. *Hint:* A pattern may be the best way to validate the product key.

GROUP PROJECTS

1. Along with your group members, read Consulting Opportunity 15.3, "To Enter or Not to Enter: That Is the Question," presented earlier in this chapter. Design an appropriate data entry system for Elsinore Industries. Your group's design should emphasize efficiency and accuracy. In addition, distinguish between data that are changeable and data that differentiate an item being entered from all others. Draw prototypes of any screen necessary to explain what you are recommending.

2. Divide your group into analysts and Elsinore Industries employees to role play. The analysts should present the new data entry system, complete with prototype displays. Ask for feedback on the design from Elsinore employees.
3. Write a brief paragraph describing how to improve the original data entry design based on the comments received.

SELECTED BIBLIOGRAPHY

Davis, G. B., and M. H. Olson. *Management Information Systems, Conceptual Foundations, Structure, and Development*, 2d ed. New York: McGraw-Hill, 1985.

Lamming, M. G., P. Brown, K. Carter, M. Eldridge, M. Flynn, G. Louie, P. Robinson, and A. Sellan. "The Design of a Human Memory Prosthesis." *Computer Journal*, Vol. 37, 1994, pp. 153–63.

Lee, Y. M., F. Cheng, Y. T. Leung. "Exploring the Impact of RFID on Supply Chain Dynamics." In *Proceedings of the 2004 Winter Simulation Conference*, pp. 1145–1152. Edited by R. G. Ingalls, M. D. Rossetti, J. S. Smith, and B.A. Peters.

Miller, G. A. "The Magical Number Seven, Plus or Minus Two: Some Limits on Our Capability for Processing Information." *Psychological Review*, Vol. 63, No. 2, March 1956, pp. 81–97.

Newman, W. N., and M. G. Lamming. *Interactive System Design*. Reading, MA: Addison-Wesley Publishing Co., 1995.

Owsowitz, S., and A. Sweetland. "Factors Affecting Coding Errors." *Rand Memorandum RM-4346-PR*. Santa Monica, CA: Rand Corporation, 1965.

Robey, D., and W. Taggart. "Human Processing in Information and Decision Support Systems." *MIS Quarterly*, Vol. 6, No. 2, June 1982, pp. 61–73.

Ryder, J. "Credit Card Validation Using LUHN Formula." Available at: www.freevbcode.com. Last accessed December 26, 2006.

ALLEN SCHMIDT, JULIE E. KENDALL, AND KENNETH E. KENDALL

ENTERING NATURALLY

Tuesday afternoon finds Anna and Chip having their weekly analysis and design review session. Chip waves toward a large stack of documents that are neatly organized on a large table. "I can't believe that we're almost finished with the design of this system," he remarks. "It's been a long process, but I'll bet we've obtained enough user feedback to ensure a high-quality system. All that's left is the design of the data entry procedures, and we'll be ready to start packaging the specs for the programmers."

"Yes," replies Anna, "the end is in sight. Let's start by examining the design of the input portion of the system."

"The ADD SOFTWARE program is online," notes Chip. "The operator will have to sight-verify each transaction. After all data fields have been edited for accuracy, a message will appear on the bottom of the display. It will prompt the operators to check the data on the display for accuracy against the form and click the **Save Record** button if correct. The operators will have a chance to make changes if the data are keyed incorrectly".

Every data field must be edited for accuracy. Chip notes, "In the long run, it's better to have complete editing for accuracy in the programs rather than to find that erroneous data have been stored on master files and printed on reports."

The strategy for field editing is to check the data in the following order:

1. Syntax—whether the data are numeric or alphabetic—and the length of the data. An example is the HARDWARE INVENTORY NUMBER, which must be eight characters in length and numeric.
2. The contents of the field, including range, limit, and values for the data. When validating the DATE PURCHASED, the month must be from 1 to 12. This check should occur only after the month has been verified as numeric.
3. Cross-reference checks between two or more data elements. To check the day portion of the DATE PURCHASED, a table of the number of days possible for each month will be used for an upper limit. This table could not be used if the month number was not between 1 and 12. Check digits are another example of a cross-reference edit.
4. External edits, such as reading a file to verify if the record to be added already exists in the file. Reading records is slower than editing, which is performed in main memory, and it should occur only after the data successfully pass all other edits.

Edit criteria have been entered on the Visible Analyst **Element Repository** display screen as the elements were added to the design. These elements include simple editing criteria and table checking. The **Notes** area may be used to enter editing criteria. The HARDWARE INVENTORY NUMBER entry includes a reference for using the modulus-11 method of verifying the check digit portion of the number. Furthermore, when adding a new computer, the COMPUTER MASTER must be read to ensure that a record does not already exist with the same HARDWARE INVENTORY NUMBER.

"I think some reports will be useful," Chip tells Anna. "The first report involves creating a final list of all the elements found both on the COMPUTER MASTER and the structural records contained in the master. The report is produced using the **Report** feature, and shows the elements, their length, pictures, and edit criteria in the **Notes** area." This report is used to create the edit criteria table, which became part of the program specifications.

Several of the elements have **Notes** areas referring to tables, as well as entries for the codes in the **Values and Meanings** area. An example is the INTERNAL BOARD element. "I'll produce a list of all tables we'll require," Anna offers. This time, the **Report Query** feature is used to produce the necessary information. A list of all elements containing notes starting with "Table of codes" is printed. Included on the list are the **Picture** and **Length,** showing the syntax of the code. With this list, tables are created.

Each table of codes is defined using Microsoft Access tables. Chip and Anna each spend time working on the tables. A mnemonic code is chosen for BOARD and DISPLAY, because these two would be easy for maintenance personnel to work with. Mnemonic codes are also used to represent the SOFTWARE CATEGORY, because these will be easy for users to remember.

"There are a wide variety of printers available," remarks Chip. "I think a significant-digit subset coding scheme would be the best here. The first digit represents the type of printer . . . laser and so on. The next two digits are for manufacturer, and the last two are a sequence number representing different model numbers."

Anna agrees. "That's good, Chip. That strategy can also be used for the campus buildings: the first digit for the campus location, and the remaining two digits representing individual buildings in the campus."

Chip designs the codes used for the BOARD table. The Microsoft Access display is shown in Figure E15.1. Two columns are used to define codes. The left column

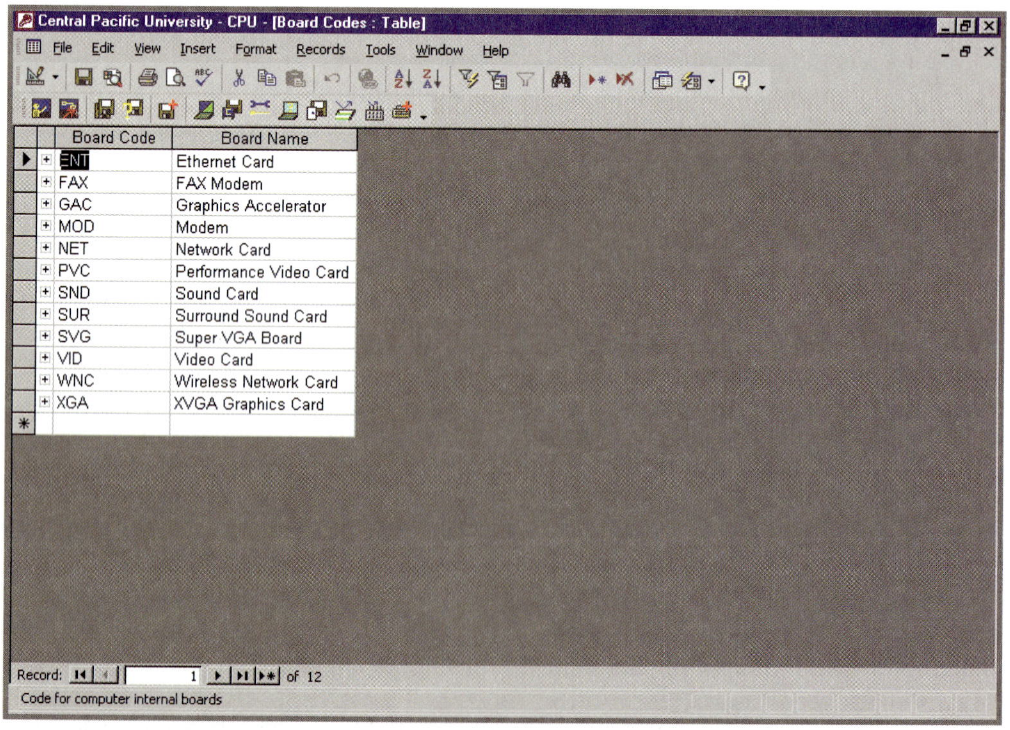

Board Code	Board Name
ENT	Ethernet Card
FAX	FAX Modem
GAC	Graphics Accelerator
MOD	Modem
NET	Network Card
PVC	Performance Video Card
SND	Sound Card
SUR	Surround Sound Card
SVG	Super VGA Board
VID	Video Card
WNC	Wireless Network Card
XGA	XVGA Graphics Card

FIGURE E15.1

BOARD TABLE defined using Microsoft Access.

contains the code, and the right column contains the meaning of the code. These entries may be modified, and new entries may be added, providing flexibility in the final system.

"Here's the SOFTWARE CATEGORY table that I created," says Anna. "This table may be easily updated as new software is developed and acquired by the university."

"That's a valuable component of the system," Chip comments. "It provides consistency for all codes and their meanings."

Chip and Anna finish their work the next morning at about 11:30. They glance around the room happily, frequently reexamining the final design. The months of analysis, design work, consultation with the users, and careful adherence to standards are finally complete.

"I feel really good about this project," says Anna.

Chip agrees, "I'm proud of the quality we put in."

EXERCISES

E-1. Modify and print the following elements with edit criteria in the **Notes** (or **Values and Meanings** for specific codes) area.

Element	*Edit Criteria*
a. SOFTWARE CATEGORY	Table of codes: Software Category Code
b. COURSE TRAINING LEVEL CODE	B - Beginning; I - Intermediate; A - Advanced
c. NETWORK CONNECTION NAME	0 - No Internet; M - Modem; D - DSL; 1 - T1 Line; W - Wireless
d. OPERATING SYSTEM	M - Macintosh; N - Windows NT; X - Windows XP; 0 - Windows 2000; U - Unix

E-2. Modify and print the following elements with edit criteria placed in the **Notes** area:

a. Element: SOFTWARE INVENTORY NUMBER
   Notes: A modulus-11 check digit must be verified when entering the number. The ADD SOFTWARE program creates the check digit. The ADD SOFTWARE program should also check the SOFTWARE MASTER file to ensure that a record with the same inventory number does not already exist.

b. Element: DATE PURCHASED
   Notes: Verify that the DATE PURCHASED is less than or equal to the current date.

c. Element: QUANTITY RECEIVED
   Notes: Verify that the QUANTITY RECEIVED is less than or equal to the QUANTITY ORDERED.

The exercises preceded by a Web icon indicate value-added material is available from the Web site at www.prenhall.com/kendall. Students can download a sample Visible Analyst Project and a Microsoft Access database that can be used to complete the exercises. Visible Analyst software can be packaged with this text for an additional fee.

d. Element: SOFTWARE UPGRADE VERSION
Notes: Ensure that the software UPGRADE VERSION is greater than the current version.

e. Element: HARD DRIVE
Notes: HARD DRIVE 2 may exist only if there is an entry for HARD DRIVE 1.

E-3. View and print the **Coded Elements Report Query.**

E-4. Use Microsoft Access to view the SOFTWARE CATEGORY CODES table. What is wrong with the design of these codes?

E-5. Use Microsoft Access to modify and print the BOARD CODES table. Add the following codes.

PCM	PCMCIA Fax Modem
WNT	Wireless Network Card
FER	Finger print Reader Card

E-6. Use Microsoft Access to modify and print the PRINTER CODES table. The format of this significant-digit subset code is as follows:
TMMSS, where

T	is the type of printer
M	is the manufacturer
S	represents a sequence number, with a higher number indicating an improved model

Values for the type of printer are:

0	Multifunction
1	Photo
2	Inkjet
3	Thermal
4	Laser
5	PostScript
6	Plotter

Values for the manufacturer are as follows:

01	IBM
02	Epson
03	Hewlett-Packard
04	Panasonic
05	Lexmark
06	Samsung
07	Canon
08	Texas Instruments

Add the following codes:

Code	*Meaning*
20301	Hewlett-Packard DeskJet D4160
30601	Lexmark X2350 3 in 1
40201	Epson Stylus Photo Cx3810 3 in 1
80305	HP Color LaserJet 3600n
90107	Canon MP830

E-7. Use Microsoft Access to modify and print the MONITOR CODES table using the mnemonic form. Add the following entries:

Code	***Meaning***
LCDM	LCD
FSCM	Flat Screen
XGAT	XGA TFT Screen
SVGA	Super VGA
PLSM	Plasma
AMTX	Active Color Matrix

E-8. After speaking with Dot Matricks and Mike Crowe, it has become apparent that the campus codes must be sortable for installing hardware and software, as well as for creating inventory sheets. Use Microsoft Access to modify and print the CAMPUS LOCATION CODES table. The first digit represents the campus location. Values are as follows:

1	Central Campus
2	Waterford Campus
3	Hillside Campus

The next three digits represent buildings in the campus, with the following building codes:

001	Administration	010	Environmental Studies
002	Admissions	011	Geology
003	Agricultural	012	Law
004	Astronomy	013	Library
005	Business	014	Mathematics
006	Chemical Engineering	015	Medicine
007	Computer Science	016	Physics
008	Education	017	Psychology
009	Engineering	018	Zoology

Use a combination (your choice) of campus and building codes to build the final table of codes. Include the meaning of the code.

QUALITY ASSURANCE THROUGH SOFTWARE ENGINEERING

16

Learning Objectives

Once you have mastered the material in this chapter you will be able to:

1. **Recognize the importance of users and analysts taking a total quality approach to the entire SDLC.**
2. **Create structure charts to design modular, top-down systems.**
3. **Use a variety of techniques to improve the quality of software design and maintenance.**
4. **Understand the importance of running a variety of tests during systems development to identify unknown problems.**

Quality has long been a concern of businesses, as it should be for systems analysts in the analysis and design of information systems. It is too risky to undertake the entire analysis and design process without using a quality assurance approach. The three approaches to quality assurance through software engineering are (1) securing total quality assurance by designing systems and software with a top-down, modular approach; (2) documenting software with appropriate tools; and (3) testing, maintaining, and auditing software.

Two thoughts guide quality assurance. The first is that the user of the information system is the single most important factor in establishing and evaluating its quality. The second is that it is far less costly to correct problems in their early stages than it is to wait until a problem is articulated through user complaints or crises.

We already have learned about the huge investment of labor and other business resources that are required to launch a system successfully. Using quality assurance throughout the process is a way to minimize risks, it helps ensure that the resulting system is what is needed and wanted, and it will demonstrably improve some aspect of business performance. This chapter provides the analyst with three major approaches to quality.

THE TOTAL QUALITY MANAGEMENT APPROACH

Total quality management (TQM) is essential throughout all the systems development steps. According to Dean and Evans (1994), the primary elements of TQM are meaningful only when occurring in an organizational context that supports a comprehensive quality effort. It is in this context that the elements of customer focus, strategic planning and leadership, continuous improvement, empowerment, and teamwork are united to change employees' behavior and, ultimately, the organization's course. Notice that the concept of quality has broadened over the years to reflect an organizational, rather than an exclusively production, approach. Instead of conceiving of quality as controlling the number of defective products produced, quality is now thought of as an evolutionary process toward perfection that is referred to as total quality management.

Systems analysts must be aware of the factors that are driving the interest in quality. It is important to realize that the increasing commitment of businesses to TQM fits extraordinarily well into the overall objectives for systems analysis and design.

SIX SIGMA

The advent of Six Sigma has changed the approach to quality management. Every systems analyst and systems user needs to be aware of Six Sigma and apply some of the principles to their systems analysis projects. Originally developed by Motorola in the 1980s, Six Sigma is more than a methodology; it is a culture built on quality. The goal of Six Sigma is to eliminate all defects. This applies to any product, service, or process. In operations management textbooks from the 1970s to the end of the century, quality control was expressed in terms of three standard deviations from the mean, or three sigma, which equals about 67,000 defects per million opportunities. Six Sigma implies a goal of only 3.4 defects per million opportunities.

Six Sigma is a top-down approach. It requires a CEO to adopt the philosophy and an executive to serve as project champion. A Six Sigma project leader is called a Black Belt. People chosen to be Black Belts can come from different levels and different pay grades, but must have project experience and must undergo special training. Black Belts are certified after they have successfully led projects. Project members are called Green Belts. Master Black Belts are Black Belts who have worked on many projects and are available as a resource to project teams. (The metaphor of the Black Belt comes from the ranking system of capabilities in martial arts. It emphasizes the importance of discipline by its adherents in all things.)

Six Sigma can be summarized as a methodology. The steps of Six Sigma are shown in Figure 16.1. Six Sigma, however, is much more than a methodology; it is a philosophy and a culture.

For more information on Six Sigma and quality management, visit the Web site for the Juran Center at the Carlson School of Management, University of Minnesota, Twin Cities (www.csom.umn.edu). In 2002 the Juran Center issued a proclamation to support and encourage quality. The authors of this book signed the charter at that time, and we agree wholeheartedly with its principles.

Joseph M. Juran had said, "All quality improvement occurs on a project-by-project basis and in no other way" (Juran, 1964). Systems analysts, project managers, and users should take that to heart.

RESPONSIBILITY FOR TOTAL QUALITY MANAGEMENT

Practically speaking, a large portion of the responsibility for the quality of information systems rests with systems users and management. Two things must happen for TQM to become a reality with systems projects. First, the full organizational support of management must exist, which is a departure from merely endorsing the newest management gimmick. Such support means establishing a

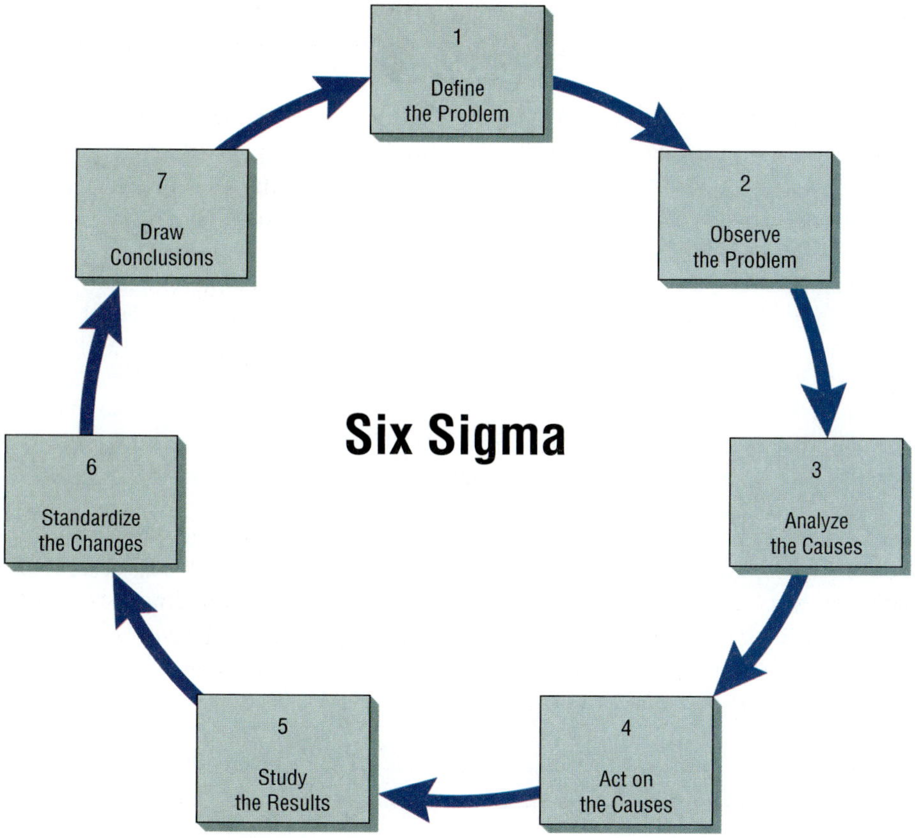

FIGURE 16.1

Every systems analyst should understand the methodology and philosophy of Six Sigma.

context for management people to consider seriously how the quality of information systems and information itself affects their work.

Early commitment to quality from the analyst and business users is necessary to achieve the goal of quality. This commitment results in exerting an evenly paced effort toward quality throughout the systems development life cycle, and it stands in stark contrast to having to pour huge amounts of effort into ironing out problems at the end of the project.

Organizational support for quality in management information systems can be achieved by providing on-the-job time for IS quality circles, which consist of six to eight organizational peers specifically charged with considering both how to improve information systems and how to implement improvements.

Through work in IS quality circles or through other mechanisms already in place, management and users must develop guidelines for quality standards of information systems. Preferably, standards will be reshaped every time a new system or major modification is to be formally proposed by the systems analysis team.

Hammering out quality standards is not easy, but it is possible and has been done. Part of the systems analyst's job is encouraging users to crystallize their expectations about information systems and their interactions with them.

Departmental quality standards must then be communicated through feedback to the systems analysis team. The team is often surprised at what has developed. Expectations typically are less complex than what experienced analysts know could be done with a system. In addition, human issues that have been overlooked or underrated by the analyst team may be designated as extremely pressing in users' quality standards. Getting users involved in spelling out quality standards for information systems will help the analyst avoid expensive mistakes in unwanted or unnecessary systems development.

CONSULTING OPPORTUNITY 16.1

THE QUALITY OF MIS IS NOT STRAINED

"Merle, come here and take a look at these end-of-the-week reports," Portia pleads. As one of the managers on the six-person IS task force/quality assurance committee, Portia has been examining for her marketing department the system output that has been produced by the prototype. The systems analysis team has asked her to review the output.

Merle Chant walks over to Portia's desk and takes a look at the prospectus she's holding. "Why, what's wrong?" he asks. "It looks okay to me. I think you're taking this task force deal too much to heart. We're supposed to get our other work done as well, you know." Merle turns to leave and returns to his desk slightly perturbed at being interrupted.

"Merle, have a little mercy. It is really silly to put up with these reports the way they are. I can't find anything I need, and then I'm supposed to tell everyone else in the department what part of the report to read. I, for one, am disappointed. This report is slipshod. It doesn't make any sense to me. It's a rehash of the output we're getting now. Actually, it looks worse. I am going to bring this up at the next task force meeting," Portia proclaims insistently.

Merle turns to face her, saying, "Quality is their responsibility, Portia. If the system isn't giving us good reports, they'll fix it when it's all together. All you're doing is making waves. You're acting as if they actually value our input. I wouldn't give them the time of day, let alone do their work for them. They're so smart, let them figure out what we need."

Portia looks at Merle blankly, then starts getting a little angry. "We've been on the task force for four weeks," she says. "You've sat in on four meetings. We're the ones who know the business. The whole idea of TQM is to tell them what we need, what we're satisfied with. If we don't tell them what we need, then we can't complain. I'm bringing it up the next time we meet."

How effective do you think Merle will be in communicating his standards of quality to the systems analysis team and members of the IS task force? Respond in a paragraph. If the systems analysts are able to perceive Merle's unwillingness to work with the task force on developing quality standards, what would you say to convince him of the importance of user involvement in TQM? Make a list of arguments supporting the use of TQM. How can the systems analysis team respond to the concerns Portia is bringing up? In a paragraph, devise a response.

STRUCTURED WALKTHROUGH

One of the strongest quality management actions the systems analysis team can take is to do structured walkthroughs routinely. Structured walkthroughs are a way of using peer reviewers to monitor the system's programming and overall development, point out problems, and allow the programmer or analyst responsible for that portion of the system to make suitable changes.

Structured walkthroughs involve at least four people: the person responsible for the part of the system or subsystem being reviewed (a programmer or analyst), a walkthrough coordinator, a programmer or analyst peer, and a peer who takes notes about suggestions.

Each person attending a walkthrough has a special role to play. The coordinator is there to ensure that the others adhere to any roles assigned to them and to ensure that any activities scheduled are accomplished. The programmer or analyst is there to listen, not to defend his or her thinking, rationalize a problem, or argue. The programmer or analyst peer is present to point out errors or potential problems, not to specify how the problems should be remedied. The notetaker records what is said so that the others present can interact without encumbrance.

Structured walkthroughs can be done whenever a portion of coding, a subsystem, or a system is finished. Just be sure that the subsystem under review is comprehensible outside of its larger context. Structured walkthroughs fit well in a total quality management approach when performed throughout the systems development life cycle. The time they take should be short—half an hour to an hour at most—which means that they must be well coordinated. Figure 16.2 shows a form that is useful in organizing the structured walkthrough and reporting its results. Because walkthroughs take time, do not overuse them.

Use structured walkthroughs as a way to obtain (and then act on) valuable feedback from a perspective that you lack. As with all quality assurance measures,

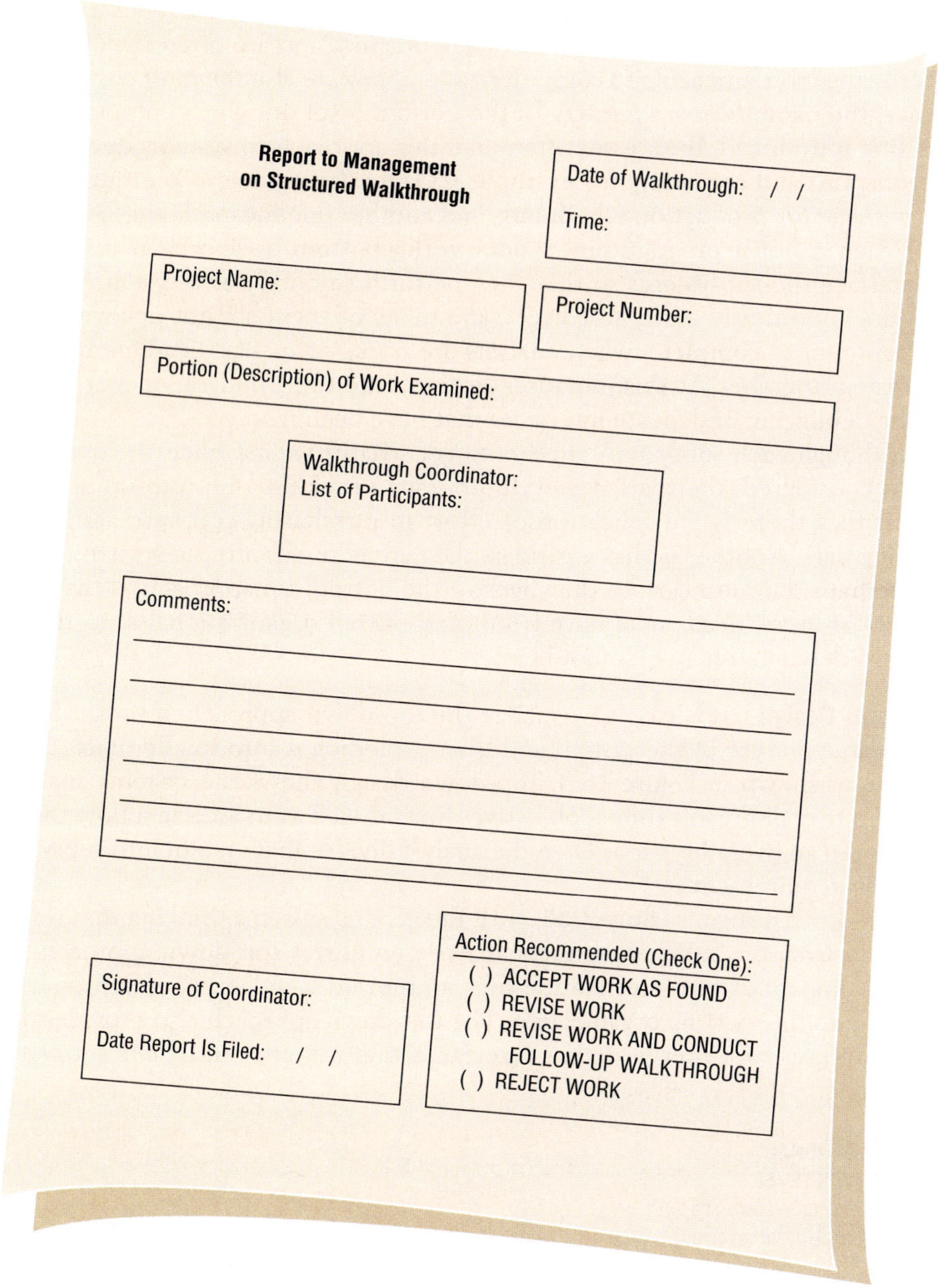

Report to Management on Structured Walkthrough

Date of Walkthrough: / /

Time:

Project Name:

Project Number:

Portion (Description) of Work Examined:

Walkthrough Coordinator:
List of Participants:

Comments:

Signature of Coordinator:

Date Report Is Filed: / /

Action Recommended (Check One):
( ) ACCEPT WORK AS FOUND
( ) REVISE WORK
( ) REVISE WORK AND CONDUCT FOLLOW-UP WALKTHROUGH
( ) REJECT WORK

FIGURE 16.2
A form to document structured walkthroughs; walkthroughs can be done whenever a portion of coding, a system, or a subsystem is complete.

the point of walkthroughs is to evaluate the product systematically on an ongoing basis rather than wait until completion of the system.

SYSTEMS DESIGN AND DEVELOPMENT

In this section, we define the bottom-up and top-down designs of systems, as well as the modular approach to programming. We discuss the advantages of each one, as well as the precautions that should be observed when employing either a top-down or modular approach. We also discuss the appropriateness of the top-down and modular approaches for aiding in quality assurance of systems projects.

Bottom-Up Design Bottom-up design refers to identifying the processes that need computerization as they arise, analyzing them as systems, and either coding the processes or purchasing packaged software to meet the immediate problem. The problems that require computerization are often on the lowest level of the organization. Problems on the lowest level of the organization are often structured and thereby the most amenable to computerization; they are also the most cost effective. Hence, the name *bottom-up* refers to the bottom level on which computerization was first introduced. Businesses often take this approach to systems development by going out and acquiring, for example, COTS software for accounting, a different package for production scheduling, and another one for marketing.

When in-house programming is done with a bottom-up approach, it is difficult to interface the subsystems so that they perform smoothly as a system. Interface bugs are enormously costly to correct, and many of them are not uncovered until programming is complete, when analysts are trying to meet a deadline in putting the system together. At this juncture, there is little time, budget, or user patience for the debugging of delicate interfaces that have been ignored.

Although each subsystem appears to get what it wants, when the overall system is considered, there are severe limitations to taking a bottom-up approach. One is that there is a duplication of effort in purchasing software and even in entering data. Another is that worthless data are entered into the system. A third, and perhaps the most serious drawback of the bottom-up approach, is that, while pockets of users' needs may have been met, overall organizational objectives are not considered and hence cannot be met.

Top-Down Design It is easy to visualize the top-down approach; it means looking at the large picture of the system and then exploding it into smaller parts or subsystems, as shown in Figure 16.3. Top-down design allows the systems analyst to ascertain overall organizational objectives first, as well as to ascertain how they are best met in an overall system. Then the analyst divides that system into subsystems and their requirements.

Top-down design is compatible with the general systems thinking that was discussed in Chapter 2. When systems analysts employ a top-down approach, they are thinking about the interrelationships and interdependencies of subsystems as they fit into the existing organization. The top-down approach also provides desirable emphasis on synergy or the interfaces that systems and their subsystems

FIGURE 16.3
Using the top-down approach to first ascertain overall organizational objectives.

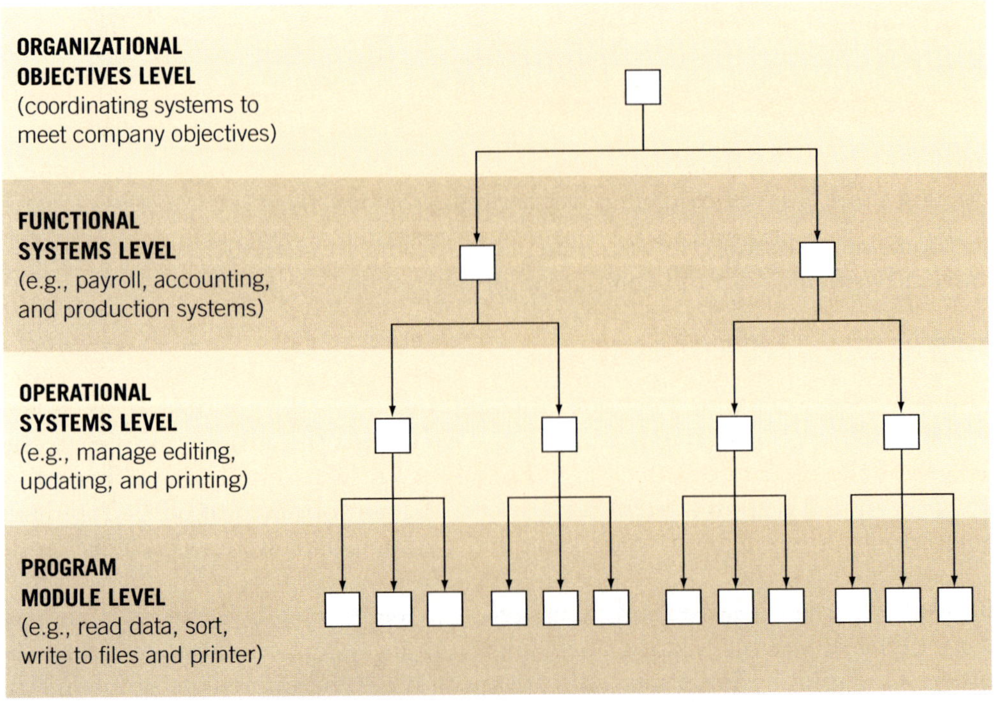

require, which is lacking in the bottom-up approach. It helps to answer the question of how teams must work together to accomplish their goals.

The advantages of using a top-down approach to systems design include avoiding the chaos of attempting to design a system all at once. As we have seen, planning and implementing management information systems is incredibly complex. Attempting to get all subsystems in place and running at once is agreeing to fail.

A second advantage of taking a top-down approach to design is that it enables separate systems analysis teams to work in parallel on different but necessary subsystems, which can save a great deal of time. The use of teams for subsystems design is particularly well suited to a total quality assurance approach.

A third advantage is that a top-down approach avoids a major problem associated with a bottom-up approach; it prevents systems analysts from getting so mired in detail that they lose sight of what the system is supposed to do.

There are some pitfalls of top-down design that the systems analyst needs to know. The first is the danger that the system will be divided into the "wrong" subsystems. Attention must be paid to overlapping needs and to the sharing of resources so that the partitioning of subsystems makes sense for the total systems picture. Furthermore, it is important that each subsystem address the correct problem. Recall that much of the information in Chapter 2 introduces you to a variety of tools that can help you correctly identify systems, subsystems, and their boundaries.

A second danger is that once subsystem divisions are made, their interfaces may be neglected or ignored. Responsibility for interfaces needs to be detailed.

A third caution that accompanies the use of top-down design is that subsystems must be reintegrated eventually. Mechanisms for reintegration need to be put in place at the beginning. One suggestion is regular information trading between subsystem teams; another is using tools that permit flexibility if changes to interrelated subsystems are required.

Total quality management and the top-down approach to design can go hand-in-hand. The top-down approach provides the systems group with a ready-made division of users into task forces (specialized teams of users) for subsystems. Task forces set up in this manner can then serve a dual function as quality circles for the management information system. The necessary structure for quality assurance is then in place, as is proper motivation for getting the subsystem to accomplish the departmental goals that are important to the users involved.

MODULAR DEVELOPMENT

Once the top-down design approach is taken, the modular approach is useful in programming. This approach involves breaking the programming into logical, manageable portions, or modules. This kind of programming works well with top-down design because it emphasizes the interfaces between modules and does not neglect them until later in systems development. Ideally, each individual module should be functionally cohesive so that it is charged with accomplishing only one function.

Modular program design has three main advantages. First, modules are easier to write and debug because they are virtually self-contained. Tracing an error in a module is less complicated, because a problem in one module should not cause problems in others.

A second advantage of modular design is that modules are easier to maintain. Modifications usually will be limited to a few modules and will not be spread over an entire program.

A third advantage of modular design is that modules are easier to grasp, because they are self-contained subsystems. Hence, a reader can pick up a code listing of a module and understand its function.

Some guidelines for modular programming include the following:

1. Keep each module to a manageable size (ideally including only one function).
2. Pay particular attention to the critical interfaces (the data and control variables that are passed to other modules).
3. Minimize the number of modules the user must modify when making changes.
4. Maintain the hierarchical relationships set up in the top-down phases.

MODULARITY IN THE WINDOWS ENVIRONMENT

Modularity is becoming increasingly important. Microsoft developed two systems to link programs in its Windows environment. The first is called Dynamic Data Exchange (DDE), which shares code by using Dynamic Link Library (DLL) files. Using DDE, a user can store data in one program—perhaps a spreadsheet such as Excel—and then use that data in another program, say a word processing package such as Word for Windows. The program that contains the original data is called the server, and the program that uses the data is called the client (another term for client host). The DDE link can be set up so that whenever the client's word processing file is opened, the data are automatically updated and any changes made to the server spreadsheet file since the word processing file was last opened are reflected. (See Chapter 17 for an extended discussion of the client/server model.)

One of the most commonly used DLL files is COMMDLG.DLL, which contains Windows' **File Open, File Save, Search,** and **Print** dialog boxes. One advantage of using this file is that programs will have the same look and feel as other Windows programs. It also speeds development, because programmers do not have to write the code contained in common DLL files.

A second approach to linking programs in Windows is called Object Linking and Embedding (OLE). This method of connecting programs is superior to DDE because it ties in application data and graphics. Whereas DDE uses a cut-and-paste approach to linking data and does not retain formatting, OLE retains all the properties of the originally created data. This object-oriented approach (see Chapter 18 for a discussion of object-oriented principles) allows the end user to remain in the client application and still edit the original data in the server application. With OLE, when an end user clicks on the embedded object, a toolbar pops up to allow visual editing.

USING STRUCTURE CHARTS TO DESIGN SYSTEMS

The recommended tool for designing a modular, top-down system is called a structure chart. A structure chart is simply a diagram consisting of rectangular boxes, which represent the modules, and connecting arrows.

Figure 16.4 shows three modules that are labeled 000, 100, and 200, and are connected using right-angle lines. Higher-level modules are numbered by 100s or 1,000s, and lower-level modules are numbered by 10s or 100s. This numbering allows programmers to insert modules using a number between the adjacent module numbers. For example, a module inserted between modules 110 and 120 would receive number 115. If two modules were inserted, the numbers might be 114 and 117. These numbering schemes vary, depending on the organizational standards used.

Off to the sides of the connecting lines, two types of arrows are drawn. The arrows with the empty circles are called data couples, and the arrows with the filled-in circles are called control flags or switches. A switch is the same as a control flag except that it is limited to two values: either yes or no. These arrows indicate that something is passed either down to the lower module or up to the upper one.

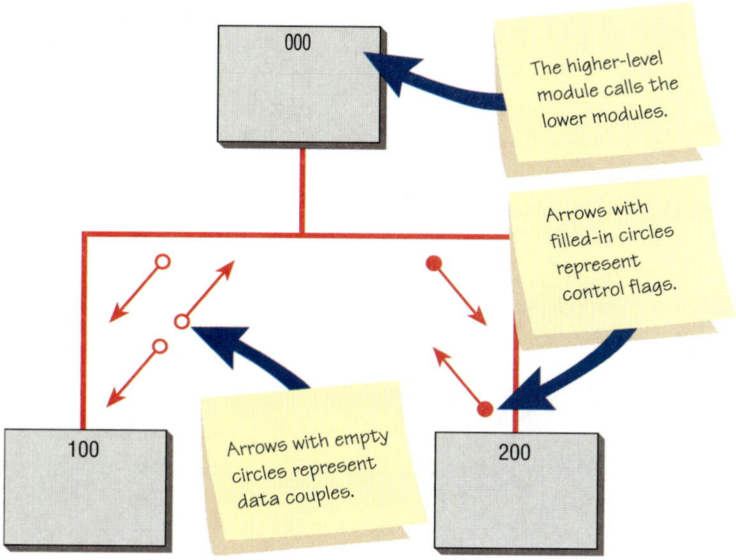

FIGURE 16.4
A structure diagram encourages top-down design using modules.

Ideally, the analyst should keep this coupling to a minimum. The fewer data couples and control flags one has in the system, the easier it is to change the system. When these modules are actually programmed, it is important to pass the least number of data couples between modules.

Even more important is that numerous control flags should be avoided. Control is designed to be passed from lower-level modules to those higher in the structure. On rare occasions, however, it will be necessary to pass control downward in the structure. Control flags govern which portion of a module is to be executed and are associated with IF . . . THEN . . . ELSE . . . and other similar types of statements. When control is passed downward, a low-level module is allowed to make a decision, and the result is a module that performs two different tasks. This result violates the ideal of a functional module: it should perform only one task.

Figure 16.5 illustrates a portion of a structure chart for adding new employees. The program reads an EMPLOYEE TRANSACTION file and verifies that each record in the file contains only acceptable data. Separate reports are printed for both valid and invalid records, providing an audit trail of all transactions. The

FIGURE 16.5
This structure chart illustrates control moving downward and also shows nonfunctional modules.

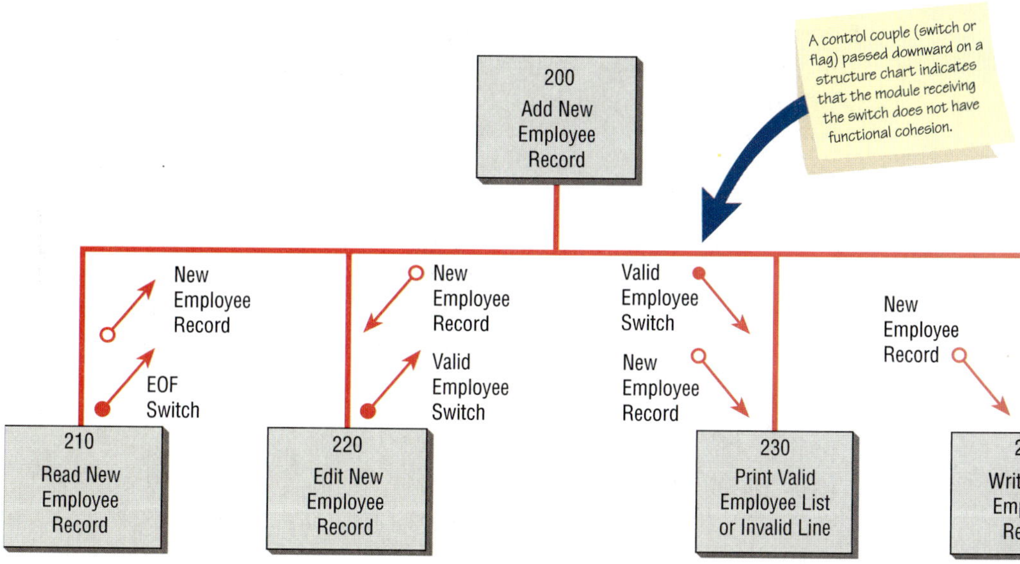

FIGURE 16.6

Pseudocode for module 230 illustrating the effect of passing a switch downward.

```
Module 230—Print Valid Employee List or Invalid Line

IF VALID EMPLOYEE SWITCH = 'Y'
    Move EMPLOYEE NUMBER to VALID EMPLOYEE LIST
    Move EMPLOYEE NAME to VALID EMPLOYEE LIST
    Move EMPLOYEE JOB TITLE to VALID EMPLOYEE LIST
    Move EMPLOYEE DEPARTMENT to VALID EMPLOYEE LIST
    Move EMPLOYEE WORK PHONE NUMBER to VALID EMPLOYEE LIST
    Move EMPLOYEE DATE HIRED to VALID EMPLOYEE LIST
    DO PRINT VALID EMPLOYEE LIST
ELSE
    Move EMPLOYEE NUMBER to INVALID LINE
    Move EMPLOYEE NAME to INVALID LINE
    Move EMPLOYEE JOB TITLE to INVALID LINE
    Move EMPLOYEE DEPARTMENT to INVALID LINE
    Move EMPLOYEE WORK PHONE NUMBER to INVALID LINE
    Move EMPLOYEE DATE HIRED to INVALID LINE
    DO PRINT INVALID LINE
ENDIF
```

report containing invalid records is sent to the user for error correction. Records that are valid are placed in a valid transaction file, which is passed to a separate program for updating the EMPLOYEE MASTER file. Module 200, ADD NEW EMPLOYEE RECORD, represents the logic of adding one record. Because module 230 is used to print both reports, a control flag must be sent down to tell the module which report to print. The logic of module 230 is thus entirely controlled by an IF statement, which is illustrated in Figure 16.6.

Figure 16.7 shows the correct way to design the structure underneath module 200, ADD NEW EMPLOYEE RECORD. Here, each print function has been

FIGURE 16.7

An improved structure chart showing control flowing upward.

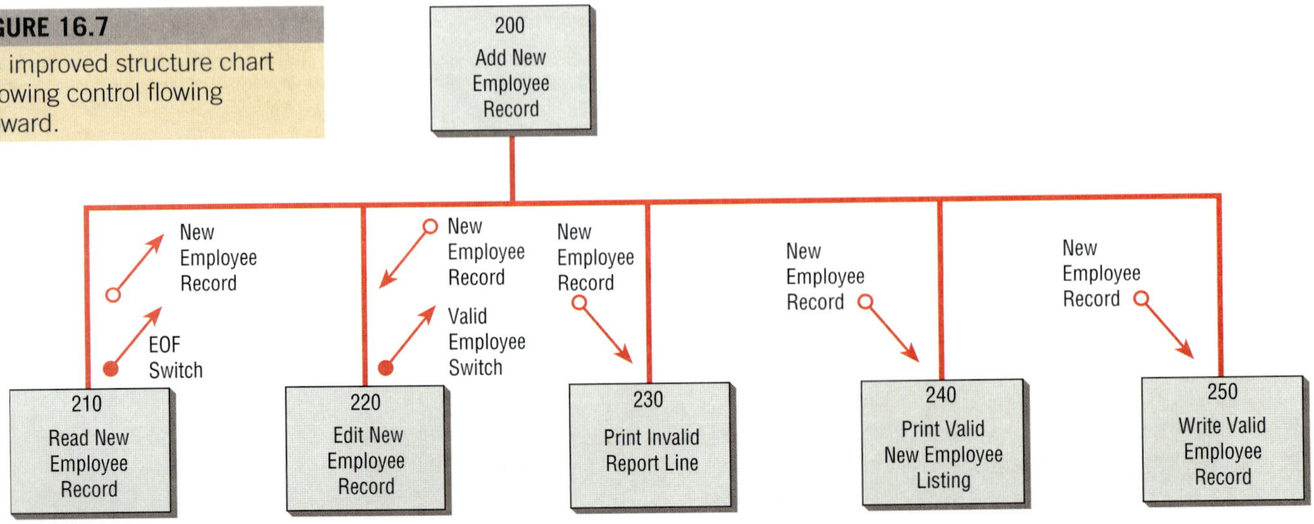

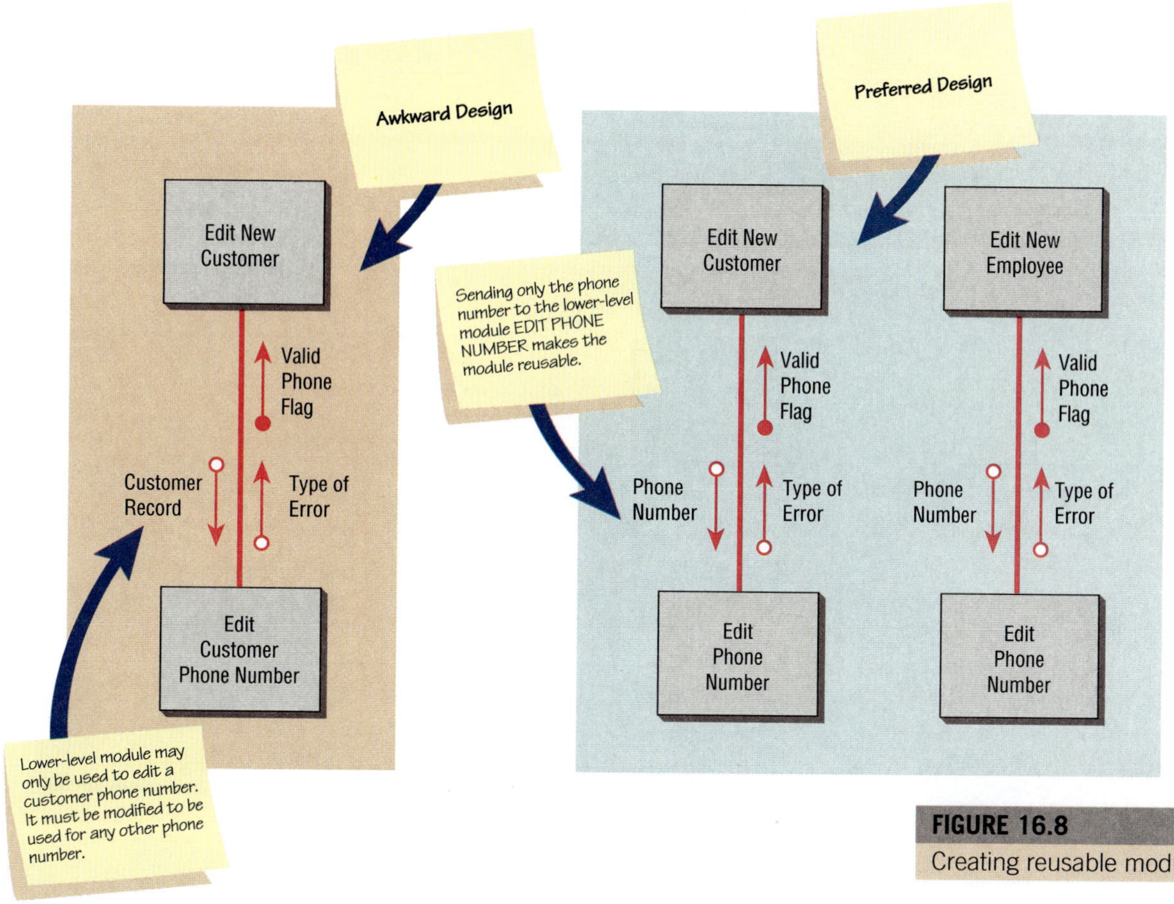

FIGURE 16.8
Creating reusable modules.

placed in a separate module, and control flags are only passed up the structure to the higher-level module.

The data that are passed through data couples must also be examined. It is best to pass only the data required to accomplish the function of the module. This approach is called data coupling. Passing excessive data is called stamp coupling, and although it is relatively harmless, it reduces the possibility of creating a reusable module.

Figure 16.8 illustrates this concept. Here, the module EDIT NEW CUSTOMER passes the CUSTOMER RECORD to the EDIT CUSTOMER PHONE NUMBER module, where PHONE NUMBER, an element found in the CUSTOMER RECORD, is validated, and a control flag is passed back to the EDIT NEW CUSTOMER module. The TYPE OF ERROR (if any), one containing an error message such as "INVALID AREA CODE" or "PHONE NUMBER IS NOT NUMERIC," is also passed upward. The message may be either printed or displayed on a screen.

Although such modules are fairly easy to create and modify every time a phone number from a different source record needs to be edited, a new module, similar to EDIT CUSTOMER PHONE NUMBER, must be created. Furthermore, if the way the phone number is being validated changes, as occurs when a new area code or an international country code must be added, each of these lower-level modules must be modified.

Because the lower-level module does not require any of the other elements on the CUSTOMER RECORD, the solution is to pass only the PHONE NUMBER to the lower-level module. The name of the module in this scenario changes to EDIT

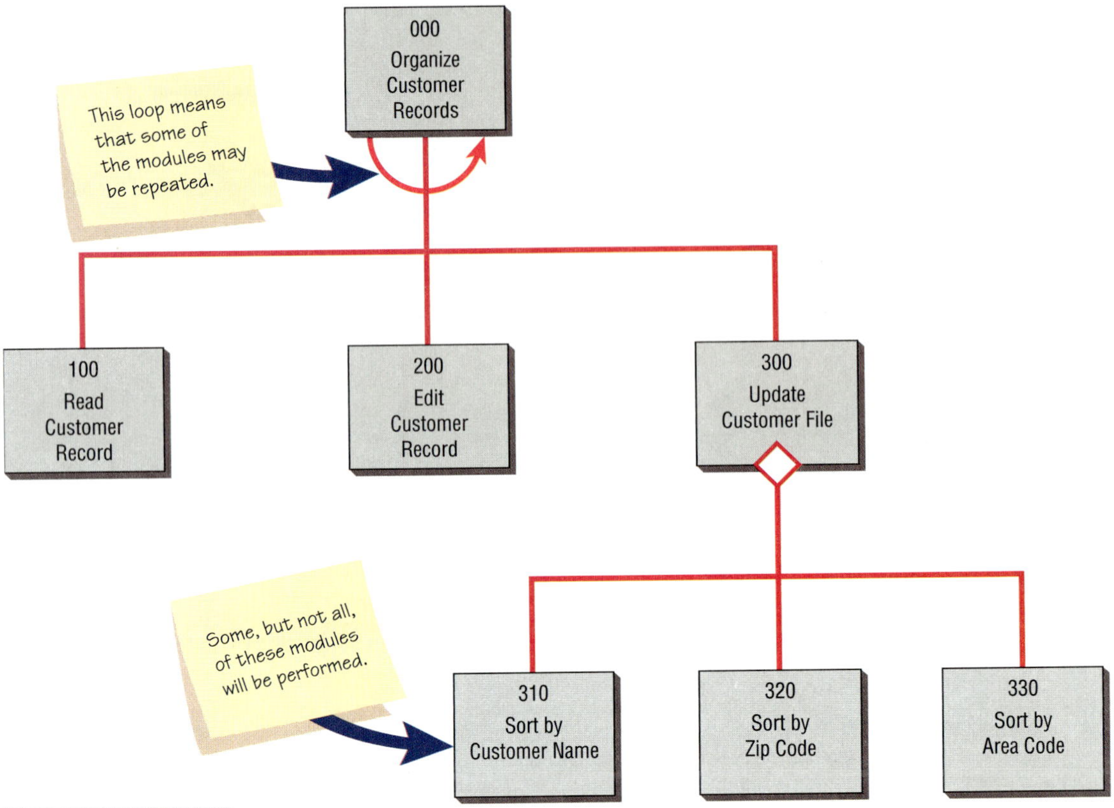

FIGURE 16.9
The loop and diamond are two symbols that indicate special action in a structure chart.

PHONE NUMBER, and it may be used to edit *any* phone number: a customer phone number or an employee phone number. The modules on the right side of the figure illustrate this concept. When the rules for validating the phone number change, only EDIT PHONE NUMBER needs to be modified, regardless of how many programs utilize that module. Often these general-purpose modules are placed in a separately compiled program called either a subprogram, function, or procedure, depending on the computer language.

Another symbol used in structure charts is the loop, as shown in Figure 16.9. This symbol indicates that some procedures found in modules 100 and 200 are to be repeated until finished. In this example it implies that READ CUSTOMER RECORD and EDIT CUSTOMER RECORD are repeated until all the customer records are completed. Then these are sorted in module 300, but as you can see, they can be sorted in three different ways: by name, zip code, or area code. In order to show that some, but not all, of the sorting will be done, another symbol, a diamond is used. Notice that the diamond doesn't indicate which of the three modules will be performed, nor does the loop indicate which modules will be repeated. They are purposely meant to be general, not specific.

DRAWING A STRUCTURE CHART

Obviously, structure charts are meant to be drawn from the top down, but where does one start to find the processes that are to become the modules? Most likely, the best place to find this information is in the data flow diagram (see Chapter 7).

When transforming a data flow diagram into a structure chart, there are several additional considerations to keep in mind. The data flow diagram will indicate

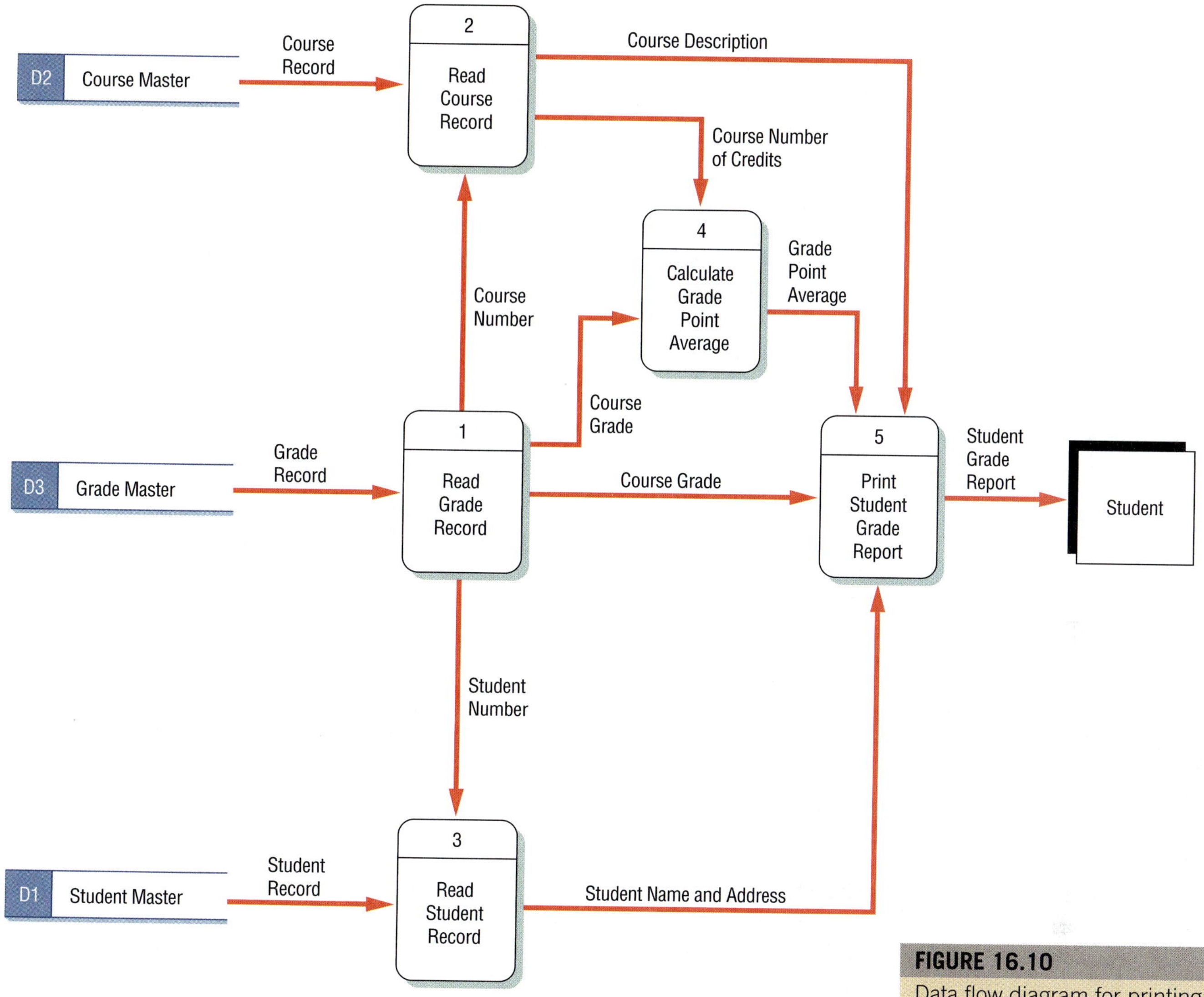

FIGURE 16.10
Data flow diagram for printing a student grade report.

the sequence of the modules in a structure chart. If one process provides input to another process, the corresponding modules must be performed in the same sequence. Figure 16.10 is a data flow diagram for preparing a student grade report. Notice that process 1, READ GRADE RECORD, provides input to process 2, READ COURSE RECORD, and to process 3, READ STUDENT RECORD. The structure chart created for this diagram is illustrated in Figure 16.11. Notice that module 110, READ GRADE RECORD, must be executed first. Processes 2 and 3 must be executed next, but because they do not provide input to each other, the order of these modules (120 and 130) in the structure chart is unimportant and may be reversed without any effect on the final results. Processes 1 and 2 provide input to process 4, CALCULATE GRADE POINT AVERAGE (also known as module 140). Process 5, PRINT STUDENT GRADE REPORT (module 150), receives data flow from all the other processes and must be the last module to be performed.

If a process explodes to a child data flow diagram, the module corresponding to the parent process will have subordinate modules that correspond to the processes found on the child diagram. Process 5, PRINT STUDENT GRADE REPORT, has four input data flows and one output, and is therefore a good candidate for a child

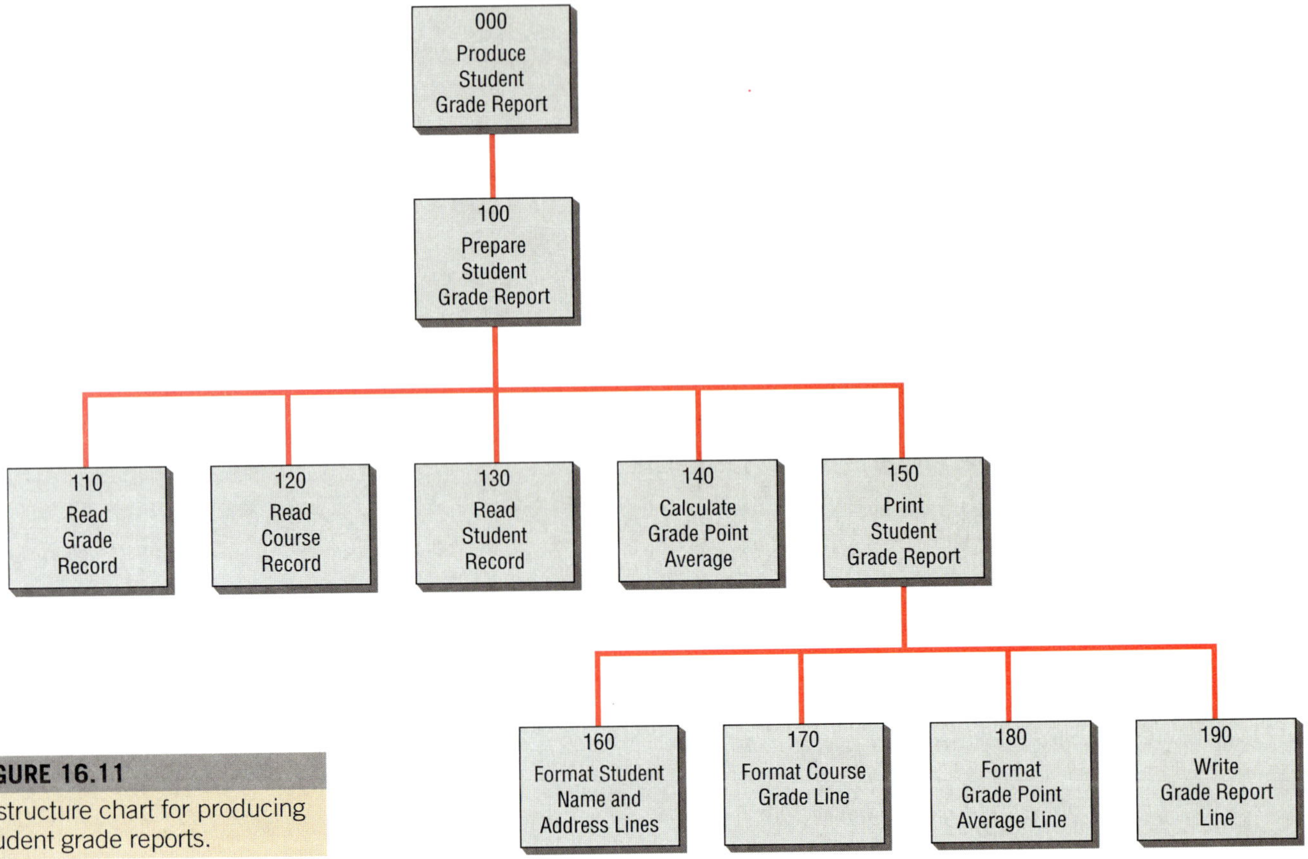

FIGURE 16.11
A structure chart for producing student grade reports.

diagram. Figure 16.12 illustrates Diagram 5, the details of process 5. The processes on Diagram 5 translate to the modules subordinate to module 150, PRINT STUDENT GRADE REPORT.

TYPES OF MODULES

Structure chart modules fall into one of three general categories: (1) control, (2) transformational (sometimes called worker), or (3) functional. When producing a structure chart that is easy to develop and modify, one should take care not to mix the different types of modules.

Control modules are usually found near the top of the structure chart and contain the logic for performing the lower-level modules. The control modules may or may not be represented on the data flow diagram. The types of statements that are usually in control modules are IF, PERFORM, and DO. Detailed statements such as ADD and MOVE are usually kept to a minimum. Control logic is usually the most difficult to design; therefore, control modules should not be very large in size. If a control module has more than nine subordinate modules, new control modules should be created that are subordinate to the original control module. The logic of a control module may be determined from a decision tree or decision table. A decision table with too many rules should be split into several decision tables, with the first table performing the second table. Each decision table would result in the creation of a control module. (See Chapter 9 for more on decision trees and tables.)

Transformational modules are those created from a data flow diagram. They usually perform only one task, although several secondary tasks may be associated with the primary task. For example, a module named PRINT CUSTOMER

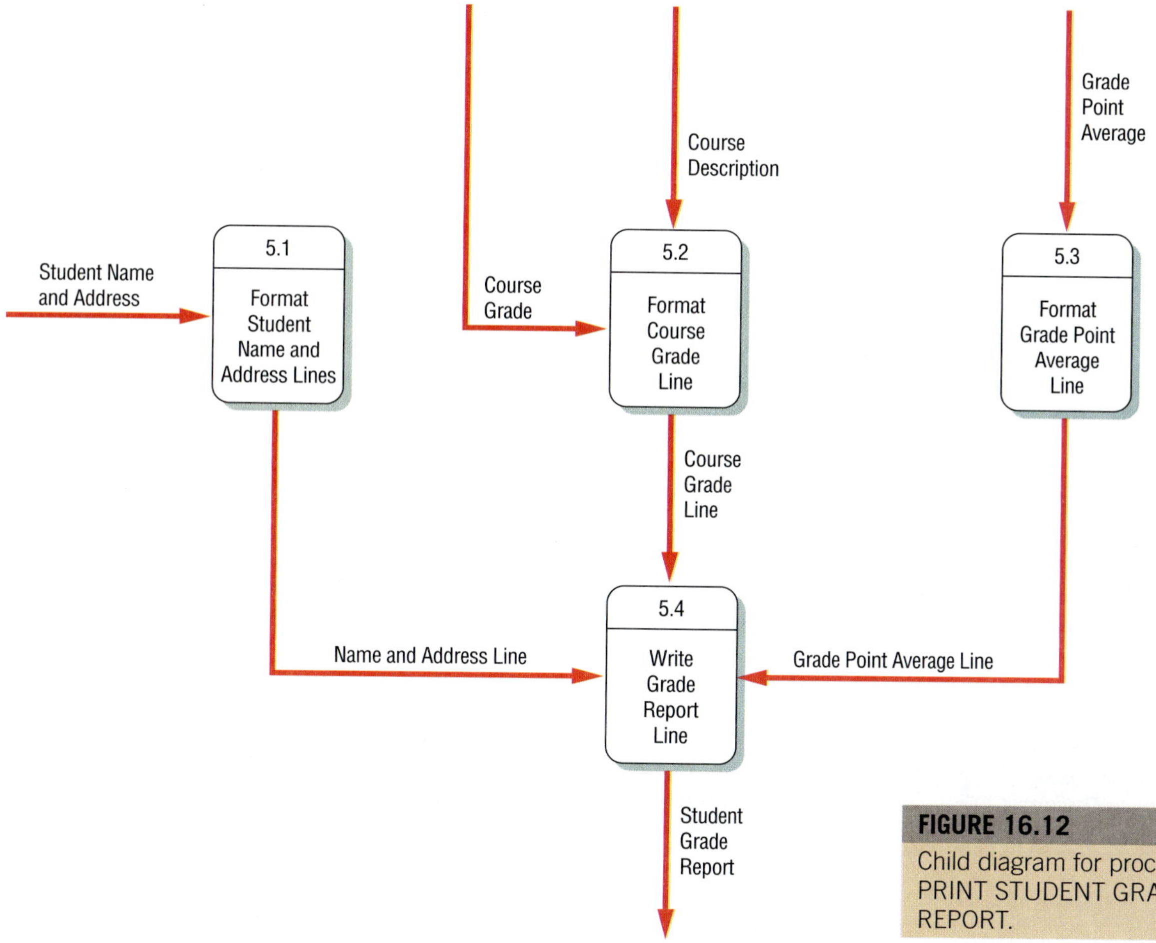

FIGURE 16.12
Child diagram for process 5, PRINT STUDENT GRADE REPORT.

TOTAL LINE may format the total line, print the line, add to the final totals, and set the customer totals to zero in preparation for accumulating the amounts of the next customer. Transformational modules usually have mixed statements, a few IF and PERFORM or DO statements, and many detailed statements such as MOVE and ADD. These modules are lower in the structure than control modules.

Functional modules are the lowest in the structure, with only a rare subordinate module beneath them. They perform only one task, such as formatting, reading, calculating, or writing. Some of these modules are found on a data flow diagram, but others may have to be added, such as reading a record or printing an error line.

Figure 16.13 represents the structure chart for adding reservations for hotel guests. Modules 000, ADD GUEST RESERVATION, and 100, ADD ROOM RESERVATION, are control modules, representing the entire program (module 000), and they provide the control necessary for making one room reservation (module 100). Module 110, DISPLAY RESERVATION SCREEN, is a functional module responsible for showing the initial reservation display. Modules 120, GET VALID ROOM RESERVATION, and 160, CONFIRM ROOM RESERVATION, are lower-level control modules.

Module 120, GET VALID ROOM RESERVATION, is performed iteratively until the reservation data are valid or until the reservation operator cancels the transaction. This type of GET VALID . . . module relieves the 100 module of a fair amount of complex code. The modules subordinate to GET VALID ROOM RESERVATION are functional modules responsible for receiving the reservation display, editing or validating the room reservation, and showing an error display if

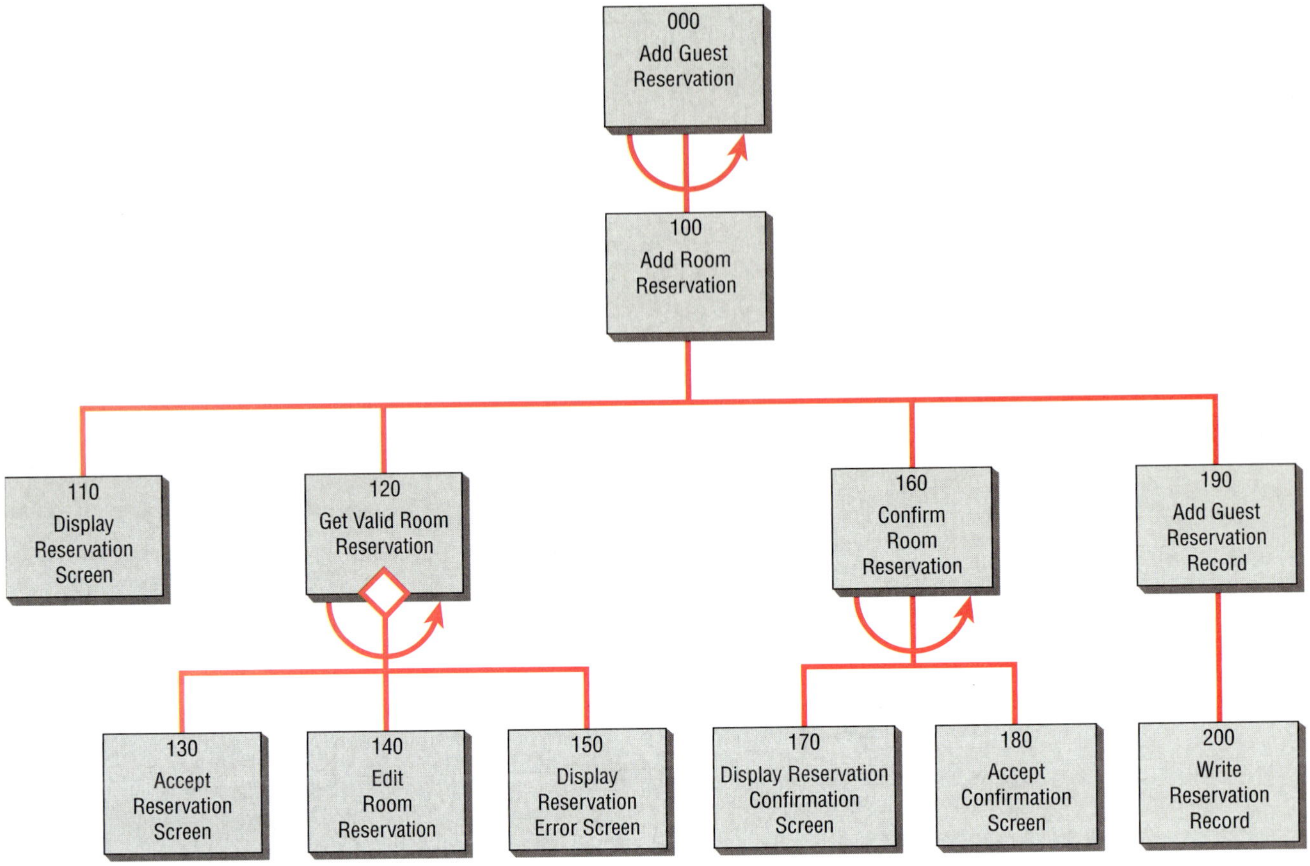

FIGURE 16.13

A structure chart for adding hotel guest reservations online.

the input data are not valid. Because these modules are in a loop, control remains in this portion of the structure until the display data are valid.

Module 160, CONFIRM ROOM RESERVATION, is also performed iteratively and allows the operator to sight-verify that the correct information has been entered. In this situation, the operator will inspect the display and press a specified key, such as the **Enter** key, if the data are correct, or a different key to modify or cancel the transaction. Again, the program will remain in these modules, looping until the operator accepts or cancels the reservation.

Module 190 is a transformational module that formats the RESERVATION RECORD and performs module 200 to write the RESERVATION RECORD. Modules 130, 140, 150, 170, 180, and 200 are functional modules, performing only one task: accepting a display, showing a display, or editing or writing a record. These modules are the easiest to code, debug, and maintain.

MODULE SUBORDINATION

A subordinate module is one lower on the structure chart called by another module higher in the structure. Each subordinate module should represent a task that is a part of the function of the higher-level module. Allowing the lower-level module to perform a task not required by the calling module is called improper subordination. In such a case, the lower module should be moved higher in the structure.

Figure 16.14 illustrates this concept using a structure chart for changing a CUSTOMER MASTER file. Examine module 120, READ CUSTOMER MASTER. It has the task of using the CUSTOMER NUMBER from the CHANGE TRANS. RECORD to obtain the matching CUSTOMER RECORD directly. If the record is

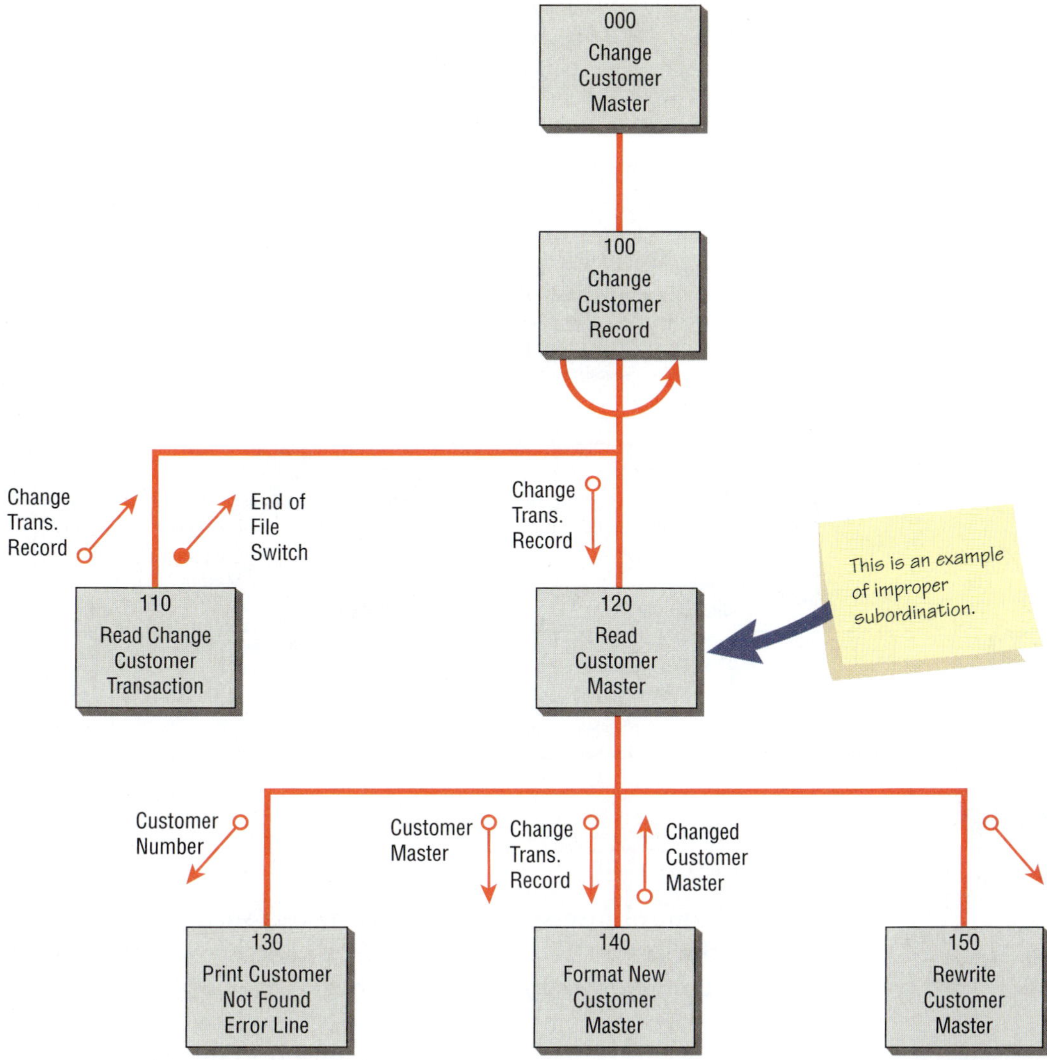

FIGURE 16.14

A structure chart illustrating the principle of improper subordination.

not found, an error line is printed. Otherwise, the CUSTOMER MASTER is changed, and the record is rewritten. This module should be a functional module, simply reading a record, but instead it has three subordinate modules. The question must be asked, "Does an error line have to be printed to accomplish reading the CUSTOMER MASTER?" Furthermore, "Does the NEW CUSTOMER MASTER have to be formatted and rewritten so as to read the CUSTOMER MASTER?" Because the answer to both questions is no, modules 130, 140, and 150 should not be subordinate to READ CUSTOMER MASTER.

Figure 16.15 shows the corrected structure chart. Control statements are moved out of the READ CUSTOMER MASTER record and into the primary control module, CHANGE CUSTOMER RECORD. READ CUSTOMER MASTER becomes a functional module (module 120).

Even when a structure chart accomplishes all the purposes for which it was drawn, the structure chart cannot stand alone as the sole design and documentation technique. First, it doesn't show the order in which the modules should be executed (a data flow diagram will accomplish that). Second, it doesn't show enough detail (pseudocode will accomplish that). The remainder of this chapter discusses these more detailed design and documentation techniques for software development using the newspaper subscription problem presented earlier, which we now view in more detail.

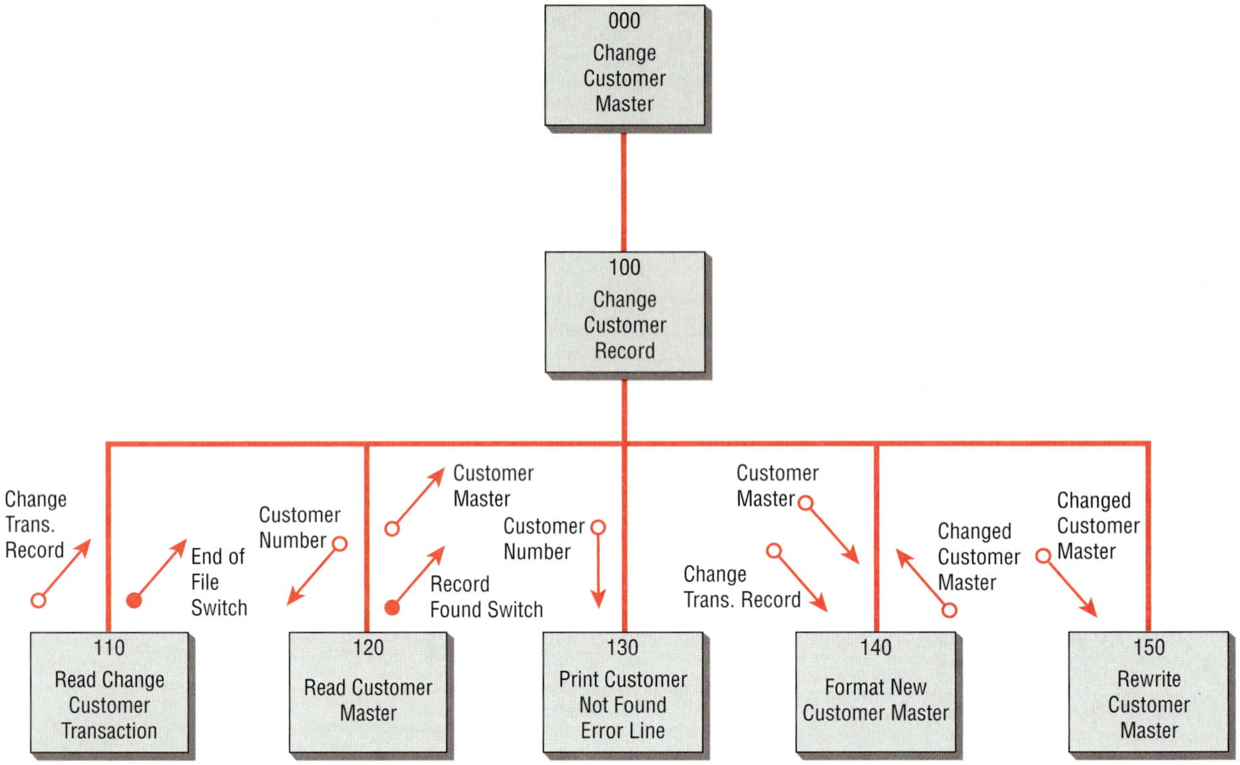

FIGURE 16.15
A corrected structure chart showing proper subordination.

SOFTWARE ENGINEERING AND DOCUMENTATION

Planning and control are essential elements of every successful system. In developing software for the system, the systems analyst should know that planning takes place in the design before programming is even begun. We need techniques to help us set program objectives, so that our programs are complete. We also need design techniques to help us break apart the programming effort into manageable modules.

It is not satisfactory, however, to try to get by with just the planning stages. After programs are completed, they must be maintained, and maintenance efforts typically outweigh the effort expended on the original design and programming.

The techniques described in the upcoming section are meant not only to be used initially in the design of software, but also in its maintenance. Because most systems are not considered disposable, they will need to be maintained. The total quality assurance effort requires that programs be documented properly.

Software and procedures are documented so that they are encoded into a format that can be easily accessed. Access to procedures is necessary for new people learning the system and as a reminder to those who use the program infrequently. Documentation allows users, programmers, and analysts to "see" the system, its software, and procedures without having to interact with it. Documentation should be prototyped before it is considered complete.

Some documentation provides an overview of the system itself, whereas procedural documentation details what must be done to run software on the system and program documentation details the program code that is used.

Turnover of information service personnel has traditionally been high in comparison with other departments, so chances are that the people who conceived of and installed the original system will not be the same ones who maintain it. Consistent, well-updated documentation will shorten the number of hours required for new people to learn the system before performing maintenance.

There are many reasons why systems and programs are undocumented or underdocumented. Some of the problems reside with the systems and programs themselves, others with systems analysts and programmers.

Some legacy systems were written before a business standardized its documentation techniques, but they are still in use (without documentation). Many other systems have tolerated major and minor modifications and patches over the years, but their documentation has not been modified to reflect them. Some systems featuring specialized programs were purchased for their important applications despite their lack of accompanying documentation.

Systems analysts may fail to document systems properly because they do not have the time or are not rewarded for time spent documenting. Some analysts do not document because they dread doing so or think it is not their real work. Furthermore, many analysts are reticent about documenting systems that are not their own, perhaps fearing reprisals if they include incorrect material about someone else's system. Documentation accomplished by means of a CASE tool during the analysis phases can address many of these problems.

There is no single standard design and documentation technique in use today. In the following sections, we discuss several different techniques that are currently in use. Each technique has its own advantages and disadvantages, because each one has unique properties.

PSEUDOCODE

In Chapter 9, we introduced the concept of structured English as a technique of analyzing decisions. Pseudocode is similar to structured English because it is not a particular type of programming code, but it can be used as an intermediate step for developing program code.

Figure 16.16 is an example of pseudocode for Chenoweth Enterprises, a newspaper conglomerate that publishes *Charlie Brown's Journal, The Steel Pier Observer,* and *Wicked*, the ever popular teen-oriented paper. The newspaper conglomerate goes through a process of updating, printing, and providing management reports for each of its newspapers. The pseudocode for this process involves a process of updating each newspaper list of subscribers, nested within the entire set of newspapers. This structure easily can be seen in the pseudocode.

The use of pseudocode is common in the industry, but lack of standardization will prevent it from being accepted by everyone. Because pseudocode is so close to program code, it is naturally favored by programmers and consequently not as favored by business analysts. Pseudocode is frequently used to represent the logic of each module on a structure chart.

The data flow diagram may be used to write the pseudocode logic. When used at a program level rather than at a system level, the data flow diagram may incorporate several additional symbols. The star (*), meaning "and," is used to indicate that both named data flows must be present. Refer to the portion of a data flow diagram that is illustrated in Figure 16.17. If the input data flows are from different processes, the presence of the "and" connector signifies that the process receiving the flow must perform some sort of file matching, either a sequential match, reading all the records from both files, or an indexed read of a second file using a key field obtained from the first file.

The plus sign enclosed in a circle (⊕) represents an exclusive "or" and indicates that one or the other data flow is present at any given time. Use of this symbol implies that the process receiving or producing the data flow must have a corresponding IF . . . THEN . . . ELSE . . . statement.

FIGURE 16.16
Using pseudocode to depict a subscription update service for a newspaper conglomerate.

```
Open Files
Read the first Newspaper.name
DO WHILE there are more Newspaper.name(s)
  PRINT Date
  PRINT Newspaper.name
  Read first Subscriber.record
  DO WHILE there are more Subscriber.record(s)
    IF Transaction = Modify.Renewal
      THEN Subs.length = Subs.length + Num.weeks
    ELSE IF Transaction = New
      THEN PERFORM Add.subscriber
      THEN Subs.length = Num.weeks
    ELSE IF Transaction = Modify.address
      THEN PERFORM Address.change
    ELSE IF Transaction = Delete.subscriber
      THEN PERFORM Prepare.refunds.update
      PERFORM Print.refund.check
      Subs.length = 0
    ELSE PERFORM Error.in.transaction
    ENDIF
    PERFORM Prepare.subscriber.list
    Read another Subscriber.record
  ENDO
  PERFORM Print.subscriber.list
  Get next Newspaper.name
ENDO
Close Files
```

PROCEDURE MANUALS

Procedure manuals are common organizational documents that most people have seen. They are the English-language component of documentation, although they may also contain program codes, flowcharts, and so on. Manuals are intended to communicate to those who use them. They may contain background comments, steps required to accomplish different transactions, instructions on how to recover from problems, and what to do next if something isn't working (troubleshooting). Many manuals are now available online, with hypertext capability that facilitates use.

A straightforward, standardized approach to creating user support documentation is desirable. To be useful, user documentation must be kept up to date. Use of the Web has revolutionized the speed with which assistance can be obtained by users. Many software developers are moving user support—complete with FAQ, help desks, technical support, and fax-back service—to the Web. In addition, many COTS software vendors include "Read Me" files with downloads or shipments of new software. These files serve a variety of purposes: they document changes, patches, or fixes for newly discovered bugs in the application that have occurred too late in its development to be included in the accompanying user's manual.

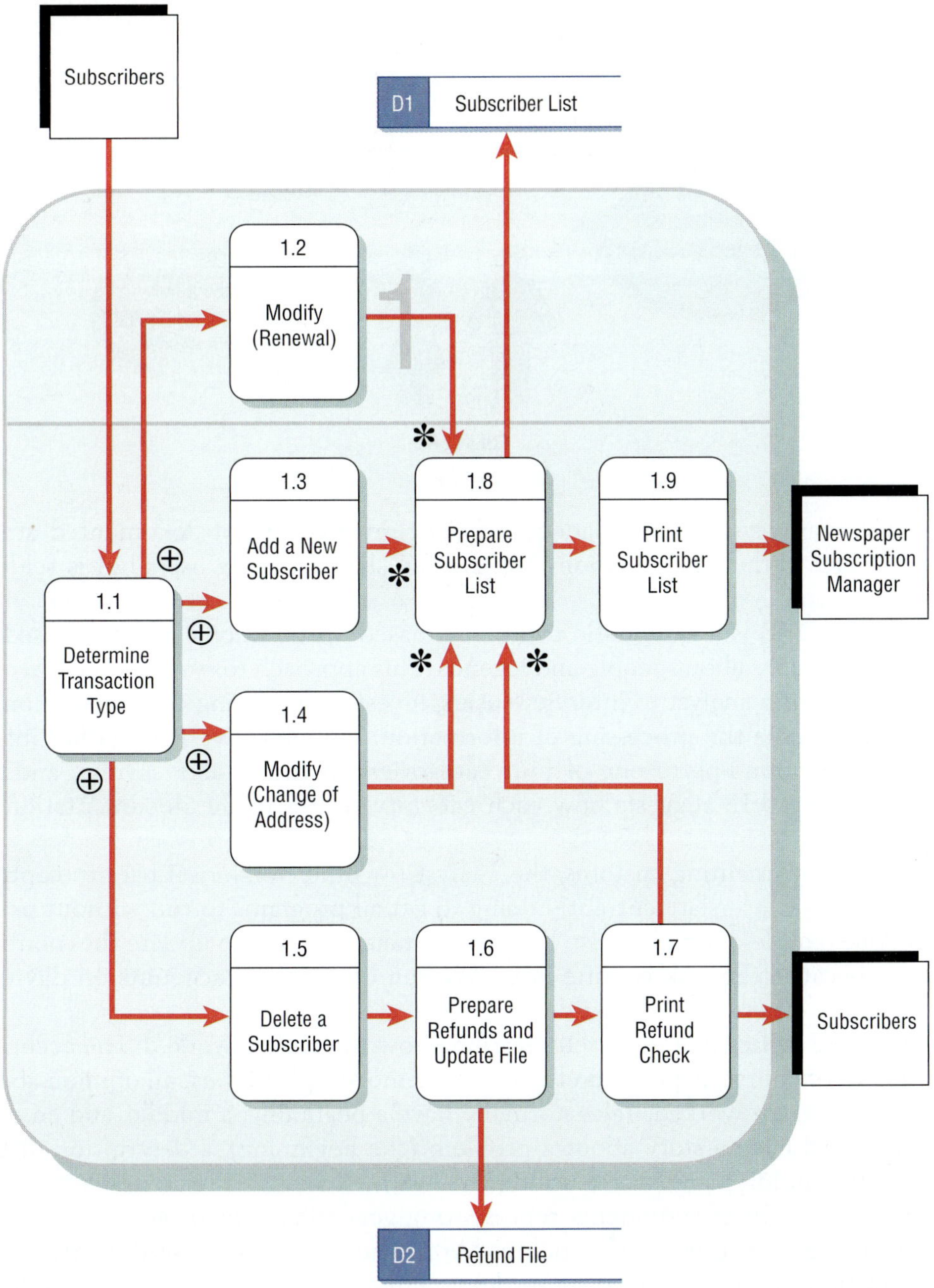

FIGURE 16.17
Special symbols are used in the data flow diagram for newspaper subscriber transaction processing to illustrate AND and OR logic.

Key sections of a manual should include an introduction, how to use the software, what to do if things go wrong, a technical reference section, an index, and information on how to contact the manufacturer. Online manuals on Web sites should also include information on downloading updates and a FAQ page. The biggest complaints with procedure manuals are that (1) they are poorly organized, (2) it is hard to find needed information in them, (3) the specific case in question does not appear in the manual, and (4) the manual is not written in plain English. In an upcoming section on testing, we discuss the importance of having users "test" systems manuals and prototype Web sites before they are finalized.

THE FOLKLORE METHOD

FOLKLORE is a systems documentation technique that was created to supplement some of the techniques just covered. Even with the plethora of techniques

FIGURE 16.18

Customs, tales, sayings, and art forms used in the FOLKLORE method of documentation apply to information systems.

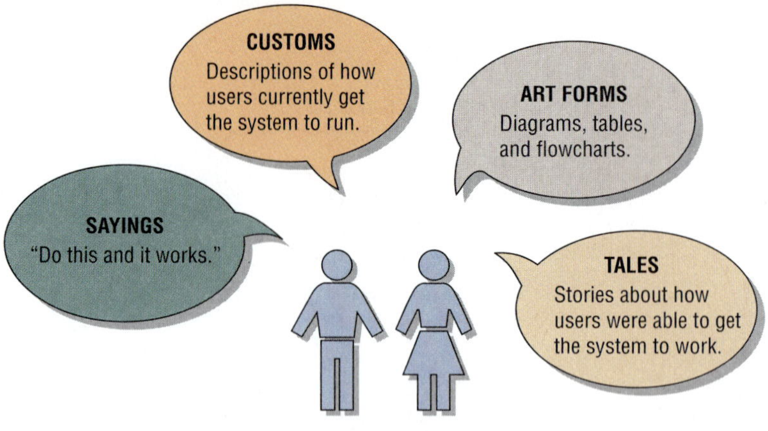

available, many systems are inadequately documented or not documented at all. FOLKLORE gathers information that is often shared among users but is seldom written down.

FOLKLORE is a systematic technique, based on traditional methods used in gathering folklore about people and legends. This approach to systems documentation requires the analyst to interview users, investigate existing documentation in files, and observe the processing of information. The objective is to gather information corresponding to one of four categories: customs, tales, sayings, and art forms. Figure 16.18 suggests how each category relates to the documentation of information systems.

When documenting customs, the analyst (or other folklorist) tries to capture in writing what users are currently doing to get all programs to run without problems. An example of a custom is: "Usually, we take two days to update the monthly records because the task is quite large. We run commercial accounts on day one and save the others for the next day."

Tales are stories that users tell regarding how the system worked. The accuracy of the tale, of course, depends on the user's memory and is at best an opinion about how the program worked. Tales normally have a beginning, a middle, and an end. So we would have a story about a problem (the beginning), a description of the effects (the middle), and the solution (the end).

Sayings are brief statements representing generalizations or advice. We have many sayings in everyday life, such as "April showers bring May flowers," or "A stitch in time saves nine." In systems documentation, we have many sayings, such as "Omit this section of code and the program will bomb," or "Always back up frequently." Users like to give advice, and the analyst should try to capture this advice and include it in the FOLKLORE documentation.

Gathering art forms is another important activity of traditional folklorists, and the systems analyst should understand its importance, too. Flowcharts, diagrams, and tables that users draw sometimes may be better or more useful than flowcharts drawn by the original system author. Analysts will often find such art posted on bulletin boards, or they may ask the users to clean out their files and retrieve any useful diagrams.

The FOLKLORE approach works because it can help fill the knowledge gap created when a program author leaves. Contributors to the FOLKLORE document do not have to document the entire system, only the parts they know about. Finally, it is fun for users to contribute, taking some of the burden from analysts. Notice that the class of recommendation systems that was discussed earlier in the text is very close to the FOLKLORE conceptualization. These systems expand the

CONSULTING OPPORTUNITY 16.2

WRITE IS RIGHT

"It's so easy to understand. I say if everybody uses pseudocode, we won't have trouble, you know, with things not being standardized," says Al Gorithm, a new programmer who will be working with your systems analysis team. Al is speaking to an informal meeting among three members of the systems analysis team, a six-person MIS task force from the advertising department, and two programmers, who were all working to develop an information system for advertising personnel.

Philip, an advertising account executive and one of the members of the MIS task force, looks up in surprise. "What is this method called?" The two programmers reply at the same time, "Pseudocode." Philip looks unimpressed and says, "That doesn't say anything to me."

Neeva Phail, one of the systems analysts, begins explaining. "It probably won't matter one way or the other what we use, if—"

Flo Chart, another systems analyst, breaks in saying, "I hate pseudocode." She looks hopefully at the programmers. "I'm sure we can agree on a better technique."

David, an older advertising executive, seems slightly upset, stating, "I learned about flowcharting from the first systems analysts we had years ago. Don't you people do that anymore? I think they work best."

What was at first a friendly meeting suddenly seems to have reached an impasse. The participants are looking at each other warily. As a systems analyst who has worked on many different projects with many different kinds of people, you realize that the group is looking to you to make some reasonable suggestions.

Based on what you know about the various documentation techniques, what technique(s) would you propose to the members of the group? How will the technique(s) you proposed overcome some of the concerns they have voiced? What process will you use to decide on appropriate techniques? Compose your answer in one page.

idea of FOLKLORE to include all kinds of recommendations, such as ratings of restaurants and movies. Through low or no-cost email on the Web, some initial barriers to gathering and sharing informal information have been overcome.

The danger of relying on FOLKLORE is that the information gathered from users may be correct, partially correct, or incorrect. Unless someone takes the time to redo program documentation entirely, however, the description of customs, tales, sayings, and art forms may be the only written information about how a set of programs work.

CHOOSING A DESIGN AND DOCUMENTATION TECHNIQUE

The techniques discussed in this chapter are extremely valuable as design tools, memory aids, productivity tools, and as a means of reducing dependencies on key staff members. The systems analyst, however, is faced with a difficult decision regarding which method to adopt. The following is a set of guidelines to help the analyst use the appropriate technique.

Choose a technique that:

1. Is compatible with existing documentation.
2. Is understood by others in the organization.
3. Allows you to return to working on the system after you have been away from it for a period of time.
4. Is suitable for the size of the system on which you are working.
5. Allows for a structured design approach if that is considered to be more important than other factors.
6. Allows for easy modification.

TESTING, MAINTENANCE, AND AUDITING

Once the analyst has designed and coded the system, testing, maintenance, and auditing of it are prime considerations.

THE TESTING PROCESS

All the system's newly written or modified application programs—as well as new procedural manuals, new hardware, and all system interfaces—must be tested thoroughly. Haphazard, trial-and-error testing will not suffice.

Testing is done throughout systems development, not just at the end. It is meant to turn up heretofore unknown problems, not to demonstrate the perfection of programs, manuals, or equipment.

Although testing is tedious, it is an essential series of steps that helps ensure the quality of the eventual system. It is far less disruptive to test beforehand than to have a poorly tested system fail after installation. Testing is accomplished on subsystems or program modules as work progresses. Testing is done on many different levels at various intervals. Before the system is put into production, all programs must be desk checked, checked with test data, and checked to see if the modules work together with one another as planned.

The system as a working whole must also be tested. Included here are testing the interfaces between subsystems, the correctness of output, and the usefulness and understandability of systems documentation and output. Programmers, analysts, operators, and users all play different roles in the various aspects of testing, as shown in Figure 16.19. Testing of hardware is typically provided as a service by vendors of equipment, who will run their own tests on equipment when it is delivered onsite.

Program Testing with Test Data Much of the responsibility for program testing resides with the original author(s) of each program. The systems analyst serves as an advisor and coordinator for program testing. In this capacity, the analyst works to ensure that correct testing techniques are implemented by programmers but probably does not personally carry out this level of checking.

At this stage, programmers must first desk check their programs to verify the way the system will work. In desk checking, the programmer follows each step in the program on paper to check whether the routine works as it is written.

Next, programmers must create both valid and invalid test data. These data are then run to see if base routines work and also to catch errors. If output from main modules is satisfactory, you can add more test data so as to check other modules. Created test data should test possible minimum and maximum values as well as all

FIGURE 16.19
Programmers, analysts, operators, and users all play different roles in testing software and systems.

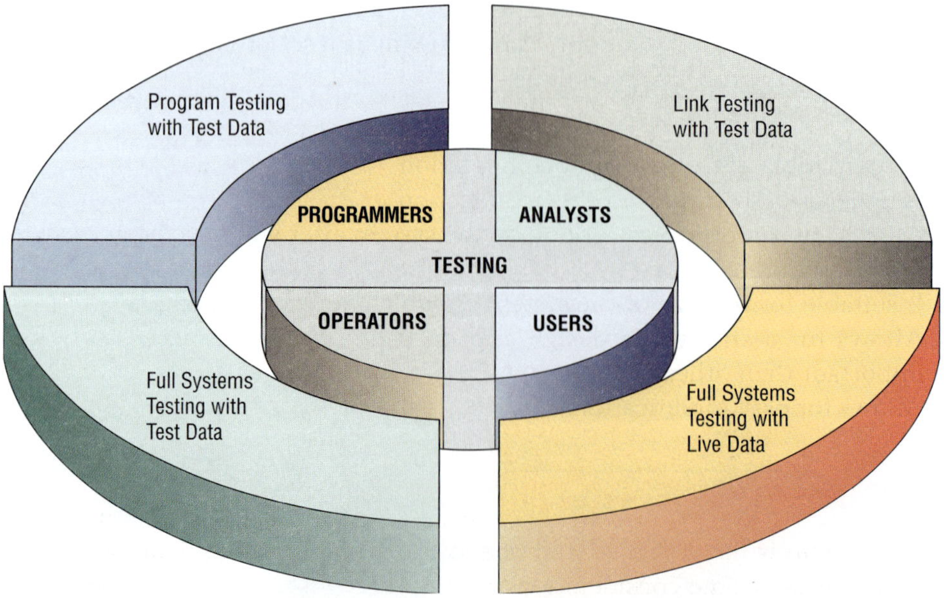

possible variations in format and codes. File output from test data must be carefully verified. It should never be assumed that data contained in a file are correct just because a file was created and accessed.

Throughout this process, the systems analyst checks output for errors, advising the programmer of any needed corrections. The analyst will usually not recommend or create test data for program testing but might point out to the programmer omissions of data types to be added in later tests.

Link Testing with Test Data When programs pass desk checking and checking with test data, they must go through link testing, which is also referred to as string testing. Link testing checks to see if programs that are interdependent actually work together as planned.

A small amount of test data, usually designed by the systems analyst to test system specifications as well as programs, is used for link testing. It may take several passes through the system to test all combinations, because it is immensely difficult to unravel problems if you try to test everything all at once.

The analyst creates special test data that cover a variety of processing situations for link testing. First, typical test data are processed to see if the system can handle normal transactions, those that would make up the bulk of its load. If the system works with normal transactions, variations are added, including invalid data used to ensure that the system can properly detect errors.

Full Systems Testing with Test Data When link tests are satisfactorily concluded, the system as a complete entity must be tested. At this stage, operators and end users become actively involved in testing. Test data, created by the systems analysis team for the express purpose of testing system objectives, are used.

As can be expected, there are a number of factors to consider when systems testing with test data:

1. Examining whether operators have adequate documentation in procedure manuals (hard copy or online) to afford correct and efficient operation.
2. Checking whether procedure manuals are clear enough in communicating how data should be prepared for input.
3. Ascertaining if work flows necessitated by the new or modified system actually "flow."
4. Determining if output is correct and whether users understand that this output is, in all likelihood, as it will look in its final form.

Remember to schedule adequate time for system testing. Unfortunately, this step often gets dropped if system installation is lagging behind the target date.

Systems testing includes reaffirming the quality standards for system performance that were set up when initial system specifications were made. Everyone involved should once again agree on how to determine whether the system is doing what it is supposed to do. This step will include measures of error, timeliness, ease of use, proper ordering of transactions, acceptable down time, and understandable procedure manuals.

Full Systems Testing with Live Data When systems tests using test data prove satisfactory, it is a good idea to try the new system with several passes on what is called live data, data that have been successfully processed through the existing system. This step allows an accurate comparison of the new system's output with what you know to be correctly processed output, as well as a good idea for testing how actual data will be handled. Obviously, this step is not possible when creating

CONSULTING OPPORTUNITY 16.3

CRAMMING FOR YOUR SYSTEMS TEST

"We're strapped for time. Just look at this projection," says Lou Scuntroll, the newest member of your systems analysis team, showing you the PERT diagram that the team has been using to project when the new system would be up and running. "We can't possibly make the July target date for testing with live data. We're running three weeks behind because of that slow equipment shipment."

As one of the systems analysts who has seen deadlines come and go on other projects, you try to remain calm and to size up the situation carefully before you speak. Slowly, you question Lou about the possibility of delaying testing.

Lou replies, "If we try to push the testing off until the first weeks of August, there are two key people from accounting who are going to be out on vacation." Lou is visibly upset at the possibility of missing the deadline.

Stan Dards, another junior member of your systems analysis team, enters Lou's office. "You two look terrible. Things are going okay, aren't they? I'm not reassigned to program a payroll application, am I?"

Lou looks up, obviously neither appreciating Stan's sense of humor nor what seems like his single-minded self-concern. "Good thing you came in when you did. We've got some big decisions to make about scheduling." Lou holds up the PERT diagram for Stan's inspection. "Notice the July test date. Notice that there is no way we can make it. Any bright ideas?"

Stan contemplates the chart momentarily, then states, "Something's got to go. Let's see here . . . maybe move testing of the accounting module to—"

Lou interrupts, saying bluntly, "Nope, already thought of that, but Stanford and Binet from accounting are out of town in August. Maybe we can skip that portion of the testing. They've been really cooperative. I don't think they'd object if we just 'do it for real' and test as we actually go into production."

"I think that's a good idea, Lou," Stan agrees, trying to make up for his earlier jokes. "We haven't had any real trouble with that, and the programmers sure are confident. That way we could stay on schedule with everything else. I vote for *not* testing the accounting portion, but just sort of winging it when it starts up."

As the most senior member of the team present, what can you do to convince Lou and Stan about the importance of testing the accounting module with live data? What can systems analysts do in planning their time to allow adequate time for testing with test and live data? What are some of the possible problems the team members may encounter if they do not test the system completely with live data before putting the system into production? Realistically, are there steps in the systems analysis and design process that can be collapsed to bring a delayed project in on time? Respond to these questions in two pages.

entirely new outputs (for instance, output from an ecommerce transaction from a new corporate Web site). As with test data, only small amounts of live data are used in this kind of system testing.

Testing is an important period for assessing how end users and operators actually interact with the system. Although much thought is given to user-system interaction (see Chapter 14), you can never fully predict the wide range of differences in the way users will actually interact with the system. It is not enough to interview users about how they are interacting with the system; you must observe them firsthand.

Items to watch for are ease of learning the system and user reaction to system feedback, including what happens when an error message is received, and what happens when the user is informed that the system is executing his or her commands. Be particularly sensitive to how users react to system response time and to the language of responses. Also listen to what users say about the system as they encounter it. Any real problems need to be addressed before the system is put into production, not just glossed over as adjustments to the system that users and operators ought to make on their own.

As mentioned earlier, procedure manuals also need to be tested. Although manuals can be proofread by support staff and checked for technical accuracy by the systems analysis team, the only real way to test them is to have users and operators try them, preferably during full systems testing with live data. Have them use accurate but not final versions of the manuals.

It is difficult to communicate procedures accurately. Too much information will be just as much a deterrent to system use as too little. Use of Web-based documents can help in this regard. Users can jump to topics of interest, and download and print what they want to keep. Consider user suggestions, and incorporate them into the final versions of Web pages, printed manuals, and other documentation.

MAINTENANCE PRACTICES

Your objective as a systems analyst should be to install or modify systems that have a reasonably useful life. You want to create a system whose design is comprehensive and farsighted enough to serve current and projected user needs for several years to come. Part of your expertise should be used to project what those needs might be and then build flexibility and adaptability into the system. The better the system design, the easier it will be to maintain and the less money the business will have to spend on maintenance.

Reducing maintenance costs is a major concern, because software maintenance alone can devour upwards of 50 percent of the total data processing budget for a business. Excessive maintenance costs reflect directly back on the system's designer, because approximately 70 percent of software errors have been attributed to inappropriate software design. From a systems perspective, it makes sense that detecting and correcting software design errors early on is less costly than letting errors remain unnoticed until maintenance is necessary.

Maintenance is performed most often to improve the existing software rather than to respond to a crisis or system failure. As users' requirements change, software and documentation should be changed as part of the maintenance work. In addition, programs might be recoded to improve on the efficiency of the original program. Over half of all maintenance is composed of such enhancement work.

Maintenance is also done to update software in response to the changing organization. This work is not as substantial as enhancing the software, but it must be done. Emergency and adaptive maintenance comprises less than half of all system maintenance.

Part of the systems analyst's job is to ensure that there are adequate channels and procedures in place to permit feedback about—and subsequent response to—maintenance needs. Users must be able to communicate problems and suggestions easily to those who will be maintaining the system. It is very discouraging if the system is not properly maintained. Solutions are to provide users email access to technical support, as well as to allow them to download product updates or patches from the Web.

The systems analyst also needs to set up a classification scheme to allow users to designate the perceived importance of the maintenance being suggested or requested. Classifying requests enables maintenance programmers to understand how users themselves estimate the importance of their requests. This viewpoint, along with other factors, can then be taken into account when scheduling maintenance.

AUDITING

Auditing is yet another way of ensuring the quality of the information contained in the system. Broadly defined, auditing refers to having an expert who is not involved in setting up or using a system examine information in order to ascertain its reliability. Whether or not information is found to be reliable, the finding on its reliability is communicated to others for the purpose of making the system's information more useful to them.

For information systems, there are generally two kinds of auditors: internal and external. Whether both are necessary for the system you design depends on what kind of system it is. Internal auditors work for the same organization that owns the information system, whereas external (also called independent) auditors are hired from the outside.

External auditors are used when the information system processes data that influences a company's financial statements. External auditors audit the system to ensure the fairness of the financial statements being produced. They may also be brought in if there is something out of the ordinary occurring that involves company employees, such as suspected computer fraud or embezzlement.

Internal auditors study the controls used in the information system to make sure that they are adequate and that they are doing what they are purported to be doing. They also test the adequacy of security controls. Although they work for the same organization, internal auditors do not report to the people responsible for the system they are auditing. The work of internal auditors is often more in-depth than that of external auditors.

SUMMARY

The systems analyst uses three broad approaches to total quality management (TQM) for analyzing and designing information systems: designing systems and software with a top-down, modular approach, designing and documenting systems and software using systematic methods, and testing systems and software so that they can be easily maintained and audited.

Six Sigma is a culture, philosophy, methodology, and approach to quality that has as its goal the elimination of all defects. The seven steps of a Six Sigma approach are: (1) define the problem; (2) observe the problem; (3) analyze the causes; (4) act on the causes; (5) study the results; (6) standardize the changes; and (7) draw conclusions.

Users are critically important for establishing and evaluating the quality of several dimensions of management information systems and decision support systems. They can be involved in the entire evolution of systems through the establishment of MIS task forces or quality circles.

TQM can be successfully implemented by taking a top-down approach to design. This approach refers to looking at overall organizational objectives first and then decomposing them into manageable subsystem requirements. Modular development makes programming, debugging, and maintenance easier to accomplish. Programming in modules is well suited to taking a top-down approach.

Two systems link programs in the Windows environment. One is DDE (Dynamic Data Exchange), which shares code by using Dynamic Link Library (DLL) files. Using DDE, a user can store data in one program and then use it in another. A second approach to linking programs in Windows is OLE (Object Linking and Embedding). Because of its object-oriented approach, this linking method is superior to DDE for linking application data and graphics.

A recommended tool for designing a top-down, modular system is called a structure chart. Two types of arrows are used to indicate the kinds of parameters that are passed between the modules. The first is called a data couple, and the second is called a control flag. Structure chart modules fall into one of three categories: control, transformational (sometimes called worker), and functional or specialized.

Part of TQM is to see that programs and systems are properly designed, documented, and maintained. Some of the structured techniques that can aid the systems analyst are pseudocode, procedure manuals, and FOLKLORE. Pseudocode is frequently used to represent the logic of each module or structure chart.

"This is a fascinating place to work. I'm sure you agree, now that you've had a chance to observe us. Sometimes I think it must be fun to be an outsider . . . don't you feel like an anthropologist discovering a new culture? I remember when I first came here. Everything was so new, so strange. Why, even the language was different. It wasn't a 'customer'; it was a 'client.' We didn't have 'departments'; we had 'units.' It's not an employee cafeteria; it's the 'canteen.' That goes for the way we work, too. We all have our different ways to approach things. I think I'm getting the hang of what Snowden expects, but every once in a while I make a mistake, too. For instance, if I can give him work on disk, he'd just as soon see it that way than get a printed report. That's why I have two computers on my desk, too! I always see you taking so many notes . . . I guess it makes sense, though. You're supposed to document what *we* do with our systems and information as well as what your team is doing, aren't you?"

HYPERCASE QUESTIONS

1. Use the FOLKLORE method to complete the documentation of the Management Information Systems Unit GEMS system. Be sure to include customs, tales, sayings, and art forms.
2. In two paragraphs, suggest a PC-based approach for capturing the elements of FOLKLORE so that it is not necessary to use a paper-based log. Make sure that your suggested solution can accommodate graphics as well as text.
3. Design input and output screens for FOLKLORE that facilitate easy entry, and provide prompting so that recall of FOLKLORE elements is immediate.

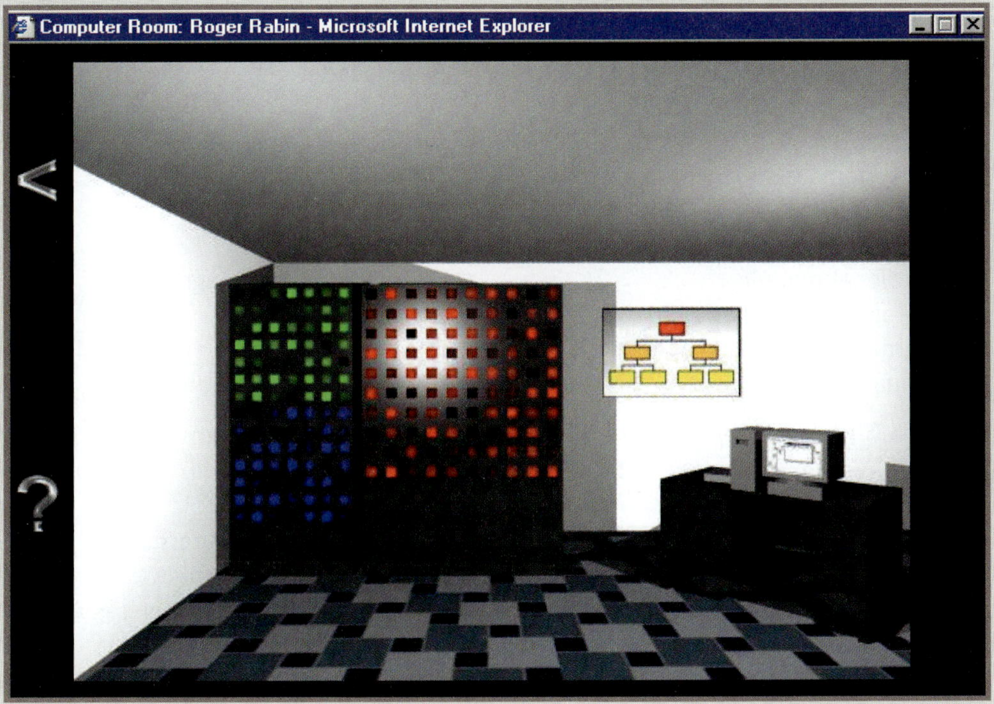

FIGURE 16.HC1

In HyperCase, use FOLKLORE to document art forms that users have created or collected to make sense of their systems.

Pseudocode can be used for structured walkthroughs. Systems analysts must choose a technique that fits in well with what was previously used in the organization and that allows flexibility and easy modification.

Testing of specific programs, subsystems, and total systems is essential to quality. Testing is done to turn up any existing problems with programs and their interfaces before the system is actually used. Testing is usually done in a bottom-up fashion, with program codes being desk checked first. Following several intermediate test steps, testing of the full system with live data (actual data that have been successfully processed with the old system) is accomplished. This testing provides an opportunity to work out any problems that arise before the system is put into production.

System maintenance is an important consideration. Well-designed software can help reduce maintenance costs. Systems analysts need to set up channels for user feedback on maintenance needs, because systems that are not maintained will fall into disuse. Web sites can help in this regard by providing access to product updates and email exchanges with technical staff.

Both internal and external auditors are used to determine the reliability of the system's information. They communicate their audit findings to others so as to improve the usefulness of the system's information.

KEYWORDS AND PHRASES

bottom-up design
control flag (switch)
control module
data couple
desk check
Dynamic Data Exchange (DDE)
Dynamic Link Library (DLL)
FOLKLORE
full systems testing with live data
full systems testing with test data
functional module
improper subordination
internal auditor
IS quality circle
link testing with test data (string testing)
modular development
Object Linking and Embedding (OLE)
program testing with test data
pseudocode
Six Sigma
software documentation
software maintenance
stamp coupling
structure chart
structured walkthrough
top-down design
total quality management (TQM)
transformational module

REVIEW QUESTIONS

1. What are the three broad approaches available to the systems analyst for attaining quality in newly developed systems?
2. Who or what is the most important factor in establishing and evaluating the quality of information systems or decision support systems? Why?
3. Define the total quality management (TQM) approach as it applies to the analysis and design of information systems.
4. What is meant by the term *Six Sigma?*
5. What is an IS quality circle?
6. Define what is meant by doing a structured walkthrough. Who should be involved? When should structured walkthroughs be done?
7. List the disadvantages to taking a bottom-up approach to design.
8. List the advantages of taking a top-down approach to design.

9. What are the three main disadvantages of taking a top-down approach to design?
10. Define modular development.
11. List four guidelines for correct modular programming.
12. How do structure charts help the analyst?
13. Name the two types of arrows used in structure charts.
14. Why do we want to keep the number of arrows to a minimum when using structure charts?
15. Why should control flags be passed upward in a structure chart?
16. List two ways that the data flow diagram helps to build a structure chart.
17. List the three categories of modules. Why are they used in structure charts?
18. How can a Web site help in maintaining the system and its documentation?
19. Give two reasons that support the necessity of well-developed systems and software documentation.
20. Define pseudocode.
21. List the four biggest complaints users voice about procedure manuals.
22. In what four categories does the FOLKLORE documentation method collect information?
23. List six guidelines for choosing a design and documentation technique.
24. Whose primary responsibility is it to test computer programs?
25. What is the difference between test data and live data?
26. What are the two types of systems auditors?

PROBLEMS

1. One of your systems analysis team members has been discouraging user input on quality standards, arguing that because you are the experts, you are really the only ones who know what constitutes a quality system. In a paragraph, explain to your team member why getting user input is critical to system quality. Use an example.
2. Draw a structure chart for the credit reporting system in Figure 16.EX1.
3. Write pseudocode for Problem 2.

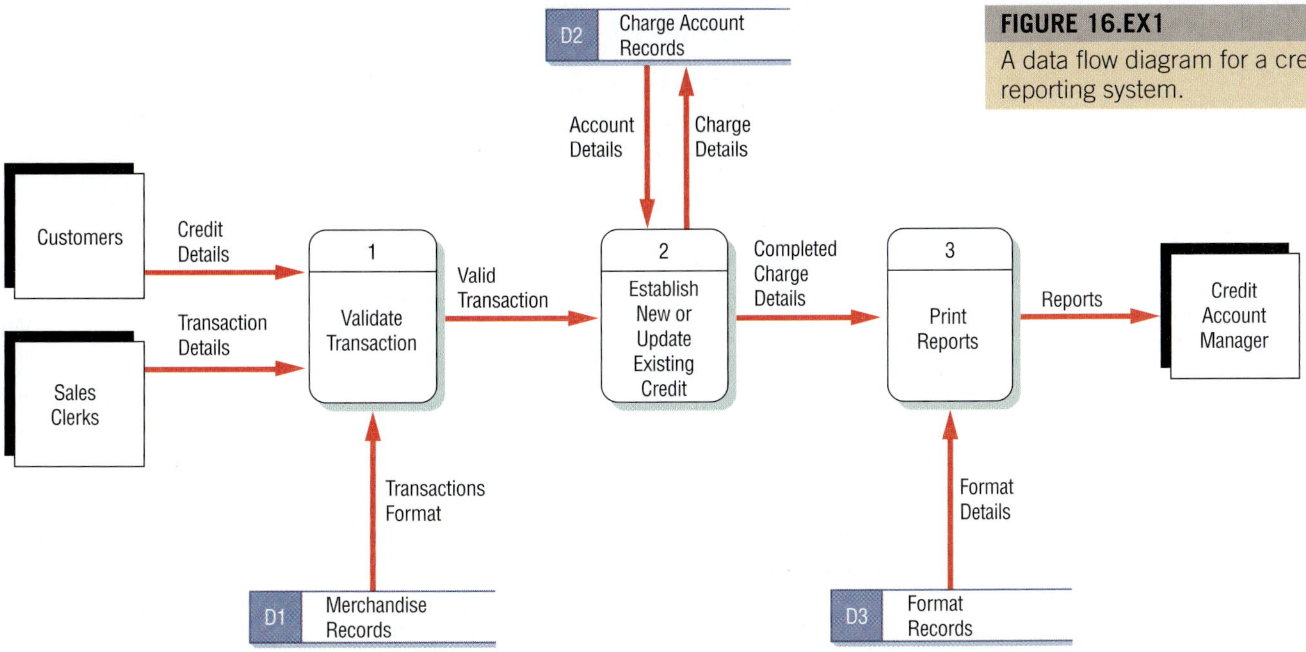

FIGURE 16.EX1
A data flow diagram for a credit reporting system.

4. Write pseudocode for the Citron Car rental policy provided in Consulting Opportunity 9.3.
5. Write a detailed table of contents for a procedure manual that explains to users how to log onto your school's computer network, as well as the school's network policies (who is an authorized user, and so on). Make sure that the manual is written with the user in mind.
6. Your systems analysis team is close to completing a system for Meecham Feeds. Roger is quite confident that the programs that he has written for Meecham's inventory system will perform as necessary, because they are similar to programs he has done before. Your team has been very busy and would ideally like to begin full systems testing as soon as possible.

   Two of your junior team members have proposed the following:
   a. Skip desk checking of the programs (because similar programs were checked in other installations; Roger has agreed).
   b. Do link testing with large amounts of data to prove that the system will work.
   c. Do full systems testing with large amounts of live data to show that the system is working.

   Respond to each of the three steps in their proposed test schedule. Use a paragraph to explain your response.
7. Propose a revised testing plan for Meecham Feeds (Problem 6). Break down your plan into a sequence of detailed steps.

GROUP PROJECTS

1. Divide your group into two subgroups. One subgroup should interview the members of the other subgroup about their experiences encountered in registering for a class. Questions should be designed to elicit information on customs, tales, sayings, and art forms that will help document the registration process at your school.
2. Reunite your group to develop a Web page for a short excerpt for a FOLKLORE manual that documents the process of registering for a class, one based on the FOLKLORE passed on in the interviews in Project 1. Remember to include examples of customs, tales, sayings, and art forms.

SELECTED BIBLIOGRAPHY

Dean, J. W., Jr., and J. R. Evans. *Total Quality.* St. Paul, MN: West, 1994.

Deming, W. E. *Management for Quality and Productivity.* Cambridge, MA: MIT Center for Advanced Engineering Study, 1981.

Evans, J. R., and W. M. Lindsay. *An Introduction to Six Sigma*. Cincinnati, OH: South-Western College Publishing, 2004.

Juran, J. M. *Managerial Breakthrough*. New York: McGraw-Hill, 1964.

Kendall, J. E., and P. Kerola. "A Foundation for the Use of Hypertext Based Documentation Techniques." *Journal of End User Computing,* Vol. 6, No. 1, Winter 1994, pp. 4–14.

Kendall, K. E., and R. Losee. "Information System FOLKLORE: A New Technique for System Documentation." *Information and Management,* Vol. 10, No. 2, 1986, pp. 103–11.

Kendall, K. E., and S. Yoo. "Pseudocode-Box Diagrams: An Approach to More Understandable, Productive, and Adaptable Software Design and Coding." *International Journal on Policy and Information,* Vol. 12, No. 1, June 1988, pp. 39–51.

Krajewski, L., L. Ritzman, and M. Malhotra. *Operations Management: Processes and Value Chains,* 8th ed. Upper Saddle River, NJ: Pearson Prentice Hall, 2007.

ALLEN SCHMIDT, JULIE E. KENDALL, AND KENNETH E. KENDALL

CHARTING THE STRUCTURE

"Here they are, as promised," Chip and Anna say triumphantly as they hand over their specifications to Mack Roe, the project programmer.

"Thanks," Mack says. "I've got a lot of work ahead."

Mack starts by creating a structure chart for each program and then each module design. The PRODUCE SOFTWARE CROSS-REFERENCE REPORT structure chart is shown in Figure E16.1. The "C" in front of each module number refers to the

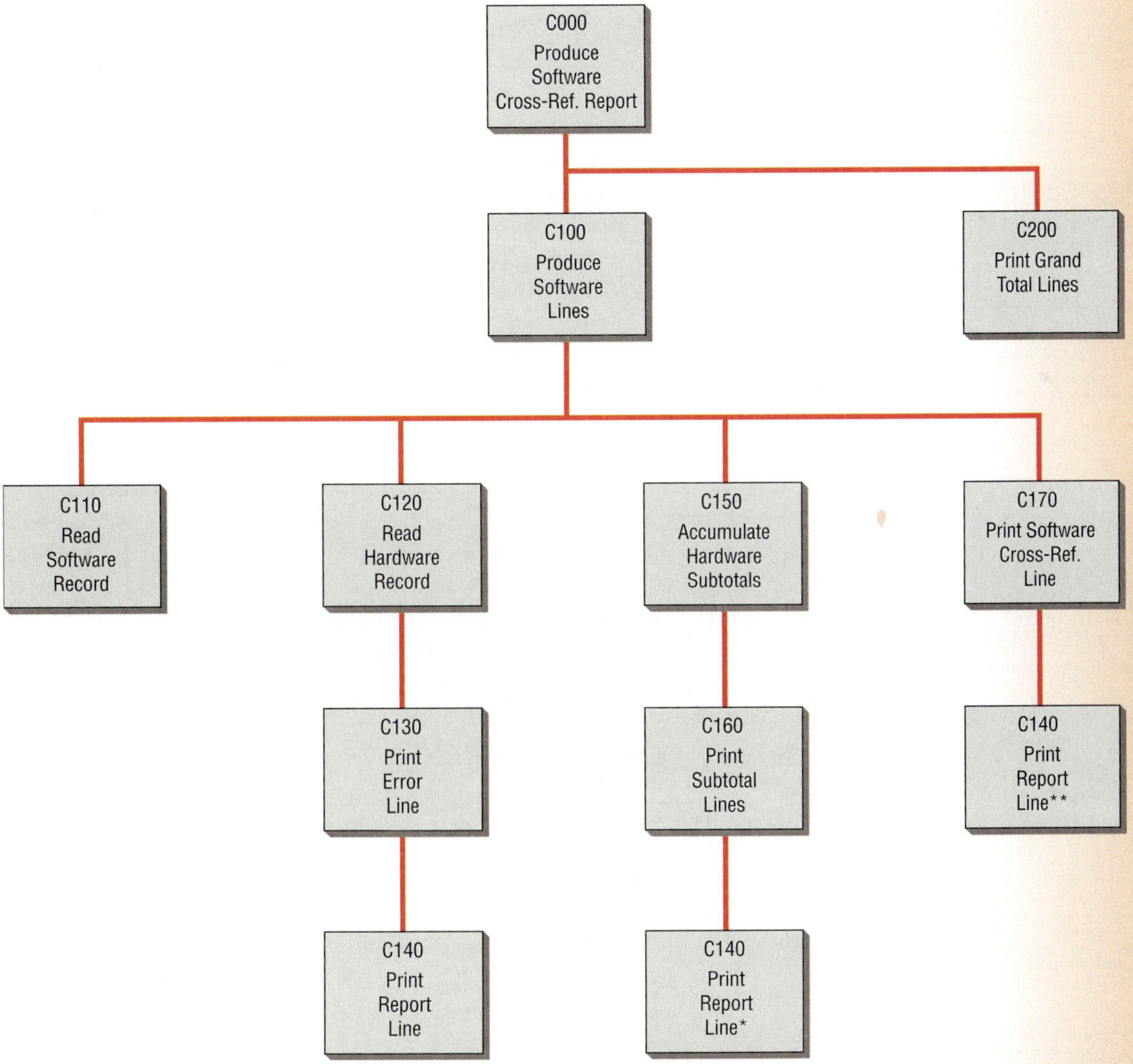

FIGURE E16.1

PRODUCE SOFTWARE CROSS-REFERENCE REPORT structure chart. The single asterisk (*) and the double asterisk (**) indicate the second and third occurrence of module C140.

CROSS-REFERENCE REPORT (a letter is required by Visible Analyst as the first character in a module name). This draft is the first one Mack uses in a structured walk-through with Dee Ziner, a senior programmer.

Dee Ziner has several important suggestions for improving the structure. She says, "Module C130, PRINT ERROR LINE, is improperly subordinate to the calling module C120, READ HARDWARE RECORD. The question may be asked, 'Must the program print an error line to accomplish reading a HARDWARE RECORD?' Because the answer is no, the module should be placed at the same level as C120, READ HARDWARE RECORD."

She continues discussing the situation with Mack, saying, "The same is true concerning module C160, PRINT SUBTOTAL LINES. That is not a function of accumulating hardware subtotals and should not be called from module C150, ACCUMULATE HARDWARE SUBTOTALS." Dee continues the walkthrough by asking the question, "May one SOFTWARE RECORD be located on many machines?" Mack responds that that is true, and another controlling module, PRINT SOFTWARE CROSS-REFERENCE LINE, is included in the structure chart.

Mack proceeds to incorporate the changes to the structure chart. When the correct hierarchy is established, the coupling is added. Careful attention is given to pass minimal data and to only pass control *up* the structure chart. The final version is illustrated in Figure E16.2. Module C116 is new, using the SOFTWARE/HARDWARE RELATION file to link one SOFTWARE RECORD to many HARDWARE RECORDS. The SOFTWARE INVENTORY NUMBER is passed down to the module, and the relation file is randomly read. The HARDWARE INVENTORY NUMBER and control switch RELATION NOT FOUND are passed up the structure.

The final structure chart has a functional shape to it. A few control modules at the top of the structure, several worker modules in the middle, and a few specialist modules at the bottom provide a general fan-out, fan-in shape. The module names are all in verb-adjective-noun form, describing what has been accomplished after the module has finished executing. For example, module C150 has the verb "accumulate," describing the work accomplished by the module. "Subtotals," a noun, are being accumulated, and "hardware" describes which subtotals are accumulated.

Each of the modules on the structure chart was described in the repository. Figure E16.3 illustrates the display describing the function for module C100, PRODUCE SOFTWARE LINES. Notice that the module description contains pseudocode depicting the logic of the module. Because PRODUCE SOFTWARE LINES is a control module, its logic should consist of looping and decision making, with minimal statements concerning processing details such as ADD or READ.

Each data and control couple on the structure chart may also be described in the repository. The **Related to** area provides a link to the repository entry that contains the details of elements contained in the data couple.

"Well, I guess that we're about done creating diagrams for the programmers," remarks Chip.

"Creating diagrams, yes," counters Anna, "but there's a bit more that we can give them."

"What do you mean?" asks Chip, with a puzzled look on his face.

"Let's use Visible Analyst to generate the database tables for Microsoft Access," exclaims Anna. "I thought we would start with one of the major entities, such as the SOFTWARE MASTER, and use the code generation feature of Visible Analyst."

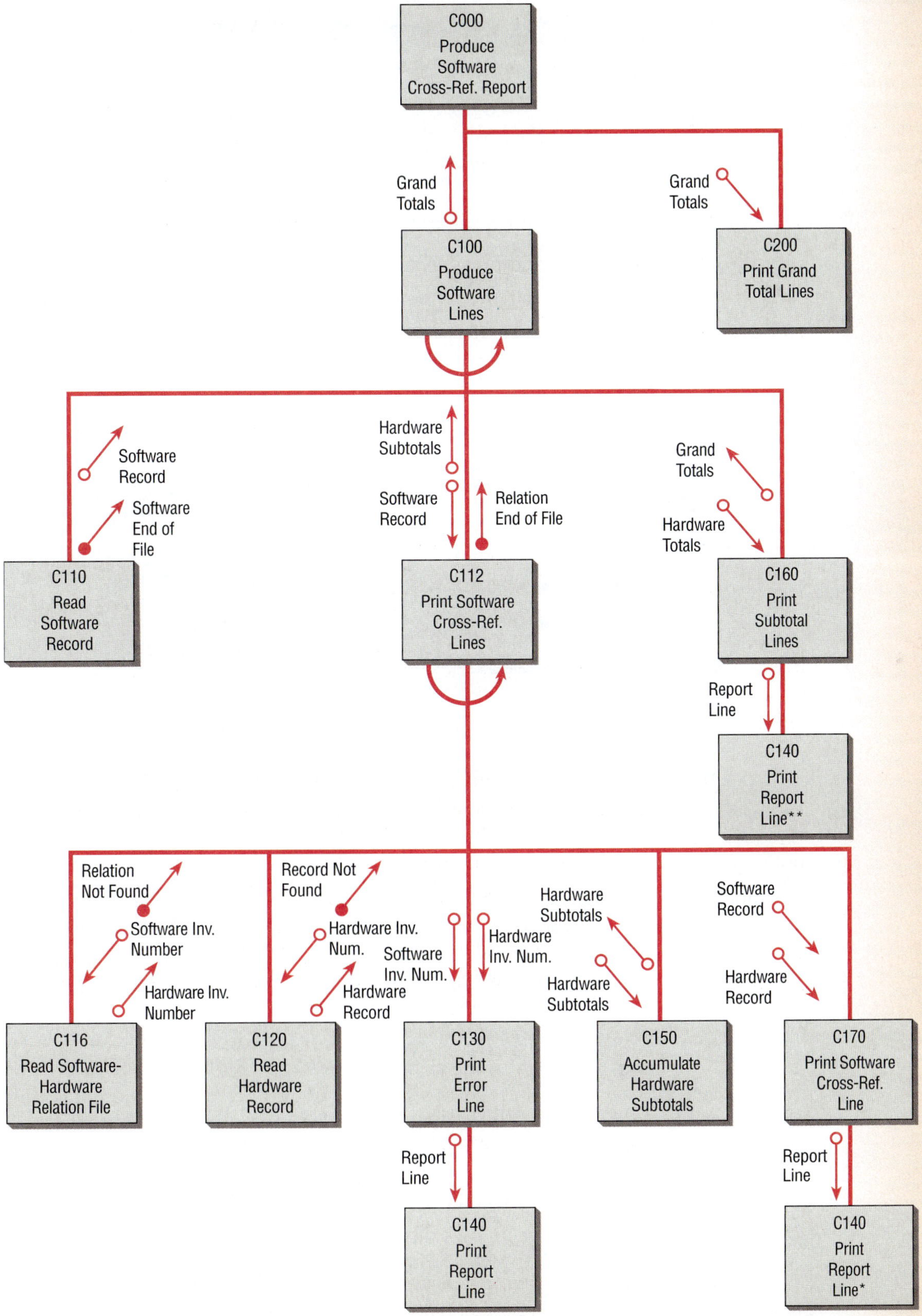

FIGURE E16.2

PRODUCE SOFTWARE CROSS-REFERENCE REPORT structure chart, with coupling. The single asterisk (*) and the double asterisk (**) indicate the second and third occurrence of module C140.

16

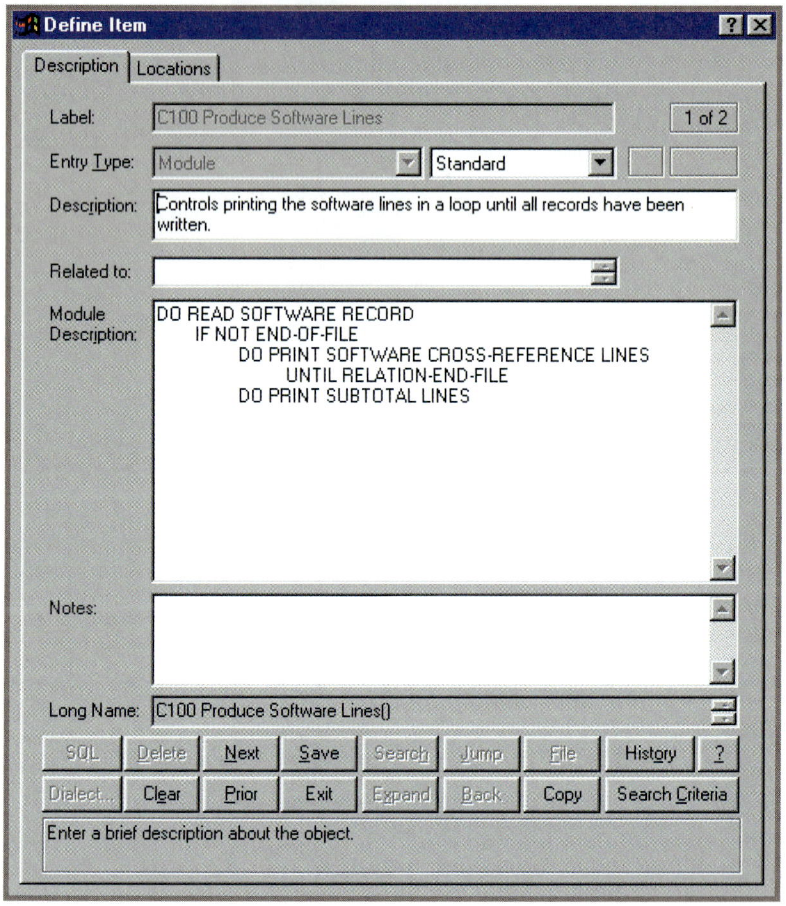

FIGURE E16.3
PRODUCE SOFTWARE LINES module repository screen.

Anna and Chip proceed to work with Visible Analyst to ensure that all the elements have been defined for the SOFTWARE MASTER. Anna clicks **Repository** and **Generate Database Schema.** They select the COMPUTER SYSTEM diagram and give the schema the same name. The entire schema for the computer system is generated.

"I'm going to copy a portion of the schema to work with just the SOFTWARE MASTER," Anna remarks to Chip. She copies the generated SQL for the SOFTWARE MASTER file. The next step is to create a blank query in Microsoft Access. Anna runs Microsoft Access and creates a new empty query. She clicks on the SQL button and pastes the SOFTWARE MASTER file into the SQL window.

"I need to change the name of the table to SOFTWARE and change the query type to Make Table," continues Anna. She gives the new table the name SOFTWARE. Anna clicks the **Run Query** button and closes the query.

"What happened?" asks Chip with a puzzled look. "I don't see any output."

Anna clicks on the **Tables** button. "Take a look at our new table!" Anna exclaims. She clicks the SOFTWARE table and design view. "Here's our structure from Visible Analyst, implemented in Microsoft Access."

"Now that is cool," beams Chip.

The analysts continue to generate tables until the design is complete.

"I think that we can leave the rest to the programming staff," remarks Anna. "We better start developing the test plans for each program."

Test plans contain details about how to determine if the programs are working correctly, and they are sent to Mack and Dee, who will create the actual test data. Invalid and valid data are included on each test file used in batch programs. The same is true for interactive systems, except that the test data are written on forms imitating the screen design. After Mack has finished testing his programs and is satisfied that they are working correctly, he challenges Dee to find any errors in the programs. In turn, Dee has Mack test her programs in a round of friendly competition. They both realize that programmers may not always catch their own errors, because they are intimately familiar with their own programs and may not recognize subtle errors in logic.

EXERCISES

E-1. View the PRODUCE SOFTWARE CROSS-REF REP structure chart. Double click on the modules to view the repository entries for some of the modules.

E-2. Modify the PRODUCE HARDWARE INVESTMENT RPT structure chart. Add the function PRINT INVESTMENT LINE in the empty rectangle provided. Subordinate to this module is PRINT HEADING LINES and WRITE REPORT LINE. Describe each function in the repository.

E-3. Modify the CHANGE COMPUTER file structure chart. Include the looping symbol and add the following modules subordinate to module 160, CHANGE COMPUTER RECORD (also see below):

A. SHOW CHANGE DISPLAY
B. ACCEPT COMPUTER CHANGES
C. VALIDATE CHANGES
D. DISPLAY ERROR MESSAGE
E. CONFIRM CHANGES

The following modules should be subordinate to module 220, PUT COMPUTER RECORD:

A. FORMAT COMPUTER RECORD
B. REWRITE COMPUTER RECORD

E-4. Modify the ADD SOFTWARE RECORD structure chart by adding a looping symbol and coupling for the connections. The following coupling should be placed on the connection line above each module (also see below):

A. Module:	DISPLAY ADD SOFTWARE SCREEN
Passed Up:	ADD SOFTWARE SCREEN
B. Module:	ACCEPT ADD SOFTWARE SCREEN
Passed Up:	EXIT INDICATOR (Control)
	ADD SOFTWARE SCREEN DATA

The exercises preceded by a Web icon indicate value-added material is available from the Web site at www.prenhall.com/kendall. Students can download a sample Visible Analyst Project and a Microsoft Access database that can be used to complete the exercises. Visible Analyst software can be packaged with this text for an additional fee.

C. Module: VALIDATE ADD SOFTWARE DATA
Passed Down: ADD SOFTWARE SCREEN DATA
Passed Up: CANCEL TRANSACTION (Control)
VALID ADD SOFTWARE DATA

D. Module: READ SOFTWARE RECORD
Passed Down: SOFTWARE INVENTORY NUMBER
Passed Up: RECORD FOUND (Control)

E. Module: VALIDATE HARDWARE REQUIREMENTS
Passed Down: ADD SOFTWARE SCREEN DATA
Passed Up: VALID DATA (Control)
ERROR MESSAGE

F. Module: DISPLAY ERROR MESSAGE
Passed Down: ERROR MESSAGE

G. Module: PUT NEW SOFTWARE RECORD
Passed Down: VALID ADD SOFTWARE DATA

H. Module: FORMAT SOFTWARE RECORD
Passed Down: VALID ADD SOFTWARE DATA
Passed Up: FORMATTED SOFTWARE RECORD

I. Module: WRITE SOFTWARE RECORD
Passed Down: FORMATTED SOFTWARE RECORD

E-5. Create the PRINT PROBLEM MACHINE REPORT structure chart. An outline of the modules follows, with each subordinate module indented:

- PRINT PROBLEM MACHINE REPORT
  - PRINT PROBLEM MACHINE LINES
    - READ MACHINE RECORD
    - DETERMINE PROBLEM MACHINE
    - PRINT PROBLEM MACHINE LINE
      - PRINT HEADING LINES
      - WRITE REPORT LINE
  - PRINT FINAL REPORT LINES
    - WRITE REPORT LINE

E-6. Create the CHANGE SOFTWARE RECORD structure chart. Modules of the program are shown with subordinate modules indented.

- CHANGE SOFTWARE FILE
  - CHANGE SOFTWARE RECORDS
    - GET SOFTWARE RECORD
      - DISPLAY SOFTWARE ID SCREEN
      - ACCEPT SOFTWARE ID SCREEN
      - FIND SOFTWARE RECORD
      - DISPLAY ERROR LINE
    - OBTAIN SOFTWARE CHANGES
      - DISPLAY CHANGE SCREEN
      - ACCEPT SOFTWARE CHANGES
      - VALIDATE CHANGES
      - DISPLAY ERROR LINE

PUT SOFTWARE RECORD
FORMAT SOFTWARE RECORD
REWRITE SOFTWARE RECORD

E-7. Create the SOFTWARE DETAILS INQUIRY structure chart. Modules are listed with subordinate modules indented.

INQUIRE SOFTWARE DETAILS
INQUIRE SOFTWARE RECORD
GET SOFTWARE RECORD
DISPLAY SOFTWARE ID SCREEN
ACCEPT SOFTWARE ID SCREEN
FIND SOFTWARE RECORD
DISPLAY ERROR LINE
DISPLAY INQUIRY SCREEN
FORMAT SOFTWARE INQUIRY SCREEN
DISPLAY SOFTWARE INQUIRY SCREEN

E-8. View the ADD COMPUTER system flowchart.

E-9. Modify the ADD SOFTWARE system flow. Add the following program rectangles below the INSTALL SOFTWARE manual process. Include input and output files and reports specified for each program.

Program:	UPDATE SOFTWARE RELATIONAL FILE
Input:	UPDATE SOFTWARE INSTALLATION LIST, document
	UPDATE INSTALLED SOFTWARE SCREEN, display
Output:	SOFTWARE RELATIONAL FILE, disk
	INSTALLED SOFTWARE TRANSACTION, disk
Program:	PRINT USER NOTIFICATION REPORT
Input:	INSTALLED SOFTWARE TRANSACTION, disk
Output:	USER NOTIFICATION REPORT, report

E-10. Create the ADD STAFF system flowchart. There are two programs: ADD STAFF and PRINT NEW STAFF LIST. Input to the ADD STAFF program is a NEW STAFF listing and an ADD NEW STAFF entry display. The STAFF MASTER file is updated and a NEW STAFF LOG file is produced. The NEW STAFF LOG file is input to the PRINT NEW STAFF LIST program, producing the NEW STAFF LIST report.

E-11. Design test data on paper to test the ADD COMPUTER program. Use Microsoft Access to test the display. Note any discrepancies.

E-12. Design test data and predicted results for the ADD SOFTWARE program. Use Microsoft Access to test the display and note whether the results conformed to your predictions.

E-13. Design test data and predicted results for the ADD TRAINING CLASS program. Use Microsoft Access to test the display and note whether the results conformed to your predictions.

E-14. Design test data on paper to test the CHANGE SOFTWARE EXPERT program. Use Microsoft Access to test the display. Note any discrepancies.

SUCCESSFULLY IMPLEMENTING THE INFORMATION SYSTEM

17

LEARNING OBJECTIVES

Once you have mastered the material in this chapter you will be able to:

1. **Comprehend the implementation of a variety of distributed systems.**
2. **Design appropriate training programs for users of the new system.**
3. **Recognize the differences among physical conversion strategies, and be able to recommend an appropriate one to a client.**
4. **Address security, disaster preparedness, and disaster recovery concerns for traditional and Web-based systems.**
5. **Understand the importance of evaluating the new system, and be able to recommend a suitable evaluation technique to a client.**

The process of ensuring that the information system is operational and then allowing users to take over its operation for use and evaluation is called implementation. The systems analyst has several approaches to implementation that should be considered as the changeover to the new system is being prepared. They include shifting more computer power to users through distributed processing, training users, converting from the old system, and evaluating the new one.

The first approach to implementation concerns the movement of computer power to individual users by setting up and shifting computer power and responsibility to groups throughout the business with the help of distributed computing.

The second approach to implementation is using different strategies for training users and personnel, using a variety of training techniques, and making sure that each user understands any new role that he or she must take on because of the new information system.

Another approach to implementation is choosing a conversion strategy. The systems analyst needs to weigh the situation and propose a conversion plan that is appropriate for the particular organization and information system.

The fourth approach to implementation involves evaluating the new or modified information system. The analyst needs to formulate performance measures to evaluate the system. Evaluations come from users, management, and analysts themselves.

IMPLEMENTING DISTRIBUTED SYSTEMS

If the reliability of a telecommunications network is high, it is possible to have distributed systems for businesses, a setup that can be conceived of as an application of telecommunications. The concept of distributed systems is used in many different ways. Here it will be taken in a broad sense so that it includes workstations that can communicate with each other and data processors, as well as different hierarchical architectural configurations of data processors that communicate with each other and that have differing data storage capabilities.

The information architecture model that will likely dominate networking in the next few years is that of the client/server. In this model, the processing functions are delegated either to clients (users) or to servers, depending on which machines are most suitable for executing the work. In this type of architecture, the client portion of a network application will run on the client system, with the server part of the application running on the file server. With a client/server model, users interact with limited parts of the application, including the user interface, data input, database queries, and report generation. Controlling user access to centralized databases, retrieving or processing data, and other functions (such as managing peripheral devices) are handled by the server.

CLIENT/SERVER TECHNOLOGY

The client/server (C/S) model, client/server computing, client/server technology, and client/server architecture all refer to a design model that can be thought of as applications running on a local area network (LAN). In very basic terms, you can picture the client requesting—and the server executing or in some way fulfilling—the request. The computers on the network are programmed to perform work efficiently by dividing up processing tasks among clients and servers. Figure 17.1 shows how a client/server model might be configured with a LAN. Note that several "clients" are depicted as user workstations.

When you think of the client/server model, you should think of a system that accentuates the users as the center of the work, with their interaction with data being the key concept. Although there are two elements working—the client and the server—it is the intent of the C/S model that users view it as one system. Indeed, the hope is that users are unaware of how the client/server network is performing its distributed processing, because it should have the look and feel of a unified system. In a peer-to-peer network, PCs can act as either the server or the client, depending on the requirements of the application.

Clients as Part of the C/S Model Using a LAN When you see the term *client*, you might be tempted to think of people or users; for example, we speak of "clients of our consulting practice." In the C/S model, however, the term *client* refers not to people but to networked machines that are typical points of entry to the client/server system that is used by humans. Therefore, clients could be networked desktop computers, a workstation, or notebook computers, or any other way in which the user can enter the system.

Using a graphical user interface (GUI), individuals typically interface directly only with the client part. Client workstations use smaller programs that reside in the client to do front-end processing (as opposed to the back-end processing, mentioned later), including communicating with the user. If an application is called a client-based application, the application resides in a client computer and cannot be accessed by other users on the network. Note that client-based applications require separate installation on each workstation if the LAN has not purchased a site license.

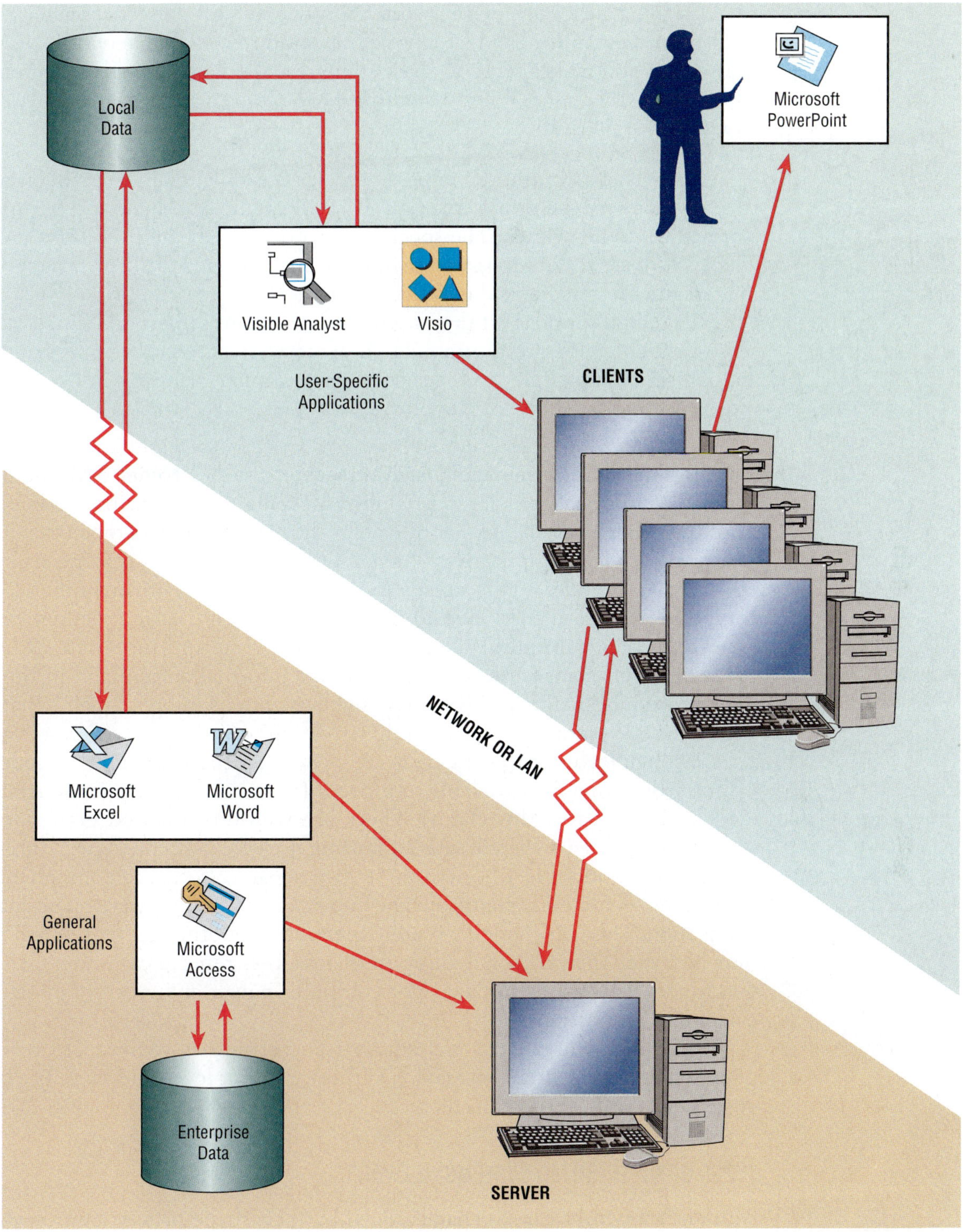

FIGURE 17.1
A client/server system configuration.

File Server. *File server* is the term used to denote a computer on a LAN that stores on its hard disk the application programs and data files for all the clients on the network. Server-based applications are types of client processing capabilities that permit the user to request network applications (programs stored on a network server rather than on a user's computer) from the server. Back-end processing (such as a physical search of a database, for instance) will usually take place on a server. If a file server crashes, client-based applications are not affected.

Designing a client/server network is a way to allocate resources in a LAN so as to distribute computing power among the computers in the network. Note, however, that it still makes sense to share some resources, which can be centralized in a file server. Client/server networks are proving to be a good, solid way to embody workgroup applications.

Print Server. A print server on a LAN is accessible to all workstations. In contrast to a file server, a print server is a PC dedicated to receiving and (temporarily) storing files to be printed. The specialized software that the print server uses first enables it to store print jobs, and then helps it to manage the distribution of printing tasks to printers hooked into the network.

Although it sounds as if they are the same as print servers and file servers, Web servers are software, not a combination of software and hardware as print servers and file servers are. Refer to the section on designing Web sites in Chapter 11 for more information about Web applications.

Weighing the Advantages and Disadvantages of the C/S Model Although many companies jumped right in and requested client/server systems, we have found from the experience of early adopters that they are not always the best solution to an organization's computing problems. Often, the systems designer is asked to endorse a C/S model that is already in the works. Just as with any other corporate computing proposal that you did not have an active part in creating, you must review the plan carefully. Will the organization's culture support a C/S model? What kinds of changes must be made in the informal culture and in the formal work procedures before a C/S model can be used to its full potential? What should your role as a systems analyst be in this situation?

Although lower processing costs are cited as a benefit of the C/S model, there is very little actual data available to prove it (even though there is some anecdotal evidence to support this claim). There are well-documented high start-up or switch-over costs associated with a movement to a C/S architecture. Applications for the C/S model must be written as two separate software components, each running on separate machines, but they must appear as if they are operating as one application. The C/S model is more expensive than other options which use terminals, rather than personal computers, to access remote computers. Using the C/S model, however, affords greater computer power and greater opportunity to customize applications.

Without the organizational support and structure required to realize the potential of putting decision-making authority at user level, and therefore closer to customers, this benefit is meaningless.

TYPES OF DISTRIBUTED SYSTEMS NETWORKS

Although networks can be characterized by their shape or topology, they are also discussed in terms of their geographic coverage and the kinds of services they offer. Standard types of networks include a wide area network (WAN) and a local area network (LAN). Local area networks are standard for linking local computers or terminals within a department, building, or several buildings of an organization. Wide area networks can serve users over several miles or across entire continents. There are four main types of distributed systems networks: hierarchical, star, ring, and bus. Each requires different hardware and software and has different capabilities.

Networking is now technically, economically, and operationally feasible for small offices as well, and it provides a solution that analysts should consider for small businesses. Network kits are sometimes called networks in a box, because

"No, I am <u>not</u> equipped with a modem connection!"

everything to set up a small network is provided for one price (usually below $200). Sometimes, software wizards to help you plan the network installation are also included in these bundles.

Networking provides advantages for small businesses when one considers the possibility for the sharing of software and the improvement of group work. Also, small businesses may be able to invest in a better-quality printer, CD-ROM drives, modems, or other peripherals, because they need fewer of them when users can share resources over the network. Most network kits exclude network operating system software, and this possibility allows the small business flexibility in using whichever one fits its requirements.

One of the costly aspects of implementing a LAN is that each time it is moved, it must be rewired. Some organizations are coping with this by setting up a high-speed, wireless local area network (WLAN). More specifically, these wireless networks are called Wi-Fi (for wireless fidelity), or alternatively the 802.11 high rate. Note that "802.11" refers to a family of specifications developed by the IEEE for wireless LAN technology. Within the 802.11 family of standards there are many specifications, including 802.11g, which applies to wireless LANs providing 204 Mbps in the 2.4-GHz band. (However, actual transmission speeds are lower when additional encryption wired equivalent privacy, or WEP, is used for security purposes.)

WLANs are comparatively cheap to set up, and they serve as a flexible technology for supporting work groups. Wireless networks can also provide mobile Internet access if PCs and other devices are equipped with adapters and are within 100 meters of an access point. Hot spots are Wi-Fi networks that are being made available in certain high-Internet traffic locations, such as college dormitories, libraries, airline clubs, and hotels, as well as in some rather unlikely public places, such as areas of Central Park, in New York City, and various coffee shops in Ireland. Some of these are commercially sponsored hot spots, and others are sponsored by local communities and municipalities to provide free Internet access.

Although this is an increasingly popular low-cost alternative, there are security concerns as well as signal integrity concerns, because Wi-Fi networks are prone to interference from systems operating nearby in the same frequency spectrum. Unfortunately, there is no way to stop or limit any additional new devices in the area. These can increase interference as well.

In order to improve the security of data transmission, Wi-Fi uses WEP, which is 802.11's optional encryption standard that most radio network interface card (NIC) and access point vendors support. Many flaws have been detected, but used in concert with traditional LAN security measures, WEP is thought to be adequate for many home and business purposes.

Many locations, in the United States and worldwide, do not have Wi-Fi or a way to connect to fixed broadband for Internet use. One of the solutions to the lack of access is the creation of the WiMax (worldwide interoperability for microwave access) family of standards. WiMax is also known as Mobile WiMax, the common term for the IEEE standard 802.16, which is the "Air Interface for Fixed Broadband Wireless Access Systems." WiMax features a greater wireless access range, a little over 30 miles, compared to about 300 feet for Wi-Fi. Broadband wireless standards are changing and evolving to 802.20.

Many major mobile service providers are offering anytime-anywhere wireless broadband access for PCs, handhelds, and other equipment over a mobile network using EV-DO (evolution data optimized). One of the current drawbacks of the technology is that, if the user is trying to get on the Web in an area with a notoriously weak signal for cell phones, the Web access will not work either.

Another type of wireless networking standard is Bluetooth. More suitable for small personal networks, Bluetooth incorporates a large variety of devices including computers, printers, handheld devices, phones, keyboards and mice, and household appliances.

Hierarchical Networks In a basic hierarchical configuration, the host—a mainframe computer—controls all the other nodes, which can include minicomputers and PCs. Note that computers on the same level do not communicate with each other. With this arrangement, large-scale computing problems are handled by the mainframe, and lesser computing demands are handled on the correct level by either minicomputers or PCs.

Star Networks Another popular configuration for distributed computing is the star network. A mainframe, PC, or workstation is designated the central node. As such, it communicates with the lesser nodes, but they cannot communicate directly with one another. A need for PCs to communicate with one another would be met by one PC sending data to the central node, which in turn would relay the data to a second PC.

Ring Networks Ring networks are another possibility for distributed computing. There is no central computer for a ring. Rather, its shape reminds us that all the nodes are of equal computing power. With the use of a ring network, all PCs can communicate directly with one another, passing along all the messages they read to their correct destinations on the ring.

Bus Configurations Another type of network for distributed processing is the bus configuration. Bus configurations work well in close quarters, such as in a suite of offices where several different devices can be hooked together using a central cable. A bus configuration allows a great deal of change by permitting users to add or remove devices quite easily. In a bus configuration, the single, central cable serves as the only path.

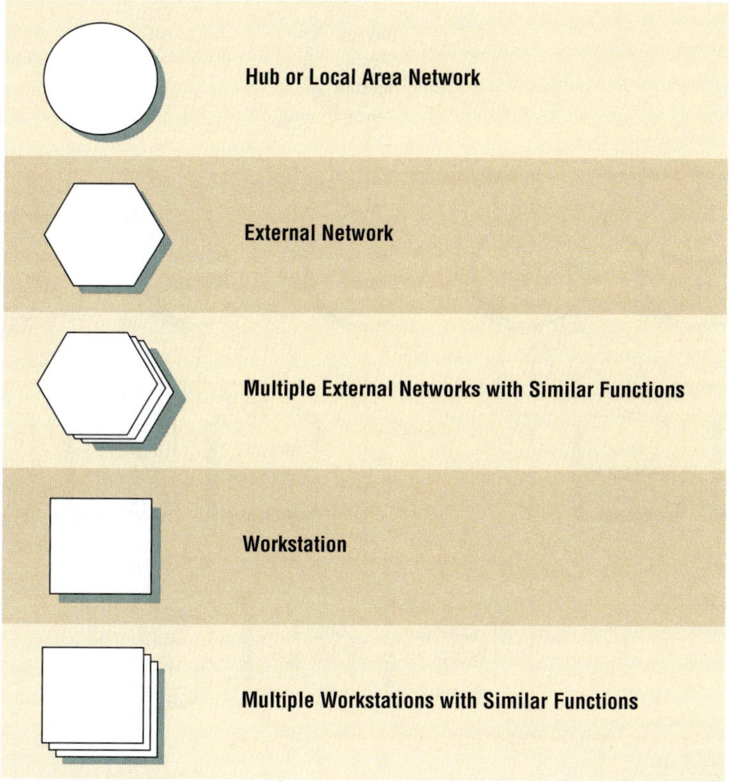

FIGURE 17.2
Use special symbols when drawing network decomposition and hub connectivity diagrams.

NETWORK MODELING

Because networking has become so important, the systems designer needs to consider network design. Whether a systems designer gets involved with decisions about token rings or Ethernet networks—or whether he or she worries about hardware such as routers and bridges that must be in place when networks meet—the systems designer must always consider the logical design of networks. Network modeling comes into play here.

CASE tools are not sufficient to help the systems designer with network modeling. It is possible to use some of a CASE tool's drawing capabilities, but forcing the data modeling tools to do network modeling does not work. Therefore, we suggest using a set of symbols such as the ones in Figure 17.2 to model the network. It is useful to have distinct symbols to distinguish among hubs, external networks, and workstations. It is also useful to adopt a convention for illustrating multiple networks and workstations.

Usually, a top-down approach is appropriate. The first step is to draw a network decomposition diagram that provides an overview of the system. Next, draw a hub connectivity diagram. Finally, explode the hub connectivity diagram to show the various workstations and how they are to be connected.

Drawing a Network Decomposition Diagram We can illustrate drawing a network decomposition model by referring once again to the World's Trend Catalog Division example from earlier chapters. Start by drawing a circle at the top and labeling it "World's Trend Network." Now draw a number of circles on the level below, as shown in Figure 17.3. These circles represent hubs for the Marketing Division and each of the three order-entry and distribution centers (the U.S. Division, the Canadian Division, and the Mexican Division).

We can extend this drawing further by drawing another level. This time, we can add the workstations. For example, the Marketing Division has two workstations

FIGURE 17.3
A network decomposition diagram for World's Trend.

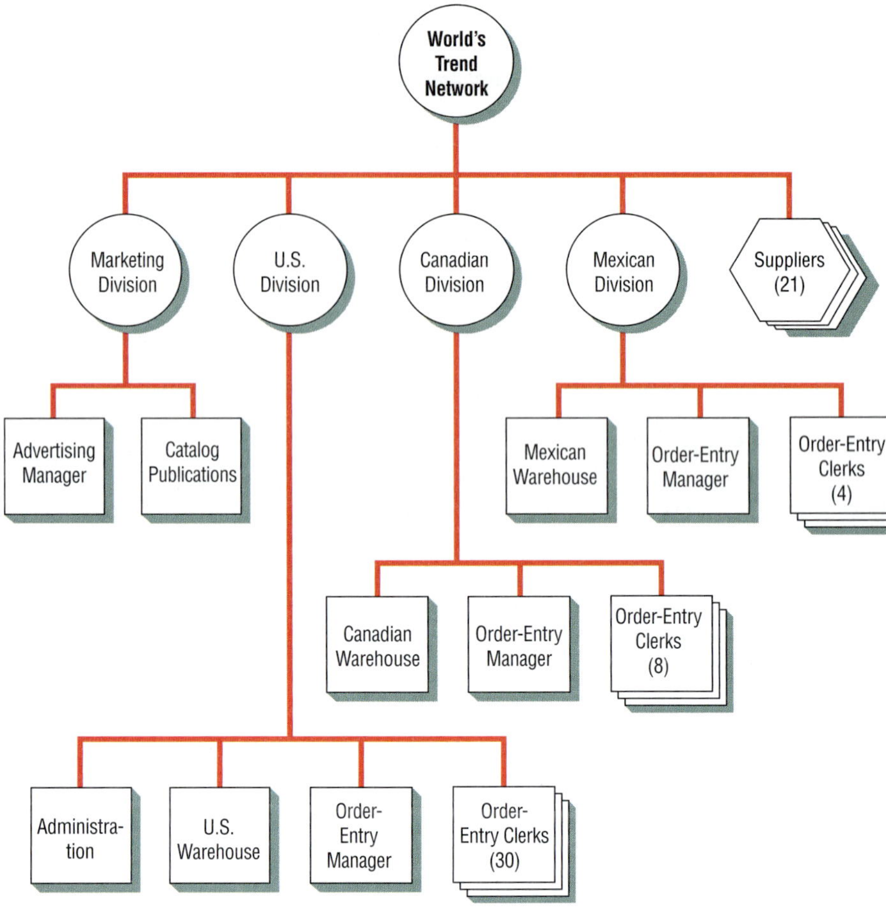

connected to it, whereas the U.S. Division has 33 workstations on its LAN (Administration, the Warehouse, the Order-Entry Manager, and 30 Order-Entry Clerks). This network is simplified for the purpose of providing a readily understandable example.

Creating a Hub Connectivity Diagram The hub connectivity diagram is useful for showing how the major hubs are connected. At World's Trend (see Figure 17.4),

FIGURE 17.4
A hub connectivity diagram for World's Trend.

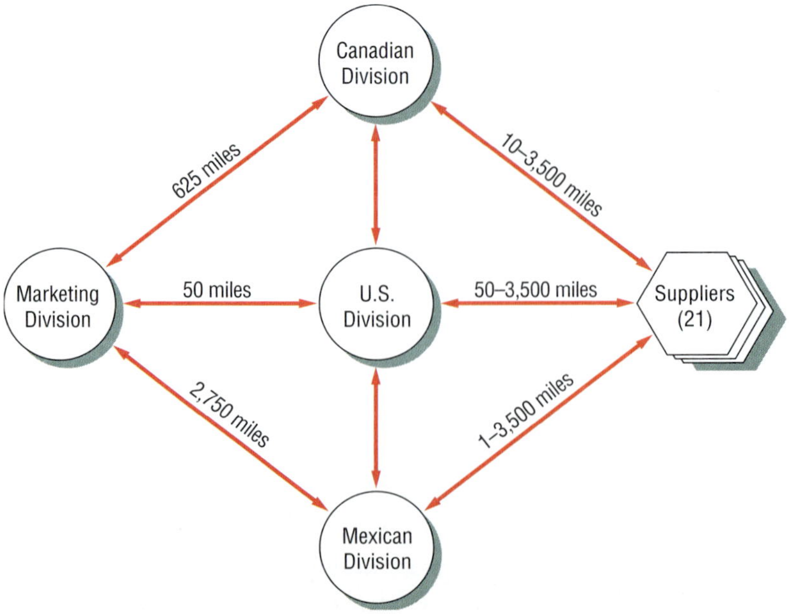

there are four major hubs that are all connected to one another. In addition, there are external hubs (suppliers) that need to be notified when inventory drops below a certain point, and so on. Each of the three country divisions are connected to the 21 suppliers; the Marketing Division, however, does not need to be connected to suppliers.

To produce an effective hub connectivity diagram, start by drawing all the hubs. Then experiment (perhaps sketching it first on a sheet of paper) to see which links are necessary. Once that is done, you can redraw the diagram so that it is attractive and communicates well to users.

Exploding the Hub Connectivity Diagram into a Workstation Connectivity Diagram The purpose of network modeling is to show the connectivity of workstations in some detail. To do so, we explode the hub connectivity diagram. Figure 17.5 shows each of the 33 workstations for the U.S. Division and how they are to be connected.

Draw the diagrams for this level by examining the third level of the network decomposition diagram. Group items such as Order-Entry Manager and Order-Entry Clerks together, because you already recognize that they must be connected. Use a special symbol to show multiple workstations and indicate in parentheses the number of similar workstations. In our example, there are 30 Order-Entry Clerks.

On the perimeter of the diagram, place workstations that must be connected to other hubs. In this way, it will be easier to represent these connections using arrows. Draw the external connections in a different color or use thicker arrows. External connections are usually long distance. For example, Administration is connected to the Marketing Division, which is 50 miles away, and also to the Canadian and Mexican Divisions. The Warehouse needs to communicate directly with the Canadian and Mexican warehouses in case it is possible to obtain the merchandise from another warehouse. The Order-Entry Manager and Order-Entry Clerks do not have to be connected to anyone outside their LAN.

Hub connectivity diagrams can be exploded to many levels. If doing so makes sense in your particular application, go ahead and draw them that way. There is no limit to the possible number of explosions.

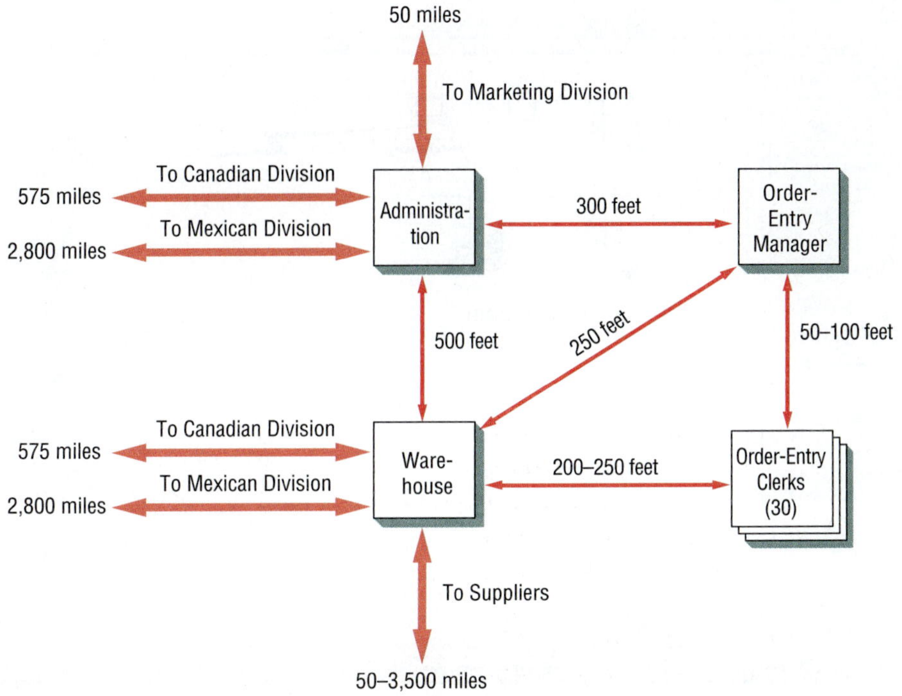

FIGURE 17.5

A workstation connectivity diagram for World's Trend.

FIGURE 17.6

Analysts can draw hub connectivity diagrams using software like Microsoft Office Visio Professional.

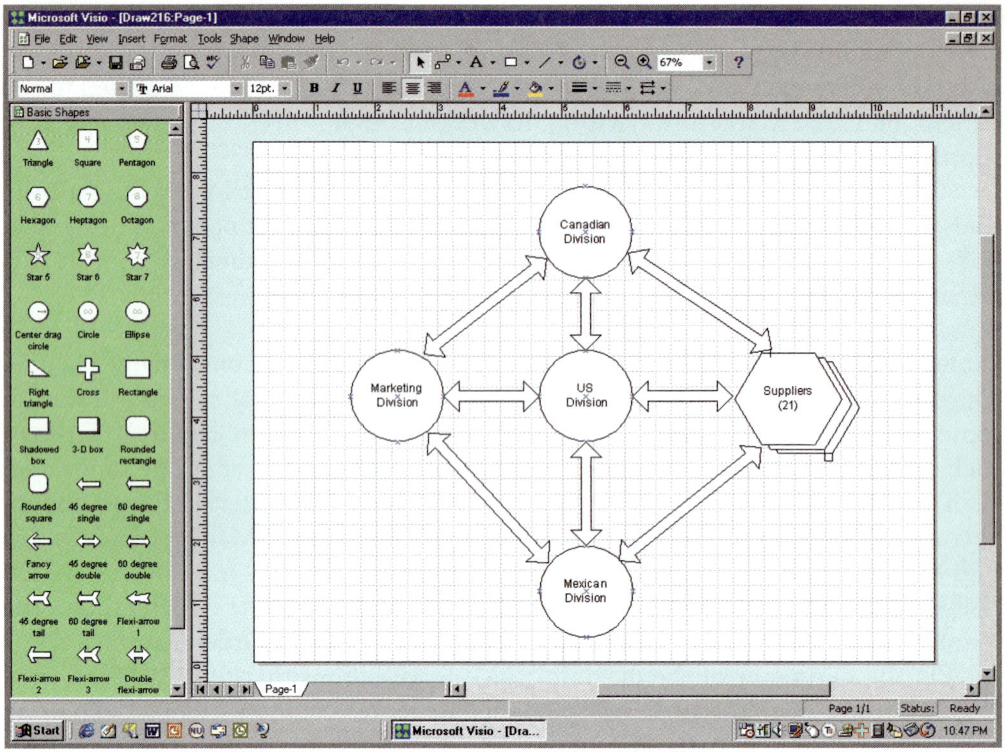

Hub connectivity and workstation connectivity diagrams can be drawn using software packages as well. Although it may be difficult if you restrict yourself to using CASE tool software, it is relatively simple if you use flexible drag and drop software, such as Microsoft Office Visio. (See Figure 17.6.)

Visio even contains stencils that depict certain pieces of equipment, if you wish to go into that much detail. Using specific stencils, an analyst could drag each symbol from the template to the piece of paper. Figure 17.7 shows how two

FIGURE 17.7

A more detailed diagram of two networks, drawn by selecting symbols from a template and dragging them to the piece of paper. This diagram was drawn using Microsoft Office Visio Professional.

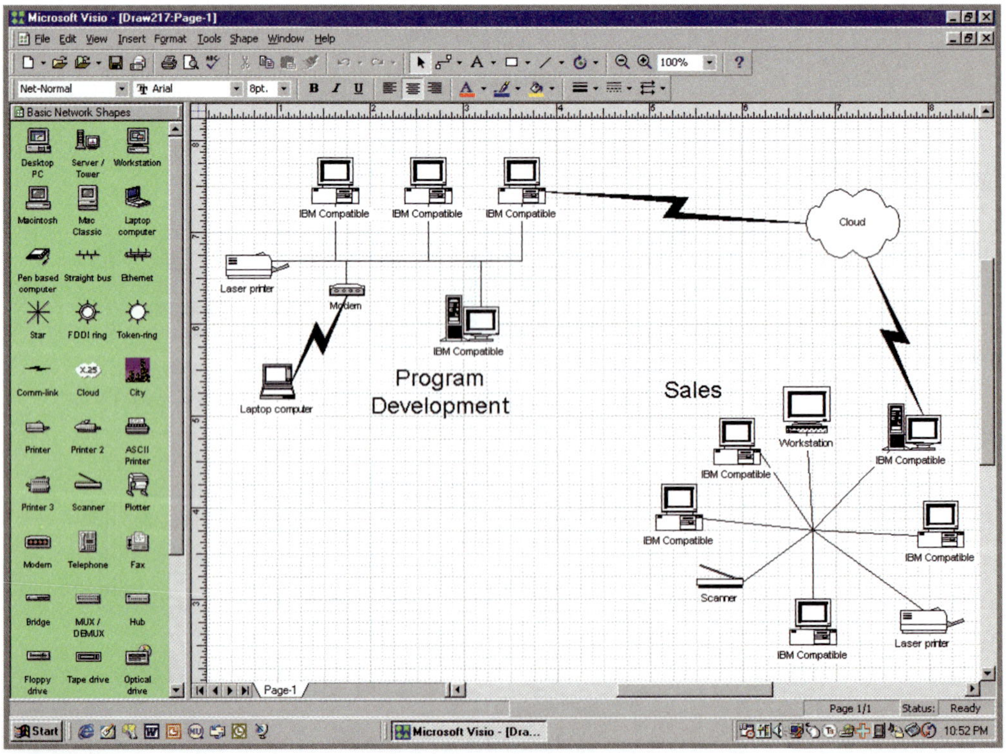

networks are set up for a software manufacturer. The top part of the figure illustrates the organization's program development sector network, and the bottom part shows the sales department network. Packages such as Microsoft Office Visio are extremely useful to the systems analyst because they save time and enhance communication by using standard symbols.

GROUPWARE

Writing applications, whether it's for an entire organization or a solitary decision maker, has also begun to change dramatically. Because much of the organization's work is actually accomplished in groups or teams, there is now a powerful movement afoot to develop special software called groupware that supports people who work together in the organization. Groupware takes advantage of the potential synergies and power available from networked PCs in LANs or WANs, or the Web. Groupware products can help group members to schedule and attend meetings, share data, create and analyze documents, communicate in unstructured ways with one another via email, hold group conferences, do image management on the departmental level, and manage and monitor workflow.

Although most software companies agree about the importance of supporting group work, they differ in their visions of what groups and individuals need for support. For example, Novell currently offers groupware features such as email, messaging, and calendaring in a networked environment. In the future, software will support users by enabling them to pull together a report containing objects gathered from anywhere on the network, regardless of what systems were used to create them. Thus, a report could have text from the annual report, bar charts from last week's sales meeting, and scanned images of hand-drawn sketches that portray the latest departmental brainstorming session. In such a case, the computer would search out the various pieces, and the software would coordinate them for use in one document.

Another approach to developing groupware has been taken by Microsoft, which is giving rudimentary workgroup capability to products such as Windows for Workgroups and Windows NT. Graphical user interfaces include an object store so that Microsoft operating systems will have built-in workgroup capabilities. In the short term, Microsoft is working with smaller developers and consultants to develop workgroup application solutions. This bottom-up approach seems to be showing successful results as well. Different groupware offers different forms of support.

Advantages of Distributed Systems Distributed systems allow the storage of data where they are not in the way of any online real-time transactions. For example, response time on inquiries might be improved if not all records need to be searched before a response is made. In addition, not all data are needed by all users all the time, so they can be stored in less-expensive media at a different site and only accessed when needed.

Use of distributed systems can also lower equipment costs, because not all parts of the system need to be able to perform all functions. Some capabilities, such as processing and storage, can be shared.

Distributed systems can also help lower costs by permitting flexibility in the choice of manufacturer, because the whole focus of networks is on communicating between nodes, and manufacturers make compatible components. This compatibility allows the user to shop for price as well as for function. Furthermore, distributed systems can be less expensive initially than large systems because it is feasible to plan for expansion without actually having to buy hardware at the time

FIGURE 17.8
There are five main advantages to creating distributed systems.

Advantages of Distributed Systems

- Allow data storage out of the way of online, real-time transactions
- Allow less expensive media for data storage when all data are not needed all the time by all users
- Lower equipment cost because not all system parts need to perform all functions
- Lower equipment cost by permitting flexibility in choice of manufacturer
- Less expensive than large systems initially because expansion can be planned for without actually purchasing hardware

the system is implemented. Developing corporate intranets is a proactive way to network organizational members, a way that can also serve as a means for cutting down on problematic aspects of the Internet (such as aimless Web surfing during corporate time, or possible security breakdowns caused by lack of firewalls) and at the same time support group work with useful applications. Extranets formed with suppliers and other important partners are also excellent ways of demonstrating that a business is outward looking and accessible. Advantages of distributed systems are given in Figure 17.8.

Disadvantages of Distributed Systems Distributed systems pose some unique problems that centralized computer systems do not. The analyst needs to weigh these problems against the advantages just presented and to raise them with the concerned business as well.

The first problem is that of network reliability. To make a network an asset rather than a liability, it must be possible to transmit, receive, process, and store data reliably. If there are too many problems with system reliability, the system will be abandoned.

Distributing greater computing power to individuals increases the threat to security because of widespread access. The need for secret passwords, secure computer rooms, and adequate security training of personnel are all concerns that multiply when distributed systems are implemented.

Systems analysts creating distributed systems need to focus on the network itself or on the synergistic aspect of distributed systems. Their power resides in their ability to interact as user workgroups share data. If the relationship between subsystems is ignored or deemphasized, you are creating more problems than you are solving. Disadvantages of distributed systems are listed in Figure 17.9.

FIGURE 17.9
There are four chief disadvantages to creating distributed systems.

Disadvantages of Distributed Systems

- Difficulty in achieving a reliable system
- Security concerns increase commensurately when more individuals have access to the system
- Analysts must emphasize the network and the interactions it provides and deemphasize the power of subsystems
- Choosing the wrong level of computing to support (i.e., individual instead of department, department instead of branch)

TRAINING USERS

Systems analysts engage in an educational process with users that is called training. Throughout the systems development life cycle, the user has been involved so that by now the analyst should possess an accurate assessment of the users who must be trained.

In the implementation of large projects, the analyst will often be managing the training rather than be personally involved in it. One of the most prized assets the analyst can bring to any training situation is the ability to see the system from the user's viewpoint. The analyst must never forget what it is like to face a new system. Those recollections can help analysts empathize with users and facilitate their training.

TRAINING STRATEGIES

Training strategies are determined by who is being trained and who will train them. The analyst will want to ensure that anyone whose work is affected by the new information system is properly trained by the appropriate trainer.

Whom to Train All people who will have primary or secondary use of the system must be trained. They include everyone from data entry personnel to those who will use output to make decisions without personally using a computer. The amount of training a system requires depends on how much someone's job will change because of the new interactions required by the revised system.

You must ensure that users of different skill levels and job interests are separated. It is certain trouble to include novices in the same training sessions as experts, because novices are quickly lost and experts are rapidly bored with basics. Both groups are then lost.

People Who Train Users For a large project, many different trainers may be used depending on how many users must be trained and who they are. Possible training sources include the following:

1. Vendors.
2. Systems analysts.
3. External paid trainers.
4. In-house trainers.
5. Other system users.

This list gives just a few of the options the analyst has in planning for and providing training.

Large vendors often provide offsite, one- or two-day training sessions on their equipment as part of the service benefits offered when corporations purchase expensive COTS software. These sessions include both lectures and hands-on training in a focused environment. They may also extend the experience with online user groups, dedicated blogs, or annual user conferences.

Because systems analysts know the organization's people and the system, they can often provide good training. The use of analysts for training purposes depends on their availability, because they also are expected to oversee the complete implementation process.

External paid trainers are sometimes brought into the organization to help with training. They may have broad experience in teaching people how to use a variety of computers, but they may not give the hands-on training that is needed for some users. In addition, they may not be able to custom-tailor their presentations enough to make them meaningful to users.

Full-time, in-house trainers are usually familiar with the skills and learning preferences of personnel and can tailor materials to their needs. One of the drawbacks of in-house trainers is that they may possess expertise in areas other than information systems and may therefore lack the depth of technical expertise that users require.

It is also possible to have any of these trainers train a small group of people from each functional area that will be using the new information system. They in turn can be used to train the remaining users. This approach can work well if the original trainees still have access to materials and trainers as resources when they themselves are providing training. Otherwise, it might degenerate into a trial-and-error situation rather than a structured one.

GUIDELINES FOR TRAINING

The analyst has four major guidelines for setting up training. They are (1) establishing measurable objectives, (2) using appropriate training methods, (3) selecting suitable training sites, and (4) employing understandable training materials.

Training Objectives Who is being trained in large part dictates the training objectives. Training objectives for each group must be spelled out clearly. Well-defined objectives are of enormous help in letting trainees know what is expected of them. In addition, objectives allow evaluation of training when it is complete. For example, operators must know such basics as turning on the machine, what to do when common errors occur, basic troubleshooting, and how to end an entry.

Training Methods Each user and operator will need slightly different training. To some extent, their jobs determine what they need to know, and their personalities, experience, and backgrounds determine how they learn best. Some users learn best by seeing, others by hearing, and still others by doing. Because it is often not possible to customize training for an individual, a combination of methods is often the best way to proceed. That way, most users are reached through one method or another.

Methods for those who learn best by seeing include demonstrations of equipment and exposure to training manuals. Those who learn best by hearing will benefit from lectures about procedures, discussions, and question-and-answer sessions among trainers and trainees. Those who learn best by doing need hands-on experience with new equipment. For jobs such as that of computer operator, hands-on experience is essential, whereas a quality assurance manager for a production line may only need to see output, learn how to interpret it, and know when it is scheduled to arrive.

Training Sites Training takes place in many different locations, some of which are more conducive to learning than others. Large computer vendors provide special offsite locations at which operable equipment is maintained free of charge. Their trainers offer hands-on experience as well as seminars in settings that allow users to concentrate on learning the new system. One of the disadvantages of offsite training is that users are away from the organizational context in which they must eventually perform.

Onsite training in the users' organization is also possible with several different kinds of trainers. The advantage is that users see the equipment placed as it will

CONSULTING OPPORTUNITY 17.1

YOU CAN LEAD A FISH TO WATER . . . BUT YOU CAN'T MAKE IT DRINK

Sam Monroe, Belle Uga, Wally Ide, and you make up a four-member systems analysis team that is developing an information system to help managers monitor and control water temperature, the number of fish released, and other factors at a large commercial fish hatchery. (They were last seen in Consulting Opportunity 6.3, when they asked you, as their fourth member, to help solve a problem involving the timely delivery of a system prototype.)

With your input, the team successfully turned the tide of the earlier dilemma, and the project has continued. Now you are discussing the training that you have begun to undertake for managers and other systems users. Due to some scheduling difficulties, you have decided to cut down on the number of different training sessions offered, which has resulted in users at a variety of levels of management and computer expertise being in the same training sessions in some instances.

Laurie Hook, one of the operators who is being trained, has been in the same training "tank" with Wade Boot, one of the managers with whom you have been working. Both Laurie and Wade have come to the team privately with different concerns.

Wade told you, "I'm mad that I have to type in my own data in the sessions. The Mississippi will freeze solid before I ever do that on my job. I've got to know *when* to expect output and how to interpret it when it comes. I'm not spending time in training sessions if I can't get that."

Laurie, who shares training sessions with Wade, also complained to your group. "We should be getting more hands-on training. All we hear is a bunch of lectures. It's like school. Not only that, but the managers in the group like to spin these 'fish stories' about what happened to them with the old system. It's boring. I want to know how to operate the thing. It's bait and switch, if you ask me. I'm not learning what you said I would, and besides, with all those bosses in there, I feel like a fish out of water."

What problems are occurring with the training sessions? How can they be addressed, given the scheduling constraints mentioned? What basic advice on setting up training sessions did your team ignore? Write a one-page response to these questions.

be when it is fully operational in the organizational context. A serious disadvantage is that trainees often feel guilty about not fulfilling their regular job duties if they remain onsite for training. Thus, full concentration on training may not be possible.

Offsite training sites are also available for a fee through consultants and vendors. Training sites can be set up in places with rented meeting space, such as a hotel, or may even be permanent facilities maintained by the trainers. These arrangements allow workers to be free from regular job demands, but they may not provide equipment for hands-on training.

Training Materials In planning for the training of users, systems analysts must realize the importance of well-prepared training materials. These materials include training manuals; training cases, in which users are assigned to work through a case that incorporates most of the commonly encountered interactions with the system; and prototypes and mock-ups of output. Users of larger systems will sometimes be able to train on elaborate Web-based simulations or software that is identical to what is being written or purchased. Most COTS software vendors provide online tutorials that illustrate basic functions, and vendors may maintain Web sites that feature pages devoted to FAQ, which can be downloaded and printed. Changes to manuals can also be gleaned from many vendors' Web sites.

Because the user's understanding of the system depends on them, training materials must be clearly written for the correct audience with a minimum of jargon. Training materials should also be well indexed and available to everyone who needs them. A summary of considerations for training objectives, methods, sites, and materials is provided in Figure 17.10.

FIGURE 17.10

Appropriate training objectives, methods, sites, and materials are contingent on many factors.

Elements	Relevant Factors
Training Objectives	Depend on requirements of user's job
Training Methods	Depend on user's job, personality, background, and experience; use combination of lecture, demonstration, hands-on, and study
Training Sites	Depend on training objectives, cost, availability; free vendor sites with operable equipment; in-house installation; rented facilities
Training Materials	Depend on user's needs; operating manuals, cases, prototypes of equipments and output; online tutorials

CONVERSION

A third approach to implementation is physically converting the old information system to the new or modified one. There are many conversion strategies available to analysts, and also a contingency approach that takes into account several user and organizational variables in deciding which conversion strategy to use. There is no single best way to proceed with conversion. The importance of adequate planning and scheduling of conversion with the strategic involvement of users (which often takes many weeks), file backup, and adequate security cannot be overemphasized.

CONVERSION STRATEGIES

The five strategies for converting from the old system to the new are given in Figure 17.11 and are as follows:

1. Direct changeover.
2. Parallel conversion.
3. Gradual, or phased, conversion.
4. Modular prototype conversion.
5. Distributed conversion.

FIGURE 17.11

Five conversion strategies for information systems.

Conversion Method	Changes over Time
Direct Changeover	
Parallel Conversion	
Gradual Conversion	
Modular Prototype Conversion	
Distributed Conversion	

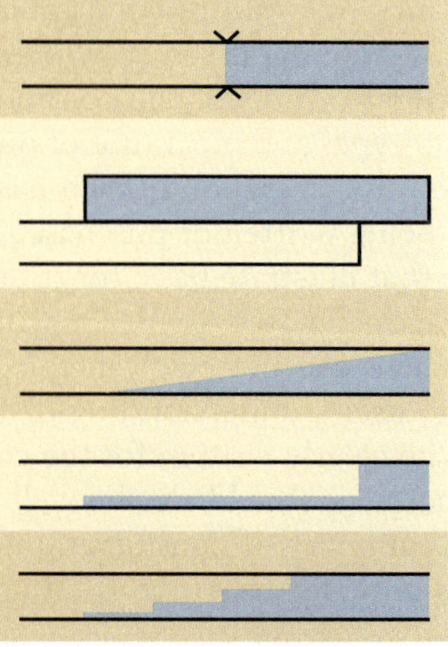

Each of the five conversion approaches is described separately in the following subsections.

Direct Changeover Conversion by direct changeover means that, on a specified date, users stop using the old system and the new system is put into use. Direct changeover can only be successful if extensive testing is done beforehand, and it works best when some delays in processing can be tolerated. Sometimes, direct changeover is done in response to a government mandate. An advantage of direct changeover is that users have no possibility of using the old system rather than the new one. Adaptation is a necessity.

Direct changeover is considered a risky approach to conversion, and its disadvantages are numerous. For instance, long delays might ensue if errors occur, because there is no alternate way to accomplish processing. In addition, disruption to the work environment may occur if users resent being forced into using an unfamiliar system without recourse. Finally, there is no adequate way to compare new results with old.

Parallel Conversion Parallel conversion refers to running the old system and the new system at the same time, in parallel. It is the most frequently used conversion approach, but its popularity may be in decline because it works best when a computerized system replaces a manual one. Both systems are run simultaneously for a specified period of time, and the reliability of results is examined. When the same results can be gained over time, the new system is put into use and the old one is stopped.

One advantage of running both systems in parallel is the possibility of checking new data against old data to catch any errors in processing in the new system. Parallel processing also offers a feeling of security to users, who are not forced to make an abrupt change to the new system.

There are many disadvantages to parallel conversion. They include the cost of running two systems at the same time and the burden on employees of virtually doubling their workload during conversion. Another disadvantage is that unless the system being replaced is a manual one, it is difficult to make comparisons between outputs of the new system and the old one. Supposedly, the new system was created to improve on the old one. Therefore, outputs from the systems should differ. Finally, it is understandable from a human perspective that employees who are faced with a choice between two systems will continue to use the old one because of their familiarity with it.

Gradual Conversion Gradual, or phased, conversion attempts to combine the best features of the two previously mentioned plans, without incurring all the risks. In this plan, the volume of transactions handled by the new system is gradually increased as the system is phased in. The advantages of this approach include allowing users to get involved with the system gradually, and the possibility of detecting and recovering from errors without a lot of down time. Disadvantages of gradual conversion include taking too long to get the new system in place and its inappropriateness for conversion of small, uncomplicated systems.

Modular Prototype Conversion Modular prototype conversion uses the building of modular, operational prototypes (as discussed in Chapter 6) to change from old systems to new in a gradual manner. As each module is modified and accepted, it is put into use. One advantage is that each module is thoroughly tested before being used. Another advantage is that users are familiar with each module as it becomes operational. Their feedback has helped determine the final attributes of the system.

However, prototyping is often not feasible, which automatically rules out this approach for many conversions. Another disadvantage is that special attention must be paid to interfaces so that the modules being built actually work as a system.

Distributed Conversion Distributed conversion refers to a situation in which many installations of the same system are contemplated, as is the case in banking or in franchises such as restaurants or clothing stores. One entire conversion is done (with any of the four approaches considered previously) at one site. When that conversion is successfully completed, other conversions are done for other sites.

An advantage of distributed conversion is that problems can be detected and contained rather than inflicted simultaneously on all sites. A disadvantage is that even when one conversion is successful, each site will have its own people and culture, along with regional and local peculiarities to work through, and they must be handled accordingly.

A contingency approach to deciding on a conversion strategy is recommended; that is, the analyst and users consider many factors in agreeing on and selecting a conversion strategy. Obviously, no particular conversion approach is equally suitable for every system implementation.

SECURITY CONCERNS FOR TRADITIONAL AND WEB-BASED SYSTEMS

Security of computer facilities, stored data, and the information generated is part of a successful conversion. Recognition of the need for security is a natural outgrowth of the belief that information is a key organizational resource, as discussed in Chapter 1. With increasingly complex transactions and many innovative exchanges, the Web has brought heightened security concerns to the IS professional's world.

It is useful to think of security of systems, data, and information on an imaginary continuum from totally secure to totally open. Although there is no such thing as a totally secure system, the actions analysts and users take are meant to move systems toward the secure end of the continuum by lessening the system's vulnerability. It should be noted that as more people in the organization gain greater computer power, gain access to the Web, or connect to intranets and extranets, security becomes increasingly difficult and complex. Sometimes, organizations will hire a security consultant to work with the systems analyst when security is crucial to successful operations.

Security is the responsibility of all those who come into contact with the system and is only as good as the most lax behavior or policy in the organization. Security has three interrelated aspects: physical, logical, and behavioral. All three must work together if the quality of security is to remain high.

PHYSICAL SECURITY

Physical security refers to securing the computer facility, its equipment, and software through physical means. It can include controlling access to the computer room by means of machine-readable badges, biometric systems, or a human sign-in/sign-out system, as well as using closed-circuit television cameras to monitor computer areas, backing up data frequently, and storing backups in a fireproof, waterproof area, often at a secure offsite location.

In addition, small computer equipment should be secured so that a typical user cannot move it, and it should be guaranteed uninterrupted power. Alarms that notify appropriate people of fire, flood, or unauthorized human intrusion must be in working order at all times.

Decisions about physical security should be made along with users when the analyst is planning for computer facilities and equipment purchases. Obviously, physical security can be much tighter if anticipated in advance of actual installation and if computer rooms are specially equipped for security when they are constructed rather than outfitted as an afterthought.

LOGICAL SECURITY

Logical security refers to logical controls in the software itself. The logical controls familiar to most users are passwords or authorization codes of some sort. When used, they permit the user with the correct password to enter the system or a particular part of a database.

Passwords, however, are treated cavalierly in many organizations. Employees have been overheard yelling a password across crowded offices, taping passwords to their display screens, and sharing personal passwords with authorized employees who have forgotten their own.

Special encryption software has been developed to protect commercial transactions on the Web, and business transactions are proliferating. Internet fraud is also up sharply, however, with few authorities trained in catching Internet criminals and a "wild west," or "last frontier," mentality clearly evidenced in those instances when authorities have been able to apprehend Web criminals.

One way for networks to cut down on the risk of exposure to security challenges from the outside world is to build a firewall or firewall system. A firewall constructs a barricade between an internal organization's network and an external (inter)network, such as the Internet. The internal network is assumed to be trustworthy and secure, whereas the Internet is not. Firewalls are intended to prevent communication into or out of the network that has not been authorized and that is not wanted. A firewall system is not a perfect remedy for organizational and Internet security; it is, however, an additional layer of security that is now widely endorsed. There is still no fully integrated way to address security problems with internal and external networks, but they do deserve analysts' attention when planning any new or improved systems.

Logical and physical controls are important but clearly not enough to provide adequate security. Behavioral changes are also necessary.

BEHAVIORAL SECURITY

The behavioral expectations of an organization are implicit in its policy manuals and even on signs posted in work rooms and lunch rooms, as we saw in Chapter 5. The behavior that organization members internalize, however, is also critical to the success of security efforts. (One reason firewalls are not attack-proof is because many attacks to information systems come from within the organization.)

Security can begin with the screening of employees who will eventually have access to computers, data, and information, to ensure that their interests are consistent with the organization's interests and that they fully understand the importance of carrying through on security procedures. Policies regarding security must be written, distributed, and updated so that employees are fully aware of expectations and responsibilities. It is typical that the systems analyst will first have contact with the behavioral aspects of security. Some organizations have written rules or policies prohibiting employees from surfing the Web during work hours, or even prohibiting Web surfing altogether, if company equipment is involved. Other corporations use software locks to limit access to Web sites that are judged to be objectionable in the workplace, such as game, gambling, or pornographic sites.

Part of the behavioral facet of security is monitoring behavior at irregular intervals to ascertain that proper procedures are being followed and to correct any behaviors that may have eroded with time. Having the system log the number of unsuccessful sign-on attempts of users is one way to monitor whether unauthorized users are attempting to sign on to the system. Periodic and frequent inventorying of equipment and software is desirable. In addition, unusually long sessions or atypical after-hours access to the system should be examined.

Employees should clearly understand what is expected of them, what is prohibited, and the extent of their rights and responsibilities. In the United States and European Union, employers are legally obligated to disclose all monitoring that is being done or that is being contemplated, and they must supply the rationale behind it. Such disclosure should include the use of video cameras, software, and phone monitoring.

Output generated by the system must be recognized for its potential to put the organization at risk in some circumstances. Controls for output include displays that can only be accessed via password, the classification of information (that is, to whom it can be distributed and when), and secure storage of printed and stored documents, no matter what their format.

In some cases, provision for shredding documents that are classified or proprietary must be made. Shredding or pulverization services can be contracted from an outside firm that, for a fee, will shred magnetic media, printer cartridges, and paper. A large corporation may shred upwards of 76,000 pounds of output in a variety of media annually.

SPECIAL SECURITY CONSIDERATIONS FOR ECOMMERCE

It is well known that intruders can violate the integrity of any computer system. As an analyst, you need to take a series of precautions to protect the computer network from both internal and external Web security threats. A number of actions and products can help you:

1. Virus protection software.
2. Email filtering products that provide policy-based email and email attachment scanning and filtering to protect companies against both incoming and outgoing email. Incoming scanning protects against spam (unsolicited email such as advertising) attacks, and outgoing scanning protects against the loss of proprietary information.
3. URL filtering products that provide employees with access to the Web by user, by groups of users, by computers, by the time, or by the day of the week.
4. Firewalls, gateways, and virtual private networks that prevent hackers from gaining backdoor access to a corporate network.
5. Intrusion detection and anti-phishing products that continually monitor usage, provide messages and reports, and suggest actions to take.
6. Vulnerability management products that assess the potential risks in a system and discover and report vulnerabilities. Some products correlate the vulnerabilities to make it easier to find the root cause of the security breach. Risk cannot be eliminated, but this software can help manage the risk by balancing security risk to the financial bottom line.
7. Security technologies such as secure socket layering (SSL) for authentication.
8. Encryption technologies such as secure electronic translation (SET).
9. Public key infrastructure (PKI) and digital certificates (obtained from a company such as Verisign). Use of digital certificates ensures that the reported sender of the message is really the company that sent the message.

PRIVACY CONSIDERATIONS FOR ECOMMERCE

The other side of security is privacy. To make your Web site more secure, you must ask the user or customer to give up some privacy.

As a Web site designer, you will recognize that the company for which you design exercises a great deal of power over the data its customers are providing. The same tenets of ethical and legal behavior apply to Web site design as to the design of any traditional application that accepts personal data from customers. The Web, however, allows the data to be collected faster and allows different data to be collected (such as the browsing habits of the customer). In general, information technology makes it possible to store more data in data warehouses, process that data, and distribute the data more widely.

Every company for which you design an ecommerce application should adopt a privacy policy. Here are some guidelines:

1. Start with a corporate policy on privacy. Make sure it is prominently displayed on the Web site so that all customers can access the policy whenever they complete a transaction.
2. Only ask for information the application requires to complete the transaction at hand. For example, is it necessary to the transaction to ask a person's age or gender?
3. Make it optional for customers to fill out personal information on the Web site. Some customers do not mind receiving targeted messages, but you should always give customers an opportunity to maintain the confidentiality of their personal data by not responding.
4. Use sources that allow you to obtain anonymous information about classes of customers. There are companies that offer audience profiling technology and technology solutions for management of advertisements, their targeting, and their delivery. They do so by maintaining a dynamic database of consumer profiles without linking them to individuals, thereby respecting customers' rights to privacy.
5. Be ethical. Avoid the latest cheap trick that permits your client to gather information about the customer in highly suspect ways. Tricks such as screen scraping (capturing remotely what is on a customer's screen) and email cookie grabbing are clear violations of privacy, and may prove to be illegal as well.

A coordinated policy of security and privacy is essential. It is essential to establish these policies and adhere to them when implementing an ecommerce application.

DISASTER RECOVERY PLANNING

No matter how diligently you and your organizational colleagues work to ensure the security and stability of systems, all employees and systems are inevitability vulnerable to some kind of natural or human-made disaster that threatens security as well as the very functioning of the business. Some disasters are quite common, such as power outages, and we can assess the probability of some disasters occurring, such as a hurricane or an earthquake. However many disasters are unexpected in their timing or their severity, perhaps even causing loss of life, creating chaos for people and the organization itself.

The fields of disaster preparedness and disaster recovery are interdependent, and they build on each other. Disaster preparedness includes what a company should do if it encounters a crisis. The field of disaster recovery is focused on how a business can continue in the aftermath of a disaster and how it can restore essential systems in the IT infrastructure. This section focuses on disaster recovery as it relates to information systems. The traditional disaster recovery process consists of planning, a walkthrough, practice drills, and recovery from the disaster.

When hit with a disaster, a company stands to lose people, money, reputation, their own assets, as well as those of their clients. It is important to do the right things to minimize potential losses. Analysts should determine what the organization's level of disaster planning is and how well articulated the role of information systems is in their disaster response and recovery plans. The key questions that analysts must ask early on are (1) whether employees know where to go, and (2) what to do in the face of a disaster. The answer to these questions will guide your further planning. Conventional wisdom provides seven elements to consider during and after a disaster. As you will see, many of them involve information systems and relate specifically to the planning required of you as a systems analyst.

1. Identify the teams responsible for managing a crisis.
2. Eliminate single points of failure.
3. Determine data replication technologies that match the organization's timetable for getting systems up and running.
4. Create detailed relocation and transportation plans.
5. Establish multiple communication channels among employees and consultants who are onsite, such as analyst teams.
6. Provide recovery solutions that include an offsite location.
7. Ensure the physical and psychological well-being of employees and others who may be physically present at the work site when a disaster hits.

The disaster preparedness plan should identify who, in the event of a disaster, is responsible for making several pivotal decisions. These include decisions about whether business operations will continue; how to support communications (both computer and voice); where people will be sent if the business is uninhabitable; where personnel will go in an emergency; seeing to the personal and psychological needs of the people present in the business and those who might be working virtually; and restoring the main computing and work environments.

Redundancy of data provides the key for eliminating single points of failure for servers running Web applications. As an analyst you can be especially helpful in setting up this type of backup and redundancy.

Some businesses are moving to storage area networks (SANs) to get away from some of the unreliability associated with physical tape backups and storage. Synchronous remote replication, also called data mirroring, for nearly real-time backup is also gaining favor. However, if companies are farther than 100 miles away from the site, the data mirroring process can be affected. Asynchronous remote replication sends data to the secondary storage location at designated time intervals. Online options are available for small businesses, too.

The organization should develop and distribute a one-page memo that contains evacuation routes and employee assembly points. This should be distributed to everyone in the organization. The three common choices are either to send employees home, to have them remain onsite, or to relocate them to a recovery facility that is set up to continue operations. The entire gamut of transportation options should be considered when developing this memo.

Organizational and analyst team members must be able to communicate in the event that their typical email is disrupted. If email is unavailable for broadcasting an emergency message, an emergency information Web page or emergency hotline can serve as viable alternatives. Recently, some software companies have started offering a suite of software tools that permits ad hoc communication by emergency response agencies that allows them to rapidly set up secure voice-over-IP, Web connectivity, and Wi-Fi hot spot capabilities. Wider availability and lower prices will undoubtedly bring these important communication capabilities to other types of organizations in the future.

To better protect the organization's backup systems and to ensure the continued, uninterrupted flow of banking transactions in the event of a disaster, new regulations in the United States stipulate that bank offsite locations must be at least 100 miles away from the original site. Since paper files and backups also present a monumental problem and are highly vulnerable to natural and human-made disasters, organizations are strongly encouraged to create a plan that helps them move toward a digital documentation project that is meant to convert all of their paper documents to electronic formats within three to five years of inception (Stephens, 2003).

Support for humans working at an organization that experiences a disaster is paramount. There must be plentiful and easily available water, especially if employees are unable to leave the site for a number of days due to outside weather conditions or partial building collapses. While food is important, water is more so. Employees should also be issued a safety kit containing water, a dust mask, a flashlight, glow sticks, and a whistle. One way to learn what should comprise a personal workspace disaster supplies kit is to go to The American Red Cross Web site (www.redcross.org), which provides details for supporting humans during disasters and providing for them in the aftermath.

OTHER CONVERSION CONSIDERATIONS

Conversion also entails other details for the analyst, which include the following:

1. Ordering equipment (up to three months ahead of planned conversion).
2. Ordering any necessary materials that are externally supplied to the information system, such as toner cartridges, paper, preprinted forms, and magnetic media.
3. Appointing a manager to supervise, or personally supervising, the preparation of the installation site.
4. Planning, scheduling, and supervising programmers and data entry personnel who must convert all relevant files and databases.

For many implementations, your chief role will be accurately estimating the time needed for each activity, appointing people to manage each subproject, and coordinating their work. For smaller projects, you will do much of the conversion work on your own. Many of the project management techniques discussed in Chapter 3, such as Gantt charts, PERT, function point analysis, and successfully communicating with team members, are useful for planning and controlling implementation.

ORGANIZATIONAL METAPHORS AND THEIR RELATIONSHIP TO SUCCESSFUL SYSTEMS

Be aware of organizational metaphors when you attempt to implement a system you have just developed. Our research has suggested that the success or failure of a system may be related to the metaphors used by organizational members.

When people in the organization describe the company as a zoo, you can infer that the atmosphere is chaotic; if it is described as a machine, everything is working in an orderly fashion. When the predominant metaphor is war, journey, or jungle, the environment is chaotic, as with the zoo. The war and journey metaphors are oriented toward an organization goal, however, whereas the zoo and jungle metaphors are not.

In addition to the machine, metaphors such as society, family, and the game all signify order and rules. Although the machine and game metaphors are goal

FIGURE 17.12
Organizational metaphors may contribute to the success or failure of an information system.

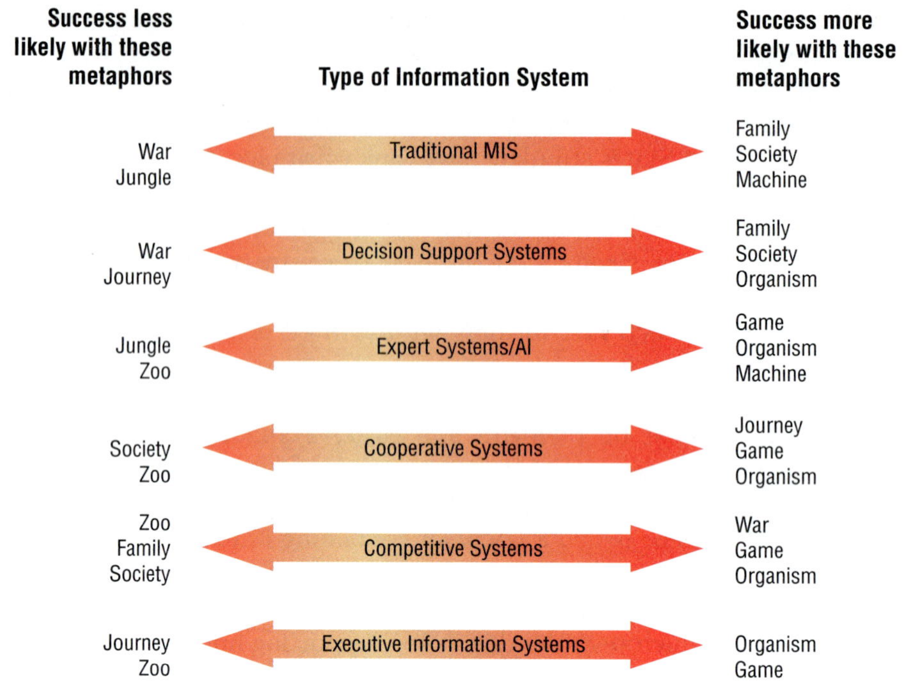

oriented, the society and zoo metaphors do not stress the company's goal, but instead allow individuals in the corporation to set their own standards and rewards. Another metaphor, organism, appears balanced between order and chaos, corporate and individual goals.

Our research suggests that the success or failure of a system may have something to do with the predominant metaphor. Figure 17.12 shows that a traditional MIS will tend to succeed when the predominant metaphor is society, machine, or family, but it might not succeed if the metaphor is war or jungle (two chaotic metaphors). Notice, however, that competitive systems will most likely succeed if the metaphor is war.

Positive metaphors appear to be game, organism, and machine. Negative metaphors appear to be jungle and zoo. The others (journey, war, society, and family) show mixed success depending on the type of information system being developed. More research needs to be done in this area. In the meantime, the systems analyst should be aware that metaphors communicated in interviews could be meaningful and may even be a contributing factor toward the success of the information system implementation.

EVALUATION

Throughout the systems development life cycle, the analyst, management, and users have been evaluating the evolving information systems and networks to give feedback for their eventual improvement. Evaluation is also called for following system implementation.

EVALUATION TECHNIQUES

In recognition that the ongoing evaluation of information systems and networks is important, many evaluation techniques have been devised. These techniques include cost-benefit analysis (as discussed in Chapter 10); models that attempt to estimate the value of a decision based on the effects of revised information using information theory, simulation, or Bayesian statistics; user evaluations that emphasize implementation problems and user involvement; and information system utility approaches that examine the properties of information.

Each type of evaluation serves a different purpose and has inherent drawbacks. Cost-benefit analysis may be difficult to apply, because information systems provide information about objectives for the first time, making it impossible to compare performance before and after implementation of the system or distributed network. The revised decision evaluation approach presents difficulty, because all variables involved with the design, development, and implementation of the information system cannot be calculated or quantified. The user involvement approach yields some insight for new projects by providing a checklist of potentially dysfunctional behavior by various organizational members, but it stresses implementation over other aspects of IS design. The information system utility approach to evaluation can be more comprehensive than the others if it is expanded and systematically applied.

THE INFORMATION SYSTEM UTILITY APPROACH

The information system utility approach for evaluating information systems can be a comprehensive and fruitful technique for measuring the success of a developed system. It also can serve as a guide in the development of any future projects the analyst might undertake.

Utilities of information include possession, form, place, and time. To evaluate the information system comprehensively, these utilities must be expanded to include actualization utility and goal utility. Then the utilities can be seen to address adequately the questions of who (possession), what (form), where (place), when (time), how (actualization), and why (goal). An example of this information utility approach can be seen in the evaluation of a blood inventory system in Figure 17.13.

FIGURE 17.13

Evaluating a blood inventory information and decision support system using the information system utility approach.

Information Systems Modules	Form Utility	Time Utility	Place Utility	Possession Utility	Actualization Utility	Goal Utility
Inventory Lists **Success**	**Good**. Acronyms used were the same as shipping codes. As systems grew, too much information was presented; this overload called for summary information.	**Good**. Reports were received at least one hour before scheduled shipments on a daily basis.	**Good**. Inventory lists were printed at the regional blood center. Lists were delivered to hospitals with the current shipments.	**Good**. The same people who originally kept manual records received these reports.	**Good**. Implementation was easy because hospitals found the inventory lists to be extremely useful.	**Good**. Information about the location of particular units was made available.
Management Summary Reports **Success**	**Good**. Summary report was designed to exact format specifications of manual summary reports developed by the blood administrator for city hospitals.	**Good**. Same as listings.	**Good**. Summary reports were printed at the center where they were needed.	**Good**. Blood administrators who originally kept manual reports received these reports.	**Good**. Blood administrators participated in the design of the reports.	**Good**. Summary reports helped reduce outdating and prevent shortages.
Short-Term Forecasting **Success**	**Good**. A forecast was issued for each blood type.	**Good**. Forecasts were updated daily.	**Good**. Printed at blood center.	**Good**. Administrators concerned with distribution and collections received the report.	**Good**. Output design could have been more participative.	**Good**. Shortages were prevented by calling in more donors.
Heuristic Allocation **Failure**	**Poor**. The people who allocated blood mistrusted the mysterious numbers produced by the computer.	**Good**. Reports were provided one hour before allocation decisions were made.	**Good**. Printed at blood center.	**Fair**. Administrators responsible for daily blood allocation received the original.	**Poor**. Too many people were involved with blood inventories to be able to participate in the design of the system.	**Poor**. This was not an immediate goal of the blood region. Shipping costs were passed on to patients.

CONSULTING OPPORTUNITY 17.2

THE SWEET SMELL OF SUCCESS

Recall that in Consulting Opportunity 3.1, "The Sweetest Sound I've Ever Sipped," you met Felix Straw. Devise a systems solution that will address the problems discussed there. (*Hint:* The technology is important, but so is the way people can use it.) Your solution should stress collaboration, flexibility, adaptability, and access. Use network diagramming to illustrate your solution. In a few paragraphs, write a rationale for why your solution should be chosen.

Possession Utility Possession utility answers the question of who should receive output, or, in other words, who should be responsible for making decisions. Information has no value in the hands of someone who lacks the power to make improvements in the system or someone who lacks the ability to use the information productively.

Form Utility Form utility answers the question of what kind of output is distributed to the decision maker. The documents must be useful for a particular decision maker in terms of the document's format and the jargon used. Acronyms and column headings must be meaningful to the user. Furthermore, information itself must be in an appropriate form. For example, the user should not have to divide one number by another to obtain a ratio. Instead, a ratio should be calculated and prominently displayed. At the other extreme is the presentation of too much irrelevant data. Information overload certainly decreases the value of an information system.

Place Utility Place utility answers the question of where the information is distributed. Information must be delivered to the location where the decision is made. More detailed reports or previous management reports should be filed or stored to facilitate future access.

Time Utility Time utility answers the question of when information is delivered. Information must arrive before a decision is made. Late information has no utility. At the other extreme is the delivery of information too far in advance of the decision. Reports may become inaccurate or may be forgotten if delivered prematurely.

Actualization Utility Actualization utility involves how the information is introduced and used by the decision maker. First, the information system has value if it possesses the ability to be implemented. Second, actualization utility implies that an information system has value if it is maintained after its designers depart, or if a one-time use of the information system obtains satisfactory and long-lasting results.

Goal Utility Goal utility answers the "why" of information systems by asking whether the output has value in helping the organization obtain its objectives. The goal of the information system must not only be in line with the goals of decision makers, but it must also reflect their priorities.

EVALUATING THE SYSTEM

An information system can be evaluated as successful if it possesses all six of these utilities. If the system module is judged as "poor" in providing one of the utilities, the entire module will be destined to fail. A partial or "fair" attainment of a utility

CONSULTING OPPORTUNITY 17.3

MOPPING UP WITH THE NEW SYSTEM

"I don't know what happened. When the new system was installed, the systems analysts made a clean getaway, as far as I can tell," says Marc Schnieder, waxing philosophic. Recall that he is owner of the Marc Schnieder Janitorial Supply Company. (You last met Marc in Consulting Opportunity 13.1, in which you helped him with his data storage needs. In the interim, he has had a new information system installed.)

"The systems analysis team asked us some questions about how we liked the new system," Marc supplies eagerly. "We didn't really know how to tell them that the output wasn't as spotless as we'd like. I mean, it's confusing. It isn't getting to the right people at the right time or anything. We never really did get into the nitty-gritty about the finished system with that consulting team. I feel as if we had to hire your group just to mop up after what they left."

After further discussions with Stan Lessink and Jill Oh, the company's chief programmers, you realize that the team that did the initial installation had no evaluation mechanism. Suggest a suitable framework for evaluating the kinds of concerns that Mr. Schnieder raised about the system. What are the problems that can occur when a system is not evaluated systematically? Respond in a paragraph.

will result in a partially successful module. If the information system module is judged as "good" in providing every utility, the module is a success.

The information system utility approach of "who, what, when, where, why, and how" used to evaluate the regional blood inventory management information system resulted in the subjective judgments concerning the utility of the information system summarized in Figure 17.13. As you can see, three of the modules were rated as "good" in each category of utility, and consequently these modules were considered successful. One module was judged a failure after the trial period. Explanations of each judgment made for the four modules are also provided.

The information system utility approach is a workable and straightforward framework for evaluating large-scale information systems projects and ongoing efforts. It also can be usefully employed as a checklist to monitor the progress of systems under development. Furthermore, evaluation following implementation allows the analyst to acquire ideas about how to proceed with future systems projects.

EVALUATING CORPORATE WEB SITES

Evaluating the corporate Web site that you are developing or maintaining is an important part of any successful implementation effort. Analysts can use the information system utility approach previously described to assess the aesthetic qualities, content, and delivery of the site. As an analyst or Webmaster, you should go one step further and analyze Web traffic.

A visitor to your Web site can generate a large amount of useful information for you to analyze. This information can be gathered automatically by capturing information about the source, including the previous Web site the user visited and the key words used to find the site; the information can also be obtained through using cookies (files left on a user's computer about when they last were on the site).

A leading Web activity monitoring package is Webtrends. Figure 17.14 is a sample report showing the most downloaded files on the Web site by day of the week. The graph displays the top five downloaded files, and the table at the bottom is a sorted list of all downloads.

An analyst or Webmaster can gain valuable information by using a service such as Webtrends. (Although some services are free, the pay services usually provide

FIGURE 17.14

A sample report from Webtrends Corporation showing the most downloadable files on the corporate Web site.

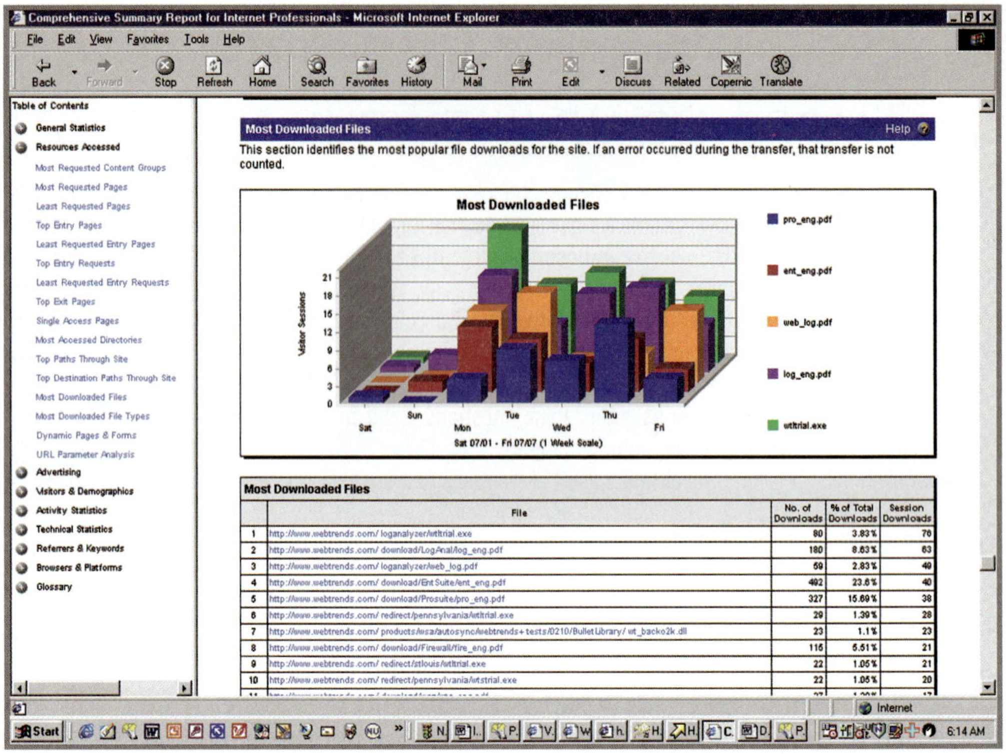

the detail needed to evaluate the site in depth. The cost is an ongoing budget item for maintaining the Web site.) Information to help you evaluate your client's site and make improvements is plentiful and easy to obtain. The seven essential items are described next.

1. **Know how often your client's Web site is visited.** The number of hits a Web site had in the last few days, the number of visitor sessions, and the number of pages visited are a few of the general things you need to know. To evaluate a site properly, you should get more detailed information about how much traffic the client's site is experiencing.
2. **Learn details about specific pages on the site.** Detailed information about pages accessed helps in evaluating both the content and the ability to navigate the site properly. It is often telling when the last page visited is a page containing the prices of your products. In addition, by knowing the top exit page, you can get statistics on the most requested pages, most requested topics, top paths a visitor takes through the client's Web site, or even the most downloadable files. If the Web site is a commercial one, shopping cart reports can show how many visitors were converted into buyers and how many abandoned their carts or failed to complete the checkout process.
3. **Find out more about the Web site's visitors.** Visitor demographics and information such as the number of visits by a particular visitor in a period of time, whether the visitor is a new or a returning one, and who the top visitors are—all are valuable information when evaluating a Web site. It is possible to get summary data about the geographic region or even the city most represented by visitors to the site.

   One service, Commerce Trends, is available from Webtrends Corporation. Figure 17.15 shows a page that compares selected statistics about visitors over time. The top graph shows unique visitors, the middle graph shows first-time visitors, and the bottom graph displays the average length of visits over time. This information allows an analyst to evaluate the Web site in terms of the

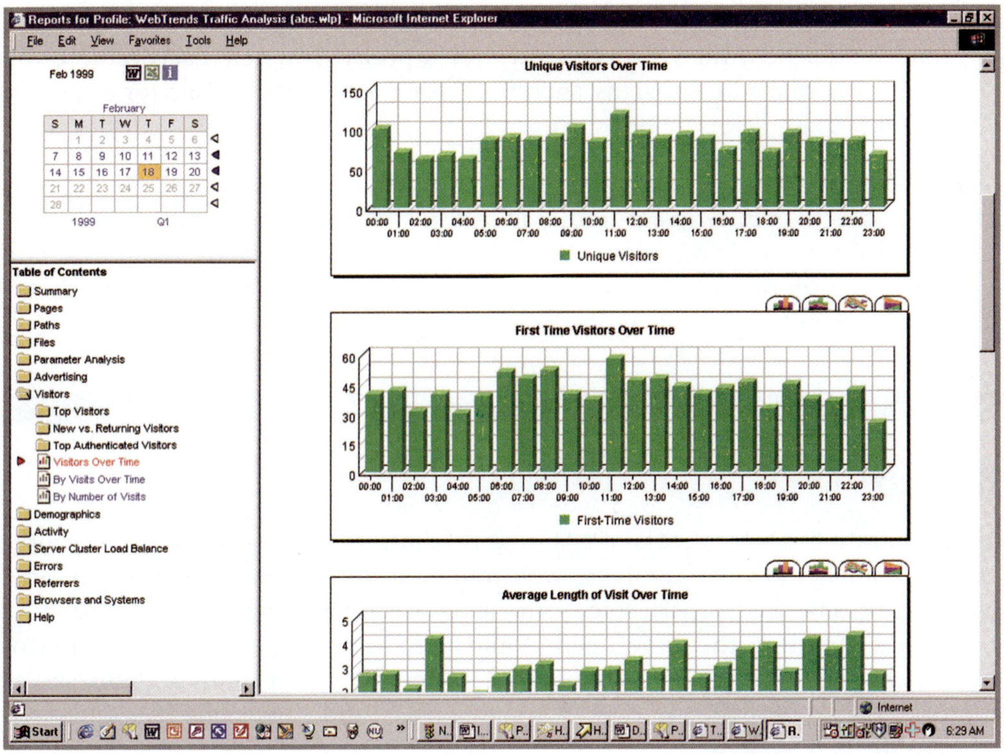

FIGURE 17.15

A report comparing statistics on visitors generated by Commerce Trends (from Webtrends Corporation).

ability to attract new visitors and keep them once they have visited the site. Notice that the calendar at the top left corner can be used to change the view from daily to weekly or monthly.

4. **Discover if visitors can properly fill out the forms you designed.** Once you attract and keep visitors, you need to know whether they are filling out forms properly and whether they understand the client's site in general. If the error rate is high, redesign the form and see what happens. Analysis of the statistics will reveal whether bad form design was to blame for errors in response.
5. **Find out who is referring Web site visitors to the client's site.** Find out which sites are responsible for referring visitors to the client's Web site. Get statistics on the top referring site, the top search engines leading to the site, and even the keywords visitors used to locate your client's Web site.

   To increase your company's Web presence, site promotion is helpful. Many available services, such as NetAnnounce Premier and NetMechanic, assist in optimizing your home page and automatically create and install metatags (HTML code that search engines use to classify a Web site). These services then submit the site to top search engines such as Google, Yahoo!, AltaVista, and Excite.

   After promoting a site, you can use Web traffic analysis to track whether the site promotion really made a difference. Because the majority of users searching for a Web site do not look beyond the first page of search results, promotion of your client's Web site is essential.
6. **Determine what browsers visitors are using.** By knowing what browsers are being used, you can add browser-specific features that improve the look and feel of the site and encourage visitors to stay longer, thereby improving the stickiness of the site. It helps to know whether visitors are using current or outdated browsers.
7. **Find out if the client's Web site visitors are interested in advertising.** Finally, find out if visitors to the site are interested in the ad campaigns you have on your site. Get reports on the success of ad banners, email campaigns, and even

offline and direct mail campaigns. You can take advantage of associate programs and send your visitors to sites for a profit. You can also evaluate the client's internal ad campaigns, such as offering a product for sale for a specific period.

Web activity services can be helpful in evaluating whether the site is meeting its stated objectives in terms of traffic, advertising effectiveness, employee productivity, and return on investment. It is one of the ways an analyst can evaluate whether the corporate Web presence is meeting management goals and whether it accurately portrays the organization's vision.

SUMMARY

Implementation is the process of ensuring that information systems and networks are operational and then involving well-trained users in their operation. In large systems projects, the primary role of the analyst is overseeing implementation by correctly estimating the time needed and then supervising the installation of equipment for information systems (which may be set up with a client/server approach over a local area network), training users, and converting files and databases to the new system.

Distributed systems take advantage of telecommunications technology and database management to interconnect people manipulating some of the same data in meaningful but different ways. As hardware and software are evaluated, the systems analyst also needs to consider the costs and benefits of employing a distributed system to fulfill user requirements.

One of the most popular ways to approach distributed systems is through the use of a client/server (C/S) model. Standard types of organizational networks include the local area network (LAN) and the wide area network (WAN). Using a top-down approach, analysts can use five symbols to help draw network decomposition and hub connectivity diagrams. Specialized software, called groupware, is written specifically to support groups or teams of workers with functional applications. Its purpose is to help group members to work together through networks.

Training users and personnel to interact with the information system is an important part of implementation, because users must usually be able to run the system without the intervention of the analyst. The analyst needs to consider who needs to be trained, who will train them, the objectives of training, the methods of instruction to be used, the training sites, and the training materials.

Conversion is also part of the implementation process. The analyst has several strategies for changing from the old information system to the new. The five conversion strategies are direct changeover, parallel conversion, phased or gradual conversion, modular prototype conversion, and distributed conversion. Taking a contingency approach to conversion strategies can help the analyst in choosing an appropriate strategy, one that suits different system and organizational variables.

Security of data and systems has taken on increased importance for analysts who are designing more ecommerce applications. Security has several facets—physical, logical, and behavioral—that must all work together. Analysts can take a number of precautions, such as virus protection software, email filtering, URL filters, firewalls, gateways, virtual private networks, intrusion detection products, secure socket layering, secure electronic translation, and the use of a public key

"As you know, Snowden is determined to implement some kind of automated tracking for the Training people. Even after having you and your team here at MRE for all of this time, though, it isn't clear to me how that will ever come about. You've probably noticed by now that people such as Tom Ketcham are pretty set in their ways, but so is Snowden, and he definitely has the upper hand. I'm not telling you anything you don't know already, am I? I think when Snowden comes back from Poland, you should be ready to show him how we can implement an automated tracking system for the Training group, but it really has to be acceptable to the new users. After all, they're the ones who have to live with it. I'll pencil you in for a meeting with Snowden two weeks from today."

HYPERCASE QUESTIONS

1. Develop an implementation plan that would be useful to the Training group in changing to an automated project tracking system. Use a paragraph to explain your approach. Be sure that what you are doing also meets Snowden's expectations.
2. In two paragraphs, discuss what *conversion* approach is appropriate for adopting a new automated project tracking system for the Training group.
3. Provide an outline of steps you would take to train the users in the Training group so that they could use their new system. In a paragraph, discuss any obstacles you see to training the users in the Training group, and also list how you would overcome these problems.

infrastructure to improve privacy, confidentiality, and the security of systems, networks, data, individuals, and organizations.

In addition, every company for which you design an ecommerce application should adopt a privacy policy following five guidelines.

Even though you take all possible measures to ensure system security, privacy, and stability, all employees and systems are vulnerable to natural or human-made disaster. Disaster recovery is focused on how a business can continue after a disaster has hit and how it can restore essential IT infrastructure.

Research suggests that systems analysts can improve the chances that newly implemented systems will be accepted if they develop systems with predominant organizational metaphors in mind. Nine main metaphors in use are society, family, machine, organism, journey, game, war, jungle, and zoo. For example, traditional MIS are more likely to succeed when metaphors such as the family, society, or machine are used, and they are less likely to succeed with organizational metaphors such as war and the jungle.

After implementation, the new information system and the approach taken (perhaps client/server technology) should be evaluated. Many different evaluation approaches are available, including cost-benefit analysis, the revised decision evaluation approach, and user involvement evaluations.

The information system utility framework is a direct way to evaluate a new system based on the six utilities of possession, form, place, time, actualization, and goal. These utilities correspond to, and answer the questions of, who, what, where, when, how, and why, so as to evaluate the utilities of the information system. Utilities can also serve as a checklist for systems under development.

KEYWORDS AND PHRASES

- audience profiling
- behavioral security
- Bluetooth
- bus configuration
- client/server model
- corporate privacy policy
- direct changeover
- disaster preparedness
- disaster recovery
- distributed conversion
- distributed processing
- email filtering products
- encryption software
- EV-DO
- file server
- firewall or firewall system
- gateway
- gradual or phased conversion
- groupware
- hierarchical network
- hits
- hub connectivity
- information system utility
  - approach to evaluation
    - possession utility
    - form utility
    - place utility
    - time utility
    - actualization utility
    - goal utility
- local area network (LAN)
- logical security
- mobile WiMax
- modular prototype conversion
- network decomposition
- network modeling
- organizational metaphors
  - zoo
  - machine
  - war
  - journey
  - jungle
  - society
  - family
  - game
  - organism
- page view
- parallel conversion
- physical security
- print server
- public key infrastructure (PKI)
- referring site
- ring network
- secure electronic translation (SET)
- secure socket layering (SSL)
- star network
- storage area networks (SANs)
- unique visitors
- URL filtering products
- virus protection software
- Web activity monitoring
- Web site promotion
- Web traffic analysis
- wide area network (WAN)
- Wi-Fi
- WiMax
- wired equivalent privacy (WEP)
- wireless local area network (WLAN)

REVIEW QUESTIONS

1. List the four approaches to implementation.
2. Describe what is meant by distributed system.
3. List all the terms provided in the text to describe a wireless local area network.
4. List two reasons that an organization might prefer to set up a WLAN rather than a LAN.
5. What are two drawbacks to the implementation of a Wi-Fi network?
6. What does WEP stand for?
7. Why is WEP recommended for use on Wi-Fi networks?
8. What are two additional names for WiMax?
9. What is a hierarchical network?
10. Draw a star network and label the nodes appropriately.
11. How does a ring network differ from a star network?
12. What is a bus configuration for distributed processing?

13. What is the client/server model?
14. Describe how a client is different from a user.
15. What is a peer-to-peer network? How does it differ from other client/server networks?
16. What is a file server?
17. What are the advantages of using a client/server approach?
18. What are the disadvantages of using a client/server approach?
19. What is the purpose of groupware?
20. Who should be trained to use the new or modified information system?
21. List the five possible sources of training for users of information systems.
22. Why is it important to have well-defined training objectives?
23. Some users learn best by seeing, others by hearing, and still others by doing. Give an example of how each kind of learning can be incorporated into a training session.
24. State an advantage and a disadvantage of onsite training sessions.
25. List the attributes of well-executed training materials for users.
26. List the five conversion strategies for converting old information systems to new ones.
27. Define the terms *physical*, *logical*, and *behavioral security*, and give an example of each one that illustrates the differences among them.
28. What are three ways to control access to a computer room?
29. Define what encryption software means.
30. What is a firewall or firewall system?
31. List five of the several measures an analyst can take to improve the security, privacy, and confidentiality of data, systems, networks, individuals, and organizations that use ecommerce Web applications.
32. List five guidelines for designing a corporate privacy policy for ecommerce applications.
33. Briefly give the differences between disaster preparedness and disaster recovery.
34. List the nine organizational metaphors and the hypothesized success of each type of system given their presence.
35. List and describe the utilities of information systems that can be used to evaluate the information system.
36. What are seven essential items that the analyst should include in performing a Web site traffic analysis?

PROBLEMS

1. Draw a local area network or some other configuration of distributed processing using the client/server approach to solve some of the data sharing problems that Bakerloo Brothers construction company is having. It wants to be able to allow teams of architects to work on blueprints at headquarters, let the construction supervisor enter last-minute changes to plans under construction from the field, and permit clients to view plans from almost anywhere. Currently, the company has a LAN for the architects who are in one city (Philadelphia) that lets them share some drawing tools and any updates that team members make with architects in other cities (New York, Terre Haute, Milwaukee, Lincoln, and Vancouver). The supervisor uses a notebook computer, cannot make any changes, and is not connected to a database. Clients view plans on displays, but sales representatives are not able to enter modifications to show them what would happen if a wall were moved or a roof line altered. (*Hint*: List the problems that the company is encountering, analyze

the symptoms, think of a solution, and then start drawing.) More than one network may be necessary, and not all problems will be amenable to a systems solution.

2. Create a disaster recovery plan for one of the networks you recommended to Bakerloo Brothers in Problem 1.
3. Cramtrack, the regional commuter train system, is trying to train users of its newly installed computer system. For the users to get the proper training, the systems analysts involved with the project sent a memo to the heads of the four departments that include both primary and secondary users. The memo said in part, "Only people who feel as if they require training need to make reservations for offsite training; all others should learn the system as they work with it on the job." Only three of a possible 42 users signed up. The analysts were satisfied that the memo effectively screened people who needed training from those who did not.
   a. In a paragraph, explain how the systems analysts got off the track in their approach to training.
   b. Outline the steps you would take to ensure that the right people at Cramtrack are trained.
   c. Suggest in a paragraph how the Web might be used to assist in training for Cramtrack.
4. A beautiful, full-color brochure arrived on Bill Cornwell's desk describing the Benny Company's offsite training program and facilities in glowing terms; it showed happy users at PCs and professional-looking trainers leaning over them with concerned looks. Bill ran excitedly into Roseann's office and told her, "We've got to use these people. This place looks terrific!" Roseann was not persuaded by the brochure, but didn't know what to say in defense of the onsite training for users that she had already authorized.
   a. In a few sentences, help Roseann argue the usefulness of onsite training with in-house trainers in contrast to offsite training with externally hired trainers.
   b. If Bill does decide on Benny Company training, what should he do to verify that this company is indeed the right place to train the company's information system users? Make a list of actions he should take.
5. "Just a little longer . . . I want to be sure this is working correctly before I change over," says Buffy, the owner of three bathroom accessories boutiques called Tub 'n Stuff. Her accountant, who helped her set up a new accounting information system, is desperately trying to persuade Buffy to change over completely to the new system. Buffy has insisted on running the old and new systems in parallel for an entire year.
   a. Briefly describe the general problems involved in using a parallel conversion strategy for implementing a new information system.
   b. In a paragraph, try to convince the owner of Tub 'n Stuff that a year of running a system in parallel is long enough. Suggest a way to end Tub 'n Stuff's dual systems that will provide enough reassurance to Buffy. (Assume the new system is reliable.)
6. Draft a plan to perform Web traffic analysis for the ecommerce application developed for Marathon Vitamin Shops. (See Consulting Opportunities 1.1, 13.2, and 14.5 for more information about the organization, their products, and their goals.) Your plan should take the form of a written report to the owner of the chain, Bill Berry. Be sure to indicate what statistics you will monitor and why they are important for Marathon Vitamin Shops to know.
7. FilmMagic, a chain of video rental stores introduced in Chapter 7, is experimenting with adding a new Web-based service to its store (similar to

www.netflix.com) that would, for a monthly fee, permit customers to choose a list of DVDs, have them sent to their home, and return them in prepaid mailers when they had finished viewing them. Based on what you know about FilmMagic, write a corporate privacy policy that would work well on their newly proposed Web site. Create a prototype screen (either with a graphics package or on a word processor) that includes appropriate language, fonts, and icons to show how your policy will appear as a page on FilmMagic's Web site.

8. Ayman's Office Supplies Company recently had a new information system installed to help its managers with inventory. In speaking with the managers, you notice that they seemed disgruntled with the system output, which is a series of displays that show current inventory, customer and supplier addresses, and so on. All screens need to be accessed through several special commands and the use of a password. The managers had several opinions about the system but had no systematic way to evaluate it.
   a. Devise a checklist or form that helps Ayman's managers evaluate the utilities of an information system.
   b. Suggest a second way to evaluate the information system. Compare it with what you did in Problem 8a.
9. Visit a number of ISPs such as Verio, Earthlink, and others. Investigate what sort of Web traffic analysis features they offer to Webmasters whose Web sites they host. Make a list of reports and statistics they offer, and write this list up as the evaluation portion of an ecommerce application systems development proposal.

GROUP PROJECTS

1. Visit six different Web sites. Choose one Web site from each of the categories below:
   a. A portal, such as Yahoo! or Excite.
   b. A news page, such as ABC News or the *New York Times.*
   c. A software company.
   d. A university Web site.
   e. An official Web site for a sports team or a theatre company.
   f. A Web site from a continent other than the one on which you live.

   Evaluate each using an information utility approach.

   Prepare a table similar to the one in Figure 17.13 with your answers. There will be one row for each of the six Web sites. Indicate the URL of the Web site. When you think you need Web traffic analysis to evaluate one of the utilities, state so in the appropriate cell of the table.
2. Examine each of the six Web sites you found for Group Project Problem 1 parts a–f. Identify whether any of the sites state a privacy policy. Use the five guidelines given earlier in the chapter to help you evaluate the usefulness of the policies you find. Using a paragraph for each of the six Web sites state:
   a. Whether you were able to identify a privacy policy and
   b. List any improvements or clarifications you would make to each privacy policy you identified.

SELECTED BIBLIOGRAPHY

American Red Cross Web site. Available at: www.redcross.org. Last accessed August 7, 2006.

Avery, M. "A Guide to Selecting and Using Business Recovery Planning Software." *Disaster Recovery Journal.* Available at www.drj.com. Last accessed November 7, 2005.

Bruno-Britz, P. "Taking Steps for Disaster Recovery." *Information Today,* Vol. 22, No. 9, October 2005, pp. 1 and 21.

Derfler, F. J., Jr., and L. Freed. *How Networks Work.* Emeryville, CA: Ziff-Davis Press, 1993.

Frey, H. "Scalable Geographic Routing Algorithms for Wireless Ad Hoc Networks." *IEEE Network,* July/August 2004, pp. 18–22.

Geier, J. "802.11 WEP: Concepts and Vulnerability." Available at: <www.80211-planet.com/tutorials/article.php/1368661>. Last accessed June 3, 2003.

Ginzberg, M. J. "Key Recurrent Issues in the MIS Implementation Process." *MIS Quarterly,* Vol. 5, No. 2, 1981, pp. 47–59.

Gross, G. "Cisco Introduces Emergency Communications Suite." *Computerworld Networking.* Available at: www.computerworld.com. Last accessed August 7, 2006.

Hawkins, S. M., D. C. Yen, and D. C. Chou. "Disaster Recovery Planning: A Strategy for Data Security." *Information Management and Computer Security,* Vol. 8, No. 5, 2000, pp. 222–229.

Hecht, J. A. "Business Continuity Management." *Communications of the AIS,* Vol. 8, Article 30, 2002.

Jessup, L. M., and J. S. Valacich. *Group Support Systems.* New York: Macmillan, 1993.

Kendall, J. E., and K. E. Kendall. "Metaphors and Methodologies: Living Beyond the Systems Machine." *MIS Quarterly,* Vol. 17, No. 2, June 1993, pp. 149–71.

Kendall, K. E. "Evaluation of a Regional Blood Distribution Information System." *International Journal of Physical Distribution and Materials Management,* Vol. 10, No. 7, 1980.

———. "Metaphors and Their Meaning for Information Systems Development." *European Journal of Information Systems,* Vol. 3, No. 1, 1994, pp. 37–47.

Kendall, K. E., J. E. Kendall, and K. C. Lee. "Understanding Disaster Recovery Planning through a Theatre Metaphor: Rehearsing for a Show that Might Never Open." *Communications of AIS,* Vol. 16, 2005, pp. 1001–1012.

Kennedy, D. "Seven Ways to Avoid Disaster in Your Disaster Recovery Planning and Procedures." *Law Practice TODAY.* Available at www.abanet.org. Last accessed November 10, 2005.

Laudon, K. C., and J. Laudon. *Management Information Systems,* 9th ed. Upper Saddle River, NJ: Prentice Hall, 2006.

O'Hara, M. T., and R. T. Watson. "Automation, Business Process Reengineering and Client Server Technology: A Three-Stage Model of Organizational Change." In V. Grover and W. J. Kittinger (eds.), *Business Process Change: Concepts, Methods, and Technologies.* Harrisburg, PA: Idea Group Publishing, 1995.

Oppliger, R. "Internet Security: Firewalls and Beyond." *Communications of the ACM,* Vol. 40, No. 5, May 1997, pp. 92–102.

Rigney, S. "Network in a Box." *PC Magazine,* Vol. 16, No. 16, September 1997.

Shaffer, G. "Coping with Change." *PC Magazine,* June 14, 1994.

Stephens, D. O. (2003) "Protecting records in the Face of Chaos, Calamity, and Cataclym," *The Information Management Journal,* Jan/Feb pp. 33–40.

Swanson, E. B. *Information System Implementation: Bridging the Gap Between Design and Utilization.* Homewood, IL: Irwin, 1988.

Zmud, R. W., and J. F. Cox. "The Implementation Process: A Change Approach." *MIS Quarterly,* Vol. 3, No. 2, 1979, pp. 35–44.

Allen Schmidt, Julie E. Kendall, and Kenneth E. Kendall

SEMPER REDUNDATE

Mack Roe walks to Anna's desk where Chip is standing and says, "The last program has been tested and incorporated into the system test. The results indicate that the system is finally complete. Every program and subsystem is working as planned. The whole system checks out. Testing has been thorough and exacting, with all the problems and program bugs satisfactorily resolved. I've reviewed the deliverables, and each one has been developed into programs. I'll leave you two to install it and then celebrate."

"That's fantastic!" Anna replies as Mack leaves. "We've been anticipating this moment for a long time. We now have the task of installing the system. I've checked with Mike Crowe, and all the hardware has arrived and has been installed. The computers have been connected in a star configuration, and the network software has been installed. Why don't we make a list of the tasks to be completed?"

"Sure," answers Chip. "We'll need to train the users on the operation of the system. It would be good to provide some general training, followed by specific training for each user. We might want to train several people—the user and a backup person—for each specific operation."

"That's all right with me," responds Anna, "but I don't think we should have a backup person for Paige Prynter. Somehow I don't think she would be fond of the idea."

"Speaking of backup," says Chip, "what about creating backups of master files and other system files? We should design an automated procedure for creating these copies."

"Yes," replies Anna. "Great idea. We also need to be concerned with system security: who can access the data, and who has clearance to update various database elements. We should also create a disaster recovery plan, just in case of things like power outages or other human-made or natural disasters."

"I agree," remarks Chip. "You never know when things might go awry. Another consideration is converting the production files from the old system to the new format. We don't want to rekey all the records from the hardware and software master files."

"Why don't we have one of the programmers write a one-time program that will convert each file from the old format to the new?" suggests Anna. "The indexes could be automatically updated, and additional fields initialized to spaces or zeros."

The programmers complete the file conversion programs in a short time. The new files are created and painstakingly verified for accuracy. This effort is rewarded with new master files that contain all the necessary records loaded with correct information.

Training is scheduled to start in the Information Center. Hy Perteks is more than willing to reserve a block of time for installing the software and providing the training sessions. Chip and Anna alternate in providing instruction, each for the portions of the system they had created.

With the training sessions concluded, the last task is the conversion of the old system to the new. The phased method is selected as the best approach. First, the computer hardware programs are installed. Records are updated with information for the additional elements included in the system design.

17

Next, the software update programs are installed. Again, updates to master file records are entered. When the records contain complete information, the inquiry screens are installed. Finally, report and menu programs are added to the system.

"The installation is a great success," exults Chip. "Everything is working correctly, without a bug in the system. I guess we should knock on wood. Have you heard any comments from the users?"

"Yes," replies Anna. "They are happy and relieved to have their new system. Mike Crowe has already started to use the preventive maintenance feature and has his students helping to tackle one lab room at a time. Cher and Dot were running through the various displays and several times commented on how easy it is to perform tasks. I paid a visit to Paige Prynter, and she asked me what she should do with all her free time."

The analysts smile at each other. Chip says, "It has been a really great project to work on."

"It certainly has," answers Anna. "The best system we've ever created here at CPU."

"I've learned a lot about the university in my short time here, too. It's a great place to work," Chip muses.

"And as long as you remember our motto, you should do fine," Anna replies. "Semper redundate," she says to Chip.

"Yeah, I see it on all the letterhead. I must admit, though, that I never took Latin in school. What does the motto actually mean?" Chip asks.

"Always backup!" Anna says securely.

EXERCISE

E-1. Use a paragraph to speculate on why the star network configuration was used. Does it matter that users are in several different rooms?

E-2. Describe procedures that should be designed to create automatic backup files. In a paragraph, be sure to consider the pros and cons of these procedures.

E-3. List security measures that should be taken to prevent unauthorized persons from using the computer system.

E-4. Outline a disaster recovery plan for the new computer system you have created for CPU. In particular focus on the teams that will be responsible for managing a crisis.

E-5. Explain in a paragraph why a phased conversion would be used to install the computer system.

OBJECT-ORIENTED SYSTEMS ANALYSIS AND DESIGN USING UML

18

Learning Objectives

Once you have mastered the material in this chapter you will be able to:

1. **Understand what object-oriented systems analysis and design is and appreciate its usefulness.**
2. **Comprehend the concepts of unified modeling language (UML), the standard approach for modeling a system in the object-oriented world.**
3. **Apply the steps used in UML to break down the system into a use case model and then a class model.**
4. **Diagram systems with the UML toolset so they can be described and properly designed.**
5. **Document and communicate the newly modeled object-oriented system to users and other analysts.**

The challenge of developing new information systems for ecommerce, wireless, and handheld applications in dynamic economic, legal, social, and physical environments calls for new analysis and design techniques. Object-oriented analysis and design can offer an approach that facilitates logical, rapid, and thorough methods for creating new systems responsive to a changing business landscape. Object-oriented techniques work well in situations in which complicated information systems are undergoing continuous maintenance, adaptation, and redesign.

Object-oriented systems describe entities as objects. Objects are part of a general concept called classes. The desire to place items into classes is not new. Describing the world as being made of up animals, vegetables, and minerals is an example of classification, although it has little scientific basis. The scientific approach includes classes of animals (such as mammals), and then divides the classes into subclasses (such as egg-laying animals and pouched mammals).

The idea behind classes is to have a reference point and describe a specific object in terms of its similarities to or differences from members of its own class. In doing so, it is more efficient for someone to say, "The koala bear is a marsupial (or pouched animal) with a large round head and furry ears," than it is to describe a koala bear by describing all of its characteristics as a mammal. It is more efficient to describe characteristics, appearance, and even behavior in this way. When you hear the word *reusable* in the object-oriented world, it means you can be more

By Julie E. Kendall, Kenneth E. Kendall, and Allen Schmidt.

efficient, because you do not have to start at the beginning to describe an object every time it is needed for software development.

When the object-oriented approach was first introduced, advocates cited reusability of the objects as the main benefit of their approach. It makes intuitive sense that the recycling of program parts should reduce the costs of development in computer-based systems. It has already proved very effective in the development of GUIs and databases. Although reusability is the main goal, maintaining systems is also very important, and by creating objects that contain both data and program code, a change in one object has a minimal impact on other objects.

In this chapter, we introduce the unified modeling language (UML), the industry standard for modeling object-oriented systems. UML toolset includes diagrams that allow you to visualize the construction of an object-oriented system. UML is a powerful tool that can greatly improve the quality of your systems analysis and design, and thereby help create higher-quality information systems. UML standards change. UML 2.0 renamed some diagrams and added new ones.

By using UML iteratively, you can achieve a greater understanding between the business and IT teams regarding the system requirements and the processes that need to occur in the system to meet those requirements. Each iteration takes a successively more detailed look at the design of the system until the things and relationships in the system are clearly and precisely defined in UML documents. The most important features of each phase may be initially defined, then added to later in the development process. Although the process is iterative, it is important to be as complete as possible initially.

When your analysis and design are done, you should have an accurate and detailed set of specifications for the classes, processes, and other artifacts in the system, which will help you avoid the expense of recoding because of poor initial planning. An artifact is a general term meaning any piece of information used or produced when developing systems. It may be a diagram, descriptive text, user instructions, code methods, programs, or any other component of the system.

OBJECT-ORIENTED CONCEPTS

Object-oriented programming differs from traditional procedural programming by examining the objects that are part of a system. Each object is a computer representation of some actual thing or event. General descriptions of the key object-oriented concepts of objects, classes, and inheritance are presented in this section, with further details on other UML concepts introduced later in this chapter.

OBJECTS

Objects are persons, places, or things that are relevant to the system we are analyzing. Objects may be customers, items, orders, and so on. Objects may also be GUI displays or text areas on the display.

CLASSES

Objects are represented by and grouped into classes that are optimal for reuse and maintainability. A class defines the set of shared attributes and behaviors found in each object in the class. For example, records for students in a course section have similar information stored for each student. The students could be said to make up a class (no pun intended). The values may be different for each student, but the type of information is the same. Programmers must define the various classes in the program they are writing. When the program runs, objects can be created from the established class. The term *instantiate* is used when an object is created from a

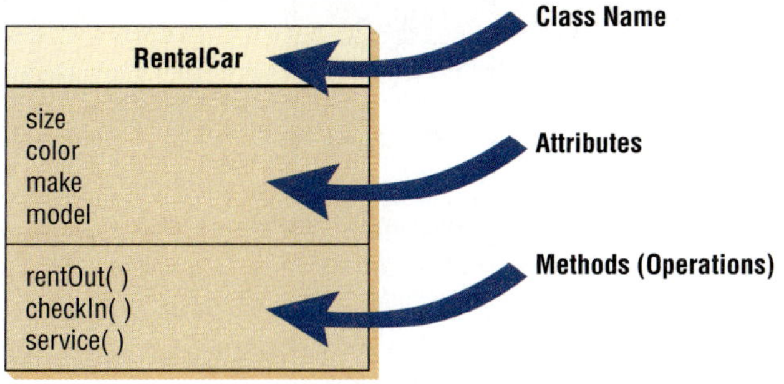

FIGURE 18.1
An example of a UML class. A class is depicted as a rectangle consisting of the class name, attributes, and methods.

class. For example, a program could instantiate a student named Peter Wellington as an object from the class labeled as student.

What makes object-oriented programming, and thus object-oriented analysis and design, different from classical programming is the technique of putting all of an object's attributes and methods within one self-contained structure, the class itself. This is a familiar occurrence in the physical world. For example, a packaged cake mix is analogous to a class since it has both the ingredients as well as instructions on how to mix and bake the cake. A wool sweater is similar to a class because it has a label with care instructions sewn into it that caution you to wash it by hand and lay it flat to dry.

Each class should have a name that differentiates it from all other classes. Class names are usually nouns or short phrases and begin with an uppercase letter. In Figure 18.1 the class is called **RentalCar.** In UML, a class is drawn as a rectangle. The rectangle contains two other important features: a list of attributes and a series of methods. These items describe a class, the unit of analysis that is a large part of what we call object-oriented analysis and design.

An attribute describes some property that is possessed by all objects of the class. Notice that the **RentalCar** class possesses the attributes of size, color, make, and model. All cars possess these attributes, but each car will have different values for its attributes. For example, a car can be blue, white, or some other color. Later on we will demonstrate that you can be more specific about the range of values for these properties. When specifying attributes, the first letter is usually lowercase.

A method is an action that can be requested from any object of the class. Methods are the processes that a class knows to carry out. Methods are also called operations. For the class of **RentalCar, rentOut( ), checkIn( ),** and **service( )** are examples of methods. When specifying methods, the first letter is usually lowercase.

INHERITANCE

Another key concept of object-oriented systems is inheritance. Classes can have children; that is, one class can be created out of another class. In UML, the original—or parent class—is known as a base class. The child class is called a derived class. A derived class can be created in such a way that it will inherit all the attributes and behaviors of the base class. A derived class, however, may have additional attributes and behaviors. For example, there might be a **Vehicle** class for a car rental company that contains attributes such as **size, color,** and **make.** The derived classes might be **Car** or **Truck,** as shown in Figure 18.2.

Inheritance reduces programming labor by using common objects easily. The programmer only needs to declare that the **Car** class inherits from the **Vehicle** class, and then provide any additional details about new attributes or behaviors that are unique to a car. All the attributes and behaviors of the **Vehicle** class are automatically and implicitly part of the **Car** class and require no additional

FIGURE 18.2

A class diagram showing inheritance. Car and Truck are specific examples of vehicles and inherit the characteristics of the more general class, **Vehicle.**

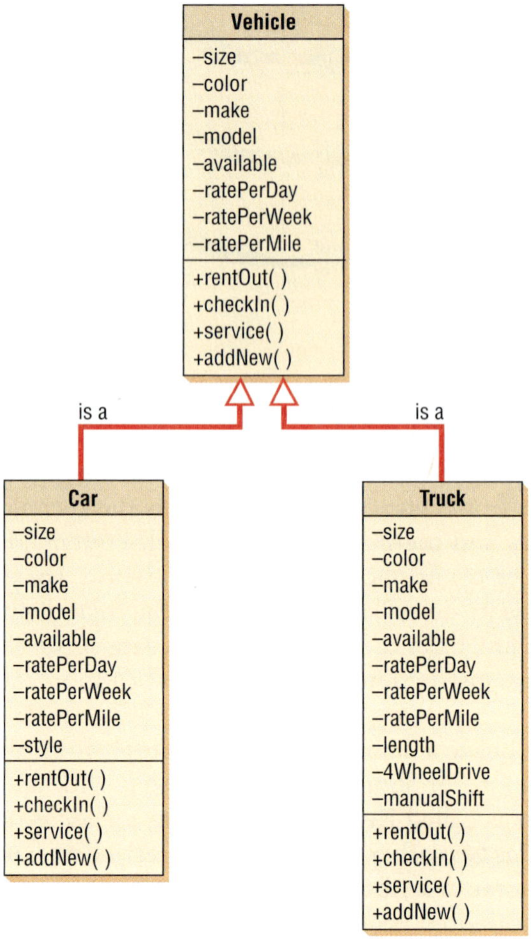

programming. This enables the analyst to define once but use many times, and is similar to data that is in the third normal form, defined only once in one database table (as discussed in Chapter 13).

In Figure 18.2, attributes are preceded by minus signs and methods are preceded by plus signs. We will discuss this in more detail later in the chapter, but for now take note that the minus signs mean that these attributes are private (not shared with other classes) and these methods are public (may be invoked by other classes).

Program code reuse has been a part of structured systems development and programming languages (such as COBOL) for many years, and there have been subprograms that encapsulate data. Inheritance, however, is a feature that is only found in object-oriented systems.

CRC CARDS AND OBJECT THINK

Now that we have covered the fundamental concepts of object-oriented systems analysis and design, we need to examine ways to create classes and objects from the business problems and systems we are facing. One way to begin enacting the object-oriented approach is to start thinking and talking in this new way. One handy approach is to develop CRC cards.

CRC stands for class, responsibilities, and collaborators. The analyst can use these concepts when beginning to talk about or model the system from an object-oriented perspective. CRC cards are used to represent the responsibilities of classes and the interaction between the classes. Analysts create the cards based on scenarios that outline system requirements. These scenarios model the behavior of the system

CONSULTING OPPORTUNITY 18.1

MAKING THE MAGIC REEL*

Fred and Ginger, owners of the FilmMagic chain of stores (which rent videos, DVDs, and video games), have always been interested in new technology. Because they keep adding new products to rent (such as DVDs and new games for PlayStation 3), their business has grown into a smash hit in several cities.

Because your home is close to their original store, you have become friends with them over the dozen years they have been in business, renting tapes and then DVDs as they make the move from the big screen to personal media. You often swap views about which movies are "must sees" and which are "bombs."

Because you have described the new object-oriented approaches you have been learning, they would like you to analyze their business using this approach. You can find a summary of FilmMagic business activities in Figure 7.15. Notice also the series of data flow diagrams in that chapter to help you conceptualize the problem and begin making the transition to Object Think.

Because you are such good friends with Fred and Ginger and because you wouldn't mind a little practical experience using O-O thinking, you agree to apply what you know and give them a report. Once you have reread the business activities for FilmMagic, provide a timely review by completing the following tasks:

- Use the CRC cards technique to list classes, responsibilities, and collaborators.
- Use the Object Think technique to list "knows" and corresponding attributes for the objects in those classes identified in the previous stage.

Write up both steps and waltz over to FilmMagic headquarters with your report in hand. Clearly, Fred and Ginger are hoping for a rave review.

*Based on a problem written by Dr. Ping Zhang of Syracuse University.

under study. If they are to be used in a group, CRC cards can be created manually on small note cards for flexibility, or they can be created using a computer.

We have added two columns to the original CRC card template: the Object Think column and the property column. The Object Think statements are written in plain English, and the property, or attribute, name is entered in its proper place. The purpose of these columns is to clarify thinking and help move toward creating UML diagrams.

INTERACTING DURING A CRC SESSION

CRC cards can be created interactively with a handful of analysts who can work together to identify the class in the problem domain presented by the business. One suggestion is to find all the nouns and verbs in a problem statement that has been created to capture the problem. Nouns usually indicate the classes in the system, and responsibilities can be found by identifying the verbs.

With your analyst group, brainstorm to identity all the classes you can. Follow the standard format for brainstorming, which is not to criticize any participant's response at this point, but rather to elicit as many responses as possible. When all classes have been identified, the analysts can then compile them, weed out the illogical ones, and write each one on its own card. Assign one class to each person in the group, who will "own" it for the duration of the CRC session.

Next, the group creates scenarios that are actually walkthroughs of system functions by taking desired functionality from the requirements document previously created. Typical systems methods should be considered first, with exceptions such as error recovery taken up after the routine ones have been covered.

As the group decides which class is responsible for a particular function, the analyst who owns the class for the session picks up that card and declares, "I need to fulfill my responsibility." When a card is held in the air, it is considered an object and can do things. The group then proceeds to refine the responsibility into smaller and smaller tasks, if possible. These tasks can be fulfilled by the object if it is

Class Name: Department
Superclasses:
Subclasses:

Responsibilities	Collaborators	Object Think	Property
Add a new department	Course	I know my name	Department Name
Provide department information		I know my department chair	Chair Name

Class Name: Course
Superclasses:
Subclasses:

Responsibilities	Collaborators	Object Think	Property
Add a new course	Department	I know my course number	Course Number
Change course information	Textbook	I know my description	Course Description
Display course information	Assignment	I know my number of credits	Credits
	Exam		

Class Name: Textbook
Superclasses:
Subclasses:

Responsibilities	Collaborators	Object Think	Property
Add a new textbook	Course	I know my ISBN	ISBN
Change textbook information		I know my author	Author
Find textbook information		I know my title	Title
Remove obsolete textbooks		I know my edition	Edition
		I know my publisher	Publisher
		I know if I am required	Required

Class Name: Assignment
Superclasses:
Subclasses:

Responsibilities	Collaborators	Object Think	Property
Add a new assignment	Course	I know my assignment number	Task Number
Change an assignment		I know my description	Task Description
View an assignment		I know how many points I am worth	Points
		I know when I am due	Due Date

FIGURE 18.3
Four CRC cards for course offerings show how analysts fill in the details for classes, responsibilities, and collaborators, as well as for object think statements and property names.

appropriate, or the group can decide that it can be fulfilled by interacting with other things. If there are no other appropriate classes in existence, the group may need to create one.

The four CRC cards depicted in Figure 18.3 show four classes for course offerings. Notice that in a class called **Course,** the systems analyst is referred to four collaborators: the department, the textbook, the course assignment, and the course exam. These collaborators are then described as classes of their own on the other CRC cards.

The responsibilities listed will eventually evolve into what are called methods in UML. The Object Think statements seem elementary, but they are conversational so as to encourage a group of analysts during a CRC session to describe as many of these statements as possible. As shown in the example, all dialog during a CRC session is carried out in the first person, so that even the **textbook** speaks: "I know my ISBN." "I know my author." These statements can then be used to describe attributes in UML. These attributes can be called by their variable names, such as **edition** and **publisher.**

THE UNIFIED MODELING LANGUAGE (UML) CONCEPTS AND DIAGRAMS

UML approach is well worth investigating and understanding, due to its wide acceptance and usage. UML provides a standardized set of tools to document the analysis and design of a software system. The UML toolset includes diagrams that allow people to visualize the construction of an object-oriented system, similar to the way a set of blueprints allows people to visualize the construction of a building. Whether you are working independently or with a large systems development team, the documentation that you create with UML provides an effective means of communication between the development team and the business team on a project.

UML consists of things, relationships, and diagrams, as illustrated in Figure 18.4. The first components, or primary elements, of UML are called things. You may prefer another word, such as object, but in UML they are called things. Structural things are most common. Structural things are classes, interfaces, use cases, and many other elements that provide a way to create models. Structural things allow the user to describe relationships. Behavioral things describe how things work. Examples of behavioral things are interactions and state machines. Group things are used to define boundaries. An example of a group thing is a package. Finally, we have annotational things, so that we can add notes to the diagrams.

Relationships are the glue that holds the things together. It is useful to think of relationships in two ways. Structural relationships are used to tie the things together in the structural diagrams. Structural relationships include dependencies, aggregations, associations, and generalizations. Structural relationships show inheritance, for example. Behavioral relationships are used in the behavioral diagrams. The four basic types of behavioral relationships are communicates, includes, extends, and generalizes.

There are two main types of diagrams in UML: structural diagrams and behavioral diagrams. Structural diagrams are used, for example, to describe the relationships between classes. They include class diagrams, object diagrams, component diagrams, and deployment diagrams. Behavioral diagrams, on the other hand, can be used to describe the interaction between people (called actors in UML) and the thing we refer to as a use case, or how the actors use the system. Behavioral diagrams include use case diagrams, sequence diagrams, communication diagrams, statechart diagrams, and activity diagrams.

In the remainder of this chapter, we first discuss use case modeling, the basis for all UML techniques. Next, we look at how a use case is used to derive activities, sequences, and classes—the most commonly used UML diagrams. Because entire books are dedicated to the syntax and usage of UML (the actual UML specification document is over 800 pages long), we provide only a brief summary of the most valuable and commonly used aspects of UML.

FIGURE 18.4

An overall view of UML and its components: Things, Relationships, and Diagrams.

UML Category	UML Elements	Specific UML Details
Things	Structural Things	Classes Interfaces Collaborations Use Cases Active Classes Components Nodes
	Behavioral Things	Interactions State Machines
	Grouping Things	Packages
	Annotational Things	Notes
Relationships	Structural Relationships	Dependencies Aggregations Associations Generalizations
	Behavioral Relationships	Communicates Includes Extends Generalizes
Diagrams	Structural Diagrams	Class Diagrams Component Diagrams Deployment Diagrams
	Behavioral Diagrams	Use Case Diagrams Sequence Diagrams Communication Diagrams Statechart Diagrams Activity Diagrams

The six most commonly used UML diagrams are:

1. A use case diagram, describing how the system is used. Analysts start with a use case diagram.
2. A use case scenario (although technically it is not a diagram) is a verbal articulation of exceptions to the main behavior described by the primary use case.
3. An activity diagram, illustrating the overall flow of activities. Each use case may create one activity diagram.
4. Sequence diagrams, showing the sequence of activities and class relationships. Each use case may create one or more sequence diagrams. An alternative to a sequence diagram is a communication diagram, which contains the same information but emphasizes communication instead of timing.
5. Class diagrams, showing the classes and relationships. Sequence diagrams are used (along with CRC cards) to determine classes. An offshoot of a class diagram is a gen/spec diagram (which stands for generalization/specialization).
6. Statechart diagrams, showing the state transitions. Each class may create a statechart diagram, which is useful for determining class methods.

How these diagrams relate to one another is illustrated in Figure 18.5. We will discuss each of these diagrams in the following sections.

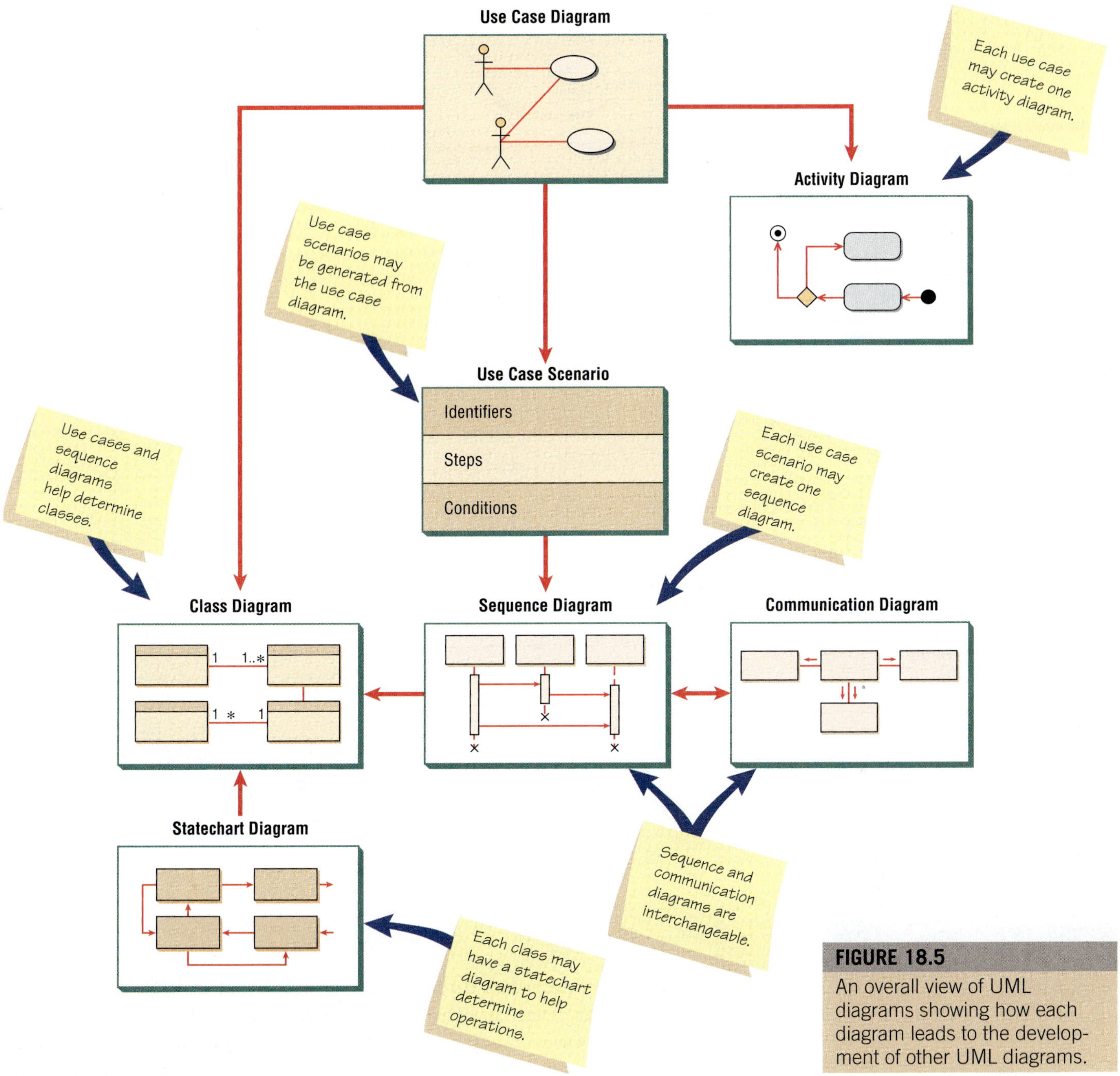

FIGURE 18.5
An overall view of UML diagrams showing how each diagram leads to the development of other UML diagrams.

USE CASE MODELING

UML is fundamentally based on an object-oriented analysis technique known as use case modeling, which was introduced in Chapter 2. A use case model describes *what* a system does without describing *how* the system does it. UML can be used to analyze the use case model, and to derive system objects and their interactions with each other and with the users of the system. Using UML techniques, you further analyze the objects and their interactions to derive object behavior, attributes, and relationships.

A use case provides developers with a view of what the users want. It is free of technical or implementation details. We can think of a use case as a sequence of transactions in a system. The use case model is based on the interactions and relationships of individual use cases.

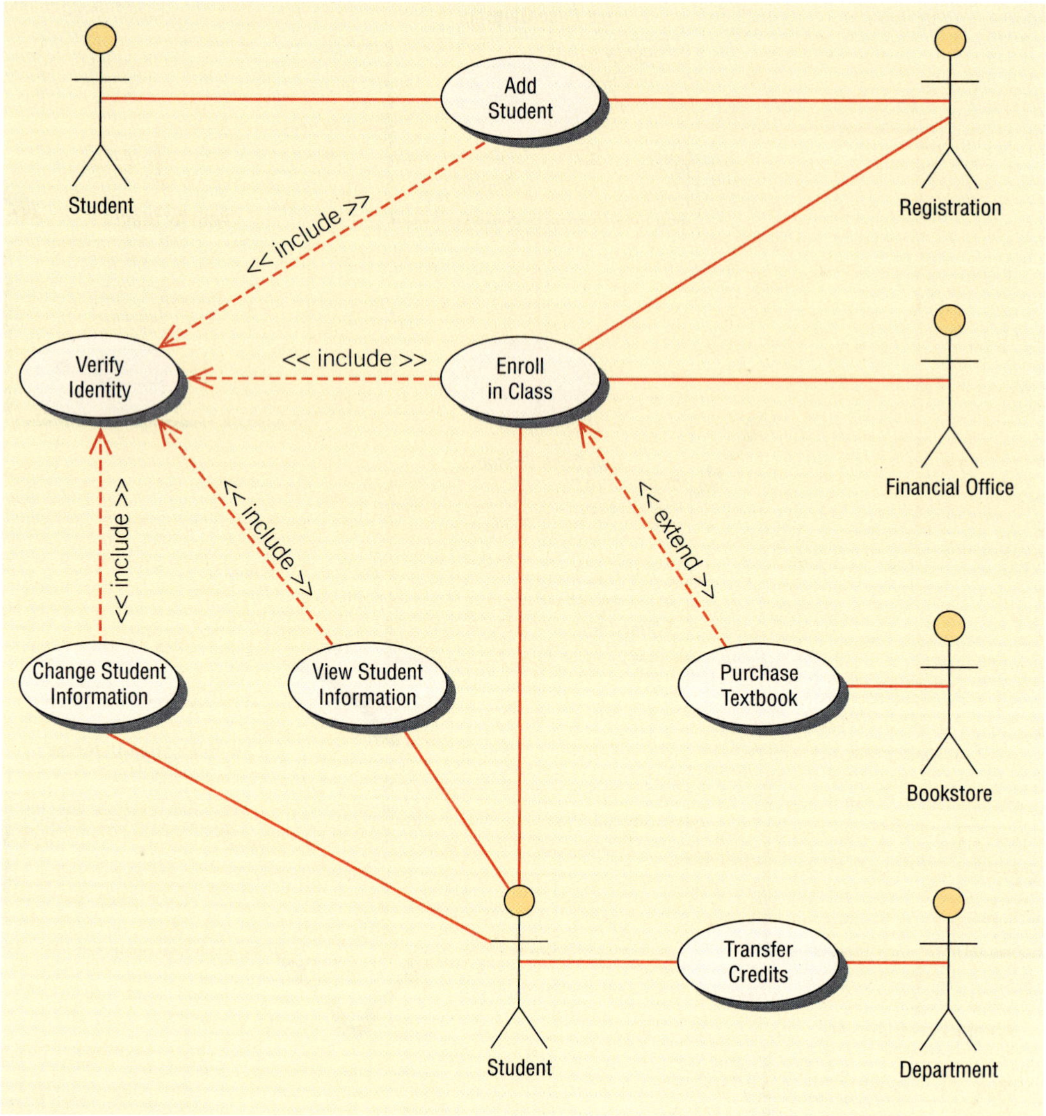

FIGURE 18.6

A use case example of student enrollment.

A use case always describes three things: an actor that initiates an event; the event that triggers a use case; and the use case that performs the actions triggered by the event. In a use case, an actor using the system initiates an event that begins a related series of interactions in the system. Use cases are used to document a single transaction or event. An event is an input to the system that happens at a specific time and place and causes the system to do something. For more information about use case symbols and how to draw use case diagrams, see Chapter 2.

Figure 18.6 is a use case example of student enrollment at a university. Notice that only the most important functions are represented. The **Add Student** use case does not indicate how to add students, the method of implementation. Students could be added in person, using the Web, using a touch-tone telephone, or any combination of these methods. The **Add Student** use case includes the **Verify Identity** use case to verify the identity of the student. The **Purchase Textbook** use case extends the **Enroll in Class** use case, and may be part of a system to enroll students in an online course.

It may seem as if the **Change Student Information** use case is a minor system feature and should not be included on the use case diagram, but because this information changes frequently, administration has a keen interest in allowing students

Use case name:	Change Student Information		
Area:	Student System	**UniqueID:**	Student UC 005
Actor(s):	Student		
Description:	Allow student to change his or her own information, such as name, home address, home telephone, campus address, campus telephone, cell phone, and other information using a secure Web site.		
Triggering Event:	Student uses Change Student Information Web site, enters student ID and password, and clicks the **Submit** button.		
Trigger type:	☒ External ☐ Temporal		

Steps Performed (Main Path)	**Information for Steps**
1. Student Logons on to the secure Web server.	Student ID, Password
2. Student record is read and password is verified.	Student Record, StudentID, Password
3. Current student personal information is displayed on the Change Student Web page.	Student Record
4. Student enters changes on the Change Student Web form and clicks **Submit** button.	Change Student Web Form
5. Changes are validated on the Web server.	Change Student Web Form
6. Change Student Journal record is written.	Change Student Web Form
7. Student record is updated on the Student Master.	Change Student Web Form, Student Record
8. Confirmation Web page is sent to the student.	Confirmation Page

Preconditions:	Student is on the Change Student Information Web page.
Postconditions:	Student has successfully changed personal information.
Assumptions:	Student has a browser and a valid user ID and password.
Requirements Met:	Allow students to be able to change personal information using a secure Web site.
Outstanding Issues:	Should the number of times a student is allowed to logon be controlled?
Priority:	Medium
Risk:	Medium

FIGURE 18.7

A use case scenario is divided into three sections: identification and initiation, steps performed, and conditions, assumptions, and questions.

to change their own personal information. The fact that the administrators deem this to be important not only justifies, but calls for, the use case to be written up.

Students would not be allowed to change grade point average, outstanding fees, and other information. This use case also includes the **Verify Identity** use case, and in this situation, it means having the student enter a user ID and password before gaining access to the system. **View Student Information** allows students to view their personal information, as well as courses and grades.

A use case scenario example is shown in Figure 18.7. Some of the areas included are optional, and may not be used by all organizations. The three main areas are:

1. Use case identifiers and initiators.
2. Steps performed.
3. Conditions, assumptions, and questions.

In the first area the use case is identified by it name, **Change Student Information,** the actor is identified as a **Student,** and the Use Case and Triggering Event are described. The second area contains a series of steps that are performed as long as no errors are encountered. Finally, in the third area, all of the pre- and postconditions and assumptions are identified. Some of these are obvious, such as the precondition that the student is on the correct Web page and the assumption that the student has a valid student ID and password. Others are not so obvious, such as the outstanding issue regarding how many times the student is allowed to logon to the system.

Use case diagrams provide the basis for creating other types of diagrams, such as class diagrams and activity diagrams. Use case scenarios are helpful in drawing sequence diagrams. Both use case diagrams and use case scenarios are powerful tools to help us understand how a system works in general.

ACTIVITY DIAGRAMS

Activity diagrams show the sequence of activities in a process, including sequential and parallel activities, and decisions that are made. An activity diagram is usually created for one use case and may show the different possible scenarios.

The symbols on an activity diagram are illustrated in Figure 18.8. A rectangle with rounded ends represents an activity, either a manual one, such as signing a legal document, or an automated one, such as a method or program.

An arrow represents an event. Events represent things that happen at a certain time and place.

A diamond represents either a decision (also called a branch) or a merge. Decisions have one arrow going into the diamond and several going out. A guard condition, showing the condition values, may be included. Merges show several events combining to form one event.

FIGURE 18.8
Specialized symbols are used to draw an activity diagram.

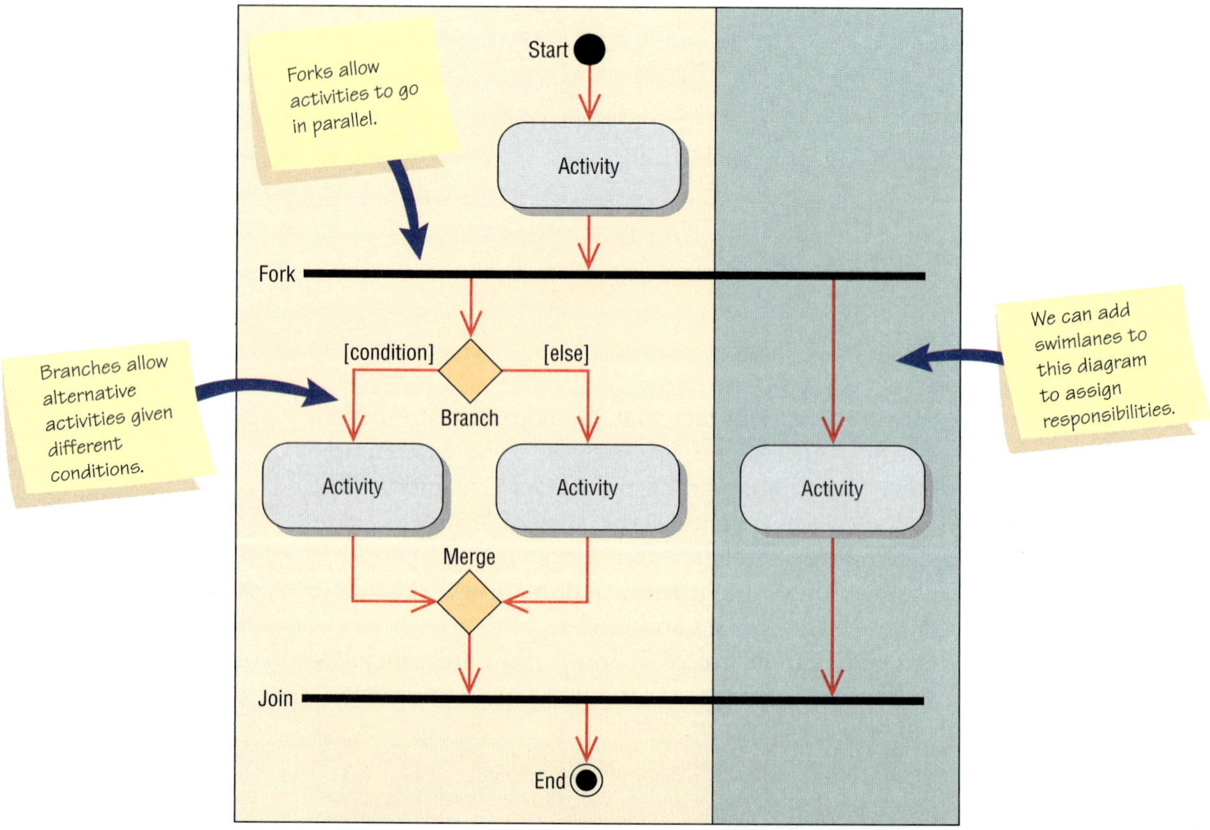

A long, flat rectangle represents a synchronization bar. These are used to show parallel activities, and may have one event going into the synchronization bar and several events going out of it, called a fork. A synchronization in which several events merge into one event is called a join.

There are two symbols that show the start and end of the diagram. The initial state is shown as a filled-in circle. The final state is shown as a black circle surrounded by a white circle.

Rectangles surrounding other symbols, called swimlanes, indicate partitioning and are used to show which activities are done on which platform, such as a browser, server, or mainframe computer; or to show activities done by different user groups. Swimlanes are zones that can depict logic as well as the responsibility of a class.

You can see an example of swimlanes in Figure 18.9, which illustrates an activity diagram for the **Change Student Information** use case. It starts with the student

FIGURE 18.9
This activity diagram shows three swimlanes: Client Web Page, Web Server, and Mainframe.

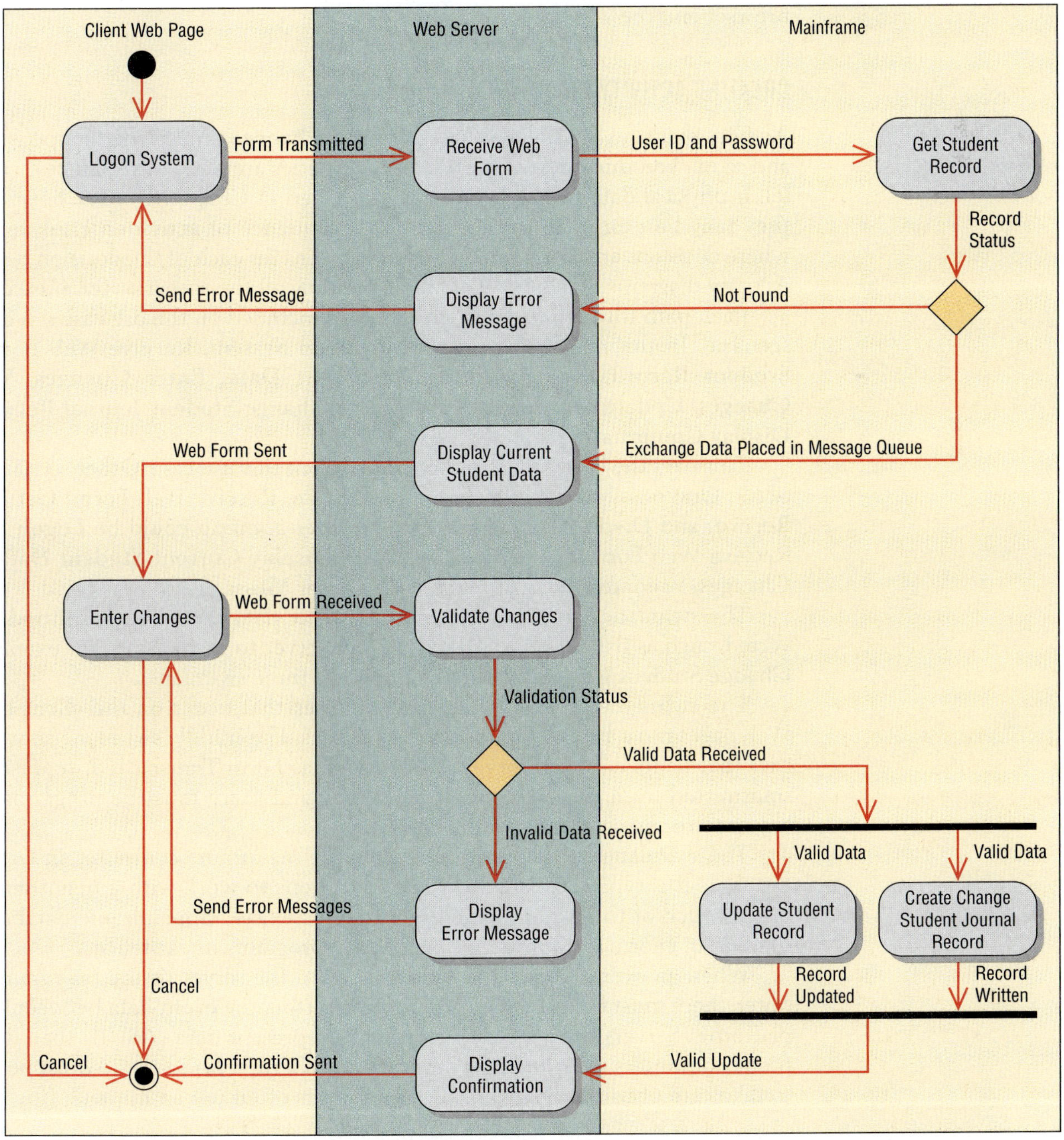

logging onto the system by filling out a Web form and clicking the **Submit** button. The form is transmitted to the Web server, which then passes the data to the mainframe computer. The mainframe accesses the STUDENT database and passes either a "Not Found" message or selected student data to the Web server.

The diamond below the **Get Student Record** state indicates this decision. If the student record has not been found, the Web server displays an error message on the Web page. If the student record has been found, the Web server formats a new Web page containing the current student data in a Web form. The student may cancel the change from either the **Logon System** or the **Enter Changes** states, and the activity halts.

If the student enters changes on the Web form and clicks the **Submit** button, the change data is transmitted to the server and a program starts running that validates the changes. If there are errors, an error message is sent to the Web page. If the data are valid, the student record is updated and a Change Student Journal Record is written. After a valid update, a confirmation Web page is sent to the browser and the activity terminates.

CREATING ACTIVITY DIAGRAMS

Activity diagrams are created by asking what happens first, what happens second, and so on. You must determine whether activities are done in sequence or in parallel. If physical data flow diagrams (as described in Chapter 7) have been created, they may be examined to determine the sequence of activities. Look for places where decisions are made, and ask what happens for each of the decision outcomes. Activity diagrams may be created by examining all the scenarios for a use case.

Each path through the various decisions included on the use case is a different scenario. In the main path would be **Logon System, Receive Web Form, Get Student Record, Display Current Student Data, Enter Changes, Validate Changes, Update Student Record, Create Change Student Journal Record,** and **Display Confirmation.**

This isn't the only scenario that comes from this use case. Other scenarios may occur. One possibility could be **Logon System, Receive Web Form, Get Student Record,** and **Display Error Message.** Another scenario could be **Logon System, Receive Web Form, Get Student Record, Display Current Student Data, Enter Changes, Validate Changes,** and **Display Error Message.**

The swimlanes are useful to show how the data must be transmitted or converted, such as from Web to server or from server to mainframe. For example, the **Change Student Record** activity diagram has three swimlanes.

The swimlane on the left shows activities that occur on the client browser. Web pages must be created for these activities. The middle swimlane shows activities that happen on the server. Events, such as **Form Transmitted,** represent data transmitted from the browser to the server, and there must be programs on the server to receive and process the client data.

The swimlane on the right represents the mainframe computer. In large organizations it is typical for many Web applications to work with a mainframe computer. Much of the data in large organizations exists on mainframe databases and there is an enormous number of mainframe programs in existence.

When an event crosses the swimlane from the server to the mainframe computer, there must be a mechanism for transmitting the event data between the two platforms. Servers use a different format to represent data (ASCII) than do mainframe computers (they use a format called EBCDIC). Middleware must be present to take care of the conversion. IBM computers often use an mqueue (for message

CONSULTING OPPORTUNITY 18.2

RECYCLING THE PROGRAMMING ENVIRONMENT

"I feel like I'm writing the same code over and over again," says Benito Pérez, a programmer working on a new automated warehouse design. "I have written so many programs lately that dealt with robotic-type things that control themselves: automated mailroom trolleys, building surveillance robots, automatic pool cleaners, automatic lawnmowers, monorail trains, and now warehouse trolleys. They are all variations on a theme."

Lisa Bernoulli, the project manager, had heard this sort of complaint for years. She replies, "Oh come on, Ben. These things aren't really that close. How can you compare a mailroom robot, an automated warehouse, and a monorail train? I'll bet less than 10 percent of the code is the same."

"Look," says Benito. "All three involve machines that have to find a starting point, follow a circuitous route, make stops for loading and unloading, and eventually go to a stopping point. All three have to make decisions at branches in their routes. All three have to avoid colliding with things. I'm tired of redesigning code that is largely familiar to me."

"Hmmm," Lisa muses as she looks over the basic requirements for the warehouse system and remembers the monorail system she and Benito had worked on last year. The requirements regarded a small-lot electronics manufacturing firm that was automating its warehouse and product movement system. The warehouse contains incoming parts, work in progress, and finished goods. The automated warehouse uses a flatbed robot trolley. This robot is a four-wheel electric cart, similar to a golf cart except that it has no seats. Flatbed robot trolleys have a flat, 6′ × 4′ cargo surface about 3′ above ground level. These trolleys have a radio communications device that provides a real-time data link to a central warehouse computer. Flatbed trolleys have two sensors: a path sensor that detects a special type of paint and a motion sensor that detects movement. These trolleys follow painted paths around the factory floor. Special paint codes mark forks and branches in the paths, trolley start and stop points, and general location points.

The facility includes three loading dock stations and 10 workstations. Each station has a video terminal or computer connected to the central computer. When products are needed or are ready to be collected from a workstation, the central computer is informed by the worker at the station. The central computer then dispatches trolleys accordingly. Each station has a drop point and a pickup point. Flatbed trolleys move about the factory picking up work at pickup points and dropping off work at drop points. The program that will run the trolleys must interact heavily with the existing job-scheduling program that helps schedule workstation tasks.

How should Lisa go about reusing Benito Pérez's work on the monorail in their current task of creating a trolley object? Explain in two paragraphs.

queue). The message queue receives data from the server programs, places it in a holding area, and calls a mainframe program, usually written in a language called CICS. This program retrieves or updates the data, and sends the results back to the message queue.

In the example activity diagram shown, the decision below the **Get Student Record** state is made on the mainframe computer. This means that the message queue receives either a "Not Found" message or the database record for the student. If the mainframe simply placed the **Record Status Received** in the message queue and the decision was evaluated on the server, the server would have to call the mainframe again to obtain the valid data. This would slow down the response to the person waiting at the browser.

Swimlanes also help to divide up the tasks in a team. Web designers would be needed for the Web pages displayed on the client browser. Other members would work with programming languages, such as Java, PERL or .NET, on the server. Mainframe CICS programmers would write programs that would work with the message queue. The analyst must ensure that the data that the various team members need is available and correctly defined. Sometimes the data in the message queue is an XML document. If an outside organization is involved, the data also might be an XML document.

The activity diagram provides a map of a use case, and allows the analyst to experiment with moving portions of the design to different platforms and ask "What if?" for a variety of decisions. The use of unique symbols and swimlanes makes this diagram one that people want to use to communicate with others.

SEQUENCE AND COMMUNICATION DIAGRAMS

An interaction diagram is either a sequence diagram or a communication diagram, which show essentially the same information. These diagrams, along with class diagrams, are used in a use case realization, which is a way to achieve or accomplish a use case.

SEQUENCE DIAGRAMS

Sequence diagrams can illustrate a succession of interactions between classes or object instances over time. Sequence diagrams are often used to illustrate the processing described in use case scenarios. In practice, sequence diagrams are derived from use case analysis and are used in systems design to derive the interactions, relationships, and methods of the objects in the system. Sequence diagrams are used to show the overall pattern of the activities or interactions in a use case. Each use case scenario may create one sequence diagram, although sequence diagrams are not always created for minor scenarios.

The symbols used in sequence diagrams are shown in Figure 18.10. Actors and classes or object instances are shown in boxes along the top of the diagram. The leftmost object is the starting object and may be a person (for which a use case actor symbol is used), window, dialog box, or other user interface. Some of the interactions are physical only, such as signing a contract. The top rectangles use indicators in the name to indicate whether the rectangle represents an object, a class, or a class and object.

objectName:	A name with a colon after it represents an object.
:class	A colon with a name after it represents a class.
objectName:class	A name, followed by a colon and another name, represents an object in a class.

A vertical line represents the lifeline for the class or object, which corresponds to the time from when it is created through when it is destroyed. An X on the bottom of the lifeline represents when the object is destroyed. A lateral bar or vertical

FIGURE 18.10
Specialized symbols used to draw a sequence diagram.

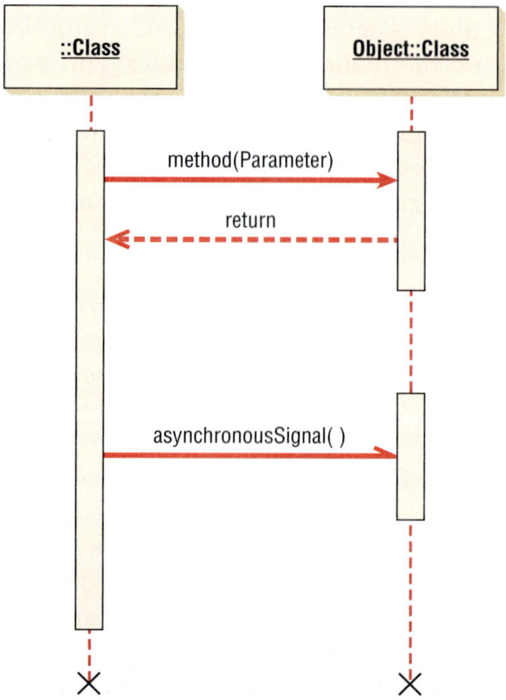

rectangle on the lifeline shows the focus of control when the object is busy doing things.

Horizontal arrows show messages or signals that are sent between the classes. Messages belong to the receiving class. There are some variations in the message arrows. Solid arrowheads represent synchronous calls, which are the most common. These are used when the sending class waits for a response from the receiving class, and control is returned to the sending class when the class receiving the message finishes executing. Half (or open) arrowheads represent asynchronous calls, or those that are sent without an expectation of returning to the sending class. An example would be using a menu to run a program. A return is shown as an arrow, sometimes with a dashed line. Messages are labeled using one of the following formats:

- The name of the message followed by empty parentheses: **messageName( ).**
- The name of the message followed by parameters in parentheses: **messageName(parameter1, parameter2 . . .)**
- The message name followed by the parameter type, parameter name, and any default value for the parameter in parentheses: **messageName(parameterType:parameterName(defaultValue).** Parameter types indicate the type of data, such as string, number, or date.
- The message may be a stereotype, such as **«Create»,** indicating that a new object is created as a result of the message.

Timing in the sequence diagram is displayed from top to bottom; the first interaction is drawn at the top of the diagram, and the interaction that occurs last is drawn at the bottom of the diagram. The interaction arrows begin at the bar of the actor or object that initiates the interaction, and they end pointing at the bar of the actor or object that receives the interaction request. The starting actor, class, or object is shown on the left. This may be the actor that initiates the activity or it may be a class representing the user interface.

Figure 18.11 is a simplified example of a sequence diagram for a use case that admits a student to a university. On the left is the **newStudentInterface** class that is used to obtain student information. The **initialize( )** message is sent to the **Student** class, which creates a new student record and returns the student number. To simplify the diagram, the parameters that are sent to the **Student** class have been omitted, but would include the student name, address, and so on. The next activity is to send a **selectDorm** message to the **Dorm** class. This message would include dorm selection information, such as a health dorm or other student requirements. The **Dorm** class returns the dorm name and room number. The third activity is to send a **selectProgram** message to the **Program** class, including the program name and other course of study information. The program advisor name is returned to the **newStudentUserInterface** class. A **studentComplete** message is sent to the **Student** class with the dorm, advisor name, and other information.

Sequence diagrams can be used to translate the use case scenario into a visual tool for systems analysis. The initial sequence diagram used in systems analysis shows the actors and classes in the system and the interactions between them for a specific process. You can use this version of the sequence diagram to verify processes with the business area experts who have assisted you in developing the system requirements. A sequence diagram emphasizes the time ordering (sequence) of messages.

During the systems design phase, the sequence diagrams are refined to derive the methods and interactions between classes. Messages from one class are used to identify class relationships. The actors in the earlier sequence diagrams are translated

FIGURE 18.11

A sequence diagram for student admission. Sequence diagrams emphasize the time ordering of messages.

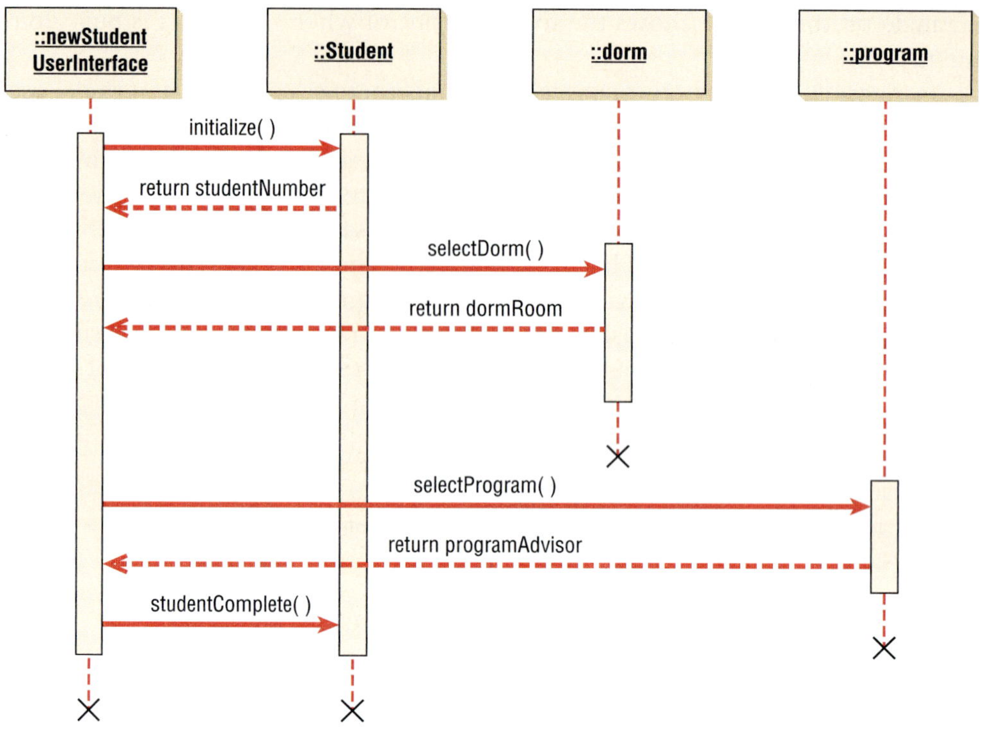

to interfaces, and class interactions are translated to class methods. Class methods used to create instances of other classes and to perform other internal system functions become apparent in the system design using sequence diagrams.

COMMUNICATION DIAGRAMS

Communication diagrams were introduced in UML 2.0. Their original name in UML 1.x was collaboration diagrams. Communication diagrams describe the interactions of two or more things in the system that perform a behavior that is more than any one of the things can do alone. For instance, a car can be broken down into several thousand individual parts. The parts are put together to form the major subsystems of the vehicle: the engine, the transmission, the brake system, and so forth. The individual parts of the car can be thought of as classes, because they have distinct attributes and functions. The individual parts of the engine form a collaboration, because they "communicate" with each other to make the engine run when the driver steps on the accelerator.

A communication diagram is made up of three parts: objects (also called participants), the communication links, and the messages that can be passed along those links. Communication diagrams show the same information as a sequence diagram but may be more difficult to read. In order to show time ordering, you must indicate a sequence number and describe the message.

A communication diagram emphasizes the organization of objects, whereas a sequence diagram emphasizes the time ordering of messages. A communication diagram will show a path to indicate how one object is linked to another.

Some UML modeling software, such as IBM's Rational Rose, will automatically convert a sequence diagram to a communication diagram or a communication diagram to a sequence diagram with the click of a button. A communication diagram for the student admission example is illustrated in Figure 18.12. Each rectangle represents an object or a class. Connecting lines show the classes that need to collaborate or work with each other. The messages sent from one class to another are shown along connecting lines. Messages are numbered to show the

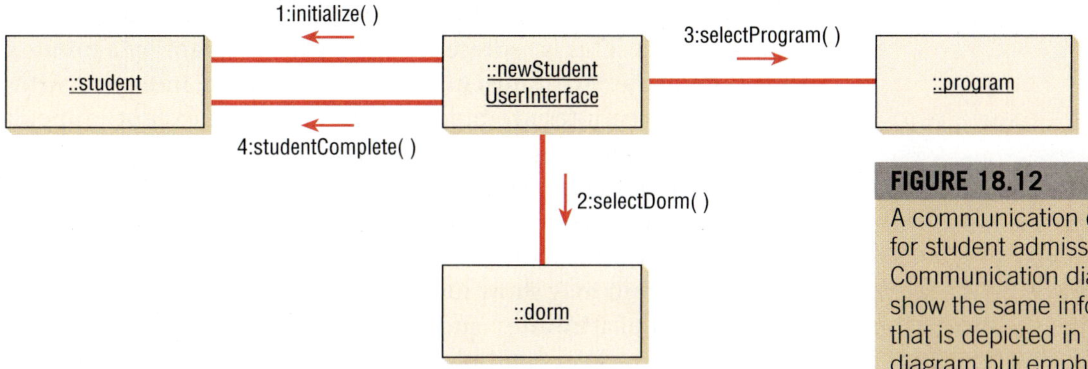

FIGURE 18.12
A communication diagram for student admission. Communication diagrams show the same information that is depicted in a sequence diagram but emphasize the organization of objects rather than the time ordering.

time sequence. Return values may also be included and numbered to indicate when they are returned within the time sequence.

CLASS DIAGRAMS

Object-oriented methodologies work to discover classes, attributes, methods, and relationships between classes. Because programming occurs at the class level, defining classes is one of the most important object-oriented analysis tasks. Class diagrams show the static features of the system and do not represent any particular processing. A class diagram also shows the nature of the relationships between classes.

Classes are represented by a rectangle on a class diagram. In the simplest format, the rectangle may include only the class name, but may also include the attributes and methods. Attributes are what the class knows about characteristics of the objects, and methods (also called operations) are what the class knows about how to do to things. Methods are small sections of code that work with the attributes.

Figure 18.13 illustrates a class diagram for course offerings. Notice that the name is centered at the top of the class, usually in boldface type. The area directly below the name shows the attributes, and the bottom portion lists the methods. The class diagram shows data storage requirements as well as processing requirements. Later in the chapter we will discuss the meaning of the diamond symbols shown in this figure.

FIGURE 18.13
A class diagram for course offerings. The filled-in diamonds show aggregation and the empty diamond shows a whole-part relationship.

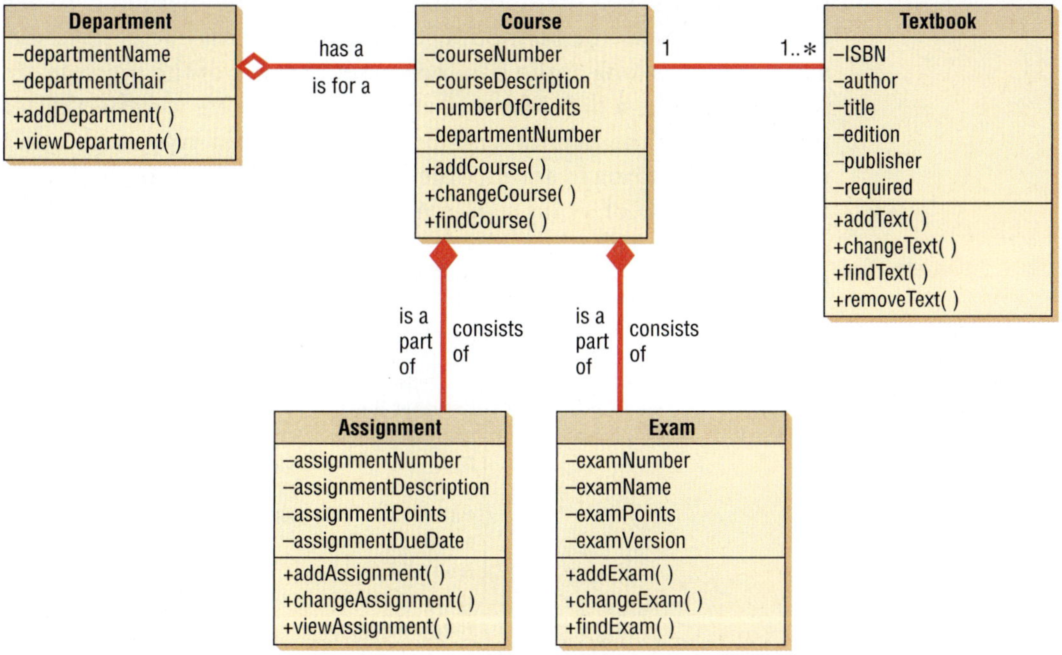

The attributes (or properties) are usually designated as private, or only available in the object. This is represented on a class diagram by a minus sign in front of the attribute name. Attributes may also be protected, indicated with a pound symbol (#). These attributes are hidden from all classes except immediate subclasses. Under rare circumstances, an attribute is public, meaning that it is visible to other objects outside its class. Making attributes private means that the attributes are only available to outside objects through the class methods, a technique called encapsulation, or information hiding.

A class diagram may show just the class name; or the class name and attributes; or the class name, attributes, and methods. Showing only the class name is useful when the diagram is very complex and includes many classes. If the diagram is simpler, attributes and methods may be included. When attributes are included, there are three ways to show the attribute information. The simplest is to include only the attribute name, which takes the least amount of space.

The type of data (such as string, double, integer, or date) may be included on the class diagram. The most complete descriptions would include an equal sign (=) after the type of data followed by the initial value for the attribute. Figure 18.14 illustrates class attributes.

If the attribute must take on one of a finite number of values, such as a student type with values of F for full-time, P for part-time, and N for nonmatriculating, these may be included in curly brackets separated by commas: **studentType:char{F,P,N}.**

Information hiding means that objects' methods must be available to other classes, so methods are often public, meaning that they may be invoked from other classes. On a class diagram, public messages (and any public attributes) are shown with a plus sign (+) in front of them. Methods also have parentheses after them, indicating that data may be passed as parameters along with the message. The message parameters, as well as the type of data, may be included on the class diagram.

There are two types of methods: standard and custom. Standard methods are basic things that all classes of objects know how to do, such as create a new object instance. Custom methods are designed for a specific class.

METHOD OVERLOADING

Method overloading refers to including the same method (or operation) several times in a class. The method signature includes the method name and the parameters included with the method. The same method may be defined more than once in a given class, as long as the parameters sent as part of the message are different; that is, there must be a different message signature. There may be a different number of parameters, or the parameters might be a different type, such as a number in one method and a string in another method. An example of method overloading may be found in the use of a plus sign in many programming languages. If the attributes on either side of the plus sign are numbers, the two numbers are added. If the attributes are strings of characters, the strings are concatenated to form one long string.

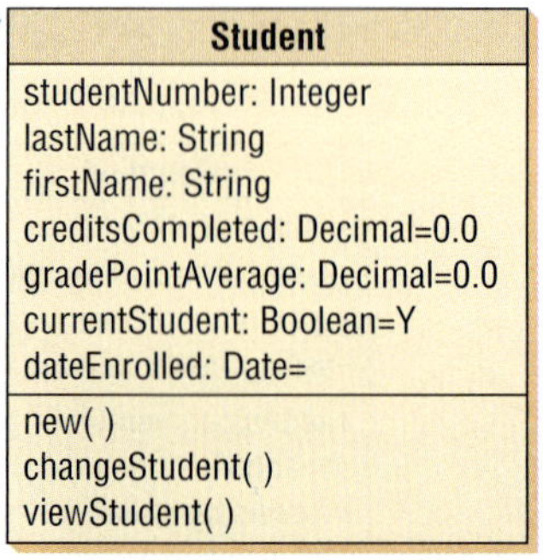

FIGURE 18.14

An extended **Student** class that shows the type of data and, in some cases, its initial value or default value.

In a bank deposit example, a deposit slip could contain just the amount of the deposit, in which case the bank would deposit the entire amount, or it could contain the deposit amount and the amount of cash to be returned. Both situations would use a deposit check method, but the parameters (one situation would also request the amount of cash to be returned) would be different.

TYPES OF CLASSES

Classes fall into four categories: entity, interface, abstract, and control. These categories are explained below.

Entity Classes Entity classes represent real-world items, such as people, things, and so on. Entity classes are the entities represented on an entity-relationship diagram. CASE tools such as Visible Analyst will allow you to create a UML entity class from an entity on an E-R diagram.

The analyst needs to determine which attributes to include in the classes. Each object has many attributes, but the class should include only those that are used by the organization. For example, when creating an entity class for a student at a college, you would need to know attributes that identify the student, such as home and campus address, as well as grade point average, total credits, and so on. If you were keeping track of the same student for an online clothing store, you would have to know basic identifying information, as well as other descriptive attributes such as measurements or color preferences.

Boundary, or Interface, Classes Boundary, or interface, classes provide a means for users to work with the system. There are two broad categories of interface classes: human and system.

A human interface may be a display, window, Web form, dialog box, menu, list box, or other display control. It may also be a touch-tone telephone, bar code, or other way for users to interact with the system. Human interfaces should be prototyped (as described in Chapter 6), and often a storyboard is used to model the sequence of interactions.

System interfaces involve sending data to or receiving data from other systems. This may include databases in the organization. If data are sent to an external organization, they are often in the form of XML files or other well-published interfaces with clearly defined messages and protocols. External interfaces are the least stable, because there is often little or no control over an external partner who may alter the format of the message or data.

XML helps to provide standardization, because an external partner may add new elements to the XML document, but a corporation transforming the data to a format that may be used to append to an internal database may simply choose to ignore the additional elements without any problems.

The attributes of these classes are those found on the display or report. The methods are those required to work with the display, or to produce the report.

Abstract Classes Abstract classes are classes that cannot be directly instantiated. Abstract classes are those that are linked to concrete classes in a generalization/specialization (gen/spec) relationship. The name of an abstract class is usually denoted in italics.

Control Classes Control, or active, classes are used to control the flow of activities, and they act as a coordinator when implementing classes. To achieve classes that are reusable, a class diagram may include many small control classes. Control classes are often derived during system design.

Often a new control class will be created just to make another class reusable. An example would be the logon process. There might be one control class that handles the logon user interface, containing the logic to check the user ID and password. The problem that arises is that the logon control class is designed for a specific logon display. By creating a logon control class that handles just the unique logon display, the data may be passed to a more general validation control class, which performs a check on user IDs and passwords received from many other control classes receiving messages from specific user interfaces. This increases reusability and isolates the logon verification methods from the user interface handling methods.

The rules for creating sequence diagrams are that all interface classes must be connected to a control class. Similarly, all entity classes must be connected to a control class. Interface classes, unlike the other two, are never connected directly to entity classes.

DEFINING MESSAGES AND METHODS

Each message may be defined using a notation similar to that described for the data dictionary (as shown in Chapter 8). The definition would include a list of the parameters passed with the message as well as the elements contained in the return message. The methods may have logic defined using structured English, a decision table, or a decision tree, as depicted in Chapter 9.

The analyst can use the techniques of horizontal balancing with any class method. All the data returned from an entity class must be obtained either from the attributes stored in the entity class, from the parameters passed on the message sent to the class, or as a result of a calculation performed by the method of the class. The method logic and parameters must be examined to ensure that the method logic has all the information required to complete its work. Horizontal balancing is further described in Chapter 7.

A CLASS EXAMPLE FOR THE WEB

Classes may also be represented using special symbols for entity, boundary (or interface), and control classes. These are called stereotypes, an extension to UML, which are special symbols that may be used during analysis, but are often used when performing object-oriented design. They allow the analyst freedom to play with the design to optimize reusability.

The different types of classes are often used when working in the systems design phase. Figure 18.15 is an example illustrating a sequence diagram representing a student viewing his or her personal and course information. In the diagram, **:View Student User Interface** is an example of an interface class; **:Student, :Section,** and **:Course** are examples of entity classes; and **:View Student Interface Controller** and **:Calculate Grade Point Average** are control classes.

The student is shown on the left as an actor, and he or she provides a **userLogon** to the **:View Student User Interface** class. This is a Web form that obtains the student's user ID and password. When the student clicks the **Submit** button, the Web form is passed to a **:View Student Interface Controller.** This class is responsible for the coordination of sending messages and receiving returned information from all the other classes.

The **:View Student Interface Controller** sends a **getStudent( )** message to the **:Student** class, which reads a database table and proceeds to return the **studentData.**

The **studentWebPage** is returned to the **:View Student User Interface,** which displays the information in the Web browser. At the bottom of the page is a **nextButton** that the student clicks to view courses. When the user clicks this

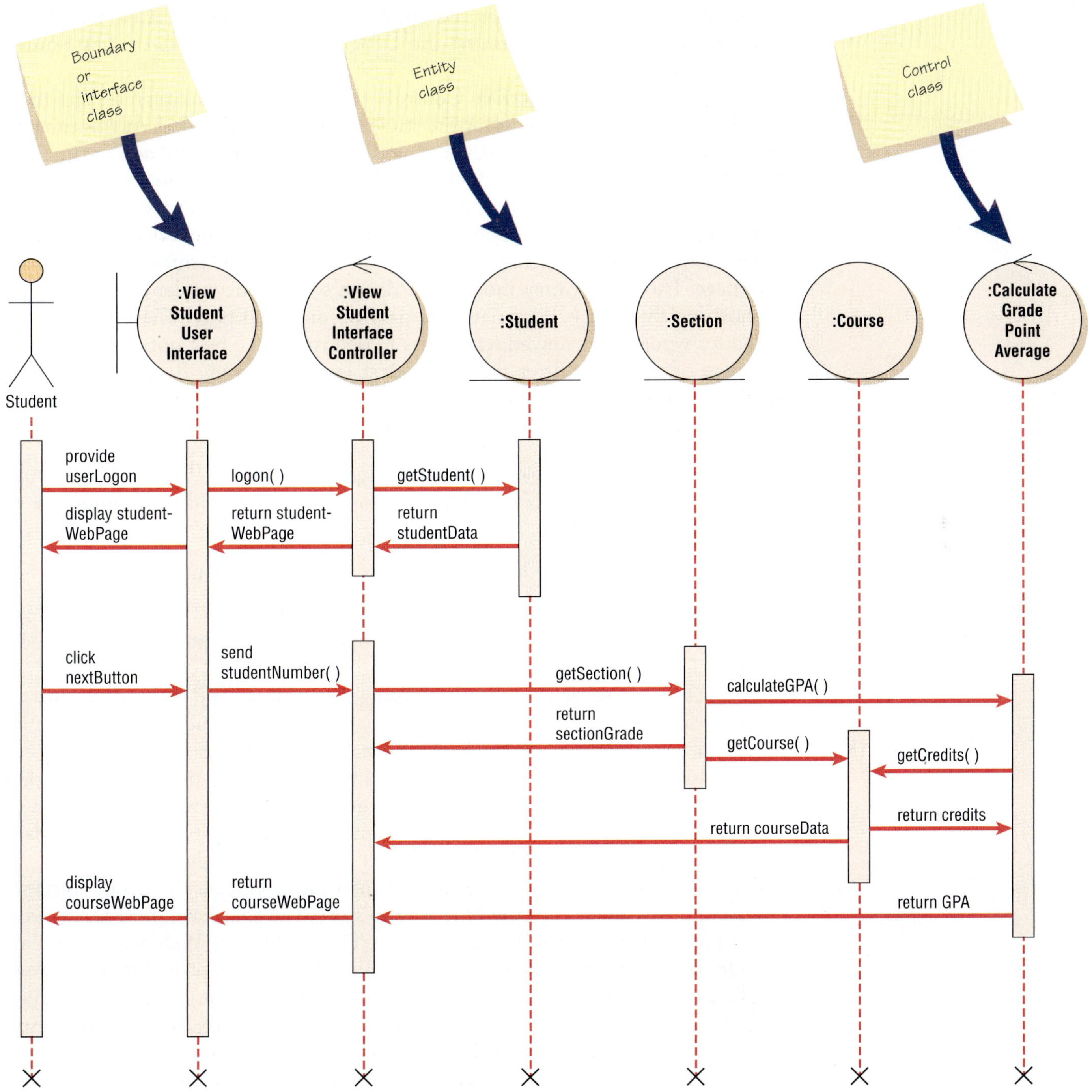

FIGURE 18.15

A sequence diagram for using two Web pages: one for student information, one for course information.

button, it sends a Web form to the **:View Student Interface Controller.** This form contains the **studentNumber( ),** sent along with the **studentWebPage,** and is used to send a message to the **:Section** class to obtain the section grade. If the **studentNumber( )** was not automatically sent, it would mean that the student would have to enter his or her **studentNumber( )** again, which would not be a satisfactory user interface because it involves redundant keying. Notice that the **:Student** class is not involved, and that the focus of control (the vertical bar that is connected to the **:Student** class) ends before the second set of activities (the horizontal arrows pointing to the right) begins. The **:View Student Interface Controller** class sends a **getSection( )** message to the **:Section** class, which returns a **sectionGrade.** The **:Section** class also sends a **calculateGPA( )** message to the **:Calculate Grade Point Average** class, which sends a message back to the **:Course** class. The **:Course** class returns the **credits,** which enables the **:Calculate Grade Point Average** class to determine the GPA and return it to the **:View Student Interface Controller.**

The **:View Student Interface Controller** would repeat sending messages to the **:Section** class until all sections for the student have been included. At this time, the **:View Student Interface Controller** would send the **courseWebPage** to the **:View Student User Interface** class, which would display the information in the browser.

Using the user interface, control, and entity classes also allows the analyst to explore and play with the design. The design mentioned above would display all the student personal information on one page and the course information on a second page. The analyst may modify the design so that the student personal information and the course information appear on one Web page. These two possible scenarios would be reviewed with users to determine the best option.

One of the difficulties for the analyst is to determine how to include the **studentNumber** after clicking the **Next** button, because the **:Student** class is no longer available. There are three ways to store and retransmit data from a Web page:

1. Include the information in the URL displaying in the address or location area of the browser. In this case, the location line might read something like the following:

    http://www.cpu.edu/student/studentinq.html?studentNumber=12345

    Everything after the question mark is data that may be used by the class methods. This means of storing data is easy to implement and is often used in search engines.

    There are several drawbacks to using this method, and the analyst must use due caution. The first concern is privacy—anyone can read the Web address. If the application involves medical information, credit card numbers, and so on, this is not a good choice. Most browsers will also display previous Web address data in subsequent sessions if the user enters the first few characters, and the information may be compromised, leading to identity theft. A second disadvantage is that the data are usually lost after the user closes the browser.
2. Store the information in a cookie, a small file stored on the client (browser) computer. Cookies are the only way to store data that have persistence, existing beyond the current browser session. This enables the Web page to display a message such as "Welcome back, Robin. If you are not Robin, click here." Cookies usually store primary key account numbers, but not credit card numbers or other private information. Cookies are limited to 20 per domain (such as www.cpu.edu) and each cookie must be 4,000 characters or less.

    The analyst must work with other business units to determine who needs to use cookies, and there must be some central control over the names used in the cookies. If the organization needs to have more than 20 cookies, a common solution is to create different domain names used by the organization, such as support.cpu.edu or instruction.cpu.edu.
3. Use hidden Web form fields. These fields usually contain data that are sent by the server, are invisible, and do not occupy any space on the Web page. In the view student information example, the **:View Student Interface Controller** class added a hidden field containing the **studentNumber** to the **studentWebPage** form along with the **nextButton.** When the student clicks the **nextButton,** the **studentNumber** is sent to the server and the **:View Student Interface Controller** knows which student to obtain course and grade information for. The data in hidden forms is not saved from one browser session to another, so privacy is maintained.

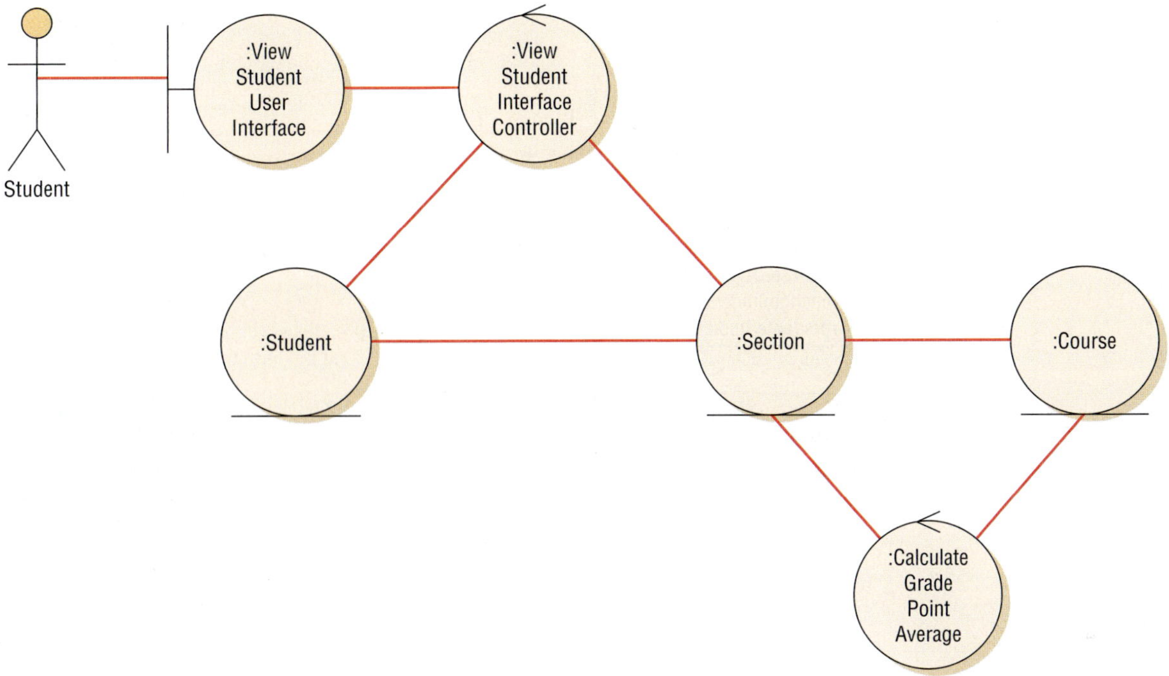

FIGURE 18.16

A class diagram for the **studentWebPage** using special class symbols.

The class symbols also may be used on class and communication diagrams. Figure 18.16 illustrates the class diagram for a student viewing personal and course information on Web pages. Each class has attributes and methods (which are not shown on diagrams using this notation).

If the class is a user interface type of class, the attributes are the controls (or fields) on the screen or form. The methods would be those that work with the screen, such as submit or reset. They might also be JavaScript for a Web page, because the code works directly with the Web page.

If the class is a control class, the attributes would be those needed to implement the class, such as variables used just in the control class. The methods would be those used to perform calculations, make decisions, and send messages to other classes.

If the class is an entity class, the attributes represent those stored for the entity and the methods working directly with the entity, such as creating a new instance, modifying, deleting, obtaining, or printing.

Web sites may use a combination of many different classes to accomplish user objectives. For example, a Web site may use JavaScript to prevalidate data, then pass data to the server control classes, which perform thorough validation, including obtaining data. The server control classes may in turn send JavaScript back to the Web page to do some formatting. It is not uncommon to have a Web application involve many classes, some of them containing only one line of code in a method, in order to achieve the goal of reusability.

RELATIONSHIPS

Relationships are connections between classes, similar to those found on an entity-relationship diagram. These are shown as lines connecting classes on a class diagram. There are two categories of relationships: associations and whole/part relationships.

Associations The simplest type of relationship is an association, or a structural connection between classes or objects. Associations are shown as a simple line on a class diagram. The end points of the line are labeled with a symbol indicating the multiplicity, which is the same as cardinality on an entity-relationship diagram.

FIGURE 18.17

Types of associations that may occur in class diagrams.

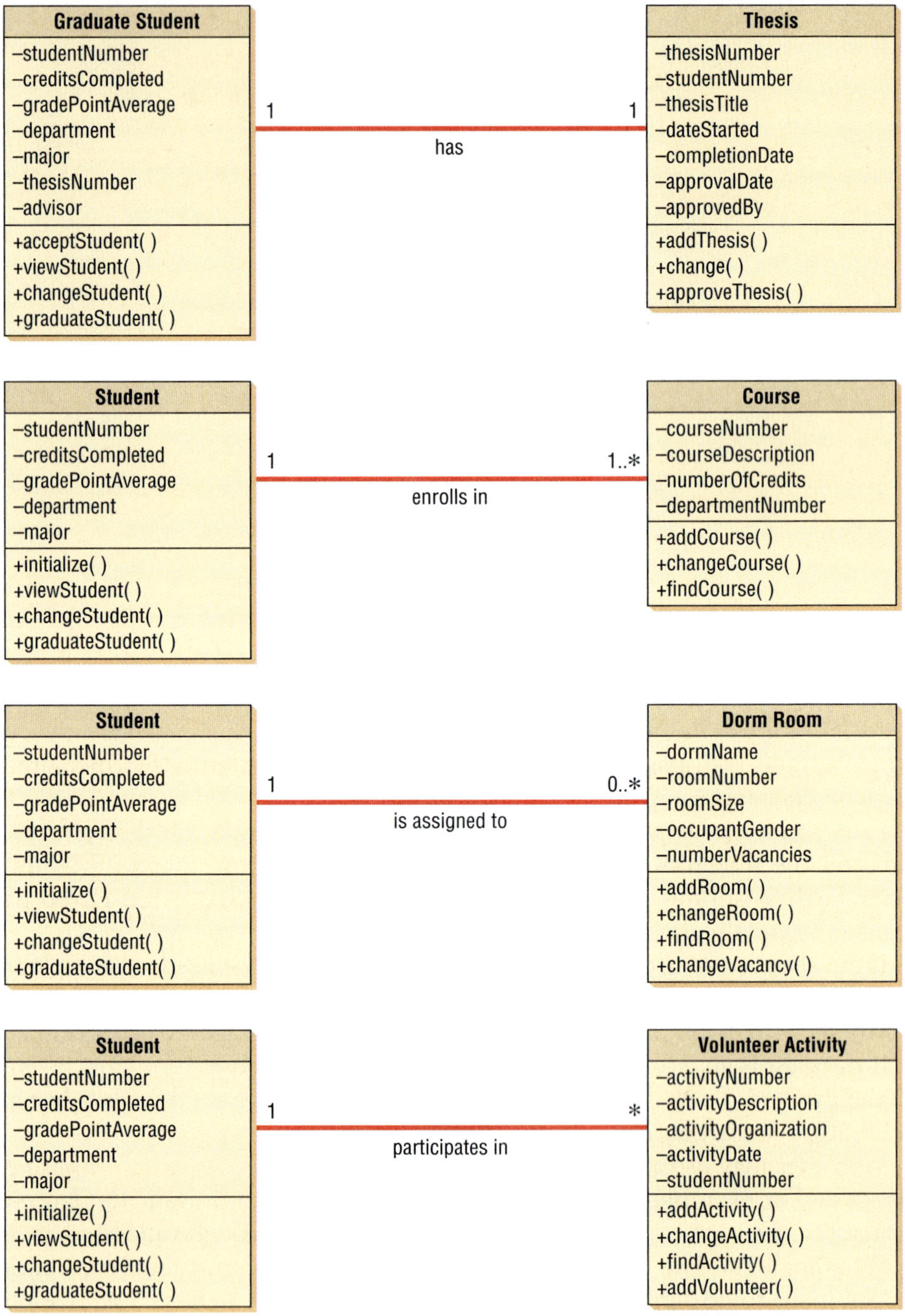

A zero represents none, a one represents one and only one, and an asterisk represents many. The notation 0..1 represents from zero to one, and the notation 1..* represents from one to many. Associations are illustrated in Figure 18.17.

Class diagrams do not restrict the lower limit for an association. For example, an association might be 5..*, indicating that a minimum of five must be present. The same is true for upper limits. For example, the number of courses a student is currently enrolled in may be 1..10, representing from one to 10 courses. It can also include a range of values separated by commas, such as 2, 3, 4. In UML model, associations are usually labeled with a descriptive name.

Association classes are those that are used to break up a many-to-many association between classes. These are similar to associative entities on an entity-relationship diagram. **Student** and **Course** have a many-to-many relationship,

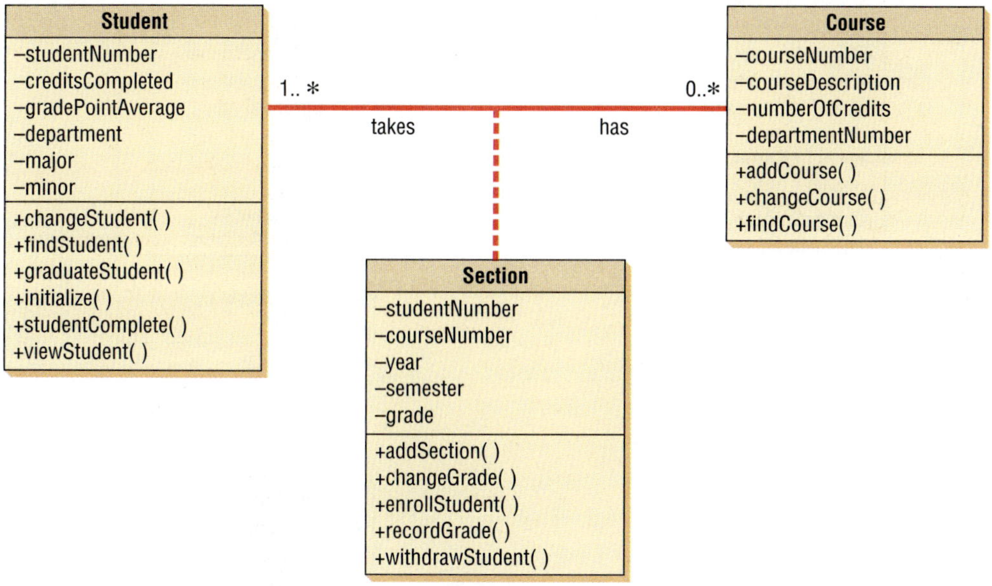

FIGURE 18.18

An example of an associative class in which a particular section defines the relationship between a student and a course.

which is resolved by adding an association class called **Section** between the classes of **Student** and **Course.** Figure 18.18 illustrates an association class called **Section,** shown with a dotted line connected to the many-to-many relationship line.

An object in a class may have a relationship to other objects in the same class, called a reflexive association. An example would be a task having a precedent task, or an employee supervising another employee. This is shown as an association line connecting the class to itself, with labels indicating the role names, such as task and precedent task.

Whole/Part Relationships Whole/part relationships are when one class represents the whole object and other classes represent parts. The whole acts as a container for the parts. These relationships are shown on a class diagram by a line with a diamond on one end. The diamond is connected to the object that is the whole. Whole/part relationships (as well as aggregation, discussed below) are shown in Figure 18.19.

A whole/part relationship may be an entity object that has distinct parts, such as a computer system that includes the computer, printer, display, and so on, or an automobile that has an engine, brake system, transmission, and so on. Whole/part relationships may also be used to describe a user interface, in which one GUI screen contains a series of objects such as lists, boxes, or radio buttons, or perhaps a header, body, and footer area. Whole/part relationships have three categories: aggregation, collection, and composition.

Aggregation. An aggregation is often described as a "has a" relationship. Aggregation provides a means of showing that the whole object is composed of the sum of its parts (other objects). In the student enrollment example, the department *has a* course and the course *is for a* department. This is a weaker relationship, because a department may be changed or removed and the course may still exist. A computer package may not be available any longer, but the printers and other components still exist. The diamond at the end of the relationship line is not filled in.

Collection. A collection consists of a whole and its members. This may be a voting district with voters or a library with books. The voters or books may change, but the whole retains its identity. This is a weak association.

FIGURE 18.19

An example of whole-part and aggregation relationships.

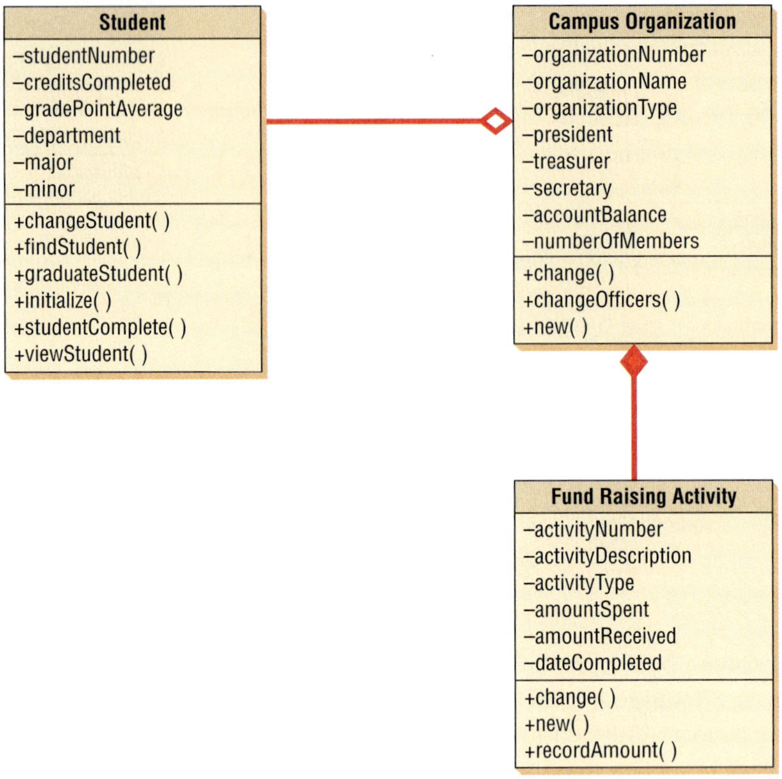

Composition. Composition, a whole/part relationship in which the whole has a responsibility for the part, is stronger relationship, and is usually shown with a filled-in diamond. Keywords for composition are one class "always contains" another class. If the whole is deleted, all parts are deleted. An example would be an insurance policy with riders. If the policy is canceled, the insurance riders are also canceled. In a database, the referential integrity would be set to delete cascading child records. In a university there is a composition relationship between a course and an assignment as well as between a course and an exam. If the course is deleted, assignments and exams are deleted as well.

GENERALIZATION/SPECIALIZATION (GEN/SPEC) DIAGRAMS

A generalization/specialization (gen/spec) diagram falls into the category of a class diagram. Sometimes it is necessary to separate out the generalizations from the specific instances. As we mentioned at the beginning of this chapter, a koala bear is part of a class of marsupials, which is part of a class of animals. Sometimes we need to distinguish whether a koala bear is an animal or a koala bear is a type of animal. Furthermore, a koala bear can be a stuffed toy animal. So we often need to clarify these subtleties.

Generalization A generalization describes a relationship between a general kind of thing and a more specific kind of thing. This type of relationship is often described as an "is a" relationship. For example, a car *is a* vehicle and a truck *is a* vehicle. In this case, vehicle is the general thing, whereas car and truck are the more specific things. Generalization relationships are used for modeling class inheritance and specialization. A general class is sometimes called a superclass, base class, or parent class; a specialized class is called a subclass, derived class, or child class.

Inheritance Several classes may have the same attributes and/or methods. When this occurs, a general class is created containing the common attributes and methods. The specialized class inherits or receives the attributes and methods of the general class. In addition, the specialized class has attributes and methods that are unique and only defined in the specialized class. Creating generalized classes and allowing the specialized class to inherit the attributes and methods helps to foster reuse, because the code is used many times. It also helps to maintain existing program code. This allows the analyst to define attributes and methods once but use them many times, in each inherited class.

One of the special features of the object-oriented approach is the creation and maintenance of large class libraries that are available in multiple languages. So, for instance, a programmer using Java, .NET, or C# will have access to a huge number of classes that have already been developed.

Polymorphism Polymorphism (meaning many forms), or method overriding (not the same as method overloading), is the capability of an object-oriented program to have several versions of the same method with the same name within a superclass/subclass relationship. The subclass inherits a parent method but may add to it or modify it. The subclass may change the type of data, or change how the method works. For example, there might be a customer who receives an additional volume discount, and the method for calculating an order total is modified. The subclass method is said to override the superclass method.

When attributes or methods are defined more than once, the most specific one (the lowest in the class hierarchy) is used. The compiled program walks up the chain of classes, looking for methods.

Abstract Classes Abstract classes are general classes and are used when gen/spec is included in the design. The general class becomes the abstract class. The abstract class has no direct objects or class instances, and is only used in conjunction with specialized classes. Abstract classes usually have attributes and may have a few methods.

Figure 18.20 is an example of a gen/spec class diagram. The arrow points to the general class, or superclass. Often the lines connecting two or more subclasses to a superclass are joined using one arrow pointing to the superclass, but these could be shown as separate arrows as well. Notice that the top level is Person, representing any person. The attributes describe qualities that all people at a university have. The methods allow the class to change the name and the address (including telephone and email address). This is an abstract class, with no instances.

Student and Employee are subclasses, because they have different attributes and methods. An employee does not have a grade point average and a student does not have a salary. This is a simple version, and does not include employees that are students and students that work for the university. If these were added, they would be subclasses of the **Employee** and **Student** classes. **Employee** has two subclasses, **Faculty** and **Administrator,** because there are different attributes and methods for each of these specialized classes.

Subclasses have special verbs to define them. These are often run-on words, using *isa* for "is a," *isakinda* for "is a kind of," and *canbea* for "can be a." There is no distinction between "is a" and "is an;" they both use *isa*.

isa	Faculty *isa* Employee
isakinda	Administrator *isakinda* Employee
canbea	Employee *canbea* Faculty

FIGURE 18.20

A gen/spec diagram is a refined form of a class diagram.

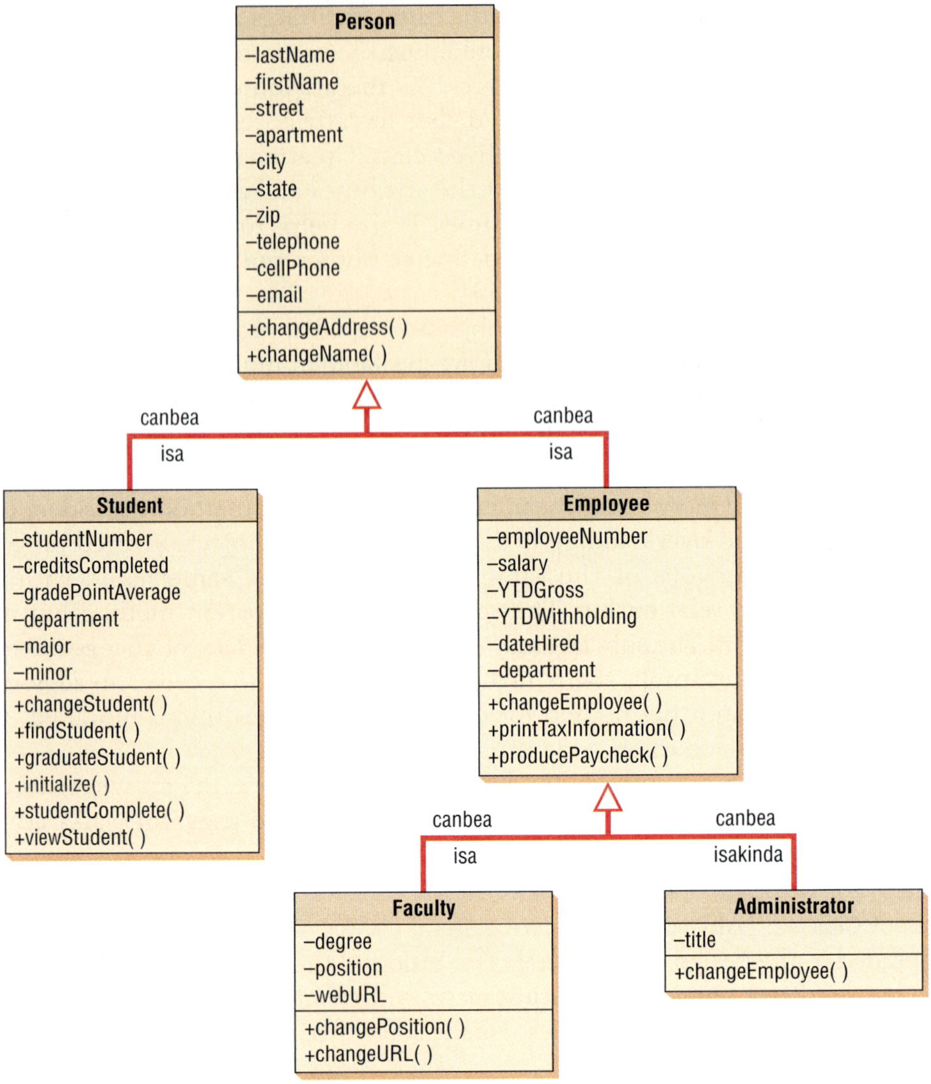

Identifying Abstract Classes You may be able to identify abstract classes by looking to see if a number of classes or database tables have the same elements, or if a number of classes have the same methods. You can create a general class by pulling out the common attributes and methods, or you might create a specialized class for the unique attributes and methods. Using a banking example, a withdrawal, a payment on a loan, or a check written, will all have the same method—they subtract money from the customer balance.

Finding Classes There are a number of ways to determine classes. They may be discovered during interviewing or JAD sessions (described in Chapter 4), during facilitated team sessions, or from brainstorming sessions. Analyzing documents and memos may also reveal classes. One of the easiest ways is to use the CRC method described previously in this chapter. The analyst should also examine use cases, looking for nouns. Each noun may lead to a candidate, or potential, class. They are called candidate classes because some of the nouns may be attributes of a class.

Each class should exist for a distinct object that has a clear definition. Ask what the class knows, the attributes; and what the class knows how to do, the methods. Identify class relationships and the multiplicity for each end of the relationship. If the relationship is many-to-many, create an intersection or associative class, similar to the associative entity in an entity-relationship diagram.

Determining Class Methods The analyst must determine class attributes and methods. Attributes are easy to identify, but the methods that work with the attributes may be more difficult. Some of the methods are standard, and are always associated with a class, such as new( ), or the «create» method, which is an extension to UML created by a person or organization, called a stereotype. The « » symbols are not simply pairs of greater than and less than symbols, but are called guillemots or chevrons.

Another useful way to determine methods is to examine a CRUD matrix (see Chapter 7). Figure 18.21 illustrates a CRUD matrix for course offerings. Each letter requires a different method. If there is a C for create, add a new( ) method. If there is a U for update, add an update( ) or change( ) method. If there is a D for delete, add a delete( ) or remove( ) method. If there is an R for read, add methods for finding, viewing, or printing. In the example shown, the **textbook** class would need a create method to add a textbook, and a read method to initiate a course inquiry, change a textbook, or find a textbook. If a textbook was replaced, an update method would be needed, and if a textbook was removed, a delete method would be required.

Messages In order to accomplish useful work, most classes need to communicate with one another. Information can be sent by an object in one class to an object in another class using a message, similar to a call in a traditional programming language. A message also acts as a command, telling the receiving class to do something. A message consists of the name of the method in the receiving class, as well as the attributes (parameters or arguments) that are passed with the method name. The receiving class must have a method corresponding to the message name.

Activity	Department	Course	Textbook	Assignment	Exam
Add Department	C				
View Department	R				
Add Course	R	C			
Change Course	R	U			
Course Inquiry	R	R	R	R	R
Add Textbook	R	R	C		
Change Textbook		R	RU		
Find Textbook		R	R		
Remove Textbook		R	D		
Add Assignment		R		C	
Change Assignment		R		RU	
View Assignment		R		R	
Add Exam		R			R
Change Exam		R			RU
View Exam		R			R

FIGURE 18.21
A CRUD matrix can be used to help determine what methods are needed. This CRUD matrix is used to determine the methods and operations for course offerings.

Since messages are sent from one class to another, they may be thought of as an output or an input. The first class must supply the parameters included with the message and the second class uses the parameters. If a physical child data flow diagram exists for the problem domain, it may help to discover methods. The data flow from one primitive process to another represents the message, and the primitive processes should be examined as candidate methods.

STATECHART DIAGRAMS

The statechart, or state transition, diagram is another way to determine class methods. It is used to examine the different states that an object may have.

A statechart diagram is created for a single class. Typically objects are created, go through changes, and are deleted or removed.

Objects exist in these various states, which are the conditions of an object at a specific time. An object's attribute values define the state that the object is in, and sometimes there is an attribute, such as Order Status (pending, picking, packaged, shipped, received, and so on) that indicates the state. A state has a name with each word capitalized. The name should be unique and meaningful to the users. A state also has entry and exit actions, the things the object must do every time it enters or leaves a given state.

An event is something that happens at a specific time and place. Events cause a change of the object state, and it is said that a transition "fires." States separate events, such as an order that is waiting to be filled, and events separate states, such as an Order Received event or an Order Complete event.

An event causes the transition, and happens when a guard condition has been met. A guard condition is something that evaluates to either true or false, and may be as simple as "Click to confirm order." It also may be a condition that occurs in a method, such as an item that is out of stock. Guard conditions are shown in square brackets next to the event label.

There are also deferred events, or events that are held until an object changes to a state that can accept them. A user keying something in when a word processor is performing a timed backup is an example of a deferred event. After the timed backup has completed, the text appears in the document.

Events fall into three different categories:

1. Signals or asynchronous messages, which occur when the calling program does not wait for a returning message, such as a feature run from a menu.
2. Synchronous messages, which are calls to functions or subroutines. The calling object stops and waits for control to be returned to it, along with an optional message.
3. Temporal events, which occur at a predetermined time. These usually do not involve an actor or any external event.

Material objects have persistence; that is, they exist for a long period of time. Airplane flights, concerts, and sporting events have shorter persistence (they may have states that transition in a shorter time). Some objects, called transient objects, do not survive the end of a session. These include main memory, Web URL (or location) data, Web pages, CICS displays, and so on. The only way to save transient objects is to store information about them, such as storing Web data in a cookie.

Each time an object changes state, some of the attributes change their values. Furthermore, each time an object's attributes change, there must be a method to change the attributes. Each of the methods would need a display or Web form to add or change the attributes. These become the interface objects. The display or

Web form would often have more controls (or fields) on them than just the attributes that change. They would usually have primary keys, identifying information (such as a name or address), and other attributes that are needed for a good user interface. The exception is a temporal event, which may use database tables or a queue containing the information.

STATE TRANSITION EXAMPLE

Consider a student enrolling at a university and the various states that they would go through. Three of the states are listed below in detail:

State:	Potential Student
Event:	Application Submitted
Method:	new( )
Attributes changed:	Number Name Address
User interface:	Student Application Web Form
State:	Accepted Student
Event:	Requirements Met
Method:	acceptStudent( )
Attributes changed:	Admission Date Student Status Return Acceptance Letter
User interface:	Accept Student Display
State:	Dorm Assigned Student
Event:	Dorm Selected
Method:	assignDorm( )
Attributes changed:	Dorm Name Dorm Room Meal Plan
User interface:	Assign Student Dorm Display

The other states are **Program Student, Current Student, Continuing Student,** and **Graduated Student.** Each state would have an event, methods, attributes changed, and a user interface associated with it. This series of states can be used to determine the attributes and methods that make up part of the class.

The states and events that trigger the changes may be represented on a statechart diagram (or a state transition diagram). The statechart diagram for **Student** is illustrated in Figure 18.22. States are represented by rectangles, and events or activities are the arrows that link the states and cause one state to change to another state. Transition events are named in the past tense, because they have already occurred to create the transition.

Statechart diagrams are not created for all classes. They are created when:

1. A class has a complex life cycle.
2. An instance of a class may update its attributes in a number of ways through the life cycle.
3. A class has an operational life cycle.
4. Two classes depend on each other.
5. The object's current behavior depends on what happened previously.

When you examine a statechart diagram, use the opportunity to look for errors and exceptions. Inspect the diagram to see whether events are happening at the wrong time. Also check that all events and states have been represented. Statechart

FIGURE 18.22
A statechart diagram showing how a student progresses from a potential student to a graduated student.

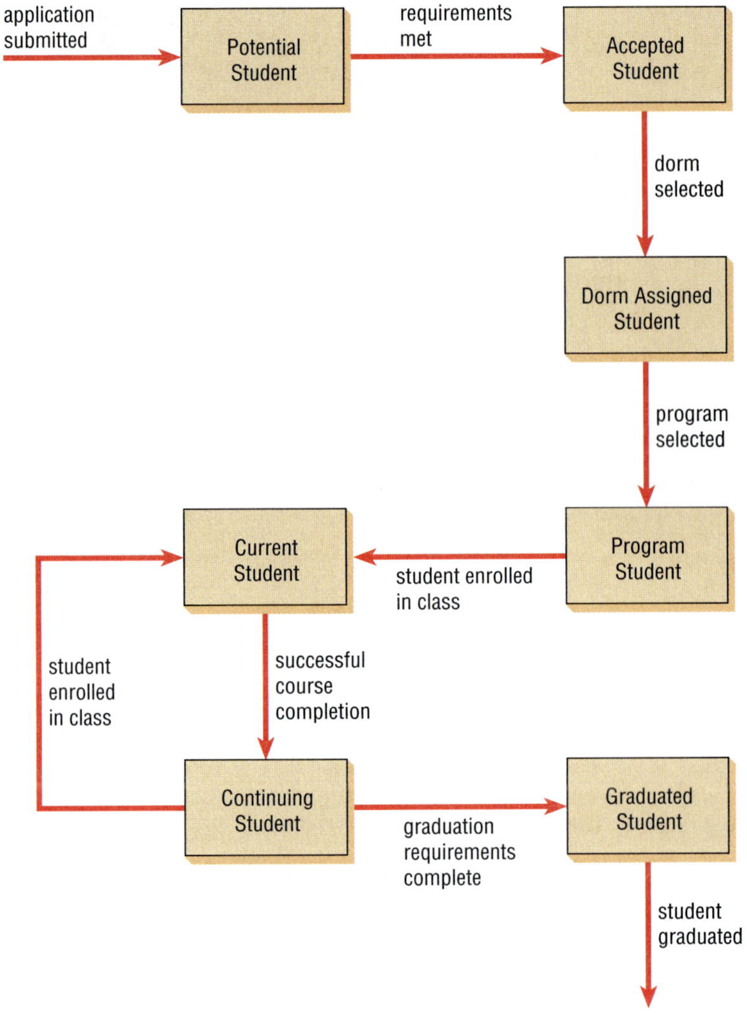

diagrams have only two problems to avoid. Check to see that a state does not have all transitions going into the state or all transitions coming out of the state.

Each state should have at least one transition in and out of it. Some statechart diagrams use the same start and terminator symbols that an activity diagram uses: a filled-in circle to represent the start, and concentric circles with the center filled in to signify the end of the diagram.

PACKAGES AND OTHER UML ARTIFACTS

Packages are containers for other UML things, such as use cases or classes. Packages can show system partitioning, indicating which classes or use cases are grouped into a subsystem, called logical packages. They may also be component packages, which contain physical system components, or use case packages, containing a group of use cases. Packages use a folder symbol with the package name either in the folder tab or centered in the folder. Packaging can occur during systems analysis, or later when the system is being designed. Packages may also have relationships, similar to class diagrams, which may include associations and inheritance.

Figure 18.23 is an example of a use case package diagram. It shows that four use cases, **Add Student, Enroll in Class, Transfer Credits,** and **View Student Information,** are part of the **Student** package. There are three use cases, **Add**

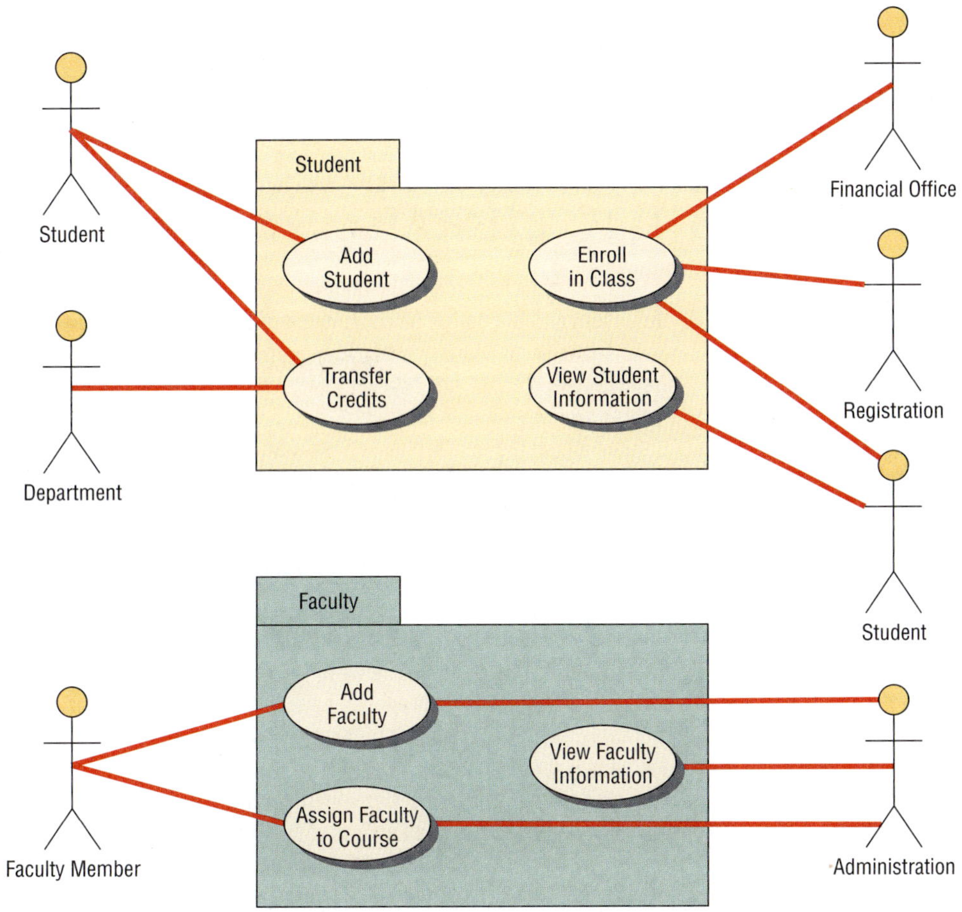

FIGURE 18.23

Use cases can be grouped into packages.

Faculty, View Faculty Information, and **Assign Faculty to Course,** that are part of the **Faculty** package.

As you continue constructing diagrams, you will want to make use of component diagrams, deployment diagrams, and annotational things. These permit different perspectives on the work being accomplished.

The component diagram is similar to a class diagram, but is more of a bird's-eye view of the system architecture. The component diagram shows the components of the system, such as a class file, a package, shared libraries, a database, and so on, and how they are related to each other. The individual components in a component diagram are considered in more detail within other UML diagrams, such as class diagrams and use case diagrams.

The deployment diagram illustrates the physical implementation of the system, including the hardware, the relationships between the hardware, and the system on which it is deployed. The deployment diagram may show servers, workstations, printers, and so on.

Annotational things give developers more information about the system. These consist of notes that can be attached to anything in UML: objects, behaviors, relationships, diagrams, or anything that requires detailed descriptions, assumptions, or any information relevant to the design and functionality of the system. The success of UML relies on the complete and accurate documentation of your system model to provide as much information as possible to the development team. Notes provide a source of common knowledge and understanding about your system to help put your developers on the same page. Notes are shown as a paper symbol with a bent corner and a line connecting them to the area that needs elaboration.

CONSULTING OPPORTUNITY 18.3

DEVELOPING A FINE SYSTEM THAT WAS LONG OVERDUE: USING OBJECT-ORIENTED ANALYSIS FOR THE RUMINSKI PUBLIC LIBRARY SYSTEM*

As Dewey Dezmal enters the high-ceilinged, wood-paneled reading room of the Ruminski Public Library, a young woman, seated at a long, oak table, pokes her head out from behind a monitor, sees him and stands, saying, "Welcome. I'm Peri Otticle, the director of the library. I understand you are here to help us develop our new information system."

Still in awe of the beauty of the old library building and the juxtaposition of so much technology amid so much history, Dewey introduces himself as a systems analyst with a small IT consulting firm, People and Objects, Inc.

"It's the first time I've been assigned to this type of project, although it's actually interesting for me, because my degree is from the Information Studies School at Upstate University. You can major in library science or IT there, so lots of my classmates went on to work in public libraries. I opted for the IT degree."

"We should work well together, then," Peri says. "Let's go to my office so we don't disturb any patrons, and I can talk you through a report I wrote."

As they pass the beautiful, winding staircase seemingly sculpted in wood, Peri notices Dewey looking at the surroundings and says, "You may wonder about the grandeur of the building, because we are a public institution. We are fortunate. Our benefactor is Valerian Ruminski. In fact, he has donated so much money to so many libraries that the staff affectionately calls him 'Valerian the Librarian.'

As they pass several patrons, Peri continues, "As you can see, it's a very busy place. And, regardless of our old surroundings, we don't dwell in the past."

Dewey reads the report Peri has handed him. One large section is titled "Summary of Patrons' Main Requirements," and the bulleted list states:

- A library patron who is registered in the system can borrow books and magazines from the system.
- The library system should periodically check (at least once per week) whether a copy of a book or journal borrowed by a patron has become overdue. If so, a notice will be sent to the patron.
- A patron can reserve a book or journal that has been lent out or is in the process of purchase. The reservation should be canceled when the patron checks out the book or journal or through a formal canceling service.

As Dewey looks up from the report, he says to Peri, "I'm beginning to understand the patron (or user) requirements. I see lots of similarities between my old university library and yours. One item I didn't see covered, though, was how you decide what the library should collect and what it should get rid of."

Peri chuckles and replies, "That's an insightful question. The library staff handles the purchase of new books and journals for the library. If something is popular, more than two copies are purchased. We can create, update, and delete information about titles and copies of books and journals, patrons, loan of materials, and reservations in the system."

Dewey looks up from his note pad and says, "I'm still a little confused. What's the difference between the terms *title* and *copy*?"

Peri responds, "The library can have several copies of a title. Title normally refers to the name of a book or journal. Copies of a title are actually lent out from the library."

Based on Dewey's interview with Peri and the requirements description in her report, as well as your own experience using library services, use UML to answer the following questions. (*Note:* It is important to make sure your solutions are logical and workable. State your assumptions clearly whenever necessary.)

1. Draw a use case diagram to represent actors and use cases in the system.
2. For each use case, describe the steps (as we did to organize the use cases).
3. Describe scenarios for the steps. In other words, create a patron and write up an example of the patron as he or she goes through each step.
4. Develop a list of things.
5. Create sequence diagrams for use cases based on steps and scenarios.
6. Complete the class diagram by determining relationships between classes and defining the attributes and methods of each class. Use the grouping thing called package to simplify the class diagram.

*Based on a problem written by Dr. Wayne Huang.

PUTTING UML TO WORK

The unified modeling language provides a useful toolset for systems analysis and design. As with any product created with the help of tools, the value of UML deliverables in a project depends on the expertise with which the systems analyst wields the tools. The analyst will initially use UML toolset to break down the system requirements into a use case model and an object model. The use case model describes the use cases and actors. The object model describes the objects and object associations, and the responsibilities, collaborators, and attributes of the objects.

1. Define the use case model.
   - Find the actors in the problem domain by reviewing the system requirements and interviewing some business experts.
   - Identify the major events initiated by the actors, and develop a set of primary use cases at a very high level that describe the events from the perspective of each actor.
   - Develop the use case diagrams to provide understanding of how the actors relate to the use cases that will define the system.
   - Refine the primary use cases to develop a detailed description of system functionality for each primary use case. Provide additional details by developing the use case scenarios that document the alternate flows of the primary use cases.
   - Review the use case scenarios with the business area experts to verify processes and interactions. Make modifications as necessary until the business area experts agree that the use case scenarios are complete and accurate.
2. Continue UML diagramming to model the system during the systems analysis phase.
   - Derive activity diagrams from use case diagrams.
   - Develop sequence and communication diagrams from use case scenarios.
   - Review the sequence diagrams with the business area experts to verify processes and interactions. Make modifications as necessary until the business area experts agree that the sequence diagrams are complete and accurate. This additional review of the graphical sequence diagrams often provides the business area experts an opportunity to rethink and refine processes in more atomic detail than the review of the use case scenarios.
3. Develop the class diagrams.
   - Look for nouns in use cases and list them. They are potential objects. Once you identify the objects, look for similarities and differences in the objects due to the objects' states or behavior, and then create classes.
   - Define the major relationships between the classes. Look for "has a" and "is a" relationships between classes.
   - Examine use case and sequence diagrams in order to determine classes.
   - Beginning with the use cases that are the most important to the system design, create class diagrams that show the classes and relationships that exist in the use cases. One class diagram may represent the classes and relationships described in several related use cases.
4. Draw statechart diagrams.
   - Develop statechart diagrams for certain class diagrams to provide further analysis of the system at this point. Use statechart diagrams to aid in understanding complex processes that cannot be fully derived by the sequence diagrams.
   - Determine methods by examining statechart diagrams. Derive state (data) class attributes from use cases, business area experts, and class methods. Indicate whether the methods and attributes of the class are public (accessible externally) or private (internal to the class). The statechart diagrams are extremely useful in modifying class diagrams.

5. Begin systems design by refining UML diagrams, and using them to derive classes and their attributes and methods.
   - Review all existing UML diagrams for the system. Write class specifications for each class that include the class attributes, methods, and their descriptions. Review sequence diagrams to identify other class methods.
   - Develop methods specifications that detail the input and output requirements for the method, along with a detailed description of the internal processing of the method.
   - Create another set of sequence diagrams (if necessary) to reflect the actual class methods and interactions with each other and the system interfaces.
   - Create class diagrams using the specialized class symbols for boundary or interface class, entity class, and control class.
   - Analyze the class diagrams to derive the system components; that is, functionally and logically related classes that will be compiled and deployed together as a .DLL, a .COM object, a Java Bean, a package, and so forth.
   - Develop deployment diagrams to indicate how your system components will be deployed in the production environment.
6. Document your system design in detail. This step is critical. The more complete the information you provide the development team through documentation and UML diagrams, the faster the development and the more solid the final production system.

THE IMPORTANCE OF USING UML FOR MODELING

UML is a powerful tool that can greatly improve the quality of your systems analysis and design, and it is hoped that the improved practices will translate into higher-quality systems.

By using UML iteratively in analysis and design, you can achieve a greater understanding between the business team and the IT team regarding the system requirements and the processes that need to occur in the system to meet those requirements.

The first iteration of analysis should be at a very high level to identify the overall system objectives and validate the requirements through use case analysis. Identifying the actors and defining the initial use case model are part of this first iteration. Subsequent iterations of analysis further refine the system requirements through the development of use case scenarios, class diagrams, sequence diagrams, statechart diagrams, and so on. Each iteration takes a successively more detailed look at the design of the system until the things and relationships in the system are clearly and precisely defined in UML documents.

When your analysis and design are complete, you should have an accurate and detailed set of specifications for the classes, scenarios, activities, and sequencing in the system. In general, you can relate the thoroughness of the analysis and design of a system to the amount of time required to develop the system and the resultant quality of the delivered product.

Often overlooked in the development of a new system is that the further a project progresses, the costlier the changes are to the business requirements of a system. Changing the design of a system using a CASE tool, or even on paper, during the analysis and design phases of a project is easier, faster, and much less expensive than doing so during the development phase of the project.

CONSULTING OPPORTUNITY 18.4

C-SHORE++

"They want the core of the customer service representative's user interface to be radically reprogrammed again!" says Bradley Vargo, the Information Systems Development Director at C-Shore Mutual Funds. "Only eight months ago, we completed a two-year development project of the Customer Service Representative System, CSR. During that entire project, we endured a parade of moving requirements. Every month, those guys in the Marketing Department would invent some competitive new customer service feature, and within a week, the CSR group would be down here with vast changes to the CSR System specifications. I thought we'd never finish that project! Now it looks as if we will have to start a new reprogramming project on a system less than a year old. We had forecast this system for a seven-year lifespan! Now I think it may be going into eternal reconstruction."

Bradley is talking with Rachael Ciupek, the senior application systems analyst responsible for the CSR system, and Bridget Ciupek, her sister and the programmer who wrote most of the user interface. "Calm down, Bradley," says Rachael. "It is not the fault of the kids in Marketing or CSR. The nature of our business has been affected by fast-paced competition. Marketing doesn't invent these changes out of boredom. They are often responding to new, computer-based customer services offered by our competition. We have to stay ahead or at least keep up, or we'll all be looking for new jobs!"

"Bradley, Rachael, I think you better know that the situation may be worse than you think," Bridget chips in. "The programmers have actually been making small changes in the CSR user interface for the past eight months anyway. The CSR users have been calling us directly and begging for help. They usually want just a small change to one isolated part of the system, but that has created a high labor drain because we have to recertify the entire system. You know how the effects of a small change can ripple through a large program. We've billed the time to program maintenance on the grounds that we thought we were just fine-tuning the completed system. Although the changes have been gradual, in eight months we've pretty much rewritten about a quarter of the CSR user interface code already. The work has not been falling off. It's still pretty steady."

"So what you're telling me," says Bradley, "is that we have system needs in this area that have been changing constantly while we tried to write specifications, tried to write program code, and tried to make a fixed solution work against a fluid problem. How can we afford to write programs if they will only last a few months without needing expensive maintenance?"

How can Bradley manage a systems development process that no longer has fixed or constant business processes as part of its goal set? Is there a way for Rachael to manage specification and control maintenance costs when programmers are constantly asked to tinker with isolated parts of a large program? Keep in mind that an important goal is to provide good support for the users' needs and the organization's business strategies.

Unfortunately, some employers are shortsighted, believing that only when a programmer or analyst is coding is that employee actually working. Some employers erroneously assume that programmer productivity can be judged solely by the amount of code produced, without recognizing that diagramming ultimately saves time and money that might otherwise be wasted if a project is prototyped without proper planning.

An analogy to building a house is very apt in this situation. Although you hire a builder to build a house, you do not want to live in a structure built without planning, one in which rooms and features are randomly added without regard to function or cost. You want a builder to build your agreed-upon design from blueprints containing specifications that have been carefully reviewed by everyone concerned. As a member of an analyst team so accurately observed, "Putting a project on paper before coding will wind up costing less in the long run. It's much cheaper to erase a diagram than it is to change coding."

When business requirements change during the analysis phase, you may have to redraw some UML diagrams. If the business requirements change during the development phase, however, a substantial amount of time and expense may be required to redesign, recode, and retest the system. By confirming your analysis and design on paper (especially through the use of UML diagrams) with users who are business area experts, you help to ensure that correct business requirements will be met when the system is completed.

SUMMARY

Object-oriented systems describe entities as objects. Objects are part of a general concept called classes, the main unit of analysis in object-oriented analysis and design. When the object-oriented approach was first introduced, advocates cited reusability of the objects as the main benefit of their approach. Although reusability is the main goal, maintaining systems is also very important.

Analysts can use CRC cards to begin the process of object modeling in an informal way. Object think can be added to the CRC cards to assist the analyst in refining responsibilities into smaller and smaller tasks. CRC sessions can be held with a group of analysts to determine classes and responsibilities interactively.

Unified modeling language (UML) provides a standardized set of tools to document the analysis and design of a software system. UML is fundamentally based on an object-oriented technique known as use case modeling. A use case model describes *what* a system does without describing *how* the system does it. A use case model partitions system functionality into behaviors (called use cases) that are significant to the users of the system (called actors). Different scenarios are created for each different set of conditions of a use case.

The main components of UML are things, relationships, and diagrams. Diagrams are related to one another. Structural things are most common; they include classes, interfaces, use cases, and many other elements that provide a way to create models. Structural things allow the user to describe relationships. Behavioral things describe how things work. Group things are used to define boundaries. Annotational things permit the analyst to add notes to the diagrams.

Relationships are the glue that holds the things together. Structural relationships are used to tie the things together in structural diagrams. Structural relationships include dependencies, aggregations, associations, and generalizations. Behavioral diagrams use the four basic types of behavioral relationships: communicates, includes, extends, and generalizes.

The toolset of UML is composed of UML diagrams. They include use case diagrams, activity diagrams, sequence diagrams, communication diagrams, class diagrams, and statechart diagrams. In addition to the diagrams, analysts can describe a use case using a use case scenario.

By using UML iteratively in analysis and design, you can achieve a greater understanding between the business team and the IT team regarding the system requirements and the processes that need to occur in the system to meet those requirements.

KEYWORDS AND PHRASES

abstract class
activity diagram
actor
aggregation
annotational thing
association
asynchronous message
boundary class
branch
class
class diagram
collaboration
communication diagram
control class
CRC cards
dependencies
deployment diagram
entity class
event
fork
generalization/specialization (gen/spec)

happy path
inheritance
join
main path
merge
message
method overloading
method overriding
object
object-oriented
package
polymorphism
primary use case
relationship
sequence diagram
state
statechart diagram
swimlane
synchronization bar
synchronous message
temporal event
unified modeling language (UML)
unified process
use case diagram
use case scenario
whole/part structure

REVIEW QUESTIONS

1. List two reasons for taking an object-oriented approach to systems development.
2. Describe the difference between a class and an object.
3. Explain the concept of inheritance in object-oriented systems.
4. What does CRC stand for?
5. Describe what Object Think adds to the CRC card.
6. What is UML?
7. What are the three major elements of UML?
8. List what the concept of structural things includes.
9. List what the concept of behavioral things includes.
10. What are the two main types of diagrams in UML?
11. List the diagrams included in structural diagrams.
12. List the diagrams included in behavioral diagrams.
13. What is it that a use case model describes?
14. Would you describe a use case model as a logical or physical model of the system? Defend your answer in a paragraph.
15. Define what an actor is in a use case diagram.
16. What three things must a use case always describe?
17. What does an activity diagram depict?
18. Write a paragraph that describes the use of swimlanes on activity diagrams.
19. What can be depicted on a sequence or communication diagram?
20. Why is defining classes such an important object-oriented analysis task?
21. What can be shown on a class diagram?
22. Define method overloading.
23. List the four categories into which classes fall.
24. What are the two categories of relationships between classes?
25. What are gen/spec diagrams used for?
26. What is another term for polymorphism?
27. What is depicted by a statechart diagram?
28. What is a package in UML approach?
29. Why is using UML for modeling important?

PROBLEMS

1. Create a series of CRC cards for World's Trend Catalog Division. Once an order is placed, the order fulfillment crew takes over and checks for availability, fills the order, and calculates the total amount of the order. Use five CRC cards, one for each of the following classes: order, order fulfillment, inventory,

product, and customer. Complete the section on classes, responsibilities, and collaborators.

2. Finish the CRC cards in Problem 1 by creating Object Think statements and property names for each of the five classes.
3. Draw a use case diagram for World's Trend Catalog Division.
4. For the FilmMagic problem in Consulting Opportunity 18.1, draw a class diagram in UML.
5. For the FilmMagic problem in Consulting Opportunity 18.1, draw statechart diagrams for (a) **Customer** and (b) **Video.**
6. Draw four pictures showing examples of four types of behavioral relationships for Joel Porter's BMW automobile dealership. What type of relationship is involved when a customer must arrange financing? Are there common activities involved when a person either leases or buys an automobile? What type of relationship is between an employee that is a manager or one that is a salesperson?
7. Draw a communication diagram for a student taking a course from a teacher, who is part of the faculty.
8. Coleman County has a phone exchange that handles calls between callers and those receiving the call. Given these three actors, draw a simple sequence diagram for making a simple phone call.
9. You are ready to begin UML modeling for the Kirt Clinic. Draw a class diagram that includes a physician, a patient, an appointment, and a patient's bill. Do not get the insurance company involved.
10. Use UML to draw examples of the four structural relationships for the Kirt Clinic.
11. Write a sample use case scenario for a patient who sees a physician in the Kirt Clinic.
12. Woody's Supermarket, a small chain of grocery stores, is building a Web site to allow customers to place orders for groceries and other items they sell. The customer places a Web order, the customer master is updated, and an order record created. The order prints at a local store, and the goods are picked from the shelves by the store employees. Customers are sent an email notification that their order is ready. When they pick up the order, frozen goods, chilled products, and other items are assembled. Draw an activity diagram showing the customer using the Web site to place an order, verification of the order, order confirmation, order details sent to the local store, and a customer email sent to the customer.
13. Sludge's Auto was introduced in Chapter 12 as an auto parts recycling center, using Ajax on Web sites for customers to browse for parts. The customer needs to know the make, model, and year of a car as well as the part. If the part is in stock, the description, condition of the part, price, and shipping cost are displayed, with the quantity available for each condition of the part, along with a picture of the part. Draw a sequence diagram using boundary, control, and entity classes for the Auto Part Query for Sludge's Auto.
14. Musixscore.com is an online service providing sheet music to customers. On the "browse music" Web page, customers select a genre of music from a drop-down list. The Web page uses Ajax to obtain a list of performers, musicians, or groups that match the genre, which is formatted as a drop-down list. When a selection is made from the performers drop-down list, the Web page uses Ajax to display a third drop-down list displaying all of the CDs or other works of the performer. When a CD is selected, the Web page uses Ajax to obtain all the songs on the CD in a fourth drop-down list. The viewer may make multiple selections. When the **Add To Shopping Cart** image is clicked, the songs

are added to the shopping cart. The viewer may change any of the drop-down lists to select additional sheet music, and the process is repeated.

a. Write a use case description for the Browse Music Score use case, representing this activity.
b. Draw a sequence diagram using boundary, control, and entity classes for the Musixscore Web page.
c. Write a list of the messages, names and the parameters, along with the data types, that would be passed to the classes and the values (with data types) that are included with the return message. Make any assumptions you need about the data.
d. Create a class diagram for the entity classes used in the sequence diagram.

SELECTED BIBLIOGRAPHY

Beck, K., and W. Cunningham. "Laboratory for Teaching Object-Oriented Thinking," OOPSLA'89, as quoted in D. Butler, CRC Card Session Tutorial. Available: <www.csc.calpoly.edu/~dbutler/tutorials/winter96/crc_b/tutorial.html>. Last accessed, February 6, 2001.

Bellin, D., and S. Suchman Simone. *The CRC Card Book*. Reading, MA: Addison-Wesley Longman, 1997.

Booch, G., I. Jacobson, and J. Rumbaugh. *The Unified Modeling Language User Guide,* 2d ed. Boston: Addison-Wesley Publishing Co., 1999.

Cockburn, A. *Writing Effective Use Cases.* Boston: Addison-Wesley Publishing Co., 2001.

Dobing, B., and J. Parsons. "How UML Is Used." *Communications of the ACM,* Vol. 49, No. 5, May 2006, pp. 109–113.

Fowler, M., and K. Scott. *UML Distilled: A Brief Guide to the Standard Object Modeling Language,* 2d ed. Boston: Addison-Wesley Publishing Co., 2000.

Kulak, D., and E. Guiney. *Use Cases: Requirements in Context*, 2d ed. Boston: Pearson Education, 2004.

Miles, R., and K. Hamilton. *Learning UML 2.0*. Cambridge, MA: 2006.

Sahraoudi, A.E.K., and T. Blum. "Using Object-Oriented Methods in a System Lifecycle Process Model." ACM SIGSOFT Software Engineering Notes, Vol. 28, No. 2, March 2003.

Unified Modeling Language Notation Guide ad/97–01–09. Santa Clara, CA: Rational Software Corporation, 1997.

GLOSSARY

Numbers in parentheses refer to the chapter in which that term is defined.

ACTOR In UML, a particular role of a user of the system. The actor exists outside the system and interacts with the system in a specific way. An actor can be a human, another system, or a device such as a keyboard or a modem. (18) *See also* use case.

AGGREGATION Often described as "has a" relationship when using UML for an object-oriented approach. Aggregations provide a means of showing that the whole object is composed of the sum of its parts (other objects). (18)

AGILE APPROACH (OR AGILE MODELING) A systems development approach that is similar to extreme programming, which has values, principles, and practices useful for systems analysts. (6)

AJAX A method using JavaScript and XML to dynamically change Web pages without displaying a new page by obtaining small amounts of data from the server. (12)

ALIAS Alternative name for a data element used by different users. Recorded in a data dictionary. (8)

APPLICATION SERVICE PROVIDER (ASP) A company that hosts application software, which is leased by other organizations for use on the Web. Applications include traditional ones as well as collaboration and data management. (17)

ASSOCIATIVE ENTITY An entity type that associates the instances of one or more entity types and contains attributes that are peculiar to the relationship between those entity instances. (2)

ATTRIBUTE Some characteristic of an entity. There can be many attributes for each entity. (13) *See also* data item.

ATTRIBUTIVE ENTITY One of the types of entities used in entity-relationship diagrams. Something useful in describing attributes, especially repeating groups. (2)

BEHAVIOR How an object acts and reacts. (18)

BIPOLAR QUESTION A subset of closed questions that can be answered in two ways only, such as yes or no, true or false, and agree or disagree. (4) *See also* closed question, open-ended question.

BROWSER Special software that runs on an Internet-connected computer enabling users to view hypertext-based Web pages on the Internet. Microsoft Internet Explorer and Netscape Communicator are examples of graphical browsers. (11)

BUBBLE DIAGRAM A simple diagram that shows data associations of data elements. Each entity is enclosed in an ellipse, and arrows are used to show the relationships. Also called a data model diagram. (13)

BUSINESS RULES Statements specific to an organization's functioning that provide a logical description of business activities. Used to help create data flow diagrams. (7)

CASE TOOLS Computer-aided software engineering tools that include computer-based automated diagramming, analyzing, and modeling capabilities.

CHILD DIAGRAM The diagram that results from exploding the process on Diagram 0 (called the parent process). (7)

CLASS A common template for a group of individual objects with common attributes and common behavior in object-oriented analysis and design and UML. (18)

CLASS DIAGRAM Used to graphically model the static structural design view of a system; illustrates the functional requirements of the system gathered by way of analysis, as well as the physical design of the system. (18)

CLIENT/SERVER ARCHITECTURE A design model that features applications running on a local area network (LAN). Computers on the network divide processing tasks among servers and clients. Clients are networked machines that are points of entry into the client/server system. (17)

CLOSED QUESTION A type of question used in interviews or on surveys that closes the possible response set available to respondents. (4) *See also* bipolar question, open-ended question.

CLOSED SYSTEM Part of general systems theory; a system that does not receive information, energy, people, or raw materials as input. Systems are never totally closed or totally open, but exist on a continuum from more closed to more open. (2) *See also* open system.

COMMAND LANGUAGE INTERFACE A type of interface that allows users to control the application with a series of keystrokes, commands, phrases, or some sequence of these three methods. (14)

COMPUTER-AIDED SOFTWARE ENGINEERING (CASE) Specialized software tools that include computer-based automated diagramming, analyzing, and modeling capabilities. (1) *See also* lower CASE tools.

CONTEXT-LEVEL DATA FLOW DIAGRAM The most basic data flow diagram of an organization showing how processes transform incoming data into outgoing information. Also called an environmental model. (2) *See also* data flow diagram.

CONTROL FLAG Used in structure charts to govern which portion of a module is to be executed, associated with IF, THEN, ELSE, and other similar types of statements. (16)

CONVERSION Physically converting the old information system to the new one. There are five conversion strategies: direct changeover, parallel conversion, phased or gradual conversion, modular prototype conversion, and distributed conversion. (17)

CRC CARDS The analyst creates Class, Responsibilities, and Collaborators cards to represent the responsibilities of classes and the interaction between the classes when beginning to model the system from an object-oriented perspective. Analysts create the cards based on scenarios that outline system requirements. (18)

CRITICAL PATH The longest path calculated using the PERT scheduling technique; the path that will cause the whole systems project to fall behind if even one day's delay is encountered on it. (3)

DASHBOARD Display for decision makers including a variety of displays of relevant performance measurements. (11)

DATA COUPLE Depiction of the passing of data between two modules on a structure chart. (16)

DATA DICTIONARY A reference work of data about data (metadata) created by the systems analyst based on data flow diagrams; collects and coordinates specific data terms, confirming what each term means to different people in the organization. (8)

DATA ELEMENT A simple piece of data, can be base or derived; should be defined in the data dictionary. (8)

DATA FLOW Data that move in the system from one place to another; input and output are depicted using an arrow with an arrowhead in data flow diagrams. (7)

DATA FLOW DIAGRAM (DFD) Graphical depiction of data processes, data flows, and data stores in a business system. (7)

DATA ITEM The smallest unit in a file or database. Used interchangeably with the word *attribute*. (13)

DATA MINING Techniques that apply algorithms for extracting patterns from data stored in data warehouses that are typically not apparent to human decision makers. Also known as knowledge data discovery (KDD). (14)

DATA REPOSITORY A centralized database that contains all diagrams, form and report definitions, data structures, data definitions, process flows and logic, and definitions of other organizational and system components; provides a set of mechanisms and structures to achieve seamless data-to-tool and data-to-data integration. (8)

DATA STORE Data that are at rest in the system; depicted using an open-ended rectangle in data flow diagrams. (7)

DATA STRUCTURE Structures composed of data elements, typically described using algebraic notation to produce a view of the elements. The analyst begins with the logical design and then designs the physical data structures. (8)

DATA WAREHOUSE A collection of data in support of management decision processes that is subject oriented, integrated, time variant, and nonvolatile. (14) *See also* data mining.

DATABASE A formally defined and centrally controlled store of electronic data intended for use in many different applications. (13)

DATABASE MANAGEMENT SYSTEM (DBMS) Software that organizes data in a database providing information storage, organization, and retrieval capacities. (13)

DECISION SUPPORT SYSTEM (DSS) An interactive information system that supports the decision-making process through the presentation of information designed specifically for the decision maker's problem-solving approach and application needs. It does not make a decision for the user. (10)

DECISION TABLE A way to examine, describe, and document structured decisions. Four quadrants are drawn to describe the conditions, identify possible decision alternatives, indicate which actions should be performed, and describe the actions. (9)

DECISION TREE A method of decision analysis for structured decisions; an appropriate approach when actions must be accomplished in a certain sequence. (9)

DEFAULT VALUE A value that a field will assume unless an explicit value is entered for it. (13)

DELIVERABLES Any of the software, documentation, procedures, user manuals, or training sessions that a systems analyst delivers to a client based on specific contractual promises. (8)

DENORMALIZATION Defining physical records not in third or higher normal forms; includes joining attributes from several relations together to avoid the cost of accessing several files. Partitioning is an intentional form of denormalization. (13)

DIGITAL SUBSCRIBER LINE (DSL) Protocols that allow high-speed data transmission over regular telephone wire. (17)

DISASTER RECOVERY PLANNING Strategic and tactical plans to aid people and systems to recover in the face of natural and human-made disasters. (17)

DISPLAY Any one of a number of display alternatives that users employ to view computer software, including monitors and liquid plasma screens. (11)

DISTRIBUTED SYSTEMS Computer systems that are distributed geographically, as well as having their processing, data, and databases distributed. One common architecture for distributed systems is a LAN-based client/server system. (17)

DOCUMENTATION Written material created by the analyst that describes how to run the software, gives an overview of the system, or details the program code used. Analysts can use a CASE tool to facilitate documentation. (16)

DROP-DOWN LIST One of many GUI design elements that permits users to click on a box that appears to drop down on the screen and list a number of alternatives, which can be subsequently chosen. (11)

ECOMMERCE Doing business electronically, including via email, Web technologies, BBS, smart cards, EFT, and EDI, among suppliers, customers, governmental agencies, and other businesses to conduct and execute transactions in business, administrative, and consumer activities. (1)

ENCAPSULATION In object-oriented analysis and design, an object is encapsulated by its behavior. An object maintains data about the real-world things it represents in a true sense. An object must be asked or told to change its own data with a message. (18)

ENCRYPTION The process of converting a message into an encrypted message by using a key so that the message cannot be read by a person. The intended receiver of the message can then use a key to decode and read the encrypted message. (13)

END USERS In an organization, noninformation system professionals who specify the business requirements for and use software applications. End users often request new or modified applications, test and approve applications, and may serve on project teams as business experts. (1)

ENTITY A person, group, department, or system that either receives or originates information or data. One of the primary symbols on a data flow diagram. (2) *See also* data flow diagram, external entity.

ENTITY-RELATIONSHIP (E-R) DIAGRAM A graphical representation of an E-R model. (8)

ENTITY TYPE A collection of entities that share common properties or characteristics. (8)

ENVIRONMENT Anything external to an organization. Multiple environments exist, such as the physical, economic, legal, and social environments. (2)

EXECUTIVE SUPPORT SYSTEM (ESS) A computer system that helps executives organize their interactions with the external environment by providing graphical and communication support. (1)

EXPERT SYSTEM (ES) A computer-based system that captures and uses the knowledge of an expert for solving a particular problem. Basic components are the knowledge base, an inference engine, and the user interface. (1)

EXTERNAL ENTITY A source or destination of data considered to be external to the system being described. Also called an entity. (7) *See also* data flow diagram.

EXTREME PROGRAMMING (XP) Extreme programming (XP) is a systems development approach that accepts what we know as good systems development practices and takes them to the extreme; has unique core practices such as short release, a 40-hour work week, an on-site customer, and pair programming. (3)

FAVICON A small icon displayed next to any bookmarked address in a browser. Copying the bookmarked link to a desktop results in a larger version of the icon being placed there. Unique favicons can be generated with a Java icon generator or with other graphics programs. (11)

FIELD A physical part of a database that can be packed with several data items; the smallest unit of named application data recognized by system software. (13)

FIREWALL Computer security software used to erect a barrier between an organization's LAN and the Internet. Although it prevents hackers from getting into an internal network, it also stops organizational members from getting direct access to the Internet. (17)

FIRST NORMAL FORM (1NF) The first step in normalizing a relation in data used in a database so that it contains no repeating groups. (13) *See also* second normal form, third normal form.

FIT Describes the way that HCI elements of the human, the computer, and the task that needs to be performed work together to improve performance and well-being. (14)

FOLKLORE A system documentation technique based on traditional methods used in gathering information about people and legends. (16)

FORM-FILL INTERFACE Part of GUI design elements that automatically prompt the user to fill in a standard form. Useful for ecommerce applications. (14)

FUNCTION POINT ANALYSIS A way to estimate project size, considering the five main components of computer systems: external inputs, external outputs, external log queries, internal logical files, and external interface files. (3)

GANTT CHART A graphical representation of a project that shows each task activity as a horizontal bar, the length of which is proportional to its time for completion. (3)

GRAPHICAL USER INTERFACE (GUI) An icon-based user interface, with features such as pull-down menus, drop-down lists, and radio buttons. (14)

HUMAN–COMPUTER INTERACTION (HCI) The aspect of a computer that enables communications and interactions between humans and the computer; the layer of the computer between humans and the computer. (14)

HYPERLINK Any highlighted word in a hypertext system that will display another document when clicked on by the user. (11)

ICON Small picture that represents an activity and function available to users when they activate it, often with a mouse click. Frequently used in GUI design. (14)

IMPLEMENTATION The last phase of the systems development life cycle, in which the analyst ensures that the system is in operation and then allows users to take over its operation and evaluation. (17)

INDEXED FILE ORGANIZATION A type of file organization that uses separate index files to locate records. (13)

INHERITANCE In object-oriented analysis and design, classes can have children. The parent class is known as the base class, and the child class is called a derived class. The derived class can be created to inherit all the attributes and behaviors of the base class. (18)

INPUT Any data, either text or numbers, that are entered into an information system for storage or processing via forms, screens, voice, or interactive Web fill-in forms. (12)

INTANGIBLE BENEFITS Benefits that accrue to the organization as a result of a new information system and that are difficult to measure, such as improving decision making, enhancing accuracy, and becoming more competitive. (10) *See also* tangible benefits, intangible costs, tangible costs.

INTANGIBLE COSTS Costs that are difficult to estimate and may not be known, including losing a competitive edge, losing a reputation for innovation, and declining company image, due to untimely or inaccessible information. (10) *See also* tangible costs, tangible benefits, intangible benefits.

INTEGRATED SERVICES DIGITAL NETWORK (ISDN) A switched network service that provides end-to-end digital connectivity for transmitting voice, data, and video simultaneously over a single line versus multiple lines. (17)

INTERNET SERVICE PROVIDER (ISP) A company that provides access to the Internet and that may provide other services, such as Web hosting and Web traffic analysis for a fee. (12)

IP (INTERNET PROTOCOL) ADDRESS The number used to represent an individual computer on a network. The format for an IP address is 999.999.999.999. (17)

JAVA An object-oriented programming language that allows dynamic applications to be run on the Internet. (11)

JOINT APPLICATION DESIGN (JAD) IBM's proprietary approach to panel interviews conducted with analysts, users, and executives to accomplish requirements analysis jointly. (4)

KEY One of the data items in a record that is used to identify a record. (13) *See also* primary key, secondary key.

LEVEL 0 DIAGRAM The explosion (or decomposition) of the context-level data flow diagram, showing from three to nine major processes, important data flows, and data stores of the system under study. (7)

LOCAL AREA NETWORK (LAN) The cabling, hardware, and software used to connect workstations, computers, and file servers located in a confined geographical area (typically within one building or campus). (15)

LOGICAL DATA FLOW DIAGRAM A diagram that focuses on the business and how the business operates; describes the business events that take place and the data required and produced by each event. (7) *See also* data flow diagram, physical data flow diagram.

LOWER CASE TOOLS CASE tools used by analysts to generate computer source code, eliminating the need for programming the system. (1) *See also* CASE tools.

MAINTENANCE Maintaining the information system to improve it or to fix problems begins in this phase of the SDLC and continues through the life of the system. Some maintenance can be done automatically through connecting to the vendor's Web site. (1)

MANAGEMENT INFORMATION SYSTEM (MIS) A computer-based system composed of people, software, hardware, and procedures that share a common database to help users interpret and apply data to the business. (1)

MASHUPS A new application created by combining two or more Web-based APIs, or application programming interfaces, together. (14)

METHOD In UML, an action that can be requested from any object of the class; the processes that a class knows how to carry out. (18)

MNEMONIC CODE Any code (often using a combination of letters and symbols) that helps the data entry person remember how to correctly enter data or helps the user remember how to use the information. (15)

NATURAL-LANGUAGE INTERFACE An interface that permits the user to speak or write in human language to interact with the computer. (14)

NORMALIZATION The transformation of complex user views and data stores to a set of smaller, stable data structures. Normalized data structures are more easily maintained than complex structures. (13)

OBJECT In the object-oriented approach, an object is a computer representation of some real-world thing or event; can have both attributes and behaviors. (18)

OBJECT CLASS A category of similar objects. Objects are grouped into classes. A class defines the set of shared attributes and behaviors found in each object in the class. (18)

OBJECT DIAGRAM A diagram that is similar to class diagrams but that portrays the state of class instances and their relationships at a point in time; shows objects and their relationships. Also shows optionality (customer can have zero or more rental contracts) and cardinality (rental contract can have only one customer). (18)

OBJECT THINK Elementary statements the analyst writes on CRC cards to begin thinking in an object-oriented way. (18)

OPEN-ENDED QUESTION A type of question used in interviews or on surveys that opens up the possible response set available to respondents. (4) *See also* bipolar question, closed question.

OPEN SOURCE SOFTWARE A development model and philosophy of distributing software free and publishing its source code, which can then be studied, shared, and modified by users and programmers. The Linux operating system is an example. (1)

OPEN SYSTEM Part of general systems theory; a system that freely receives information, energy, people, or raw materials as input. Systems are never totally closed or totally open, but exist on a continuum from more closed to more open. (2) *See also* closed system.

OUTPUT Information delivered to users through the information system by way of intranets, extranets, or the Web, on printed reports, on displays, or via audio. (11)

PACKAGE In UML, things can be grouped together in packages, which can be considered physical subsystems. Systems are implemented and deployed in packages. (18)

PAIR PROGRAMMING A core practice of the agile approach wherein two programmers who choose to work together both do the programming, run the tests, and talk to one another about ways to efficiently and effectively get the job done. (3)

PERT DIAGRAM A tool used to determine critical activities for a project. It can be used to improve a project schedule and evaluate progress. It stands for Program Evaluation Review Technique. (3)

PHYSICAL DATA FLOW DIAGRAM A DFD that shows how a system will be implemented, including the hardware, software, people, and files involved. (7) *See also* logical data flow diagram.

PLUG-IN Additional software (often developed by a third party) that can be used with another program; for example, RealNetworks' Real Player or Macromedia Flash are used as plug-ins in Web browsers to play streaming audio or video and view vector-based animation. (11)

PODCASTING The technique of putting downloadable audio files on the Web. (11)

POLYMORPHISM Alternative behaviors among derived classes in object-oriented approaches. When several classes inherit both attributes and behaviors, the behavior of a derived class might be different from its base class or its sibling-derived classes. (18)

PRESENT VALUE The total amount that a series of future payments is worth now; a way to assess the economic outlays and revenues of the information system over its economic life and compare costs today with future benefits. (10)

PRIMARY KEY A key that uniquely identifies a record. (13) *See also* key, secondary key.

PROBES Follow-up questions primarily used during interviews between analysts and users. (4) *See also* closed question, open-ended question.

PROBLEM DEFINITION A formal statement of the problem, including (1) the issues of the present situation, (2) the objectives for each issue, (3) the requirements that must be included in all proposed systems, and (4) the constraints that limit system development.

PROCESS The activities that transform or change data in an information system. They can be either manual or automated. Signified by a rounded rectangle in a data flow diagram. (2)

PROJECT CHARTER A written document describing the expected results of the systems project (deliverables) and the time frame for delivery; it essentially becomes a contract between the chief analyst (or project manager) and their analysis team with the organizational users requesting the new system. (3)

PROJECT MANAGEMENT The art and science of planning a project, estimating costs and schedules, managing risk, and organizing and overseeing a team. Many software packages exist to support project management tasks. (3)

PROJECT MANAGER A person responsible for overseeing the planning, costing, scheduling, and team organization of a (often systems) project. Frequently, it is a role played by a systems analyst. (3)

PROTOTYPING A rapid, interactive process between users and analysts to create and refine portions of a new system; it can be used as part of the systems development life cycle (SDLC) for requirements determination or as an alternative to the SDLC. (6) *See also* rapid application development.

PSEUDOCODE A technique to create computer instructions that are the intermediate step between English and program code; used to represent the logic of each module on a structure chart. (16) *See also* structure chart.

PULL-DOWN MENU One of many GUI design elements that provides an onscreen menu of command options that appear after the user selects the command name on a menu bar. (14).

QUERIES Questions users pose to the database concerning data within it. Each query involves an entity, an attribute, and a value. (14)

RADIO BUTTON One of many GUI design elements that provides a round option button in a dialog box. Buttons are mutually exclusive, because a user can choose only one radio button option within the group of options displayed. (11)

RAPID APPLICATION DEVELOPMENT (RAD) An object-oriented approach to systems development that includes a method of development as well as software tools. (6) *See also* prototyping.

RECORD A collection of data items that have something in common with the entity described. (13)

RELATIONAL DATABASE MODEL Represents data in the database as two-dimensional tables called relations. As long as both tables share a common data element, the database can relate any one file or table to data in another file or table. (13)

RELATIONSHIP Association between entities (sometimes referred to as data association); can take the form of one-to-one, one-to-many, many-to-one, or many-to-many. (13)

REPEATING GROUP The existence of many of the same elements in the data structure. (8) *See also* data structure.

RUBY ON RAILS A combination programming language and code generator for creating Web applications. (11)

SAMPLING Systematically selecting representative elements of a population. Analysts sample hard data, archival data, and people during information requirements determination. (5)

SECOND NORMAL FORM (2NF) When normalizing data for a database, the analyst ensures that all nonkey attributes are fully dependent on the primary key. All partial dependencies are removed and placed in another relation. (13) *See also* first normal form, third normal form.

SECONDARY KEY A key that cannot uniquely identify a record; can be used to select a group of records that belong to a set. (13)

SEQUENCE DIAGRAM In UML, a sequence diagram illustrates a succession of interactions between object instances over time. Often used to illustrate the processing described in use case scenarios. (18)

SIX SIGMA A culture built on quality; the goal is to eliminate all defects. (16)

STATECHART DIAGRAM In UML, a way to further refine requirements. (18)

STRUCTURE CHART A tool for designing a modular, top-down system consisting of rectangular boxes and connecting arrows. (16). *See also* control flag, data couple.

STRUCTURED ENGLISH A technique for analyzing structured decisions based on structure logic and simple English statements, such as add, multiply, and move. (9)

STRUCTURED OBSERVATION OF THE ENVIRONMENT (STROBE) A systematic observational method for classifying and interpreting organizational elements that influence decision making. Based on mise-en-scène film criticism. (5)

STRUCTURED WALKTHROUGH A systematic peer review of the system's programming and overall development that points out problems and allows the programmer or analyst to make suitable changes. (16)

SUPPLY CHAIN MANAGEMENT An organization's effort to integrate their suppliers, distributors, and customer management requirements into one unified process. Ecommerce applications can improve supply chain management. (17)

SWIMLANES Zones used in activity diagrams to indicate partitioning; can show which activities are done on which platform and by which user group; can also depict system logic. (18)

SYSTEM A collection of subsystems that are interrelated and interdependent, working together to accomplish predetermined goals and objectives. All systems have input, processes, output, and feedback. Examples are a computer information system and an organization. (2) *See also* closed system, open system.

SYSTEMS ANALYST The person who systematically assesses how businesses function by examining the inputting and processing of data and the outputting of information with the intent of improving organizational processes. (1)

SYSTEMS DEVELOPMENT LIFE CYCLE (SDLC) A seven-phase approach to systems analysis and design that holds that systems are best developed through the use of a specific cycle of analyst and user activities. (1)

SYSTEMS DEVELOPMENT METHODOLOGY Any accepted approach for analyzing, designing, implementing, testing, maintaining, and evaluating an information system. (1) *See also* systems development life cycle.

SYSTEMS PROPOSAL A written proposal that summarizes the systems analyst's work in the business up to that point and includes recommendations and alternatives to solve the identified systems problems. (10)

SYSTEMS TESTING The sixth phase in the SDLC (along with maintenance). Uses both test data and eventually live data to measure errors, timeliness, ease of use, proper ordering of transactions, acceptable down time, understanding procedure manuals, and other aspects of the new system. (16)

TANGIBLE BENEFITS Advantages measurable in dollars that accrue to the organization through the use of the information systems. (10) *See also* intangible benefits, intangible costs, tangible costs.

TANGIBLE COSTS The costs in dollars that can be accurately projected by the systems analyst, including the cost of computers, resources, analysts' and programmer's time, and other employees' salaries, to develop a new system. (10) *See also* intangible costs, tangible benefits, intangible benefits.

TECHNOLOGY ACCEPTANCE MODEL (TAM) A research-based way for analysts to organize their thinking about whether users will accept and use information technology, typically including perceived usefulness and perceived ease of use. (14)

THINGS In UML, things describe the objects of object-oriented analysis and design. The two most often used groupings of things are structural things and behavioral things. (18)

THIRD NORMAL FORM (3NF) A form in which any transitive dependencies are removed. A transitive dependency is one in which nonkey attributes are dependent on other nonkey attributes. (13) *See also* first normal form, second normal form.

TRANSACTION PROCESSING SYSTEM (TPS) A computerized information system developed to process large amounts of data for routine business transactions, such as payroll and inventory. (1)

UNIFIED MODELING LANGUAGE (UML) UML provides a standardized set of tools to document the object-oriented analysis and design of a software system. (18)

USABILITY A way for designers to evaluate the systems and interfaces they create with an eye toward addressing as many HCI concerns as thoroughly as possible. (14)

USE CASE In UML, a sequence of transactions in a system; the purpose is to produce something of value to an actor in the system; focuses on what the system does rather than on how it does it. The use case model is based on the interactions and relationships of individual use cases. In a use case, an actor using the system initiates an event that begins a related series of interactions in the system. (18)

VALIDATION SOFTWARE Software that checks whether data input to the information system is valid. Although validating input is largely done through software that is the programmer's responsibility, it is the analyst's responsibility to know what common problems might invalidate a transaction. (15)

VOICE OVER INTERNET PROTOCOL (VoIP) The routing of voice data over the Internet. (10)

WEBMASTER The person responsible for updating and maintaining a Web site; often initially the systems analyst during development of ecommerce applications. (12)

XML SCHEMAS A precise way to define the content of an XML document; may include the exact number of times an element can occur, the type of data within elements, limits on the data, and the number of places to the left and right of a decimal number. (8)

XP *See* extreme programming and agile modeling. (3)

ACRONYMS

API	application programming interface
ASP	application service provider
B2B	business-to-business
B2C	business-to-consumer
CARE	computer-assisted reengineering
CASE	Computer-Aided Software Engineering
CDROM	compact disk read-only memory
CD-RW	compact disk read write
CSCWS	computer-supported collaborative work system
CSS	Cascading Style Sheets
DBMS	database management system
DDE	Dynamic Data Exchange
DFD	data flow diagram
DHTML	dynamic HTML
DLL	dynamic link library
DSL	digital subscriber line
DSS	decision support system
DTD	Document Type Definition
DVD	digital versatile disk
E-R	entity-relationship
EIS	executive information system
ERD	entity-relationship diagram
ERP	enterprise resource planning
ES	expert system
ESS	executive support system
FAQ	frequently asked questions
FPC	function point count
FTP	file transfer protocol
GIF	graphic interchange format
GUI	graphical user interface
HCI	human–computer interaction
HTML	hypertext markup language
http://	hypertext transfer protocol
ISDN	Integrated Services Digital Network
ISP	Internet service provider
JAD	joint application design
JPEG	Joint Photographic Experts Group
LAN	local area network
MIS	management information system
OCR	optical character recognition
OLE	Object Linking and Embedding
PDA	personal digital assistant
PERT	Program Evaluation and Review Techniques
PHP	hypertext preprocessor; an open source programming language
PKI	public key infrastructure
RAD	rapid application development
SAN	storage area network
SDLC	systems development life cycle
SET	secure electronic translation
SQL	structured query language
SSL	secure socket layering
STROBE	structured observation of the environment
TAM	Technology Acceptance Model
TPS	transaction processing system
TQM	total quality management
UML	unified modeling language
URL	uniform resource locator
VB.NET	Visual Basic .NET, a microsoft programming environment
VoIP	Voice over Internet Protocol
VPN	virtual private network
WAN	wide area network
WAP	wireless application protocol
WiMax	worldwide interoperability for microwave access
WMP	Windows Media Photo
WWW	World Wide Web
XP	extreme programming
XSLT	extensible stylesheet language transformations

INDEX

NOTE: Page numbers followed by an italic *f* indicate figures.

SYMBOLS

* (asterisk), 288, 550, 649, 734
{ } (braces), 271
[ ] (brackets), 271
≪ ≫ (chevrons), 739
— (dash), 316
= (equal sign), 271, 728
> (greater than), 287, 309
< (less than), 287
– (minus sign), 712
+ (plus sign), 271, 288, 649, 712
# (pound symbol), 728
/ (slash), 555

A

Above-line captions, 435, 436*f*
Abstract classes, 729, 737–38
Access
  form sections, 434, 435*f*
  WLANs, 394, 552, 676
Accommodating disabled workers, 543
Account numbers, 593
Accuracy
  codes, 555
  data entry in ecommerce, 616–17
  decision tables, 318–19
  FOLKLORE documentation, 652, 653
  form completion, 437
  graphical screen displays, 400
  input objectives, 433
  process specifications, 324–25
Action entries, 314–19
Action language, 545
Actions
  decision tables, 313–19
  decision trees, 320, 321
Active listening, 189
Active tags, 608
Activity diagrams
  creation, 722–23
  definition, 716
  overview, 720–22
Activity planning, 68–74
Actors
  definition, 39
  sequence diagram symbols, 724
  UML concepts, 715
  use case modeling, 39–42
  use case scenarios, 43–5
Actualization utility, 696
Adaptive maintenance, 657
Add-ons, 344–45
ADD statement, 644, 645
Ad hoc queries, 491, 509
Adobe Acrobat, 384
Adobe LifeCycle Form Manager, 441
Advertising, 699–700
Agent of change, 9
Aggregations, 735
Agile modeling
  basic activities, 189–190, 191*f*
  core practices, 190, 191*f*
  lessons learned, 195–97
  overview, 20, 86, 185
  processes and tools, 190–95
  project management, 86–95
  resource control variables, 190
  versus structured methods, 197–203
  tasks in typical day, 192
  values and principles, 186–89, 191*f*, 196
AHP. *See* Analytical hierarchy processing (AHP)
AI. *See* Artificial intelligence
Ajax (Asynchronous JavaScript and XML)
  electronic and Web form design, 455–57
  feedback types, 560, 561
  output production, 415–16
  overview, 7
  Web partitioning, 247
  Web site design, 404
Ajax spreadsheet, 457
Ajax Write, 457
Alarms, 688
Algebraic notation, 271
Aliases, 275
Alphabetic derivation codes, 592–93
Alphabetic elements, 277
Alphabetic sorting, 395
ALT attribute, 409
Alteration effects, 385
Alternative systems, 359–60
Altova, 616
American Express, 517, 614
American Red Cross, 693
Americans with Disabilities Act, 457, 543
Ampersands, 573
Analogies, 368
Analysis phase, 69
Analyst's playscripts, 156–57
Analytical hierarchy processing (AHP), 349–50
AND condition, 572
AND operator, 569
"and" phrasing, 309, 649
Anecdotal evidence, 203
Anecdotes, 368
Animation, 385
Annotational things, 715, 743
Answering questions, 368, 408
Antenna, 608
Applets, 565
Application programming interfaces (APIs), 566
Application service provider (ASP)
  benefits and drawbacks, 345*f*, 347–48
  software evaluation, 347–48
  vendor support, 348
Area charts, 363–64
Arial font, 446
Arithmetic means, 353
Arithmetic operations, 569–70, 571*f*
Arrow
  activity diagrams, 720
  data flow diagrams, 218*f*, 219, 223
  electronic and Web form design, 444, 447
  gen/spec diagrams, 737
  sequence diagrams, 725
  structure charts, 638, 639*f*
Art forms, 652
Artificial intelligence (AI), 2–3, 350
ASCII format, 722
Ask.com, 546
ASP. *See* Application service provider (ASP)
Associate programs, 700
Associations, 516, 733–35
Associative entities, 36, 37–38
Asterisks (*), 288, 550, 649, 734
Asynchronous JavaScript and XML. *See* Ajax
Asynchronous messages, 740
Atom, 387
Attention deficit disorder, 543
Attitude, 187, 535–36
Attractiveness, 433, 437–38
Attributes
  boundary classes, 729
  class diagrams, 727, 728
  class method determination, 739
  database anomalies, 505–6
  database concepts, 481*f*, 482, 485, 486
  database use steps, 510, 512*f*
  definition, 485
  entity classes, 729
  entity-relationship symbols, 484*f*
  file types, 488
  normalization process, 495–501
  object-oriented concepts, 710–11
  print report design guidelines, 397–98
  query types, 567–70
  relational structure terminology, 491
  sampling, 146
  software decisions, 349, 350
  state chart diagrams, 740–41
  Web site graphics, 409
  XML documentation, 288–89
Attributive entities, 36–37, 38
Audacity, 385
Audience, 366, 368, 400
Audio feedback, 560–61
Audio output
  display screens, 382, 383*f*
  feedback, 385
  hearing impaired employees, 544
Auditing, 657–58
Authorization codes, 689
Autism, 543
Autocomplete features, 617
Automation
  data capture computer tasks, 602–4
  data dictionaries, 268
  ecommerce email feedback, 563
  feasibility, 66
  scanned forms, 440

B

Back-end processing, 673
Background design, 409, 458–59
Background information, 110–11
Backup protection, 693
Balloons, 562
Banking systems, 693
Bar charts, 365–66, 400*f*
Bar codes, 607–8
Base classes, 711
Base elements, 230–31, 283, 325
Batch validation, 560
Beeping, 560
Behavioral diagrams, 715, 716*f*
Behavioral relationships
  overview, 40–41
  UML concepts, 715, 716*f*
Behavioral security, 689–90
Behavioral things, 715
Below-line captions, 435, 436*f*
Benchmarking, 341
Benefits, 351–60
Best-fitting lines, 352–53
Bias, 144, 394–98
Big bosses, 92
Biomedical engineering, 543, 544
Bipolar questions, 113
Black Belt project leader, 632
Black circles, 721
Blinking cursors, 445
BlipIt, 195
Blipstar, 566
Block sequence codes, 594, 595*f*
Blogdigger, 388
Bloglines, 388
Blogs, 412–13
Bluetooth® communication, 552, 676
Body section
  electronic and Web form design, 441
  paper form design, 434, 435*f*
Bogozo Real Estate, 566
Bold font, 446, 727
Bookmarked sites, 412
Books
  revisions, 388
  Web site design resources, 405

Boolean logic
  ecommerce navigation, 565
  query design, 569, 570, 571*f*
Bordered boxes, 447
Bottleneck, 604
BottomFeeder, 388
Bottom-up design, 635–36, 681
Boundary classes, 729
Boxed captions, 435, 436*f*
Boxed tables, 362
Braces ({ }), 271, 568
Brackets ([ ]), 271
Braille keyboards, 544
Brainstorming, 713
Branches, 720
Breadboarding, 173
Break-even analysis, 355–56, 359, 362
Bright colors, 460
Broken links, 407, 408*f*
Browsers
  Web site design, 403, 404
  Web site evaluation, 699
Browsing, Internet, 351
B2C ecommerce applications, 440
Bubble diagrams, 493, 495*f*
Bugs. *See also* Errors
  agile development roles, 92
  agile versus structured methods, 198
  bottom-up design, 636
  generated code, 18
  importance of maintenance, 15
  modular development, 637
  Six Sigma approach, 632
  software warranties, 348
Building blocks, 346
Bulletin boards, 154, 563
Bullets, 409
Bus configurations, 676
Business forms. *See* Forms
Business knowledge, 82
Business rule formats, 307
Buttons. *See also specific types*
  GUI design, 447, 448, 449
  Intranet/Internet design, 461
  tab control dialog boxes, 457, 458
  Web site design, 409, 410
Buying hardware, 343

C

Cache, 409
Calculator layout, 543
Canadian postal codes, 600
Canceled transactions, 557
Candidate keys, 486
Captioning
  electronic and Web forms, 441, 446
  paper form design, 435–37
Cartoons, 408
Cascading style sheets. *See* CSS
CASE. *See* Computer-Aided Software Engineering tools
CASE repository, 17–18
Case structures, 309, 310*f*
Cash-flow analysis
  criteria for use, 359
  example, 358*f*
  overview, 357
Catalog numbers, 385
Catalogs, form, 151
Causal relationships, 352
CD-ROM output, 383*f*, 386
CD-RW output, 383*f*
Central cables, 676
Central tendency, 127
Change
  agents, 9
  agile modeling, 188
  data capture decisions, 602
  line graphs, 363–64
Channels, 387
Charters, project, 85–86
Charts. *See specific types*
Check boxes, 447, 450
Check constraints, 505
Check digits, 486, 611–13
Check-off captions, 436–37
Chevron symbol (≪ ≫), 739
Child classes, 711
Child diagrams
  data flow–structure chart conversion, 643–44
  examples, 237, 239*f*, 244–45*f*
  general data flow diagram development, 221–23, 225
  physical data flow diagram development, 231
Child tables, 505
CICS, 723
Cipher codes, 595–96
Circle buttons, 447
Circle charts, 366
Circle symbol
  activity diagrams, 721
  decision trees, 320
  entity-relationship models, 36, 484
Clarification notes, 435–36
Class diagrams
  associations, 734
  definition, 716
  example, 733*f*
  overview, 727
  symbols, 727
  UML use, 745
Classes
  class diagrams, 727
  CRC cards, 712–15
  definition, 20, 709
  determination, 738–39
  names, 728
  overview, 710–11, 712*f*
  purpose, 709–10
  sequence diagram symbols, 724
  types, 729–30
  Web example, 730–33
Classification
  codes, 593–94, 595*f*
  maintenance tasks, 657
ClearCase, 195
Client-based applications, 672
Client/server (C/S) model
  advantages and disadvantages, 674
  LAN configuration, 672–74
  modularity in Windows, 638
  overview, 672
  RAD tools, 183
Closedness, organizational, 29
Closed questions
  interviews, 112–14
  questionnaires, 122, 123–26
Clothing, 159
Clustering, 516
Clutter
  forms, 438
  screens, 402, 416, 445
Coaches, 92
COBOL, 80
Codes
  dialog design, 555, 557
  effective data entry, 591–601
Coding
  agile development approach, 87, 189, 190
  code generation, 18–19
  modular development, 637–38
Cognitive styles, 537–41, 565
Collaboration diagrams, 726–27
Collaborative filtering, 350, 351
Collections, 735
Colloquial language, 391
Color
  blindness, 459, 544
  dialog design, 554
  electronic and Web form design, 444, 449, 458–60
  intranet/Internet feedback, 461
  office decor, 159
  of paper, 397
Column charts, 364–65
Column projection, 508–509, 510*f*
Column totals, 437
Command buttons, 449
Command-language interfaces, 550–51
COMMDLG.DLL file, 638
Comments section
  electronic and Web forms, 441, 443
  paper forms, 434, 435*f*
Commerce Trends, 698–99
Commercial off-the-shelf (COTS) software
  advantages and disadvantages, 345*f*, 346, 347
  examples, 346
  needs evaluation, 345, 346–51
  prototyping, 178–179
  support documentation, 650
  team management, 84
  training materials, 685
  user help types, 562
  vendor support, 348
  Web site content, 408–9
Communicates relationships, 40*f*, 41
Communication
  agile approach overview, 87, 89, 94
  agile approach principles, 189
  agile approach values, 186
  agile versus structured methods, 200
  CASE tools, 16–17
  dashboard features, 401
  data flow diagram use, 250
  decision trees versus decision tables, 321
  dialog design, 554
  disaster recovery, 692–93
  email output, 386–387
  joint application design, 120
  logical data flow diagrams, 227
  maintenance tips, 657
  presentation organization, 368
  system analyst's qualities, 9
  systems proposal development, 361–66
  team management, 82–83
  testing with live data, 656–57
  use case modeling benefits, 45–46
  user stories, 192–94
Communication diagrams, 726–27
Comparative operators, 569, 571*f*
Completeness, decision table, 318–19
Completion dates
  agile approach, 87–88, 95, 199
  estimation, 76
Component diagrams, 743
Component packages, 742
Composite keys, 487, 505
Compositions, 736
Composition tests, 610–11
Computer-Aided Software Engineering (CASE) tools
  agile versus structured methods, 199
  classification, 17–19
  fit-performance-well-being interaction, 535
  network modeling, 677
  overview, 16
  purpose, 16–17
Computer-assisted form design, 438–40
Computer-based project scheduling, 74–76
Computer-generated information, 1
Computer hardware
  acquisition considerations, 342–45
  agile approach costs, 88
  conversion considerations, 693
  cost-benefit systems analysis, 351–60
  needs assessment, 339–45
  physical security, 688–89
  selection steps, 340*f*
  sizes, 342
Computer-supported collaborative work systems (CSCWS), 2, 4
Compuware Track Record, 195
ComUnit, 195
Concatenated keys, 487, 505
Concealing information, 595–96
Conceptual schemas, 490
Concise codes, 598–99
Conclusion, presentation, 368
Conditional forecasts, 352
Condition alternatives, 313–19
Conditions
  decision tables, 313–19
  decision trees, 320, 321
Confidence, 461
Confidence coefficient, 147
Confidence level, 147
Confidence, speaking, 368
Consistent data, 233, 433
Consistent design
  dialog design, 557–58
  electronic and Web forms, 443
  interfaces, 547
  Web sites, 411
Constant information, 397
Construction phase, 183
Construx, 76
Consultants, 92
Consulting role, 8
Content, Web site, 408–9
Context-level data flow diagram
  development, 220–21
  example, 235*f*, 242*f*
  overview, 32–34
  use case modeling, 42
Context-sensitive help, 443, 444*f*, 562
Continuous elements, 276–77
Contradictions, 318
Contrasting colors, 458, 459
Control
  electronic and Web forms, 449–51
  overview, 68
  paper-based forms, 440–41
  timing, 68–74
Control breaks, 397
Control classes, 729–30
Control flags, 638, 639
Controlling forms, 440–41
Control modules, 644
Convenience samples, 145
Conversion, 686–688, 693–94
Cookies, 617, 691, 732
Corel Designer, 84
CorelDraw Graphics Suite, 84
Corporate blogs, 412
Corporate information, 110–11, 154
CORVID, 350

Costar, 76
Cost concerns
agile development, 87, 88, 202
ASP benefits and drawbacks, 347, 348
benefits of virtual organizations, 29
commercial software, 346
cost-benefit systems analysis, 351–60, 695
C/S pros and cons, 674
data mining approach, 517
data warehouse costs, 514
display output advantages, 383
distributed system advantages, 681
economic feasibility, 67
hardware acquisition considerations, 343–44, 351–60
joint application design, 118, 120
maintenance costs, 657
networking considerations, 675
output method selection, 381
output technology considerations, 394
system maintenance, 15
COTS. *See* Commercial off-the-shelf software
Courage, 187
Cover letters, 360
C++, 80
CRC cards, 712–15
Create, Read, Update, and Delete (CRUD) acronym, 229, 504, 739
Creativity, 121, 203
Credit cards
concise codes, 599
customer profiles, 607
data mining patterns, 517
input validation, 613–14
Criterium DecisionPlus, 349
Critical path, 72, 74
Critiquing Web sites, 406
Cross-reference checks, 611, 615
Crow's foot notation, 34, 483*f*, 484
CRUD. *See* Create, Read, Update, and Delete acronym
Cryptograms, 595
Crystal Ball 2000, 349
CSCWS. *See* Computer-supported collaborative work systems
C/S model. *See* Client/server model
CSS
output production, 413, 414
Web site design, 403, 406, 410
Cue cards, 562
Culture, organizational
agile approach risks, 201–2
joint application design, 121
overview, 49
Six Sigma approach, 632, 633*f*
Cursors
dialog design, 556–57
disabled users, 544–45
screen forms, 441, 445
Customers
agile development practices, 189, 190
agile development risks, 202–3
agile development roles, 91
audio files, 385
concealing codes, 595–96
data mining approach, 517–18
ecommerce data entry, 617
ecommerce privacy, 691
output technology considerations, 390–91
planning game, 93
push technology, 389
Custom methods, 728
Customs, 652
Custom software
advantages and disadvantages, 345*f*, 346
bottom-up approach, 636
needs assessment, 346
Cutover phase, 183
CVS, 195

D

Daily scrum, 197
Dash (—), 316
Dashboards, 400–2, 541
Dashboard Widgets, 402
Dashed lines, 449, 500
Data. *See also* Information
dashboard design, 401, 402
data capture decisions, 601–2
ecommerce cautions, 85
feasibility studies, 63
forecasting models, 352
input validation, 608–16
retrieval steps, 506–11
sampling design, 144
testing procedures, 655–57
Database design
databases versus data warehouses, 512–18
denormalization, 511–12
general database concepts, 480–92
master file/database relations guidelines, 503–6
normalization, 492–503
overview, 479
use procedures, 506–11
Database management system (DBMS), 480
Databases
versus data warehouses, 513–14
definition, 479
electronic form control, 450
management information system users, 3
output production, 413
overview, 480
query by example, 570–73
structured query language, 573
system development life cycle, 13
Web site partitioning, 247
Data capture
effective/efficient, 608
forms, 150–52
Web site evaluation, 697
Data couples, 638–47
Data dictionaries
categories, 268
creation, 268–69, 279–282
data elements, 274–77
data flows, 269–271
data stores, 277–79
data structures, 271–74
function, 282
need for, 268
normalization example, 493, 494*f*
output bias, 396
overview, 267–68
process specifications, 306, 307, 312–313, 324*f*, 325
use of, 282–89
Data elements
data dictionaries, 274–77, 281
file types, 488
normalization examples, 493, 495*f*
Data entry
accurate form completion, 437
alternative interfaces, 552, 553
coding guidelines, 591–604
data capture, 601–8
dialog design, 554–56
ecommerce environments, 616–17
form-fill interfaces, 549–50
input validation, 608–16
keyboard design, 542–43
Data flow
context-level data flow diagrams, 33
data dictionaries, 269–71
Data flow diagrams
advantages, 218
agile versus structured methods, 199
CASE tools, 16, 17
communication of use, 250
conversion to structure charts, 642–45
data dictionaries, 269*f*, 279, 280*f*, 283–84
development, 220–25
examples, 32–39
logical, 225–37
overview, 217
physical, 225, 238–46
process specifications, 306, 307*f*, 321*f*, 323–27
pseudocode logic, 649
system development life cycle phases, 13
Web site designs, 246–50
Data gathering. *See also specific methods*
activity planning and control, 69–70
agile versus structured methods, 199–200
Data hygiene, 518
Data items
normalization process, 495
overview, 485
values, 486*f*
Data mining, 511, 513
Data model diagrams, 493, 495*f*
Data redundancy. *See* Redundancy
Data repositories, 268–69
Data storage. *See* Storage
Data stores
data dictionaries, 269*f*, 277–79, 281–82, 283*f*
data flow diagram development, 219, 221, 224
physical data flow diagrams, 229–30
Data structures, 271–274, 312*f*, 313
Data warehouses
data mining, 516–18
online analytic processing, 514–16
overview, 512–14
Date codes, 601
DBMS. *See* Database management system
DDE. *See* Dynamic Data Exchange
Deadlines. *See* Completion dates
Decimal points, 555
Decisioneering, 349
Decision making
animation output, 385
data capture, 601–2
data mining, 516
display design guidelines, 399–401
documentation techniques, 653
hardware inventory, 341
hardware selection, 340*f*
observation of managers, 155–57
organizational managers, 47–48
output design objectives, 380–81
physical security, 689
report analysis, 149
software selection, 340*f*, 349–51
Decision structures, 309, 310*f*
Decision support systems (DSS)
function, 2
overview, 3
software evaluation, 348–50
Decision tables
advanced types, 319
completeness and accuracy, 318
control modules, 644
versus decision trees, 321
development, 315–18
examples, 316–18
overview, 313–14
selection, 322
Decision trees
versus decision tables, 321
drawing instructions, 320–21
overview, 319
selection, 323
Defaults, 555–56
Deferred events, 740
Delays, processing, 561
Deleting records, 505
Deletion anomalies, 506
Delivery, presentation, 368
Delphi studies, 352
Demo, 197
Demonstrations, 384
Denormalization, 511–12, 515*f*
Deployment diagrams, 743
Derived classes, 711
Derived elements, 231, 277, 284
Design
agile approach practices, 189–90
forms, 433–41
network modeling, 677–81
normalization process, 502
SDLC phases, 13, 69
Design, output
bias effects, 394–98
blog design, 412–13
display design guidelines, 398–403
objectives, 379–81
output content, 381
technologies, 381–94
Web sites, 403–13
Design, systems
alternative methods, 20–21
bottom-up approach, 635–36
importance, 7
project management, 81–86
top-down approach, 636–37
Design, Web sites. *See* Web sites
Desks, 157–58
Desktops, 402–3
Detailed reports, 381, 396
Detailed results section, 361
Deviation column charts, 365, 366*f*
DevPartner Code Review, 195
DHTML, 404
Diagrams. *See specific types*
Diagram 0
data dictionary creation, 279
data flow diagram development, 221, 222*f*, 235–36, 238*f*
examples, 243*f*
Dialog
effective communication, 554
operation and consistency, 557
overview, 554
user action, 555–57
Dialog boxes, 546–47

Diamond-shaped question structure, 116, 117*f*
Diamond symbol, 642, 720, 722, 735
Dictionaries, 77, 600
Dictionaries, data
categories, 268
creation, 268–69, 279–82
data elements, 274–77
data flows, 269–71
data stores, 277–79
data structures, 271–74
function, 282
need for, 268
normalization example, 493, 494*f*
output bias, 396
overview, 267–68
process specifications, 306, 307, 312–13, 324*f*, 325
use of, 282–89
Differentiation data, 602
Digital certificates, 690
Digital sounds, 385
DinoTech Web site, 407*f*, 565, 566*f*
Direct changeover, 686*f*, 687
Direct mail, 517, 518, 593
Disabled users, 411, 542–45, 553
Disaster recovery, 691–93
Discount rates, 358, 359*f*
Discrete elements, 276, 277
Display screens
CSS styles, 414
design guidelines, 398–403
form design, 441–60, 549–50
output design, 381, 382–84, 394
visually impaired users, 542, 544
Distance collaboration, 384
Distributed conversion, 686*f*, 688
Distributed systems
advantages, 681–82
C/S model, 672–74
disadvantages, 682
groupware, 681
network modeling, 677–81
network types, 674–76, 677*f*
overview, 672
Divisions, 411
DLL. *See* Dynamic Link Library
Documentation
data flow diagram use, 250
form-fill interface advantages, 550
importance, 648
lack of, 649
quality assurance, 648–53
system development life cycle, 14
UML use, 746
use case data flow diagrams, 232
use case scenarios, 42–43
Document type definition (DTD), 287–89, 616
Dollar values, 358–59
Domain integrity, 505
Domains, 491
DO statement, 644, 645
Double square symbol, 218*f*, 219
Dragon NaturallySpeaking, 553*f*
Drop-down lists
dialog design, 556
form control, 450
GUI design, 447–48, 548
input validation, 615
normalization process, 502
DSS. *See* decision support systems
DTD. *See* Document type definition
Dummy activities, 72–73
DVD output, 383*f*, 386
Dynamic Data Exchange (DDE), 638
Dynamic Link Library (DLL), 638
Dynamic Web pages, 453–57
Dyslexia, 543

E

Earthquakes, 691–93
Ease of use, 348*f*, 536
EBCDIC format, 722
Ecommerce applications
accurate data entry, 616–17
custom software needs, 346
design considerations, 563–66
development personnel's qualifications, 8
feasibility impact grid, 64, 65
integration, 5
intranet/Internet design, 461
privacy concerns, 691
security concerns, 690
team management, 85
Economic feasibility, 67
Editing characters, 555
802.11 standards, 675, 676
Electronic form design software, 438–40
Electronic output, 382, 383, 386–88
Elemental symbols, 385
ELSE rule, 319
Email
disaster recovery, 692
display screen drawbacks, 384
ecommerce feedback, 563
filtering products, 690
interview preparation, 111
output options, 386–87
questionnaire administration, 131
Embezzlement, 658
Emergency maintenance, 657
Emergency situations, 691–93
Encryption software, 689, 690
English, structured
conventions, 309–12
examples, 311*f*, 313*f*, 322*f*
horizontal balancing, 325–26
overview, 308–9
selection, 322
Enhancement work, 657
Enter key, 449
Enterprise resource planning (ERP) systems
integration, 5
organizations as systems, 32
software evaluation, 346
Entities
context-level data flow diagrams, 33
database concepts, 481–85
data flow diagram development, 220–25
data flow diagram symbols, 218*f*, 219
definition, 34, 481
file types, 488
master file design, 503–4
normalization examples, 493, 494*f*
query types, 567–70
Entity classes, 729
Entity integrity constraints, 505
Entity-relationship (E-R) models
database concepts, 482*f*, 483–85
examples, 34–39
overview, 34
record key determination, 502–3
requirements, 39
symbols, 483*f*
Entity subtypes, 481–82
Entry sequence, 461
Environmental model. *See* Context-level data flow diagram
Environments
audio feedback, 561
definition, 29
hearing impaired users, 542
metaphors, 693–94
observation, 157–62
organizations as systems, 29
output technology considerations, 394
eOmniForm.com, 440
Equal sign (=), 271, 728
E-R. *See* Entity-relationship models
Ergonomics
keyboard issues, 542, 605
surveys, 537, 538*f*
ERP. *See* Enterprise resource planning systems
Errors. *See also* Bugs
data flow diagrams, 223–25
feedback types, 560
form completion, 437
interface considerations, 553
sequence codes, 592–93
statechart diagrams, 741–42
testing procedures, 654–57
validating input, 608–16
ESS. *See* Executive support systems
Estimating models, 76
Ethics, 10, 518, 691
ETHICS approach, 20–21
European Union (EU), 533, 554
Evaluation
agile development risks, 203
computer hardware, 341–45
SDLC phases, 14
software, 345–51
structured walkthrough technique, 634–35
system implementation, 694–700
users' response to prototypes, 180–81
vendor support, 344–45
Web site design, 405, 406*f*, 697–701
EV-DO (evolution data optimized), 676
Event modeling, 231–32
Event response charts, 451–53
Event response tables, 231
Events, 740
Evolutionary agents, 389
Exception reports, 381, 395, 396
Executive sponsors, 118, 157–58
Executive summaries, 360
Executive support systems (ESS), 2, 4
Exit option, 557
Expedia.com, 454
Experience, work, 82
Experimentation, with prototype, 180
Expert Choice software, 60, 349
Expert systems
function, 2
overview, 3–4
software decisions, 350
Expiration date, credit card, 614
Exploration phase, 94*f*, 95
Exsys CORVID, 350
Extended-entry tables, 315, 319
Extends relationships, 40*f*, 41
Extensible markup language (XML)
Ajax design, 455
data dictionary uses, 284–89
input validation, 616
output production, 413–16
RSS feeds, 387
system interfaces, 729
Extensible style language transformation (XSLT), 413*f*, 415
Extensions, 404
External auditors, 658
External entities. *See* Entities
External events, 43
External hubs, 679
External interface files, 77
External logical files, 77–79
External output, 381
External paid trainers, 683–84
External quality, 88
External queries, 77
External style sheets, 410–11
Extranets, 682
Extreme programming
versus agile modeling, 186–89, 192
development tools, 194–95

F

Failed projects, 86
FAQ, 104, 408
Favicon, 412
Favorites, 412
Faxes, 617
Feasibility
definition of objectives, 64–66
determination of resources, 66–68
judgment, 68
overview, 63–64
Feasibility impact grid (FIG), 64–66
Feedback
agile modeling principles, 188
agile modeling values, 186–87
audio output, 385
ecommerce considerations, 563–65, 617
graphical user interfaces, 551
human–computer interaction, 558–63
identification of systems problems, 58
importance, 558
Internet/intranet design, 461
live test data, 656
maintenance, 657
message boxes, 449
modified keyboards, 542
organizations as systems, 28, 29
prototype development, 175
users' evaluation of prototype, 181
FeedDEMON, 388
Feedster, 388
Female population, 459
Fields
database concepts, 485
dialog design, 555–56
electronic and Web form design, 446–51, 453, 459
form-fill interfaces, 549–50
input validation, 610, 614–15
master file design, 504
scanned forms, 439–40
FIG. *See* Feasibility impact grid
Figures, 361. *See also specific types*
Files
database advantages, 480
database use steps, 506–11
data storage approaches, 479
organization, 489–90
overview, 488
relational structure terminology, 491
types, 488, 489*f*
File servers, 672–73
Fill-in forms
design guidelines, 434–37
interfaces, 549–50
Intranet/Internet design, 460–61
Filtering information, 200–1
Financial issues
agile development, 87, 88, 202
ASP benefits and drawbacks, 347, 348

Financial issues (*continued*)
benefits of virtual organizations, 29
commercial software, 346
cost-benefit systems analysis, 351–60, 695
C/S pros and cons, 674
data mining approach, 517
data warehouse costs, 514
display output advantages, 383
distributed system advantages, 681
economic feasibility, 67
hardware acquisition considerations, 343–44, 351–60
joint application design, 118, 120
maintenance costs, 657
networking considerations, 675
output method selection, 381
output technology considerations, 394
system maintenance, 15
Firefox, 387, 388, 404, 453
Firewalls, 689, 690
First normal form (1NF), 496–98
First-of-a-series prototype, 172*f*, 173
Fishbone diagrams, 93–94
Fit, 534, 535*f*, 545*f*
Flat-panel displays, 414
Flexibility
dashboard design, 402
ecommerce navigation, 565
output bias, 396
output design, 382, 383
software evaluation, 348*f*
Flow, form, 434
Folder symbol, 742
FOLKLORE method, 651–53
Fonts
consistent design, 557
display screen design, 384
form attractiveness, 438, 445–46
push technology, 389
Web site design, 410
Footnotes, 362
Forecasting models, 352–54
Foreground, 458–59
Foreign keys, 500, 502, 503
Form-fill interfaces, 549–50
FormFlow, 444*f*, 549*f*
Form flow, 434, 437, 443
Form number, 441
Forms
definition, 433
design guidelines, 433–41
dialog design, 555
display design, 441–60
ecommerce feedback, 563–64
effective/efficient data capture, 604–5, 606–7
interfaces, 549–50
main sections, 434
objectives, 433
output technology considerations, 394
overview, 433
print design guidelines, 396, 397
process specification format, 306–7
structured walkthroughs, 635*f*
usability surveys, 538*f*
Web site design, 405, 406*f*, 441–60
Web site evaluation, 699
Web site partitioning, 247
Form utility, 696
40-hour work week
agile versus structured methods, 200–1
core agile practices, 90, 190
core agile values, 196
Fraud, 658, 689
FTP, 404
Fun, 411
Functional attributes, 397
Function codes, 598
Function point count (FPC), 77, 79
Functions, 306, 642
Funnel question structure, 116

G

Gadgets, 403
Game metaphor, 693–94
Gantt charts, 70–71, 72*f*
Gateways, 690
GDSS. *See* Group decision support systems
General classes, 736, 737, 738
Generalizations, 736
Generalizes relationships, 40*f*, 41–42
General Motors, 517
Gen/spec diagrams, 716, 729, 736–40
Geocoding, 566
Geographical checks, 611
Gesturing, 368
GIF file, 404, 409
Glyph symbols, 598
Goal setting, 83–84
Goal utility, 696
Google, 408, 565
Google Earth, 457
Google maps, 566
Google Suggest, 457
Gradual conversion, 686*f*, 687
Graphical judgment, 352
Graphical user interfaces (GUI)
classification codes, 594
client/server model, 672
efficient/effective data capture, 603–4
electronic and Web form design, 446–49, 457–58
input validation, 614–15
menus, 548
overview, 551–52
Graphics. *See specific types*
Graphs. *See also specific types*
break-even analysis, 356*f*
cognitive styles, 537, 540–41
dashboard design, 401, 402
display design guidelines, 400
graphical judgment, 352*f*
incorrectly drawn, 367
moving averages, 353*f*
output bias, 395–396
payback periods, 356*f*
systems proposal creation, 362–66
Greater than (>) symbol, 287
Green Belt project members, 632
Group decision support systems (GDSS)
function, 2
overview, 4
RAD workshop, 182
Group things, 715
Groupware, 681
Guard condition, 720, 740

H

Halo effect, 127
Handheld devices
accurate form completion, 437
alternative interfaces, 552
output design, 383
recent developments, 6
Web site design, 403
Hands-on experiences, 684
Hard data, 149
Hardware
acquisition considerations, 342–45
agile approach costs, 88
conversion considerations, 693
cost-benefit systems analysis, 351–60
needs assessment, 339–45
physical security, 688–89
selection steps, 340*f*
sizes, 342
Hashed file organization, 490
HCI. *See* Human–computer interaction (HCI)
Headings
electronic and Web form design, 441
paper form design, 434, 435*f*
Web site design, 410
Headphones, 544
Hearing impairments, 542, 544
Help. *See* User help
Hidden fields, 450–51, 732
Hierarchical databases, 490
Hierarchical networks, 676
Historical data, 352
Historical reports, 381
HollywoodVideo.com, 351
Holograms, 397
Home keys, 542
Home pages, 351, 403, 410
Hooks, 368
Horizontal balancing, 325–27, 730
Horizontal check-off captions, 437
Hot spots, 409, 675
Hourglass icon, 558
HTML
definition, 404*f*
Web site design, 403
versus XML, 285
http://, 404*f*
httpUnit, 195
Hub connectivity, 678–81
Human–computer interaction (HCI)
best practices, 545
cognitive styles, 537–41
dialog design, 554–57, 558*f*
ecommerce considerations, 563–66
interfaces, 545–54
overview, 10–11, 533–34
performance and well-being effects, 534–36
physical considerations, 543–45
query design, 567–73
systems development life cycle, 11
technology acceptance model, 536
test data, 656
usability, 536–37
user feedback, 558–63
Human information overload, 200–1
Human interfaces, 729
Humility, 187
Humor, 368
Hurricanes, 691–93
HyperCase® Experiences, 22, 50–51, 97–98, 119, 132, 155, 163–64, 205, 251, 290, 328, 350, 357, 369, 417, 463, 520, 574, 619, 659, 701
Hyperlinks
detailed feedback, 562
dialog design, 554
user movement, 443
Web and electronic form design tips, 443
Web versus paper forms, 441

I

IBM Rational Rose, 726
IBM VisualAge, 195
Icons
dialog design, 554
electronic and Web form design, 446, 448*f*
standards, 557
Identification
data entry codes, 592, 593
form sections, 434, 435*f*
Idle times, 341
IEXMLTLS, 615
IF . . . ELSE statements, 615
IF statement, 644, 645
IF-THEN-ELSE statements, 309, 313
IF-THEN statements, 320
Illiteracy, 543
Image maps, 449
Implementation phase
conversion issues, 686–88, 693–94
data gathering, 70
distributed systems, 672–82
evaluation guidelines, 694–700
rapid application development, 182–83, 184–85
security concerns, 688–93
systems development life cycle, 14
user training, 682–85, 686*f*
Includes relationships, 40*f*, 41
Indentation, 287
Index fields, 504
Indexing, 510
Info Harvest, 349
Information. *See also* Data
computer-generated versus manually produced, 1
dynamic Web pages, 453
external sources, 351
importance, 1
observation of environment, 159
output bias, 395
overload, 200–1, 380
print report design conventions, 397
software decisions, 351
systems development life cycle phases, 12
Information gathering. *See* Data gathering
Information systems
graphical models, 32–39
hierarchy, 2*f*
implications of management hierarchy, 48–49
systems development life cycle phases, 13–16
types, 2–4
Information system utility approach, 695–96
Inheritance, 711–12, 737
In-house trainers, 684
Inner join, 508
Innovation, 201–3, 341
Input
data dictionary creation, 280–81, 282*f*
data flow diagram development, 221–25
feedback types, 559–61
form design guidelines, 433–41
function point analyses, 77
horizontal balancing, 325, 326
mobility problems, 544–45
organizations as systems, 28, 30–31
output quality, 433

process specification format, 307
validation, 608–16
Input/output forms. *See* Form-fill interfaces
Inquiry programs, 554
Insert anomalies, 505–506
Installation
feedback, 561
network wizards, 675
support, 344
Instantiated program, 710–11
Instructions
audio type, 385
dialog design, 554
display design guidelines, 398
electronic and Web forms, 441, 443
paper form sections, 434, 435*f*
Intangible benefits, 355
Intangible costs, 355–56
Integration, 4–7, 346, 362
Integrity constraints, 504–5
Intelligent agents, 6, 351
Interaction diagrams, 724–27
Interactive information gathering, 109. *See also specific methods*
Interface classes, 729
Interface data flows, 222
Interface objects, 740
Interfaces
dialog design, 554–57
disabled users, 542–45
ecommerce considerations, 563–66
feedback, 558–65
prototype development, 177
system development life cycle phases, 13
top-down design, 637
types, 545–54
Internal auditors, 657–58
Internal data flow, 269
Internal logical files, 77
Internal output, 381
Internal quality, 88
Internal schemas, 490
International Standards Organization. *See* ISO standards
Internet
design tips, 460–61
dialog design, 554
external information sources, 351
fraud, 689
surfing, 689
Internet Explorer, 453
Interval scales, 127
Interviews
agile versus structured methods, 199–200
overview, 109–10
preparation, 110–12
question sequence, 114–16
question types, 111, 112–14
report, 116–18
sample sizes, 148
Intranet design, 460–61, 554
Introduction, presentation, 368
Intuit, 401*f*
Intuitive navigation, 565
Invalid values, 611
Inventories
behavioral security, 690
computer hardware, 340–41
form completion, 437
Inverse video, 445
Investigation
overview, 148–49
qualitative documents, 153–55
quantitative documents, 149–52
"is a" relationships, 736
ISO standards, 537, 597
IS quality circles, 633, 637
Italics, 729
Iterations
agile development phase, 94*f*, 95
data dictionaries and process specifications, 312, 313
structured English conventions, 309, 310*f*
iTunes, 385

J

JAD. *See* Joint application design
Java
agile development tools, 195
function point analysis, 80, 404
rollover menus, 565
JavaScript
Ajax, 415
display screen output, 402
dynamic Web pages, 453, 454–55
feedback types, 560
input validation, 615
rollover menus, 565
Web site design, 411
JBuilder, 195
JetForm, 444*f*, 549*f*
Jmeter, 195
Joining records, 506–508
Joint application design (JAD)
benefits, 121
drawbacks, 121–22
meeting location, 120
overview, 118
participants, 118, 120
structured analysis of activities, 120
supporting conditions, 118
Jokes, 368
Journey metaphor, 693
JPEG, 404, 409
Judgment models, 352
Jungle metaphor, 693, 694
JUnit, 195
JUnitPerf, 195
Juran Center, 632

K

KDD. *See* Knowledge data discovery
Keyboards
data entry methods, 605
dialog design, 556
sensory impaired users, 542–43, 544
unicode, 597
Key combinations, 548
Keys
determination, 502–3
master file design, 504
normalization process, 493–501
overview, 486–87
Keys, graph, 363
Knowledge acquisition, 350
Knowledge-based systems. *See* Expert systems
Knowledge data discovery (KDD), 511, 516–18
Knowledge engineers, 4
Knowledge search, 200
Knowledge work systems (KWS)
efficiency, 197–203
function, 2
overview, 3
Kodak Photo CD process, 608

L

Labels, 447, 607
Labor costs, 605–6, 607
Language
blog design, 412–13
output technology designs, 390–91
qualitative document analysis, 153
questionnaire creation, 125–26
systems alternative proposal section, 361
unicode, 597
user interfaces, 545
Web site design, 411
LANs. *See* Local area networks
Late projects, 70
Lateral bars, 724–25
Latin characters, 597
Laws, 392, 393–94, 543
Layers, 453
Layout, form, 438
Leader, team
characteristics, 82
Scrum method, 196
Six Sigma approach, 632
Leasing hardware, 343–44, 394
Least square lines, 352–53
Legacy systems, 649
Leniency, 127
Less than (<) symbol, 287, 309
Libraries, 394, 603, 737
Lighting, 159
LIKE parameter, 573
Limit setting, 395
Linear flow, 225
Line captions, 435, 436*f*, 437
Line graphs, 363–64
Line weights, 438
Linked lists, 489–90
Links, broken, 407, 408*f*
Link testing, 655
List boxes, 447–48
Listening, 189
Live data, 655–57
Local area networks (LAN)
clients in C/S model, 672–74
cost factors, 675
overview, 674
Logical data flow diagrams, 225–37
Logical data structures, 273–74
Logical packages, 742
Logical process specifications, 323–24
Logical security, 689
Logon control classes, 730
Looping, 312, 560
Loop symbol, 642
Lower CASE tools, 18–19
Luhn formula, 614

M

Machine metaphor, 693–94
Macintosh operating system, 446
Magnetic ink character recognition (MICR), 606–7
Mailings, 383, 593
Mainframes, 480
Maintenance, system
agile approach, 94*f*, 95–96
CASE tools, 17
importance, 14–15, 648
modular development, 637
quality assurance, 657
system development life cycle, 14, 15
vendor support, 344*f*
Male population, 459
Manageable modules, 175
Management information systems (MIS)
feasibility impact grid, 64, 65
function, 2
overview, 3
Managers
clothing, 158
decision-making tasks, 47–48
desk placement, 157–58
hardware inventories, 340
hierarchy, 46–48
information systems implications, 48–49
observation, 155–57
output technology considerations, 392
project initiation, 58
project selection, 63
Six Sigma approach, 632
systems perspective, 30–31
TQM responsibilities, 632–33
Manuals, 154, 650–51, 656
Manufacturers' specifications, 342
Manuscript revisions, 388
Many-to-many relationships, 483*f*, 502–3, 734
Many-to-one relationships
entity-relationship models, 35–36, 483*f*, 484
normalization process, 495–96, 502
notation, 484
referential integrity, 505
Mapping software, 408
MapQuest, 408
Margins, 384
Marketing databases, 518
Mark-sense forms, 606*f*, 607
Martin, James, 183
Mashups, 566
Master Black Belt project leaders, 632
Master files, 488, 489, 503–6
Matching records, 556
Materials requirements planning (MRP), 32
Mcommerce, 6
Mean, 353
Measurement scales, 126–27, 203, 355
Memory, 341
Memos, 153–54
Menus
dialog design, 556
electronic and Web form design, 441, 443, 453
interface types, 547–48
Web site design, 410
Merges, 720
Message boxes, 449
Message queue, 722–23
Messages
class diagrams, 728
communication diagrams, 726
definition, 730
overview, 739–40
sequence diagrams, 725–26
Metacodes, 607
Metadata
database concepts, 481, 487–88
data dictionaries, 267
Metaphors
conversion considerations, 693–94
output technology considerations, 391
qualitative documents, 153
Web site design, 408
Metatags, 411, 699
Method of least squares, 352–53
Methods
class diagrams, 727
definition, 711, 730
determination, 739
overlapping, 728–29
polymorphism, 737
UML concepts, 715

Method signature, 728
MICR. *See* Magnetic ink character recognition
Microsoft Access, 183, 346, 447*f*, 488, 571–72*f*
Microsoft Excel, 346, 353, 446*f*, 539*f*
Microsoft FrontPage, 563, 565
Microsoft .NET, 183, 195
Microsoft Office, 457–58, 547
Microsoft Outlook, 75
Microsoft PowerPoint, 385, 457*f*
Microsoft Project, 74–75
Microsoft Visio, 407, 408*f*, 681
Microsoft Visio Professional, 556*f*, 680*f*
Microsoft Visual Basic, 183
Microsoft Visual Studio Analyzer, 195
Microsoft Visual Studio .NET, 195
Microsoft Word, 346, 384
Middle managers, 47, 48
Middleware, 722
Minispecs. *See* Process specifications
Minus signs (−), 712, 728
MIS. *See* Management information systems
Mise-en-scène analyses, 157
Mnemonic codes, 597, 599
Mobile WiMax, 676
Mobility problems, 544–45, 553
Model numbers, 340
Modem Media, 405*f*
Modems, 410
Modifications
  coding guidelines, 601
  COTS software disadvantages, 347
  disabled employees, 543
  dynamic Web pages, 454
  modular development, 637
  prototype development, 176–77
Modular development
  conversion, 687–88
  overview, 637–38
  prototypes, 175
  structure charts, 638–47, 648*f*
  testing, 654
  Windows environment, 638
Modular prototype conversion, 686*f*, 687–88
Modulus numbers, 611–12, 613*f*
Money concerns
  agile development, 87, 88, 202
  ASP benefits and drawbacks, 347, 348
  benefits of virtual organizations, 29
  commercial software, 346
  cost-benefit systems analysis, 351–60, 695
  C/S pros and cons, 674
  data mining approach, 517
  data warehouse costs, 514
  display output advantages, 383
  distributed system advantages, 681
  economic feasibility, 67
  hardware acquisition considerations, 343–44, 351–60
  joint application design, 118, 120
  maintenance costs, 657
  networking considerations, 675
  output method selection, 381
  output technology considerations, 394
  system maintenance, 15
Monitoring, employee, 690
Motivation, 82, 84, 536
Mouse, 548, 556
MOVE statements, 312–13, 644, 645
Movie reviews, 388
Moving averages, 353
MP3 files, 385
Mqueue, 722–23
MRP. *See* Materials requirements planning
Multinational Web site, 411
Multipliers, 359
Multiview, 21
Music, 385, 386
MY MSN, 388
My Yahoo!, 388

N

Name tag, 287
Naming process, 219, 306, 711
Natural disasters, 691–93
Natural-language interfaces, 546
Navigation
  consistency, 557
  ecommerce considerations, 565–66
  event response charts, 453
  Web site design, 411
Navigation bars, 565
Nested instructions, 309*f*, 311
Nested menus, 548
NetAnnounce Premier, 699
Netflix.com, 351
NetMechanic, 699
NetMeeting, 195
Net Perceptions, 351
Network databases, 490
Network decomposition diagrams, 677–78, 679
Networks
  distributed system disadvantages, 682
  groupware, 681
  kits, 674–75
  modeling, 677–81
  types, 674–76
Neural nets, 350
News
  external information sources, 351
  pull technology, 388–89
  push technology, 389
  RSS feed, 388
NewsIsFree, 388
Newsletter, 388, 389
NEWSMONSTER, 388
Nominal scales, 126–27
Nonoperational prototype, 172*f*, 173
Nonverbal symbolism, 49
Normalization
  definition, 492
  example, 493–501
  steps, 492–93
Norms, 83
Notification manager software, 6
Nouns, 713
Novell, 681
Novices, 683
Null values, 505
Number formats, 275–76
Numeric codes, 600
Numeric keypads, 542–43
Numeric weights, 351
Nunit, 195

O

OAS. *See* Office automation systems
OASIS newsletter, 388*f*
Object identifiers (OIDs), 487
Objectives
  bottom-up design, 636
  data entry, 591
  effectiveness of databases, 480
  feasibility studies, 64–66
  forms, 433
  interview preparation, 111
  normalization process, 495
  output design, 379–81
  problem definition in project initiation, 59–60
  sampling design, 144
  systems development life cycle, 11–12
  top-down design, 636
  training guidelines, 684
  Web site design, 407
Object Linking and Embedding (OLE), 638
Object menus, 548
Object-oriented approach (OOA)
  activity diagrams, 720–23
  basic concepts, 710–12
  class diagrams, 727–40
  CRC cards, 712–14
  modularity in Windows, 638
  Object Think statements, 712–14
  overview, 709–10
  packages, 742–43
  process specifications, 305
  rapid application development, 183
  sequence and communication diagrams, 723–27
  statechart diagrams, 740–42
  systems development life cycle phases, 12
  UML approach, 715–16, 717*f*
  UML artifacts, 742–43
  use case modeling, 717–20
Object-oriented (O-O) analysis and design, 19–20
Objects
  associations, 735
  class overview, 710–11
  communication diagrams, 726
  CRC cards, 712–15
  definition, 20, 709
  inheritance overview, 711–12
  overview, 710
  sequence diagram symbols, 724
  statechart diagrams, 740–41
Object Think statements, 713–15
Observation
  agile versus structured methods, 200
  decision makers, 155–57
  physical environment, 157–62
  systems proposal, 360
  users with prototypes, 180, 181*f*
OCLC. *See* Online computer library center
OCR. *See* Optical character recognition
Office Assistant (Microsoft), 547
Office automation systems (OAS), 2, 3
Office equipment, 158–59
Office location, 157
Offsite training, 684, 685
OIDs. *See* Object identifiers
OLAP. *See* Online analytic processing
OLE. *See* Object Linking and Embedding
OmniForm, 439–40
One-click navigation, 565
100-percent stacked column charts, 365, 366
1NF. *See* First normal form
One-time costs, 356
One-to-many relationships
  entity-relationship models, 35–36, 483*f*, 484
  normalization process, 495–96, 502
  notation, 484
  referential integrity, 505
One-to-one relationships
  denormalization, 512
  entity-relationship models, 34, 35–36, 483*f*, 484
  entity subtypes, 482
  notation, 484
One-to-zero relationships, 484
Online analytic processing (OLAP)
  databases versus data warehouses, 513
  denormalization, 511
  overview, 514, 515
Online computer library center (OCLC), 603
Online help, 562
Online manuals, 651
Online newspapers, 351
Onsite customers, 90, 190, 195, 200
Onsite training, 684–85
OOA. *See* Object-oriented approach
Open-ended questions
  interviews, 112
  questionnaires, 122, 123, 124*f*, 126*f*
Open-ended rectangle symbol, 218*f*, 219
Openness, organizational, 29
Open reactions, 180
Open source software, 6–7
Operational feasibility, 67–68
Operations. *See* Methods
Operations managers, 47, 48
Optical character recognition (OCR), 605
Option buttons, 447
Option groups, 447
Oracle, 346
Oral presentations. *See* Presentations
OR condition, 572
Order fulfillment, 617
Order status updates, 617
Organic design house, 405*f*
Organism metaphor, 694
Organizational boundaries, 28
Organizational closedness, 29
Organizational culture
  agile approach risks, 201–2
  joint application design, 121
  overview, 49
  Six Sigma approach, 632, 633*f*
Organizational goals, 63
Organizational narratives, 157
Organizational openness, 29
Organizational politics, 85
Organizations
  blogs, 412
  culture, 49
  hardware inventory, 340
  interrelatedness and interdependence, 28–29
  management hierarchy, 46–48
  overview, 27–28
  project initiation, 58–59
  project selection, 63
OR operator, 569, 570
Orphan records, 505
"or" phrasing, 309
Outer join, 508
Outlines, 360, 565
Output
  behavioral security, 690
  data dictionary creation, 280–81, 282*f*
  definition, 379
  form, 379
  function point analyses, 77

general data flow diagram development, 221–25
horizontal balancing, 325, 326
organizations as systems, 28, 30–31
physical data flow diagram development, 230
production, 413–16
reliance on quality input, 433
test data, 655
Output design
bias effects, 394–98
blog design, 412–13
display design guidelines, 398–403
objectives, 379–81
output content, 381
technologies, 381–94
Web sites, 403–13
Outsourcing, 347–48

P

Packaged software. *See* Commercial off-the-shelf software
Packages, 742–43
Packed decimal format, 276
Page numbers, 397
Pair programming
agile modeling lessons, 195
agile modeling practices, 190
agile modeling values, 186
agile versus structured methods, 198
overview, 90–91
Pairwise comparisons, 349–50
Palette Grabber, 404
Palm Desktop, 75
Paper, 397, 439
Parallel conversion, 686*f*, 687
Parameter queries, 572*f*, 573
Parentheses, 271, 569
Parent processes, 221, 222, 223*f*
Parent tables, 505
Parkinson's law, 199
Participants, 726
Partitioning
data flow diagrams, 232–34, 240–41, 245–46
electronic and Web form design, 443
process specifications, 324
Web sites, 246–50
Passive tags, 608
Passwords, 689
Patched-up prototype, 172*f*, 173
Patterns, 516–17
Pattern validation methods, 615
Payback periods
break-even analysis, 356
criteria for use, 359
line graph display, 364
table displays, 362
Payment records, 150*f*
Pdf files, 384
Peer-to-peer networks, 672
PeopleSoft, 179
Perceived ease of use, 536
Perceived usefulness, 536
PerfMon, 195
Performance
effectiveness, 348*f*
efficiency, 348*f*
HCI effects, 534–36
measures, 401, 402
reports, 149–50
PERFORM statement, 644, 645
Permalinks, 413
Personal computer formats, 275, 276*f*
Personal digital assistants (PDAs), 6, 552
Personal information managers (PIM), 75–76
Personalized home pages, 351
Personalized output, 380
PERT diagrams, 71–74, 75, 547*f*
PgDn keys, 443
Phone digit layout, 543
Photographs, 409
PHP, 404*f*
Physical data flow diagrams, 225, 228–42, 248*f*
Physical data structures, 273–74
Physical process specifications, 324
Physical security, 688–89
Pie charts, 366, 401
Pilot groups, 125–26
Pilots, 173
PIM. *See* Personal information managers
pipe symbol (|), 36
Pivot tables, 537–39
Pixels, 403
PKI. *See* Public key infrastructure
Places, 457–58
Place utility, 696
Planning
agile development practices, 93–94
disaster recovery, 692
software engineering, 648
Web site design, 406–12
Playscripts, 156–57
Pluck, 388
Plug-ins, 404*f*, 406
Plus sign (+), 271, 288, 649, 712, 728
Podcasts, 383*f*, 385
PodProducer, 385
Poetry, 368
Point-and-click interfaces. *See* Graphical user interfaces
Pointers, 489, 490
Pointing devices, 552
Policy handbooks, 155, 689, 691
Polymorphism, 737
Population samples, 145
Pop-up menus, 548
Pop-up windows, 443, 444*f*
Possession utility, 696
Postconditions, 45
Posters, 154
Pound symbol (#), 728
PowerBuilder, 80
Precedent tasks, 484
Preconditions, 45
Preparation dates, 397
Preprinted forms, 397
Presentation language, 545
Presentations
audio output, 385
database process, 511
display design guidelines, 398–99
equipment, 120
output bias, 395
systems proposal, 366–68
Web site design, 410–11
Present value analysis, 358–59
Primary actors, 40
Primary keys
database anomalies, 505–6
database concepts, 486, 488
integrity constraints, 505
normalization example, 502, 503
Primitive processes, 223, 323
Printed output
costs, 383
design, 396–98
output technologies, 381, 382, 383*f*, 394
processing delays, 561
Print servers, 674
Privacy, 608, 691, 732
Probability samples, 145
Probes, 114
Problem solving
process specification format, 307
project initiation, 58–62
system analyst's qualities, 9
systems development life cycle, 11–12
Procedure manuals, 650–51, 656
Procedures, 642, 648–53
Processes
context-level data flow diagrams, 32
data flow diagram errors, 224–25
data flow diagram symbols, 219
data flow–structure chart conversion, 643
definition, 28
interrelatedness in organizations, 28
Processing delays, 561
Process names, 306
Process numbers, 306
Process specifications
accuracy, 324–25
data dictionaries, 312–13, 324*f*, 325
data flow diagrams, 306, 307*f*, 321*f*, 323–27
format, 306–8
goals, 306
overview, 305–6
partitioning, 324
physical and logical, 323–24
processes not requiring specifications, 306
Product backlog, 197
Productionizing phase, 94*f*, 95
Production reports, 149
Productivity
agile approach costs, 88
agile versus structured methods, 197–202
CASE tools, 16
project goals, 83–84
UML importance, 747
Professional development. *See* Training
Profiles, customer, 517–18, 607, 691
Programmers
agile development roles, 91, 92
COTS software considerations, 347
function point analyses, 80
hours worked, 90
structured walkthroughs, 634
system development life cycle, 14
team assembly, 82
teams in agile approach, 90–91
testing roles, 654*f*
Programming
agile development approach, 87, 189, 190
code generation, 18–19
modular development, 637–38
Programming, pair
agile modeling lessons, 195
agile modeling practices, 190
agile modeling values, 186
agile versus structured methods, 198
overview, 90–91
Project champion approach, 21
Project charters, 85–86
Project goals, 83–84
Projection, 508–9, 510*f*
Project management
agile development, 86–95
analysis and design activities, 81–86
computer-based project scheduling, 74–76
feasibility, 63–68
function point analyses, 76–81
overview, 57
planning and control, 68–74
project initiation, 57–63
project selection, 62–63
Project managers, 76, 81
Project Web, 195
Promotion, Web site, 411–12
Proportionality, 395
Proposals, systems
components, 360–61
cost-benefit analysis, 351–60
creation, 361–66
hardware and software needs, 339–51
overview, 339
presentation, 366–68
system analyst's role, 13
Proposal summaries, 361
Props, 158
Prototyping
advantages, 178
as alternative to SDLC, 174–75
conversion, 688
COTS software, 178–79
disadvantages, 177–78
graphical screen designs, 400
output bias, 396
overview, 20, 171–72
prototype development, 175–79
rapid application development, 181–85
systems proposal, 360
types, 172–75
users' role, 179–81
Proximity cards, 608
Pseudocode, 649, 650*f*, 651*f*
Public domain music, 385
Public key infrastructure (PKI), 690
Public speaking, 368
Pull-down menus, 548, 556, 594
Pull technologies, 387, 388–89
Pulverization services, 690
Purchasing hardware, 343
Purposiveness, 380
Purposive samples, 145
Push technologies, 351, 387, 389
PVCS, 195
Pyramid question structure, 114–15

Q

QBE. *See* Query by example
Qualified employees/applicants, 543
Qualitative documents, 153–55
Quality assurance
agile approach, 88–89, 188
auditing, 657–58
data entry, 591
documentation, 648–53
maintenance, 657
output's reliance on input, 433
overview, 631
paper, 397
software evaluation, 348*f*
structure charts, 638–47, 648*f*
testing, 653–57
TQM approach, 631–38
Quantitative documents, 149–52
Quantity, output, 380

Queries
databases versus data warehouses, 513
design guidelines, 567–73
Query by example (QBE), 570–73
Question-and-answer interfaces, 546–47
Question marks, 288
Questionnaires
administration, 130–31
agile versus structured methods, 200
considerations, 122–23
design, 128–30
mark-sense forms, 607
overview, 122
question writing tips, 123–26
scales, 126–27
systems proposal, 360
usability, 537, 538*f*
users' attitudes, 536
Questions
interviews, 112–16
questionnaire creation, 123–26, 128–30
systems proposal presentation, 368
Web site design, 408
Quotations, 368, 413
QWERTY keyboard, 542

R

RAD. *See* Rapid application development
RAD design workshop phase, 182, 184*f*
Radio buttons
dialog design, 556
form control, 449–50
GUI design, 447
input validation, 615
Radio frequency identification (RFID), 608
Random number codes, 592
Random samples, 145
Range tests, 611
Rapid application development (RAD)
disadvantages, 185
overview, 181
phases, 182–83
purpose, 183–84
versus SDLC, 183–85
software tools, 183
systems development life cycle phases, 12
Rational Rose, 726
Rational Visual Test Tools, 195
Readers, 608
"Read Me" files, 650
Realistic images, 385
Reality, 481
RealTime, 195
Reasonableness tests, 611
Recommendations section, 361
Recommendation systems, 350–51
Records
database anomalies, 505–6
database concepts, 485, 488–90
database use steps, 506–11
dialog design, 556
example, 486*f*
integrity constraints, 504–5
quantitative document analysis, 150
relational structure terminology, 491
Rectangle symbol
activity diagrams, 720, 721
class diagrams, 727
data flow diagrams, 218*f*, 219
entity-relationship symbols, 483–84
sequence diagrams, 724, 725
Red, 461
Redundancy
database anomalies, 505–6
decision tables, 318–19
denormalization, 511–12
Referential integrity, 505
Referring sites, 699
Reflexive associations, 735
Relational databases
design considerations, 503–6
normalization, 494–3
overview, 490–91, 492*f*
recent changes, 480
Relationships. *See also specific types*
categories, 733–36
database concepts, 483–84
UML concepts, 715, 716*f*
Reliability, 127
Renting hardware, 344, 394
Repetition, 408, 495
Report files, 488
Reports
inclusion of codes, 601
output bias, 396
output content, 381
print design, 396–98
push technology, 389
transaction file function, 488
Repositories. *See* Data repositories
Request processing, 561–62
Requirements planning phase, 182
Resources
agile modeling controls, 190
agile modeling lessons, 196
determination, 66–68
Web site design, 404
Respondents, 123, 130–31
Restricted databases, 505
Retail stores, 385
Reusability, 710
Revealing information, 596–97
Revised decision evaluation approach, 695
Revision dates, 441
RFID. *See* Radio frequency identification
Right mouse button, 548
Ring networks, 676
Risk management, 80–81
Risk taking, 93–94, 201–3
Roles databases, 439*f*
Rollover menus, 565
Row selection, 509, 511*f*
Row totals, 437
RSSBANDIT, 388
RSS file, 385, 386–87
Ruby on Rails language, 7
Rules, 505

S

Safety kits, 693
Sales reports, 149
Sampling
design, 144–46
overview, 143–44
questionnaire administration, 130
rationale, 144
sample size, 146–48
systems proposal, 360
workload estimates, 341
Sans serif font, 446
SAP, 346
Satisfaction surveys, 536
Sayings, 652
Scale models, 173
Scales, 126–27
Scanned forms, 439–40
ScanSoft, 439–40
Scheduling
activity planning, 68–74
computer-based, 74–76
risk in agile approach, 93–94
Schemas, 289, 490, 491*f*, 615
Scope, 89
Screening employees, 689
Screen magnifiers, 544
Screen output
CSS styles, 414
design guidelines, 398–403
form design, 441–60, 549–50
output design, 381, 382–84, 394
visually impaired users, 542, 544
Screen reading software, 411
Screen resolutions, 383, 403, 410
Screen savers, 351
Screen scraping, 691
Scripts, 385
Scrolling text boxes, 461
Scrum, 196–97, 200
SDLC. *See* Systems development life cycle
Search engines, 408, 411, 699
Search functions, 565
Secondary actors, 40
Secondary keys, 487, 488
Second normal form (2NF), 498, 499*f*
Secure socket layering (SSL), 690
Security
Ajax design, 457
ASP drawbacks, 348
concealing codes, 595–96
data flow diagram partitioning, 233–34
ecommerce projects, 85
implementation issues, 688–93
input validation, 609
internal auditors' tasks, 658
print report design, 397
Web site partitioning, 247
WLAN concerns, 675–76
SELECT DISTINCTROW keyword, 573
Selected features prototype, 172*f*, 173–74
Selecting projects, 62–63
Selection, 312, 509, 511*f*
Self-administration, of questionnaires, 131
Self-discipline, 10
Self-join relationships, 484, 508
Self-validating codes. *See* Check digits
Sensory impairments, 542–43
Sequence codes, 592, 594, 595*f*
Sequence diagrams
versus communication diagrams, 726
definition, 716
example, 730–32
overview, 724
symbols, 724–25
Sequences, 516
Sequential organization, 489
Sequential structures, 309, 310*f*, 312
Server-based applications, 673
Servers. *See* Client/server (C/S) model
Service employees, 437
Shaded boxes, 444
Shaded buttons, 449
Shapes, icon, 446
SHARPREADER, 388
Shipping charges, 461
Shopping carts, 461, 698
Shortcut abbreviations, 548
Shorthand symbols, 161
Short release
agile versus structured methods, 199
core agile practices, 90, 190, 195
Shredding documents, 690
Siftware, 513, 516
Signature section, 434, 435*f*
Significant-digit subset codes, 596–97
Sign-on attempts, 690
Simple random samples, 145
Simple sequence codes, 592
Simplicity
agile modeling, 186, 188
display design guidelines, 398
electronic and Web form design, 441–43, 444
input objectives, 433
Simulations, 685
Single-digit miskeys, 612
Site maps, 565
Site promotion, 699
Six Sigma, 632, 633*f*
Slash (/), 555
Sliders, 448–49
Slope, 353
Small businesses, 674–75
SmallTalk, 195
Smartcards, 608
Society metaphor, 694
Soft Systems Methodology, 21
Software
agile development tools, 194–95
behavioral security, 689
code generation, 18
cost-benefit analysis, 351–60
C/S model pros and cons, 674
data capture automation, 602–4
disaster recovery, 692
documentation and quality assurance, 648–53
form design packages, 438–40
groupware tasks, 681
hub connectivity, 680
input validation, 609–16
logical security, 689
needs assessment, 345–51
print report design guidelines, 396
quality assurance, 648–53
RAD tools, 183
registration key codes, 557
selection steps, 340*f*
system development life cycle phases, 13–14
tab control dialog boxes, 458
training materials, 685
vendor support, 344*f*, 348
visual displays of databases, 540
Web site design, 403, 407, 411, 458
weighted objectives, 60
Software forums, 563
Sortable codes, 600
Sorted information, 395, 510, 513*f*
Sound, 385, 542
SourceForge.net, 195
Spatial orientation, 385
Speaking guidelines, 368
Specialized classes, 736, 737, 738
Specialty forms, 437
Speech software, 544, 552, 553
Spell checkers, 77
Spin buttons, 448–49
Spiral model, 20
Spooling, 488
Spreadsheets, 359
Sprint, 197
Sprint backlog, 197

SQL. *See* Structured query language
Square nodes, 320
SSL. *See* Secure socket layering
Stability, 599
Staffing, 79–80, 85
Stakeholders, 44
Stamp coupling, 641
Standard methods, 728
Standards, 198, 633
Star networks, 676
Star symbol, 649
Statechart diagrams
  definition, 716
  example, 741–42
  overview, 740–41
  UML use, 745
Stationers, 437
Stereotypes, 730–32
Stickiness, 408
Storage
  approaches, 479
  distributed system advantages, 681
  ecommerce data entry, 617
  electronic and Web form design, 449–50
  importance, 479
  input validation, 611
  output technology considerations, 392–93
  Web pages, 732
Story cards, 93
Strategic managers
  decision-making tasks, 47–48
  function, 47
  information systems implications, 48–49
  output technology considerations, 392
  systems perspective, 30–31
Stratified samples, 145–46
STROBE (structured observation of the environment), 157–62
Structural diagrams, 715, 716*f*
Structural relationships, 715, 716*f*
Structural things, 715
Structure charts, 638–47, 648*f*
Structured decisions
  analysis technique selection, 321–23
  decision tables, 313–19
  decision trees, 319–21
  structured English, 308–13
  system development life cycle phases, 13
Structured English
  conventions, 309–12
  examples, 311*f*, 313*f*, 322*f*
  horizontal balancing, 325–26
  overview, 308–9
  selection, 322
Structured logic, 308, 309
Structured observation of the environment. *See* STROBE
Structured query language (SQL), 573
Structured walkthroughs, 634–35
Structure, Web site, 407
Stylistic attributes, 398
Stylus, 552
Subcultures, organizational, 49
Subordinate modules, 646–47, 648*f*
Subprograms
  function, 306
  process specification format, 307
  structure charts, 642
Summary
  blogs, 413
  reports, 381, 396
Supporting actors, 40
Supporting experts, 9
Support services
  hardware, 344–45
  software, 348
Surveys
  administration, 130–31
  agile versus structured methods, 200
  considerations, 122–23
  design, 128–30
  mark-sense forms, 607
  overview, 122
  question writing tips, 123–26
  scales, 126–27
  systems proposal, 360
  usability, 537, 538*f*
  users' attitudes, 536
Swimlanes, 721, 722, 723
Switches, 638, 639
Symbols. *See also specific symbols*
  activity diagrams, 720–22
  animation output, 385
  associations, 733–34
  class diagrams, 727
  data dictionaries, 271, 276
  data flow diagrams, 218–19
  entity-relationships, 483*f*
  network modeling, 677–79, 677*f*
  packages, 742
  pseudocode logic, 649, 651*f*
  sequence diagrams, 724–25
  STROBE, 161
  structure charts, 638, 642
  whole/part relationships, 735
  XML tags, 287
Symmetry, 320
Synchronization bar, 721
Synchronous messages, 740
Syntax rules, 551
Syntax tests, 614
Systematic sampling, 145
System control, 28, 29
System interfaces, 729
System maintenance
  agile approach, 94*f*, 95–96
  CASE tools, 17
  importance, 14–15, 648
  modular development, 637
  quality assurance, 657
  system development life cycle, 14, 15
  vendor support, 344*f*
Systems. *See* Information systems
Systems alternatives section, 361
Systems analysis and design
  alternative methods, 20–21
  bottom-up approach, 635–36
  importance, 7
  project management, 81–86
  top-down approach, 636–37
Systems analysts
  CASE tools, 16–17
  definition, 8
  ecommerce job qualifications, 8
  forecasting requirements, 352
  project initiation, 59–60
  qualities, 9–10, 11
  role, 7–10, 654*f*
  team members, 82
  training issues, 683
Systems development life cycle (SDLC)
  versus agile modeling, 192
  CASE tools, 17, 18*f*
  human–computer interaction, 11
  illustration, 10*f*
  overview, 10
  phases, 10–16
  prototyping as alternative to, 174–75
  versus rapid application development, 183–85
Systems projects. *See* Project management
Systems proposal
  components, 360–61
  cost-benefit analysis, 351–60
  creation, 361–66
  hardware and software needs, 339–51
  overview, 339
  presentation, 366–68
  system analyst's role, 13

T

Tab control dialog boxes, 457–58, 557, 558*f*
Tableau Software, 540–41
Table captions, 437
Table files, 488
Table of contents, 360, 565
Tables. *See also specific types*
  cognitive styles, 537–39
  database anomalies, 505–6
  database integrity constraints, 504–5
  database normalization process, 502–3
  relational data structures, 490–91
  systems proposal development, 361–62
  Web site design, 411
Tablet PCs, 552
Tales, 652
TAM. *See* Technology acceptance model
Tangible benefits, 354–55
Tangible costs, 355
Team, project
  agile approach risks, 201–2
  assembly, 81–82
  communication strategies, 82–83
  COTS software, 84
  ecommerce projects, 85
  groupware, 681–82
  motivation, 84
  productivity goals, 83–84
  programmers in agile approach, 90–91
  Scrum methods, 196–97
  top-down design, 637
Technical feasibility, 67
Technology acceptance model (TAM), 536
Telephones, 385, 543, 562
Templates
  ecommerce feedback, 563
  electronic form design, 439*f*
  hub connectivity, 680*f*
  Web site design, 406
Temporal events, 43, 740, 741
Temporary data stores, 219
Tensions, 82
Testers, 92
Testing
  agile approach, 87, 92, 189
  quality assurance, 653–57
  system development life cycle, 14
Text
  electronic and Web form design, 447, 449
  searches, 600
  Web site design, 409, 411
Text boxes
  form control, 449–50
  GUI design, 447
  Intranet/Internet design, 461
Themes, 408
Things, 715, 716*f*
Third normal form (3NF), 499–501, 507
Three-clicks rule, 411, 443
Tick marks, 435
Timeboxing, 75–76, 200
Time/timing
  activity planning and control, 68–74
  agile approach, 87–88, 190, 198, 199, 200
  agile approach risks, 202
  Ajax benefits, 455
  bar chart depiction, 365–66
  completion dates, 76
  databases versus data warehouses, 513
  data entry bottlenecks, 604
  data entry methods, 605
  data flow diagram partitioning, 232
  direct changeover, 687
  estimated workloads, 341, 342*f*
  hardware acquisition considerations, 343–44
  hardware evaluation, 341
  joint application design, 121
  lack of documentation, 649
  line graph depictions, 363–64
  output design objectives, 380–81
  output technology considerations, 392
  physical data flow diagrams, 230
  present value analysis, 358–59
  processing delays, 561
  project scheduling, 74–76
  project selection, 63
  prototype development, 175–76
  prototyping versus SDLC, 174
  sequence diagrams, 725
  structured walkthroughs, 634
  Web page loading, 410
Time utility, 696
Title pages, 360
Titles
  blogs, 413
  dialog design, 554
  graphs, 363
  print reports, 397
  tables, 362
  Web site design, 409
TiVo.com, 351
Toll-free catalog numbers, 385
Toll roads, 608
Top-down approach
  overview, 636–37
  process specifications, 305
  structure charts, 638–47
Total quality management (TQM), 631–38
Totals calculation, 510, 513*f*
Totals section
  example, 437, 438*f*
  form sections, 434, 435*f*
Touch screens, 543, 552, 553
TPS. *See* Transaction processing systems
TQM. *See* Total quality management
Trackers, 92
Training
  agile development risks, 202
  agile versus structured methods, 199
  implementation issues, 683–85, 686*f*
  improved fit, 534
  output bias, 396
  vendor support, 344*f*
  video output purposes, 384
Training the neural net, 350
Transaction data stores, 230

Transaction files, 488
Transaction processing
systems (TPS)
feasibility impact grid, 64, 65
function, 2
overview, 2–3
Transcription, 437
Transformational modules, 644–46
Transient objects, 740
Transition effects, 385
Transitive dependency, 498,
499, 506
Transposed digits, 612–13
Trends
bar chart depictions, 365–66
column chart depictions, 364
data mining patterns, 516–17
display design guidelines, 400
estimation, 352–54
line graph depictions, 363–64
printer options, 382
TrueTime, 195
Trust, 82, 187
Tuples, 491
Turnaround documents, 381, 382*f*
Turnover, employee, 648
Tutorials, 561, 685
2NF. *See* Second normal form
Type fonts, 438
Typing, 542, 555–56

U

UML. *See* Unified modeling
language
Unadjusted function points
(UFP), 79
Unauthorized people, 609
Unconditional forecasting, 352
Underline, 309, 311*f*
Undue hardship, 543
Unicode, 276, 597–98
Unified modeling language (UML)
activity diagrams, 720–23
artifacts, 742–43
class diagrams, 727–40
importance, 746–47
object-oriented concepts, 710–12
overview, 709, 715–16
packages, 742–43
procedures, 744–46
sequence and communication
diagrams, 723–27
statechart diagrams, 740–42
use case modeling, 717–20,
746–47
Uniformity, 601
Unique codes, 600
Unique constraints, 505
Unobtrusive information gathering,
143. *See also specific methods*
UPC codes, 608
Update anomalies, 506
Upper CASE tools, 17–18
URL, 404*f*, 691
Usability, 536–37, 538*f*
Use case diagrams, 716
Use case modeling
benefits, 45–46
data flow diagrams, 232, 233*f*
definition of use case model, 745
diagram development, 42
example, 43, 718–20
overview, 39, 717–18
symbols, 39–40
unified modeling language,
717–20, 746–47
use case relationships,
40–42
Use case packages, 742
Use case realization, 724
Use case scenarios
benefits, 46
definition, 716
documentation, 42–43
examples, 43–45
overview, 42
User design phase, 183
User help
detailed feedback, 562
dialog design, 554
electronic and Web forms,
441, 443
procedure manuals, 650
standard design, 557
varieties, 562–63
User interfaces
dialog design, 554–57
disabled users, 542–45
ecommerce considerations,
563–66
feedback, 558–65
prototype development, 177
system development life cycle
phases, 13
top-down design, 637
types, 545–54
User involvement approach, 695
User movement
electronic and Web form
design, 443
form-fill interfaces, 549
Web site design, 398–99
Users
attitude toward computers, 536
CASE tools, 16–17
cognitive styles, 537–41, 565
dialog action, 555–57
disabled, 411, 542–45
display screen advantages, 383
ecommerce privacy, 691
hardware inventory, 340
human–computer interaction
benefits, 10–11
maintenance feedback, 657
operational feasibility, 67–68
output bias, 394–98
output design objectives, 380
presentation audience, 368
procedure manuals, 650–51
prototyping role, 179–81
prototyping versus SDLC, 174
RAD phases, 182
security concerns, 689–90
systems development life cycle
phases, 11–12, 14
testing roles, 654*f*
testing with live data, 655–57
TQM responsibilities, 632–33
training issues, 682–85
User stories, 192–94
User views, 490, 506
Uses relationships, 40*f*, 41
Utility bills, 381

V

VA. *See* Visible Analyst (VA)
Validity
input data, 608–18
scales, 127
Value adjustment factor (VAF), 79
Values
agile modeling, 186–87,
191*f*, 196
data items, 485, 486*f*
electronic and Web form design,
448–51
entity integrity constraints, 505
input validation, 611
output bias, 395
query types, 567–70
Varchar data, 275
Variable information, 397
Variable-length records, 485
VB .NET, 404*f*
VBScript, 402
VBUnit, 195
Vendors
commercial software
disadvantages, 347
concealing codes, 595–96
hardware evaluation, 341, 342
hardware support, 344–45
output technology
considerations, 394
software support, 348
training concerns, 683, 684, 685
Verbal symbolism, 49
Verbs, 713, 737
Verdana font, 446
Verification codes, 614
Verisign, 690
Vertical lines, 724
Video output, 384–85
Viewing area, 458
Virtual organizations, 29–30
Virtual private networks, 690
Virtual teams, 29–30
Virus protection software, 690
Visa cards, 614
Visible Analyst (VA)
data stores, 278, 279*f*
entity classes, 729
overview, 16
Visitor demographics, 698–99
Visual C++, 183
Visual Intercept, 195
Visually impaired users, 411,
542, 544
Visual Source Safe, 195
Voice files, 385
Voice, presentation, 368
Voice recognition software.
See Speech software
Volume, 356
Volume capacity, hardware, 341
Vulnerability management
products, 690

W

WANs. *See* Wide area networks
War metaphor, 693
Warranties, 344, 348
WAV files, 385
Web-based forms, 151
Web-based output, 381
Web-based simulations, 685
Webcasters, 389
Web Developer, 404, 405*f*
Web editor, 403
Web interfaces. *See* Interfaces
Web logs. *See* Blogs
Webmaster, 404*f*
Web servers, 674
Web sites
dialog design, 555
display screen drawbacks,
383–84
evaluation guidelines,
697–700
feedback types, 559–61
filtering products, 690
form design, 441–60
general design guidelines,
403–13, 502
online manuals, 651
partitioning, 246–50
qualitative analysis, 154
storage, 732
video output, 384
Web surfing, 689, 690
Web surveys, 128*f*, 131
Web systems, 5
Web terms, 404*f*
Webtrends, 697, 698*f*
Webtrends Corporation,
698–99
Weighting methods, 613
Well-being, 535–36
WEP (wired equivalent
privacy), 676
What-if analyses, 352
WHERE keyword, 573
Whiteboard, 195
White circles, 721
Whole/part relationships,
735–36
Wide area networks (WANs),
674, 675
Widgets, 402–3
Wiki Wiki, 195
WiMax (worldwide interoperability
for microwave access), 676
Windows for Workgroups, 681
Windows Media Player, 385, 404*f*,
409, 459*f*
Windows NT, 681
Windows operating system,
446, 638
Wireless local area networks
(WLANs)
access, 394, 552, 676
overview, 675–76
Wireless system integration, 6
Wizards
network installation, 675
overview, 562
question-and-answer
interfaces, 547
Wizz RSS, 388
WLANs. *See* Wireless local area
networks
WOPR Placebar Customizer, 458
Word choice, 125–26
Word processing, 547
Word wrap, 449
Work experience, 82
Working models, 173
Workloads, 341, 342*f*
Workshops, 182
Workstation connectivity, 677–81
Worldwide interoperability for
microwave access.
See WiMax
W-2 form, 393
WYSIWYG, 396

X

XML. *See* Extensible markup
language
XML Spy, 615
XSLT. *See* Extensible style language
transformation

Y

Y intercepts, 353

Z

Zero-to-many relationships, 484
Zero-to-one relationships, 484
Zip codes, 593
Zoned decimal format, 276
Zoo metaphor, 693–94

Prentice Hall

Management Information Systems Titles

MIS:

Jessup/Valacich, *Information Systems Today 3/e © 2008*
Kroenke, *Using MIS © 2007*
Kroenke, *Experiencing MIS © 2008*
Laudon/Laudon, *Management Information Systems 9/e © 2006*
Laudon/Laudon, *Essentials of Business Information Systems 7/e © 2007*
Luftman et al., *Managing the IT Resource © 2004*
Malaga, *Information Systems Technology © 2005*
Martin et al., *Managing IT 5/e © 2005*
McLeod/Schell, *Management Information Systems 10/e © 2007*
McNurlin/Sprague, *Information Systems Management In Practice 7/e © 2006*
Miller, *MIS: Decision Making with Application Software (Cases) 3/e © 2007*
Senn, *Information Technology 3/e © 2004*

Database Management:

Bordoloi/Bock, *Oracle SQL © 2004*
Bordoloi/Bock, *SQL for SQL Server © 2004*
Frost/Day/VanSlyke, *Database Design and Development: A Visual Approach © 2006*
Hoffer/Prescott/McFadden, *Modern Database Management 8/e © 2007*
Kroenke, *Database Concepts 3/e © 2007*
Kroenke, *Database Processing 10/e © 2006*
Perry/Post, *Introduction to Oracle 10g © 2007*
Perry/Post, *Introduction to SQL 2005 © 2007*

Systems Analysis and Design:

Hoffer/George/Valacich, *Modern Systems Analysis and Design 5/e © 2008*
Kendall/Kendall, *Systems Analysis and Design 7/e © 2008*
Valacich/George/Hoffer, *Essentials of Systems Analysis and Design 3/e © 2006*

Object-Oriented Systems Analysis and Design:

George/Batra/Valacich/Hoffer, *Object-Oriented Systems Analysis and Design 2/e © 2007*
Stumpf/Teague, *Object-Oriented Systems Analysis and Design with UML © 2005*